CompTIA® Network+® N10-005 In Depth

Tamara Dean

COURSE TECHNOLOGY
CENGAGE Learning®

Australia • Brazil • Japan • Korea • Mexico • Singapore • Spain • United Kingdom • United States

CompTIA® Network+® N10-005 In Depth

Tamara Dean

Vice President, Careers & Computing: Dave Garza

Publisher and General Manager, Course Technology PTR: Stacy Hiquet

Executive Editor: Stephen Helba

Associate Director of Marketing: Sarah Panella

Acquisitions Editors: Nick Lombardi and Heather Hurley

Managing Editor: Marah Bellegarde

Manager of Editorial Services: Heather Talbot

Senior Product Manager: Michelle Ruelos Cannistraci

Developmental Editor: Ann Shaffer

Editorial Assistant: Sarah Pickering

Vice President, Marketing: Jennifer Ann Baker

Senior Marketing Manager: Mark Hughes

Senior Production Director: Wendy Troeger

Production Manager: Andrew Crouth

Senior Content Project Manager: Andrea Majot

Art Director: Jackie Bates

Media Editor: William Overocker

Cover Designer: Mike Tanamachi

Cover Photo or Illustration: Veer.com

Library of Congress Control Number: 2012939939

ISBN-13: 978-1-285-07657-7

ISBN-10: 1-285-07657-5

Course Technology
20 Channel Center Street
Boston, MA 02210
USA

Cengage Learning is a leading provider of customized learning solutions with office locations around the globe, including Singapore, the United Kingdom, Australia, Mexico, Brazil, and Japan. Locate your local office at: **international.cengage.com/region**

Cengage Learning products are represented in Canada by Nelson Education, Ltd.

For your lifelong learning solutions, visit **www.cengage.com/coursetechnology**

Visit our corporate website at **cengage.com**

Printed in the United States of America
1 2 3 4 5 6 7 16 15 14 13 12

Table of Contents

Preface

Knowing how to install, configure, and troubleshoot a computer network is a highly marketable and exciting skill. This book first introduces the fundamental building blocks that form a modern network, such as protocols, media, topologies, and hardware. It then provides in-depth coverage of the most important concepts in contemporary networking, such as TCP/IP, Ethernet, wireless transmission, virtual networks, and security. After reading the book and completing the end-of-chapter exercises, you will be prepared to select the best network design, hardware, and software for your environment. You will also have the skills to build a network from scratch and maintain, upgrade, troubleshoot, and manage an existing network. Finally, you will be well prepared to pass CompTIA's Network+ certification exam.

Because some technical topics can be difficult to grasp, this book explains concepts logically and in a clear, approachable style. In addition, concepts are reinforced by real-world examples of networking issues from a professional's standpoint. Each chapter opens with an On the Job story from a network engineer. These real-world examples make this book a practical learning tool. The numerous tables and illustrations, along with the glossaries, appendices, and study questions, make the book a valuable reference for any networking professional.

Intended Audience

This book is intended to serve the needs of students and professionals who are interested in mastering fundamental, vendor-independent networking concepts. No previous networking experience is necessary to begin learning from this book, although knowledge of basic computer principles is helpful. Those seeking to pass CompTIA's Network+ certification exam will find the text's content, approach, and numerous study questions especially helpful. For more information on Network+ certification, visit CompTIA's Web site at *www.comptia.org*.

The book's pedagogical features are designed to provide a truly interactive learning experience, preparing you for the challenges of the highly dynamic networking industry.

Chapter Descriptions

The following list summarizes the topics covered in each chapter of this book:

Chapter 1, "An Introduction to Networking," begins by answering the question "What is a network?" Next, it presents the fundamental types of networks and describes the elements that constitute the most popular type, the client/server network. This chapter also introduces career options for those interested in mastering networking skills.

Chapter 2, "Networking Standards and the OSI Model," describes the organizations that set standards in the networking industry, including those that oversee wiring codes, network access methods, and Internet addressing. It also discusses the OSI model, which is the industry standard for conceptualizing communication between computers on a network.

Chapter 3, "Transmission Basics and Networking Media," describes signaling techniques used on modern networks, including those used over coaxial cable, twisted pair cable, and fiber-optic cable. It also covers the characteristics—including cost, materials, and connector types—for physical media that can be used to carry signals. Finally, it describes structured cabling standards and best practices for installing network cables.

Chapter 4, "Introduction to TCP/IP Protocols," introduces you to the most popular set of protocols used by networks today, TCP/IP. Functions and interactions between each TCP/IP core protocol are described in the context of the TCP/IP model and the OSI model. This chapter also explains IPv4 and IPv6 addressing and host and domain naming conventions.

Chapter 5, "Topologies and Ethernet Standards," discusses the variety of physical and logical topologies found on LANs (local area networks), with an emphasis on the most popular and fault-tolerant types. Next it describes several Ethernet standards, from the older 10-Mbps to the very latest 10-Gbps transmission rates.

Chapter 6, "Network Hardware, Switching, and Routing," examines the hardware associated with a network, including NICs (network interface cards), hubs, routers, bridges, gateways, and switches. It describes how switches and routers deliver information over a network. In Chapter 6, you will also learn how to install network hardware.

Chapter 7, "Wide Area Networks," expands on your knowledge of networks by examining WAN (wide area network) topologies and transmission methods, such as T-carriers, ISDN, DSL, and broadband cable.

Chapter 8, "Wireless Networking," covers every popular wireless LAN and WAN networking standard, including its frequency range, maximum transmission distance, and maximum throughput. Here you'll also learn how data are converted to electromagnetic waves and how obstacles can impair wireless communication. Finally, this chapter teaches you how to perform a wireless site survey, install and configure a wireless access point, and troubleshoot wireless connectivity problems.

Chapter 9, "In-Depth TCP/IP Networking," explores advanced concepts related to TCP/IP-based networking, such as subnetting, CIDR (Classless Interdomain Routing), and NAT (Network Address Translation). It also details commands useful for evaluating devices and troubleshooting connections that use TCP/IP.

Chapter 10, "Virtual Networks and Remote Access," introduces you to virtualization, in which one physical computer can host several virtual workstations and servers. It describes how virtual machines interact with each other and with the network to obtain addresses and communicate.

Chapter 10 also explains how remote clients can access shared resources and how VPNs (virtual private networks) allow geographically distant clients to exchange data securely.

Chapter 11, "Network Security," discusses critical network security techniques, including the use of firewalls, encryption, intrusion detection, and enterprise-wide security policies. Network security is a major concern when designing and maintaining modern networks, which typically use open protocols and connect to public networks such as the Internet.

Chapter 12, "Voice and Video over IP," describes the latest uses of packet-switched networks: delivering voice and video signals. These signals used to be carried over telephony or television networks only, but improvements in data networks' scale and speed have resulted in a convergence of data, voice, and video over the same transmission paths. You'll learn about the infrastructure, protocols, and equipment necessary to carry and receive such services over converged networks.

Chapter 13, "Troubleshooting Network Problems," approaches the tasks of troubleshooting and maintaining networks in a logical, practical manner. Further, this chapter teaches you how to use several software and hardware troubleshooting tools. A mastery of troubleshooting is not only critical for qualifying for Network+ certification, but is also a highly valued skill in the workplace.

Chapter 14, "Ensuring Integrity and Availability," explains how to keep network resources available and connections reliable despite threats such as power outages or hardware and software failures. In this chapter, you will find information about malware protection, fault-tolerant storage, data backups, and disaster recovery planning.

Chapter 15, "Network Management," concludes the book by describing several aspects of network management, including documentation, policies and regulations, asset management, and change management. This chapter builds on all the knowledge you've gained about network fundamentals, design, maintenance, and troubleshooting.

The appendices at the end of this book serve as references for the networking professional:

Appendix A, "Network+ Examination Objectives," provides a complete list of the latest Network+ certification exam objectives, including the percentage of the exam's content they represent and which chapters in the book cover material associated with each objective.

Appendix B, "Network+ Practice Exam," offers a practice exam containing 100 questions similar in content and presentation to those you will find on CompTIA's Network+ examination.

Appendix C, "Visual Guide to Connectors," provides a visual connector reference chart for quick identification of connectors and receptacles used in contemporary networking.

Appendix D, "Answers to Chapter Review Questions," provides the answers to the questions found at the end of each chapter so you can check your understanding.

Appendix E, "Glossary," is a comprehensive listing of all the key terms defined throughout the book.

Appendix F, "Answers to Network+ Practice Exam Questions," presents the answers to the 100 questions found in Appendix B.

Appendix G, "Network Operating System Basics," summarizes how network operating systems interact with clients; manage shared resources; and organize files, objects, and directories. In Appendix G, you will also find an overview of the features of the most common network operating systems, Windows Server 2008 R2, UNIX, and Linux. Although knowledge of network operating systems is not explicitly listed in the Network+ examination objectives, as a network administrator, you will need to understand how they function.

New to This Edition

- Content maps completely to CompTIA's Network+ N10-005 exam
- New chapter, "Virtual Networks and Remote Access," covers virtualization, virtual machines, virtual NICs, virtual switches, cloud computing, as well as remote access and VPNs
- Added content on wireless WAN technology, including HSPA+, LTE, and cellular networks
- Increased emphasis on network security
- Expanded coverage of IPv6, including IPv6 subnetting
- Comparison of TCP/IP model with OSI model
- Discussions from the previous edition enhanced by new tables and figures

Features

To aid you in fully understanding networking concepts, this book includes many features designed to enhance your learning experience.

Chapter Objectives—Each chapter begins with a list of the concepts to be mastered within that chapter. This list provides you with both a quick reference to the chapter's contents and a useful study aid.

Illustrations and Tables—Numerous full-color illustrations of network media, methods of signaling, protocol behavior, hardware, topology, software screens, peripherals, and components help you visualize common network elements, theories, and concepts. In addition, the many tables included provide details and comparisons of both practical and theoretical information.

Chapter Summaries—Each chapter's text is followed by a summary of the concepts introduced in that chapter. These summaries provide a helpful way to revisit the ideas covered in each chapter.

Review Questions—The end-of-chapter assessment begins with a set of review questions that reinforce the ideas introduced in each chapter. Many questions are situational. Rather than simply asking you to repeat what you've learned, these questions help you evaluate and apply the material you have learned. Answering these questions will ensure that you have mastered the important concepts and provide valuable practice for taking CompTIA's Network+ exam.

Text and Graphic Conventions

Wherever appropriate, additional information and exercises have been added to this book to help you better understand the topic at hand. The following icons are used throughout the text to alert you to additional materials:

The Note icon draws your attention to helpful material related to the subject being described.

The Tip icon highlights helpful pointers on completing particular tasks.

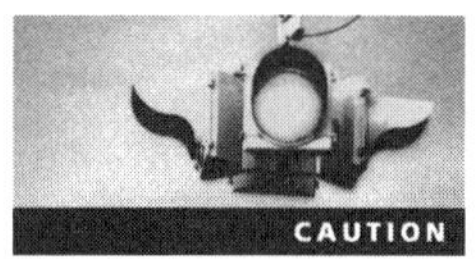

The Caution icon alerts you to specific dangers related to networking technologies.

All of the content that relates to CompTIA's Network+ Certification exam, whether it is a page or a sentence, is highlighted with a Net+ icon and the relevant objective number in the margin. This unique feature highlights the important information at a glance, so you can pay extra attention to the certification material.

State of the Information Technology (IT) Field

Organizations depend on computers and information technology to thrive and grow. Globalization, or connecting with customers and suppliers around the world, is a direct result of the widespread use of the Internet. Rapidly changing technology further affects how companies do business and keeps the demand for skilled and certified IT workers strong across industries. Every sector of the economy requires IT professionals who can establish, maintain, troubleshoot, and extend their business systems.

Despite the economic downturn that began in 2007, employment in IT has rebounded early and with vigor. The latest *Occupational Outlook Handbook* from the Bureau of Labor Statistics (part of the United States Department of Labor) predicts that employment of network and computer systems specialists will increase by 28 percent between 2010 and 2020. This rate is double the predicted national average for all occupations. Median pay for jobs in this sector is almost $70,000.

In any industry, a skilled workforce is important for continually driving business. Finding highly skilled IT workers can be a struggle for employers, given that technologies change approximately every two years. With such a quick product life cycle, IT workers must strive to keep up with these changes to continually bring value to their employers.

Certifications

Different levels of education are required for the many jobs in the IT industry. Additionally, the level of education and type of training required varies from employer to employer, but the need for qualified technicians remains a constant. As technology changes and advances in the industry evolve, many employers prefer candidates who already have the skills to implement these new technologies. Traditional degrees and diplomas do not identify the skills that a job applicant possesses. Companies are relying increasingly on technical certifications to adequately identify a job applicant's skills. Technical certifications are a way for employers to ensure the quality and skill qualifications of their computer professionals, and they can offer job seekers a competitive edge over their competition.

Certifications fall into one of two categories: vendor-neutral and vendor-specific. Vendor-neutral certifications are those that test for the skills and knowledge required in specific industry job roles and do not subscribe to a vendor's specific technology solutions. Some examples of vendor-neutral certifications include all of the CompTIA certifications, Project Management Institute's certifications, and Security Certified Program certifications. Vendor-specific certifications validate the skills and knowledge necessary to be successful while utilizing a specific vendor's technology solution. Some examples of vendor-specific certifications include those offered by Microsoft, IBM, and Cisco.

As employers struggle to fill open IT positions with qualified candidates, certifications are a means of validating the skill sets necessary to be successful within organizations. In most careers, salary and compensation is determined by experience and education, but in the IT field, the number and type of certifications an employee earns also determine salary and wage increases. For example, according to CompTIA, companies such as Cisco, Dell, EDS, Geek Squad, HP, Office Depot, Ricoh, Sharp, and Xerox recommend or require their networking technicians achieve Network+ certification.

Certification provides job applicants with more than just a competitive edge over their noncertified counterparts competing for the same IT positions. Some institutions of higher education grant college credit to students who successfully pass certification exams, moving them further along in their degree programs. Certification also gives individuals who are interested in careers in the military the ability to move into higher positions more quickly. And many advanced certification programs accept, and sometimes require, entry-level certifications as part of their exams. For example, Cisco and Microsoft accept some CompTIA certifications as prerequisites for their certification programs.

Career Planning

Finding a career that fits a person's personality, skill set, and lifestyle is challenging and fulfilling, but can often be difficult. What are the steps individuals should take to find that dream career? Is IT interesting to you? Chances are, that if you are reading this book, this question has already been answered. What is it about IT that you like? The world of work in the IT industry is vast. Some questions to ask yourself: Are you a person who likes to work alone, or do you like to work in a group? Do you like speaking directly with customers, or do you prefer to stay behind the scenes? Does your lifestyle encourage a lot of travel, or do you need to stay in one location? All of these factors influence your job decision. Inventory assessments are a good first step to learning more about you, your interests, work values, and abilities. A variety of Web sites can offer assistance with career planning and assessments.

What's New with CompTIA Network+ Certification

With its N10-005 Network+ exam, CompTIA has emphasized more hands-on experience and expanded the scope of the exam to include the latest network technologies. Objectives that used to require only identifying protocols, devices, and standards now require demonstrating an ability to install and configure connectivity devices or to apply protocols and standards. Some objectives, such as knowledge of virtual network components and cellular data networks, are new. A few older technologies have been dropped from the objectives. However, bear in mind that some legacy protocols and standards appear in the objectives' list of acronyms, and the Network+ exam could refer to them.

As with the previous Network+ exam, the N10-005 version includes many scenario-based questions. Mastering, rather than simply memorizing, the material in this book will help you succeed on the exam and on the job.

Here are the domains covered on the new Network+ exam:

Domain	% of Examination
Domain 1.0 Networking Concepts	21%
Domain 2.0 Network Installation and Configuration	23%
Domain 3.0 Network Media and Topologies	17%
Domain 4.0 Network Management	20%
Domain 5.0 Network Security	19%

How to Become CompTIA Certified

This training material can help you prepare for and pass a related CompTIA certification exam or exams. To achieve CompTIA certification, you must register for and pass a CompTIA certification exam or exams.

To become CompTIA certified, you must:

1. Select a testing center and certification exam provider. For more information, please visit the following Web site: *http://certification.comptia.org/getCertified/steps_to_certification.aspx*
2. Register for and schedule a time to take the CompTIA certification exam(s) at a convenient location.
3. Take and pass the CompTIA certification exam(s).

For more information about CompTIA's certifications, such as their industry acceptance, benefits, or program news, please visit *http://certification.comptia.org/getCertified*

CompTIA is dedicated to advancing industry growth through its educational programs, market research, networking events, professional certifications, and public policy advocacy.

CompTIA is a not-for-profit information technology trade association. CompTIA's certifications are designed by subject matter experts from across the IT industry. Each CompTIA certification is vendor neutral, covers multiple technologies, and requires demonstration of skills and knowledge widely sought after by the IT industry.

To contact CompTIA with any questions or comments, please call 866-835-8020, ext. 2 or visit the Customer Support Center on the CompTIA Web site at *www.comptia.org/contactus.aspx*.

Network+ Test Preparation Materials

CompTIA Network+ N10-005 In Depth is packed with tools to help students prepare for CompTIA's N10-005 Network+ exam, released in 2011. This book includes the Network+ icon in the margins highlighting relevant content, a table in Appendix A explaining where each exam objective is covered in the book, and a 100-question practice exam in Appendix B.

About the Author

Tamara Dean has worked in the field of networking for nearly 20 years, most recently as a networking consultant, and before that, as the manager of Internet services and data center operations for a regional ISP. She has managed LANs at the University of Wisconsin and at a pharmaceutical firm, worked as a telecommunications analyst for the FCC, and cofounded a local radio station. Well-published in networking, Ms. Dean also authored *Guide to Telecommunications Technology* for Cengage Learning.

Acknowledgments

As with any large undertaking, this book is the result of many contributions and collaborative efforts. It would not exist without the help of friends, family, fellow networking professionals, and Course Technology/Cengage Learning staff. I'm again indebted to Nick Lombardi, Acquisitions Editor, and Stephen Helba, Executive Editor, for championing this book. Thanks to Michelle Ruelos Cannistraci, Senior Product Manager, and Andrea Majot, Senior Content Product Manager, for coordinating all aspects of the book's production and making sure it advanced swiftly and smoothly. Many thanks to Ann Shaffer, Developmental Editor and friend, for juggling multiple deadlines with grace and for insisting on coherence, clarity, and precision throughout each draft. Thanks to Susan Pedicini, Quality Assurance expert, for scrutinizing every page with stunning attention to detail and alerting me to errors and inconsistencies. With this edition, I am indebted to Reddy Sreemannarayana and Suwathiga Velayutham of Integra Communications, who guided the book from final edits to finished product, and to Copy Editor Karen Annett for watching all the details. Thanks to Abby Reip for obtaining photos and permissions.

I'm also grateful to instructors who have used this text and offered suggestions for improvement: Tom Gibson – Wichita Technical Institute, Nancy Jones – Coastline College, Katherine Oser – Central Texas College, Jane Perschbach – Central Texas College, Stephan Shelton – Wichita Technical Institute, and Richard Smolenski – Westwood College.

For sharing their expertise, thanks to networking professionals Marcin Antkiewicz, Michael Bleacher, Martin Brown, David Butcher, Peyton Engel, Todd Fisher Wallin, Tom Johnson, Thom Jones, Brooke Noelke, Jane Perschbach, Jeff Shuckra, Paul Snapp, and Greg Tomsho. Thanks to Paul and Janet Dean for encouragement and support. My deepest gratitude goes to David Klann, who generously offered suggestions and always, with good cheer, paused his Perl scripting for impromptu discussions of esoteric networking topics.

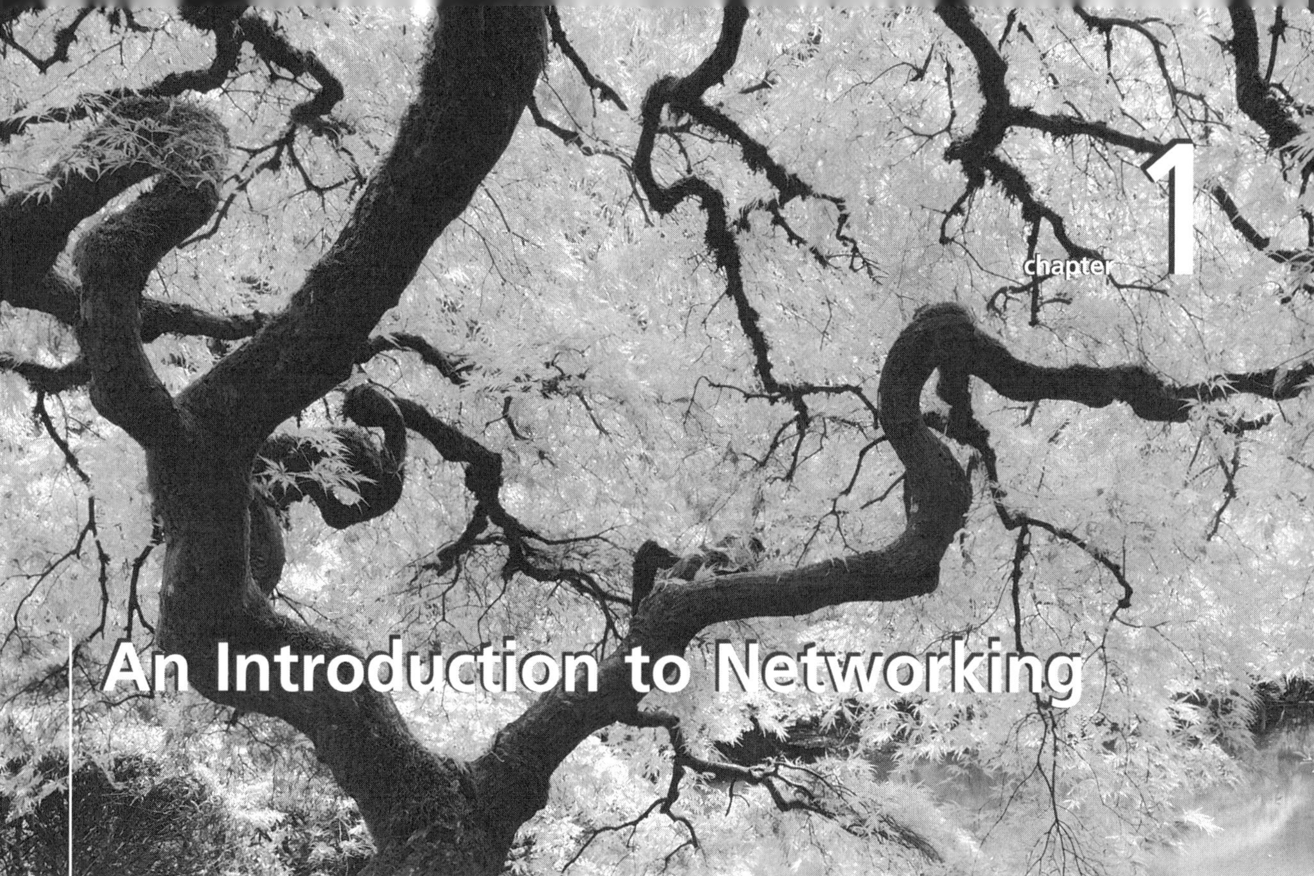

After reading this chapter and completing the exercises, you will be able to:

- List the advantages of networked computing relative to stand-alone computing
- Distinguish between client/server and peer-to-peer networks
- List elements common to all client/server networks
- Describe several specific uses for a network
- Identify some of the certifications available to networking professionals
- Identify the kinds of skills and specializations that will help you excel as a networking professional

I was the chief information officer for a large political research firm that served the president of the United States. I was also teaching at a local community college as an adjunct. Some students just stood out. They were hungry for knowledge. After 15 years of teaching, I could spot the other kind—students who were just there for a grade. Those students seemed to think they didn't have to work hard in school because they would learn what they needed on the job. Others really wanted to get their money's worth out of school and learn all they could.

I noticed one student who was always the last one out of class because she was trying to solve some problem or another. The material wasn't coming easy to her, but I could tell she was curious, and that meant that she was learning things she hadn't intended to learn. I hired her to work for the political research firm because she never rested until she solved any problem she set out to resolve. Before she even finished college, she was making $45,000 a year at her new job. She was the hardest working member of my staff and I constantly gave her new responsibilities.

After only two years, I left to go to another company, but I didn't worry about leaving because I knew my former student could handle it. She became the youngest CIO in the history of the firm. Hard work and a lust for learning were the keys to her success.

Michael Bleacher
Assistant Dean, School of Technology and School of Business
Westwood College

Loosely defined, a **network** is a group of computers and other devices (such as printers) that are connected by some type of transmission media. Variations on the elements of a network and the way it is designed, however, are nearly infinite. A network can be as small as two computers connected by a cable in a home office or as large as several thousand computers connected across the world via a combination of cable, phone lines, and cellular links. In addition to connecting personal computers, networks might link mainframe computers, printers, plotters, fax machines, and phone systems. They might communicate through copper wires, fiber-optic cable, or radio waves. This chapter introduces you to the fundamental characteristics of networks.

Why Use Networks?

Using networks offers advantages relative to using a **stand-alone computer**—that is, a computer that is not connected to other computers and that uses software applications and data stored on its local disks. Most important, networks enable multiple users to share devices

(for example, printers) and data (such as spreadsheet files), which are collectively known as the network's **resources**. Sharing devices saves money. For example, rather than buying 20 printers for 20 staff members, a company can buy one printer and have those 20 staff members share it over a network. Sharing devices also saves time. For example, it's faster for coworkers to share data over a network than to copy data to a removable storage device and physically transport the storage device from one computer to another—an outdated file-sharing method commonly referred to as a **sneakernet** (presumably because people wore sneakers when walking from computer to computer). Before networks, transferring data via floppy disks was the only possible way to share data.

Networks also allow you to manage, or administer, resources on multiple computers from a central location. Imagine you work in the Information Technology (IT) Department of a multinational bank and must verify that each of 5000 employees around the globe uses the same version of a database program. Without a network, you would have to visit every employee's machine to check and install the proper software. With a network, however, you could provide employees with access to the database program on a single computer using a Web page. Because they allow you to share devices and administer computers centrally, networks increase productivity. It's not surprising, then, that virtually all organizations depend on their networks to stay competitive.

Types of Networks

Computers can be positioned on a network in different ways relative to each other. They can have different levels of control over shared resources. They can also be made to communicate and share resources according to different schemes. The following sections describe two fundamental network models: peer-to-peer and client/server.

Net+

Peer-to-Peer Networks

3.5 The simplest form of a network is a **peer-to-peer network**. In a peer-to-peer network, every computer can communicate directly with every other computer. By default, no computer on a peer-to-peer network has more authority than another. However, each computer can be configured to share only some of its resources and prevent access to other resources. Traditional peer-to-peer networks typically consist of two or more general-purpose personal computers, with modest processing capabilities. Every computer is capable of sending and receiving information to and from every other computer, as shown in Figure 1-1.

The following are advantages of using traditional peer-to-peer networks:

- They are simple to configure. For this reason, they may be used in environments in which time or technical expertise is scarce.
- They are often less expensive to set up and maintain than other types of networks. This fact makes them suitable for environments in which saving money is critical.

The following are disadvantages of using traditional peer-to-peer networks:

- They are not very flexible. As a peer-to-peer network grows larger, adding or changing significant elements of the network may be difficult.

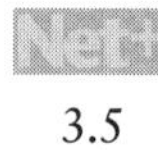
3.5

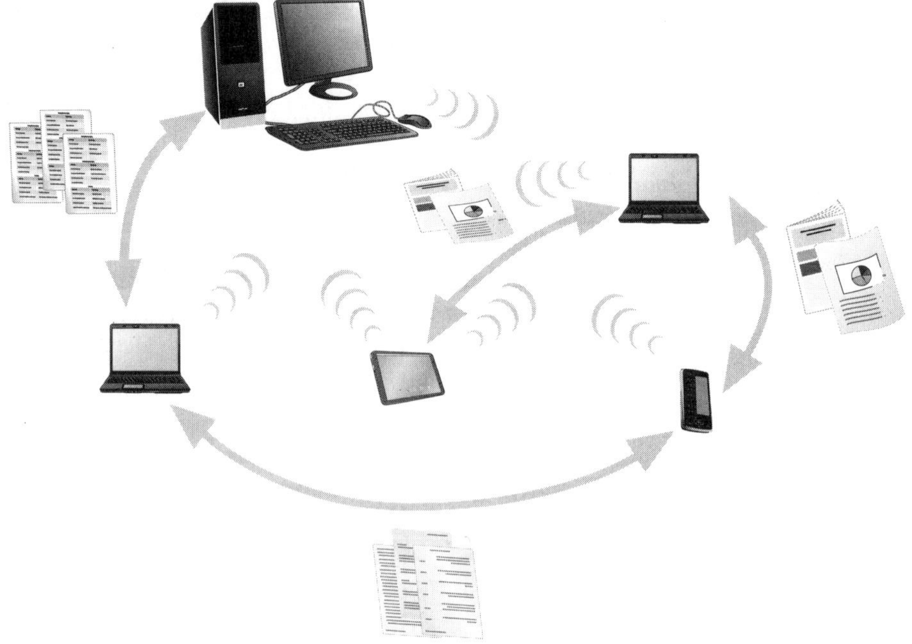

Figure 1-1 Resource sharing on a simple peer-to-peer network

- They are also not necessarily secure—meaning that in simple installations, data and other resources shared by network users can be easily discovered and used by unauthorized people.
- They are not practical for connecting more than a handful of computers because they do not always centralize resources.

For example, if your computer is part of a peer-to-peer network that includes five other computers, and computer users store their spreadsheets and word-processing files on their own hard disks, whenever your colleagues want to edit your files, they must access your machine on the network. If one colleague saves a changed version of one of your spreadsheets on her hard disk, you'll find it difficult to keep track of which version is the most current. As you can imagine, the more computers you add to a peer-to-peer network, the more difficult it becomes to find and manage resources.

A common way to share resources on a peer-to-peer network is by modifying the file-sharing controls via the computer's operating system. For example, you could choose to create a directory on your computer's hard disk called "SharedDocs" and then configure the directory to allow all networked computers to read its files. On a peer-to-peer network, each user is responsible for configuring her computer to allow access to certain resources and prevent access to others. In other words, resource sharing is not controlled by a central computer or authority. Because access depends on many different users, it might not be uniform or secure.

Although traditional peer-to-peer networks are typically small and contained within a home or office, examples of very large peer-to-peer networks have emerged to take advantage of the Internet. These newer types of peer-to-peer networks (commonly called **P2P networks**)

3.5 link computers from around the world to share files between each others' hard disks. Unlike the older style of peer-to-peer network, they require specialized software (besides the computer's operating system) to allow resource sharing. Examples of these networks include Gnutella, Bitcoin, and the original Napster. In 2001, Napster, which allowed users around the globe to share music files, was forced to cease operation due to charges of copyright infringement from musicians and music producers. Later, the service was redesigned to provide legitimate music file-sharing services. A company called BitTorrent has made a unique high-speed peer-to-peer communications method (also called BitTorrent) the foundation of its business. The company specializes in allowing companies and individuals to share video, audio, software, and games over the Internet. Although BitTorrent's peer-to-peer technology is legal, its use for distributing illegal or copyrighted materials has generated several lawsuits against the company.

Client/Server Networks

Another way of designing a network is to use a central computer, known as a **server**, to facilitate communication and resource sharing between other computers on the network, which are known as **clients**. Clients take the form of personal computers, also known as **workstations**, or mobile devices, such as smartphones. A network that uses a server to enable clients to share data, data storage space, and devices is known as a **client/server network**. The term **client/server architecture** is sometimes used to refer to the design of a network in which clients rely on servers for resource sharing and processing.

In terms of resource sharing and control, you can compare the client/server network with a public library. Just as a librarian manages the use of books and other media by patrons, a server manages the use of shared resources by clients. For example, if a patron does not have the credentials to check out books, the librarian prevents the patron from doing so. Similarly, a server allows only authorized clients to access its resources.

Every computer on a client/server network acts as a client or a server. (It is possible, but uncommon, for some computers to act as both.) Clients on a network can still run applications from and save data to their local hard disk. But by connecting to a server, they also have the option of using shared applications, data, and devices. Clients on a client/server network do not share their resources directly with each other, but rather use the server as an intermediary. Clients and servers communicate through connectivity devices such as switches or routers. These devices are covered in detail in Chapter 6.

Figure 1-2 illustrates how resources are shared on a client/server network.

To function as a server, a computer must be running an **NOS (network operating system)**.

An NOS is a special type of software designed to do the following:

- Manage data and other resources for a number of clients.
- Ensure that only authorized users access the network.
- Control which type of files a user can open and read.
- Restrict when and from where users can access the network.
- Dictate which rules computers will use to communicate.
- Supply applications to clients.

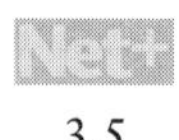
3.5

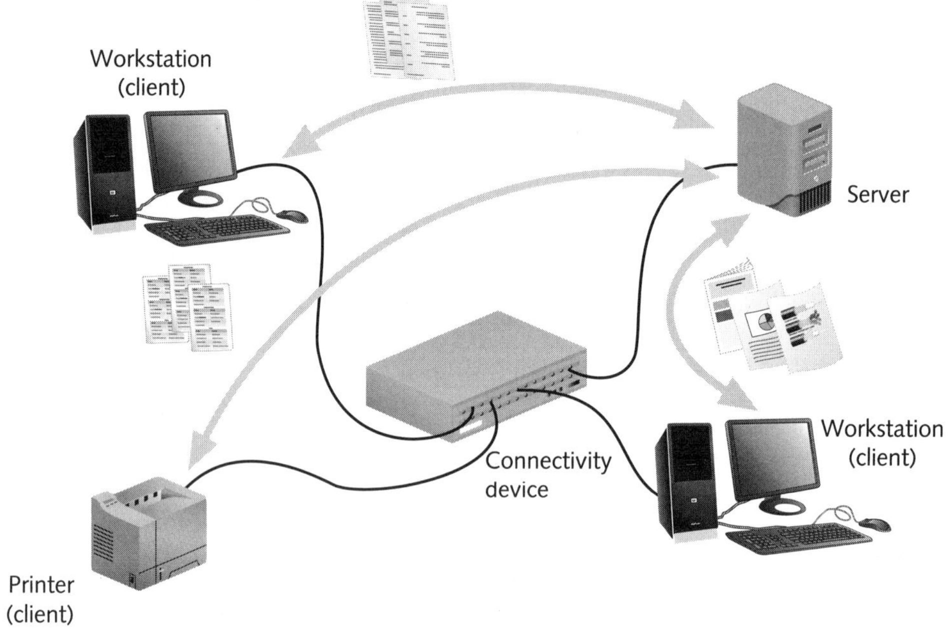

Figure 1-2 Resource sharing on a client/server network

Examples of popular network operating systems include various forms of UNIX and Linux, Microsoft Windows Server 2008 R2, and Mac OS X Server. By contrast, a stand-alone computer, or a client computer, uses an operating system, such as Windows 7 or a version of Linux, UNIX, or Mac OS, and has authority for managing resources on other computers.

Usually, servers have more memory, processing, and storage capacity than clients. They may even be equipped with special hardware designed to provide network management functions beyond that provided by the network operating system. For example, a server might contain an extra hard disk and specialized software so that if the primary hard disk fails, the secondary hard disk automatically takes its place.

Although client/server networks are typically more complex in their design and maintenance than peer-to-peer networks, they offer many advantages over peer-to-peer networks, such as:

- User logon accounts and passwords for anyone on a server-based network can be assigned in one place.
- Access to multiple shared resources (such as data files or printers) can be centrally granted to a single user or groups of users.
- Problems on the network can be monitored, diagnosed, and often fixed from one location.
- Servers are optimized to handle heavy processing loads and dedicated to handling requests from clients, enabling faster response time.
- Because of their efficient processing and larger disk storage, servers can connect more than a handful of computers on a network.

3.5 Together, these advantages make client/server networks easier to manage, more secure, and more powerful than peer-to-peer networks. They are also more **scalable** than peer-to-peer networks. In other words, it is easier to add computers and other devices to a client/server network.

Because client/server networks are by far the most popular type of network, most of the concepts covered in this book and on the Network+ exam pertain to client/server networks. Next, you will learn how networks are classified according to size.

LANs, MANs, and WANs

As its name suggests, a **LAN (local area network)** is a network of computers and other devices that is confined to a relatively small space, such as one building or even one office. Small LANs first became popular in the early 1980s. At that time, LANs might have consisted of a handful of computers connected in a peer-to-peer fashion. Today's LANs are typically much larger and more complex client/server networks.

Often, separate LANs are interconnected and rely on several servers running many different applications and managing resources other than data. For example, imagine an office building in which each of a company's departments runs its own LAN and all the LANs are connected. This network may contain dozens of servers, hundreds of workstations, and several shared storage devices, printers, plotters, fax machines, and even telephone interfaces. Figure 1-3 roughly depicts this type of network (in reality, the network would probably contain many more clients). As you progress through this book, you will learn about the devices on this network and how they communicate. After completing this book, you'll understand how to integrate clients, servers, and connectivity devices so as to create networks that are reliable, secure, and manageable.

Networks may extend beyond the boundaries of a building. A network that is larger than a LAN and connects clients and servers from multiple buildings—for example, a handful of government offices surrounding a state capitol building—is known as a **MAN (metropolitan area network)**. Because of the distance it covers, a MAN may use different transmission technology and media than a LAN.

A network that connects two or more geographically distinct LANs or MANs is called a **WAN (wide area network)**. Because such networks carry data over longer distances than LANs, WANs may use different transmission methods and media than LANs. Most MANs can also be described as WANs; in fact, network engineers are more likely to refer to all networks that cover a broad geographical range as WANs.

WANs commonly connect separate offices in the same organization, whether they are across town or across the world from each other. For example, imagine you work for a nationwide plumbing supply company that keeps its inventory in warehouses in Topeka, Kansas, and Panama City, Florida. Suppose also that the company's headquarters is located in New York. When a customer calls and asks whether you have five faucets of a certain type available to ship overnight, you need to check the inventory databases for both the Topeka and Panama City warehouses. Thanks to your WAN, the data are accessible from your New York desktop. Twice a day, the warehouses' inventory software automatically updates a database located on a central server in New York via WAN links that connect the locations.

WANs are also used to connect LANs that belong to different organizations. For example, all the public universities within a state might combine and share their resources via a WAN. The largest and most varied WAN in the world is the **Internet**. Figure 1-4 depicts a simple WAN.

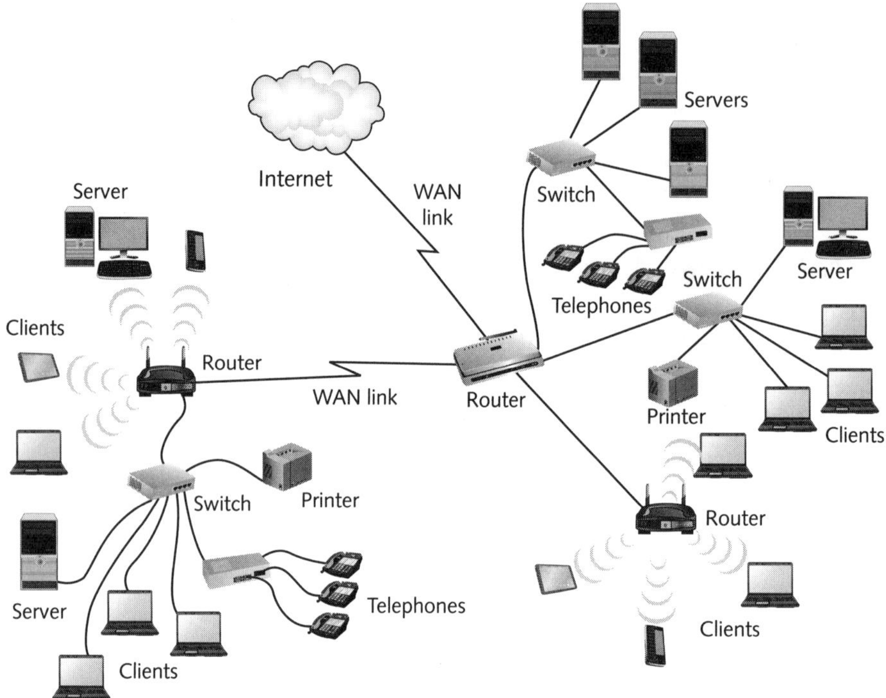

Figure 1-3 Interconnected LANs

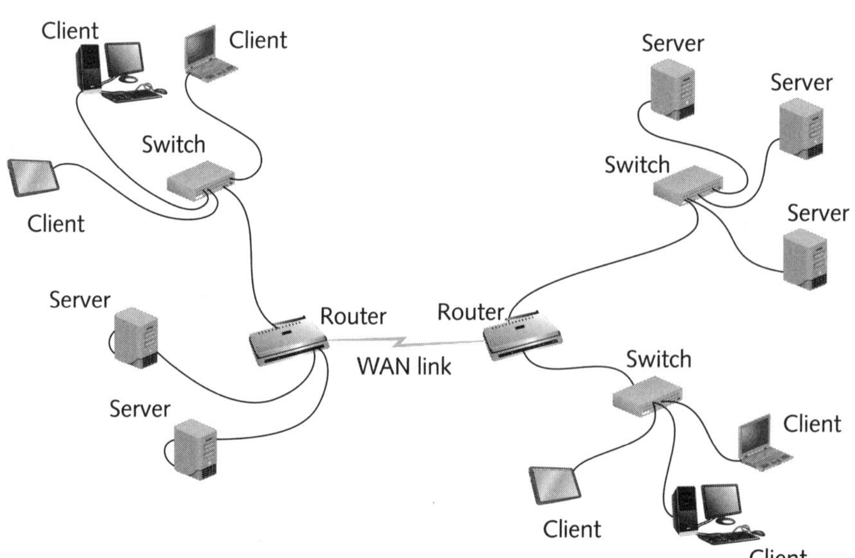

Figure 1-4 A simple WAN

Elements Common to Client/Server Networks

3.5

You have learned that networks, no matter how simple or complex, provide some benefits over stand-alone computers. They also share terminology and common building blocks, some of which you have already encountered. The following list provides a more complete rundown of basic elements common to all client/server networks. You will learn more about these topics throughout this book:

- *Client*—A computer on the network that requests resources or services from another computer on a network; in some cases, a client could also act as a server. The term client may also refer to the human **user** of a client workstation or to client software installed on the workstation.
- *Server*—A computer on the network that manages shared resources; servers usually have more processing power, memory, and hard disk space than clients. They run network operating software that can manage not only data, but also users, groups, security, and applications on the network.
- *Workstation*—A personal computer (such as a desktop or laptop), which may or may not be connected to a network; most clients are workstation computers.
- *NIC (network interface card)*—The device (pronounced *nick)* inside a computer that connects a computer to the network media, thus allowing it to communicate with other computers; many companies (such as Intel, Linksys, and Netgear) manufacture NICs, which come with a variety of specifications that are tailored to the requirements of the workstation and the network. Some connect to the **motherboard**, which is the main circuit that controls the computer, some are integrated as part of the motherboard, and others connect via an external port. NICs are also known as **network adapters**. Figure 1-5 depicts a NIC connected to a computer's motherboard.

Because different PCs and network types require different kinds of NICs, you cannot assume that a NIC that works in one workstation will work in another.

Figure 1-5 A NIC (network interface card)

3.5

- *NOS (network operating system)*—The software that runs on a server and enables the server to manage data, users, groups, security, applications, and other networking functions. Examples include various types of UNIX and Linux operating systems, Microsoft Windows Server 2008 R2, and Mac OS X Server.
- *Host*—A computer that enables resource sharing by other computers on the same network.
- *Node*—A client, server, or other device that can communicate over a network and that is identified by a unique number, known as its network **address**.
- *Connectivity device*—A specialized device that allows multiple networks or multiple parts of one network to connect and exchange data. A small client/server network can operate without connectivity devices. However, medium- and large-sized LANs use them to extend the network and to connect with WANs. WANs use them to connect with the Internet and with other WANs.
- *Segment*—A part of a network. Usually, a segment is composed of a group of nodes that use the same communications channel for all their traffic.
- *Backbone*—The part of a network to which segments and significant shared devices (such as routers, switches, and servers) connect. A backbone is sometimes referred to as "a network of networks" because of its role in interconnecting smaller parts of a LAN or WAN. Figure 1-6 shows a LAN with its backbone highlighted in yellow.
- *Topology*—The physical layout of a computer network. Topologies vary according to the needs of the organization and available hardware and expertise. Networks can be arranged in a ring, bus, or star formation, and the star formation is the most common. Hybrid combinations of these patterns are also possible. Figure 1-7 illustrates these network topologies, which you must understand to design and troubleshoot networks.
- *Protocol*—A standard method or format for communication between networked devices. For example, some protocols ensure that data are transferred in sequence and without error from one node on the network to another. Other protocols

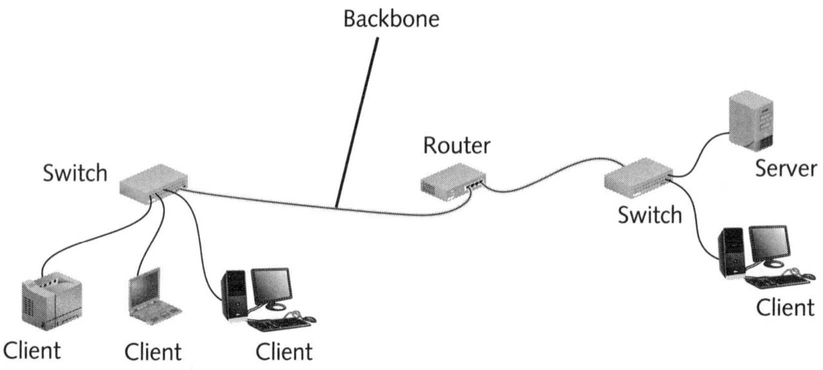

Figure 1-6 A LAN backbone

Net+
3.5

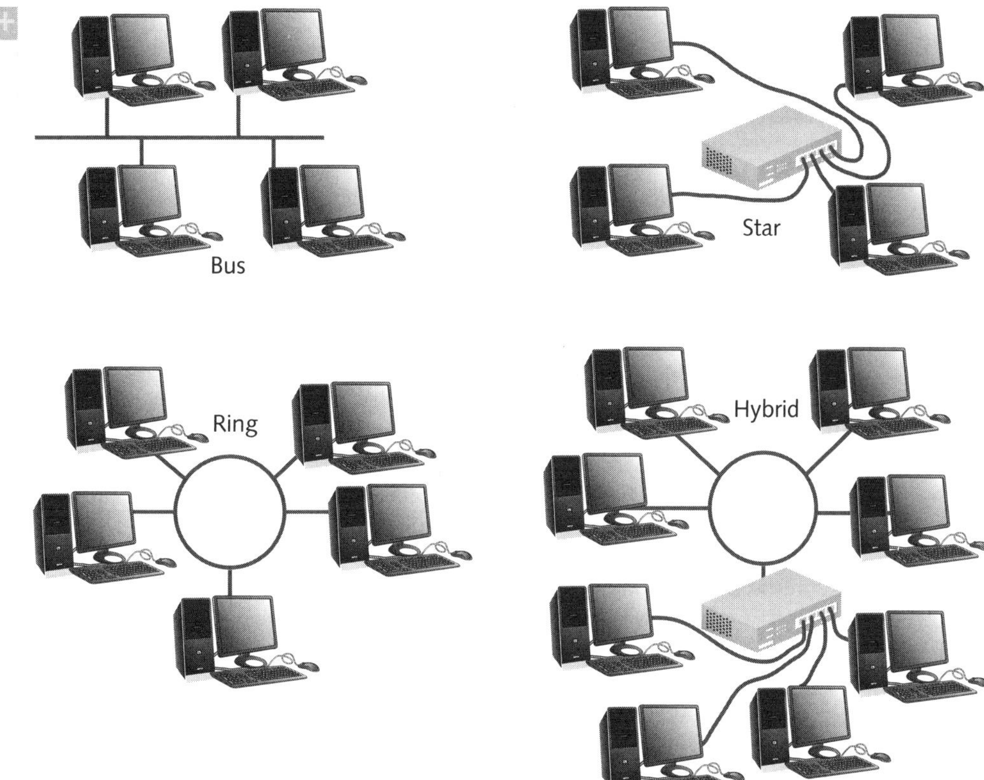

Figure 1-7 Common network topologies

ensure that data belonging to a Web page are formatted to appear correctly in a Web browser window. Still others encode passwords and keep data transmissions secure.

- *Packet*—A distinct unit of data exchanged between nodes on a network. Breaking a large stream of data into many packets allows a network to deliver that data more efficiently and reliably.
- *Addressing*—The scheme for assigning a unique identifying number to every node on the network. The type of addressing used depends on the network's protocols and network operating system. Each network device must have a unique address so that data can be transmitted reliably to and from that device.
- *Transmission media*—The means through which data are transmitted and received. Transmission media may be physical, such as wire or cable, or atmospheric (wireless), such as radio waves. Figure 1-8 shows several examples of transmission media. Chapter 3, which explains physical transmission media in detail, offers additional images of network cabling.

Now that you are familiar with basic network terminology, you are ready to appreciate the many uses of computer networks.

Net+ 3.5

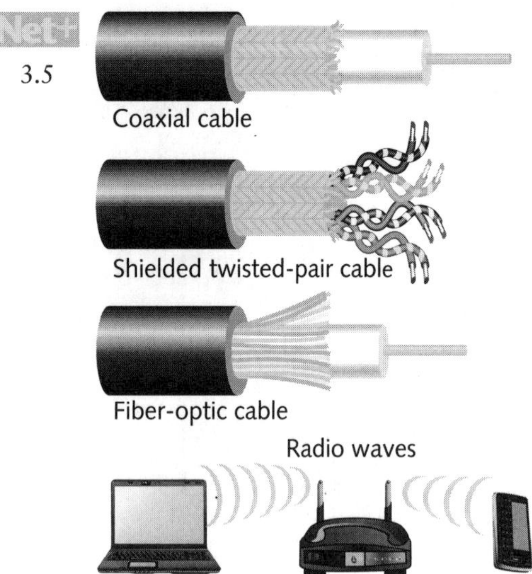

Figure 1-8 Examples of network transmission media

How Networks Are Used

The functions provided by a network are usually referred to as **network services**. Any network manager will tell you that the network service with the highest visibility is e-mail. If your company's e-mail system fails, users will notice within minutes—and they will not be shy about informing you of the failure. Although e-mail may be the most visible network service, other services can be just as vital. Printer sharing, file sharing, Internet access and Web site delivery, remote access capabilities, the provision of voice (telephone) and video services, and network management are all critical business functions provided through networks. In large organizations, separate servers may be dedicated to performing each of these functions. In offices with only a few users and little network traffic, one server may perform all functions.

File and Print Services

The term **file services** refers to a server's ability to share data files, applications (such as word-processing or spreadsheet programs), and disk storage space. A server that provides file services is called a **file server**. File services accounted for the first use of networks and remain the foundation of networking today, for a number of reasons. As mentioned earlier, it is easier and faster to store shared data at a central location than to copy files to disks and then pass the disks around. Data stored at a central location is typically more secure because a network administrator can take charge of backing up this data, rather than relying on individual users to make their own copies. In addition, using a file server to run applications for multiple users requires the purchase of fewer copies of the application and less maintenance work for the network administrator.

Using **print services** to share printers across a network also saves time and money. A high-capacity printer can cost thousands of dollars, but can handle the printing tasks of an entire

department, thereby eliminating the need to buy a desktop printer for each worker. With one printer, less time is spent on maintenance and management. If a shared printer fails, the network administrator can diagnose the problem from a workstation anywhere on the network using the network operating system's printer control functions. Often, the administrator can solve the problem without even visiting the printer.

Access Services

A network's access services allow remote users to connect to the network. (The term **remote user** refers to a person working on a computer on a different network or in a different geographical location from the LAN's server.) Less frequently, access services allow network users to connect to machines outside the network. Most network operating systems include built-in access services that enable users to dial in to a **remote access server**, log on to the network, and take advantage of the network just as if they were logged on to a workstation on the office LAN. A remote access server may also be known as simply an **access server**.

Organizations might use access services to provide LAN connectivity for workers at home, workers on the road, and workers at small satellite offices where dedicated WAN connections are not cost effective. In addition, access services can allow staff from other organizations (such as a software or hardware vendor) to help diagnose a network problem. For example, suppose you work for a clothing manufacturer that uses embroidery software to control the machines that sew insignias on shirts and hats. You are an expert on networking, but less adept with the automated embroidery software. When the software causes problems, you turn to the software vendor for help. But suppose the vendor's technician can't solve the problem except by logging on to your network. In that case, it is much more efficient and less expensive to allow the technician to dial in to your network through a remote access server than to fly the technician to your office.

It is important to remember that remote access servers—no matter which platform (hardware or operating system software) they run on—allow external users to use network resources and devices just as if they were logged on to a workstation in the office. From a remote location, users can print files to shared printers, log on to hosts, retrieve mail from an internal messaging system, or run queries on internal databases. Because they can be accessed by the world outside the local network, remote access servers necessitate strict security measures.

Communications Services

Today's networks can help users communicate in many ways: e-mail, telephone, video, fax, cell phone, smartphone (for example, an iPhone), and personal digital assistant (for example, a BlackBerry). Using the same network to deliver multiple types of communications services is known as **convergence**. A similar term, **unified communications**, refers to the centralized management of multiple network-based communications. For example, your company might use one software program to manage intraoffice phone calls, long-distance phone calls, cell phone calls, voice mail, faxes, and text messaging for all the users on your network. Chapter 12 describes how networks deliver these services.

The oldest network communications services are **mail services**, which coordinate the storage and transfer of e-mail between users on a network. The computer responsible for mail services is called a **mail server**. Mail servers are usually connected to the Internet, but when clients only need to exchange e-mail within their organization, their mail server may be isolated on their LAN.

In addition to simply sending, receiving, and storing mail, mail servers can do the following:

- Intercept or filter unsolicited e-mail, known as **spam**.
- Find objectionable content in e-mails and do something about that content, such as flagging it to make the recipient aware of it.
- Route messages according to particular rules. For example, if a technical support representative has not opened a customer's message within 15 minutes of delivery, a mail server could automatically forward the message to a supervisor.
- Provide a Web-based client for checking e-mail.
- Notify administrators or users if certain events occur, such as a user's mailbox exceeding its maximum amount of space on a server.
- Schedule e-mail transmission, retrieval, storage, and maintenance functions.
- Communicate with mail servers on other networks so that mail can be exchanged between users who do not connect to the same LAN.

To supply these services, a mail server runs specialized mail server software, examples of which include Sendmail and Microsoft Exchange Server. Because of their critical nature and heavy use, maintaining a mail server in any sizable organization requires a significant commitment of technical support and administration resources.

Internet Services

You have probably connected to the Internet without knowing or caring about all of the services running behind the scenes. But in fact, many servers are working together to bring Web pages to your desktop. For example, a **Web server** is a computer installed with the appropriate software to supply Web pages to many different clients upon demand. The most popular Web server software is Apache. It's used to deliver more than 60 percent of Web pages on the Internet.

Supplying Web pages is only one type of Internet service. Other **Internet services** include file transfer capabilities, Internet addressing schemes, security filters, and a means for directly logging on to other computers on the Internet.

Management Services

When networks were small and simple, a single network administrator could manage the entire network. For instance, suppose a user called to report a problem logging on to the network and that the administrator diagnosed the problem as an addressing conflict (that is, two workstations having the same network address). In a very small network, the conflicting workstations might be located right around the corner from each other, and one address could be changed quickly. In another example, if a manager needed to report the number of copies of Adobe Photoshop in use in a certain department, the network administrator could probably get the desired information by just walking through the department and checking the various workstations.

As networks grow larger and more complex, however, they become more difficult to manage. Using network management services can help you keep track of a large network. Network **management services** centrally administer management tasks on the network, such as ensuring that no more than 20 workstations are using Adobe Photoshop at one time in an organization

that purchased a 20-user license for the software. Some organizations dedicate a number of servers to network management functions, with each server performing only one or two unique services.

Numerous services fall under the category of network management. Some of the most important ones include the following:

- ***Traffic monitoring*** *and control*—Determining how much **traffic**, or data transmission activity, is taking place on a network and notifying administrators when the network becomes overloaded. In general, the larger the network, the more critical it is to monitor traffic.
- ***Load balancing***—Distributing data transfer activity evenly so that no single device becomes overwhelmed. Load balancing is especially important for networks in which it's difficult to predict the number of requests that will be issued to a server, as is the case with Web servers.
- *Hardware diagnosis and failure alert*—Determining when a network component fails and automatically notifying the network administrator through an e-mail or text message.
- ***Asset management***—Collecting and storing data on the number and types of software and hardware assets in an organization's network. With asset management software, a server can electronically examine each client's software and hardware and automatically save the data in a database. Other types of assets might be identified and tracked using RFID (Radio Frequency Identification) tags, which emit a wireless signal at all times. Wireless detection devices connected to a network can track the locations of RFID-tagged devices. For example, a hospital might use RFID tags to keep track of the wheelchairs, beds, and IV pumps that circulate throughout its campus. Before asset management services, inventory data had to be gathered manually and typed into spreadsheets.
- ***License tracking***—Determining how many copies of a single application are currently in use on the network and ensuring that number does not exceed the number of licenses purchased. This information is important for legal reasons, as software companies are vigilant about illegally copying software or using more than the authorized number of copies.
- ***Security auditing***—Evaluating what security measures are currently in force and notifying the network administrator if a security breach occurs.
- ***Software distribution***—Automatically transferring a file or installing an application from the server to a client on the network. The installation process can be started from either the server or the client. Several options are available when distributing software, such as warning users about updates, writing changes to a workstation's system files, and restarting the workstation after the update.
- ***Address management***—Centrally managing a finite number of network addresses for an entire network. Usually this task can be accomplished without manually modifying the client workstation configurations.
- ***Backup and restoration of data***—Backing up critical data files to a secure storage area and then restoring data if the original files are lost or deleted. Often backups are performed according to a formulaic schedule. Backup and data restoration services

provide centralized management of data backup on multiple servers and on-demand restoration of files and directories.

Network management services will be covered in depth later in the book. For now, it is enough to be aware of the variety of services and the importance of this growing area of networking.

Becoming a Networking Professional

If you search online employment services, you'll probably find hundreds of postings for computer professionals. Of course, the level of expertise required for each of these jobs differs. Some companies simply need "warm bodies" to ensure that a higher-level engineer is notified if a critical network segment fails; other companies are looking for people to plan their global information technology strategies. Needless to say, the more extensive your skills, the better your chances for landing a lucrative and interesting job in networking. To prepare yourself to enter this job market, master a number of general networking technologies. Only then should you pick a few areas that interest you and study those specialties. Hone your communication and teamwork skills, and stay abreast of emerging technologies. Consider the tremendous advantages of attaining professional certification and getting to know others in your field. The following sections offer suggestions on how to approach a career in networking.

Mastering the Technical Challenges

Although computer networking is a varied field, some general technical skills will serve you well no matter which specialty you choose. Because you are already interested in computers, you probably enjoy an aptitude for logical and analytical thinking. You probably also want to acquire these skills:

- Installing, configuring, and troubleshooting network server software and hardware
- Installing, configuring, and troubleshooting network client software and hardware
- Understanding the characteristics of different transmission media
- Understanding network design
- Understanding network protocols
- Understanding how users interact with the network
- Constructing a network with clients, servers, media, and connectivity devices

Because you can expand your networking knowledge in almost any direction, you should pay attention to the general skills that interest you most, then pick one or two of those areas and concentrate on them. The following specialties are currently in high demand:

- Network security
- Convergence (the delivery of voice, video, and data over a single network)
- In-depth knowledge about one or more NOSs: UNIX, Linux, Mac OS X Server, or Microsoft Windows Server 2008 R2
- Network management

- Wireless network design
- Configuration and optimization of routers and switches
- Centralized data storage and management for large-scale environments

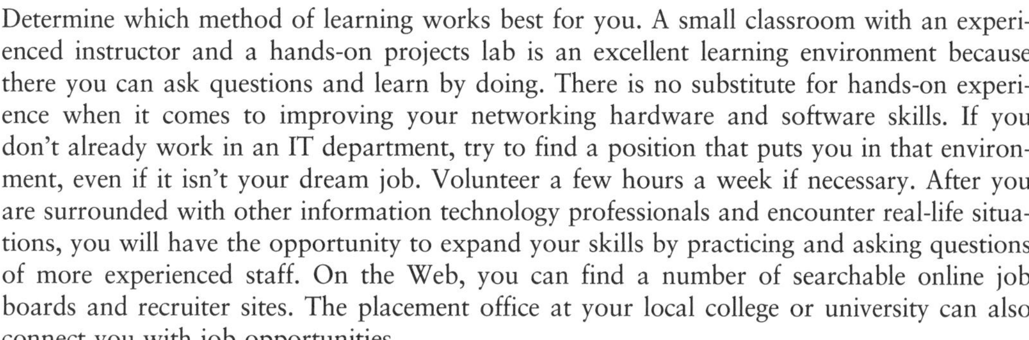
Determine which method of learning works best for you. A small classroom with an experienced instructor and a hands-on projects lab is an excellent learning environment because there you can ask questions and learn by doing. There is no substitute for hands-on experience when it comes to improving your networking hardware and software skills. If you don't already work in an IT department, try to find a position that puts you in that environment, even if it isn't your dream job. Volunteer a few hours a week if necessary. After you are surrounded with other information technology professionals and encounter real-life situations, you will have the opportunity to expand your skills by practicing and asking questions of more experienced staff. On the Web, you can find a number of searchable online job boards and recruiter sites. The placement office at your local college or university can also connect you with job opportunities.

Developing Your Soft Skills

Knowing how to configure a router or install UNIX will serve you well, but advanced soft skills will help you stand out. The term **soft skills** refers to those skills that are not easily measurable, such as customer relations, oral and written communications, dependability, teamwork, and leadership abilities. Some soft skills might appear to be advantages in any profession, but they are especially important when you must work in teams, in challenging technical circumstances, and under tight deadlines—requirements that apply to most networking projects. For this reason, soft skills merit closer examination:

- *Customer relations*—Perhaps one of the most important soft skills, customer relations involve an ability to listen to customers' frustrations and desires and then empathize, respond, and guide customers to their goals without acting arrogant. Bear in mind that some of your customers will not appreciate or enjoy technology as much as you do, and they will value your patience as you help them. The better your customer relations, the more respected and popular you will be as a network professional.
- *Oral and written communications*—You may understand the most complicated technical details about a network, but if you cannot communicate them to colleagues and clients, the significance of your knowledge is diminished. Imagine that you are a networking consultant who is competing with several other firms to overhaul a metropolitan hospital's network, a project that could generate millions of dollars for your company. You may have designed the best solution and have it clearly mapped out in your head, but your plan is useless if you can't describe it clearly. The hospital's planning committee will accept whichever proposal makes the most sense to them—that is, the proposal whose suggestions and justifications are plainly communicated.
- *Dependability*—This characteristic will help you in any career. However, in the field of networking, where breakdowns or glitches can occur at any time of day or night and only a limited number of individuals have the expertise to fix them, being dependable is critical. Your career will benefit when you are the one who is available to address a problem, even if you don't always know the answer immediately.

- *Teamwork*—Individual computer professionals often have strong preferences for a certain type of hardware or software. Some technical people like to think that they have all of the answers. For these and other reasons, teamwork in IT departments is sometimes lacking. To be the best networking professional in your department, you must be open to new ideas, encourage cooperation among your colleagues, and allow others to help you and make suggestions.
- *Leadership abilities*—As a networking professional, you will sometimes need to make difficult or unpopular decisions under pressure. You may need to persuade opinionated colleagues to try a new product, tell a group of angry users that what they want is not possible, or manage a project with nearly impossible budgetary and time restrictions. In all of these situations, you will benefit from having strong leadership skills.

After your career in networking begins, you will discover which soft skills you already possess and which ones you need to cultivate. The important thing is that you realize the importance of these attributes and are willing to devote the time necessary to develop them.

Pursuing Certification

Certification is the process of mastering material pertaining to a particular hardware system, operating system, programming language, or software application, then proving your mastery by passing a series of exams. Certification programs are developed and administered either by a manufacturer or a professional organization such as **CompTIA** (**Computing Technology Industry Association**). You can pursue a number of different certifications, depending on your specialty interest. For example, if you want to become a PC technician, you should attain **A+** certification. If you want to specialize in Microsoft product support and development, pursue **MCITP** (**Microsoft Certified IT Professional**) certification. To specialize in the configuration and management of Cisco Systems' switches and routers, work toward Cisco's **CCNA** (**Cisco Certified Network Associate**) or go for their most difficult and prestigious distinction, **CCIE** (**Cisco Certified Internetwork Expert**) certification, which requires candidates to pass lab exams. To prove a mastery of many aspects of networking, you can choose to become Network+ certified. **Network+** (**Net+**) is a professional certification established by CompTIA that verifies broad, vendor-independent networking technology skills, such as an understanding of protocols, topologies, networking hardware, and network troubleshooting. Network+ may also be a stepping stone to more advanced certifications. The material in this book addresses the knowledge objectives you must understand to qualify for Network+ certification.

Certification is a popular career development tool for job seekers and a measure of an employee's qualifications for employers. Following are a list of benefits to becoming certified:

- *Better salary*—Professionals with certification can usually ask for higher salaries than those who aren't certified. Employers will also want to retain certified employees, especially if they helped pay for their training, and will offer incentives to keep certified professionals at the company.
- *Greater opportunities*—Certification may qualify you for additional degrees or more advanced technical positions.

- *Professional respect*—After you have proven your skills with a product or system, your colleagues and clients will gain great respect for your ability to solve problems with that system or product. They will therefore feel confident asking you for help.
- *Access to better support*—Many manufacturers reward certified professionals with less-expensive, more detailed, and more direct access to their technical support.

Finding a Job in Networking

With the proper credentials and demonstrated technical knowledge, you will qualify for a multitude of positions in networking. For this reason, you can and must be selective when searching for a job. Following are some ways to research your possibilities:

- *Search the Web*—Because your job will deal directly with technology, it makes sense to use technology to find it. Companies in the computer industry recruit intensively on the Web, either through searchable job databases or through links on their company Web sites. Most job database Web sites do not charge for their services, but may require you to register with them. One popular general Web job database is Monster at *www.monster.com*. IT-specific job sites include Dice at *www.dice.com*, Slashdot Jobs at *jobs.slashdot.org*, and *computerjobs.com*. A simple Web search could yield dozens more.
- *Check your local newspaper's Web site*—Although many employers list job openings through national online services, some with specific, local opportunities might advertise only in a local or regional newspaper's online classifieds. It's worth checking the Web site of your newspaper for these types of listings.
- *Visit a career center*—Regardless of whether you are a registered university or college student, you can use career center services to find a list of job openings in your area. Companies that are hiring pay much attention to the collegiate career centers because of the number of job seekers served by these centers. Visit the college or university campus nearest you and search through its career center listings.
- *Network*—Find like-minded professionals with whom you can discuss job possibilities. You may meet these individuals through training classes, conferences, professional organizations, or career fairs. Let them know that you are looking for a job, and specify exactly what kind of job you want. If they can't suggest any leads for you, ask these people if they have other colleagues who might.
- *Attend career fairs*—Most metropolitan areas host career fairs for job seekers in the information technology field, and some large companies host their own job fairs. Even if you aren't sure you want to work for any of the companies represented at a job fair, attend the job fair to research the market. You can find out which skills are in high demand in your area and which types of companies are hiring the most networking professionals. You can also meet other people in your field who may offer valuable advice based on their employment experience.
- *Enlist a recruiter*—Many recruiting agencies deal strictly with clients in the technical fields. By signing up with such a recruiting agency, you may have access to job opportunities that you didn't know existed. You might also take advantage of a temporary assignment, to see if the fit between you and an employer is mutually beneficial, before accepting a permanent job with that employer.

Joining Professional Associations

Joining an organization can connect you with people who have similar interests, provide new opportunities for learning, allow you to access specialized information, and give you more tangible assets such as free goods. Specifically, a networking professional organization might offer its own publications, technical workshops and conferences, free software, prerelease software, and access to expensive hardware labs.

You can choose from several prominent professional organizations in the field of networking. Because the field has grown so quickly, with so many areas in which to specialize, no single professional organization stands out as the most advantageous or highly respected. You will have to decide whether an organization is appropriate for you. Among other things, you will want to consider the organization's total membership, membership benefits, membership dues, technical emphasis, and whether it hosts a local chapter. Many organizations host student chapters on university campuses. You may also want to find a professional association that caters to your demographic group (such as Women in Technology International, if you are female). Table 1-1 lists some professional organizations and their Web sites.

Table 1-1 Some networking organizations

Professional organization	Web site
Association for Computing Machinery (ACM)	www.acm.org
Association of Information Technology Professionals	www.aitp.org
IEEE Computer Society	www.computer.org
Network Professional Association	www.npanet.org
Women in Technology International (WITI)	www.witi.org

Chapter Summary

- A network is a group of computers and other devices (such as printers) that are connected by some type of transmission media, such as copper or fiber-optic cable or radio waves, in the case of wireless transmission.
- All networks offer advantages relative to using a stand-alone computer. Networks enable multiple users to share devices and data. Sharing resources saves time and money. Networks also allow you to manage, or administer, resources on multiple computers from a central location.
- In a peer-to-peer network, every computer can communicate directly with every other computer. By default, no computer on a peer-to-peer network has more authority than another. However, each computer can be configured to share only some of its resources and keep other resources inaccessible.
- Traditional peer-to-peer networks are usually simple and inexpensive to set up. However, they are not necessarily flexible or secure.

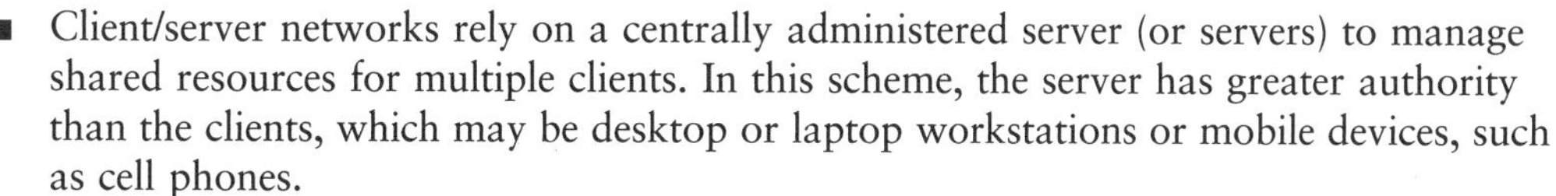

- Client/server networks rely on a centrally administered server (or servers) to manage shared resources for multiple clients. In this scheme, the server has greater authority than the clients, which may be desktop or laptop workstations or mobile devices, such as cell phones.
- Client/server networks are more complex and expensive to install than peer-to-peer networks. However, they are more easily managed, more scalable, and typically more secure. They are by far the most popular type of network in use today.
- Servers typically possess more processing power, hard disk space, and memory than client computers. To manage access to and use of shared resources, among other centralized functions, a server requires a network operating system.
- A LAN (local area network) is a network of computers and other devices that is confined to a relatively small space, such as one building or even one office.
- LANs can be interconnected to form WANs (wide area networks), which traverse longer distances and may use different transmission methods and media than LANs. The Internet is the largest example of a WAN.
- Client/server networks share some common elements, including clients, servers, workstations, transmission media, connectivity devices, protocols, addressing, topology, NICs, packets, network operating systems, hosts, backbones, segments, and nodes.
- Networks provide a wide range of services, including printing, file sharing, Internet access, remote access, communicating in multiple forms, and network management.
- File and print services provide the foundation for networking. They enable multiple users to share data, applications, storage areas, and printers.
- Networks use access services to allow remote users to connect to the network or network users to connect to machines outside the network.
- Communications services provided by networks include e-mail, telephone, video, fax, messaging, and voice mail.
- Mail services (running on mail servers) allow users on a network to exchange and store e-mail. Most mail packages also provide filtering, routing, scheduling, notification, and connectivity with other mail systems.
- Internet services such as Web servers and browsers, file transfer capabilities, addressing schemes, and security filters enable organizations to connect to and use the global Internet.
- Network management services centrally administer and simplify complicated management tasks on the network, such as asset management, security auditing, hardware problem diagnosis, backup and restore services, license tracking, load balancing, and data traffic control.
- To prepare yourself for a networking career, master a number of broad networking skills, such as installing and configuring client and server hardware and software. Then pick a few areas that interest you, such as network security or voice/data integration, and study those specialties.
- Certification is the process of mastering material pertaining to a particular hardware system, operating system, programming language, or other software program, then proving your mastery by passing a series of exams. The benefits of certification can

include a better salary, more job opportunities, greater professional respect, and better access to technical support.

- To excel in the field of networking, hone your soft skills, such as customer relations, oral and written communications, dependability, teamwork, and leadership abilities.
- Joining an association for networking professionals can connect you with like-minded people, give you access to workshops and technical publications, allow you to receive discounted or free software, and perhaps even help you find a job in the field.

Key Terms

A+ The professional certification established by CompTIA that verifies knowledge about PC operation, repair, and management.

access server *See* remote access server.

address A number that uniquely identifies each workstation and device on a network. Without unique addresses, computers on the network could not reliably communicate.

address management The process of centrally administering a finite number of network addresses for an entire LAN. Usually this task can be accomplished without touching the client workstations.

addressing The scheme for assigning a unique identifying number to every workstation and device on the network. The type of addressing used on a network depends on its protocols and network operating system.

asset management The process of collecting and storing data on the number and types of software and hardware assets in an organization's network. The data collection is automated by electronically examining each network client from a server.

backbone The part of a network to which segments and significant shared devices (such as routers, switches, and servers) connect. A backbone is sometimes referred to as "a network of networks" because of its role in interconnecting smaller parts of a LAN or WAN.

backing up The process of copying critical data files to a secure storage area. Often, backups are performed according to a formulaic schedule.

CCIE (Cisco Certified Internetwork Expert) An elite certification that recognizes expert-level installation, configuration, management, and troubleshooting skills on networks that use a range of Cisco Systems' devices.

CCNA (Cisco Certified Network Associate) A professional certification that attests to one's skills in installing, configuring, maintaining, and troubleshooting medium-sized networks that use Cisco Systems' switches and routers.

certification The process of mastering material pertaining to a particular hardware system, operating system, programming language, or other software program, then proving your mastery by passing a series of exams.

Cisco Certified Internetwork Expert *See* CCIE.

Cisco Certified Network Associate *See* CCNA.

client A computer on the network that requests resources or services from another computer on a network. In some cases, a client could also act as a server. The term *client* may also refer to the user of a client workstation or a client software application installed on the workstation.

client/server architecture A network design in which client computers use a centrally administered server to share data, data storage space, and devices.

client/server network A network that uses centrally administered computers, known as servers, to enable resource sharing for and to facilitate communication between the other computers on the network.

CompTIA (Computing Technology Industry Association) An association of computer resellers, manufacturers, and training companies that sets industry-wide standards for computer professionals. CompTIA established and sponsors the A+ and Network+ (Net+) certifications.

Computing Technology Industry Association *See* CompTIA.

connectivity device One of several types of specialized devices that allows two or more networks or multiple parts of one network to connect and exchange data.

convergence The use of data networks to carry voice (or telephone), video, and other communications services in addition to data.

file server A specialized server that enables clients to share applications and data across the network.

file services The functions of a file server that allow users to share data files, applications, and storage areas.

host A computer that enables resource sharing by other computers on the same network.

Internet A complex WAN that connects LANs and clients around the globe.

Internet services The services that enable a network to communicate with the Internet, including Web servers and browsers, file transfer capabilities, Internet addressing schemes, security filters, and a means for directly logging on to other computers.

LAN (local area network) A network of computers and other devices that is confined to a relatively small space, such as one building or even one office.

license tracking The process of determining the number of copies of a single application that are currently in use on the network and whether the number in use exceeds the authorized number of licenses.

load balancing The process of distributing data transfer activity evenly so that no single device is overwhelmed.

local area network *See* LAN.

mail server A server that manages the storage and transfer of e-mail messages.

mail services The network services that manage the storage and transfer of e-mail between users on a network. In addition to sending, receiving, and storing mail, mail services can include filtering, routing, notification, scheduling, and data exchange with other mail servers.

MAN (metropolitan area network) A network that is larger than a LAN, typically connecting clients and servers from multiple buildings, but within a limited geographic area. For example, a MAN could connect multiple city government buildings around a city's center.

management services The network services that centrally administer and simplify complicated management tasks on the network. Examples of management services include license tracking, security auditing, asset management, address management, software distribution, traffic monitoring, load balancing, and hardware diagnosis.

MCITP (Microsoft Certified IT Professional) A professional certification established by Microsoft that demonstrates in-depth knowledge about Microsoft products.

metropolitan area network *See* MAN.

Microsoft Certified IT Professional *See* MCITP.

motherboard The main circuit board that controls a computer.

network A group of computers and other devices (such as printers) that are connected by and can exchange data via some type of transmission media, such as a cable, a wire, or the atmosphere.

network adapter *See* NIC.

Network+ (Net+) The professional certification established by CompTIA that verifies broad, vendor-independent networking technology skills, such as an understanding of protocols, topologies, networking hardware, and network troubleshooting.

network interface card *See* NIC.

network operating system *See* NOS.

network services The functions provided by a network.

NIC (network interface card) The device that enables a workstation to connect to the network and communicate with other computers. NICs are manufactured by several different companies and come with a variety of specifications that are tailored to the workstation's and the network's requirements. NICs are also called network adapters.

node A computer or other device connected to a network, which has a unique address and is capable of sending or receiving data.

NOS (network operating system) The software that runs on a server and enables the server to manage data, users, groups, security, applications, and other networking functions. The most popular network operating systems are UNIX, Linux, and Microsoft Windows Server 2008 R2.

P2P network *See* peer-to-peer network.

packet A discrete unit of information sent from one node on a network to another.

peer-to-peer network A network in which every computer can communicate directly with every other computer. By default, no computer on a peer-to-peer network has more authority than another. However, each computer can be configured to share only some of its resources and keep other resources inaccessible to other nodes on the network.

print services The network service that allows printers to be shared by several users on a network.

protocol A standard method or format for communication between network devices. For example, some protocols ensure that data are transferred in sequence and without error from one node on the network to another. Other protocols ensure that data belonging to a Web page are formatted to appear correctly in a Web browser window. Still others encode passwords and keep data transmissions secure.

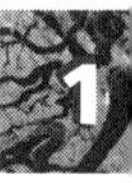

remote access server A server that runs communications services that enable remote users to log on to a network. Also known as an access server.

remote user A person working on a computer on a different network or in a different geographical location from the LAN's server.

resources The devices, data, and data storage space provided by a computer, whether stand-alone or shared.

restoring The process of retrieving files from a backup. It is necessary to restore files if the original files are lost or deleted.

scalable The property of a network that allows you to add nodes or increase its size easily.

security auditing The process of evaluating security measures currently in place on a network and notifying the network administrator if a security breach occurs.

segment A part of a network. Usually, a segment is composed of a group of nodes that share the same communications channel for all their traffic.

server A computer on the network that manages shared resources. Servers usually have more processing power, memory, and hard disk space than clients. They run network operating software that can manage not only data, but also users, groups, security, and applications on the network.

sneakernet A way of exchanging data between computers that are not connected on a network. The term "sneakernet" was coined before the widespread use of networks, when data was copied from a computer to a removable storage device such as a floppy disk, carried (presumably by someone wearing sneakers) to another computer, then copied from the storage device onto the second computer.

soft skills The skills such as customer relations, oral and written communications, dependability, teamwork, and leadership abilities, which are not easily measured, but are nevertheless important in a networking career.

software distribution The process of automatically transferring a data file or installing a software application from the server to a client on the network.

spam Unsolicited, unwanted e-mail.

stand-alone computer A computer that uses applications and data only from its local disks and that is not connected to a network.

topology The physical layout of computers on a network.

traffic The data transmission and processing activity taking place on a computer network at any given time.

traffic monitoring The process of determining how much data transfer activity is taking place on a network or network segment and notifying administrators when a segment becomes overloaded.

transmission media The means through which data are transmitted and received. Transmission media may be physical, such as wire or cable, or wireless, such as radio waves.

unified communications The centralized management of multiple types of network-based communications, such as voice, video, fax, and messaging services.

user A person who uses a computer.

WAN (wide area network) A network that spans a long distance and connects two or more LANs.

Web server A computer that manages Web site services, such as supplying a Web page to multiple users on demand.

wide area network *See* WAN.

workstation A computer that runs a desktop operating system and connects to a network.

Review Questions

1. Which of the following enables multiple users to share devices and data?
   a. Workstations
   b. Clients
   c. Stand-alone computers
   d. Networks
2. What network design offers simplicity in configuration and low costs to set up and maintain?
   a. Client/server
   b. Peer-to-peer
   c. Bus topology
   d. Wide area network (WAN)
3. Which of the following is an advantage of a client/server network?
   a. They are simple to configure.
   b. They can connect more than a handful of computers on a network.
   c. They are often suitable for environments in which saving money is critical.
   d. They avoid scalability.
4. What term describes the phenomenon of offering multiple types of communications services on the same network?
   a. Unified communications
   b. Convergence
   c. Hybrid network topology
   d. Client/server architecture
5. Which network function is the oldest and still most frequently used?
   a. Internet services
   b. Print services
   c. Remote access services
   d. Mail services

6. True or false? The simplest form of a network is a client/server network.
7. True or false? A segment is part of a network usually composed of a group of nodes that use the same communications channel for all their traffic.
8. True or false? General technical skills are not useful in assisting networking professionals who choose to specialize in a particular area.
9. True or false? Soft skills refer to those skills that are easily measurable.
10. True or false? The Association for Computing Machinery (ACM) is the most advantageous and highly respected professional organization in the industry today.
11. A(n) ________________ is a group of computers and other devices that are connected by some type of transmission media.
12. In a(n) ________________ network, every computer can communicate directly with every other computer.
13. Client/server networks are more ________________ than peer-to-peer networks, meaning client/server networks can be more easily added onto and extended than peer-to-peer networks.
14. The functions provided by a network are usually referred to as ________________.
15. The process of proving your mastery in material pertaining to a particular hardware system, operating system, programming language, or software application by passing a series of exams is known as ________________.

chapter 2

Networking Standards and the OSI Model

After reading this chapter and completing the exercises, you will be able to:

- Identify organizations that set standards for networking
- Describe the purpose of the OSI model and each of its layers
- Explain specific functions belonging to each OSI model layer
- Understand how two network nodes communicate through the OSI model
- Discuss the structure and purpose of data packets and frames
- Describe the two types of addressing covered by the OSI model

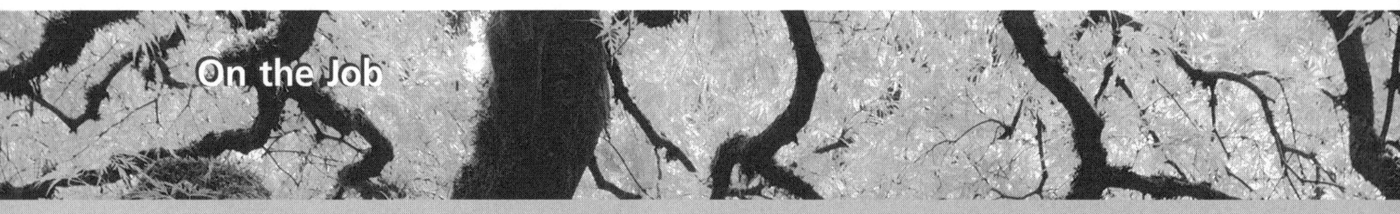

On the Job

While I was working as a junior project manager in the Technology Solutions Department for a large corporation, I was assigned to work on a network infrastructure project. At the time, I had no training as a network engineer, and was instead responsible for small- to medium-sized technology projects as they related to a business unit that spanned five states. For this new project, our goal was to change the network's topology in a way that would allow the network to grow over time for the least amount of money, and to keep the network up-to-date with the latest trends within the industry.

As with most projects, a budget was set at the beginning. This budget allowed us to hire a professional vendor to complete the wiring and cabling installations. The network engineers who worked for the vendor were experts on everything related to wiring and cabling. However, before they could get very far, our budget was aggressively reduced. Suddenly, we could no longer afford the cabling experts. Instead, senior managers decided that work would be completed by our company's own junior IT technicians, people who were better suited to printer paper jam resolution than recabling an entire network. They knew nothing about hierarchical cable structure, maximum cable distances, or endpoint terminations.

This ignorance of basic networking standards had dire consequences on our project's budget and timeline. But the problem wasn't just that the IT people doing the work lacked the proper knowledge. As the project manager, with no systematic knowledge of networking standards, I was also hampered in my ability to keep things on track.

Part of a successful project manager's job is recognizing the need for subject matter experts, or at least being able to understand where to find key pieces of information related to the project and then interpreting that information as it relates to the project. In my case, a simple understanding of a set of telecommunications standards, or TIA/EIA-568, would have been indispensable in completing the network topology change project.

Our in-house team began the project on a vacant floor that was to become new employee office space. We unknowingly exceeded cable runs, terminated wall outlet connection points incorrectly, and generally did a poor installation job. Only after new client computers were installed and exhibited a variety of connection issues did we realize our installation was most likely the culprit. We soon understood that our lack of prior planning and our ignorance of industry standards were to blame. Through painful trial and error, we gained an in-depth knowledge of telecommunications structured cabling and the tools needed to implement a network topology change, but with the cost of this knowledge was a lot of time on a ladder removing ceiling tiles and working late into the night to ensure clients were able to effectively run their applications at the start of the next workday.

Tom Johnson
Segment Account Manager, Defense Industry

When trying to grasp a new theoretical concept, it often helps to form a picture of that concept in your mind. In the field of chemistry, for example, even though you can't see a water molecule, you can represent it with a simple drawing of two hydrogen atoms and one oxygen atom. Similarly, in the field of networking, even though you can't see the communication that occurs between two nodes on a network, you can use a model to depict how the communication takes place. The model commonly used to describe network communications is called the OSI (Open Systems Interconnection) model.

In this chapter, you will learn about the standards organizations that have helped create the various conventions (such as the OSI model) used in networking. Next, you'll be introduced to the seven layers of the OSI model and learn how they interact. You will then take a closer look at what goes on in each layer. Finally, you will learn to apply those details to a practical networking environment. Granted, learning the OSI model is not the most exciting part of becoming a networking expert. Thoroughly understanding it, however, is essential to proficient network design and troubleshooting.

Networking Standards Organizations

Standards are documented agreements containing technical specifications or other precise criteria that stipulate how a particular product or service should be designed or performed. Many different industries use standards to ensure that products, processes, and services suit their purposes. For example, the construction industry follows standards to ensure a building's safety and accessibility, such as those defining the width and slope of wheelchair ramps. The airline industry adheres to standards that specify the precise contents of jet fuel.

Because of the wide variety of hardware and software in use today, standards are especially important in the world of networking. Without standards, it would be very difficult to design a network because you could not be certain that software or hardware from different manufacturers would work together. For example, if one manufacturer designed a network cable with a 1-centimeter-wide plug and another company manufactured a wall plate with a 0.8-centimeter-wide opening, you would not be able to insert the plug into the wall plate.

When purchasing networking equipment, therefore, you want to verify that equipment meets the standards your network requires. However, bear in mind that standards define the *minimum* acceptable performance of a product or service—not the ideal. So, for example, you might purchase two different network cables that comply with the minimum standard for transmitting at a certain speed, but one cable might exceed that standard, allowing for better network performance. In the case of network cables, exceeding minimum standards often follows from the use of quality materials and careful production techniques.

Because the computer industry grew so quickly out of several technical disciplines, many different organizations evolved to oversee its standards. In some cases, a few organizations are responsible for a single aspect of networking. For example, both the American National Standards Institute (ANSI) and IEEE are involved in setting standards for wireless networks. Whereas ANSI prescribes the kind of NIC (network interface card) that the consumer needs to accept a wireless connection, IEEE prescribes, among other things, how the network will ensure that different parts of a communication sent through the atmosphere arrive at their destination in the correct sequence.

A complete list of the standards that regulate computers and networking would fill an encyclopedia. Although you don't need to know the fine points of every standard, you should be familiar with the groups that set networking standards and the critical aspects of standards required by your network.

ANSI

ANSI (American National Standards Institute) is an organization composed of more than a thousand representatives from industry and government who together determine standards for the electronics industry and other fields, such as chemical and nuclear engineering, health and safety, and construction. ANSI also represents the United States in setting international standards. This organization does not dictate that manufacturers comply with its standards, but requests voluntarily compliance. Of course, manufacturers and developers benefit from compliance, because compliance assures potential customers that the systems are reliable and can be integrated with an existing infrastructure. New electronic equipment and methods must undergo rigorous testing to prove they are worthy of ANSI's approval.

You can purchase ANSI standards documents online from ANSI's Web site *(www.ansi.org)* or find them at a university or public library. You need not read complete ANSI standards to be a competent networking professional, but you should understand the breadth and significance of ANSI's influence.

EIA and TIA

Two related standards organizations are EIA and TIA. **EIA (Electronic Industries Alliance)** is a trade organization composed of representatives from electronics manufacturing firms across the United States. EIA not only sets standards for its members, but also helps write ANSI standards and lobbies for legislation favorable to the growth of the computer and electronics industries.

In 1988, one of the EIA's subgroups merged with the former United States Telecommunications Suppliers Association (USTSA) to form **TIA (Telecommunications Industry Association).** TIA focuses on standards for information technology, wireless, satellite, fiber optics, and telephone equipment. Both TIA and EIA set standards, lobby governments and industry, and sponsor conferences, exhibitions, and forums in their areas of interest.

Probably the best known standards to come from the TIA/EIA alliance are its guidelines for how network cable should be installed in commercial buildings, known as the "TIA/EIA 568-B Series." You'll learn about following these guidelines while terminating cables in Chapter 3. You can find out more about TIA from its Web site, *www.tiaonline.org,* and EIA from its Web site, *www.eia.org.*

IEEE

The **IEEE (Institute of Electrical and Electronics Engineers)**, or "I-triple-E," is an international society composed of engineering professionals. Its goals are to promote development and education in the electrical engineering and computer science fields. To this end, IEEE hosts numerous symposia, conferences, and local chapter meetings and publishes papers designed to educate members on technological advances. It also maintains a standards board that establishes its own standards for the electronics and computer industries and contributes to the work of other standards-setting bodies, such as ANSI.

IEEE technical papers and standards are highly respected in the networking profession. Among other places, you will find references to IEEE standards in the manuals that accompany NICs. You can purchase IEEE documents online from IEEE's Web site (*www.ieee.org*) or find them in a university or public library.

ISO

ISO (**International Organization for Standardization**), headquartered in Geneva, Switzerland, is a collection of standards organizations representing 162 countries. ISO's goal is to establish international technological standards to facilitate global exchange of information and barrier-free trade. Given the organization's full name, you might expect it to be called *IOS,* but ISO is not meant to be an acronym. In fact, *iso* is the Greek word for *equal.* Using this term conveys the organization's dedication to standards.

ISO's authority is not limited to the information-processing and communications industries. It also applies to the fields of textiles, packaging, distribution of goods, energy production and utilization, shipbuilding, and banking and financial services. The universal agreements on screw threads, bank cards, and even the names for currencies are all products of ISO's work. In fact, fewer than 3000 of ISO's more than 18,500 standards apply to computer-related products and functions. You can find out more about ISO at its Web site: *www.iso.org.*

ITU

The **ITU** (**International Telecommunication Union**) is a specialized United Nations agency that regulates international telecommunications, including radio and TV frequencies, satellite and telephony specifications, networking infrastructure, and tariffs applied to global communications. It also provides developing countries with technical expertise and equipment to advance those nations' technological bases.

The ITU was founded in Paris in 1865. It became part of the United Nations in 1947 and relocated to Geneva, Switzerland. Its standards arm contains members from 193 countries and publishes detailed policy and standards documents that can be found on its Web site: *www.itu.int.* Typically, ITU documents pertain more to global telecommunications issues than to industry technical specifications. However, the ITU is deeply involved with the implementation of worldwide Internet services. As in other areas, the ITU cooperates with several different standards organizations, such as ISOC (discussed next), to develop these standards.

ISOC

ISOC (**Internet Society**), founded in 1992, is a professional membership society that helps to establish technical standards for the Internet. Some current ISOC concerns include the rapid growth of the Internet and keeping it accessible, information security, and the need for stable addressing services and open standards across the Internet. ISOC's membership consists of more than 44,000 Internet professionals from over 80 chapters around the world.

ISOC oversees groups with specific missions, such as the **IAB** (**Internet Architecture Board**). IAB is a technical advisory group of researchers and technical professionals interested in overseeing the Internet's design and management. As part of its charter, IAB is responsible for Internet growth and management strategy, resolution of technical disputes, and standards oversight.

Another ISOC group is the **IETF (Internet Engineering Task Force)**, the organization that sets standards for how systems communicate over the Internet—in particular, how protocols operate and interact. Anyone can submit a proposed standard for IETF approval. The standard then undergoes elaborate review, testing, and approval processes. On an international level, IETF works with the ITU to help give technical standards approved in the United States international acceptance. You can learn more about ISOC and its member organizations, IAB and IETF, at their Web site: *www.isoc.org*.

IANA and ICANN

You have learned that every computer on a network must have a unique address. On the Internet, this is especially important because millions of different computers must be available to transmit and receive data at any time. Addresses used to identify computers on the Internet and other TCP/IP-based networks are known as **IP (Internet Protocol) addresses.** To ensure that every Internet-connected device has a unique IP address, organizations across the globe rely on centralized authorities.

In early Internet history, a nonprofit group called the **IANA (Internet Assigned Numbers Authority)** kept records of available and reserved IP addresses and determined how addresses were doled out. Starting in 1997, IANA coordinated its efforts with three **RIRs (Regional Internet Registries)**: ARIN (American Registry for Internet Numbers), APNIC (Asia Pacific Network Information Centre), and RIPE (Reseaux IP Europeens). An RIR is a not-for-profit agency that manages the distribution of IP addresses to private and public entities. In the late 1990s, the United States Department of Commerce (DOC), which funded IANA, decided to overhaul IP addressing and domain name management. The DOC recommended the formation of **ICANN (Internet Corporation for Assigned Names and Numbers)**, a private, nonprofit corporation. ICANN is now ultimately responsible for IP addressing and domain name management. Technically speaking, however, IANA continues to perform the system administration.

Individuals and businesses do not typically obtain IP addresses directly from an RIR or IANA. Instead, they lease a group of addresses from their **ISP (Internet service provider)**, a business that provides organizations and individuals with access to the Internet and often, other services, such as e-mail and Web hosting. An ISP, in turn, arranges with its RIR for the right to use certain IP addresses on its network. The RIR obtains its right to dole out those addresses from ICANN. In addition, the RIR coordinates with IANA to ensure that the addresses are associated with devices connected to the ISP's network. You can learn more about IANA and ICANN at their Web sites, *www.iana.org* and *www.icann.org*, respectively.

The OSI Model

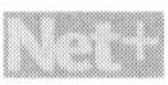
1.1

In the early 1980s, ISO began work on a universal set of specifications that would enable computer platforms across the world to communicate openly. The result was a helpful model for understanding and developing computer-to-computer communications over a network. This model, called the **OSI (Open Systems Interconnection) model,** divides network communications into seven layers: Physical, Data Link, Network, Transport, Session, Presentation, and Application. At each layer, protocols perform services unique to that layer. While performing

those services, the protocols also interact with protocols in the layers directly above and below. In addition, at the top of the OSI model, Application layer protocols interact with the software
1.1 you use (such as an e-mail or spreadsheet program). At the bottom, Physical layer services act on the networking cables and connectors to issue and receive signals.

You have already learned that protocols are the rules by which computers communicate. A protocol is simply a set of instructions written by a programmer to perform a function or group of functions. Some protocols are included with a computer's operating system. Others are files installed with software programs. Chapter 4 covers protocols in depth; however, some protocols are briefly introduced in the following sections to better explain what happens at each layer of the OSI model.

The OSI model is a theoretical representation of what happens between two nodes communicating on a network. It does not prescribe the type of hardware or software that should support each layer. Nor does it describe how software programs interact with other software programs or how software programs interact with humans. Every process that occurs during network communications can be associated with a layer of the OSI model, so you should be familiar with the names of the layers and understand the key services and protocols that belong to each.

Networking professionals often devise a mnemonic way of remembering the seven layers of the OSI model. One strategy is to make a sentence using words that begin with the same first letter of each layer, starting with either the lowest (Physical) or the highest (Application) layer. For example, you might choose to remember the phrase "Programmers Dare Not Throw Salty Pretzels Away." Quirky phrases are often easiest to remember.

The path that data takes from one computer to another through the OSI model is illustrated in Figure 2-1. First, a user or device initiates a data exchange through the Application layer. The Application layer separates data into **PDUs (protocol data units)**, or discrete amounts of data. From there, Application layer PDUs progress down through OSI model layers 6, 5, 4, 3, 2, and 1 before being issued to the network medium—for example, the wire. The data traverses the network until it reaches the second computer's Physical layer. Then at the receiving computer the data progresses up the OSI model until it reaches the second computer's Application layer. This transfer of information happens in milliseconds.

Logically, however, each layer communicates with the same layer from one computer to another. In other words, the Application layer protocols on one computer exchange information with the Application layer protocols of the second computer. Protocols from other layers do not attempt to interpret Application layer data. In the following sections, the OSI model layers are discussed from highest to lowest, beginning with the Application layer, where the flow of information is initiated.

Bear in mind that the OSI model is a generalized and sometimes imperfect representation of network communication. In some cases, network functions can be associated with more than one layer of the model, and in other cases, network operations do not require services from every layer.

Net+ 1.1

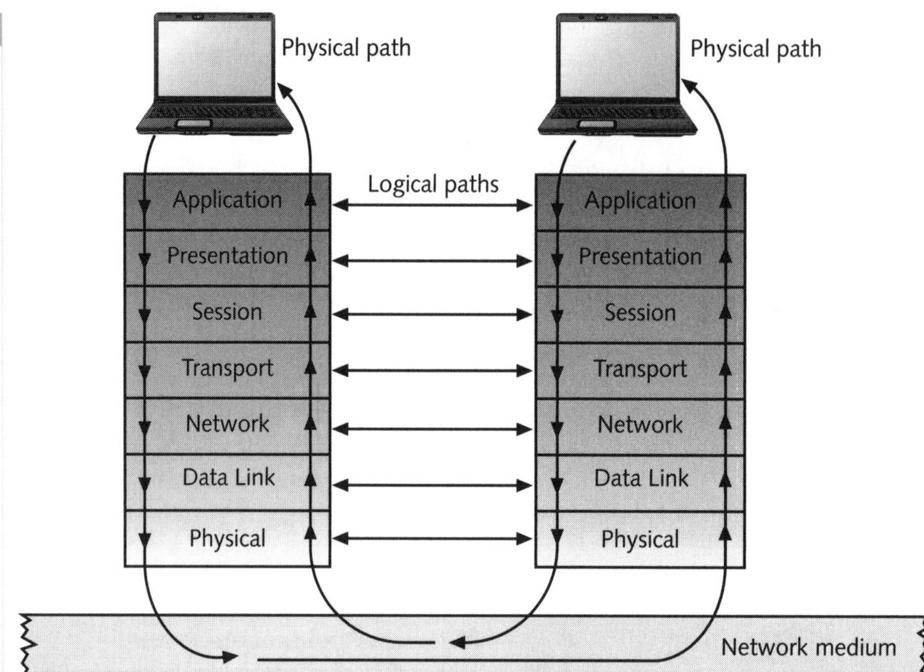

Figure 2-1 Flow of data through the OSI model

Application Layer

The top, or seventh, layer of the OSI model is the **Application layer**. Contrary to what its name implies, the Application layer does not include software programs, such as Microsoft Word or Firefox. Instead, the Application layer facilitates communication between such programs and lower-layer network services. Services at this layer enable the network to interpret a program's request and the program to interpret data sent from the network. Through Application layer protocols, programs negotiate their formatting, procedural, security, synchronization, and other requirements with the network. Note that not all these requirements are *fulfilled* by Application layer protocols. They are merely agreed upon at this stage.

Net+ 1.1 1.2 1.6

For example, when you choose to open a Web page in Firefox, an Application layer protocol called **HTTP (Hypertext Transfer Protocol)** formats and sends your request from your client's browser (a software application) to the server. It also formats and sends the Web server's response back to your client's browser. Figure 2-2 illustrates how the Application layer services operate in this example.

Suppose you choose to view the Library of Congress's Web site. You type *www.loc.gov/index.html* in Firefox and press Enter. At that point, Firefox's **API (application programming interface)**, a set of routines that make up part of the software, transfers your request to the HTTP protocol. HTTP prompts lower-layer protocols to establish a connection between your computer and the Web server. Next, HTTP formats your request for the Web page and sends the request to the Web server. One part of the HTTP request includes a command that begins with "GET" and tells the server what page you want to retrieve. Other parts of the request indicate what version

Net+
1.1
1.2
1.6

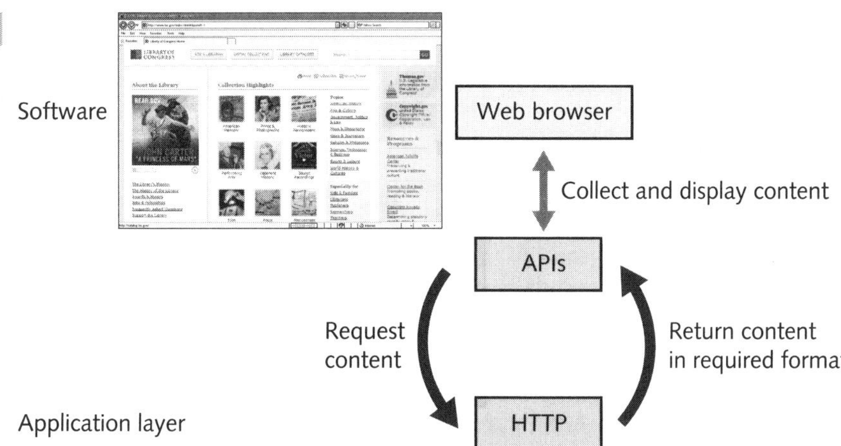

Figure 2-2 Application layer functions while retrieving a Web page

of HTTP you're using, what types of graphics and what language your browser can accept, and what browser version you're using, among other things.

After receiving your computer's HTTP request, the Web server responsible for *www.loc.gov* responds, also via HTTP. Its response includes the text and graphics that make up the Web page, plus specifications for the content contained in the page, the HTTP version used, the type of HTTP response, and the length of the page. However, if the Web page is unavailable, the host, *www.loc.gov,* sends an HTTP response containing an error message, such as "Error 404 - File Not Found."

After receiving the Web server's response, your workstation uses HTTP to interpret this response so that Firefox can present the *www.loc.gov/index.html* Web page in a format you'll recognize, with neatly arranged text and images. Note that the information issued by one node's HTTP protocol is designed to be interpreted by the other node's HTTP protocol. However, as you will learn in later sections, HTTP requests cannot traverse the network without the assistance of lower-layer protocols.

Presentation Layer

Net+ Protocols at the **Presentation layer** accept Application layer data and format it so that one
1.1 type of application and host can understand data from another type of application and host. In other words, the Presentation layer serves as a translator. If you have spent any time working with computer graphics, you have probably heard of the GIF, JPG, and TIFF methods of compressing and encoding graphics. MPEG and QuickTime are two popular methods of compressing and encoding audio and video data. The popular audio format MP3, for example, uses MPEG compression. It can turn a music track that would require 30 MB of space on a CD into a file no larger than 3 MB—or even smaller, if lower quality were acceptable. In the previous example of requesting a Web page, the Presentation layer protocols would interpret the JPG files transmitted within the Web server's HTTP response.

Presentation layer services also manage data encryption (such as the scrambling of passwords) and decryption. For example, if you look up your bank account status via the Internet, you are using a secure connection, and Presentation layer protocols will encrypt your account data before it is transmitted. On your end of the network, the Presentation layer will decrypt the

1.1 data as it is received. You will learn more about Presentation layer protocols, such as SSL (Secure Sockets Layer) and TLS (Transport Layer Security), in Chapter 11. Figure 2-3 offers an example of how Presentation layer services perform while retrieving a secure Web page.

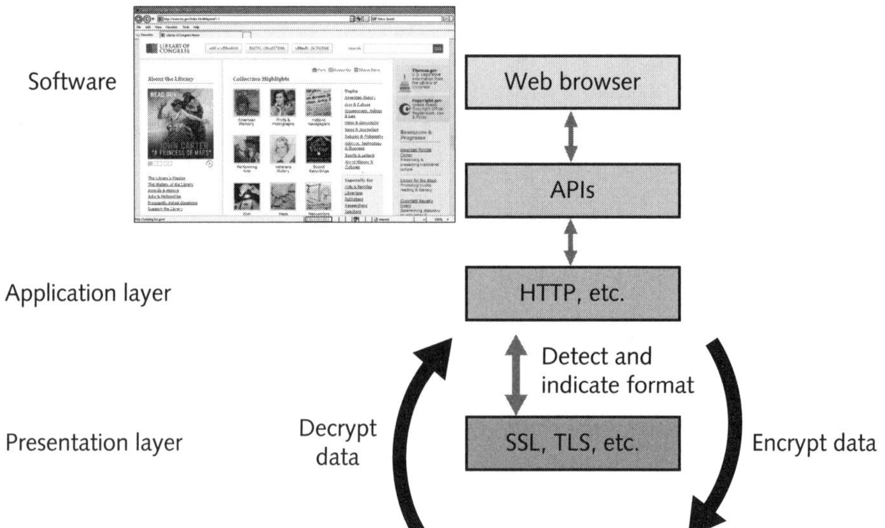

Figure 2-3 Presentation layer services while retrieving a secure Web page

Session Layer

Protocols in the **Session layer** coordinate and maintain communications between two nodes on the network. The term **session** refers to a connection for ongoing data exchange between two parties. Historically, it was used in the context of terminal and mainframe communications, in which the **terminal** is a device with little (if any) of its own processing or disk capacity that depends on a host to supply it with software and processing services. Today, the term *session* is often used in the context of a connection between a remote client and an access server or between a Web browser client and a Web server. When thinking in terms of the OSI model, however, this is misleading. Modern networks don't make use of Session layer protocols for routine data exchange, such as Web page retrieval or file sharing. Yet applications that require precisely coordinated data exchanges, such as videoconferencing or voice (telephone) communication, still use Session layer protocols.

Among the Session layer's functions are establishing and keeping alive the communications link for the duration of the session, keeping the communication secure, synchronizing the dialogue between the two nodes, determining whether communications have been cut off, and, if so, figuring out where to restart transmission, and terminating communications. Session layer services also set the terms of communication by deciding which node communicates first and how long a node can communicate. If a connection is lost, the Session layer protocols will detect that and initiate attempts to reconnect. If they cannot reconnect after a certain period of time, they will close the session and inform your client software that communication has ended. Finally, the Session layer monitors the identification of session participants, ensuring that only the authorized nodes can access the session.

1.1 Figure 2-4 illustrates how Session layer protocols establish and manage a call between two Internet phones at different locations.

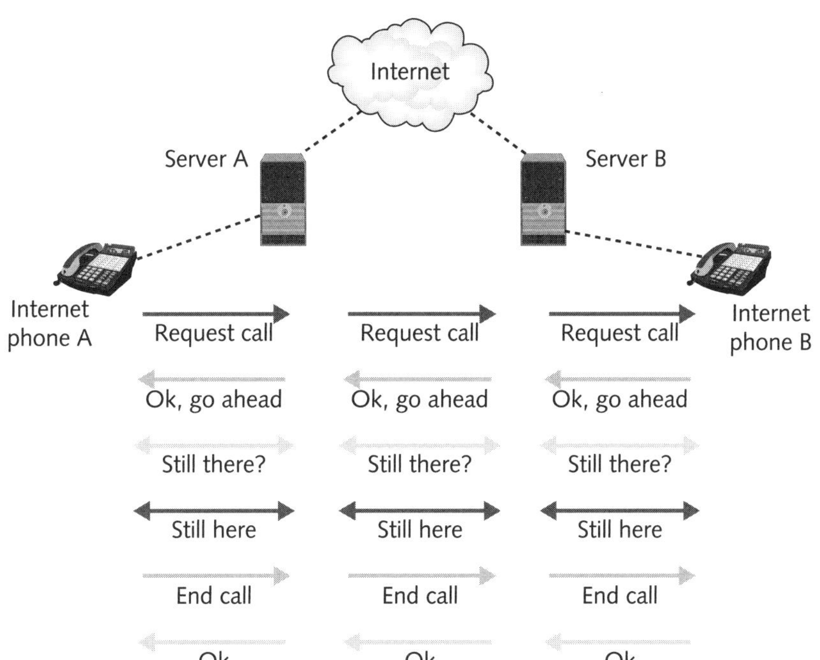

Figure 2-4 Session layer protocols managing voice communications

Transport Layer

1.1 Protocols in the **Transport layer** accept data from the Session layer and manage end-to-end
1.2 delivery of data. That means they can ensure that the data are transferred from point A to
1.6 point B reliably, in the correct sequence, and without errors. Without Transport layer services, data could not be verified or interpreted by its recipient. Transport layer protocols also handle **flow control**, which is the process of gauging the appropriate rate of transmission based on how fast the recipient can accept data. Dozens of different Transport layer protocols exist, but most modern networks, such as the Internet, rely on only a few. In the example of retrieving a Web page, a Transport layer protocol called TCP (Transmission Control Protocol) takes care of reliably transmitting the HTTP protocol's request from client to server and vice versa. You will learn more about this significant protocol later in this book.

Some Transport layer protocols take steps to ensure that data arrives exactly as it was sent. Such protocols are **connection oriented** because they establish a connection with another node before they begin transmitting data. TCP is one example of a connection-oriented protocol. In the case of requesting a Web page, the client's TCP protocol first sends a **SYN (synchronization)** packet request for a connection to the Web server. The Web server responds with a **SYN-ACK (synchronization-acknowledgment)** packet, or a confirmation, to indicate that it's willing to make a connection. Then, the client responds with its own **ACK (acknowledgment)**. Through this three-step process, also known as a **three-way handshake**, a connection is established. Only after TCP establishes this connection does it transmit the HTTP request for a Web page.

1.1
1.2
1.6

Acknowledgments are also used in subsequent communications to ensure that data was properly delivered. For every data unit a node sends, its connection-oriented protocol expects an acknowledgment from the recipient. For example, after a client's TCP protocol issued an HTTP request, it would expect to receive an acknowledgment from the Web server proving that the data arrived. If data isn't acknowledged within a given time period, the client's protocol assumes the data was lost and retransmits it.

To ensure data integrity further, connection-oriented protocols such as TCP use a checksum. A **checksum** is a unique character string that allows the receiving node to determine if an arriving data unit exactly matches the data unit sent by the source. Checksums are added to data at the source and verified at the destination. If at the destination a checksum doesn't match what the source predicted, the destination's Transport layer protocols ask the source to retransmit the data. As you will learn, protocols at other layers of the OSI model also use checksums.

1.1
1.2

Not all Transport layer protocols are concerned with reliability. Those that do not establish a connection before transmitting and make no effort to ensure that data is delivered free of errors are called **connectionless** protocols. A connectionless protocol's lack of sophistication makes it more efficient than a connection-oriented protocol and renders it useful in situations in which data must be transferred quickly, such as live audio or video transmissions over the Internet. In these cases, connection-oriented protocols—with their acknowledgments, checksums, and flow control mechanisms—would add overhead to the transmission and potentially bog it down. In a video transmission, for example, this could result in pictures that are incomplete or aren't updated quickly enough to coincide with the audio.

In addition to ensuring reliable data delivery, Transport layer protocols break large data units received from the Session layer into multiple smaller units, called **segments**. This process is known as **segmentation**. On certain types of networks, segmentation increases data transmission efficiency. In some cases, segmentation is necessary for data units to match a network's **MTU** (**maximum transmission unit**), the largest data unit it will carry. Every network type specifies a default MTU (though its size can be modified to some extent by a network administrator). For example, by default, Ethernet networks cannot accept packets with data payloads larger than 1500 bytes. Suppose an application wants to send a 6000-byte unit of data. Before this data unit can be issued to an Ethernet network, it must be segmented into units no larger than 1500 bytes. To learn a network's MTU size (and thereby determine whether it needs to segment packets), Transport layer protocols perform a discovery routine upon establishing a connection with the network. Thereafter, the protocols will segment each data unit as necessary until closing the connection.

Segmentation is similar to the process of breaking down words into recognizable syllables that a child uses when learning to read. **Reassembly** is the process of reconstructing the segmented data units. To continue the reading analogy, when a child understands the separate syllables, he can combine them into a word—that is, he can reassemble the parts into a whole. To learn how reassembly works, suppose that you asked this question in history class: "Ms. Jones? How did poor farming techniques contribute to the Dust Bowl?" but that the words arrived at Ms. Jones's ear as "poor farming techniques Ms. Jones? how did to the Dust Bowl? contribute." On a network, the Transport layer recognizes this kind of disorder and rearranges the data pieces so that they make sense.

Sequencing is a method of identifying segments that belong to the same group of subdivided data. Sequencing also indicates where a unit of data begins, as well as the order in which groups of data were issued and, therefore, should be interpreted. While establishing a connection, the

1.1
1.2
Transport layer protocols from two devices agree on certain parameters of their communication, including a sequencing scheme. For sequencing to work properly, the Transport layer protocols of two nodes must synchronize their timing and agree on a starting point for the transmission.

Figure 2-5 illustrates the concept of segmentation and reassembly.

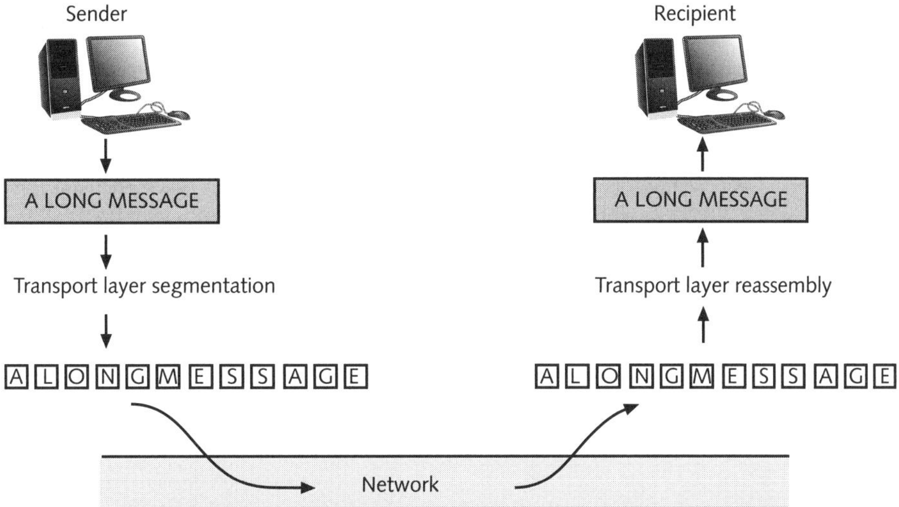

Figure 2-5 Segmentation and reassembly

1.1
1.2
1.6
Figure 2-6 depicts the information contained in an actual TCP segment used to request the Web page *www.loc.gov/index.html*. After reading this section, you should recognize much of the segment's contents. After learning more about protocols later in this book, you will understand the meaning of everything contained in a TCP segment.

```
Transmission Control Protocol, Src Port: http (80), Dst Port: 1958 (1958), Seq: 3043958669, Ack: 937013559, Len: 0
  Source port: http (80)
  Destination port: 1958 (1958)
  Sequence number: 3043958669
  Acknowledgment number: 937013559
  Header length: 24 bytes
⊟ Flags: 0x0012 (SYN, ACK)
    0... .... = Congestion Window Reduced (CWR): Not set
    .0.. .... = ECN-Echo: Not set
    ..0. .... = Urgent: Not set
    ...1 .... = Acknowledgment: Set
    .... 0... = Push: Not set
    .... .0.. = Reset: Not set
    .... ..1. = Syn: Set
    .... ...0 = Fin: Not set
  Window size: 5840
  Checksum: 0x206a (correct)
⊟ Options: (4 bytes)
    Maximum segment size: 1460 bytes
```

Figure 2-6 A TCP segment

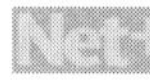

Network Layer

1.1 The primary function of protocols at the **Network layer**, the third layer in the OSI model, is
1.2 to translate network addresses into their physical counterparts and decide how to route data
1.3 from the sender to the receiver. Addressing is a system for assigning unique identification
1.6 numbers to devices on a network. Each node has two types of addresses.

One type of address is called a network address. **Network addresses** follow a hierarchical addressing scheme and can be assigned through operating system software. They are hierarchical because they contain subsets of data that incrementally narrow down the location of a node, just as your home address is hierarchical because it provides a country, state, zip code, city, street, house number, and person's name. Network layer address formats differ depending on which Network layer protocol the network uses. Network addresses are also called **Network layer addresses, logical addresses**, or **virtual addresses**. The second type of address assigned to each node is called a physical address, discussed in detail in the next section.

For example, a computer running on a TCP/IP network might have a Network layer address of 10.34.99.12 and a physical address of 0060973E97F3. In the classroom example, this addressing scheme is like saying that "Ms. Jones" and "United States citizen with Social Security number 123-45-6789" are the same person. Even though there may be other people named "Ms. Jones" in the United States, only one person has the Social Security number 123-45-6789. Within the confines of your classroom, however, there is only one Ms. Jones, so you can be certain the correct person will respond when you say, "Ms. Jones?" There's no need to use her Social Security number.

Network layer protocols accept the Transport layer segments and add logical addressing
1.1 information in a network header. At this point, the data unit becomes a packet. Network
layer protocols also determine the path from point A on one network to point B on another
network by factoring in:

- Delivery priorities (for example, packets that make up a phone call connected through the Internet might be designated high priority, whereas a mass e-mail message is low priority)
- Network congestion
- Quality of service (for example, some packets may require faster, more reliable delivery)
- Cost of alternative routes

The process of determining the best path is known as routing. More formally, to **route** means to intelligently direct data based on addressing, patterns of usage, and availability. Because the Network layer handles routing, **routers**—the devices that connect network segments and direct data—belong in the Network layer.

Although there are numerous Network layer protocols, one of the most common, and the one
1.1 that underlies most Internet traffic, is the **IP** (**Internet Protocol**). In the example of requesting a
1.2 Web page, IP is the protocol that instructs the network where the HTTP request is coming from
1.6 and where it should go. Figure 2-7 depicts the data found in an IP packet used to contact the
Web site *www.loc.gov/index.html*. Notice the Network layer addresses, or IP addresses, in the first line of the packet. The first, labeled "src Addr" reveals the unique IP address of the computer issuing the transmission. The next, labeled "DST Add," indicates the unique IP address of the receiving computer. Chapter 4 illustrates IP packets and describes them in more detail.

On TCP/IP-based networks (such as the Internet), Network layer protocols can perform
an additional function called fragmentation. In **fragmentation**, a Network layer protocol
1.1 (such as IP) subdivides the segments it receives from the Transport layer into smaller
1.2 packets. If this process sounds familiar, it's because fragmentation accomplishes the same
1.6 task at the Network layer that segmentation performs at the Transport layer. It ensures that packets issued to the network are no larger than the network's maximum transmission unit size. However, if a Transport layer protocol performs segmentation, fragmentation may not be necessary. For greater network efficiency, segmentation is preferred. Not all Transport layer protocols are designed to accomplish segmentation. If a Transport layer protocol cannot perform segmentation, Network layer protocols will perform fragmentation, if needed.

```
⊟Internet Protocol, src Addr: 140.147.249.7 (140.147.249.7), Dst Add: 10.11.11.51 (10.11.11.51)
    Version: 4
    Header length: 20 bytes
  ⊞ Differentiated Services Field: 0x00 (DSCP 0x00: Default; ECN: 0x00)
    Total Length: 44
    Identification: 0x0000 (0)
  ⊟ Flags: 0x04
      .1.. = Don't fragment: Set
      ..0. = More fragments: Not Set
    Fragment offset: 0
    Time to live: 64
    Protocol: TCP 0x06
    Header checksum: 0x9ff3 (correct)
    Source: 140.147.249.7 (140.147.249.7)
    Destination: 10.11.11.51 (10.11.11.51)
```

Figure 2-7 An IP packet

Net+

Data Link Layer

1.1 In the second layer of the OSI model, the **Data Link layer**, protocols divide data they receive
1.2 from the Network layer into distinct frames that can then be transmitted by the Physical layer. A **frame** is a structured package for moving data that includes not only the raw data, or "payload," but also the sender's and receiver's network addresses, and error checking and control information. The addresses tell the network where to deliver the frame, whereas the error checking and control information ensure that the frame arrives without any problems.

To understand the function of the Data Link layer fully, pretend for a moment that computers communicate as humans do. Suppose you are in Ms. Jones's large classroom, which is full of noisy students, and you need to ask the teacher a question. To get your message through, you might say, "Ms. Jones? Can you explain more about the effects of railroads on commerce in the mid-nineteenth century?" In this example, you are the sender (in a busy network) and you have addressed your recipient, Ms. Jones, just as the Data Link layer addresses another computer on the network. In addition, you have formatted your thought as a question, just as the Data Link layer formats data into frames that can be interpreted by receiving computers.

Net+ What happens if the room is so noisy that Ms. Jones hears only part of your question? For
1.1 example, she might receive "on commerce in the late-nineteenth century?" This kind of
1.2 error can happen in network communications as well (because of wiring problems, for example). The Data Link layer protocols find out that information has been dropped and ask the first computer to retransmit its message—just as in a classroom setting Ms. Jones might say, "I didn't hear you. Can you repeat the question?" The Data Link layer accomplishes this task through a process called error checking.

Error checking is accomplished by a 4-byte **FCS (frame check sequence)** field, whose purpose is to ensure that the data at the destination exactly match the data issued from the source. When the source node transmits the data, it performs an algorithm (or mathematical routine) called a **CRC (cyclic redundancy check)**. CRC takes the values of all of the preceding fields in the frame and generates a unique 4-byte number, the FCS. When the destination node receives the frame, its Data Link layer services unscramble the FCS via the same CRC algorithm and ensure that the frame's fields match their original form. If this comparison fails, the receiving node assumes that the frame has been damaged in transit and requests that the source node retransmit the data. Note that the receiving node, and not the sending node, is responsible for detecting errors.

In addition, the sender's Data Link layer waits for acknowledgment from the receiver's Transport layer that data was received correctly. If the sender does not get this acknowledgment within a prescribed period of time, its Data Link layer gives instruction to retransmit the information. The Data Link layer never tries to figure out what went wrong. Similarly, as in a busy classroom, Ms. Jones will probably say, "Pardon me?" rather than, "It sounds as if you might have a question about railroads, and I heard only the last part of it, which dealt with commerce, so I assume you are asking about commerce and railroads; is that correct?" Obviously, the former method is more efficient.

Another communications mishap that might occur in a noisy classroom or on a busy network is a glut of communication requests. For example, at the end of class, 20 people might ask Ms. Jones 20 different questions at once. Of course, she can't pay attention to all of them simultaneously. She will probably say, "One person at a time, please," then point to one student who asked a question. This is just like what the Data Link layer does for the Physical layer. One node on a network (a Web server, for example) may receive multiple requests that include many frames of data each. The Data Link layer controls the flow of this information, allowing the NIC to process data without error.

In fact, the IEEE has divided the Data Link layer into two sublayers, as shown in Figure 2-8. The reason for this change was to allow higher-layer protocols (for example, those operating in the Network layer) to interact with Data Link layer protocols without regard for Physical layer specifications.

Net+ The upper sublayer of the Data Link layer, called the **LLC (Logical Link Control) sublayer**,
1.1 provides an interface to the Network layer protocols, manages flow control, and issues
1.2 requests for transmission for data that have suffered errors. The **MAC (Media Access Con-**
1.3 **trol) sublayer**, the lower sublayer of the Data Link layer, manages access to the physical medium. It appends the **physical address** of the destination computer onto the data frame. The physical address is a fixed number associated with a device's network interface. It is assigned to each NIC at the factory and stored in the NIC's on-board memory. Because this

Net+
1.1
1.2

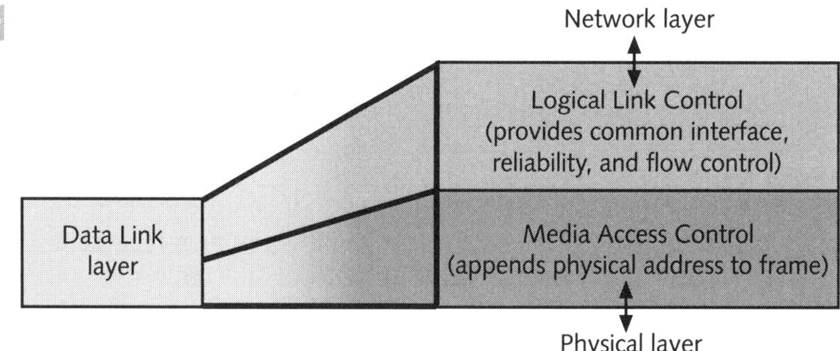

Figure 2-8 The Data Link layer and its sublayers
© Cengage Learning 2013

Net+ address is appended by the MAC sublayer of the Data Link layer, it is also known as a **MAC**
1.1 **address** or a **Data Link layer address.** Sometimes, it's also called a **hardware address.**

1.2
1.3 You can find a NIC's physical address through your computer's protocol configuration utility or by simply looking at the NIC. The physical address will be stamped directly onto the NIC's circuit board or on a sticker attached to some part of the NIC, as shown in Figure 2-9. In Hands-On Project 2-3 at the end of this chapter, you will have a chance to discover your computer's physical address using both these methods.

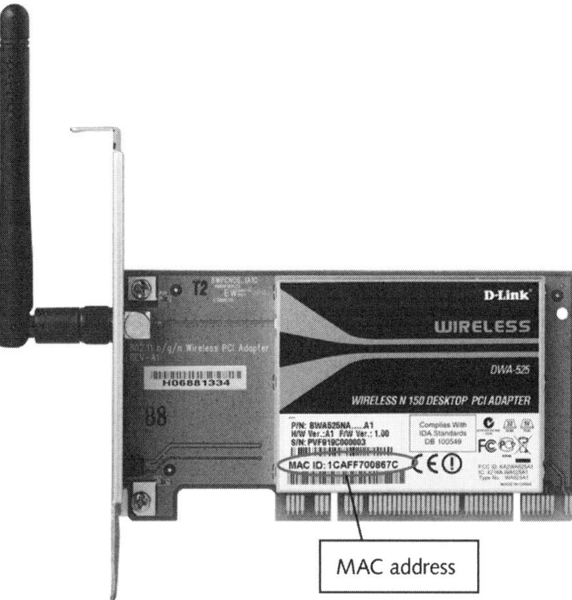

Figure 2-9 A NIC's physical address
Courtesy of D-Link North America

Physical addresses contain two parts. The first part, known as the **OUI (Organizationally Unique Identifier)**, is a character sequence assigned by IEEE that identifies the NIC's manufacturer. For example, a series of Ethernet NICs manufactured by the 3Com Corporation

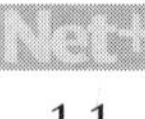

1.1
1.2
1.3

begins with the hexadecimal characters "00608C," while a series of Ethernet NICs manufactured by Intel begins with "00AA00." Some manufacturers have several different OUIs. IEEE also uses the term **company_id** to refer to the OUI. Traditionally, this portion of a physical address is sometimes called the **block ID.**

The remaining characters in a physical address, known as the **extension identifier**, identify the interface. Vendors such as 3Com and Intel assign each NIC a unique extension identifier, based on the NIC's model and manufacture date. By assigning unique extension identifiers, companies ensure that no two NICs share the same physical address. Extension identifiers may also be known as **device IDs.**

In traditional physical addressing schemes, the OUI is six characters (or 24 bits) long and the extension identifier is also six characters long. Together, the OUI and extension identifier form a whole physical address. For example, IBM might assign one of its NICs the extension identifier 005499. The combination of the IBM OUI and this extension identifier result in a unique, 12-character, or 48-bit address of 00608C005499.

Physical addresses are frequently depicted as hexadecimal numbers separated by colons—for example, 00:60:8C:00:54:99.Whereas the traditional MAC addressing scheme assigns interfaces a 48-bit address, IEEE's newer **EUI-64 (Extended Unique Identifier-64)** standard calls for a 64-bit physical address. In the EUI-64 standard, the OUI portion is 24 bits in length. A 40-bit extension identifier makes up the rest of the physical address to total 64 bits.

Hexadecimal, or base 16, is a numeral system that uses 0 through 9 to represent its first 10 numbers, then uses the letters A through F to represent the next six numbers, as shown below. (The system we use for everyday counting is base 10, or decimal, notation.)

Decimal: 0 1 2 3 4 5 6 7 8 9 10 11 12 13 14 15

Hexadecimal: 0 1 2 3 4 5 6 7 8 9 A B C D E F

In hexadecimal notation, the decimal number 12 is represented by the letter C, for example. Starting with the decimal number 16, hexadecimal notation uses a 1 to represent the previous 15 digits and begins counting again at 0. In other words, a decimal number 16 is represented as 10 in hexadecimal and a decimal number 32 is represented as 20 in hexadecimal, or 2 x 16 + 0 x 1.

You can convert a hexadecimal number to a decimal number by multiplying the decimal equivalent of the digit in each position by its hexadecimal value for that position. Each value is an exponential value of 16. For instance, the value at position 3 equals 16^3, or 4096. The value associated with positions is shown below (note that positions can extend beyond the 4th position):

Hexadecimal position: 4 3 2 1 0

Hexadecimal value: 65536 4096 256 16 1

The decimal equivalent of the hexadecimal number C0F is 12 x 256 + 0 x 16 + 15 x 1, or 3072 + 0 + 15, or 3087.

In computer science, hexadecimal notation (sometimes called, simply, "hex") is used as a shorter, readable version of the binary numbers that computers interpret. Chapters 3 and 4 describe binary notation in more detail.

If you know a computer's physical address, you can determine which company manufactured
1.1 its NIC by looking up its block ID. IEEE maintains a database of block IDs and their manu-
1.2 facturers, which is accessible via the Web. At the time of this writing, the database search
1.3 page could be found at *http://standards.ieee.org/regauth/oui/index.shtml.*

Figure 2-10 provides a simple view of a frame created at the Data Link layer. Notice the fields reserved for the physical, or MAC, addresses belonging to the transmission's destination and source nodes. The purpose of the preamble field in this frame is to synchronize signaling between nodes. You will learn more about Ethernet frames in Chapter 5.

Preamble	Destination's physical address	Source's physical address	Type	Data	FCS
8 Bytes	6 Bytes	6 Bytes	2 Bytes	46–1500 Bytes	6 Bytes

Figure 2-10 A frame

Because of their hardware addressing function, NICs can be said to perform in the Data Link layer of the OSI model. However, they also perform services in the Physical layer, which is described next.

Physical Layer

1.1 The **Physical layer** is the lowest, or first, layer of the OSI model. Protocols at the Physical layer accept frames from the Data Link layer and generate signals as changes in voltage at the NIC. (Signals are made of electrical impulses that, when issued in a certain pattern, represent information.) When the network uses copper as its transmission medium, these signals are also issued over the wire as voltage. In the case of fiber-optic cable, signals are issued as light pulses. When a network uses wireless transmission, the signals are sent from antennas as electromagnetic waves.

When receiving data, Physical layer protocols detect and accept signals, which they pass on to the Data Link layer. Physical layer protocols also set the data transmission rate and monitor data error rates. However, even if they recognize an error, they cannot perform error correction. When you install a NIC in your desktop PC and connect it to a cable, you are establishing the foundation that allows the computer to be networked. In other words, you are providing a Physical layer.

Simple connectivity devices such as hubs and repeaters operate at the Physical layer. NICs operate at both the Physical layer and at the Data Link layer. As you would expect, physical network problems, such as a severed wire or a broken connectivity device, affect the Physical layer. Similarly, if you insert a NIC but fail to seat it deeply enough in the computer's main circuit board, your computer will experience network problems at the Physical layer.

Most of the functions that network administrators are most concerned with happen in the first four layers of the OSI model: Physical, Data Link, Network, and Transport. Therefore, the bulk of material in this book and on the Network+ exam relates to these four layers. Software programmers, on the other hand, are more apt to be concerned with what happens at the Application, Presentation, and Session layers.

Applying the OSI Model

1.1 Now that you have been introduced to the seven layers of the OSI model, you can take a
1.2 closer look at exactly how the layers interact. For reference, Table 2-1 summarizes the functions of the seven OSI model layers. The bookmark attached to the back cover of this book also lists functions and protocols belonging to each layer.

Table 2-1 Functions of the OSI layers

OSI model layer	Function
Application (Layer 7)	Provides interface between software applications and a network for interpreting applications' requests and requirements
Presentation (Layer 6)	Allows hosts and applications to use a common language; performs data formatting, encryption, and compression
Session (Layer 5)	Establishes, maintains, and terminates user connections
Transport (Layer 4)	Ensures accurate delivery of data through flow control, segmentation and reassembly, error correction, and acknowledgment
Network (Layer 3)	Establishes network connections; translates network addresses into their physical counterparts and determines routing
Data Link (Layer 2)	Packages data in frames appropriate to network transmission method
Physical (Layer 1)	Manages signaling to and from physical network connections

Communication Between Two Systems

Based on what you have learned about the OSI model, it should be clear to you that data issued from a software application are not in the same form as the data that your NIC sends to the network. At each layer of the OSI model, some information—for example, a format specification or a network address—is added to the original data. After it has followed the path from the Application layer to the Physical layer, data are significantly transformed, as shown in Figure 2-11. The following paragraphs describe this process in detail.

To understand how data change, it is useful to trace the steps in a typical client/server exchange, such as retrieving a mail message from a mail server. Suppose that you connect to your company's network from your home computer via a broadband Internet connection, log on, start your e-mail application, and then click a button in the e-mail application to retrieve your mail from the server. At that point, Application layer services on your computer accept data from your mail application and formulate a request meant for the mail server software. They add an application header to the data that the program wants to send. The application header contains information about the e-mail application's requirements, so that the mail server can fulfill its request properly. The Application layer transfers the request to the Presentation layer, in the form of a protocol data unit (PDU).

The Presentation layer first determines whether and how it should format or encrypt the data request received from the Application layer. For example, if your mail client requires encryption, the Presentation layer protocols will add that information to the PDU in a presentation header. If your e-mail message contains graphics or formatted text, that information will also be added.

Net+
1.1
1.2

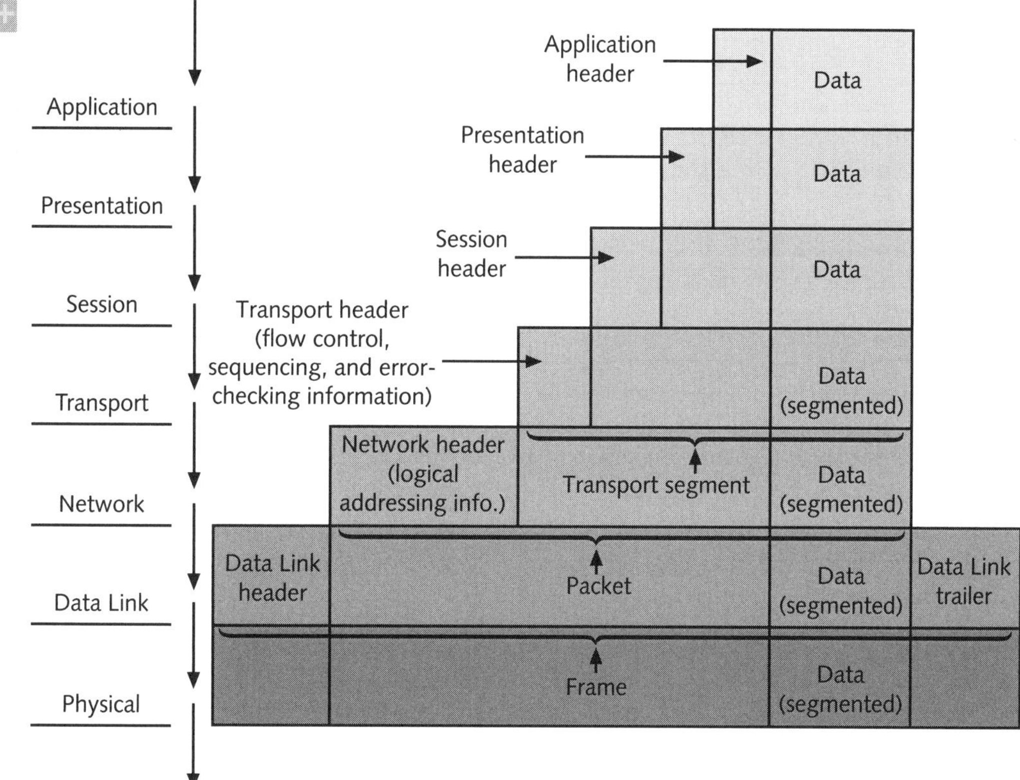

Figure 2-11 Data transformation through the OSI model

Then, the Presentation layer sends its PDU to the Session layer, which adds a session header that contains information about how your home computer communicates with the network. For example, the session header might indicate that your Internet connection can only transmit and receive data at 512 Kbps. The Session layer then passes the PDU to the Transport layer.

At the Transport layer, the PDU—your request for mail and the headers added by previous layers—is broken down into smaller pieces of data, or segments. The segments' maximum size is dictated by the type of network transmission method in use (for example, Ethernet). Suppose your mail request PDU is too large to be a single segment. In that case, Transport layer protocols subdivide it into two or more smaller segments and assign sequence identifiers to all of the smaller segments. This information becomes part of the transport header. Protocols also add checksum, flow control, and acknowledgment data to the transport header. The Transport layer then passes these segments, one at a time, to the Network layer.

Next, Network layer protocols add logical addressing information to the segments, so that your request will be properly routed to the mail server and the mail server will respond to your computer. This information is contained in the network header. With the addition of network address information, the pieces of data are called packets. The Network layer then passes the packets to the Data Link layer.

At the Data Link layer, protocols add a header to the front of each packet and a trailer to the
1.1 end of each packet to make frames. (The trailer indicates where a frame ends.) In other
1.2 words, the Data Link layer protocols **encapsulate** the Network layer packets. Encapsulation is frequently compared with placing an envelope within a larger envelope. This analogy conveys the idea that the Data Link layer does not attempt to interpret any information added in the Network layer, but simply surrounds it.

Using frames reduces the possibility of lost data or errors on the network because built into each frame is a way of checking for errors. After verifying that the data have not been damaged, the Data Link layer then passes the frames to the Physical layer.

Finally, your request for mail, in the form of many frames, hits the NIC at the Physical layer. The Physical layer does not interpret the frames or add information to the frames; it simply transmits them over the broadband connection to your LAN, across your office network, and to the mail server after the binary digits (bits), or ones and zeroes, have been converted to electrical pulses. As the frames arrive at the mail server, the server's Physical layer accepts the frames and transfers them to the Data Link layer. The mail server begins to unravel your request, reversing the process just described, until it responds to your request with its own transmission, beginning from its Application layer.

The terms *frame, packet, datagram,* and *PDU* are sometimes used interchangeably to refer to a small piece of data formatted for network transmission. Technically, however, a *packet* is a piece of information that contains network addressing information, and a *frame* is a piece of data enclosed by a Data Link layer header and trailer. *Datagram* is synonymous with packet. *PDU* generically refers to a unit of data at any layer of the OSI model. However, networking professionals sometimes use the term *packet* to refer to *frames, PDUs,* and Transport layer segments alike.

Net+

Frame Specifications

1.1 You have learned that frames are composed of several smaller components, or fields. The
1.2 characteristics of these components depend on the type of network on which the frames run
3.7 and on the standards that they must follow. By far, the most popular type of networking technology in use today is Ethernet, which uses Ethernet frames. You'll learn much more about Ethernet in Chapter 5, but the following serves as an introduction, as well as a comparison between this favored network type and its historical rival, token ring.

Ethernet is a networking technology originally developed at Xerox in the early 1970s and improved by Digital Equipment Corporation, Intel, and Xerox. There are four different types of Ethernet frames. The most popular form of Ethernet is characterized by the unique way in which devices share a common transmission channel, described in the IEEE 802.3 standard.

A much less-common networking technology, **token ring**, was developed by IBM in the 1980s. It relies upon direct links between nodes and a ring topology. Nodes pass around **tokens**, special control frames that indicate to the network when a particular node is about to transmit data. Although this networking technology is nearly obsolete, there is a remote chance that you might work on a token ring network. The IEEE has defined token ring technology in its 802.5 standard.

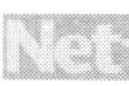

Ethernet frames are different from token ring frames, and the two will not interact with each
1.1 other on a network. In fact, most LANs do not support more than one frame type because
1.2 devices cannot support more than one frame type per physical interface, or NIC. (NICs can,
3.7 however, support multiple protocols.) Although you can conceivably transmit both token
ring and Ethernet frames on a network, Ethernet interfaces cannot interpret token ring frames, and vice versa. Normally, LANs use *either* Ethernet or token ring, and almost all contemporary LANs use Ethernet.

It is important to know what frame type (or types) your network environment requires. You will use this information when installing network operating systems, configuring servers and client workstations, installing NICs, troubleshooting network problems, and purchasing network equipment.

IEEE Networking Specifications

In addition to frame types and addressing, IEEE networking specifications apply to connectivity, networking media, error-checking algorithms, encryption, emerging technologies, and more. All of these specifications fall under the IEEE's Project 802, an effort to standardize physical and logical elements of a network. IEEE developed these standards before the OSI model was standardized by ISO, but IEEE's 802 standards can be applied to the layers of the OSI model. Table 2-2 describes just some of the IEEE 802 specifications. The Network+ certification exam includes questions about IEEE 802 specifications, with an emphasis on the technologies described by 802.3 and 802.11.

Table 2-2 **IEEE 802 standards**

Standard	Name	Topic
802.1	Bridging and Management	Routing, bridging, and network-to-network communications
802.2	Logical Link Control	Error and flow control over data frames
802.3	Ethernet	All forms of Ethernet media and interfaces
802.5	Token Ring LAN	All forms of token ring media and interfaces
802.11	Wireless LANs	Standards for wireless networking for many different broadcast frequencies and usage techniques
802.15	Wireless PANs	The coexistence of wireless personal area networks with other wireless devices in unlicensed frequency bands
802.16	Broadband Wireless MANs	The atmospheric interface and related functions associated with broadband wireless connectivity; also known as WiMAX
802.17	Resilient Packet Rings	Access method, physical layer specifications, and management of shared packet-based transmission on resilient rings (such as SONET)
802.20	Mobile Broadband Wireless Access	Packet handling and other specifications for multivendor, mobile high-speed wireless transmission, nicknamed "mobile WiMAX"
802.22	Wireless Regional Area Networks	Wireless, broadcast-style network to operate in the UHF/VHF frequency bands formerly used for TV channels

Chapter Summary

- Standards are documented agreements containing precise criteria that are used as guidelines to ensure that materials, products, processes, and services suit their purpose. Standards also help to ensure interoperability between software and hardware from different manufacturers.
- Some of the significant standards organizations are ANSI, EIA/TIA, IEEE, ISO, ITU, ISOC, IANA, and ICANN.
- ISO's OSI (Open Systems Interconnection) model represents communication between two computers on a network. It divides networking architecture into seven layers: Physical, Data Link, Network, Transport, Session, Presentation, and Application. Each layer has its own set of functions and interacts with the layers directly above and below it.
- Protocols in the Application layer, the seventh layer of the OSI model, enable software programs to negotiate their formatting, procedural, security, synchronization, and other requirements with the network.
- Protocols in the Presentation layer, the sixth OSI model layer, serve as translators between the application and the network, using a common language for different hosts and applications to exchange data.
- Protocols in the Session layer, the fifth OSI model layer, coordinate and maintain links between two devices for the duration of their communication. They also synchronize dialogue, determine whether communications have been cut off, and, if so, figure out where to restart transmission.
- The primary function of protocols in the Transport layer, the fourth OSI model layer, is to oversee end-to-end data delivery. In the case of connection-oriented protocols, this means data are delivered reliably. They verify that data are received in the same sequence in which they were sent. They are also responsible for flow control, segmentation, and reassembly of packets. Connectionless Transport layer protocols do not offer such guarantees.
- Protocols in the Network layer, the third OSI model layer, manage logical addressing and determine routes based on addressing, patterns of usage, and availability. Routers belong to the Network layer because they use this information to intelligently direct data from sender to receiver.
- Network layer addresses, also called logical or virtual addresses, are assigned to devices through operating system software. They are composed of hierarchical information, so they can be easily interpreted by routers and used to direct data to their destination.
- The primary function of protocols at the Data Link layer, the second layer of the OSI model, is to organize data they receive from the Network layer into frames that contain error-checking routines and can then be transmitted by the Physical layer.
- The Data Link layer is subdivided into the Logical Link Control and MAC sublayers. The LLC sublayer ensures a common interface for the Network layer protocols. The MAC sublayer is responsible for adding physical address data to frames.

- Physical addresses (also known as MAC addresses) are 48- or 64-bit unique identifiers assigned to each network interface. They consist of an OUI (Organizationally Unique Identifier), which is assigned to manufacturers by IEEE, and an extension identifier, a unique number assigned to each NIC by the manufacturer.
- Protocols at the Physical layer generate and detect signals so as to transmit and receive data over a network medium. These protocols also set the data transmission rate and monitor data error rates, but do not provide error correction.
- A data request from a software program is received by the Application layer protocols and is transferred down through the layers of the OSI model until it reaches the Physical layer (the network cable, for example). At that point, data is sent to its destination over the network medium, and the Physical layer protocols at the destination send it back up through the layers of the OSI model until it reaches the Application layer.
- Data frames are small blocks of data with control, addressing, and handling information attached to them. Frames are composed of several fields. The characteristics of these fields depend on the type of network on which the frames run and the standards that they must follow. Ethernet and token ring networks use different frame types, and one type of network cannot interpret the others' frames.
- In addition to frame types and addressing schemes, the IEEE networking specifications apply to connectivity, networking media, error-checking algorithms, encryption, emerging technologies, and more. All of these specifications fall under the IEEE's Project 802, an effort to standardize the elements of networking.
- Significant IEEE 802 standards are 802.3, which describes Ethernet; 802.11, which describes wireless networking; and 802.16, which describes broadband wireless metropolitan area networks.

Key Terms

802.2 The IEEE standard for error and flow control in data frames.

802.3 The IEEE standard for Ethernet networking devices and data handling (using the CSMA/CD access method).

802.5 The IEEE standard for token ring networking devices and data handling.

802.11 The IEEE standard for wireless networking.

ACK (acknowledgment) A response generated at the Transport layer of the OSI model that confirms to a sender that its frame was received. The ACK packet is the third of three in the three-step process of establishing a connection.

acknowledgment *See* ACK.

American National Standards Institute *See* ANSI.

ANSI (American National Standards Institute) An organization composed of more than 1000 representatives from industry and government who together determine standards for the electronics industry in addition to other fields, such as chemical and nuclear engineering, health and safety, and construction.

API (application programming interface) A set of routines that make up part of a software application.

Application layer The seventh layer of the OSI model. Application layer protocols enable software programs to negotiate formatting, procedural, security, synchronization, and other requirements with the network.

application programming interface *See* API.

block ID *See* OUI.

checksum A method of error checking that determines if the contents of an arriving data unit match the contents of the data unit sent by the source.

company_id *See* OUI.

connection oriented A type of Transport layer protocol that requires the establishment of a connection between communicating nodes before it will transmit data.

connectionless A type of Transport layer protocol that services a request without requiring a verified session and without guaranteeing delivery of data.

CRC (cyclic redundancy check) An algorithm (or mathematical routine) used to verify the accuracy of data contained in a data frame.

cyclic redundancy check *See* CRC.

Data Link layer The second layer in the OSI model. The Data Link layer bridges the networking media with the Network layer. Its primary function is to divide the data it receives from the Network layer into frames that can then be transmitted by the Physical layer.

Data Link layer address *See* MAC address.

device ID *See* extension identifier.

EIA (Electronic Industries Alliance) A trade organization composed of representatives from electronics manufacturing firms across the United States that sets standards for electronic equipment and lobbies for legislation favorable to the growth of the computer and electronics industries.

Electronic Industries Alliance *See* EIA.

encapsulate The process of wrapping one layer's PDU with protocol information so that it can be interpreted by a lower layer. For example, Data Link layer protocols encapsulate Network layer packets in frames.

Ethernet A networking technology originally developed at Xerox in the 1970s and improved by Digital Equipment Corporation, Intel, and Xerox. Ethernet, which is the most common form of network transmission technology, follows the IEEE 802.3 standard.

EUI-64 (Extended Unique Identifier-64) The IEEE standard defining 64-bit physical addresses. In the EUI-64 scheme, the OUI portion of an address is 24 bits in length. A 40-bit extension identifier makes up the rest of the physical address to total 64 bits.

Extended Unique Identifier-64 *See* EUI-64.

extension identifier A unique set of characters assigned to each NIC by its manufacturer. In the traditional, 48-bit physical addressing scheme, the extension identifier is 24 bits long. In EUI-64, the extension identifier is 40 bits long.

FCS (frame check sequence) The field in a frame responsible for ensuring that data carried by the frame arrives intact. It uses an algorithm, such as CRC, to accomplish this verification.

flow control A method of gauging the appropriate rate of data transmission based on how fast the recipient can accept data.

fragmentation A Network layer service that subdivides segments it receives from the Transport layer into smaller packets.

frame A package for data that includes not only the raw data, or "payload," but also the sender's and recipient's addressing and control information. Frames are generated at the Data Link layer of the OSI model and are issued to the network at the Physical layer.

frame check sequence *See* FCS.

hardware address *See* MAC address.

HTTP (Hypertext Transfer Protocol) An Application layer protocol that formulates and interprets requests between Web clients and servers.

Hypertext Transfer Protocol *See* HTTP.

IAB (Internet Architecture Board) A technical advisory group of researchers and technical professionals responsible for Internet growth and management strategy, resolution of technical disputes, and standards oversight.

IANA (Internet Assigned Numbers Authority) A nonprofit, United States government-funded group that was established at the University of Southern California and charged with managing IP address allocation and the Domain Name System. The oversight for many of IANA's functions was given to ICANN in 1998; however, IANA continues to perform Internet addressing and Domain Name System administration.

ICANN (Internet Corporation for Assigned Names and Numbers) The nonprofit corporation currently designated by the United States government to maintain and assign IP addresses.

IEEE (Institute of Electrical and Electronics Engineers) An international society composed of engineering professionals. Its goals are to promote development and education in the electrical engineering and computer science fields.

IETF (Internet Engineering Task Force) An organization that sets standards for how systems communicate over the Internet (for example, how protocols operate and interact).

Institute of Electrical and Electronics Engineers *See* IEEE.

International Organization for Standardization *See* ISO.

International Telecommunication Union *See* ITU.

Internet Architecture Board *See* IAB.

Internet Assigned Numbers Authority *See* IANA.

Internet Corporation for Assigned Names and Numbers *See* ICANN.

Internet Engineering Task Force *See* IETF.

Internet Protocol *See* IP.

Internet Protocol address *See* IP address.

Internet service provider *See* ISP.

Internet Society *See* ISOC.

IP (Internet Protocol) A core protocol in the TCP/IP suite that operates in the Network layer of the OSI model and provides information about how and where data should be delivered. IP is the subprotocol that enables TCP/IP to internetwork.

IP address (Internet Protocol address) The Network layer address assigned to nodes to uniquely identify them on a TCP/IP network. IPv4 addresses consist of 32 bits divided into four octets, or bytes. IPv6 addresses are composed of eight 16-bit fields, for a total of 128 bits.

ISO (International Organization for Standardization) A collection of standards organizations representing 162 countries with headquarters located in Geneva, Switzerland. Its goal is to establish international technological standards to facilitate the global exchange of information and barrier-free trade.

ISOC (Internet Society) A professional organization with members from 90 chapters around the world that helps to establish technical standards for the Internet.

ISP (Internet service provider) A business that provides organizations and individuals with Internet access and often, other services, such as e-mail and Web hosting.

ITU (International Telecommunication Union) A United Nations agency that regulates international telecommunications and provides developing countries with technical expertise and equipment to advance their technological bases.

LLC (Logical Link Control) sublayer The upper sublayer in the Data Link layer. The LLC provides a common interface and supplies reliability and flow control services.

logical address *See* network address.

Logical Link Control sublayer *See* LLC (Logical Link Control) sublayer.

MAC address *See* physical address.

MAC (Media Access Control) sublayer The lower sublayer of the Data Link layer. The MAC appends the physical address of the destination computer onto the frame.

maximum transmission unit *See* MTU.

Media Access Control sublayer *See* MAC (Media Access Control) sublayer.

MTU (maximum transmission unit) The largest data unit a network (for example, Ethernet or token ring) will accept for transmission.

network address A unique identifying number for a network node that follows a hierarchical addressing scheme and can be assigned through operating system software. Network addresses are added to data packets and interpreted by protocols at the Network layer of the OSI model.

Network layer The third layer in the OSI model. Protocols in the Network layer translate network addresses into their physical counterparts and decide how to route data from the sender to the receiver.

Network layer address *See* network address.

Open Systems Interconnection model *See* OSI (Open Systems Interconnection) model.

Organizationally Unique Identifier *See* OUI.

OSI (Open Systems Interconnection) model A model for understanding and developing computer-to-computer communication developed in the 1980s by ISO. It divides networking functions among seven layers: Physical, Data Link, Network, Transport, Session, Presentation, and Application.

OUI (Organizationally Unique Identifier) A 24-bit character sequence assigned by IEEE that appears at the beginning of a network interface's physical address and identifies the NIC's manufacturer.

PDU (protocol data unit) A unit of data at any layer of the OSI model.

physical address A 48- or 64-bit network interface identifier that includes two parts: the OUI, assigned by IEEE to the manufacturer, and the extension identifier, a unique number assigned to each NIC by the manufacturer.

Physical layer The lowest, or first, layer of the OSI model. Protocols in the Physical layer generate and detect signals so as to transmit and receive data over a network medium. These protocols also set the data transmission rate and monitor data error rates, but do not provide error correction.

Presentation layer The sixth layer of the OSI model. Protocols in the Presentation layer translate between the application and the network. Here, data are formatted in a schema that the network can understand, with the format varying according to the type of network used. The Presentation layer also manages data encryption and decryption, such as the scrambling of system passwords.

protocol data unit *See* PDU.

reassembly The process of reconstructing data units that have been segmented.

Regional Internet Registry *See* RIR.

RIR (Regional Internet Registry) A not-for-profit agency that manages the distribution of IP addresses to private and public entities. ARIN is the RIR for North, Central, and South America and sub-Saharan Africa. APNIC is the RIR for Asia and the Pacific region. RIPE is the RIR for Europe and North Africa.

route To intelligently direct data between networks based on addressing, patterns of usage, and availability of network segments.

router A device that connects network segments and directs data based on information contained in the data packet.

segment A unit of data that results from subdividing a larger protocol data unit.

segmentation The process of decreasing the size of data units when moving data from a network that can handle larger data units to a network that can handle only smaller data units.

sequencing The process of assigning a placeholder to each piece of a data block to allow the receiving node's Transport layer to reassemble the data in the correct order.

session A connection for data exchange between two parties. The term *session* may be used in the context of Web, remote access, or terminal and mainframe communications, for example.

Session layer The fifth layer in the OSI model. The Session layer establishes and maintains communication between two nodes on the network. It can be considered the "traffic cop" for communications, such as videoconferencing, that require precisely coordinated data exchange.

standard A documented agreement containing technical specifications or other precise criteria that are used as guidelines to ensure that materials, products, processes, and services suit their intended purpose.

SYN (synchronization) The packet one node sends to request a connection with another node on the network. The SYN packet is the first of three in the three-step process of establishing a connection.

SYN-ACK (synchronization-acknowledgment) The packet a node sends to acknowledge to another node that it has received a SYN request for connection. The SYN-ACK packet is the second of three in the three-step process of establishing a connection.

synchronization *See* SYN.

synchronization-acknowledgment *See* SYN-ACK.

Telecommunications Industry Association *See* TIA.

terminal A device with little (if any) of its own processing or disk capacity that depends on a host to supply it with applications and data-processing services.

three-way handshake A three-step process in which Transport layer protocols establish a connection between nodes. The three steps are: Node A issues a SYN packet to node B, node B responds with SYN-ACK, and node A responds with ACK.

TIA (Telecommunications Industry Association) A subgroup of the EIA that focuses on standards for information technology, wireless, satellite, fiber optics, and telephone equipment. Probably the best known standards to come from the TIA/EIA alliance are its guidelines for how network cable should be installed in commercial buildings, known as the "TIA/EIA 568-B Series."

token A special control frame that indicates to the rest of the network that a particular node has the right to transmit data.

token ring A networking technology developed by IBM in the 1980s. It relies upon direct links between nodes and a ring topology, using tokens to allow nodes to transmit data.

Transport layer The fourth layer of the OSI model. In the Transport layer, protocols ensure that data are transferred from point A to point B reliably and without errors. Transport layer services include flow control, acknowledgment, error correction, segmentation, reassembly, and sequencing.

virtual address *See* network address.

Review Questions

1. Which of the following is the acceptable performance level of a product or service as defined by a standard?
   a. maximum
   b. minimum
   c. standard
   d. ideal
2. What international society is composed of engineering professionals with a goal of promoting the development and education in the electrical engineering and computer science fields?
   a. ANSI
   b. IEA
   c. IEEE
   d. ISO
3. Which OSI model layer accepts data from the Session layer and manages end-to-end delivery of data?
   a. Network
   b. Physical
   c. Data link
   d. Transport
4. Which type of address contains subsets of data that incrementally narrow down the location of a node?
   a. network
   b. physical
   c. logical
   d. segmented
5. Which OSI model layer divides data received from the Network layer into distinct frames that can then be transmitted by the Physical layer?
   a. Transport
   b. Application
   c. Session
   d. Data Link
6. True or false? Standards help to assure network designers that hardware and software from different manufacturers will work together.
7. True or false? The OSI model is a physical representation of what happens between two nodes communicating on a network.

8. True or false? Software applications such as Microsoft Word and Excel may be found in the OSI model's Application layer.
9. True or false? The OSI model's Presentation layer serves as a translator.
10. True or false? Most LANs will support both Ethernet and token ring frames.
11. The ANSI (American National Standards Institute) organization does not dictate that manufacturers comply with its standards, but requests ________________ compliance.
12. A(n) ________________ is a not-for-profit agency that manages the distribution of IP addresses to private and public entities.
13. A helpful model for understanding and developing computer-to-computer communications over a network is known as the ________________ model.
14. A user or device initiates a data exchange through the OSI ________________ layer.
15. ________________ occurs when OSI Data Link layer protocols add a header to the front of each packet and a trailer to the end of each packet to make frames.

After reading this chapter and completing the exercises, you will be able to:

- Explain basic data transmission concepts, including full duplexing, attenuation, latency, and noise
- Describe the physical characteristics of coaxial cable, STP, UTP, and fiber-optic media
- Compare the benefits and limitations of different networking media
- Explain the principles behind and uses for serial cables
- Identify wiring standards and the best practices for cabling buildings and work areas

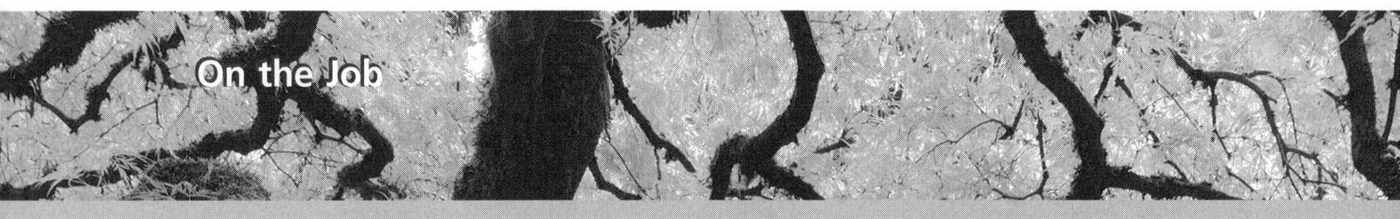

On the Job

I was asked to consult on a network problem concerning slow speeds and dead network jacks. The business was located in a building that was configured for two rental spaces with a single entrance. After entering the front door, I encountered a door to one set of offices on the right and the same on the left. Straight ahead was a door to the mechanical rooms.

When I removed the wall plates, I found that the installer had untwisted the pairs by at least one inch on all of the jacks. On some of the nonfunctional wall jacks, the pairs were untwisted three inches or more and stuffed haphazardly into the wall box.

The next mystery was the single 12-port switch, which didn't make sense because I was now able to get link on 19 wall sockets. This meant that it was time to start removing ceiling tiles and following wires. Fortunately, all of the wires came together in a bundle that exited into the ceiling above the entry way. From there, most of the bundle turned and went toward the mechanical room, where the fiber-modem and 12-port switch were located. Unfortunately, a few of the wires went toward the other rental space. The other set of offices were not currently rented, and so were not accessible without contacting the landlord. The landlord was hesitant to give access to the other space. He insisted that the problem could not have anything to do with the wiring in that part of the building, because his nephew, who was an electrician, had done all of the network cabling in the building. Instead, the landlord insisted that the tenants must have messed up the wall jacks on their side.

After tracing cable after cable above the suspended ceiling, I finally found another network switch hiding on top of one of the ceiling tiles. All of the cable terminations had around two inches of the pairs untwisted to make it easier to install the RJ-45 terminals.

I replaced all of the terminals on the cables at the hidden switch. All of the client's wall jacks were now able to achieve link and connect, transferring at 100 Mbps full-duplex.

Todd Fisher Wallin
Operations Coordinator, Driftless Community Radio

Just as highways and streets provide the foundation for automobile travel, networking media provide the physical foundation for data transmission. Media are the physical or atmospheric paths that signals follow. The first networks transmitted data over thick coaxial cables. Today, when not transmitted through the air, as in wireless networks, data are commonly transmitted over a type of cable that resembles telephone cords. It's sheathed in flexible plastic and contains twisted copper wire inside. For long-distance network connections, fiber-optic cable is preferred. Today, however, organizations are more often sending signals through the atmosphere to form wireless networks, which are covered in Chapter 8. Because networks are always evolving and demanding greater speed, versatility, and reliability, networking media change rapidly.

Network problems often occur at or below the Physical layer. Therefore, understanding the characteristics of various networking media is critical to designing and troubleshooting networks. You also need to know how data are transmitted over the media. This chapter discusses physical networking media and the details of data transmission. You'll learn what it takes to make data transmission dependable and how to correct some common transmission problems.

Transmission Basics

In data networking, the term **transmit** means to issue signals along a network medium such as a cable. **Transmission** refers to either the process of transmitting or the progress of signals after they have been transmitted. In other words, you could say, "My NIC transmitted a message, but because the network is slow, the transmission took 10 seconds to reach the server." In fact, NICs both transmit and receive signals, which means they are a type of **transceiver**.

Long ago, people transmitted information across distances via smoke or fire signals. Needless to say, many different methods of data transmission have evolved since that time. The transmission techniques in use on today's networks are complex and varied. In the following sections, you will learn about some fundamental characteristics that define today's data transmission. In later chapters, you will learn about more subtle and specific differences between types of data transmission.

Analog and Digital Signaling

One important characteristic of data transmission is the type of signaling involved. On a data network, information can be transmitted via one of two signaling methods: analog or digital.

Computers generate and interpret digital signals as electrical current, the pressure of which is measured in **volts**. The strength of an electrical signal is directly proportional to its voltage. Thus, when network engineers talk about the strength of a signal, they often refer to the signal's **voltage**. Once the electrical signal leaves a computer, it can travel over copper cabling as electrical current, over fiber-optic cable as light pulses, or through the air as electromagnetic waves.

Analog data signals are also generated as voltage. However, in **analog** signals, voltage varies continuously and appears as a wavy line when graphed over time, as shown in Figure 3-1.

An analog signal, like other waveforms, is characterized by four fundamental properties: amplitude, frequency, wavelength, and phase. A wave's **amplitude** is a measure of its strength at any given point in time. On a wave graph, the amplitude is the height of the wave at any point in time. In Figure 3-1, for example, the wave has an amplitude of 5 volts at .25 seconds, an amplitude of 0 volts at .5 seconds, and an amplitude of -5 volts at .75 seconds.

Whereas amplitude indicates an analog wave's strength, **frequency** is the number of times that a wave's amplitude cycles from its starting point, through its highest amplitude and its lowest amplitude, and back to its starting point over a fixed period of time. Frequency is expressed in cycles per second, or **hertz (Hz)**, named after German physicist Heinrich Hertz, who experimented with electromagnetic waves in the late nineteenth century. For example, in Figure 3-1, the wave cycles to its highest then lowest amplitude and returns to its starting point once in 1 second. Thus, the frequency of that wave would be 1 cycle per second, or 1 Hz—which, as it turns out, is an extremely low frequency.

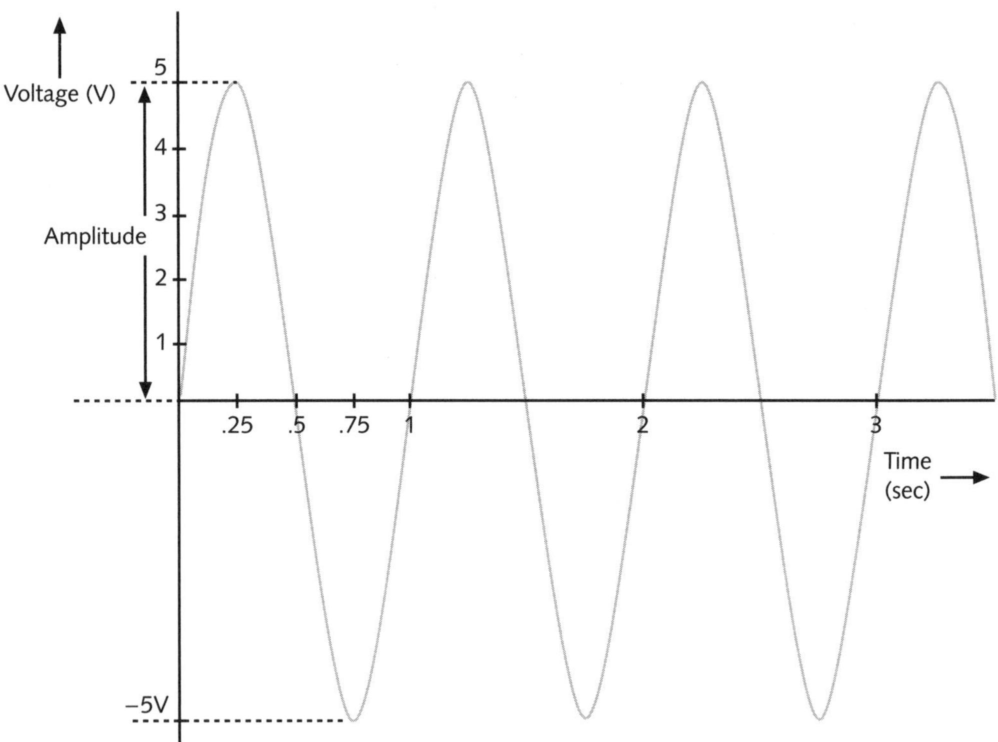

Figure 3-1 An example of an analog signal

Frequencies used to convey speech over telephone wires fall in the 300 to 3300 Hz range. Humans can hear frequencies between 20 and 20,000 Hz. An FM radio station may use a frequency between 850,000 Hz (or 850 kHz) and 108,000,000 Hz (or 108 MHz) to transmit its signal through the air. You will learn more about radio frequencies used in networking later in this chapter.

The distance between corresponding points on a wave's cycle—for example, between one peak and the next—is called its **wavelength**. Wavelengths can be expressed in meters or feet. A wave's wavelength is inversely proportional to its frequency. In other words, the higher the frequency, the shorter the wavelength. For example, a radio wave with a frequency of 1,000,000 cycles per second (1 MHz) has a wavelength of 300 meters, whereas a wave with a frequency of 2,000,000 Hz (2 MHz) has a wavelength of 150 meters.

The term **phase** refers to the progress of a wave over time in relationship to a fixed point. Suppose two separate waves have identical amplitudes and frequencies. If one wave starts at its lowest amplitude at the same time the second wave starts at its highest amplitude, these waves will have different phases. More precisely, they will be 180 degrees out of phase (using the standard assignment of 360 degrees to one complete wave). Had the second wave also started at its lowest amplitude, the two waves would be in phase. Figure 3-2 illustrates waves with identical amplitudes and frequencies whose phases are 90 degrees apart.

One benefit to analog signals is that, because they are more variable than digital signals, they can convey greater subtleties with less energy. For example, think of the difference between your voice and a digitally simulated voice, such as the automated service that some libraries

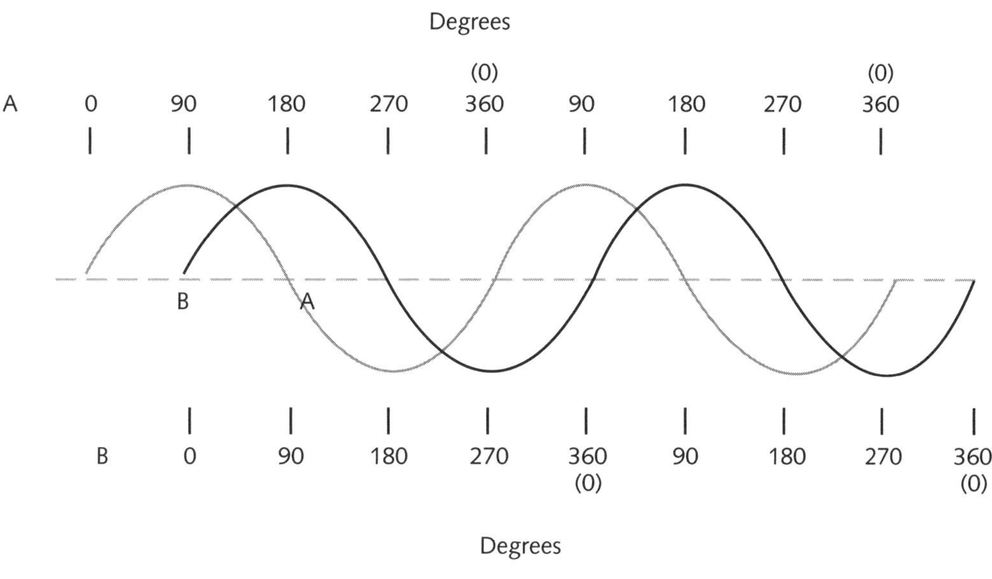

Figure 3-2 Waves with a 90-degree phase difference

use to notify you when a book you have requested is available. A digitally simulated voice has a poorer quality than your own voice—that is, it sounds more like a machine. It can't convey the full range of tones and subtle inflections that you expect in a human voice. Only very high-quality digital signals—for example, those used to record music on compact discs—can achieve such accuracy.

One drawback to analog signals is that their voltage is varied and imprecise. Thus, analog transmission is more susceptible to transmission flaws such as **noise**, or any type of interference that may degrade a signal, than digital signals. If you have tried to listen to AM radio on a stormy night, you have probably heard the crackle and static of noise affecting the signal.

Now contrast the analog signals pictured in Figures 3-1 and 3-2 to a digital signal, as shown in Figure 3-3. **Digital** signals are composed of pulses of precise, positive voltages and zero voltages. A pulse of positive voltage represents a 1. A pulse of zero voltage (in other words, the lack of any voltage) represents a 0. The use of 1s and 0s to represent information is characteristic of a **binary** system. Every pulse in the digital signal is called a binary digit, or **bit**.

A bit can have only one of two possible values: 1 or 0. Eight bits together form a **byte**. In broad terms, one byte carries one piece of information. For example, the byte 01111001 means 121 on a digital network.

Computers read and write information—for example, program instructions, routing information, and network addresses—in bits and bytes. When a number is represented in binary form (for example, 01111001), each bit position, or placeholder, in the number represents a specific multiple of 2. Because a byte contains 8 bits, it has eight placeholders. When counting placeholders in a byte, you move from right to left. The placeholder farthest to the right is known as the zero position, the one to its left is in the first position, and so on. The placeholder farthest to the left is in the seventh position, as shown in Figure 3-4.

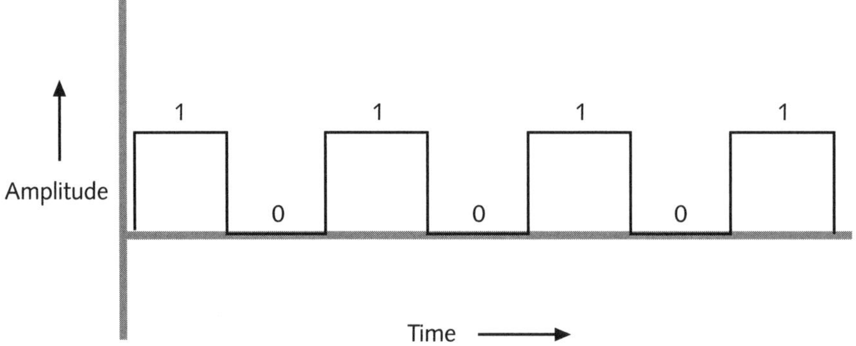

Figure 3-3 An example of a digital signal

Bit position:	7	6	5	4	3	2	1	0
Binary exponential:	2^7	2^6	2^5	2^4	2^3	2^2	2^1	2^0
Value if bit = 1:	128	64	32	16	8	4	2	1

Figure 3-4 Components of a byte

To find the decimal value of a bit, you multiply the 1 or 0 (whichever the bit is set to) by 2^x, where x equals the bit's position. For example, the 1 or 0 in the zero position must be multiplied by 2 to the 0 power, or 2^0, to determine its value. Any number (other than zero) raised to the power of 0 has a value of 1. Thus, if the zero-position bit is 1, it represents a value of 1×2^0, or 1×1, which equals 1. If a 0 is in the zero position, its value equals 0×2^0, or 0×1, which equals 0. In every position, if a bit is 0, that position represents a decimal number of 0.

To convert a byte to a decimal number, determine the value represented by each bit, then add those values together. If a bit in the byte is 1 (in other words, if it's "on"), the bit's numerical equivalent in the coding scheme is added to the total. If a bit is 0, that position has no value and nothing is added to the total. For example, the byte 11111111 equals: $1 \times 2^7 + 1 \times 2^6 + 1 \times 2^5 + 1 \times 2^4 + 1 \times 2^3 + 1 \times 2^2 + 1 \times 2^1 + 1 \times 2^0$, or 128 + 64 + 32 + 16 + 8 + 4 + 2 + 1. Its decimal equivalent, then, is 255. In another example, the byte 00100100 equals: $0 \times 2^7 + 0 \times 2^6 + 1 \times 2^5 + 0 \times 2^4 + 0 \times 2^3 + 1 \times 2^2 + 0 \times 2^1 + 0 \times 2^0$, or 0 + 0 + 32 + 0 + 0 + 4 + 0 + 0. Its decimal equivalent, then, is 36.

Figure 3-4 illustrates placeholders in a byte, the exponential multiplier for each position, and the different decimal values that are represented by a 1 in each position.

To convert a decimal number to a byte, you reverse this process. For example, the decimal number 8 equals 2^3, which means a single "on" bit would be indicated in the fourth bit position as follows: 00001000. In another example, the decimal number 9 equals 8 + 1, or $2^3 + 2^0$, and would be represented by the binary number 00001001.

The binary numbering scheme may be used with more than eight positions. However, in the digital world, bytes form the building blocks for messages, and bytes always include eight positions. In a data signal, multiple bytes are combined to form a message. If you were to peek at the 1s and 0s used to transmit an entire e-mail message, for example, you might see millions of 0s and 1s passing by. A computer can quickly translate these binary numbers into codes, such as ASCII or JPEG, that express letters, numbers, and pictures.

Converting between decimal and binary numbers can be done by hand, as shown previously, or by using a scientific calculator, such as the one available with any of the Windows operating systems. Take, for example, the number 131. To convert it to a binary number:

1. Click the **Start** button, select **All Programs**, select **Accessories**, and then select **Calculator**. The Calculator window opens.
2. On a computer running Windows XP or Windows Vista, click **View**, then click **Scientific**. On a computer running Windows 7, click **View**, then click **Programmer**. Verify that the **Dec** option button is selected.
3. Type **131**, and then click the **Bin** option button. The binary equivalent of the number 131, 10000011, appears in the display window.

You can reverse this process to convert a binary number to a decimal number.

4. Close the Calculator window.

If you're connected to the Internet and using a Web browser, you can quickly convert binary and decimal numbers by using Google calculator. Go to *www.google.com,* then type in the number you want to convert, plus the format, in the search text box. For example, to convert the decimal number 131 into binary form, type "131 in binary" (without the quotation marks), and then press Enter. You see the following result: 131 = 0b10000011. The prefix "0b" indicates that the number is in binary format. To convert a binary number into decimal form, type "0b" (without the quotation marks) before the binary number. For example, entering "0b10000011 in decimal" (without the quotation marks) would return the number 131.

Because digital transmission involves sending and receiving only a pattern of 1s and 0s, represented by precise pulses, it is more reliable than analog transmission, which relies on variable waves. In addition, noise affects digital transmission less severely. On the other hand, digital transmission requires many pulses to transmit the same amount of information that an analog signal can transmit with a single wave. Nevertheless, the high reliability of digital transmission makes this extra signaling worthwhile. In the end, digital transmission is more efficient than analog transmission because it results in fewer errors and, therefore, requires less overhead to compensate for errors.

Overhead is a term used by networking professionals to describe the nondata information that must accompany data for a signal to be properly routed and interpreted by the network.

For example, the Data Link layer header and trailer, the Network layer addressing information, and the Transport layer flow-control information added to a piece of data in order to send it over the network are all part of the transmission's overhead.

It's important to understand that in both the analog and digital worlds, a variety of signaling techniques are used. For each technique, standards dictate what type of transmitter, communications channel, and receiver should be used. For example, the type of transmitter (NIC) used for computers on a LAN and the way in which this transmitter manipulates electric current to produce signals is different from the transmitter and signaling techniques used with a satellite link. Although not all signaling methods are covered in this book, you will learn about the most common methods used for data networking.

Data Modulation

Data relies almost exclusively on digital transmission. However, in some cases the type of connection your network uses may be capable of handling only analog signals. For example, telephone lines are designed to carry analog signals. If you connect to your ISP's network via a telephone line, the data signals issued by your computer must be converted into analog form before they get to the phone line. Later, they must be converted back into digital form when they arrive at the ISP's access server. A modem accomplishes this translation. The word **modem** reflects this device's function as a *mod*ulator/*dem*odulator—that is, it modulates digital signals into analog signals at the transmitting end, then demodulates analog signals into digital signals at the receiving end.

Data modulation is a technology used to modify analog signals to make them suitable for carrying data over a communication path. In **modulation**, a simple wave, called a carrier wave, is combined with another analog signal to produce a unique signal that gets transmitted from one node to another. The carrier wave has preset properties (including frequency, amplitude, and phase). Its purpose is to help convey information; in other words, it's only a messenger. Another signal, known as the information or data wave, is added to the carrier wave. When the information wave is added, it modifies one property of the carrier wave (for example, the frequency, amplitude, or phase). The result is a new, blended signal that contains properties of both the carrier wave and added data. When the signal reaches its destination, the receiver separates the data from the carrier wave.

Modulation can be used to make a signal conform to a specific pathway, as in the case of **FM (frequency modulation)** radio, in which the data must travel along a particular frequency. In frequency modulation, the frequency of the carrier signal is modified by the application of the data signal. In **AM (amplitude modulation)**, the amplitude of the carrier signal is modified by the application of the data signal. Modulation may also be used to issue multiple signals to the same communications channel and prevent the signals from interfering with one another. Figure 3-5 depicts an unaltered carrier wave, a data wave, and the combined wave as modified through frequency modulation. Later in this book, you will learn about networking technologies, such as DSL (digital subscriber line), that make use of modulation.

Net+

Simplex, Half-Duplex, and Duplex

3.1 Data transmission, whether analog or digital, may also be characterized by the direction in which the signals travel over the media. In cases in which signals may travel in only one direction, the transmission is considered **simplex**. An example of simplex communication is

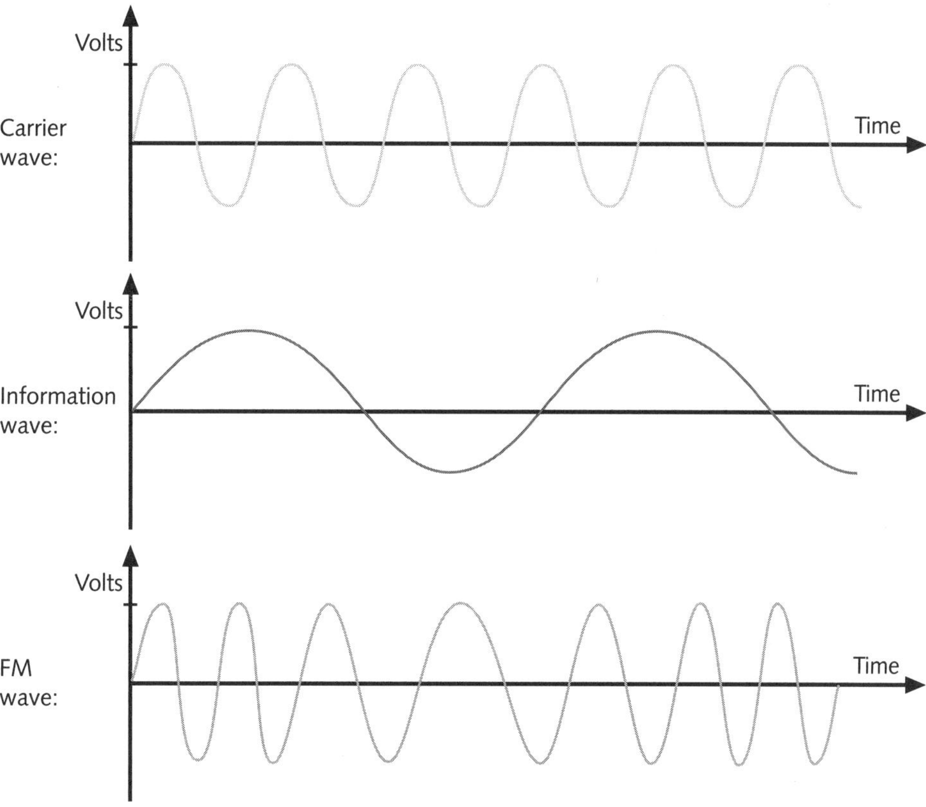

Figure 3-5 A carrier wave modified through frequency modulation

Net+ 3.1 a football coach calling out orders to his team through a megaphone. In this example, the coach's voice is the signal, and it travels in only one direction—away from the megaphone's mouthpiece and toward the team. Simplex is sometimes called one-way, or unidirectional, communication.

In **half-duplex** transmission, signals may travel in both directions over a medium but in only one direction at a time. Half-duplex systems contain only one channel for communication, and that channel must be shared for multiple nodes to exchange information. For example, a walkie-talkie or an apartment's intercom system that requires you to press a "talk" button to allow your voice to be transmitted uses half-duplex transmission. If you visit a friend's apartment building, you press the "talk" button to send your voice signals to his apartment. When your friend responds, he presses the "talk" button in his apartment to send his voice signal in the opposite direction over the wire to the speaker in the lobby where you wait. If you press the "talk" button while he's talking, you will not be able to hear his voice transmission. In a similar manner, some networks operate with only half-duplex capability.

When signals are free to travel in both directions over a medium simultaneously, the transmission is considered **full-duplex**. Full-duplex may also be called bidirectional transmission or, sometimes, simply **duplex**. When you call a friend on the telephone, your connection is an example of a full-duplex transmission because your voice signals can be transmitted to

3.1 your friend at the same time your friend's voice signals are transmitted in the opposite direction to you. In other words, both of you can talk and hear each other simultaneously.

Figure 3-6 compares simplex, half-duplex, and full-duplex transmissions.

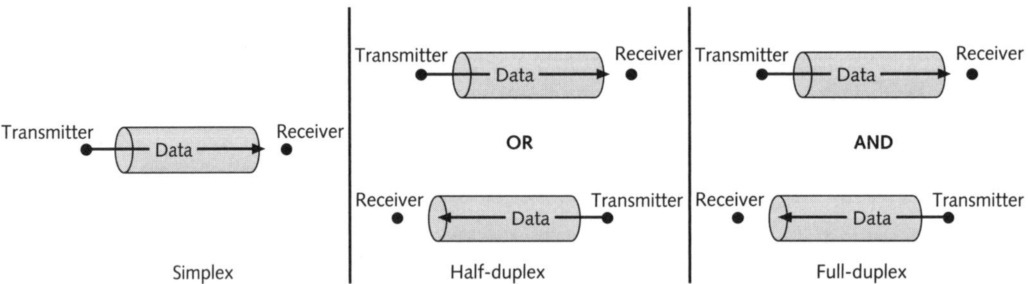

Figure 3-6 Simplex, half-duplex, and full-duplex transmission

Full-duplex transmission is also used on data networks. For example, Ethernet networks achieve full-duplex transmission using multiple channels on the same medium. A **channel** is a distinct communication path between nodes, much as a lane is a distinct transportation path on a freeway. Channels may be separated either logically or physically. You will learn about logically separate channels in the next section.

An example of physically separate channels occurs when one wire within a network cable is used for transmission while another wire is used for reception. In this example, each separate wire in the medium allows half-duplex transmission. When combined in a cable, they form a medium that provides full-duplex transmission. Full-duplex capability increases the speed with which data can travel over a network. In some cases—for example, when providing telephone service over the Internet—full-duplex data networks are a requirement.

Many network devices, such as modems and NICs, allow you to specify whether the device should use half- or full-duplex communication. It's important to know what type of transmission a network supports before installing network devices on that network. Modern NICs use full-duplex by default. If you configure a computer's NIC to use half-duplex while the rest of the network is using full-duplex, for example, that computer will not be able to communicate on the network.

Multiplexing

A form of transmission that allows multiple signals to travel simultaneously over one medium is known as **multiplexing**. To carry multiple signals, the medium's channel is logically separated into multiple smaller channels, or **subchannels**. Many different types of multiplexing are available, and the type used in any given situation depends on what the media, transmission, and reception equipment can handle. For each type of multiplexing, a device that can combine many signals on a channel, a **multiplexer (mux)**, is required at the transmitting end of the channel. At the receiving end, a **demultiplexer (demux)** separates the combined signals and regenerates them in their original form. Networks rely on multiplexing to increase the amount of data that can be transmitted in a given time span over a given bandwidth.

Net+ 3.1

One type of multiplexing, **TDM (time division multiplexing)**, divides a channel into multiple intervals of time, or time slots. It then assigns a separate time slot to every node on the network and, in that time slot, carries data from that node. For example, if five stations are connected to a network over one wire, five different time slots are established in the communications channel. Workstation A may be assigned time slot 1, workstation B time slot 2, workstation C time slot 3, and so on. Time slots are reserved for their designated nodes regardless of whether the node has data to transmit. If a node does not have data to send, nothing is sent during its time slot. This arrangement can be inefficient if some nodes on the network rarely send data. Figure 3-7 shows a simple TDM model.

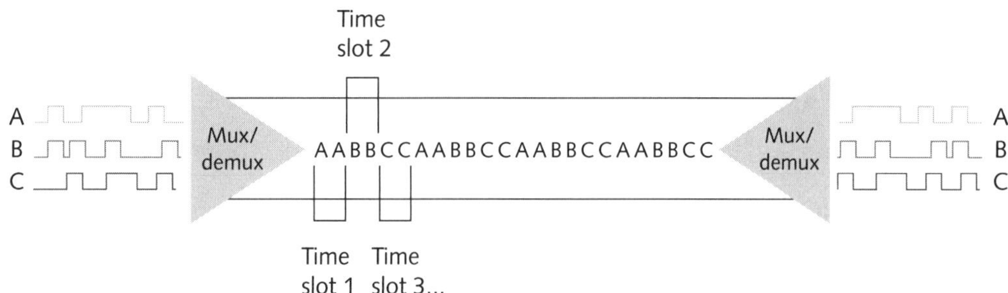

Figure 3-7 Time division multiplexing

Statistical multiplexing is similar to time division multiplexing, but rather than assigning a separate slot to each node in succession, the transmitter assigns slots to nodes according to priority and need. This method is more efficient than TDM, because in statistical multiplexing time slots are unlikely to remain empty. To begin with, in statistical multiplexing, as in TDM, each node is assigned one time slot. However, if a node doesn't use its time slot, statistical multiplexing devices recognize that and assign its slot to another node that needs to send data. The contention for slots may be arbitrated according to use or priority or even more sophisticated factors, depending on the network. Most important, statistical multiplexing maximizes available bandwidth on a network. Figure 3-8 depicts a simple statistical multiplexing system.

Figure 3-8 Statistical multiplexing

FDM (frequency division multiplexing) is a type of multiplexing that assigns a unique frequency band to each communications subchannel. Signals are modulated with different carrier frequencies, then multiplexed to simultaneously travel over a single channel. The first use of FDM was in the early twentieth century when telephone companies discovered they could send multiple voice signals over a single cable. That meant that, rather than stringing separate lines for each residence (and adding to the urban tangle of wires), they could send

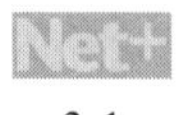
3.1 as many as 24 multiplexed signals over a single neighborhood line. Each signal was then demultiplexed before being brought into the home.

Now, telephone companies also multiplex signals on the phone line that enters your residence. Voice communications use the frequency band of 300–3400 Hz (because this matches approximately the range of human hearing), for a total bandwidth of 3100 Hz. But the potential bandwidth of one phone line far exceeds this. Telephone companies implement FDM to subdivide and send signals in the bandwidth above 3400 Hz. Because the frequencies can't be heard, you don't notice the data transmission occurring while you talk on the telephone. Figure 3-9 provides a simplified view of FDM, in which waves representing three different frequencies are carried simultaneously by one channel.

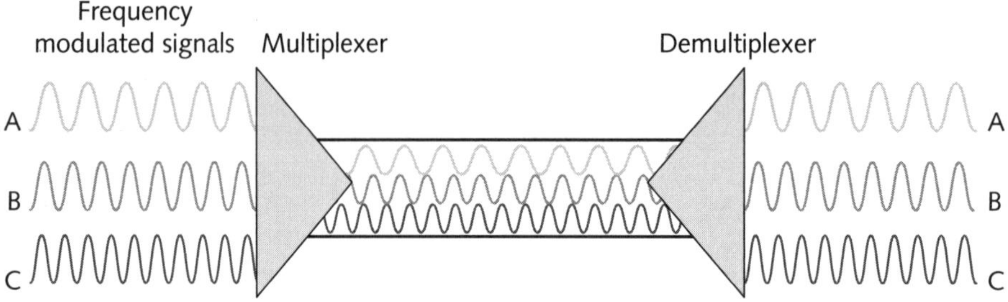

Figure 3-9 Frequency division multiplexing

Different forms of FDM exist. One type is used in cellular telephone transmission and another by DSL Internet access (you'll learn more about DSL in Chapter 7).

WDM (wavelength division multiplexing) is a technology used with fiber-optic cable, which enables one fiber-optic connection to carry multiple light signals simultaneously. Using WDM, a single fiber can transmit as many as 20 million telephone conversations at one time. WDM can work over any type of fiber-optic cable.

In the first step of WDM, a beam of light is divided into up to 40 different carrier waves, each with a different wavelength (and, therefore, a different color). Each wavelength represents a separate transmission channel capable of transmitting up to 10 Gbps. Before transmission, each carrier wave is modulated with a different data signal. Then, through a very narrow beam of light, lasers issue the separate, modulated waves to a multiplexer. The multiplexer combines all of the waves, in the same way that a prism can accept light beams of different wavelengths and concentrate them into a single beam of white light. Next, another laser issues this multiplexed beam to a strand of fiber within a fiber-optic cable. The fiber carries the multiplexed signals to a receiver, which is connected to a demultiplexer. The demultiplexer acts as a prism to separate the combined signals according to their different wavelengths (or colors). Then, the separate waves are sent to their destinations on the network. If the signal risks losing strength between the multiplexer and demultiplexer, an amplifier might be used to boost it. Figure 3-10 illustrates WDM transmission.

Most modern fiber-optic networks use a type of WDM called **DWDM (dense wavelength division multiplexing)**. In DWDM, a single fiber in a fiber-optic cable can carry between 80 and 160 channels. It achieves this increased capacity because it uses more wavelengths for signaling. In other words, there is less separation between the usable carrier waves in

Net+
3.1

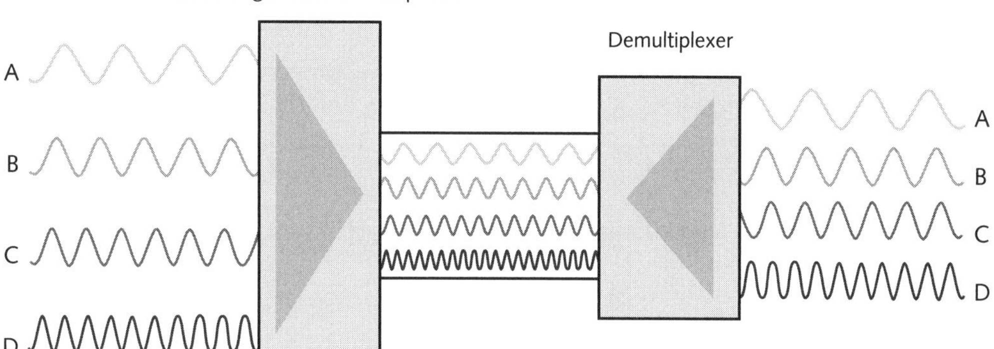

Figure 3-10 Wavelength division multiplexing

DWDM than there is in the original form of WDM. Because of its extraordinary capacity, DWDM is typically used on high-bandwidth or long-distance WAN links, such as the connection between a large ISP and its (even larger) network service provider.

Relationships Between Nodes

So far you have learned about two important characteristics of data transmission: the type of signaling (analog or digital) and the direction in which the signal travels (simplex, half-duplex, full-duplex, or multiplex). Another important characteristic is the number of senders and receivers, as well as the relationship between them. In general, data communications may involve a single transmitter with one or more receivers, or multiple transmitters with one or more receivers. The remainder of this section introduces the most common relationships between transmitters and receivers.

When a data transmission involves only one transmitter and one receiver, it is considered a **point-to-point** transmission. An office building in Dallas exchanging data with another office in St. Louis over a WAN connection is an example of point-to-point transmission. In this case, the sender only transmits data that is intended to be used by a specific receiver.

By contrast, **point-to-multipoint** transmission involves one transmitter and multiple receivers. Point-to-multipoint arrangements can be separated into two types: broadcast and nonbroadcast. **Broadcast** transmission involves one transmitter and multiple, *undefined* receivers. For example, a radio station indiscriminately transmitting a signal from its antenna on a tower to thousands of cars with radio antennas uses broadcast transmission. A broadcast transmission sends data to any and all receivers, without regard for which receiver can use it. Broadcast transmissions are frequently used on both wired and wireless networks because they are simple and quick. They are used to identify certain nodes, to send data to certain nodes (even though every node is capable of picking up the transmitted data, only the destination node will actually do it), and to send announcements to all nodes.

When more tailored data transfer is desired, a network might use **nonbroadcast point-to-multipoint transmission**. In this scenario, a node issues signals to multiple, *defined* recipients. For example, a network administrator could schedule the LAN transmission of an instructional video that only she and all of her team's workstations could receive.

3.1

Figure 3-11 contrasts point-to-point and point-to-multipoint transmissions.

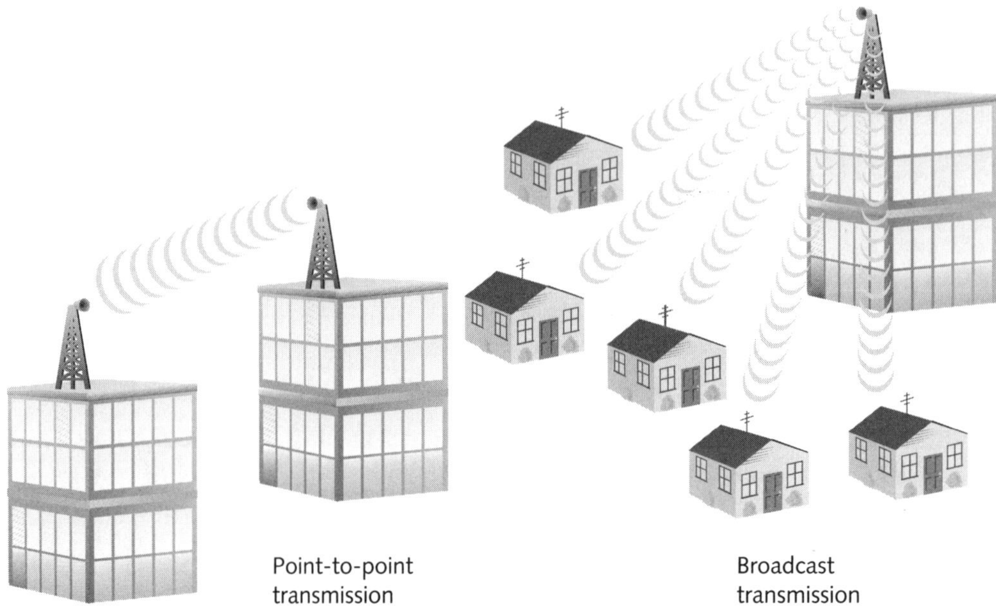

Figure 3-11 Point-to-point versus broadcast transmission

Throughput and Bandwidth

One data transmission characteristic often discussed and analyzed by networking professionals is throughput. **Throughput** is the measure of how much data is transmitted during a given period of time. It may also be called **capacity** or bandwidth (though as you will learn, bandwidth is technically different from throughput). Throughput is commonly expressed as a quantity of bits transmitted per second, with prefixes used to designate different throughput amounts. For example, the prefix *kilo* combined with the word *bit* (as in *kilobit*) indicates 1000 bits per second. Rather than talking about a throughput of 1000 bits per second, you typically say the throughput was 1 kilobit per second (1 Kbps). Table 3-1 summarizes the terminology and abbreviations used when discussing different throughput amounts.

Table 3-1 Throughput measures

Quantity	Prefix	Complete example	Abbreviation
1 bit per second	n/a	**1 bit per second**	bps
1000 bits per second	kilo	**1 kilobit per second**	Kbps
1,000,000 bits per second	mega	**1 megabit per second**	Mbps
1,000,000,000 bits per second	giga	**1 gigabit per second**	Gbps
1,000,000,000,000 bits per second	tera	**1 terabit per second**	Tbps

3.1 As an example, a residential broadband Internet connection might be rated for a maximum throughput of 1.544 Mbps. A fast LAN might transport up to 10 Gbps of data. Contemporary networks commonly achieve throughputs of 10 Mbps, 100 Mbps, 1 Gbps, or higher. Applications that require significant throughput include videoconferencing and telephone signaling. By contrast, instant messaging and e-mail, for example, require much less throughput.

Be careful not to confuse bits and bytes when discussing throughput. Although data storage quantities are typically expressed in multiples of bytes, data transmission quantities (in other words, throughput) are more commonly expressed in multiples of bits per second. When representing different data quantities, a small *b* represents bits, whereas a capital *B* represents bytes. To put this into context, a modem may transmit data at 56.6 Kbps (kilobits per second); a data file may be 56 KB (kilobytes) in size. Another difference between data storage and data throughput measures is that in data storage the prefix *kilo* means 2 to the 10th power, *or* 1024, *not* 1000.

Often, the term *bandwidth* is used interchangeably with throughput, and in fact, this may be the case on the Network+ certification exam. Bandwidth and throughput are similar concepts, but strictly speaking, **bandwidth** is a measure of the difference between the highest and lowest frequencies that a medium can transmit. This range of frequencies, which is expressed in Hz, is directly related to throughput. For example, if the Federal Communications Commission (FCC) told you that you could transmit a radio signal between 870 and 880 MHz, your allotted bandwidth (literally, the width of your frequency band) would be 10 MHz.

Baseband and Broadband

Baseband is a transmission form in which (typically) digital signals are sent through direct current (DC) pulses applied to the wire. This direct current requires exclusive use of the wire's capacity. As a result, baseband systems can transmit only one signal, or one channel, at a time. Every device on a baseband system shares the same channel. When one node is transmitting data on a baseband system, all other nodes on the network must wait for that transmission to end before they can send data. Baseband transmission supports half-duplexing, which means that computers can both send and receive information on the same length of wire. In some cases, baseband also supports full duplexing.

Ethernet is an example of a baseband system found on many LANs. In Ethernet, each device on a network can transmit over the wire—but only one device at a time. For example, if you want to save a file to the server, your NIC submits your request to use the wire; if no other device is using the wire to transmit data at that time, your workstation can go ahead. If the wire is in use, your workstation must wait and try again later. Of course, this retrying process happens so quickly that you don't even notice the wait.

Broadband is a form of transmission in which signals are modulated as radio frequency (RF) analog waves that use different frequency ranges. Unlike baseband, broadband technology does not encode information as digital pulses.

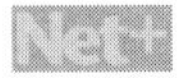

As you may know, broadband transmission is used to bring cable TV to your home. Your cable TV connection can carry at least 25 times as much data as a typical baseband system
3.1 (like Ethernet) carries, including many different broadcast frequencies on different channels. In traditional broadband systems, signals travel in only one direction—toward the user. To allow users to send data as well, cable systems allot a separate channel space for the user's transmission and use amplifiers that can separate data the user issues from data the network transmits. Broadband transmission is generally more expensive than baseband transmission because of the extra hardware involved. On the other hand, broadband systems can span longer distances than baseband.

In the field of networking, some terms have more than one meaning, depending on their context. *Broadband* is one of those terms. The *broadband* described in this chapter is the transmission system that carries RF signals across multiple channels on a coaxial cable, as used by cable TV. This definition was the original meaning of broadband. However, *broadband* has evolved to mean any of several different network types that use digital signaling to transmit data at very high transmission rates.

Transmission Flaws

2.2 Both analog and digital signals are susceptible to degradation between the time they are
3.1 issued by a transmitter and the time they are received. One of the most common transmission flaws affecting data signals is noise.

Noise As you learned earlier, noise is any undesirable influence that may degrade or distort a signal. Many different types of noise may affect transmission. A common source of noise is **EMI (electromagnetic interference)**, or waves that emanate from electrical devices or cables carrying electricity. Motors, power lines, televisions, copiers, fluorescent lights, microwave ovens, manufacturing machinery, and other sources of electrical activity (including a severe thunderstorm) can cause EMI. One type of EMI is **RFI (radio frequency interference)**, or electromagnetic interference caused by radio waves. (Often, you'll see EMI referred to as EMI/RFI.) Strong broadcast signals from radio or TV antennas can generate RFI. When EMI noise affects analog signals, this distortion can result in the incorrect transmission of data, just as if static prevented you from hearing a radio station broadcast. However, this type of noise affects digital signals much less. Because digital signals do not depend on subtle amplitude or frequency differences to communicate information, they are more apt to be readable despite distortions caused by EMI noise.

Another form of noise that hinders data transmission is cross talk. **Cross talk** occurs when a signal traveling on one wire or cable infringes on the signal traveling over an adjacent wire or
3.1 cable. When cross talk occurs between two cables, it's called **alien cross talk.** When it occurs between wire pairs near the source of a signal, it's known as **NEXT (near end cross talk).** One potential cause of NEXT is an improper termination—for example, one in which wire insulation has been damaged or wire pairs have been untwisted too far.

If you've ever been on the phone and heard the conversation on your second line in the background, you have heard the effects of cross talk. In this example, the current carrying a signal on the second line's wire imposes itself on the wire carrying your line's

Net+ 3.1 signal, as shown in Figure 3-12. The resulting noise, or cross talk, is equal to a portion of the second line's signal. Cross talk in the form of overlapping phone conversations is bothersome, but does not usually prevent you from hearing your own line's conversation. In data networks, however, cross talk can be extreme enough to prevent the accurate delivery of data.

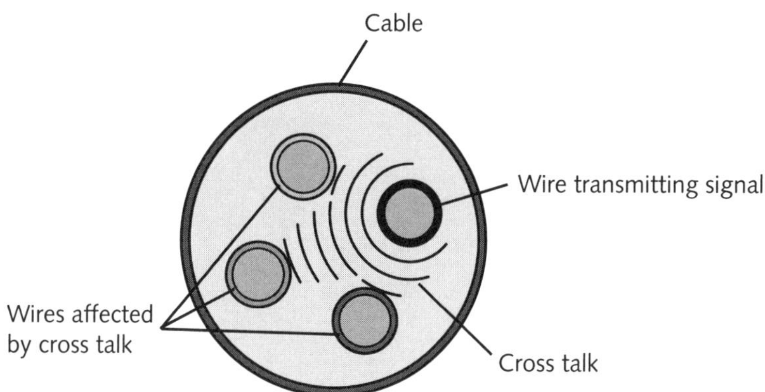

Figure 3-12 Cross talk between wires in a cable

In every signal, a certain amount of noise is unavoidable. However, engineers have designed a number of ways to limit the potential for noise to degrade a signal. One way is simply to ensure that the strength of the signal exceeds the strength of the noise. Proper cable design and installation are also critical for protecting against noise's effects. Note that all forms of noise are measured in decibels (dB).

Attenuation Another transmission flaw is **attenuation**, or the loss of a signal's strength as it travels away from its source. Just as your voice becomes fainter as it travels farther, so do signals fade with distance. To compensate for attenuation, both analog and digital signals are boosted en route. However, the technology used to boost an analog signal is different from that used to boost a digital signal. Analog signals pass through an **amplifier**, an electronic device that increases the voltage, or strength, of the signals. When an analog signal is amplified, the noise that it has accumulated is also amplified. This indiscriminate amplification causes the analog signal to worsen progressively. After multiple amplifications, an analog signal may become difficult to decipher. Figure 3-13 shows an analog signal distorted by noise and then amplified once.

When digital signals are repeated, they are actually retransmitted in their original form, without the noise they might have accumulated previously. This process is known as **regeneration**. A device that regenerates a digital signal is called a **repeater**. Figure 3-14 shows a digital signal distorted by noise and then regenerated by a repeater. Amplifiers and repeaters belong to the Physical layer of the OSI model. Both are used to extend the length of a network. Because most networks are digital, they typically use repeaters.

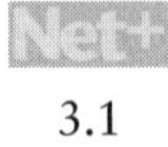

3.1

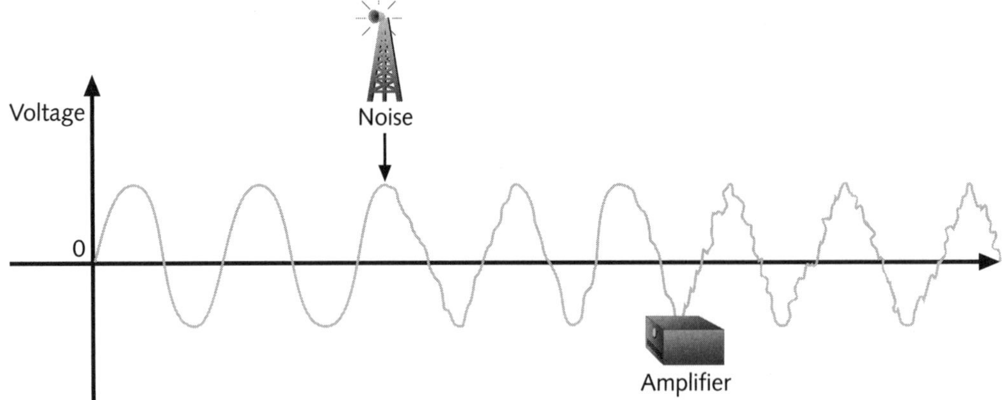

Figure 3-13 An analog signal distorted by noise and then amplified

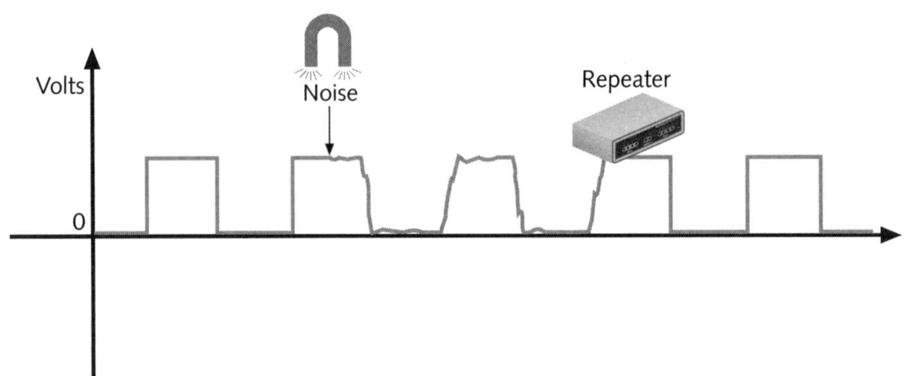

Figure 3-14 A digital signal distorted by noise and then repeated

Latency In an ideal world, networks could transmit data instantaneously between sender and receiver, no matter how great the distance between the two. However, in the real world every network is subjected to a delay between the transmission of a signal and its eventual receipt. For example, when you press a key on your computer to save a file to a network server, the file's data must travel through your NIC, the network wire, one or more connectivity devices, more cabling, and the server's NIC before it lands on the server's hard disk. Although electrons travel rapidly, they still have to travel, and a brief delay takes place between the moment you press the key and the moment the server accepts the data. This delay is called **latency**.

The length of the cable involved affects latency, as does the existence of any intervening connectivity device, such as a router. Different devices affect latency to different degrees. For example, modems, which must modulate both incoming and outgoing signals, increase a connection's latency far more than hubs, which simply repeat a signal. The most common

3.1 way to measure latency on data networks is by calculating a packet's RTT (**round-trip time**), or the length of time it takes for a packet to go from sender to receiver, then back from receiver to sender. RTT is usually measured in milliseconds.

Latency causes problems only when a receiving node is expecting some type of communication, such as the rest of a data stream it has begun to accept. If that node does not receive the rest of the data stream within a given time period, it assumes that no more data are coming. This assumption may cause transmission errors on a network. When you connect multiple network segments and thereby increase the distance between sender and receiver, you increase the network's latency. To constrain the latency and avoid its associated errors, each type of cabling is rated for a maximum number of connected network segments, and each transmission method is assigned a maximum segment length.

Common Media Characteristics

3.1 Now that you are familiar with data-signaling characteristics, you are ready to learn more about the physical and atmospheric paths that these signals traverse. When deciding which kind of transmission media to use, you must match your networking needs with the characteristics of the media. This section describes the characteristics of several types of physical media, including throughput, cost, noise immunity, size and scalability, and connectors and media converters. The medium used for wireless transmission, the atmosphere, is discussed in detail in Chapter 8.

Throughput

Perhaps the most significant factor in choosing a transmission method is its throughput. All media are limited by the laws of physics that prevent signals from traveling faster than the speed of light. Beyond that, throughput is limited by the signaling and multiplexing techniques used in a given transmission method. Using fiber-optic cables allows faster throughput than copper or wireless connections. Noise and devices connected to the transmission medium can further limit throughput. A noisy circuit spends more time compensating for the noise and, therefore, has fewer resources available for transmitting data.

Cost

Cost is another significant factor in choosing a network medium. However, the precise costs of using a particular type of cable or wireless connection can be difficult to pinpoint. For example, although a vendor might quote you the cost per foot for new network cabling, you might also have to upgrade some hardware on your network to use that type of cabling. Thus, the cost of upgrading your media would actually include more than the cost of the cabling itself. Not only do media costs depend on the hardware that already exists in a network, but they also depend on the size of your network and the cost of labor in your area (unless you plan to install the cable yourself). The following variables can all influence the final cost of implementing a certain type of media:

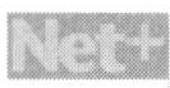

3.1

- *Cost of installation*—Can you install the media yourself, or must you hire contractors to do it? Will you need to move walls or build new conduits or closets? Will you need to lease lines from a service provider?
- *Cost of new infrastructure versus reusing existing infrastructure*—Can you use existing wiring? In some cases, for example, installing all new Category 6 UTP wiring may not pay off if you can use existing Category 5 UTP wiring. If you replace only part of your infrastructure, will it be easily integrated with the existing media?
- *Cost of maintenance and support*—Reuse of an existing cabling infrastructure does not save any money if it is in constant need of repair or enhancement. Also, if you use an unfamiliar media type, it may cost more to hire a technician to service it. Will you be able to service the media yourself, or must you hire contractors to service it?
- *Cost of a lower transmission rate affecting productivity*—If you save money by reusing existing slower connections, are you incurring costs by reducing productivity? In other words, are you making staff wait longer to save and print reports or exchange e-mail?
- *Cost of downtime*—If a cabling system is poorly installed and needs fixing, or if an inexpensive solution needs to be replaced in just a few years, at least some of your organization's users will not be able to work. Even at a small office, a few hours of downtime can cost a business several thousand dollars in lost productivity. For an organization that relies on its network for taking orders or providing services, the toll could be much higher.
- *Cost of obsolescence*—Are you choosing media that may become passing fads, requiring rapid replacement? Will you be able to find reasonably priced connectivity hardware that will be compatible with your chosen media for years to come?

When planning a new cabling installation or replacing existing infrastructure, a good rule of thumb is to choose a solution that will last at least 10 years. A long-term solution, such as choosing the latest high-quality cabling that can handle throughput 10 times faster than your existing network uses, might cost more than a short-term solution initially, but will likely cost less over its life of use.

Net+

Noise Immunity

2.2 3.1 As you learned earlier, noise can distort data signals. The extent to which noise affects a signal depends partly on the transmission media. Some types of media are more susceptible to noise than others. The type of media least susceptible to noise is fiber-optic cable because it does not use electric current, but light waves, to conduct signals.

On most networks, noise is an ever-present threat, so you should take measures to limit its impact on your network. For example, install cabling well away from powerful electromagnetic forces. If your environment still leaves your network vulnerable, choose a type of transmission media that helps to protect the signal from noise. For example, wireless signals are more apt to be distorted by EMI/RFI than signals traveling over a cable. It is also possible to use antinoise algorithms to protect data from being corrupted by noise. If these measures

don't ward off interference, in the case of wired media, you may need to use a metal **conduit**,
2.2 or pipeline, to contain and further protect the cabling.

3.1

Size and Scalability

2.6 Three specifications determine the size and scalability of networking media: maximum nodes
3.1 per segment, maximum segment length, and maximum network length. In cabling, each of these specifications is based on the physical characteristics of the wire and the electrical characteristics of data transmission. The maximum number of nodes per segment depends on attenuation and latency. Each device added to a network segment causes a slight increase in the signal's attenuation and latency. To ensure a clear, strong, and timely signal, you must limit the number of nodes on a segment.

The maximum segment length depends on attenuation and latency plus the segment type. A network can include two types of segments: populated and unpopulated. A **populated segment** is a part of a network that contains end nodes. For example, a switch connecting users in a classroom is part of a populated segment. An **unpopulated segment**, also known as a **link segment**, is a part of the network that does not contain end nodes, but simply connects two networking devices such as routers.

Segment lengths are limited because after a certain distance, a signal loses so much strength that it cannot be accurately interpreted. The maximum distance a signal can travel and still be interpreted accurately is equal to a segment's maximum length. Beyond this length, data loss is apt to occur. As with the maximum number of nodes per segment, maximum segment length varies between different cabling types. The same principle of data loss applies to maximum network length, which is the sum of the network's segment lengths.

Connectors and Media Converters

3.1 **Connectors** are the pieces of hardware that connect the wire to the network device, be it a
3.2 file server, workstation, switch, or printer. Every networking medium requires a specific kind of connector. The type of connectors you use will affect the cost of installing and maintaining the network, the ease of adding new segments or nodes to the network, and the technical expertise required to maintain the network. The connectors you are most likely to encounter on modern networks are illustrated throughout this chapter and shown together in Appendix C.

Connectors are specific to a particular media type, but that doesn't prevent one network from using multiple media. Some connectivity devices are designed to accept more than one type of media. If you are working with a connectivity device that can't, you can integrate the two media types by using media converters. A **media converter** is a piece of hardware that enables networks or segments running on different media to interconnect and exchange signals. For example, suppose a segment leading from your company's data center to a group of workstations uses fiber-optic cable, but the workgroup hub can only accept twisted pair (copper) cable. In that case, you could use a media converter to interconnect the hub with the fiber-optic cable. The media converter completes the physical connection and also converts the electrical signals from the copper cable to light wave signals that can traverse the fiber-optic cable, and vice versa. Such a media converter is shown in Figure 3-15.

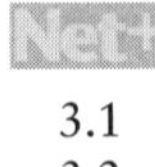

3.1
3.2

Figure 3-15 Copper wire-to-fiber media converter
Courtesy of Omnitron Systems Technology

The terms *wire* and *cable are* used synonymously in some situations. Strictly speaking, however, *wire* is a subset of *cabling,* because the *cabling* category may also include fiber-optic cable, which is almost never called wire. The exact meaning of the term *wire* depends on context. For example, if you said, in a somewhat casual way, "We had 6 gigs of data go over the wire last night," you would be referring to whatever transmission media helped carry the data—whether fiber, radio waves, coax, or UTP.

Now that you understand data transmission and the factors to consider when choosing a transmission medium, you are ready to learn about different types of transmission media. To qualify for Network+ certification, you must know the characteristics and limitations of each type of media, how to install and design a network with each type, how to troubleshoot networking media problems, and how to provide for future network growth with each option.

Coaxial Cable

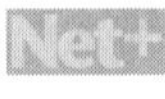

3.1 **Coaxial cable**, called "coax" for short, was the foundation for Ethernet networks in the 1980s and remained a popular transmission medium for many years. Over time, however, twisted pair and fiber-optic cabling have replaced coax in modern LANs. If you work on long-established networks or cable systems, however, you might have to work with coaxial cable.

Coaxial cable consists of a central metal core (often copper) surrounded by an insulator, a braided metal shielding, called **braiding** or **shield**, and an outer cover, called the **sheath** or jacket. Figure 3-16 depicts a typical coaxial cable. The core may be constructed of one solid metal wire or several thin strands of metal wire. The core carries the electromagnetic signal, and the braided metal shielding acts as both a shield against noise and a ground for the signal. The insulator layer usually consists of a plastic material such as PVC (polyvinyl chloride) or Teflon. It protects the core from the metal shielding because if the two made contact, the

3.1 wire would short-circuit. The sheath, which protects the cable from physical damage, may be PVC or a more expensive, fire-resistant plastic.

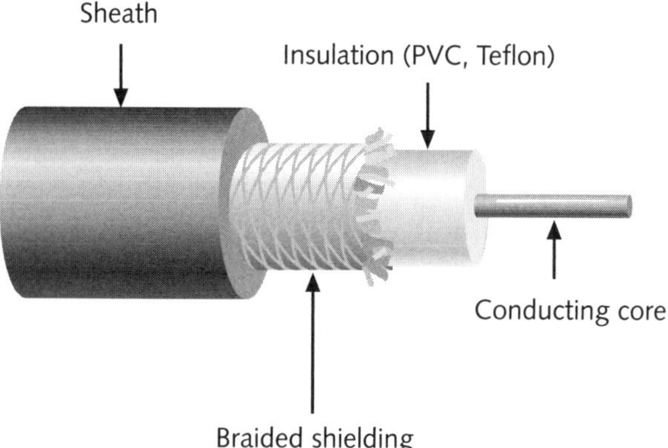

Figure 3-16 Coaxial cable

Because of its shielding, most coaxial cable has a high resistance to noise. It can also carry signals farther than twisted pair cabling before amplification of the signals becomes necessary (although not as far as fiber-optic cabling). On the other hand, coaxial cable is more expensive than twisted pair cable because it requires significantly more raw materials to manufacture.

Coaxial cabling comes in hundreds of specifications, although you are likely to see only two or three types of coax in use on data networks. All types have been assigned an RG specification number. (RG stands for *radio guide,* which is appropriate because coaxial cabling is used to guide radio frequencies in broadband transmission.) The significant differences between the cable types lie in the materials used for their shielding and conducting cores, which in turn influence their transmission characteristics, such as **impedance** (or the resistance that contributes to controlling the signal, as expressed in ohms), attenuation, and throughput. Each type of coax is suited to a different purpose. When discussing the size of the conducting core in a coaxial cable, we refer to its **American Wire Gauge (AWG)** size. The larger the AWG size, the smaller the diameter of a piece of wire. Following is a list of coaxial cable specifications used with data networks:

- *RG-6*—A type of coaxial cable that is characterized by an impedance of 75 ohms and contains an 18 AWG conducting core. The core is usually made of solid copper. RG-6 coaxial cables are used, for example, to deliver broadband cable Internet service and cable TV, particularly over long distances. If a service provider such as Comcast or Charter supplies you with Internet service, the cable entering your home is RG-6.
- *RG-8*—A type of coaxial cable characterized by a 50-ohm impedance and a 10 AWG core. RG-8 provided the medium for the first Ethernet networks, known as **Thicknet**. You will never find Thicknet on new networks, but you might find it on older networks.

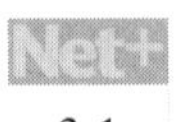

3.1

- *RG-58*—A type of coaxial cable characterized by a 50-ohm impedance and a 24 AWG core. RG-58 was a popular medium for Ethernet LANs in the 1980s. With a smaller diameter than RG-8, RG-58 is more flexible and easier to handle and install. Its core is typically made of several thin strands of copper. The Ethernet standard that relies on RG-58 coax is called **Thinnet** because it is thinner than Thicknet cables. Like Thicknet, Thinnet is almost never used on modern networks, although you might encounter it on networks installed in the 1980s.
- *RG-59*—A type of coaxial cable characterized by a 75-ohm impedance and a 20 or 22 AWG core, usually made of braided copper. Less expensive but suffering from greater attenuation than the more common RG-6 coax, RG-59 is still used for relatively short connections, for example, when distributing video signals from a central receiver to multiple monitors within a building.

3.1
3.2

The two coaxial cable types commonly used in networks today, RG-6 and RG-59, can terminate with one of two connector types: an F-Type connector or a BNC connector. **F-Type connectors** attach to coaxial cable so that the pin in the center of the connector is the conducting core of the cable. Therefore, F-Type connectors require that the cable contain a solid metal core. After being attached to the cable by crimping or compression, connectors are threaded and screw together like a nut-and-bolt assembly. A male F-Type connector, or plug, attached to coax is shown in Figure 3-17. A corresponding female F-Type connector, or jack, would be coupled with the male connector. F-Type connectors are most often used with RG-6 cables.

Figure 3-17 F-Type connector
Courtesy of MCM Electronics, Inc.

BNC stands for Bayonet Neill-Concelman, a term that refers to both a style of connection and its two inventors. (Sometimes the term *British Naval Connector* is also used.) A **BNC connector** is crimped, compressed, or twisted onto a coaxial cable. It connects to another BNC connector via a turning-and-locking mechanism—this is the bayonet coupling referenced in its name. Unlike an F-Type connector, male BNC connectors do not use the central conducting core of the coax as part of the connection, but provide their own conducting pin. BNC was once the standard for connecting coaxial-based Ethernet segments. Today, though, you're more likely to find BNC connectors used with RG-59 coaxial cable. Less commonly, they're also used with RG-6. Figure 3-18 shows a BNC connector that is not attached to a cable.

3.1
3.2

Figure 3-18 BNC connector
© Igor Smichkov/Shutterstock.com

When sourcing connectors for coaxial cable, you need to specify the type of cable you are using. For instance, when working with RG-6 coax, choose an F-Type connector made specifically for RG-6 cables. That way, you'll be certain that the connectors and cable share the same impedance rating. If impedance ratings don't match, data errors will result and network performance will suffer.

Next, you will learn about a medium you are more likely to find on modern LANs, twisted pair cable.

Twisted Pair Cable

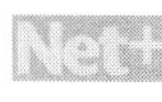
3.1

Twisted pair cable consists of color-coded pairs of insulated copper wires, each with a diameter of 0.4 to 0.8 mm (approximately the diameter of a straight pin). Every two wires are twisted around each other to form pairs, and all the pairs are encased in a plastic sheath, as shown in Figure 3-19. The number of pairs in a cable varies, depending on the cable type.

The more twists per foot in a pair of wires, the more resistant the pair will be to cross talk. Higher-quality, more-expensive twisted pair cable contains more twists per foot. The number of twists per meter or foot is known as the **twist ratio**. Because twisting the wire pairs more tightly requires more cable, however, a high twist ratio can result in greater attenuation. For optimal performance, cable manufacturers must strike a balance between minimizing cross talk and reducing attenuation.

Net+ 3.1

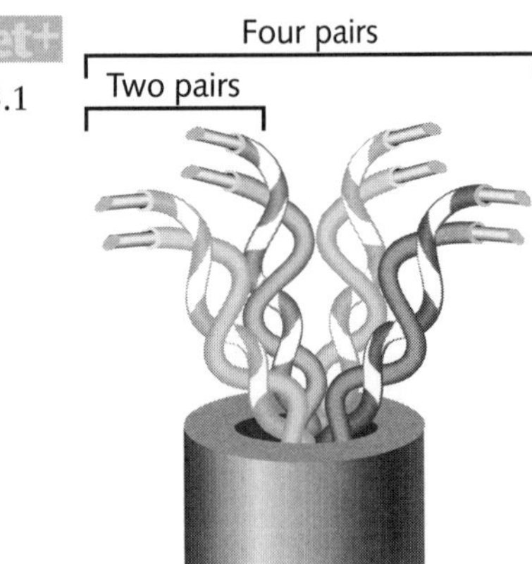

Figure 3-19 Twisted pair cable

Because twisted pair is used in such a wide variety of environments and for a variety of purposes, it comes in hundreds of different designs. These designs vary in their twist ratio, the number of wire pairs that they contain, the grade of copper used, the type of shielding (if any), and the materials used for shielding, among other things. A twisted pair cable may contain from 1 to 4200 wire pairs. Modern networks typically use cables that contain four wire pairs, in which one pair is dedicated to sending data and another pair is dedicated to receiving data.

In 1991, two standards organizations, the TIA/EIA, finalized their specifications for twisted pair wiring in a standard called "TIA/EIA 568." Since then, this body has continually revised the international standards for new and modified transmission media. Its standards now cover cabling media, design, and installation specifications. The TIA/EIA 568 standard divides twisted pair wiring into several categories. The types of twisted pair wiring you will hear about most often are **Cat** (category) 3, 5, 5e, 6, and 6a, and Cat 7. All of the category cables fall under the TIA/EIA 568 standard. Modern LANs use Cat 5 or higher wiring.

Twisted pair cable is relatively inexpensive, flexible, and easy to install, and it can span a significant distance before requiring a repeater (though not as far as coax). Twisted pair cable easily accommodates several different topologies, although it is most often implemented in star or star-hybrid topologies. All twisted pair cable falls into one of two categories: STP (shielded twisted pair) or UTP (unshielded twisted pair).

STP (Shielded Twisted Pair)

STP (shielded twisted pair) cable consists of twisted-wire pairs that are not only individually insulated, but also surrounded by a shielding made of a metallic substance such as foil. Some STP use a braided copper shielding. The shielding acts as a barrier to external electromagnetic forces, thus preventing them from affecting the signals traveling over the wire inside the shielding. It also contains the electrical energy of the signals inside. The shielding may be grounded to enhance its protective effects. The effectiveness of STP's shield depends on the level and type of environmental noise, the thickness and material used for the shield, the grounding mechanism, and the symmetry and consistency of the shielding. Figure 3-20 depicts an STP cable.

3.1

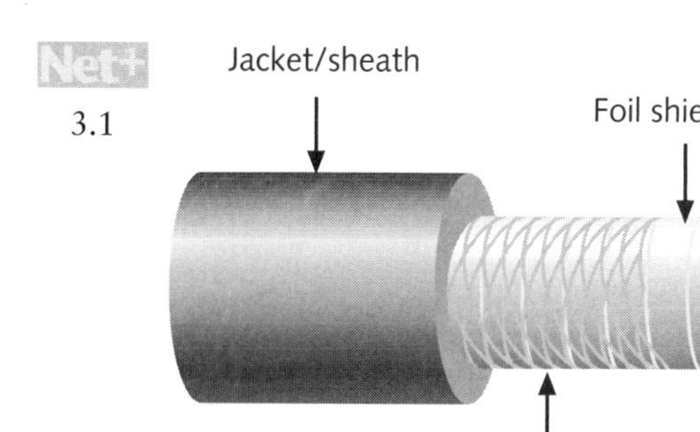

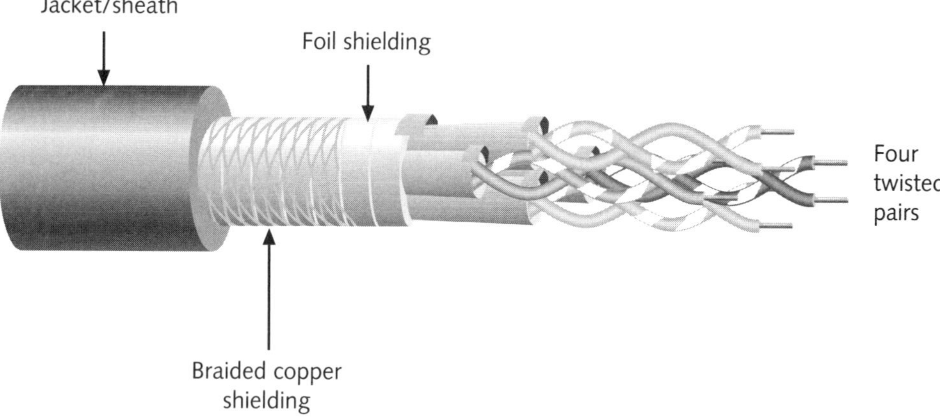

Figure 3-20 STP cable

UTP (Unshielded Twisted Pair)

UTP (unshielded twisted pair) cabling consists of one or more insulated wire pairs encased in a plastic sheath. As its name implies, UTP does not contain additional shielding for the twisted pairs. As a result, UTP is both less expensive and less resistant to noise than STP. Figure 3-21 depicts a typical UTP cable.

Figure 3-21 UTP cable

Earlier, you learned that the TIA/EIA consortium designated standards for twisted pair wiring. To manage network cabling, you need to be familiar with the standards for use on modern networks, particularly Cat 5 or higher. Note that Cat 4 cabling exists, too, but it is rarely used.

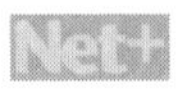

3.1

- *Cat 3 (Category 3)*—A form of UTP that contains four wire pairs and can carry up to 10 Mbps of data with a possible bandwidth of 16 MHz. Cat 3 was used for 10-Mbps Ethernet or 4-Mbps token ring networks. You will rarely find it on any modern network, however.
- *Cat 5 (Category 5)*—A form of UTP that contains four wire pairs and supports up to 1000 Mbps throughput and a 100-MHz signal rate. Figure 3-22 depicts a typical Cat 5 UTP cable with its twisted pairs untwisted, allowing you to see their matched color coding. For example, the wire that is colored solid orange is twisted around the wire that is part orange and part white to form the pair responsible for transmitting data.

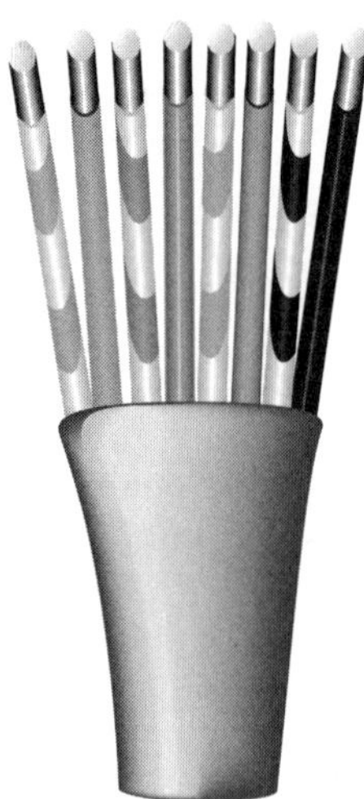

Figure 3-22 A Cat 5 UTP cable with pairs untwisted

It can be difficult to tell the difference between four-pair Cat 3 cables and four-pair Cat 5 or Cat 5e cables. However, some visual clues can help. On Cat 5 cable, the jacket is usually stamped with the manufacturer's name and cable type, including the Cat 5 specification. A cable whose jacket has no markings is more likely to be Cat 3. Also, pairs in Cat 5 cables have a significantly higher twist ratio than pairs in Cat 3 cables. Although Cat 3 pairs might be twisted as few as three times per foot, Cat 5 pairs are twisted at least 12 times per foot. Other clues, such as the date of installation (old cable is more likely to be Cat 3), looseness of the jacket (Cat 3's jacket is typically looser than Cat 5's), and the extent to which pairs are untwisted before a termination (Cat 5 can tolerate only a small amount of untwisting) are also helpful, though less definitive.

- *Cat 5e (Enhanced Category 5)*—A higher-grade version of Cat 5 wiring that contains high-quality copper offers a high twist ratio and uses advanced methods for reducing cross talk. Cat 5e can support a signaling rate as high as 350 MHz, more than triple the capability of regular Cat 5.
- *Cat 6 (Category 6)*—A twisted pair cable that contains four wire pairs, each wrapped in foil insulation. Additional foil insulation covers the bundle of wire pairs, and a fire-resistant plastic sheath covers the second foil layer. The foil insulation provides

excellent resistance to cross talk and enables Cat 6 to support a 250-MHz signaling
3.1 rate and at least six times the throughput supported by regular Cat 5.

- *Cat 6a (Augmented Category 6)*—A higher-grade version of Cat 6 wiring that reduces attenuation and cross talk and allows for potentially exceeding traditional network segment length limits. Cat 6a is capable of a 500-MHz signaling rate and can reliably transmit data at multi-gigabit per second rates. Cat 6a cabling is backward compatible with Cat 5, Cat 5e, and Cat 6 cabling, which means that it can replace lower-level cabling without requiring connector or equipment changes.

- *Cat 7 (Category 7)*—A twisted pair cable that contains multiple wire pairs, each surrounded by its own shielding, then packaged in additional shielding beneath the sheath. One advantage to Cat 7 cabling is that it can support signal rates up to 1 GHz. However, it requires different connectors than other versions of UTP because its twisted pairs must be more isolated from each other to ward off cross talk. Because of its added shielding, Cat 7 cabling is also larger and less flexible than other versions of UTP cable. Cat 7 is less common than Cat 5, Cat 6, or Cat 6a on modern networks.

Technically, because Cat 6 and Cat 7 contain wires that are individually shielded, they are not unshielded twisted pair. Instead, they are more similar to shielded twisted pair.

UTP cabling may be used with any one of several IEEE Physical layer networking standards that specify throughput maximums of 10, 100, 1000, and even 10,000 Mbps. These standards are described in detail in Chapter 5.

Comparing STP and UTP

STP and UTP share several characteristics. The following list highlights their similarities and differences:

- *Throughput*—STP and UTP can both transmit data at 10 Mbps, 100 Mbps, 1 Gbps, and 10 Gbps, depending on the grade of cabling and the transmission method in use.
- *Cost*—STP and UTP vary in cost, depending on the grade of copper used, the category rating, and any enhancements. Typically, STP is more expensive than UTP because it contains more materials and it has a lower demand. It also requires grounding, which can lead to more expensive installation. High-grade UTP can be expensive, too, however. For example, Cat 6a costs more per foot than Cat 5 cabling.

- *Connector*—STP and UTP use **RJ-45 (registered jack 45)** modular connectors and
3.1 data jacks, which look similar to analog telephone connectors and jacks. However,
3.2 telephone connections follow the **RJ-11 (registered jack 11)** standard. Figure 3-23
shows a close-up of an RJ-45 connector for a cable containing four wire pairs. For comparison, this figure also shows a traditional RJ-11 phone line connector. All types of Ethernet that rely on twisted pair cabling use RJ-45 connectors.

- *Noise immunity*—Because of its shielding, STP is more noise resistant than UTP. On
3.1 the other hand, signals transmitted over UTP may be subject to filtering and balancing techniques to offset the effects of noise.

- *Size and scalability*—The maximum segment length for both STP and UTP is 100 m, or 328
3.1 feet, on Ethernet networks that support data rates from 1 Mbps to 10 Gbps. These
2.6 accommodate a maximum of 1024 nodes. (However, attaching so many nodes to a segment is very impractical, as it would slow traffic and make management nearly impossible.)

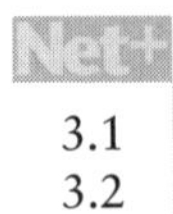

3.1
3.2

Figure 3-23 RJ-45 and RJ-11 connectors
Gary Herrington Photography

Net+

Terminating Twisted Pair Cable

2.6 Imagine you have been sent to one of your employer's remote offices and charged with
3.1 upgrading all the old Cat 3 patch cables in a data closet with new, Cat 6a patch cables. A
3.2 **patch cable** is a relatively short (usually between 3 and 25 feet) length of cabling with
4.2 connectors at both ends. Based on the company's network documentation, you brought 50 premade cables with RJ-45 plugs on both ends, which you purchased from an online cable vendor. At the remote location, however, you discover that its data closet actually contains 60 patch cables that need replacing. No additional premade cables are available at that office, and you don't have time to order more. Luckily, you have brought your networking tool kit with spare RJ-45 plugs and a spool of Cat 6a cable. Knowing how to properly terminate Cat 6a cables allows you to make all the new patch cables you need and complete your work. Even if you are never faced with this situation, it's likely that at some point you will have to replace an RJ-45 connector on an existing cable. This section describes how to terminate twisted pair cable.

Proper cable termination is a basic requirement for two nodes on a network to communicate. Beyond that, however, poor terminations can lead to loss or noise—and consequently, errors—in a signal. Closely following termination standards, then, is critical. TIA/EIA has specified two different methods of inserting twisted pair wires into RJ-45 plugs: TIA/EIA 568A and TIA/EIA 568B. Functionally, there is no difference between the standards. You only have to be certain that you use the same standard on every RJ-45 plug and jack on your network, so that data is transmitted and received correctly. Figure 3-24 depicts pin numbers and assignments (or pinouts) for the TIA/EIA 568A standard when used on an Ethernet network. Figure 3-25 depicts pin numbers and assignments for the TIA/EIA 568B standard.

Although networking professionals commonly refer to wires in Figures 3-24 and 3-25 as *transmit* and *receive,* their original *T* and *R* designations stand for *Tip* and *Ring,* terms that come from early telephone technology but are irrelevant today.

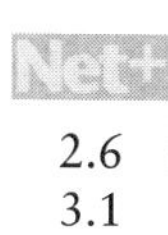

2.6
3.1
3.2
4.2

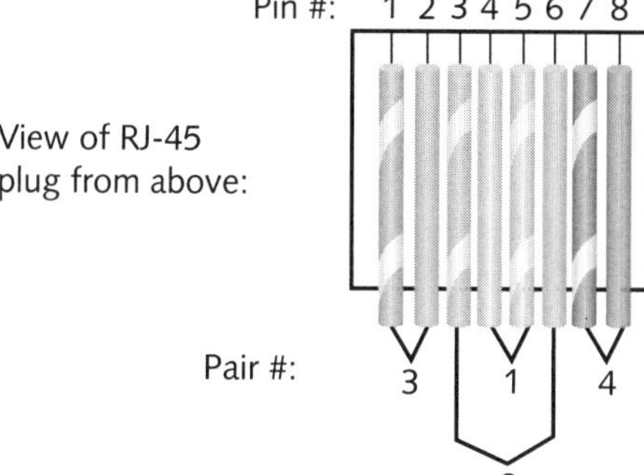

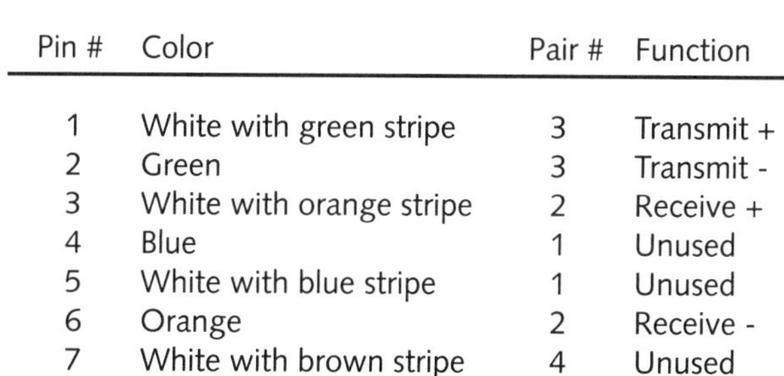

Pin #	Color	Pair #	Function
1	White with green stripe	3	Transmit +
2	Green	3	Transmit -
3	White with orange stripe	2	Receive +
4	Blue	1	Unused
5	White with blue stripe	1	Unused
6	Orange	2	Receive -
7	White with brown stripe	4	Unused
8	Brown	4	Unused

Figure 3-24 TIA/EIA 568A standard terminations

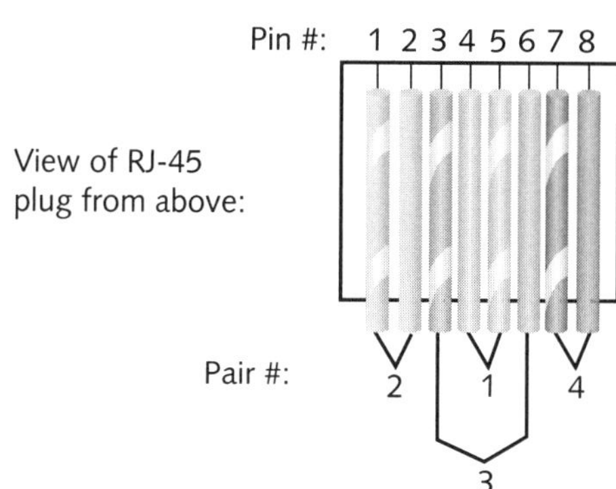

Pin #	Color	Pair #	Function
1	White with orange stripe	2	Transmit +
2	Orange	2	Transmit -
3	White with green stripe	3	Receive +
4	Blue	1	Unused
5	White with blue stripe	1	Unused
6	Green	3	Receive -
7	White with brown stripe	4	Unused
8	Brown	4	Unused

Figure 3-25 TIA/EIA 568B standard terminations

If you terminate the RJ-45 plugs at both ends of a patch cable identically, following one of the TIA/EIA 568 standards, you will create a **straight-through cable.** A straight-through
2.6 cable is so named because it allows signals to pass "straight through" from one end to the
3.1 other. This is the type used to connect a workstation to a router, for example.
3.2
4.2 However, in some cases you may want to reverse the pin locations of some wires—for example, when you want to connect two workstations without using a connectivity device or when you want to connect two hubs through their data ports. This can be accomplished through the use of a **crossover cable**, a patch cable in which the termination locations of the transmit and receive wires on one end of the cable are reversed, as shown in Figure 3-26. In this example, the TIA/EIA 568B standard is used on the left side, whereas the TIA/EIA 568A standard is used on the right side. Notice that only pairs 2 and 3 are switched, because those are the pairs sending and receiving data.

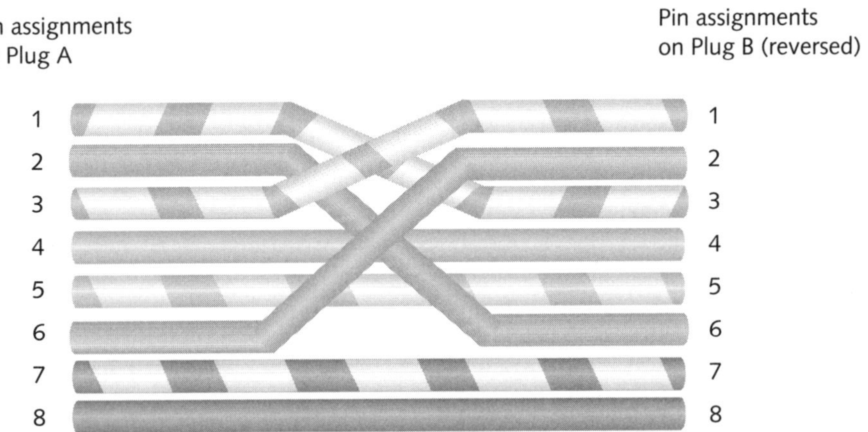

Figure 3-26 RJ-45 terminations on a crossover cable

Modern NICs and switches are equipped with an autosense function that enables them to detect the way wires are terminated in a plug and adapt their transmit and receive signaling accordingly. Therefore, crossover cables are only necessary if you are connecting computers or connectivity devices with older interfaces that lack the autosense feature. Connecting two brand-new computers with a straight-through patch cable enables them to communicate directly.

The tools you'll need to terminate a twisted pair cable with an RJ-45 plug are a wire cutter, wire stripper, and crimping tool, which are pictured in Figures 3-27, 3-28, and 3-29, respectively. (In fact, you can find a single device that contains all three of these tools.)

Following are the steps to create a straight-through patch cable using Cat 5e twisted pair cable. To create a crossover cable, you would simply reorder the wires in Step 4 to match Figure 3-26. The process of fixing wires inside the connector is called crimping, and it is a skill that requires practice—so don't be discouraged if the first cable you create doesn't

2.6
3.1
3.2
4.2

Figure 3-27 Wire cutter
© iStockphoto/Dave White

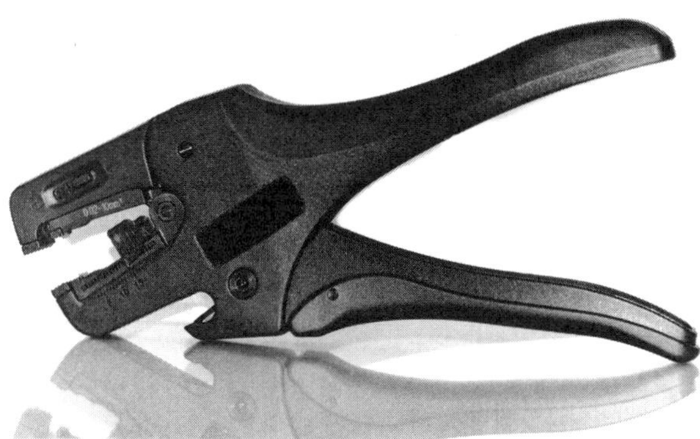

Figure 3-28 Wire stripper
© Francesco81/Shutterstock.com

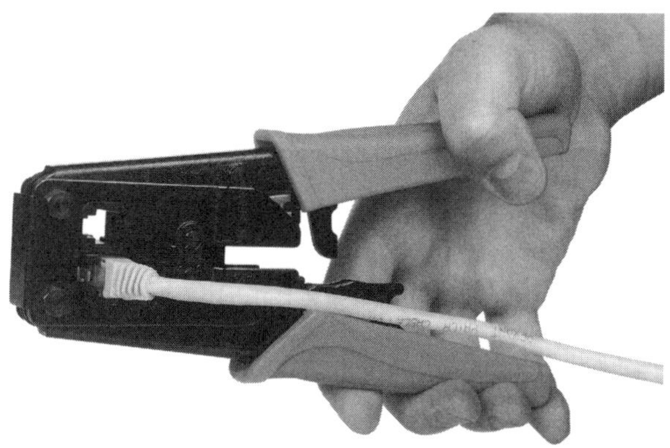

Figure 3-29 Crimping tool
© Olga Drabovich/Shutterstock.com

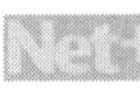

reliably transmit and receive data. You'll get to practice making cables in the end-of-chapter Hands-On Projects:

2.6

3.1 1. Using the wire cutter, make a clean cut at both ends of the twisted pair cable.

3.2

4.2 2. Using the wire stripper, remove the sheath off of one end of the twisted pair cable, beginning at approximately 1 inch from the end. Be careful to neither damage nor remove the insulation that's on the twisted pairs inside.

3. In addition to the four wire pairs, inside the sheath you'll find a string. Cut the string, then separate the four wire pairs in the full 1 inch of exposed cabling. Carefully unwind each pair and straighten each wire.
4. To make a straight-through cable, align all eight wires on a flat surface, one next to the other, ordered according to their colors and positions listed in Figure 3-25. (It might be helpful first to "groom"—or pull steadily across the length of—the unwound section of each wire to straighten it out and help it stay in place.)
5. Measure ½" from the end of the wires, and cleanly cut the wires at this length. Keeping the wires in line and in order, gently slide them into their positions in the RJ-45 plug. (The sheath should extend into the plug about 3/8".)
6. After the wires are fully inserted, place the RJ-45 plug in the crimping tool and press firmly to crimp the wires into place. (Be careful not to rotate your hand or the wire as you do this, otherwise only some of the wires will be properly terminated.) Crimping causes the internal RJ-45 pins to pierce the insulation of the wire, thus creating contact between the two conductors.
7. Now remove the RJ-45 connector from the crimping tool. Examine the end and see whether each wire appears to be in contact with the pin. It may be difficult to tell simply by looking at the connector. The real test is whether your cable will successfully transmit and receive signals.
8. Repeat Steps 2 through 7 for the other end of the cable. After completing Step 7 for the other end, you will have created a straight-through patch cable.

Even after you feel confident making your own cables, it's a good idea to verify that they can transmit and receive data at the necessary rates using a cable tester. Cable testing is discussed in Chapter 13.

Now that you have learned about transmission media that use copper wires to conduct signals, you are ready to learn how signals are transmitted over glass fibers.

Fiber-Optic Cable

3.1

Fiber-optic cable, or simply *fiber*, contains one or several glass or plastic fibers at its center, or **core**. Data is transmitted via pulsing light sent from a laser (in the case of 1- and 10-gigabit technologies) or an LED (light-emitting diode) through the central fibers. Surrounding the fibers is a layer of glass or plastic called **cladding**. The cladding has a different density from the glass or plastic in the strands. It reflects light back to the core in patterns that vary depending on the transmission mode. This reflection allows the fiber to bend around corners without diminishing the integrity of the light-based signal. Outside the cladding, a plastic buffer protects the cladding and core. Because the buffer is opaque, it also absorbs any light that might escape. To

Net+
3.1

prevent the cable from stretching, and to protect the inner core further, strands of Kevlar (a polymeric fiber) surround the plastic buffer. Finally, a plastic sheath covers the strands of Kevlar. Figure 3-30 shows a fiber-optic cable with multiple, insulated fibers.

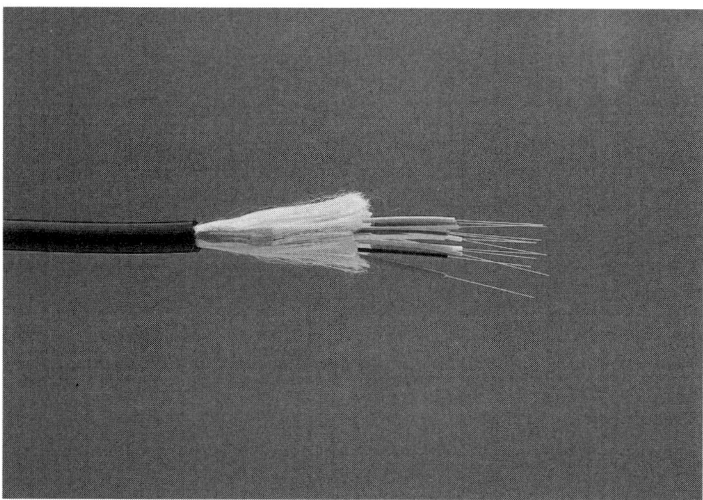

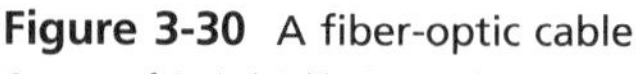

Figure 3-30 A fiber-optic cable
Courtesy of Optical Cable Corporation

Like twisted pair and coaxial cabling, fiber-optic cabling comes in a number of different varieties, depending on its intended use and the manufacturer. For example, fiber-optic cables used to connect the facilities of large telephone and data carriers may contain as many as 1000 fibers and be heavily sheathed to prevent damage from extreme environmental conditions. At the other end of the spectrum, fiber-optic patch cables for use on LANs may contain only two strands of fiber and be pliable enough to wrap around your hand. Because each strand of glass in a fiber-optic cable transmits in one direction only—in simplex fashion—two strands are needed for full-duplex communication. One solution is to use a **zipcord cable**, in which two strands are combined side by side in conjoined jackets, as depicted in Figure 3-31. You'll find zipcords where fiber-optic cable spans relatively short distances, such as connecting a server and switch. A zipcord may come with one of many types of connectors on its ends, as described later in this section.

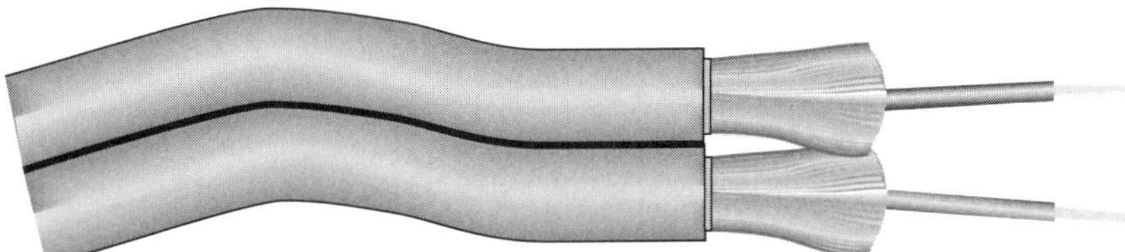

Figure 3-31 Zipcord fiber-optic patch cable
© Cengage Learning 2013

Fiber-optic cable provides the following benefits over copper cabling:

- Extremely high throughput
- Very high resistance to noise

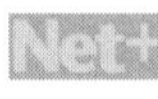

3.1

- Excellent security
- Ability to carry signals for much longer distances before requiring repeaters than copper cable
- Industry standard for high-speed networking

The most significant drawback to the use of fiber is that covering a certain distance with fiber-optic cable is more expensive than using twisted pair cable. Also, fiber-optic cable requires special equipment to splice, which means that quickly repairing a fiber-optic cable in the field (given little time or resources) can be difficult. Fiber's characteristics are summarized in the following list:

- *Throughput*—Fiber has proved reliable in transmitting data at rates that can reach 100 gigabits (or 100,000 megabits) per second per channel. Fiber's amazing throughput is partly due to the physics of light traveling through glass. Unlike electrical pulses traveling over copper, the light experiences virtually no resistance. Therefore, light-based signals can be transmitted at faster rates and with fewer errors than electrical pulses. In fact, a pure glass strand can accept up to 1 billion laser light pulses per second. Its high throughput capability makes it suitable for network backbones and for serving applications that generate a great deal of traffic, such as video or audio conferencing.
- *Cost*—Fiber-optic cable is the most expensive transmission medium. Because of its cost, most organizations find it impractical to run fiber to every desktop. Not only is the cable itself more expensive than copper cabling, but fiber-optic transmitters and connectivity equipment can cost as much as five times more than those designed for UTP networks. In addition, hiring skilled fiber cable installers costs more than hiring twisted pair cable installers.

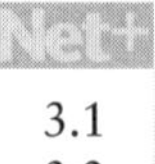

3.1
3.2

- *Connectors*—With fiber cabling, you can use any of 10 different types of connectors. Figures 3-32, 3-33, 3-34, and 3-35 show four of the most common connector types: the **SC (subscriber connector** or **standard connector)**, **ST (straight tip)**, **LC (local connector)**, and **MT-RJ (mechanical transfer registered jack)**. Existing fiber networks might use ST or SC connectors. However, LC and MT-RJ connectors are used on the very latest fiber-optic technology. LC and MT-RJ connectors are preferable to ST and SC connectors because of their smaller size, which allows for a higher density of connections at each termination point. The MT-RJ connector is unique because it contains two strands of fiber in a single **ferrule**, which is a short tube within a connector that encircles the fiber and keeps it properly aligned. With two strands in each ferrule, a single MT-RJ connector provides for full-duplex signaling. Linking

Figure 3-32 SC (subscriber connector or standard connector)
Courtesy of SENKO Advanced Components Inc.

3.1
3.2

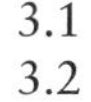

Figure 3-33 ST (straight tip) connector
Courtesy of SENKO Advanced Components Inc.

Figure 3-34 LC (local connector)
Courtesy of SENKO Advanced Components Inc.

Figure 3-35 MT-RJ (mechanical transfer register jack) connector
Courtesy of SENKO Advanced Components Inc.

devices that require different connectors is simple because you can purchase fiber-optic cables with different connector types at each end.

- *Noise immunity*—Because fiber does not conduct electrical current to transmit signals, 3.1 it is unaffected by EMI. Its impressive noise resistance is one reason why fiber can span such long distances before it requires repeaters to regenerate its signal.
- *Size and scalability*—Depending on the type of fiber-optic cable used, segment lengths vary from 150 to 40,000 meters. This limit is due primarily to **optical loss**, or the degradation of the light signal after it travels a certain distance away from its source (just as the light of a flashlight dims after a certain number of feet). Optical loss accrues over long distances and grows with every connection point in the fiber

3.1 network. Dust or oil in a connection (for example, from people handling the fiber while splicing it) can further exacerbate optical loss. Some types of fiber-optic cable can carry signals 40 miles while others are suited for distances under a mile. The distance a cable can carry light depends partly on the light's wavelength. It also depends on whether the cable is single mode or multimode.

SMF (Single-Mode Fiber)

SMF (single-mode fiber) consists of a narrow core of 8 to 10 microns in diameter. Laser-generated light travels a single path over the core, reflecting very little. Because it reflects little, the light does not disperse as the signal travels along the fiber. This continuity allows single-mode fiber to accommodate the highest bandwidths and longest distances (without requiring repeaters) of all network transmission media. Figure 3-36 depicts a simplified version of how signals travel over single-mode fiber. Single-mode fiber can carry signals many miles before the signals require repeating. Therefore, it is preferred for connecting WAN locations and service provider facilities, for example. The Internet backbone depends on single-mode fiber. However, because of its relatively high cost, single-mode fiber is rarely used for shorter connections, such as those between a server and switch.

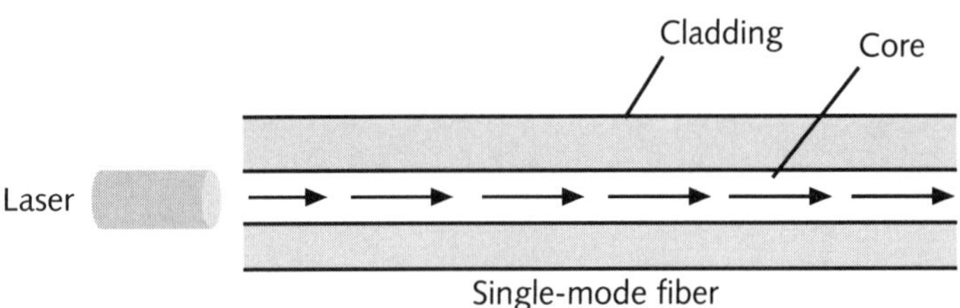

Figure 3-36 Transmission over single-mode fiber-optic cable

MMF (Multimode Fiber)

MMF (multimode fiber) contains a core with a larger diameter than single-mode fiber, usually 50 or 62.5 microns, over which many pulses of light generated by a laser or LED travel at different angles. Signals traveling over multimode fiber experience greater attenuation than those traversing single-mode fiber. Therefore, multimode fiber is not suited to distances longer than a few miles. On the other hand, multimode fiber is less expensive to install. It is often found on cables that connect a router to a switch or a server on the backbone of a network. In cases where fiber connects desktop workstations to the network, multimode fiber is preferred because of its lower cost. Figure 3-37 depicts a simplified view of how signals travel over multimode fiber.

Fiber-Optic Converters

Converters are required to connect networks using multimode fiber with networks using single-mode fiber. They are also required to connect the fiber- and copper-based parts of a network. The bidirectional converter accepts the signal from one part of the network and regenerates before issuing it to the next part. Figure 3-38 shows a converter that connects

Net+
3.1

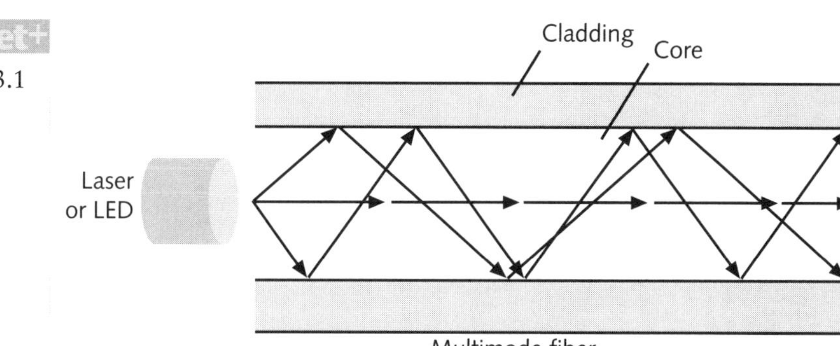

Figure 3-37 Transmission over multimode fiber-optic cable

single-mode and multimode portions of a network. Refer to Figure 3-15 to see a converter that connects multimode fiber with an Ethernet network using UTP. Figure 3-39 shows a fiber to coax converter.

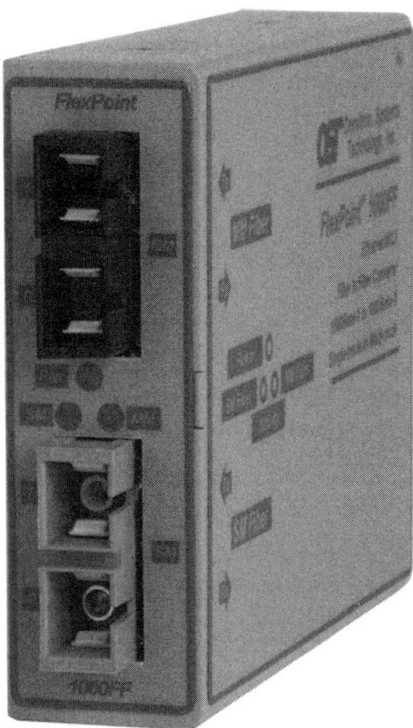

Figure 3-38 Single-mode to multimode converter
Courtesy of Omnitron Systems Technology

Serial Cables

So far you have learned about the kinds of physical media used between connectivity devices and with nodes on a LAN or WAN. This section describes a type of cable that can be used to connect directly to a device such as a router, server, or switch. **Serial** refers to a style of data

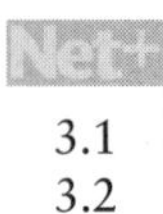

3.1
3.2

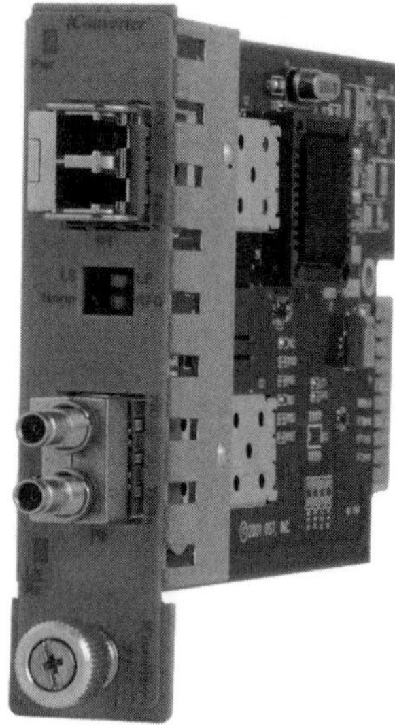

Figure 3-39 Fiber to coax converter
Courtesy of Omnitron Systems Technology

transmission in which the pulses that represent bits follow one another along a single transmission line. In other words, they are issued sequentially, not simultaneously. A **serial cable** is one that carries serial transmissions. Several types of serial cables exist.

Net+ 3.2 EIA/TIA has codified a popular serial data transmission method known as **RS-232 (Recommended Standard 232)**. This Physical layer standard specifies, among other things, signal voltage and timing, plus the characteristics of compatible interfaces. Different connector types comply with this standard, including RJ-45 connectors, **DB-9 connectors**, and **DB-25 connectors**. You are already familiar with RJ-45 plugs. Figures 3-40 and 3-41 illustrate male DB-9 and DB-25 connectors, respectively. Notice that the arrangement of the pins on both connectors resembles a sideways letter D. Also notice that a DB-9 connector contains 9 contact points and a DB-25 connector contains 25.

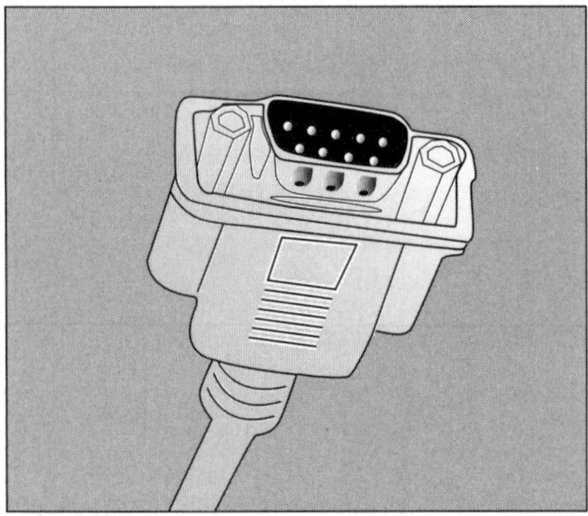

Figure 3-40 DB-9 connector

3.2

Figure 3-41 DB-25 connector

For many years, serial cables were used to connect external modems with workstations. However, as an administrator on today's networks, you're more likely to use an RS-232 connection between a workstation and a router to make your workstation act as a console for configuring and managing that router. In fact, a higher-end router designed for use in your data center (not the kind of router you'd use at home) usually comes with an RS-232-compatible cable. The serial interface on the back of the connectivity device is often labeled "Console." This is not to say that a serial cable is the only way of connecting to a router for configuring and managing it. However, if the router is brand new, if the network is malfunctioning, or if for some other reason the device cannot obtain an IP address, you need to access it directly and not via a network connection.

You can find RS-232 cables with different types of connectors at either end. For example, many Cisco routers come with a console port that's RJ-45 compliant. If you wanted to connect such a router to your laptop's DB-9 serial port, you could find an RS-232 cable with an RJ-45 plug on one end and a DB-9 plug on the other.

The fact that a serial cable terminates in an RJ-45 connector does not mean it will work if plugged into a device's RJ-45 Ethernet port! When using a serial cable with an RJ-45 connector, be certain to plug it into the appropriate serial interface.

In addition to using different connector types, the termination points on RS-232 cables can be arranged in various ways, depending on the cable's purpose. Earlier you learned about the difference between straight-through and crossover cables in the context of terminating twisted pair cables. An RS-232 cable, whether it uses DB-9, DB-25, or RJ-45 connectors, can also be straight-through. You also have the option of reversing the transmit and receive pins on one end, thereby making it into a crossover cable. Among other things, you could use such a crossover cable to directly connect two routers via their serial interfaces.

You'll learn more about connectivity devices such as routers and switches in Chapter 6. The following section describes how to arrange physical networking media between end users and connectivity devices on a LAN or WAN.

Structured Cabling

2.6
3.8

Organizations that pay attention to their **cable plant**—the hardware that makes up the enterprise-wide cabling system—are apt to experience fewer Physical layer network problems, smoother network expansions, and simpler network troubleshooting. Following the cabling standards and best practices described in this chapter can help.

If you were to tour hundreds of data centers and equipment rooms at established enterprises, you would see similar cabling arrangements. That's because most organizations follow a cabling standard. One popular standard is TIA/EIA's joint 568 Commercial Building Wiring Standard, also known as **structured cabling**, for uniform, enterprise-wide, multivendor cabling systems. The standard suggests how networking media can best be installed to maximize performance and minimize upkeep. Structured cabling applies no matter what type of media or transmission technology a network uses. (It does, however assume a network based on the star topology.) In other words, it's designed to work just as well for 10-Mbps networks as it does for 10-Gbps networks. Structured cabling is based on a hierarchical design that begins where a telecommunications company's service enters a building and ends at a user's workstation. Figure 3-42 illustrates the different components of structured cabling in an enterprise from a bird's-eye view. Figure 3-43 gives a glimpse of how structured cabling appears within a building (in this case, one that is not part of a larger, enterprise-wide network). Detailed descriptions of the components referenced in these figures follow:

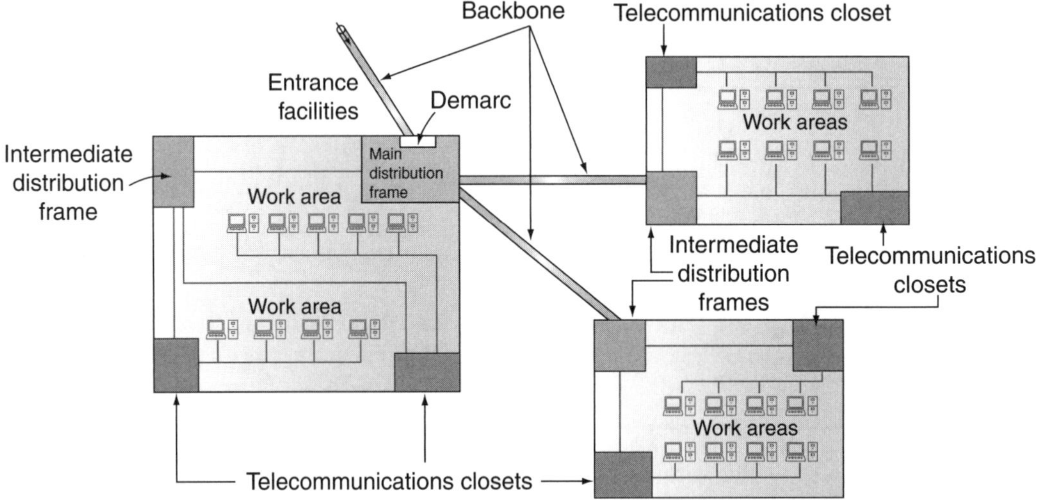

Figure 3-42 TIA/EIA structured cabling in an enterprise

- ***Entrance facilities***—The facilities necessary for a service provider (whether it is a local phone company, Internet service provider, or long-distance carrier) to connect with another organization's LAN or WAN. Entrance facilities may include fiber-optic cable and multiplexers, coaxial cable, UTP, satellite or wireless transceivers, and other devices or cabling. If the entrance facilities are supplied by a telecommunications carrier and rely on UTP, they may come in the form of 25-pair wire. As the name suggests, **25-pair wire** is a bundle of 25 wire pairs. As you might expect, **100-pair**

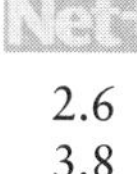

2.6
3.8

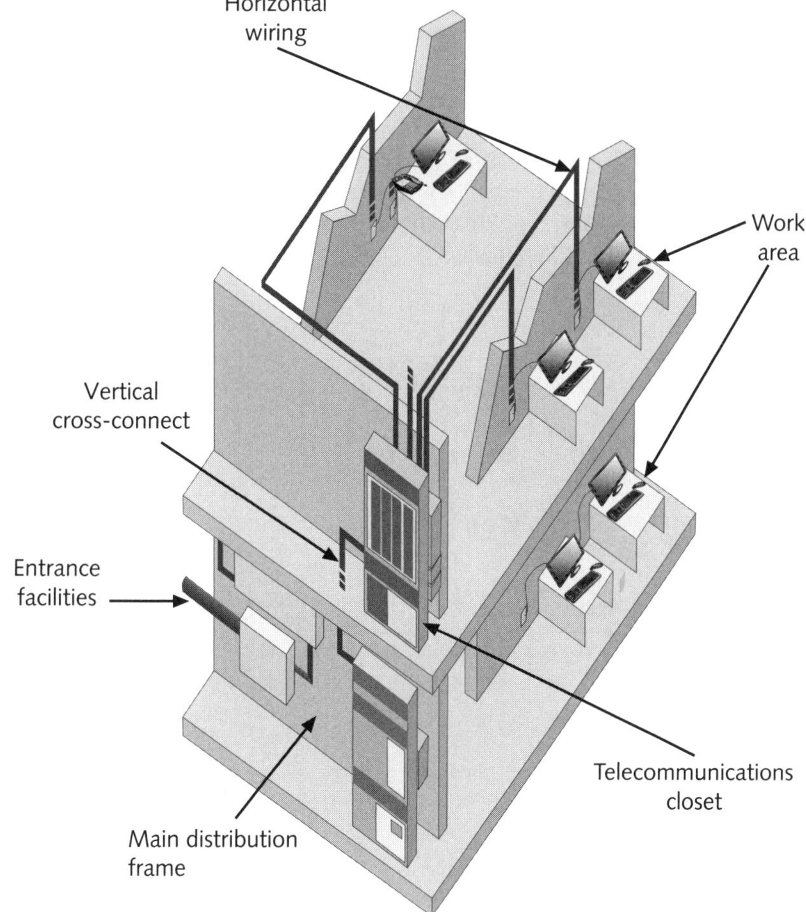

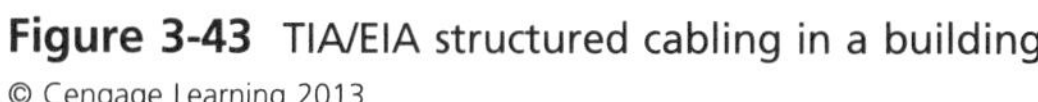

Figure 3-43 TIA/EIA structured cabling in a building

wire contains 100 twisted wire pairs. More commonly, however, entrance facilities depend on fiber-optic cable. The entrance facility designates where the telecommunications service provider accepts responsibility for the (external) connection. The point of division between the service provider's network and the internal network is also known as the **demarcation point** (or **demarc**).

- *MDF (main distribution frame)*—Also known as the **main cross-connect**, the first point of interconnection between an organization's LAN or WAN and a service provider's facility. An MDF typically includes connectivity devices, such as switches and routers, and media, such as fiber-optic cable, capable of the greatest throughput. Often, it also houses an organization's main servers. In an enterprise-wide network, equipment in an MDF connects to equipment housed in another building's IDF. Sometimes the MDF is simply known as the computer room or equipment room.

- *Cross-connect facilities*—The points where circuits interconnect with other circuits. For
3.8 example, when an MDF accepts UTP from a service provider, the wire pairs terminate at a
4.2 punch-down block. A **punch-down block** is a panel of data receptors into which twisted

3.8
4.2

pair wire is inserted, or punched down, to complete a circuit. Punch-down blocks were for many years the standard method of terminating telephone circuits. The type used on data networks is known as the **110 block**. 110 blocks are available in several different capacities. That is, "110" does not represent the number of wire pairs the block can terminate. From a punch-down block, wires are distributed to a **patch panel**, a wall-mounted panel of data receptors. Figure 3-44 shows a patch panel and Figure 3-45 shows a punch-down block. A patch panel allows the insertion of patch cables. Note that cross-connect facilities are not limited to the MDF and may be used in other equipment rooms that are part of a building's cable infrastructure.

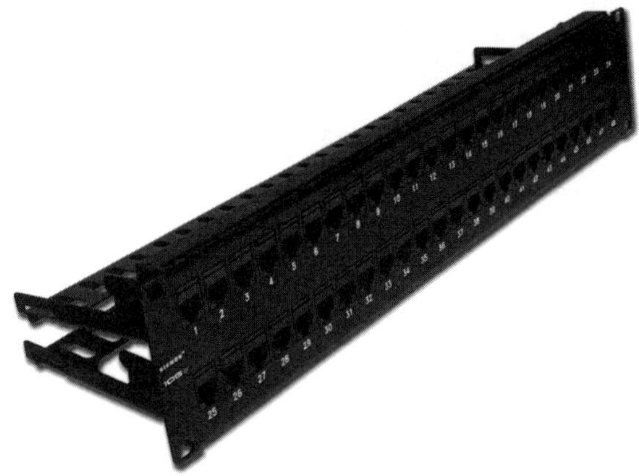

Figure 3-44 Patch panel
Courtesy of Siemon

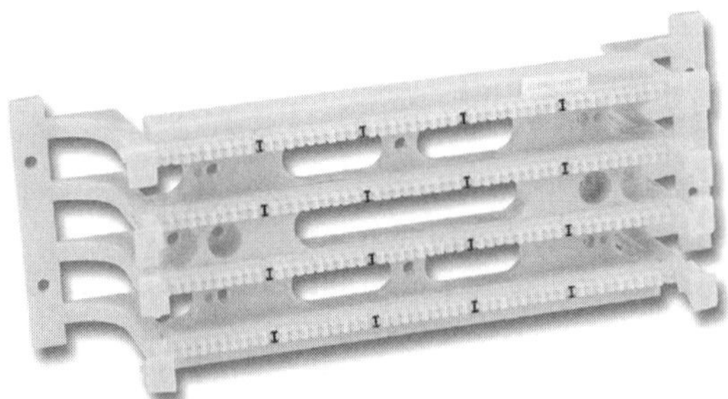

Figure 3-45 Punch-down block
Courtesy of Siemon

Net+

2.6
3.8

- *IDF (intermediate distribution frame)*—A junction point between the MDF and concentrations of fewer connections—for example, those that terminate in a telecommunications closet.
- *Backbone wiring*—The cables or wireless links that provide interconnection between entrance facilities and MDFs, MDFs and IDFs, and IDFs and telecommunications closets. One component of the backbone is given a special term: **vertical cross-connect**.

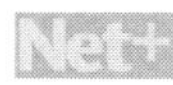

A vertical cross-connect runs between a building's floors. For example, it might
2.6 connect an MDF and IDF or IDFs and telecommunications closets (described next)
3.8 within a building. The TIA/EIA standard designates distance limitations for backbones of varying cable types, as specified in Table 3-2. On modern networks, backbones are usually composed of fiber-optic or UTP cable.

- *Telecommunications closet*—Also known as a "telco room," it contains connectivity for groups of workstations in its area, plus cross-connections to IDFs or, in smaller organizations, an MDF. Large organizations may have several telco rooms per floor, but the TIA/EIA standard specifies at least one per floor. Telecommunications closets typically house patch panels, punch-down blocks, and connectivity devices for a work area. Because telecommunications closets are usually small, enclosed spaces, good cooling and ventilation systems are important to maintaining a constant temperature.
- *Horizontal wiring*—This is the wiring that connects workstations to the closest telecommunications closet. TIA/EIA recognizes three possible cabling types for horizontal wiring: STP, UTP, or fiber-optic cable. The maximum allowable distance for horizontal wiring is 100 m. This span includes 90 m to connect a data jack on the wall to the telecommunications closet plus a maximum of 10 m to connect a workstation to the data jack on the wall. Figure 3-46 depicts a horizontal wiring configuration.

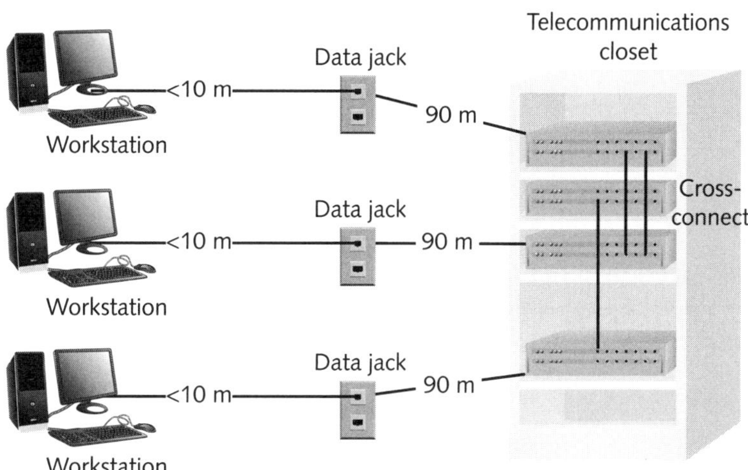

Figure 3-46 Horizontal wiring

- *Work area*—An area that encompasses all patch cables and horizontal wiring necessary to connect workstations, printers, and other network devices from their NICs to the telecommunications closet. The TIA/EIA standard calls for each wall jack to contain at least one voice and one data outlet, as pictured in Figure 3-47. Realistically, you will encounter a variety of wall jacks. For example, in a student computer lab lacking phones, a wall jack with a combination of voice and data outlets is unnecessary.

2.6
3.8

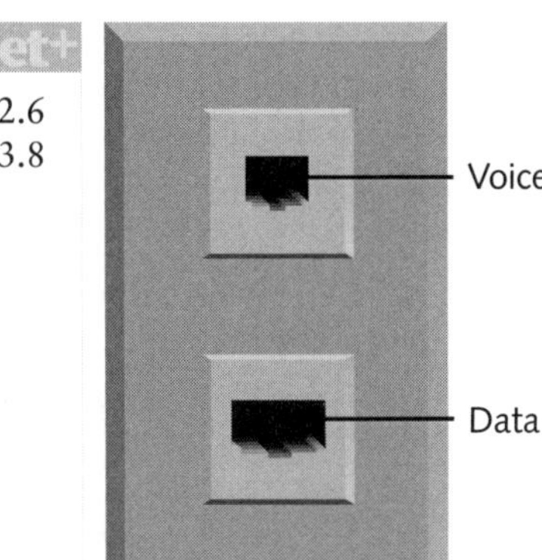

Figure 3-47 A standard TIA/EIA outlet

Table 3-2 TIA/EIA specifications for backbone cabling

Cable type	Cross-connects to telecommunications closet	MDF or IDF to telecommunications closet	Cross-connects to IDF or MDF
UTP	800 m (voice specification)	500 m	300 m
Single-mode fiber	3000 m	500 m	1500 m
Multimode fiber	2000 m	500 m	1500 m

Figure 3-48 illustrates a cable installation using UTP from the telecommunications closet to the work area.

Knowing the standards for cabling a building or enterprise is key, but until you have practiced terminating, running, and testing cables, this knowledge is only theoretical. The following section provides some practical information that you can apply when working with physical networking media.

Best Practices for Cable Installation and Management

3.8

So far, you have read about the variety of cables used in networking and the limitations inherent in each. You may worry that with hundreds of varieties of cable, choosing the correct one and making it work with your network is next to impossible. The good news is that if you follow both the manufacturers' installation guidelines and the TIA/EIA standards, you are almost guaranteed success. Many network problems can be traced to poor cable installation techniques. For example, if you don't crimp twisted pair wires in the correct position in an RJ-45 connector, the cable will fail to transmit or receive data (or both—in which case, the cable will not function at all). Installing the wrong grade of cable can either cause your network to fail or render it more susceptible to damage.

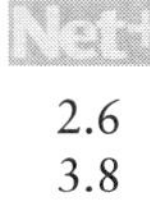
2.6
3.8

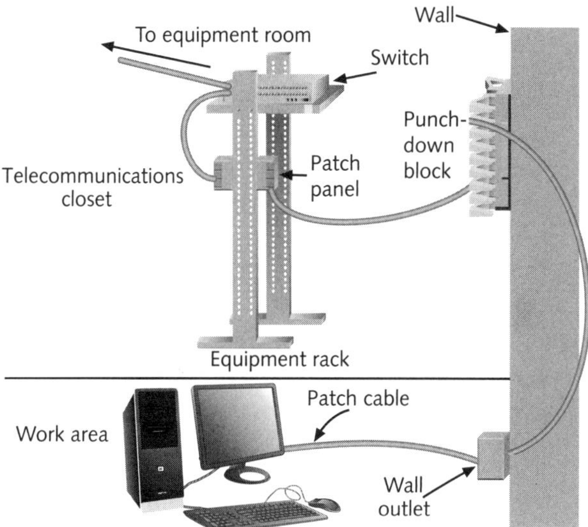

Figure 3-48 A typical UTP cabling installation

3.1
3.6

The art of proper cabling could fill an entire book. If you plan to specialize in cable installation, design, or maintenance, you should invest in a reference dedicated to this topic. As a network professional, you will likely occasionally add new cables to a room or telecommunications closet, repair defective cable ends, or install a data outlet. Following are some cable installation tips that will help prevent Physical layer failures:

- Do not untwist twisted pair cables more than one-half inch before inserting them into the punch-down block.
- Do not leave more than 1 inch of exposed (stripped) cable before a twisted pair termination. Doing so will increase the possibility for cross talk and data errors.
- Pay attention to the bend radius limitations for the type of cable you are installing. **Bend radius** is the radius of the maximum arc into which you can loop a cable before you will impair data transmission. Generally, a twisted pair cable's bend radius is equal to or greater than four times the diameter of the cable. Be careful not to exceed it.
- Use a cable tester to verify that each segment of cabling you install transmits data reliably. This practice will prevent you from later having to track down errors in multiple, long stretches of cable. Chapter 13, which covers troubleshooting network problems, explains the tools and methods needed to test cable continuity.
- Avoid cinching cables so tightly that you squeeze their outer covering, a practice that leads to difficult-to-diagnose data errors.
- Avoid laying cable across the floor where it might sustain damage from rolling chairs or foot traffic. If you must take this tack, cover the cable with a cable protector.

- Install cable at least 3 feet away from fluorescent lights or other sources of EMI. This
2.2 will reduce the possibility for noise to affect your network's signals.
- 3.1 Always leave some slack in cable runs. Stringing cable too tightly risks connectivity
3.6 and data transmission problems.
- If you run cable in the **plenum**, the area above the ceiling tile or below the subflooring, make sure the cable sheath is plenum-rated, and consult with local electric installation codes to be certain you are installing it correctly. A plenum-rated cable is more fire resistant, and if burned, produces less smoke than other cables.
- Pay attention to grounding requirements and follow them religiously.

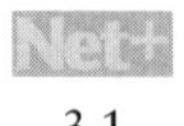

- Adhering to structured cabling hierarchies is only part of a smart cable management
strategy. You or your network manager should also specify standards for the types of
3.1 cable used by your organization and maintain a list of approved cabling vendors.
3.6 Keep a supply room stocked with spare parts so that you can easily and quickly
3.8 replace defective parts.

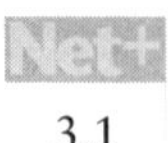

- Create documentation for your cabling plant, including the locations, installation
dates, lengths, and grades of installed cable. Label every data jack, punch-down block,
3.1 and connector. Use color-coded cables for different purposes (cables can be purchased
3.6 in a variety of sheath colors). For example, you might want to use pink for patch
4.5 cables, green for horizontal wiring, and gray for vertical (backbone) wiring. Be certain
to document your color schemes.
- Keep your cable plant documentation in a centrally accessible location and be certain to update it as you change the network. The more you document, the easier it will be to move or add cable segments.
- Finally, create a plan for expanding your cabling plant. For example, if your organization is rapidly enlarging, consider replacing your backbone with fiber and leave plenty of space in your telecommunications closets for more racks.

Chapter Summary

- Information can be transmitted via two methods: analog or digital. Analog signals are continuous waves that result in variable and inexact transmission. Digital signals are based on electrical or light pulses that represent information encoded in binary form.
- In half-duplex transmission, signals can travel in both directions over a medium but in only one direction at a time. When signals can travel in both directions over a medium simultaneously, the transmission is considered full-duplex.
- A form of transmission that allows multiple signals to travel simultaneously over one medium is known as multiplexing. In multiplexing, the single medium is logically separated into multiple channels, or subchannels.
- Throughput is the amount of data that the medium can transmit during a given period of time. Throughput is usually measured in bits per second and depends on the physical nature of the medium.
- Baseband is a form of transmission in which digital signals are sent through direct current pulses applied to the wire. Baseband systems can transmit only one signal, or

one channel, at a time. Broadband, on the other hand, uses modulated analog frequencies to transmit multiple signals over the same wire.

- Noise is interference that distorts an analog or digital signal. It may be caused by electrical sources, such as power lines, fluorescent lights, copiers, and microwave ovens, or by broadcast signals.
- Analog and digital signals both suffer attenuation, or loss of signal, as they travel farther from their sources. To compensate, analog signals are amplified, and digital signals are regenerated through repeaters.

- Every network is susceptible to a delay between the transmission of a signal and its receipt. This delay is called latency. The length of the cable contributes to latency, as does the presence of any intervening connectivity device.
- Coaxial cable consists of a central metal conducting core (often copper) surrounded by a plastic insulator, a braided metal shielding, and an outer plastic cover called the sheath. The conducting core carries the electromagnetic signal, and the shielding acts as both a protection against noise and a ground for the signal. The insulator layer protects the copper core from the metal shielding. The sheath protects the cable from physical damage.
- Most networks no longer rely on coaxial cable; however, if you obtain Internet service from a cable company, the cable that enters your home will be a type of coax known as RG-6.
- Twisted pair cable consists of color-coded pairs of insulated copper wires, each with a diameter of 0.4 to 0.8 mm, twisted around each other and encased in plastic coating.
- STP (shielded twisted pair) cable consists of twisted-wire pairs that are not only individually insulated, but also surrounded by a shielding made of a metallic substance such as foil to reduce the effects of noise on the signal.
- UTP (unshielded twisted pair) cabling consists of one or more insulated wire pairs encased in a plastic sheath. As its name suggests, UTP does not contain additional shielding for the twisted pairs. As a result, UTP is both less expensive and less resistant to noise than STP.
- Fiber-optic cable contains one or several glass or plastic fibers in its core. Data is transmitted via pulsing light sent from a laser or light-emitting diode through the central fiber(s). Outside the fiber(s), cladding reflects light back to the core in different patterns that vary depending on the transmission mode.
- Fiber-optic cable provides the benefits of very high throughput, very high resistance to noise, and excellent security.
- Fiber cable variations fall into two categories: single mode and multimode. Single-mode fiber uses a small-diameter core, over which light travels mostly down its center, reflecting very few times. This allows single-mode fiber to accommodate high throughput over long distances without requiring repeaters.
- MMF (multimode fiber) uses a core with a larger diameter, over which many pulses of light travel at different angles. Multimode fiber is less expensive than SMF (single-mode fiber).
- Serial communication is often used on short connections between devices when a network is not available. For example, you might use an RS-232 serial cable to connect your laptop to a router so that you can configure the router from your laptop.

- TIA/EIA's 568 Commercial Building Wiring Standard, also known as structured cabling, provides guidelines for uniform, enterprise-wide, multivendor cabling systems. Structured cabling is based on a hierarchical design that begins with a service provider's facilities and ends at users' workstations.
- The best practice for installing cable is to follow the TIA/EIA 568 specifications and the manufacturer's recommendations. Be careful not to exceed a cable's bend radius, untwist wire pairs more than one-half inch, or remove more than one inch of insulation from copper wire. Install plenum-rated cable in ceilings and floors, and run cabling away from where it might suffer physical damage. Maintain clear, comprehensive documentation on your cable plant.

Key Terms

1 gigabit per second (Gbps) 1,000,000,000 bits per second.

1 kilobit per second (Kbps) 1000 bits per second.

1 megabit per second (Mbps) 1,000,000 bits per second.

1 terabit per second (Tbps) 1,000,000,000,000 bits per second.

100-pair wire UTP supplied by a telecommunications carrier that contains 100 wire pairs.

110 block Part of an organization's cross-connect facilities, a type of punch-down block designed to terminate Cat 5 or better twisted pair wires.

25-pair wire UTP supplied by a telecommunications carrier that contains 25 wire pairs.

alien cross talk EMI interference induced on one cable by signals traveling over a nearby cable.

AM (amplitude modulation) A modulation technique in which the amplitude of the carrier signal is modified by the application of a data signal.

American Wire Gauge *See* AWG.

amplifier A device that boosts, or strengthens, an analog signal.

amplitude A measure of a signal's strength.

amplitude modulation *See* AM.

analog A signal that uses variable voltage to create continuous waves, resulting in an inexact transmission.

attenuation The extent to which a signal has weakened after traveling a given distance.

augmented Category 6 *See* Cat 6a.

AWG (American Wire Gauge) A standard rating that indicates the diameter of a wire, such as the conducting core of a coaxial cable.

bandwidth A measure of the difference between the highest and lowest frequencies that a medium can transmit.

baseband A form of transmission in which digital signals are sent through direct current pulses applied to a wire. This direct current requires exclusive use of the wire's capacity, so baseband systems can transmit only one signal, or one channel, at a time. Every device on a baseband system shares a single channel.

bend radius The radius of the maximum arc into which you can loop a cable before you will cause data transmission errors. Generally, a twisted pair cable's bend radius is equal to or greater than four times the diameter of the cable.

binary A system founded on using 1s and 0s to encode information.

bit (binary digit) A bit equals a single pulse in the digital encoding system. It may have only one of two values: 0 or 1.

BNC (Bayonet Neill-Concelman, or British Naval Connector) A standard for coaxial cable connectors named after its coupling method and its inventors.

BNC connector A coaxial cable connector type that uses a twist-and-lock (or bayonet) style of coupling. It may be used with several coaxial cable types, including RG-6 and RG-59.

braiding A braided metal shielding used to insulate some types of coaxial cable.

broadband A form of transmission in which signals are modulated as radio frequency analog pulses with different frequency ranges. Unlike baseband, broadband technology does not involve binary encoding. The use of multiple frequencies enables a broadband system to operate over several channels and, therefore, carry much more data than a baseband system.

broadcast A transmission that involves one transmitter and multiple, undefined receivers.

byte Eight bits of information. In a digital signaling system, broadly speaking, 1 byte carries one piece of information.

cable plant The hardware that constitutes the enterprise-wide cabling system.

capacity *See* throughput.

Cat Abbreviation for the word *category* when describing a type of twisted pair cable. For example, Category 5 unshielded twisted pair cable may also be called Cat 5.

Cat 3 (Category 3) A form of UTP that contains four wire pairs and can carry up to 10 Mbps, with a possible bandwidth of 16 MHz. Cat 3 was used for 10-Mbps Ethernet or 4-Mbps token ring networks.

Cat 5 (Category 5) A form of UTP that contains four wire pairs and supports up to 100-Mbps throughput and a 100-MHz signal rate.

Cat 5e (Enhanced Category 5) A higher-grade version of Cat 5 wiring that contains high-quality copper, offers a high twist ratio, and uses advanced methods for reducing cross talk. Enhanced Cat 5 can support a signaling rate of up to 350 MHz, more than triple the capability of regular Cat 5.

Cat 6 (Category 6) A twisted pair cable that contains four wire pairs, each wrapped in foil insulation. Additional foil insulation covers the bundle of wire pairs, and a fire-resistant plastic sheath covers the second foil layer. The foil insulation provides excellent resistance to cross talk and enables Cat 6 to support a signaling rate of 250 MHz and at least six times the throughput supported by regular Cat 5.

Cat 6a (Augmented Category 6) A higher-grade version of Cat 6 wiring that further reduces attenuation and cross talk and allows for potentially exceeding traditional network segment length limits. Cat 6a is capable of a 500-MHz signaling rate and can reliably transmit data at multi-gigabit per second rates.

Cat 7 (Category 7) A twisted pair cable that contains multiple wire pairs, each separately shielded then surrounded by another layer of shielding within the jacket. Cat 7 can support up to a 1-GHz signal rate. But because of its extra layers, it is less flexible than other forms of twisted pair wiring.

Category 3 *See* Cat 3.

Category 5 *See* Cat 5.

Category 6 *See* Cat 6.

Category 7 *See* Cat 7.

channel A distinct communication path between two or more nodes, much like a lane is a distinct transportation path on a freeway. Channels may be separated either logically (as in multiplexing) or physically (as when they are carried by separate wires).

cladding The glass or plastic shield around the core of a fiber-optic cable. Cladding reflects light back to the core in patterns that vary depending on the transmission mode. This reflection allows fiber to bend around corners without impairing the light-based signal.

coaxial cable A type of cable that consists of a central metal conducting core, which might be solid or stranded and is often made of copper, surrounded by an insulator, a braided metal shielding, called braiding, and an outer cover, called the sheath or jacket. Coaxial cable, called "coax" for short, was the foundation for Ethernet networks in the 1980s. Today it's used to connect cable Internet and cable TV systems.

conduit The pipeline used to contain and protect cabling. Conduit is usually made from metal.

connectors The pieces of hardware that connect the wire to the network device, be it a file server, workstation, switch, or printer.

core The central component of a cable designed to carry a signal. The core of a fiber-optic cable, for example, consists of one or several glass or plastic fibers. The core of a coaxial copper cable consists of one large or several small strands of copper.

crossover cable A twisted pair patch cable in which the termination locations of the transmit and receive wires on one end of the cable are reversed.

cross talk A type of interference caused by signals traveling on nearby wire pairs infringing on another pair's signal.

DB-9 connector A type of connector with nine pins that's commonly used in serial communication that conforms to the RS-232 standard.

DB-25 connector A type of connector with 25 pins that's commonly used in serial communication that conforms to the RS-232 standard.

demarc *See* demarcation point.

demarcation point (demarc) The point of division between a telecommunications service carrier's network and a building's internal network.

demultiplexer (demux) A device that separates multiplexed signals once they are received and regenerates them in their original form.

demux *See* demultiplexer

dense wavelength division multiplexing *See* DWDM.

digital As opposed to analog signals, digital signals are composed of pulses that can have a value of only 1 or 0.

duplex *See* full-duplex.

DWDM (dense wavelength division multiplexing) A multiplexing technique used over single-mode or multimode fiber-optic cable in which each signal is assigned a different wavelength for its carrier wave. In DWDM, little space exists between carrier waves in order to achieve extraordinary high capacity.

electromagnetic interference *See* EMI.

EMI (electromagnetic interference) A type of interference that may be caused by motors, power lines, televisions, copiers, fluorescent lights, or other sources of electrical activity.

Enhanced Category 5 *See* Cat 5e.

entrance facilities The facilities necessary for a service provider (whether it is a local phone company, Internet service provider, or long-distance carrier) to connect with another organization's LAN or WAN.

FDM (frequency division multiplexing) A type of multiplexing that assigns a unique frequency band to each communications subchannel. Signals are modulated with different carrier frequencies, then multiplexed to simultaneously travel over a single channel.

ferrule A short tube within a fiber-optic cable connector that encircles the fiber strand and keeps it properly aligned.

fiber-optic cable A form of cable that contains one or several glass or plastic fibers in its core. Data is transmitted via pulsing light sent from a laser or light-emitting diode (LED) through the central fiber (or fibers). Fiber-optic cables offer significantly higher throughput than copper-based cables. They may be single-mode or multimode and typically use wave-division multiplexing to carry multiple signals.

FM (frequency modulation) A method of data modulation in which the frequency of the carrier signal is modified by the application of the data signal.

frequency The number of times that a signal's amplitude changes over a fixed period of time, expressed in cycles per second, or hertz (Hz).

frequency division multiplexing *See* FDM.

frequency modulation *See* FM.

F-Type connector A connector used to terminate coaxial cable used for transmitting television and broadband cable signals.

full-duplex A type of transmission in which signals may travel in both directions over a medium simultaneously. May also be called, simply, "duplex."

half-duplex A type of transmission in which signals may travel in both directions over a medium, but in only one direction at a time.

hertz (Hz) A measure of frequency equivalent to the number of amplitude cycles per second.

IDF (intermediate distribution frame) A junction point between the MDF and concentrations of fewer connections—for example, those that terminate in a telecommunications closet.

impedance The resistance that contributes to controlling an electrical signal. Impedance is measured in ohms.

intermediate distribution frame *See* IDF.

latency The delay between the transmission of a signal and its receipt.

LC (local connector) A connector used with single-mode or multimode fiber-optic cable.

link segment *See* unpopulated segment.

local connector *See* LC.

main cross-connect *See* MDF.

main distribution frame *See* MDF.

MDF (main distribution frame) Also known as the main cross-connect, the first point of interconnection between an organization's LAN or WAN and a service provider's facility.

mechanical transfer registered jack *See* MT-RJ.

media converter A device that enables networks or segments using different media to interconnect and exchange signals.

MMF (multimode fiber) A type of fiber-optic cable that contains a core with a diameter between 50 and 100 microns, through which many pulses of light generated by a light-emitting diode (LED) travel at different angles.

modem A device that modulates analog signals into digital signals at the transmitting end for transmission over telephone lines, and demodulates digital signals into analog signals at the receiving end.

modulation A technique for formatting signals in which one property of a simple carrier wave is modified by the addition of a data signal during transmission.

MT-RJ (mechanical transfer registered jack) A connector used with single-mode or multimode fiber-optic cable.

multimode fiber *See* MMF.

multiplexer A device that separates a medium into multiple channels and issues signals to each of those subchannels.

multiplexing A form of transmission that allows multiple signals to travel simultaneously over one medium.

near end cross talk *See* NEXT.

NEXT (near end cross talk) Cross talk, or the impingement of the signal carried by one wire onto a nearby wire, that occurs between wire pairs near the source of a signal.

noise The unwanted signals, or interference, from sources near network cabling, such as electrical motors, power lines, and radar.

nonbroadcast point-to-multipoint transmission A communications arrangement in which a single transmitter issues signals to multiple, defined recipients.

optical loss The degradation of a light signal on a fiber-optic network.

overhead The nondata information that must accompany data for a signal to be properly routed and interpreted by the network.

patch cable A relatively short section (usually between 3 and 25 feet) of cabling with connectors on both ends.

patch panel A wall-mounted panel of data receptors into which cross-connect patch cables from the punch-down block are inserted.

phase A point or stage in a wave's progress over time.

plenum The area above the ceiling tile or below the subfloor in a building.

point-to-multipoint A communications arrangement in which one transmitter issues signals to multiple receivers. The receivers may be undefined, as in a broadcast transmission, or defined, as in a nonbroadcast transmission.

point-to-point A data transmission that involves one transmitter and one receiver.

populated segment A network segment that contains end nodes, such as workstations.

punch-down block A panel of data receptors into which twisted pair wire is inserted, or punched down, to complete a circuit.

radio frequency interference *See* RFI.

Recommended Standard 232 *See* RS-232.

regeneration The process of retransmitting a digital signal. Regeneration, unlike amplification, repeats the pure signal, with none of the noise it has accumulated.

registered jack 11 *See* RJ-11.

registered jack 45 *See* RJ-45.

repeater A device used to regenerate a signal.

RFI (radio frequency interference) A kind of interference that may be generated by broadcast signals from radio or TV antennas.

RG-6 A type of coaxial cable with an impedance of 75 ohms and that contains an 18 AWG core conductor. RG-6 is used for television, satellite, and broadband cable connections.

RG-8 A type of coaxial cable characterized by a 50-ohm impedance and a 10 AWG core. RG-8 provided the medium for the first Ethernet networks, which followed the now-obsolete 10BASE-5 standard.

RG-58 A type of coaxial cable characterized by a 50-ohm impedance and a 24 AWG core. RG-58 was a popular medium for Ethernet LANs in the 1980s, used for the now-obsolete 10BASE-2 standard.

RG-59 A type of coaxial cable characterized by a 75-ohm impedance and a 20 or 22 AWG core, usually made of braided copper. Less expensive but suffering greater attenuation than the more common RG-6 coax, RG-59 is used for relatively short connections.

RJ-11 (registered jack 11) The standard connector used with unshielded twisted pair cabling (usually Cat 3 or Level 1) to connect analog telephones.

RJ-45 (registered jack 45) The standard connector used with shielded twisted pair and unshielded twisted pair cabling.

round-trip time *See* RTT.

RS-232 (Recommended Standard 232) A Physical layer standard for serial communications, as defined by EIA/TIA.

RTT (round-trip time) The length of time it takes for a packet to go from sender to receiver, then back from receiver to sender. RTT is usually measured in milliseconds.

SC (subscriber connector or standard connector) A connector used with single-mode or multimode fiber-optic cable.

serial A style of data transmission in which the pulses that represent bits follow one another along a single transmission line. In other words, they are issued sequentially, not simultaneously.

serial cable A cable, such as an RS-232 type, that permits serial data transmission.

sheath The outer cover, or jacket, of a cable.

shield *See* braiding.

shielded twisted pair *See* STP.

simplex A type of transmission in which signals may travel in only one direction over a medium.

single-mode fiber *See* SMF.

SMF (single-mode fiber) A type of fiber-optic cable with a narrow core that carries light pulses along a single path data from one end of the cable to the other end. Data can be transmitted faster and for longer distances on single-mode fiber than on multimode fiber. However, single-mode fiber is more expensive.

ST (straight tip) A connector used with single-mode or multimode fiber-optic cable.

standard connector *See* SC.

statistical multiplexing A method of multiplexing in which each node on a network is assigned a separate time slot for transmission, based on the node's priority and need.

STP (shielded twisted pair) A type of cable containing twisted-wire pairs that are not only individually insulated, but also surrounded by a shielding made of a metallic substance such as foil.

straight-through cable A twisted pair patch cable in which the wire terminations in both connectors follow the same scheme.

straight tip *See* ST.

structured cabling A method for uniform, enterprise-wide, multivendor cabling systems specified by the TIA/EIA 568 Commercial Building Wiring Standard. Structured cabling is based on a hierarchical design using a high-speed backbone.

subchannel One of many distinct communication paths established when a channel is multiplexed or modulated.

subscriber connector *See* SC.

TDM (time division multiplexing) A method of multiplexing that assigns a time slot in the flow of communications to every node on the network and, in that time slot, carries data from that node.

telecommunications closet Also known as a "telco room," the space that contains connectivity for groups of workstations in a defined area, plus cross-connections to IDFs or, in smaller organizations, an MDF. Large organizations may have several telecommunications closets per floor, but the TIA/EIA standard specifies at least one per floor.

Thicknet An IEEE Physical layer standard for achieving a maximum of 10-Mbps throughput over coaxial copper cable. Thicknet is also known as 10Base-5. Its maximum segment length is 500 meters, and it relies on a bus topology.

Thinnet An IEEE Physical layer standard for achieving 10-Mbps throughput over coaxial copper cable. Thinnet is also known as 10Base-2. Its maximum segment length is 185 meters, and it relies on a bus topology.

throughput The amount of data that a medium can transmit during a given period of time. Throughput is usually measured in megabits (1,000,000 bits) per second, or Mbps. The physical nature of every transmission media determines its potential throughput.

time division multiplexing *See* TDM.

transceiver A device that transmits and receives signals.

transmission In networking, the application of data signals to a medium or the progress of data signals over a medium from one point to another.

transmit To issue signals to the network medium.

twist ratio The number of twists per meter or foot in a twisted pair cable.

twisted pair A type of cable similar to telephone wiring that consists of color-coded pairs of insulated copper wires, each with a diameter of 0.4 to 0.8 mm, twisted around each other and encased in plastic coating.

unpopulated segment A network segment that does not contain end nodes, such as workstations. Unpopulated segments are also called link segments.

unshielded twisted pair *See* UTP.

UTP (unshielded twisted pair) A type of cabling that consists of one or more insulated wire pairs encased in a plastic sheath. As its name implies, UTP does not contain additional shielding for the twisted pairs. As a result, UTP is both less expensive and less resistant to noise than STP.

vertical cross-connect Part of a network's backbone that supplies connectivity between a building's floors. For example, vertical cross-connects might connect an MDF and an IDF or IDFs and telecommunications closets within a building.

volt The measurement used to describe the degree of pressure an electrical current exerts on a conductor.

voltage The pressure (sometimes informally referred to as the strength) of an electrical current.

wavelength The distance between corresponding points on a wave's cycle. Wavelength is inversely proportional to frequency.

wavelength division multiplexing *See* WDM.

WDM (wavelength division multiplexing) A multiplexing technique in which each signal on a fiber-optic cable is assigned a different wavelength, which equates to its own subchannel. Each wavelength is modulated with a data signal. In this manner, multiple signals can be simultaneously transmitted in the same direction over a length of fiber.

zipcord cable A relatively short fiber-optic cable in which two strands are arranged side by side in conjoined jackets, enabling full-duplex communication.

Review Questions

1. What terms characterize data transmission by the direction signals may travel over media?
   a. noise, throughput, attenuation, and latency
   b. amplitude, frequency, wavelength, and phase
   c. simplex, half-duplex, full-duplex, and duplex
   d. multiplexing
2. Which of the following describes the loss of signal strength as the signal travels away from its source?
   a. noise
   b. crosstalk
   c. attenuation
   d. latency
3. What is the most significant factor in choosing a transmission method?
   a. noise
   b. throughput
   c. cost
   d. scalability
4. What type of cable consists of one or more insulated wire pairs encased in a plastic sheath?
   a. coaxial
   b. STP (shielded twisted pair)
   c. UTP (unshielded twisted pair)
   d. fiber
5. What type of fiber-optic cable uses a small-diameter core?
   a. mini-mode
   b. unimode
   c. multimode
   d. single-mode
6. True or false? Digital signals are composed of pulses of precise, positive voltages and zero voltages.
7. True or false? Throughput is the measure of how much data is transmitted during a given period of time.
8. True or false? Broadband is a transmission form in which (typically) digital signals are sent through direct current (DC) pulses applied to the wire.
9. True or false? Because of its shielding, most coaxial cable has a high resistance to noise.

10. True or false? A layer of glass or plastic surrounding the fibers in fiber-optic cable is called cladding.

11. ________________ is a term used by networking professionals to describe the nondata information that must accompany data for a signal to be properly routed and interpreted by the network.

12. In ________________, a simple wave, called a carrier wave, is combined with another analog signal to produce a unique signal that is transmitted from one node to another.

13. A form of transmission that allows multiple signals to travel simultaneously over one medium is known as ________________.

14. If you terminate the RJ-45 plugs at both ends of a patch cable identically, following one of the TIA/EIA 568 standards, you will create a(n) ________________ cable.

15. ________________ is the Physical layer standard that specifies, among other things, signal voltage and timing, plus the characteristics of compatible interfaces.

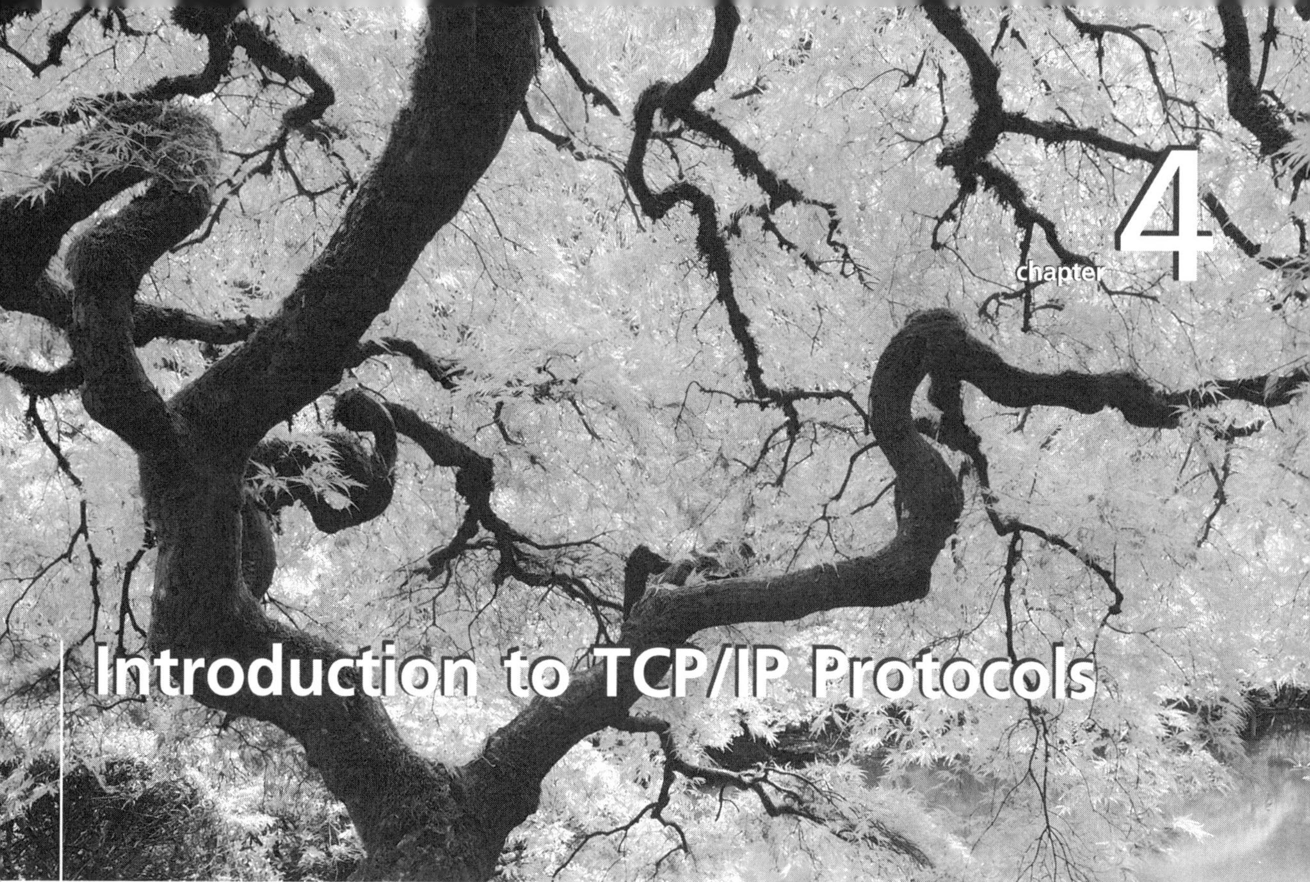

chapter 4

Introduction to TCP/IP Protocols

After reading this chapter and completing the exercises, you will be able to:

- Identify and explain the functions of the core TCP/IP protocols
- Explain the TCP/IP model and how it corresponds to the OSI model
- Discuss addressing schemes for TCP/IP in IPv4 and IPv6 and explain how addresses are assigned automatically using DHCP (Dynamic Host Configuration Protocol)
- Describe the purpose and implementation of DNS (Domain Name System)
- Identify the well-known ports for key TCP/IP services
- Describe how common Application layer TCP/IP protocols are used

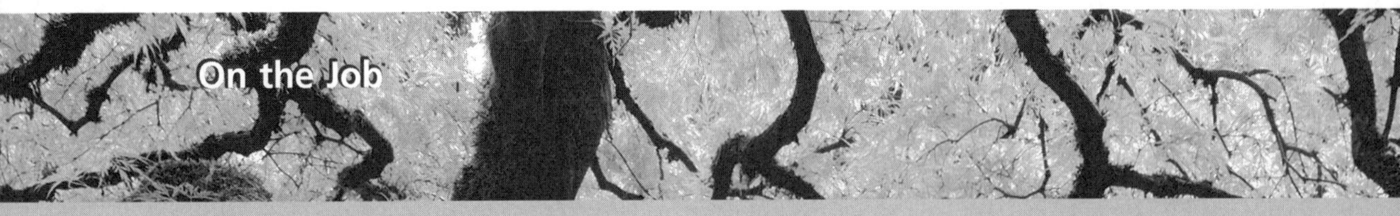

On the Job

I woke up to a message from an on-call engineer, Bill, saying, "Help, I am out of ideas for DNS troubleshooting!" Twenty minutes later, as I walked into the office, he recited a chaotic list of all the troubleshooting steps he took and every possible problem that could have caused the issue at hand. We took a walk to the vending machines so I could get caffeine and the story.

Dying server hardware forced Bill to move a number of services to new hardware. DNS was scheduled to be last, as the configuration was simple, and moving it was supposed to be a quick and easy task. Everything seemed to work fine, but queries for all of the Internet and a test internal domain were not being answered. The OS configuration and DNS server settings all seemed fine, but no matter what we tweaked, the service did not work right.

Because Bill knew more about DNS than I did, there was little reason for a detailed walk-through of the configurations. I took a quick look, in hope of finding something obvious that he had missed, but the configuration was sound. Since no trivial fix was available, I reverted to basic troubleshooting mode and started to work through a simple list of items to check: "ping localhost, ping the interface, ping the router, and a host beyond it...."

The last check returned "connect: Network is unreachable." A quick glance at the route table explained the issue: There was no default route. Without a way to forward traffic, no host outside of a few statically defined internal networks were reachable, including all of the root DNS servers.

The fix was simple and, once the service was restored, I helped a bit with moving other services. Another set of eyes is an invaluable asset during late-night work, and I had to work off all that caffeine.

Marcin Antkiewicz

In Chapter 1, you learned that a protocol is a rule that governs how computers on a network exchange data and instructions. Without protocols, devices could not interpret the signals sent by other devices, and data would go nowhere. In Chapter 2, you learned about the tasks associated with each layer of the OSI model, such as formatting, addressing, and error correction. You also learned that these tasks are performed by protocols. In this chapter, you will learn about the most commonly used networking protocols, their components, and their functions. This chapter is not an exhaustive study of protocols, but rather a practical guide to applying them. At the end of the chapter, you will have the opportunity to customize how your networked computer uses protocols. You will also analyze realistic networking scenarios pertaining to protocols and devise your own solutions. Because protocols form the foundation of network communications, you must fully understand them to manage a network effectively.

In the networking industry, the term *protocol* is sometimes used to refer to a group, or suite, of individual protocols that work together. In the sections that follow, you will learn about the protocol suite that is used on virtually all networks today—TCP/IP. As a network professional, you may occasionally encounter obsolete protocol suites that are not detailed in this chapter. But you will definitely encounter TCP/IP both on the job and in the Network+ certification exam. To be successful, you need to understand TCP/IP in depth.

Characteristics of TCP/IP (Transmission Control Protocol/ Internet Protocol)

1.6 **TCP/IP** (**Transmission Control Protocol/Internet Protocol**) is not simply one protocol, but rather a suite of specialized protocols—including TCP, IP, UDP, ARP, and many others—called **subprotocols**. Most network administrators refer to the entire group as "TCP/IP," or sometimes simply "IP." For example, a network administrator might say, "Our network only runs IP" when she means that all of the network's services rely on TCP/IP subprotocols.

TCP/IP's roots lie with the United States Department of Defense, which developed TCP/IP for its Advanced Research Projects Agency network (ARPANET, the precursor to today's Internet) in the late 1960s. UNIX and Linux have always relied on TCP/IP. The most recent versions of all other network operating systems also use TCP/IP as their default protocol. Though other protocol suites exist, TCP/IP has become the standard thanks to several advantages:

- *It is open, rather than proprietary*—TCP/IP is not owned by a company, which means you do not need to purchase a license to use it. It costs nothing and its code can be edited and modified by any programmer.
- *It is flexible*—The TCP/IP suite of protocols can run on virtually any platform and connect dissimilar operating systems and devices.
- *It is **routable***—TCP/IP transmissions carry Network layer addressing information that can be interpreted by routers to determine the best path for directing data over a network. Not all protocols are routable. Only routable protocols are suitable for large networks.

TCP/IP is a broad topic with numerous technical, historical, and practical aspects. Advanced TCP/IP topics are covered in Chapter 9. If you want to become an expert on TCP/IP, consider investing in a book or study guide solely devoted to this suite of protocols.

The TCP/IP Model

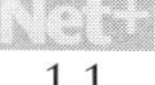

The TCP/IP suite of protocols can be divided into four layers that roughly correspond
1.1 to the seven layers of the OSI model, as depicted in Figure 4-1 and described in the
1.6 following list.

Net+ 1.1 1.6

TCP/IP model	Protocols and services	OSI model
Application	HTTP, FTP, Telnet, NTP, DHCP, PING	Application
		Presentation
		Session
Transport	TCP, UDP	Transport
Internet	IP, ARP, ICMP, IGMP	Network
Network Interface	Ethernet	Data Link
		Physical

Figure 4-1 The TCP/IP model compared with the OSI model

- *Application layer*—Roughly equivalent to the Application, Presentation, and Session layers of the OSI model. Applications gain access to the network through this layer, via protocols such as HTTP (Hypertext Transfer Protocol), FTP (File Transfer Protocol), Telnet, NTP (Network Time Protocol), DHCP (Dynamic Host Configuration Protocol), and PING (Packet Internet Groper), to name only some.
- *Transport layer*—Roughly corresponds to the Transport layer of the OSI model. This layer holds the Transmission Control Protocol (TCP) and User Datagram Protocol (UDP), which provide flow control, error checking, and sequencing.
- *Internet layer*—Equivalent to the Network layer of the OSI model. This layer holds the Internet Protocol (IP), Internet Control Message Protocol (ICMP), Internet Group Management Protocol (IGMP), and Address Resolution Protocol (ARP). These protocols handle routing and address resolution.
- *Network Interface layer (*or *Link layer)*—Roughly equivalent to the Data Link and Physical layers of the OSI model. Functions in this layer handle formatting of data and transmission to the network interface.

Unlike the OSI model, the TCP/IP model grew to describe how protocols work *after* the protocols were widely in use. For this reason, it is sometimes considered more practical than the OSI model, which is considered more theoretical. Understanding what functions belong to each layer of the models will come in handy when you're troubleshooting problems. For example, a simple test might indicate that a transmission is breaking down at the Transport layer. Although you might not know the cause of the problem, narrowing down its scope in this way will lead you and your colleagues to the next step in assessing and fixing the problem.

The TCP/IP Core Protocols

Net+ 1.6

Certain subprotocols of the TCP/IP suite, called **TCP/IP core protocols**, operate in the Transport or Network layers of the OSI model and provide basic services to protocols in other layers. As you might guess, TCP and IP are the most significant protocols in the TCP/IP suite. These and other core protocols are introduced in the following sections.

Net+

TCP (Transmission Control Protocol)

1.6 **TCP (Transmission Control Protocol)** operates in the Transport layer of the TCP/IP and OSI models and provides reliable data delivery services. TCP is a connection-oriented subprotocol, which means that a connection must be established between communicating nodes before this protocol will transmit data. As an analogy, suppose you were standing by a lake trying to communicate with a friend in a boat floating 100 yards offshore on a foggy afternoon. You need to give her an urgent message about a storm that's fast approaching. You could shout at her, but you might not know whether she heard you correctly, if at all. To be certain she gets your message, it would be better to call her cell phone and talk. Similar to completing a phone call and making sure your friend answers and can hear you before you tell her about the storm, in data communications, TCP is the protocol that ensures a connection has been made before it allows the message to continue.

TCP further ensures reliable data delivery through sequencing and checksums. In the analogy of communicating with a friend offshore, this would be similar to asking her to confirm that she understood your warning. Without TCP's connection and its sequencing and checksum measures, data would be transmitted indiscriminately. If not for TCP, a host would issue data without knowing whether the destination node was offline, for example, or whether the data became corrupt during transmission. This would be like shouting a lot of warnings to your offshore friend without making sure she understood—and then walking away.

Finally, TCP provides flow control to ensure that a node is not flooded with data. In the case of communicating with a friend in a boat, this would be like speaking slowly enough over the phone so that she can hear every word and understand your message.

Figure 4-2 depicts the format of a TCP segment, the entity that becomes encapsulated by the IP packet in the Network layer (and, thus, becomes the IP packet's data). Fields belonging to a TCP segment are defined in Table 4-1.

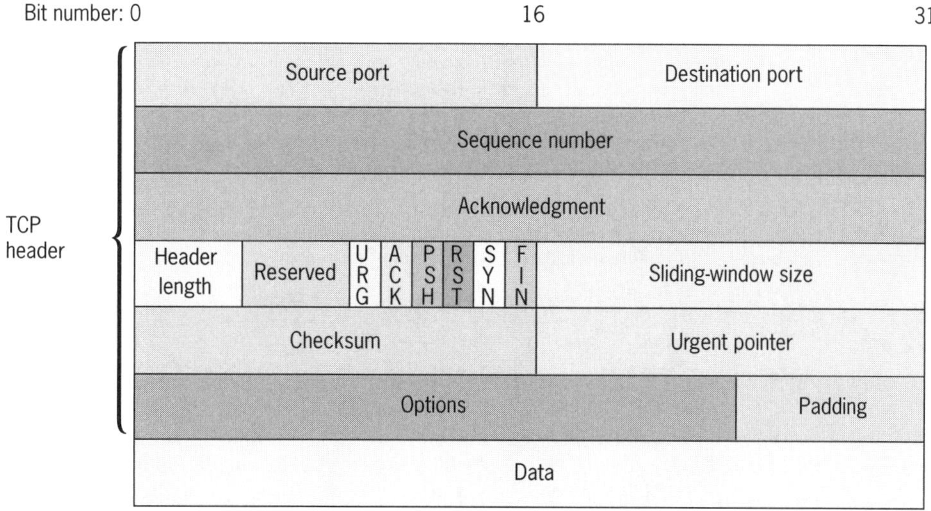

Figure 4-2 A TCP segment

Net+ 1.6

Table 4-1 Fields in a TCP segment

Field	Length	Function
Source port	16 bits	Indicates the port number at the source node. A **port number** is the address on a host where an application makes itself available to incoming or outgoing data.
Destination port	16 bits	Indicates the port number at the destination node.
Sequence number	32 bits	Identifies the data segment's position in the stream of data segments already sent.
Acknowledgment number (ACK)	32 bits	Confirms receipt of the data via a return message to the sender.
TCP header length	4 bits	Indicates the length of the TCP header.
Reserved	6 bits	A field reserved for later use.
Flags	6 bits	A collection of six 1-bit fields that signal special conditions through flags. The following flags are available for the sender's use: • URG—If set to *1*, the Urgent pointer field contains information for the receiver. • ACK—If set to *1*, the Acknowledgment field contains information for the receiver. (If set to *0*, the receiver will ignore the Acknowledgment field.) • PSH—If set to *1*, it indicates that data should be sent to an application without buffering. • RST—If set to *1*, the sender is requesting that the connection be reset. • SYN—If set to *1*, the sender is requesting a synchronization of the sequence numbers between the two nodes. This code is used when TCP requests a connection to set the initial sequence number. • FIN—If set to *1*, the segment is the last in a sequence and the connection should be closed.
Sliding-window size (or window)	16 bits	Indicates how many bytes the sender can issue to a receiver while acknowledgment for this segment is outstanding. This field performs flow control, preventing the receiver from being deluged with bytes. For example, suppose a server indicates a sliding window size of 4000 bytes. Also suppose the client has already issued 1000 bytes, 250 of which have been received and acknowledged by the server. That means that the server is still buffering 750 bytes. Therefore, the client can only issue 3250 additional bytes before it receives acknowledgment from the server for the 750 bytes.
Checksum	16 bits	Allows the receiving node to determine whether the TCP segment became corrupted during transmission.
Urgent pointer	16 bits	Indicates a location in the data field where urgent data resides.
Options	0–32 bits	Specifies special options, such as the maximum segment size a network can handle.
Padding	Variable	Contains filler information to ensure that the size of the TCP header is a multiple of 32 bits.
Data	Variable	Contains data originally sent by the source node. The size of the Data field depends on how much data need to be transmitted, the constraints on the TCP segment size imposed by the network type, and the limitation that the segment must fit within an IP packet.

1.6

In the Chapter 2 discussion of Transport layer functions, you learned how TCP establishes connections for HTTP requests. You also saw an example of TCP segment data from an actual HTTP request. However, you might not have understood what all of the data meant. Now that you know the function of each TCP segment field, you can interpret its contents. Figure 4-3 offers another look at the TCP segment.

```
Transmission Control Protocol, Src Port: http (80), Dst Port: 1958 (1958), Seq: 3043958669, Ack: 937013559, Len: 0
   Source port : http (80)
   Destination port: 1958 (1958)
   Sequence number: 3043958669
   Acknowledgment number: 937013559
   Header length: 24 bytes
⊟ Flags:_ 0xx0012 (SYN, ACK)
     0... .... = Congestion Window Reduced (CWR): Not set
     .0.. .... = ECN-Echo: Not set
     ..0. .... = Urgent: Not set
     ...1 .... = Acknowledgment: Set
     .... 0... = Push: Not set
     .... .0.. = Reset: Not set
     .... ..1. = Syn: Set
     .... ...0 = Fin: not set
   window size: 5840
   Checksum: 0x206a (correct)
⊟ Options: (4bytes)
     Maximum segment size: 1460 bytes
```

Figure 4-3 TCP segment data

Suppose the segment in Figure 4-3 was sent from computer B to computer A. Begin interpreting the segment at the Source port line. Notice the segment was issued from computer B's port 80, the port assigned to HTTP by default. It was addressed to port 1958 on computer A. The sequence number for this segment is 3043958669. The next segment that computer B expects to receive from computer A will have the sequence number of 937013559 because this is what computer B has entered in the Acknowledgment field. By simply having a value, the Acknowledgment field performs its duty of letting a node know that its last communication was received. By indicating a sequence number, the Acknowledgment field does double-duty. Next, look at the Header length field. It indicates that the TCP header is 24 bytes long—4 bytes larger than its minimum size—which means that some of the available options were specified or the padding space was used.

In the flags category, notice that there are two unfamiliar flags: Congestion Window Reduced and ECN-Echo. These are optional flags that can be used to help TCP react to and reduce traffic congestion. They are only available when TCP is establishing a connection. However, in this segment, they are not set. Of all the possible flags in the Figure 4-3 segment, only the ACK and SYN flags are set. This means that computer B is acknowledging the last segment it received from computer A and also negotiating a synchronization scheme for sequencing. The window size is 5840, meaning that computer B can accept 5840 more bytes of data from computer A even while this segment remains unacknowledged. The Checksum field indicates the valid outcome of the error-checking algorithm used to verify the segment's header. In this case, the checksum is 0x206a. When computer A receives this segment, it will

1.6 perform the same algorithm, and if the result is 0x206a, it will know the TCP header arrived without damage. Finally, this segment uses its option field to specify a maximum TCP segment size of 1460 bytes.

Note that a computer doesn't "see" the TCP segment as it's shown in Figure 4-3. This figure was obtained by using a data analyzer program that translates each packet into a user-friendly form. From the computer's standpoint, the TCP segment is encoded as hexadecimal characters. The computer does not need any labels to identify the fields because as long as TCP/IP protocol standards are followed, it knows exactly where each byte of data is located.

The TCP segment pictured in Figure 4-3 is part of the process of establishing a connection between computer B and computer A. In fact, it is the second segment of three used to establish a TCP connection. In the first step of establishing this connection, computer A issues a message to computer B with its SYN bit set, indicating the desire to communicate and synchronize sequence numbers. In its message, it sends a random number that will be used to synchronize the communication. In Figure 4-4, for example, this number is 937013558. (Its ACK bit is usually set to 0.) After computer B receives this message, it responds with a segment whose ACK and SYN flags are both set. In computer B's transmission, the ACK field contains a number that equals the sequence number computer A originally sent plus 1. As Figure 4-4 illustrates, computer B sends the number 937013559. In this manner, computer B signals to computer A that it has received the request for communication and further, it expects computer A to respond with the sequence number 937013559. In its SYN field, computer B sends its own random number (in Figure 4-4, this number is 3043958669), which computer A will use to acknowledge that it received computer B's transmission. Next, computer A issues a segment whose sequence number is 937013559 (because this is what

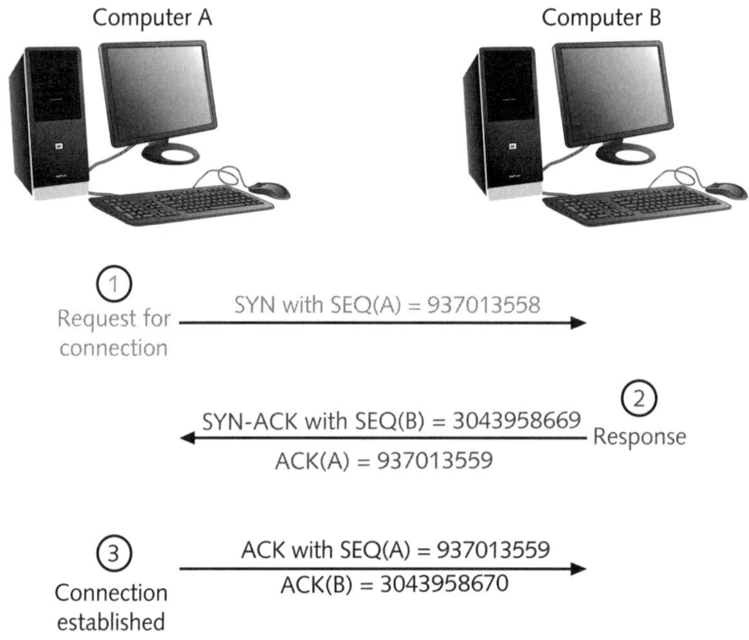

Figure 4-4 Establishing a TCP connection

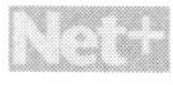

1.6 computer B indicated it expects to receive). In the same segment, computer A also communicates a sequence number via its Acknowledgment field. This number equals the sequence number that computer B sent plus 1. In the example shown in Figure 4-4, computer A expects 3043958670 to be the sequence number of the next segment it receives from computer B. Thus, in its next communication (not shown in Figure 4-4), computer B will respond with a segment whose sequence number is 937013560. The two nodes continue communicating this way until computer A issues a segment whose FIN flag is set, indicating the end of the transmission.

TCP is not the only core protocol at the Transport layer. A similar but less complex protocol, UDP, is discussed next.

UDP (User Datagram Protocol)

UDP (User Datagram Protocol), like TCP, belongs to the Transport layer of the TCP/IP and OSI models. Unlike TCP, however, UDP is a connectionless transport service. In other words, UDP offers no assurance that packets will be received in the correct sequence. In fact, this protocol does not guarantee that the packets will be received at all. Furthermore, it provides no error checking or sequencing. In the analogy of trying to communicate from shore to a friend on a boat, this would be like shouting into the fog without making sure she heard you correctly, if at all.

UDP's lack of sophistication makes it more efficient than TCP. It can be useful in situations in which a great volume of data must be transferred quickly, such as live audio or video transmissions over the Internet. In these cases, TCP—with its acknowledgments, checksums, and flow-control mechanisms—would only add more overhead to the transmission. UDP is also more efficient for carrying messages that fit within one data packet.

In contrast to a TCP header's 10 fields, the UDP header contains only four fields: Source port, Destination port, Length, and Checksum. Use of the Checksum field in UDP is optional. Figure 4-5 depicts a UDP segment. Contrast its header with the much larger TCP segment header shown in Figure 4-2.

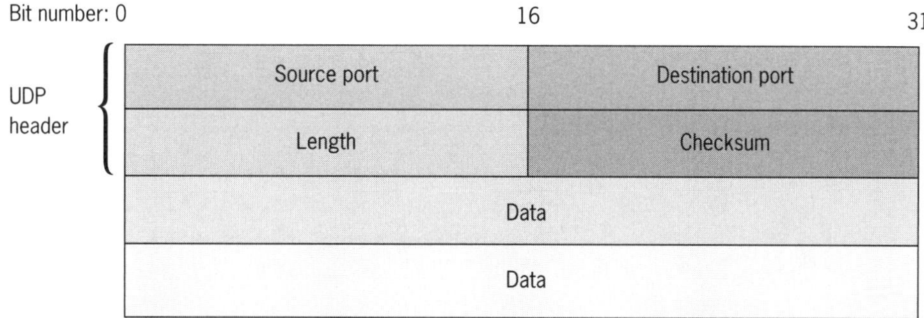

Figure 4-5 A UDP segment

Now that you understand the functions of and differences between TCP and UDP, you are ready to learn more about IP (Internet Protocol).

Net+

IP (Internet Protocol)

1.6 IP (Internet Protocol) belongs to the Internet layer of the TCP/IP model and the Network layer of the OSI model. It provides information about how and where data should be delivered, including the data's source and destination addresses. IP is the subprotocol that enables TCP/IP to **internetwork**—that is, to traverse more than one LAN segment and more than one type of network through a router.

As you know, at the Network layer of the OSI model, data are formed into packets, also known as **datagrams**. The IP packet acts as an envelope for data and contains information necessary for routers to transfer data between different LAN segments.

Two versions of the IP protocol are used on networks today. **IPv4**, which was introduced over 30 years ago, is still the standard on most networks. IPv4 is an unreliable, connectionless protocol, which means that it does not guarantee delivery of data. However, higher-level protocols of the TCP/IP suite, such as TCP, use IPv4 to ensure that data packets are delivered to the right addresses.

The newer version of IP, **IPv6**, also known as **IP next generation**, or **IPng**, was released in 1998. Most new applications, servers, clients, and network devices support IPv6. However, due to the cost of upgrading infrastructure, many organizations have hesitated to upgrade from IPv4. Switching to IPv6 has advantages. IPv6 offers better security and better prioritization provisions than IPv4, plus automatic IP address configuration. But perhaps the most valuable advantage IPv6 offers is its promise of billions and billions of additional IP addresses through its new addressing scheme.

IPv4 Packets Due to the added information it carries, IPv6 uses different packets than IPv4. The following sections describe both types of packets in detail. Figure 4-6 depicts an IPv4 packet. Its fields are explained in Table 4-2.

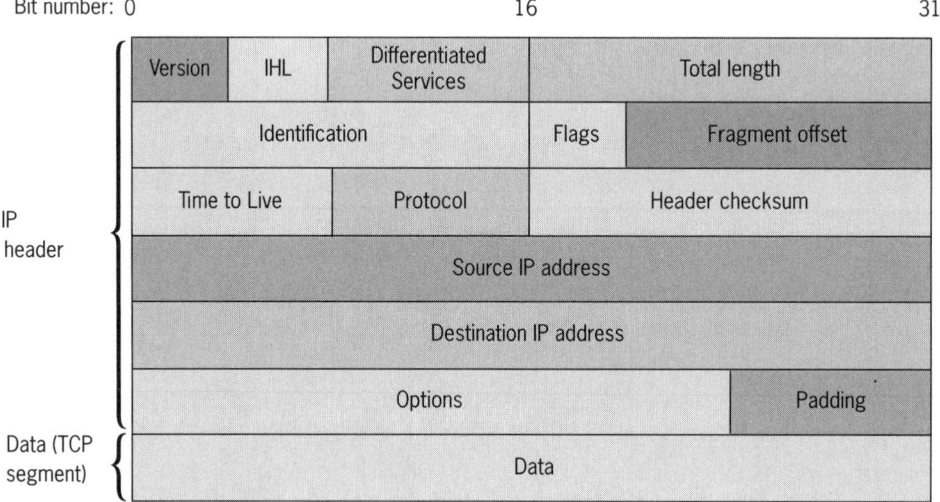

Figure 4-6 An IPv4 packet

Net+ 1.6

Table 4-2 Fields in an IPv4 packet

Field	Length	Function
Version	4 bits	Identifies the version number of the protocol—for example, IPv4 or IPv6. The receiving workstation looks at this field first to determine whether it can read the incoming data. If it cannot, it will reject the packet.
Internet header length (IHL)	4 bits	Identifies the number of 4-byte (or 32-bit) blocks in the IPv4 header. The most common header length is composed of five groupings, as the minimum length of an IPv4 header is 20 4-byte blocks. This field indicates to the receiving node where data will begin (immediately after the header ends).
Differentiated Services (DiffServ)	8 bits	Informs routers the level of precedence they should apply when processing the incoming packet. Differentiated Services allows up to 64 values and a wide range of priority handling options.
Total length	16 bits	Identifies the total length of the IP packet, including the header and data, in bytes. An IP packet, including its header and data, cannot exceed 65,535 bytes.
Identification	16 bits	Identifies the message to which a packet belongs and enables the receiving node to reassemble fragmented messages. This field and the following two fields, Flags and Fragment offset, assist in reassembly of fragmented packets.
Flags	3 bits	Indicates whether a message is fragmented and, if it is fragmented, whether this packet is the last in the fragment.
Fragment offset	13 bits	Identifies where the packet fragment belongs in the incoming set of fragments.
Time to Live (TTL)	8 bits	Indicates the maximum duration that the packet can remain on the network before it is discarded. Although this field was originally meant to represent units of time, on modern networks it represents the number of times a packet has been forwarded by a router, or the number of router **hops** it has endured. Therefore, TTL is often called the **hop limit**. The TTL for packets is variable and configurable, but is usually set at 32 or 64. Each time a packet passes through a router, its TTL is reduced by 1. When a router receives a datagram with a TTL equal to 1, it discards that packet (or more precisely, the frame to which it belongs).
Protocol	8 bits	Identifies the type of Transport layer protocol that will receive the datagram (for example, TCP or UDP).
Header checksum	16 bits	Allows the receiving node to calculate whether the IP header has been corrupted during transmission. If the checksum accompanying the message does not have the proper value when the packet is received, the packet is presumed to be corrupt and is discarded.
Source IP address	32 bits	Identifies the full IP address of the source node.
Destination IP address	32 bits	Indicates the full IP address of the destination node.
Options	Variable	May contain optional routing and timing information.
Padding	Variable	Contains filler bits to ensure that the header is a multiple of 32 bits.
Data	Variable	Includes the data originally sent by the source node, plus information added by TCP in the Transport layer.

In the Chapter 2 discussion of the OSI model's Network layer functions, you were introduced to IP and the data contained in its packets. You also saw an example of IPv4 packet data from an actual HTTP request. However, you might not have understood what all of

1.6 the data meant. Now that you are familiar with the fields of an IPv4 packet, you can interpret its contents. Figure 4-7 offers another look at the IPv4 packet.

```
⊟Internet Protocol, Src Addr: 140.147.249.7 (140.147.249.7), Dst Addr: 10.11.11.51 (10.11.11.51)
    Version: 4
    Header length: 20 bytes
  ⊞Differentiated Services Field: 0x00 (DSCP 0x00: Default; ECN 0x00)
    Total Length: 44
    Identification: 0x0000 (0)
  ⊟Flags: 0x04
      .1.. = Don't fragment: Set
      ..0. = More fragments: Not set
    Fragment offset: 0
    Time to live: 64
    Protocol: TCP (0x06)
    Header checksum: 0x9ff3 (correct)
    Source: 140.147.249.7 (140.147.249.7)
    Destination: 10.11.11.51 (10.11.11.51)
```

Figure 4-7 IPv4 packet data

Begin interpreting the datagram in Figure 4-7 with the Version field, which indicates that this transmission relies on version 4 of the Internet Protocol. Next, notice that the datagram has a header length of 20 bytes. Because this is the minimum size for an IP header, you can deduce that the datagram contains no options or padding. In the Differentiated Services field, no options for priority handling are set, which is not unusual in routine data exchanges such as retrieving a Web page. The total length of the datagram is given as 44 bytes. This makes sense when you consider that its header is 20 bytes and the TCP segment that it encapsulates is 24 bytes. Considering that the maximum size of an IP packet is 65,535 bytes, this is a very small packet.

Next in the IP datagram is the Identification field, which uniquely identifies the packet. This packet, the first one issued from computer B to computer A in the TCP connection exchange, is identified in hexadecimal notation as 0x0000. In the Flags field, which indicates whether this packet is fragmented, the Don't fragment option is set with a value of 1. So you know that this packet is not fragmented. And because it's not fragmented, the fragment offset field does not apply and is set to 0.

This datagram's TTL (Time to Live) is set to 64. That means that if the packet were to keep traveling across a network, it would be allowed 64 more hops before it was discarded. The Protocol field is next. It indicates that encapsulated within the packet is a TCP segment. TCP is always indicated by the hexadecimal string of 0x06. The next field provides the correct header checksum answer, which is used by the recipient of this packet to determine whether the header was damaged in transit. Finally, the last two fields in the packet show the logical addresses for its source and destination.

IPv6 Packets As you have learned, IPv6 was designed to offer better prioritization, better security, and a much larger range of IP addresses than IPv4. The fields in an IPv6 packet header, explained in Table 4-3 and shown in Figure 4-8, reflect those enhancements.

Net+
1.6

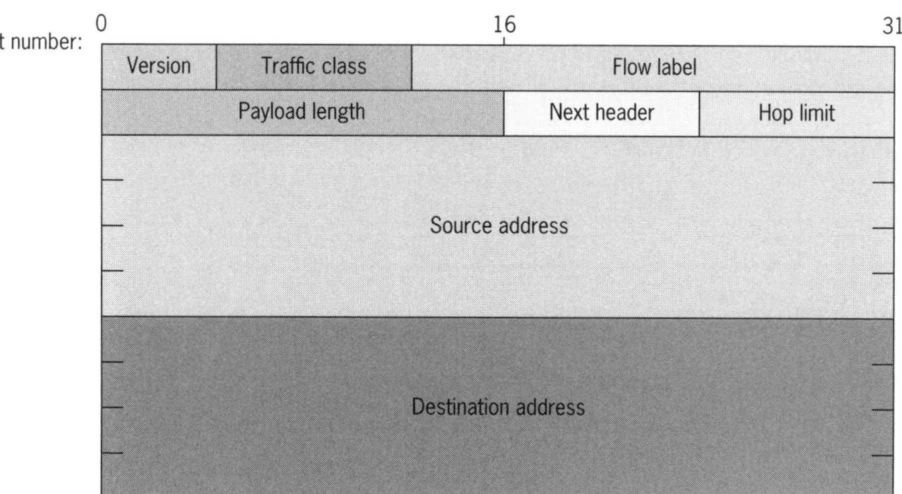

Figure 4-8 An IPv6 packet header

Table 4-3 Fields in an IPv6 packet

Field	Length	Function
Version	4 bits	Indicates what IP version the packet uses.
Traffic class	8 bits	Identifies the packet's priority. It is similar, but not the same as the Type of service field in IPv4 packets.
Flow label	20 bits	Indicates which **flow**, or sequence of packets issued from one source to one or multiple destinations, the datagram belongs to. Routers interpret flow information to ensure that packets belonging to the same transmission arrive together. Flow information may also help with traffic prioritization.
Payload length	16 bits	Indicates the size of the payload, or data carried by the packet. Unlike the Total length field in IPv4 packets, the Payload length in IPv6 packets does not refer to the size of the whole packet.
Next header	8 bits	Identifies the type of header that immediately follows the IP packet header, usually TCP or UDP.
Hop limit	8 bits	Indicates the number of times that the packet can be forwarded by routers on the network, similar to the TTL field in IPv4 packets. When the hop limit reaches 0, the packet is discarded.
Source address	128 bits	Identifies the full IP address of the transmitting node.
Destination address	128 bits	Identifies the full IP address of the receiving node.

If you compare the fields and functions listed in Table 4-3 with those listed for the IPv4 packet in Table 4-2, you'll notice some similarities and some differences. For example, both packets begin with a 4-bit Version field. Other fields, such as the TTL in IPv4 and the Hop limit in IPv6, are similar, but slightly different. One striking difference between the two versions is that IPv6 packets accommodate the much longer IPv6 addresses.

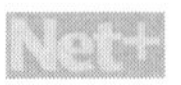

1.6 Figure 4-9 shows the contents of an actual IPv6 packet header. This packet formed part of a message issued by PING, a common diagnostic tool that is described in detail later in this chapter. First in the header comes the Version field, which indicates that this transmission relies on version 6 of the Internet Protocol, expressed in binary format as 0110. (Recall from Chapter 2's discussion of binary conversion that 0110 would be 0 x 8 + 1 x 4 + 1 x 2 + 0 x 1, or 6, in decimal format.)

```
Internet Protocol Version 6, Src: 2001:470:1f10:1a6::2 (2001:470:1f10:1a6::2), Dst: 2001:470:1f10:1a6::1 (2001:470:1f10:1a6::1)
  0110 .... = Version: 6
  .... 0000 0000 .... .... .... .... .... = Traffic class: 0x00000000
  .... .... .... 0000 0000 0000 0000 0000 = Flowlabel: 0x00000000
  Payload length: 64
  Next header: ICMPv6 (0x3a)
  Hop limit: 64
  Source: 2001:470:1f10:1a6::2 (2001:470:1f10:1a6::2)
  Destination: 2001:470:1f10:1a6::1 (2001:470:1f10:1a6::1)
```

Figure 4-9 IPv6 packet data

Next, notice that the Traffic class and Flow label field are both set to 0x0000000. That means values for these fields have not been specified. Without Traffic class or Flow label information, routers receiving this packet will not prioritize it or make any guarantees that it will reach its destination at the same time as any other packets. For many types of traffic, this is perfectly acceptable.

Next in the IPv6 header comes the Payload field, with a value of 64, which means the packet carries 64 bits of data. Considering that IPv6 packets may carry payloads as large as 64 KB, this is a very small packet. The Next header field in this packet indicates that the data in the payload belongs to an ICMP transmission. (ICMP is also described later in this chapter.) The IPv6 datagram's Hop limit is set to 64. That means that if the packet were to keep traveling across a network, it could be forwarded by routers 64 times before it was discarded. Finally, the last two fields in the packet show the IP addresses for the packet's source and destination, 2001:470:1f10:1a6::2 and 2001:470:1f10:1a6::1, respectively.

It's useful to understand the differences between IPv4 and IPv6 transmissions before learning about other TCP/IP protocols. For example, the protocols described in the next two sections, IGMP and ARP, are used only on IPv4 networks. The functions they provide have become part of the IPv6 protocol and no longer need to be provided by separate Network layer protocols.

IGMP (Internet Group Management Protocol)

Another core TCP/IP protocol is **IGMP** (**Internet Group Management Protocol** or **Internet Group Multicast Protocol**). IGMP operates at the Network layer of the OSI model and manages multicasting on networks running IPv4. **Multicasting** is a transmission method that allows one node to send data to a defined group of nodes. Whereas most data transmission occurs on a point-to-point basis, multicasting is a point-to-multipoint method. And unlike a broadcast transmission, a multicast transmission does not necessarily issue transmissions to every node on a segment. Multicasting can be used for teleconferencing or videoconferencing over the Internet, for example. Routers use IGMP to determine which nodes belong to a certain multicast group and to transmit data to all nodes in that group. Network nodes use IGMP to join or leave multicast groups at any time.

ARP (Address Resolution Protocol)

ARP (**Address Resolution Protocol**) is a Network layer protocol used with IPv4 that obtains the MAC (physical) address of a host, or node, and then creates a database that maps the MAC address to the host's IP address. If one node needs to know the MAC address of another node on

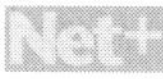

the same network, the first node issues a broadcast message to the network, using ARP, that
1.6 essentially says, "Will the computer with the IP address 1.2.3.4 please send me its MAC
address?" In the context of networking, a broadcast is a transmission that is simultaneously sent to all nodes on a particular network segment. The node that has the IP address 1.2.3.4 then broadcasts a reply that contains the physical address of the destination host.

To make ARP more efficient, computers save recognized MAC-to-IP address mappings on their hard disks in a database known as an **ARP table** (also called an **ARP cache**). After a computer has saved this information, the next time it needs the MAC address for another device, it finds the address in its ARP table and does not need to broadcast another request. Although the precise format of ARP tables may vary from one operating system to another, the essential contents of the table and its purpose remain the same. A sample ARP table is shown in Figure 4-10.

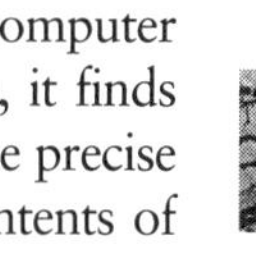

```
IP Address          Hardware Address     Type

123.45.67.80        60:23:A6:F1:C4:D2    Static
123.45.67.89        20:00:3D:21:E0:11    Dynamic
123.45.67.73        A0:BB:77:C2:25:FA    Dynamic
```

Figure 4-10 Sample ARP table

An ARP table can contain two types of entries: dynamic and static. **Dynamic ARP table entries** are created when a client makes an ARP request that cannot be satisfied by data already in the ARP table. **Static ARP table entries** are those that someone has entered manually using the ARP utility. The ARP utility, accessed via the arp command from a Windows command prompt or a UNIX or Linux shell prompt, provides a way of obtaining information from and manipulating a device's ARP table. For example, you can view a Windows workstation's ARP table by typing `arp -a` at the command line and pressing Enter. ARP can be a valuable troubleshooting tool for discovering the identity of a machine whose IP address you know, or for identifying the problem of two machines trying to use the same IP address.

ICMP (Internet Control Message Protocol)

Whereas IP helps direct data to its correct destination, **ICMP (Internet Control Message Protocol)** is a Network layer core protocol that reports on the success or failure of data delivery. It can indicate when part of a network is congested, when data fails to reach its destination, and when data has been discarded because the allotted time for its delivery (its TTL) expired. ICMP announces these transmission failures to the sender, but ICMP cannot correct any of the errors it detects; those functions are left to higher-layer protocols, such as TCP. However, ICMP's announcements provide critical information for troubleshooting network problems.

IPv6 relies on **ICMPv6 (Internet Control Message Protocol version 6)** to perform the functions that ICMP, IGMP, and ARP perform in IPv4. In other words, ICMPv6 detects and reports data transmission errors, discovers other nodes on a network, and manages multicasting.

IPv4 Addressing

You have learned that networks recognize two kinds of addresses: logical (or Network layer)
1.2 and physical (or MAC, or hardware) addresses. Physical addresses are assigned to a device's
1.3 NIC at the factory by its manufacturer. Logical addresses can be manually or automatically
1.6 assigned and must follow rules set by the protocol standards. In the TCP/IP protocol suite, IP

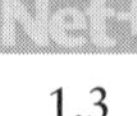

is the protocol responsible for logical addressing. For this reason, addresses on TCP/IP-based
1.3 networks are often called IP addresses. IP addresses are assigned and used according to very
1.6 specific parameters.

Each IP address is a unique 32-bit number, divided into four **octets**, or sets of 8 bits, that are separated by periods. Because 8 bits equals 1 byte, each octet is a byte, and an IP address is thus composed of 4 bytes. An example of a valid IP address is 144.92.43.178.

An IP address contains two types of information: network and host. From the first octet, you can determine the **network class**. In traditional IP addressing, three types of network classes are used for LANs: Class A, Class B, and Class C. (In Chapter 9, however, you'll learn about developments that allow networks to circumvent such class designations.) Table 4-4 summarizes characteristics of the three commonly used classes of TCP/IP-based networks.

In addition, Class D and Class E addresses do exist, but are rarely used. Class D addresses, which begin with an octet whose value is between 224 and 239, are reserved for multicasting. IETF (Internet Engineering Task Force) reserves Class E addresses, which begin with an octet whose value is between 240 and 254, for experimental use. You should never assign Class D or Class E addresses to devices on your network.

Certain octets in an IP address are reserved for special functions. The number 0 is reserved to act as a placeholder when referring to an entire group of computers on a network—for example, 10.0.0.0 represents all of the devices whose first octet is 10. The number 255, when used in the host portion of an address, indicates a broadcast transmission. Sending a message to the address 147.82.255.255, for example, sends a message to all devices connected to the 147.82.0.0 network.

Table 4-4 Commonly used TCP/IP classes

Network class	Beginning octet	Number of networks	Maximum addressable hosts per network
A	1–126	126	16,777,214
B	128–191	> 16,000	65,534
C	192–223	> 2,000,000	254

A portion of each IP address contains clues about the network class. An IP address whose first octet is in the range of 1–126 belongs to a Class A network. All IP addresses for devices on a Class A segment share the same first octet, or bits 0 through 7, as shown in Figure 4-11. For example, nodes with the following IP addresses may belong to the same Class A network: 23.78.110.109, 23.164.32.97, 23.48.112.43, and 23.108.37.22. In this example, 23 is the **network ID**. The second through fourth octets (bits 8 through 31) in a Class A address identify the host.

An IP whose first octet is in the range of 128–191 belongs to a Class B network. All IP addresses for devices on a Class B segment share the first two octets, or bits 0 through 15. For example, nodes with the following IP addresses may belong to the same Class B network: 168.34.88.29, 168.34.55.41, 168.34.73.49, and 168.34.205.113. In this example, 168.34 is the network ID. The third and fourth octets (bits 16 through 31) on a Class B network identify the host, as shown in Figure 4-11.

Net+
1.3
1.6

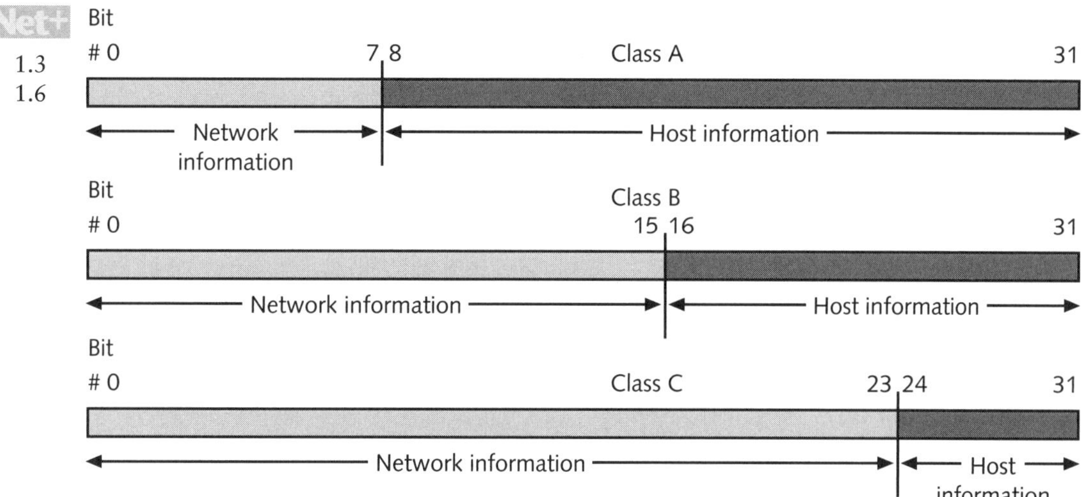

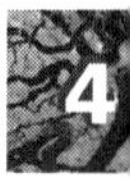

Figure 4-11 IPv4 addresses and their classes

An IP address whose first octet is in the range of 192–223 belongs to a Class C network. All IP addresses for devices on a Class C segment share the first three octets, or bits 0 through 23. For example, nodes with the following addresses may belong to the same Class C network: 204.139.118.7, 204.139.118.54, 204.139.118.14, and 204.139.118.31. In this example, 204.139.118 is the network ID. The fourth octet (bits 24 through 31) on a Class C network identifies the host, as shown in Figure 4-11.

Internet founders intended the use of network classes to provide easy organization and a sufficient quantity of IP addresses on the Internet. However, their goals haven't necessarily been met. Class A addresses were distributed liberally to large companies and government organizations who were early users of the Internet, such as IBM. Some organizations reserved many more addresses than they had devices. Class B addresses were distributed to midsized organizations and Class C addresses to smaller organizations, such as colleges. Today, many Internet addresses go unused, but cannot be reassigned because an organization has reserved them. Although potentially more than 4.3 billion Internet addresses are available, the demand for such addresses grows exponentially every year. To respond to this demand, a new addressing scheme was developed that can supply the world with enough addresses to last well into this century. IP version 6 (IPv6) incorporates this new addressing scheme. You will learn more about IPv6 addressing later in this chapter.

In addition, some IP addresses are reserved for special functions, like broadcasts, and cannot be assigned to machines or devices. Notice that 127 is not a valid first octet for any IPv4 address. The range of addresses beginning with 127 is reserved for a device communicating with itself, or performing loopback communication. Thus, the IP address 127.0.0.1 is called a **loopback address**. Attempting to contact this IP number—in other words, attempting to contact your own machine—is known as a **loopback test**. (In fact, when you transmit to any IP address beginning with the 127 octet, you are communicating with your own machine.) A loopback test can prove useful when troubleshooting problems with a workstation's TCP/IP communications. If you receive a positive response from a loopback test, you know that the TCP/IP core protocols are installed and in use on your workstation.

The command used to view IP information on a Windows workstation is ***ipconfig***. To view your current IP information on a Windows workstation:

1.3
1.6
4.3

1. Click the **Start** button, select **All Programs**, select **Accessories**, and then select **Command Prompt**. The Command Prompt window opens.
2. At the command prompt, type **`ipconfig /all`** and press **Enter**. Your workstation's IP address information is displayed, similar to the information shown in Figure 4-12.

```
Windows IP Configuration

        Host Name . . . . . . . . . . . . : Studentx
        Primary Dns Suffix  . . . . . . . :
        Node Type . . . . . . . . . . . . : Unknown
        IP Routing Enabled. . . . . . . . : No
        WINS Proxy Enabled. . . . . . . . : No

Ethernet adapter Local Area Connection:

        Connection-specific DNS Suffix  . : jones
        Description . . . . . . . . . . . : Realtek RTL8139/810x Family Fast Ethern
 NIC
        Physical Address. . . . . . . . . : 00-08-0D-E7-2F-0C
        Dhcp Enabled. . . . . . . . . . . : Yes
        Autoconfiguration Enabled . . . . : Yes
        IP Address. . . . . . . . . . . . : 10.11.11.100
        Subnet Mask . . . . . . . . . . . : 255.255.255.0
        Default Gateway . . . . . . . . . : 10.11.11.1
        DHCP Server . . . . . . . . . . . : 10.11.11.1
        DNS Servers . . . . . . . . . . . : 10.11.11.1
                                            206.141.192.60
                                            206.141.193.55
        Lease Obtained. . . . . . . . . . : Thursday, October 26, 2013 6:24:51 PM
        Lease Expires . . . . . . . . . . : Friday, October 27, 2013 6:24:51 PM

Ethernet adapter Wireless Network Connection:

        Media State . . . . . . . . . . . : Media disconnected
        Description . . . . . . . . . . . : Toshiba Wireless LAN Mini PCI Card
        Physical Address. . . . . . . . . : 00-02-2D-85-DF-11
```

Figure 4-12 Results of the `ipconfig /all` command on a Windows workstation

3. Type **`exit`** and press **Enter** to close the Command Prompt window.

To view and edit IP information on a computer running a version of the UNIX or Linux operating system, use the **`ifconfig`** command. (Note that `ipconfig` and `ifconfig` differ by only one letter.) Simply type `ifconfig -a` at the shell prompt to view all the information about your TCP/IP connections and addresses, as shown in Figure 4-13. In this figure, the IP address is labeled `inet addr`.

```
bash-3.00% ifconfig -a
eth0      Link encap:Ethernet  HWaddr 00:02:8A:A4:F8:C8
          inet addr:10.1.1.100  Bcast:10.1.1.255  Mask:255.255.255.0
          UP BROADCAST NOTRAILERS RUNNING MULTICAST  MTU:1500  Metric:1
          RX packets:0 errors:0 dropped:0 overruns:0 frame:0
          TX packets:0 errors:0 dropped:0 overruns:0 carrier:0
          collisions:0 txqueuelen:1000
          RX bytes:0 (0.0 b)  TX bytes:0 (0.0 b)

lo        Link encap:Local Loopback
          inet addr:127.0.0.1  Mask:255.0.0.0
          UP LOOPBACK RUNNING  MTU:16436  Metric:1
          RX packets:0 errors:0 dropped:0 overruns:0 frame:0
          TX packets:0 errors:0 dropped:0 overruns:0 carrier:0
          collisions:0 txqueuelen:0
          RX bytes:0 (0.0 b)  TX bytes:0 (0.0 b)

bash-3.00%
```

Figure 4-13 Results of the `ifconfig -a` command on a UNIX workstation

Now that you have learned the most important characteristics of IP addresses, you are ready to learn more about how computers interpret these addresses.

Net+

Binary and Dotted Decimal Notation

1.3 So far, all of the IP addresses in this section have been represented in dotted decimal nota-
1.6 tion. **Dotted decimal notation**, the most common way of expressing IP addresses, refers to the "shorthand" convention used to represent IP addresses and make them easy for people to read. In dotted decimal notation, a decimal number between 0 and 255 represents each binary octet, for a total of 256 possibilities. A period, or dot, separates each decimal. An example of a dotted decimal IP address is 131.65.10.18.

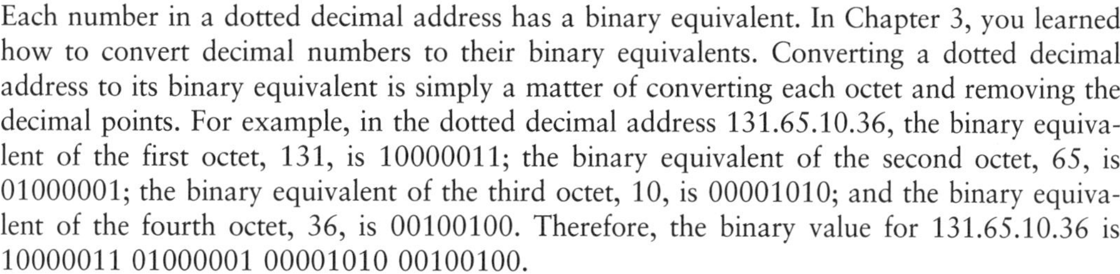

Each number in a dotted decimal address has a binary equivalent. In Chapter 3, you learned how to convert decimal numbers to their binary equivalents. Converting a dotted decimal address to its binary equivalent is simply a matter of converting each octet and removing the decimal points. For example, in the dotted decimal address 131.65.10.36, the binary equivalent of the first octet, 131, is 10000011; the binary equivalent of the second octet, 65, is 01000001; the binary equivalent of the third octet, 10, is 00001010; and the binary equivalent of the fourth octet, 36, is 00100100. Therefore, the binary value for 131.65.10.36 is 10000011 01000001 00001010 00100100.

Subnet Mask

In addition to an IP address, every device on a network running IPv4 is assigned a subnet mask. A **subnet mask** is a special 32-bit number that, when combined with a device's IP address, informs the rest of the network about the segment or network to which the device is attached. That is, it identifies the device's **subnet**. Like IP addresses, subnet masks are composed of four octets (32 bits) and can be expressed in either binary or dotted decimal notation. Subnet masks are assigned in the same way that IP addresses are assigned—either manually, within a device's TCP/IP configuration, or automatically, through a service such as DHCP (described in detail later in this chapter). A more common term for subnet mask is **net mask**, and sometimes simply **mask**, as in "a device's mask."

You might wonder why a network node even needs a subnet mask, given that the first octet of its IP address indicates its network class. The answer lies with **subnetting**, a process of subdividing a single class of networks into multiple, smaller logical networks, or segments.

Network managers create subnets to manage and separate network traffic and to make the best use of a limited number of IP addresses. Methods of subnetting are discussed in detail in Chapter 9. For now, it is enough to know that regardless of whether a network is subnetted, its devices are assigned a subnet mask.

On networks that use subnetting, the subnet mask varies depending on the way the network is subnetted. On networks that do not use subnetting, however, the subnet masks take on a default value, as shown in Table 4-5. To qualify for Network+ certification, you should be familiar with the default subnet masks associated with each network class.

Table 4-5 Default subnet masks

1.3
1.6

Network class		Default subnet mask
A	1–126	255.0.0.0
B	128–191	255.255.0.0
C	192–223	255.255.255.0

IPv6 Addressing

1.3
1.6

Up to this point, you have learned about IP addressing according to the IPv4 scheme. This section introduces you to addressing in IPv6 and explains the differences between addressing in IPv4 and addressing in IPv6. For Network+ certification, you will need to understand both addressing schemes.

The most notable difference between IP addresses in IPv4 and IPv6 is their size. Whereas IPv4 addresses are composed of 32 bits, IPv6 addresses are composed of eight 16-bit fields, for a total of 128 bits. The added fields and the larger address size result in an increase of 2^{96} (or 4 billion times 4 billion times 4 billion) available IP addresses in the IPv6 addressing scheme. The addition of more IP addresses not only allows every interface on every Internet-connected device to have a unique number, but also eliminates the need for IP address conservation. With the increasing number of network-enabled devices, including handheld computers, telephones, home security systems, traffic cameras, and even pet-tracking systems, the limited quantity of IPv4 addresses posed a serious bottleneck.

A second difference between IPv4 and IPv6 addresses is the way they are represented. Whereas each octet in an IPv4 address contains decimal numbers separated by a period (for example, 123.45.67.89), each field in an IPv6 address is typically represented in hexadecimal numbers separated by a colon. (Keep in mind that the computer still reads the binary version of this address, and if you wanted, you could also write an IPv6 address in binary format.) An example of a valid IPv6 address is FE22:00FF:002D:0000:0000:0000:3012:CCE3.

Because many IPv6 addresses will contain multiple fields that have values of 0, two methods of shorthand for representing these fields have been established. One method eliminates all leading zeros—that is, zeros that precede another hexadecimal digit—within a field. For example, the field 00FF could also be written FF and the field 0000 could be written 0. Thus, FE22:00FF:002D:0000:0000:0000:3012:CCE3 can be written as FE22:FF:2D:0:0:0:3012:CCE3. A second type of shorthand substitutes :: for any number of multiple, zero-value fields. Thus, FE22:00FF:002D:0000:0000:0000:3012:CCE3 can also be written as FE22:FF:2D::3012:CCE3.

The substitution of multiple zero-value fields can only be performed once within an address; otherwise, you cannot tell how many fields the :: symbol represents. For example, the IPv6 address 2001:0:0:34D0:0:0:9F77:2854 could *not* be abbreviated 2001::34D0::9F77:2854. It could instead be abbreviated 2001::34D0:0:0:9F77:2854 *or* 2001:0:0:34D0::9F77:2854.

An important address to memorize is the IPv6 loopback address. Recall that in IPv4 the loopback address has a value of 127.0.0.1. In IPv6, however, the loopback address has a value of 0:0:0:0:0:0:0:1. Abbreviated, the IPv6 loopback address becomes ::1.

Net+
A third difference between the two types of IP addresses is that in IPv6, addresses can reflect the
1.3 scope of a transmission's recipients—for example, a single node, a group, or a special kind of
1.6 group. One type of IPv6 address is a **unicast address**, or an address that represents a single interface on a device. A unicast address is the type of address that would be assigned, for example, to a workstation's network adapter. If you wanted to save a file from your laptop onto your company's server using IPv6, that transmission would call for a unicast address. Also, the loopback address is a unicast address.

A **multicast address** represents multiple interfaces (often on multiple devices). Multicast addresses are useful for transmitting the same data to many different devices simultaneously, as in point-to-multipoint communications. IPv6 allows for the specification of several types of multicast groups. For example, the global multicast group, which directs data to all reachable nodes, is akin to the broadcast transmission in IPv4. The link-local multicast group includes computers that share the same link as the transmitting node.

An **anycast address** represents any one interface from a group of interfaces, any one of which can accept a transmission. Anycast addresses could be useful for identifying all of the routers that belong to one ISP, for example. In this instance, an Internet transmission destined for one of that ISP's servers could be accepted by the first available router in the anycast group. The result is that the transmission finishes faster than if it had to wait for one specific router interface to become available. At this time, anycast addresses are not designed to be assigned to hosts, such as servers or workstations.

A fourth significant difference between IPv4 and IPv6 addressing is that in IPv6, each address contains a **Format Prefix**, or a variable-length field at the beginning of the address that indicates what type of address it is—unicast, multicast, or anycast. A link-local unicast address begins with the hexadecimal string FE80. A site-local unicast address begins with FEC0. A multicast address begins with the following hexadecimal string: FF0x, where *x* is a character that corresponds to a group scope ID. For example, the Format Prefix for a link-local multicast address is FF02, while the Format Prefix for a global multicast address is FF0E.

Virtually all modern network devices and operating systems can transmit and receive data using both IPv4 and IPv6. Using both on one network is known as a **dual-stack** approach. Dual-stack networks are common because even as organizations upgrade to IPv6, their customers, partners, and suppliers with interconnected networks might lag behind and require IPv4 support. Several methods exist to accommodate IPv6 traffic on IPv4 networks. Although a thorough explanation of each method is beyond the scope of this book, Chapter 9 will describe IPv6 and IPv4 networking in greater detail.

Assigning IP Addresses

You have learned that several government-sponsored organizations—including IANA, ICANN,
1.3 and RIRs—cooperate to dole out IP addresses to ISPs and other network providers around the world. You also learned that most companies and individuals obtain IP addresses from their ISPs and not directly from the government's higher authorities. This section describes how an organization assigns its group of IP addresses to networked devices so that they can communicate over the Internet.

1.3 Whether connecting to the Internet or to another computer within a LAN, every node on a TCP/IP network must have a unique IP address. Suppose client B joins a network and takes an IP address that is already in use by client A, which is on the same subnet. In that case, client B will receive an error message and its TCP/IP services will be disabled. client A may also receive an error message, but can continue to function normally.

You can modify a client's TCP/IP properties to assign it an IP address manually. A manually assigned IP address is called a **static IP address** because it does not change automatically. It changes only when you reconfigure the client's TCP/IP properties. Unfortunately, due to human error, static IP addressing can easily result in the duplication of address assignments. So rather than assigning IP addresses manually, most network administrators rely on a network service to automatically assign them. An IP address that is assigned to a device upon request and is changeable is known as a **dynamic IP address**. The most common method for automatically assigning IPv4 addresses is using the Dynamic Host Configuration Protocol (DHCP).

DHCP (Dynamic Host Configuration Protocol)

1.3 **DHCP (Dynamic Host Configuration Protocol)** is an automated means of assigning a unique
1.6 IP address to devices on a network. In DHCP, a **DHCP server** manages IP address assignment.
2.3 The server maintains information about which addresses are allowable, which are available, and which have already been associated with a host. DHCP belongs to the Application layer of the TCP/IP and OSI models. Reasons for implementing DHCP include the following:

- *To reduce the time and planning spent on IP address management*—Central management of IP addresses eliminates the need for network administrators to edit the TCP/IP configuration on every network workstation, printer, or other device.
- *To reduce the potential for errors in assigning IP addresses*—With DHCP, almost no possibility exists that a workstation will be assigned an invalid address or that two workstations will attempt to use the same IP address. (Occasionally, the DHCP server software may make a mistake.)
- *To enable users to move their workstations and printers without having to change their TCP/IP configuration*—As long as a workstation is configured to obtain its IP address from a DHCP server and that server is available, the workstation can be attached anywhere on the network and receive a valid address.
- *To make IP addressing transparent for mobile users*—A person visiting your office, for example, could attach to your network and receive an IP address without having to change his laptop's configuration.

DHCP Leasing Process With DHCP, a device borrows, or leases, an IP address while it is attached to the network. In other words, it uses the IP address on a temporary basis for a specified length of time. On most networks, a client obtains its DHCP-assigned address as soon as it logs on to a network. The length of time a **lease** remains in effect depends on DHCP server and client configurations. Leases that expire must be renegotiated for the client to remain on the network. Alternatively, users can force a lease termination at the client, or a network administrator can force lease terminations at the server.

Configuring the DHCP service involves identifying a **DHCP scope**, or a range of addresses that can be leased to any network device on a particular segment, plus a list of excluded addresses, if any exist. As a network administrator, you configure the duration of the lease

Net+ to be as short or as long as necessary, from a matter of minutes to forever. After the DHCP server is running, the client and server take the following steps to negotiate the client's first
1.3 lease. (Note that the following example applies to a workstation, but devices such as net-
1.6 worked printers may also take advantage of DHCP.)
2.3

1. When the client workstation is powered on and its NIC detects a network connection, it sends out a DHCP discover packet in broadcast fashion via the UDP protocol to the DHCP server.
2. Every DHCP server on the same subnet as the client receives the broadcast request. Each DHCP server responds, in broadcast fashion, to offer an available IP address, while simultaneously withholding that address from other clients. The response message includes the available IP address, subnet mask, IP address of the DHCP server, and lease duration. (Because the client doesn't have an IP address, the DHCP server cannot send the information directly to the client.)
3. The client accepts the first IP address that it receives, responding with a broadcast message that essentially confirms to the DHCP server that it wants to accept the address. Because this message is broadcast, all other DHCP servers that might have responded to the client's original query see this confirmation and return the IP addresses they had reserved for the client to their pool of available addresses.
4. When the selected DHCP server receives the confirmation, it replies to the client with an acknowledgment message. It also provides more information, such as DNS, subnet mask, or gateway addresses that the client might have requested.

The preceding steps involve the exchange of only four packets and, therefore, do not usually increase the time it takes for a client to log on to the network. Figure 4-14 depicts the DHCP leasing process. The client and server do not have to repeat this exchange until the

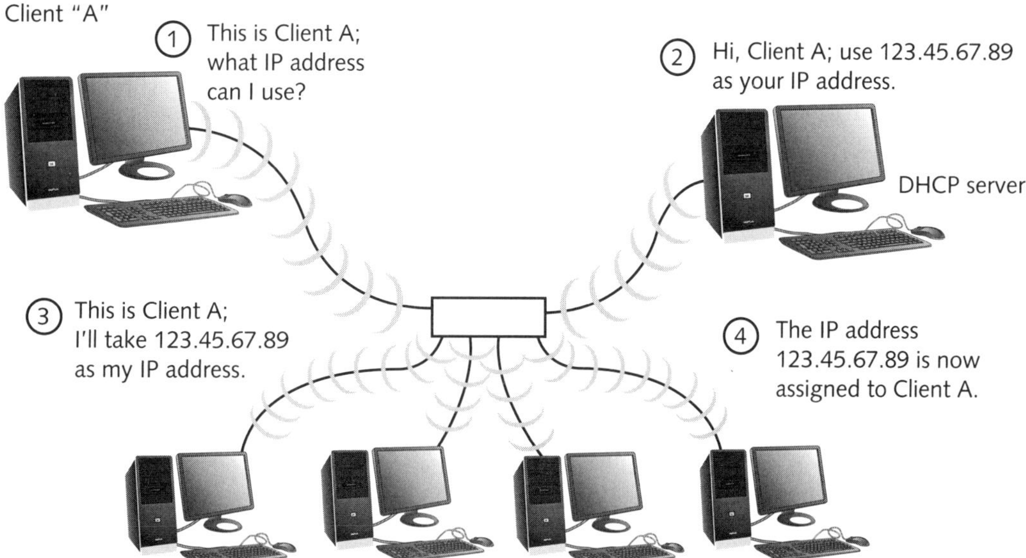
Client "A"
1 This is Client A; what IP address can I use?
2 Hi, Client A; use 123.45.67.89 as your IP address.
DHCP server
3 This is Client A; I'll take 123.45.67.89 as my IP address.
4 The IP address 123.45.67.89 is now assigned to Client A.

Figure 4-14 The DHCP leasing process

Net+ lease is terminated. The IP address remains in the client's TCP/IP settings so that even after
1.3 the client shuts down and reboots, it can use this information and not have to request a new
1.6 address. However, if the device is moved to another network, it will be assigned different IP
2.3 address information suited to that network.

4.3 **Terminating a DHCP Lease** A DHCP lease may expire based on the period established for it in the server configuration, or it may be manually terminated at any time from either the client's TCP/IP configuration or the server's DHCP configuration. In some instances, a user must terminate a lease. For example, if a DHCP server fails and another is installed to replace it, the clients that relied on the first DHCP server need to release their old leases (and obtain new leases from the new server).

To release TCP/IP settings on a client running a Windows operating system:

1. Click the **Start** button, click **All Programs**, click **Accessories**, and then click **Command Prompt**. The Command Prompt window opens.
2. At the command prompt, type `ipconfig /release` and then press **Enter**. Your TCP/ IP configuration values are cleared, and both the IP address and subnet mask revert to 0.0.0.0.
3. Type `exit` and press **Enter** to close the Command Prompt window.

Releasing old DHCP information is the first step in the process of obtaining a new IP address. To obtain a new IP address on a Windows workstation:

1. If you are not already at a command prompt, click the **Start** button, click **All Programs**, click **Accessories**, and then click **Command Prompt**. The Command Prompt window opens.
2. At the command prompt, type `ipconfig /renew` and then press **Enter**. Your client follows the DHCP leasing process, which reestablishes its TCP/IP configuration values. These values will be appropriate for the network to which you are attached.
3. Type `exit` and press **Enter** to close the Command Prompt window.

Occasionally your client's attempt to renew or obtain a new DHCP-assigned address will fail. For example, you might receive a message indicating that the DHCP server is unreachable. This error could result from one of many problems: Your client might be disconnected from the network, whether because a cable is unplugged or faulty or because its protocols are not installed or configured properly; your client or server's DHCP services could be improperly configured; or the DHCP server might be down.

The type of DHCP used on IPv4 networks can also be called **DHCPv4**. The type used with IPv6 is known as **DHCPv6**, and it operates in the same way as the version used for IPv4, described previously. However, because IPv6 comes with automatic addressing capabilities, DHCP addressing services are optional on IPv6 networks.

DHCP services run on several types of devices. The installation and configurations for each type of server vary; for specifics, refer to the DHCP server software or NOS manual. To qualify for Network+ certification, you need not know the intricacies of installing and configuring DHCP server software. You do, however, need to know what DHCP does and how it accomplishes it. You also need to understand the advantages of using dynamic IP addresses rather than static addresses.

Net+ Private and Link-Local Addresses

1.3 You have already learned about some addresses, such as the loopback address and broadcast addresses, which are reserved for special uses. In addition to these, Internet authorities have designated IP address ranges that can be used for private addresses. **Private addresses** allow hosts in an organization to communicate across its internal network. Private addresses cannot be routed on a public network, such as the Internet. Private addresses differ from **public addresses** in that the latter are assigned to an organization by Internet authorities and can be used to identify hosts on the Internet.

The following IPv4 address ranges are reserved for private addresses:

10.0.0.0 through 10.255.255.255

172.16.0.0 through 172.31.255.255

192.168.0.0 through 192.168.255.255

With private addressing, Company A can assign its workstations the IP addresses 10.5.5.2 through 10.5.5.22; meanwhile, across town, Company B might assign its workstations IP addresses 10.5.5.5 through 10.5.5.15. Although the companies are using some of the same IP addresses internally, because these addresses are not used beyond the companies' networks, no conflicts will occur as a result. When the workstations at either company need to communicate over the Internet, each is assigned a different, Internet-routable IP address. You will learn more about why and how this is accomplished in Chapter 9.

Using private addresses can extend the number of available IPv4 addresses on an organization's network. Private addresses also allow computers on an organization's network to communicate if a DHCP server is unavailable to assign routable addresses. Operating systems come equipped with a way to automatically assign each node a provisional IP address if this occurs. This provisional address, capable of transmitting and receiving data only on a local network segment, is known as the **link-local address**. A link-local address is a special kind of private address. With a link-local address, a computer can communicate across a LAN segment or communicate directly with another computer when the two are connected with a cable, for example. However, link-local addresses are not routable and do not allow nodes to communicate beyond their segments. In other words, clients with link-local addresses separated by a router could not exchange data. Were they connected to the same switch, they could.

Even though their use is restricted, link-local addresses must still follow standards to avoid network transmission trouble. IANA (Internet Assigned Numbers Authority) has designated ranges of IP addresses for use as link-local addresses. For IPv4, the range is 169.254.0.0 through 169.254.254.255. Link-local addresses in IPv6 always begin with FE80.

Zeroconf (Zero Configuration) is the collection of protocols that assigns link-local addresses, performs DNS functions (described later in this chapter), and discovers services, such as print services, available to the node. Because Zeroconf is part of a computer's operating software, the assignment happens without the need to register or check with a central authority. In the case of a network whose DHCP is temporarily unavailable, when the DHCP server is available once again, Zeroconf services release its assigned IP address and allow the client to receive a DHCP-assigned address.

With Zeroconf, IPv4 addresses are assigned through **IPv4LL (IP version 4 Link Local)**, a protocol that manages automatic address assignment among locally connected nodes. In IPv4LL,

1.3

when computer A joins the network, it randomly chooses an IP address in the range from 169.254.1.0 to 169.254.254.255. Before using its chosen address to communicate, computer A sends a message, via the ARP protocol, to the rest of its subnet indicating its desire to use that IP address. But suppose computer B is already using the address. In that case, computer B will respond to computer A's message with a broadcast that alerts every other node on the subnet that the IP address is already in use. Computer A will then randomly select a different IP address. However, if, after a brief period of time, no other node responds to the first node's announcement, computer A will issue a broadcast message that informs the rest of the subnet that it has assigned itself the address it chose initially.

Zeroconf is especially useful with network printers. Some printers don't come with interfaces that enable a network administrator to easily configure TCP/IP variables. If they support Zeroconf, printers can connect to the network and be ready to communicate with no human intervention. Virtually all modern printers come with Zeroconf support.

Zeroconf is also part of modern client and network operating systems. The version of Zeroconf services used by most Linux operating systems is known as **Avahi**. Apple's version of Zeroconf is called **Bonjour**. The service that provides link-local addressing on Windows clients is known as **APIPA** (**Automatic Private IP Addressing**).

To check whether a computer running a Windows operating system is using APIPA:

1. Click the **Start** button, click **All Programs**, click **Accessories**, and then select **Command Prompt**. The Command Prompt window opens.
2. At the command prompt, type `ipconfig /all` and then press **Enter**. If the Autoconfiguration Enabled option is set to Yes, your computer is using APIPA.

Even if your network does not need or use APIPA, leaving it enabled is not necessarily problematic because APIPA is designed to first check for the presence of a DHCP server and allow the DHCP server to assign addresses. In addition, if a computer's IP address has been assigned statically, APIPA does not reassign a new address. It only works with clients configured to use DHCP. APIPA can be disabled, however, by editing the Windows operating system's Registry.

Sockets and Ports

1.5
1.6

Just as a device requires a unique address to send and receive information over the network, a process also requires a unique address. Every process on a machine is assigned a port number. If you compare IP addressing with the addressing system used by the postal service, and you equate a host's IP address to the address of a building, a port number is similar to an apartment number within that building.

A process's port number plus its host machine's IP address equals the process's **socket**. For example, the standard port number for the Telnet service is 23. On a host whose IPv4 address is 10.43.3.87, the socket address for Telnet is 10.43.3.87:23. In other words, the host assumes that any requests coming into port number 23 are Telnet requests (that is, unless you reconfigure the host to change the default Telnet port). Notice that a port number is expressed as a number following a colon after an IP address. In this example, 23 is not considered an additional octet, but simply a pointer to a port. Sockets form virtual connections between a process on one computer and the same process running on another computer.

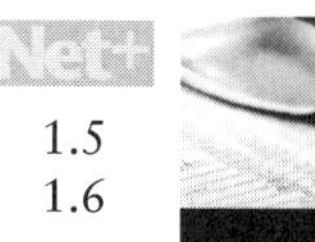
1.5
1.6

Because port numbers are used by Transport layer protocols, they apply whether your network uses IPv4 or IPv6.

The use of port numbers simplifies TCP/IP communications and ensures that data are transmitted to the correct application. When a client requests communications with a server and specifies port 23, for example, the server knows immediately that the client wants a Telnet session. No extra data exchange is necessary to define the session type, and the server can initiate the Telnet service without delay. The server will connect to the client's Telnet port—by default, port 23—and establish a virtual circuit. Figure 4-15 depicts this process.

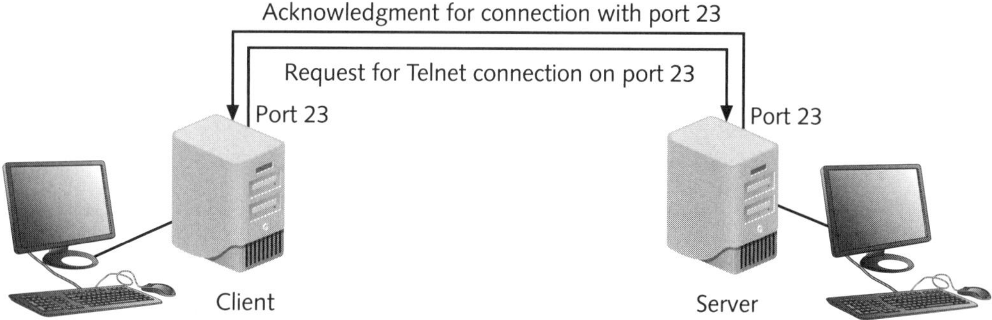

Figure 4-15 A virtual connection for the Telnet service

Port numbers range from 0 to 65535 and are divided by IANA into three types: Well Known Ports, Registered Ports, and Dynamic and/or Private Ports. **Well Known Ports** are in the range from 0 to 1023 and are assigned to processes that only the operating system or an administrator of the system can access. These were the first ports assigned to processes, and so the earliest TCP/IP protocols, such as TCP, UDP, Telnet, and FTP, use Well Known Ports. Table 4-6 lists some of these Well Known Ports. **Registered Ports** are in the range from 1024 to 49151. These ports are accessible to network users and processes that do not have special administrative privileges. Default assignments of these ports (for example, by a software program) must be registered with IANA. **Dynamic Ports** and/or **Private Ports** are those ranging from 49152 to 65535 and are open for use without restriction.

Although you do not need to memorize every port number for the Network+ certification exam, you may be asked about the port numbers associated with common services, such as Telnet, FTP, and HTTP. Knowing them will also help you in configuring and troubleshooting networks using TCP/IP.

Port numbers are assigned either by the operating system or by software programs that rely on them. Servers maintain an editable, text-based file of port numbers and their associated services. If you have administrative privileges—that is, if you know the logon id and password that allows you to modify any aspect of a system—you can change which port number a service uses. For example, you could change the default port number for Telnet on your server

1.5
1.6

from 23 to 2330. Changing a default port number is rarely a good idea, however, because it violates the standard and means that processes programmed to use a standard port will not be able to communicate with your machine. Nevertheless, some network administrators who are preoccupied with security may change their servers' port numbers in an attempt to confuse people with malicious intent who try connecting to their devices through conventional sockets.

Table 4-6 Commonly used TCP/IP port numbers

Port number	Process name	Protocol used	Description
20	FTP-DATA	TCP	File transfer—data
21	FTP	TCP	File transfer—control
22	SSH	TCP	Secure Shell
23	TELNET	TCP	Telnet
25	SMTP	TCP	Simple Mail Transfer Protocol
53	DNS	TCP and UDP	Domain Name System
67 (client to server) and 68 (server to client)	DHCPv4	UDP	Dynamic Host Configuration Protocol version 4
69	TFTP	UDP	Trivial File Transfer Protocol
80	HTTP	TCP and UDP	Hypertext Transfer Protocol
110	POP3	TCP	Post Office Protocol 3
123	NTP	TCP	Network Time Protocol
143	IMAP	TCP	Internet Message Access Protocol
443	HTTPS	TCP	Secure implementation of HTTP
546 (client to server) and 547 (server to client)	DHCPv6	UDP	Dynamic Host Configuration Protocol version 6
3389	RDP	TCP	Remote Desktop Protocol

Host Names and DNS (Domain Name System)

1.7

Much of TCP/IP addressing involves numbers—often long, complicated numbers. Computers can manage numbers easily. However, most people can remember words better than numbers. Imagine if you had to identify your friends' and families' Social Security numbers whenever you wanted to write a note or talk to them. Communication would be frustrating at the very least, and perhaps even impossible—especially if you're the kind of person who has trouble remembering even your own Social Security number. Similarly, people prefer to associate names with networked devices rather than remember IP addresses. For this reason, the Internet authorities established a naming system for all nodes on the Internet.

Every device on the Internet is technically known as a host. Every host can take a **host name**, a name that describes the device. For example, someone named Jasmine McDonald might name her workstation "Jasmine." If the computer is reserved for a specific purpose, you may

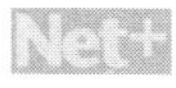

1.7 want to name it accordingly. For example, a company that offers free software downloads through the FTP service might call its host machine "ftpserver."

Domain Names

Every host is a member of a **domain**, or a group of computers that belongs to the same organization and has part of their IP addresses in common. A domain is identified by its domain name. Usually, a **domain name** is associated with a company or other type of organization, such as a university, government organization, or company. For example, IBM's domain name is ibm.com, and the United States Library of Congress's domain name is loc.gov.

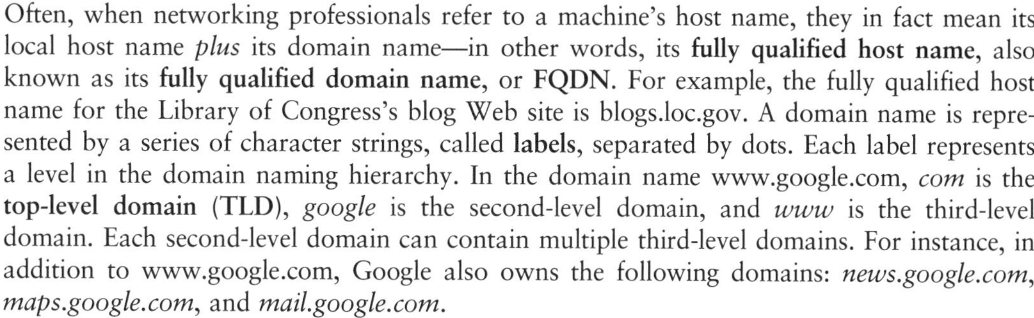

Often, when networking professionals refer to a machine's host name, they in fact mean its local host name *plus* its domain name—in other words, its **fully qualified host name**, also known as its **fully qualified domain name**, or **FQDN**. For example, the fully qualified host name for the Library of Congress's blog Web site is blogs.loc.gov. A domain name is represented by a series of character strings, called **labels**, separated by dots. Each label represents a level in the domain naming hierarchy. In the domain name www.google.com, *com* is the **top-level domain** (**TLD**), *google* is the second-level domain, and *www* is the third-level domain. Each second-level domain can contain multiple third-level domains. For instance, in addition to www.google.com, Google also owns the following domains: *news.google.com*, *maps.google.com*, and *mail.google.com*.

Domain names must be registered with an Internet naming authority that works on behalf of ICANN. ICANN has established conventions for domain naming so that certain TLDs apply to every type of organization that uses the Internet. Table 4-7 lists some well-known ICANN-approved TLDs. The first eight TLDs listed in this table were established in the mid-1980s. Of these, no restrictions exist on the use of the .com, .org, and .net TLDs, but ICANN does restrict what type of hosts can be associated with the .arpa, .mil, .int, .edu, and .gov TLDs.

In addition to those listed in Table 4-7, ICANN has approved over 240 **country code TLDs** to represent different countries and territories across the globe. For example, .ca is the country code TLD assigned to Canada and .jp is the country code TLD assigned to Japan. Organizations are not required to use country code TLDs. For example, although Cisco's headquarters are located in the United States, the company's domain name is *www.cisco.com*, not *www.cisco.us*. On the other hand, some United States organizations do use the .us suffix. For example, the domain name for the Garden City, New York, public school district is *www.gardencity.k12.ny.us*. A complete list of current TLDs can be found at *www.iana.org/domains/root/db/*.

NOTE

In 2011, ICANN decided to loosen its restrictions on TLD names and allow organizations to apply for a new TLD composed of almost any alphanumeric string, including one that uses characters not found in the English language. Applying for a new TLD costs $185,000, and each application will undergo a rigorous evaluation.

After an organization reserves a domain name, the rest of the world's computers know to associate that domain name with the organization to which it is assigned, and no other organization can legally use it. For example, you might apply for a domain name made up of your first and last names. If your name is Evgeny Simonovsky, you might request the domain name evgenysimonovsky.com. After you have reserved the domain, hosts across the Internet

1.7

Table 4-7 Some well-known top-level domains

Domain suffix	Type of organization
ARPA	Reverse lookup domain (special Internet function)
COM	Commercial
EDU	Educational
GOV	Government
ORG	Noncommercial organization (such as a nonprofit agency)
NET	Network (such as an ISP)
INT	International Treaty Organization
MIL	United States military organization
BIZ	Businesses
INFO	Unrestricted use
AERO	Air-transport industry
COOP	Cooperatives

would associate that name with your network. No other parties in the world could use evgenysimonovsky.com in naming computers that they allow to connect to the Internet.

Host and domain names are subject to some restrictions. Domain names may consist of any alphanumeric combination up to a maximum of 253 characters, and can include hyphens, underscores, or periods in the name, but no other special characters. The interesting part of host and domain naming relates to how all Internet-connected machines in the world know which names belong to which machines. Before tackling the entire world, however, you can start by thinking about how one company might deal with its local host names, as explained in the following section.

Host Files

The first incarnation of the Internet (ARPAnet) was used by fewer than 1000 hosts. The entire network relied on one ASCII text file called HOSTS.TXT to associate host names with IP addresses. This file was generically known as a **host file**. Growth of the Internet soon made this simple arrangement impossible to maintain—the host file would require constant changes, searching through one file from all over the nation would strain the Internet's bandwidth capacity, and the entire Internet would fail if the file were accidentally deleted.

However, in rare cases you may still encounter this older system of using a text file to associate internal host names with their IP addresses. Figure 4-16 provides an example of such a file. Notice that each host is matched by one line identifying the host's name and IP address. In addition, a third field, called an **alias**, provides a nickname for the host. An alias allows a user within an organization to address a host by a shorter name than the full host name. Typically, the first line of a host file begins with a pound sign and contains comments about the file's columns. A pound sign may precede comments anywhere in the host file. In addition to identifying hosts on other networks, each host file indicates the local host's address.

1.7

In Figure 4-16, the local host is presumed to exist on the cengage.com domain. Note that the local host's address points to the loopback address, first for IPv6 and in the next line, for IPv4.

```
# Host database
#
# This file contains the mappings of IP addresses to host names and the
# aliases for each host name. In the presence of the domain name service,
# this file may not be consulted.
#
# Comments (such as these) may be inserted on individual lines or
# following the machine name denoted by a '#' symbol.
#
#
# Address   Host name                          Alias

::1         localhost.cengage.com              localhost
127.0.0.1   localhost.cengage.com              localhost


69.32.133.79      www.cengage.com              Web
69.32.134.163     ftp.cengage.com              FTP
69.32.146.63      gale.cengage.com             Gale
69.32.132.117     poweron.cengage.com          TechSupport
```

Figure 4-16 Sample host file

On a computer running UNIX or Linux, a host file is called **hosts** and is located in the /etc directory. On a Windows computer, a host file is also called hosts (with no file extension) and is located in the Windows\system32\drivers\etc folder.

A simple host file can satisfy the needs of a small organization; however, it is not sufficient for large organizations, much less for the Internet. Instead, an automated solution is mandatory.

DNS (Domain Name System)

In the mid-1980s, computer scientists responsible for the Internet's growth devised a hierarchical way of associating domain names with IP addresses, called the **DNS (Domain Name System** or **Domain Name Service**). DNS refers to both the Application layer service that accomplishes this association and also to the organized system of computers and databases that makes this association possible. The DNS service does not rely on one file or even one server, but rather on many computers across the globe. These computers are related in a hierarchical manner, with 13 computers, known as **root servers**, acting as the ultimate authorities. Because it is distributed, DNS will not fail catastrophically if one or a handful of servers experience errors.

To direct traffic efficiently, the DNS service is divided into three components: resolvers, name servers, and namespace. **Resolvers** are any hosts on the Internet that need to look up domain name information. The resolver client is built into TCP/IP applications such as HTTP. If you point your Web browser to *http://www.loc.gov*, your HTTP client software initiates the resolver service to find the IP address for *www.loc.gov*. If you have visited the site before,

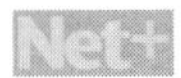
1.7

the information may exist in a local **DNS cache**, a database stored on your computer that indicates what IP address is associated with the *www.loc.gov* host name. If the information is not stored locally, the resolver service queries your machine's designated name server to find the IP address for *www.loc.gov*.

Name servers, or **DNS servers**, are servers that contain databases of associated names and IP addresses and provide this information to resolvers on request. If one name server cannot resolve the domain name to its IP address, it passes the query to a higher-authority name server. For example, suppose you are trying to open the *www.loc.gov* Web page from a workstation on your company's network. Further, suppose this is the first time you've visited the Library of Congress online. Upon discovering it does not have the information saved locally, your client's resolver service queries the closest name server for the IP address associated with *www.loc.gov*. That name server is probably connected to your LAN. If your LAN's name server cannot supply the IP address for *www.loc.gov*, it queries a higher-level name server. In other words, your company's name server sends a request to the name server at the company's Internet service provider (ISP). If that name server does not have the information in its database, it queries a name server elsewhere on the Internet that acts as the ISP's naming authority. This process, depicted in Figure 4-17, continues until the request is granted.

The term **namespace** refers to the database of Internet IP addresses and their associated names. Namespace is not a single file that you can open and view like a store's inventory database. Rather, it is an abstract concept that describes how the name servers of the world share DNS information. You can think of DNS namespace as a giant, distributed address book for every computer in the world. Just as you might keep an address book of close friends and family on your computer, but rely on a different source, such as an Internet lookup service, to find contact information for people you don't know, the DNS namespace does not store every piece of information in one place. Instead, it relies on multiple sources to resolve host names and IP addresses.

The structure of the namespace reflects DNS's hierarchical nature. It is divided into **DNS zones**, or portions for which one organization is assigned authority to manage. For example, network administrators at the Library of Congress are responsible for managing the namespace for all hosts in the loc.gov domain. If you obtained your own domain name, you would be responsible for managing its namespace. A zone may consist of only one domain. Higher-level zones, such as those associated with TLDs, however, may contain several domains. For example, the .gov zone contains every domain name that ends in .gov.

Information about hosts in a DNS zone is contained in a **zone file**. Each zone file contains **resource records** that describe one piece of information in the DNS database. In the address book analogy, a zone file would be similar to the contact list you keep on your computer (your zone) and a resource record would contain the phone number, address, and e-mail address for one of your friends. By storing resource records in its zone file, every name server holds a piece of the DNS namespace.

Resource records come in many different types, depending on their function. For example, an **address resource record** is a type of resource record that maps the IP address of an Internet-connected device to its domain name. Each record contains a name field to identify the domain name of the machine to which the record refers, a type field to identify the type of resource record involved, a class field to identify the class to which the record belongs (usually "IN" or "Internet"), a Time to Live field to identify how long the record should be saved in temporary

Net+
1.7

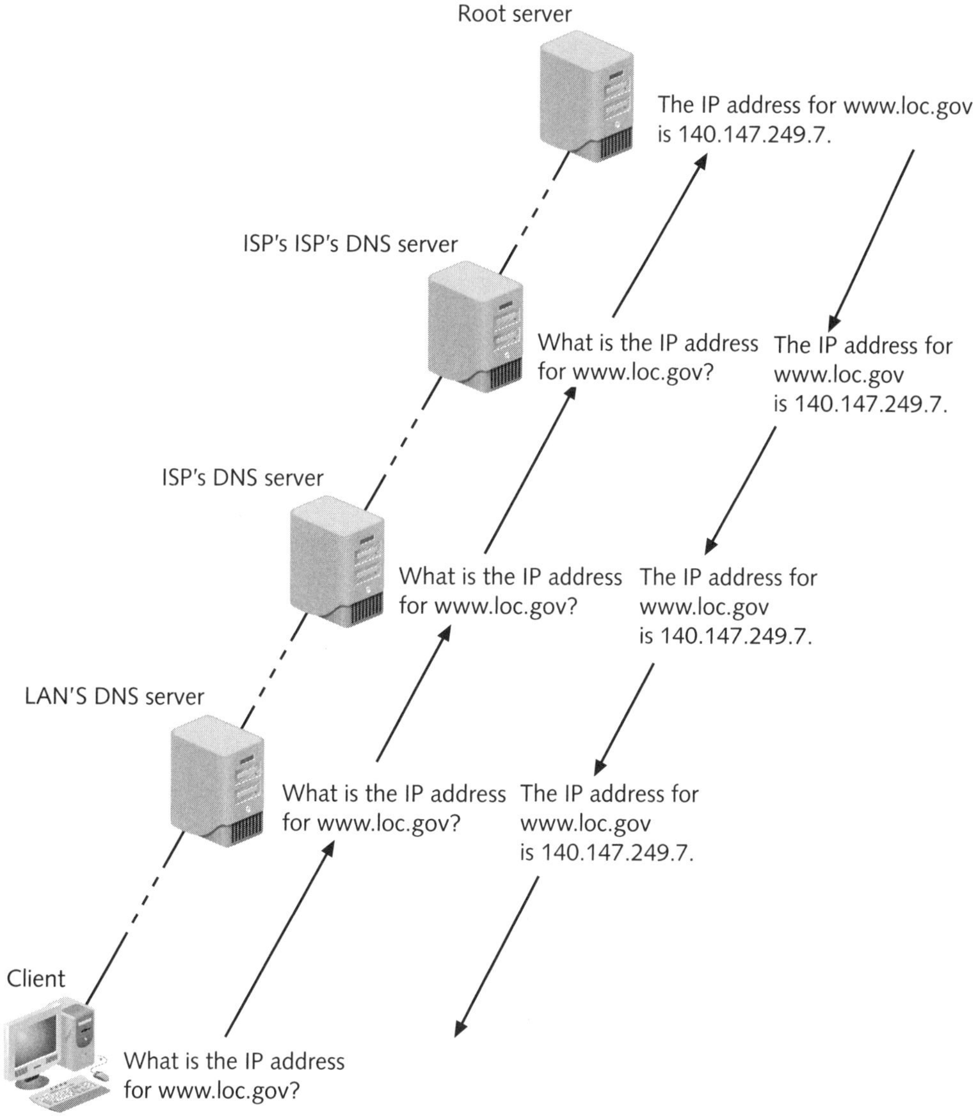

Root server

The IP address for www.loc.gov is 140.147.249.7.

ISP's ISP's DNS server

What is the IP address for www.loc.gov?

The IP address for www.loc.gov is 140.147.249.7.

ISP's DNS server

What is the IP address for www.loc.gov?

The IP address for www.loc.gov is 140.147.249.7.

LAN'S DNS server

What is the IP address for www.loc.gov?

The IP address for www.loc.gov is 140.147.249.7.

Client

What is the IP address for www.loc.gov?

Figure 4-17 Domain name resolution

memory, a data length field to identify how much data the record contains, and the actual record data. Approximately 20 types of resource records are currently used. Table 4-8 lists the types of DNS records you will encounter most often.

In the following address resource record, gmail.com is the host domain name, IN stands for the Internet record class, A identifies the record type as "address," and 74.125.225.22 is the host's IP address:

```
gmail.com. IN A 74.125.225.22
```

At one time, network administrators manually maintained resource records for their networks' hosts. Now, however, modern clients update their resource records dynamically.

Table 4-8 Common DNS record types

1.7

Type	Name	Description
A	Address record	A host's IPv4 address
AAAA	Address record	A host's IPv6 address
CNAME	Canonical name record	Another name for the host
MX	Mail exchange record	Identifies a mail server
PTR	Pointer record	Points to a canonical name

This saves time and eliminates the possibility for human error in modifying DNS information. Clients can be configured to trigger a DNS update when they receive a new IP address (for example, through DHCP), when their host names change, or when they connect to a network. Alternatively, a user can force a DNS record update by issuing a command. For example, typing `ipconfig /registerdns` at a Windows operating system command prompt while logged on as an administrator forces an update of the client's registered DNS information. In the Hands-On Projects at the end of this chapter, you will have the chance to view your locally cached DNS information—including multiple resource records—clear the cache, and then view it again after resolving names with IP addresses.

Configuring DNS

Any host that must communicate with other hosts on the Internet needs to know how to find its name server. Although small organizations might use only one name server, most organizations rely on two name servers—a primary and a secondary name server—to help ensure Internet connectivity. The secondary name server relies on the primary name server as its authority. To ensure that records between the servers match, the secondary server initiates a **zone transfer**, copying the primary name server's zone file to the secondary name server. If the primary name server experiences a failure, devices on the network attempt to use the secondary name server. Assuming the zone transfer was successful, the secondary name server should operate just as the primary name server would, and clients will not notice the difference. Each device on the network relies on the name servers and, therefore, must know how to find them.

On most networks, the DHCP service automatically assigns clients the appropriate addresses for their primary and secondary name servers. However, occasionally you might want to manually configure these values. For example, specifying your preferred DNS server address when connecting to a public network, such as a wireless network at a café, can protect your computer from attempts to assign a rogue DNS server—that is, one operated by a hacker who could take advantage of your computer's trust to steal private information.

To view or change the name server information on a Windows 7 workstation:

1. Click the **Start** button, type **`ncpa.cpl`** in the Search programs and files text box, and then press **Enter**. The Network Connections window opens.
2. Right-click the icon that represents your network adapter, and click **Properties** on the shortcut menu. A User Account Control dialog box may appear, asking if you want to allow the following program to make changes. Click **Yes** to proceed. Your adapter's Network Connection Properties window appears.

1.7

3. Under the "This connection uses the following items" heading, select **Internet Protocol Version 4 (TCP/IPv4)**, and then click **Properties.** The Internet Protocol version 4 (TCP/IPv4) Properties dialog box opens, as shown in Figure 4-18.

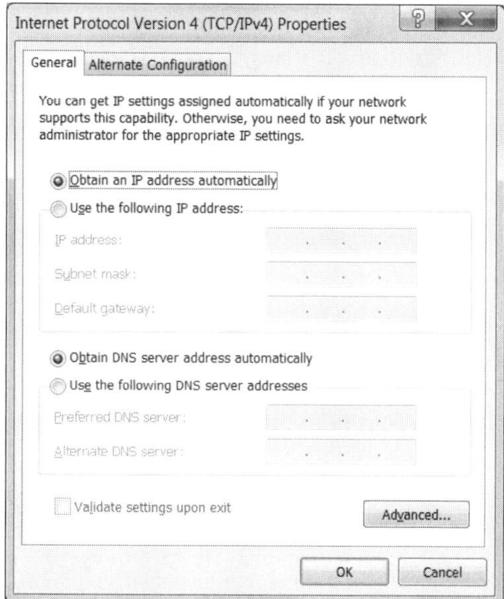

Figure 4-18 Windows 7 Internet Protocol Version 4 (TCP/IPv4) Properties dialog box

4. If you want to specify the DNS server your workstation relies on, rather than allowing DHCP to supply the DNS server address, verify that the General tab is still selected, and then click the **Use the following DNS server addresses** button.
5. Enter the IP address for your primary DNS server in the Preferred DNS server space and the address for your secondary DNS server in the Alternate DNS server space.
6. Click **OK**, click **Close** to save your changes, and then close the Network Connections window.

DDNS (Dynamic DNS)

DNS is a reliable way of locating a host as long as the host's IP address remains relatively constant over time—that is, if it's static. However, many Internet users subscribe to a type of Internet service in which their IP address changes periodically. For a user who only wants to send and receive e-mail and surf the Web, frequently changing IP addresses is not problematic. But for a user who wants to host a Web site, for example, it can be. To maintain the association between his Web site's host or domain name and an IP address, such a user must change his computer's DNS record and propagate this change across the Internet each time the IP address changes. When IP addresses change frequently, manually changing DNS records becomes unmanageable.

A solution is to use **DDNS (Dynamic DNS)**. In DDNS, a service provider runs a program on the user's computer that notifies the service provider when the user's IP address changes.

1.7 Upon notification, the service provider's server launches a routine that automatically updates the DNS record for that user's computer. The DNS record update becomes effective throughout the Internet in a matter of minutes.

Note that DDNS does not take the place of DNS, but is an additional service, available for a small fee. DDNS is a good option for home or small office users who maintain Web sites but do not want to pay the additional (often high) cost of reserving a static IP address. However, because of the slight delay in DNS record propagation caused each time an IP address changes, larger organizations typically prefer to pay more for a statically assigned IP address.

Associating host and domain names with computers on a TCP/IP-based network is performed by the Application layer protocol DNS. The following section describes other important Application layer protocols.

Application Layer Protocols

1.6 In addition to the core Transport and Internet layer protocols, the TCP/IP suite encompasses several Application layer protocols. These protocols work over TCP or UDP plus IP, translating user requests into a format the network can read. In Chapter 2, you learned about an Application layer protocol central to using the Web, HTTP. And earlier in this chapter, you learned about an Application layer protocol used for automatic address assignment, DHCP. The following sections describe some additional Application layer protocols. Throughout this book, and especially in Chapter 9, you'll encounter even more TCP/IP Application layer protocols.

Telnet

Telnet is a terminal emulation protocol used to log on to remote hosts using the TCP/IP protocol suite. Using Telnet, a TCP connection is established via port 23 and keystrokes on the user's machine act like keystrokes on the remotely connected machine. Often, Telnet is used to connect two dissimilar systems, such as PCs and UNIX machines. Through Telnet, you can control a remote host over a network. For example, network managers can use Telnet to log on to a router from a computer elsewhere on their LAN and modify the router's configuration. Telnet, however, is notoriously insecure (meaning that someone with malicious intent could easily falsify the credentials Telnet requires to log on to a device successfully), so telnetting to a router across a public network would not be wise. Other, more secure methods of remotely connecting to a host have replaced Telnet for that reason. A popular alternative, known as SSH, is described in Chapter 11, which focuses on security.

FTP (File Transfer Protocol)

FTP (File Transfer Protocol) is an Application layer protocol used to send and receive files via TCP/IP using ports 20 and 21. In FTP exchanges, a host running the FTP server portion accepts commands from another host running the FTP client portion. FTP clients come with a set of simple commands that make up their user interfaces. To exchange data, the client depends on an FTP server that is always waiting for requests. After a client connects to the FTP server, FTP data are exchanged via TCP, which means that FTP provides some assurance of delivery.

1.6 FTP commands will work from your operating system's command prompt; they do not require special client software. As a network professional, you may need to use these commands to download software (such as NOS patches or client updates) from hosts. For example, if you need the latest version of the Fedora Linux distribution, you can use FTP from your workstation's command prompt to download the compressed software from a Fedora-authorized FTP server to your hard disk. To do so, you can start the FTP utility by typing ftp from your operating system command (or shell) prompt. The command prompt turns into the FTP prompt, `FTP>`. From there, you can run FTP commands. Alternatively, if you know what operation you want to perform, you can connect directly to an FTP server. For example, to connect directly to the Fedora FTP server at Boston University (one of several that provides the software via FTP), type `ftp fedora.bu.edu`, and then press Enter. If the host is running, it responds with a greeting and a request for you to log on.

Many FTP hosts, especially those whose purpose is to provide software updates, accept anonymous logons. This means that when prompted for a username, you need only type the word *anonymous* (in lowercase letters) and press Enter. When prompted for a password on an anonymous FTP site, you can typically use your e-mail address. The host's logon screen should indicate whether this is acceptable. On the other hand, if you are logging on to a private FTP site, you must obtain a valid username and password from the site's network administrator to make a successful connection.

After you have successfully connected to a host, additional commands allow you to manage the connection and manipulate files. To view a list of the variables you can use with FTP, type `ftp help` and press Enter.

Graphical FTP clients, such as WS_FTP, CuteFTP, and FileZilla, have rendered the command-line method of FTPing files less common. In many cases, you can also accomplish FTP file transfers directly from a modern Web browser. To do this, you need only point your browser to the FTP host. From there, you can move through directories and exchange files just as you would navigate the files and directories on your desktop or LAN server.

As with Telnet, a more secure version of the FTP protocol has been developed. This protocol, known as SFTP, is discussed in Chapter 11.

FTP and Telnet share some similarities, including their reliance on TCP and their ability to log on to a remote host and perform commands on that host. However, they differ in that, when you use Telnet, the commands you type require a syntax that is relative to your local workstation. When you use FTP, the commands you type require a syntax that is relative to the remote host to which you have logged on. Also, Telnet has no built-in commands for transferring files between the remote host and your workstation.

TFTP (Trivial File Transfer Protocol)

TFTP (Trivial File Transfer Protocol) is another TCP/IP Application layer protocol that enables file transfers between computers, but it is simpler (or more trivial) than FTP. TFTP communicates via port 69. A significant difference between FTP and TFTP is that TFTP relies on UDP at the Transport layer. Its use of UDP means that TFTP is connectionless and does not guarantee reliable delivery of data. Also, TFTP does not require users to log on to the

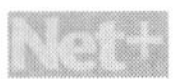

1.6 remote host with an ID and password in order to gain access to a directory and transfer files. Instead, when you enter the TFTP command, your computer issues a simple request to access the host's files. The remote host responds with an acknowledgment, and then the two computers begin transferring data. Each time a packet of data is transmitted to the host, the local workstation waits for an acknowledgment from the host before issuing another packet. In this way, TFTP overcomes some of the limitations of relying on a connectionless Transport layer protocol. A final difference between FTP and TFTP is that the latter does not allow directory browsing. In FTP, you can connect to a host and navigate through all the directories you've been granted access to view.

TFTP is useful when you need to load data or programs on a computer that lacks a hard drive—that is, on a **diskless workstation**. For example, suppose a TFTP server holds Microsoft Excel. When a client issues a TFTP request for that program, the server would transmit the program files to the workstation's memory. After the user completes his Excel work, the program files would be released from his workstation's memory. In this situation, the fact that TFTP does not require a user to log on to a host is an advantage. It makes the transfer of program files quick and easy. As you can imagine, however, not requiring a logon also presents a security risk, so TFTP servers must be carefully placed and monitored on a network.

NTP (Network Time Protocol)

NTP (Network Time Protocol) is a simple but important Application layer protocol used to synchronize the clocks of computers on a network. NTP communicates via port 123 and depends on UDP for Transport layer services. Time is critical in routing to determine the most efficient path for data over a network. Time synchronization across a network is also important for time-stamped security methods and maintaining accuracy and consistency between multiple storage systems. NTP is a protocol that benefits from UDP's quick, connectionless nature at the Transport layer. NTP is time sensitive and cannot wait for the error checking that TCP would require.

Net+

PING (Packet Internet Groper)

4.3 **PING (Packet Internet Groper)** is a utility that can verify that TCP/IP is installed, bound to the NIC, configured correctly, and communicating with the network. It is often employed simply to determine whether a host is responding (or "up"). PING uses ICMP services to send echo request and echo reply messages that determine the validity of an IP address. These two types of messages work in much the same way that sonar operates. First, a signal, called an **echo request**, is sent out to another computer. The other computer then rebroadcasts the signal, in the form of an **echo reply**, to the sender. The process of sending this signal back and forth is known as **pinging**.

You can ping either an IP address or a host name. For example, to determine whether the *www.loc.gov* site is responding, you could type `ping www.loc.gov` and press Enter. Alternately, you could type `ping 140.147.249.7` (the IP address of this site at the time this book was written) and press Enter. If the site is operating correctly, you receive a response that includes multiple replies from that host. If the site is not operating correctly, you will receive a response indicating that the request timed out or that the host was not found. You could also receive a "request timed out" message if your workstation is not properly connected to the network, or if the network is malfunctioning. Your ping test might also be

4.3 unsuccessful if the organization whose host you tried to contact prevents its network devices from accepting or responding to PING commands for security reasons. Figure 4-19 gives examples of a successful and an unsuccessful ping test.

```
C:\>ping 140.147.249.7

Pinging 140.147.249.7 with 32 bytes of data:

Reply from 140.147.249.7: bytes=32 time=47ms TTL=243
Reply from 140.147.249.7: bytes=32 time=46ms TTL=243
Reply from 140.147.249.7: bytes=32 time=46ms TTL=243
Reply from 140.147.249.7: bytes=32 time=48ms TTL=243

Ping statistics for 140.147.249.7:
    Packets: Sent = 4, Received = 4, Lost = 0 (0% loss),
Approximate round trip times in milli-seconds:
    Minimum = 46ms, Maximum = 48ms, Average = 46ms

C:\>ping 22.34.129.87

Pinging 22.34.129.87 with 32 bytes of data:

Request timed out.
Request timed out.
Request timed out.
Request timed out.

Ping statistics for 22.34.129.87:
    Packets: Sent = 4, Received = 0, Lost = 4 (100% loss),

C:\>
```

Figure 4-19 Output from successful and unsuccessful PING tests

By pinging the loopback address, 127.0.0.1, you can determine whether your workstation's TCP/IP services are running. By pinging a host on another subnet, you can determine whether the problem lies with a connectivity device between the two subnets.

For example, suppose that you have recently moved your computer from the Accounting Department to the Advertising Department, and now you cannot access the Web. The first test you should perform is pinging the loopback address. If that test is successful, then you know that your workstation's TCP/IP services are running correctly. Next, you might try pinging your neighbor's machine. If you receive a positive response, you know that your network connection is working. You should then try pinging a machine on another subnet that you know is connected to the network—for example, a computer in the IT Department. If this test is unsuccessful, it is possible that you do not have the correct settings in your TCP/IP configuration or that something is wrong with your network's connectivity (for example, a router may be malfunctioning).

As with other TCP/IP commands, PING can be used with a number of different options, or **switches**, and the syntax of the command may vary depending on the operating system. But a ping command always begins with the word *ping* followed by a hyphen (-) and a switch, followed by a variable pertaining to that switch. The following are some useful PING switches:

- `-?`—Displays the help text for the ping command, including its syntax and a full list of switches.
- `-a`—When used with an IP address, resolves the address to a host name.

4.3

- -n—Allows you to specify a number of echo requests to send. For example, if you want to ping the Library of Congress site with only two echo requests (rather than the standard four that a Windows operating system uses), you could type the following command: `ping -n 2 www.loc.gov`.
- -r—When used with a number from 1 to 9, displays the route taken during ping hops.

To view the proper syntax and a list of switches available for PING, type ping at the command prompt on a Windows-based computer or at the shell prompt on a UNIX or Linux system.

The PING utility as described previously works with networks running IPv4. On IPv6 networks, you must use a different version of the command that operates similarly. On Linux computers running IPv6, the **ping6** utility will issue ICMP packets to determine whether a host is available. For Windows computers, the command is `ping -6` followed by the host or IP address. If the destination host does not run IPv6, however, your attempt will be unsuccessful. For example, typing `ping -6 ipv6.google.com` and pressing Enter at the command prompt on a Windows computer running IPv6 would result in the reply shown in Figure 4-20. Typing `ping -6 www.google.com`, a host not running IPv6, would result in an error message.

```
C:\>ping -6 ipv6.google.com

Pinging ipv6.l.google.com [2607:f8b0:4001:c01::63] with 32 bytes of data:
Reply from 2607:f8b0:4001:c01::63: time=268ms
Reply from 2607:f8b0:4001:c01::63: time=290ms
Reply from 2607:f8b0:4001:c01::63: time=312ms
Reply from 2607:f8b0:4001:c01::63: time=130ms

Ping statistics for 2607:f8b0:4001:c01::63:
    Packets: Sent = 4, Received = 4, Lost = 0 (0% loss),
Approximate round trip times in milli-seconds:
    Minimum = 130ms, Maximum = 312ms, Average = 250ms

C:\>_
```

Figure 4-20 Output from successful `ping -6` command on a Windows computer

Chapter Summary

- Protocols define the standards for communication between nodes on a network. The term *protocol* can refer to a group, or suite, of individual protocols that work together to accomplish data translation, data handling, error checking, and addressing.
- Protocols vary by transmission efficiency, utilization of resources, ease of setup, compatibility, and ability to travel between one LAN segment and another. Protocols that can span more than one LAN are routable, which means they carry Network layer addressing information that can be interpreted by a router.
- TCP/IP is the most popular protocol suite because of its low cost, open nature, ability to communicate between dissimilar platforms, and the fact that it is routable. It is a de facto standard on the Internet and is the protocol of choice on LANs.

- The TCP/IP model is a practical way of categorizing protocols and services used on a TCP/IP network. Its Application layer roughly translates to the Application, Presentation, and Session layers of the OSI model. Its Transport layer is equivalent to the OSI model's Transport layer. Its Internet layer is analogous to the OSI model's Network layer. Its Network Interface layer, or Link layer, roughly equals the OSI model's Data Link and Physical layers.
- TCP (Transmission Control Protocol) belongs to the Transport layer of the TCP/IP and OSI models. TCP is a connection-oriented subprotocol; it requires a connection to be established between communicating nodes before it will transmit data. TCP provides reliability through checksum, flow control, and sequencing information.

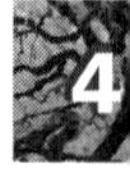

- UDP (User Datagram Protocol), like TCP, is a Transport layer protocol. UDP is a connectionless service and offers no delivery guarantees. But UDP is more efficient than TCP and useful in applications that require fast data transmission, such as videoconferencing.
- IP (Internet Protocol) belongs to the Internet layer of the TCP/IP model and the Network layer of the OSI model. It provides information about how and where data should be delivered.
- ARP (Address Resolution Protocol) belongs to the Internet layer of the TCP/IP model and the Network layer of the OSI model. It obtains the MAC (physical) address of a host, or node, and then creates a local database that maps the MAC address to the host's IP (logical) address.
- In IPv4, each IP address is a unique 32-bit number, divided into four octets (or bytes). Every IP address contains two types of information: network and host.
- In traditional IPv4 addressing, all nodes on a Class A network share the first octet of their IP numbers, a number between 1 and 126. Nodes on a Class B network share the first two octets, and all their IP addresses begin with a number between 128 and 191. Class C network IP numbers share the first three octets, with their first octet being a number between 192 and 223.
- Although computers read IPv4 addresses in binary form, humans usually read them in dotted decimal notation, in which a decimal number represents each octet and every number is separated by a period.
- A subnet mask is a 32-bit number that indicates whether and how a network has been subnetted—that is, subdivided into multiple smaller networks—and indicates the difference between network and host information in an IPv4 address. Subnetting is implemented to more easily manage network traffic and conserve a limited number of IPv4 addresses.
- IPv6 (IP version 6) is the latest version of IP. Its addresses are composed of eight 16-bit fields and total 128 bits. The larger address size results in an additional 2^{96} available IP addresses compared with the earlier version, IPv4. IPv6 provides several other benefits over IPv4, including a more efficient header, better overall security, better prioritization allowances, and automatic IP address configuration.
- IP addresses assigned manually are called static IP addresses; however, using static IP addresses allows for the possibility of assigning the same address to more than one device.
- Dynamic IP address assignment can be achieved using DHCP (Dynamic Host Configuration Protocol). DHCP essentially eliminates duplicate-addressing problems.

- The IPv4 addresses in the ranges 10.0.0.0 through 10.255.255.255, 172.16.0.0 through 172.31.255.255, and 192.168.0.0 through 192.168.255.255 are reserved for private addresses, or those used only within an organization's network. These addresses cannot be used to identify hosts on the Internet.
- A link-local address is a special kind of private address automatically assigned by an operating system to allow a node to communicate over its local subnet if a routable IP address is not available. ICANN has established the range of 169.254.0.0 through 169.254.254.255 as potential link-local IPv4 addresses. IPv6 link-local addresses begin with FE80. Zeroconf is a collection of protocols that manages link-local addressing.
- A socket is a logical address assigned to a specific process running on a host. It forms a virtual circuit between the processes on two networked hosts. The socket's address represents a combination of the host's IP address and the port number associated with a process.
- Every host is identified by a host name and belongs to a domain. A domain is a group of hosts that share a domain name and have part of their IP addresses in common.
- Every domain is identified by its domain name. Usually, a domain name is associated with a company or other type of organization, such as a university or military unit. Domain names must be reserved with an ICANN-approved domain registrar.
- DNS (Domain Name System or Domain Name Service) is a hierarchical way of tracking domain names and their addresses. The DNS database does not rely on one file or even one server, but rather is distributed over several key computers across the Internet to prevent catastrophic failure if one or a few computers go down.
- Name servers or DNS servers contain databases of names and their associated IP addresses. If one name server cannot resolve the IP address, the query passes to a higher-level name server. Each name server manages a group of machines called a zone. DNS relies on the hierarchical zones and zone files to distribute naming information.
- Some key TCP/IP Application layer protocols include Telnet (for logging on to hosts), FTP and TFTP (for transferring files between hosts), NTP (for synchronizing time between hosts), and PING (for sending echo requests and echo replies that can indicate whether a host is responding).

Key Terms

Address Resolution Protocol *See* ARP.

address resource record A type of DNS data record that maps the IP address of an Internet-connected device to its domain name.

alias A nickname for a node's host name. Aliases can be specified in a local host file.

anycast address A type of address specified in IPv6 that represents a group of interfaces, any one of which (and usually the first available of which) can accept a transmission. At this time, anycast addresses are not designed to be assigned to hosts, such as servers or workstations, but rather to routers.

APIPA (Automatic Private IP Addressing) A service available on computers running one of the Windows operating systems that automatically assigns the computer's network interface a link-local IP address.

ARP (Address Resolution Protocol) A core protocol in the TCP/IP suite that belongs in the Network layer of the OSI model. ARP obtains the MAC (physical) address of a host, or node, and then creates a local database that maps the MAC address to the host's IP (logical) address.

ARP cache *See* ARP table.

ARP table A database of records that maps MAC addresses to IP addresses. The ARP table is stored on a computer's hard disk where it is used by the ARP utility to supply the MAC addresses of network nodes, given their IP addresses.

Automatic Private IP Addressing *See* APIPA.

Avahi A version of Zeroconf available for use with the Linux operating system.

Bonjour Apple's implementation of the Zeroconf group of protocols.

country code TLD A top-level domain that corresponds to a country. For example, the country code TLD for Canada is .ca, and the country code TLD for Japan is .jp.

datagram *See* data packet.

DDNS (Dynamic DNS) A method of dynamically updating DNS records for a host. DDNS client computers are configured to notify a service provider when their IP addresses change, then the service provider propagates the DNS record change across the Internet automatically.

DHCP (Dynamic Host Configuration Protocol) An Application layer protocol in the TCP/IP suite that manages the dynamic distribution of IP addresses on a network. Using DHCP to assign IP addresses can nearly eliminate duplicate-addressing problems.

DHCP scope The predefined range of addresses that can be leased to any network device on a particular segment.

DHCP server A server that manages IP address assignment, maintaining information about which addresses are allowable, which are available, and which have already been associated with a host.

DHCPv4 The version of DHCP used with IPv4. DHCPv4 uses port number 67 for client-to-server communications and port number 68 for server-to-client communications.

DHCPv6 The version of DHCP used with IPv6. DHCPv6 uses port number 546 for client-to-server communications and port number 547 for server-to-client communications.

diskless workstation A workstation that doesn't contain a hard disk, but instead relies on a small amount of read-only memory to connect to a network and to pick up its system files.

DNS (Domain Name System or Domain Name Service) A hierarchical way of tracking domain names and their addresses, devised in the mid-1980s. The DNS database does not rely on one file or even one server, but rather is distributed over several key computers across the Internet to prevent catastrophic failure if one or a few computers go down. DNS is a TCP/IP service that belongs to the Application layer of the OSI model.

DNS cache A database on a computer that stores information about IP addresses and their associated host names. DNS caches can exist on clients as well as on name servers.

DNS server *See* name server.

DNS zone A portion of the DNS namespace for which one organization is assigned authority to manage.

domain A group of computers that belong to the same organization and have part of their IP addresses in common.

domain name The symbolic name that identifies a domain. Usually, a domain name is associated with a company or other type of organization, such as a university or military unit.

Domain Name Service *See* DNS.

Domain Name System *See* DNS.

dotted decimal notation The shorthand convention used to represent IPv4 addresses and make them more easily readable by humans. In dotted decimal notation, a decimal number between 0 and 255 represents each binary octet. A period, or dot, separates each decimal.

dual-stack A type of network that supports both IPv4 and IPv6 traffic.

dynamic ARP table entry A record in an ARP table that is created when a client makes an ARP request that cannot be satisfied by data already in the ARP table.

Dynamic DNS *See* DDNS.

Dynamic Host Configuration Protocol *See* DHCP.

Dynamic Host Configuration Protocol version 4 *See* DHCPv4.

Dynamic Host Configuration Protocol version 6 *See* DHCPv6.

dynamic IP address An IP address that is assigned to a device upon request and may change when the DHCP lease expires or is terminated. BOOTP and DHCP are two ways of assigning dynamic IP addresses.

Dynamic Ports TCP/IP ports in the range of 49,152 through 65,535, which are open for use without requiring administrative privileges on a host or approval from IANA.

echo reply The response signal sent by a device after another device pings it.

echo request The request for a response generated when one device pings another device.

File Transfer Protocol *See* FTP.

flow A sequence of packets issued from one source to one or many destinations. Routers interpret flow information to ensure that packets belonging to the same transmission arrive together. Flow information may also help with traffic prioritization.

Format Prefix A variable-length field at the beginning of an IPv6 address that indicates what type of address it is (for example, unicast, anycast, or multicast).

FQDN (fully qualified domain name) A host name plus domain name that uniquely identifies a computer or location on a network.

FTP (File Transfer Protocol) An Application layer protocol used to send and receive files via TCP/IP.

fully qualified domain name *See* FQDN.

fully qualified host name *See* FQDN.

hop A term used to describe each trip a unit of data takes from one connectivity device to another. Typically, *hop* is used in the context of router-to-router communications.

hop limit *See* TTL.

host file A text file that associates TCP/IP host names with IP addresses.

host name A symbolic name that describes a TCP/IP device.

hosts The name of the host file used on UNIX, Linux, and Windows systems. On a UNIX- or Linux-based computer, hosts is found in the /etc directory. On a Windows-based computer, it is found in the %systemroot%\system32\drivers\etc folder.

ICMP (Internet Control Message Protocol) A core protocol in the TCP/IP suite that notifies the sender that something has gone wrong in the transmission process and that packets were not delivered.

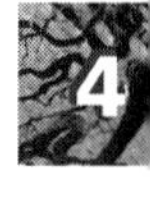

ICMPv6 The version of ICMP used with IPv6 networks. ICMPv6 performs the functions that ICMP, IGMP, and ARP perform in IPv4. It detects and reports data transmission errors, discovers other nodes on a network, and manages multicasting.

ifconfig A TCP/IP configuration and management utility used with UNIX and Linux systems.

IGMP (Internet Group Management Protocol or Internet Group Multicast Protocol) A TCP/IP protocol used on IPv4 networks to manage multicast transmissions. Routers use IGMP to determine which nodes belong to a multicast group, and nodes use IGMP to join or leave a multicast group.

Internet Control Message Protocol *See* ICMP.

Internet Control Message Protocol version 6 *See* ICMPv6

Internet Group Management Protocol *See* IGMP.

Internet Group Multicast Protocol *See* IGMP.

internetwork To traverse more than one LAN segment and more than one type of network through a router.

IP datagram *See* IP packet.

IP next generation *See* IPv6.

IP packet The IP portion of a TCP/IP frame that acts as an envelope for data, holding information necessary for routers to transfer data between subnets.

IP version 4 Link Local *See* IPv4LL.

ipconfig The utility used to display TCP/IP addressing and domain name information in the Windows client operating systems.

IPng *See* IPv6.

IPv4 IP version 4, the Internet Protocol standard released in the 1980s and still commonly used on modern networks. It specifies 32-bit addresses composed of four octets. It lacks the security, automatic addressing, and prioritization benefits of IPv6. It also suffers from a limited number of addresses, a problem that can be resolved by using IPv6 instead.

IPv4LL (IP version 4 Link Local) A protocol that manages automatic address assignment among locally connected nodes. IPv4LL is part of the Zeroconf group of protocols.

IPv6 (IP version 6) A newer standard for IP addressing that is gradually replacing the current IPv4 (IP version 4). Most notably, IPv6 uses a newer, more efficient header in its packets and allows for 128-bit source and destination IP addresses. The use of longer addresses will allow for many more IP addresses to be in circulation. IPv6 also provides automatic addressing, better security, and prioritization features.

label A character string that represents a domain (either top-level, second-level, or third-level).

lease The agreement between a DHCP server and client on how long the client can use a DHCP-assigned IP address. DHCP services can be configured to provide lease terms equal to any amount of time.

link-local address An IP address that is automatically assigned by an operating system to allow a node to communicate over its local subnet if a routable IP address is not available. ICANN has established the range of 169.254.0.0 through 169.254.254.255 as potential link-local IPv4 addresses. IPv6 link-local addresses begin with FE80.

loopback address An IP address reserved for communicating from a node to itself (used mostly for troubleshooting purposes). The IPv4 loopback address is always cited as 127.0.0.1, although in fact, transmitting to any IP address whose first octet is 127 will contact the originating device. In IPv6, the loopback address is represented as ::1.

loopback test An attempt to contact one's own machine for troubleshooting purposes. In TCP/IP-based networking, a loopback test can be performed by communicating with an IPv4 address that begins with an octet of 127. Usually, this means pinging the address 127.0.0.1.

mask *See* subnet mask.

multicast address A type of address in the IPv6 that represents multiple interfaces, often on multiple nodes. An IPv6 multicast address begins with the following hexadecimal field: FF0*x*, where *x* is a character that identifies the address's group scope.

multicasting A means of transmission in which one device sends data to a specific group of devices (not necessarily the entire network segment) in a point-to-multipoint fashion.

name server A server that contains a database of TCP/IP host names and their associated IP addresses. A name server supplies a resolver with the requested information. If it cannot resolve the IP address, the query passes to a higher-level name server.

namespace The database of Internet IP addresses and their associated names distributed over DNS name servers worldwide.

net mask *See* subnet mask.

network class A classification for TCP/IP-based networks that pertains to the network's potential size and is indicated by an IP address's network ID and subnet mask. Network Classes A, B, and C are commonly used by clients on LANs; network Classes D and E are reserved for special purposes.

network ID The portion of an IP address common to all nodes on the same network or subnet.

Network Time Protocol *See* NTP.

NTP (Network Time Protocol) A simple Application layer protocol in the TCP/IP suite used to synchronize the clocks of computers on a network. NTP depends on UDP for Transport layer services.

octet One of the 4 bytes that are separated by periods and together make up an IPv4 address.

Packet Internet Groper *See* PING.

ping To send an echo request signal from one node on a TCP/IP-based network to another, using the PING utility. *See also* PING.

PING (Packet Internet Groper) A TCP/IP troubleshooting utility that can verify that TCP/IP is installed, bound to the NIC, configured correctly, and communicating with the network. PING uses ICMP to send echo request and echo reply messages that determine the validity of an IP address.

ping6 The version of the PING utility used on Linux computers that run IPv6.

port number The address on a host where an application makes itself available to incoming data.

private address An IP address used only on an organization's internal network. Certain IP address ranges are reserved for private addresses. Private addresses cannot be used to communicate over the Internet.

Private Port *See* Dynamic Ports.

public address An IP address that is valid for use on public networks, such as the Internet. An organization assigns its hosts public addresses from the range of addresses assigned to it by Internet numbering authorities.

Registered Ports The TCP/IP ports in the range of 1024 to 49,151. These ports are accessible to network users and processes that do not have special administrative privileges. Default assignments of these ports must be registered with IANA.

resolver Any host on the Internet that needs to look up domain name information.

resource record The element of a DNS database stored on a name server that contains information about TCP/IP host names and their addresses.

root server A DNS server maintained by ICANN and IANA that is an authority on how to contact the top-level domains, such as those ending with .com, .edu, .net, .us, and so on. ICANN oversees the operation of 13 root servers around the world.

routable The protocols that can span more than one LAN because they carry Network layer and addressing information that can be interpreted by a router.

socket A logical address assigned to a specific process running on a computer. Some sockets are reserved for operating system functions.

static ARP table entry A record in an ARP table that someone has manually entered using the ARP utility. Static ARP table entries remain the same until someone manually modifies them with the ARP utility.

static IP address An IP address that is manually assigned to a device and remains constant until it is manually changed.

subnet A part of a network in which all nodes shares a network addressing component and a fixed amount of bandwidth.

subnet mask In IPv4 addressing, a 32-bit number that, when combined with a device's IP address, indicates what kind of subnet the device belongs to.

subnetting The process of subdividing a single class of network into multiple, smaller networks.

subprotocols The specialized protocols that work together and belong to a protocol suite.

switch The letters or words added to a command that allow you to customize a utility's output. Switches are usually preceded by a hyphen or forward slash character.

TCP (Transmission Control Protocol) A core protocol of the TCP/IP suite. TCP belongs to the Transport layer and provides reliable data delivery services.

TCP/IP (Transmission Control Protocol/Internet Protocol) A suite of networking protocols that includes TCP, IP, UDP, and many others. TCP/IP provides the foundation for data exchange across the Internet.

TCP/IP core protocols The major subprotocols of the TCP/IP suite, including IP, TCP, and UDP.

Telnet A terminal emulation protocol used to log on to remote hosts using the TCP/IP protocol. Telnet resides in the Application layer of the OSI model.

TFTP (Trivial File Transfer Protocol) A TCP/IP Application layer protocol that enables file transfers between computers. Unlike FTP, TFTP relies on UDP at the Transport layer and does not require a user to log on to the remote host.

Time to Live *See* TTL.

TLD (top-level domain) The highest-level category used to distinguish domain names—for example, .org, .com, and .net. A TLD is also known as the domain suffix.

top-level domain *See* TLD.

Transmission Control Protocol *See* TCP.

Transmission Control Protocol/Internet Protocol *See* TCP/IP.

Trivial File Transfer Protocol *See* TFTP.

TTL (Time to Live) A number that indicates the maximum duration that a packet can remain on the network before it is discarded. Although this field was originally meant to represent units of time, on modern networks it represents the number of router hops a datagram has endured. The TTL for datagrams is variable and configurable, but is usually set at 32 or 64. Each time a datagram passes through a router, its TTL is reduced by 1. When a router receives a datagram with a TTL equal to 1, the router discards that datagram.

UDP (User Datagram Protocol) A core protocol in the TCP/IP suite that sits in the Transport layer of the OSI model. UDP is a connectionless transport service.

unicast address A type of IPv6 address that represents a single interface on a device.

User Datagram Protocol *See* UDP.

Well Known Ports The TCP/IP port numbers 0 to 1023, so named because they were long ago assigned by Internet authorities to popular services (for example, FTP and Telnet), and are, therefore, well known and frequently used.

Zero configuration *See* Zeroconf.

Zeroconf (Zero configuration) A collection of protocols that assigns link-local addresses, performs DNS functions, and discovers services, such as print services, available to the node.

zone file A text file associated with a DNS zone that contains resource records identifying domains and their IP addresses.

zone transfer In DNS, the act of copying a primary name server's zone file to the secondary name server to ensure that both contain the same information.

Review Questions

1. Which TCP/IP core protocol operates in the Network layer of the OSI model and provides information about how and where data should be delivered?
   a. TCP
   b. UDP
   c. IP
   d. ICMP
2. Which IPv4 network class address contains a first octet in the range of 128-191?
   a. Class A
   b. Class B
   c. Class C
   d. Class D
3. How many bits are in an IPv6 address?
   a. 32
   b. 64
   c. 128
   d. 256
4. In the domain name `www.google.com`, which of the following describes the label for `com`?
   a. top-level domain (TLD)
   b. second-level domain
   c. third-level domain
   d. host-level domain
5. Which protocol that resides at the Application layer is used to log on to remote hosts using the TCP/IP protocol?
   a. Ping
   b. FTP
   c. NNTP
   d. Telnet
6. True or false? ARP maps host IP addresses to MAC addresses.
7. True or false? BOOTP provides a way to manually assign static IP addresses.
8. True or false? In IPv6, the loopback address has a value of 0:0:0:0:0:0:0:1, which is abbreviated as ::1.
9. True or false? The term namespace refers to the database of Internet IP addresses and their associated names.

10. True or false? DNS (Domain Name System or Domain Name Service) is a hierarchical way of associating domain names with IP addresses.

11. Protocols that can span more than one LAN are ________________,which means that they carry Network layer addressing information that can be interpreted by a router.

12. In ________________, a decimal number between 0 and 255 represents each binary octet, for a total of 256 possibilities. A period, or dot, separates each decimal.

13. A(n) ________________ is a special 32-bit number that, when combined with a device's IP address, informs the rest of the network about the segment or network to which the device is attached.

14. If a DHCP server is not available ________________, is a service available on computers running one of the Windows operating systems that automatically assigns the computer's network interface a link-local IP address.

15. A(n) ________________ is a logical address assigned to a specific process that is running on a computer. Some are reserved for operating system functions.

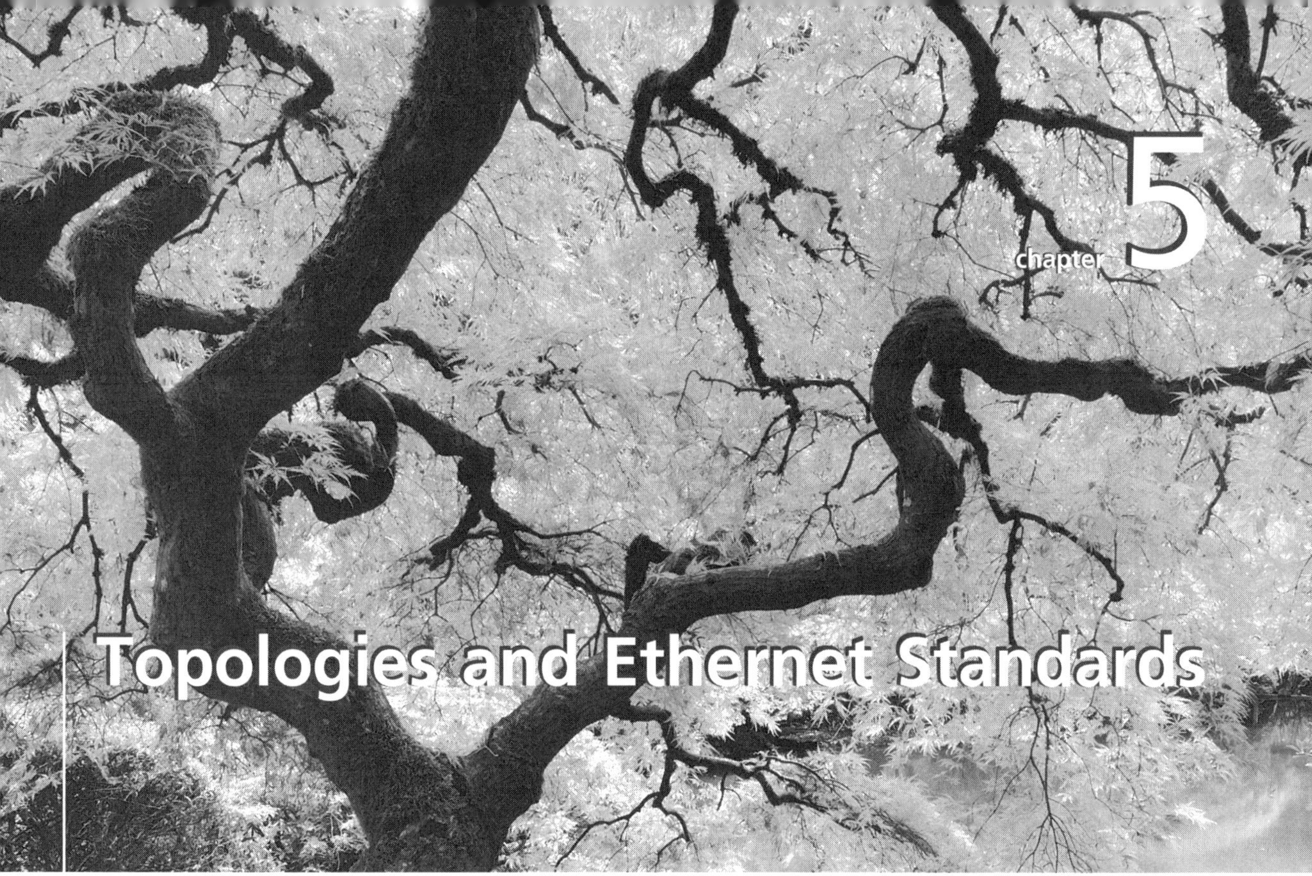

After reading this chapter and completing the exercises, you will be able to:

- Describe the basic and hybrid LAN topologies, and their uses, advantages, and disadvantages
- Describe the backbone structures that form the foundation for most networks
- Compare the different types of switching used in data transmission
- Explain how nodes on Ethernet networks share a communications channel
- Identify the characteristics of several Ethernet standards

To a large extent, topologies and technologies have converged in today's networks, a fact that ultimately makes our IT design choices a little easier. However, it helps to know where we came from to better understand where we are going and why.

As the IT director for a community college, I was tasked with keeping about 1000 computers in four buildings up and running. Our network backbone was a distributed FDDI ring topology running over fiber-optic cable connecting all four buildings. Workstations and servers were connected via 10Base-T Ethernet hubs and switches over Cat 5 cable. One morning, we were alerted to the fact that users in Building 2 had lost connectivity to other buildings, and that no devices in Building 2 could be contacted from other buildings. A faulty FDDI concentrator was found to be the culprit.

At this point, I had a decision to make: Replace the faulty FDDI concentrator at the whopping cost of over $6000, or replace the distributed backbone FDDI ring topology with a collapsed backbone star topology using Ethernet switches for about $2000 and some design and cabling work. The former solution was easier to implement because it only required replacing one piece of equipment and no change to the design. However, a star topology with a collapsed backbone using Ethernet switches would bring our network into the twenty-first century. In addition, by updating the design, we were future-proofing our network rather than depending on more expensive 1990s technology. To me, it was a no-brainer. We spent a long Saturday afternoon, ultimately working into the wee hours of Sunday morning, reconfiguring the fiber-optic cables to work with our new collapsed backbone design. But, for the peace of mind, easier management, and better performance, it was well worth it.

Greg Tomsho
Former IT Director, Catawba Valley Community College

Just as an architect must decide where to place walls and doors, where to install electrical and plumbing systems, and how to manage traffic patterns through rooms to make a building more livable, a network architect must consider many factors, both seen and unseen, when designing a network. This chapter details some basic elements of network architecture: physical and logical topologies. These elements are crucial to understanding networking design, troubleshooting, and management, all of which are discussed later in this book.

In this chapter, you will also learn about the most commonly used network access method, Ethernet, including its many Physical layer standards. After you master the physical and logical fundamentals of network architecture, you will have all the tools necessary to design a network as elegant as the Taj Mahal.

Simple Physical Topologies

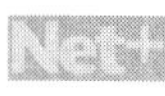

3.5 **Physical topology** refers to the physical layout of the media, nodes, and devices on a network. It depicts a network in broad scope. It does not specify device types, connectivity methods, addressing schemes, or other specific details. Physical topologies are divided into three fundamental shapes: bus, ring, and star. These shapes can be mixed to create hybrid topologies.

Before you design a network, you need to understand physical topologies because they are integral to the type of network (for example, Ethernet), cabling infrastructure, and transmission media you use. You must also understand a network's physical topology to troubleshoot its problems or change its infrastructure. A thorough knowledge of physical topologies is necessary to obtain Network+ certification.

Physical topologies and logical topologies (discussed later) are two different networking concepts. You should be aware that when used alone, the word *topology* often refers to a network's *physical* topology.

Bus

A **bus topology** consists of a single cable, called the **bus**, that connects all nodes on a network without intervening connectivity devices. A bus topology can support only one channel for communication; as a result, every node shares the bus's total capacity. Most bus networks—for example, Thinnet and Thicknet—use coaxial cable as their physical medium. Bus networks rely on a **passive topology**, which means each node passively listens for, then accepts, data directed to it. When one node wants to transmit data to another node, it broadcasts an alert to the entire network, informing all nodes that a transmission is being sent; the destination node then picks up the transmission. Nodes other than the sending and receiving nodes ignore the message.

For example, suppose that you want to send an instant message to your friend Diane, who works across the hall, asking whether she wants to have lunch with you. You click the Send button after typing your message, and the data stream that contains your message is sent to your NIC. Your NIC then sends a message across the shared wire that essentially says, "I have a message for Diane's computer." The message passes by every NIC between your computer and Diane's computer until Diane's computer recognizes that the message is meant for it and responds by accepting the data.

At the ends of each bus network are 50-ohm resistors known as terminators. **Terminators** stop signals after they have reached the end of the wire. Without these devices, signals on a bus network would travel endlessly between the two ends of the network—a phenomenon known as **signal bounce**—and new signals could not get through. To understand this concept, imagine that you and a partner, standing at opposite sides of a canyon, are yelling to each other. When you call out, your words echo; when your partner replies, his words also echo. Now imagine that the echoes never fade. After a short while, you could not continue conversing because all of the previously generated sound waves would still be bouncing around, creating too much noise for you to hear anything else. On a network, terminators prevent this problem by halting the transmission of old signals. A bus network must also be grounded at one end to help remove static electricity that could adversely affect the signal. Figure 5-1 depicts a terminated bus network.

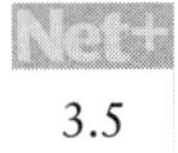

3.5

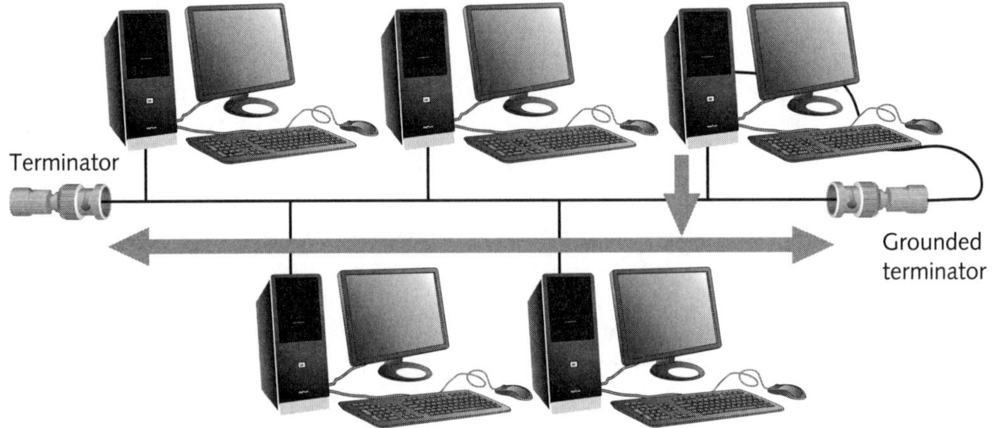

Figure 5-1 A terminated bus topology network

Although networks based on a bus topology are relatively inexpensive to set up, they do not scale well. As you add more nodes, the network's performance degrades. Because of the single-channel limitation, the more nodes on a bus network, the more slowly the network will transmit and deliver data. A bus topology is rarely practical for networks with more than a dozen workstations.

Bus networks are also difficult to troubleshoot because it is a challenge to identify fault locations. To understand why, think of the game called "telephone," in which one person whispers a phrase into the ear of the next person, who whispers the phrase into the ear of another person, and so on, until the final person in line repeats the phrase aloud. The vast majority of the time, the phrase recited by the last person bears little resemblance to the original phrase. When the game ends, it's hard to determine precisely where in the chain the individual errors cropped up. Similarly, errors may occur at any intermediate point on a bus network, but at the receiving end it's possible to tell only that an error occurred. Finding the source of the error can prove very difficult.

A final disadvantage to bus networks is that they are not very fault tolerant. **Fault tolerance** is the capability for a component or system to continue functioning despite damage or malfunction. On bus networks, any single break or a defect affects the entire network.

Because they have poor fault tolerance, do not scale well, and are difficult to troubleshoot, pure bus topologies do not form the basis of modern networks. Understanding their faults, however, will help you recognize the advantages of the more popular topologies in use today.

Ring

In a **ring topology**, each node is connected to the two nearest nodes so that the entire network forms a circle, as shown in Figure 5-2. Data are transmitted clockwise in one direction around the ring. Each workstation accepts and responds to packets addressed to it, then forwards the other packets to the next workstation in the ring. Each workstation acts as a repeater for the transmission. The fact that all workstations participate in delivery makes the

Net+ 3.5 ring topology an **active topology**. This is one way a ring topology differs from a bus topology. A ring topology also differs in that it has no "ends" and data stop at their destination. In most ring networks, twisted pair or fiber-optic cabling is used as the physical medium.

Figure 5-2 A ring topology network

One drawback of a simple ring topology is that a single malfunctioning workstation can disable the network. For example, suppose that you and five colleagues share a pure ring topology LAN in your small office. You decide to send an instant message to Cesar, who works three offices away, telling him you found his lost glasses. Between your office and Cesar's office are two other offices, and two other workstations on the ring. Your instant message must pass through the two intervening workstations' NICs before it reaches Cesar's computer. If one of these workstations has a malfunctioning NIC, your message will never reach Cesar.

In addition, just as in a bus topology, the more workstations that must participate in data transmission, the slower the response time. Consequently, pure ring topologies are not very flexible or scalable. Contemporary LANs rarely use pure ring topologies.

Star

In a **star topology**, every node on the network is connected through a central device. Years ago, the connecting device would have been a hub. On modern networks, the connecting device is a router or switch. Figure 5-3 depicts a typical star topology. Star topologies are usually built with twisted pair or fiber-optic cabling. Any single cable on a star network connects only two devices (for example, a workstation and a switch), so a cabling problem will affect

3.5 two nodes at most. Devices such as workstations or printers transmit data to the connectivity device, which then retransmits the signal to the network segment containing the destination node.

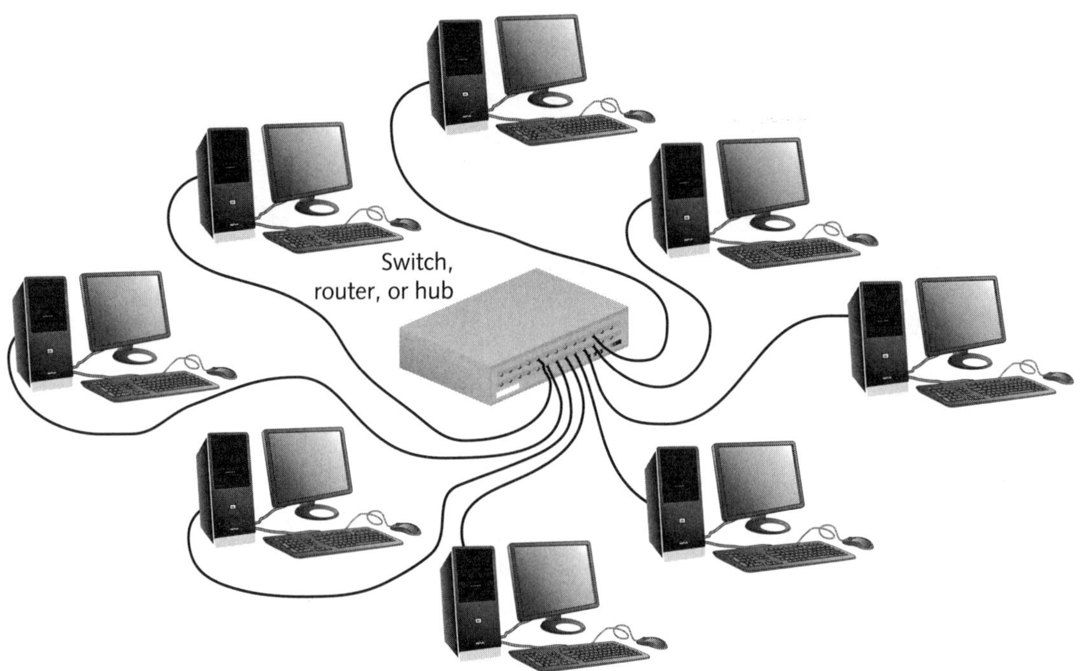

Figure 5-3 A star topology network

Star topologies require more cabling than ring or bus networks. However, because each node is separately connected to a central connectivity device, they are more fault tolerant. A single malfunctioning workstation cannot disable an entire star network. A failure in the central connectivity device can take down a LAN segment, though.

Because they include a centralized connection point, star topologies are also flexible. Nodes can easily be moved and segments can be isolated or interconnected with other networks. Star networks are, therefore, scalable. For this reason, and because of their fault tolerance, the star topology has become the most popular fundamental layout used in contemporary LANs. Single star networks are commonly interconnected with other networks through switches or routers to form more complex topologies. Modern Ethernet networks are based on the star topology.

Star networks can support a maximum of only 1024 addressable nodes on a logical network. For example, if you have a campus with 3000 users, hundreds of networked printers, and scores of other devices, you must strategically create smaller logical networks. Even if you had 1000 users and *could* put them on the same logical network, you wouldn't, because doing so would result in poor performance and difficult management. Instead, you would use routers or switches to separate segments. You'll learn more about such techniques later in this chapter and in Chapter 6.

Hybrid Topologies

3.5 Except in very small networks, you will rarely encounter a network that follows a pure bus, ring, or star topology. Simple topologies are too restrictive, particularly if the LAN must accommodate a large number of devices. More likely, you will work with a complex combination of these topologies, known as a **hybrid topology**. Two kinds of hybrid topologies are explained in the following sections.

Star-Wired Ring

The **star-wired ring topology** uses the physical layout of a star in conjunction with the ring logical topology. In Figure 5-4, which depicts this architecture, the solid lines represent a physical connection and the dotted lines represent the flow of data. Data are sent around the star in a circular pattern. This hybrid topology benefits from the fault tolerance of the star topology, as data transmission does not depend on each workstation to act as a repeater. Token ring networks, as specified in IEEE 802.5, use this hybrid topology.

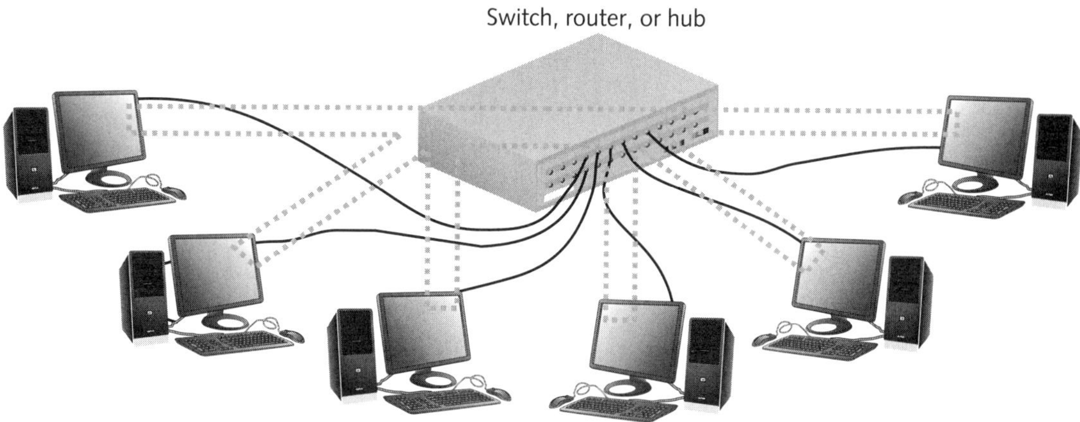

Figure 5-4 A star-wired ring topology network

Star-Wired Bus

Another popular hybrid topology combines the star and bus formations. In a **star-wired bus topology**, groups of workstations are star-connected to connectivity devices and then networked via a single bus, as shown in Figure 5-5. With this design, you can cover longer distances and easily interconnect or isolate different network segments. One drawback is that this option is more expensive than using the star topology alone because it requires more cabling and potentially more connectivity devices. However, compared with the benefits, these drawbacks are negligible. The star-wired bus topology forms the basis for modern Ethernet networks, which commonly use switches or routers as the connectivity devices.

Net+ 3.5

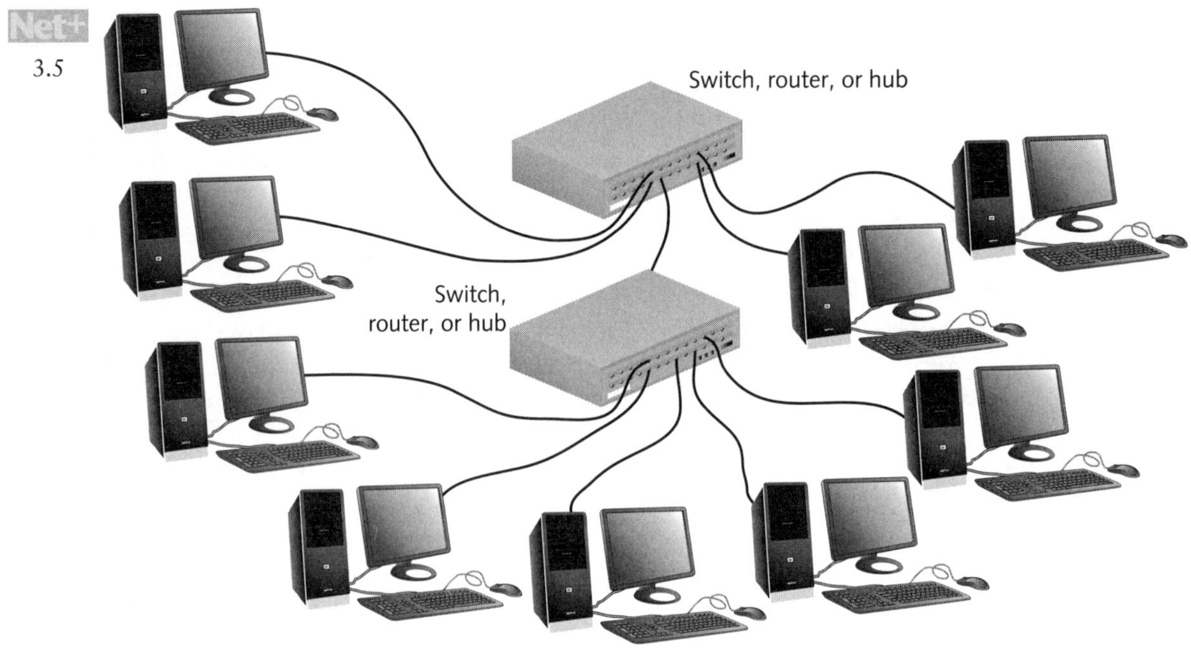

Figure 5-5 A star-wired bus topology network

Logical Topologies

Net+ 3.5

The term **logical topology** refers to the way in which data are transmitted between nodes, rather than the physical layout of the paths that data take. A network's logical topology will not necessarily match its physical topology.

The most common logical topologies are bus and ring. In a bus logical topology, signals travel from one network device to all other devices on the network or network segment. They may or may not travel through an intervening connectivity device (as in a star topology network). A network that uses a bus physical topology also uses a bus logical topology. In addition, networks that use either the star or star-wired bus physical topologies also result in a bus logical topology. Ethernet networks use the bus logical topology.

The fact that all nodes connected to a bus network can communicate directly via broadcast transmissions makes them part of a single **broadcast domain**. Similarly, all nodes connected to a single repeating device or switch belong to a broadcast domain—that is, unless the switch is specially configured to separate broadcast domains. Routers and other devices that operate at Layer 3 separate broadcast domains.

For designing and troubleshooting Ethernet networks, it is necessary to understand that all of a segment's broadcast traffic is transmitted to all of the segment's nodes. As an example, suppose you connect your laptop to your company's Ethernet network. In an attempt to contact a DHCP server and obtain an IP address, your laptop issues a DHCP discover packet in broadcast fashion. Therefore, the packet is sent to every workstation connected to the same Ethernet segment as your laptop, even though the request wasn't meant for them.

3.5 In addition, if one device has a malfunctioning NIC that is issuing bad or excessive packets, those packets will be detected by the NICs of all devices on the same segment. The result is a waste of available bandwidth and potential transmission errors. As you will learn, however, modern Ethernet networks can overcome such drawbacks through speed and design techniques.

In contrast to a bus logical topology, in a ring logical topology, signals follow a circular path between sender and receiver. Networks that use a pure ring topology, such as the now-obsolete token ring networks, use a ring logical topology. As shown by the dashed lines in Figure 5-4, the ring logical topology is also used by the star-wired ring hybrid physical topology because signals follow a circular path, even as they travel through a connectivity device.

Backbone Networks

As you learned in Chapter 1, a network backbone is the part of a network to which segments and significant shared devices connect. Backbones usually are capable of more throughput than the media connecting nodes with connectivity devices. This added capacity is necessary because backbones carry more traffic. For example, LANs in large organizations commonly rely on a fiber-optic backbone but continue to use Cat 5 or better UTP to connect nodes with switches or routers.

Although even the smallest LAN technically has a backbone, on an enterprise-wide network, backbones are more complex and more difficult to plan. In networking, the term **enterprise** refers to an entire organization, including its local and remote offices, a mixture of computer systems, and a number of departments. Enterprise-wide computing must, therefore, take into account the breadth and diversity of a large organization's computer needs. The backbone is the most significant building block of enterprise-wide networks. It may take one of several different shapes, as described in the following sections.

Serial Backbone

A **serial backbone** is the simplest kind of backbone. It consists of two or more devices connected to each other by a single medium in a daisy-chain fashion. In networking, a **daisy chain** is simply a linked series of devices. Switches can be connected in a daisy chain to extend a network. For example, suppose you manage a small star-wired bus topology network in which a single switch serves a workgroup of eight users. When new employees are added to that department and you need more network connections, you could connect a second switch to the first switch in a daisy-chain fashion. The new switch would offer open ports for new users. Because the star-wired hybrids provide for modular additions, daisy-chaining is a logical solution for growth. Also, because switches can easily be connected through cables attached to their ports, a LAN's infrastructure can be expanded with little additional cost.

Switches are not the only devices that can be connected in a serial backbone. In fact, gateways and routers also commonly form part of the backbone. Figure 5-6 illustrates a serial backbone network, in which the backbone is indicated by a dashed line.

When designing and troubleshooting serial backbone networks, it's important to remember that only so many repeating devices can be connected in a serial fashion. Therefore, the distance you can span between connected repeating devices is limited. Later in this chapter, you will learn

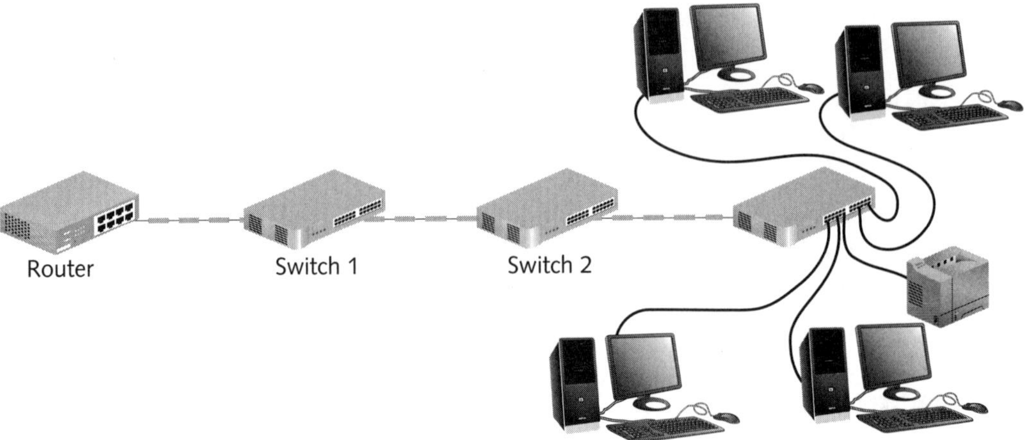

Figure 5-6 A serial backbone

about the maximum number of repeating devices and segments for each type of Ethernet network. Exceeding the maximum network length will adversely affect the performance of a LAN. If you extend a LAN beyond its recommended size, intermittent and unpredictable data transmission errors will result. Similarly, if you daisy-chain a topology with limited bandwidth, you risk overloading the channel and generating still more data errors.

Modern networks of any size don't depend on simple serial backbones. Instead, they use a more scalable and fault-tolerant framework such as a distributed backbone.

Distributed Backbone

A **distributed backbone** consists of a number of intermediate connectivity devices connected to one or more central connectivity devices, such as switches or routers, in a hierarchy, as shown in Figure 5-7. In Figure 5-7, the dashed lines represent the backbone. This kind of topology allows for simple expansion and limited capital outlay for growth because more layers of devices can be added to existing layers. For example, suppose that you are the network administrator for a small publisher's office. You might begin your network with a distributed backbone consisting of two switches that supply connectivity to your 20 users, 10 on each switch. When your company hires more staff, you can connect another switch to one of the existing switches, and use the new switch to connect the new staff to the network.

A more complicated distributed backbone connects multiple LANs or LAN segments using routers, as shown in Figure 5-8. In this example, the routers form the highest layer of the backbone to connect the LANs or LAN segments.

A distributed backbone also provides network administrators with the ability to segregate workgroups and, therefore, manage them more easily. For example, it adapts well to an enterprise-wide network confined to a single building, in which certain switches can be assigned according to the floor or department. Note that it's possible for distributed backbones to include repeating devices linked in a daisy-chain fashion. This arrangement requires the same length considerations that serial backbones demand. Another possible problem in this design relates to the potential single points of failure, such as the devices

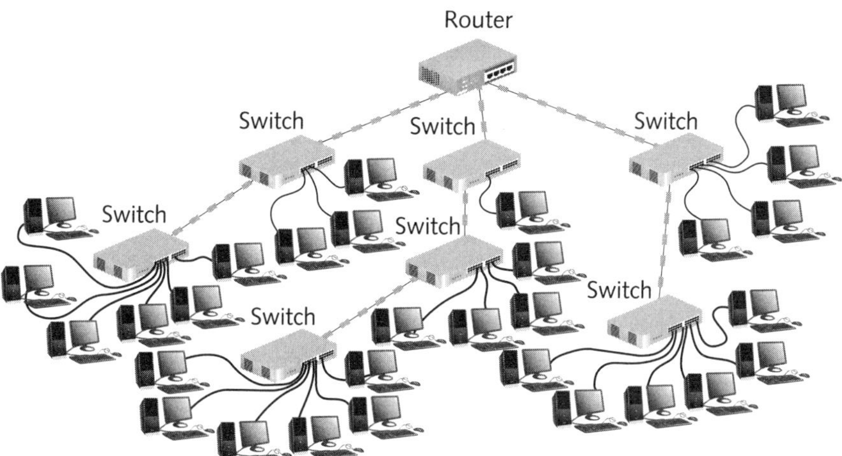

Figure 5-7 A simple distributed backbone

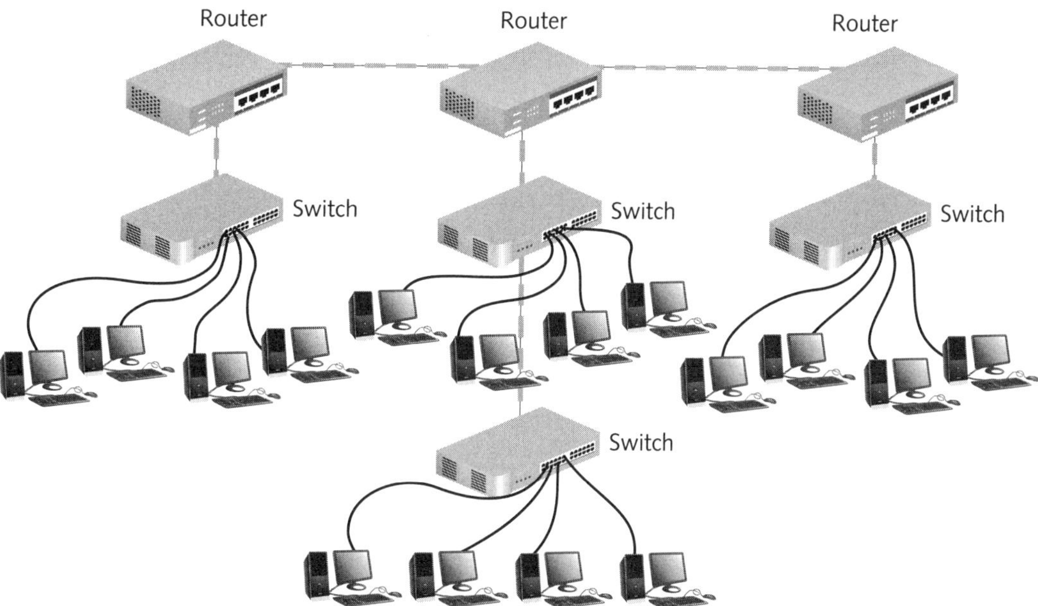

Figure 5-8 A distributed backbone connecting multiple LANs

at the uppermost layers. Despite these potential drawbacks, implementing a distributed backbone network can be relatively simple, quick, and inexpensive.

Collapsed Backbone

The **collapsed backbone** topology uses a router or switch as the single central connection point for multiple subnetworks, as shown in Figure 5-9. Contrast Figure 5-9 with Figure 5-8, in which multiple LANs are connected via a distributed backbone. In a collapsed backbone, a single router or switch is the highest layer of the backbone. The router or switch that makes up the collapsed backbone must contain multiprocessors to handle the heavy traffic going through it. This is risky because a failure in the central router or switch can bring down the entire network. In addition, because routers cannot move traffic as quickly as switches, using a router may slow data transmission.

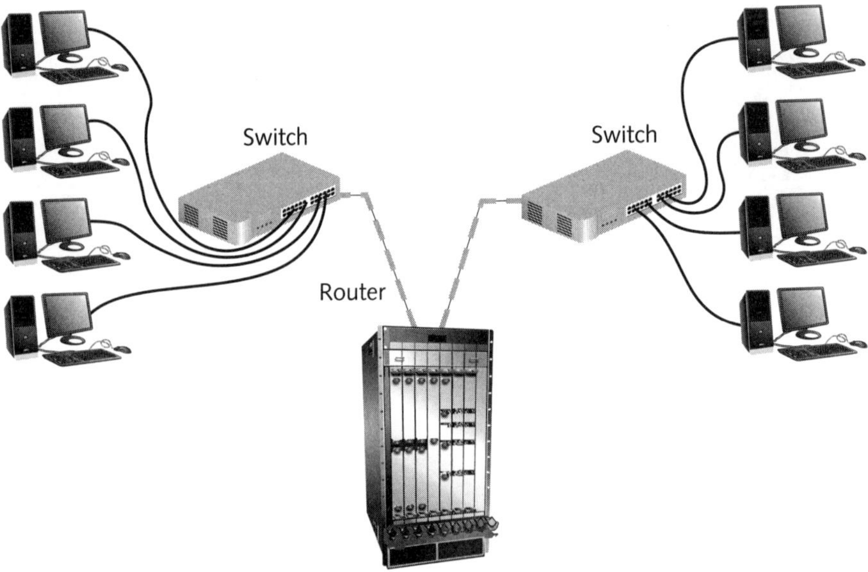

Figure 5-9 A collapsed backbone

Nevertheless, a collapsed backbone topology offers substantial advantages. Most significantly, this arrangement allows you to interconnect different types of subnetworks. You can also centrally manage maintenance and troubleshooting chores.

Parallel Backbone

A **parallel backbone** is the most robust type of network backbone. This variation of the collapsed backbone arrangement consists of more than one connection from the central router or switch to each network segment. In a network with more than one router or switch, the parallel backbone calls for duplicate connections between those connectivity devices as well. Figure 5-10 depicts a simple parallel backbone topology. As you can see, each switch is connected to the router by two cables, and the two routers are also connected by two cables.

The most significant advantage of using a parallel backbone is that its redundant (duplicate) links ensure network connectivity to any area of the enterprise. Parallel backbones are more expensive than other enterprise-wide topologies because they require much more cabling than the others. However, they make up for the additional cost by offering increased performance and better fault tolerance.

As a network administrator, you might choose to implement parallel connections to only some of the most critical devices on your network. For example, if the first and second switches in

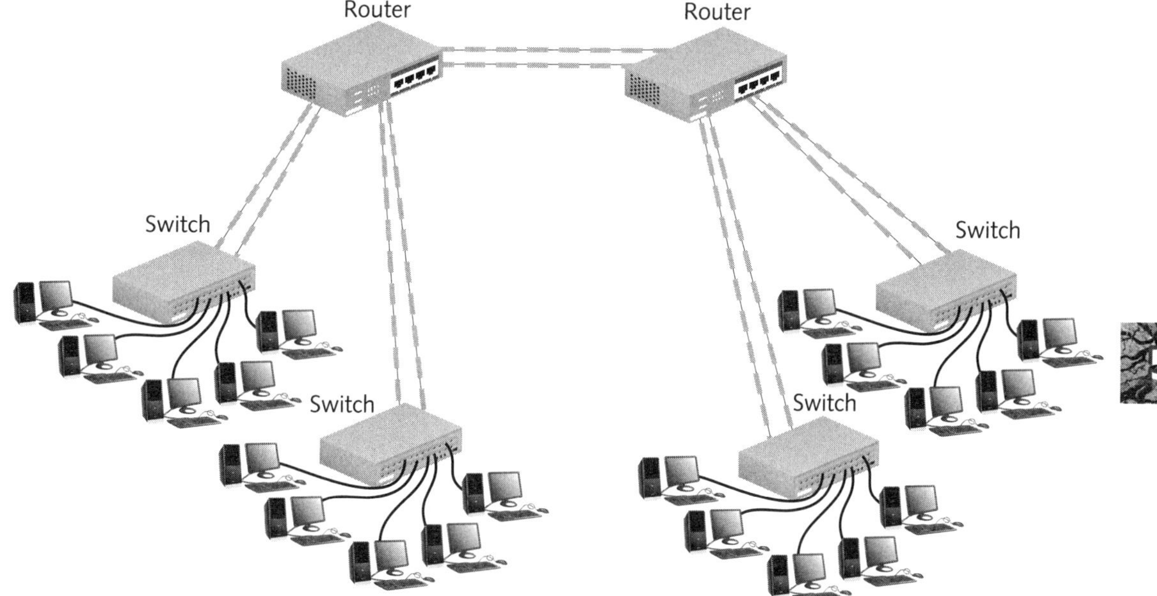

Figure 5-10 A parallel backbone

Figure 5-10 connected your Facilities and Payroll Departments to the rest of the network, and your organization could never afford to lose connectivity with those departments, you might use a parallel structure for those links. If the third and fourth switches in Figure 5-10 connected your organization's Recreation and Training Departments to the network, you might decide that parallel connections were unnecessary for these departments. By selectively implementing the parallel structure, you can lower connectivity costs and leave available additional ports on the connectivity devices.

Bear in mind that an enterprise-wide LAN or WAN may include different combinations of physical topologies and backbone designs. Now that you understand how networks may be arranged, both physically and logically, you are ready to learn more about how connections between nodes are established.

Switching

3.4 **Switching** is a component of a network's logical topology that determines how connections are created between nodes. Three switching methods are used on modern networks: circuit switching, packet switching, and multiprotocol label switching.

Circuit Switching

In **circuit switching**, a connection is established between two network nodes before they begin transmitting data. Bandwidth is dedicated to this connection and remains available until the users terminate communication between the two nodes. While the nodes remain connected, all data follow the same path initially selected by the switch. Traditional telephone calls—that is, calls not carried over TCP/IP networks—for example, typically use a circuit-switched connection.

Because circuit switching monopolizes its piece of bandwidth while the two stations remain connected, even when no actual communication is taking place, it can result in a waste of
3.4 available resources. However, some network applications benefit from such a reserved path. For example, live audio or videoconferencing might not tolerate the time delay it would take to reorganize data packets that have taken separate paths through another switching method. Several WAN technologies, such as ISDN, T1 services, and ATM (described in Chapter 7), also use circuit switching.

Packet Switching

By far the most popular method for connecting nodes on a network is packet switching. **Packet switching** breaks data into packets before they are transported. Packets can travel any path on the network to their destination because, as you learned in Chapter 4, each packet contains the destination address and sequencing information. Consequently, packets can attempt to find the fastest circuit available at any instant. They need not follow each other along the same path, nor must they arrive at their destination in the same sequence as when they left their source.

To understand this technology, imagine that you work in Washington, D.C., and you organized a field trip for 50 colleagues to the National Air and Space Museum. You gave the museum's exact address to your colleagues and told them to leave precisely at 7:00 a.m. from your office building several blocks away. You did not tell your coworkers which route to take. Some might choose the subway, others might hail a taxicab, and still others might choose to drive their own cars or even walk. All of them will attempt to find the fastest route to the museum. But if a group of six decides to take a taxicab and only four people fit in that taxi, the next two people have to wait for another taxi. Or, a taxi might get caught in rush hour traffic and be forced to find an alternate route. Thus, the fastest route might not be obvious the moment everyone departs. But no matter which transportation method your colleagues choose, all will arrive at the museum and reassemble as a group. This analogy illustrates how packets travel in a packet-switched network.

When packets reach their destination node, the node reassembles them based on their control information. Because of the time it takes to reassemble the packets into a message, packet switching requires speedy connections if it's used for live audio or video transmission. Even connections as slow as a dial-up Internet service, however, are sufficiently fast to send and receive typical network data, such as e-mail messages, spreadsheet files, or even software programs from a server to a client. The greatest advantage to packet switching lies in the fact that it does not waste bandwidth by holding a connection open until a message reaches its destination, as circuit switching does. Ethernet networks and the Internet are the most common examples of packet-switched networks.

MPLS (Multiprotocol Label Switching)

3.5 Another type of switching, **MPLS (multiprotocol label switching)**, was introduced by the IETF in 1999. As its name implies, MPLS enables multiple types of Layer 3 protocols to travel over any one of several connection-oriented Layer 2 protocols. As you have learned, IP is the most commonly used Layer 3 protocol, and so MPLS most often supports IP. MPLS can operate over Ethernet frames, but is more often used with other Layer 2 protocols, like those designed for WANs. In fact, one of its benefits is the ability to use packet-switched technologies over

3.5 traditionally circuit-switched networks. MPLS can also create end-to-end paths that act like circuit-switched connections.

In addition, MPLS addresses some limitations of traditional packet switching. For example, on an IP-based network, each router along the data's path must interpret the IP datagram's header to discover its destination address, and then perform a route lookup to determine where to forward the packet next. As you can imagine, stopping to process this information at every router slows transmission. In MPLS, the first router that receives a packet adds one or more labels to the Layer 3 datagram. (Collectively, the MPLS labels are sometimes called a shim because of their placement between Layer 3 and Layer 2 information. Also, MPLS is sometimes said to belong to "Layer 2.5.") Then the network's Layer 2 protocol header is added, as shown in Figure 5-11.

Labels added during MPLS include special addressing and, sometimes, prioritization information. Routers then need only interpret the MPLS labels, which can point to exclusive, predefined data paths. Network engineers have significant control in setting these paths. Consequently, MPLS offers potentially faster transmission than traditionally packet-switched or circuit-switched networks. Because it can add prioritization information, MPLS can also offer better **QoS (quality of service)**. QoS is a specification that guarantees delivery of data within a certain time frame. These advantages make MPLS especially well suited to WANs.

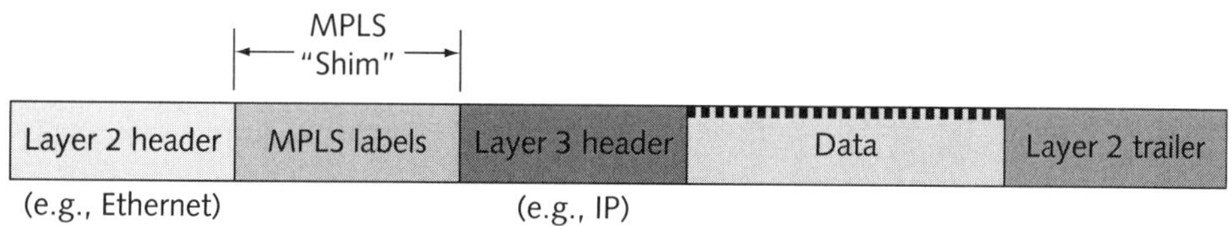

Figure 5-11 MPLS shim within a frame

Now that you are familiar with the various methods of establishing paths between nodes, you are ready to investigate Ethernet, a Layer 2 standard used on nearly every LAN.

Ethernet

3.7 Ethernet is a flexible technology that can run on a variety of network media and offers excellent throughput at a reasonable cost. Because of its many advantages Ethernet is, by far, the most popular network technology used on modern LANs.

Ethernet has evolved through many variations, and its speed and reliability continue to improve. As a result of this history, it supports many different versions—so many, in fact, that you might find the many variations a little confusing. However, all Ethernet networks have at least one thing in common—their access method, which is known as CSMA/CD.

Net+ CSMA/CD (Carrier Sense Multiple Access with Collision Detection)

3.7 A network's **access method** is its method of controlling how network nodes access the communications channel. In comparing a network with a highway, the on-ramps would be one part of the highway's access method. A busy highway might use stoplights at each on-ramp to allow only one person to merge into traffic every five seconds. After merging, cars must drive within lanes, and each lane is limited as to how many cars it can hold at one time. All of these highway controls are designed to avoid collisions and help drivers get to their destinations. On networks, similar restrictions apply to the way in which multiple computers share a finite amount of bandwidth on a network. These controls make up the network's access method.

All Ethernet networks, independent of their speed or frame type, use an access method called **CSMA/CD (Carrier Sense Multiple Access with Collision Detection)**. To understand Ethernet, you must first understand CSMA/CD. Take a minute to think about the full name *Carrier Sense Multiple Access with Collision Detection.* The term *Carrier Sense* refers to the fact that Ethernet NICs listen on the network and wait until they detect (or sense) that no other nodes are transmitting data over the signal (or carrier) on the communications channel before they begin to transmit. The term *Multiple Access* refers to the fact that several Ethernet nodes can be connected to a network and can monitor traffic, or access the media, simultaneously.

In CSMA/CD, when a node wants to transmit data it must first access the transmission media and determine whether the channel is free. If the channel is not free, it waits and checks again after a very brief amount of time. If the channel is free, the node transmits its data. Any node can transmit data after it determines that the channel is free. But what if two nodes simultaneously check the channel, determine that it's free, and begin to transmit? When this happens, their two transmissions interfere with each other; this is known as a **collision**.

The last part of CSMA/CD, the term *collision detection,* refers to the way nodes respond to a collision. In the event of a collision, the network performs a series of steps known as the collision detection routine. If a node's NIC determines that its data have been involved in a collision, it immediately stops transmitting. Next, in a process called **jamming**, the NIC issues a special 32-bit sequence that indicates to the rest of the network nodes that its previous transmission was faulty and that those data frames are invalid. After waiting, the NIC determines if the line is again available; if it is available, the NIC retransmits its data.

On heavily trafficked network segments, collisions are fairly common. It is not surprising that the more nodes there are transmitting data on a segment, the more collisions that will take place. (Although a collision rate greater than 5 percent of all traffic is unusual and may point to a problematic NIC or poor cabling on the network.) When an Ethernet segment grows to include a particularly large number of nodes, you may see performance suffer as a result of collisions. This "critical mass" number depends on the type and volume of data that the network regularly transmits. Collisions can corrupt data or truncate data frames, so it is important that the network detect and compensate for them. Figure 5-12 depicts the way CSMA/CD regulates data flow to avoid and, if necessary, detect collisions.

Net+ On an Ethernet network, a **collision domain** is the portion of a network in which collisions
1.4 occur if two nodes transmit data at the same time. When designing an Ethernet network, it's
3.7 important to note that because repeaters simply regenerate any signal they receive, they repeat collisions just as they repeat data. Thus, connecting multiple parts of a network with

Net+
1.4
3.7

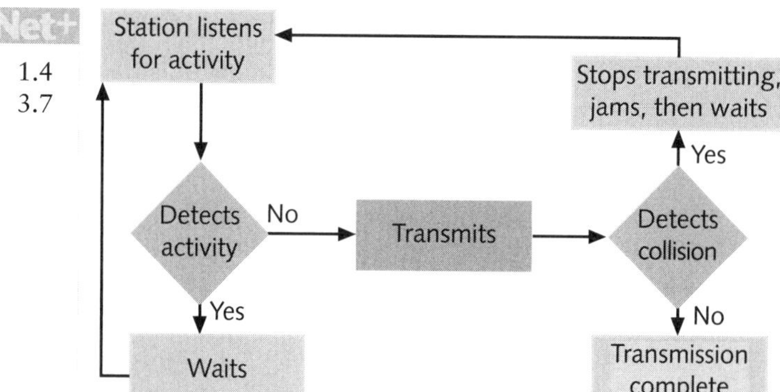

Figure 5-12 CSMA/CD process

repeaters or hubs results in a larger collision domain. Switches and routers, however, separate collision domains.

Collision domains differ from broadcast domains in that collision domains define a logically shared space for Layer 2 communications. Also, by default, switches do not separate broadcast domains. Figure 5-13 illustrates the difference between broadcast domains and collision domains.

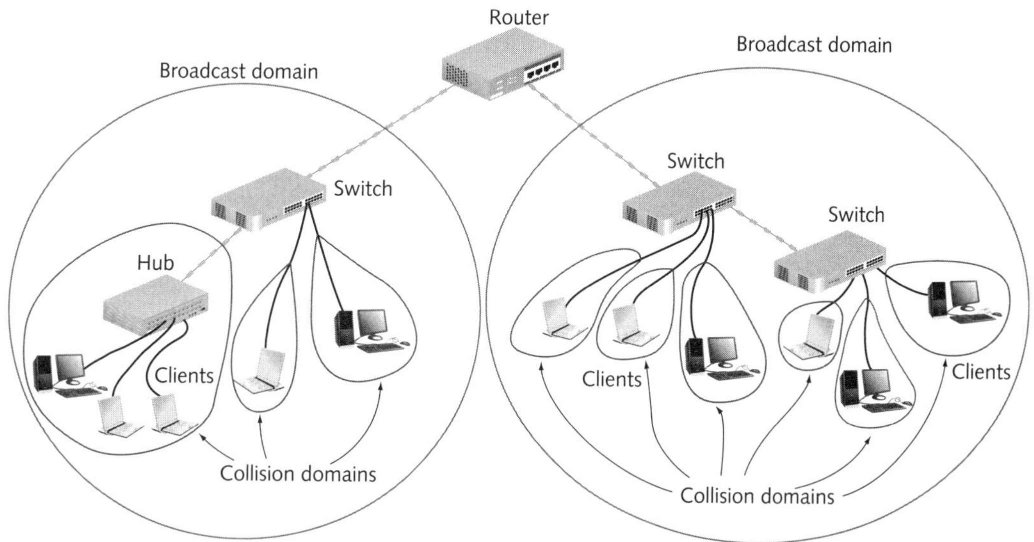

Figure 5-13 Broadcast domains and collision domains

Collision domains play a role in the Ethernet cabling distance limitations. For example, if two nodes on the same segment are positioned beyond the maximum recommended segment length, data propagation delays will be too long for CSMA/CD to be effective. A **data propagation**

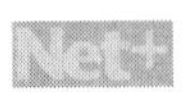

delay is the length of time data take to travel from one point on the segment to another point. When data take a long time, CSMA/CD's collision detection routine cannot identify collisions
1.4 3.7 accurately. In other words, one node on the segment might begin its CSMA/CD routine and determine that the channel is free even though a second node has begun transmitting because the second node's data are taking so long to reach the first node.

At rates of 100 or 1000 Mbps, data travel so quickly that NICs can't always keep up with the collision detection and retransmission routines. For example, because of the speed employed on a 100-Mbps Ethernet network, the window of time for the NIC to both detect and compensate for the error is much less than that of a 10-Mbps network. To minimize undetected collisions, 100-Mbps networks can support only a maximum of three network segments connected with two repeating devices, such as hubs, whereas 10-Mbps buses can support a maximum of five network segments connected with four repeating devices. This shorter path reduces the highest potential propagation delay between nodes. Although it's important to know about limitations related to repeating devices, practically speaking, today's enterprise networks, which use switches and routers, will rarely be affected by these limitations.

Ethernet Standards for Copper Cable

3.7 Recall that IEEE Physical layer standards specify how signals are transmitted to the media. The following sections describe the standards for several types of Ethernet networks. Bear in mind that the technologies described by IEEE standards differ significantly in how they encode signals at the Physical layer. The specifics of encoding methods are beyond the scope of this book. However, encoding methods affect a standard's maximum throughput, segment length, and wiring requirements—and these are the details you need to understand for designing networks and installing cable.

In Ethernet technology, the most common theoretical maximum data transfer rates are 10 Mbps, 100 Mbps, 1 Gbps, and 10 Gbps. Actual data transfer rates on a network will vary, just as you might average 22 miles per gallon (mpg) driving your car to work and back, even though the manufacturer rates the car's gas mileage at 28 mpg.

10Base-T 10Base-T was a popular Ethernet networking standard that replaced the older Thicknet and Thinnet technologies. In 10Base-T, the *10* represents its maximum throughput of *10 Mbps*, the *Base* indicates that it uses *baseband transmission*, and the *T* stands for *twisted pair*, the medium it uses. On a 10Base-T network, one pair of wires in the UTP cable is used for transmission, while a second pair of wires is used for reception. These two pairs of wires allow 10Base-T networks to provide full-duplex transmission. A 10Base-T network requires Cat 3 or better UTP.

Nodes on a 10Base-T Ethernet network connect to a central network device in a star fashion. As is typical of a star topology, a single network cable connects only two devices. This characteristic makes 10Base-T networks more fault tolerant than older networks that used the bus topology. Use of the star topology also makes 10Base-T networks easier to troubleshoot because you can isolate problems more readily when every device has a separate connection to the LAN.

Net+ 3.7 10Base-T follows the **5-4-3 rule** of networking. This rule says that, between two communicating nodes, the network cannot contain more than five network segments connected by four repeating devices, and no more than three of the segments may be populated (at least two must be unpopulated). The maximum distance that a 10Base-T segment can traverse is 100 meters. To go beyond that distance, Ethernet star segments must be connected by additional connectivity devices to form more complex topologies. This arrangement can connect a maximum of five sequential network segments, for an overall distance between communicating nodes of 500 meters. Figure 5-14 depicts a 10Base-T Ethernet network with maximum segment lengths.

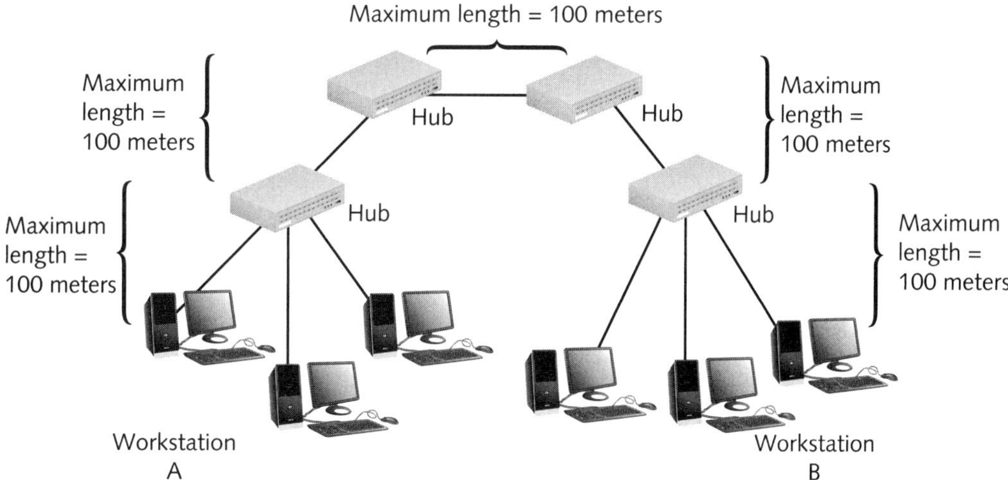

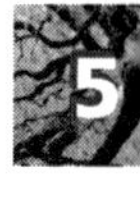

Figure 5-14 A 10Base-T network

100Base-T (Fast Ethernet) As networks expanded and handled heavier traffic, Ethernet's long-standing 10-Mbps limitation proved a bottleneck. The need for faster LANs that could use the same infrastructure as the popular 10Base-T technology was met by 100Base-T, also known as **Fast Ethernet**. 100Base-T, specified in the IEEE **802.3u** standard, enables LANs to run at a 100-Mbps data transfer rate, a tenfold increase from that provided by 10Base-T, without requiring a significant investment in new infrastructure. 100Base-T uses baseband transmission and the same star topology as 10Base-T. It also uses the same RJ-45 modular connectors. Depending on the type of 100Base-T technology used, it may require Cat 3, Cat 5, or better UTP.

As with 10Base-T, nodes on a 100Base-T network are configured in a star topology. However, unlike 10-Mbps Ethernet networks, 100Base-T networks do not follow the 5-4-3 rule. Because of their faster response requirements, to avoid data errors they require communicating nodes to be even closer. 100Base-T buses can support a maximum of three network segments connected with two repeating devices. Each segment length is limited to 100 meters. Thus, the overall maximum length between nodes is limited to 300 meters, as shown in Figure 5-15.

Net+
3.7

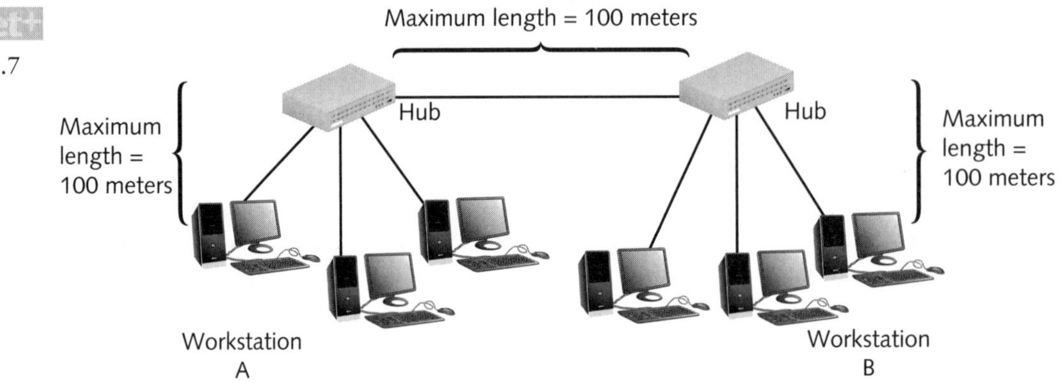

Figure 5-15 A 100Base-T network

The most common standard for achieving 100-Mbps throughput over twisted pair is **100Base-TX**. Compared with 10Base-T, it sends signals 10 times faster and condenses the time between digital pulses as well as the time a station must wait and listen for a signal. 100Base-TX requires Cat 5 or better unshielded twisted pair cabling. Within the cable, it uses the same two pairs of wire for transmitting and receiving data that 10Base-T uses. Therefore, like 10Base-T, 100Base-TX is also capable of full-duplex transmission. Full duplexing can potentially double the effective bandwidth of a 100Base-T network to 200 Mbps.

1000Base-T Because of increasing volumes of data and numbers of users who need to access this data quickly, even 100 Mbps has not met the throughput demands of many networks. Ethernet technologies designed to transmit data at 1 Gbps are collectively known as **Gigabit Ethernet. 1000Base-T** is a standard for achieving throughputs 10 times faster than Fast Ethernet over copper cable, as described in IEEE's **802.3ab** standard. In *1000Base-TX, 1000* represents *1000 megabits per second (Mbps),* or 1 gigabit per second (Gbps). *Base* indicates that it uses *baseband transmission*, and *T* indicates that it relies on *twisted pair wiring.*

1000Base-T achieves its higher throughput by using all four pairs of wires in a Cat 5 or better cable to both transmit and receive signals, whereas 100Base-T uses only two of the four pairs. 1000Base-T also uses a different data encoding scheme than 100Base-T networks use. However, the standards can be combined on the same network and you can purchase NICs that support 10 Mbps, 100 Mbps, and 1 Gbps via the same connector jack. Because of this compatibility, and the fact that 1000Base-T can use existing Cat 5 cabling, the 1-gigabit technology can be added gradually to an existing 100-Mbps network with minimal interruption of service. The maximum segment length on a 1000Base-T network is 100 meters. It allows for only one repeater. Therefore, the maximum distance between communicating nodes on a 1000Base-T network is 200 meters.

10GBase-T In 2006, IEEE released its **802.3an** standard for transmitting 10 Gbps over twisted pair, **10GBase-T**. This standard was a breakthrough in pushing the limits of the twisted pair medium. To achieve such dramatic data transmission rates, however, 10GBase-T segments require Cat 6, Cat 6a, or Cat 7 cabling. Still, as with other twisted pair Ethernet standards, the maximum segment length for 10GBase-T is 100 meters. The primary benefit of the 10GBase-T

Net+ 3.7 standard is that it makes very fast data transmission available at a much lower cost than using fiber-optic cable. 10GBase-T would probably not be used to connect two office locations across town because of its distance limitations. However, it could be used to connect network devices or to connect servers or workstations to a LAN. This type of implementation would easily allow the use of converged services, such as video and voice, at every desktop.

Yet long before IEEE developed a 10GBase-T standard for twisted pair cable, it had established standards for achieving high data rates over fiber-optic cable. In fact, fiber optic is the best medium for delivering high throughput. The following section details the IEEE standards that apply to these high-speed networks.

Ethernet Standards for Fiber-Optic Cable

100Base-FX The **100Base-FX** standard specifies a network capable of 100-Mbps throughput that uses baseband transmission and fiber-optic cabling. 100Base-FX requires multimode fiber containing at least two strands of fiber. In half-duplex mode, one strand is used for data transmission while the other strand is used for reception. In full-duplex implementations, both strands are used for both sending and receiving data. 100Base-FX has a maximum segment length of 412 meters if half-duplex transmission is used and 2000 meters if full-duplex is used. The standard allows for a maximum of one repeater to connect segments. The 100Base-FX standard uses a star topology, with its repeaters connected in a bus fashion.

100Base-FX, like 100Base-T, is also considered Fast Ethernet and is described in IEEE's 802.3u standard. Organizations switching, or migrating, from UTP to fiber media can combine 100Base-TX and 100Base-FX within one network. To do this, transceivers (for example, NICs) in computers and connectivity devices must have both RJ-45 and SC, ST, LC, or MT-RJ ports. Alternatively, a 100Base-TX to 100Base-FX media converter may be used at any point in the network to interconnect the different media and convert the signals of one standard to signals that work with the other standard.

1000Base-LX IEEE has specified three different types of 1000Base, or 1-gigabit, Ethernet technologies for use over fiber-optic cable in its **802.3z** standard.

Probably the most common 1-gigabit Ethernet standard in use today is **1000Base-LX.** The *1000* in 1000Base-LX stands for *1000-Mbps*—or 1-Gbps—throughput. *Base* stands for *baseband transmission,* and *LX* represents its reliance on *long* wavelengths of 1300 nanometers. (A nanometer equals 0.000000001 meters, or about the width of six carbon atoms in a row.) 1000Base-LX has a longer reach than any other 1-gigabit technology available today. It relies on either single-mode or multimode fiber. With multimode fiber (62.5 microns in diameter), the maximum segment length is 550 meters. When used with single-mode fiber (8 microns in diameter), 1000Base-LX can reach 5000 meters. 1000Base-LX networks can use one repeater between segments. Because of its potential length, 1000Base-LX is *an* excellent choice for long backbones—connecting buildings in a MAN, for example, or connecting an ISP with its telecommunications carrier.

1000Base-SX **1000Base-SX** is similar to 1000Base-LX in that it has a maximum throughput of 1 Gbps. However, it relies on only multimode fiber-optic cable as its medium. This makes it less expensive to install than 1000Base-LX. Another difference is that 1000Base-SX uses short wavelengths of 850 nanometers—thus, the *SX,* which stands for *short.* The maximum segment length for 1000Base-SX depends on two things: the diameter of the fiber and the modal bandwidth used to transmit signals. **Modal bandwidth** is a measure of the highest frequency of

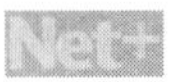

3.7 signal a multimode fiber can support over a specific distance and is measured in MHz-km. It is related to the distortion that occurs when multiple pulses of light, although issued at the same time, arrive at the end of a fiber at slightly different times. The higher the modal bandwidth, the longer a multimode fiber can carry a signal reliably.

When used with fibers whose diameters are 50 microns each, and with the highest possible modal bandwidth, the maximum segment length on a 1000Base-SX network is 550 meters. When used with fibers whose diameters are 62.5 microns each, and with the highest possible modal bandwidth, the maximum segment length is 275 meters. Only one repeater may be used between segments. Therefore, 1000Base-SX is best suited for shorter network runs than 1000Base-LX—for example, connecting a data center with a telecommunications closet in an office building.

10-Gigabit Fiber-Optic Standards

As you have learned, the throughput potential for fiber-optic cable is extraordinary, and engineers continue to push its limits. In 2002, IEEE published its **802.3ae** standard for fiber-optic Ethernet networks transmitting data at 10 Gbps. Several variations were described by the standard, but all share some characteristics in common. For example, all of the fiber-optic 10-gigabit options rely on a star topology and allow for only one repeater. (As you will learn in later chapters, however, switches, and not repeaters, are more commonly used with high-speed data links.) In addition, all 10-gigabit standards operate under full-duplex mode only. The 10-gigabit fiber-optic standards differ significantly in the wavelength of light each uses to issue signals and, as a result, their maximum allowable segment length differs also.

10GBase-SR and 10GBase-SW The 10-gigabit options with the shortest segment length are **10GBase-SR** and **10GBase-SW**. By now you can guess that the *10G* stands for the standard's maximum throughput of *10 gigabits per second* and *Base* stands for *baseband transmission. S* stands for *short reach.* The fact that one of the standards ends with *R* and the other ends with *W* reflects the type of Physical layer encoding each uses. Simply put, 10GBase-SR is designed to work with fiber connections on LANs, and 10GBase-SW is designed to work with WAN links that use a highly reliable fiber-optic ring technology called SONET. You'll learn more about SONET in Chapter 7.

10GBase-SR and 10GBase-SW rely on multimode fiber and transmit signals with wavelengths of 850 nanometers. As with the 1-gigabit standards, the maximum segment length on a 10GBase-SR or 10GBase-SW network depends on the diameter of the fibers used. It also depends on the modal bandwidth used. For example, if 50-micron fiber is used with the maximum possible modal bandwidth, the maximum segment length is 300 meters. If 62.5-micron fiber is used with the maximum possible modal bandwidth, a 10GBase-SR or 10GBase-SW segment can be 66 meters long. Either way, this 10-gigabit Ethernet technology is best suited for connections within a data center or building, as its distance is the most limited.

10GBase-LR and 10GBase-LW Another standard defined in IEEE 802.3ae is **10GBase-LR** and **10GBase-LW**, in which the *10G* stands for *10 gigabits per second, Base* stands for *baseband transmission,* and *L* stands for *long reach.* 10GBase-LR and 10GBase-LW networks carry signals with wavelengths of 1310 nanometers through single-mode fiber. Their maximum segment length is 10,000 meters. As is the case with the previously described 10-gigabit standard, in 10GBase-LW the *W* reflects its unique method of encoding that allows it to work over SONET WAN links. 10GBase-LR and 10GBase-LW technology is suited to WAN or MAN implementations.

3.7 **10GBase-ER and 10GBase-EW** For the longest fiber-optic segments, network administrators choose **10GBase-ER** or **10GBase-EW**. In this standard, *E* stands for *extended reach*. 10GBase-ER and 10GBase-EW require single-mode fiber, through which they transmit signals with wavelengths of 1550 nanometers. These standards allow for segments up to 40,000 meters, or nearly 25 miles, long. The 10GBase-EW standard specifies encoding that makes it compatible with the SONET transmission format. Given their long-distance capabilities, 10GBase-ER and 10GBase-EW are best suited for use on WANs.

NSPs and ISPs use 10-gigabit Ethernet where traffic is aggregated and customers demand fast data transfer. As with any new technology, however, when 10-gigabit Ethernet becomes more economical, more organizations will adopt it for their WANs and LANs. Even faster Ethernet networks are on the way. IEEE has recently ratified standards for 40- and 100-gigabit Ethernet.

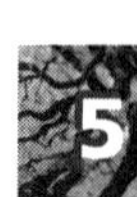

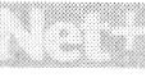

Summary of Common Ethernet Standards

3.7

To obtain Network+ certification, you must be familiar with the different characteristics and limitations of each type of network discussed in this chapter. To put this information in context, Table 5-1 summarizes the characteristics and limitations for common Physical layer networking standards, including Ethernet networks that use twisted pair cable and fiber-optic cable. In addition to the varying specifications below, remember that all of these standards rely on a star or star-bus hybrid network topology.

Table 5-1 Common Ethernet standards

Standard	Maximum transmission speed (Mbps)	Maximum distance per segment (m)	Physical media
10Base-T	10	100	Cat 3 or better UTP
100Base-TX	100	100	Cat 5 or better UTP
1000Base-T	1000	100	Cat 5 or better UTP (Cat 5e is preferred)
10GBase-T	10,000	100	Cat 6 or Cat 7 (preferred)
100Base-FX	100	2000	MMF
1000Base-LX	1000	550 5000	MMF SMF
1000Base-SX	1000	Up to 550, depending on modal bandwidth and fiber core diameter	MMF
10GBase-SR and 10GBase-SW	10,000	Up to 300, depending on modal bandwidth and fiber core diameter	MMF
10GBase-LR and 10GBase-LW	10,000	10,000	SMF
10GBase-ER and 10GBase-EW	10,000	40,000	SMF

Net+ 3.7

In this chapter, you have learned about several varieties of Ethernet as well as their throughputs, distances, and media requirements. You should recognize that multiple Ethernet specifications may be found on a single LAN. For example, one switch might serve a number of clients with Fast Ethernet (100Base-T), while the routers that form the LAN's backbone might communicate over 1-gigabit Ethernet (1000Base-T). On a WAN, even more varieties might be used. For example, two NSPs might exchange a high volume of traffic using 10-gigabit Ethernet. That level of service, characterized by very high throughput and reliability, is commonly called **Carrier Ethernet**. Specifications for Carrier Ethernet include techniques for exceeding the normal 10-gigabit distance limitations shown in Table 5-1. Detailing these techniques is beyond the scope of this book, however.

Figure 5-16 provides a simplified example of how more than one type of Ethernet may be used on a network. Note that the connections between the company and its ISP and between the ISP and its NSP are identified, generically, as WAN links. After reading Chapter 7, you'll understand what type of links might fit there.

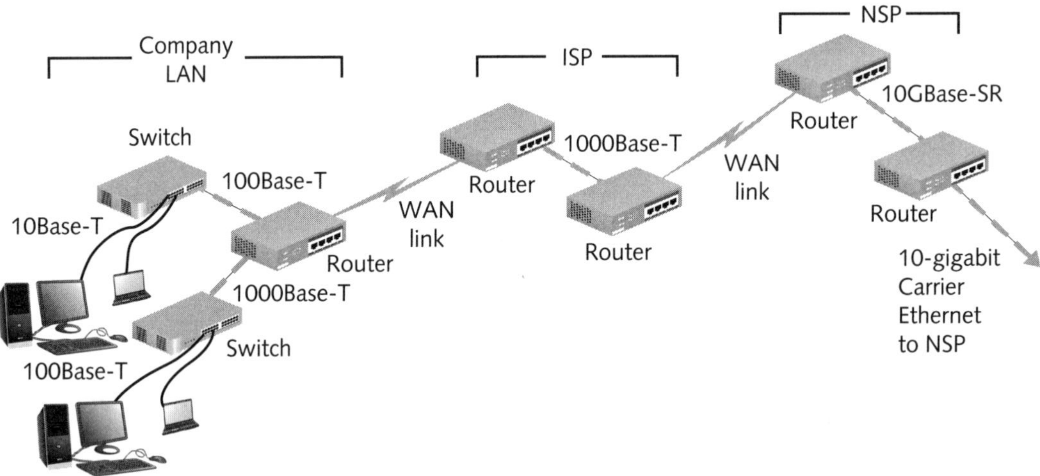

Figure 5-16 Multiple types of Ethernet on a WAN

Ethernet Frames

Chapter 2 introduced you to data frames, the packages that carry higher-layer data and control information that enable data to reach their destinations without errors and in the correct sequence. Ethernet networks may use any of four kinds of data frames: Ethernet_802.2 (Raw), Ethernet_802.3 (Novell proprietary), Ethernet II (DIX), and Ethernet_SNAP. This variety of Ethernet frame types came about as different organizations released and revised Ethernet standards during the 1980s, changing as LAN technology evolved. Each frame type differs slightly in the way it codes and decodes packets of data traveling from one device to another.

Physical layer standards, such as 100Base-T, have no effect on the type of framing that occurs in the Data Link layer. Thus, Ethernet frame types have no relation to the topology or cabling characteristics of the network. Framing also takes place independently of the higher-level layers. Theoretically, all frame types could carry any one of many higher-layer protocols. But as you'll learn in the following discussion, not all frame types are well suited to carrying all kinds of traffic.

Using and Configuring Frames

A node's Data Link layer services must be properly configured to expect the types of frames it might receive. You can use multiple frame types on a network, but a node configured to use only one frame type cannot communicate with another node that uses a different frame type. If a node receives an unfamiliar frame type, it will not be able to decode the data contained in the frame, nor will it be able to communicate with nodes configured to use that frame type. For this reason, it is important for LAN administrators to ensure that all devices use the same, correct frame type. These days, virtually all networks use the Ethernet II frame type. But in the 1990s, before this uniformity evolved, the use of different NOSs or legacy hardware often required managing devices to interpret multiple frame types.

Frame types can be specified through a device's NIC configuration software. To make matters easier, most NICs can automatically sense what types of frames are running on a network and adjust themselves to that specification. This feature is called autodetect, or autosense. Workstations, networked printers, and servers added to an existing network can all take advantage of autodetection. Even if your devices use the autodetect feature, you should nevertheless know what frame types are running on your network so that you can troubleshoot connectivity problems.

Frame Fields

All Ethernet frame types share many fields in common. For example, every Ethernet frame contains a 7-byte preamble and a 1-byte start-of-frame delimiter. The **preamble** signals to the receiving node that data are incoming and indicates when the data flow is about to begin. The **SFD (start-of-frame delimiter)** identifies where the data field begins. Preambles and SFDs are not included, however, when calculating a frame's total size.

Each Ethernet frame also contains a 14-byte header, which includes a destination address, a source address, and an additional field that varies in function and size, depending on the frame type. The destination address and source address fields are each 6 bytes long. The destination address identifies the recipient of the data frame, and the source address identifies the network node that originally sent the data. Recall that any network device can be identified by its physical address, also known as a hardware address or MAC (Media Access Control) address. The source address and destination address fields of an Ethernet frame use the MAC address to identify where data originated and where it should be delivered.

Also, all Ethernet frames contain a 4-byte FCS (frame check sequence) field. Recall that the function of the FCS field is to ensure that the data at the destination exactly match the data issued from the source using the CRC (cyclic redundancy check) algorithm. Together, the FCS and the header make up the 18-byte "frame" for the data. The data portion of an Ethernet frame may contain from 46 to 1500 bytes of information (and recall that this includes the Network layer datagram). If fewer than 46 bytes of data are supplied by the higher layers, the source node fills out the data portion with extra bytes until it totals 46 bytes. The extra bytes are known as **padding** and have no significance other than to fill out the frame. They do not affect the data being transmitted.

Adding the 18-byte framing portion plus the smallest possible data field of 46 bytes equals the minimum Ethernet frame size of 64 bytes. Adding the framing portion plus the largest possible data field of 1500 bytes equals the maximum Ethernet frame size of 1518 bytes. No matter what frame type is used, the size range of 64 to 1518 total bytes applies to all Ethernet frames.

Because of the overhead present in each frame and the time required to perform CSMA/CD, the use of larger frame sizes on a network generally results in faster throughput. To some extent, you cannot control your network's frame sizes. You can, however, help improve network performance by properly managing frames. For example, network administrators should strive to minimize the number of broadcast frames on their networks because broadcast frames tend to be very small and, therefore, inefficient. Also, running more than one frame type on the same network can result in inefficiencies because it requires devices to examine each incoming frame to determine its type. Given a choice, it's most efficient to support only one frame type on a network.

Ethernet II (DIX)

Ethernet II, used on virtually all modern networks, is an Ethernet frame type developed by DEC, Intel, and Xerox (abbreviated as DIX) before the IEEE began to standardize Ethernet. The Ethernet II frame type (or DIX, as it is sometimes called) is distinguished by other Ethernet frame types in that it contains a 2-byte type field. This type field identifies the Network layer protocol (such as IP or ARP) contained in the frame. For example, if a frame were carrying an IP datagram, its type field would contain 0x0800, the type code for IP.

Because of its support for multiple Network layer protocols and because it uses fewer bytes as overhead than other frame types, Ethernet II is the type most commonly used on contemporary Ethernet networks. Figure 5-17 depicts an Ethernet II frame.

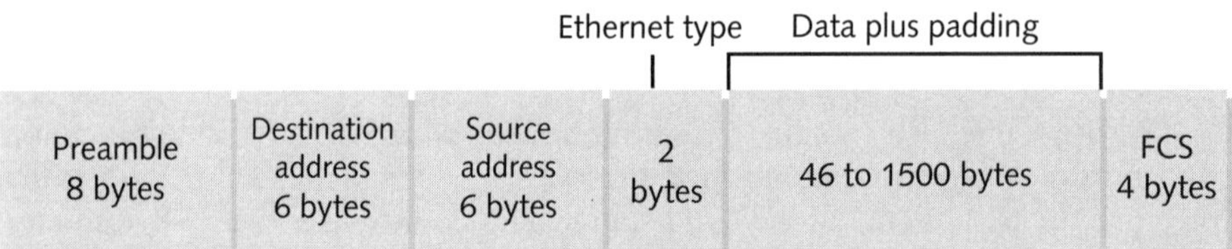

Figure 5-17 Ethernet II (DIX) frame

PoE (Power over Ethernet)

Net+ 2.1 In 2003, IEEE released its **802.3af** standard, which specifies a method for supplying electrical power over Ethernet connections, also known as **PoE** (**Power over Ethernet**). Although the standard is relatively new, the concept is not. In fact, your home telephone receives power from the telephone company over the lines that enter your residence. This power is necessary for dial tone and ringing. On an Ethernet network, carrying power over signaling connections can be useful for nodes that are far from traditional power receptacles or need a constant, reliable power source. For example, a wireless access point at an outdoor theater, a telephone used to receive digitized voice signals, an Internet gaming station in the center of a mall, or a critical router at the core of a network's backbone can all benefit from PoE.

The PoE standard specifies two types of devices: PSE (power sourcing equipment) and PDs (powered devices). **PSE (power sourcing equipment)** refers to the device that supplies the

power; usually this device depends on backup power sources (in other words, not the electrical grid maintained by utilities). **PDs (powered devices)** are those that receive the power from
2.1 the PSE. PoE requires Cat 5 or better copper cable. In the cable, electric current may run over an unused pair of wires or over the pair of wires used for data transmission in a 10Base-T, 100Base-TX, 1000Base-T, or 10GBase-T network. The standard allows for both approaches; however, on a single network, the choice of current-carrying pairs should be consistent between all PSE and PDs.

Not all connectivity devices are capable of issuing power. To use PoE, you must purchase a switch or router that supports it, like the switch shown in Figure 5-18. Also, not all end nodes are capable of receiving PoE. The IEEE standard has accounted for that possibility by requiring all PSE to first determine whether a node is PoE-capable before attempting to supply it with power. That means that PoE is compatible with current 802.3 installations.

Figure 5-18 PoE-capable switch

On networks that demand PoE but don't have PoE-capable equipment, you can add PoE adapters, like the ones shown in Figure 5-19. One type of adapter connects to a switch or router to allow it to supply power. The other adapter attaches to a client, such as an outdoor camera, to receive power over the Ethernet connection.

Figure 5-19 PoE adapters

Chapter Summary

- A physical topology is the basic physical layout of a network's media, nodes, and connectivity devices. Physical topologies are categorized into three fundamental shapes: bus, ring, and star.
- A bus topology consists of a single cable connecting all nodes on a network without intervening connectivity devices. At either end of a bus network, 50-ohm resistors (terminators) stop signals after they have reached their destination. Without terminators, signals on a bus network experience signal bounce and LAN performance suffers. Modern networks do not use a pure bus topology.
- In a ring topology, each node is connected to the two nearest nodes so that the entire network forms a circle. Data are transmitted in one direction around the ring. Each workstation accepts and responds to packets addressed to it, then forwards the other packets to the next workstation in the ring.
- In a star topology, every node on the network is connected through a central device, such as a switch or router. Any single cable on a star network connects only two devices, so a cabling problem will affect only two nodes. A source node transmits data to a connectivity device, which then retransmits the information to the rest of the network segment where the destination node can pick it up.
- Star topology networks are more fault tolerant than bus topology networks because a failure in one part of the network will not necessarily affect transmission on the entire network.
- Few LANs use the simple physical topologies in their pure form. More often, LANs employ a hybrid of more than one simple physical topology. The star-wired ring topology uses the physical layout of a star and the token-passing data transmission method. Data are sent around the star in a circular pattern. Token ring networks, as specified in IEEE 802.5, use this hybrid topology.
- In a star-wired bus topology, groups of workstations are star-connected to connectivity devices and then networked via a single bus. This design can cover longer distances than a simple star topology and easily interconnect or isolate different network segments. The star-wired bus topology commonly forms the basis for Ethernet and Fast Ethernet networks.
- Switches, routers, or hubs that service star-wired bus or star-wired ring topologies can be daisy-chained to form a more complex hybrid topology. However, daisy chains of repeating devices can only extend a network so far before data errors are apt to occur. In this case, maximum segment and network length limits must be carefully maintained.
- Network logical topologies describe how signals travel over a network. The two main types of logical topologies are bus and ring. Ethernet networks use a bus logical topology, and token ring networks use a ring logical topology.
- Network backbones may follow serial, distributed, collapsed, or parallel topologies. In a serial topology, two or more internetworking devices are connected to each other by a single cable in a daisy chain. This is the simplest type of backbone.

- A distributed backbone consists of a number of intermediate connectivity devices connected to one or more central devices in a hierarchy. This topology allows for easy network management and scalability.
- The collapsed backbone topology uses a router or switch as the single central connection point for multiple subnetworks. This is risky because an entire network could fail if the central device fails. Also, if the central connectivity device becomes overtaxed, performance on the entire network suffers.
- A parallel backbone is a variation of the collapsed backbone arrangement that consists of more than one connection from the central router or switch to each network segment and parallel connections between routers and switches, if more than one is present. Parallel backbones are the most expensive, but also the most fault-tolerant, type of backbone.

- Switching manages the filtering and forwarding of packets between nodes on a network. Every network relies on one or more types of switching, including circuit switching, packet switching, or MPLS (multiprotocol label switching).
- Packet switching separates data into packets before they are transported. Packets can travel any path on the network to their destination and attempt to find the fastest circuit available at any instant. They need not follow the same path, nor must they arrive at their destination in the same sequence as when they left their source.
- MPLS (multiprotocol label switching) enables multiple types of Layer 3 protocols to travel over any one of several connection-oriented Layer 2 protocols. In MPLS, the first router that receives a packet adds one or more labels to the Layer 3 datagram in a shim. Then the network's Layer 2 protocol header is added. MPLS offers potentially faster transmission with better quality of service guarantees.
- Ethernet employs a network access method called CSMA/CD (Carrier Sense Multiple Access with Collision Detection). All Ethernet networks, independent of their speed or frame type, use CSMA/CD.
- On heavily trafficked Ethernet segments, collisions are common. The more nodes that are transmitting data on a network segment, the more collisions will take place. When an Ethernet segment grows to a particular number of nodes, performance may suffer as a result of collisions.
- A collision domain is the portion of a network where collisions occur if two nodes transmit data at the same time. Repeaters, which simply regenerate signals they receive, repeat collisions, too. Thus, connecting multiple segments with repeaters results in a larger collision domain. Switches and routers, however, separate collision domains.
- Using switches enables network managers to separate a network segment into smaller logical segments, each independent of the other and supporting its own traffic. The use of switched Ethernet increases the effective bandwidth of a network segment because at any given time fewer workstations vie for the access to a shared channel.
- 10Base-T is a Physical layer specification for an Ethernet network that is capable of 10-Mbps throughput and uses baseband transmission and twisted pair media. It has a maximum segment length of 100 meters. It follows the 5-4-3 rule, which allows up to five segments between two communicating nodes, permits up to four repeating devices, and allows up to three of the segments to be populated.

- 100Base-T (also called Fast Ethernet) is a Physical layer specification for an Ethernet network that is capable of 100-Mbps throughput and uses baseband transmission and twisted pair media. It has a maximum segment length of 100 meters and allows up to three segments connected by two repeating devices.
- 1000Base-T (also called Gigabit Ethernet) is a Physical layer specification for an Ethernet network that is capable of 1000-Mbps (1-Gbps) throughput and uses baseband transmission and twisted pair media. It has a maximum segment length of 100 meters and allows only one repeating device between segments.
- 10GBase-T is Physical layer specification for transmitting 10 Gbps over twisted pair cable. It relies on Cat 6 or better wiring and has a maximum segment length of 100 meters.
- 100Base-FX is a Physical layer specification for a network that can achieve 100-Mbps throughput using baseband transmission running on multimode fiber. Its maximum segment length is 2000 meters.
- 1-Gbps Physical layer standards for fiber-optic networks include 1000Base-SX and 1000Base-LX. Because 1000Base-LX reaches farther and uses a longer wavelength, it is the more popular of the two. 1000Base-LX can use either single-mode or multimode fiber-optic cable; its segments can be up to 550 or 5000 meters, respectively. 1000Base-SX uses only multimode fiber and can span up to 550 meters, depending on modal bandwidth and fiber core diameter.
- 10-Gbps Physical layer standards include 10GBase-SR and 10GBase-SW (short reach), which rely on multimode fiber-optic cable and can span a maximum of 300 meters; 10GBase-LR and 10GBase-LW (long reach), which rely on single-mode fiber and can span a maximum of 10,000 meters; and 10GBaseER and 10GBase-EW (extended reach), which also use single-mode fiber and can span up to 40,000 meters. Standards marked with a *W* mean they are specially encoded to operate over SONET links.
- Networks may use one (or a combination) of four kinds of Ethernet data frames. Each frame type differs slightly in the way it codes and decodes packets of data from one device to another. Most modern networks rely on Ethernet II (DIX) frames.

Key Terms

10Base-T A Physical layer standard for networks that specifies baseband transmission, twisted pair media, and 10-Mbps throughput. 10Base-T networks have a maximum segment length of 100 meters and rely on a star topology.

10GBase-ER A Physical layer standard for achieving 10-Gbps data transmission over single-mode, fiber-optic cable. In 10GBase-ER, the *ER* stands for *extended reach*. This standard specifies a star topology and segment lengths up to 40,000 meters.

10GBase-EW A variation of the 10GBase-ER standard that is specially encoded to operate over SONET links.

10GBase-LR A Physical layer standard for achieving 10-Gbps data transmission over single-mode, fiber-optic cable using wavelengths of 1310 nanometers. In 10GBase-LR, the *LR* stands for *long reach*. This standard specifies a star topology and segment lengths up to 10,000 meters.

10GBase-LW A variation of the 10GBase-LR standard that is specially encoded to operate over SONET links.

10GBase-SR A Physical layer standard for achieving 10-Gbps data transmission over multimode fiber using wavelengths of 850 nanometers. The maximum segment length for 10GBase-SR can reach up to 300 meters, depending on the fiber core diameter and modal bandwidth used.

10GBase-SW A variation of the 10GBase-SR standard that is specially encoded to operate over SONET links.

10GBase-T A Physical layer standard for achieving 10-Gbps data transmission over twisted pair cable. Described in its 2006 standard 802.3an, IEEE specifies Cat 6 or Cat 7 cable as the appropriate medium for 10GBase-T. The maximum segment length for 10GBase-T is 100 meters.

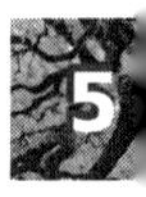

100Base-FX A Physical layer standard for networks that specifies baseband transmission, multimode fiber cabling, and 100-Mbps throughput. 100Base-FX networks have a maximum segment length of 2000 meters. 100Base-FX may also be called Fast Ethernet.

100Base-T A Physical layer standard for networks that specifies baseband transmission, twisted pair cabling, and 100-Mbps throughput. 100Base-T networks have a maximum segment length of 100 meters and use the star topology. 100Base-T is also known as Fast Ethernet.

100Base-TX A type of 100Base-T network that uses two wire pairs in a twisted pair cable, but uses faster signaling to achieve 100-Mbps throughput. It is capable of full-duplex transmission and requires Cat 5 or better twisted pair media.

1000Base-LX A Physical layer standard for networks that specifies 1-Gbps transmission over fiber-optic cable using baseband transmission. 1000Base-LX can run on either single-mode or multimode fiber. The *LX* represents its reliance on long wavelengths of 1300 nanometers. 1000Base-LX can extend to 5000-meter segment lengths using single-mode, fiber-optic cable. 1000Base-LX networks can use one repeater between segments.

1000Base-SX A Physical layer standard for networks that specifies 1-Gbps transmission over fiber-optic cable using baseband transmission. 1000Base-SX runs on multimode fiber. Its maximum segment length is 550 meters. The *SX* represents its reliance on short wavelengths of 850 nanometers. 1000Base-SX can use one repeater.

1000Base-T A Physical layer standard for achieving 1 Gbps over UTP. 1000Base-T achieves its higher throughput by using all four pairs of wires in a Cat 5 or better twisted pair cable to both transmit and receive signals. 1000Base-T also uses a different data encoding scheme than that used by other UTP Physical layer specifications.

5-4-3 rule A guideline for 10-Mbps Ethernet networks stating that between two communicating nodes, the network cannot contain more than five network segments connected by four repeating devices, and no more than three of the segments may be populated.

802.3ab The IEEE standard that describes 1000Base-T, a 1-gigabit Ethernet technology that runs over four pairs of Cat 5 or better cable.

802.3ae The IEEE standard that describes 10-gigabit Ethernet technologies, including 10GBase-SR, 10GBase-SW, 10GBase-LR, 10GBase-LW, 10GBase-ER, and 10GBase-EW.

802.3af The IEEE standard that specifies a way of supplying electrical Power over Ethernet (PoE). 802.3af requires Cat 5 or better UTP or STP cabling and uses power sourcing equipment to supply current over a wire pair to powered devices. PoE is compatible with existing 10Base-T, 100Base-TX, 1000Base-T, and 10GBase-T implementations.

802.3an The IEEE standard that describes 10GBase-T, a 10-Gbps Ethernet technology that runs on Cat 6 or Cat 7 twisted pair cable.

802.3u The IEEE standard that describes Fast Ethernet technologies, including 100Base-TX.

802.3z The IEEE standard that describes 1000Base (or 1-gigabit) Ethernet technologies, including 1000Base-LX and 1000Base-SX.

access method A network's method of controlling how nodes access the communications channel. For example, CSMA/CD (Carrier Sense Multiple Access with Collision Detection) is the access method specified in the IEEE 802.3 (Ethernet) standard.

active topology A topology in which each workstation participates in transmitting data over the network. A ring topology is considered an active topology.

broadcast domain Logically grouped network nodes that can communicate directly via broadcast transmissions. By default, switches and repeating devices such as hubs extend broadcast domains. Routers and other Layer 3 devices separate broadcast domains.

bus The single cable connecting all devices in a bus topology.

bus topology A topology in which a single cable connects all nodes on a network without intervening connectivity devices.

Carrier Ethernet A level of Ethernet service that is characterized by very high throughput and reliability and is used between carriers, such as NSPs.

Carrier Sense Multiple Access with Collision Detection *See* CSMA/CD.

circuit switching A type of switching in which a connection is established between two network nodes before they begin transmitting data. Bandwidth is dedicated to this connection and remains available until users terminate the communication between the two nodes.

collapsed backbone A type of backbone that uses a router or switch as the single central connection point for multiple subnetworks.

collision In Ethernet networks, the interference of one node's data transmission with the data transmission of another node sharing the same segment.

collision domain The portion of an Ethernet network in which collisions could occur if two nodes transmit data at the same time. Switches and routers separate collision domains.

CSMA/CD (Carrier Sense Multiple Access with Collision Detection) A network access method specified for use by IEEE 802.3 (Ethernet) networks. In CSMA/CD, each node waits its turn before transmitting data to avoid interfering with other nodes' transmissions. If a node's NIC determines that its data have been involved in a collision, it immediately stops transmitting. Next, in a process called jamming, the NIC issues a special 32-bit sequence that indicates to the rest of the network nodes that its previous transmission was faulty and that those data frames are invalid. After waiting, the NIC determines if the line is again available; if it is available, the NIC retransmits its data.

daisy chain A group of connectivity devices linked together in a serial fashion.

data propagation delay The length of time data take to travel from one point on the segment to another point. On Ethernet networks, CSMA/CD's collision detection routine cannot operate accurately if the data propagation delay is too long.

distributed backbone A type of backbone in which a number of intermediate connectivity devices are connected to one or more central connectivity devices, such switches or routers, in a hierarchy.

enterprise An entire organization, including local and remote offices, a mixture of computer systems, and a number of departments. Enterprise-wide computing takes into account the breadth and diversity of a large organization's computer needs.

Ethernet II The original Ethernet frame type developed by Digital Equipment Corporation, Intel, and Xerox, before the IEEE began to standardize Ethernet. Ethernet II is distinguished from other Ethernet frame types in that it contains a 2-byte type field to identify the upper-layer protocol contained in the frame. It supports TCP/IP and other higher-layer protocols.

Fast Ethernet A type of Ethernet network that is capable of 100-Mbps throughput. 100Base-T and 100Base-FX are both examples of Fast Ethernet.

fault tolerance The capability for a component or system to continue functioning despite damage or malfunction.

Gigabit Ethernet A type of Ethernet network that is capable of 1000-Mbps, or 1-Gbps, throughput.

hybrid topology A physical topology that combines characteristics of more than one simple physical topology.

jamming A part of CSMA/CD in which, upon detecting a collision, a station issues a special 32-bit sequence to indicate to all nodes on an Ethernet segment that its previously transmitted frame has suffered a collision and should be considered faulty.

logical topology A characteristic of network transmission that reflects the way in which data are transmitted between nodes. A network's logical topology may differ from its physical topology. The most common logical topologies are bus and ring.

MPLS (multiprotocol label switching) A type of switching that enables any one of several Layer 2 protocols to carry multiple types of Layer 3 protocols. One of its benefits is the ability to use packet-switched technologies over traditionally circuit-switched networks. MPLS can also create end-to-end paths that act like circuit-switched connections.

modal bandwidth A measure of the highest frequency of signal a multimode fiber-optic cable can support over a specific distance. Modal bandwidth is measured in MHz-km.

multiprotocol label switching *See* MPLS.

packet switching A type of switching in which data are broken into packets before being transported. In packet switching, packets can travel any path on the network to their destination because each packet contains a destination address and sequencing information.

padding The bytes added to the data (or information) portion of an Ethernet frame to ensure this field is at least 46 bytes in size. Padding has no effect on the data carried by the frame.

parallel backbone A type of backbone that consists of more than one connection from the central router or switch to each network segment.

passive topology A network topology in which each node passively listens for, then accepts, data directed to it. A bus topology is considered a passive topology.

PD (powered device) On a network using Power over Ethernet, a node that receives power from power sourcing equipment.

physical topology The physical layout of the media, nodes, and devices on a network. A physical topology does not specify device types, connectivity methods, or addressing schemes. Physical topologies are categorized into three fundamental shapes: bus, ring, and star. These shapes can be mixed to create hybrid topologies.

PoE (Power over Ethernet) A method of delivering current to devices using Ethernet connection cables.

Power over Ethernet *See* PoE.

power sourcing equipment *See* PSE.

powered device *See* PD.

preamble The field in an Ethernet frame that signals to the receiving node that data are incoming and indicates when the data flow is about to begin.

PSE (power sourcing equipment) On a network using Power over Ethernet, the device that supplies power to end nodes.

QoS (quality of service) The result of specifications for guaranteeing data delivery within a certain period of time after their transmission.

quality of service *See* QoS.

ring topology A network layout in which each node is connected to the two nearest nodes so that the entire network forms a circle. Data are transmitted in one direction around the ring. Each workstation accepts and responds to packets addressed to it, then forwards the other packets to the next workstation in the ring.

serial backbone A type of backbone that consists of two or more internetworking devices connected to each other by a single cable in a daisy chain.

SFD (start-of-frame delimiter) A 1-byte field that indicates where the data field begins in an Ethernet frame.

signal bounce A phenomenon, caused by improper termination on a bus-topology network, in which signals travel endlessly between the two ends of the network, preventing new signals from getting through.

star topology A physical topology in which every node on the network is connected through a central connectivity device. Any single physical wire on a star network connects only two devices, so a cabling problem will affect only two nodes. Nodes transmit data to the device, which then retransmits the data to the rest of the network segment where the destination node can pick it up.

star-wired bus topology A hybrid topology in which groups of workstations are connected in a star fashion to connectivity devices that are networked via a single bus.

star-wired ring topology A hybrid topology that uses the physical layout of a star and the token-passing data transmission method.

start-of-frame delimiter *See* SFD.

switching A component of a network's logical topology that manages how packets are filtered and forwarded between nodes on the network.

terminator A resistor that is attached to each end of a bus-topology network and that causes the signal to stop rather than reflect back toward its source.

Review Questions

1. Which of the following describes a ring topology?
   a. A single cable connects all nodes on a network without intervening connectivity devices.
   b. Each node is connected to the two nearest nodes so that the entire network forms a circle.
   c. Every node on the network is connected through a central device, such as a hub, router, or switch.
   d. Signals follow a circular path between sender and receiver.

2. A star-wired bus is referred to as which of the following topology types?
   a. physical
   b. logical
   c. hybrid
   d. backbone
3. Which of the following has a backbone network topology that uses a router or switch as the single central connection point for multiple subnetworks?
   a. serial
   b. distributed
   c. collapsed
   d. parallel
4. What switching technique establishes a connection between two network nodes before transmitting data?
   a. Circuit switching
   b. Message switching
   c. Packet switching
   d. MPLS (Multiple Label Switching)
5. Which of the following is a 10-gigabit per second Ethernet fiber-optic standard?
   a. 10GBase-ER
   b. 10Base-T
   c. 10GBase-T
   d. 100Base-FX
6. True or false? The most common logical topologies are bus and ring.
7. True or false? A serial backbone consists of two or more devices connected to each other by a single medium in a daisy-chain fashion.
8. True or false? The most popular method for connecting nodes on a network is circuit switching.

9. True or false? On heavily trafficked Ethernet network segments, collisions are fairly common.
10. True or false? The various Ethernet standards for copper cable utilize encoding methods that affect maximum throughput, segment length, and wiring requirements.
11. A physical ________________ is the physical layout of a network's media, nodes, and connectivity devices.
12. A characteristic of network transmission that reflects the way in which data are transmitted between nodes is known as the ________________.
13. All Ethernet networks use the ________________ access method.
14. The ________________ frame type is distinguished from other Ethernet frame types in that it contains a 2-byte type field.
15. The IEEE 802.3af standard, which specifies a method for supplying electrical power over Ethernet connections, is also known as ________________.

Network Hardware, Switching, and Routing

After reading this chapter and completing the exercises, you will be able to:

- Identify the functions of LAN connectivity hardware
- Install, configure, and differentiate between network devices, such as NICs, hubs, bridges, switches, routers, and gateways
- Explain the advanced features of a switch and understand popular switching techniques, including VLAN management
- Explain the purposes and properties of routing
- Describe common IPv4 and IPv6 routing protocols

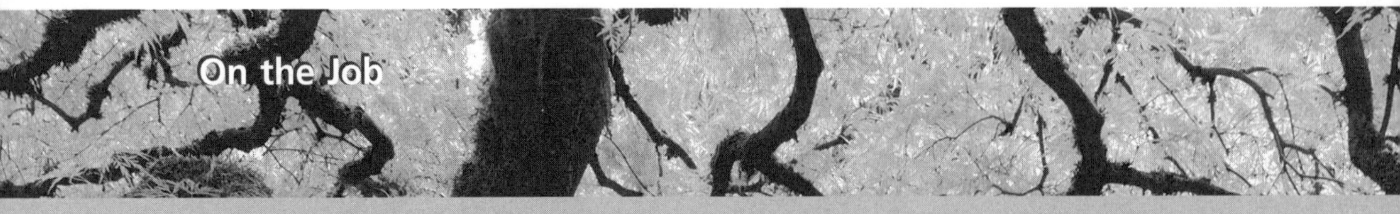

On the Job

I recently provided the technical expertise to build a new FM radio station in rural Wisconsin. In addition to specifying and installing microphones, speakers, and sound boards, I also designed and created the station's network. Within the station's building, the network connects studios, office computers, and a Voice over IP (VoIP) telephone system. Beyond the building, the network sends the station's broadcast signal to its antenna.

When I set up the radio station network, I decided to separate different kinds of network traffic. To do this, I chose to create VLANs, rather than creating multiple physical networks, for several reasons, not the least of which is the cost of acquiring and maintaining multiple network switches. Managing multiple subnets on a single device has simplified deployment and long-term maintenance.

The VLANs are set up as follows:

- VLAN 101 (IP address subnet 10.10.1.0/24) is the transmitter network.
- VLAN 201 (IP address subnet 10.20.1.0/24) is the studio network.
- VLAN 301 (IP address subnet 10.30.1.0/24) is the office network.
- VLAN 401 (IP address subnet 10.40.1.0/24) is the telephone network.

Using VLANs allows the station to keep general Internet traffic off the latency-sensitive studio subnet. The systems on the studio subnet include the audio automation players and the analog-to-digital audio encoders. These computers receive and send digital audio over the network and demand timely delivery of packets. Further, these computers do not need to access Internet resources. We chose to isolate these systems from the others using VLANs (and access lists) to help guarantee the timely delivery of audio data.

Meanwhile, placing our VoIP telephones on a separate VLAN prevents studio audio traffic, as well as the general office and Internet traffic, from interfering with the telephone system traffic.

David Klann
WDRT 91.9FM

In Chapter 3, you learned how data is transmitted. Now, you need to know how data arrives at its destination. To understand this process, it's helpful to compare data transmission with the means by which the United States Postal Service delivers mail: Mail trucks, airplanes, and delivery staff serve as the transmission system that moves information from place to place. Machines and personnel at the post office interpret addresses on the envelopes and either deliver the mail to a transfer point or to your home. Inefficiencies in mail delivery, such as letters being misdirected to the wrong transfer point, frustrate both the sender and the receiver of the mail and increase the overall cost of delivery.

In data networks, the task of directing information efficiently to the correct destination is handled by connectivity devices, primarily switches and routers. In this chapter, you will learn about these devices and their roles in managing data traffic. Material in this chapter relates mostly to functions occurring in the Data Link and Network layers of the OSI model. Some material also relates to the Physical layer. You will learn the concepts involved in moving data from place to place, including issues related to switching and routing protocols. You will also see pictures of the switches and routers that make data transfer possible. (It's important for you to have an accurate mental image of this equipment because, in a cluttered data closet, it may prove difficult to identify the hardware underneath the wiring.) In addition, you will learn more about network interface cards, which serve as the workstation's link to the network and are often the source of connectivity problems.

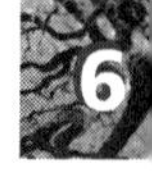

NICs (Network Interface Cards)

1.2 NICs (network interface cards, also called network adapters or network cards) enable a workstation, server, printer, connectivity device, or other node to receive and transmit data over the network media. NICs contain a transceiver, which transmits and receives data signals. As you learned in Chapter 2, NICs belong to both the Physical layer and Data Link layer of the OSI model because they issue data signals to a wire or into the air and assemble or disassemble data frames. They also interpret physical addressing information to ensure data is delivered to its proper destination. In addition, they perform the routines that determine which node has the right to transmit data over a network at any given instant—CSMA/CD on an Ethernet network, for example.

Advances in NIC technology are making this hardware smarter than ever. Many NICs can also perform prioritization, network management, buffering, and traffic-filtering functions. On most clients, NICs do not, however, analyze information added by the protocols in Layers 3 through 7 of the OSI model. For example, they could not determine whether the frames they transmit and receive use IP datagrams or a different Layer 2 protocol. Nor could they determine whether the Presentation layer has encrypted the data in those packets.

Because NICs are common to every networking device and every network, knowing as much as possible about them will prove useful. The following section describes several types of NICs, their functions, and their features.

Types of NICs

2.6 As you design or troubleshoot a network, you will need to know the characteristics of the NICs used by its clients, servers, and connectivity devices. For example, when you order a switch, you'll have to specify the network interfaces that match your network's speed and cabling connectors. NICs come in a variety of types depending on the following:

- Access method (for example, Ethernet)
- Network transmission speed (for example, 100 Mbps versus 1 Gbps)
- Connector interfaces (for example, RJ-45 versus SC)
- Number of connector interfaces, or ports

2.6

- Method of interfacing with the computer's motherboard (for example, on-board, expansion slot, or peripheral) and interface standard (for example, PCIe or USB)
- Manufacturer (popular NIC manufacturers include 3Com, Adaptec, D-Link, IBM, Intel, Kingston, Linksys, Netgear, SMC, and Western Digital, to name just a few)
- Support for enhanced features, such as PoE, buffering, or traffic management

The following section describes one category of NICs, those that are installed on an expansion board inside a computer.

Expansion Board NICs If you have worked with PCs or studied for CompTIA's A+ exam, you are probably familiar with the concept of a bus. A computer's **bus** is the circuit, or signaling pathway, used by the motherboard to transmit data to the computer's components, including its memory, processor, hard disk, and NIC. (A computer's bus may also be called its **system bus** or **main bus**.) Buses differ according to their capacity. The capacity of a bus is defined principally by the width of its data path (expressed in bits) and its clock speed (expressed in MHz). A data path size equals the number of bits that it can transmit in parallel at any given time. In the earliest PCs, buses had an 8-bit data path. Later, manufacturers expanded buses to handle 16 bits of data, then 32 bits. Most new desktop computers use buses capable of exchanging 64 bits of data, and some are even capable of 128 bits. As the number of bits of data that a bus can handle increases, so too does the speed of the devices attached to the bus.

A computer's bus can be expanded to include devices other than those found on the motherboard. The motherboard contains **expansion slots**, or openings with multiple electrical contacts, that allow devices such as NICs, modems, or sound cards to connect to the computer's expanded bus. The devices are found on a circuit board called an **expansion card** or **expansion board**. Inserting an expansion board into an expansion slot establishes an electrical connection between the expansion board and the motherboard. Thus, the device connected to the expansion board becomes connected to the computer's main circuit and part of its bus. With expansion boards connected to its main circuit, a computer can centrally control the device.

Multiple bus types exist, and to become part of a computer's bus, an expansion board must use the same bus type. By far, the most popular expansion board NIC today is one that uses a PCIe bus. **PCIe (Peripheral Component Interconnect Express)** is a 32-bit bus capable of transferring data at up to 1 Gbps per data path, or lane, in full-duplex transmission. It was introduced in 2004 and has continued to evolve ever since, offering efficient data transfer, support for quality of service distinctions, and error reporting and handling. PCIe slots vary depending on the number of lanes they support: An x1 slot supports a single lane, an x2 slot supports two lanes, and so on. Each lane offers a full-duplex throughput of up to 1 Gbps. A PCIe slot can support up to 32 lanes. Figure 6-1 depicts a PCIe expansion board NIC.

You can easily determine the type of bus your PC uses by reading the documentation that came with the computer. Someday, however, you may need to replace a NIC on a PC whose documentation is missing. To verify the type of bus a PC uses, you can look inside the PC case. (Later in this chapter, you will learn how to open a computer case, check the computer's bus, and install a NIC safely.) If a motherboard supports more than one kind of expansion slot, refer to the NIC and PC manufacturers' guidelines for information on the preferred type of NIC. If possible, you should choose a NIC that matches the most modern bus on the motherboard. Although you may be able to use the older bus and NIC types

Net+
2.6

Figure 6-1 PCIe expansion board NIC
Courtesy of Intel Corporation

without any adverse effects, some NICs will not work in an older bus if a faster, newer bus is available on the motherboard.

Peripheral NICs Some devices, such as flash drives or NICs, are attached to the computer's bus externally rather than internally. PCMCIA (Personal Computer Memory Card International Association), USB (Universal Serial Bus), CompactFlash, or FireWire (IEEE 1394) slots can all be used to connect peripherals such as NICs. Externally attached NICs are portable and simple to install. Typically, you only need to plug an externally attached adapter into the port to complete the physical installation. Installing and configuring software may also be required. In contrast, to install an expansion board NIC, you need to turn off and unplug the computer, remove its cover, insert the board into an expansion slot, fasten the board in place, replace the cover, turn on the computer, and then install or configure necessary software. A wireless USB NIC is shown in Figure 6-2.

Figure 6-2 A USB NIC
© Charles B. Ming Onn / Shutterstock.com

Net+ 2.6

On-Board NICs Not all devices are connected to a computer's motherboard via an expansion slot or peripheral bus. Some are connected directly to the motherboard using **on-board ports**. For example, the electrical connection that controls a computer's mouse operates through an on-board port, as does the connection for its keyboard and monitor. Most new computers also use **on-board NICs**, or NICs that are integrated into the motherboard. Such NICs use the same kinds of bus interfaces as expansion board NICs—for example, PCIe. A significant advantage to using an on-board NIC is that it saves space, freeing expansion slots for additional peripherals. Figure 6-3 shows a workstation's motherboard with two on-board NICs.

Figure 6-3 Motherboard with on-board NICs
Courtesy of EVGA USA

NICs are designed for use with either wired or wireless networks. Wireless NICs, which contain antennas to send and receive signals, can be found for all of the bus types discussed in this chapter. Installation and configuration for wireless NICs is the same as for wired NICs.

Installing and Configuring NICs

Most new clients, servers, and connectivity devices will arrive with their NICs preinstalled and functional. However, someday you might want to upgrade the NIC in a client workstation to one that can handle faster transmission speeds or add NICs to your server, for example. In that case, you need to know how to install NICs properly.

To install a NIC, you must first install the hardware, and then install the software that shipped with it. The following sections explain how to install and configure NICs.

Installing NIC Hardware It's always advisable to start by reading the manufacturer's documentation that accompanies the NIC hardware. The following steps generally apply to any kind of expansion card NIC installation in a desktop computer, but your experience may vary.

To install an expansion card NIC:

1. Make sure that your toolkit includes a Phillips-head screwdriver, a ground strap, and a ground mat to protect the internal components from electrostatic discharge. Also, make sure that you have ample space in which to work, whether on the floor, a desk, or a table.

2.6

2. Turn off the computer's power switch, and then unplug the computer. In addition to endangering you, opening a PC while it's turned on can damage the PC's internal circuitry. Also unplug attached peripherals and the network cable, if necessary.
3. Attach the ground strap to your wrist and make sure that it's connected to the ground mat underneath the computer.
4. Open the computer's case. Desktop computer cases are attached in several different ways. They might use four or six screws to attach the housing to the back panel, or they might not use any screws and slide off instead. Remove all necessary screws and then remove the computer's case.
5. Select a slot on the computer's motherboard where you will insert the NIC. Make sure that the slot matches the type of expansion card you have. Remove the metal slot cover for that slot from the back of the PC. Some slot covers are attached with a single screw; after removing the screw, you can lift out the slot cover. Other slot covers are merely metal parts with perforated edges that you can punch or twist out with your hands.
6. Insert the NIC by lining up its slot connector with the slot and pressing it firmly into the slot. Don't be afraid to press down hard, but make sure the expansion card is properly aligned with the slot when you do so. If you have correctly inserted the NIC, it should not wiggle near its base. A loose NIC causes connectivity problems. Figure 6-4 shows a close-up of a NIC firmly seated in its slot.

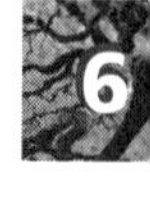

Figure 6-4 A properly inserted expansion board NIC
Gary Herrington Photography

7. The metal bracket at the end of the NIC should now be positioned where the metal slot cover was located before you removed the slot cover. Attach the bracket with a screw to the back of the computer cover to secure the NIC in place.

2.6

8. Make sure that you have not loosened any cables or cards inside the PC or left any screws or debris inside the computer.
9. Replace the cover on the computer and reinsert the screws that you removed in Step 4, if applicable. Also reinsert any cables you removed.
10. Plug in the computer and turn it on. Proceed to configure the NIC's software, as discussed later in this chapter.

Physically installing a peripheral NIC is much easier than installing an expansion card NIC. In general, you simply insert the device into the appropriate slot. Make sure that the card is firmly inserted. If you can wiggle it, you need to realign it or push it in farther.

On servers and other high-powered computers, you may need to install multiple NICs. For the hardware installation, you can simply repeat the installation process for the first NIC, choosing a different slot. The trick to using multiple NICs on one machine lies in correctly configuring the software for each NIC. Simple NIC configuration is covered in the following section. The precise steps involved in configuring NICs will depend on the computer's operating system.

Installing and Configuring NIC Software Even if your computer runs an operating system with plug-and-play technology, you must ensure that the correct device driver is installed for the NIC and that it is configured properly. A **device driver** (sometimes called, simply, a **driver**) is software that enables an attached device to communicate with the computer's operating system. When you purchase a computer that already contains a peripheral, the device drivers should already be installed. However, when you add hardware, the proper device driver must be installed. Operating systems come with a multitude of built-in device drivers. In most cases, after you physically install new hardware and restart, the operating system automatically recognizes the hardware and installs the device's drivers. Each time a computer starts up, the device drivers for all its connected peripherals are loaded into RAM so that the computer can communicate with those devices at any time.

In other cases, the operating system might not contain appropriate device drivers for the hardware you have added. This section describes how to install and configure NIC software on a Windows 7 operating system that does not already use the correct and current device driver. Regardless of which operating system you use, you should first refer to the NIC's documentation because your situation may vary. Read the NIC documentation carefully to make sure you are installing the appropriate drivers. Installing a device driver designed for Windows XP on a Windows 7 computer, for example, probably won't work.

To install NIC software from a Windows 7 interface, you need access to the Windows 7 software and the device drivers specific to the NIC. These drivers can be found online, at the NIC manufacturer's Web site, or on a disk shipped with the NIC. If you choose to download the drivers from a Web site, make sure that you get the appropriate drivers for your operating system and NIC type. Also, make sure that the drivers you download are the most current version, sometimes called "shipping drivers," and not beta-level, or unsupported, drivers.

To install and configure NIC software:

1. Physically install the NIC, and then restart the computer. Log on to the computer as a user with administrator privileges.
2. As long as you haven't disabled the plug-and-play capabilities, Windows 7 should automatically detect the new hardware. Upon detecting the NIC, it should also install

2.6

the NIC's driver. In many cases, you need not install any other software or adjust the configuration for the NIC to operate properly.

3. There are certain situations in which you might want to change or update the device driver that the operating system has chosen. To do this, click the **Start button**, then select **Control Panel**. The Control Panel window opens.
4. Click **System and Security**. The System and Security window opens.
5. Click **System**. The System window opens.
6. Click **Device Manager**. A User Account Control window may appear, requesting your permission to continue.
7. If necessary, click **Yes** to continue. The Device Manager window opens, displaying a list of installed devices.
8. Double-click the **Network adapters** icon. A list of installed NICs appears.
9. Double-click the adapter for which you want to install new device drivers.
10. Click the **Driver** tab. Details about your NIC's current driver appear, as shown in Figure 6-5.

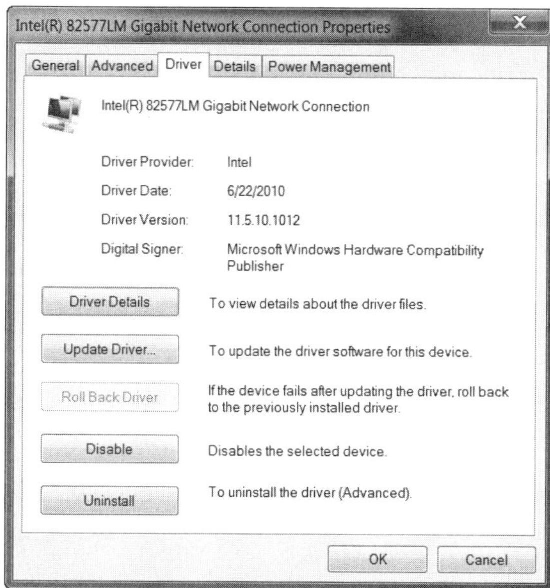

Figure 6-5 Network adapter properties dialog box with Driver tab selected

11. Click **Update Driver**. The Update Driver Software window opens, prompting you to choose whether to search automatically for updated driver software or browse your computer for driver software.
12. Make sure that the disk with the correct driver on it is inserted or that you know where on your hard disk you saved the driver. Click **Browse my computer for driver software**.

13. In the Search for driver software in this location text box, enter the drive and directory information for your driver or click the **Browse** button and navigate to the directory
2.6 that contains your driver, and then click **OK**.
14. Click **Next** to continue. Wait while Windows 7 searches your drive for a driver that matches your network card. (If the disk sent with the NIC contains drivers for more than one type of NIC, you are asked to select the precise model you are using. After making your choice, click **OK**.)
15. Windows 7 will find the appropriate driver for your NIC and install it onto your hard disk. Later, it informs you that it has successfully updated your driver software. To continue, click **Close**. Then close all windows.

Installing NIC drivers on a UNIX or Linux workstation depends somewhat on the version you are running. For example, versions of Linux that support plug-and-play technology normally detect a connected NIC and automatically install the correct drivers. The first NIC the operating system detects is called, by default, eth0. If a second NIC is present, it is called eth1. Because they provide the network interface, eth0 and eth1 are called, in UNIX and Linux terminology, simply, interfaces.

Net+ After installing a NIC, you might need to modify its transmission characteristics—for example, whether it uses full duplexing, whether it can detect a network's speed, or even its MAC
2.1
2.6 address. In almost all cases, NIC settings can be changed through the operating system. For example, on a Windows 7 workstation, access the network adapter properties by following Steps 1 through 9 described earlier for updating a NIC's device driver. Clicking the Advanced tab rather than the Driver tab allows you to modify many characteristics about your NIC.

On a Linux workstation, a popular utility called **ethtool** allows you to view and change NIC settings. Although ethtool doesn't ship with all versions of Linux, it is compatible with any installation and can be downloaded from reputable Internet sources. To display the properties of a computer's first network interface, as shown in Figure 6-6, type `ethtool eth0` at a Linux command prompt and press Enter.

In the example shown in Figure 6-6, the line `Supports auto-negotiation: Yes` indicates that the network interface is configured to automatically sense, or autonegotiate, the speed at which it should transmit and receive data on the network. Suppose, however, that your Linux workstation is connecting to an older connectivity device whose network interface expects 100-Mbps throughput and cannot detect and follow any different network speed. In that case, you could use ethtool to force your NIC to turn off its autonegotiate capability and only transmit and receive data at the speed that the device expects. The command `ethtool -s eth0 speed 100 autoneg off` would accomplish this. To list all the options you can use with the command, type `ethtool -h` and press Enter.

Net+ **Verifying NIC Functionality** After you have installed and configured a NIC, you
2.6 need to ensure that it connects properly to the network. A simple test, of course, is to check whether the client, server, or connectivity device can communicate with the network. If it can't, you need to find out why.

One way to diagnose a malfunctioning NIC is to use the configuration utility provided by the NIC's manufacturer. NIC configuration utilities allow you to test the NIC's physical components and connectivity. Most of the tests can be performed without additional hardware. However, to perform the entire group of the diagnostic tests on the NIC's utility disk, you must have a loopback plug. A **loopback plug** (also called a **loopback adapter**) is a

Net+ 2.1 2.6

```
Settings for eth0:
        Supported ports: [ TP ]
        Supported link modes:   10baseT/Half 10baseT/Full
                                100baseT/Half 100baseT/Full
                                1000baseT/Full
        Supported pause frame use: No
        Supports auto-negotiation: Yes
        Advertised link modes:  10baseT/Half 10baseT/Full
                                100baseT/Half 100baseT/Full
                                1000baseT/Full
        Advertised pause frame use: No
        Advertised auto-negotiation: Yes
        Speed: 100Mb/s
        Duplex: Full
        Port: Twisted Pair
        PHYAD: 2
        Transceiver: internal
        Auto-negotiation: on
        MDI-X: off
        Supports Wake-on: pumbg
        Wake-on: g
        Current message level: 0x00000001 (1)
                               drv
        Link detected: yes
```

Figure 6-6 Linux network interface properties shown by the `ethtool` command

Net+ 2.6 4.2

connector that plugs into a port, such as an RJ-45 port, and crosses over the transmit line to the receive line so that outgoing signals can be redirected into the computer for testing. One connectivity test, called a loopback test, requires you to install a loopback plug into the NIC's media connector. Note that none of the connectivity tests should be performed on a computer connected to a live network. If a NIC fails its connectivity tests, it is probably configured incorrectly. If a NIC fails a physical component test, it might need to be replaced.

The word *loopback* implies that signals are routed back toward their source, rather than toward an external destination. When used in the context of NICs, the loopback test refers to a check of the adapter's ability to transmit and receive signals. Recall that the term loopback is also used in the context of TCP/IP protocol testing. In that context, pinging the loopback address provides you with information on TCP/IP functionality.

Net+ 2.6

Another way to learn about your NIC's functionality is simply by looking at it. Most NICs have LEDs that indicate whether they are communicating with the network. The precise location, type, and meaning of LED indicators vary from one manufacturer to another. The only way to know for certain what your NIC's LEDs are trying to tell you is to read the documentation. In general, a steady or blinking green LED indicates that the NIC is functional and has a connection to the network. Sometimes this light is labeled LNK. Blinking yellow or orange LEDs may indicate that the NIC is transmitting or receiving data. The transmit and receive LEDs on some ports are labeled TX and RX, respectively. If they exist, red LEDs may indicate a problem with the NIC or its ability to connect to the network.

2.6
4.3

In addition to viewing its LEDs and using a loopback plug to test a NIC's functionality, you can also check a NIC's connectivity with simple commands. As you learned in Chapter 4, pinging the loopback address—127.0.0.1 on a computer running IPv4 or ::1 on a computer running IPv6—will indicate whether an interface is functional. On a computer running a Windows operating system, typing `ipconfig /all` at a command prompt will provide information about your interfaces. On a computer running Linux or UNIX, the `ifconfig -a` command will do the same.

So far, you have learned about a variety of NICs and how to install and configure them on clients. The next section describes network interfaces commonly used in connectivity devices such as switches and routers.

Modular Interfaces

2.1
2.6

It makes sense to purchase workstations or servers with on-board NICs already installed; however, customizing network interfaces on connectivity devices can be more practical on a large network. For example, suppose you were creating a network for a new, fast-growing business. At first, the business might need only two fiber-optic connections for its backbone and 24 RJ-45, Gigabit Ethernet connections for its clients and servers. In the future, however, the business might plan to bring fiber-optic connectivity to every desktop. Rather than ordering a switch that contains exactly this number and type of on-board interfaces, you could order a switch that allows you to change and upgrade its interfaces at any time. The switch would contain sockets that allow one of many types of modular interfaces to be plugged in. Such interfaces are easily inserted into the sockets to connect with its motherboard, also called a **backplane**. A hardware component that can be changed in this manner, without disrupting operations, is known as **hot-swappable**. Using hot-swappable interfaces means you don't have to purchase a new switch, open the chassis of the existing switch, causing network downtime and risking hardware damage, or even turn off the switch to upgrade the network. Modular interfaces can also be found on some expansion board NICs and media converters.

GBIC (Gigabit interface converter), pronounced *jee-bick*, is a standard type of modular interface designed in the 1990s for Gigabit Ethernet connections. GBICs may contain RJ-45 or fiber-optic cable ports (such as LC, SC, or ST). Figure 6-7 shows a GBIC that can be used on a 1000Base-T network.

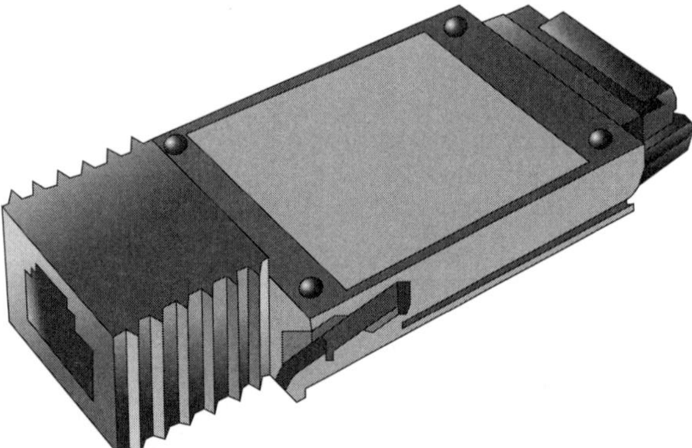

Figure 6-7 GBIC (Gigabit interface converter) with an RJ-45 port

Net+ A newer modular interface has made the GBIC largely obsolete. **SFPs (small form-factor plug-
2.1 gable) transceivers** provide the same function as a GBIC, but allow more ports per inch—in
2.6 other words, they are more compact. For this reason, they are also sometimes known as **mini
GBICs** or **SFP GBICs**. Current SFP standards enable these transceivers to send and receive data at rates up to 10 Gbps. Figure 6-8 shows an SFP with ports for fiber-optic cable connectors, one for transmitting and another for receiving data.

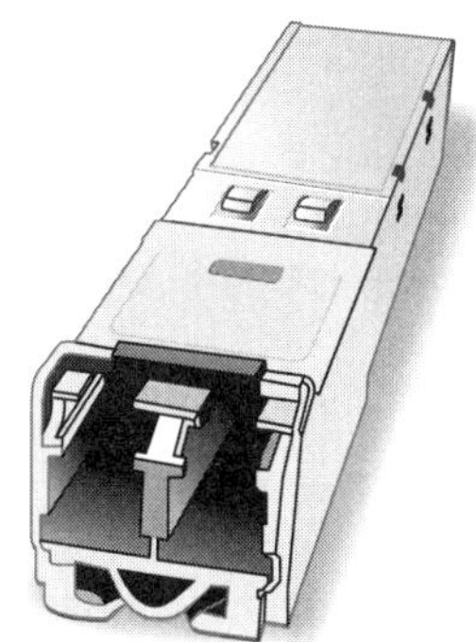

Figure 6-8 SFP (small form-factor pluggable) transceiver for use with fiber connections

Installing a GBIC or SFP is simply a matter of sliding the transceiver into a socket on the back of the connectivity device. Most SFPs come with a tab or latch system of locking them into place. They are also keyed so that they will slide into the socket only when they are aligned properly. The switch or router need not be powered down when you add or remove transceivers. However, do not attach cables before inserting a transceiver, and always remove the cables before removing a transceiver. Figure 6-9 illustrates how a fiber-optic SFP is installed in a switch, for example.

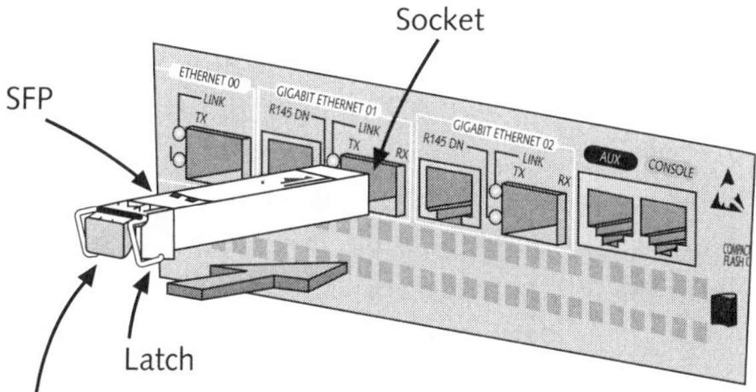

Figure 6-9 Installing an SFP in a switch

Some SFPs contain management interfaces separate from the switch's configuration utility. For example, the 10-Gbps SFP on a router could have its own IP address. A network administra-
2.1 tor could use the Telnet utility to connect to the SFP and configure its ports to use a particular
2.6 speed or routing protocol without accessing the router's operating system.

Repeaters and Hubs

Now that you have learned about the many types of network interfaces and how to install
1.2 and configure them, you are ready to learn about connectivity devices. As you'll recall, the telecommunications closet is the area containing the connectivity equipment for work areas and sometimes entire floors of a building. Within the telecommunications closet, horizontal cabling from the workstations attaches to punch-down blocks, patch panels, hubs, switches, routers, and bridges. In older installations, telecommunications closets may house repeaters. Repeaters are the simplest type of connectivity devices that regenerate a digital signal.

Repeaters operate in the Physical layer of the OSI model and, therefore, have no means to interpret the data they retransmit. For example, they cannot improve or correct a bad or erroneous signal; they simply regenerate a signal over an entire segment. It is up to the receiver to recognize and accept its data.

A repeater is limited not only in function, but also in scope. A repeater contains one input port and one output port, so it is capable only of receiving and repeating a single data stream. Furthermore, repeaters are suited only to bus topology networks. A repeater allows you to extend a network inexpensively. However, because of repeaters' limitations and the decreasing costs of other connectivity devices, repeaters are not used on modern networks. Instead, clients in a workgroup area are more likely to be connected by switches or routers, which are discussed later in this chapter.

At its most primitive, a **hub** is a repeater with more than one output port. A hub typically contains multiple data ports into which the patch cables for network nodes, such as workstations, printers, and servers, are connected. Like repeaters, hubs operate at the Physical layer of the OSI model. A hub accepts signals from a transmitting node and repeats those signals to all other connected nodes in a broadcast fashion. Most hubs also contain one port, called an **uplink port**, that allows the hub to connect to another hub or other connectivity device. On Ethernet networks, hubs can serve as the central connection point for branches of a star or star-based hybrid topology. As you learned in Chapter 5, all devices connected to a hub share the same amount of bandwidth and the same collision domain. The more nodes participating in the same collision domain, the higher the likelihood of transmission errors and slower performance.

Hubs were a mainstay of network connectivity on small networks of the 1980s and 1990s. However, because of their limited features and the fact that they merely repeat signals within a single collision domain, hubs were replaced by routers and switches. To understand how switches operate, it is helpful to learn about bridges first.

Bridges

Bridges are devices that connect two network segments by analyzing incoming frames and
1.2 making decisions about where to direct them based on each frame's MAC address. They operate at the Data Link layer of the OSI model. Bridges resemble repeaters, in that they have a

1.2 single input and a single output port. They differ from repeaters in that they can interpret physical addressing information.

Historically speaking, a significant advantage to using bridges over repeaters or hubs was that bridges are protocol independent. For instance, all bridges can connect an Ethernet segment carrying IP-based traffic with an Ethernet segment carrying traffic that uses a different Network layer protocol. Some bridges can also connect two segments using different Data Link and Physical layer protocols—for example, an Ethernet segment with a token ring segment, or a wire-bound Ethernet segment with a wireless Ethernet segment.

Because they only review Data Link layer information, bridges can move data more rapidly than older routers, for example, which must examine Network layer protocol information. On the other hand, bridges take longer to transmit data than either repeaters or hubs because bridges actually analyze each frame, whereas repeaters and hubs do not.

Another advantage to using bridges over simple repeating devices is that they can extend an Ethernet network without further extending a collision domain, or segment. In other words, by inserting a bridge into a network, you can add length beyond the maximum limits that apply to segments. Finally, bridges can help improve network performance because they can be programmed to filter out certain types of frames (for example, unnecessary broadcast frames, whose transmissions squander bandwidth).

To translate between two segment types, a bridge reads a frame's destination MAC address and decides to either forward or filter it. If the bridge determines that the destination node is on another segment on the network, it forwards (retransmits) the packet to that segment. If the destination address belongs to the same segment as the source address, the bridge filters (discards) the frame. As nodes transmit data through the bridge, the bridge establishes a **filtering database** (also known as a **forwarding table**) of known MAC addresses and their locations on the network. The bridge uses its filtering database to determine whether a packet should be forwarded or filtered, as illustrated in Figure 6-10.

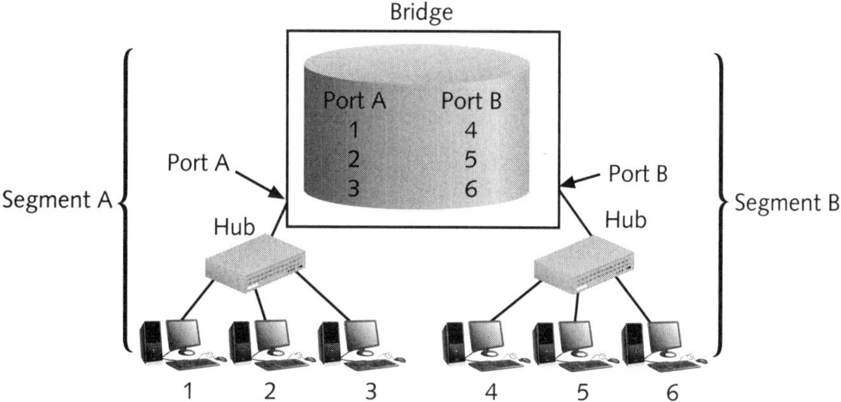

Figure 6-10 A bridge's use of a filtering database

Using Figure 6-10 as an example, imagine that you sit at workstation 1 on segment A of the LAN, and your colleague Cory sits at workstation 2 on segment A. When you attempt to send data to Cory's computer, your transmission goes through your segment's hub and then to the

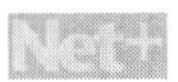

1.2

bridge. The bridge reads the MAC address of Cory's computer. It then searches its filtering database to determine whether that MAC address belongs to the same segment you are on or whether it belongs to a different segment. The bridge can determine only that the MAC address of Cory's workstation is associated with its port A. If the MAC address belongs to a different segment, the bridge forwards the data to that segment, whose corresponding port identity is also in the filtering database. In this case, however, your workstation and Cory's workstation reside on the same LAN segment, so the data is filtered (that is, ignored) and your message is delivered to Cory's workstation through segment A's hub.

Conversely, if you want to send data to your supervisor's computer, which is workstation 5 in Figure 6-10, your transmission first passes through segment A's hub and then on to the bridge. The bridge reads the MAC address for your supervisor's machine (the destination address in your data stream) and searches for the port associated with that machine. In this case, the bridge recognizes workstation 5 as being connected to port B, and it forwards the data to that port. Subsequently, the segment B hub ensures delivery of the data to your supervisor's computer.

After you install a new bridge, it uses one of several methods to learn about the network and discover the destination address for each packet it handles. After it discovers this information, it records the destination node's MAC address and its associated port in its filtering database. Over time, it discovers all nodes on the network and constructs database entries for each.

Stand-alone bridges became popular in the 1980s and early 1990s. And although bridging technology evolved to create more sophisticated bridge devices, switches and routers also evolved. Equipment manufacturers have improved the speed and functionality of routers and switches while lowering their cost, leaving bridges to become extinct. Although bridges are rarely found on modern LANs, understanding the concept of bridging is essential to understanding how switches work. For example, the bridging process pictured in Figure 6-10 applies to every port on a switch. The next section introduces switches and explains their functions.

Switches

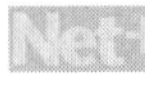

1.2
1.4

Switches are connectivity devices that subdivide a network into smaller logical pieces, or segments. Traditional switches operate at the Data Link layer of the OSI model, while modern switches can operate at Layer 3 or even Layer 4. As with bridges, switches interpret MAC address information. In fact, they can be described as multiport bridges. Figure 6-11 depicts two switches. On the right is a 24-port switch, useful for connecting nodes in a workgroup, and on the left is a high-capacity switch that contains multiple redundant features (such as duplicate SFPs) and offers security, automated traffic management, and even routing functions. Switches vary greatly in size and function, so there's no such thing as a "typical" switch. Most switches have at least an internal processor, an operating system, memory, and several ports that enable other nodes to connect to it.

Because they have multiple ports, switches can make better use of limited bandwidth and prove more cost efficient than bridges. Each port on the switch acts like a bridge, and each device connected to a switch effectively receives its own dedicated channel. In other words, a switch can turn a shared channel into several channels. From the Ethernet perspective, each dedicated channel represents a collision domain. Because a switch limits the number of devices in a collision domain, it limits the potential for collisions.

1.4

Figure 6-11 Switches
Courtesy of Juniper Networks, Inc.; © Vtls / Shutterstock.com

Switches have historically been used to replace hubs and ease traffic congestion in LAN workgroups. Some network administrators have replaced backbone routers with switches because switches provide at least two advantages: better security and better performance. By their nature, switches provide better security than many other devices because they isolate one device's traffic from other devices' traffic. And because switches provide separate channels for (potentially) every device, performance stands to gain. Applications that transfer a large amount of traffic and are sensitive to time delays, such as videoconferencing applications, benefit from the full use of the channel's capacity. In addition, hardware and software in a switch are optimized for fast data forwarding.

Switches have their disadvantages, too. Although they contain buffers to hold incoming data and accommodate bursts of traffic, they can become overwhelmed by continuous, heavy traffic. In that event, the switch cannot prevent data loss. Also, although higher-layer protocols, such as TCP, detect the loss and respond with a timeout, others, such as UDP, do not. For packets using such protocols, the number of collisions mounts, and eventually all network traffic grinds to a halt. Therefore, plan placement of switches carefully to match backbone capacity and traffic patterns.

Although a large LAN's backbone switch might be expensive and complex, switches for small office or home networks are inexpensive and simple to install and configure. The next section describes how to install a simple switch.

Switch Installation

2.1 As with any networking equipment, the best way to ensure that you install a switch properly
2.6 is to follow the manufacturer's guidelines. Small workgroup switches are normally simple to

Net+ 2.1 2.6

install. Many operate properly upon being added to a network. The following steps describe, in general, how to connect multiple nodes to a small switch, and then how to connect that switch to another connectivity device. These instructions assume you're using Cat 5 or better UTP cables to connect devices to the switch.

1. Make sure the switch is situated where you are going to keep it after all the cables are connected.
2. Before connecting any cables to the switch's ports, plug it in and turn it on. Also, when connecting a node to a switch, the node should not be turned on. Otherwise, data irregularities can occur, forcing you to reset the switch.
3. The switch's power light should illuminate. Most switches perform self-tests when turned on, and blinking lights indicate that these tests are in progress. Wait until the tests are completed (as indicated by a steady, green power light).
4. If you are using a small, inexpensive switch, you might not have to configure it and you can skip to Step 5. However, you might need to assign an IP address to the switch, change the administrator password, or set up management functions. You can configure a switch by accessing its configuration page over the network via a Web browser or at the command prompt. Refer to your switch's instructions for more information on its configuration utility.
5. Using a straight-through patch cable, connect the node's NIC to one of the switch's ports, as shown in Figure 6-12. If you intend to connect this switch to another connectivity device, do not connect patch cables from nodes to the uplink port or to the port adjacent to the uplink port. On most switches, the uplink port is directly wired to its adjacent port inside the device.

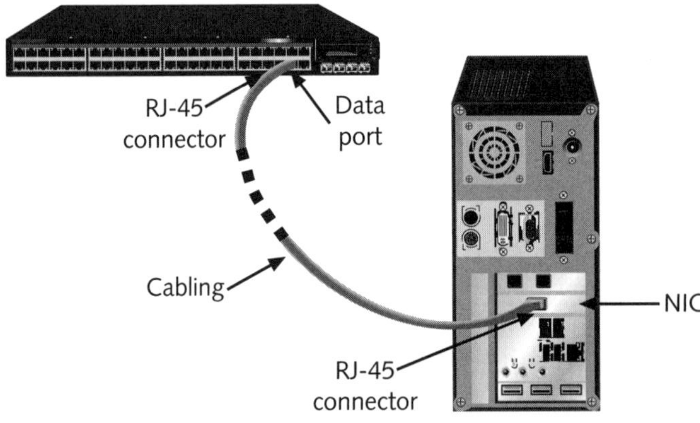

Figure 6-12 Connecting a workstation to a switch

Because most switches have the capability to automatically detect and adjust to the transmit and receive wire terminations in a plug, it usually doesn't matter whether you use a straight-through or crossover cable to connect a switch with nodes or a switch with another connectivity device.

6. After all the nodes have been connected to the switch, if you do not plan to connect the switch to another connectivity device, you can turn on the nodes. After the nodes con-
2.1 nect to the network through the newly installed switch, check to verify that the switch's
2.6 link and traffic lights for each port act as they should, according to the switch's documentation. Then make sure the nodes can access the network as planned.
7. To connect the switch to a larger network, you can insert one end of a crossover patch cable into the switch's uplink port, then insert the other end of the cable into a data port on the other connectivity device. Alternately, you can insert one end of a straight-through cable into one of the switch's data ports, then insert the other end of the straight-through cable into another device's data port. After connecting the switch to another device, the switch senses the activity on its uplink port, evidenced by its blinking traffic light.

Figure 6-13 illustrates a typical way of using a small switch on a small office or home network. In this example, the switch connects a group of nodes, including workstations, server, and printer, with each other and with an Internet connection.

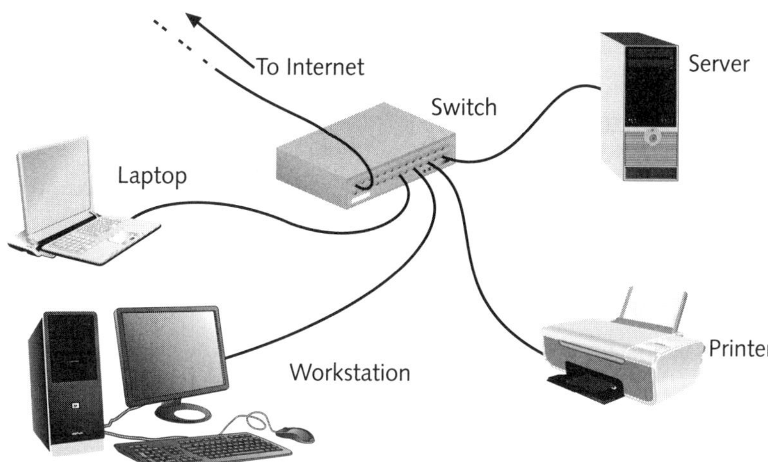

Figure 6-13 A switch on a small network

Now that you understand the purposes and placement of switches in a network, you are ready to learn more about how they perform their functions.

Switching Methods

1.4 Switches differ in how they interpret incoming frames and determine what to do with the frames. Although four switching modes exist, the two basic methods discussed in the following sections are most popular.

Cut-Through Mode

A switch running in **cut-through mode** reads a frame's header and decides where to forward the data before it receives the entire packet. Recall that the first 14 bytes of a frame constitute its header, which contains the destination MAC address.

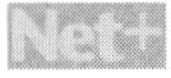

1.4 This information is sufficient for the switch to determine which port should get the frame and begin transmitting the frame (without bothering to read the rest of the frame and check its accuracy).

What if the frame becomes corrupt? Because the cut-through mode does not allow the switch to read the frame check sequence before it begins transmitting, it can't verify data integrity in that way. On the other hand, cut-through switches can detect **runts**, or erroneously shortened packets. Upon detecting a runt, the switch waits to transmit that packet until it determines its integrity. It's important to remember, however, that runts are only one type of data flaw. Cut-through switches *cannot* detect corrupt packets; indeed, they may increase the number of errors found on the network by propagating flawed packets.

The most significant advantage of the cut-through mode is its speed. Because it does not stop to read the entire data packet, a cut-through switch can forward information much more rapidly than a store-and-forward switch can (as described in the next section). The time-saving advantages to cut-through switching become insignificant, however, if the switch is flooded with traffic. In this case, the cut-through switch must buffer (or temporarily hold) data, just like a store-and-forward switch. Cut-through switches are best suited to small workgroups in which speed is important and the relatively low number of devices minimizes the potential for errors.

Store-and-Forward Mode In **store-and-forward mode**, a switch reads the entire data frame into its memory and checks it for accuracy before transmitting the information. Although this method is more time consuming than the cut-through method, it allows store-and-forward switches to transmit data more accurately. Store-and-forward mode switches are more appropriate for larger LAN environments because they do not propagate data errors. In contrast, cut-through mode switches do forward errors, so they may contribute to network congestion if a particular segment is experiencing a number of collisions. In large environments, a failure to check for errors can result in problematic traffic congestion.

Store-and-forward switches can also transfer data between segments running different transmission speeds. For example, a high-speed network printer that serves 50 students could be attached to a 100-Mbps port on the switch, thereby allowing all of the student workstations to connect to 10-Mbps ports on the same switch. With this scheme, the printer can quickly service multiple jobs. This characteristic makes store-and-forward mode switches preferable in mixed-speed environments.

VLANs and Trunking

1.4 In addition to improving bandwidth usage compared with lower-layer devices, switches can cre-
2.1 ate **VLANs (virtual local area networks)**, or logically separate networks within networks, by grouping a number of ports into a broadcast domain. **802.1q** is the IEEE standard that specifies how VLAN information appears in frames and how switches interpret that information.

As you know, a broadcast domain is a combination of ports that make up a Layer 2 segment. Ports in a broadcast domain rely on a Layer 2 device, such as a switch, to forward broadcast frames among them. In contrast to a collision domain, ports in the same broadcast domain do not share a single channel. (Recall that switches separate collision domains.) In the context of TCP/IP networking, a broadcast domain is also known as a subnet. Figure 6-14 illustrates a simple VLAN design.

Net+
1.4
2.1

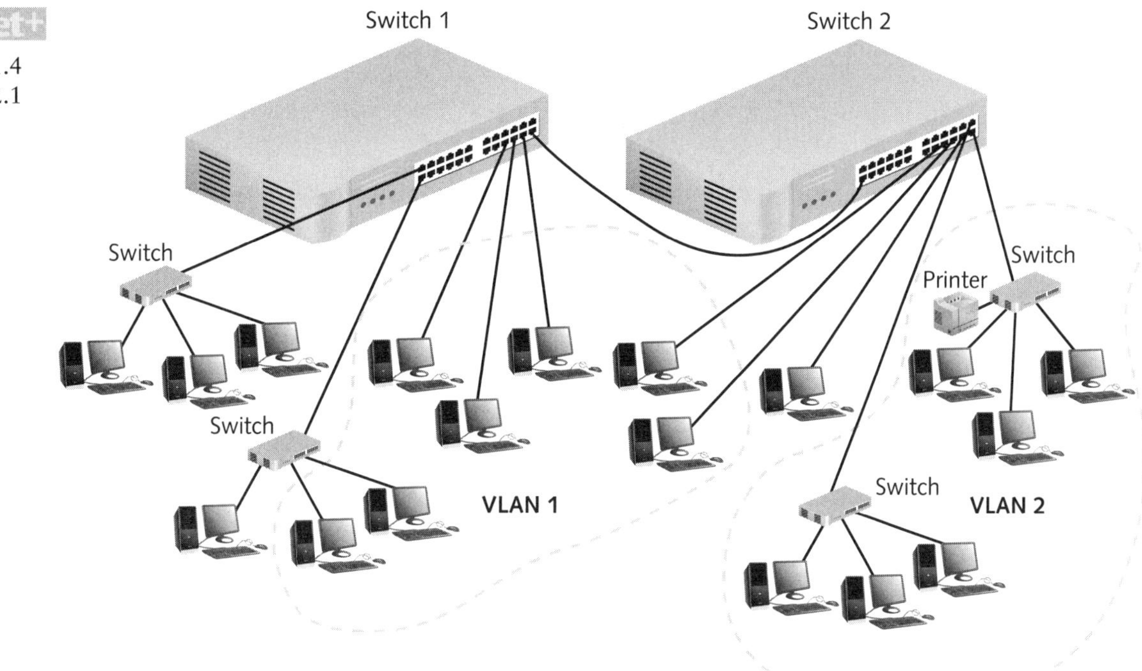

Figure 6-14 A simple VLAN design

Network engineers value VLANs for their flexibility. They can include ports from more than one switch or segment. Any type of end node can belong to one or more VLANs. VLANs can link geographically distant users over a WAN, and they can create small workgroups within LANs. Reasons for using VLANs include:

- Separating groups of users who need special security or network functions
- Isolating connections with heavy or unpredictable traffic patterns
- Identifying groups of devices whose data should be given priority handling
- Containing groups of devices that rely on legacy protocols incompatible with the majority of the network's traffic.
- Separating a very large network into smaller, more manageable subnets

One case in which a company might want to implement a VLAN is to allow visitors access to minimal network functions—for example, an Internet connection—without allowing the possibility of access to the company's data stored on servers. In another example, companies that use their packet-switched networks to carry telephone calls often group all of the voice traffic on a separate VLAN to prevent this unique and potentially heavy traffic from adversely affecting routine client/server tasks.

A switch is typically preconfigured with one default VLAN that includes all its ports. This default VLAN cannot be renamed or deleted. You can create additional VLANs by properly configuring a switch's operating system software. The critical step in creating VLANs is to indicate which VLAN each port belongs to. In addition, you can specify security parameters,

Net+ 1.4 2.1 filtering instructions (if the switch should not forward any frames from a certain segment, for example), performance requirements for certain ports, and network addressing and management options. Options vary according to the switch manufacturer and model. In the Hands-On Projects at the end of this chapter, you will have the opportunity to create and configure VLANs on a Cisco switch.

Once you create a VLAN, you also maintain it via the switch's software. Figure 6-15 illustrates the result of a `show vlan` command on a Cisco switch on a large enterprise-wide network. The `show vlan` command is used to list the current VLANs recognized by a switch, and it is unique to Cisco-brand switches (and a few others that mimic that company's conventions). Other manufacturers' switch software includes similar maintenance commands.

Figure 6-15 lists 13 VLANs configured on the network. VLAN number 1 and VLANs 1002 through 1005 are defaults preestablished on the Cisco switch, but not actually used. The first half of the command output shows each VLAN's number, name, status, and which ports belong to it. For example, VLAN number 18, which is named "VLAN0018," is active and contains the ports "Gi1/3" and "Gi2/3." A port called "Gi1/3," in this case, refers to the third port on the first module of this Gigabit Ethernet switch.

The second half of the command output provides additional information about each VLAN, including the type of network it operates on. In this example, all VLANs that are active and not preestablished defaults use Ethernet, which is indicated by the "enet" type. Each VLAN is assigned a different SAID, or security association identifier, which indicates to other connectivity devices which VLAN a transmission belongs to. By default, Cisco switches assign a VLAN a SAID of 100,000 plus the VLAN number. Also, in this example each VLAN is configured to transmit and receive frames with a maximum transmission unit (MTU) size of 1500 bytes, which is the default selection. Rarely do network administrators change this variable.

One potential problem in creating VLANs is that by grouping together certain nodes, you are not merely including those nodes—you are also excluding another group. This means you can potentially cut off a group from the rest of the network. For example, suppose your company's IT director demands that you assign all executive workstations to their own VLAN, and that you configure the network's switch to group these users' computers into a VLAN. After this change, users would be able to exchange data with each other, but they would not be able to download data from the file server or download mail from the mail server, because these servers are not included in their VLAN. To allow different VLANs to exchange data, you need to connect those VLANs with a router or Layer 3 switch.

A single switch can manage traffic belonging to several VLANs. In fact, one switch's interface can carry the traffic of VLANs configured on multiple switches, thanks to a technique known as **trunking**. The term *trunk* originated in the telephony field, where it referred to an aggregation of logical connections over one physical connection. For instance, a trunk carried signals for many residential telephone lines in the same neighborhood over one cable. Similarly, in the context of switching, a trunk is a single physical connection between switches through which many logical VLANs can transmit and receive data.

To keep the data belonging to each VLAN separate, each frame is identified with a VLAN identifier, or tag, added to its header, according to specifications in the 802.1q standard. Trunking protocols assign and interpret these tags, thereby managing the distribution of frames through a trunk. The most popular protocol for exchanging VLAN information over trunks is Cisco's **VTP (VLAN trunking protocol)**. VTP allows one switch on a network to centrally manage all VLANs.

Net+
1.4
2.1

```
VLAN Name                             Status    Ports
---- -------------------------------- --------- -------------------------------
1    default                          active    Te1/1, Te1/2, Gi1/5, Gi1/6
                                                Te2/1, Te2/2, Gi2/5, Gi2/6
                                                Gi4/3, Gi5/12, Gi6/12, Gi6/19
                                                Gi8/11, Gi8/19, Gi9/4
5    VLAN0005                         active
13   VLAN0013                         active    Gi3/2, Gi3/3, Gi3/4, Gi8/12
14   VLAN0014                         active    Gi4/1, Gi4/2, Gi4/4, Gi9/12
16   VLAN0016                         active    Gi5/8
18   VLAN0018                         active    Gi1/3, Gi2/3
19   VLAN0019                         active    Gi5/11, Gi6/11
104  VLAN0104                         active    Gi1/4, Gi2/4, Gi3/5, Gi3/6
                                                Gi4/5, Gi4/6, Gi5/1, Gi5/2
                                                Gi5/3, Gi5/4, Gi5/5, Gi5/6
                                                Gi5/7, Gi5/9, Gi5/10, Gi5/13
                                                Gi5/14, Gi5/15, Gi5/16, Gi5/17
                                                Gi5/18, Gi5/19, Gi5/20, Gi5/21
                                                Gi5/22, Gi5/23, Gi5/24, Gi6/1
                                                Gi6/2, Gi6/3, Gi6/4, Gi6/5
                                                Gi6/6, Gi6/7, Gi6/9, Gi6/10
                                                Gi6/13, Gi6/14, Gi6/15, Gi6/16
                                                Gi6/17, Gi6/18, Gi6/20, Gi6/21
                                                Gi6/22, Gi6/23, Gi6/24, Gi7/6
                                                Gi7/8, Gi7/11, Gi7/12, Gi7/19
                                                Gi8/8, Gi8/24, Gi9/1, Gi9/2
                                                Gi9/3, Gi9/13
105  VLAN0105                         active    Gi7/24, Gi9/5, Gi9/6, Gi9/7
                                                Gi9/8, Gi9/10, Gi9/11, Gi9/14
                                                Gi9/16, Gi9/18, Gi9/19, Gi9/20
                                                Gi9/21, Gi9/22, Gi9/23, Gi9/24
                                                Gi10/1, Gi10/2, Gi10/4, Gi10/5
                                                Gi10/6, Gi10/8, Gi10/9, Gi10/10
                                                Gi10/11, Gi10/12, Gi10/13
                                                Gi10/14, Gi10/15, Gi10/16
                                                Gi10/17, Gi10/18, Gi10/19
                                                Gi10/20, Gi10/21, Gi10/22
                                                Gi10/23, Gi10/24
106  VLAN0106                         active    Gi6/8
107  VLAN0107                         active    Gi7/1, Gi7/2, Gi7/3, Gi7/4
                                                Gi7/5, Gi7/7, Gi7/9, Gi7/10
                                                Gi7/13, Gi7/14, Gi7/16, Gi7/17
                                                Gi7/18, Gi7/21, Gi7/22, Gi8/1
                                                Gi8/2, Gi8/3, Gi8/4, Gi8/5
                                                Gi8/6, Gi8/7, Gi8/9, Gi8/10
                                                Gi8/13, Gi8/14, Gi8/16, Gi8/17
                                                Gi8/18, Gi8/21, Gi8/22
108  VLAN0108                         active    Gi7/15, Gi7/20, Gi7/23, Gi8/15
                                                Gi8/20, Gi8/23
109  VLAN0109                         active
601  VLAN0601                         active
1002 fddi-default                     act/unsup
1003 token-ring-default               act/unsup
1004 fddinet-default                  act/unsup
1005 trnet-default                    act/unsup

VLAN Type  SAID       MTU   Parent RingNo BridgeNo Stp  BrdgMode Trans1 Trans2
---- ----- ---------- ----- ------ ------ -------- ---- -------- ------ ------
1    enet  100001     1500  -      -      -        -    -        0      0
5    enet  100005     1500  -      -      -        -    -        0      0
13   enet  100013     1500  -      -      -        -    -        0      0
14   enet  100014     1500  -      -      -        -    -        0      0
16   enet  100016     1500  -      -      -        -    -        0      0
18   enet  100018     1500  -      -      -        -    -        0      0
19   enet  100019     1500  -      -      -        -    -        0      0
104  enet  100104     1500  -      -      -        -    -        0      0
105  enet  100105     1500  -      -      -        -    -        0      0
106  enet  100106     1500  -      -      -        -    -        0      0
107  enet  100107     1500  -      -      -        -    -        0      0
108  enet  100108     1500  -      -      -        -    -        0      0
109  enet  100109     1500  -      -      -        -    -        0      0
601  enet  100601     1500  -      -      -        -    -        0      0
1002 fddi  101002     1500  -      -      -        -    -        0      0
1003 tr    101003     1500  -      -      -        -    -        0      0
1004 fdnet 101004     1500  -      -      -        ieee -        0      0
1005 trnet 101005     1500  -      -      -        ibm  -        0      0
```

Figure 6-15 Result of the `show vlan` command on a Cisco switch

Net+ As when creating VLANs, you create and maintain trunks through the switch's operating system software. A port on a switch is configured as either an access port or a trunk port. An **access**
1.4 2.1 **port** is used for connecting nodes that can only exchange information with the switch. For example, a server connected to an access port cannot recognize which VLAN it belongs to, nor can it recognize other VLANs on the same switch. A **trunk port** is the interface on a switch capable of managing traffic among multiple VLANs. Thus, a trunk is a link between two switches' trunk ports. Figure 6-16 illustrates how a trunk connects and conveys information about VLANs.

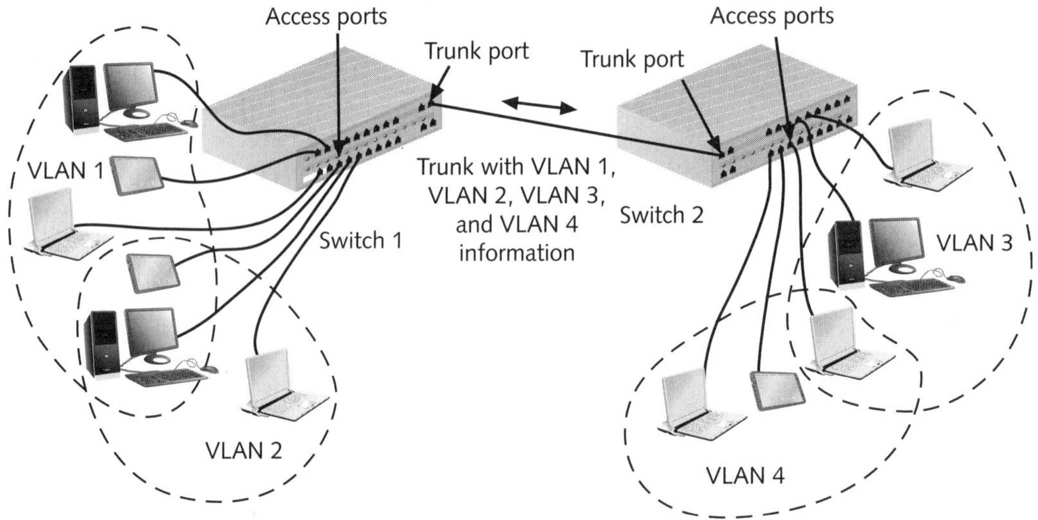

Figure 6-16 Trunk for multiple VLANs

VLAN configuration can be complex. It requires careful planning to ensure that all users and devices that need to exchange data can do so after the VLAN is in operation. It also requires contemplating how the VLAN switch will interact with other devices. For example, if you want users from different VLANs to be able to communicate, you need to connect those VLANs through a Layer 3 device, such as a router or a higher-layer switch, like the ones discussed later in this chapter.

Net+ STP (Spanning Tree Protocol)

1.4 Suppose you design an enterprise-wide network with several switches interconnected via their
2.5 uplink ports in a hybrid star-bus topology. To make the network more fault tolerant, you install multiple, or redundant, switches at critical junctures. Redundancy allows data the option of traveling through more than one switch toward its destination and makes your network less vulnerable to hardware malfunctions. For example, if one switch suffers a power supply failure, traffic can reroute through a second switch. Your network might look something like the one pictured in Figure 6-17. (In reality, of course, many more nodes would connect to the switches.)

A potential problem with the network shown in Figure 6-17 has to do with traffic loops. What if the server attached to switch A issues a broadcast frame, which switch A then reissues to all of its ports (other than the port to which the server is attached)? In that case, switch A will issue the broadcast frame to switches B, C, and D, which will then reissue the

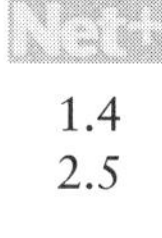
1.4
2.5

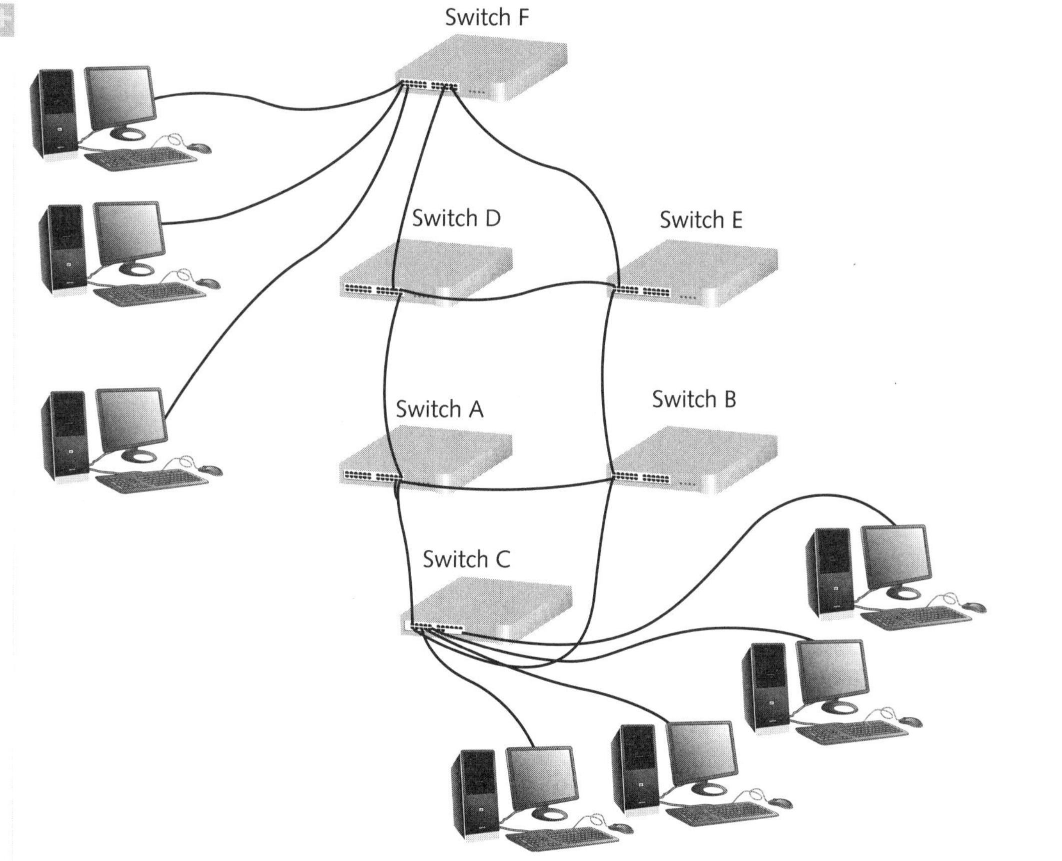

Figure 6-17 Enterprise-wide switched network

broadcast frame back to switch A and to each other, and so on. If no mechanism exists to stop this broadcast storm, the high traffic volume will severely impair network performance. To eliminate the possibility of this and other types of traffic loops, switches and bridges use **STP (Spanning Tree Protocol)**.

1.2
1.4

STP is defined in IEEE standard **802.1D** and functions in the Data Link layer. It prevents traffic loops by calculating paths that avoid potential loops and by artificially blocking the links that would complete a loop. In addition, STP can adapt to changes in the network. For instance, if a switch is removed, STP will recalculate the best loop-free data paths between the remaining switches.

In the following explanation of STP, you can substitute *switch* wherever the word *bridge* is used. As you have learned, a switch is really just a glorified bridge. STP terminology refers to a Layer 2 device as a *bridge*.

First, STP selects a **root bridge**, or master bridge, which will provide the basis for all subsequent path calculations. The term *root bridge* makes sense when you consider the protocol's

method, "spanning tree." Only one root bridge exists on a network, and from it a series of
1.4 logical branches, or data paths, emanate. STP selects the root bridge based on its **BID (Bridge**
2.1 **ID)**, which is a combination of a 2-byte priority field and the bridge's MAC address. To
2.5 begin with, all bridges on the network share the same priority number, and so the bridge
with the lowest MAC address becomes the root bridge.

Next, on every other bridge on the network, STP examines the possible paths between that bridge and the root bridge. Then it chooses the shortest of these paths—that is, the path that will carry data to its target fastest. Furthermore, STP stipulates that only one port and one intermediary bridge can forward frames from the root bridge to the destination bridge.

Finally, STP disables links that are not part of the shortest path. To do so, it blocks all ports other than the designated forwarding port from transmitting or receiving network traffic. (The ports can, however, continue to receive information from STP.) Figure 6-18 illustrates a switched network with certain paths selected and others blocked by STP. In this drawing, for example, traffic from the root bridge would only be forwarded to switch D via switch A. Even though switch D is physically connected to switches E, F, and A, STP has limited the logical pathway to go through switch A. If switch A were to fail, STP would choose a different logical pathway for frames destined for switch D.

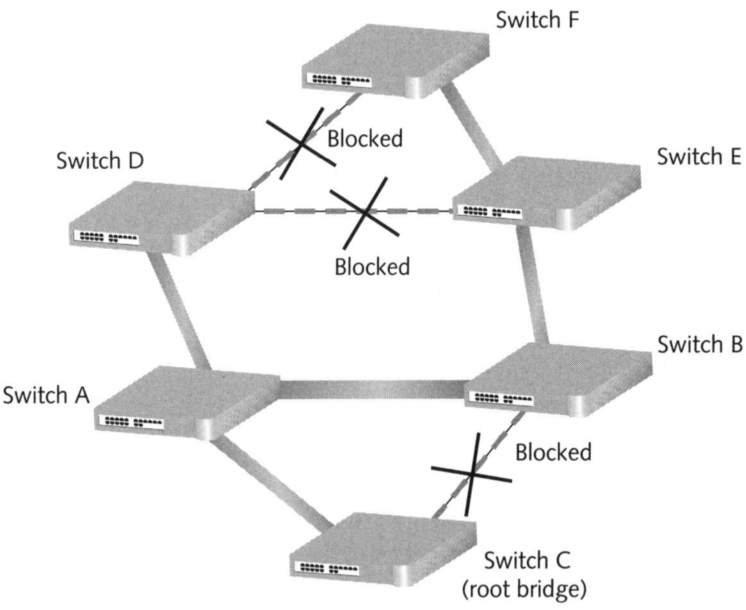

Figure 6-18 STP-selected paths on a switched network

STP was introduced in the 1980s, and since then, network developers have repeatedly modified it to improve and customize its functioning. The original STP is considered too slow for today's networks. For instance, it could take up to two minutes to detect and account for a link failure. With that kind of lag time, older versions of STP would bog down network transmissions, especially where high-volume, speed-dependent traffic, like telephone or video signals, is involved. Newer versions of STP, such as **RSTP (Rapid Spanning Tree Protocol)**,

defined in IEEE's **802.1w** standard, can detect and correct for link failures in milliseconds.
1.4 Some switch manufacturers, such as Cisco and Extreme Networks, have designed proprietary
2.1 versions of STP that are optimized to work most efficiently on their equipment.

2.5 When installing switches on your network, you do not need to enable or configure STP (or the more current version that came with your switch). It will come with the switch's operating software and should function smoothly by default and without intervention. However, if you want to designate preferred paths between bridges or choose a special root bridge, for example, STP allows you to alter its default prioritization.

Content and Multilayer Switches

1.2 You have learned that switches operate in Layer 2 of the OSI model, routers operate in Layer 3,
1.4 and hubs operate in Layer 1. You also learned that the distinctions between bridges, switches, and routers are blurring. Indeed, many networks already use switches that can operate at Layer 3 (Network layer), similar to a router. Manufacturers have also made switches that operate at Layer 4 (Transport layer). A switch capable of interpreting Layer 3 data is called a **Layer 3 switch** (and sometimes called a **routing switch**). Similarly, a switch capable of interpreting Layer 4 data is called a **Layer 4 switch**. Switches that operate anywhere between Layer 4 and Layer 7 are also known as **content switches** or **application switches**.

Among other things, the ability to interpret higher-layer data enables switches to perform advanced filtering, statistics keeping, and security functions. But the features of Layer 3 and Layer 4 switches vary widely depending on the manufacturer and the price. (This variability is exacerbated by the fact that key players in the networking trade have not agreed on standards for these switches.) In fact, it's often hard to distinguish between a Layer 3 switch and a router. In some cases, the difference comes down to what the manufacturer has decided to call the device in order to sell more of it. But in general, Layer 3 and Layer 4 switches, similar to Layer 2 switches, are optimized for fast Layer 2 data handling.

Higher-layer switches can cost three times more than Layer 2 switches, and are typically used as part of a network's backbone. They would not be appropriate for use on a small, contained LAN or to connect a group of end users to the network.

Despite the fact that the boundaries between switches and routers blur, it's important to understand the key functions of traditional routers, which are still used on many WANs and enterprise-wide networks today. The following section discusses routers and routing in detail.

Routers

A **router** is a multiport connectivity device that directs data between nodes on a network.
1.2 Routers can integrate LANs and WANs running at different transmission speeds and using a
1.4 variety of protocols. Simply put, when a router receives an incoming packet, it reads the packet's logical addressing information. Based on this, it determines to which network the packet must be delivered. Then, it determines the shortest path to that network. Finally, it forwards the packet to the next hop in that path. Routers operate at the Network layer (Layer 3) of the OSI model. They can be devices dedicated to routing, off-the-shelf computers configured to perform routing services, or even a desktop computer with two NICs configured to route packets.

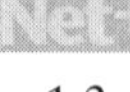

Recall that Network layer protocols direct data from one segment or type of network to another. Logical addressing, using protocols such as IP, also occurs at this layer. Conse-
1.2
1.4
quently, unlike bridges and Layer 2 switches, routers are protocol dependent. In other words, they must be designed or configured to recognize a certain Network layer protocol before they can forward data transmitted using that protocol. Broadly speaking, routers are slower than switches or bridges because they take time to interpret information in Layers 3 and higher.

Traditional stand-alone LAN routers are being replaced by Layer 3 switches that support the routing functions. However, despite competition from Layer 3 switches, routers are finding niches in specialized applications such as linking large Internet nodes or completing digitized telephone calls. The concept of routing, and everything described in the remainder of this section, applies to both routers and Layer 3 switches.

Router Characteristics and Functions

1.4 A router's strength lies in its intelligence. Not only can routers keep track of the locations of certain nodes on the network, as switches can, but they can also determine the shortest, fastest path between two nodes. For this reason, and because they can connect dissimilar network types, routers are powerful, indispensable devices on large LANs and WANs. The Internet, for example, relies on a multitude of routers across the world.

A typical router has an internal processor, an operating system, memory, input and output jacks for different types of network connectors (depending on the network type), and, usually, a management console interface. Three examples of routers are shown in Figure 6-19, with the most complex on the left and the simplest on the right. High-powered, multiprotocol routers may have several slot bays to accommodate multiple network interfaces. At the other end of the scale are simple, inexpensive routers often used in small offices and homes. As with the simple switches described in the previous section, these simple routers can be added to a network and function properly without significant configuration.

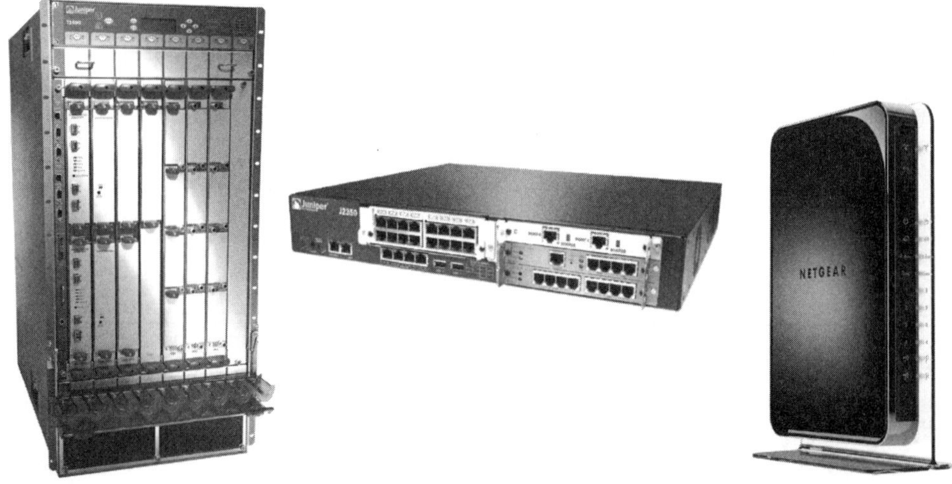

Figure 6-19 Routers

Courtesy of Juniper Networks, Inc. (left and center images); Courtesy of NETGEAR (right image)

1.4 A router is a very flexible device. Although any one can be specialized for a variety of tasks, all routers can do the following:

- Connect dissimilar networks.
- Interpret Layer 3 addressing and other information (such as quality of service indicators).
- Determine the best path for data to follow from point A to point B.
- Reroute traffic if a primary path is down but another path is available.

In addition to performing these basic functions, routers may perform any of the following optional functions:

- Filter out broadcast transmissions to alleviate network congestion.
- Prevent certain types of traffic from getting to a network, enabling customized segregation and security.
- Support simultaneous local and remote connectivity.
- Provide high network fault tolerance through redundant components such as power supplies or network interfaces.
- Monitor network traffic and report statistics.
- Diagnose internal or other connectivity problems and trigger alarms.

Routers are often categorized according to the scope of the network they serve. A router that directs data between nodes on an autonomous LAN (or one owned and operated by a single organization) is known as an **interior router**. Such routers do not direct data between an employee's workstation and a Web server on the Internet. They can, however, direct data between an employee's workstation and his supervisor's workstation in an office down the hall. Another type of router is an **exterior router**. Exterior routers direct data between nodes external to a given autonomous LAN. Routers that operate on the Internet backbone are exterior routers. Between interior and exterior routers are **border routers** (or **gateway routers**). Such routers connect an autonomous LAN with a WAN. For example, the router that connects a business with its ISP is a border router.

Routers rely on **routing tables** to identify which routers serve which hosts. A routing table is a database stored in the router's memory that maintains information about where hosts are located and the most efficient way to reach them. (You will learn more about routing tables in Chapter 9.) Routers may use one of two methods for directing data on the network: static or dynamic routing. **Static routing** is a technique in which a network administrator configures a router to use specific paths between nodes. Static routes can be specified in a routing table. However, because it does not account for occasional network congestion, failed connections, or device moves, static routing is not optimal. If a router or a segment connected to a router is moved, the network administrator must reprogram the static router's tables. Static routing requires human intervention, so it is less efficient and accurate than dynamic routing.

Dynamic routing, on the other hand, automatically calculates the best path between two nodes and accumulates this information in the routing table. If congestion or failures affect the network, a router using dynamic routing can detect the problems and reroute data through a different path. As a part of dynamic routing, by default, when a router is added to a network, routing protocols update its routing tables. Most networks primarily use

Net+ dynamic routing, but may include some static routing to indicate, for example, a router of last resort, the router that accepts all unroutable packets.

1.4
2.1 On small office or home LANs, routers are simple to install. Setting up the hardware connections is similar to installing a workgroup switch, as described earlier in this chapter. A router, however, requires additional configuration. For small office and home routers, a Web-based configuration interface leads you through the setup process.

However, because of their customizability, routers can be a challenge to install on sizable networks. Typically, an engineer must be very familiar with routing technology to figure out how to place and configure a router to best advantage. Figure 6-20 gives you some idea of how routers fit into a LAN environment. If you plan to specialize in network design or management, you should research router types and their capabilities further.

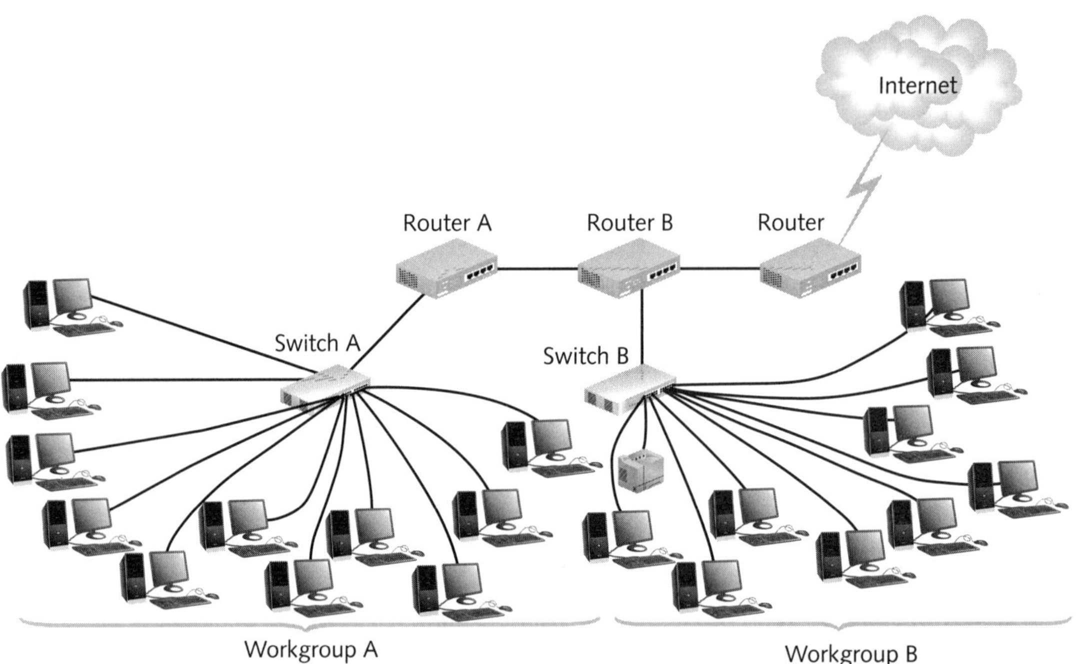

Figure 6-20 The placement of routers on a LAN

In the setup depicted in Figure 6-20, if a workstation in workgroup A wants to print to the printer in workgroup B, it creates a transmission containing the address of the workgroup B printer. Then, it sends its packets to switch A. When switch A receives the transmission, it checks the MAC address for the printer and determines that the message needs to be forwarded. It forwards the message to router A. Router A examines the destination network address in each packet and consults its router table to find out where the packet needs to go and then determines the most efficient way of delivering the message. In this example, it sends the data to router B. Before it forwards the data, however, router A increments (increases) the number of hops tallied in all the packets. Each time a packet passes through a router, it has made a hop. Packets can only take a certain number of hops before they are discarded.

After it increments the number of hops tallied in each packet, router A forwards the data to
1.4 router B. Router B increments each packet's hop count, reads each packet's destination net-
2.1 work address, and sends them to switch B. Based on the destination MAC address in the
packets, switch B delivers the transmission to workgroup B. The printer picks up the message, and then begins printing.

Routing Protocols

1.4 Finding the best route for data to take across the network is one of the most valued and sophisticated functions performed by a router. The term **best path** refers to the most efficient route from one node on a network to another. The best path in a particular situation depends on the number of hops between nodes, the current network activity, the unavailable links, the network transmission speed, and the topology. To determine the best path, routers communicate with each other through **routing protocols**. Keep in mind that routing protocols are *not* the same as routable protocols, such as TCP/IP, although routing protocols may piggyback on routable protocols. Routing protocols are used only to collect data about current network status and contribute to the selection of the best paths. From these data, routers create routing tables, which act as a type of road map for future packet forwarding. You'll learn more about routing tables in Chapter 9.

The method by which a routing protocol chooses the best path for data is known as its **routing metric**. Some of the factors that routing metrics may weigh include:

- Number of hops (network segments crossed)
- Throughput on a potential path
- Delay, or latency, on a potential path
- Load, or the traffic or processing burden sustained by a router in the path
- MTU (maximum transmission unit), or the largest packet size allowable by routers in the path
- **Cost**, or a value assigned to a particular route as judged by the network administrator; the more desirable the path, the lower its cost
- Reliability of a potential path, based on historical performance

In addition to its ability to find the best path, a routing protocol can be characterized according to its router **convergence time**, the time it takes for a router to recognize a best path in the event of a change or network outage. Its overhead, or the burden placed on the underlying network to support the routing protocol, is also a distinguishing feature.

To attain Network+ certification, you should be familiar with the most common routing protocols: RIP, RIPv2, BGP, OSPF, IS-IS, and EIGRP. (Additional routing protocols exist, but a discussion of these exceeds the scope of this book.) These six common routing protocols are described in the following sections and summarized in Table 6-1.

Distance-Vector: RIP, RIPv2, BGP Routing protocols can be divided into three types: distance-vector, link-state, or a hybrid of distance-vector and link-state. The types differ in how they assess route information and determine the best path for data. **Distance-vector** routing protocols decide on the basis of the distance to a destination. Some distance-vector routing protocols only factor in the number of hops to the destination, while others

1.4 take into account latency and other network traffic characteristics. Furthermore, distance-vector routing protocols periodically exchange their route information with neighboring routers. However, routers relying on this type of routing protocol must accept the data they receive from their neighbors. They cannot, for example, independently assess network conditions two hops away.

RIP (Routing Information Protocol), a distance-vector routing protocol, is the oldest routing protocol. RIP factors in only the number of hops between nodes when determining the best path from one point to another. It does not consider network congestion or link speed, for example. RIP is an **IGP (Interior Gateway Protocol)**, which means that it can only route data within an autonomous (internal) network. For example, RIP and other IGPs cannot route packets from a LAN across the Internet to another LAN.

Routers using RIP broadcast their routing tables every 30 seconds to other routers, regardless of whether the tables have changed. This broadcasting creates excessive network traffic, especially if a large number of routes exist. If the routing tables change, it may take several minutes before the new information propagates to routers at the far reaches of the network; thus, the convergence time for RIP is poor. However, one advantage to RIP is its stability. For example, RIP prevents routing loops from continuing indefinitely by limiting the number of hops a packet can take between its source and its destination to 15. If the number of hops in a path exceeds 15, the network destination is considered unreachable. Thus, RIP does not work well in very large network environments in which data may have to travel through more than 15 routers to reach their destination (for example, on the Internet). Also, compared with other routing protocols, RIP is slower and less secure.

Developers have improved RIP since its release in 1988 and informally renamed the original RIP RIPv1 (Routing Information Protocol version 1). The latest version, **RIPv2 (Routing Information Protocol version 2)**, generates less broadcast traffic and functions more securely than RIPv1. Still, RIPv2 cannot exceed 15 hops, and it is less commonly used than some link-state routing protocols discussed later.

A distance-vector routing protocol suited to WANs is **BGP (Border Gateway Protocol)**. Unlike RIP, BGP communicates using BGP-specific messages that travel between routers over TCP sessions. Using BGP, routers can determine best paths based on many different factors. In addition, network administrators can configure BGP to follow policies that might, for example, avoid a certain router or instruct a group of routers to prefer one particular route over other available routes. BGP is the most complex of the routing protocols mentioned in this chapter. Because it is an **EGP (Exterior Gateway Protocol)** and can span multiple, autonomous networks, it is the routing protocol of choice for Internet traffic. BGP is used by border and exterior routers. If you maintain networks for an ISP or large telecommunications company, you will need to understand BGP.

Link-State: OSPF, IS-IS A **link-state** routing protocol is one that enables routers across a network to share information, after which each router can independently map the network and determine the best path between itself and a packet's destination node. (By contrast, recall that distance-vector routing protocols require routers to rely on their neighbors for data path information.)

OSPF (Open Shortest Path First) is a link-state routing protocol used on interior or border routers. It was introduced as an improvement to RIP and can coexist with RIP (or RIPv2) on a network. Unlike RIP, OSPF imposes no hop limits on a transmission path. Also, OSPF

Net+ uses a more complex algorithm for determining best paths than RIP uses. Under optimal
1.4 network conditions, the best path is the most direct path between two points. If excessive traffic levels or an outage preclude data from following the most direct path, a router may determine that the most efficient path actually goes through additional routers. Because OSPF is a link-state routing protocol, each router running OSPF maintains a database of the other routers' links. If OSPF learns of the failure of a given link, the router can rapidly compute an alternate path. This calculation demands more memory and CPU power than RIP would, but it keeps network bandwidth to a minimum and provides a very fast convergence time, often invisible to the users. OSPF is supported by all modern routers. Therefore, it is commonly used on LANs that rely on a mix of routers from different manufacturers.

Another link-state routing protocol, which uses a best-path algorithm similar to OSPF's, is **IS-IS (Intermediate System to Intermediate System)**. IS-IS was originally codified by ISO, which referred to routers as "intermediate systems," thus the protocol's name. Unlike OSPF, however, IS-IS, a type of IGP, is designed for use on interior routers only. Also, it differs in that it supports two Layer 3 protocols: IP or an ISO-specific protocol. IS-IS is much less common than OSPF.

Hybrid: EIGRP Some routing protocols reflect characteristics of both link-state and distance-vector routing protocols and are known as hybrid routing protocols. The most popular example is **EIGRP (Enhanced Interior Gateway Routing Protocol)**. This routing protocol, used on interior or border routers, was developed in the mid-1980s by Cisco Systems. It has a fast convergence time and a low network overhead, and is easier to configure and less CPU-intensive than OSPF. EIGRP also offers the benefits of supporting multiple protocols and limiting unnecessary network traffic between routers. It accommodates very large and heterogeneous networks, but is only supported by Cisco routers. On LANs that use exclusively Cisco routers, EIGRP is generally preferred over OSPF.

Table 6-1 Summary of common routing protocols

Routing protocol	Type	Location
RIP (Routing Information Protocol)	Distance-vector	Interior
RIPv2 (Routing Information Protocol version 2)	Distance-vector	Interior
BGP (Border Gateway Protocol)	Distance-vector	Exterior
OSPF (Open Shortest Path First)	Link-state	Interior or exterior
IS-IS (Intermediate System to Intermediate System)	Link-state	Interior
EIGRP (Enhanced Interior Gateway Routing Protocol)	Hybrid	Exterior or Interior

You have learned about a router's essential features, including how it functions, how it fits into a network, and how it communicates with other routers. Because routers are such critical backbone devices, this book discusses them in more detail in several chapters. For example, you will learn about routers in the context of wireless networks in Chapter 8 and about the roles routers play in transmitting voice and video signals in Chapter 12. The following section introduces gateways, which share some similarities with routers and may even exist on routers.

Gateways and Other Multifunction Devices

Gateway is a term that can refer to one of many similar kinds of devices or interfaces in networking, so it's important to understand the context in which the term is used. In broad terms, **gateways** are combinations of networking hardware and software that connect two dissimilar kinds of networks. Specifically, they may connect two systems that use different formatting, communications protocols, or architecture. Unlike the connectivity hardware discussed earlier in this chapter, gateways actually repackage information so that it can be read by another system. To accomplish this task, gateways must operate at multiple layers of the OSI model. They communicate with an application, establish and manage sessions, translate encoded data, and interpret logical and physical addressing data.

Gateways can reside on servers, microcomputers, connectivity devices (such as routers), or mainframes. They are almost always designed for one category of gateway functions. In addition, they transmit data more slowly than bridges or routers (which are not acting as gateways) because of the complex translations they conduct. At a slower speed, gateways have the potential to cause extreme network congestion. In certain situations, however, only a gateway will suffice.

During your networking career, you will most likely hear gateways discussed in the context of Internet connections and e-mail systems. Popular types of gateways, including e-mail gateways, are described in the following list:

- *E-mail gateway*—A gateway that translates messages from one type of e-mail system to another. For example, an e-mail gateway allows networks that use Sendmail mail server software to exchange mail with networks that use Microsoft Exchange Server software.
- *Internet gateway*—A gateway that allows and manages access between LANs and the Internet. An Internet gateway can restrict the kind of access LAN users have to the Internet, and vice versa.
- *LAN gateway*—A gateway that allows segments of a LAN running different protocols or different network models to communicate with each other. A router, a single port on a router, or even a server may act as a LAN gateway. The LAN gateway category might also include remote access servers that allow dial-up connectivity to a LAN.
- *Voice/data gateway*—A gateway that connects the part of a network that handles data traffic with the part of a network that handles voice traffic. Voice applications have drastically different requirements than data applications. For example, before a voice signal can be transmitted over a data network, it needs to be digitized and compressed. When it reaches a voice receiver, such as a telephone, it has to be uncompressed and regenerated as recognizable speech, without delays. All these functions require specialized protocols and processes. A voice/data gateway can translate between these unique network segments and traditional data network segments.
- *Firewall*—A gateway that selectively blocks or filters traffic between networks. As with any other type of gateway, **firewalls** may be devices optimized for performing their tasks or computers installed with software necessary to accomplish those tasks. Because firewalls are integral to network security, they are discussed in detail in Chapter 11.

Chapter Summary

- Network adapters come in a variety of types depending on access method (Ethernet), network transmission speed (for example, 100 Mbps versus 1 Gbps), connector interfaces (for example, SC versus RJ-45), number of ports, type of compatible motherboard or device, and manufacturer.
- Newer computers may come with PCIe expansion board NICs, which attach to the motherboard via an expansion slot, or on-board NICs (especially in the case of laptops), which are integrated into the motherboard. Peripheral NICs, such as those that connect via USB port, can also be used.
- NICs are designed to be used with either wire-bound or wireless connections. A wireless NIC uses an antenna to exchange signals with the network. This type of connectivity suits environments in which cabling cannot be installed or where roaming clients must be supported.

- Modular interfaces such as GBICs (Gigabit interface converters) and SFP (small form-factor pluggable) transceivers enable network administrators to add and remove network connections to and from connectivity devices without negatively affecting operations.
- Repeaters are the connectivity devices that perform the regeneration of a digital signal. They belong to the Physical layer of the OSI model; therefore, they do not have any means to interpret the data they are retransmitting.
- At its most primitive, a hub is a multiport repeater. A hub contains multiple data ports into which the patch cables for network nodes are connected. The hub accepts signals from a transmitting node and repeats those signals to all other connected nodes in a broadcast fashion, thereby creating a single collision domain. Most hubs also contain one port, called an uplink port, which allows the hub to connect to another hub or other connectivity device.
- Bridges resemble repeaters in that they have a single input and a single output port, but they can interpret the data they retransmit. Bridging occurs at the Data Link layer of the OSI model. Bridges read the destination's MAC address information and decide whether to forward (retransmit) a packet to another segment on the network or, if the destination address belongs to the same segment as the source address, discard it.
- As nodes transmit data through the bridge, the bridge establishes a filtering database of known MAC addresses and their locations on the network. The bridge uses its filtering database to determine whether a packet should be forwarded or filtered.
- Switches subdivide a network into smaller, logical pieces. They operate at the Data Link layer (Layer 2) of the OSI model and can interpret MAC address information. In this respect, switches resemble bridges.
- Switches are generally secure because they isolate one device's traffic from other devices' traffic. Because switches provide separate channels for potentially every device, they allow applications that transfer a large amount of traffic and that are sensitive to time delays, such as videoconferencing, to make full use of the network's capacity.
- A switch running in cut-through mode reads a frame's header and decides where to forward the data before it receives the entire packet. In store-and-forward mode,

switches read the entire data frame into their memory and check it for accuracy before transmitting it. Although this method is more time consuming than the cut-through method, it allows store-and-forward switches to transmit data more accurately.

- Switches can create VLANs (virtual local area networks) by logically grouping several ports into a broadcast domain. The ports do not have to reside on the same switch or even on the same network segment. VLANs can isolate nodes and their traffic for security, easier management, or better performance. Multiple VLANs can be carried over single switch interfaces using VLAN trunking.
- On networks with several interconnected switches, STP (Spanning Tree Protocol) prevents traffic loops (and, as a consequence, broadcast storms) by calculating paths that avoid potential loops and by artificially blocking the links that would complete a loop.
- Manufacturers are producing switches that can operate at Layer 3 (Network layer) and Layer 4 (Transport layer) of the OSI model, making them act more like routers. The ability to interpret higher-layer data enables switches to perform advanced filtering, statistics keeping, and security functions.
- A router is a multiport device that can connect dissimilar LANs and WANs running at different transmission speeds, using a variety of protocols. Routers interpret logical addresses and determine the best path between nodes. They operate at the Network layer (Layer 3) or higher of the OSI model.
- Static routing is a technique in which a network administrator programs a router to use specific paths between nodes. Dynamic routing automatically calculates the best path between two nodes and accumulates this information in a routing table. If congestion or failures affect the network, a router using dynamic routing can detect the problems and reroute data through a different path. Most modern networks use dynamic routing.
- To determine the best path, routers communicate with each other through routing protocols. Different routing protocols use different routing metrics to choose the best path.
- Routing metrics may factor in the number of hops between nodes, throughput, delay, MTU, cost, load, and reliability.
- Distance-vector routing protocols determine the best route for data based on the distance to a destination. Some distance-vector routing protocols only factor in the number of hops to the destination, while others take into account latency and other network traffic characteristics.
- A link-state routing protocol enables routers across a network to share information, after which each router can independently map the network and determine the best path between itself and a packet's destination node.
- Some routing protocols reflect characteristics of both link-state and distance-vector routing protocols and are known as hybrid routing protocols.
- RIP (Routing Information Protocol), a distance-vector routing protocol, is the slowest and least secure and limits transmissions to 15 hops. RIPv2 makes up for some of the original RIP's overhead and security limitations, but its forwarding remains limited to 15 hops. RIP belongs to the IGP (Interior Gateway Protocol) category of protocols that can forward data only within an autonomous LAN.

- BGP (Border Gateway Protocol), used primarily for routing over Internet backbones, uses the most complex best-path calculation of all the commonly used routing protocols. It's considered a border routing protocol.
- OSPF (Open Shortest Path First) is a link-state routing protocol used on interior or border routers. It was introduced as an improvement to RIP and can coexist with RIP (or RIPv2) on a network. Unlike RIP, OSPF imposes no hop limits on a transmission path. Also, OSPF uses a more complex algorithm for determining best paths than RIP uses.
- IS-IS uses virtually the same methods as OSPF to calculate best paths, is less common, and is limited to interior routers.
- EIGRP (Enhanced Interior Gateway Routing Protocol) is a hybrid EGP type of routing protocol and is a Cisco standard commonly used on LANs that use exclusively Cisco routers.
- Gateways are combinations of networking hardware and software that connect two dissimilar kinds of networks. Specifically, they may connect two systems that use different formatting, communications protocols, or architecture. To accomplish this task, they must operate at multiple layers of the OSI model.
- Several different network devices can perform functions at multiple layers of the OSI model, including e-mail gateways, Internet gateways, LAN gateways, firewalls, and voice/data gateways.

Key Terms

802.1D The IEEE standard that describes, among other things, bridging and STP (Spanning Tree Protocol).

802.1q The IEEE standard that specifies how VLAN and trunking information appear in frames and how switches and bridges interpret that information.

802.1w The IEEE standard that describes RSTP (Rapid Spanning Tree Protocol), which evolved from STP (Spanning Tree Protocol).

access port The interface on a switch used for an end node. Devices connected to access ports are unaware of VLAN information.

application switch A switch that provides functions between Layer 4 and Layer 7 of the OSI model.

backplane A synonym for motherboard, often used in the context of switches and routers.

best path The most efficient route from one node on a network to another. Under optimal network conditions, the best path is the most direct path between two points. However, when traffic congestion, segment failures, and other factors create obstacles, the most direct path might not be the best path.

BGP (Border Gateway Protocol) A distance-vector routing protocol capable of considering many factors in its routing metrics. BGP, an Exterior Gateway Protocol, is the routing protocol used on Internet backbones.

BID (Bridge ID) A combination of a 2-byte priority field and a bridge's MAC address, used in STP (Spanning Tree Protocol) to select a root bridge.

Border Gateway Protocol *See* BGP.

border router A router that connects an autonomous LAN with an exterior network—for example, the router that connects a business to its ISP.

bridge A connectivity device that operates at the Data Link layer (Layer 2) of the OSI model and reads header information to forward packets according to their MAC addresses. Bridges use a filtering database to determine which packets to discard and which to forward. Bridges contain one input and one output port and separate network segments.

Bridge ID *See* BID.

bus The type of circuit used by a computer's motherboard to transmit data to components. Most new Pentium computers use buses capable of exchanging 32 or 64 bits of data. As the number of bits of data a bus handles increases, so too does the speed of the device attached to the bus.

content switch A switch that provides functions between Layer 4 and Layer 7 of the OSI model.

convergence time The time it takes for a router to recognize a best path in the event of a change or network outage.

cost In the context of routing metrics, the value assigned to a particular route as judged by the network administrator. The more desirable the path, the lower its cost.

cut-through mode A switching mode in which a switch reads a frame's header and decides where to forward the data before it receives the entire packet. Cut-through mode is faster, but less accurate, than the other switching method, store-and-forward mode.

device driver The software that enables an attached device to communicate with the computer's operating system.

distance-vector The simplest type of routing protocols, these determine the best route for data based on the distance to a destination. Some distance-vector routing protocols, like RIP, only factor in the number of hops to the destination, while others take into account latency and other network traffic characteristics.

driver *See* device driver.

dynamic routing A method of routing that automatically calculates the best path between two nodes and accumulates this information in a routing table. If congestion or failures affect the network, a router using dynamic routing can detect the problems and reroute data through a different path. Modern networks primarily use dynamic routing.

EGP (Exterior Gateway Protocol) A routing protocol that can span multiple, autonomous networks. BGP and EIGRP are examples of Exterior Gateway Protocols.

EIGRP (Enhanced Interior Gateway Routing Protocol) A routing protocol developed in the mid-1980s by Cisco Systems that has a fast convergence time and a low network overhead, but is easier to configure and less CPU-intensive than OSPF. EIGRP also offers the benefits of supporting multiple protocols and limiting unnecessary network traffic between routers.

Enhanced Interior Gateway Routing Protocol *See* EIGRP.

ethtool A popular tool for viewing and modifying network interface properties on Linux computers.

expansion board A circuit board used to connect a device to a computer's motherboard.

expansion card *See* expansion board.

expansion slot A receptacle on a computer's motherboard that contains multiple electrical contacts into which an expansion board can be inserted.

Exterior Gateway Protocol *See* EGP.

exterior router A router that directs data between nodes outside a given autonomous LAN, for example, routers used on the Internet's backbone.

filtering database A collection of data created and used by a bridge that correlates the MAC addresses of connected workstations with their locations. A filtering database is also known as a forwarding table.

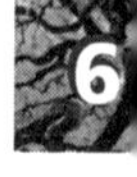

firewall A device (either a router or a computer running special software) that selectively filters or blocks traffic between networks. Firewalls are commonly used to improve data security.

forwarding table *See* filtering database.

gateway A combination of networking hardware and software that connects two dissimilar kinds of networks. Gateways perform connectivity, session management, and data translation, so they must operate at multiple layers of the OSI model.

gateway router *See* border router.

GBIC (Gigabit interface converter) A standard type of modular interface designed in the 1990s for Gigabit Ethernet connections. GBICs may contain RJ-45 or fiber-optic cable ports (such as LC, SC, or ST). They are inserted into a socket on a connectivity device's backplane.

Gigabit interface converter *See* GBIC.

hot-swappable The feature of a component that allows it to be installed or removed without disrupting operations.

hub A connectivity device that retransmits incoming data signals to its multiple ports. Typically, hubs contain one uplink port, which is used to connect to a network's backbone.

IGP (Interior Gateway Protocol) A routing protocol, such as RIP, that can only route data within an autonomous (internal) network.

interior router A router that directs data between nodes on an autonomous LAN.

Intermediate System to Intermediate System *See* IS-IS.

Interior Gateway Protocol *See* IGP.

IS-IS (Intermediate System to Intermediate System) A link-state routing protocol that uses a best-path algorithm similar to OSPF's. IS-IS was originally codified by ISO, which referred to routers as "intermediate systems," thus the protocol's name. Unlike OSPF, IS-IS is designed for use on interior routers only.

Layer 3 switch A switch capable of interpreting data at Layer 3 (Network layer) of the OSI model.

Layer 4 switch A switch capable of interpreting data at Layer 4 (Transport layer) of the OSI model.

link-state A type of routing protocol that enables routers across a network to share information, after which each router can independently map the network and determine the best path between itself and a packet's destination node.

loopback adapter *See* loopback plug.

loopback plug A connector used for troubleshooting that plugs into a port (for example, a serial, parallel, or RJ-45 port) and crosses over the transmit line to the receive line, allowing outgoing signals to be redirected back into the computer for testing.

main bus *See* bus.

mini GBIC *See* SFP.

on-board NIC A NIC that is integrated into a computer's motherboard, rather than connected via an expansion slot or peripheral bus.

on-board port A port that is integrated into a computer's motherboard.

Open Shortest Path First *See* OSPF.

OSPF (Open Shortest Path First) A routing protocol that makes up for some of the limitations of RIP and can coexist with RIP on a network.

PCIe (PCI Component Interconnect Express) A 32-bit bus standard capable of transferring data at up to 1 Gbps per data path, or lane, in full-duplex transmission. PCIe is commonly used for expansion board NICs.

PCI Component Interconnect Express *See* PCIe.

Rapid Spanning Tree Protocol *See* RSTP.

RIP (Routing Information Protocol) The oldest routing protocol that is still widely used, RIP is a distance-vector protocol that uses hop count as its routing metric and allows up to only 15 hops. It is considered an IGP. Compared with other, more modern, routing protocols, RIP is slower and less secure.

RIPv2 (Routing Information Protocol version 2) An updated version of the original RIP routing protocol, which makes up for some of its predecessor's overhead and security flaws. However, RIPv2's packet forwarding is still limited to a maximum 15 hops.

root bridge The single bridge on a network selected by the Spanning Tree Protocol to provide the basis for all subsequent path calculations.

router A multiport device that operates at Layer 3 of the OSI model and uses logical addressing information to direct data between networks or segments. Routers can connect dissimilar LANs and WANs running at different transmission speeds and using a variety of Network layer protocols. They determine the best path between nodes based on traffic congestion, available versus unavailable routes, load balancing targets, and other factors.

Routing Information Protocol *See* RIP.

Routing Information Protocol version 2 *See* RIPv2.

routing metric The method used by routing protocols to determine the best path for data to follow over a network. Routing metrics may be calculated using any of several variables, including number of hops, bandwidth, delay, MTU, cost, and load.

routing protocols The means by which routers communicate with each other about network status. Routing protocols determine the best path for data to take between nodes.

routing switch *See* Layer 3 switch.

routing table A database stored in a router's memory that maintains information about the location of hosts and best paths for forwarding packets to them.

RSTP (Rapid Spanning Tree Protocol) As described in IEEE's 802.1w standard, a version of the Spanning Tree Protocol that can detect and correct for network changes much more quickly.

runt An erroneously shortened packet.

SFP (small form-factor pluggable) transceiver A standard hot-swappable network interface used to link a connectivity device's backplane with fiber-optic or copper cabling. SFPs are known as mini GBICs because they perform a similar function as GBICs, but have a smaller profile. Current SFP standards enable them to send and receive data at up to 10 Gbps.

SFP GBIC *See* SFP.

Spanning Tree Protocol *See* STP.

static routing A technique in which a network administrator programs a router to use specific paths between nodes. Because it does not account for occasional network congestion, failed connections, or device moves and requires manual configuration, static routing is not optimal.

store-and-forward mode A method of switching in which a switch reads the entire data frame into its memory and checks it for accuracy before transmitting it. Although this method is more time consuming than the cut-through method, it allows store-and-forward switches to transmit data more accurately.

STP (Spanning Tree Protocol) A switching protocol defined in IEEE 802.1D. STP operates in the Data Link layer to prevent traffic loops by calculating paths that avoid potential loops and by artificially blocking links that would complete a loop. Given changes to a network's links or devices, STP recalculates its paths.

switch A connectivity device that logically subdivides a network into smaller, individual collision domains. A switch operates at the Data Link layer of the OSI model and can interpret MAC address information to determine whether to filter (discard) or forward packets it receives.

system bus *See* bus.

trunk port The interface on a switch capable of managing traffic from multiple VLANs.

trunking The aggregation of multiple logical connections in one physical connection between connectivity devices. In the case of VLANs, a trunk allows two switches to manage and exchange data between multiple VLANs.

uplink port A port on a connectivity device, such as a hub or switch, used to connect it to another connectivity device.

virtual local area network *See* VLAN.

VLAN (virtual local area network) A network within a network that is logically defined by grouping its devices' switch ports in the same broadcast domain. A VLAN can consist of any type of network node in any geographic location and can incorporate nodes connected to different switches.

VLAN trunking protocol *See* VTP.

VTP (VLAN trunking protocol) Cisco's protocol for exchanging VLAN information over trunks. VTP allows one switch on a network to centrally manage all VLANs.

Review Questions

1. Which bus type allows a NIC to be attached externally?
   a. PCI
   b. PCIe
   c. PCMCIA
   d. ISA
2. Which device acts most like a router?
   a. OSI model Layer 1 repeater
   b. OSI model Layer 2 hub
   c. OSI model Layer 2 bridge
   d. OSI model Layer 3 switch
3. Which term identifies a router category that directs data between nodes on an autonomous LAN?
   a. interior router
   b. exterior router
   c. border router
   d. gateway router
4. Which routing technique programs a router to use specific paths between nodes?
   a. dynamic routing
   b. static routing
   c. interior routing
   d. exterior routing
5. Which routing protocol is commonly used on LANs that use exclusively Cisco routers?
   a. RIPv2
   b. OSPF
   c. BGP
   d. EIGRP
6. True or false? All NICs are engineered to work in an older bus regardless of whether a faster, new bus is available on the motherboard.
7. True or false? A computer's port is the circuit, or signaling pathway, used by the motherboard to transmit data to the computer's components, including its memory, processor, hard disk and NIC.
8. True or false? Bridges can move data more rapidly than older routers.
9. True or false? Routers are protocol dependent.

10. True or false? Routing protocols are the same as routable protocols, such as TCP/IP.
11. A(n) ________________ is the connectivity device that performs the regeneration of a digital signal.
12. A(n) ________________ is a multiport repeater
13. A(n) ________________ is a device that connects two network segments by analyzing incoming frames and making decisions about where to direct them based on each frame's MAC address.
14. A switch running in ________________ mode reads a frame's header and decides where to forward the data before it receives the entire packet.
15. ________________ are combinations of networking hardware and software that connect two dissimilar kinds of networks.

chapter 7

Wide Area Networks

After reading this chapter and completing the exercises, you will be able to:

- Identify a variety of uses for WANs
- Explain different WAN topologies, including their advantages and disadvantages
- Compare the characteristics of WAN technologies, including their switching type, throughput, media, security, and reliability
- Describe several WAN transmission and connection methods, including PSTN, ISDN, T-carriers, DSL, broadband cable, broadband over powerline, ATM, and SONET

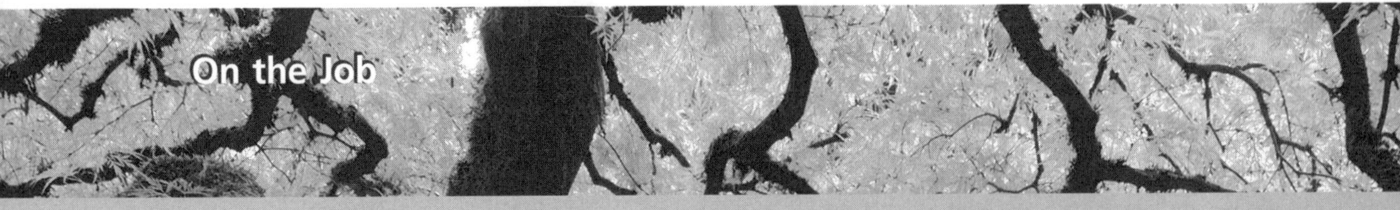

On the Job

I worked for a major global airline. We had centralized servers and a massive SQL Server database. The three distributed reservations centers were located in Orlando, Houston, and Denver. The database was highly fluid, with fares changing on every flight for every seat that was booked. In addition to the reservations systems, we had databases for managing crew, equipment, and maintenance schedules that all had to talk to each other. Synchronization had to occur in real time, of course, because the changes affected moving aircraft and people all around the world.

Our data center was really something cool. It was right out of a movie. We could see every company aircraft on a huge world map, along with all the aircraft from the FAA feed from every airline around the world. This was kind of like seeing the traffic snarls on today's smarter GPS devices. Our data center also had to identify the data traffic load on the wide area network (WAN) load and balance it carefully. Our technicians had to be trained on how to look at the data traffic, which looked remarkably similar to the airplanes on the map!

I'm sure you've been at the airport when they announce that a flight is oversold. Although some airlines intentionally overbook flights, WAN traffic imbalances can also lead to double booking. This is how it could happen:

A customer from England books a flight from London to New York on the Internet. This transaction generates traffic that taps the database and finds the one remaining seat. If the traffic is congested along the communications channel, the reservation for that seat might be snapped up by another customer talking with an agent in Denver microseconds before the confirmation comes in from London. All the servers must communicate the unavailability of the seat that has just been reserved, but even real time is a little slower than the speed of light. This is due to lag at the big routers that form the Internet backbone.

Fortunately, this doesn't happen very often because computers can project how many seats will go out empty based on many different factors, such as weather and historical metrics. In today's cutthroat game of international air travel, any advantage can give an airline the edge it needs to be profitable for that quarter. Load balancing is a critical job that computers can't always handle. We need sharp technicians to make this happen.

Michael Bleacher
Assistant Dean, School of Technology and School of Business
Westwood College

Now that you understand the basic transmission media, network models, and networking hardware associated with LANs (local area networks), you need to expand that knowledge to encompass WANs (wide area networks). As you have learned, a WAN is a network that connects two or more geographically distinct LANs. You might assume that WANs are the same as LANs, only bigger. Although a WAN is based on the same principles as a LAN, including reliance on the OSI model, its distance requirements affect its entire infrastructure. As a result, WANs differ from LANs in many respects.

To understand the difference between a LAN and WAN, think of the hallways and stairs of your house as LAN pathways. These interior passages allow you to go from room to room. To reach destinations outside your house, however, you need to use sidewalks and streets. These public thoroughfares are analogous to WAN pathways—except that WAN pathways are not necessarily public.

This chapter discusses the technical differences between LANs and WANs and describes in detail WAN transmission media and methods. It also notes the potential pitfalls in establishing and maintaining WANs. WANs are significant concerns for organizations attempting to meet the needs of telecommuting workers, global business partners, and Internet-based commerce. To pass the Network+ certification exam, you must be familiar with the variety of WAN options.

WAN Essentials

A WAN is a network that traverses some distance and usually connects LANs, whether across the city or across the nation. You are probably familiar with at least one WAN—the Internet, which is the largest WAN in existence. However, the Internet is not a typical WAN. Many WANs arise from the simple need to connect one location to another. As an organization grows, the WAN might grow to connect more and more sites, located across a city or around the world. Only an organization's information technology budget and aspirations limit the dimensions of its WAN.

Any business or government institution with sites scattered over a wide geographical area needs a way to exchange data between those sites. Each of the following scenarios demonstrates a need for a WAN:

- A bank with offices around the state needs to connect those offices to gather transaction and account information into a central database. Furthermore, it needs to connect with global financial clearinghouses to, for example, conduct transactions with other institutions.
- Regional sales representatives for a national pharmaceutical company need to submit their sales figures to a file server at the company's headquarters and receive e-mail from the company's mail server.
- An automobile manufacturer in Detroit contracts out its plastic parts manufacturing to a Delaware-based company. Through WAN links, the auto manufacturer can video conference with the plastics manufacturer, exchange specification data, and even examine the parts for quality from a remote location.
- A clothing manufacturer sells its products over the Internet to customers throughout the world.

Although all of these businesses need WANs, they might not need the same kinds of WANs. Depending on the traffic load, budget, geographical breadth, and commercially available technology, each might implement a different transmission method. For every business need, a few appropriate WAN connection types might exist. However, many WAN technologies can coexist on the same network.

WANs and LANs have several fundamental properties in common. Both are designed to enable communication between clients and hosts for resource sharing. In general, both use the same protocols from Layers 3 and higher of the OSI model. And both networks typically carry digitized data via packet-switched connections.

However, LANs and WANs often differ at Layers 1 and 2 of the OSI model in access methods, topologies, and, sometimes, media. They also differ in the extent to which the organization that uses the network is responsible for the network. LANs that depend on wire-bound transmission use a building's internal cabling, such as twisted pair, which runs from work areas to the walls, through plenum areas, and to a telecommunications closet. Such wiring is private; it belongs to the building owner. In contrast, WANs typically send data over publicly available communications networks, which are owned by local and long-distance telecommunications carriers. Such carriers, which are privately owned corporations, are also known as **NSPs (network service providers)**. Some large NSPs based in the United States include AT&T, Verizon, and Sprint. Customers lease connections from these carriers, with payments based on the amount of bandwidth they need. For best throughput and quality, organizations lease **dedicated** lines, or continuously available communications channels, from a telecommunications provider, such as a local telephone company or ISP. Dedicated lines come in a variety of types that are distinguished by their capacity and transmission characteristics.

The individual geographic locations connected by a WAN are known as WAN sites. A **WAN link** is a connection between one WAN site (or point) and another site (or point). Most WAN links are point-to-point, connecting one site to only one other site. That is, the link does not connect one site to several other sites, in the way that LAN routers connect multiple segments or workstations. Nevertheless, one location may be connected to more than one location by multiple WAN links. Figure 7-1 illustrates the difference between WAN and LAN connectivity.

The following section describes different topologies used on WANs.

WAN Topologies

3.5

WAN topologies resemble LAN topologies, but their details differ because of the distance they must cover, the larger number of users they serve, and the heavy traffic they often handle. For example, WAN topologies connect sites via dedicated and, usually, high-speed links. As a consequence, WANs use different connectivity devices. For example, to connect two buildings via high-speed T1 carrier lines, each location must use a special type of terminating device, a multiplexer, plus a router. And because WAN connections require routers or other Layer 3 devices to connect locations, their links are not capable of carrying nonroutable protocols. The following sections describe common WAN topologies and special considerations for using each.

3.5

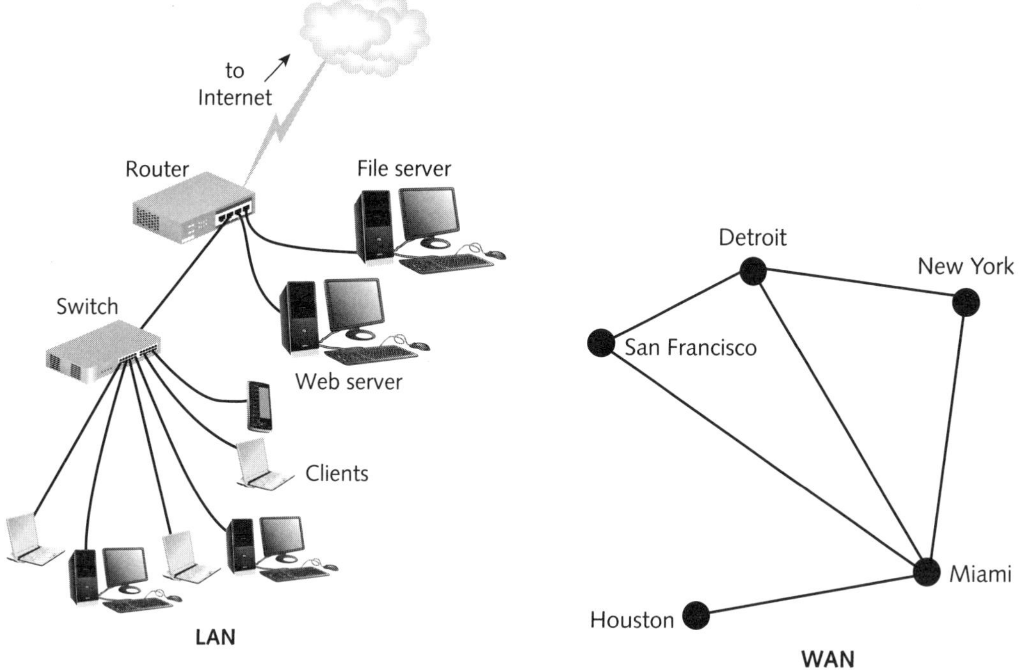

Figure 7-1 Differences in LAN and WAN connectivity

Bus

A WAN in which each site is directly connected to no more than two other sites in a serial fashion is known as a **bus topology WAN**. A bus topology WAN is similar to a bus topology LAN in that each site depends on every other site in the network to transmit and receive its traffic. However, bus topology LANs use computers with shared access to one cable, whereas the WAN bus topology uses different locations, each one connected to another one through point-to-point links.

A bus topology WAN is often the best option for organizations with only a few sites and the capability to use dedicated circuits. Some examples of dedicated circuits include T1, DSL, and ISDN connections, all of which are detailed later in this chapter. Dedicated circuits make it possible to transmit data regularly and reliably. Figure 7-2 depicts a bus topology WAN using T1 and DSL connections.

Bus WAN topologies are suitable for only small WANs. Because all sites between the sending and receiving location must participate in carrying traffic, this model does not scale well. The addition of more sites can cause performance to suffer. Also, a single failure on a bus topology WAN can take down communications between all sites.

Ring

In a **ring topology WAN**, each site is connected to two other sites so that the entire WAN forms a ring pattern, as shown in Figure 7-3. This architecture is similar to the simple ring topology used on a LAN, except that a WAN ring topology connects locations rather than local nodes.

Net+ 3.5

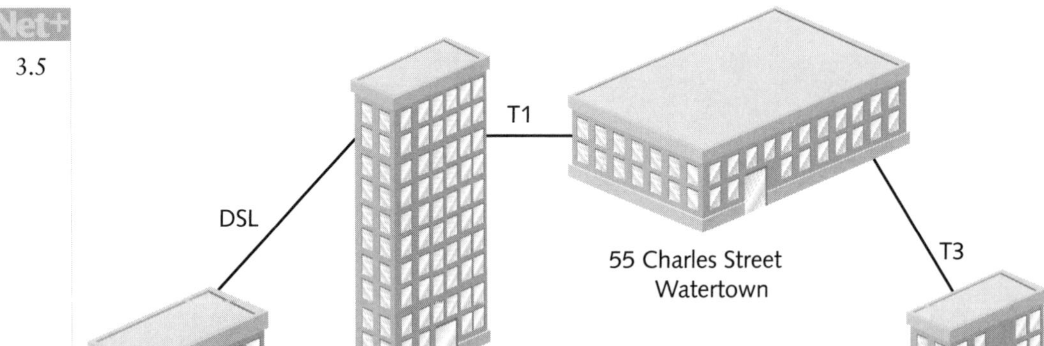

Figure 7-2 A bus topology WAN

Also, on most modern WANs, a ring topology relies on redundant rings to carry data. Using redundant rings means that a ring topology WAN cannot be taken down by the loss of one site; instead, if one site fails, data can be rerouted around the WAN in a different direction. On the other hand, expanding ring-configured WANs can be difficult, and it is more expensive than expanding a bus topology WAN. For these reasons, WANs that use the ring topology are only practical for connecting fewer than four or five locations.

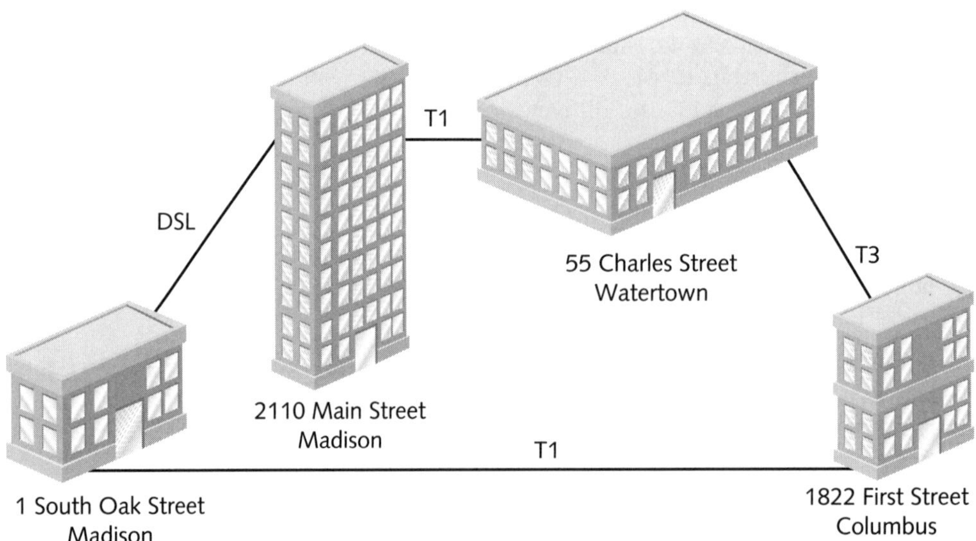

Figure 7-3 A ring topology WAN

Star

3.5 The **star topology WAN** mimics the arrangement of a star topology LAN. A single site acts as the central connection point for several other points, as shown in Figure 7-4. This arrangement provides separate routes for data between any two sites. That means that if a single connection fails, only one location loses WAN access. For example, if the T3 link between the Oak Street and Main Street locations fails, the Watertown and Columbus locations can still communicate with the Main Street location because they use different routes. In a bus or ring topology, however, a single connection failure would halt all traffic between all sites. Another advantage of a star WAN is that when all of its dedicated circuits are functioning, a star WAN provides shorter data paths between any two sites.

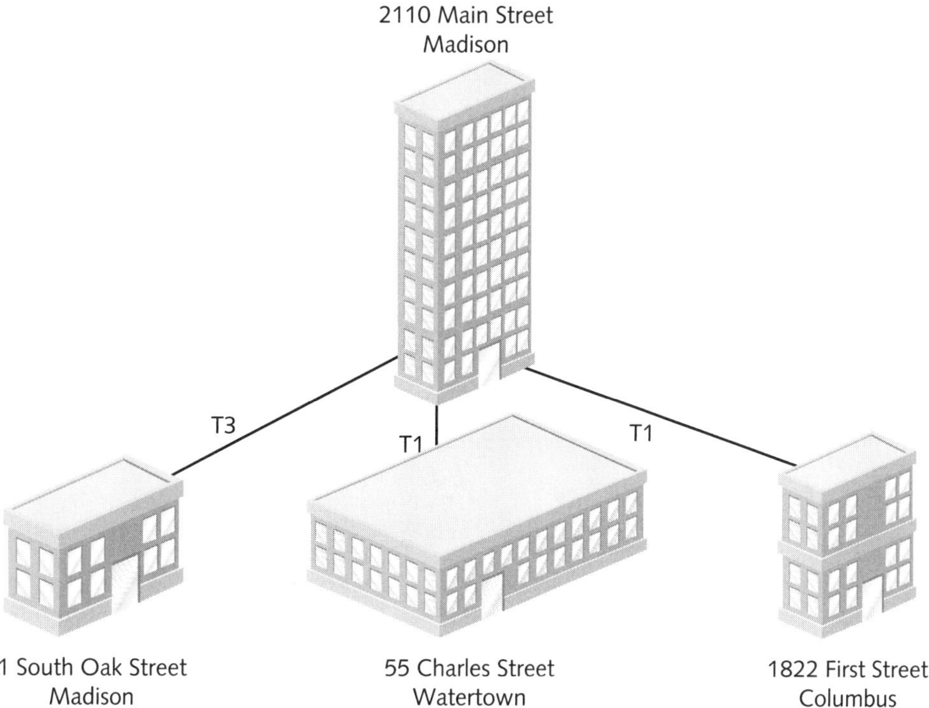

Figure 7-4 A star topology WAN

Extending a star WAN is relatively simple and less costly than extending a bus or ring topology WAN. For example, if the organization that uses the star WAN pictured in Figure 7-4 wanted to add a Maple Street, Madison, location to its topology, it could simply lease a new dedicated circuit from the Main Street office to its Maple Street office. None of the other offices would be affected by the change. If the organization were using a bus or ring WAN topology, however, two separate dedicated connections would be required to incorporate the new location into the network.

As with star LAN topologies, the greatest drawback of a star WAN is that a failure at the central connection point can bring down the entire WAN. In Figure 7-4, for example, if the Main Street office suffered a catastrophic fire, the entire WAN would fail. Similarly, if

3.5 the central connection point is overloaded with traffic, performance on the entire WAN will be adversely affected.

Mesh

A **mesh topology WAN** incorporates many directly interconnected sites. Because every site is interconnected, data can travel directly from its origin to its destination. If one connection suffers a problem, routers can redirect data easily and quickly. Mesh WANs are the most fault-tolerant type of WAN because they provide multiple routes for data to follow between any two points. For example, if the Madison office in Figure 7-5 suffered a catastrophic fire, the Dubuque office could still send and transmit data to and from the Detroit office by going directly to the Detroit office. If both the Madison and Detroit offices failed, the Dubuque and Indianapolis offices could still communicate.

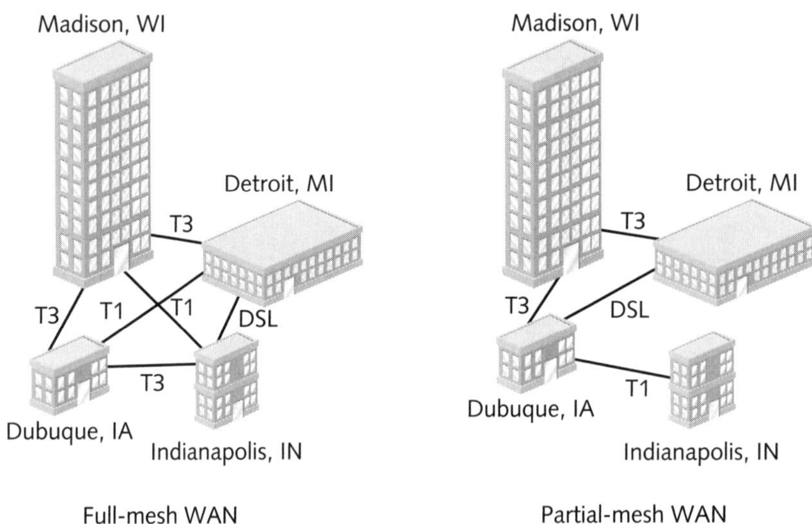

Figure 7-5 Full-mesh and partial-mesh WANs

The type of mesh topology in which every WAN site is directly connected to every other site is called a **full-mesh WAN**. One drawback to a full-mesh WAN is the cost. If more than a few sites are involved, connecting every site to every other requires leasing a large number of dedicated circuits. As WANs grow larger, the expense multiplies. To reduce costs, a network administrator might choose to implement a **partial-mesh WAN**, in which only critical WAN sites are directly interconnected and secondary sites are connected through star or ring topologies, as shown in Figure 7-5. Partial-mesh WANs are more common in today's business world than full-mesh WANs because they are more economical.

Tiered

In a **tiered topology WAN**, sites connected in star or ring formations are interconnected at different levels, with the interconnection points being organized into layers to form hierarchical groupings. Figure 7-6 depicts a tiered WAN. In this example, the Madison, Detroit, and New

York offices form the upper tier, and the Dubuque, Indianapolis, Toronto, Toledo, Washington,
3.5 and Boston offices form the lower tier. If the Detroit office suffers a failure, the Toronto and Toledo offices cannot communicate with any other nodes on the WAN, nor can the Washington, Boston, and New York locations exchange data with the other six locations. Yet the Washington, Boston, and New York locations can still exchange data with each other, as can the Indianapolis, Dubuque, and Madison locations.

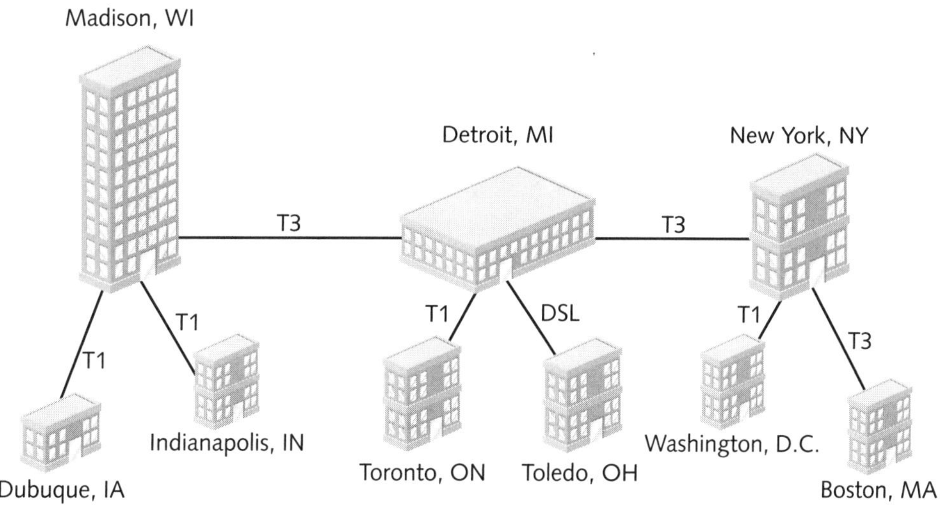

Figure 7-6 A tiered topology WAN

Variations on this topology abound. Indeed, flexibility makes the tiered approach quite practical. A network architect can determine the best placement of top-level routers based on traffic patterns or critical data paths. In addition, tiered systems allow for easy expansion and inclusion of redundant links to support growth. On the other hand, their enormous flexibility means that creation of tiered WANs requires careful consideration of geography, usage patterns, and growth potential.

Now that you understand the fundamental shapes that WANs may take, you are ready to learn about specific technologies and types. WAN technologies discussed in the following sections differ in terms of speed, reliability, cost, distance covered, and security. Also, some are defined by specifications at the Data Link layer, whereas others are defined by specifications at the Physical layer of the OSI model. As you learn about each technology, pay attention to its characteristics and think about its possible applications. To qualify for Network+ certification, you must be familiar with the variety of WAN connection types and be able to identify the networking environments that each suits best.

PSTN

PSTN, which stands for **Public Switched Telephone Network**, refers to the network of lines
3.4 and carrier equipment that provides telephone service to most homes and businesses. PSTN may also be called **POTS (plain old telephone service)**. The PSTN encompasses the entire

3.4

telephone system, from the wires that enter homes and businesses to the network centers that connect different regions of a country.

Originally, the PSTN carried only analog traffic. All of its lines were copper wires, and switching was handled by operators who manually connected calls upon request. Today, switching is computer controlled, and nearly all of the PSTN uses digital transmission. Signals may deliver voice, video, or data traffic and travel over fiber-optic or twisted pair copper cable, microwave, and satellite connections.

This chapter includes examples of PSTN-based network technologies that enable users to connect to WANs. In Chapter 12, you'll learn about technologies that have replaced the PSTN's original function as a voice carrier. Boundaries between the PSTN and computer networks have blurred. To appreciate how these spheres overlap, it's helpful to understand how the PSTN provided WAN connectivity when the Internet first became popular in the 1990s. At that time, most home users logged on to the Internet via a dial-up connection.

A **dial-up** connection is one in which a user connects her computer, via a modem, to a distant network and stays connected for a finite period of time. Unlike other types of WAN connections, dial-up connections provide a fixed period of access to the network, just as the phone call you make to a friend has a fixed length, determined by when you initiate and terminate the call. The term *dial-up* usually refers to a connection that uses a PSTN line.

When computers connect to a public or private data network via the PSTN, modems are almost always necessary because even today, certain elements of the PSTN can't handle digital transmission. Recall that a modem converts a computer's digital pulses into analog signals before it issues them to the telephone line, then converts the analog signals back into digital pulses at the receiving computer's end. Between the modems at either end, a signal travels through a carrier's network of switches and, possibly, long-distance connections.

Tracing the path of a dial-up connection is one good way to learn about the traditional PSTN. Imagine you are vacationing at a remote cabin in Alaska and the only way to connect to the Internet is via the phone line. You decide to dial into your ISP to pick up e-mail using an older laptop's 56-Kbps modem. To do so, you first initiate a call through your computer's dial-up software, which instructs your modem to dial the number for your ISP's remote access server. Next, your modem attempts to establish a connection. It converts the digital signal from your laptop into an analog signal that travels over the phone line to the local telephone company's network until it reaches the **CO (central office)**. A CO is the place where a telephone company terminates lines and switches calls between different locations. Between your vacation cabin and the nearest CO, signals might go through one or more of the telephone company's remote switching facilities. Modern remote switching facilities (sometimes called pedestals, because of their shape) usually contain digital equipment to convert the analog signal back to a digital signal before forwarding it to the CO.

Whether at a remote switching facility or at the CO, your signal is converted back to digital pulses. If the cabin and the ISP share the same CO, the signal is switched from your incoming connection directly to the ISP. In most cases, the ISP would have a dedicated connection to a CO. If so, your signal is issued over this dedicated connection multiplexed together with many other signals.

Yet it's likely that your vacation cabin doesn't share the same CO as your ISP. In that case, the first part of the process is the same as if you were at home—you initiate a call and connect to the local telephone company's CO, and along the way, your signal is converted to digital pulses.

Net+ 3.4 However, this time your signal cannot go straight to your ISP because your ISP doesn't have a connection in that carrier's CO. Instead, the local telephone company that serves the cabin's geographical area forwards the signal from its local CO to a regional CO through a dedicated connection between the two. This regional office most likely connects to a much larger regional or national WAN. The signal travels over the WAN to the regional CO closest to your ISP. That regional office directs the signal to your ISP's local CO, or straight to the ISP's network. Figure 7-7 illustrates the path a signal might take in a long-distance dial-up connection. Notice

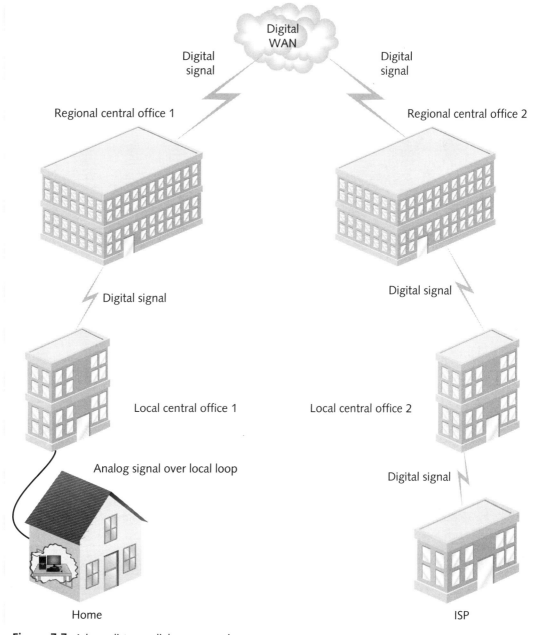

Figure 7-7 A long-distance dial-up connection

3.4 that in this figure, the WAN to which regional offices connect is represented as a cloud. On networking diagrams, packet-switched networks (including the Internet) are depicted as clouds, because of the indeterminate nature of their traffic patterns.

The portion of the PSTN that connects any residence or business to the nearest CO is known as the **local loop**, or the **last mile** (though it is not necessarily a mile long), and is illustrated in Figure 7-8. It's the part of the PSTN most likely to still use copper wire and carry analog signals. That's because extending fiber-optic cable or high-speed wireless connections to every residence and business is costly. However, fully digital connections do exist. No matter what kind of media is used, the end of the local loop, and also the end of the carrier's responsibility for the network, is the customer's demarcation point, where wires terminate at an **NIU** (**network interface unit**).

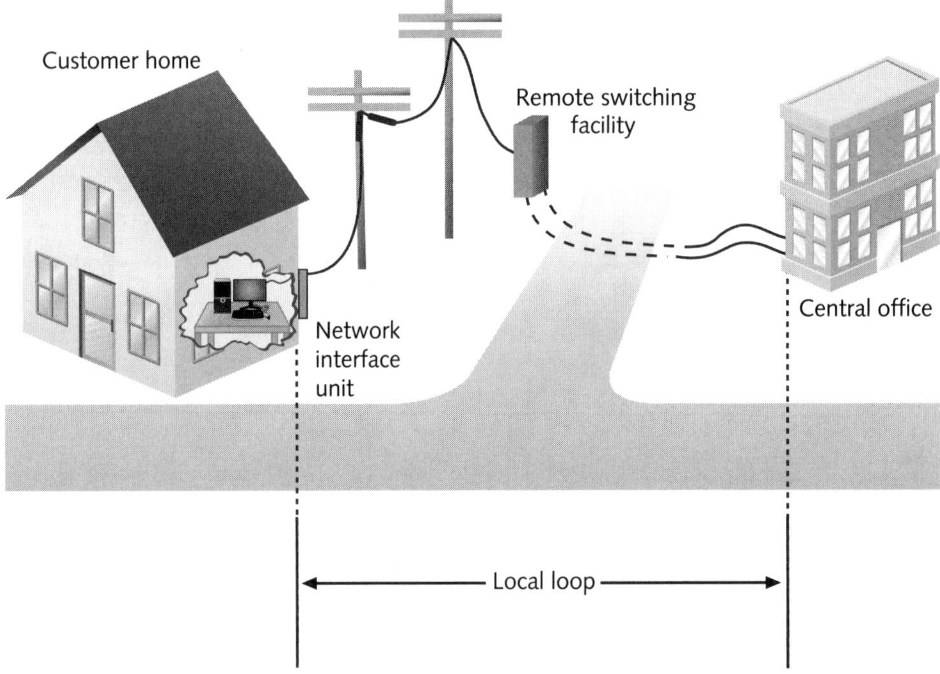

Figure 7-8 Local loop portion of the PSTN

An example of a digital local loop is a service called **FTTH** (**fiber to the home**), which simply means that a telephone company connects residential users to its network with fiber-optic cable. A more generic term is **FTTP** (**fiber to the premises**), which refers to the use of a fiber-optic cable to connect either a residence or a business. Fiber-optic local loops may be part of a **PON** (**passive optical network**), a network in which a carrier uses fiber-optic cabling to connect with multiple endpoints—for example, several homes in a neighborhood or many businesses on a city block. The word *passive* applies because in a PON no repeaters or other connectivity devices intervene between a carrier and its customer.

In the point-to-multipoint structure of a PON, the single endpoint at the carrier's central office is known as the network's **OLT** (**optical line terminal**). The OLT is a device with multiple optical ports, or PON interfaces, similar to interfaces on a router. In fact, a router can be equipped with a special OLT interface card. The OLT contains a splitter that subdivides

Net+ 3.4 the capacity of each port into up to 32 logical channels, one per subscriber. Physically, the PON consists of fiber-optic distribution cable leading to the vicinity of its many customers—for example, to the edge of a city block where multiple businesses will use its services or to a building of multiple residential subscribers. There, as shown in Figure 7-9, the fiber-optic connection terminates at an **ONU (optical network unit)**. The ONU distributes signals to multiple endpoints via fiber-optic cable, in the case of FTTP, or via copper or coax cable.

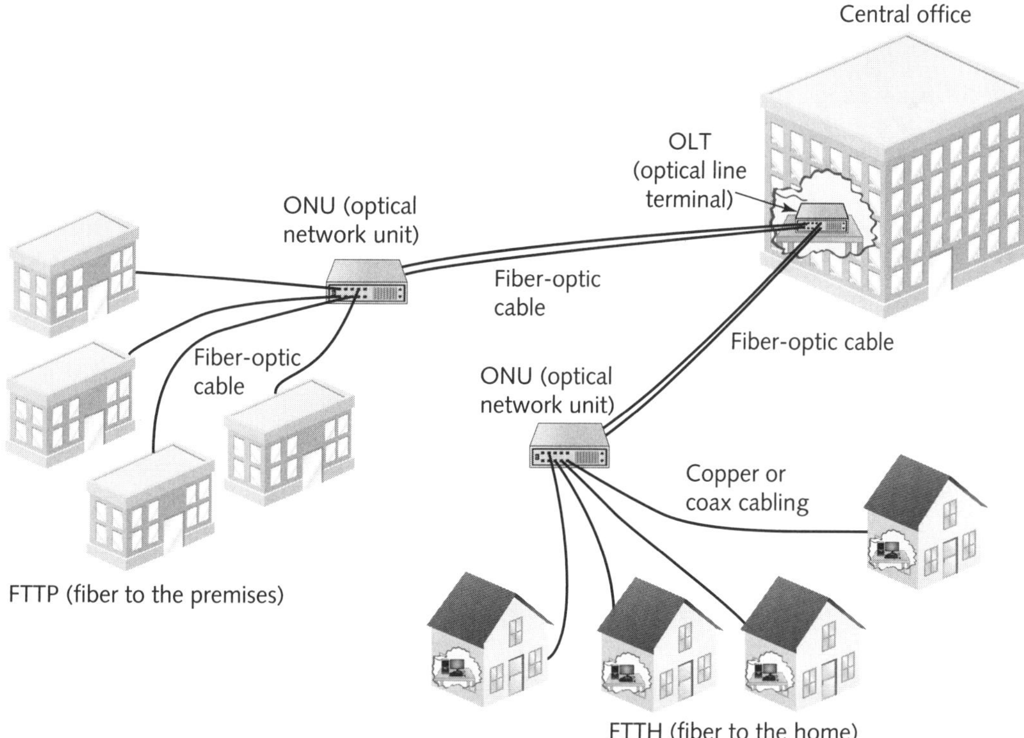

Figure 7-9 Passive optical network (PON)

PONs can handle one of several transmission technologies, including Ethernet, ATM, and SONET (discussed later in this chapter). The carrier controls which standard and how much throughput it delivers to each customer. As you can imagine, fiber-optic connections to a business or residence dramatically increase potential throughput and, therefore, the range of services available to customers. Video- and Voice-over-IP services benefit significantly from FTTP.

Several WAN technologies use the public telephone network. One of the first to do so was X.25.

X.25 and Frame Relay

3.4 X.25 is an analog, packet-switched technology designed for long-distance data transmission and standardized by the ITU in the mid-1970s. The original standard for X.25 specified a maximum of 64-Kbps throughput, but by 1992 the standard was updated to include

3.4 maximum throughput of 2.048 Mbps. It was originally developed as a more reliable alternative to the voice telephone system for connecting mainframe computers and remote terminals. Later, it was adopted as a method of connecting clients and servers over WANs.

The X.25 standard specifies protocols at the Physical, Data Link, and Network layers of the OSI model. It provides excellent flow control and ensures data reliability over long distances by verifying the transmission at every node. Unfortunately, this verification also renders X.25 comparatively slow and unsuitable for time-sensitive applications, such as audio or video. On the other hand, X.25 benefits from being a long-established, well-known, and low-cost technology. X.25 was never widely adopted in the United States, but was accepted by other countries and was for a long time the dominant packet-switching technology used on WANs around the world.

Recall that, in packet switching, packets belonging to the same data stream may follow different, optimal paths to their destination. As a result, packet switching uses bandwidth more efficiently and allows for faster transmission than if each packet in the data stream had to follow the same path, as in circuit switching. Packet switching is also more flexible than circuit switching because packet sizes may vary.

Frame relay is a digital version of X.25 that also relies on packet switching. ITU and ANSI standardized frame relay in 1984. However, because of a lack of compatibility with other WAN technologies at the time, frame relay did not become popular in the United States and Canada until the late 1980s. Frame relay protocols operate at the Data Link layer of the OSI model and can support multiple different Network and Transport layer protocols. The name is derived from the fact that data is separated into frames, which are then relayed from one node to another without any verification or processing.

An important difference between frame relay and X.25 is that frame relay does not guarantee reliable delivery of data. X.25 checks for errors and, in the case of an error, either corrects the damaged data or retransmits the original data. Frame relay, on the other hand, simply checks for errors. It leaves the error correction up to higher-layer protocols. Partly because it doesn't perform the same level of error correction that X.25 performs (and, thus, has less overhead), frame relay supports higher throughput than X.25. It offers throughputs between 64 Kbps and 45 Mbps. A frame relay customer chooses the amount of bandwidth he requires and pays for only that amount.

Both X.25 and frame relay rely on virtual circuits. **Virtual circuits** are connections between network nodes that, although based on potentially disparate physical links, logically appear to be direct, dedicated links between those nodes. One advantage to virtual circuits is their configurable use of limited bandwidth, which can make them more efficient. Several virtual circuits can be assigned to one length of cable or even to one channel on that cable. A virtual circuit uses the channel only when it needs to transmit data. Meanwhile, the channel is available for use by other virtual circuits.

X.25 and frame relay may be configured as **SVCs (switched virtual circuits)** or **PVCs (permanent virtual circuits)**. SVCs are connections that are established when parties need to transmit, then terminated after the transmission is complete. PVCs are connections that are established before data need to be transmitted and maintained after the transmission is complete. Note that in a PVC, the connection is established only between the two points (the sender and receiver); the connection does not specify the exact route the data will travel.

Net+ 3.4 Thus, in a PVC, data may follow any number of paths from point A to point B. For example, a transmission traveling over a PVC from Baltimore to Phoenix might go from Baltimore to Washington, D.C., to Chicago, then to Phoenix; the next transmission over that PVC, however, might go from Baltimore to Boston to St. Louis to Denver to Phoenix.

PVCs are *not* dedicated, individual links. When you lease an X.25 or frame relay circuit from your local carrier, your contract reflects the endpoints you specify and the amount of bandwidth you require between those endpoints. The service provider guarantees a minimum amount of bandwidth, called the **CIR (committed information rate)**. Provisions usually account for bursts of traffic that occasionally exceed the CIR. When you lease a PVC, you share bandwidth with the other X.25 and frame relay users on the backbone. PVC links are best suited to frequent and consistent data transmission.

The advantage to leasing a frame relay circuit over leasing a dedicated service is that you pay for only the amount of bandwidth required. Another advantage is that frame relay is less expensive than some other WAN technologies, depending on your location and its network availability. Also, frame relay is a long-established worldwide standard. Figure 7-10 illustrates a WAN using frame relay.

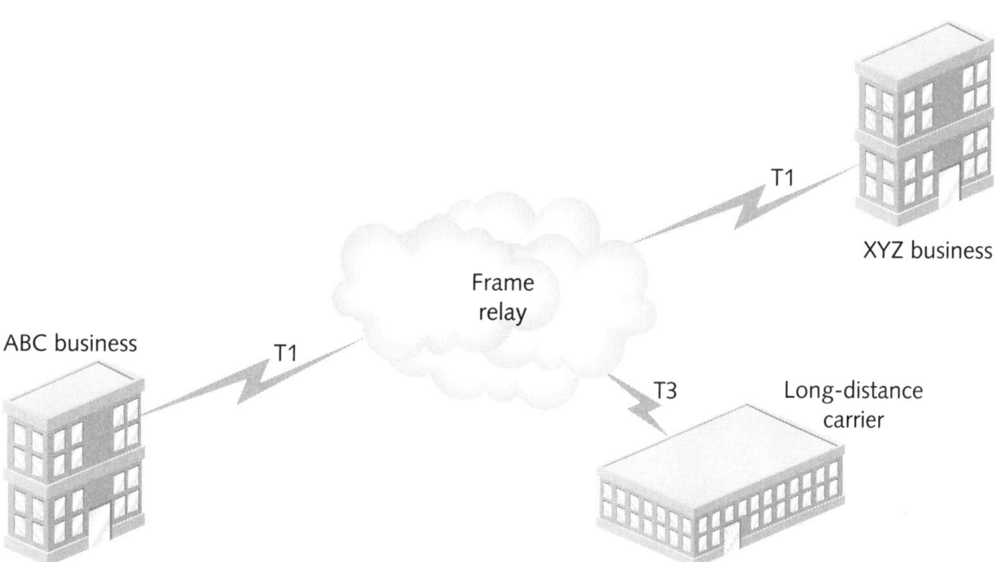

Figure 7-10 A WAN using frame relay

On the other hand, because frame relay and X.25 use shared lines, their throughput remains at the mercy of variable traffic patterns. In the middle of the night, data over your frame relay network may zip along at 1.544 Mbps; during midday, when everyone is surfing the Web, it may slow down to less than your CIR. In addition, frame relay circuits are not as private (and potentially not as secure) as dedicated circuits. Nevertheless, because they use the same connectivity equipment as T-carriers, they can easily be upgraded to T-carrier dedicated lines. In all but the most remote locations, frame relay connections have been replaced with newer WAN technologies such as those described in the next section.

ISDN

3.4

ISDN (Integrated Services Digital Network) is an international standard, originally established by the ITU in 1984, for transmitting digital data over the PSTN. In North America, a standard ISDN implementation wasn't finalized until 1992 because telephone switch manufacturers couldn't agree on compatible technology for supporting ISDN. The technology's uncertain start initially made telephone companies reluctant to invest in it, and ISDN didn't catch on as quickly as predicted. However, in the 1990s ISDN finally became a popular method of connecting WAN locations to exchange both data and voice signals.

ISDN specifies protocols at the Physical, Data Link, and Transport layers of the OSI model. These protocols handle signaling, framing, connection setup and termination, routing, flow control, and error detection and correction. ISDN relies on the PSTN for its transmission medium. Connections can be either dial-up or dedicated. Dial-up ISDN is distinguished from the workstation dial-up connections discussed previously because it relies exclusively on digital transmission. In other words, it does not convert a computer's digital signals to analog before transmitting them over the PSTN. Also, ISDN is distinguished because it can simultaneously carry as many as two voice calls and one data connection on a single line. Therefore, ISDN can eliminate the need to pay for separate phone lines to support faxes, modems, and voice calls at one location.

All ISDN connections are based on two types of channels: B channels and D channels. The **B channel** is the "bearer" channel, employing circuit-switching techniques to carry voice, video, audio, and other types of data over the ISDN connection. A single B channel has a maximum throughput of 64 Kbps (although it is sometimes limited to 56 Kbps by the ISDN provider). The number of B channels in a single ISDN connection may vary. The **D channel** is the "data" channel, employing packet-switching techniques to carry information about the call, such as session initiation and termination signals, caller identity, call forwarding, and conference calling signals. A single D channel has a maximum throughput of 16 or 64 Kbps, depending on the type of ISDN connection. Each ISDN connection uses only one D channel.

In North America, two types of ISDN connections are commonly used: **BRI (Basic Rate Interface)** and PRI (Primary Rate Interface). BRI uses two B channels and one D channel, as indicated by the notation 2B+D. The two B channels are treated as separate connections by the network and can carry voice and data or two data streams simultaneously and separate from each other. In a process called **bonding**, these two 64-Kbps B channels can be combined to achieve an effective throughput of 128 Kbps—the maximum amount of data traffic that a BRI connection can accommodate. Most consumers who subscribe to ISDN from home use BRI, which is the most economical type of ISDN connection.

Figure 7-11 illustrates how a typical BRI link supplies a home consumer with an ISDN link. From the telephone company's lines, the ISDN channels connect to a Network Termination 1 device at the customer's site. The **NT1 (Network Termination 1)** device connects the twisted pair wiring at the customer's building with the ISDN terminal equipment via RJ-11 (standard telephone) or RJ-45 data jacks. The ISDN **TE (terminal equipment)** may include cards or stand-alone devices used to connect computers to the ISDN line (similar to a network adapter used on Ethernet networks).

So that the ISDN line can connect to analog equipment, the signal must first pass through a terminal adapter. A **TA (terminal adapter)** converts digital signals into analog signals for use

Net+ 3.4

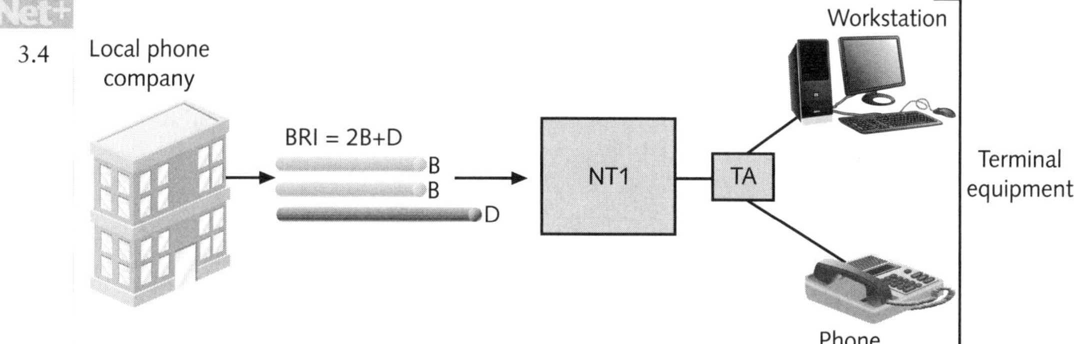

Figure 7-11 A BRI link

with ISDN phones and other analog devices. (Terminal adapters are sometimes called ISDN modems, though they are not, technically, modems.) Typically, telecommuters who want more throughput than their analog phone line can offer choose BRI as their ISDN connection. For a home user, the terminal adapter would most likely be an ISDN router, whereas the terminal equipment could be an Ethernet card in the user's workstation plus, perhaps, a phone.

NOTE

The BRI configuration depicted in Figure 7-11 applies to installations in North America only. Because transmission standards differ in Europe and Asia, different numbers of B channels are used in ISDN connections in those regions.

PRI (Primary Rate Interface) uses 23 B channels and one 64-Kbps D channel, as represented by the notation 23B+D. PRI is less commonly used by individual subscribers than BRI is, but it may be selected by businesses and other organizations that need more throughput. As with BRI, the separate B channels in a PRI link can carry voice and data, independently of each other or bonded together. The maximum potential throughput for a PRI connection is 1.544 Mbps.

PRI and BRI connections may be interconnected on a single network. PRI links use the same kind of equipment as BRI links, but require the services of an extra network termination device, called an **NT2 (Network Termination 2)**, to handle the multiple ISDN lines. Figure 7-12 depicts a typical PRI link as it would be installed in North America.

Individual customers who need to transmit more data than a typical modem can handle or who want to use a single line for both data and voice may use ISDN lines. ISDN, although not available in every location of the United States, can be purchased from most local telephone companies. Costs vary depending on the customer's location. PRI is more expensive than BRI. Dial-up ISDN service is less expensive than dedicated ISDN service. In some areas, ISDN providers charge customers additional usage fees based on the total length of time they remain connected. One disadvantage of ISDN is that it can span a distance of only 18,000 linear feet before repeater equipment is needed to boost the signal. For this reason, it is only feasible to use for the local loop portion of the WAN link.

Net+ 3.4

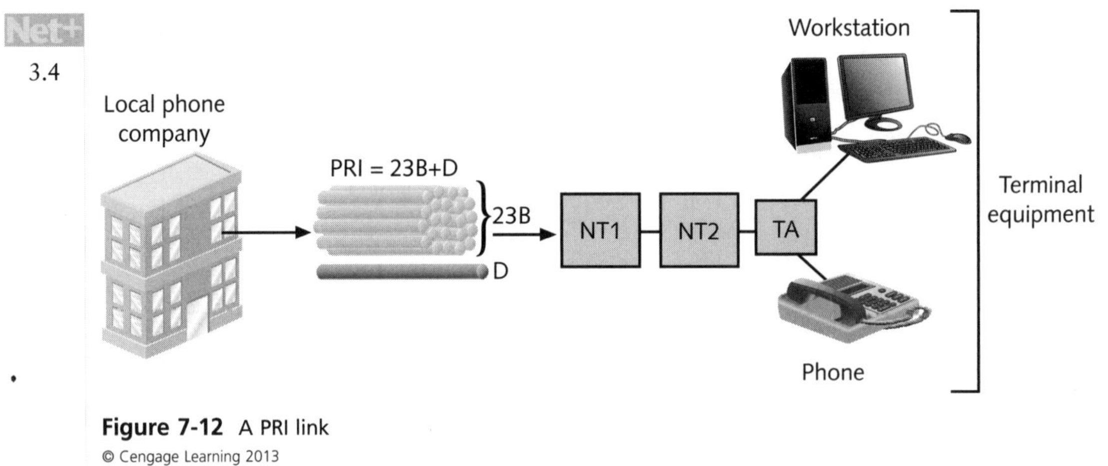

Figure 7-12 A PRI link

T-Carriers

Net+ 3.4

Another WAN transmission method that grew from a need to transmit digital data at high speeds over the PSTN is T-carrier technology, which includes T1s, fractional T1s, and T3s. **T-carrier** standards specify a method of signaling, which means they belong to the Physical layer of the OSI model. A T-carrier uses TDM (time division multiplexing) over two wire pairs (one for transmitting and one for receiving) to divide a single channel into multiple channels. For example, multiplexing enables a single T1 circuit to carry 24 channels, each capable of 64-Kbps throughput; thus, a T1 has a maximum capacity of 24 × 64 Kbps, or 1.544 Mbps. Each channel may carry data, voice, or video signals. The medium used for T-carrier signaling can be ordinary copper wire, fiber-optic cable, or wireless links.

AT&T developed T-carrier technology in 1957 in an effort to digitize voice signals and thereby enable such signals to travel longer distances over the PSTN. Before that time, voice signals, which were purely analog, were expensive to transmit over long distances because of the number of connectivity devices needed to keep the signal intelligible. In the 1970s, many businesses installed T1s to obtain more voice throughput per line. In the 1990s, with increased data communication demands, such as Internet access and geographically dispersed offices, T1s became a popular way to connect WAN sites.

The next section describes the various types of T-carriers, and then the chapter moves on to describe T-carrier connectivity.

Types of T-Carriers

A number of T-carrier varieties are available to businesses today, as shown in Table 7-1. The most common T-carrier implementations are T1 and, for higher bandwidth needs, T3. A T1 circuit can carry the equivalent of 24 voice or data channels, giving a maximum data throughput of 1.544 Mbps. A T3 circuit can carry the equivalent of 672 voice or data channels, giving a maximum data throughput of 44.736 Mbps (its throughput is typically rounded up to 45 Mbps for the purposes of discussion).

Net+ 3.4

Table 7-1 Carrier specifications

Signal level	Carrier	Number of T1s	Number of channels	Throughput (Mbps)
DS0	—	1/24	1	.064
DS1	T1	1	24	1.544
DS1C	T1C	2	48	3.152
DS2	T2	4	96	6.312
DS3	T3	28	672	44.736
DS4	T4	168	4032	274.176
DS5	T5	240	5760	400.352

The speed of a T-carrier depends on its signal level. The **signal level** refers to the T-carrier's Physical layer electrical signaling characteristics as defined by ANSI standards in the early 1980s. **DS0 (digital signal, level 0)** is the equivalent of one data or voice channel. All other signal levels are multiples of DS0.

You may hear *signal level* and *carrier* terms used interchangeably—for example, DS1 and T1. In fact, T1 is the implementation of the DS1 standard used in North America and most of Asia. In Europe, the standard high-speed carrier connections are E1 and E3. Like T1s and T3s, E1s and E3s use time division multiplexing. However, an **E1** allows for 30 channels and offers 2.048-Mbps throughput. An **E3** allows for 480 channels and offers 34.368-Mbps throughput. Using special hardware, T1s can interconnect with E1s and T3s with E3s for international communications.

As a networking professional, you are likely to work with T1 or T3 lines. In addition to knowing their capacity, you should be familiar with their costs and uses. T1s are commonly used by businesses to connect branch offices or to connect to a carrier, such as an ISP. Telephone companies also use T1s to connect their smaller COs. ISPs may use multiple T1s or T3s, depending on their size, to connect to their Internet carriers.

Because a T3 provides 28 times more throughput than a T1, some organizations find that multiple T1s—rather than a single T3—can accommodate their throughput needs. For example, suppose a university research laboratory needs to transmit molecular images over the Internet to another university, and its peak throughput need (at any given time) is 10 Mbps. The laboratory would require seven T1s (10 Mbps divided by 1.544 Mbps equals 6.48 T1s). Leasing seven T1s would prove much less expensive for the university than leasing a single T3.

The cost of T1s varies from region to region. On average, leasing a full T1 might cost approximately $500 to install, plus an additional $300 to $800 per month in access fees. The longer the distance between the provider (such as an ISP or a telephone company) and the subscriber, the higher a T1's monthly charge. For example, a T1 between Houston and New York will cost more than a T1 between Washington, D.C., and New York. Similarly, a T1 from a suburb of New York to the city center will cost more than a T1 from the city center to a business three blocks away.

3.4

For organizations that do not need as much as 1.544-Mbps throughput, a fractional T1 might be a better option. A **fractional T1** lease allows organizations to use only some of the channels on a T1 line and be charged according to the number of channels they use. Thus, fractional T1 bandwidth can be leased in multiples of 64 Kbps. A fractional T1 is best suited to businesses that expect their traffic to grow and that may require a full T1 eventually, but can't currently justify leasing a full T1.

T3s are more expensive than T1s and are used by more data-intensive businesses—for example, computer consulting firms that provide online data backups and warehousing for a number of other businesses or large long-distance carriers. A T3 might cost as much as $1000 to install, plus monthly service fees based on usage. If a customer uses the full T3 bandwidth of 45 Mbps, for example, the monthly charges might be as high as $10,000. Of course, T-carrier costs will vary depending on the service provider, your location, and the distance covered by the T3.

Net+

T-Carrier Connectivity

3.1
3.4
3.8

The approximate costs mentioned previously include monthly access and installation, but not connectivity hardware. Every T-carrier line requires connectivity hardware at both the customer site and the local telecommunications provider's switching facility. Connectivity hardware may be purchased or leased. If your organization uses an ISP to establish and service your T-carrier line, you might lease the connectivity equipment. If you lease the line directly from the local carrier and you anticipate little change in your connectivity requirements over time, however, you might want to purchase the hardware.

T-carrier lines require specialized connectivity hardware that cannot be used with other WAN transmission methods. In addition, T-carrier lines require different media, depending on their throughput. In the following sections, you will learn about the physical components of a T-carrier connection between a customer site and a local carrier.

Wiring As mentioned earlier, the T-carrier system is based on AT&T's original attempt to digitize existing long-distance PSTN lines. T1 technology can use UTP or STP (unshielded or shielded twisted pair) copper wiring—in other words, plain telephone wire—coaxial cable, microwave, or fiber-optic cable as its transmission media. However, because the digital signals require a clean connection (that is, one less susceptible to noise and attenuation), STP is preferable to UTP. For T1s using STP, repeaters must regenerate the signal approximately every 6000 feet. Twisted pair wiring cannot adequately carry the high throughput of multiple T1s or T3 transmissions. Thus, for multiple T1s, fiber-optic cabling is the medium of choice.

Termination In Chapter 3, you learned how to terminate UTP cable in an RJ-45 connector, the type used for most patch cables on LANs. However, when copper cabling is used to carry T1 traffic, it terminates in an **RJ-48** connector. RJ-48 and RJ-45 connectors are the same size and contain the same number of pins, but wire pairs used to carry T1 traffic are terminated differently in an RJ-48, as shown in Figure 7-13. T1 traffic uses pins 1 and 2 for the receive pair and pins 4 and 5 for the transmit pair.

As with LAN patch cables, T1 cables can be straight-through, in which case pinouts at both ends match those pictured in Figure 7-13. Straight-through cables might be used at a carrier's facility to connect a patch panel with a T1 router interface. T1 crossover cables also exist. In a crossover cable, the transmit and receive pairs are reversed, as shown in Figure 7-14. A T1 crossover cable could be used to connect two connectivity devices, such as CSUs/DSUs (discussed later) or WAN interface cards that act as CSU/DSUs.

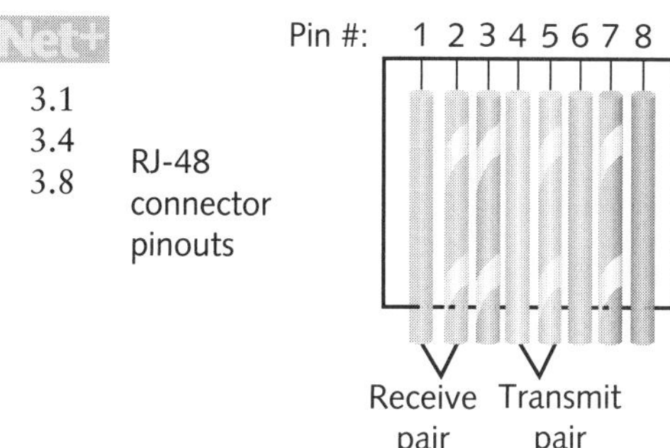

Figure 7-13 T1 wire terminations in an RJ-48 connector

Figure 7-14 T1 crossover cable terminations

At the customer's demarc (demarcation point), either inside or outside the building, RJ-48 connectors terminate in a **smart jack**, a type of NIU. In addition to terminating the line, a smart jack functions as a monitoring point for the connection. If the line between the carrier and customer experiences significant data errors, the smart jack will report this fact to the carrier. Technicians can also check the status of the line at the smart jack. Most include LEDs associated with transmitted and received signals. For example, a steady green light on the display indicates no connectivity problems, whereas a flickering light indicates data errors. A power light indicates whether or not the smart jack is receiving any signal. Figure 7-15 shows a smart jack (or network interface) designed to be used with a T1.

The smart jack is not capable of interpreting data, however. For that, the T-carrier signals depend on a CSU/DSU.

CSU/DSU (Channel Service Unit/Data Service Unit) Although CSUs (**channel**
3.4 **service units**) and DSUs (**data service units**) are actually two separate devices, they are typically
3.8 combined into a single stand-alone device or an interface card called a CSU/DSU. The **CSU/**
DSU is the connection point for a T1 line. The CSU provides termination for the digital signal
and ensures connection integrity through error correction and line monitoring. The DSU

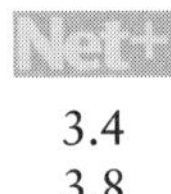
3.4
3.8

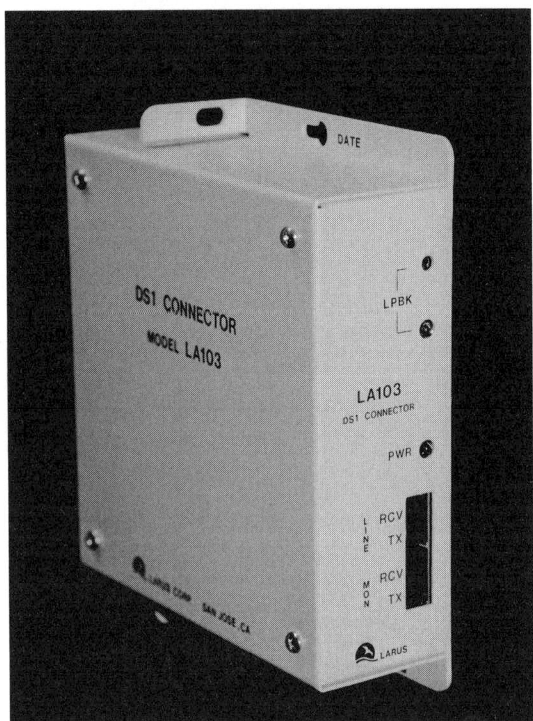

Figure 7-15 A T1 smart jack
Photo courtesy of CXR Larus Corporation, San Jose, CA

converts the T-carrier frames into frames the LAN can interpret and vice versa. It also connects T-carrier lines with terminating equipment. Finally, a DSU usually incorporates a multiplexer. (In some T-carrier installations, the multiplexer can be a separate device connected to the DSU.) For an incoming T-carrier line, the multiplexer separates its combined channels into individual signals that can be interpreted on the LAN. For an outgoing T-carrier line, the multiplexer combines multiple signals from a LAN for transport over the T-carrier. After being demultiplexed, an incoming T-carrier signal passes on to devices collectively known as terminal equipment. Examples of terminal equipment include switches, routers, or telephone exchange devices that accept only voice transmissions (such as a telephone switch).

Figure 7-16 shows a stand-alone CSU/DSU.

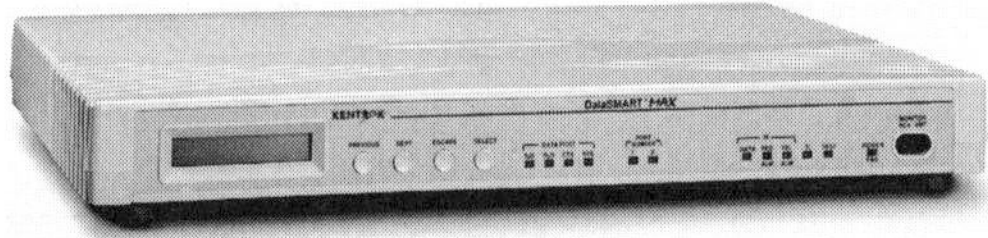

Figure 7-16 A CSU/DSU
Kentrox, Inc.

Figure 7-17 depicts a typical use of smart jacks and CSU/DSUs with a point-to-point T1-connected WAN. In the following sections, you will learn how routers and switches integrate with CSU/DSUs and multiplexers to connect T-carriers to a LAN.

Net+
3.4
3.8

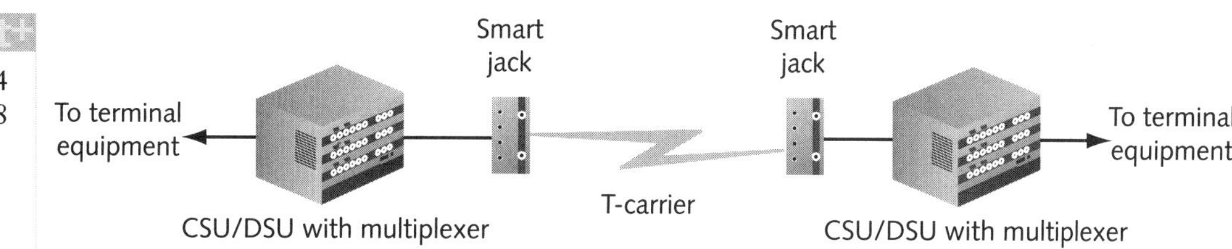

Figure 7-17 A point-to-point T-carrier connection

Terminal Equipment On a typical T1-connected data network, the terminal equipment consists of switches or routers. Usually, a router or Layer 3 or higher switch is the best option because these devices can translate between different Layer 3 protocols that might be used on the WAN and LAN. The router or switch accepts incoming signals from a CSU/DSU and, if necessary, translates Network layer protocols, then directs data to its destination exactly as it does on any LAN.

On some implementations, the CSU/DSU is not a separate device, but is integrated with the router or switch as an expansion card. Compared with a stand-alone CSU/DSU, which must connect to the terminal equipment via a cable, an integrated CSU/DSU offers faster signal processing and better network performance. In most cases, it is also a less-expensive and lower-maintenance solution than using a separate CSU/DSU device. Figure 7-18 illustrates one way a router with an integrated CSU/DSU can be used to connect a LAN with a T1 WAN link.

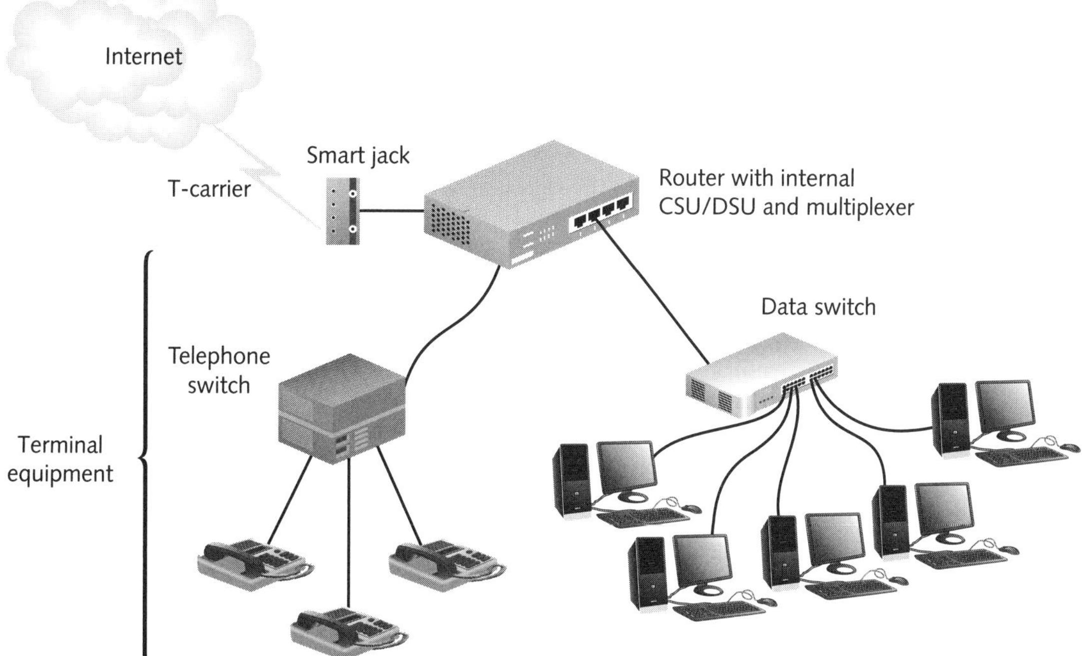

Figure 7-18 A T-carrier connecting to a LAN through a router

DSL (Digital Subscriber Line)

3.4 DSL (**digital subscriber line**) is a WAN connection method introduced by researchers at Bell Laboratories in the mid-1990s. It operates over the PSTN and competes directly with ISDN and T1 services, as well as broadband cable services, which are discussed later in this chapter. Like ISDN, DSL can span only limited distances without the help of repeaters and is, therefore, best suited to the local loop portion of a WAN link. Also, like ISDN and T-carriers, DSL can support multiple data and voice channels over a single line.

DSL uses data modulation techniques at the Physical layer of the OSI model to achieve extraordinary throughput over regular telephone lines. To understand how DSL and voice signals can share the same line, it's helpful to note that telephone lines carry voice signals over a very small range of frequencies, between 300 and 3300 Hz. This leaves higher, inaudible frequencies unused and available for carrying data. Also recall that in data modulation, a data signal alters the properties of a carrier signal. Depending on its version, DSL connection may use a modulation technique based on amplitude or phase modulation. However, in DSL, modulation follows more complex patterns than the modulation you learned about earlier in this book. The details of DSL modulation techniques are beyond the scope of this book. However, you should understand that the types of modulation used by a DSL version affect its throughput and the distance its signals can travel before requiring a repeater. The following section describes the different versions of DSL.

Types of DSL

The term **xDSL** refers to all DSL varieties, of which at least eight currently exist. The better-known DSL varieties include ADSL (Asymmetric DSL), G.Lite (a version of ADSL), HDSL (High Bit-Rate DSL), SDSL (Symmetric or Single-Line DSL), VDSL (Very High Bit-Rate DSL), and SHDSL (Single-Line High Bit-Rate DSL)—the *x* in *xDSL* is replaced by the variety name. DSL types can be divided into two categories: asymmetrical and symmetrical.

To understand the difference between these two categories, you must understand the concepts of downstream and upstream data transmission. The term **downstream** refers to data traveling from the carrier's switching facility to the customer. **Upstream** refers to data traveling from the customer to the carrier's switching facility. In some types of DSL, the throughput rates for downstream and upstream traffic differ. In other words, if you were connected to the Internet via a DSL link, you could download images from the Internet more rapidly than you could upload them because the downstream throughput would be greater. A technology that offers more throughput in one direction than in the other is considered **asymmetrical**. In asymmetrical communications, downstream throughput is higher than upstream throughput. Asymmetrical communication is well suited to users who receive more information from the network than they send to it—for example, people watching videoconferences or people surfing the Web. ADSL and VDSL are examples of **asymmetrical DSL**.

Conversely, **symmetrical** technology provides equal capacity for data traveling both upstream and downstream. Symmetrical transmission is suited to users who both upload and download significant amounts of data—for example, a bank's branch office that sends large volumes of account information to the central server at the bank's headquarters and, in turn, receives large amounts of account information from the central server at the bank's headquarters. HDSL, SDSL, and SHDSL are examples of **symmetrical DSL**.

Net+
3.4

DSL versions also differ in the type of modulation they use. Some, such as the popular full-rate ADSL and VDSL, create multiple narrow channels in the higher frequency range to carry more data. For these versions, a splitter must be installed at the carrier and at the customer's premises to separate the data signal from the voice signal before it reaches the terminal equipment (for example, the phone or the computer). G.Lite, a slower and less-expensive version of ADSL, eliminates the splitter but requires the use of a filter to prevent high-frequency DSL signals from reaching the telephone. Other types of DSL, such as HDSL and SDSL, cannot use the same wire pair that is used for voice signals. Instead, these types of DSL use the extra pair of wires contained in a telephone cable (that are otherwise typically unused).

The types of DSL also vary in terms of their capacity and maximum line length. A VDSL line that carries as much as 52 Mbps in one direction and as much as 6.4 Mbps in the opposite direction can extend only a maximum of 1000 feet between the customer's premises and the carrier's switching facility. This limitation might suit businesses located close to a telephone company's CO (for example, in the middle of a metropolitan area), but it won't work for most individuals. The most popular form of DSL, ADSL, provides a maximum of 6.144 Mbps downstream and a maximum of 640 Kbps upstream. However, the distance between the customer and the central office affects the actual throughput a customer experiences. Close to the central office, DSL achieves its highest maximum throughput. The farther away the customer's premises, the lower the throughput. In the case of ADSL, a customer 9000 feet from the central office can potentially experience ADSL's maximum potential throughput of 6.144 Mbps downstream. At 18,000 feet away, the farthest allowable distance, the customer will experience as little as 1.544-Mbps throughput. Still, this throughput and this distance (approximately 3.4 miles) renders ADSL suitable for most telecommuters. Table 7-2 compares current specifications for six DSL types.

Table 7-2 Comparison of DSL types

DSL type	Maximum upstream throughput (Mbps)	Maximum downstream throughput (Mbps)	Distance limitation (feet)
ADSL ("full rate")	0.640	6.144	18,000
G.Lite (a type of ADSL)	0.512	1.544	25,000
HDSL or HDSL-2	1.544 or 2.048	1.544 or 2.048	18,000 or 12,000
SDSL	1.544	1.544	12,000
SHDSL	2.36 or 4.7	2.36 or 4.7	26,000 or 18,000
VDSL	1.6, 3.2, or 6.4	12.9, 25.9, or 51.8	1000–4500

Published distance limitations and throughput can vary from one service provider to another, depending on how far the provider is willing to guarantee a particular level of service. In addition, service providers may limit each user's maximum throughput based on terms of the service agreement. For example, in 2011 AT&T capped the total amount of data transfer allowed for each of its DSL subscribers to 150 GB per month. The company instituted the new policy in response to a dramatic spike in downstream bandwidth usage due to Netflix streaming—in particular, online gaming. In fact, in 2010, Netflix accounted for nearly 30 percent of all downstream Internet traffic requested by fixed users in the United States.

3.4 In addition to their data modulation techniques, capacity, and distance limitations, DSL types vary according to how they use the PSTN. Next, you will learn about how DSL connects to a business or residence over the PSTN.

DSL Connectivity

This section follows the path of an ADSL connection from a home computer, through the local loop, and to the telecommunications carrier's switching facility. Although variations exist, this describes the most common implementation of DSL.

Suppose you have an ADSL connection at home. One evening you open your Web browser and request the home page of your favorite sports team to find the last game's score. As you know, the first step in this process is establishing a TCP connection with the team's Web server. Your TCP request message leaves your computer's NIC and travels over your home network to a DSL modem. A **DSL modem** is a device that modulates outgoing signals and demodulates incoming DSL signals. Thus, it contains receptacles to connect both to your incoming telephone line and to your computer or network connectivity device. Because you are using ADSL, the DSL modem also contains a splitter to separate incoming voice and data signals. The DSL modem may be external or internal (as an expansion card, for example) to the computer. If external, it may connect to a computer's NIC via an RJ-45, USB, or wireless interface. If your home network contains more than one computer and you want all computers to share the DSL bandwidth, the DSL modem must connect to a device such as a switch or router, instead of just one computer. In fact, rather than using two separate devices, you could buy a router that combines DSL modem functionalities with the ability to connect multiple computers and share DSL bandwidth. A DSL modem is shown in Figure 7-19.

Figure 7-19 A DSL modem

Courtesy of Zoom Telephonics, Inc.

When your request arrives at the DSL modem, it is modulated according to the ADSL specifications. Then, the DSL modem forwards the modulated signal to your local loop—the lines that connect your home with the rest of the PSTN. For the first stretch of the local loop, the signal continues over four-pair UTP wire. At some distance less than 18,000 feet, it is combined with other modulated signals in a telephone switch, usually at a remote switching facility. (To accept DSL signals, your telecommunications carrier must have newer digital switching equipment. In the few remaining locales where carriers have not updated their switching equipment, DSL service is not available.)

Inside the carrier's remote switching facility, a splitter separates your line's data signal from any voice signals that are also carried on the line. Next, your request is sent to a device called

Net+ a **DSLAM** (**DSL access multiplexer**), which aggregates multiple DSL subscriber lines and con-
3.4 nects them to the carrier's CO. Finally, your request is issued from your carrier's network to the Internet backbone, as pictured in Figure 7-20. The request travels over the Internet until it reaches your sports team's Web server. Barring line problems and Internet congestion, the entire journey happens in a fraction of a second. After your team's Web server accepts the connection request, the data follow the same path, but in reverse.

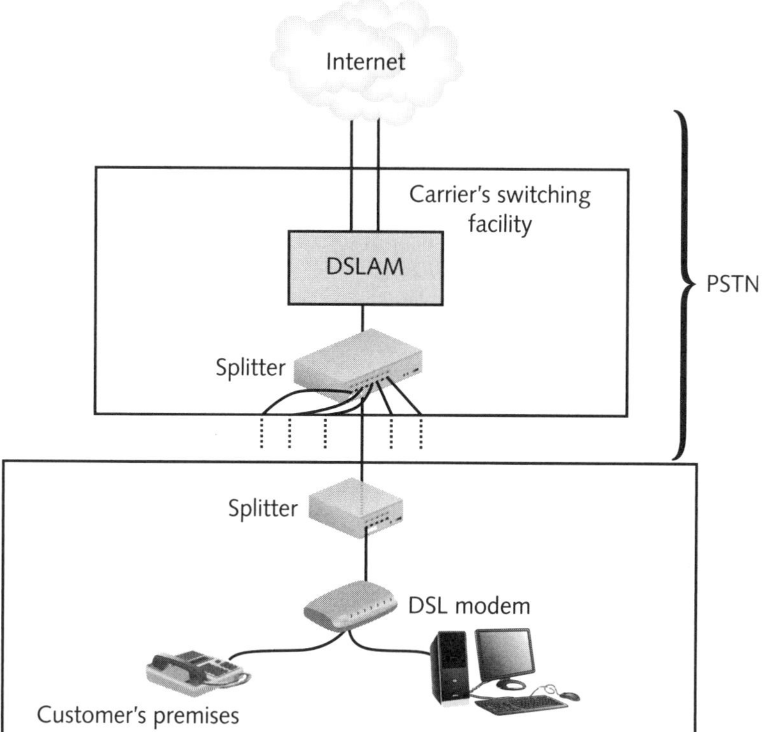

Figure 7-20 A DSL connection

Telecommunications carriers and manufacturers have positioned DSL as a competitor for T1, ISDN, and broadband cable services. The installation, hardware, and monthly access costs for DSL are slightly less than those for ISDN lines and significantly less than the cost for T1s. (At the time of this writing, ADSL costs approximately $30 per month in the United States, though prices vary by speed and location.) Generally speaking, DSL throughput rates, especially upstream, are lower than broadband cable, its main competition among residential customers.

Broadband Cable

While local and long-distance phone companies strive to make DSL the preferred method of
3.4 Internet access for consumers, cable companies are pushing their own connectivity option. This option, called **broadband cable** or **cable modem access**, is based on the coaxial cable

3.4 wiring used for TV signals. Such wiring can theoretically transmit as much as 150 Mbps downstream and as much as 10 Mbps upstream. Thus, broadband cable is an asymmetrical technology. However, actual broadband cable throughput is typically limited (or throttled) by the cable companies and further diminished by the fact that physical connections are shared. Customers might be allowed, at most, 10 Mbps downstream and 2 Mbps upstream throughput. During peak times of use, they might see data rates of 3 Mbps downstream and 1 Mbps upstream, for example. The asymmetry of broadband cable makes it a logical choice for users who want to surf the Web or download data from a network.

Broadband cable connections require that the customer use a special **cable modem**, a device that modulates and demodulates signals for transmission and reception via cable wiring. Cable modems operate at the Physical and Data Link layer of the OSI model, and, therefore, do not manipulate higher-layer protocols, such as IP. The cable modem then connects to a customer's PC via an RJ-45, USB, or wireless interface to a NIC. Alternately, the cable modem could connect to a connectivity device, such as a switch or router, thereby supplying bandwidth to a LAN rather than to just one computer. It's also possible to use a device that combines cable modem functionality with a router; this single device can then provide both the broadband cable connection and the capability of sharing the bandwidth between multiple nodes. Figure 7-21 provides an example of a cable modem.

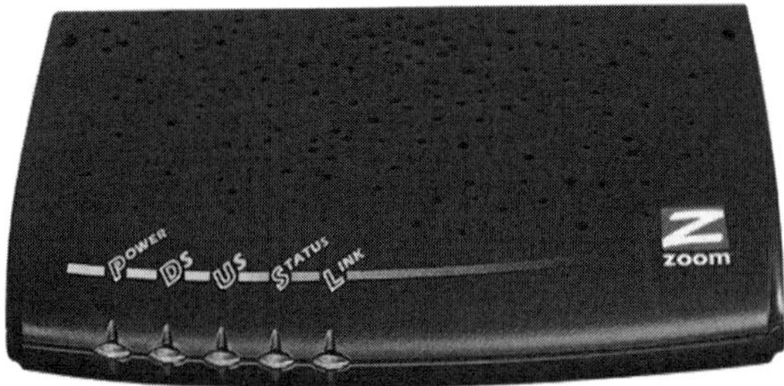

Figure 7-21 A cable modem

Courtesy of Zoom Telephonics, Inc.

Before customers can subscribe to broadband cable, however, their local cable company must have the necessary infrastructure. Traditional cable TV networks supply the infrastructure for downstream communication (the TV programming), but not for upstream communication. To provide Internet access through its network, the cable company must have upgraded its equipment to support bidirectional, digital communications. For starters, the cable company's network wiring must be replaced with **HFC (hybrid fiber-coax)**, an expensive fiber-optic link that can support high frequencies. The HFC connects the cable company's offices to a node location near the customer. Most large cable companies, such as Comcast and Charter, long ago upgraded their infrastructure to use HFC. Either fiber-optic or coaxial cable may connect the node to the customer's business or residence via a connection known as a **cable drop**. All cable drops for the cable subscribers in the same neighborhood connect to the local node. These nodes then connect to the cable company's central office, which is known as its head-end. At the head-end, the cable company can connect to the Internet through a variety of means (often via fiber-optic cable) or it can pick up digital satellite or microwave transmissions. The head-end can transmit data to as many as 1000 subscribers, in a one-to-many communication system. Figure 7-22 illustrates the infrastructure of a cable system.

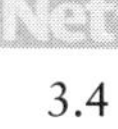
3.4

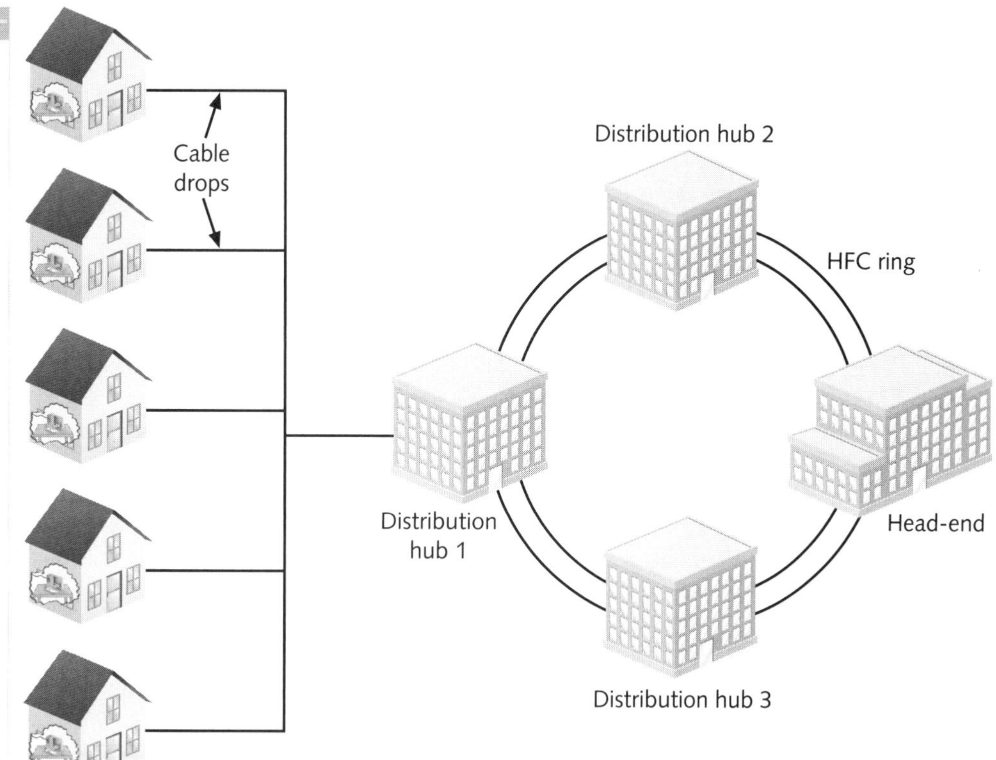

Figure 7-22 Cable infrastructure

Like DSL, broadband cable provides a dedicated, or continuous, connection that does not require dialing up a service provider. Unlike DSL, broadband cable requires many subscribers to share the same local line, thus raising concerns about security and actual (versus theoretical) throughput. For example, if your cable company supplied you and five of your neighbors with broadband cable services, your neighbors could, with some technical prowess, capture the data that you transmit to the Internet. (Modern cable networks provide encryption for data traveling to and from customer premises; however, these encryption schemes can be thwarted.) Moreover, the throughput of a cable line is fixed. As with any fixed resource, the more one claims, the less that is left for others. In other words, the greater the number of users sharing a single line, the less throughput available to each individual user. Cable companies counter this perceived disadvantage by rightly claiming that at some point (for example, at a remote switching facility or at the DSLAM interface), a telecommunications carrier's DSL bandwidth is also fixed and shared among a group of customers.

In the United States, broadband cable access costs approximately $45 per month for customers who already subscribe to cable TV service. Broadband cable is less often used in businesses than DSL, primarily because most office buildings do not contain a coaxial cable infrastructure.

BPL (Broadband over Powerline)

3.1
3.4

In addition to coaxial, twisted pair, and fiber-optic cable, power lines can be used to deliver broadband Internet service. Starting around the year 2000, electric utilities began offering **BPL (broadband over powerline)**, or high-speed Internet access, over the electrical grid. The service promised potential for connecting remote users who might not be within reach of DSL or cable services, but who were connected to the power lines, to finally receive high-speed Internet access. BPL is shared among multiple customers, which limits practical throughputs to no more than 1 Mbps. Each customer accesses the network using a modem plugged into an electrical outlet. BPL requires users to be within 2 km of a repeater.

BPL didn't take off as planned, however, and promise for the service's widespread deployment peaked in the mid-2000s. Standards were subjected to opposition from many telecommunications groups and took a long time to develop. Necessary infrastructure upgrades, including numerous repeaters, cost more than anticipated. Also, signals transmitted via power lines are subject to much more noise than those carried by DSL or cable services. And finally, amateur radio operators who claimed its frequencies interfered with their signals protested the service. Most U.S. utility companies that invested in BPL have abandoned it. Installations do exist, however, in some European countries.

ATM (Asynchronous Transfer Mode)

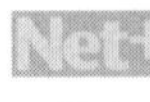
3.4

So far, you have learned about several WAN transmission methods, such as ISDN, T-carriers, and DSL, which achieve high throughput by manipulating signals at the Physical layer. You also learned about some, such as X.25 and frame relay, that operate at the Data Link layer. **ATM (Asynchronous Transfer Mode)** is a third WAN technology that functions at the Data Link layer. Its ITU standard prescribes both network access and signal multiplexing techniques. **Asynchronous** refers to a communications method in which nodes do not have to conform to any predetermined schemes that specify the timing of data transmissions. In asynchronous communications, a node can transmit at any instant, and the destination node must accept the transmission as it comes. To ensure that the receiving node knows when it has received a complete frame, asynchronous communications provide start and stop bits for each character transmitted. When the receiving node recognizes a start bit, it begins to accept a new character. When it receives the stop bit for that character, it ceases to look for the end of that character's transmission. Asynchronous data transmission, therefore, occurs in random stops and starts.

ATM was first conceived by researchers at Bell Labs in the early 1980s, but it took a dozen years before standards organizations could reach an agreement on its specifications. ATM may run over fiber-optic cable or Cat 5 or better UTP or STP cable. Though less popular now than in the late 1990s, ATM may still be found on WANs, particularly those owned by large, public telecommunications carriers.

Like Ethernet, ATM specifies Data Link layer framing techniques. But what sets ATM apart from Ethernet is its fixed packet size. In ATM, a packet is called a **cell** and always consists of 48 bytes of data plus a 5-byte header. This fixed-sized, 53-byte packet allows ATM to provide predictable network performance. However, recall that a smaller packet size requires more overhead. In fact, ATM's smaller packet size does decrease its potential throughput, but the efficiency of using cells compensates for that loss.

3.4 Like X.25 and frame relay, ATM relies on virtual circuits. On an ATM network, switches determine the optimal path between the sender and receiver and then establish this path before the network transmits data. Because ATM packages data into cells before transmission, each of which travels separately to its destination, ATM is typically considered a packet-switching technology. At the same time, the use of virtual circuits means that ATM provides the main advantage of circuit switching—that is, a point-to-point connection that remains reliably available to the transmission until it completes, making ATM a connection-oriented technology.

Establishing a reliable connection allows ATM to guarantee a specific QoS (quality of service) for certain transmissions. ATM networks can supply four QoS levels, from a "best effort" attempt for noncritical data to a guaranteed, real-time transmission for time-sensitive data. This is important for organizations using networks for time-sensitive applications, such as video and audio transmissions. For example, a company that wants to use its physical connection between two offices located at opposite sides of a state to carry voice phone calls might choose the ATM network technology with the highest possible QoS. On the other hand, the company might assign a low QoS to routine e-mail messages exchanged between the two offices. Without QoS guarantees, cells belonging to the same message may arrive in the wrong order or too slowly to be properly interpreted by the receiving node.

ATM's developers have made certain it is compatible with other leading network technologies. Its cells can support multiple types of higher-layer protocols. In addition, the ATM networks can be integrated with Ethernet or token ring networks through the use of **LANE** (**LAN Emulation**). LANE encapsulates incoming Ethernet or token ring frames, then converts them into ATM cells for transmission over an ATM network.

ATM's throughput potential rivals any other described in this chapter, ranging from 25 Mbps to 622 Mbps. When leasing ATM connections, you can choose to pay for only as much throughput as you think you'll need. This also allows you to tailor your desired QoS.

Currently, ATM is relatively expensive, is rarely used on small LANs, and is almost never used to connect typical workstations to a network. Gigabit Ethernet, a cheaper technology, has replaced ATM on many networks. In addition to its lower cost, Gigabit Ethernet is a more natural upgrade for the multitude of Fast Ethernet users. It overcomes the QoS issue by simply providing a larger pipe for the greater volume of traffic using the network. Although ATM caught on among the very largest carriers in the late 1990s, most networking professionals have followed the Gigabit Ethernet standard rather than spending extra dollars on ATM infrastructure.

Where ATM is still used, it's often deployed over the popular SONET WAN technology, discussed next.

SONET (Synchronous Optical Network)

3.4 **SONET** (**Synchronous Optical Network**) is a high-bandwidth WAN signaling technique developed by Bell Communications Research in the 1980s, and later standardized by ANSI and ITU. SONET specifies framing and multiplexing techniques at the Physical layer of the OSI model. Its four key strengths are that it can integrate many other WAN technologies, it

3.4 offers fast data transfer rates, it allows for simple link additions and removals, and it provides a high degree of fault tolerance. (The word *synchronous* as used in the name of this technology means that data being transmitted and received by nodes must conform to a timing scheme. A clock maintains time for all nodes on a network. A receiving node in synchronous communications recognizes that it should be receiving data by looking at the time on the clock.)

Perhaps the most important SONET advantage is that it provides interoperability. Before SONET, telecommunications carriers that used different signaling techniques (or even the same technique but different equipment) could not be assured that their networks could communicate. Now, SONET is often used to aggregate multiple T1s, T3s, or ISDN lines. SONET is also used as the underlying technology for ATM transmission. Furthermore, because it can work directly with the different standards used in different countries, SONET has emerged as the best choice for linking WANs between North America, Europe, and Asia. Internationally, SONET is known as **SDH (Synchronous Digital Hierarchy)**.

SONET's extraordinary fault tolerance results from its use of a double-ring topology over fiber-optic cable. In this type of layout, one ring acts as the primary route for data, transmitting in a clockwise direction. The second ring acts as a backup, transmitting data counterclockwise around the ring. If, for example, a backhoe operator severs the primary ring, SONET would automatically reroute traffic to the backup ring without any loss of service. This characteristic, known as **self-healing**, makes SONET very reliable. (To lower the potential for a single accident to sever both rings, the cables that make up each ring should not lay adjacent to each other.) Figure 7-23 illustrates a SONET ring and its dual-fiber connections.

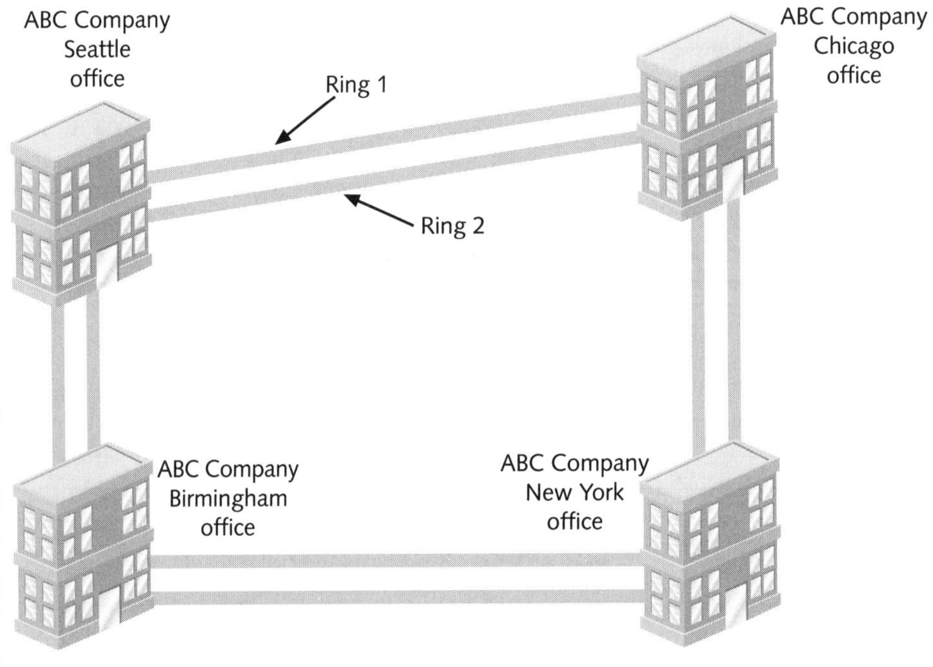

Figure 7-23 A SONET ring

Net+ 3.4 A SONET ring begins and ends at the telecommunications carrier's facility. In between, it connects an organization's multiple WAN sites in a ring fashion. It may also connect with multiple carrier facilities for additional fault tolerance. Companies can lease an entire SONET ring from a telecommunications carrier, or they can lease part of a SONET ring—for example, a circuit that offers T1 throughput—to take advantage of SONET's reliability.

At both the carrier and the customer premises, a SONET ring terminates at a multiplexer. A multiplexer combines individual SONET signals on the transmitting end, and another multiplexer separates combined signals on the receiving end. On the transmitting end, multiplexers accept input from different network types (for example, a T1 or ISDN line) and format the data in a standard SONET frame. That means that many different devices might connect to a SONET multiplexer, including, for example, a private telephone switch, a T1 multiplexer, and an ATM data switch. On the receiving end, multiplexers translate the incoming signals back into their original format. Most SONET multiplexers allow for easy additions or removals of connections to the SONET ring, which makes this technology easily adaptable to growing and changing networks. Figure 7-24 shows the devices necessary to connect a WAN site with a SONET ring. This is the simplest type of SONET connection; however, variations abound.

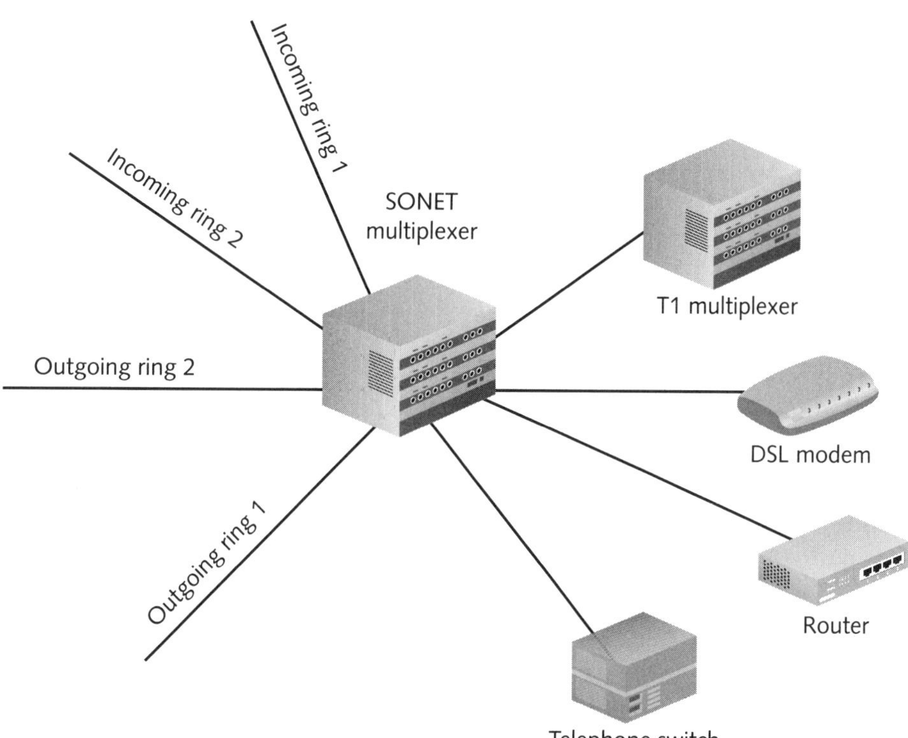

Figure 7-24 SONET connectivity

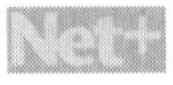
3.4 The data rate of a particular SONET ring is indicated by its **OC (Optical Carrier)** level, a rating that is internationally recognized by networking professionals and standards organizations. OC levels in SONET are analogous to the digital signal levels of T-carriers. Table 7-3 lists the OC levels and their maximum throughput.

SONET technology is typically not implemented by small or medium-sized businesses because of its high cost. It is commonly used, for example, by large companies; long-distance companies linking metropolitan areas and countries; ISPs that want to guarantee fast, reliable access to the Internet; or telephone companies connecting their COs. SONET is particularly suited to audio, video, and imaging data transmission. As you can imagine, given its reliance on fiber-optic cable and its redundancy requirements, SONET technology is expensive to implement.

Table 7-3 SONET OC levels

OC level	Throughput (Mbps)
OC1	51.84
OC3	155.52
OC12	622
OC24	1244
OC48	2488
OC96	4976
OC192	9953
OC768	39,813

WAN Technologies Compared

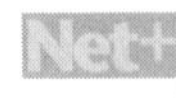
3.4 You have learned that WAN links offer a wide range of throughputs, from 56 Kbps for a PSTN dial-up connection to potentially 39.8 Gbps for a full-speed SONET connection. Table 7-4 summarizes the media and throughputs offered by each technology discussed in this chapter. Bear in mind that each technology's transmission techniques (for example, switching for frame relay versus point-to-point for T1) will affect real throughput, so the maximum transmission speed is a theoretical limit. Actual transmission speeds will vary. In addition, this table omits wireless and satellite WAN technologies, which are discussed in the next chapter.

Net+ 3.4

Table 7-4 A comparison of WAN technology throughputs

WAN technology	Typical media	Maximum throughput
Dial-up over PSTN	UTP or STP	56 Kbps theoretical; actual limit is 53 Kbps
X.25	UTP/STP (DS1 or DS3)	64 Kbps or 2.048 Mbps
Frame relay	UTP/STP (DS1 or DS3)	45 Mbps
BRI (ISDN)	UTP/STP (PSTN)	128 Kbps
PRI (ISDN)	UTP/STP (PSTN)	1.544 Mbps
T1	UTP/STP (PSTN), microwave, or fiber-optic cable	1.544 Mbps
Fractional T1	UTP/STP (PSTN), microwave, or fiber-optic cable	n times 64 Kbps (where *n* = number of channels leased)
T3	Microwave link or fiber-optic cable	45 Mbps
xDSL	UTP/STP (PSTN)	Theoretically, 1.544 Mbps–52 Mbps (depending on the type), but typical residential DSL throughputs are limited to 1.5 Mbps
Broadband cable	Hybrid fiber-coaxial cable	Theoretically, 56 Mbps downstream, 10 Mbps upstream, but actual throughputs are approximately 1.5–3 Mbps upstream and 256–768 Kbps downstream
BPL	Power line	Up to 1 Mbps actual throughput
ATM	Fiber-optic cable, UTP/STP (PSTN)	25 Mbps to 622 Mbps (depending on the customer's preferred bit rate)
SONET	Fiber-optic cable	51, 155, 622, 1244, 2488, 4976, 9952, or 39813 Mbps (depending on the OC level)

Chapter Summary

- WANs are distinguished from LANs by the fact that WANs traverse a wider geographical area. They usually employ point-to-point, dedicated communications rather than point-to-multipoint communications. They also use different connectivity devices, depending on the WAN technology in use.
- A WAN in which each site is connected in a serial fashion to no more than two other sites is known as a bus topology WAN. This topology often provides the best solution for organizations with only a few sites and access to dedicated circuits.
- In a ring topology WAN, each site is connected to two other sites so that the entire WAN forms a ring pattern. This architecture is similar to the LAN ring topology, except that most ring topology WANs have the capability to reverse the direction data travel to avoid a failed site.
- In the star topology WAN, a single site acts as the central connection point for several other points. This arrangement allows one connection to fail without affecting other connections. Therefore, star topology WANs are more fault tolerant than bus or ring WANs.

- A mesh topology WAN consists of many directly interconnected sites. In partial-mesh WANs, only some of the WAN sites are directly interconnected. In full-mesh WANs, every site is directly connected to every other site. The full-mesh topology is the most fault tolerant and also the most expensive WAN topology to implement.
- A tiered topology WAN is one in which sites that are connected in star or ring formations are interconnected at different levels, with the interconnection points being organized into layers to form hierarchical groupings.
- The PSTN (Public Switched Telephone Network) is the network of lines and carrier equipment that provides telephone service to most homes and businesses. It was originally composed of analog lines alone, but now also uses digital transmission over fiber-optic or copper twisted pair cable, microwave, and satellite connections. The local loop portion of the PSTN is still primarily UTP; it is this portion that limits throughput on the PSTN. The PSTN provides the foundation for several types of WAN connections, including dial-up networking, X.25, frame relay, T-carriers, and DSL.
- FTTP (fiber to the premises) refers to the use of a fiber-optic cable to complete a carrier's connection to a subscriber, whether residential or business. FTTP can be found on PONs (passive optical networks), which are point-to-multipoint networks. In PONs, a single port on a carrier's OLT (optical line terminal) is capable of carrying 32 channels, each assigned to a customer. Fiber connects the OLT port with an ONU (optical network unit) near a group of subscribers. From the ONU, fiber-optic or copper cabling brings services to multiple customers.
- X.25 is an analog, packet-switched technology optimized for reliable, long-distance data transmission. It can support 2-Mbps throughput. X.25 was originally developed and used for communications between mainframe computers and remote terminals.
- Frame relay, like X.25, relies on packet switching, but carries digital signals. It does not analyze frames to check for errors, but simply relays them from node to node, so frame relay supports higher bandwidth than X.25, offering a maximum of 45-Mbps throughput.
- Both X.25 and frame relay are configured as PVCs (permanent virtual circuits), or point-to-point connections over which data may follow different paths. When leasing an X.25 or frame relay circuit from a telecommunications carrier, a customer specifies endpoints and the amount of bandwidth required between them.
- ISDN (Integrated Services Digital Network) is an international standard for protocols at the Physical, Data Link, and Transport layers that allows the PSTN to carry digital signals. ISDN lines may carry voice and data signals simultaneously but require an ISDN phone to carry voice traffic and an ISDN router and ISDN terminal adapter to carry data.
- Two types of ISDN connections are commonly used by consumers in North America: BRI (Basic Rate Interface) and PRI (Primary Rate Interface). Both use a combination of bearer channels (B channels) and data channels (D channels). The B channel transmits and receives data or voice from point to point. The D channel carries information about the call, such as session initiation and termination signals, caller identity, call forwarding, and conference calling signals.
- BRI uses two 64-Kbps circuit-switched B channels and a 16-Kbps D channel. The maximum throughput for a BRI connection is 128 Kbps. PRI uses 23 B channels and

one 64-Kbps D channel. The maximum potential throughput for a PRI connection is 1.544 Mbps. Individual subscribers rarely use PRI, preferring BRI instead, but PRI may be used by businesses and other organizations that need more throughput.

- T-carrier technology uses TDM (time division multiplexing) to divide a single channel into multiple channels for carrying voice, data, video, or other signals. Devices at the sending end arrange the data streams (multiplex), then devices at the receiving end filter them back into separate signals (demultiplex).
- The most common T-carrier implementations are T1 and T3. A T1 circuit can carry the equivalent of 24 voice channels, giving a maximum data throughput of 1.544 Mbps. A T3 circuit can carry the equivalent of 672 voice channels, giving a maximum data throughput of 44.736 Mbps.
- The signal level of a T-carrier refers to its Physical layer electrical signaling characteristics, as defined by ANSI standards. DS0 is the equivalent of one data or voice channel. All other signal levels are multiples of DS0.
- T1 technology can use UTP or STP, preferably the latter. However, twisted pair wiring cannot adequately carry the high throughput of multiple T1s or T3 transmissions. For T3 transmissions, fiber-optic cable or microwave connections are necessary.

- Incoming T-carrier lines terminate in RJ-48 connectors at a smart jack at the customer's demarc. Next, signals are processed by a CSU/DSU. The CSU/DSU ensures connection integrity through error correction and line monitoring and converts the T-carrier frames into frames the LAN can interpret, and vice versa. It also connects T-carrier lines with terminating equipment. A CSU/DSU often includes a multiplexer.
- DSL (digital subscriber line) is a WAN connection method that uses advanced phase or amplitude modulation in the higher (inaudible) frequencies on a phone line to achieve throughputs of up to 51.8 Mbps. DSL comes in eight different varieties, each of which is either asymmetrical or symmetrical. In asymmetrical transmission, more data can be sent in one direction than in the other direction. In symmetrical transmission, throughput is equal in both directions. The most popular form of DSL is ADSL.
- DSL technology creates a dedicated circuit. At the consumer end, a DSL modem connects computers and telephones to the DSL line. At the carrier end, a DSLAM (DSL access multiplexer) aggregates multiple incoming DSL lines before connecting them to the Internet or to larger carriers.
- Broadband cable is a dedicated service that relies on the cable wiring used for TV signals. The service can theoretically provide as much as 36-Mbps downstream and 10-Mbps upstream throughput, though actual throughput is much lower.
- Broadband cable connections require that the customer use a special cable modem to transmit and receive signals over coaxial cable wiring. In addition, cable companies must have replaced their coaxial cable plant with hybrid fiber-coax cable to support bidirectional, digital communications.
- In some locations, users can access the Internet using BPL (broadband over powerline). The service is shared among multiple customers, which limits practical throughputs to no more than 1 Mbps. Each customer accesses the network using a modem plugged into an electrical outlet. BPL requires users to be within 2 km of a repeater.

- ATM (Asynchronous Transfer Mode) is a Data Link layer standard that relies on fixed packets, called cells, consisting of 48 bytes of data plus a 5-byte header. It's a connection-oriented technology based on virtual circuits. Having a reliable connection enables ATM to guarantee QoS (quality of service) levels for designated transmissions.
- SONET (Synchronous Optical Network) is a high-bandwidth WAN signaling technique that specifies framing and multiplexing techniques at the Physical layer of the OSI model. Its four key strengths are that it can integrate many other WAN technologies (for example, T-carriers, ISDN, and ATM technology), it offers fast data transfer rates, it allows for simple link additions and removals, and it provides a high degree of fault tolerance. Internationally, SONET is known as SDH.
- SONET depends on fiber-optic transmission media and uses multiplexers to connect to network devices (such as routers or telephone switches) at the customer's end. A typical SONET network takes the form of a dual-ring topology. If one ring breaks, SONET technology automatically reroutes traffic along a backup ring. This characteristic, known as self-healing, makes SONET very reliable.

Key Terms

ADSL (Asymmetric DSL) A variation of DSL that offers more throughput when data travel downstream, downloading from a local carrier's switching facility to the customer, than when data travel upstream, uploading from the customer to the local carrier's switching facility.

asymmetrical The characteristic of a transmission technology that affords greater bandwidth in one direction (either from the customer to the carrier, or vice versa) than in the other direction.

asymmetrical DSL *See* ADSL.

asynchronous A transmission method in which data being transmitted and received by nodes do not have to conform to any timing scheme. In asynchronous communications, a node can transmit at any time and the destination node must accept the transmission as it comes.

Asynchronous Transfer Mode *See* ATM.

ATM (Asynchronous Transfer Mode) A Data Link layer technology originally conceived in the early 1980s at Bell Labs and standardized by the ITU in the mid-1990s. ATM relies on fixed packets, called cells, that each consist of 48 bytes of data plus a 5-byte header. ATM relies on virtual circuits and establishes a connection before sending data. The reliable connection ensured by ATM allows network managers to specify QoS levels for certain types of traffic.

B channel In ISDN, the "bearer" channel, so named because it bears traffic from point to point.

Basic Rate Interface *See* BRI.

bonding The process of combining more than one bearer channel of an ISDN line to increase throughput. For example, BRI's two 64-Kbps B channels are bonded to create an effective throughput of 128 Kbps.

BPL (broadband over powerline) High-speed Internet access delivered over the electrical grid.

BRI (Basic Rate Interface) A variety of ISDN that uses two 64-Kbps bearer channels and one 16-Kbps data channel, as summarized by the notation 2B+D. BRI is the most common form of ISDN employed by home users.

broadband cable A method of connecting to the Internet over a cable network. In broadband cable, computers are connected to a cable modem that modulates and demodulates signals to and from the cable company's head-end.

broadband over powerline *See* BPL.

bus topology WAN A WAN in which each location is connected to no more than two other locations in a serial fashion.

cable drop The fiber-optic or coaxial cable that connects a neighborhood cable node to a customer's house.

cable modem A device that modulates and demodulates signals for transmission and reception via cable wiring.

cable modem access *See* broadband cable.

cell A packet of a fixed size. In ATM technology, a cell consists of 48 bytes of data plus a 5-byte header.

central office *See* CO.

channel service unit *See* CSU.

CIR (committed information rate) The guaranteed minimum amount of bandwidth selected when leasing a frame relay circuit. Frame relay costs are partially based on CIR.

CO (central office) The location where a local or long-distance telephone service provider terminates and interconnects customer lines.

committed information rate *See* CIR.

CSU (channel service unit) A device used with T-carrier technology that provides termination for the digital signal and ensures connection integrity through error correction and line monitoring. Typically, a CSU is combined with a DSU in a single device, a CSU/DSU.

CSU/DSU A combination of a CSU (channel service unit) and a DSU (data service unit) that serves as the connection point for a T1 line at the customer's site. Most modern CSU/DSUs also contain a multiplexer. A CSU/DSU may be a separate device or an expansion card in another device, such as a router.

D channel In ISDN, the "data" channel is used to carry information about the call, such as session initiation and termination signals, caller identity, call forwarding, and conference calling signals.

data service unit *See* DSU.

dedicated A continuously available link or service that is leased through another carrier. Examples of dedicated lines include ADSL, T1, and T3.

dial-up A type of connection in which a user connects to a distant network from a computer and stays connected for a finite period of time. Most of the time, the term *dial-up* refers to a connection that uses a PSTN line.

digital subscriber line *See* DSL.

downstream A term used to describe data traffic that flows from a carrier's facility to the customer. In asymmetrical communications, downstream throughput is usually much higher than upstream throughput. In symmetrical communications, downstream and upstream throughputs are equal.

DS0 (digital signal, level 0) The equivalent of one data or voice channel in T-carrier technology, as defined by ANSI Physical layer standards. All other signal levels are multiples of DS0.

DSL (digital subscriber line) A dedicated WAN technology that uses advanced data modulation techniques at the Physical layer to achieve extraordinary throughput over regular phone lines. DSL comes in several different varieties, the most common of which is Asymmetric DSL (ADSL).

DSL access multiplexer *See* DSLAM.

DSL modem A device that demodulates an incoming DSL signal, extracting the information and passing it to the data equipment (such as telephones and computers) and modulates an outgoing DSL signal.

DSLAM (DSL access multiplexer) A connectivity device located at a telecommunications carrier's office that aggregates multiple DSL subscriber lines and connects them to a larger carrier or to the Internet backbone.

DSU (data service unit) A device used in T-carrier technology that converts the digital signal used by bridges, routers, and multiplexers into the digital signal used on cabling. Typically, a DSU is combined with a CSU in a single device, a CSU/DSU.

E1 A digital carrier standard used in Europe that offers 30 channels and a maximum of 2.048-Mbps throughput.

E3 A digital carrier standard used in Europe that offers 480 channels and a maximum of 34.368-Mbps throughput.

fiber to the home *See* FTTH.

fiber to the premises *See* FTTP.

fractional T1 An arrangement that allows a customer to lease only some of the channels on a T1 line.

frame relay A digital, packet-switched WAN technology whose protocols operate at the Data Link layer. The name is derived from the fact that data is separated into frames, which are then relayed from one node to another without any verification or processing. Frame relay offers throughputs between 64 Kbps and 45 Mbps. A frame relay customer chooses the amount of bandwidth he requires and pays for only that amount.

FTTH (fiber to the home) A service in which a residential customer is connected to his carrier's network with fiber-optic cable.

FTTP (fiber to the premises) A service in which a residential or business customer is connected to his carrier's network using fiber-optic cable.

full-mesh WAN A version of the mesh topology WAN in which every site is directly connected to every other site. Full-mesh WANs are the most fault-tolerant type of WAN.

head-end A cable company's central office, which connects cable wiring to many nodes before it reaches customers' sites.

HFC (hybrid fiber-coax) A link that consists of fiber cable connecting the cable company's offices to a node location near the customer and coaxial cable connecting the node to the customer's house. HFC upgrades to existing cable wiring are required before current TV cable systems can provide Internet access.

hybrid fiber-coax *See* HFC.

Integrated Services Digital Network *See* ISDN.

ISDN (Integrated Services Digital Network) An international standard that uses PSTN lines to carry digital signals. It specifies protocols at the Physical, Data Link, and Transport layers of the OSI model. ISDN lines may carry voice and data signals simultaneously. Two types of ISDN connections are used in North America: BRI (Basic Rate Interface) and PRI (Primary Rate Interface). Both use a combination of bearer channels (B channels) and data channels (D channels).

LAN Emulation *See* LANE.

LANE (LAN Emulation) A method for transporting token ring or Ethernet frames over ATM networks. LANE encapsulates incoming Ethernet or token ring frames, then converts them into ATM cells for transmission over an ATM network.

last mile *See* local loop.

local loop The part of a phone system that connects a customer site with a telecommunications carrier's switching facility.

mesh topology WAN A type of WAN in which several sites are directly interconnected. Mesh WANs are highly fault tolerant because they provide multiple routes for data to follow between any two points.

network interface unit *See* NIU.

network service provider *See* NSP.

Network Termination 1 *See* NT1.

Network Termination 2 *See* NT2.

NIU (network interface unit) The point at which PSTN-owned lines terminate at a customer's premises. The NIU is usually located at the demarc.

NSP (network service provider) A carrier that provides long-distance (and often global) connectivity between major data-switching centers across the Internet. AT&T, Verizon, and Sprint are all examples of network service providers in the United States. Customers, including ISPs, can lease dedicated private or public Internet connections from an NSP.

NT1 (Network Termination 1) A device used on ISDN networks that connects the incoming twisted pair wiring with the customer's ISDN terminal equipment.

NT2 (Network Termination 2) An additional connection device required on PRI to handle the multiple ISDN lines between the customer's network termination connection and the local phone company's wires.

OC (Optical Carrier) An internationally recognized rating that indicates throughput rates for SONET connections.

OLT (optical line terminal) A device located at the carrier's endpoint of a passive optical network. An OLT contains multiple optical ports, or PON interfaces and a splitter that subdivides the capacity of each port into up to 32 logical channels, one per subscriber.

ONU (optical network unit) In a passive optical network, the device near the customer premises that terminates a carrier's fiber-optic cable connection and distributes signals to multiple endpoints via fiber-optic cable, in the case of FTTP, or via copper or coax cable.

Optical Carrier *See* OC.

optical line terminal *See* OLT.

optical network unit *See* ONU.

partial-mesh WAN A version of a mesh topology WAN in which only critical sites are directly interconnected and secondary sites are connected through star or ring topologies. Partial-mesh WANs are less expensive to implement than full-mesh WANs.

passive optical network *See* PON.

permanent virtual circuit *See* PVC.

plain old telephone service (POTS) *See* PSTN.

PON (passive optical network) A network in which a carrier uses fiber-optic cabling to connect with multiple endpoints—for example, many businesses on a city block. The word *passive* applies because in a PON no repeaters or other connectivity devices intervene between a carrier and its customer.

POTS *See* PSTN.

PRI (Primary Rate Interface) A type of ISDN that uses 23 bearer channels and one 64-Kbps data channel, represented by the notation 23B+D. PRI is less commonly used by individual subscribers than BRI, but it may be used by businesses and other organizations needing more throughput.

Primary Rate Interface *See* PRI.

PSTN (Public Switched Telephone Network) The network of lines and carrier equipment that provides telephone service to most homes and businesses. Now, except for the local loop, nearly all of the PSTN uses digital transmission. Its traffic is carried by fiber-optic or copper twisted pair cable, microwave, and satellite connections.

Public Switched Telephone Network *See* PSTN.

PVC (permanent virtual circuit) A point-to-point connection over which data may follow any number of different paths, as opposed to a dedicated line that follows a predefined path. X.25, frame relay, and some forms of ATM use PVCs.

registered jack 48 *See* RJ-48.

ring topology WAN A type of WAN in which each site is connected to two other sites so that the entire WAN forms a ring pattern.

RJ-48 (registered jack 48) A standard for terminating wires in an eight-pin connector. RJ-48 is the preferred connector type for T1 connections that rely on twisted pair wiring.

SDH (Synchronous Digital Hierarchy) The international equivalent of SONET.

self-healing A characteristic of dual-ring topologies that allows them to automatically reroute traffic along the backup ring if the primary ring becomes severed.

signal level An ANSI standard for T-carrier technology that refers to its Physical layer electrical signaling characteristics. DS0 is the equivalent of one data or voice channel. All other signal levels are multiples of DS0.

smart jack A termination for T-carrier wire pairs that is located at the customer demark and which functions as a connection protection and monitoring point.

SONET (Synchronous Optical Network) A high-bandwidth WAN signaling technique that specifies framing and multiplexing techniques at the Physical layer of the OSI model. It can integrate many other WAN technologies (for example, T-carriers, ISDN, and ATM technology) and allows for simple link additions and removals. SONET's topology includes a double ring of fiber-optic cable, which results in very high fault tolerance.

star topology WAN A type of WAN in which a single site acts as the central connection point for several other points. This arrangement provides separate routes for data between any two sites; however, if the central connection point fails, the entire WAN fails.

SVC (switched virtual circuit) A logical, point-to-point connection that relies on switches to determine the optimal path between sender and receiver. ATM technology uses SVCs.

switched virtual circuit *See* SVC.

symmetrical A characteristic of transmission technology that provides equal throughput for data traveling both upstream and downstream and is suited to users who both upload and download significant amounts of data.

symmetrical DSL A variation of DSL that provides equal throughput both upstream and downstream between the customer and the carrier.

synchronous A transmission method in which data being transmitted and received by nodes must conform to a timing scheme.

Synchronous Digital Hierarchy *See* SDH.

Synchronous Optical Network *See* SONET.

T1 A digital carrier standard used in North America and most of Asia that provides 1.544-Mbps throughput and 24 channels for voice, data, video, or audio signals. T1s rely on time division multiplexing and may use shielded or unshielded twisted pair, coaxial cable, fiber optics, or microwave links.

T3 A digital carrier standard used in North America and most of Asia that can carry the equivalent of 672 channels for voice, data, video, or audio, with a maximum data throughput of 44.736 Mbps (typically rounded up to 45 Mbps for purposes of discussion). T3s rely on time division multiplexing and require either fiber-optic or microwave transmission media.

T-carrier The term for any kind of leased line that follows the standards for T1s, fractional T1s, T1Cs, T2s, T3s, or T4s.

TA (terminal adapter) A device used to convert digital signals into analog signals for use with ISDN phones and other analog devices. TAs are sometimes called ISDN modems.

TE (terminal equipment) The end nodes (such as computers and printers) served by the same connection (such as an ISDN, DSL, or T1 link).

terminal adapter *See* TA.

terminal equipment *See* TE.

tiered topology WAN A type of WAN in which sites that are connected in star or ring formations are interconnected at different levels, with the interconnection points being organized into layers to form hierarchical groupings.

upstream A term used to describe data traffic that flows from a customer's site to a carrier's facility. In asymmetrical communications, upstream throughput is usually much lower than downstream throughput. In symmetrical communications, upstream and downstream throughputs are equal.

virtual circuit A connection between network nodes that, although based on potentially disparate physical links, logically appears to be a direct, dedicated link between those nodes.

WAN link A point-to-point connection between two nodes on a WAN.

X.25 An analog, packet-switched WAN technology optimized for reliable, long-distance data transmission and standardized by the ITU in the mid-1970s. The X.25 standard specifies protocols at the Physical, Data Link, and Network layers of the OSI model. It provides excellent flow control and ensures data reliability over long distances by verifying the transmission at every node. X.25 can support a maximum of only 2-Mbps throughput.

xDSL The term used to refer to all varieties of DSL.

Review Questions

1. Which WAN topology is only practical for connecting fewer than four or five locations?
   a. star
   b. mesh
   c. ring
   d. partial-mesh
2. What is the primary reason that small or medium-sized business typically do not implement SONET technology for an Internet connection?
   a. high cost
   b. marginal security
   c. complexity
   d. lack of availability
3. Which type of DSL would a bank's branch office that sends large volumes of account information to the central server at the bank's headquarters and, in turn, receives large amounts of account information from the central server at the bank's headquarters require?
   a. ADSL
   b. HDSL
   c. G.Lite
   d. VDSL
4. What advantage is gained from ATM's fixed-size, 53-byte packet?
   a. increased throughput
   b. less overhead
   c. predictable network performance
   d. low costs for small networks

5. Which WAN technology is the best choice for linking WANs between North America, Europe, and Asia?
   a. SONET
   b. Frame relay
   c. ATM
   d. Broadband
6. True or false? WANs typically send data over publicly available communications networks.
7. True or false? A bus WAN topology scales well.
8. True or false? Broadband cable is a symmetrical technology.
9. True or false? The speed of a T-carrier depends on its signal level.
10. True or false? WANs and LANs have several fundamental properties in common.

11. A(n) ________________ topology WAN incorporates many directly interconnected sites and data can travel directly from its origin to its destination.
12. In a(n) ________________ topology WAN, sites connected in star or ring formations are interconnected at different levels, with the interconnection points being organized into layers to form hierarchical groupings.
13. A(n) ________________ refers to the network of lines and carrier equipment that provides telephone service to most homes and businesses.
14. The ________________ standard specifies protocols at the Physical, Data Link, and Network layers of the OSI model.
15. All ISDN connections are based on two types of channels. The ________________ channel employs packet-switching techniques to carry information about the call, such as session initiation and termination signals, caller identity, call forwarding, and conference calling signals.

Wireless Networking

After reading this chapter and completing the exercises, you will be able to:

- Explain how nodes exchange wireless signals
- Identify potential obstacles to successful wireless transmission and their repercussions, such as interference and reflection
- Understand WLAN (wireless LAN) architecture
- Specify the characteristics of popular WLAN transmission methods, including 802.11 a/b/g/n
- Install and configure wireless access points and their clients
- Describe wireless WAN technologies, including 802.16 (WiMAX), HSPA+, LTE, and satellite communications

On the Job

When Isthmus Publishing was attempting to gain better bandwidth than its current DSL access allowed, we decided on WiMAX. We acquired and installed hardware that allowed non-line-of-sight connectivity. A solid connection was made and worked flawlessly for several months. We were so pleased with the new access that we canceled our DSL service as being redundant and slow.

At the same time, a new building was being erected directly in the path of our line of sight. Initially, this posed no problems at all. Then, one day, our Internet access was agonizingly slow at best and nonfunctional at worst. We spent many hours on the rooftop adjusting the radio antenna in an attempt to restore service to the previous levels, all to no avail. Since our previous DSL connection had been shut down, we had little Web access, sporadic email delivery, and no way to process credit card payments in a timely fashion.

We quickly tried to reestablish a DSL subscription; it had become apparent that a secondary backup connection was essential to ensure business operations. In the meantime, we kept working with the supplier of the WiMAX connection.

Eventually, we figured out that the metallic content in the reflective glass of the new building across the street created the disruption. The ISP installed new hardware that allowed us to send our signal to a rooftop 180 degrees in the opposite direction; the signal would then be sent to them from that other customer's antenna. Service was restored, all systems returned to normal, and we have had no problems since.

We still, however, keep DSL around as a backup.

Thom Jones
Isthmus Publishing

Air provides an intangible means of transporting data over networks. For decades, radio and TV stations have transmitted analog signals through the air. Such analog signals are also capable of carrying data. Networks that transmit signals through the air via radio frequency (RF) waves are known as **wireless** networks or **WLANs** (**wireless local area networks**). Wireless transmission media are now common in business and home networks and necessary in some specialized network environments. In addition to providing the basis for LAN transmissions, wireless signals can traverse long distances using microwave, satellite, and cellular links. In this chapter, you'll learn how data travel through the air and how to make it happen on your network.

The Wireless Spectrum

All wireless signals are carried through the air by electromagnetic waves. The **wireless spectrum** is a continuum of the electromagnetic waves used for data and voice communication. On the spectrum, waves are arranged according to their frequencies, from lowest to highest. The wireless spectrum (as defined by the FCC, which controls its use) spans frequencies between 9 KHz and 300 GHz. Each type of wireless service can be associated with one area of the wireless spectrum. AM broadcasting, for example, sits near the low-frequency end of the wireless communications spectrum, using frequencies between 535 and 1605 KHz. Infrared waves belong to a wide band of frequencies at the high-frequency end of the spectrum, between 300 GHz and 300,000 GHz. Most wireless networks use frequencies around 2.4 GHz or 5 GHz and some use frequencies around 3.7 GHz. Figure 8-1 shows the wireless spectrum and roughly identifies the range of frequencies associated with major wireless services. Later in this chapter, you will learn specifically which frequencies each technology uses.

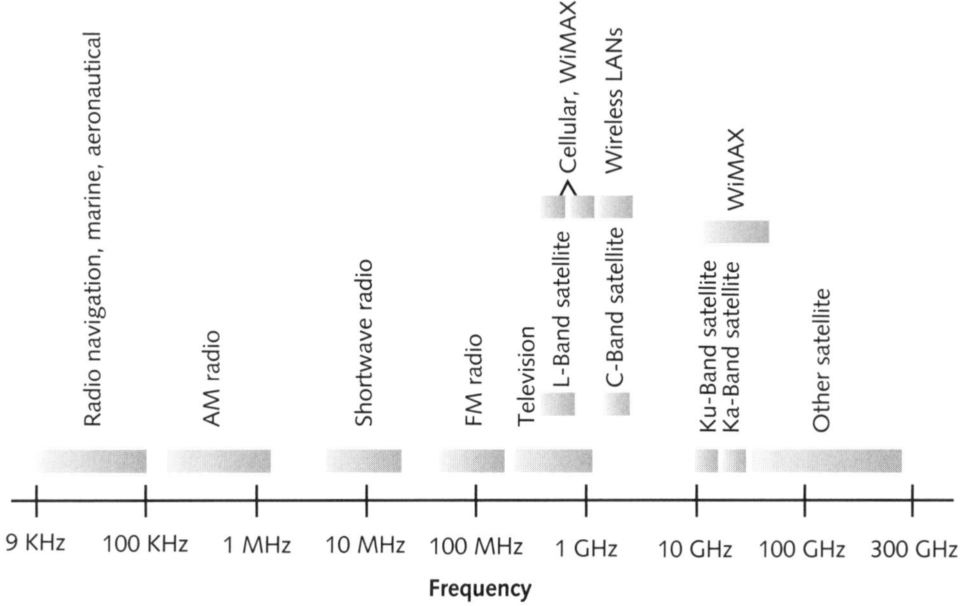

Figure 8-1 The wireless spectrum

In the United States, the collection of frequencies available for communication—also known as "the airwaves"—is considered a natural resource available for public use. The FCC grants organizations in different locations exclusive rights to use each frequency. It also determines what frequency ranges can be used for what purposes. Of course, signals propagating through the air do not necessarily remain within one nation. Therefore, it is important for countries across the world to agree on wireless communications standards. ITU is the governing body that sets standards for international wireless services, including frequency allocation, signaling, and protocols used by wireless devices; wireless transmission and reception equipment; satellite orbits; and so on. If governments and companies did not adhere to ITU standards, chances are that a wireless device could not be used outside the country in which it was manufactured.

Characteristics of Wireless Transmission

In previous chapters, you learned about signals that travel over a physical medium, such as a copper or fiber-optic cable. Wired and wireless signals share many similarities, including use of the same Layer 3 and higher protocols, for example. However, the nature of the atmosphere makes wireless transmission vastly different from wired transmission. Because the air provides no fixed path for signals to follow, signals travel without guidance. Contrast this to guided media, such as UTP or fiber-optic cable, which do provide a fixed signal path. The lack of a fixed path requires wireless signals to be transmitted, received, controlled, and corrected differently from wired signals.

Just as with wired signals, wireless signals originate from electrical current traveling along a conductor. The electrical signal travels from the transmitter to an antenna, which then emits the signal, as a series of electromagnetic waves, to the atmosphere. The signal propagates through the air until it reaches its destination. At the destination, another antenna accepts the signal, and a receiver converts it back to current. Figure 8-2 illustrates this process.

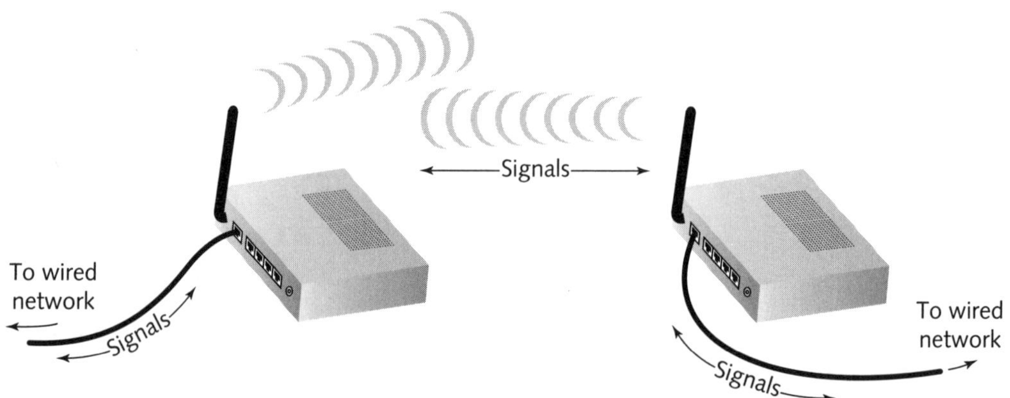

Figure 8-2 Wireless transmission and reception

Notice that antennas are used for both the transmission and reception of wireless signals. As you would expect, to exchange information, two antennas must be tuned to the same frequency. In communications terminology, this means they share the same channel.

Antennas

Each type of wireless service requires an antenna specifically designed for that service. The service's specifications determine the antenna's power output, frequency, and radiation pattern. An antenna's **radiation pattern** describes the relative strength over a three-dimensional area of all the electromagnetic energy the antenna sends or receives.

A **directional antenna** issues wireless signals along a single direction. This type of antenna is used when the source needs to communicate with one destination, as in a point-to-point link. A satellite downlink (for example, the kind used to receive digital TV signals) uses directional antennas. In contrast, an **omnidirectional antenna** issues and receives wireless signals with equal strength and clarity in all directions. This type of antenna is used when many different receivers must be able to pick up the signal, or when the receiver's location is highly mobile. TV and radio stations use omnidirectional antennas, as do most towers that transmit cellular signals.

The geographical area that an antenna or wireless system can reach is known as its **range**. Receivers must be within the range to receive accurate signals consistently. Even within an antenna's range, however, signals may be hampered by obstacles and rendered unintelligible.

Net+ Signal Propagation

2.4 Ideally, a wireless signal would travel directly in a straight line from its transmitter to its intended receiver. This type of propagation, known as **LOS (line-of-sight)**, uses the least amount of energy and results in the reception of the clearest possible signal. However, because the atmosphere is an unguided medium and the path between a transmitter and a receiver is not always clear, wireless signals do not usually follow a straight line. When an obstacle stands in a signal's way, the signal may pass through the object or be absorbed by the object, or it may be subject to any of the following phenomena: reflection, diffraction, or scattering. The object's geometry governs which of these three phenomena occurs.

Reflection in wireless signaling is no different from reflection of other electromagnetic waves, such as light. The wave encounters an obstacle and reflects—or bounces back—toward its source. For this reason, when assessing wireless transmission, reflection is also called **bounce**. A wireless signal will bounce off objects whose dimensions are large compared with the signal's average wavelength. In the context of a wireless LAN, which may use signals with wavelengths between 1 and 10 meters, such objects include walls, floors, ceilings, and the Earth. In addition, signals reflect more readily off conductive materials, like metal, than insulators, like concrete.

In **diffraction**, a wireless signal splits into secondary waves when it encounters an obstruction. The secondary waves continue to propagate in the direction in which they were split. If you could see wireless signals being diffracted, they would appear to be bending around the obstacle. Objects with sharp edges—including the corners of walls and desks—cause diffraction.

Scattering is the diffusion, or the reflection in multiple different directions, of a signal. Scattering occurs when a wireless signal encounters an object that has small dimensions compared with the signal's wavelength. Scattering is also related to the roughness of the surface a wireless signal encounters. The rougher the surface, the more likely a signal is to scatter when it hits that surface. In an office building, objects such as chairs, books, and computers cause scattering of wireless LAN signals. For signals traveling outdoors, rain, mist, hail, and snow may all cause scattering.

Because of reflection, diffraction, and scattering, wireless signals follow a number of different paths to their destination. Such signals are known as **multipath** signals. Figure 8-3 illustrates multipath signals caused by these three phenomena.

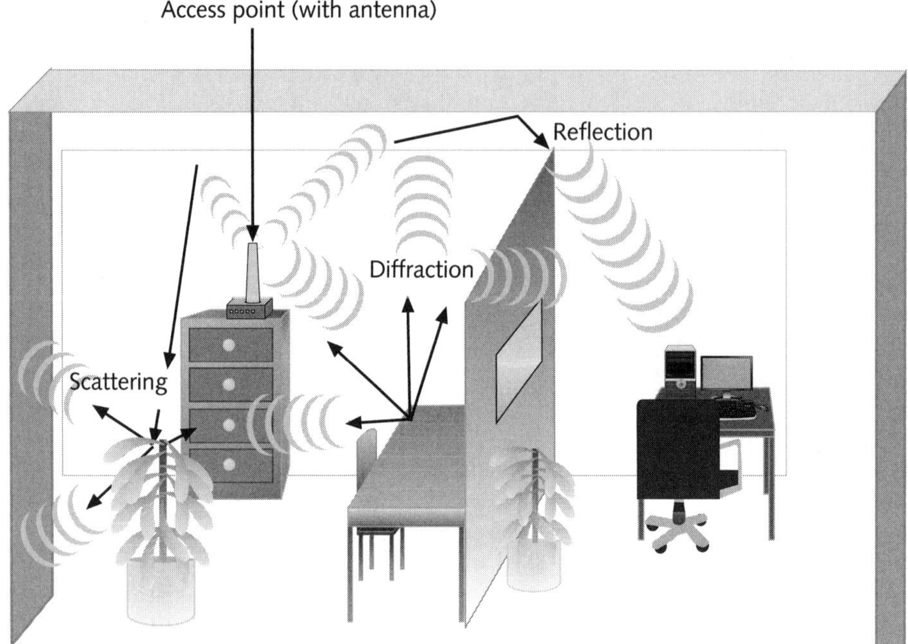

Figure 8-3 Multipath signal propagation

Net+ 2.4

The multipath nature of wireless signals is both a blessing and a curse. On one hand, because signals bounce off obstacles, they have a better chance of reaching their destination. In environments such as an office building, wireless services depend on signals bouncing off walls, ceilings, floors, and furniture so that they may eventually reach their destination. Imagine how inconvenient and inefficient it would be, for example, to make sure you were standing within clear view of a transmitter to receive a text message.

The downside to multipath signaling is that, because of their various paths, multipath signals travel different distances between their transmitter and a receiver. Thus, multiple instances of the same signal can arrive at a receiver at different times. This may cause signals to be misinterpreted, resulting in data errors. Error-correction algorithms will detect the errors and the sender will have to retransmit the signal. The more errors that occur, the slower the throughput. Environments such as manufacturing plants, which contain myriad reflective surfaces, experience greater throughput degradation than relatively open spaces, such as homes.

Signal Degradation

No matter what paths wireless signals take, they are bound to run into obstacles. When they do, the original signal issued by the transmitter will experience **fading**, or a variation in signal strength as a result of some of the electromagnetic energy being scattered, reflected, or diffracted after being issued by the transmitter. Multipath signaling is a significant cause of fading. Because of fading, the strength of the signal that reaches the receiver is lower than the transmitted signal's strength. This makes sense because as more waves are reflected, diffracted, or scattered by obstacles, fewer are likely to reach their destination on time and without errors. Excessive fading can cause dropped calls or slow data transmission.

2.4

As with wired signals, wireless signals also experience attenuation. After a signal is transmitted, the farther it moves away from the transmission antenna the more it weakens. Just as with wired transmission, wireless signals are amplified (if analog) or repeated (if digital) to strengthen the signal so that it can be clearly received. The difference is that the intermediate points through which wireless signals are amplified or repeated are transceivers connected to antennas.

However, attenuation is not the most severe flaw affecting wireless signals. Wireless signals are also susceptible to noise. As you learned in Chapter 3, noise is also known as EMI (electromagnetic interference), or, in the context of wireless communications, interference. Interference is a significant problem for wireless communications because the atmosphere is saturated with electromagnetic waves. For example, wireless LANs may be affected by cellular phones, hands-free headsets, microwaves, machinery, or overhead lights.

Interference can distort and weaken a wireless signal in the same way that noise distorts and weakens a wired signal. However, because wireless signals cannot depend on a conduit or shielding to protect them from extraneous EMI, they are more vulnerable to noise. The extent of interference that a wireless signal experiences depends partly on the density of signals within a geographical area. Signals traveling through areas in which many wireless communications systems are in use—for example, the center of a metropolitan area—are the most apt to suffer interference.

Frequency Ranges

For many years, wireless networks relied on frequencies in the range of 2.4–2.4835 GHz, more commonly known as the **2.4-GHz band**, to send and receive signals. This band offers 11 communications channels that are unlicensed in the United States. An unlicensed frequency is one for which the FCC does not require users to register their service and reserve it for their sole use. Because the 2.4-GHz band also carries cordless telephone and other types of signals, it is highly susceptible to interference. For example, on your home wireless network, your tablet computer might lose connectivity when your cordless telephone rings. One way to guard against this type of interference is to make sure your access point and cordless telephone use different channels within the 2.4-GHz band.

Wireless LANs and WANs may instead use the **5-GHz band**, which comprises four frequency bands: 5.1 GHz, 5.3 GHz, 5.4 GHz, and 5.8 GHz. It consists of 24 unlicensed bands, each 20-MHz wide. Because the 5-GHz band is also used by weather and military radar communications in the United States, WLAN equipment using this range of frequencies must be able to monitor and detect radar signals and, if one is detected, switch to a different channel automatically.

Narrowband, Broadband, and Spread-Spectrum Signals

Transmission technologies differ according to how much of the wireless spectrum their signals use. An important distinction is whether a wireless service uses narrowband or broadband signaling. In **narrowband**, a transmitter concentrates the signal energy at a single frequency or in a very small range of frequencies. In contrast to narrowband, broadband uses a relatively wide band of the wireless spectrum. Broadband technologies, as a result of their wider frequency bands, offer higher throughputs than narrowband technologies.

The use of multiple frequencies to transmit a signal is known as **spread-spectrum** technology because the signal is spread out over the wireless spectrum. In other words, a signal never stays continuously within one frequency range during its transmission. One result of spreading a signal over a wide frequency band is that it requires less power per frequency than narrowband signaling. This distribution of signal strength makes spread-spectrum signals less likely to interfere with narrowband signals traveling in the same frequency band.

Spread-spectrum signaling, originally used with military wireless transmissions in World War II, remains a popular way of making wireless transmissions more secure. Because signals are split across several frequencies according to a sequence known only to the authorized transmitter and receiver, it is much more difficult for unauthorized receivers to capture and decode spread-spectrum signals. To generic receivers, signals issued via spread-spectrum technology appear as unintelligible noise.

One specific implementation of spread spectrum is **FHSS (frequency hopping spread spectrum)**. In FHSS transmission, a signal jumps between several different frequencies within a band in a synchronization pattern known only to the channel's receiver and transmitter, as shown in Figure 8-4. FHSS devices in the U.S. split the 2.4–2.4835 band into 79 distinct frequencies.

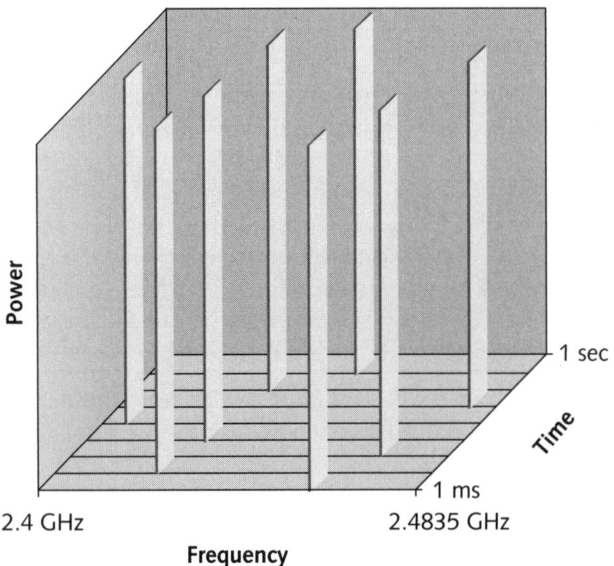

Figure 8-4 FHSS (frequency hopping spread spectrum)

Another type of spread-spectrum signaling is called **DSSS (direct-sequence spread spectrum)**. In DSSS, a signal's bits are distributed over an entire frequency band at once, as shown in

Figure 8-5. Each bit is coded so that the receiver can reassemble the original signal upon receiving the bits. Most wireless LAN standards specify some form of DSSS modulation.

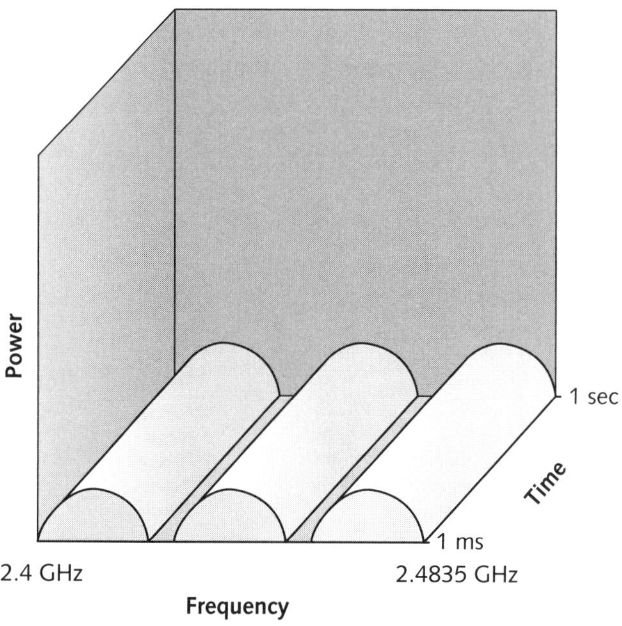

Figure 8-5 DSSS (direct-sequence spread spectrum)

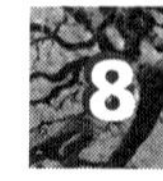

Fixed vs. Mobile

Each type of wireless communication falls into one of two categories: fixed or mobile. In **fixed** wireless systems, the locations of the transmitter and receiver do not move. The transmitting antenna focuses its energy directly toward the receiving antenna. This results in a point-to-point link. One advantage of fixed wireless is that, because the receiver's location is predictable, energy need not be wasted issuing signals across a large geographical area. Thus, more energy can be used for the signal. Fixed wireless links are used in some data and voice applications. For example, a service provider may obtain data services through a fixed link with a satellite. In cases in which a long distance or difficult terrain must be traversed, fixed wireless links are more economical than cabling.

Many types of communications are unsuited to fixed wireless, however. For example, a waiter who uses a wireless handheld computer to transmit orders to the restaurant's kitchen could not use a service that requires him to remain in one spot to send and receive signals. Instead, wireless LANs, along with cellular telephone, paging, and many other services use mobile wireless systems. In **mobile** wireless, the receiver can be located anywhere within the transmitter's range. This allows the receiver to roam from one place to another while continuing to pick up its signal.

Now that you understand some characteristics of wireless transmission, you are ready to learn about the way most wireless LANs are structured. Later, you'll learn about their access methods and how to install wireless connectivity devices.

WLAN (Wireless LAN) Architecture

Net+ 2.2 2.6

Because they are not bound by cabling paths between nodes and connectivity devices, wireless networks are not laid out using the same topologies as wired networks. They have their own, different layouts. Smaller wireless networks, in which a small number of nodes closely positioned need to exchange data, can be arranged in an ad hoc fashion. In an **ad hoc** WLAN, wireless nodes, or **stations**, transmit directly to each other via wireless NICs without an intervening connectivity device, as shown in Figure 8-6.

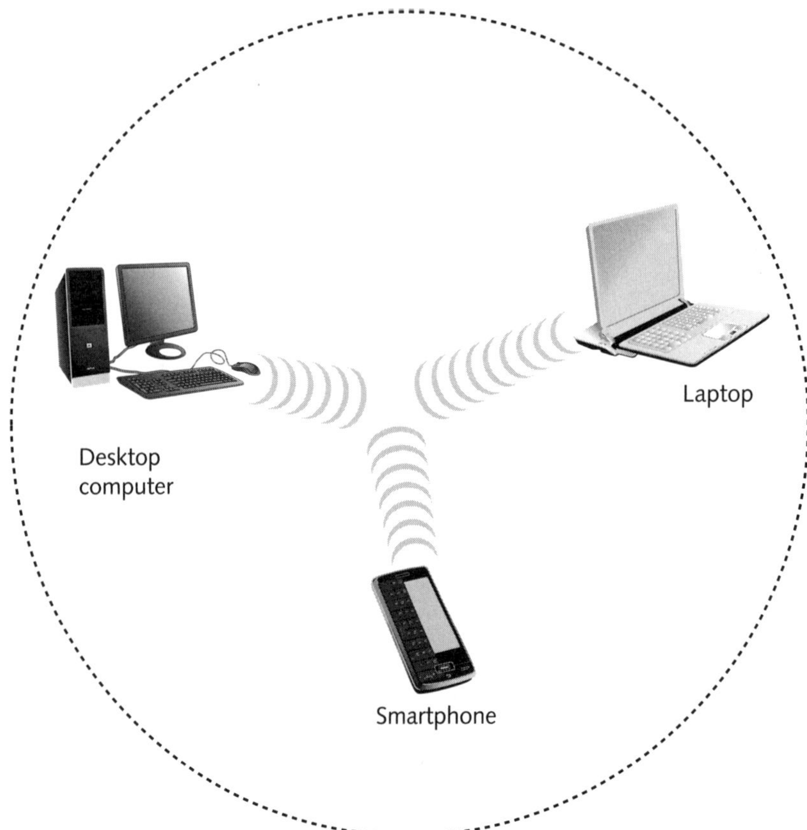

Figure 8-6 An ad hoc WLAN

However, an ad hoc arrangement would not work well for a WLAN with many users or whose users are spread out over a wide area, or where obstacles could stand in the way of signals between stations. Instead of communicating directly with each other in ad hoc mode, nearly all WLANs use the infrastructure mode, which depends on an intervening connectivity device called a wireless access point. A **wireless access point (WAP)**—also known simply as an **access point,** or an **AP**—is a device that accepts wireless signals from multiple nodes and retransmits them to the rest of the network. Access points may also be known as **base stations**. Access points for use on small office or home networks often include routing functions. As such, they may also be called **wireless routers** or **wireless gateways**.

Net+ 2.2 2.6

To cover its intended range, an access point must have sufficient power and be strategically placed so that stations can communicate with it. For instance, if an access point serves a group of workstations in several offices on one floor in a building, it should probably be located in an open area near the center of that floor. And like other wireless devices, access points contain an antenna connected to their transceivers. An **infrastructure WLAN** is shown in Figure 8-7.

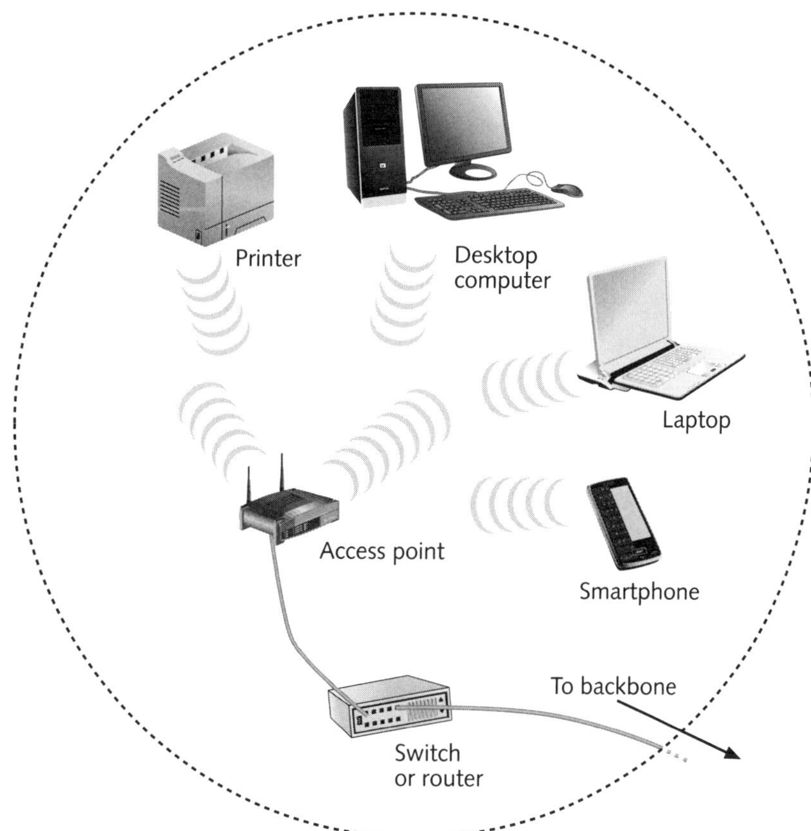

Figure 8-7 An infrastructure WLAN

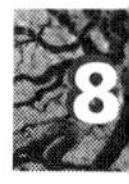

It's common for a WLAN to include several access points. The number of access points depends on the number of stations a WLAN connects. The maximum number of stations each access point can serve varies from 10 to 100, depending on the wireless technology used. Exceeding the recommended maximum leads to a greater incidence of errors and slower overall transmission.

Mobile networking allows wireless nodes to roam from one location to another within a certain range of their access point. This range depends on the wireless access method, the equipment manufacturer, and the office environment. As with other wireless technologies, WLAN signals are subject to interference and obstruction that cause multipath signaling. Therefore, a building with many thick, concrete walls, for example, will limit the effective range of a WLAN more severely than an open area divided into cubicles. In most WLAN scenarios, stations must remain within 300 feet of an access point to maintain optimal transmission speeds.

2.2
2.6

In addition to connecting multiple nodes within a LAN, wireless technology can be used to connect two different parts of a LAN or two separate LANs. Such connections typically use a fixed link with directional antennas between two access points, as shown in Figure 8-8. Because point-to-point links only have to transmit in one direction, they can apply more energy to signal propagation than mobile wireless links. As a result of applying more energy to the signal, their maximum transmission distance is greater. In the case of connecting two WLANs, access points could be as far as 1000 feet apart.

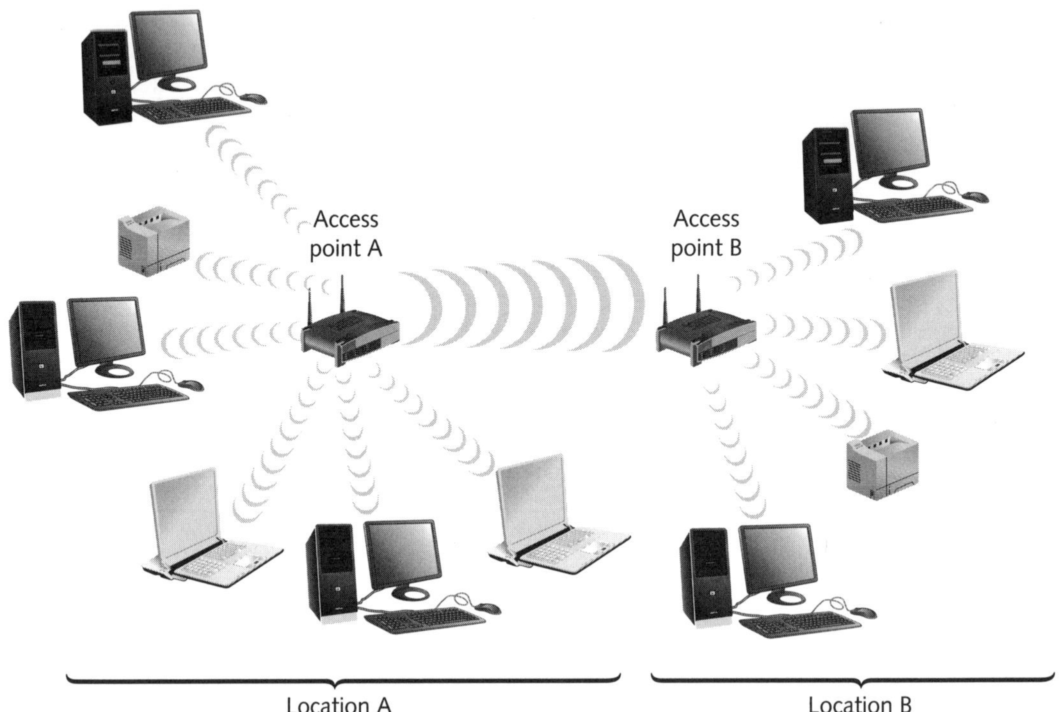

Figure 8-8 Wireless LAN interconnection

WLANs support the same protocols (for example, TCP/IP) and operating systems (for example, UNIX, Linux, or Windows) as wired LANs. This compatibility ensures that wireless and wired transmission methods can be integrated on the same network. Only the signaling techniques differ between wireless and wired portions of a LAN. However, techniques for generating and encoding wireless signals vary from one WLAN standard to another. The following section describes the most popular WLAN Physical and Data Link layer standards.

802.11 WLANs

3.3

Similar to the development of wired network access technologies, the evolution of wireless access methods did not follow one direct and cooperative path, but grew from the efforts of multiple vendors and organizations. Now, the industry accepts a handful of different

3.3 wireless technologies. Each wireless technology is defined by a standard that describes unique functions at both the Physical and the Data Link layers of the OSI model. These standards differ in their specified signaling methods, geographic ranges, and frequency usages, among other things. Such differences make certain technologies better suited to home networks and others better suited to networks at large organizations. The most popular wireless standards used on contemporary LANs are those developed by IEEE's 802.11 committee.

IEEE released its first wireless network standard in 1997. Since then, its WLAN standards committee, also known as the 802.11 committee, has published several distinct standards related to wireless networking. Each IEEE wireless network access standard is named after the 802.11 task group (or subcommittee) that developed it. The four IEEE 802.11 task groups that have generated notable wireless standards are 802.11b, 802.11a, 802.11g, and 802.11n. Collectively, these four 802.11 standards are known as **Wi-Fi**, for wireless fidelity, and they share many characteristics. For example, although some of their Physical layer services vary, all four use half-duplex signaling. In other words, a wireless station using one of the 802.11 techniques can either transmit or receive, but cannot do both simultaneously (assuming the station has only one transceiver installed, as is usually the case). In addition, all 802.11 networks follow the same access method, as described in the following section.

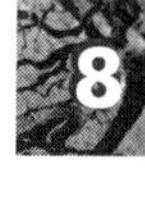

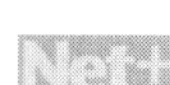

Access Method

3.3 In Chapter 2, you learned that the MAC sublayer of the Data Link layer is responsible for
3.7 appending physical addresses to a data frame and for governing multiple nodes' access to a single medium. As with 802.3 (Ethernet), the 802.11 MAC services append 48-bit (or 6-byte) physical addresses to a frame to identify its source and destination. The use of the same physical addressing scheme allows 802.11 networks to be easily combined with other IEEE 802 networks, including Ethernet networks. However, because wireless devices are not designed to transmit and receive simultaneously, and, therefore, cannot quickly detect collisions, 802.11 networks use a different access method than Ethernet networks.

802.11 standards specify the use of **CSMA/CA (Carrier Sense Multiple Access with Collision Avoidance)** to access a shared medium. Using CSMA/CA, a station on an 802.11 network checks for existing wireless transmissions before it begins to send data. If the source node detects no transmission activity on the network, it waits a brief, random amount of time, and then sends its transmission. If the source does detect activity, it waits a brief period of time before checking the channel again. The destination node receives the transmission and, after verifying its accuracy, issues an acknowledgment (ACK) packet to the source. If the source receives this acknowledgment, it assumes the transmission was properly completed. However, interference or other transmissions on the network could impede this exchange. If, after transmitting a message, the source node fails to receive acknowledgment from the destination node, it assumes its transmission did not arrive properly, and it begins the CSMA/CA process anew. Compared with CSMA/CD (Carrier Sense Multiple Access with Collision Detection), CSMA/CA minimizes, but does not eliminate, the potential for collisions. The use of ACK packets to verify every transmission means that 802.11 networks require more overhead than 802.3 networks. Therefore, a wireless network with a theoretical maximum throughput of 10 Mbps will, in fact, transmit less data per second than a wired Ethernet network with the same theoretical maximum

throughput. In reality, most wireless networks tend to achieve between one-third and one-half of their theoretical maximum throughput. For example, one type of 802.11 network,
3.3 802.11g, is rated for a maximum of 54 Mbps; most 802.11g networks achieve between
3.7 20 and 25 Mbps. As described later in this chapter, however, the 802.11n standard includes several techniques for reducing overhead and making the technology's actual throughput match its theoretical throughput.

One way to ensure that packets are not inhibited by other transmissions is to reserve the medium for one station's use. In 802.11, this can be accomplished through the optional **RTS/CTS (Request to Send/Clear to Send)** protocol. RTS/CTS enables a source node to issue an RTS signal to an access point requesting the exclusive opportunity to transmit. If the access point agrees by responding with a CTS signal, the access point temporarily suspends communication with all stations in its range and waits for the source node to complete its transmission. RTS/CTS is not routinely used by wireless stations, but for transmissions involving large packets (those more subject to damage by interference), RTS/CTS can prove more efficient. On the other hand, using RTS/CTS further decreases the overall efficiency of the 802.11 network. Figure 8-9 illustrates the CSMA/CA process.

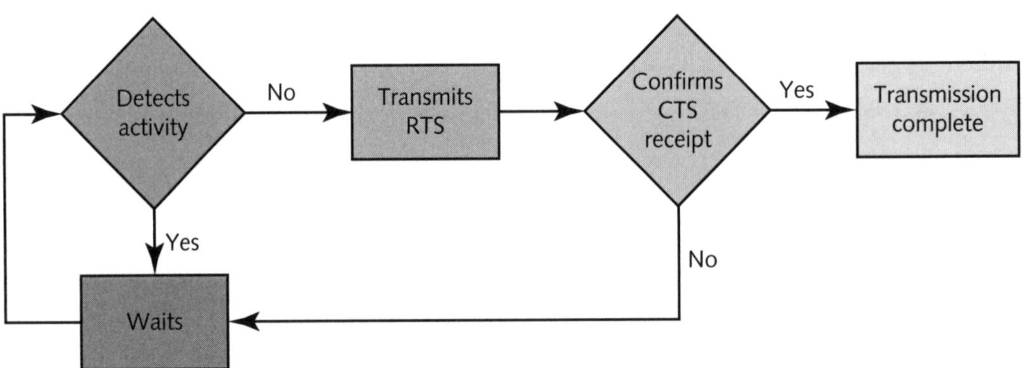

Figure 8-9 CSMA/CA (Carrier Sense Multiple Access with Collision Avoidance)

Association

2.2 Suppose you have just purchased a new laptop with a wireless NIC that supports one of the
3.3 802.11 wireless standards. When you bring your laptop to a local Internet café and turn it on, your laptop soon prompts you to log on to the café's wireless network to gain access to the Internet. This seemingly simple process, known as **association**, involves a number of packet exchanges between the café's access point and your computer. Association is another function of the MAC sublayer described in the 802.11 standard.

As long as a station is on and has its wireless protocols running, it periodically surveys its surroundings for evidence of an access point, a task known as **scanning**. A station can use either active scanning or passive scanning. In **active scanning**, the station transmits a special frame, known as a **probe**, on all available channels within its frequency range. When an access point finds the probe frame, it issues a probe response. This response contains all the information a station needs to associate with the access point, including a status code and station ID number for that station. After receiving the probe response, a station

Net+ can agree to associate with that access point. The final decision to associate with an access
2.2 point, at least for the first time, usually requires the consent of the user. Once association
3.3 is complete, the two nodes begin communicating over the frequency channel specified by
the access point.

In **passive scanning**, a wireless station listens on all channels within its frequency range for a special signal, known as a **beacon frame**, issued from an access point. The beacon frame contains information that a wireless node requires to associate itself with the access point. For example, the frame indicates the network's transmission rate and the **SSID (service set identifier)**, a unique character string used to identify an access point. After detecting a beacon frame, the station can choose to associate with that access point. The two nodes agree on a frequency channel and begin communicating.

When setting up a WLAN, most network administrators use the access point's configuration utility to assign a unique SSID, rather than the default SSID provided by the manufacturer. This can contribute to better security and easier network management. For example, the access point used by employees in the Customer Service Department of a company could be assigned the SSID "CustSvc". In IEEE terminology, a group of stations that share an access point are said to be part of one **BSS (basic service set)**. The identifier for this group of stations is known as a **BSSID (basic service set identifier)**.

Some WLANs are large enough to require multiple access points. A group of access points connected to the same LAN are known collectively as an **ESS (extended service set)**. BSSs that belong to the same ESS share a special identifier, called an **ESSID (extended service set identifier)**. In practice, many networking professionals don't distinguish between the terms *SSID* and *ESSID*. They simply configure every access point in a group or LAN with the same SSID.

Within an ESS, a client can associate with any one of many access points that use the same ESSID. That allows users to roam about an office without losing wireless network service. In fact, **roaming** is the term applied to a station moving from one BSS to another without losing connectivity.

Figure 8-10 illustrates a network with only one BSS; Figure 8-11 shows a network encompassing multiple BSSs that form an ESS.

Clients running Windows 7 or modern versions of Linux will first attempt to associate with a known access point. For example, suppose the SSID for your access point at home is "SpaceInvader". When you visit a café on the other side of the city, your laptop will recognize that the "SpaceInvader" SSID doesn't exist in that location. Instead, your laptop's operating system will detect the presence of other access points in the area. If the café has an access point, for example, it will offer you the option of associating with that access point. Suppose the café is in a busy metropolitan area where every business on the block has its own access point. In that case, the operating system (or the NetworkManager program, if you are running Linux) will present you with a list of all access points within range. Further, your client software will prioritize the access point with the strongest signal and the lowest error rate compared with others. Note that a station does not necessarily prioritize the *closest* access point. For example, suppose another user brings his own access point to the café and his access point has a signal that is twice as strong as the café's access point. In that case, even if the new access point is farther away, your laptop will recognize the other user's access point as the best option. When you are presented with this option, however, you would be

Net+
2.2
3.3

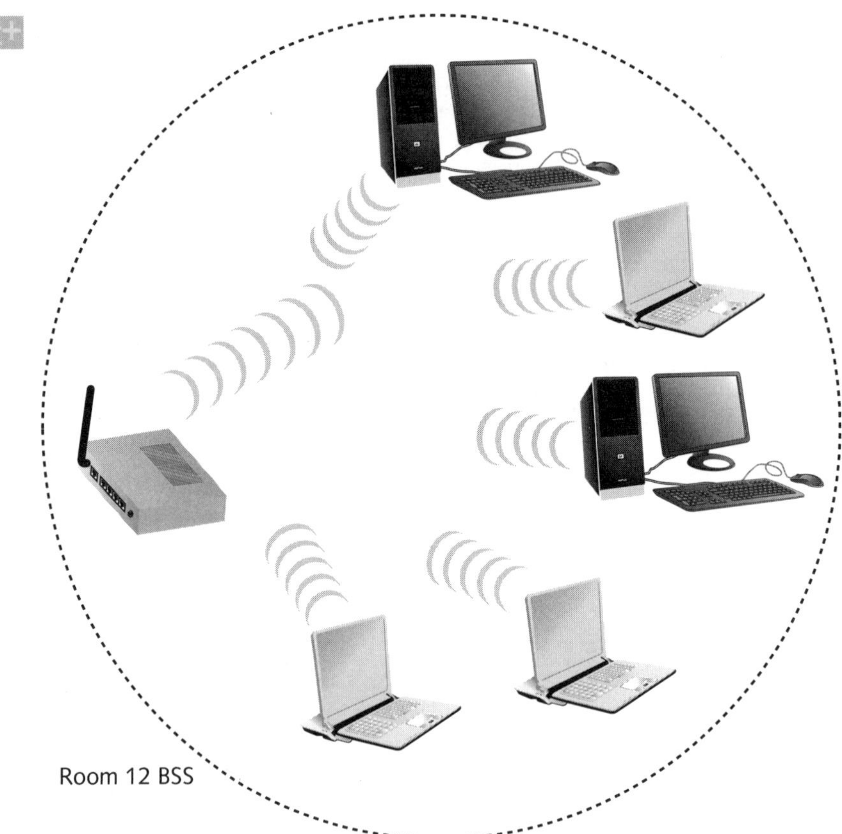

Figure 8-10 A network with a single BSS

wise to not confirm the association. If a client is configured to indiscriminately connect with the access point whose signal is strongest, that client is susceptible to being compromised by a powerful, rogue access point. If your system associates with this unauthorized access point, the person controlling that access point could steal your data or gain access to another network that trusts your system. Rogue access points can exist inadvertently, too, as when a user brings his own access point to work or uses software to turn his workstation into an access point.

On a network with several authorized access points in an ESS, however, a station must be able to associate with any access point while maintaining network connectivity. Suppose that when you begin work in the morning at your desk, your laptop associates with an access point located in a telco room down the hall. Later, you need to give a presentation in the company's main conference room on another floor of your building. Without your intervention, your laptop will choose a different access point as you travel to the conference room (perhaps more than one, depending on the size of your company's building and network).

Connecting to a different access point requires reassociation. **Reassociation** occurs when a mobile user moves out of one access point's range and into the range of another, as described in the previous example. It might also happen if the initial access point is experiencing a high rate of errors. On a network with multiple access points, network managers can take advantage

Net+
2.2
3.3

Figure 8-11 A network with multiple BSSs forming an ESS

of the stations' scanning feature to automatically balance transmission loads between those access points.

Net+
3.3

Frames

You have learned about some types of overhead required to manage access to the 802.11 wireless networks—for example, ACKs, probes, and beacons. For each function, the 802.11 standard specifies a frame type at the MAC sublayer. These multiple frame types are divided into three groups: control, management, and data. Management frames are those involved in association and reassociation, such as the probe and beacon frames. Control frames are those related to medium access and data delivery, such as the ACK and RTS/CTS frames. Data frames are those that carry the data sent between stations. An 802.11 data frame is illustrated in Figure 8-12. (Details of control and management frames are beyond the scope

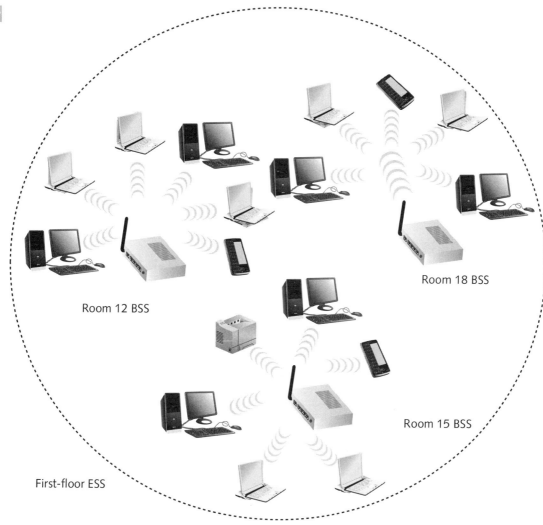

3.3 of this book.) Glancing at the 802.11 data frame, its significant overhead—that is, the large quantity of fields added to the data field—becomes apparent. These fields are explained next.

802.11 frame:

Frame control (2 bytes)	Duration (2 bytes)	Address 1 (6 bytes)	Address 2 (6 bytes)	Address 3 (6 bytes)	Sequence control (2 bytes)	Address 4 (6 bytes)	Data (0–2312 bytes)	Frame check sequence (6 bytes)

MAC header

802.3 (Ethernet) frame:

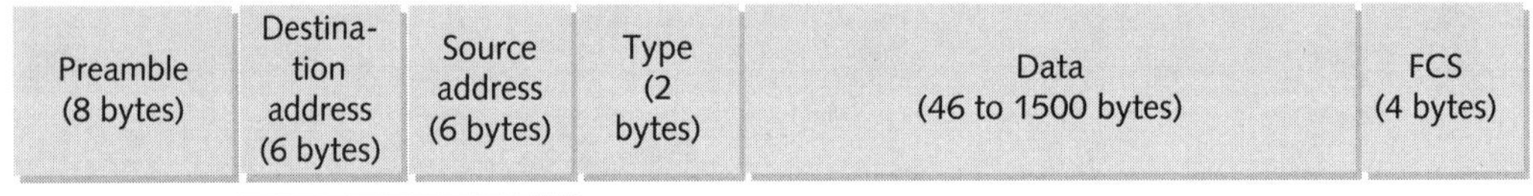

Figure 8-12 Basic 802.11 data frame compared with an 802.3 (Ethernet) frame

Compare the 802.11 data frame with the Ethernet data frame also shown in Figure 8-12. Notice that the wireless data frame contains four address fields, rather than two. These four addresses are the source address, transmitter address, receiver address, and destination address. The transmitter and receiver addresses refer to the access point or another intermediary device (if used) on the wireless network. The source and destination addresses have the same meaning as they do in the Ethernet II frame.

Another unique characteristic of the 802.11 data frame is its Sequence Control field. This field is used to indicate how a large packet is fragmented—that is, subdivided into smaller packets for more reliable delivery. Recall that on wired TCP/IP networks, error checking occurs at the Transport layer of the OSI model and packet fragmentation, if necessary, occurs at the Network layer. However, in 802.11 networks, error checking and packet fragmentation is handled at the MAC sublayer of the Data Link layer. By handling fragmentation at a lower layer, 802.11 makes its transmission—which is less efficient and more error-prone—transparent to higher layers. This means 802.11 nodes are more easily integrated with 802.3 networks and prevent the 802.11 segments of an integrated network from slowing down the 802.3 segments.

The Frame Control field in an 802.11 data frame holds information about the protocol in use, the type of frame being transmitted, whether the frame is part of a larger, fragmented packet, whether the frame is one that was reissued after an unverified delivery attempt, what type of security the frame uses, and so on. Security is a significant concern with WLANs because access points are typically more vulnerable than devices on a wired network. Wireless security is discussed in detail along with other network security topics in Chapter 11.

Although 802.11b, 802.11a, 802.11g, and 802.11n share all of the MAC sublayer characteristics described in the previous sections, they differ in their modulation methods, frequency usage,

3.3 and ranges. In other words, each varies at the Physical layer. In addition, 802.11n modifies the way frames are used at the MAC sublayer. The following sections summarize those differences.

802.11b

In 1999, the IEEE released its **802.11b** standard, which uses the 2.4–2.4835-GHz frequency range, better known as the 2.4-GHz band, and separates it into 22-MHz channels. 802.11b provides a theoretical maximum of 11-Mbps throughput; actual throughput is typically around 5 Mbps. To ensure this throughput, wireless nodes must stay within 100 meters (or approximately 330 feet) of an access point or each other, in the case of an ad hoc network. Among all the 802.11 standards, 802.11b was the first to take hold. It is also the least expensive of all the 802.11 WLAN technologies. However, most network administrators have replaced 802.11b with a faster standard, such as 802.11n.

802.11a

Although the 802.11a task group began its standards work before the 802.11b group, 802.11a was released *after* 802.11b. The **802.11a** standard differs from 802.11b and 802.11g in that it uses channels in the 5-GHz band and provides a maximum theoretical throughput of 54 Mbps, though its effective throughput falls generally between 11 and 18 Mbps. 802.11a's high throughput is attributable to its use of higher frequencies, its unique method of modulating data, and more available bandwidth. Perhaps most significant is that the 5-GHz band is not as congested as the 2.4-GHz band. Thus, 802.11a signals are less likely to suffer interference from microwave ovens, cordless phones, motors, and other (incompatible) wireless LAN signals. However, higher-frequency signals require more power to transmit, and they travel shorter distances than lower-frequency signals. The average geographic range for an 802.11a antenna is 20 meters, or approximately 66 feet. As a result, 802.11a networks require a greater density of access points between the wired LAN and wireless clients to cover the same distance that 802.11b networks cover. The additional access points, as well as the nature of 802.11a equipment, make this standard more expensive than either 802.11b or 802.11g. For this and other reasons, 802.11a is rarely preferred.

802.11g

IEEE's **802.11g** WLAN standard is designed to be just as affordable as 802.11b while increasing its maximum theoretical throughput from 11 Mbps to 54 Mbps through different data modulation techniques. The effective throughput of 802.11g ranges generally from 20 to 25 Mbps. An 802.11g antenna has a geographic range of 100 meters (or approximately 330 feet).

802.11g, like 802.11b, uses the 2.4-GHz frequency band. In addition to its high throughput, 802.11g benefits from being compatible with 802.11b networks. Thus, if a network administrator installed 802.11b access points on her LAN three years ago, this year she could add 802.11g access points and laptops, and the laptops could roam between the ranges of the 802.11b and 802.11g access points without an interruption in service.

802.11n

In 2009, IEEE ratified the **802.11n** standard. However, it was in development for years before that, and as early as mid-2007, manufacturers were selling 802.11n-compatible transceivers in their networking equipment. The primary goal of IEEE's 802.11n committee was to create

3.3 a wireless standard that provided much higher effective throughput than the other 802.11 standards. By all accounts, they succeeded. 802.11n boasts a maximum throughput of 600 Mbps, making it a threat to Fast Ethernet and a realistic platform for telephone and video signals. IEEE also specified that the 802.11n standard must be backward compatible with the 802.11a, b, and g standards.

802.11n may use either the 2.4-GHz or 5-GHz frequency range. It employs the same data modulation techniques used by 802.11a and 802.11g. However, it differs dramatically from the other three 802.11 standards in how it manages frames, channels, and encoding. These differences, which allow 802.11n to achieve its high throughput, include the following innovations:

- ***MIMO (multiple input-multiple output)***—In 802.11n, multiple antennas on an access point may issue a signal to one or more receivers. As you learned earlier, signals issued by an omnidirectional antenna will propagate in a multipath fashion. Therefore, multiple signals cannot be expected to arrive at the same receiver in concert. To account for this, in MIMO the phases of these signals are adjusted when they reach a receiving station, and the strength of the multiple signals are summed. To properly adjust phases, MIMO requires stations to update access points with information about their location. Among 802.11 equipment, this function is only available with 802.11n-capable transceivers. In addition to increasing the network's throughput, MIMO can increase an access point's range. Figure 8-13 shows an 802.11n access point with three antennas.

Figure 8-13 802.11n access point with three antennas
Courtesy of Oleksiy Mark/www.Shutterstock.com

- ***Channel bonding***—In 802.11n, two adjacent 20-MHz channels can be combined, or bonded, to make a 40-MHz channel, as shown in Figure 8-14. In fact, bonding two 20-MHz channels more than doubles the bandwidth available in a single 20-MHz channel. That's because the small amount of bandwidth normally reserved as buffers against interference at the top and bottom of the 20-MHz channels can be assigned to carry data instead. Because the 5-GHz band contains more channels and is less crowded (at least, for now), it's better suited to channel bonding than the 2.4-GHz band.

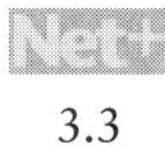

3.3

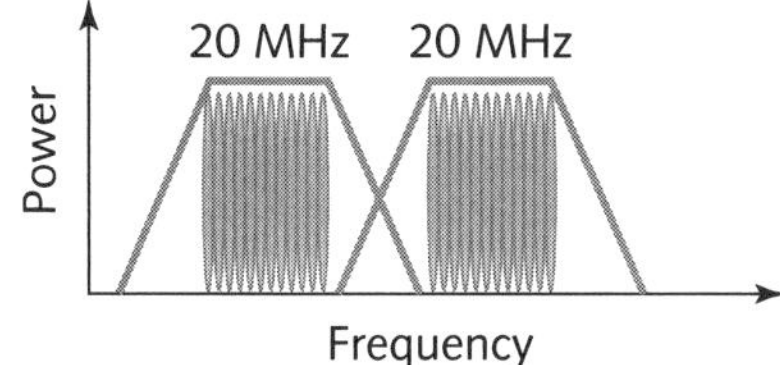

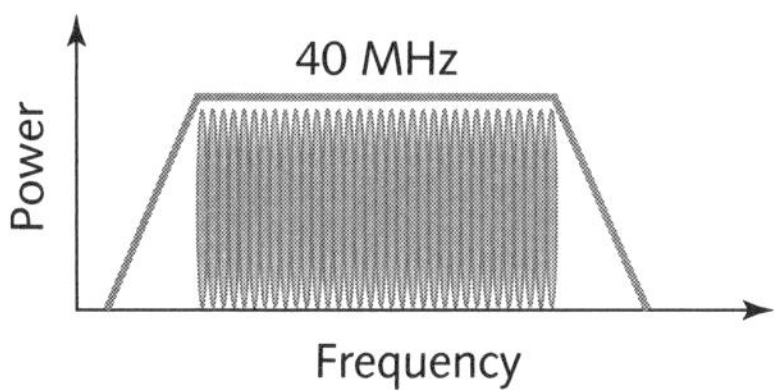

Figure 8-14 Channel bonding

- *Higher modulation rates*—As mentioned earlier, 802.11n uses the same type of data modulation used by 802.11a and 802.11g. This modulation technique allows for a single channel to be subdivided into multiple, smaller channels. Simply put, 802.11n makes more efficient use of these smaller channels and is capable of choosing from different encoding methods. 802.11n also allows for shortening the period of time transceivers wait between issuing each bit of data (which is necessary to prevent interference).
- *Frame aggregation*—802.11n networks can use one of two techniques for combining multiple frames (of the type shown in Figure 8-12) into one larger frame. Combining multiple frames reduces overhead. Suppose four small data frames are combined into one larger frame. Each larger frame will have only one copy of the same addressing information that would appear in the smaller frames. Proportionally, the data field takes up more of the aggregated frame's space. In addition, replacing four small frames with one large frame means an access point and station will have to exchange one-quarter the number of statements to negotiate media access and error control. To take advantage of frame aggregation, the maximum frame size for 802.11n is 64 KB, compared with the maximum 802.11a, b, and g frame size of 4 KB. The potential disadvantage with using larger frames is the increased probability of errors when transmitting larger blocks of data. Figure 8-15 illustrates the relatively low overhead of an aggregated 802.11n frame.

Figure 8-15 Aggregated 802.11n frame

3.3 Note that not all of the techniques listed here will be used in every 802.11n implementation. Further, reaching maximum throughput depends on the number and type of these strategies used. It also depends on whether the network uses the 2.4-GHz or 5-GHz band. Considering these factors, an 802.11n network's actual throughputs will vary between 65 to 500 Mbps.

As mentioned earlier, 802.11n is compatible with all three earlier versions of the 802.11 standard. However, in mixed environments, some of the new standard's techniques for improving throughput will not be possible. To ensure the fastest data rates on your 802.11n LAN, it's optimal to use only 802.11n-compatible devices.

To qualify for Network+ certification, you need to understand the differences between the 802.11 wireless standards. A summary of these WLAN standards is shown in Table 8-1.

Table 8-1 Wireless standards

Standard	Frequency range	Theoretical maximum throughput	Effective throughput (approximate)	Average geographic range
802.11b	2.4 GHz	11 Mbps	5 Mbps	100 meters (or approximately 330 feet)
802.11a	5 GHz	54 Mbps	11–18 Mbps	20 meters (or approximately 66 feet)
802.11g	2.4 GHz	54 Mbps	20–25 Mbps	100 meters (or approximately 330 feet)
802.11n	2.4 GHz or 5 GHz	65 to 600 Mbps	65 to 600 Mbps	Up to 400 meters (or approximately 1310 feet) if MIMO is used

The actual geographic range of any wireless technology depends on several factors, including the power of the antenna, physical barriers or obstacles between sending and receiving nodes, and interference in the environment. Therefore, although a technology is rated for a certain average geographic range, it may actually transmit signals in a shorter or longer range.

Implementing a WLAN

Now that you understand how wireless signals are exchanged, what can hinder them, and which Physical and Data Link layer standards they may follow, you are ready to
2.2 put these ideas into practice. This section first describes how to design small WLANs,
2.6 the types you might use at home or in a small office. It also describes how larger, enterprise-wide WANs are formed. Next it walks you through installing and configuring access points and clients. Finally, it details the pitfalls of implementing WLANs and how to avoid them.

Net+

Determining the Design

2.2 You have learned that WLANs may be arranged as ad hoc or infrastructure networks. You
2.6 also know that infrastructure WLANs are far more common. This section assumes your WLAN follows the infrastructure model, and as such, will include access points.

A home or small office network might call for only one access point. In this case, the access point, often combined with switching and routing functions, connects wireless clients to the LAN and acts as their gateway to the Internet. Note that the access point functions independently from the Internet access technology. In other words, configuring your home or small office WLAN follows the same principles no matter whether you connect to the Internet using broadband cable or DSL.

Figure 8-16 illustrates the typical arrangement of a home or small office WLAN. Notice that the access point (or wireless router) is connected to the cable or DSL modem using an RJ-45 cable. The cable is inserted into the access point's WAN port, which is set apart from the other data ports and might be labeled "Internet" or remain unlabeled. The additional ports on the access point allow for wired access to the router. An access point that does not include routing or switching functions would lack these extra ports and act much like a wireless hub.

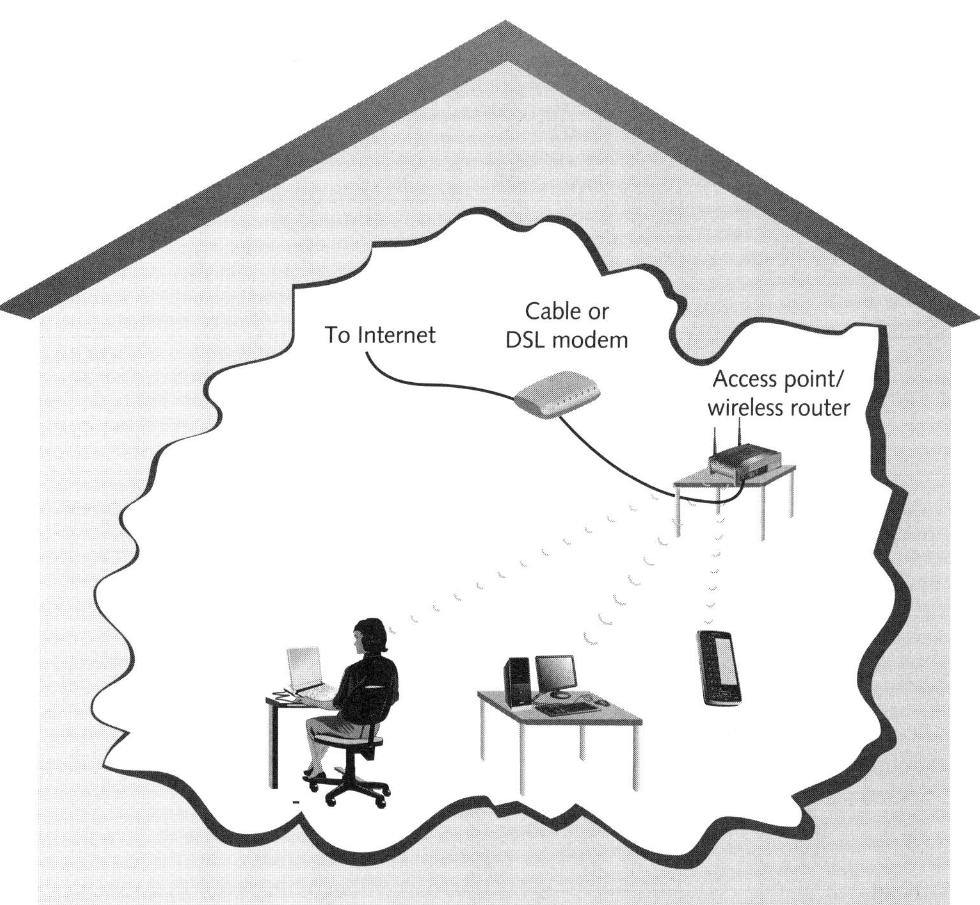

Figure 8-16 Home or small office WLAN arrangement

Placement of an access point on a WLAN must take into account the typical distances
2.2 between the access point and its clients. If your small office spans three floors, for instance,
2.6 and clients are evenly distributed among the floors, you might choose to situate the access point on the second floor. Recall that 802.11b and g signals can extend a maximum of 330 feet and still deliver data reliably, while 802.11n signals can, using MIMO, extend a maximum of 1310 feet. Also consider the type and number of obstacles between the access point and clients. For example, if your three-story building is constructed like a bunker with massive concrete floors, you might consider installing a separate access point on each floor. For best signal coverage, place the access point in a high spot, such as on a shelf or rack or in a drop ceiling. Also, make sure it's not close to potential sources of interference, including cordless phones and microwave ovens.

Larger WLANs warrant a more systematic approach to access point placement. Before placing access points in every telco room, it's wise to conduct a site survey. A **site survey** assesses client requirements, facility characteristics, and coverage areas to determine an access point arrangement that will ensure reliable wireless connectivity within a given area. For example, suppose you are the network manager for a large organization whose wireless clients are distributed over six floors of a building. On two floors, your organization takes up 2000 square feet of office space, but on the other four floors, your offices are limited to only 200 square feet. In addition, clients move between floors regularly. Other building occupants are also running wireless networks. As part of a site survey, you should study building blueprints to help identify potential obstacles and clarify the distances your network needs to span on each floor. The site survey will indicate whether certain floors require multiple access points. Visually inspecting the floors will also help determine coverage areas and best access point locations. Measuring the signal coverage and strength from other WLANs will inform your decision about the optimal strength and frequency for your wireless signals.

A site survey also includes testing proposed access point locations. In testing, a "dummy" access point is carried from location to location while a wireless client connects to it and measures its range and throughput. (Some companies sell software specially designed to conduct such testing.) Most important is testing wireless access from the farthest corners of your space. Also, testing will reveal unforeseen obstacles, such as EMI issued from lights or heavy machinery.

After a site survey has identified and verified the optimal quantity and location of access points, you are ready to install them. Recall that to ensure seamless connectivity from one coverage area to another, all access points must belong to the same ESS and share an ESSID. Configuring access points, including assigning ESSIDs, is described in the next section.

Figure 8-17 shows an example of an enterprise-wide WLAN.

When designing an enterprise-wide WLAN, you must consider how the wireless portions of the LAN will integrate with the wired portions. Access points connect the two. But an access point may perform other functions as well. It may provide security features, by, for example, including and excluding certain clients. It may participate in VLANs, allowing mobile clients to move from one access point's range to another while belonging to the same virtual LAN. Every wireless client's MAC address can be associated with an access point and each access point can be associated with a port on a switch. When these ports are grouped together in a VLAN, it doesn't matter with which access point a client associates. Because the client stays

Net+
2.2
2.6

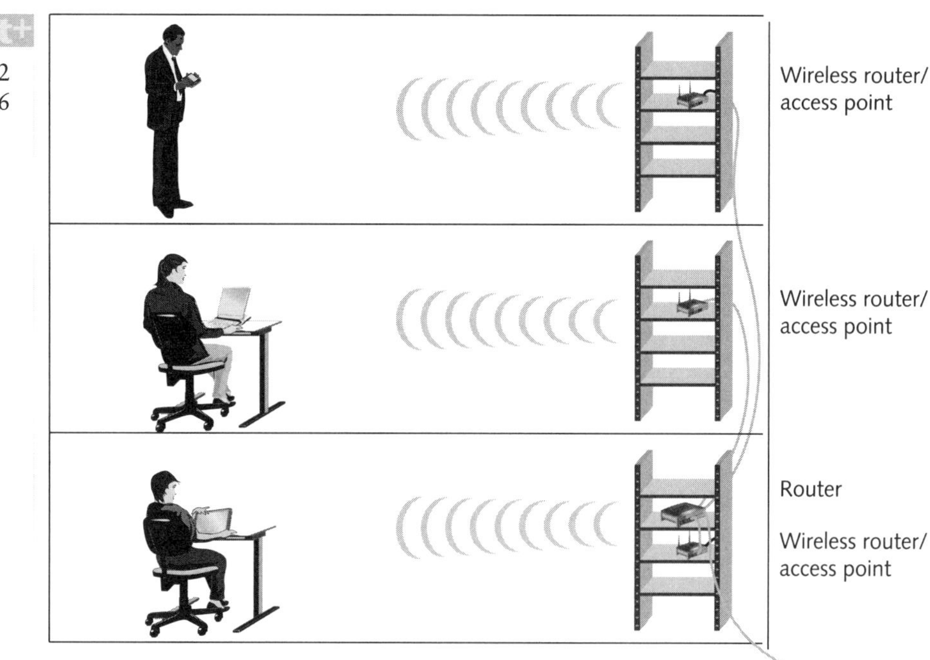

Figure 8-17 Enterprise-wide WLAN

in the same grouping, it can continue to communicate with the network as if it had remained in one spot.

Configuring Wireless Connectivity Devices

You have learned that access points provide wireless connectivity for mobile clients on an infrastructure WLAN. Access points vary in which wireless standards they support, antenna strength, and optional features such as support for voice signals or the latest security measures. You can find a small access point or wireless router suitable for home or small-office use for less than $50. More sophisticated or specialized access points—for example, those designed for rugged outdoor use, as on city streets or at train platforms—cost much more. However, as wireless networking has become commonplace, sophistication in even the least expensive devices has increased.

Each access point comes with an installation program on CD-ROM or DVD that guides you through the setup process. The process for installing such devices is similar no matter the manufacturer or model. The variables you will set during installation include:

- Administrator password
- SSID
- Whether or not DHCP is used; note that most network administrators do not configure their wireless access point as a DHCP server and, in fact, doing so when another DHCP server is already designated will cause addressing problems on the network

- Whether or not the SSID is broadcast
- 2.2 2.6 Security options such as which type, and, for each type, what credentials are necessary to associate with the access point

In the Hands-On Projects at the end of this chapter, you will have the chance to install and configure one popular wireless router/access point.

If something goes awry during your wireless router configuration, you can force all of the variables you changed to be reset. Wireless routers feature a reset button on their back panel. To reset the wireless router, first unplug it. Then, using the end of a paper clip, depress the reset button while you plug it in. Continue holding down the button for at least 30 seconds (this time period varies among manufacturers; check your wireless router's documentation for the duration yours requires). At the end of this period, the wireless router's values will be reset to the manufacturer's defaults.

After successfully configuring your access point/wireless router, you are ready to introduce it to the network. In the case of a small office or home WLAN, this means using a patch cable to connect the device's WAN port and your cable or DSL modem's LAN port. Afterward, clients should be able to associate with the access point and gain Internet access. The following section describes how to configure clients to connect to your WLAN.

Configuring Wireless Clients

Wireless access configuration varies from one type of client to another. In general, as long as an access point is broadcasting its SSID, clients in its vicinity will detect it and offer the user the option to associate with it. If the access point uses encryption, you will need to know the type of encryption and provide the right credentials to associate with it successfully. In the Hands-On Projects at the end of this chapter, you'll have the chance to explore wireless client configuration on a computer running Windows 7.

As with Windows operating systems, most Linux and UNIX clients provide a graphical interface for configuring their wireless interfaces. Because each version differs somewhat from the others, describing the steps required for each graphical interface is beyond the scope of this book. However, **iwconfig**, a command-line function for viewing and setting wireless interface parameters, is common to nearly all versions of Linux and UNIX. Following is a basic primer for using the `iwconfig` command. For more detailed information, type `man iwconfig` at any Linux or UNIX command-line prompt.

Before using iwconfig, make sure your wireless NIC is installed and that your Linux or UNIX workstation is within range of a working access point. You must also be logged in as root or a user with root-equivalent privileges. (Root on UNIX or Linux systems is comparable to an administrative user on Windows systems.) Next, open a terminal session (i.e., Command Prompt window), type `iwconfig` at the prompt, and then press Enter. The iwconfig output should look similar to that shown in Figure 8-18. Notice that in this example, "eth0" represents an interface that is not wireless (that is, a wired NIC), while "eth1" represents the wireless interface. The "lo" portion of the output indicates the loopback interface. On your computer, the wireless NIC might have a different designation. Also notice that iwconfig reveals characteristics of your access point's signal, including its frequency, power, and signal and noise levels.

Net+
2.2
2.6

```
% iwconfig
lo        no wireless extensions.

eth0      no wireless extensions.

eth1      IEEE 802.11abgn  ESSID:"CLASS_1"
          Mode:Managed  Frequency:2.412 GHz  Access Point: 00:0F:66:8E:19:89
          Bit Rate:54 Mb/s   Tx-Power:14 dBm
          Retry long limit:7   RTS thr:off   Fragment thr:off
          Power Management:on
          Link Quality=60/70  Signal level=-50 dBm
          Rx invalid nwid:0  Rx invalid crypt:0  Rx invalid frag:0
          Tx excessive retries:0  Invalid misc:747   Missed beacon:0
```

Figure 8-18 Output from `iwconfig` command

Using the `iwconfig` command, you can modify the SSID of the access point you choose to associate with, as well as many other variables. Some examples are detailed below. The syntax of the following examples assumes your workstation has labeled your wireless NIC "eth1":

- `iwconfig eth1 essid CLASS_1`—This command instructs the wireless interface to associate with an access point whose SSID (or ESSID, as shown in this command) is CLASS_1.
- `iwconfig eth1 mode Managed`—This command instructs the wireless interface to operate in infrastructure mode (as opposed to ad hoc mode).
- `iwconfig eth1 channel auto`—This command instructs the wireless interface to automatically select the best channel for wireless data exchange.
- `iwconfig eth1 freq 2.422G`—This command instructs the wireless interface to communicate on the 2.422-GHz frequency.
- `iwconfig eth1 key 6e225e3931`—This command instructs the wireless interface to use the hexadecimal number 6e225e3931 as its key for secure authentication with the access point. (6e225e3931 is only an example; on your network you will choose your own key.)

In this and the previous section, you have learned how to configure wireless clients and access points. The following section summarizes some key points about setting up wireless networks properly.

Net+

Avoiding Pitfalls

2.2 You might have had the frustrating experience of not being able to log on to a network, even
2.4 though you were sure you'd typed in your username and password correctly. Maybe it turned out that your Caps Lock key was on, changing your case-sensitive password. Or maybe you were trying to log on to the wrong server. On every type of network, many variables must be accurately set on clients, servers, and connectivity devices in order for communication to succeed. Wireless networks add a few more variables. As a reminder, following are some wireless configuration pitfalls to avoid:

- *SSID mismatch*—Your wireless client must specify the same SSID as the access point it's attempting to associate with. As you have learned, you may instruct clients to search for any available access point (or clients might be configured to do this by default). However, if the access point does not broadcast its SSID, or if your workstation is not configured to look for access points, you will have to enter the SSID during client configuration. Also bear in mind that SSIDs are case sensitive. That is, CLASS_1 does not equal Class_l. SSID mismatch will result in failed association.
- *Incorrect encryption*—Your wireless client must be configured to (a) use the same type of encryption as your access point, and (b) use a key or passphrase that matches the access point's. If either of these is incorrect, your client cannot authenticate with the access point.
- *Incorrect channel or frequency*—You have learned that the access point establishes the channel and frequency over which it will communicate with clients. Clients, then, automatically sense the correct channel and frequency. However, if you have instructed your client to use only a channel or frequency different from the one your access point uses, association will fail to occur.
- *Standard mismatch (802.11 a/b/g/n)*—If your access point is set to communicate only via 802.11g, even if the documentation says it supports 802.11b and 802.11g, clients must also follow the 802.11g standard. Clients may also be able to detect and match the correct type of 802.11 standard. However, if they are configured to follow only one standard, they will never find an access point broadcasting via a different standard.
- *Incorrect antenna placement*—On a network, many factors can cause data errors and a resulting decrease in performance. As you have learned, the most popular WLAN standards require clients to be within 330 feet of an access point's antenna for reliable data delivery. Beyond that distance, communication might occur, but data errors become more probable. Also remember to place your antenna in a high spot for best signal reception.
- *Interference*—If intermittent and difficult-to-diagnose wireless communication errors occur, interference might be the culprit. Check for sources of EMI, such as fluorescent lights, heavy machinery, cordless phones, and microwaves in the data transmission path.

Wireless WANs

3.4 The best 802.11n signal can travel approximately a quarter of a mile. But other types of wireless networks can connect stations over longer distances. For example, in some large cities dozens of surveillance cameras trained on municipal buildings and parks beam video images

Net+ to a central public safety headquarters. Meanwhile, in developing countries, wireless signals
deliver lectures and training videos to students in remote, mountainous regions. In rural areas
3.4 of the U.S., elderly patients at home wear medical monitoring devices, such as blood pressure
sensors and blood glucose meters, which use wireless networks to convey the information to
their doctors hundreds of miles away. Such networks can even alert paramedics in case of an
emergency. All of these are examples of wireless WANs. Unlike wireless LANs, wireless
WANs are designed for high-throughput, long-distance digital data exchange.

As in asymmetrical wired broadband, on wireless WANs downstream data transmission is typically faster than upstream transmission. Downstream, also called **downlink** in the context of wireless transmission, represents the connection between a carrier's antenna and a client's transceiver—for example, a smartphone. Upstream, also called **uplink** in the context of wireless transmission, refers to the connection between a client's transceiver and the carrier's antenna.

The following sections describe a variety of ways wireless clients can communicate across a city or state.

802.16 (WiMAX)

In 2001, IEEE standardized a new wireless technology under its **802.16** (wireless MAN) committee. Since that time, IEEE has released several versions of the 802.16 standard. Collectively, the 802.16 standards are known as **WiMAX**, which stands for **Worldwide Interoperability for Microwave Access**, the name of a group of manufacturers, including Intel and Nokia, who banded together to promote and develop 802.16 products and services. WiMAX was envisioned as a wireless alternative to DSL and T-carrier services for homes and businesses. It achieves much faster throughput than T-carriers at a lower cost for end users. Notable features of this standard include:

- Line-of-sight transmission between two antennas for use with fixed clients or non-line-of-sight transmission between multiple antennas for use with mobile clients
- Use of frequencies in the 2 to 11 GHz range or the 11 to 66 GHz, either licensed or nonlicensed; most WiMAX installations in the U.S. use the 2.3-, 2.5-, or 3.65-GHz bands
- Use of MIMO
- Ability to transmit and receive signals up to 50 km, or approximately 30 miles, when antennas are fixed or up to 15 km, or approximately 10 miles, when they are mobile
- QoS (quality of service) provisions

To date, the most popular IEEE 802.16 version is **802.16e**, which was approved in 2005. This was the first version of the standard that allowed for mobile clients. 802.16e connections can theoretically reach throughputs of up to 70 Mbps. A newer version of WiMAX, based on the **802.16m** standard, also known as **WiMAX 2**, was released in 2011. With higher throughput, less latency, and better support for IP telephony than previous WiMAX versions, 802.16m is positioned to compete favorably with cellular data services. And because it is backward compatible with 802.16e equipment, customers and carriers can easily transition to the newer version. Its maximum downlink throughput is 120 Mbps and its maximum uplink throughput is 60 Mbps. Future improvements to WiMAX are in the works, with throughputs of 1 Gbps predicted.

Net+ 3.4 In practice, since WiMAX is a shared technology, actual throughputs for all versions are lower than the published maximums. For example, a typical non-line-of-sight client using 802.16e actually experiences 4-Mbps downlink throughput instead of 70 Mbps. Also, as you would expect, the highest throughput is possible only over the shortest distances between transceivers in a line-of-sight arrangement. For example, 802.16e will not achieve its maximum 70 Mbps across a 30-mile span. Furthermore, some service providers cap the maximum bandwidth each customer is allowed to use and might offer a maximum downlink rate of 1 Mbps.

Still, WiMAX provides much greater throughput than Wi-Fi and T1s. Also, its range extends much farther than any of the 802.11 standards. For these reasons, WiMAX is considered more appropriate for use on MANs and WANs. It offers an alternative to DSL and broadband cable for business and residential customers who want high-speed Internet access or business customers who want an alternative to T-carriers. It's well suited to rural customers, for example, who might be in an area lacking copper or fiber-optic cabling infrastructure. WiMAX also provides network access for mobile computerized devices, including smartphones, laptops, and PDAs in metropolitan areas. Finally, WiMAX can act as the **backhaul** link, or an intermediate connection between subscriber networks and a telecommunications carrier's network. Figure 8-19 illustrates three uses for WiMAX, including a residential customer, mobile users, and a backhaul link.

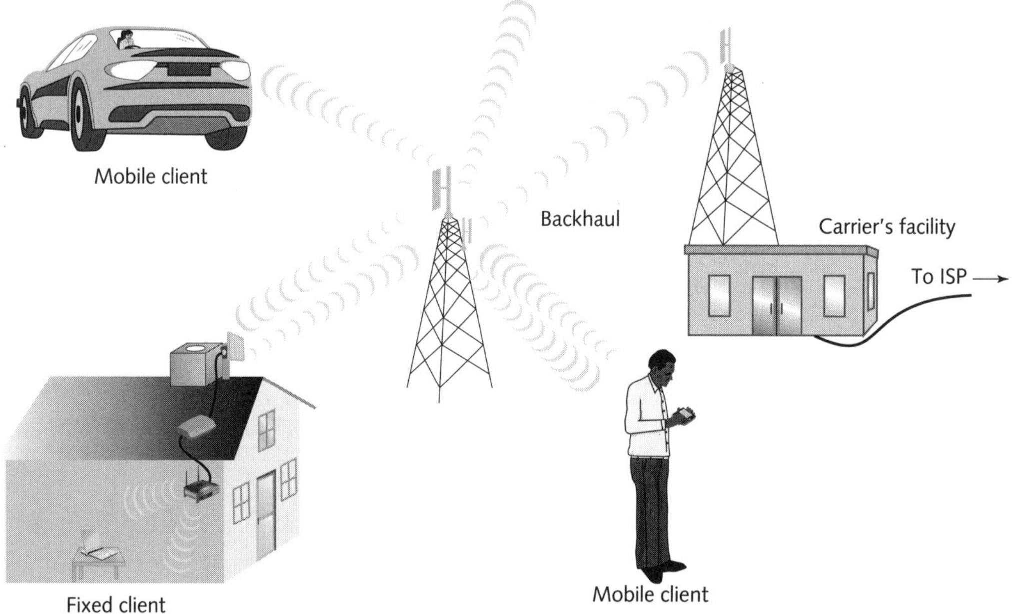

Figure 8-19 WiMAX network

As shown in Figure 8-19, in residential or small business WiMAX, the carrier installs a small antenna on the roof or even inside the building. This antenna is connected to a device similar to a cable or DSL modem for clients to access the LAN. The connectivity device could be incorporated along with the antenna in the same housing or might be separate. If separate,

3.4 the device typically attaches to the antenna with coaxial cable. It's often combined with a router. The customer's antenna communicates in a non-line-of-sight fashion with the service provider's antenna. If the service provider's facility is far away, it might use multiple antennas on towers that communicate in a line-of-sight manner, as shown in Figure 8-19. Figures 8-20 and 8-21 depict the type of antenna used at a customer's location and the type of antenna used by service providers on their towers.

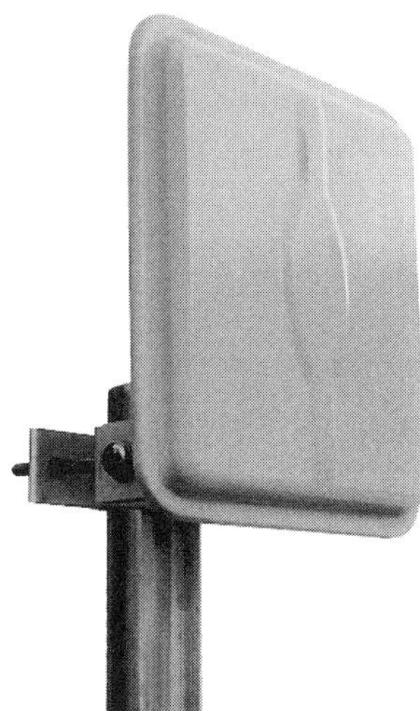

Figure 8-20 WiMAX residential antenna
Courtesy of Laird Technologies

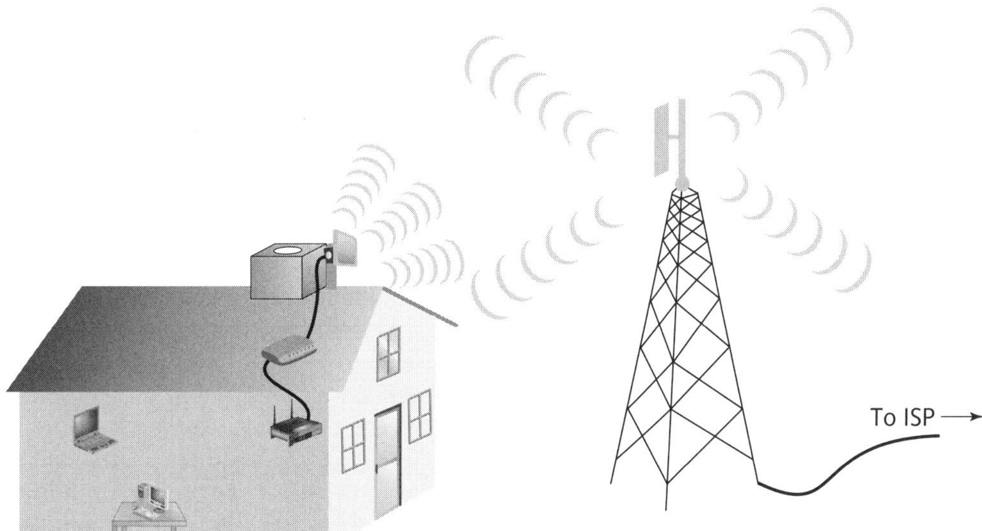

Figure 8-21 WiMAX service provider's antenna

3.4

In some installations, as when a WiMAX provider serves a metropolitan area, the customer's antenna and connectivity device are eliminated. Instead, each computer communicates directly via its on-board WiMAX transceiver with an antenna such as the one shown in Figure 8-21.

In the United States, companies such as Clearwire have established WiMAX networks in several cities using licensed frequency bands. For example, Clearwire has registered with the FCC for the sole use of channels in the 2.5-GHz band in the Chicago metropolitan area. Because the band is licensed, it suffers little interference, and Clearwire can guarantee a certain level of service. In Tokyo, WiMAX will provide Internet access to riders on fast-moving subway trains. On a citywide network, WiMAX makes more sense than Wi-Fi. However, WiMAX has received significant competition from quickly evolving cellular data services, described next.

Cellular

Cellular networks were initially designed to provide analog phone service. However, since the first mobile phones became available to consumers in the 1970s, cellular services have changed dramatically. In addition to voice signals, cellular networks now deliver text messages, Web pages, music, and videos to smartphones and handheld devices. This section describes current cellular data technology and explains the role it plays in wide area networking.

To put today's services in context, it's useful to understand that each leap in cellular technology has been described as a new generation. Each successive generation has brought a greater range of services, better quality, and higher throughputs. For example, first-generation, or **1G**, services from the 1970s and 1980s were analog. Second-generation, or **2G**, services, which reigned in the 1990s, used digital transmission and paved the way for texting and media downloads on mobile devices. Still, data transmission on 2G systems didn't exceed 240 Kbps. With the third generation, or **3G**, released in the early 2000s, data rates rose to 384 Kbps and data (but not voice) communications used packet switching. The latest generation is **4G**. It is characterized by an all-IP, packet-switched network for both data and voice transmission. 4G standards, released in 2008, also specify throughputs of 100 Mbps for fast-moving mobile clients, such as those in cars, and 1 Gbps for slow-moving mobile clients, such as pedestrians. WiMAX, though not strictly a cellular-based technology, is considered 4G because of its high-speed, packet-switched characteristics. Later in this section, you will learn about other 3G and 4G systems.

Although their access methods and features might differ, all cellular networks share a similar infrastructure in which coverage areas are divided into **cells**. Each cell is served by an antenna and its base station, or cell site. At the base station, a controller assigns mobile clients frequencies and manages communication with them. In network diagrams, cells are depicted as hexagons. Multiple cells share borders to form a network in a honeycomb pattern, as shown in Figure 8-22. Antennas are positioned at three corners of each cell, radiating and providing coverage over three equidistant lobes. When a client passes from one coverage area to another, his mobile device begins communicating with a different antenna. His communication might change frequencies or even carriers between cells. The transition, which normally happens without the user's awareness, is known as **handoff.**

3.4

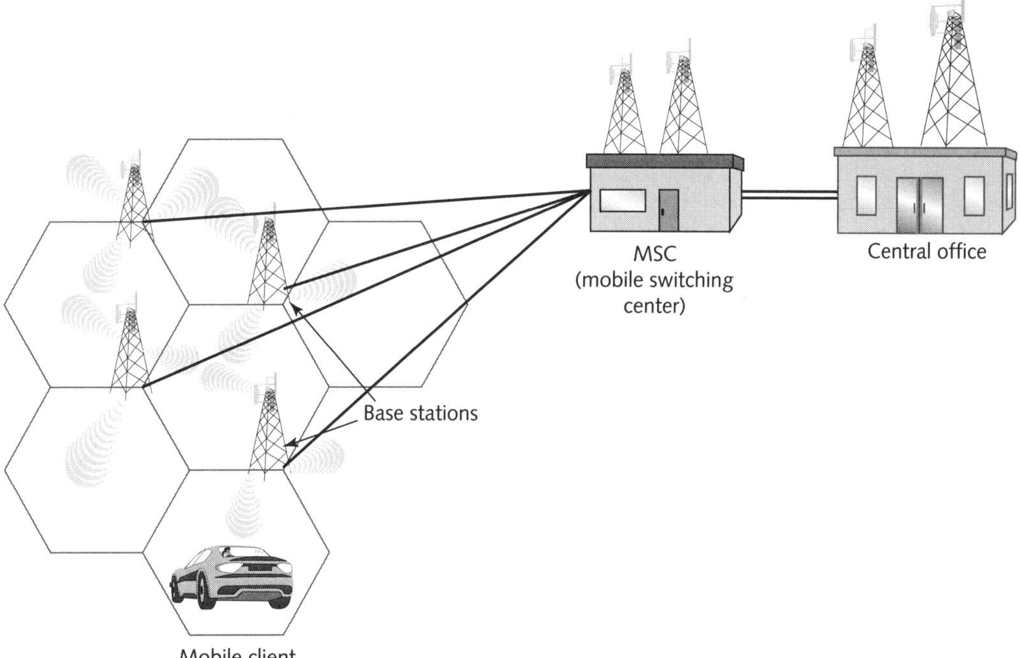

Figure 8-22 Cellular network

Cell sizes vary from roughly 1000 feet to 12 miles in diameter. The size of a cell depends on the network's access method and the region's topology, population, and amount of cellular traffic. An urban area with dense population and high volume of data and voice traffic might use cells with a diameter of only 2000 feet, their antennas mounted on tall buildings. In sparsely populated rural areas, with antennas mounted on isolated hilltop towers, cells might span more than 10 miles. In theory, the division of a network into cells provides thorough coverage over any given area. In reality, cells are misshapen due to terrain, EMF, and antenna radiation patterns. Some edges overlap and others don't meet up, leaving gaps in coverage.

As shown in Figure 8-22, each base station is connected to an **MSC (mobile switching center)**, also called an **MTSO (mobile telecommunications switching office)** by a wireless link or fiber-optic cabling. The MSC might be located inside a telephone company's central office or it might stand alone and connect to the central office via another fiber-optic cabling or a microwave link. At the MSC, the mobile network intersects with the wired network. Equipment at an MSC manages mobile clients, monitoring their location and usage patterns, and switches cellular calls. It also assigns each mobile client an IP address. With 4G cellular services, a client's IP address remains the same from cell to cell and from one carrier's territory to another. In 3G cellular services, however, client IP addresses may change when the user transitions to a different carrier's service area. From the switching center, packets sent from cellular networks are routed to wired data networks through the PSTN or private backbones using WAN technologies you learned about in Chapter 7.

Cellular networking is a complex topic, with rapidly evolving encoding and access methods, changing standards, and innovative vendors vying to dominate the market. This chapter does not

Net+ 3.4 detail the various encoding and access methods used on cellular networks. However, to qualify for Network+ certification, you should understand the basic infrastructure of a cellular network and the cellular technologies frequently used for data networking, beginning with HSPA+.

HSPA+ (High Speed Packet Access Plus) is a 3G technology released in 2008 that uses MIMO and sophisticated encoding techniques to achieve a maximum 84-Mbps downlink throughput and 11-Mbps uplink throughput in its current release. Soon, the downlink data rate is expected to increase to 336 Mbps. To achieve such speeds, HSPA+ will use limited channels more efficiently and incorporate more antennas in MIMO transmission. Approximately 170 HSPA+ networks exist around the globe. However, faster and more flexible technologies, such as LTE, are likely to overtake HSPA+ in popularity.

LTE (Long Term Evolution) is a 4G technology that uses a different access method than HSPA+ to achieve downlink data rates of up to 1 Gbps and uplink rates up to 500 Mbps. LTE is currently the fastest wireless broadband service available in the U.S. While Sprint embraced WiMAX early on for its wireless broadband services, other carriers, such as AT&T and Verizon, passed on WiMAX to adopt LTE service. WiMAX 2 and LTE now coexist and compete for market share in the U.S.

Table 8-2 summarizes wireless WAN services described in this section. Note that this does not represent a complete list of wireless broadband services—for example, older 2G and 3G cellular technologies are excluded.

Table 8-2 Characteristics of some wireless WAN services

Technology	Voice switching	Data switching	Maximum theoretical downlink throughput	Maximum theoretical uplink throughput
3G–HSPA+	Circuit	Packet	84 Mbps (with promises of 336 Mbps)	11 Mbps
(N/A)–WiMAX (802.16e)	Packet	Packet	70 Mbps	70 Mbps
4G–WiMAX 2 (802.16m)	Packet	Packet	120 Mbps (with promises of 1 Gbps for fixed clients)	60 Mbps
4G–LTE	Packet	Packet	1 Gbps	500 Mbps

Satellite

In 1945, Arthur C. Clarke (the author of *2001: A Space Odyssey*) wrote an article in which he described the possibility of communication between manned space stations that continually orbited the Earth. Other scientists recognized the worth of using satellites to convey signals from one location on Earth to another. By the 1960s, the United States was using satellites to transmit telephone and television signals across the Atlantic Ocean. Since then, the proliferation of this technology and reductions in its cost have made satellite transmission appropriate and available for transmitting consumer voice, video, music, and data.

For many years, satellites have been used to transmit live broadcasts of events happening around the world. Satellites are also used to deliver digital television and radio signals, voice and video signals, and cellular and paging signals. More recently, they have become a means of providing data services to mobile clients, such as travelers in flight or on ships at sea, who are beyond the reach of WiMAX, HSPA+, or LTE.

Net+ 3.4 **Satellite Orbits** Most satellites circle the Earth 22,300 miles above the equator in a geosynchronous orbit. **Geosynchronous earth orbit (GEO)** means that satellites orbit the Earth at the same rate as the Earth turns. Consequently, at every point in their orbit, the satellites maintain a constant distance from a specific point on the Earth's equator. Because satellites are generally used to relay information from one point on Earth to another, information sent to Earth from a satellite first has to be transmitted to the satellite from Earth in an uplink from an Earth-based transmitter to an orbiting satellite. Often, the uplink signal information is scrambled (in other words, its signal is encoded) before transmission to prevent unauthorized interception. At the satellite, a **transponder** receives the uplink signal, then transmits it to an Earth-based receiver in a downlink. A typical satellite contains 24 to 32 transponders. Each satellite uses unique frequencies for its downlink. These frequencies, as well as the satellite's orbit location, are assigned and regulated by the FCC. Back on Earth, the downlink is picked up by a dish-shaped antenna. The dish shape concentrates the signal so that it can be interpreted by a receiver. Figure 8-23 provides a simplified view of satellite communication.

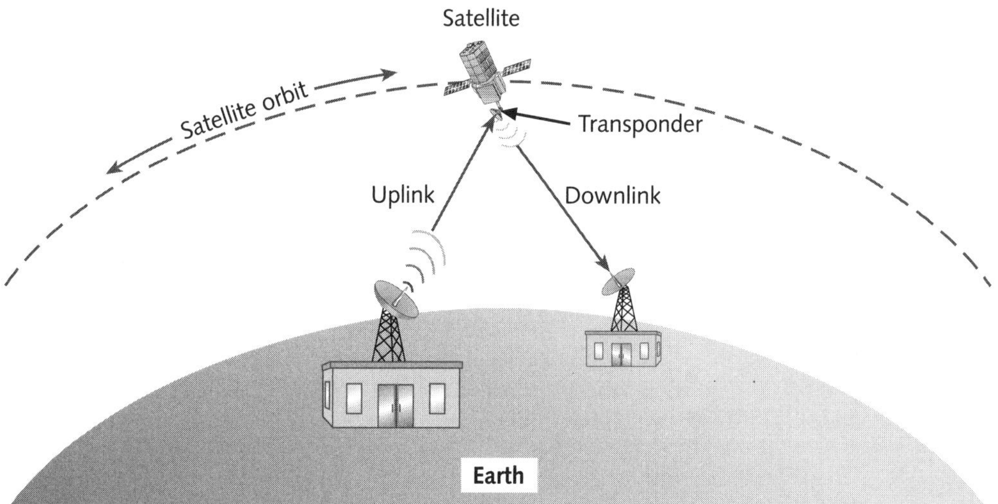

Figure 8-23 Satellite communication

Geosynchronous earth orbiting satellites are the type used by the most popular satellite data service providers. This technology is well established, and is the least expensive of all satellite technology. Also, because they remain in a fixed position relative to the Earth's surface, stationary receiving dishes on Earth can be counted on to receive satellite signals reliably.

Satellite Frequencies Satellites transmit and receive signals in any of following five frequency bands, which are roughly defined as:

- *L-band*—1.5–2.7 GHz
- *S-band*—2.7–3.5 GHz
- *C-band*—3.4–6.7 GHz
- *Ku-band*—12–18 GHz
- *Ka-band*—18–40 GHz

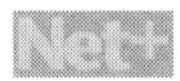

3.4 Within each band, frequencies used for uplink and downlink transmissions differ. This variation helps ensure that signals traveling in one direction (for example from a satellite to the Earth) do not interfere with signals traveling in the other direction (for example, signals from the Earth to a satellite).

Satellite Internet Services A handful of companies offer high-bandwidth Internet access via GEO satellite links. Each subscriber uses a small satellite antenna and receiver, or satellite modem, to exchange signals with the service provider's satellite network. Clients may be fixed, such as rural dwellers who are too remote for DSL, or mobile subscribers, such as travelers on ocean-going yachts.

Clients are able to exchange signals with satellites as long as they have a line-of-sight path, or an unobstructed view of the sky. To establish a satellite Internet connection, each subscriber must have a dish antenna, which is approximately two feet high by three feet wide, installed in a fixed position. In North America, these dish antennas are pointed toward the Southern Hemisphere (because the geosynchronous satellites travel over the equator). The dish antenna's receiver is connected, via cable, to a modem. This modem uses either a PCI or USB interface to connect with the subscriber's computer.

As with several other wireless WAN technologies, satellite services are typically asymmetrical and bandwidth is shared among many subscribers. Throughputs vary and are controlled by the service provider. Typical downlink rates range from 1 to 2 Mbps and uplink rates reach approximately 300 Kbps. Compared with other wireless WAN options, satellite services are slower and suffer more latency. In addition, client equipment is more expensive than that required by WiMAX, HSPA+, or LTE. Given these drawbacks, satellite data service is preferred only in circumstances that allow few alternatives or in cases where satellite receiving equipment is already installed.

Chapter Summary

- The wireless spectrum is a continuum of the electromagnetic waves used for data and voice communication. Each type of wireless service can be associated with one area, or frequency band, of the wireless spectrum.
- Most cordless telephones and many WLANs (wireless LANs) use frequencies in the 2.4-GHz band. Other WLANs use a range of frequencies near 5 GHz. The 5-GHz band offers more unlicensed channels and less potential interference.
- Wireless signals originate from electrical current traveling along a conductor. The electrical signal travels from the transmitter to an antenna, which then emits the signal, as a series of electromagnetic waves, to the atmosphere. The signal propagates through the air until it reaches its destination. At the destination, another antenna accepts the signal, and a receiver converts it back to current.
- To exchange information, two antennas must be tuned to the same frequency. In communications terminology, this means they share the same channel.
- The geographical area that an antenna or wireless system can reach is known as its range. Receivers must be within the range to receive accurate signals consistently.

- Wireless transmission is susceptible to interference from EMI. Signals are also affected by obstacles in their paths, which cause them to reflect, diffract, or scatter. A large number of obstacles can prevent wireless signals from reaching their destination.
- Because of reflection, diffraction, and scattering, wireless signals follow a number of different paths to their destination. Such signals are known as multipath signals.
- Each type of wireless communication falls into one of two categories: fixed or mobile. In fixed wireless systems, the locations of the transmitter and receiver do not move. In mobile wireless, the receiver can be located anywhere within the transmitter's range. This allows the receiver to roam from one place to another while continuing to pick up its signal.
- In an ad hoc WLAN, wireless nodes, or stations, transmit directly to each other via wireless NICs without an intervening connectivity device.
- Modern WLANs operate in infrastructure mode. They rely on access points that transmit and receive signals to and from wireless stations and connectivity devices. Access points may connect stations to a LAN or multiple network segments to a backbone. They are often combined with routers.
- Wireless standards vary by frequency, methods of signal, and geographic range. The IEEE 802.11 committee has ratified four notable wireless standards: 802.11b, 802.11a, 802.11g, and 802.11n.
- All four 802.11 standards share characteristics at the MAC sublayer level, including the CSMA/CA access method, frame formats, and methods of association between access points and stations.
- 802.11b operates in the 2.4-GHz band, uses DSSS (direct-sequence spread spectrum), and is characterized by a maximum theoretical throughput of 11 Mbps (though actual throughput is typically half of that).
- 802.11a, ratified after 802.11b, operates in the 5-GHz band and is incompatible with 802.11b or g. It's characterized by a maximum theoretical throughput of 54 Mbps, though actual throughput is much less.
- 802.11g, which operates in the 2.4-GHz band and is compatible with 802.11b, is characterized by a maximum theoretical throughput of 54 Mbps, though actual throughput is much less.
- 802.11n offers significantly faster throughput than any previously adopted 802.11 standard. Techniques such as MIMO (multiple input-multiple output), channel bonding, frame aggregation, and higher modulation rates allow 802.11n to achieve between 65 and 600 Mbps actual throughput. MIMO also dramatically increases the range of 802.11n access points. 802.11n is backward compatible with 802.11b, a, and g, though mixed environments cannot take advantage of all of 802.11n's speed enhancements.
- Most home and small office WLANs depend on a single access point, which should be centrally located to provide reliable wireless service to clients at any location.
- Designing an enterprise-wide WLAN involves choosing the appropriate quantity of access points and knowing where to position them. A site survey helps by assessing the network's client requirements, facility characteristics, and coverage areas.
- You can install and configure an access point using setup software provided by the manufacturer, or by directly connecting to the device's operating software. At a

minimum, you should change the access point's SSID (service set identifier) and administrator password. If the access point acts as a router, or Internet gateway, you must provide your Internet account credentials. In addition, you probably want to choose a method of secure authentication, modify the LAN TCP/IP properties, and perhaps change the channel and mode of communication.

- Client setup for WLANs can be very simple, if you allow the client to find an access point and choose default values for associating with it. If the access point requires secure authentication, you must at least configure the client to meet those credentials.
- For correct functioning on your WLAN, make sure clients and access points agree on an SSID, security settings, and channels. Also make sure access points are positioned far from sources of interference and that client locations do not exceed the maximum range for the type of wireless technology you use.
- IEEE 802.16 (WiMAX) is a wireless broadband technology designed for residential or business subscribers who may be fixed or mobile. The 802.16e standard can use frequencies from 2 to 66 GHz and may issue signals in a line-of-sight or non-line-of-sight manner. WiMAX can achieve throughputs of up to 70 Mbps at the shortest ranges. Its signals can travel up to 30 miles in a line-of-sight arrangement.
- WiMAX 2, specified in IEEE's 802.16m standard, is a 4G technology that achieves theoretical throughputs of 330 Mbps with lower latency and better quality for VoIP applications than previous WiMAX versions. 802.16m has been approved as a true 4G technology. Manufacturers expect it to reach throughputs of 1 Gbps in the near future.
- Cellular networks provide data services to mobile clients over packet-switched networks. Though there are many types of cellular networks, all share an infrastructure in which coverage areas are divided into cells that are serviced by antennas and base stations. Base stations communicate with MSCs (mobile switching centers), which connect the cellular network with the PSTN and other WANs.
- Two types of high-speed cellular data services are currently vying for market share: HSPA+ (High Speed Packet Access Plus) and LTE (Long Term Evolution). Both are considered 4G technologies. LTE can already achieve downlink throughputs of up to 1 Gbps, which makes it more attractive than WiMAX as well.
- Geosynchronous satellites are used to provide wireless data services to mobile or fixed clients. Satellite-based services are most appropriate for rural clients who cannot receive DSL or cable broadband or by users on planes or ships at sea, where other wireless broadband services can't reach.

Key Terms

1G The first generation of mobile phone services, popular in the 1970s and 1980s, which were entirely analog.

2.4-GHz band The range of radio frequencies from 2.4 to 2.4835 GHz. The 2.4-GHz band, which allows for 11 unlicensed channels, is used by WLANs that follow the popular 802.11b and 802.11g standards. However, it is also used for cordless telephone and other transmissions, making the 2.4-GHz band more susceptible to interference than the 5-GHz band.

2G Second-generation mobile phone service, popular in the 1990s. 2G was the first standard to use digital transmission, and as such, it paved the way for texting and media downloads on mobile devices.

3G Third-generation mobile phone service, released in the early 2000s, that specifies throughputs of 384 Kbps and packet switching for data (but not voice) communications.

4G Fourth-generation mobile phone service that is characterized by an all-IP, packet-switched network for both data and voice transmission. 4G standards, released in 2008, also specify throughputs of 100 Mbps for fast-moving mobile clients, such as those in cars, and 1 Gbps for slow-moving mobile clients, such as pedestrians.

5-GHz band A range of frequencies that comprises four frequency bands: 5.1 GHz, 5.3 GHz, 5.4 GHz, and 5.8 GHz. It consists of 24 unlicensed bands, each 20-MHz wide. The 5-GHz band is used by WLANs that follow the 802.11a and 802.11n standards.

802.11a The IEEE standard for a wireless networking technique that uses multiple frequency bands in the 5-GHz frequency range and provides a theoretical maximum throughput of 54 Mbps. 802.11a's high throughput, compared with 802.11b, is attributable to its use of higher frequencies, its unique method of encoding data, and more available bandwidth.

802.11b The IEEE standard for a wireless networking technique that uses DSSS (direct-sequence spread spectrum) signaling in the 2.4–2.4835-GHz frequency range (also called the 2.4-GHz band). 802.11b separates the 2.4-GHz band into 14 overlapping 22-MHz channels and provides a theoretical maximum of 11-Mbps throughput.

802.11g The IEEE standard for a wireless networking technique designed to be compatible with 802.11b while using different encoding techniques that allow it to reach a theoretical maximum capacity of 54 Mbps. 802.11g, like 802.11b, uses the 2.4-GHz frequency band.

802.11n The IEEE standard for a wireless networking technique that may issue signals in the 2.4- or 5-GHz band and can achieve actual data throughput between 65 and 600 Mbps. It accomplishes this through several means, including MIMO, channel bonding, and frame aggregation. 802.11n is backward compatible with 802.11a, b, and g.

802.16 An IEEE standard for wireless MANs. 802.16 networks may use frequencies between 2 and 66 GHz. Their antennas may operate in a line-of-sight or non-line-of-sight manner and cover 50 kilometers (or approximately 30 miles). 802.16 connections can achieve a maximum throughput of 70 Mbps, though actual throughput diminishes as the distance between transceivers increases. Several 802.16 standards exist. Collectively, they are known as WiMAX.

802.16e Currently, the most widely implemented version of WiMAX. With 802.16e, IEEE improved the mobility and QoS characteristics of the technology, making it better suited to VoIP and mobile phone users. 802.16e is capable of 70-Mbps throughput, but because bandwidth is shared and service providers cap data rates, most users actually experience 1–4 Mbps throughput.

802.16m Also known as WiMAX 2, the IEEE standard for a version of 802.16 that achieves theoretical throughputs of 330 Mbps with lower latency and better quality for VoIP applications than previous WiMAX versions. 802.16m has been approved as a true 4G technology. Manufacturers expect it to reach throughputs of 1 Gbps in the near future.

access point A device used on wireless LANs that transmits and receives wireless signals to and from multiple nodes and retransmits them to the rest of the network segment. Access points can connect a group of nodes with a network or two networks with each other. They may use directional or omnidirectional antennas.

active scanning A method used by wireless stations to detect the presence of an access point. In active scanning, the station issues a probe to each channel in its frequency range and waits for the access point to respond.

ad hoc A type of wireless LAN in which stations communicate directly with each other (rather than using an access point).

AP *See* access point.

association In the context of wireless networking, the communication that occurs between a station and an access point to enable the station to connect to the network via that access point.

backhaul An intermediate connection between subscriber networks and a telecommunications carrier's network.

base station *See* access point.

basic service set *See* BSS.

basic service set identifier *See* BSSID.

beacon frame In the context of wireless networking, a frame issued by an access point to alert other nodes of its existence.

bounce *See* reflection.

BSS (basic service set) In IEEE terminology, a group of stations that share an access point.

BSSID (basic service set identifier) In IEEE terminology, the identifier for a BSS (basic service set).

Carrier Sense Multiple Access with Collision Avoidance *See* CSMA/CA.

cell In a cellular network, an area of coverage serviced by an antenna and base station.

channel bonding In the context of 802.11n wireless technology, the combination of two 20-MHz frequency bands to create one 40-MHz frequency band that can carry more than twice the amount of data that a single 20-MHz band could. It's recommended for use only in the 5-GHz range because this band has more available channels and suffers less interference than the 2.4-GHz band.

CSMA/CA (Carrier Sense Multiple Access with Collision Avoidance) A network access method used on 802.11 wireless networks. In CSMA/CA, before a node begins to send data it checks the medium. If it detects no transmission activity, it waits a brief, random amount of time, and then sends its transmission. If the node does detect activity, it waits a brief period of time before checking the channel again. CSMA/CA does not eliminate, but minimizes, the potential for collisions.

diffraction In the context of wireless signal propagation, the phenomenon that occurs when an electromagnetic wave encounters an obstruction and splits into secondary waves. The secondary waves continue to propagate in the direction in which they were split. If you could see wireless signals being diffracted, they would appear to be bending around the obstacle. Objects with sharp edges—including the corners of walls and desks—cause diffraction.

direct-sequence spread spectrum *See* DSSS.

directional antenna A type of antenna that issues wireless signals along a single direction, or path.

downlink In the context of wireless transmission, the connection between a carrier's antenna and a client's transceiver—for example, a smartphone.

DSSS (direct-sequence spread spectrum) A transmission technique in which a signal's bits are distributed over an entire frequency band at once. Each bit is coded so that the receiver can reassemble the original signal upon receiving the bits.

ESS (extended service set) A group of access points and associated stations (or basic service sets) connected to the same LAN.

ESSID (extended service set identifier) A special identifier shared by BSSs that belong to the same ESS.

extended service set *See* ESS.

extended service set identifier *See* ESSID.

fading A variation in a wireless signal's strength as a result of some of the electromagnetic energy being scattered, reflected, or diffracted after being issued by the transmitter.

FHSS (frequency hopping spread spectrum) A wireless signaling technique in which a signal jumps between several different frequencies within a band in a synchronization pattern known to the channel's receiver and transmitter.

fixed A type of wireless system in which the locations of the transmitter and receiver are static. In a fixed connection, the transmitting antenna focuses its energy directly toward the receiving antenna. This results in a point-to-point link.

frequency hopping spread spectrum *See* FHSS.

GEO (geosynchronous earth orbit) The term used to refer to a satellite that maintains a constant distance from a point on the equator at every point in its orbit. Geosynchronous orbit satellites are the type used to provide satellite Internet access.

geosynchronous earth orbit *See* GEO.

handoff The transition that occurs when a cellular network client moves from one antenna's coverage area to another.

High Speed Packet Access Plus *See* HSPA+.

HSPA+ (High Speed Packet Access Plus) A 3G mobile wireless technology released in 2008 that uses MIMO and sophisticated encoding techniques to achieve a maximum 84-Mbps downlink throughput and 11-Mbps uplink throughput in its current release. Advances in more efficiently using limited channels and incorporating more antennas in MIMO promise to push the maximum downlink data rate to 336 Mbps.

infrastructure WLAN A type of WLAN in which stations communicate with an access point and not directly with each other.

iwconfig A command-line utility for viewing and setting wireless interface parameters on Linux and UNIX workstations.

line-of-sight *See* LOS.

Long Term Evolution *See* LTE.

LOS (line-of-sight) A wireless signal or path that travels directly in a straight line from its transmitter to its intended receiver. This type of propagation uses the least amount of energy and results in the reception of the clearest possible signal.

LTE (Long Term Evolution) A 4G cellular network technology that achieves downlink data rates of up to 1 Gbps and uplink rates up to 500 Mbps. AT&T and Verizon have adopted LTE for their high-speed wireless data networks.

MIMO (multiple input-multiple output) In the context of 802.11n wireless networking, the ability for access points to issue multiple signals to stations, thereby multiplying the signal's strength and increasing their range and data-carrying capacity. Because the signals follow multipath propagation, they must be phase-adjusted when they reach their destination.

mobile A type of wireless system in which the receiver can be located anywhere within the transmitter's range. This allows the receiver to roam from one place to another while continuing to pick up its signal.

mobile switching center *See* MSC.

mobile telecommunications switching office *See* MSC.

MSC (mobile switching center) A carrier's facility to which multiple cellular base stations connect. An MSC might be located inside a telephone company's central office or it might stand alone and connect to the central office via fiber-optic cabling or a microwave link. Equipment at an MSC manages mobile clients, monitoring their location and usage patterns, and switches cellular calls. It also assigns each mobile client an IP address.

MTSO (mobile telecommunications switching office) *See* MSC.

multipath The characteristic of wireless signals that follow a number of different paths to their destination (for example, because of reflection, diffraction, and scattering).

multiple input-multiple output *See* MIMO.

narrowband A type of wireless transmission in which signals travel over a single frequency or within a specified frequency range.

omnidirectional antenna A type of antenna that issues and receives wireless signals with equal strength and clarity in all directions. This type of antenna is used when many different receivers must be able to pick up the signal, or when the receiver's location is highly mobile.

passive scanning In the context of wireless networking, the process in which a station listens to several channels within a frequency range for a beacon issued by an access point.

probe In 802.11 wireless networking, a type of frame issued by a station during active scanning to find nearby access points.

radiation pattern The relative strength over a three-dimensional area of all the electromagnetic energy an antenna sends or receives.

range The geographical area in which signals issued from an antenna or wireless system can be consistently and accurately received.

reassociation In the context of wireless networking, the process of a station establishing a connection (or associating) with a different access point.

reflection In the context of wireless, the phenomenon that occurs when an electromagnetic wave encounters an obstacle and bounces back toward its source. A wireless signal will bounce off objects whose dimensions are large compared with the signal's average wavelength.

Request to Send/Clear to Send *See* RTS/CTS.

roaming In wireless networking, the process that describes a station moving between BSSs without losing connectivity.

RTS/CTS (Request to Send/Clear to Send) An exchange in which a wireless station requests the exclusive right to communicate with an access point and the access point confirms that it has granted that request.

scanning The process a wireless station undergoes to find an access point. *See also* active scanning and passive scanning.

scattering The diffusion of a wireless signal that results from hitting an object that has smaller dimensions compared with the signal's wavelength. Scattering is also related to the roughness of the surface a wireless signal encounters. The rougher the surface, the more likely a signal is to scatter when it hits that surface.

service set identifier *See* SSID.

site survey In the context of wireless networking, an assessment of client requirements, facility characteristics, and coverage areas to determine an access point arrangement that will ensure reliable wireless connectivity within a given area.

spread spectrum A type of wireless transmission in which lower-level signals are distributed over several frequencies simultaneously. Spread-spectrum transmission is more secure than narrowband.

SSID (service set identifier) A unique character string used to identify an access point on an 802.11 network.

station An end node on a network; used most often in the context of wireless networks.

transponder The equipment on a satellite that receives an uplinked signal from Earth, amplifies the signal, modifies its frequency, then retransmits it (in a downlink) to an antenna on Earth.

uplink In the context of wireless transmission, the connection between a client's transceiver and a carrier's antenna.

WAP (wireless access point) *See* access point.

Wi-Fi *See* 802.11.

WiMAX *See* 802.16.

WiMAX 2 *See* 802.16m.

wireless A type of signal made of electromagnetic energy that travels through the air.

wireless access point *See* access point.

wireless gateway An access point that provides routing functions and is used as a gateway.

wireless LAN *See* WLAN.

wireless router An access point that provides routing functions.

wireless spectrum A continuum of electromagnetic waves used for data and voice communication. The wireless spectrum (as defined by the FCC, which controls its use) spans frequencies between 9 KHz and 300 GHz. Each type of wireless service can be associated with one area of the wireless spectrum.

WLAN (wireless LAN) A LAN that uses wireless connections for some or all of its transmissions.

Worldwide Interoperability for Microwave Access (WiMAX) *See* 802.16a.

Review Questions

1. Which antenna type issues and receives wireless signals with equal strength and clarity in all directions?

   a. radiant

   b. omnidirectional

   c. directional

   d. unidirectional

2. Which frequency band is used by weather and military radar communications in the United States, requiring that WLAN equipment in this range be able to monitor and detect radar signals and, if one is detected, switch to a different channel automatically?

   a. 1.2-GHz

   b. 2.4-GHz

   c. 5-GHz

   d. 50-GHz

3. Which term describes the use of multiple frequencies to transmit a signal?

   a. spread-spectrum technology

   b. multipath

   c. narrowband

   d. full-duplexing

   Answer: a

4. What innovation in the 802.11n standard combines two adjacent 20-MHz channels to make a 40-MHz channel that achieves high throughput?

   a. MIMO (multiple input-multiple output)

   b. channel bonding

   c. higher modulation rates

   d. frame aggregation

5. Which IEEE standard makes more sense on a citywide network, but has received significant competition from quickly evolving cellular data services?

   a. satellite

   b. Wi-Fi

   c. WiMAX

   d. broadband

6. True or false? Attenuation is the most severe flaw affecting wireless signals.
7. True or false? As long as a receiver is within the range to receive accurate signals consistently, signals will remain intelligible.
8. True or false? In most WLAN scenarios, stations must remain within 600 feet of an access point to maintain optimal transmission speeds.
9. True or false? WiMAX is not available to residential customers.
10. True or false? Within each band, frequencies used for uplink and downlink transmissions are the same.
11. In ________________ wireless, the receiver can be located anywhere within the transmitter's range.
12. One specific implementation of spread spectrum is ________________, in which a signal jumps between several different frequencies within a band in a synchronization pattern that is known only to the channel's receiver and transmitter
13. A(n) ________________ assesses client requirements, facility characteristics, and coverage areas to determine an access point arrangement that will ensure reliable wireless connectivity within a given area.

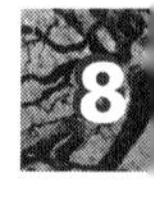

14. Collectively, the 802.16 standards are known as ________________.
15. In ________________, a wireless station listens on all channels within its frequency range for a special signal, known as a beacon frame, issued from an access point.

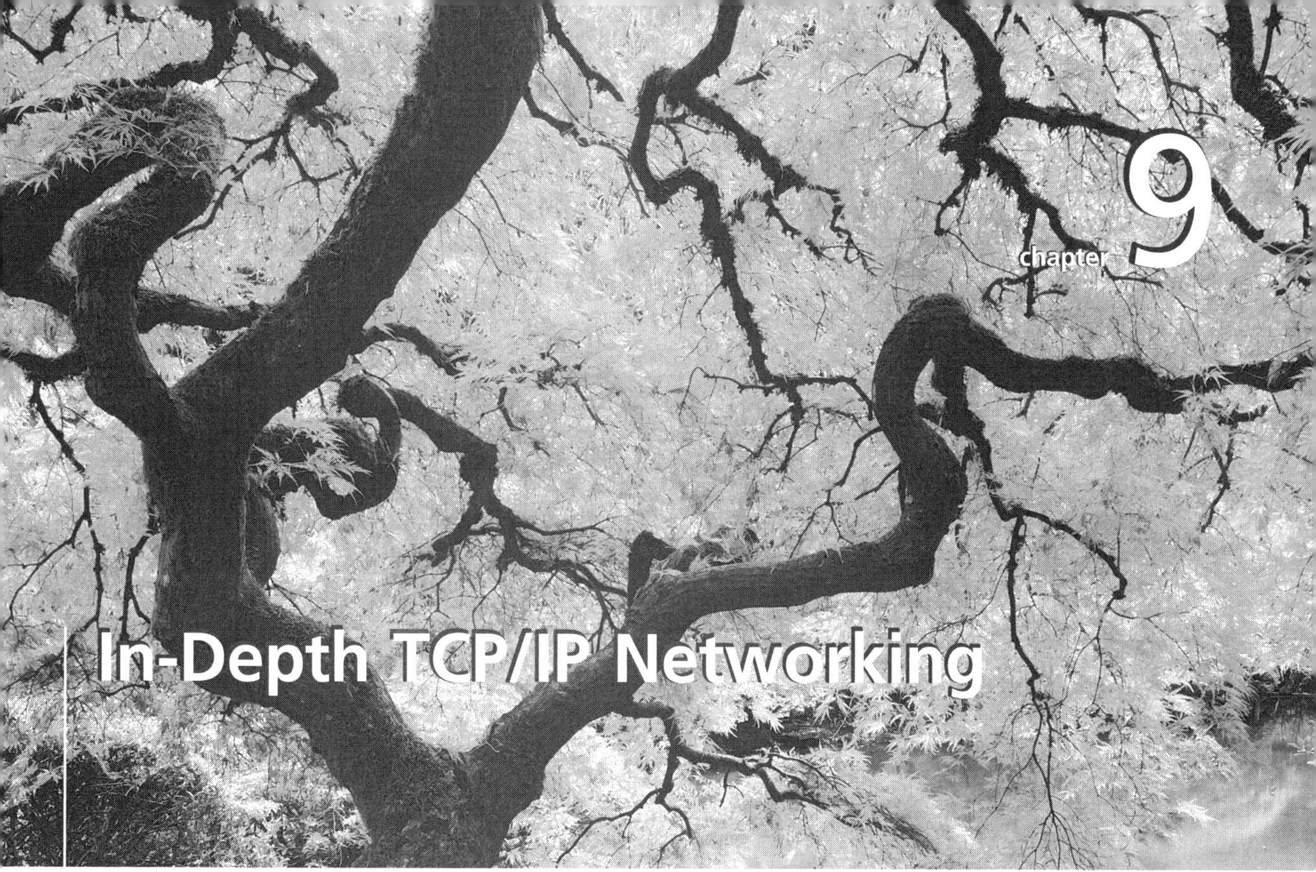

After reading this chapter and completing the exercises, you will be able to:

- Describe methods of network design unique to TCP/IP networks, including subnetting, CIDR, and address translation
- Explain the differences between public and private TCP/IP networks
- Describe protocols used between mail clients and mail servers, including SMTP, POP3, and IMAP4
- Employ multiple TCP/IP utilities for network discovery and troubleshooting

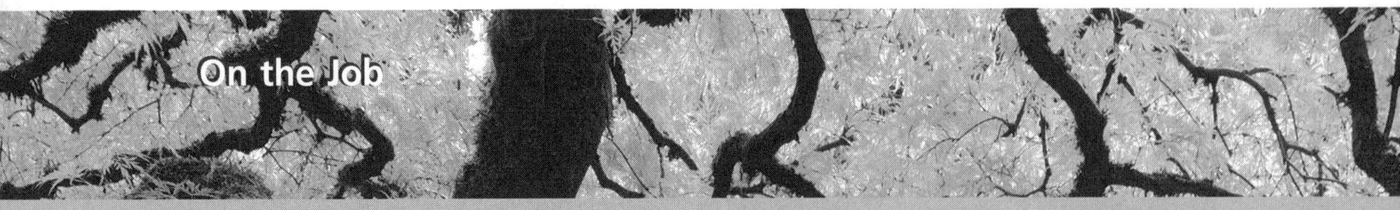

My company provided a full networking kit so I could work from my home office through a VPN. Everything worked well for over a year, until a newly hired coworker came to my location for on-the-job training.

I had wired my laptop and printer to two of the four available switched ports on the router, which also offered wireless access. The coworker's laptop had built-in wireless, so we turned it on, tested it (perfect!), and both went to work. The problems began almost immediately.

The first problem we noticed was that our previously smooth-running applications began to pause for random lengths of time, and then resume. As we became busier, the pauses became freezes and timeouts. Work became impossible. The training session switched to network troubleshooting.

Whenever a previously functioning network becomes unreliable, even from apparently trivial changes like adding a new host, my initial troubleshooting approach is to return to the previous configuration. I switched off the new laptop's wireless radio, and everything returned to normal. With the radio on, the intermittent problems returned.

I quickly ruled out obvious potential conflicts, such as a duplicate IP address. I switched the second laptop to a wired connection. No improvement. The router's error log showed no errors.

My suspicions now turned to the VPN. With a single VPN session, or no VPN sessions, simultaneous access to random sites on the Internet worked perfectly. The second VPN session triggered the problems. I contacted the IT Department head, who agreed we had encountered a router limitation. Namely, its NAT (Network Address Translation) capabilities were not sophisticated enough to maintain the proper status and state of two simultaneous VPN sessions.

Any VPN-capable router can support a single worker in a home office. A second (or subsequent) VPN session can only be reliably established if the router has been designed to support it. We solved the problem by replacing the router with a model from a different manufacturer.

David Butcher
Client Services Director

In Chapter 4, you learned about core protocols and subprotocols in the TCP/IP protocol suite, addressing schemes, and host and domain naming. You also learned that TCP/IP is a complex and highly customizable protocol suite. This chapter builds on these basic concepts, examining how TCP/IP-based networks are designed and analyzed. It also describes the services and applications that TCP/IP-based networks commonly support. If you are unclear about the concepts related to IP addressing or binary-to-decimal conversion, take time to review Chapter 4 before reading this chapter.

Designing TCP/IP-Based Networks

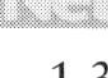

1.3 By now, you understand that most modern networks rely on the TCP/IP protocol suite, not only for Internet connectivity, but also for transmitting data over private connections. Before proceeding with TCP/IP network design considerations, it's useful to briefly review some TCP/IP fundamentals. For example, you have learned that IP is a routable protocol, and that on a network using TCP/IP each interface is associated with a unique IP address. Some nodes may use multiple IP addresses. For example, on a router that contains two NICs, each NIC can be assigned a separate IP address. Or, on a Web server that hosts multiple Web sites—such as one managed by an ISP—each Web service associated with a site can have a different IP address.

In Chapter 4, you learned about two versions of IP: IPv4 and IPv6. Recall that IPv4 addresses consist of four 8-bit octets (or bytes) that can be expressed in either binary (for example, 10000011 01000001 00001010 00100100) or dotted decimal (for example, 131.65.10.36) notation. Many networks assign IP addresses and host names dynamically, using DHCP, rather than statically. In addition, every IPv4 address can be associated with a network class—A, B, C, D, or E (though Class D and E addresses are reserved for special purposes). A node's network class provides information about the segment or network to which the node belongs. The following sections explain how network and host information in an IPv4 address can be manipulated to subdivide networks into smaller segments.

Subnetting

Subnetting separates a network into multiple logically defined segments, or subnets. Networks are commonly subnetted according to geographic locations (for example, the floors of a building connected by a LAN, or the buildings connected by a WAN), departmental boundaries, or technology types. Where subnetting is implemented, each subnet's traffic is separated from every other subnet's traffic. A network administrator might separate traffic to accomplish the following:

- *Enhance security*—Subnetworks must be connected via routers or other Layer 3 devices. As you know, these devices do not retransmit incoming frames to all other nodes on the same segment (as a hub does). Instead, they forward frames only as necessary to reach their destination. Because every frame is not indiscriminately retransmitted, the possibility for one node to tap into another node's transmissions is reduced.
- *Improve performance*—For the same reason that subnetting enhances security, it also improves performance on a network. When data is selectively retransmitted, unnecessary transmissions are kept to a minimum. Subnetting is useful for limiting the amount of broadcast traffic—and, therefore, the amount of potential collisions on Ethernet networks—by decreasing the size of each broadcast domain. The more efficient use of bandwidth results in better overall network performance.

1.3

- *Simplify troubleshooting*—For example, a network administrator might subdivide an organization's network according to geography, assigning a separate subnet to the nodes in the downtown office, west-side office, and east-side office of her company. Suppose one day the network has trouble transmitting data only to a certain group of IP addresses—those located on the west-side office subnet. When troubleshooting, rather than examining the whole network for errors or bottlenecks, the network administrator needs only to see that the faulty transmissions are all associated with addresses on the west-side subnet to know that she should zero in on that subnet.

To understand how and why subnetting is implemented, it's useful to first review IPv4 addressing conventions on a network that does not use subnetting.

Classful Addressing in IPv4 In Chapter 4, you learned about the first and simplest type of IPv4 addressing, which is known as **classful addressing** because it adheres to network class distinctions. Recall that all IPv4 addresses consist of network and host information. In classful addressing, the network information portion of an IPv4 address (the network ID) is limited to the first 8 bits in a Class A address, the first 16 bits in a Class B address, and the first 24 bits in a Class C address. Host information is contained in the last 24 bits for a Class A address, the last 16 bits in a Class B address, and the last 8 bits in a Class C address. Figure 9-1, which should look familiar from Chapter 4's discussion of IP addressing, illustrates how network and host information is separated in classful IPv4 addressing. Figure 9-2 offers some sample IPv4 addresses separated into network and host information according to the classful addressing convention.

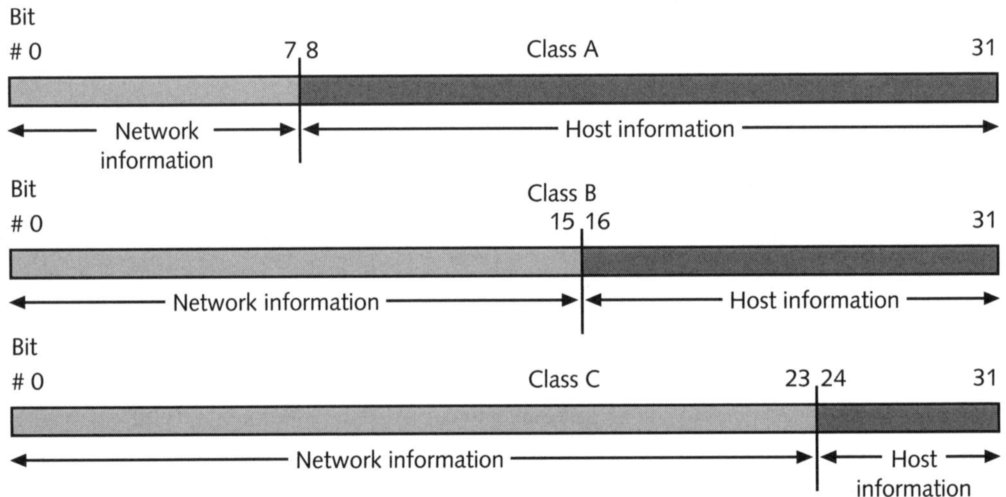

Figure 9-1 Network and host information in classful IPv4 addressing

Adhering to a fixed network ID size ultimately limits the number of hosts a network can include. For example, leasing an entire Class C network of addresses gives you only 254 usable IPv4 addresses. In addition, using classful addressing makes it difficult to separate traffic from various parts of a network. As you have learned, separating traffic offers many

1.3

Sample Class A network address: 114.56.204.33
network information = 114
host information = 56.204.33

Sample Class B network address: 147.12.38.81
network information = 147.12
host information = 38.81

Sample Class C network address: 214.57.42.7
network information = 214.57.42
host information = 7

Figure 9-2 Sample IPv4 addresses with classful addressing

practical benefits. For example, if an organization used an entire Class B network of addresses, it could have up to 65,534 hosts all on one network segment. Imagine the challenges involved in managing such a highly populated network, not to mention the poor performance that would result. In 1985, because of the difficulty of managing a whole network class of addresses and the dwindling supply of usable IPv4 addresses, computer scientists introduced subnetting.

Depending on the source, you may find the term *network ID* used interchangeably with the terms **network number** or **network prefix**.

IPv4 Subnet Masks Subnetting depends on the use of subnet masks to identify how a network is subdivided. A subnet mask indicates where network information is located in an IPv4 address. The bits in a subnet mask that are assigned the number 1 indicate that corresponding bits in an IPv4 address contain network information. The bits that are assigned the number 0 indicate that corresponding bits in an IP address contain host information. For example, a subnet mask of 11111111 11111111 11111111 00000000, or 255.255.255.0 in dotted decimal notation, indicates that the first three octets of all IP addresses belonging to that subnet will contain network information. The last octet will contain host information. As you have learned, 255.255.255.0 is the default subnet mask for Class C IPv4 addresses.

Each network class is associated with a default subnet mask, as shown in Table 9-1. For example, by default, a Class A address's first octet (or 8 bits) represents network information and is composed of all 1s. That means that if you work on a network whose hosts are configured with a subnet mask of 11111111 00000000 00000000 00000000, or 255.0.0.0, you know that the network is using Class A addresses. Furthermore, you can tell that the network is not using subnetting because 255.0.0.0 is the default subnet mask for a Class A network. If the network had been subnetted, the subnet mask would be modified.

To calculate a host's network ID given its IPv4 address and subnet mask, you follow a logical process of combining bits known as **ANDing**. In ANDing, a bit with a value of 1 plus another bit with a value of 1 results in a 1. A bit with a value of 0 plus any other bit results in a 0. If you think of 1 as "true" and 0 as "false," the logic of ANDing makes sense.

1.3

Table 9-1 **Default IPv4 subnet masks**

Network class	Default subnet mask (binary)	Number of bits used for network information	Default subnet mask (dotted decimal)
A	11111111 00000000 00000000 00000000	8	255.0.0.0
B	11111111 11111111 00000000 00000000	16	255.255.0.0
C	11111111 11111111 11111111 00000000	24	255.255.255.0

Adding a true statement to a true statement still results in a true statement. But adding a true statement to a false statement results in a false statement. ANDing logic is demonstrated in Table 9-2, which provides every possible combination of having a 1 or 0 bit in an IPv4 address or subnet mask.

Table 9-2 ANDing

IP address bit	1	1	0	0
Subnet mask bit	1	0	1	0
Resulting bit	1	0	0	0

A sample IPv4 host address, its default subnet mask, and its network ID are shown in Figure 9-3 in both binary and dotted decimal notation. Notice that the address's fourth octet could have been composed of any combination of 1s and 0s, and the network ID's fourth octet would still be all 0s.

	IP address:	11000111	00100010	00100010	01111111	199.34.89.127
and	Subnet mask:	11111111	11111111	11111111	00000000	255.255.255.0
Equals	Network ID:	11000111	00100010	00100010	00000000	199.34.89.0

Figure 9-3 Example of calculating a host's network ID

At this point, you should understand how to determine a host's network ID given its IPv4 address and subnet mask. This section explained how to apply ANDing logic to an IPv4 address plus a *default* subnet mask, but it works just the same way for networks that are subnetted and have different subnet masks, as you will soon learn. Before learning how to create subnets, however, it is necessary to understand the types of addresses that cannot be used as subnet masks or host addresses.

Special Addresses As you learned in Chapter 4, certain types of IP addresses cannot be assigned to a network interface on a node or used as subnet masks. Table 9-3 lists some of the IPv4 addresses and ranges reserved for special functions.

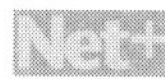

Table 9-3 IPv4 addresses reserved for special functions

1.3

IPv4 address(es)	Function
127.0.0.1	Loopback
10.0.0.0 through 10.255.255.255	Private
172.16.0.0 through 172.31.255.255	Private
192.168.0.0 through 192.168.255.255	Private
169.254.1.0 through 169.254.254.255	Link local
Addresses whose host information = 255 (for example, 199.34.89.255)	Broadcast
Addresses whose host information = 0 (for example, 199.34.89.0)	Network ID

For example, in IPv4, the address 127.0.0.1 is reserved for the loopback address. Some addresses are reserved as private or link local addresses. Another special IP address is the broadcast address for a network or segment. In a broadcast address, the octet(s) that represent the host information are set to equal all 1s, or in decimal notation, 255. In the example in Figure 9-3, the broadcast address would be 199.34.89.255. If a workstation on that network sent a message to the address 199.34.89.255, it would be issued to every node on the segment.

Still another type of special address is the network ID. In a network ID, as you know, bits available for host information are set to 0. Therefore, a workstation on the sample network used in Figure 9-3 could not be assigned the IP address 199.34.89.0 because that address is the network ID. When using classful IPv4 addressing, a network ID always ends with an octet of 0 (and may have additional, preceding octets equal to 0). However, when subnetting is applied and a default subnet mask is no longer used, a network ID may have other decimal values in its last octet(s).

Because the octets equal to 0 and 255 are reserved, only the numbers 1 through 254 can be used for host information in an IPv4 address. Thus, on a network that followed the example in Figure 9-3, the usable host addresses would range from 199.34.89.1 to 199.34.89.254. If you subnetted this network, the range of usable host addresses would be different.

As in IPv4, in IPv6 certain addresses are reserved for special functions and cannot be assigned to a subnet or a node's network interface. For example, in Chapter 4, you learned that the IPv6 loopback address is 0:0:0:0:0:0:0:1, or, in compressed notation, ::1. Link local addresses in IPv6 always begin with FE80. Multicast addresses in IPv6 always begin with FF.

The next section describes how IPv4 subnets are created and how you can determine the range of usable host addresses on a subnet. Later in the chapter, you will learn how subnetting differs in IPv6.

IPv4 Subnetting Techniques Subnetting alters the rules of classful IPv4 addressing. To create a subnet, you must borrow bits that would represent host information in classful addressing and use those bits to instead represent network information. By doing so, you reduce the number of bits available for identifying hosts. Consequently, you reduce the number of usable host addresses per subnet. The number of hosts and subnets available after subnetting is related to how many host information bits you borrow for network information.

1.3 Table 9-4 illustrates the numbers of subnets and hosts that can be created by subnetting a Class B network. Notice the range of subnet masks that can be used instead of the default Class B subnet mask of 255.255.0.0. Also compare the listed numbers of hosts per subnet to the 65,534 hosts available on a Class B network that does not use subnetting.

Table 9-4 IPv4 Class B subnet masks

Subnet mask	Number of subnets on network	Number of hosts per subnet
255.255.192.0 or 1111111 1111111 1100000 0000000	2	16,382
255.255.224.0 or 1111111 1111111 1110000 0000000	6	8190
255.255.240.0 or 1111111 1111111 1111000 0000000	14	4094
255.255.248.0 or 1111111 1111111 1111100 0000000	30	2046
255.255.252.0 or 1111111 1111111 1111110 0000000	62	1022
255.255.254.0 or 1111111 1111111 11111110 00000000	126	510
255.255.255.0 or 1111111 1111111 11111111 00000000	254	254
255.255.255.128 or 1111111 1111111 1111111 10000000	510	126
255.255.255.192 or 1111111 1111111 1111111 11000000	1022	62
255.255.255.224 or 1111111 1111111 1111111 11100000	2046	30
255.255.255.240 or 1111111 1111111 1111111 11110000	4094	14
255.255.255.248 or 1111111 1111111 1111111 11111000	8190	6
255.255.255.252 or 1111111 1111111 1111111 11111100	16,382	2

Table 9-5 illustrates the numbers of subnets and hosts that can be created by subnetting a Class C network. Notice that a Class C network allows for fewer subnets than a Class B network. This is because Class C addresses have fewer host information bits that can be borrowed for network information. In addition, fewer bits are left over for host information, which leads to a lower number of hosts per subnet than the number available to Class B subnets.

Table 9-5 IPv4 Class C subnet masks

Subnet mask	Number of subnets on network	Number of hosts per subnet
255.255.255.192 or 1111111 1111111 1111111 1100000	2	62
255.255.255.224 or 1111111 1111111 1111111 1110000	6	30
255.255.255.240 or 1111111 1111111 1111111 1111000	14	14
255.255.255.248 or 1111111 1111111 1111111 1111100	30	6
255.255.255.252 or 1111111 1111111 1111111 1111110	62	2

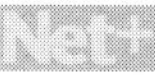
Calculating IPv4 Subnets Now that you have seen the results of subnetting, you are
1.3 ready to try subnetting an IPv4 network. Suppose you have leased the Class C network whose network ID is 199.34.89.0 and you want to divide it into six subnets to correspond to the six different departments in your company. The formula for determining how to modify a default subnet mask is:

$$2^n-2 = Y$$

where n equals the number of bits in the subnet mask that must be switched from 0 to 1, and Y equals the number of subnets that result.

Notice that this formula subtracts 2 from the total number of possible subnets—that is, from the calculation of 2 to the power of the number of the bits that equal 1. That's because in traditional subnetting, bit combinations of all 0s or all 1s are not allowed for identifying subnets—just as host addresses ending in all 0s or all 1s are not allowed because of addresses reserved for the network ID and broadcast transmissions. (However, in the next section of this chapter, you will learn why this equation doesn't apply to all modern networks.)

Because you want six separate subnets, the equation becomes $6 = 2^n - 2$.

Because $6 + 2 = 8$ and $8 = 2^3$, you know that the value of n equals 3. Therefore, three additional bits in the default subnet mask for your Class C network must change from 0 to 1.

As you know, the default subnet mask for a Class C network is 255.255.255.0, or 11111111 11111111 11111111 00000000. In this default subnet mask, the first 24 bits indicate the position of network information.

Changing three of the default subnet mask's bits from host to network information leaves you with a subnet mask of 11111111 111111111 11111111 11100000. In this modified subnet mask, the first 27 bits indicate the position of network information.

Converting from binary to the more familiar dotted decimal notation, this subnet mask becomes 255.255.255.224. When you configure the TCP/IP properties of clients on your network, you would specify this subnet mask.

Now that you have calculated the subnet mask, you still need to assign IP addresses to nodes based on your new subnetting scheme. Recall that you have borrowed 3 bits from what used to be host information in the IP address. That leaves 5 bits instead of 8 available in the last octet of your Class C addresses to identify hosts.

Adding the values of the last 5 bits, 16 + 8 + 4 + 2 + 1, equals 31, for a total of 32 potential addresses (0 through 31). However, as you have learned, one address is reserved for the network ID and cannot be used. Another address is reserved for the broadcast ID and cannot be used. Thus, using 5 bits for host information allows a maximum of 30 different host addresses for each of the six subnets. So, in this example, you can have a maximum of 6 x 30, or 180, unique host addresses on the network.

Table 9-6 lists the network ID, broadcast address, and usable host addresses for each of the six subnets in this sample Class C network. Together, the additional bits used for subnet information plus the existing network ID are known as the **extended network prefix**.

The extended network prefix for each subnet is based on which of the additional (borrowed) network information bits are set to equal 1. For example, in subnet number 1, only the third bit of the three is set to 1, making the last octet of the extended network prefix 00100000,

Net+

Table 9-6 Subnet information for six subnets in a sample IPv4 Class C network

1.3

Subnet number	Extended network prefix	Broadcast address	Usable host addresses
1	199.34.89.32 or 11000111 00100010 01011001 00100000	199.34.89.63 or 11000111 00100010 01011001 00111111	199.34.89.33 through 199.34.89.62
2	199.34.89.64 or 11000111 00100010 01011001 01000000	199.34.89.95 or 11000111 00100010 01011001 01011111	199.34.89.65 through 199.34.89.94
3	199.34.89.96 or 11000111 00100010 01011001 01100000	199.34.89.127 or 11000111 00100010 01011001 01111111	199.34.89.97 through 199.34.89.126
4	199.34.89.128 or 11000111 00100010 01011001 10000000	199.34.89.159 or 11000111 00100010 01011001 10011111	199.34.89.129 through 199.34.89.158
5	199.34.89.160 or 11000111 00100010 01011001 10100000	199.34.89.191 or 11000111 00100010 01011001 10111111	199.34.89.161 through 199.34.89.190
6	199.34.89.192 or 11000111 00100010 01011001 11000000	199.34.89.223 or 11000111 00100010 01011001 11011111	199.34.89.193 through 199.34.89.222

or in decimal notation, 32. In subnet number 2, only the second bit is set to 1, making the last octet of the extended network prefix 01000000, or 64.

Class A, Class B, and Class C networks can all be subnetted. But because each class reserves a different number of bits for network information, each class has a different number of host information bits that can be used for subnet information. The number of hosts and subnets on your network will vary depending on your network class and the way you use subnetting. Enumerating the dozens of subnet possibilities based on different arrangements and network classes is beyond the scope of this book. However, several Web sites provide excellent tools that help you calculate subnet information. One such site is *www.subnetmask.info*.

If you use subnetting on your LAN, only your LAN's devices need to interpret your devices' subnetting information. Routers external to your LAN, such as those on the Internet, pay attention to only the network portion of your devices' IP addresses when transmitting data to them. As a result, devices external to a subnetted LAN (such as routers on the Internet) can direct data to those LAN devices without interpreting the LAN's subnetting information.

Figure 9-4 illustrates a situation in which a LAN running IPv4 has been granted the Class C range of addresses that begin with 199.34.89. The network administrator has subnetted this Class C network into six smaller networks with the network IDs listed in Table 9-5. As you know, routers connect different network segments via their physical interfaces. In the case of subnetting, a router must interpret IP addresses from different subnets and direct data from one subnet to another. Each subnet corresponds to a different port on the router.

When a router on the internal LAN needs to direct data from a machine with the IP address of 199.34.89.73 to a machine with the IP address of 199.34.89.114, its interpretation of the workstations' subnet masks (255.255.255.224) plus the host information in the IP addresses tell the router that they are on different subnets. The router forwards data between the two subnets (or ports). In this figure, the devices connecting subnets to the router are labeled

Net+ 1.3

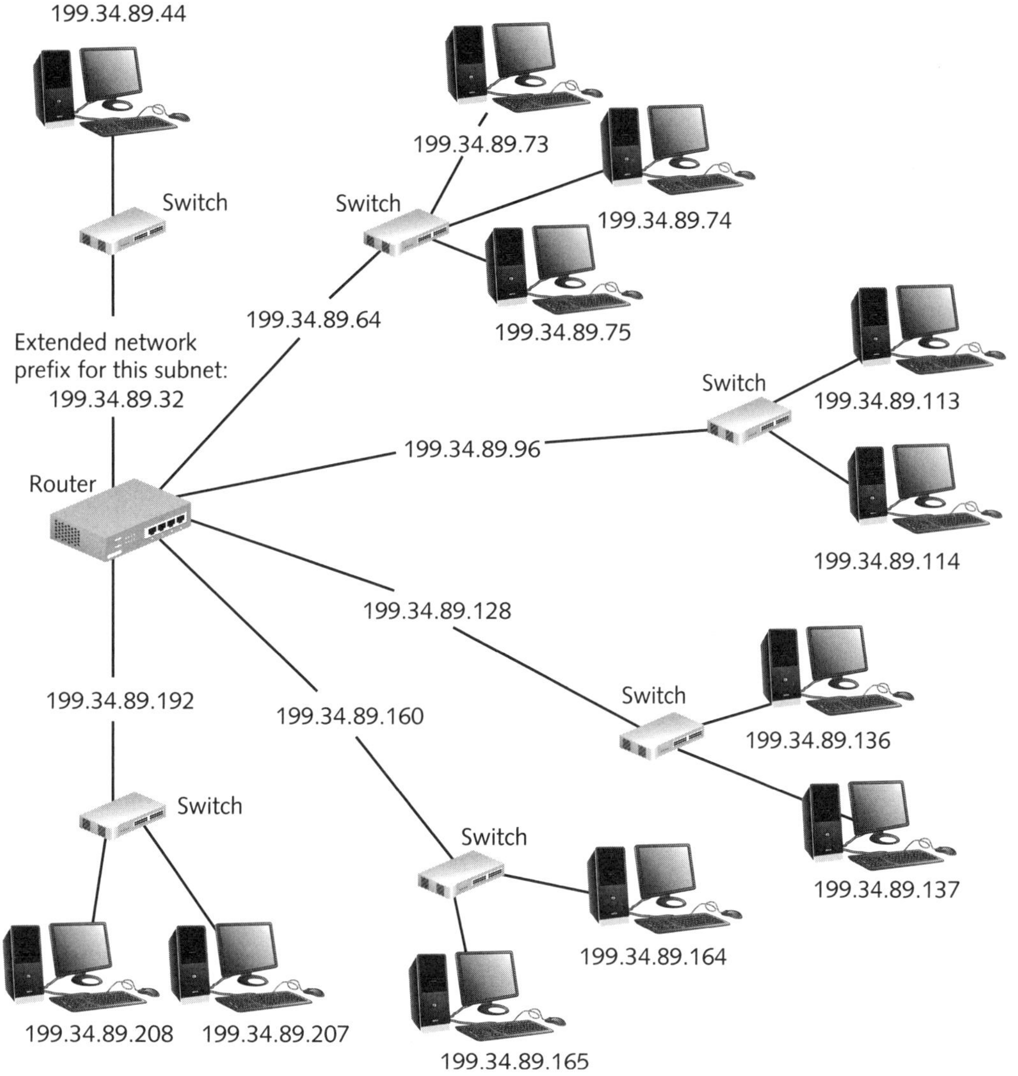

Figure 9-4 A router connecting several subnets

switches, but they could also be routers or access points. Alternatively, nodes having different extended network prefixes could be directly connected to the router so that each subnet is associated with only one device, though this is an unlikely configuration.

When a server on the Internet attempts to deliver a Web page to the machine with IP address 199.34.89.73, however, the Internet router does not use the subnet mask information. It only knows that the machine is on a Class C network beginning with a network ID of 199.34.89. That's all the information it needs to reach the organization's router. After the data enters the organization's LAN, the LAN's router then interprets the subnet mask information as if it were transmitting data internally to deliver data to the machine with IP address 199.34.89.73. Because subnetting does not affect how a device is addressed by

external networks, a network administrator does not need to inform Internet authorities
1.3 about new segments created via subnetting.

You have learned how to subdivide an IPv4 network into multiple smaller segments through subnetting. Next, you'll learn about more contemporary variations on this method.

CIDR (Classless Interdomain Routing)

By 1993, the Internet was growing exponentially, and the demand for IP addresses was growing with it. The IETF (Internet Engineering Task Force) recognized that additional measures were necessary to increase the availability and flexibility of IP addresses. In response to this need, the IETF devised **CIDR (Classless Interdomain Routing)**, which is sometimes called **classless routing** or **supernetting**. CIDR (pronounced *cider*) is not exclusive of subnetting; it merely provides additional ways of arranging network and host information in an IP address. In CIDR, conventional network class distinctions do not exist.

For example, the previous section described subdividing a Class C network into six subnets of 30 addressable hosts each. To achieve this, the subnet boundary (or length of the extended network prefix) was moved to the right—from the default 24th bit to the 27th bit—into what used to be the host information octet. In CIDR, a subnet boundary can move to the left. Moving the subnet boundary to the left allows you to use more bits for host information and, therefore, generate more usable IP addresses on your network. A subnet created by moving the subnet boundary to the left is known as a **supernet**. Figure 9-5 contrasts examples of a Class C **supernet mask** with a subnet mask.

Sample subnet mask:

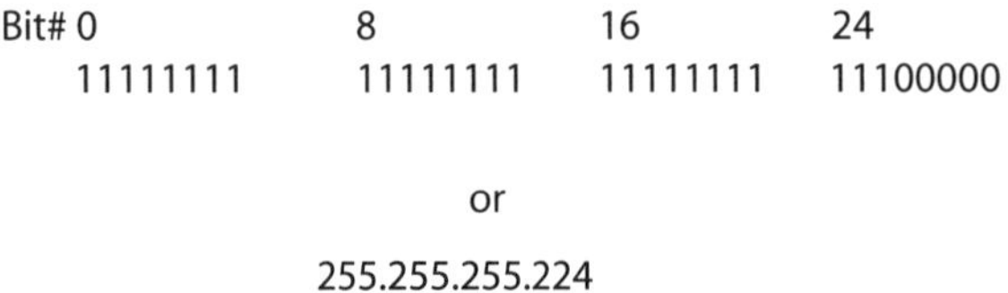

Sample supernet mask:

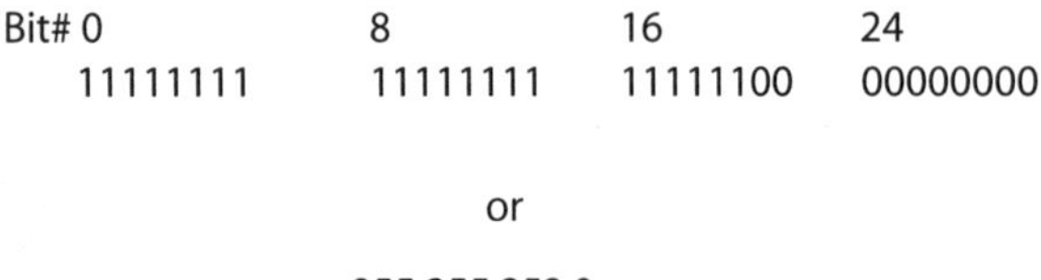

Figure 9-5 Subnet mask and supernet mask

Notice that in Figure 9-5, 27 bits are used for network information in the subnet mask, whereas only 22 bits are used for network information in the supernet mask.

Suppose that you have leased the Class C range of IPv4 addresses that shares the network ID 199.34.89.0 and, because of growth in your company, you need to greatly increase the number of host addresses this network allows by default. By changing the default subnet mask of

1.3 255.255.255.0 (11111111 11111111 11111111 00000000) to 255.255.252.0 (11111111 11111111 11111100 00000000), as shown in Figure 9-5, you can make available two extra bits for host information. Adding the values of the last 10 bits, 512 + 256 + 128 + 64 + 32 + 16 + 8 + 4 + 2 + 1, equals 1023, which leads to 1024 (0 through 1023) potential host addresses on each subnet. However, as you know, two addresses are reserved and, therefore, are unusable as host addresses. Thus, the actual number of host addresses available on this subnet is 1022.

In this example, you have subtracted information from the host portion of the IP address. Therefore, the IP addresses that result from this subnetting scheme will be different from the IP addresses you would use if you had left the network ID untouched (as in the subnetting example used in the previous section). The calculation for the new network ID is shown in Figure 9-6. For this sample subnetted Class C network, the potential host addresses fall in the range of 199.34.88.1 to 199.34.91.254. The broadcast address is 199.34.91.255.

	IP address:	11000111	00100010	01011001	01111111	199.34.89.127
and	Subnet mask:	11111111	11111111	11111100	00000000	255.255.252.0
Equals	Network ID:	11000111	00100010	01011000	00000000	199.34.88.0

Figure 9-6 Calculating a host's network ID on a supernetted network

With CIDR also came a new shorthand for denoting the position of subnet boundaries, known as **CIDR notation** (or **slash notation**). CIDR notation takes the form of the network ID followed by a forward slash (/), followed by the number of bits that are used for the extended network prefix. For example, for the Class C network whose network ID is 199.34.89.0 and which was divided into six subnets, the slash notation would be 199.34.89.0/27 because 27 bits of the subnets' addresses are used for the extended network prefix. The CIDR notation for the Class C network used as an example of supernetting earlier in this section would be 199.34.89.0/22. In CIDR terminology, the forward slash, plus the number of bits used for the extended network prefix—for example, /22—is known as a **CIDR block.**

To take advantage of classless routing, your network's routers must be able to interpret IP addresses that don't adhere to conventional network class parameters. Routers that rely on older routing protocols, such as RIP, are not capable of interpreting classless IP addresses.

Subnetting in IPv6

In Chapter 4, you learned that IPv6 addresses are composed of 128 bits, compared with IPv4's 32-bit addresses. That means 2^{128} addresses are available in IPv6, compared with IPv4's 2^{32} available addresses. Given so many addresses, an ISP can offer each of its customers an entire IPv6 subnet, or thousands of addresses, rather than a handful of IPv4 addresses that must be shared among all the company's nodes. That's only one example of how subnetting helps network administrators manage the enormous volume of IPv6 addresses.

Subnetting in IPv6 is simpler than subnetting in IPv4. One substantial difference is that unlike IPv4 addressing, IPv6 addressing does not use classes. There are no IPv6 equivalent to IPv4's Class A, Class B, or Class C networks. Every IPv6 address is classless. Furthermore, subnet masks are not used in IPv6.

Net+ 1.3 Recall that a unicast address is an address assigned to a single interface on the network. Also recall that every unicast address can be represented in binary form, but is more commonly written as eight blocks of four hexadecimal characters separated by colons. For example, 2608:FE10:1:A:002:50FF:FE2B:E708 is a valid IPv6 address. In every unicast address, the last four blocks, which equate to the last 64 bits, identify the interface. (On many IPv6 networks, those 64 bits are based on the interface's EUI-64 MAC address.) The first four blocks indicate the 64-bit **subnet prefix**, as shown in Figure 9-7. Interfaces that share a subnet prefix belong to the same subnet.

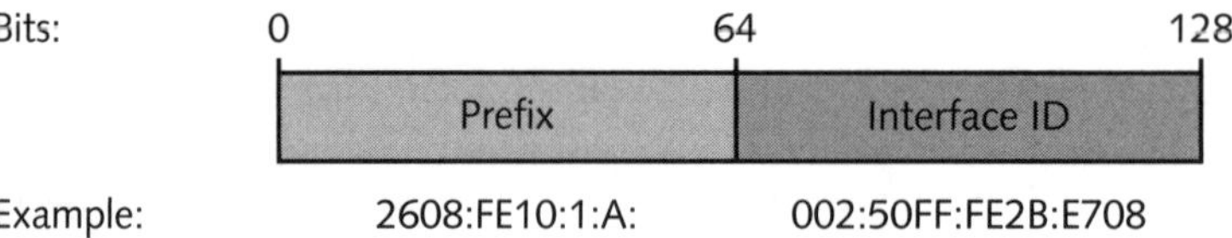

Figure 9-7 Subnet prefix and interface ID in an IPv6 address

In the IPv6 address 2608:FE10:1:A:002:50FF:FE2B:E708, the subnet prefix is 2608:FE10:1:A and the interface ID is 002:50FF:FE2B:E708. You may see subnet prefixes represented as, for example, 2608:FE10:1:A::/64, where the number of bits that identify a subnet follow a slash. However, technically speaking, a subnet is always represented by the leftmost 64 bits in an address, making the slash notation unnecessary. Given 64 bits for network information and 64 bits for interface information, a single IPv6 subnet is capable of supplying 18,446,744,073,709,551,616 IPv6 addresses.

Besides subdividing IPv6 interfaces according to subnet, IPv6 enables network administrators to more generally group interfaces that belong to the same route by specifying a **route prefix**. Because route prefixes vary in length, the slash notation is necessary when defining them. For example, the route prefix indicated by 2608:FE10::/32 includes all subnets whose prefixes begin with 2608:FE10 and, consequently, all interfaces whose IP addresses begin with 2608:FE10.

As shown in Figure 9-8, a national NSP might assign a regional ISP a block of addresses that share a 32-bit route prefix, such as 2608:FE10::/32. That regional ISP, in turn, might assign a local ISP a block of addresses that share the same 48-bit route prefix, such as 2608:FE10:1::/48. Finally, the local ISP could assign one of its large business customers a subnet—that is, a block of IPv6 addresses that share the same 64-bit subnet prefix, such as 2608:FE10:1:A::/64.

Now that you have learned how subnets are handled differently in IPv4 and IPv6 addressing, you are ready to take a closer look at gateways, which play a critical role in all networks.

Internet Gateways

As you have learned, a gateway is a combination of software and hardware that enables two different network segments to exchange data. A gateway facilitates communication between different networks or subnets. Because one device on the network cannot send data directly to a device on another subnet, a gateway must intercede and hand off the information. Every device on a TCP/IP-based network has a **default gateway**—that is, the gateway that first interprets its outbound requests to other subnets, and then interprets its inbound requests from other subnets.

Net+ 1.3

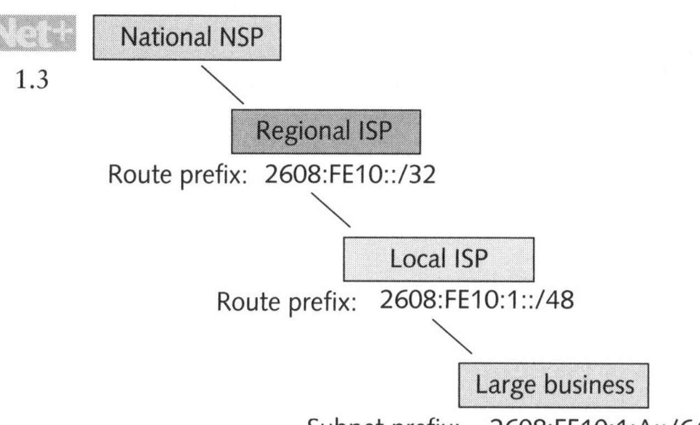

Figure 9-8 Hierarchy of IPv6 routes and subnets

A gateway is analogous to your local post office, which gathers your outbound mail and decides where to forward it. It also handles your inbound mail on its way to your mailbox. Just as a large city has several local post offices, a large organization will have several gateways to route traffic for different groups of devices. Each node on the network can have only one default gateway; that gateway is assigned either manually or automatically (in the latter case, through a service such as DHCP). Of course, if your network includes only one segment and you do not connect to the Internet, your devices would not need a default gateway because traffic would not need to cross the network's boundary.

In many cases, a default gateway is not a separate device, but rather a network interface on a router. For this reason, you may hear the term **default router** used to refer to a default gateway. By using a router's network interfaces as gateways, one router can supply multiple gateways. Each default gateway is assigned its own IP address. In Figure 9-9, workstation 10.3.105.23 (workstation A) uses the 10.3.105.1 gateway to process its requests, and workstation 10.3.102.75 (workstation B) uses the 10.3.102.1 gateway for the same purpose.

On a network running IPv4, an Internet gateway is usually assigned an IP address that ends with an octet of .1. Similarly, in IPv6, default gateway addresses usually end in ::1.

Default gateways may connect multiple internal networks, or they may connect an internal network with external networks, such as WANs or the Internet. Routers that connect multiple networks must maintain a routing table to determine where to forward information. When a router is used as a gateway, it must maintain routing tables as well.

The Internet contains a vast number of routers and gateways. If each gateway had to track addressing information for every other gateway on the Internet, it would be overtaxed. Instead, each handles only a relatively small amount of addressing information, which it uses to forward data to another gateway that knows more about the data's destination. Like routers on an internal network, Internet gateways maintain default routes to known addresses to expedite data transfer. The gateways that make up the Internet backbone are called **core gateways**.

Net+ 1.3

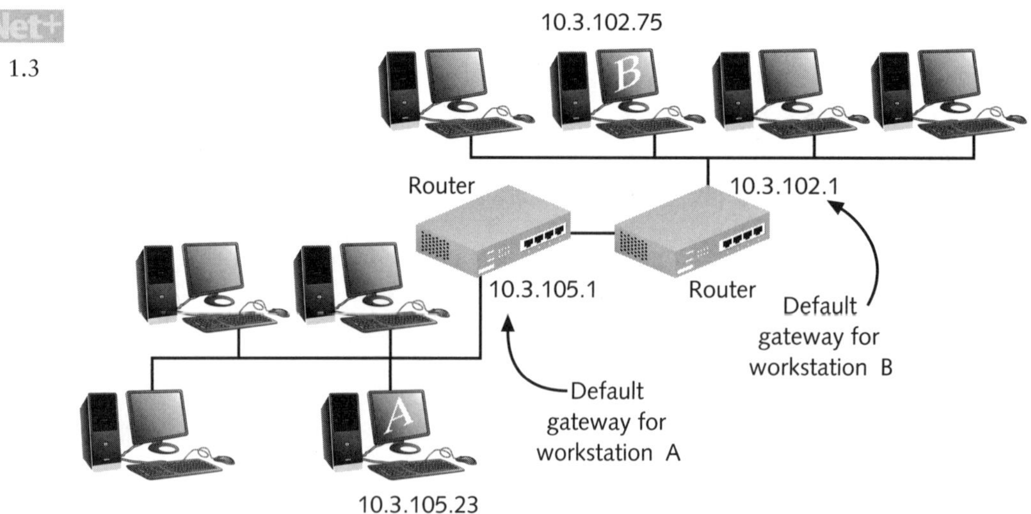

Figure 9-9 The use of default gateways

Net+

Address Translation

2.1 An organization's default gateway can also be used to "hide" the organization's internal IP addresses and keep them from being recognized on a public network. A **public network** is one that any user may access with little or no restrictions. The most familiar example of a public network is the Internet. A citywide kiosk system may also be considered a public network. Conversely, a **private network** is a network whose access is restricted to only clients or machines with proper credentials. Virtually all business LANs and WANs are private networks.

On private networks, hiding IP addresses allows network managers more flexibility in assigning addresses. Clients behind a gateway may use any IP addressing scheme, regardless of whether it is recognized as legitimate by the Internet authorities. But as soon as those clients need to connect to the Internet, they must have a legitimate IP address to exchange data. When the client's transmission reaches the default gateway, the gateway opens the IP datagram and replaces the client's private IP address with an Internet-recognized IP address. This process is known as **NAT (Network Address Translation)**. A few types of NAT are available to network administrators. Before learning how each works, though, it's helpful to know more about the reasons for address translation.

One reason for using address translation is to overcome the limitations of a low quantity of IPv4 addresses. In the early days of the Internet, businesses could lease large blocks of IP addresses, enough to assign a separate Internet-routable address to each device and client on their WAN. However, as more hosts joined the Internet, the scarcity of IPv4 addresses became a problem. Today a small business with 25 hosts, for example, might only be able to lease one IP address from its ISP. Yet the business still needs to allow all its hosts access to the Internet. With address translation, all 25 hosts can share a single Internet-routable IP address.

Net+ 2.1

Another reason for using address translation is to add a marginal amount of security to a private network when it is connected to a public network. Because a transmission is assigned a new IP address each time it reaches the public sphere, those outside an organization cannot trace the origin of the transmission back to the specific network node that sent it. However, the IP address assigned to a transmission by the gateway must be an Internet-authorized IP address; thus, it can be traced back to the organization that leased the address.

NAT is also possible in IPv6. However, the problem that NAT is primarily designed to solve, a scarcity of Internet routable addresses, is not a problem in IPv6. Thus, NAT is unnecessary on networks that run only IPv6.

A third reason for using address translation is to enable a network administrator to develop her own network addressing scheme that does not conform to a scheme dictated by ICANN. For example, suppose you are the network administrator for a private elementary school. You maintain the school's entire network, which, among other things, includes 50 client workstations. Suppose half of these clients are used by students in the classrooms or library and half are used expressly by staff. To make your network management easier, you might decide to assign each workstation an IPv4 address whose first octet begins with the number 10 and whose second octet is the number of the classroom or office where the computer is located.

For example, the principal's workstation, which is located in the administrative cubicles in Room 135, might have an IP address of 10.135.1.10. A workstation used by students in the classroom in Room 235 might be assigned an IP address of 10.235.1.12. These IP addresses would be used strictly for communication between devices on the school's network. When staff or students wanted to access the Internet, their workstations would need to have access to IP addresses that are legitimate for use on the Internet.

If you have leased at least 50 Internet-valid IP addresses from your ISP, you can assign each client a corresponding IP address for use on the Internet. For example, the student workstation in room 235 with a private IP address of 10.235.1.12 might be assigned an Internet-valid IP address of 168.11.124.110. The principal's workstation might be assigned an Internet-valid IP address of 168.11.124.113. This type of address translation is known as **SNAT (Static Network Address Translation)**. It is considered static because each client is associated with one private IP address and one public IP address that never changes. SNAT is useful when operating a mail server, for example, whose address must remain the same for clients to reach it at any time. Figure 9-10 illustrates SNAT.

Now suppose that, because the school has limited funds and does not require that all clients be connected to the Internet at all times, you decide to lease only eight IP numbers from your ISP. You then configure your gateway to translate the school's private IP addresses to addresses that can be used on the Internet. Each time a client attempts to reach the Internet, the gateway would replace its source address field in the datagram with one of the eight legitimate IP addresses. Because any Internet-valid IP address might be assigned to any client's outgoing transmission, this technique is known as **DNAT (Dynamic Network Address Translation)**. It may also be called **IP masquerading**.

You might wonder how an Internet host can respond to a client on a private network using DNAT, if all the clients on that network share a small pool of addresses. For example, when a

Net+ 2.1

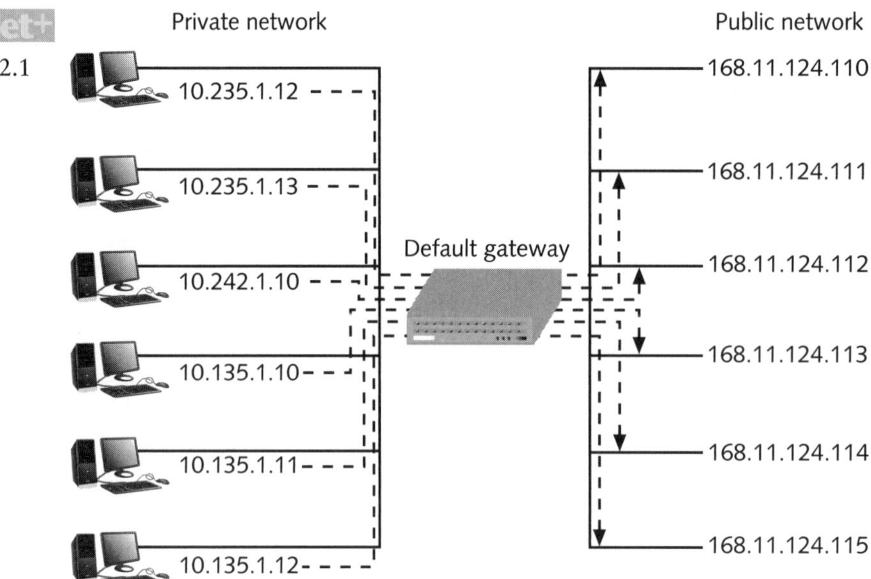

Figure 9-10 SNAT (Static Network Address Translation)

student at the elementary school opens a browser and requests the Library of Congress Web page, how will the Web server know which student workstation should receive the response? In fact, to accomplish DNAT, a gateway performs **PAT (Port Address Translation)**. With PAT, each client session with a server on the Internet is assigned a separate TCP port number. When the client issues a request to the server, its datagram's source address includes this port number. When the Internet server responds, its datagram's destination address includes the same port number. This allows the gateway to send the response to the appropriate client. PAT is the most common type of address translation used on small office and home networks.

Figure 9-11 illustrates the use of PAT where one Internet-recognized IP address is shared by four clients.

You have learned that NAT separates private and public transmissions on a TCP/IP network. Further, you have learned that gateways conduct the network translation. On most networks, this refers to a router acting as a gateway. However, the gateway might instead operate on a network host. For example, on Windows operating systems, **ICS (Internet Connection Sharing)** can be used to translate network addresses and allow clients to share an Internet connection. Using ICS, a computer with Internet access, called the **ICS host**, is configured to translate requests to and from the Internet on behalf of other computers on the network. To do this, it acts as a DHCP server, DNS resolver, and NAT gateway for clients on its LAN. The ICS host requires two network connections: one that connects to the Internet, which could be dial-up, DSL, ISDN, or broadband cable, and one that connects to the LAN. If the network uses a dial-up connection to the Internet, the ICS host connects to the Internet on demand—that is, when other computers on the network issue a request to the Internet.

When ICS is enabled on a LAN, the network adapter on the ICS host that connects to the LAN is assigned an IP address of 192.168.0.1. Clients on the small office or home office LAN must be set up to obtain IP addresses automatically. The ICS host then assigns clients

2.1

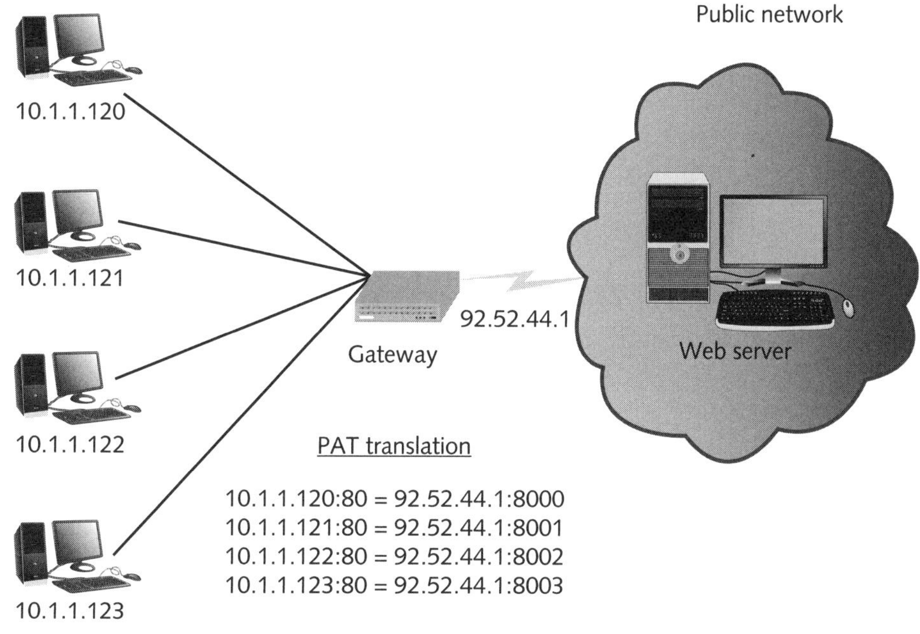

Figure 9-11 PAT (Port Address Translation)

IP addresses in the range of 192.168.0.2 through 192.168.0.254. If you are already using this range of addresses on your network (for example, in a NAT scheme), you might experience problems establishing or using ICS.

When designing a network to share an Internet connection, most network administrators prefer using a router or switch rather than ICS because ICS typically requires more configuration. It also requires the ICS host to be available whenever other computers need Internet access. However, in the unlikely event that a router or switch is not available, ICS is an adequate alternative for sharing an Internet connection among multiple clients.

TCP/IP Mail Services

1.6

As a network administrator, you will need to understand how mail services work so that you can set up and support mail clients or install and configure a mail server.

All Internet mail services rely on the same principles of mail delivery, storage, and pickup, though they may use different types of software to accomplish these functions. You have learned that mail servers communicate with other mail servers to deliver messages across the Internet. They send, receive, and store messages. They may also filter messages according to content, route messages according to configurable conditions such as timing or priority, and make available different types of interfaces for different mail clients. The most popular mail server programs are Sendmail and Microsoft Exchange Server.

1.6

Mail clients send messages to and retrieve messages from mail servers. They may also provide ways of organizing messages (using folders or mailboxes), filter messages according to content or sender information, set message priority, create and use distribution lists, send file attachments, and interpret graphic and HTML content. Hundreds of different types of mail clients exist. Examples of popular mail client software include Thunderbird and Microsoft Outlook. Other mail services, such as Gmail, are Web-based. In that case, the e-mail servers and clients communicate through special TCP/IP Application layer protocols. These protocols, all of which operate on Macintosh, Windows, UNIX, and Linux systems, are discussed in the following sections.

SMTP (Simple Mail Transfer Protocol)

SMTP (Simple Mail Transfer Protocol) is the protocol responsible for moving messages from one mail server to another over TCP/IP-based networks. SMTP belongs to the Application layer of the OSI model and relies on TCP at the Transport layer. It operates from port 25. (That is, requests to receive mail and send mail go through port 25 on the SMTP server.) SMTP, which provides the basis for Internet e-mail service, relies on higher-level programs for its instructions. Although SMTP comes with a set of human-readable (text) commands that you could conceivably use to transport mail from machine to machine, this method would be laborious, slow, and prone to error. Instead, other services, such as the Sendmail software for UNIX and Linux systems, provide more friendly and sophisticated mail interfaces that rely on SMTP as their means of transport.

SMTP is a simple subprotocol, incapable of doing anything more than transporting mail or holding it in a queue. In the post office analogy of data communications, SMTP is like the mail carrier who picks up his day's mail load at the post office and delivers it to the homes on his route. The mail carrier does not worry about where the mail is stored overnight or how it gets from another city's post office to his post office. If a piece of mail is undeliverable, he simply holds onto it; the mail carrier does not attempt to figure out what went wrong. In Internet e-mail transmission, higher-level mail protocols such as POP and IMAP, which are discussed later in this chapter, take care of these functions.

When you configure clients to use e-mail, you need to identify the user's SMTP server. (Sometimes, this server is called the mail server.) Each e-mail program specifies this setting in a different place. Assuming that your client uses DNS, you do not have to identify the IP address of the SMTP server—only the name. For example, if a user's e-mail address is *jdoe@usmail.com,* his SMTP server is probably called *"usmail.com."* You do not have to specify the TCP/IP port number used by SMTP because both the client workstation and the server assume that SMTP requests and responses flow through port 25.

MIME (Multipurpose Internet Mail Extensions)

The standard message format specified by SMTP allows for lines that contain no more than 1000 ASCII characters. That means if you relied solely on SMTP, you couldn't include pictures or even formatted text in an e-mail message. SMTP sufficed for mail transmissions in the early days of the Internet. However, its limitations prompted IEEE to release **MIME (Multipurpose Internet Mail Extensions)** in 1992. MIME is a standard for encoding and interpreting binary files, images, video, and non-ASCII character sets within an e-mail message. MIME identifies each element of a mail message according to content type. Some content types are text, graphics, audio, video, and multipart. The multipart content type indicates that a message contains more than one type of data, for example, some of the message's content is formatted as text, some as a binary file, and some as a graphics file.

MIME does not replace SMTP, but works in conjunction with it. It encodes different content types so that SMTP is fooled into thinking it is transporting an ASCII message stream. Most modern e-mail clients and servers support MIME.

Net+ POP (Post Office Protocol)

1.6 **POP (Post Office Protocol)** is an Application layer protocol used to retrieve messages from a mail server. The most current and commonly used version of the POP protocol is **POP3 (Post Office Protocol, version 3)**, which relies on TCP and operates over port 110. With POP3, mail is delivered and stored on a mail server until a user connects—via an e-mail client—to the server to retrieve his messages. As the user retrieves his messages, the messages are downloaded to his workstation. After they are downloaded, the messages are typically deleted from the mail server. You can think of POP3 as a store-and-forward type of service. Mail is stored on the POP3 server and forwarded to the client on demand. One advantage to using POP3 is that it minimizes the use of server resources because mail is deleted from the server after retrieval. Another advantage is that virtually all mail server and client applications support POP3. However, the fact that POP3 downloads messages rather than keeping them on the server can be a drawback for some users.

POP3's design makes it best suited to users who retrieve their mail from the same workstation all the time. Users who move from machine to machine are at a disadvantage because POP3 does not normally allow users to keep the mail on the server after they retrieve it. Thus, the mail is not accessible from other workstations. For example, suppose a consultant begins his day at his company's office and retrieves his e-mail on the workstation at his desk. Then, he spends the rest of the day at a client's office, where he retrieves messages on his laptop. When he comes home, he checks his e-mail from his home computer. Using POP3, his messages would be stored on three different computers. A few options exist for circumventing this problem (such as downloading messages from the mail server to a file server on a LAN), but a more thorough solution has been provided by a new, more sophisticated e-mail protocol called IMAP, described next.

IMAP (Internet Message Access Protocol)

IMAP (Internet Message Access Protocol) is a mail retrieval protocol that was developed as a more sophisticated alternative to POP3. The most current version of IMAP is version **4**, or, **IMAP4**. IMAP4 can replace POP3 without the user having to change e-mail programs. The single biggest advantage IMAP4 has over POP3 is that users can store messages on the mail server, rather than always having to download them to a local machine. This feature benefits users who may check mail from different workstations. In addition, IMAP4 provides the following features:

- *Users can retrieve all or only a portion of any mail message*—The remainder can be left on the mail server. This feature benefits users who move from machine to machine and users who have slow connections to the network or minimal free hard drive space.
- *Users can review their messages and delete them while the messages remain on the server*—This feature preserves network bandwidth, especially when the messages are long or contain attached files, because the data need not travel over the wire from the

1.6

server to the client's workstation. For users with a slow modem connection, deleting messages without having to download them represents a major advantage over POP3.

- *Users can create sophisticated methods of organizing messages on the server*—A user might, for example, build a system of folders to contain messages with similar content. Also, a user might search through all of the messages for only those that contain one particular keyword or subject line.
- *Users can share a mailbox in a central location*—For example, if several maintenance personnel who use different workstations need to receive the same messages from the Facilities Department head but do not need e-mail for any other purpose, they can all log on with the same ID and share the same mailbox on the server. If POP3 were used in this situation, only one maintenance staff member could read the message; she would then have to forward or copy it to her colleagues.

Although IMAP4 provides significant advantages over POP3, it also comes with a few disadvantages. For instance, IMAP4 servers require more storage space and usually more processing resources than POP servers do. By extension, network managers must keep a closer watch on IMAP4 servers to ensure that users are not consuming more than their fair share of space on the server. In addition, if the IMAP4 server fails, users cannot access the mail left there. IMAP4 does allow users to download messages to their own workstations, however.

Now that you have learned more about e-mail, you are ready to learn about utilities that will help you analyze TCP/IP-based networks.

Additional TCP/IP Utilities

As with any type of communication, many potential points of failure exist in the TCP/IP transmission process, and these points increase with the size of the network and the distance of the transmission. Fortunately, TCP/IP comes with a complete set of utilities that can help you track down most TCP/IP-related problems without using expensive software or hardware to analyze network traffic. You should be familiar with the use of the following tools and their switches, not only because the Network+ certification exam covers them, but also because you will regularly need these diagnostics in your work with TCP/IP networks. Each of the tools described in this section works with systems running IPv4 or IPv6.

In Chapter 4, you learned about three very important TCP/IP utilities—Telnet, ARP, and ping. The following sections present additional TCP/IP utilities that can help you discover information about your node and network. Later, in the Hands-On Projects at the end of this chapter, you'll have an opportunity to try some of these utilities.

Nearly all TCP/IP utilities can be accessed from the command prompt on any type of server or client running TCP/IP. However, the syntax of these commands may differ, depending on your client's operating system. For example, the default command that traces the path of packets from one host to another is known as `traceroute` in UNIX, as `tracepath` in some modern versions of Linux, and as `tracert` in the Windows operating systems. Similarly, the options used with each command may differ according to the operating system. For example, when working on a UNIX or Linux system, you can limit the maximum number of router hops the traceroute command allows by using the `-m` switch. On a Windows-based system, the -h switch accomplishes the same thing. The following sections cover the proper command syntax for Windows, UNIX, and Linux systems.

Net+ Ipconfig

4.3 Earlier in this book, you used the ipconfig utility to determine the TCP/IP configuration of a Windows 7 workstation. Ipconfig is the TCP/IP administration utility for use with Windows operating systems. If you work with these operating systems, you will frequently use this tool to view a computer's TCP/IP settings. Ipconfig is a command-line utility that provides information about a network adapter's IP address, subnet mask, and default gateway.

To use the ipconfig utility from a Windows workstation, for example, click the Start button, point to All Programs, click Accessories, and then click Command Prompt to open the Command Prompt window. At the command prompt, type `ipconfig` and press Enter. You should see TCP/IP information for your computer, similar to the output shown in Figure 9-12. (Actual output will vary depending on the number and type of interfaces on your computer and the type of network to which it's attached.)

```
Administrator: Command Prompt
C:\Windows\system32>ipconfig

Windows IP Configuration


Wireless LAN adapter Wireless Network Connection:

   Media State . . . . . . . . . . . : Media disconnected
   Connection-specific DNS Suffix  . :

Ethernet adapter Local Area Connection:

   Connection-specific DNS Suffix  . :
   Link-local IPv6 Address . . . . . : fe80::a9a7:bda:651f:2799%8
   IPv4 Address. . . . . . . . . . . : 10.11.11.101
   Subnet Mask . . . . . . . . . . . : 255.255.255.0
   Default Gateway . . . . . . . . . : 10.11.11.1

Tunnel adapter Local Area Connection* 7:

   Connection-specific DNS Suffix  . :
   IPv6 Address. . . . . . . . . . . : 2001:0:4137:9e50:34b5:2dc1:f5f4:f49a
   Link-local IPv6 Address . . . . . : fe80::34b5:2dc1:f5f4:f49a%10
   Default Gateway . . . . . . . . . : ::

Tunnel adapter Local Area Connection* 9:

   Media State . . . . . . . . . . . : Media disconnected
   Connection-specific DNS Suffix  . :

Tunnel adapter Local Area Connection* 10:

   Media State . . . . . . . . . . . : Media disconnected
   Connection-specific DNS Suffix  . :

Tunnel adapter Local Area Connection* 11:

   Media State . . . . . . . . . . . : Media disconnected
   Connection-specific DNS Suffix  . :

Tunnel adapter Local Area Connection* 12:

   Connection-specific DNS Suffix  . :
   Link-local IPv6 Address . . . . . : fe80::5efe:10.11.11.101%14
   Default Gateway . . . . . . . . . :

C:\Windows\system32>
```

Figure 9-12 Output of an `ipconfig` command on a Windows workstation

In addition to being used alone to list information about the TCP/IP configuration, the ipconfig utility can be used with switches to manage a computer's TCP/IP settings. For example, if you wanted to view complete information about your TCP/IP settings,

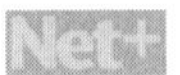
4.3

including your MAC address, subnet mask, when your DHCP lease expires, and so on, you could type: `ipconfig /all`. Note that the syntax of this command differs slightly from other TCP/IP utilities. With `ipconfig`, a forward slash (/) precedes the command switches, rather than a hyphen. The following list describes some popular switches that can be used with the `ipconfig` command:

- `/?`—Displays a list of switches available for use with the `ipconfig` command
- `/all`—Displays complete TCP/IP configuration information for each network interface on that device
- `/release`—Releases DHCP-assigned addresses for all of the device's network interfaces
- `/renew`—Renews DHCP-assigned addresses for all of the device's network interfaces

When using the `ipconfig` command, you must be logged in as an administrator to change your workstation's IP configuration.

Ifconfig

Chapter 4 also introduced you to the ifconfig utility, which is the TCP/IP configuration and management utility used on UNIX and Linux systems. As with ipconfig on Windows systems, ifconfig enables you to modify TCP/IP settings for a network interface, release and renew DHCP-assigned addresses, or simply check the status of your machine's TCP/IP settings. Ifconfig is also a utility that runs when a UNIX or Linux system starts, to establish the TCP/IP configuration for that computer.

Similar to the TCP/IP configuration utilities used with other operating systems, ifconfig can be used alone or with switches to reveal more customized information. For example, if you want to view the TCP/IP information associated with every interface on a device, you could type: `ifconfig -a`. The output would resemble the output shown in Figure 9-13. Notice that the syntax of the `ifconfig` command uses a hyphen (-) before some of the switches and no preceding character for other switches. The following list describes some of the popular switches you can use with `ifconfig`. To view a complete list of options, read the `ifconfig` man pages.

- `-a`—Applies the command to all interfaces on a device; can be used with other switches
- `down`—Marks the interface as unavailable to the network
- `up`—Reinitializes the interface after it has been taken "down," so that it is once again available to the network

Other ifconfig switches, such as those that apply to DHCP settings, vary according to the type and version of the UNIX or Linux system you use.

Netstat

The **netstat** utility displays TCP/IP statistics and details about TCP/IP components and connections on a host. Information that can be obtained from the `netstat` command includes

4.3

```
bill@lab-2 ~ $ ifconfig -a
eth0: flags=4099<UP,BROADCAST,MULTICAST>  mtu 1500  metric 1
        ether 00:21:86:a1:9e:97  txqueuelen 1000  (Ethernet)
        RX packets 840251  bytes 1154908740 (1.0 GiB)
        RX errors 0  dropped 0  overruns 0  frame 0
        TX packets 527337  bytes 52280636 (49.8 MiB)
        TX errors 0  dropped 0 overruns 0  carrier 0  collisions 0
        device interrupt 20  memory 0xfc100000-fc120000

lo: flags=73<UP,LOOPBACK,RUNNING>  mtu 16436  metric 1
        inet 127.0.0.1  netmask 255.0.0.0
        inet6 ::1  prefixlen 128  scopeid 0x10<host>
        loop  txqueuelen 0  (Local Loopback)
        RX packets 517899  bytes 39147630 (37.3 MiB)
        RX errors 0  dropped 0  overruns 0  frame 0
        TX packets 517899  bytes 39147630 (37.3 MiB)
        TX errors 0  dropped 0 overruns 0  carrier 0  collisions 0

sit0: flags=128<NOARP>  mtu 1480  metric 1
        sit  txqueuelen 0  (IPv6-in-IPv4)
        RX packets 0  bytes 0 (0.0 B)
        RX errors 0  dropped 0  overruns 0  frame 0
        TX packets 0  bytes 0 (0.0 B)
        TX errors 0  dropped 0 overruns 0  carrier 0  collisions 0

wlan0: flags=4163<UP,BROADCAST,RUNNING,MULTICAST>  mtu 1500  metric 1
        inet 192.168.1.18  netmask 255.255.255.0  broadcast 192.168.1.255
        inet6 fe80::216:ebff:fe05:86e2  prefixlen 64  scopeid 0x20<link>
        ether 00:16:eb:05:86:e2  txqueuelen 1000  (Ethernet)
        RX packets 572551  bytes 718725120 (685.4 MiB)
        RX errors 0  dropped 0  overruns 0  frame 0
        TX packets 382519  bytes 71994123 (68.6 MiB)
        TX errors 0  dropped 0 overruns 0  carrier 0  collisions 0

bill@lab-2 ~ $
```

Figure 9-13 Detailed information available through ifconfig

the port on which a particular TCP/IP service is running, regardless of whether a remote node is logged on to a host; which network connections are currently established for a client; how many packets have been handled by a network interface since it was activated; and how many data errors have occurred on a particular network interface. As you can imagine, with so much information available, the netstat utility makes a powerful diagnostic tool.

For example, suppose you are a network administrator in charge of maintaining file, print, Web, and Internet servers for an organization. You discover that your Web server, which has multiple processors, sufficient hard disk space, and multiple NICs, is suddenly taking twice as long to respond to HTTP requests. Of course, you would want to check the server's memory resources as well as its Web server software to determine that nothing is wrong with either of those. In addition, you can use the netstat utility to determine the characteristics of the traffic going into and out of each NIC. You may discover that one network card is consistently handling 80 percent of the traffic, even though you had configured the server to share traffic equally among the two. This fact may lead you to run hardware diagnostics on the NIC, and perhaps discover that its on-board processor has failed, making it much slower than the other NIC. Netstat provides a quick way to view traffic statistics, without having to run a more complex traffic analysis program, such as Wireshark.

If you use the `netstat` command without any switches, it will display a list of all the active TCP/IP connections on your machine, including the Transport layer protocol used (UDP or TCP), packets sent and received, IP address, and state of those connections.

4.3 However, like other TCP/IP commands, `netstat` can be used with a number of different switches. A `netstat` command begins with the word `netstat` followed by a space, then a hyphen and a switch, followed by a variable pertaining to that switch, if required. For example, `netstat -a` displays all current TCP and UDP connections from the issuing device to other devices on the network, as well as the source and destination service ports. The `netstat -r` command allows you to display the routing table on a given machine. The following list describes some of the most common switches used with the netstat utility:

- `-a`—Provides a list of all available TCP and UDP connections, even if they are simply listening and not currently exchanging data
- `-e`—Displays details about all the packets that have been sent over a network interface
- `-n`—Lists currently connected hosts according to their port and IP address (in numerical form)
- `-p`—Allows you to specify what type of protocol statistics to list; this switch must be followed by a protocol specification (TCP or UDP)
- `-r`—Provides a list of routing table information
- `-s`—Provides statistics about each packet transmitted by a host, separated according to protocol type (IP, TCP, UDP, or ICMP)

Figure 9-14 illustrates the output of a `netstat -a` command.

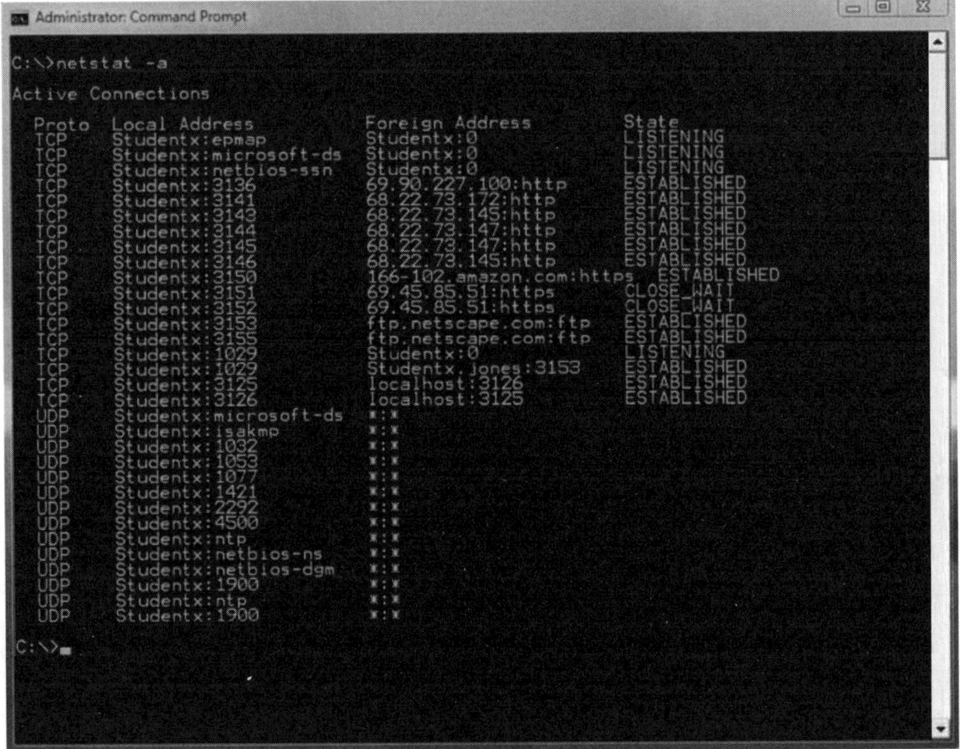

Figure 9-14 Output of a `netstat -a` command

Net+ Nbtstat

4.3 **NetBIOS** is a protocol that runs in the Session and Transport layers of the OSI model and associates NetBIOS names with workstations. NetBIOS alone is not routable because it does not contain Network layer information. However, when encapsulated in another protocol such as TCP/IP, it can be routed. On networks that run NetBIOS over TCP/IP, the **nbtstat** utility can provide information about NetBIOS statistics and resolve NetBIOS names to their IP addresses. In other words, if you know the NetBIOS name of a workstation, you can use nbtstat to determine its IP address.

Nbtstat is useful only on networks that run Windows-based operating systems and NetBIOS. UNIX and Linux systems do not use NetBIOS, so nbtstat is not useful on these computers. Since most networks run pure TCP/IP (and not NetBIOS over TCP/IP), nbtstat has limited use as a TCP/IP diagnostic utility.

As with netstat, nbtstat offers a variety of switches that you can use to tailor the output of the command. For example, you can type `nbtstat-A ip_address` to determine what machine is registered to a given IP address. The following list details popular switches used with the `nbtstat` command. Notice that they are case sensitive; the `-a` switch has a different meaning than the `-A` switch.

- `-a`—Displays a machine's name table given its NetBIOS name; the name of the machine must be supplied after the `-a` switch
- `-A`—Displays a machine's name table given its IP address; the IP address of the machine must be supplied after the `-A` switch
- `-r`—Lists statistics about names that have been resolved to IP addresses by broadcast and by WINS; this switch is useful for determining whether a workstation is resolving names properly or for determining whether WINS is operating correctly
- `-s`—Displays a list of all the current NetBIOS sessions for a machine; when used with this switch, the `nbtstat` command attempts to resolve IP addresses to NetBIOS names in the listing; if the machine has no current NetBIOS connections, the result of this command will indicate that fact

Hostname, Host, and Nslookup

In Chapter 4, you learned that each client on a network is identified by a host name. If you aren't sure what host name has been assigned to a client, you can discover it by using the **hostname** utility. At the command prompt of a computer running a Windows, UNIX, or Linux operating system, type `hostname` and then press Enter. The utility responds with the client's host name. If you have administrator privileges on a client, you may also use the hostname utility to change its host name as follows: type `hostname` *`new_hostname`*, where *`new_hostname`* is the name you want to assign to the host, and then press Enter.

If you already know a host's name and want to learn its IP address, you can use the **host** utility. When used without any switches, host simply returns either the IP address of a host if its host name is specified or its host name if its IP address is specified. For example, on a Linux workstation, you can type `/usr/bin/host www.cengage.com` and press Enter to discover the IP address associated with the host whose name is `www.cengage.com`. Or, you could type `/usr/bin/host 69.32.133.79` and press Enter to discover that the host name associated with this IP address is *www.cengage.com.* The host command comes with Linux and UNIX distributions. If your computer uses a Windows operating system, you'll need to download a third-party version of host.

4.3

A utility that is similar to host but has more flexibility is nslookup. **Nslookup** allows you to query the DNS database from any computer on the network and find the host name of a device by specifying its IP address, or vice versa. This ability is useful for verifying that a host is configured correctly or for troubleshooting DNS resolution problems. For example, if you wanted to find out whether the host whose name is *www.cengage.com* is operational, you could type: `nslookup www.cengage.com` and press Enter. Figure 9-15 shows the result of running a simple `nslookup` command at a Linux shell prompt.

Notice that the command provides not only the host's IP address, but also the primary DNS server name and address that holds the record for this name. To find the host name of a device whose IP address you know, type: `nslookup` *`ip_address`* and press Enter. In this case, the response would include not only the host name for that device, but also its IP address and the IP address and host name of its primary DNS server.

```
bill@lab-2 ~ $ nslookup www.cengage.com
Server:         127.0.0.1
Address:        127.0.0.1#53

Non-authoritative answer:
www.cengage.com canonical name = cengage.com.
Name:   cengage.com
Address: 69.32.133.79

bill@lab-2 ~ $ 
```

Figure 9-15 Output of a simple `nslookup` command

Nslookup can reveal much more than just the IP address or host name of a device. Typing just `nslookup` (without any switches), and then pressing Enter starts the nslookup utility, and the command prompt changes to a `>`. You can then use additional commands to find out more about the contents of the DNS database. For example, on a computer running UNIX you could view a list of all the host name and IP address correlations on a particular DNS server by typing `ls`. Or you could specify five seconds as the period to wait for a response by typing `timeout=5`. (The default is 10 seconds.) Many other nslookup options exist. On a UNIX or Linux system, you can find the complete list of the nslookup options in the nslookup man pages. On a Windows-based system, you can view them by typing `nslookup ?` at the command prompt. To exit the nslookup utility and return to the normal command prompt, type `exit`.

Dig

A TCP/IP utility similar to nslookup is **dig**, which stands for **domain information groper**. As with nslookup, dig allows you to query a DNS database and find the host name associated with a specific IP address or vice versa. Also similar to nslookup, dig is useful for helping network administrators diagnose DNS problems. However, both in its simplest form and when used with one or more of its multiple switches, the dig utility can provide more detailed information than nslookup. An example of a simple dig command is `dig www.cengage.com`, the output of which is shown in Figure 9-16. Compare this output to the simple nslookup command

4.3 output shown in Figure 9-15. Whereas the simple nslookup command returned the IP address for the host name, the simple dig command returned specifics about the resource records associated with the host name *www.cengage.com*. The domain name is in the first column, followed by the record's Time to Live, then its type code (for example, A for an address record or MX for a mail record), and finally, a data field indicating the IP address or other domain name with which the primary domain name is associated. A summary of this particular query, including the time it took for the `dig` command to return the data, is shown at the bottom of the output.

```
bill@lab-2 ~ $ dig www.cengage.com

; <<>> DiG 9.8.1 <<>> www.cengage.com
;; global options: +cmd
;; Got answer:
;; ->>HEADER<<- opcode: QUERY, status: NOERROR, id: 13502
;; flags: qr rd ra; QUERY: 1, ANSWER: 2, AUTHORITY: 6, ADDITIONAL: 0

;; QUESTION SECTION:
;www.cengage.com.               IN      A

;; ANSWER SECTION:
www.cengage.com.        5       IN      CNAME   cengage.com.
cengage.com.            5       IN      A       69.32.133.79

;; AUTHORITY SECTION:
cengage.com.            5       IN      NS      whindsns6.ohcinmason.com.
cengage.com.            5       IN      NS      tlauns3.ohcinmason.com.
cengage.com.            5       IN      NS      tlauns5.ohcinmason.com.
cengage.com.            5       IN      NS      dns4.gale.com.
cengage.com.            5       IN      NS      tlauns4.ohcinmason.com.
cengage.com.            5       IN      NS      dns3.gale.com.

;; Query time: 0 msec
;; SERVER: 127.0.0.1#53(127.0.0.1)
;; WHEN: Wed Jan  4 17:23:39 2013
;; MSG SIZE  rcvd: 207

bill@lab-2 ~ $
```

Figure 9-16 Output of a simple `dig` command

The dig utility comes with over two dozen switches, making it much more flexible than nslookup. For example, in a `dig` command you can specify the DNS server to query and the type of DNS record(s) for which you want to search, a timeout period for the query, a port (other than the default port 53) on the DNS server to query, and many other options. Look for the complete list of dig command switches and the syntax needed to use each in the dig man pages. The dig utility is included with UNIX and Linux operating systems. If your computer runs a Windows-based operating system, however, you must obtain the code for the dig utility from a third party and install it on your system.

Traceroute (Tracert)

Suppose you work in technical support for a large company and one afternoon you receive calls from several employees complaining about slow Internet connections. With only that knowledge, you can't say whether the problem lies with your company's LAN (for example, a workgroup or backbone switch or router), default gateway, WAN connection, your service provider's CO, or a major ISP. However, simply by using one of the commands listed in this section, you can better assess where network performance is degraded.

Net+ 4.3

The **traceroute** utility (known as **tracert** on Windows-based systems and **tracepath** on some Linux systems) uses ICMP ECHO requests to trace the path from one networked node to another, identifying all intermediate hops between the two nodes. To find the route, the traceroute utility transmits a series of UDP datagrams to a specified destination, using either the IP address or the host name to identify the destination. The first three datagrams that traceroute transmits have their TTL (Time to Live) set to 1. Because the TTL determines how many more network hops a datagram can make, datagrams with a TTL of 1 expire as they hit the first router. When they expire, they are returned to the source—in this case, the node that began the traceroute. In this way, traceroute obtains the identity of the first router. After it learns about the first router in the path, traceroute transmits a series of datagrams with a TTL of 2. The process continues for the next router in the path, and then the third, fourth, and so on, until the destination node is reached. Traceroute also returns the amount of time it took for the datagrams to reach each router in the path.

A traceroute test might stop before reaching the destination, however. This happens for one of two reasons: Either the device that traceroute is attempting to reach is down, or it does not accept ICMP transmissions. The latter is usually the case with firewalls. Therefore, if you are trying to trace a route to a host situated behind a firewall, your efforts will be thwarted. (Because ping uses ICMP transmissions, the same limitations exist for that utility.) Furthermore, traceroute cannot detect router configuration problems or detect whether a router uses different send and receive interfaces. In addition, routers might not decrement the TTL value correctly at each stop in the path. Therefore, traceroute is best used on a network with which you are already familiar. If you are reasonably certain that devices in the path between your host and a destination host do not block ICMP transmissions, traceroute can help you diagnose network congestion or network failures. You can then use your judgment and experience to compare the actual test results with what you anticipate the results should be.

The simplest form of the `traceroute` command (on a UNIX or Linux system) is `traceroute` *`ip_address`* or `traceroute` *`host_name`*. On some versions of Linux, it's `tracepath` *`ip_address`* or `tracepath` *`host_name`*. On computers that use a Windows-based operating system, the proper syntax is `tracert` *`ip_address`* or `tracert` *`host_name`*.

When run on a UNIX system, the command will return a list as shown in Figure 9-17. Tracert and tracepath output looks virtually identical.

```
Terminal
bill@lab-3 ~ $ traceroute www.cengage.com
traceroute to www.cengage.com (69.32.133.79), 30 hops max, 60 byte packets
 1  209.59.211.51 (209.59.211.51)  0.054 ms  0.042 ms  0.038 ms
 2  * * *
 3  * * *
 4  te0-0-0-7.ccr22.bos01.atlas.cogentco.com (38.97.106.33)  0.515 ms  0.533 ms *
 5  * * *
 6  * te0-1-0-7.ccr22.ord03.atlas.cogentco.com (154.54.1.98)  23.356 ms te0-0-0-1.ccr22.ord03.atlas.
cogentco.com (154.54.29.18)  23.353 ms
 7  sprint.ord03.atlas.cogentco.com (154.54.10.38)  23.785 ms  24.318 ms  24.294 ms
 8  sl-timewarner-369661-0.sprintlink.net (144.223.14.202)  33.893 ms  33.931 ms  34.294 ms
 9  * * *
10  * * *
11  * * tluser.thomsonlearning.com (69.32.128.159)  39.705 ms
12  * * *
13  itp3-132-09.thomsonlearning.com (69.32.132.9)  39.989 ms  39.976 ms *
14  * * *
15  itp3-132-09.thomsonlearning.com (69.32.132.9)  39.955 ms !H  1741.002 ms !H  39.969 ms !H
bill@lab-3 ~ $
```

Figure 9-17 Output of a `traceroute` command

Net+ 4.3 As with other TCP/IP commands, `traceroute` has a number of switches that may be used with the command. The command begins with either `traceroute`, `tracert`, or `tracepath` (depending on the operating system your computer uses), followed by a hyphen, a switch, and a variable pertaining to a particular switch, if required. For example, on a Windows-based system, `tracert -4` forces the utility to use only IPv4 transmission. The following list describes some of the popular tracert switches:

- `-d`—Instructs the `tracert` command not to resolve IP addresses to host names
- `-h`—Specifies the maximum number of hops the packets should take when attempting to reach a host (the default is 30); this switch must be followed by a specific number of hops (for example, `tracert -h 12` would indicate a maximum of 12 hops)
- `-w`—Identifies a timeout period for responses; this switch must be followed by a variable to indicate the number of milliseconds the utility should wait for a response

Mtr (my traceroute)

Mtr (my traceroute) is a route discovery and analysis utility that comes with UNIX and Linux operating systems. It combines the functions of the ping and traceroute utilities and delivers an easy-to-read chart as its output. By issuing the `mtr` command, you instruct your computer to first determine the path between your client and the host you specify, and then successively send ICMP ECHO requests to every hop on the route. In return, you learn about the devices in the path and whether and how promptly they respond. After letting the command run for a while, you also learn the devices' shortest, longest, and average response times and the extent of packet loss for each hop. This can reveal what portions of a network are suffering poor performance or even faults.

The simplest form of the `mtr` command is `mtr` *`ip_address`* or `mtr` *`host_name`*. After you enter the command, `mtr` will run continuously until you stop it by pressing Ctrl+C or unless you add an option to the command to limit its number of probes.

As you might guess, `mtr` can be used with a number of switches to refine the command's functioning and output. The command begins with `mtr`, followed by a hyphen, a switch, and a variable pertaining to a particular switch, if required. For example, entering `mtr -c 2` limits the number of ICMP ECHO requests to two. The following list defines some mtr switches:

- `-c`—Specifies how many ICMP ECHO requests to issue (in this case, *c* stands for count).
- `-r`—Used with the `-c` switch, `-r` instructs `mtr` to generate a report and then exit after a certain number of probes.
- `-n`—Instructs `mtr` to not use DNS—that is, to display only IP addresses and not host names.
- `-i`—Used with a specific number of seconds to specify the period of time between ICMP ECHO requests; the default value is one second.

Figure 9-18 illustrates the output of the command `mtr -c 100 -r www.cengage.com`. In other words, an `mtr` command that will send 100 ICMP ECHO requests along the path to the host *www.cengage.com* and will issue the results in report format. Notice that the "Snt" column displays the quantity of ICMP ECHO requests sent.

HOST: Work_1	Loss%	Snt	Last	Avg	Best	Wrst	StDev
1. my.office.com	0.0%	100	1.4	1.3	0.8	2.6	0.4
2. adsl-12-34-56-254.dsl.chcgil.net	0.0%	100	9.5	9.6	8.8	11.5	0.5
3. dist1-vlan62.chcgil.sbcglobal.net	5.0%	100	9.4	9.6	8.8	12.0	0.5
4. bb1-g7-0.chcgil.ameritech.net	0.0%	100	10.3	28.7	8.5	210.0	45.3
5. ex2-p1-0.eqchil.sbcglobal.net	0.0%	100	9.3	25.1	8.8	222.2	47.8
6. asn209-qwest.eqchil.sbcglobal.net	0.0%	100	9.2	31.2	9.0	266.5	55.6
7. cer-core-01.inet.qwest.net	3.0%	100	9.7	10.8	9.0	26.5	3.1
8. jfk-edge-23.inet.qwest.net	0.0%	100	32.1	32.3	31.1	35.0	0.6
9. 65.115.48.146	0.0%	100	71.1	72.5	69.1	261.4	19.4
10. academic.cengage.com	0.0%	100	70.0	70.3	69.4	73.0	0.6

Figure 9-18 Output of the `mtr` command

Bear in mind that, as with traceroute, mtr results might be misleading if certain devices on the network are prevented from responding to ICMP traffic. Even if a router does accept ICMP traffic, it will likely assign such requests lowest priority. A small percentage of packet loss in the middle of a route might merely reflect the fact that a router is busy and therefore slower at handling less-important traffic. In addition, beware that mtr generates a significant amount of traffic on a network. By running the mtr utility, you might slow network performance.

A program similar to mtr, **pathping**, is available as a command-line utility in Windows operating systems. The switches available for use with `pathping` are similar to those available with `mtr`. However, the `pathping` output differs slightly. `Pathping` displays the path first, then issues hundreds of ICMP ECHO requests before revealing any reply or packet loss statistics.

Net+

Route

1.4 In Chapter 6, you learned that a routing table is a file on a networked host (for example, a
2.1 workstation or router) that contains information about the paths that data will take between
4.3 that host and other network nodes. When a client or connectivity device is added to a network, it discovers best paths and adds them to its routing table. You also learned that in dynamic routing, routers gather information about the network and incorporate that information in their routing tables even as the network changes.

The **route** utility allows you to view a host's routing table. On a UNIX or Linux system, type `route` and then press Enter at the command prompt to view the routing table. On a Windows-based system, type `route print` and then press Enter. On a Cisco-brand router or another brand that uses Cisco command conventions, type `show ip route` and press Enter. Routing tables on network clients typically have no more than a few unique entries, including the default gateway and loopback address. However, routing tables on Internet backbone routers, such as those operated by ISPs, maintain hundreds of thousands of entries.

The routing table in Figure 9-19 is an example of one that might be found on a UNIX host.

1.4
2.1
4.3

```
Kernel IP routing table
Destination       Gateway        Genmask          Flags Metric Ref Use   Iface
223.37.128.0      0.0.0.0        255.255.255.0     U      0     0  4580  eth0
127.0.0.1         0.0.0.0        255.0.0.0         U      0     0  1360  lo
0.0.0.0           223.37.128.1   0.0.0.0           UG     0     0  3780  eth0
```

Figure 9-19 Sample routing table

Table 9-7 explains the fields belonging to routing tables on UNIX or Linux systems. The `route print` command used on a computer running a Windows operating system does not provide as much information and displays it in a different format.

Table 9-7 Fields in routing table on a UNIX host

Destination	The destination host's identity
Gateway	The destination host's gateway
Genmask	The destination host's netmask number
Flags	Additional information about the route, including whether it's usable (U), whether it's a gateway (G), and whether, as is the case with the loopback entry, only a single host can be reached via that route (H)
Metric	The cost of the route—that is, how efficiently it carries traffic
Ref	The number of references to the route that exist—that is, the number of routes that rely on this route
Use	The number of packets that have traversed the route
Iface	The type of interface the route uses

In fact, the `route` command allows you to do much more than simply view a host's routing table. With it you may also add, delete, or modify routes. Following are some options available for use with the route command:

- `add`—Adds a route to the routing table; this switch must be followed by information about the route, for example, `route add default gw 123.45.67.1 ethl` instructs the host to add a route that uses the gateway with an address of 123.45.67.1 on the eth1 interface.
- `del`—Deletes a route from the routing table; this option must be followed by information about the route.
- `change`—Changes an existing route; this switch must be followed by information about the route to be changed (available on Windows systems only).
- `-p`—Makes a route persistent, or reappear after a system is restarted (available on Windows systems only).

To learn about more `route` command options and the correct syntax for each, type `man route` and press Enter on a UNIX or Linux system. On a Windows system, type `route ?`
1.4
2.1 and press Enter.

4.3 Most routers and other types of hosts optimize their routing tables without human intervention. If you choose to modify a routing table, be careful to not eliminate or damage a necessary route or cause routing loops. You risk degrading network performance or even cutting off network access to some or all clients.

Chapter Summary

- Subnetting separates one network or segment into multiple logically defined segments, or subnets. A network administrator might subnet a network to achieve simpler troubleshooting, enhanced security, improved performance, and easier network management.
- A subnet mask provides clues about the location of network information in an IP address. Bits in a subnet mask that equal 1 indicate that corresponding bits in an IP address contain network information. Bits in a subnet mask that equal 0 indicate that corresponding bits in an IP address contain host information.
- To create subnets, some of an IP address's bits (which by default represent host information) are changed to represent network information instead. The change is indicated by a change in the subnet mask's bits.
- If you use subnetting on your LAN, only your LAN's devices need to interpret your devices' subnetting information. External routers, such as those on the Internet, pay attention to only the network portion of your devices' IP addresses—not their subnet masks—when transmitting data to them.
- A newer variation on traditional subnetting is provided by CIDR (Classless Interdomain Routing). CIDR offers additional ways of arranging network and host information in an IP address. In CIDR, conventional network class distinctions do not exist.
- CIDR allows the creation of supernets, or subnets established by using bits that normally would be reserved for network class information. By moving the subnet boundary to the left, more bits are made available for host information, thus increasing the number of usable host addresses on a subnetted network.
- Subnetting in IPv6 is simple. In every unicast address, the last four blocks, which equate to the last 64 bits, identify the interface. (On many IPv6 networks, those 64 bits are based on the interface's EUI-64 MAC address.) The first four blocks indicate the 64-bit subnet prefix. For example, in the IPv6 address 2608:FE10:1:A:002:50FF:FE2B:E708, the subnet prefix is 2608:FE10:1:A and the interface ID is 002:50FF:FE2B:E708.
- Besides subdividing IPv6 interfaces according to subnet, IPv6 enables network administrators to more generally group interfaces that belong to the same route by specifying a route prefix. Because route prefixes vary in length, slash notation is necessary when defining them.
- Gateways facilitate communication between different subnets. Because one device on the network cannot send data directly to a device on another subnet, a gateway (usually in the form of a router interface) must intercede and hand off the information.

- Every device on a TCP/IP-based network has a default gateway, the gateway that first interprets its outbound requests to other subnets, and then interprets its inbound requests from other subnets.
- Internet gateways maintain default routes to known addresses to expedite data transfer. The gateways that make up the Internet backbone are called core gateways.
- NAT (Network Address Translation) allows a network administrator to "hide" IP addresses assigned to nodes on a private network. In NAT, gateways assign transmissions valid Internet IP addresses when the transmission is sent to the Internet.
- SNAT (Static Network Address Translation) establishes a one-to-one correlation between each private IP address and Internet-recognized IP address.
- DNAT (Dynamic Network Address Translation) allows one or more Internet-recognized IP addresses to be shared by multiple clients. To achieve this type of address translation, a gateway assigns ports to each client's sessions, in a technique known as PAT (Port Address Translation). This is the most common type of address translation on small office and home networks.
- ICS (Internet Connection Sharing) is a service included with Windows operating systems that allows a network of computers to share a single Internet connection through an ICS host computer.
- All Internet mail services rely on the same principles of mail delivery, storage, and pickup, though they may use different types of software to accomplish these functions.
- Mail client software can communicate with various types of mail server software because the TCP/IP Application layer protocols used for this communication are standard.
- SMTP (Simple Mail Transfer Protocol) is responsible for moving messages from one e-mail server to another over TCP/IP-based networks. SMTP operates through port 25, with requests to receive mail and send mail going through that port on the SMTP server. SMTP is used in conjunction with either POP or IMAP. MIME operates over SMTP to enable mail messages to contain non-ASCII content, such as graphics, audio, video, and binary files. Most modern e-mail clients support MIME encoding.
- POP (Post Office Protocol) is a mail retrieval protocol. The most current and commonly used version of POP is called POP3. Using POP3, messages are downloaded from the mail server to a client workstation each time the user retrieves messages.
- IMAP (Internet Message Access Protocol) is another mail retrieval protocol. Its most current version is IMAP4. IMAP4 differs from POP3 in that it allows users to store messages on the mail server, rather than always having to download them to the local machine. This is an advantage for users who do not always check mail from the same computer.
- Typing `ipconfig` at the command prompt of a system running a Windows operating system reveals the TCP/IP settings for that computer.
- Ifconfig is the utility that establishes and allows management of TCP/IP settings on a UNIX or Linux system.
- The netstat utility displays TCP/IP statistics and the state of current TCP/IP components and connections. It also displays ports, which can signal whether services are using the correct ports.

- The nbtstat utility provides information about NetBIOS names and their addresses. If you know the NetBIOS name of a workstation, you can use nbtstat to determine the workstation's IP address.
- The hostname utility allows you to view or change a client's host name.
- The host utility, which comes with Linux and UNIX operating systems, allows you to find out either the host name of a node given its IP address or the IP address of a node given its host name.
- The nslookup utility is a more flexible version of the host utility. It allows you to look up the DNS host name of a network node by specifying the node's IP address, or vice versa. Nslookup is useful for troubleshooting host configuration and DNS resolution problems.
- The dig utility, similar to nslookup, queries the network's DNS database to return information about a host given its IP address, or vice versa. In its simplest form, or when used with one of its many switches, dig provides more information than nslookup.
- The traceroute utility, known as tracert on Windows-based systems and tracepath on some Linux systems, uses ICMP to trace the path from one networked node to another, identifying all intermediate hops between the two nodes. This utility is useful for determining router or subnet connectivity problems.
- Mtr is a TCP/IP utility that combines the functions of traceroute and ping to reveal not only the path data takes between two hosts, but also statistics about the path, such as how promptly router interfaces respond and the extent of packet loss at each hop.
- The route command allows you to view a host's routing table and add, delete, or modify preferred routes.

Key Terms

ANDing A logical process of combining bits. In ANDing, a bit with a value of 1 plus another bit with a value of 1 results in a 1. A bit with a value of 0 plus any other bit results in a 0.

CIDR (Classless Interdomain Routing) An IP addressing and subnetting method in which network and host information is manipulated without adhering to the limitations imposed by traditional network class distinctions. CIDR is also known as classless routing or supernetting. Older routing protocols, such as RIP, are not capable of interpreting CIDR addressing schemes.

CIDR block In CIDR notation, the number of bits used for an extended network prefix. For example, the CIDR block for 199.34.89.0/22 is /22.

CIDR notation In CIDR, a method of denoting network IDs and their subnet boundaries. Slash notation takes the form of the network ID followed by a slash (/), followed by the number of bits that are used for the extended network prefix.

classful addressing An IP addressing convention that adheres to network class distinctions, in which the first 8 bits of a Class A address, the first 16 bits of a Class B address, and the first 24 bits of a Class C address are used for network information.

Classless Interdomain Routing *See* CIDR.

classless routing *See* CIDR.

core gateway A gateway that operates on the Internet backbone.

default gateway The gateway that first interprets a device's outbound requests, and then interprets its inbound requests to and from other subnets. In a Postal Service analogy, the default gateway is similar to a local post office.

default router *See* default gateway.

dig (domain information groper) A TCP/IP utility that queries the DNS database and provides information about a host given its IP address or vice versa. Dig is similar to the nslookup utility, but provides more information, even in its simplest form, than nslookup can.

DNAT (Dynamic Network Address Translation) A type of address translation in which a limited pool of Internet-valid IP addresses is shared by multiple private network hosts.

domain information groper *See* dig.

Dynamic Network Address Translation *See* DNAT.

extended network prefix The combination of an IP address's network ID and subnet information. By interpreting the address's extended network prefix, a device can determine the subnet to which an address belongs.

host A TCP/IP utility that at its simplest returns either the IP address of a host if its host name is specified or its host name if its IP address is specified.

hostname A TCP/IP utility used to show or modify a client's host name.

ICS (Internet Connection Sharing) A service provided with Windows operating systems that allows one computer, the ICS host, to share its Internet connection with other computers on the same network.

ICS host On a network using the Microsoft Internet Connection Sharing service, the computer whose Internet connection other computers share. The ICS host must contain two network interfaces: one that connects to the Internet and one that connects to the LAN.

IMAP (Internet Message Access Protocol) A mail retrieval protocol that improves on the shortcomings of POP. The single biggest advantage IMAP4 has relative to POP is that it allows users to store messages on the mail server, rather than always having to download them to the local machine. The most current version of IMAP is version 4 (IMAP4).

IMAP4 (Internet Message Access Protocol, version 4) The most commonly used form of the Internet Message Access Protocol (IMAP).

Internet Connection Sharing *See* ICS.

Internet Message Access Protocol *See* IMAP.

Internet Message Access Protocol, version 4 *See* IMAP4.

IP masquerading *See* DNAT.

MIME (Multipurpose Internet Mail Extensions) A standard for encoding and interpreting binary files, images, video, and non-ASCII character sets within an e-mail message.

mtr (my traceroute) A route discovery and analysis utility that comes with UNIX and Linux operating systems. Mtr combines the functions of the ping and traceroute commands and delivers an easily readable chart as its output.

Multipurpose Internet Mail Extensions *See* MIME.

my traceroute *See* mtr.

NAT (Network Address Translation) A technique in which IP addresses used on a private network are assigned a public IP address by a gateway when accessing a public network.

nbtstat A TCP/IP troubleshooting utility that provides information about NetBIOS names and their addresses. If you know the NetBIOS name of a workstation, you can use nbtstat to determine its IP address.

NetBIOS A protocol that runs in the Session and Transport layers of the OSI model and associates NetBIOS names with workstations. NetBIOS alone is not routable because it does not contain Network layer information. However, when encapsulated in another protocol such as TCP/IP, it can be routed.

netstat A TCP/IP troubleshooting utility that displays statistics and the state of current TCP/IP connections. It also displays ports, which can signal whether services are using the correct ports.

Network Address Translation *See* NAT.

network number *See* network ID.

network prefix *See* network ID.

nslookup A TCP/IP utility that allows you to look up the DNS host name of a network node by specifying its IP address, or vice versa. This ability is useful for verifying that a host is configured correctly and for troubleshooting DNS resolution problems.

PAT (Port Address Translation) A form of address translation that uses TCP port numbers to distinguish each client's transmission, thus allowing multiple clients to share a limited number of Internet-recognized IP addresses.

pathping A command-line utility that combines the functionality of the tracert and ping commands (similar to UNIX's mtr command) and comes with Windows operating systems.

POP (Post Office Protocol) An Application layer protocol used to retrieve messages from a mail server. When a client retrieves mail via POP, messages previously stored on the mail server are downloaded to the client's workstation, and then deleted from the mail server.

POP3 (Post Office Protocol, version 3) The most commonly used form of the Post Office Protocol.

Port Address Translation *See* PAT.

Post Office Protocol *See* POP.

Post Office Protocol, version 3 *See* POP3.

private network A network whose access is restricted to only clients or machines with proper credentials.

public network A network that any user can access with no restrictions. The most familiar example of a public network is the Internet.

route A utility for viewing or modifying a host's routing table.

route prefix The prefix in an IPv6 address that identifies a route. Because route prefixes vary in length, slash notation is used to define them. For example, the route prefix indicated by 2608:FE10::/32 includes all subnets whose prefixes begin with 2608:FE10 and, consequently, all interfaces whose IP addresses begin with 2608:FE10.

Simple Mail Transfer Protocol *See* SMTP.

slash notation *See* CIDR notation.

SMTP (Simple Mail Transfer Protocol) The Application layer TCP/IP subprotocol responsible for moving messages from one e-mail server to another.

SNAT (Static Network Address Translation) A type of address translation in which each private IP address is correlated with its own Internet-recognized IP address.

Static Network Address Translation *See* SNAT.

subnet prefix The 64-bit prefix in an IPv6 address that identifies a subnet. A single IPv6 subnet is capable of supplying 18,446,744,073,709,551,616 IPv6 addresses.

supernet In IPv4, a type of subnet that is created by moving the subnet boundary to the left and using bits that normally would be reserved for network class information.

supernet mask A 32-bit number that, when combined with a device's IPv4 address, indicates the kind of supernet to which the device belongs.

supernetting *See* CIDR.

tracepath A version of the traceroute utility found on some Linux distributions.

traceroute (tracert) A TCP/IP troubleshooting utility that uses ICMP to trace the path from one networked node to another, identifying all intermediate hops between the two nodes. Traceroute is useful for determining router or subnet connectivity problems. On Windows-based systems, the utility is known as tracert.

Review Questions

1. What is a disadvantage of classful addressing?
   a. security
   b. poor performance
   c. troubleshooting mechanisms
   d. network traffic separation
2. Which term describes an IP address that cannot be assigned to a network interface on a node or used as subnet mask?
   a. host ID
   b. MAC ID
   c. router ID
   d. network ID
3. Which term describes a network that any user may access with little or no restrictions?
   a. open source
   b. public
   c. proprietary
   d. private

4. Which mail retrieval protocol allows users to store messages on the mail server, rather than always having to download them to the local machine?
   a. SMTP (Simple Mail Transfer Protocol)
   b. IMAP (Internet Message Access Protocol)
   c. POP (Post Office Protocol)
   d. MIME

5. Which Windows command is used to reveal a computer's TCP/IP settings?
   a. `ifconfig`
   b. `ipconfig`
   c. `nbtstat`
   d. `nslookup`

6. True or false? In classful addressing, only Class A and Class B addresses are recognized.

7. True or false? Class A, Class B, and Class C networks can all be subnetted.

8. True or false? The ipconfig utility is the TCP/IP configuration and management utility used on UNIX and Linux systems.

9. True or false? If you know the NetBIOS name of a workstation, you can use `nbtstat` to determine its IP address.

10. True or false? The `route` utility traces the path from one networked node to another, identifying all intermediate hops between the two nodes.

11. ________________ separates a network into multiple logically defined segments, or subnets.

12. ________________ is an IP addressing and subnetting method in which network and host information is manipulated without adhering to the limitations imposed by traditional network class distinctions.

13. The ________________ process occurs when the client's transmission reaches the default gateway, the gateway opens the IP datagram and replaces the client's private IP address with an Internet-recognized IP address.

14. ________________ can be used to translate network addresses and allow clients to share an Internet connection.

15. ________________ is a standard for encoding and interpreting binary files, images, video, and non-ASCII character sets within an e-mail message.

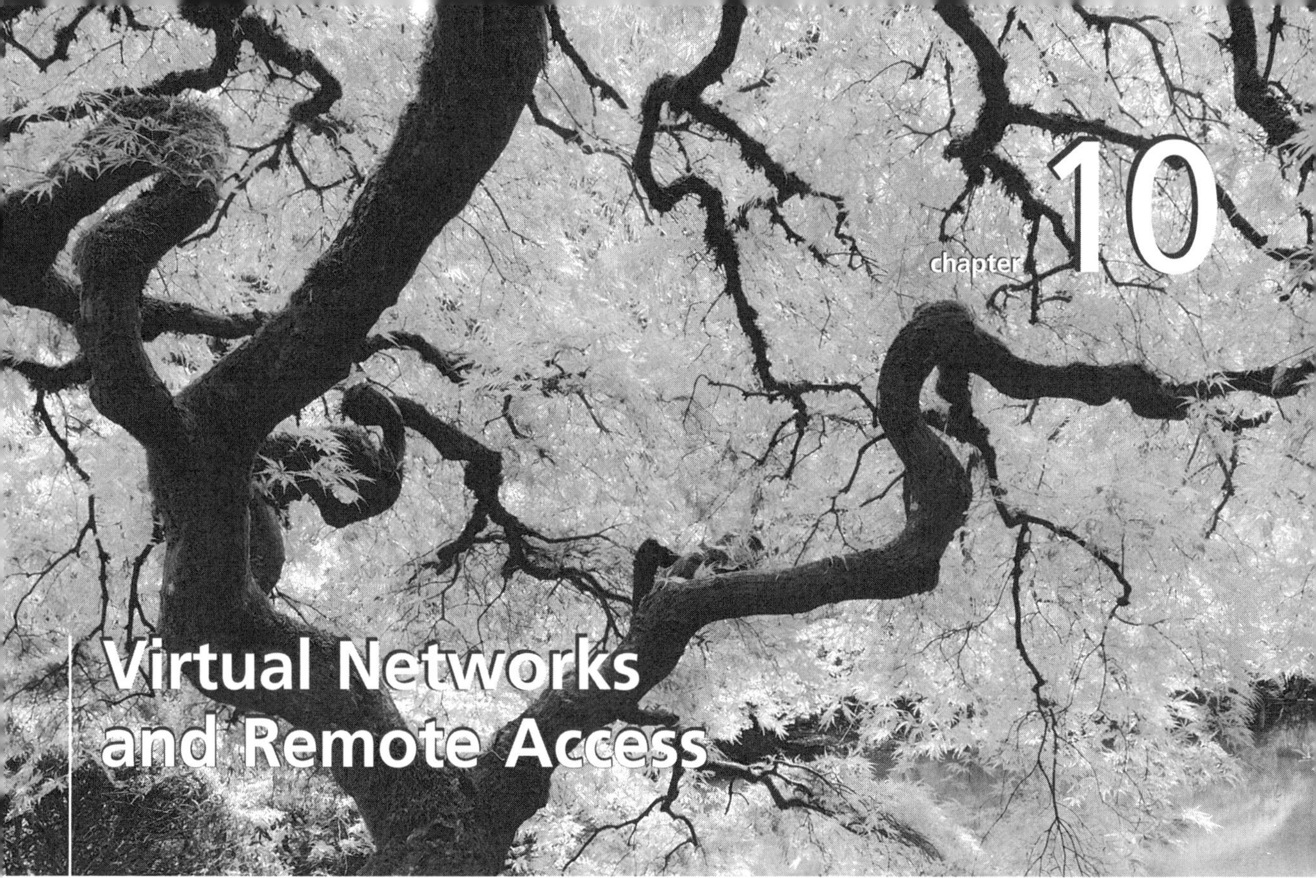

chapter 10

Virtual Networks and Remote Access

After reading this chapter and completing the exercises, you will be able to:

- Explain virtualization and identify characteristics of virtual network components
- Create and configure virtual servers, adapters, and switches as part of a network
- Describe techniques for incorporating virtual components in VLANs
- Explain methods for remotely connecting to a network, including dial-up networking, virtual desktops, and thin clients
- Discuss VPNs (virtual private networks) and the protocols they rely on
- Identify the features and benefits of cloud computing and NaaS (Network as a Service)

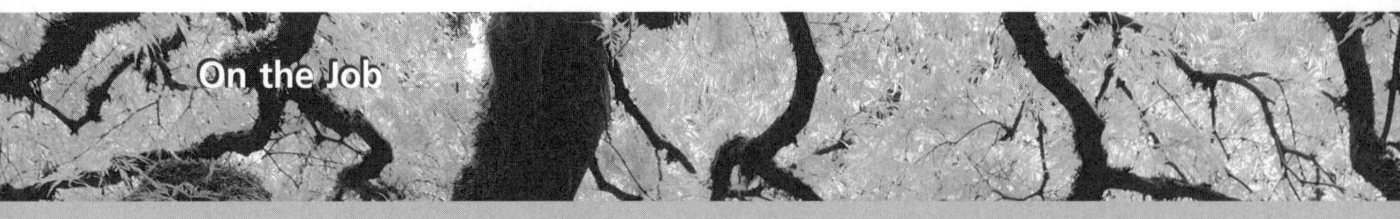

Josh studies in his Army quarters in Afghanistan while Kira works on her course from her Navy station in Spain. Both of these students are in the same class, but worlds apart. Distance education has created opportunities for many students, including those in the United States military who can remain on active duty while attending college. These active military students function in a diverse range of IT environments. Although some might be stationed on fully equipped military bases with computer labs and educational centers, others might be isolated in war zones with only their personal PCs and an Internet connection. However, cloud computing and computer virtualization give even the most isolated students the opportunity to complete the same hands-on activities as their counterparts sitting in a physical college computer lab.

In the traditional computer lab, students log on to a client or server to complete the projects outlined in a textbook. In the lab, students have access to multiple computers, each configured to a specific operating system. A contractual agreement for virtual machine hosting between Central Texas College and a hosting provider makes it possible for both distance and traditional students to perform the assigned course lab tasks without actually being physically present in the lab. By using virtual machines at a remote site, every student can log on to a virtual machine instance and remotely control the computer, the network topologies and its equipment, and the required applications in real time. Through cloud computing, students can store data, use applications, and access services available for all enrolled students regardless of their location in the world. In this way, cloud computing creates equal opportunities for learning and provides a portable IT learning environment for the military men and women currently serving their country.

Jane Perschbach, Ph.D.
Professor, Computer Science, Central Texas College

So far the clients, servers, network adapters, and connectivity devices you have learned about have been "real"—that is, you can touch them and each exists as a single entity. However, you have also learned about some elements of networks that are intangible, such as VLANs. This chapter describes a variety of virtual networking elements. It introduces you to a realm of networking where software pretends to be hardware, where servers and switches cannot be touched, but exist only as files on another computer. You will also learn how to combine physical and virtual components on the same network. Integrating virtual components offers great flexibility in creating, configuring, and managing networks. It also helps to conserve resources, potentially saving money and energy.

Virtualization

Net+ 1.9

Virtualization is the emulation of a computer, operating system environment, or application on a physical system. It's a broad term that encompasses many possibilities. In the following sections, you will learn about a type of virtualization that allows you to, for example, create a logically defined Linux client on your Windows 7 workstation or a virtual Windows Server 2008 R2 server on your UNIX server. In fact, using a virtualization program, you can create dozens of different **VMs (virtual machines)**, whether **virtual workstations** or **virtual servers**, on one computer. Together, all the VMs on a single computer share the same CPU, hard disk, memory, and network interfaces. Yet each VM functions independently, with its own logically defined hardware resources, operating system, applications, and network interfaces. A VM can be configured to use not only a different operating system, but also a different type of CPU, storage drive, or NIC than the physical computer it resides on. VMs exist as files on the hard disk of the physical computer. These files contain the operating system, applications, data, and configurations for the VMs.

Meanwhile, to users, a VM appears and acts no differently from a physical computer running the same software. For example, suppose you are the network administrator at an ISP and you establish separate virtual mail servers for five companies on one physical computer. When an employee at one company checks his e-mail, he has no idea that he is accessing the same physical computer that an employee at another company uses to check her e-mail.

In this type of virtualization, the physical computer is known as a **host** while each VM is known as a **guest**. The software that allows you to define VMs and manages resource allocation and sharing among them is known as a **virtual machine manager**, or, more commonly, a **hypervisor**. Figure 10-1 illustrates some of the elements of virtualization.

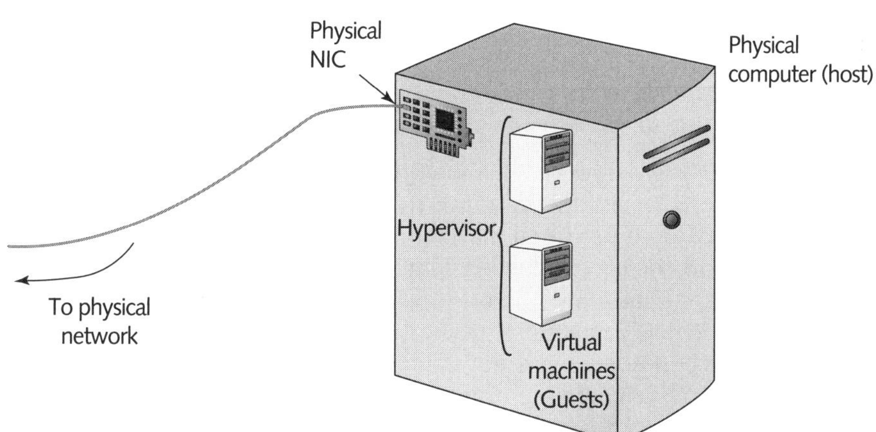

Figure 10-1 Elements of virtualization

Virtualization offers several advantages, including the following:

- *Efficient use of resources*—Physical clients or servers devoted to one function typically use only a fraction of their capacity. Without virtualization, a company might purchase six computers to run six different services—for example, mail server, DNS server, DHCP server, file server, remote access server, and database server. Each service might demand no more than 15% of its computer's processing power and memory. Using virtualization, however, a single, powerful computer can support all six services.

- *Cost and energy savings*—Organizations save money by purchasing fewer physical machines. They also save electricity because there are fewer computers drawing power and less demand for air conditioning in the computer room. Some institutions with thousands of users, such as Stanford University, are using virtualization as a way to conserve energy and are promoting it as part of campuswide sustainability efforts.
- *Fault and threat isolation*—In a virtual environment, the isolation of each guest system means that a problem with one guest does not affect the others. For example, an instructor might create multiple instances of an operating system and applications on a single computer that's shared by several classes. That allows each student to work on his own instance of the operating system environment. Any configuration errors or changes he makes on his guest machine will not affect other students. In another example, a network administrator who wants to try a beta version of an application might install that application on a guest machine rather than his host, in case the untested software causes problems. Furthermore, because a VM is granted limited access to hardware resources, security attacks on a guest may have little effect on a host or the physical network to which it's connected.
- *Simple backups, recovery, and replication*—Virtualization software enables network administrators to save snapshots, or images, of a guest machine. The images can later be used to re-create that machine on another host or on the same host. This feature allows for simple backups and quick recovery. It also makes it easy to create multiple, identical copies of one VM. Some virtualization programs even allow you to save snapshot files of VMs that can be imported into a competitor's virtualization program.

Not every type of client or server is a good candidate for virtualization, however. Potential disadvantages to creating multiple guests on a single host machine include the following:

- *Compromised performance*—When multiple virtual machines contend for finite physical resources, one virtual machine could monopolize those resources and impair the performance of other virtual machines on the same computer. In theory, careful management and resource allocation should prevent this. In practice, however, it is unwise to force a critical application—for example, a factory's real-time control systems or a hospital's emergency medical systems—to share resources and take that risk. Imagine a brewery that uses computers to measure and control tank levels, pressure, flow, and temperature of liquid ingredients during processing. These functions are vital for product quality and safety. In this example, where specialty software demands real-time, error-free performance, it makes sense to devote all of a computer's resources to this set of functions, rather than share that computer with the brewery's human resources database server, for example. In addition to multiple guest systems vying for limited physical resources, the hypervisor also requires some overhead.
- *Increased complexity*—Although virtualization reduces the number of physical machines to manage, it increases complexity and administrative burden in other

ways. For instance, a network administrator who uses virtual servers and switches must thoroughly understand virtualization software. In addition, managing addressing and switching for multiple VMs is more complex than doing so for physical machines. (You will learn more about these techniques later in this chapter.) Finally, because VMs are so easy to set up, they may be created capriciously or as part of experimentation, and then forgotten. As a result, extra VMs may litter a server's hard disk, consume resources, and unnecessarily complicate network management. By contrast, abandoned physical servers might only take up rack space.

- *Increased licensing costs*—Because every instance of commercial software requires its own license, every VM that uses such software comes with added cost. In some cases, the added cost brings little return. For example, an instructor might want to create four instances of Windows 7 on a single computer to supply four students with their own operating system environment. To comply with Microsoft's licensing restrictions, the instructor will have to purchase four copies of Windows 7. Depending on the instructor's intentions, it might make more sense, instead, to share one copy of Windows 7 and separate each student's files and settings by using four different logon IDs.
- *Single point of failure*—If a host machine fails, all its guest machines will fail, too. For example, an organization that creates VMs for its mail server, DNS server, DHCP server, file server, remote access server, and database server on a single physical computer would lose all of those services if the computer went down. Wise network administrators implement measures such as clustering and automatic failover to prevent that from happening. You'll learn more about these techniques in Chapter 14.

Most of the potential disadvantages in this list can be mitigated through thoughtful network design and virtualization control. You can choose from several virtualization programs to create and manage VMs. **VMware** is the most widely implemented virtualization software today. The company provides several different products, some designed for managing virtual workstations on a single host and others capable of managing hundreds of virtual servers across a WAN. Competing virtualization products include Microsoft's **Hyper-V**, **KVM (Kernel-based Virtual Machine)**, Oracle's **VirtualBox**, and Citrix's **Xen**. All provide similar functionality, but differ in features, interfaces, and ease of use. In this chapter, you will see sample screen shots from some of these virtualization programs and get a sense for how they function. In the Hands-On Projects at the end of this chapter, you will have the chance to install a popular virtualization program and create and network VMs.

Virtual Network Components

1.9

It is possible to create a virtual network that consists solely of virtual machines on a physical server. More practical and common, however, are networks that combine physical and virtual elements. Earlier you were introduced to VMs. In this section, you will learn how VMs connect to each other and to a physical network.

Net+

Virtual Machines and Adapters

1.9 A VM's software and hardware characteristics are assigned when it is created in the virtualization program. As you have learned, these characteristics can differ completely from those of the host machine. Popular virtualization programs offer step-by-step wizards that make creating VMs easy. One of the first steps is choosing an image of the guest's operating system. Operating system images are available for download online or can be obtained on a disc from software vendors. For example, if you are running a virtualization program on your Windows 7 workstation, you might choose to install a guest machine based on an Ubuntu Linux image you download from Ubuntu's Web site. After choosing the guest operating system, you can customize characteristics of the VM, including memory and hard disk size, processor type, and NIC type, to name a few. Figure 10-2 shows a screen from the VMware VM creation wizard that allows you to specify the amount of memory allocated to a VM.

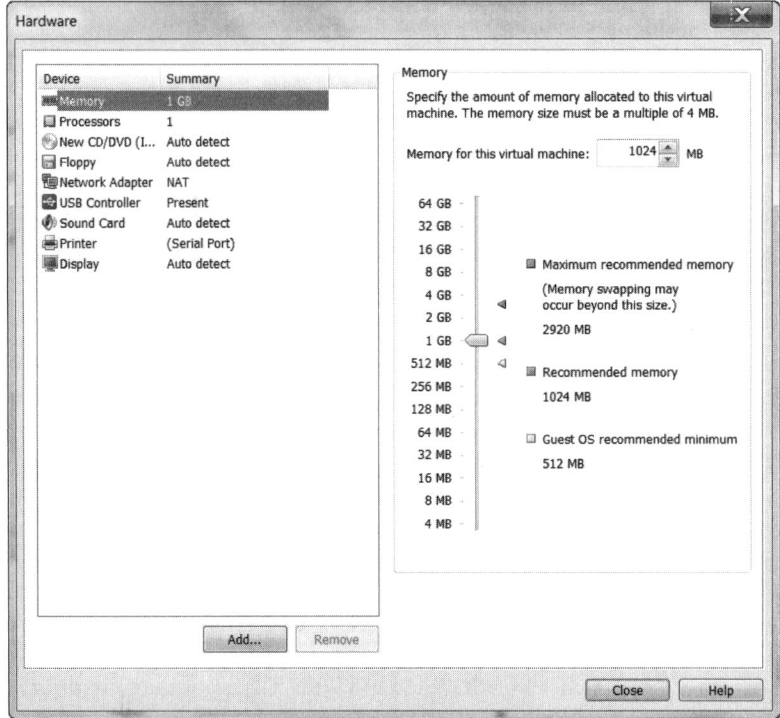

Figure 10-2 Specifying a VM's memory in VMware

To connect to a network, a virtual machine requires a **virtual adapter**, or **vNIC** (**virtual network interface card**). Just like a physical NIC, a vNIC operates at the Data Link layer and provides the computer with network access. Each VM can have several vNICs, no matter how many NICs the host machine has. The maximum number of vNICs on a VM depends on the limits imposed by the virtualization program. For example, VirtualBox allows up to eight vNICs per virtual machine.

1.9 Figure 10-3 shows a dialog box from the VMware wizard that allows you to customize properties of a virtual workstation's vNIC. One of many options you can configure for each NIC is its inbound and outbound transmission speeds. For example, you could select transmission speeds that simulate a T1 or broadband cable connection.

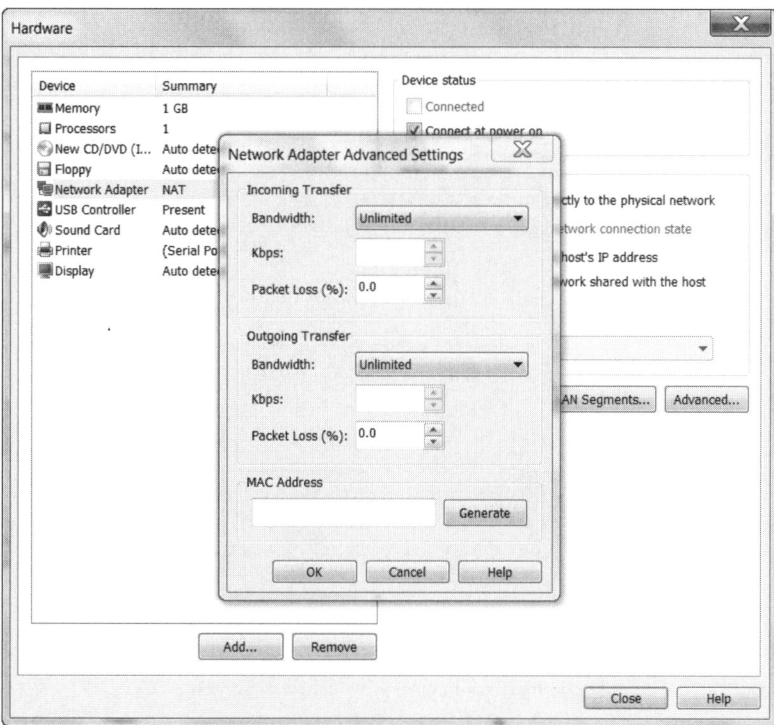

Figure 10-3 Customizing vNIC properties in VMware

Upon creation, each vNIC is automatically assigned a MAC address. Also, by default, every virtual machine's vNIC is connected to a port on a virtual switch, as described next.

Virtual Switches and Bridges

As soon as the first virtual machine's vNIC is selected, the hypervisor creates a connection between that VM and the host. Depending on the virtualization software, this connection might be called a bridge or a switch. (Recall that every port on a physical switch can be considered a bridge; thus, a switch is essentially a collection of bridges.) A **virtual switch** is a logically defined device that operates at the Data Link layer to pass frames between nodes. **Virtual bridges**, or ports on a virtual switch, connect vNICs with a network, whether virtual or physical. Thus, a virtual switch or bridge allows VMs to communicate with each other and with nodes on a physical LAN or WAN. When virtual switches or bridges are used to connect vNICs with physical NICs for physical network access, the physical NIC can be considered an uplink. Just like an uplink connection between two physical switches, the physical NIC connects a group of switched nodes to another network segment.

1.9

Virtual switches or bridges reside in the RAM of the physical computers that act as their hosts, while their configuration resides in a separate file on the host's hard disk. One host can support multiple virtual switches. The hypervisor controls the virtual switches and its ports, or bridges.

Figure 10-4 illustrates a host machine with two physical NICs that supports several virtual machines and their vNICs. A virtual switch connects the vNICs to the network.

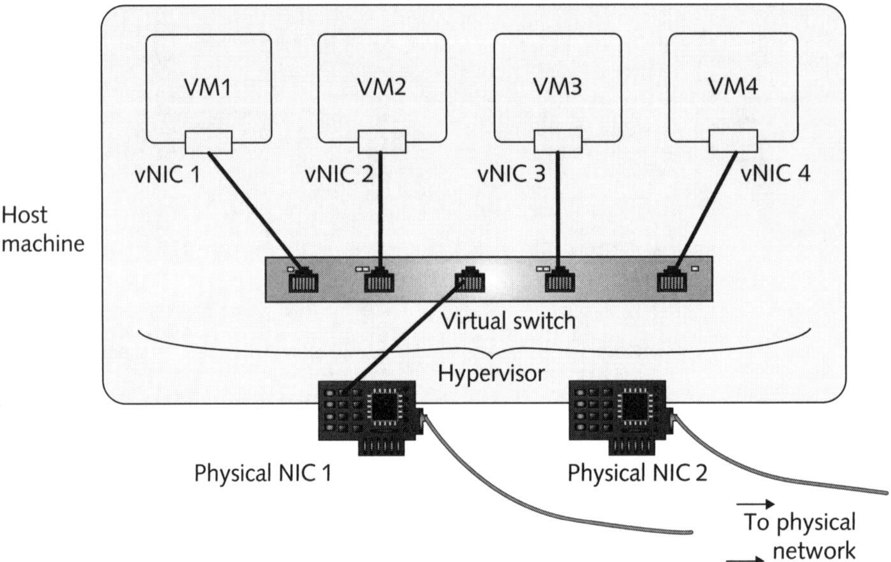

Figure 10-4 Virtual servers on a single host connected with a virtual switch

Recall from Chapter 6 that physical switches exchange traffic through routers. The same holds true for virtual switches. Suppose you created two virtual switches, switch A and switch B, on one host machine. Traffic between VMs on switch A and VMs on switch B could not pass directly between switches A and B. Instead, the virtual switches would have to exchange data through a router, whether virtual or physical, as shown in Figure 10-5. In fact, the router could simply be another virtual machine on the host configured to forward packets. Naturally, virtual switches on different host machines also have to communicate through routers.

Virtual switches offer many possibilities for customizing and managing network traffic, as you will discover later in this chapter. First, however, it's necessary to understand the different ways in which virtual interfaces can appear on and communicate with a network.

Network Connection Types

Earlier you learned that when creating a virtual interface on a VM, you choose its characteristics, such as speed. In addition, you are asked to identify what type of network connection, or networking mode, the vNIC will use. In the VMware or VirtualBox virtualization programs, you make this choice when you create or reconfigure a vNIC. In Hyper-V, you make

1.9

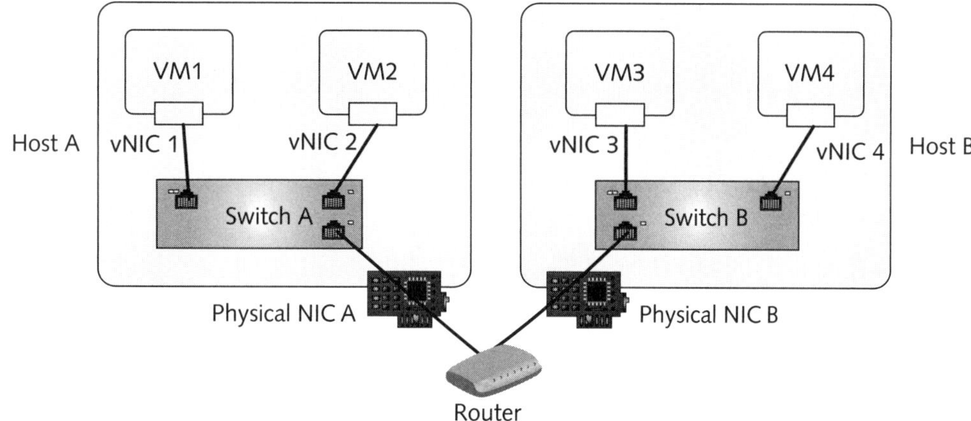

Figure 10-5 Virtual switches exchanging traffic through routers

the choice through the Virtual Network Manager. The most frequently used network connection types include bridged, NAT, and host-only, as described next.

Bridged In bridged mode, a vNIC accesses a physical network using the host machine's NIC, as shown in Figure 10-6. In other words, the virtual interface and the physical interface are bridged. If your host machine contains multiple physical adapters—for example, a wireless NIC and a wired NIC—you can choose which physical adapter to use as the bridge when you configure the virtual adapter.

Although a bridged vNIC communicates through the host's adapter, it obtains its own IP address, default gateway, and netmask from a DHCP server on the physical LAN. For example, suppose your DHCP server is configured to assign addresses in the range of 192.168.1.128 through 192.168.1.253 to nodes on your LAN. The router might assign your host machine's physical NIC an IP address of 192.168.1.131. A guest on your host might obtain an IP address of 192.168.1.132. A second guest on that host might obtain an IP address of 192.168.1.133, and so on.

When connected using bridged mode, a VM appears to other nodes as just another client or server on the network. Other nodes communicate directly with the machine without realizing it is virtual.

In VMware and VirtualBox, you can choose the bridged connection type when you create or configure the virtual adapter. In KVM, you create a bridge between the VM and your physical NIC when you modify the vNIC's settings. In Hyper-V, you create a bridged connection type by assigning VMs to an external network switch. Figure 10-7 shows the Hardware dialog box that appears while creating a virtual machine in VMware with the Bridged networking connection type selected.

VMs that must be available at a specific address, such as mail servers or Web servers, should be assigned bridged network connections. VMs that other nodes do not need to access directly can be configured to use the NAT networking mode.

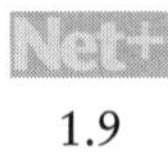

1.9

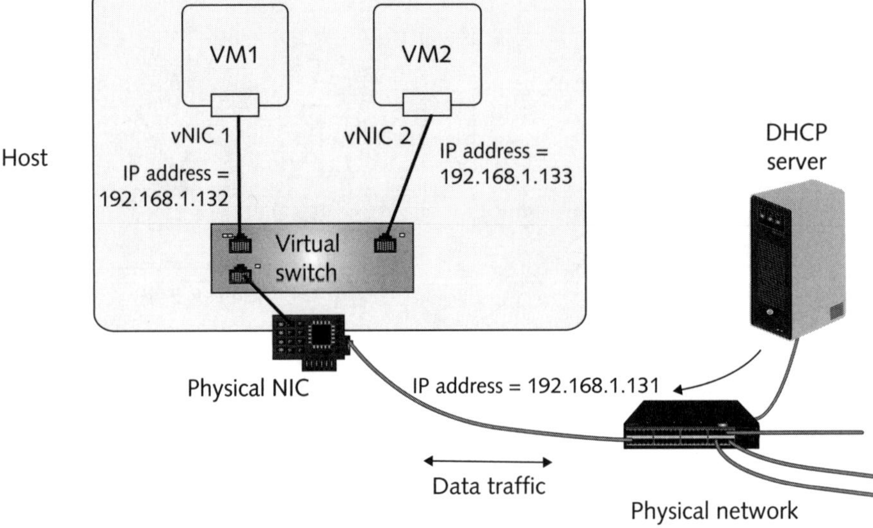

Figure 10-6 vNIC accessing a network in bridged mode

© Cengage Learning 2013

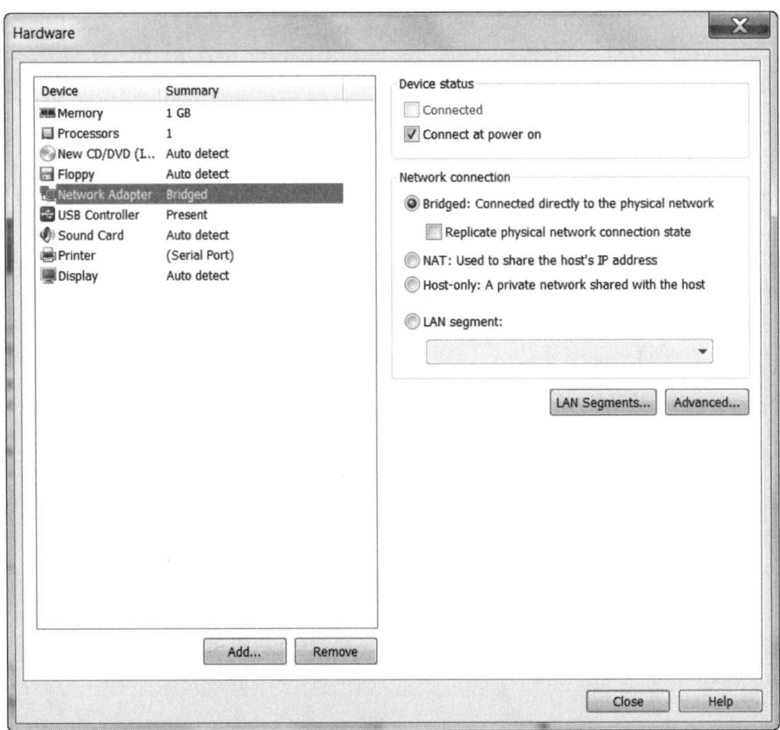

Figure 10-7 Selecting the Bridged option for a vNIC in VMware

© Cengage Learning 2013

1.9

NAT In the NAT networking mode, a vNIC relies on the host machine to act as a NAT device. In other words, the VM obtains IP addressing information from its host, rather than a server or router on the physical network. To accomplish this, the virtualization software acts as a DHCP server. A vNIC operating in NAT mode can still communicate with other nodes on the network and vice versa. However, other nodes communicate with the host machine's IP address to reach the VM; the VM itself is invisible to other nodes. Figure 10-8 illustrates a VM operating in NAT mode.

NAT is the default network connection type selected when you create a VM in VMware, VirtualBox, or KVM. In Hyper-V, the NAT connection type is created by assigning VMs to an internal network. Figure 10-9 shows the networking modes dialog box in VirtualBox, with the NAT option selected.

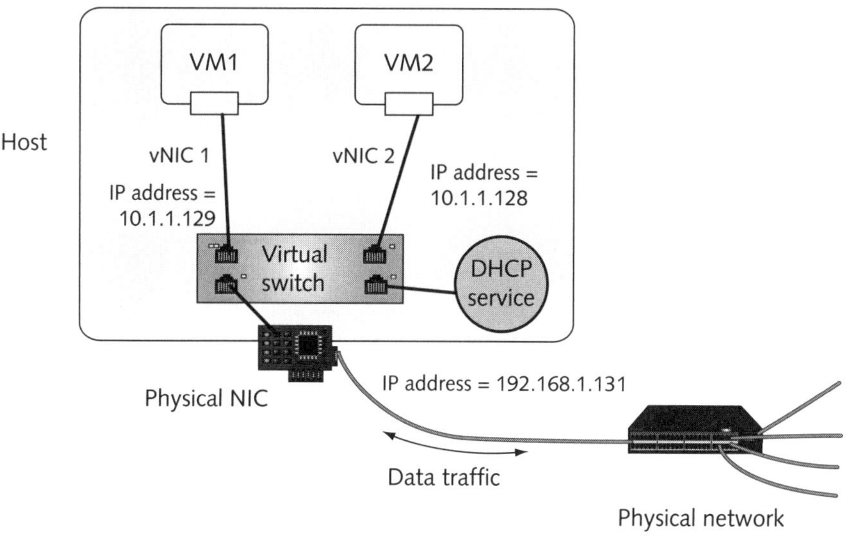

Figure 10-8 vNIC accessing a network in NAT mode

Once you have selected the NAT configuration type, you can configure the pool of IP addresses available to the VMs on a host. For example, suppose, as shown in Figure 10-8, your host machine has an IP address of 192.168.1.131. You might configure your host's DHCP service to assign IP addresses in the range of 10.1.1.128 through 10.1.1.253 to the VMs you create on that host. Because these addresses will never be evident beyond the host, you have flexibility in choosing their IP address range.

The NAT network connection type is appropriate for VMs that do not need to be accessed at a known address by other network nodes. For example, virtual workstations that are mainly used to check e-mail, share files, or surf the Web are good candidates for NAT network connections.

Host-Only In host-only networking mode, VMs on one host can exchange data with each other and with their host, but they cannot communicate with any nodes beyond the host. In other words, the vNICs never receive or transmit data via the host machine's physical NIC. In host-only mode, as in NAT mode, VMs use the DHCP service in the host's virtualization software to obtain IP address assignments.

Net+
1.9

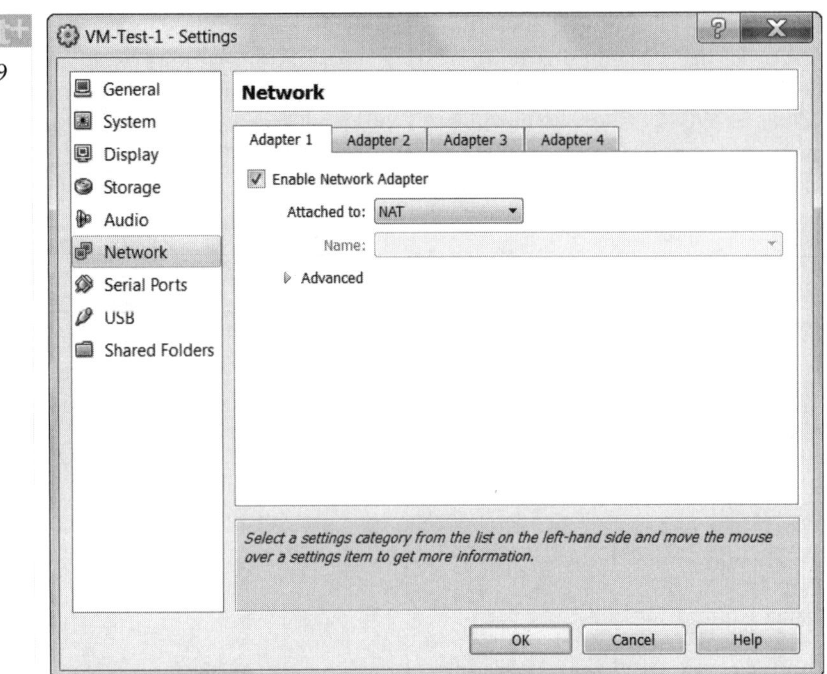

Figure 10-9 Selecting the NAT option for a vNIC in VirtualBox
© Cengage Learning 2013

Figure 10-10 illustrates how the host-only option creates an isolated virtual network. Host-only mode is appropriate for test networks or if you simply need to install a different operating system on your workstation to use a program that is incompatible with your host's operating system. For example, suppose a project requires you to create diagrams in Microsoft Visio and your workstation runs Red Hat Linux. You could install a Windows 7 VM solely for the purpose of installing and running Visio.

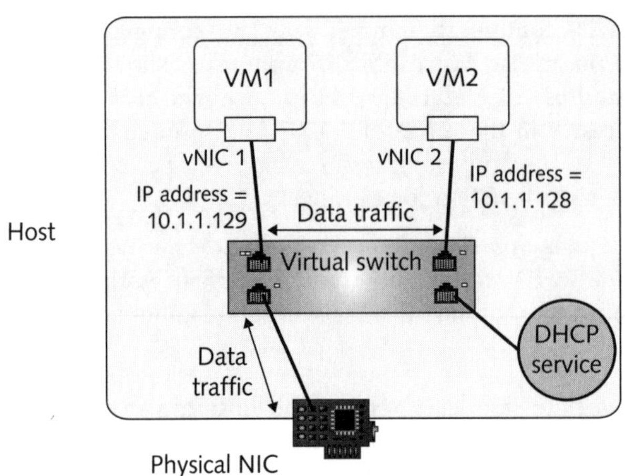

Figure 10-10 Host-only network configuration
© Cengage Learning 2013

Net+ 1.9 Obviously, because host-only mode prevents VMs from exchanging data with a physical network, this choice cannot work for virtual servers that need to be accessed by clients across a LAN. Nor can it be used for virtual workstations that need to access LAN or WAN services, such as e-mail or Web pages. Host-only networking is less commonly used than NAT or bridged mode networking.

You can choose host-only networking when you create or configure a VM in VMware or VirtualBox. In Hyper-V, the host-only connection type is created by assigning VMs to a private virtual network. In KVM, host-only is not a predefined option, but must be assigned to a vNIC via the command-line interface.

Virtualization software gives you the flexibility of creating several different networking types on one host machine. For example, on one host you could create a host-only, or private, network to test multiple versions of Linux. On the same host, you could create a group of Windows Server 2008 R2 servers that are connected to your physical LAN using the bridged connection type. Or, rather than specifying one of the four networking connection types described previously, you could also create a VM that contains a vNIC but is not connected to any nodes, whether virtual or physical. Preventing the VM from communicating with other nodes keeps it completely isolated. This might be desirable when testing unpredictable software or an image of untrusted origin.

Virtual Appliances

Imagine you're a busy network administrator, and your company's IT director has asked you to provide a complete e-mail and collaboration solution for everyone connected to the WAN. Traditionally, someone in your situation would research and obtain trial versions of the leading software, install the software on test machines, and evaluate each program over a period of weeks. You might struggle to get your hardware and operating system to work correctly with the software. Or you might wonder whether certain problems with the new software are related to the way you configured it. However, virtualization offers an alternative. Instead of installing the program on a test server, you could install a **virtual appliance**, or an image that includes the appropriate operating system, software, hardware specifications, and application configuration necessary for the package to run properly. Virtual appliances may be virtual workstations, but more commonly they are virtual servers. Each virtual appliance varies in its features and complexity. Popular functions include firewall and other security measures, network management, e-mail solutions, and remote access. Other virtual appliances are customized instances of operating systems designed to suit the needs of particular users.

Now that you are familiar with the elements that make up a virtual network, you are ready to learn techniques for managing them as part of an enterprise-wide network.

Virtual Networks and VLANs

2.1 Ask a networking professional about his virtual network and he'll probably wonder exactly what you're talking about. The term could be shorthand for a VLAN defined on a physical switch or a VPN (discussed later in this chapter), or it could simply refer to any network that connects virtual machines. For example, in its Hyper-V offering, Microsoft refers to network connection types as virtual networks. In this section, *virtual network* is used generally to refer to ways in which virtual machines can be connected with other virtual and physical network nodes.

2.1 Virtual networks resemble physical networks in many aspects. The same concerns regarding addressing, performance, security, and fault tolerance apply. In some cases—for example, when it comes to backups, troubleshooting, and software updates—virtual network management is nearly identical to physical network management. In other cases, management differs only slightly. For example, in the previous section, you learned that a DHCP server is part of virtualization software. Running on a host, it dynamically assigns IP addresses for virtual machines in NAT and host-only modes just as a DHCP server on a physical network assigns addresses for its physical clients. However, despite all the similarities between physical and virtual networks, an important difference arises when managing virtual machines in VLANs.

Recall from Chapter 6 that VLANs are subnets, or broadcast domains, logically defined on a physical switch. VLANs allow network administrators to separate network traffic for better performance, customized address management, and security. On a network that uses virtual machines, VLANs will typically include those VMs.

You also know that to create a VLAN you modify a physical switch's configuration. However, to add VMs to a VLAN defined on a physical network, you modify a *virtual* switch's configuration. In other words, VMs are not added to a preexisting VLAN on the physical switch that manages that VLAN. The following example describes a common way of incorporating VMs in VLANs. Because virtualization programs vary, the steps required and the nomenclature used will differ depending on what program you use. However, the concepts are the same.

Suppose you work at a small company whose network consists of four VLANs defined on its primary backbone switch. The VLANs subdivide traffic by group as follows: Management, Research, Test, and Public. On the network, they are defined as VLAN 120, VLAN 121, VLAN 122, and VLAN 123, respectively. To consolidate resources, your company is migrating its five physical file servers to virtual file servers on a single host using a VMware program called vSphere. The hypervisor portion of vSphere and the interface that allows you to manage virtual machines and the virtual networks they belong to is called VMware ESXi Server.

As you create the five virtual servers on your new host server, you configure each of their vNICs to operate in bridged mode. Furthermore, you decide to assign each virtual server a static IP address. After creation, the five virtual servers are connected to the same virtual switch. By default, each vNIC is assigned a single port, or bridge, on the virtual switch. (If you create multiple vNICs for your servers, each vNIC would connect to a separate port.) Because the vNICs operate in bridged mode, the virtual servers can access the physical network through the host's physical interface. Likewise, nodes on the physical network can access the virtual servers through the host's physical interface.

Next, you install applications on your virtual servers and customize software and NOS parameters. Finally, you are ready to add the servers to the appropriate VLANs. In this example, suppose all five servers belong to the Management, Research, and Test VLANs, and only one of them belongs to the Public VLAN.

In VMware, vNICs can be assigned to port groups. Grouping ports allows you to apply certain characteristics to multiple vNICs easily and quickly. Notably, all the vNICs in a port group can be assigned to one VLAN with a single command. For example, the vNICs for all five file servers will be assigned to port groups 120, 121, and 122. The vNIC for one file server will also be assigned to port group 123. Next, you associate each of the port groups

2.1 with a VLAN. For example, you would associate port group 120 with VLAN 120, port group 121 with VLAN 121, and so on.

Notice that multiple vNICs can be assigned to a single port group. Also, a single vNIC can be assigned to multiple port groups. (Depending on your network management strategy, however, you might find it simpler to create multiple vNICs so that each vNIC is associated with a different port group, or VLAN.) In other virtualization programs, vNICs are assigned to VLANs by associating them directly with a VLAN number or with a bridge that is, in turn, associated with a VLAN.

Recall from Chapter 6 that a single physical interface can carry the traffic of multiple VLANs through trunking. Therefore, the host's physical NIC must be configured to operate in trunking mode for VLAN information to pass through. In other words, it must be capable of carrying the traffic of multiple VLANs. Virtualization software refers to the physical NIC, acting as an interface for VLANs, as a trunk.

Now that you have created virtual servers connected to a virtual switch, created port groups on the switch and assigned vNICs to those port groups, associated those port groups with VLANs, and ensured that your host's physical NIC is configured to act as a trunk, all traffic tagged for VLAN 120 will be transmitted to all five file servers, for example, and all traffic tagged for VLAN 123 will only be seen by one file server.

Figure 10-11 illustrates this example of multiple virtual servers connected to multiple VLANs.

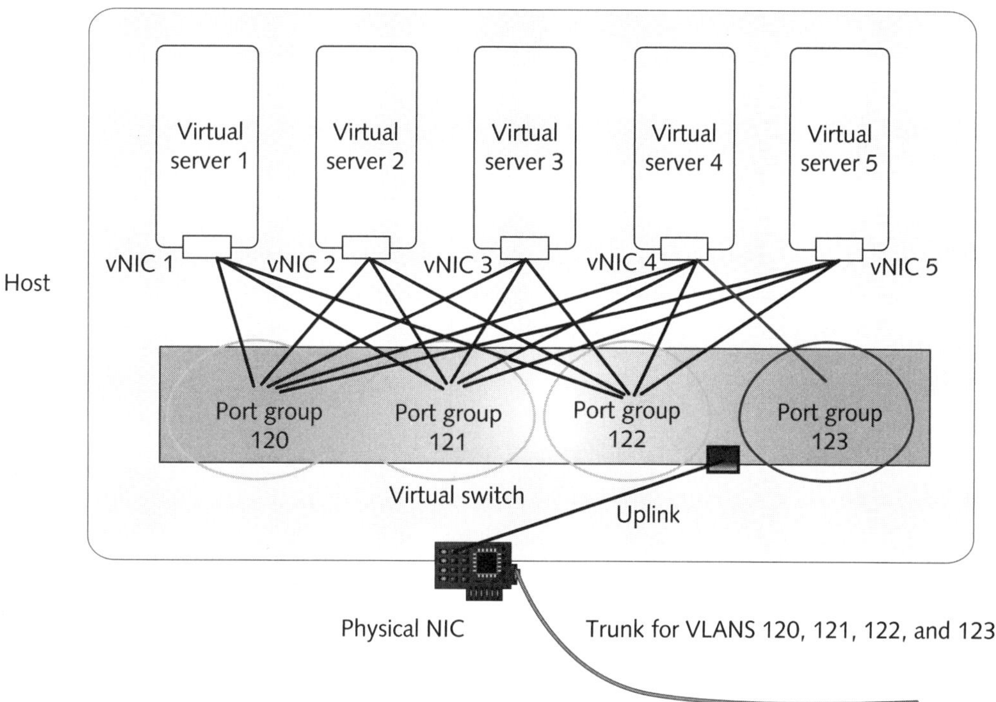

Figure 10-11 Multiple virtual servers connected to multiple VLANs

2.1 The virtual network for a company that manages multiple virtual file servers and multiple VLANs would likely be more complicated than the example described in this section. For instance, as a network administrator you might ensure high performance by using two physical NICs on the host and associating a virtual server's vNIC with both. You might instruct the virtualization software to balance loads between multiple vNICs on a busy server. You might create multiple virtual switches on the host to further separate traffic. You might even create duplicates of your virtual servers on a second physical host to ensure availability. For now, however, it is enough to understand the essential concepts of using VLANs in a combined virtual and physical network.

Remote Access and Virtual Computing

5.2 In Chapter 7, you learned about connecting nodes over long distances to form WANs. Most of the connectivity examples in that chapter assumed that the WAN locations had continuous, dedicated access to the network. For example, when a user in Phoenix wants to open a document on a server in Dallas, she needs only to find the Dallas server on her network, open a directory on the Dallas server, and then open the file. The server is available to her at any time because the Phoenix and Dallas offices are always connected and sharing resources over the WAN. However, this is not the only way to share resources over a WAN. For remote users, such as employees on the road, distance learning students, telecommuters, military personnel overseas, or staff in small, branch offices, intermittent access with a choice of connectivity methods is often more appropriate.

As a remote user, you can connect to a network via **remote access**, a service that allows a client to connect with and log on to a LAN or WAN in a different geographical location. After connecting, a remote client can access files, applications, and other shared resources, such as printers, like any other client on the LAN or WAN. To communicate via remote access, the client and host need a transmission path plus the appropriate software to complete the connection and exchange data.

Many remote access methods exist, and they vary according to the type of transmission technology, clients, hosts, and software they can or must use. Popular remote access techniques, including dial-up networking, Microsoft's RAS (Remote Access Service) or RRAS (Routing and Remote Access Service), and VPNs (virtual private networks), are described in the following sections. You will also learn about common remote access protocols.

Net+ Dial-Up Networking

3.4 In Chapter 7, you learned about the PSTN and ways in which it connects users to networks,
5.2 including dial-up. **Dial-up networking** refers to dialing directly into a private network's or ISP's remote access server to log on to a network. Dial-up clients can use PSTN, X.25, or ISDN transmission methods. However, the term *dial-up networking* usually refers to a connection between computers using the PSTN—that is, regular telephone lines. To accept client connections, the remote access server is attached to a group of modems, all of which are associated with one phone number. The client must run dial-up software (normally available with the operating system) to initiate the connection. At the same time, the remote access server runs specialized software to accept and interpret the incoming signals. When it receives a request for connection, the remote access server software presents the remote user with a prompt for his **credentials**—typically, his username and password. The server compares his

Net+ credentials with those in its database, in a process known as **authentication**. If the credentials
3.4 match, the user is allowed to log on to the network. Thereafter, the remote user can perform the
5.2 same functions he could perform while working at a client computer in the office. With the
proper server hardware and software, a remote access server can offer multiple users simultaneous remote access to the LAN. Though far less popular than it was in the 1990s, some Internet subscribers still use dial-up networking to connect to their ISP. In the Hands-On Projects at the end of this chapter, you will have the opportunity to configure a dial-up networking connection.

Dial-up networking technology is proven reliable and its software comes with virtually every operating system. Within the United States, the dial-up configuration for one location differs little from the dial-up configuration in another location. However, a dial-up connection via the PSTN comes with significant disadvantages, with the worst being its low throughput. Currently, manufacturers of PSTN modems advertise a connection speed of 56 Kbps. But the 56-Kbps maximum is only a *theoretical* threshold that assumes a pristine connection between the initiator and the receiver. Splitters, fax machines, or other devices that a signal must navigate between the sender and receiver all reduce the actual throughput. The number of switching facilities and modems through which your phone call travels also affects throughput. Each time the signal passes through a switch or is converted from analog to digital or digital to analog, it loses a little throughput. If you're surfing the Web, for example, by the time a Web page returns to you, the connection may have lost from 5 to 30 Kbps, and your effective throughput might have been reduced to 30 Kbps or less. In addition, the FCC (Federal Communications Commission), the regulatory agency that sets standards and policy for telecommunications transmission and equipment in the United States, limits the use of PSTN lines to 53 Kbps to reduce the effects of cross talk. Thus, you will never actually achieve full 56-Kbps throughput using a dial-up connection over the PSTN.

Nor can traditional dial-up networking provide the quality required by many network applications. The quality of a WAN connection is largely determined by how many data packets it loses or that become corrupt during transmission, how quickly it can transmit and receive data, and whether it drops the connection altogether. Dial-up networking compares unfavorably with other WAN connection methods on all accounts. To compensate for its relatively poor quality, most protocols employ error-checking techniques. For example, TCP/IP depends on acknowledgments of the data it receives. In addition, newer PSTN links are digital, and digital lines are more reliable than the older analog lines. Such digital lines reduce the quality problems that once plagued purely analog PSTN connections.

From a network administrator's point of view, dial-up networking also requires a significant amount of maintenance to make sure clients can always connect to a pool of modems. One way to limit the maintenance burden is for an organization to contract with an ISP to supply remote access services. In this arrangement, clients dial into the ISP's remote access server, and then the ISP connects the incoming clients with the organization's network.

The dial-up networking software that Microsoft provided with its Windows 95, 98, NT, and 2000 client operating systems is called **RAS (Remote Access Service)**. RAS requires software installed on both the client and server, a server configured to accept incoming clients, and a client with sufficient privileges (including username and password) on the server to access its resources. In the Windows 2000 Server, XP, Vista, Server 2003, Server 2008, and Server 2008 R2 operating systems, RAS is part of a more comprehensive remote access package called the RRAS (Routing and Remote Access Service). RRAS is described in the following section.

Net+

Remote Access Servers

5.2 The preceding section described dial-up networking, a type of remote access method defined by its direct, PSTN-based connection method. However, users who previously depended on dial-up connections are increasingly adopting broadband connections, such as DSL and cable. This section and following sections describe services that can accept remote access connections from a client, no matter what type of Internet access it uses.

As you have learned, remote access allows a client that is not directly attached to a LAN or WAN to connect and log on to that network. A remote client attempting to connect to a LAN or WAN requires a server to accept its connection and grant it privileges to the network's resources. Many types of remote access servers exist. Some are devices dedicated to this task, such as Cisco's AS5800 access servers. These devices run software that, in conjunction with their operating system, performs authentication for clients and communicates via dial-up networking protocols. Other types of remote access servers are computers running special software that enables them to accept incoming client connections and grant clients access to resources.

RRAS (Routing and Remote Access Service) is Microsoft's remote access software, available with the Windows Server 2003, Server 2008, and Server 2008 R2 network operating systems and the Windows XP, Vista, and 7 desktop operating systems. RRAS enables a computer to accept multiple remote client connections over any type of transmission path. It also enables the server to act as a router, determining where to direct incoming packets across the network. Further, RRAS incorporates multiple security provisions to ensure that data cannot be intercepted and interpreted by anyone other than the intended recipient and to ensure that only authorized clients can connect to the remote access server.

Figure 10-12 illustrates how clients connect with a remote access server to log on to a LAN.

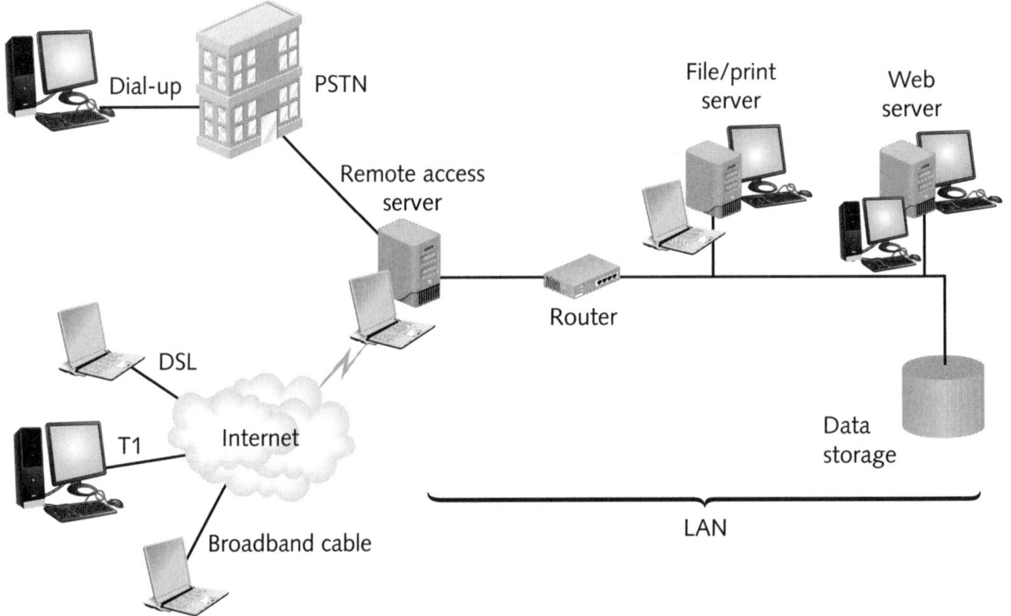

Figure 10-12 Clients connecting with a remote access server

Remote access servers depend on several types of protocols to communicate with clients, as described in the following section.

Remote Access Protocols

5.2 To exchange data, remote access servers and clients require special protocols. The **SLIP (Serial Line Internet Protocol)** and **PPP (Point-to-Point Protocol)** are two protocols that enable a workstation to connect to another computer using a serial connection (in the case of dial-up networking, *serial connection* refers to a modem). Such protocols are necessary to transport Network layer traffic over serial interfaces, which belong to the Data Link layer of the OSI model. Both SLIP and PPP encapsulate higher-layer networking protocols, such as TCP and IP, in their lower-layer data frames.

SLIP is an earlier and less-sophisticated version of the protocol than PPP. For example, SLIP can carry only IP packets, whereas PPP can carry many different types of Network layer packets. Because of its primitive nature, SLIP requires significantly more setup than PPP. When using SLIP, you typically must specify the IP addresses for both your client and for your server in your dial-up networking profile. PPP, on the other hand, can automatically obtain this information as it connects to the server. PPP also performs error correction and data compression, but SLIP does not. In addition, SLIP does not support data encryption, which makes it less secure than PPP. For all these reasons, PPP is the preferred communications protocol for remote access communications.

Another difference between SLIP and PPP is that SLIP supports only asynchronous data transmission, whereas PPP supports both asynchronous and synchronous transmission. As you learned earlier, in synchronous transmission, data must conform to a timing scheme, whereas asynchronous transmission may stop and start sporadically. In fact, asynchronous transmission was designed for communication that happens at random intervals, such as sending the keystrokes of a person typing on a remote keyboard. Thus, it is well suited for use on modem connections.

When PPP is used over an Ethernet network (no matter what the connection type), it is known as **PPPoE (PPP over Ethernet)**. PPPoE is the standard for connecting home computers to an ISP via DSL or broadband cable. When you sign up for broadband cable or DSL service, the ISP supplies you with connection software that is configured to use PPPoE. Figure 10-13 illustrates how the protocols discussed in this section and commonly used to establish a broadband Internet connection fit in the OSI model. (The Application layer protocol RDP, discussed in the following section, is only used when remotely controlling computers. Several different Application layer protocols, including HTTP or FTP, could be substituted for RDP in Figure 10-13.)

Remote Virtual Computing

So far, you have learned about dial-up networking and remote access servers, which are designed to allow many clients to log on to a network from afar. Sometimes, however, it's necessary for one workstation to remotely access and control another workstation. For example, suppose a traveling salesperson must submit weekly sales figures to her home office every Friday afternoon. While out of town, she discovers a problem with her spreadsheet program, which should automatically calculate her sales figures (for example, the percentage of a monthly quota she's reached for any given product) after she enters the raw data. She calls the home office, and a support technician attempts to resolve her issue on the phone.

5.2

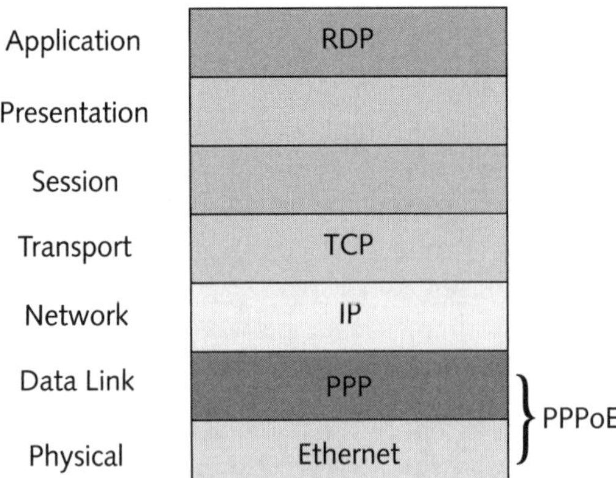

Figure 10-13 Protocols used in a remote access Internet connection

When this doesn't work, the technician may decide to run a remote virtual computing program and "take over" the salesperson's laptop (via a WAN link) to troubleshoot the spreadsheet problem. Every keystroke and mouse click the technician enters on his workstation is then issued to the salesperson's laptop. After the problem is resolved, the technician can disconnect from the salesperson's laptop.

Remote virtual computing allows a user on one computer, called the client, to control another computer, called the host or server, across a network connection. The connection could be a dedicated WAN link (such as a T1), an Internet connection, or even a dial-up connection established directly between the client's modem and the host's modem. Also, the host must be configured to allow access from the client by setting username or computer name and password credentials. A host may allow clients a variety of privileges, from merely viewing the screen to running programs and modifying data files on the host's hard disk. After connecting, if the remote user has sufficient privileges, she can send keystrokes and mouse clicks to the host and receive screen output in return. In other words, to the remote user, it appears as if she is working on the LAN- or WAN-connected host. Remote virtual computing software is specially designed to require little bandwidth. A workstation that uses such software to access a LAN is often called a **thin client** because very little hard disk space or processing power is required of the workstation.

Advantages to using remote virtual computing are that it is simple to configure and can run over any type of connection. This benefits anyone who must use dial-up connections or who must run processor-intensive applications such as databases. In this scenario, the data processing occurs on the host without the data having to traverse the connection to the remote workstation. Another advantage to remote virtual computing is that a single host can accept simultaneous connections from multiple clients. For example, a presenter can use this feature to establish a virtual conference in which several attendees log on to the host and watch the presenter manipulate the host computer's screen and keyboard.

Many types of remote virtual computing software exist, and they differ marginally in their capabilities, security mechanisms, and supported platforms. Three popular programs, discussed

5.2 next, are Microsoft Remote Desktop, VNC (Virtual Network Computing), and Citrix's ICA (Independent Computing Architecture).

Remote Desktop **Remote Desktop** is the remote virtual computing software that comes with Windows client and server operating systems. Remote Desktop relies on **RDP (Remote Desktop Protocol)**, which is an Application layer protocol that uses TCP/IP to transmit graphics and text quickly. RDP also carries session, licensing, and encryption information. RDP clients also exist for other operating systems, such as Linux, so you can connect from those clients to a Windows computer running Remote Desktop. Older versions of Windows operating systems, including Vista, may require additional software for Remote Desktop to work properly.

VNC (Virtual Network Computing) **VNC (Virtual Network Computing)** is an open source system designed to allow one workstation to remotely manipulate and receive screen updates from another workstation. **Open source** is the term for software whose code is publicly available for use and modification. As a result, anyone can change the software to enhance it or fix problems and share their modified version with others.

As with Remote Desktop's protocols, VNC's protocols operate at the Application layer. VNC packages have been developed for multiple computer platforms, including all modern versions of Windows, UNIX, Linux, and Mac OS X. In addition, VNC functions across platforms. That is, you can use a VNC client (or viewer, as it's known in VNC terms) on a Windows 7 workstation to access a VNC server running Ubuntu Linux. VNC is unique among remote virtual networking systems in this ability.

Besides its open source status, VNC boasts the ability to support multiple sessions on a single computer. One drawback of VNC compared with Remote Desktop is that its screen refresh rate is somewhat slower. However, software engineers have modified VNC to use compression techniques that expedite its data transmission. In addition, security has historically been a concern with VNC, but techniques have also evolved to mitigate this concern. Some popular versions of VNC include RealVNC, Tight VNC, and UltraVNC.

ICA (Independent Computing Architecture) Another system for remote virtual computing that supports multiple simultaneous server connections is Citrix System's XenApp. With the Citrix option, remote workstations rely on proprietary software known as an **ICA (Independent Computing Architecture)** client to connect with a remote access server and exchange keystrokes, mouse clicks, and screen updates. Running XenApp, the remote access server makes applications available to clients and manages their connections. Citrix's ICA client can work with virtually any operating system or application. Its ease of use and broad compatibility make the ICA client a popular method for supplying widespread remote access across an organization. Potential drawbacks to this method include the relatively high cost of Citrix's products and the complex nature of its server software configuration.

VPNs (Virtual Private Networks)

5.2 **VPNs (virtual private networks)** are wide area networks that are logically defined over public transmission systems. To allow access to only authorized users, traffic on a VPN is isolated from other traffic on the same public lines. For example, a national insurance provider could establish a private WAN that uses Internet connections but serves only its agent offices across

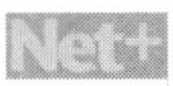

5.2 the country. By relying on the public transmission networks already in place, VPNs provide a way of constructing a convenient and relatively inexpensive WAN. In the example of a national insurance provider, the company gains significant savings by having each office connect to the Internet separately rather than leasing point-to-point connections between each office and the national headquarters.

The software required to establish VPNs is usually inexpensive, and in some cases is included with other widely used software. For example, in Windows Server 2008 R2, RRAS allows you to create a simple VPN. It turns a Windows server into a remote access server and allows clients to dial into it. Alternately, clients could dial into an ISP's remote access server, then connect with the VPN managed by RRAS. Third-party software companies also provide VPN programs that work with Windows, UNIX, Linux, and Macintosh OS X Server network operating systems. Or VPNs can be created simply by configuring special protocols on the routers or firewalls that connect each site in the VPN. This is the most common implementation of VPNs on UNIX-based networks.

Two important considerations when designing a VPN are interoperability and security. To ensure a VPN can carry all types of data in a private manner over any kind of connection, special VPN protocols encapsulate higher-layer protocols in a process known as **tunneling**. You can say that these protocols create the virtual connection, or **tunnel**, between two VPN endpoints.

Based on the kinds of endpoints they connect, VPNs can be classified according to two models: site-to-site and client-to-site. In a **site-to-site VPN**, tunnels connect multiple sites on a WAN, as shown in Figure 10-14. At each site, a VPN gateway encrypts and encapsulates data to exchange over the tunnel with another VPN gateway. Meanwhile, clients, servers, and other hosts communicate with the VPN gateway and do not have to run special VPN software. They simply send and receive data to and from the VPN gateway.

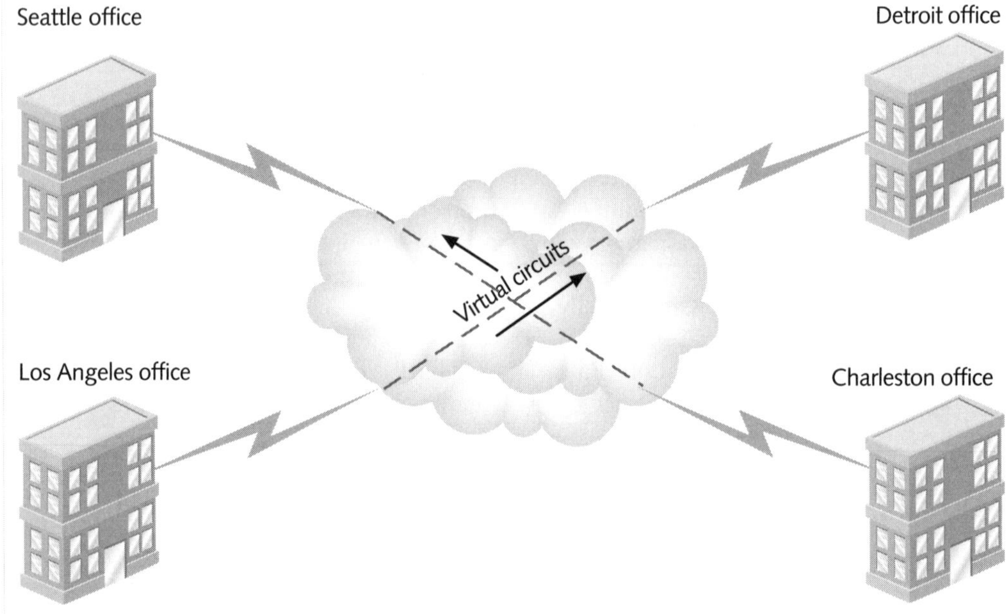

Figure 10-14 Site-to-site VPN

In a **client-to-site VPN**, clients, servers, and other hosts establish tunnels with a private
5.2 network using a remote access server or VPN gateway, as shown in Figure 10-15. Each client on a client-to-site VPN must run VPN software to create the tunnel for, and encrypt and encapsulate data. This is the type of VPN typically associated with remote access.

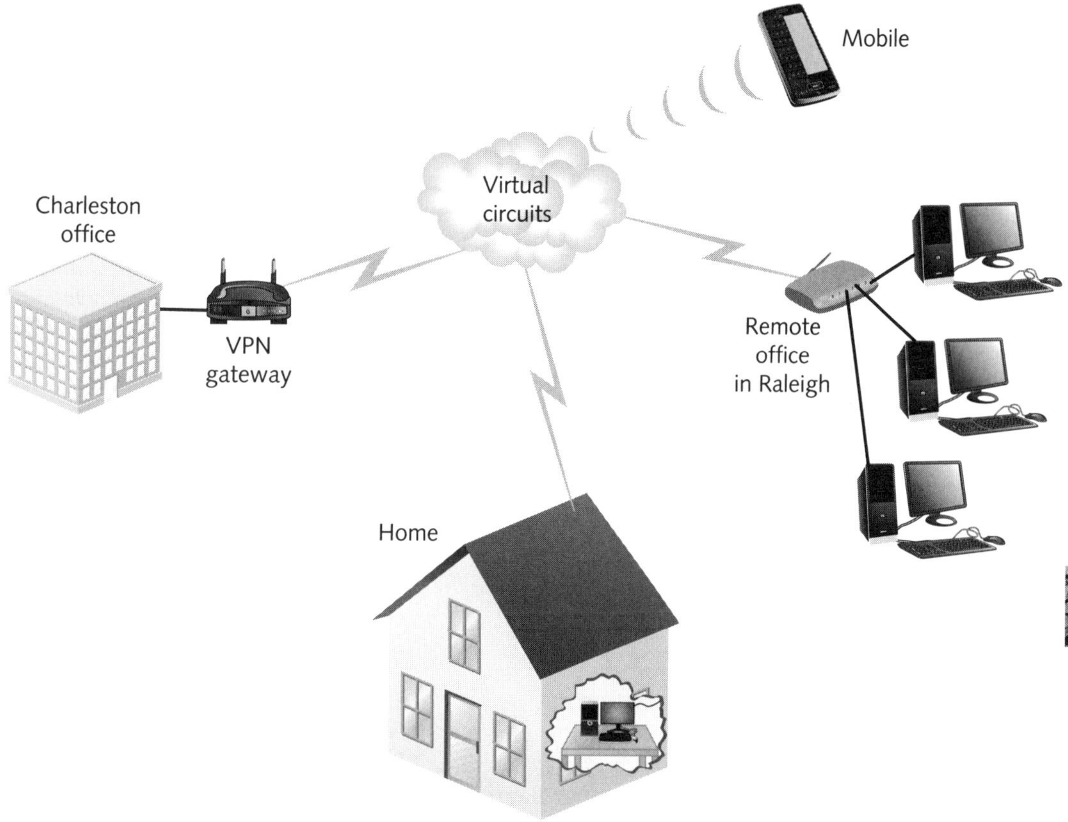

Figure 10-15 Client-to-site VPN

An enterprise-wide VPN can include elements of both the client-to-site and site-to-site models. The beauty of VPNs is that they are tailored to a customer's distance, user, and bandwidth needs, so, of course, every one is unique. However, all share the characteristics of privacy achieved over public transmission facilities using encryption and encapsulation.

As you have learned, encapsulation involves one protocol adding a header to data received from a higher-layer protocol. A VPN tunneling protocol operates at the Data Link layer and encapsulates Network layer packets, no matter what Network layer protocol is used. Two major types of tunneling protocols are used on contemporary VPNs: PPTP or L2TP.

PPTP (Point-to-Point Tunneling Protocol) is a Layer 2 protocol developed by Microsoft that expands on PPP by encapsulating it so that any type of PPP data can traverse the Internet masked as an IP transmission. PPTP supports the encryption, authentication, and access services provided by RRAS. Users can either dial directly into an RRAS access server that's part of the VPN, or they can dial into their ISP's remote access server first, then connect to a VPN.

5.2 Either way, data is transmitted from the client to the VPN using PPTP. Windows, UNIX, Linux, and Macintosh clients are all capable of connecting to a VPN using PPTP. PPTP is easy to install, and is available at no extra cost with Microsoft networking services. However, it provides less-stringent security than other tunneling protocols.

Another VPN tunneling protocol is **L2TP (Layer 2 Tunneling Protocol)**, based on technology developed by Cisco and standardized by the IETF. It encapsulates PPP data in a similar manner to PPTP, but differs in a few key ways. Unlike PPTP, L2TP is a standard accepted and used by multiple different vendors, so it can connect a VPN that uses a mix of equipment types—for example, a Juniper router, a Cisco router, and a Netgear router. Also, L2TP can connect two routers, a router and a remote access server, or a client and a remote access server.

Another important advantage to L2TP is that tunnel endpoints do not have to reside on the same packet-switched network. In other words, an L2TP client could connect to a router running L2TP on an ISP's network. The ISP could then forward the L2TP frames to another VPN router or gateway, without interpreting the frames. This L2TP tunnel, although not direct from node to node, remains isolated from other traffic. Because of its many advantages, L2TP is more commonly used than PPTP.

PPTP and L2TP are not the only protocols that can be used to carry VPN traffic. For networks in which security is critical, it is advisable to use protocols that can provide both tunneling and data encryption. Such protocols are discussed in detail in Chapter 11, which focuses on network security.

Cloud Computing

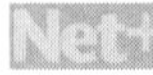
1.9 On network diagrams, the Internet is frequently depicted as a cloud. This representation arose from the packet-switched nature of data transmission over the Internet. In packet switching, as you know, each datagram can follow one of many paths to reach its destination. More recently, the cloud on networking diagrams has grown to take on new meanings, thanks in large part to the marketing efforts of network service providers. **Cloud computing** refers to the flexible provision of data storage, applications, or services to multiple clients over a network. The term includes a broad range of offerings, from hosting Web sites to delivering specialized applications to providing virtual servers for collaboration or software development. However, all cloud computing is distinguished by the following:

- *Self-service and on demand*—Services, applications, and storage in a cloud are available to users at any time, upon the user's request. For example, if you subscribe to Google's Gmail or Google Docs service, you can log on and access your mail and documents whenever you choose.
- *Elastic*—The term **elastic** in cloud computing means that services and storage capacity can be quickly and dynamically—sometimes even automatically—scaled up or down. For example, if your database server on the cloud grows and needs additional hard disk space, it can expand without you having to alert the service provider. In fact, your server can be configured in such a way as to require no intervention in this case. The amount of space you can add and the flexibility with which it can be added depend on your agreement with the service provider. Elastic also means that storage

Net+
1.9

space can be reduced, and that applications and clients can be added or removed, upon demand.

- *Support for multiple platforms*—Clients of all types, including smartphones, laptops, desktops, thin clients, and tablet computers, can access services, applications, and storage in a cloud, no matter what operating system they run or where they are located, as long as they have a network connection.
- *Resource pooling and consolidation*—In the cloud, as on host computers that contain multiple virtual machines, resources such as disk space, applications, and services are consolidated. That means one cloud computing provider can host hundreds of Web sites for hundreds of different customers on just a few servers. This is an example of a **multitenant** model, in which multiple customers share storage locations or services without knowing it. In another example of resource pooling, a single backup program might ensure that the Web sites are backed up several times a day.
- *Metered service*—Whether the cloud provides applications, desktops, storage, or services, its use is measured. A service provider might limit or charge by the amount of bandwidth, processing power, storage space, or client connections available to customers.

An organization that develops software might choose to keep its test platform on a server in the cloud, rather than on a server in its computer room. Suppose it employs dozens of developers on one project, and these developers, half of them working from home, are located in six different countries. By contracting with a cloud services organization to host its server, the software company can ensure continuous, easy access for its developers, no matter where they are or what type of computer they use. Developers can load any kind of software on the server and test it from afar. If more hard disk space is needed, that can be dynamically allocated. In addition, the cloud services provider can make sure the development server is secure and regularly backed up. In this case, cloud computing removes the burden of managing the server from the company's IT personnel. Figure 10-16 illustrates this type of cloud computing.

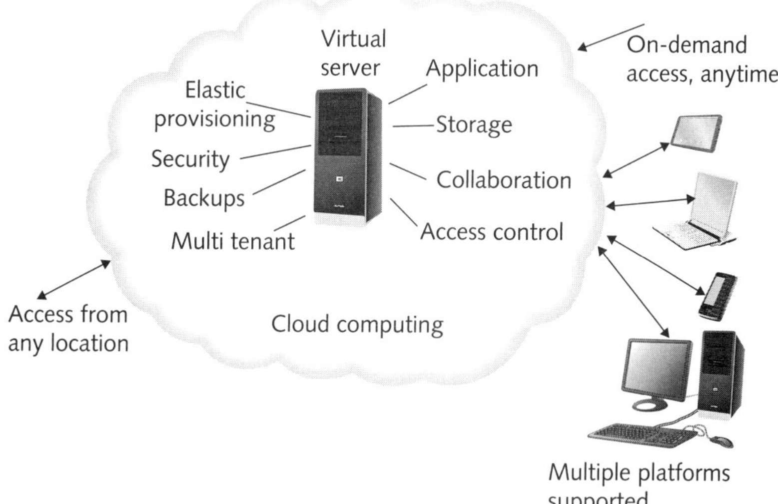

Figure 10-16 Example of cloud computing

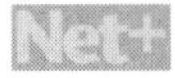
1.9

You probably recognize that the characteristics of cloud computing resemble those associated with virtualization. In fact, most cloud service providers use virtualization software to supply multiple platforms to multiple users. For example, industry leaders Rackspace and Amazon (in its Elastic Compute Cloud, or EC2, service) use Xen virtualization software to create virtual environments for their customers.

In addition to virtual servers, cloud computing can provide **virtual desktops**, which are desktop operating environments hosted virtually, on a different physical computer from the one the user interacts with. The term cloud computing also includes **NaaS (Network as a Service)**, in which a service provider offers its customers a complete set of networking services. For example, the owner of a start-up specialty foods company with few employees and zero technical expertise might choose to outsource all of the company's networking functions, such as mail, Web, DNS, DHCP, and remote access services, plus LAN and WAN connectivity, to a cloud computing service provider. Some IT professionals use a term with even broader meaning, **XaaS**, which stands for **Anything as a Service**, or sometimes **Everything as a Service**. In that model, the cloud assumes functions that go beyond networking, including, for example, monitoring, storage, applications, and virtual desktops.

Cloud services may be managed and delivered by a service provider over public transmission lines, such as the Internet, on a **public cloud**. Most of the examples in this section take place in public clouds. However, an organization with sufficient technical expertise on staff might establish a **private cloud** on its own servers in its own data center. This arrangement allows an organization to use existing hardware and connectivity, potentially saving money. It might also be preferable where network administrators want to ensure that resources are secure. Despite public cloud service providers' warranties of privacy and security, these remain significant concerns for many potential customers.

Chapter Summary

- Virtualization is the emulation of a computer, operating system environment, or application on a physical system. One host computer can support many VMs (virtual machines). VMs, also called guests, share the physical computer's CPU, hard disk, memory, and network interfaces. Yet each functions independently, with its own logically defined hardware resources, operating system, applications, and network interfaces.
- VMs exist as files on the hard disk of the physical computer. These files contain the operating system, applications, data, and configurations for the VMs.
- The software that allows you to define VMs and manages resource allocation and sharing among them is known as a virtual machine manager, or, more commonly, a hypervisor. Hypervisors are part of all virtualization programs, of which VMware is the most popular. Other virtualization programs include Hyper-V, KVM (Kernel-based Virtual Machine), and VirtualBox.
- Advantages of virtualization include efficient use of resources; cost and energy savings, which can contribute to sustainability; fault and threat isolation; and simple backups, recovery, and replication.
- Potential disadvantages of virtualization include compromised performance, increased complexity, increased licensing fees, and a single point of failure.

- To connect to a network, a virtual machine requires a virtual adapter, or vNIC (virtual NIC). Just like a physical NIC, a vNIC operates at the Data Link layer and provides the computer with network access. Each VM may have several vNICs, no matter how many NICs the host machine has.
- A virtual switch is a logically defined device that operates at the Data Link layer. Ports on a virtual switch connect vNICs with a network, whether virtual or physical, through the host's physical NIC. A virtual switch allows VMs to communicate with each other and with nodes on a physical LAN or WAN.
- Virtual switches reside in the RAM of the physical computers that act as their hosts, while their configuration resides in a separate file on the host's hard disk. One host can support multiple virtual switches. The hypervisor controls the virtual switches. In Hyper-V, a virtual switch is called a virtual network.
- When you configure a vNIC, you are asked to identify what type of network connection or networking mode the adapter will use. The most frequently used network connection types include bridged, NAT, and host-only.
- In bridged mode, a vNIC accesses a physical network using the host machine's NIC and obtains its own IP address, default gateway, and netmask from a DHCP server on the physical LAN. When connected using bridged mode, a VM appears to other nodes as just another client or server on the network. Bridged mode is best used for VMs that must be available at a specific address, such as mail servers or Web servers.
- In the NAT networking mode, a VM relies on the host machine to act as a NAT device. It obtains IP addressing information from the DHCP service in the host's virtualization software. A vNIC operating in NAT mode can still communicate with other nodes on the network and vice versa. However, other nodes communicate with the host machine's IP address to reach the VM; the VM itself is invisible to other nodes. NAT networking mode is appropriate for clients that do not need to be addressed directly and at a specific address by other nodes.

- In host-only networking mode, VMs on one host can exchange data with each other and with their host, but they cannot communicate with any nodes beyond the host to create an isolated, all-virtual network. In host-only mode, as in NAT mode, VMs use the DHCP service in the host's virtualization software to obtain IP address assignments. Host-only networking mode is best used for test environments.
- A virtual appliance is an image that includes the appropriate operating system, software, hardware specifications, and application configuration necessary for the package to run properly. Popular uses for virtual appliances include firewall and other security measures, network management, e-mail solutions, and remote access.
- VLANs are subnets logically defined on a physical switch that allow network administrators to separate network traffic for better performance, customized address management, and security. On a network that uses virtual machines, VLANs will typically include those VMs.
- To add VMs to a VLAN defined on a physical network, you modify a *virtual* switch's configuration. In other words, VMs are not added to a preexisting VLAN on the physical switch that manages that VLAN.

- In VMware, vNICs are associated with port groups, which can be assigned to VLANs. Multiple vNICs can be assigned to a single port group. Also, a single vNIC can be assigned to multiple port groups. In other virtualization programs, vNICs are assigned to VLANs by associating them directly with a VLAN number or with a bridge that is, in turn, associated with a VLAN.
- For VLANs to include vNICs, the host machine's physical NIC must be configured to operate in trunking mode. In other words, it must be capable of carrying the traffic of multiple VLANs. Virtualization software refers to the physical NIC, acting as an interface for VLANs, as a trunk.
- As a remote user, you can connect to a LAN or WAN in one of several ways: dial-up networking, connecting to a remote access server, remote virtual computing, or through a VPN (virtual private network).
- Dial-up networking involves a remote client dialing into a remote access server and connecting via a PSTN, X.25, or ISDN connection. The client must run dial-up software to initiate the connection, and the server runs specialized remote access software to accept and interpret the incoming signals.
- Remote access servers accept incoming connections from remote clients, authenticate users, allow them to log on to a LAN or WAN, and exchange data by encapsulating higher-layer protocols, such as TCP and IP in specialized protocols such as PPP. The Microsoft RRAS (Routing and Remote Access Service) is the remote access software that comes with the Windows operating systems.
- To exchange data, remote access servers and clients must communicate through special Data Link layer protocols, such as PPP (Point-to-Point Protocol) or SLIP (Serial Line Internet Protocol), that encapsulate higher-layer protocols, such as TCP and IP. PPP is the preferred protocol. When PPP is used on an Ethernet network, as is the case with most modern broadband Internet connections, it is called PPP over Ethernet, or PPPoE.
- Remote virtual computing uses specialized client and host software to allow a remote user to connect via modem to a workstation that is part of a LAN. Once the connection is made, the remote user can control that workstation, performing functions just as if she were directly connected to the LAN.
- Remote Desktop is a remote virtual computing client and server package that comes with Windows operating systems. VNC (Virtual Network Computing) refers to an open source system that enables a remote client (or viewer) workstation to manipulate and receive screen updates from a host. ICA (Independent Computing Architecture) provides the basis for Citrix Systems' proprietary remote virtual computing software.
- By creating a VPN (virtual private network), you can construct a WAN from existing public transmission systems. A VPN offers connectivity only to an organization's users, while keeping the data secure and isolated from other (public) traffic. To accomplish this, VPNs may be software or hardware based. Either way, they depend on secure protocols and transmission methods to keep data private.
- To make sure a VPN can carry all types of data in a private manner over any kind of connection, special VPN protocols encapsulate higher-layer protocols via tunneling.

Common tunneling protocols include PPTP (Point-to-Point Tunneling Protocol) and L2TP (Layer 2 Tunneling Protocol). Additional VPN protocols are discussed in Chapter 11, which focuses on network security.

- Cloud computing refers to the flexible provision of data storage, applications, or services to multiple clients over a network. Cloud computing consolidates resources and allows users from anywhere using any kind of client to access them. Further, cloud computing is elastic (that is, it can be quickly and easily scaled up or down). It is also metered, meaning that usage can be measured. Finally, it is available on demand.
- In NaaS (Network as a Service), a service provider offers its customers a complete set of networking services. XaaS, which stands for "Anything as a Service" or sometimes "Everything as a Service," includes functions that go beyond networking, including, for example, monitoring, storage, applications, and virtual desktops.
- Cloud services may be managed and delivered by a service provider over public transmission lines, such as the Internet, on a public cloud, or on an organization's servers and internal network in a private cloud.

Key Terms

Anything as a Service *See* XaaS.

authentication The process of comparing and matching a client's credentials with the credentials in the NOS user database to enable the client to log on to the network.

client-to-site VPN A type of VPN in which clients, servers, and other hosts establish tunnels with a private network using a remote access server or VPN gateway. Each client on a client-to-site VPN must run VPN software to create the tunnel for, and encrypt and encapsulate data.

cloud computing The flexible provision of data storage, applications, or services to multiple clients over a network. Cloud computing consolidates resources and is elastic, metered, self-service, multiplatform, and available on demand.

credentials A user's unique identifying characteristics that enable him to authenticate with a server and gain access to network resources. The most common credentials are a username and a password.

dial-up networking The process of dialing into a remote access server to connect with a network, be it private or public.

elastic A characteristic of cloud computing that means services can be quickly and dynamically—sometimes even automatically—scaled up or down.

Everything as a Service *See* XaaS.

guest In the context of virtualization, a virtual machine operated and managed by a virtualization program.

host In the context of virtualization, the physical computer on which virtualization software operates and manages guests.

Hyper-V Microsoft's virtualization software package. Hyper-V operates with Windows Server 2008 and Windows Server 2008 R2.

hypervisor The element of virtualization software that manages multiple guest machines and their connections to the host (and by association, to a physical network). A hypervisor is also known as a virtual machine manager.

ICA (Independent Computing Architecture) The software from Citrix Systems, Inc., that, when installed on a client, enables the client to connect with a host computer and exchange keystrokes, mouse clicks, and screen updates. Citrix's ICA client can work with virtually any operating system or application.

Kernel-based Virtual Machine *See* KVM.

KVM (Kernel-based Virtual Machine) An open source virtualization package designed for use with Linux systems.

L2TP (Layer 2 Tunneling Protocol) A protocol that encapsulates PPP data, for use on VPNs. L2TP is based on Cisco technology and is standardized by the IETF. It is distinguished by its compatibility among different manufacturers' equipment; its ability to connect between clients, routers, and servers alike; and also by the fact that it can connect nodes belonging to different Layer 3 networks.

Layer 2 Tunneling Protocol *See* L2TP.

multitenant A feature of cloud computing in which multiple customers share storage locations or services without knowing it.

NaaS (Network as a Service) A type of cloud computing that offers clients a complete set of networking services—for example, mail, Web, DNS, DHCP, and remote access services, plus LAN and WAN connectivity.

Network as a Service *See* NaaS.

open source The term that describes software whose code is publicly available for use and modification.

Point-to-Point Protocol *See* PPP.

Point-to-Point Protocol over Ethernet *See* PPPoE.

Point-to-Point Tunneling Protocol *See* PPTP.

PPP (Point-to-Point Protocol) A communications protocol that enables a workstation to connect to a server using a serial connection. PPP can support multiple Network layer protocols and can use both asynchronous and synchronous communications. It performs compression and error correction and requires little configuration on the client workstation.

PPPoE (Point-to-Point Protocol over Ethernet) PPP running over an Ethernet network.

PPTP (Point-to-Point Tunneling Protocol) A Layer 2 protocol developed by Microsoft that encapsulates PPP data for transmission over VPN connections. PPTP operates with Windows RRAS access services and can accept connections from multiple different clients. It is simple, but less secure than other modern tunneling protocols.

private cloud An arrangement in which shared and flexible data storage, applications, or services are managed on and delivered via an organization's internal network.

public cloud An arrangement in which shared and flexible data storage, applications, or services are managed centrally by service providers and delivered over public transmission lines, such as the Internet. Rackspace and Amazon (with its EC2 offering) are leading public cloud service providers.

RAS (Remote Access Service) The dial-up networking software provided with Microsoft Windows 95, 98, NT, and 2000 client operating systems. RAS requires software installed on both the client and server, a server configured to accept incoming clients, and a client with sufficient privileges (including username and password) on the server to access its resources. In more recent versions of Windows, RAS has been incorporated into the RRAS (Routing and Remote Access Service).

RDP (Remote Desktop Protocol) An Application layer protocol that uses TCP/IP to transmit graphics and text quickly over a remote client-host connection. RDP also carries session, licensing, and encryption information.

remote access A method for connecting and logging on to a LAN from a workstation that is remote, or not physically connected, to the LAN.

Remote Access Service *See* RAS.

Remote Desktop A feature of Windows operating systems that allows a computer to act as a remote host and be controlled from a client running another Windows operating system.

Remote Desktop Protocol *See* RDP.

Routing and Remote Access Service (RRAS) The software included with Windows operating systems that enables a server to act as a router, firewall, and remote access server. Using RRAS, a server can provide network access to multiple remote clients.

RRAS *See* Routing and Remote Access Service.

Serial Line Internet Protocol *See* SLIP.

site-to-site VPN A type of VPN in which VPN gateways at multiple sites encrypt and encapsulate data to exchange over a tunnel with other VPN gateways. Meanwhile, clients, servers, and other hosts on a site-to-site VPN communicate with the VPN gateway.

SLIP (Serial Line Internet Protocol) A communications protocol that enables a workstation to connect to a server using a serial connection. SLIP can support only asynchronous communications and IP traffic and requires some configuration on the client workstation. SLIP has been made obsolete by PPP.

thin client A client that relies on another host for the majority of processing and hard disk resources necessary to run applications and share files over the network.

tunnel A secured, virtual connection between two nodes on a VPN.

tunneling The process of encapsulating one type of protocol in another. Tunneling is the way in which higher-layer data is transported over VPNs by Layer 2 protocols.

virtual adapter *See* vNIC.

virtual appliance An image that includes the appropriate operating system, software, hardware specifications, and application configuration necessary for a prepackaged solution to run properly on a virtual machine.

virtual bridge An interface connecting a vNIC with a virtual or physical network, or a port on a virtual switch.

virtual desktop A desktop operating environment that is hosted virtually, on a different physical computer from the one the user interacts with.

virtual machine *See* VM.

virtual machine manager *See* hypervisor.

Virtual Network Computing *See* VNC.

virtual network interface card *See* vNIC.

virtual private network *See* VPN.

virtual server A server that exists as a virtual machine, created and managed by virtualization software on a host, or physical, computer.

virtual switch A logically defined device that is created and managed by virtualization software and that operates at the Data Link layer. Ports on a virtual switch connect virtual machines with a network, whether virtual or physical, through the host's physical NIC.

virtual workstation A workstation that exists as a virtual machine, created and managed by virtualization software on a host, or physical, computer.

VirtualBox A virtualization software platform from Oracle.

virtualization The emulation of a computer, operating system environment, or application on a physical system.

VM (virtual machine) A computer that exists in emulation on a physical computer, or host machine. Multiple VMs may exist on one host where they share the physical computer's CPU, hard disk, memory, and network interfaces.

VMware A vendor that supplies the most popular types of workstation and server virtualization software. Used casually, the term *VMware* may also refer to the virtualization software distributed by the company.

VNC (Virtual Network Computing) An open source system that enables a remote client (or viewer) workstation to manipulate and receive screen updates from a host. Examples of VNC software include RealVNC, TightVNC, and UltraVNC.

vNIC (virtual network interface card) A logically defined network interface associated with a virtual machine.

VPN (virtual private network) A logically constructed WAN that uses existing public transmission systems. VPNs can be created through the use of software or combined software and hardware solutions. This type of network allows an organization to carve out a private WAN through the Internet, serving only its offices, while keeping the data secure and isolated from other (public) traffic.

XaaS (Anything as a Service, or Everything as a Service) A type of cloud computing in which the cloud assumes functions beyond networking, including, for example, monitoring, storage, applications, and virtual desktops.

Xen An open source virtualization software platform from Citrix Systems.

Review Questions

1. What term refers to the flexible provision of data storage, applications, or services to multiple clients over a network?
   a. virtual private networking
   b. cloud computing
   c. virtual computing
   d. remote virtual computing

2. In what type of VPN do clients, servers, and other hosts establish tunnels with a private network using a remote access server or VPN gateway?
    a. client-to-client
    b. site-to-client
    c. client-to-site
    d. site-to-site
3. What term in cloud computing means that services and storage capacity can be quickly and dynamically—sometimes even automatically—scaled up or down?
    a. multitenant
    b. flexible
    c. reactive
    d. elastic
4. Which VPN protocol is a standard accepted and used by many different vendors, so it can connect a VPN that uses a mix of equipment types—for example, a Juniper router, a Cisco router, and a Netgear router?
    a. PPTP
    b. PPP
    c. L2TP
    d. SLIP

5. What type of network connection is appropriate for VMs that do not need to be accessed at a known address by other network nodes?
    a. host-only
    b. NAT
    c. VPN
    d. bridged
6. True or false? Virtual switches or bridges reside in the RAM of the physical computers that act as their hosts, while their configuration resides in a separate file on the host's hard disk.
7. True or false? Because guest systems in a virtual environment cannot be completely isolated, it is important that each guest system be configured to interact with all of the guest systems on a host computer.
8. True or false? If you are running a virtualization program on a Windows 7 workstation, you can install a guest machine based on an Ubuntu Linux image you download from Ubuntu's Web site.

9. True or false? From a network administrator's point of view, dial-up networking requires a significant amount of maintenance to ensure that clients can always connect to a pool of modems.

10. True or false? Just like a physical NIC, a vNIC operates at the Data Link layer and provides the computer with network access.

11. A(n) ________________ is a subnet that is logically defined on a physical switch that allows network administrators to separate network traffic for better performance, customized address management, and security.

12. A(n) ________________ is an image that includes the appropriate operating system, software, hardware specifications, and application configuration necessary for the package to run properly.

13. ________________ is an earlier and less-sophisticated remote access protocol version than PPP.

14. A type of cloud computing that offers clients a complete set of networking services, such as mail, Web, DNS, DHCP, and remote access services, plus LAN and WAN connectivity is a(n) ________________.

15. When a remote access server receives a request for connection, the remote access server software presents the remote user with a prompt for ________________, which is typically the username and password.

After reading this chapter and completing the exercises, you will be able to:

- Identify security threats and vulnerabilities in LANs and WANs and design security policies that minimize risks
- Explain security measures for network hardware and design, including firewalls, intrusion detection systems, and scanning tools
- Understand methods of encryption, such as SSL and IPSec, that can secure data in storage and in transit
- Describe how user authentication protocols, such as PKI, RADIUS, TACACS+, Kerberos, CHAP, MS-CHAP, and EAP function
- Use network operating system techniques to provide basic security
- Understand wireless security protocols, such as WEP, WPA, and 802.11i

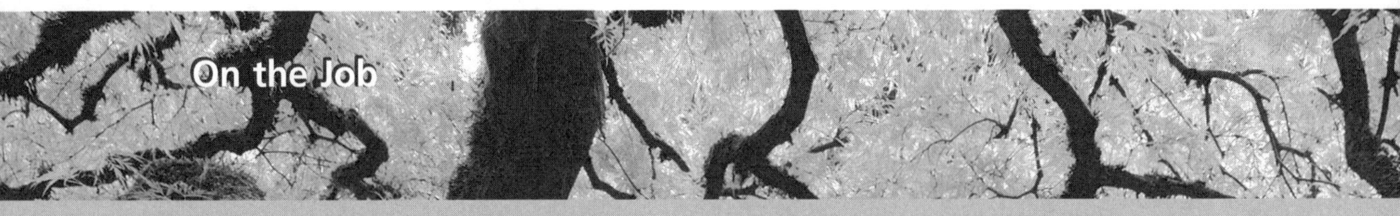

Security often involves synthesizing tidbits of information from many disparate sources in order to form an accurate picture of what has happened. My team once responded to a report that desktop computers at a biomedical corporation were crashing, with their hard drives erased, apparently, by a virus that circumvented the company's antivirus protections.

While examining an affected PC, we noticed that a few processes were still running—thanks to the fact that the operating system generally won't allow the deletion of files that are in use. Among these processes were several instances of svchost.exe. Closer examination revealed that one of these had the same name as the legitimate Windows executable, but was in fact an impostor: a saboteur was at work.

Using a disassembler, we determined that, every minute, the Trojan checked a folder on a server for the presence of a command file, whose contents it would execute. We built a program to monitor that directory and archive copies of any files that appeared; our program also recorded the user account that put the file there and the name of the system from which this was done.

The account had domain administrator privileges, and this led us to examine the domain's login scripts, where we found the code that installed the Trojan on users' workstations. We wrote a second program to record the MAC address of the system when it registered its name with the DHCP server and inspect the ARP tables from the network's switches in order to find the physical port to which it was connected. Then, with a building wiring diagram, we were able to track the culprit to a specific cubicle.

Finding the source of this problem involved knowledge about network infrastructure, operating systems, administration techniques, programming, and reverse-engineering. This is an extreme example, to be sure, but real-world security problems seldom confine themselves to a single technical area of specialization.

Peyton Engel
Technical Architect, CDW Corporation

In the early days of computing, when secured mainframes acted as central hosts and data repositories were accessed only by dumb terminals with limited rights, network security was all but unassailable. As networks have become more geographically distributed and heterogeneous, however, the risk of their misuse has also increased. Consider the largest, most heterogeneous network in existence: the Internet. Because it contains millions of points of entry, millions of servers, and millions of miles of transmission paths, it leads to millions of attacks on private networks every day. The threat of an outsider accessing an organization's network via the Internet, and then stealing or destroying data, is very real. In this chapter, you will learn about numerous threats to your network's data and infrastructure, how to manage those vulnerabilities, and, perhaps most important, how to convey the importance of network security to the rest of your organization through an effective security policy. If you choose to specialize in network security, consider attaining CompTIA's Security+ certification, which requires deeper knowledge of the topics covered in this chapter.

Security Assessment

5.4 Before spending time and money on network security, you should examine your network's security risks. As you learn about each risk facing your network, consider the effect that a loss or breach of data, programs, or access would have on your network. The more serious the potential consequences, the more attention you need to pay to the security of your network.

Different types of organizations have different levels of network security risk. For example, if you work for a large savings and loan institution that allows its clients to view their current loan status online, you must consider a number of risks associated with data and access. If someone obtained unauthorized access to your network, all of your customers' personal financial data could be vulnerable. On the other hand, if you work for a local car wash that uses its internal LAN only to track assets and sales, you may be less concerned if someone gains access to your network because the implications of unauthorized access to your data are less dire. When considering security risks, the fundamental questions are: "What is at risk?" and "What do I stand to lose if it is stolen, damaged, or eradicated?"

Every organization should assess its security risks by conducting a **posture assessment**, which is a thorough examination of each aspect of the network to determine how it might be compromised. Posture assessments should be performed at least annually and preferably quarterly. They should also be performed after making any significant changes to the network. For each threat listed in the following sections, your posture assessment should rate the severity of its potential effects, as well as its likelihood. A threat's consequences may be severe, potentially resulting in a network outage or the dispersal of top-secret information, or it may be mild, potentially resulting in a lack of access for one user or the dispersal of a relatively insignificant piece of corporate data. The more devastating a threat's effects and the more likely it is to happen, the more rigorously your security measures should address it.

If your IT Department has sufficient skills and time for routine posture assessments, they can be performed in-house. A qualified consulting company can also assess the security of your network. If the company is accredited by an agency that sets network security standards, the assessment qualifies as a **security audit**.

Certain customers—for example, a military agency—might require your company to pass an accredited security audit before they'll do business with you. Regulators require some types of companies, such as accounting firms, to host periodic security audits. But even if an audit is optional, the advantage of having an objective third party analyze your network is that he might find risks that you overlooked because of your familiarity with your environment. Security audits might seem expensive, but if your network hosts confidential and critical data, they are well worth the cost.

In the next section, you will learn about security risks associated with people, hardware, software, and Internet access.

Security Risks

5.4 To understand how to manage network security, you first need to know how to recognize threats that your network could suffer. And to do that, you must be familiar with the terms coined by network security experts. A ***hacker***, in the original sense of the word, is someone who masters the inner workings of computer hardware and software in an effort to better understand them. To be called a hacker used to be a compliment, reflecting extraordinary computer skills. Today, *hacker* is used more generally to describe individuals who gain unauthorized access to systems or networks with or without malicious intent.

A weakness of a system, process, or architecture that could lead to compromised information or unauthorized access is known as a **vulnerability**. The means of taking advantage of a vulnerability is known as an **exploit**. For example, in Chapter 8 you learned about the possibility for unauthorized, or rogue, access points to make themselves available to wireless clients. Once unsuspecting clients associate with such access points, the hacker can steal data in transit or access information on the client's system. When the rogue access point masquerades as a valid access point, using the same SSID (service set identifier) and potentially other identical settings, the exploit is known as the **evil twin**. This exploit takes advantage of a vulnerability inherent in wireless communications in which SSIDs are openly broadcast and Wi-Fi clients scan for connections.

A **zero-day exploit** is one that takes advantage of a software vulnerability that hasn't yet become public, and is known only to the hacker who discovered it. Zero-day exploits are particularly dangerous because the vulnerability is exploited before the software developer has the opportunity to provide a solution for it. Most vulnerabilities, however, are well known. Throughout this chapter, you will learn about several kinds of exploits and how to prevent or counteract security threats.

As you read about each vulnerability, think about how it could be prevented, whether it applies to your network (and if so, how damaging it might be), and how it relates to other security threats. Keep in mind that malicious and determined intruders may use one technique, which then allows them to use a second technique, which then allows them to use a third technique, and so on. For example, a hacker might discover someone's username by watching her log on to the network; the hacker might then use a password-cracking program to access the network, where he might plant a program that generates an extraordinary volume of traffic that essentially disables the network's connectivity devices.

Risks Associated with People

By some estimates, human errors, ignorance, and omissions cause more than half of all security breaches sustained by networks. One of the most common methods by which an intruder gains access to a network is to simply ask users for their passwords. For example, the intruder might pose as a technical support analyst who needs to know the password to troubleshoot a problem. This strategy is commonly called **social engineering** because it involves manipulating social relationships to gain access. A related practice is **phishing**, in which a person attempts to glean access or authentication information by posing as someone who needs that information. For example, a hacker might send an e-mail asking you to submit your user ID and password to a Web site whose link is provided in the message, claiming

5.4

that it's necessary to verify your account with a particular online retailer. Following are some additional risks associated with people:

- Intruders or attackers using social engineering or snooping to obtain user passwords
- An administrator incorrectly creating or configuring user IDs, groups, and their associated rights on a file server, resulting in file and logon access vulnerabilities
- Network administrators overlooking security flaws in topology or hardware configuration
- Network administrators overlooking security flaws in the operating system or application configuration
- Lack of proper documentation and communication of security policies, leading to deliberate or inadvertent misuse of files or network access
- Dishonest or disgruntled employees abusing their file and access rights
- An unused computer or terminal being left logged on to the network, thereby providing an entry point for an intruder
- Users or administrators choosing easy-to-guess passwords
- Authorized staff leaving computer room doors open or unlocked, allowing unauthorized individuals to enter
- Staff discarding disks or backup tapes in public waste containers
- Administrators neglecting to remove access and file rights for employees who have left the organization
- Vendors or business partners who are granted temporary access to private networks
- Users writing their passwords on paper, then placing the paper in an easily accessible place (for example, taping it to a monitor or keyboard)

Human errors account for so many security breaches because taking advantage of them is often an easy way to circumvent network security.

Risks Associated with Transmission and Hardware

This section describes security risks inherent in the Physical, Data Link, and Network layers of the OSI model. Recall that the transmission media, NICs, network access methods (for example, Ethernet), switches, routers, access points, and gateways reside at these layers. At these levels, security breaches require more technical sophistication than those that take advantage of human errors. For instance, to eavesdrop on transmissions passing through a switch, an intruder must use a device such as a protocol analyzer, connected to one of the switch's ports. In the middle layers of the OSI model, it is somewhat difficult to distinguish between hardware and software techniques. For example, because a router acts to connect one type of network to another, an intruder might take advantage of the router's security flaws by sending a flood of TCP/IP transmissions to the router, thereby disabling it from carrying legitimate traffic.

The following risks are inherent in network hardware and design:

- Transmissions can be intercepted. One type of attack that relies on intercepted transmissions is known as a **man-in-the-middle attack**. It can take one of several forms, but in all cases a person redirects or captures secure transmissions as they

5.4

occur. For example, in the case of an evil twin attack, a hacker could intercept transmissions between clients and the rogue access point, and, for instance, learn users' passwords or even supply users with a phony Web site that looks valid but presents clickable options capable of harming their systems.

- Networks that use leased public lines, such as T1 or DSL connections to the Internet, are vulnerable to eavesdropping at a building's demarc (demarcation point), at a remote switching facility, or in a central office.
- Repeating devices broadcast traffic over the entire segment, thus making transmissions more widely vulnerable to sniffing. By contrast, switches provide logical point-to-point communications, which limit the availability of data transmissions to the sending and receiving nodes. Still, intruders could physically connect to a switch or router and intercept the traffic it receives and forwards.
- Unused switch, router, or server ports can be exploited and accessed by hackers if they are not disabled. A router's configuration port, accessible by Telnet, might not be adequately secured. Network administrators can test how vulnerable their servers, routers, switches, and other devices are by using a **port scanner**, or software that searches the node for open ports. The network administrator can then secure those ports revealed by the scan to be vulnerable. Later in this chapter, you'll learn about port scanning tools.
- If routers are not properly configured to mask internal subnets, users on outside networks (such as the Internet) can read the private addresses.
- If routers aren't configured to drop packets that match certain, suspicious characteristics, they are more vulnerable to attack.
- Access servers used by remote users might not be carefully secured and monitored.
- Computers hosting very sensitive data might coexist on the same subnet with computers open to the general public.
- Passwords for switches, routers, and other devices might not be sufficiently difficult to guess, changed frequently, or worse, might be left at their default value.

Imagine that a hacker wants to bring a library's database and mail servers to a halt. Suppose also that the library's database is public and can be searched by anyone on the Web. The hacker might begin by scanning ports on the database server to determine which ones have no protection. If she found an open port on the database server, the hacker might connect to the system and deposit a program that would, a few days later, damage operating system files. Or, she could launch a heavy stream of traffic that overwhelms the database server and prevents it from functioning. She might also use her newly discovered access to determine the root password on the system, gain access to other systems, and launch a similar attack on the library's mail server, which is attached to the database server. In this way, even a single mistake on one server (not protecting an open port) can open vulnerabilities on multiple systems.

Risks Associated with Protocols and Software

Like hardware, networked software is only as secure as you configure it to be. This section describes risks inherent in the higher layers of the OSI model, such as the Transport, Session, Presentation, and Application layers. As noted earlier, the distinctions between hardware and software risks are somewhat blurry because protocols and hardware operate in tandem.

Net+ 5.4 For example, if a router is improperly configured, a hacker could exploit the openness of TCP/IP to gain access to a network. NOSs (network operating systems) and application software present different risks. In many cases, their security is compromised by a poor understanding of file access rights or simple negligence in configuring the software. Remember—even the best encryption, computer room door locks, security policies, and password rules make no difference if you grant the wrong users access to critical data and programs.

The following are some risks pertaining to networking protocols and software:

- Certain TCP/IP protocols are inherently insecure. For example, IP addresses can be falsified, checksums can be thwarted, UDP requires no authentication, and TCP requires only weak authentication. FTP is notorious for its vulnerabilities. In a famous exploit, **FTP bounce**, hackers take advantage of this insecure protocol. When a client running an FTP utility requests data from an FTP server, it specifies an IP address and port number for the data's destination. Normally, the client specifies its own IP address. However, it is possible for the client to specify any port on any host's IP address. By commanding the FTP server to connect to a different computer, a hacker can scan the ports on other hosts and transmit malicious code. To thwart FTP bounce attacks, most modern FTP servers will not issue data to hosts other than the client that originated the request.
- Trust relationships between one server and another might allow a hacker to access the entire network because of a single flaw.
- NOSs might contain "back doors" or security flaws that allow unauthorized users to gain access to the system. Unless the network administrator performs regular updates, a hacker may exploit these flaws.
- **Buffer overflow** is a vulnerability in all operating systems. Buffers, which temporarily store information in memory, are not strictly limited to the areas allocated to them on the hard disk. Someone who wants to harm a system can write a program that forces the buffer's size beyond its allotted space and saves data into adjacent memory areas. In this way, the malicious program can change the way the computer operates.

- If the NOS allows server operators to exit to a command prompt, intruders could run destructive command-line programs.
- Administrators might accept the default security options after installing an operating system or application. Often, defaults are not optimal. For example, the default username that enables someone to modify anything in Windows Server 2008 R2 is called *Administrator*. This default is well known, so if you leave the default username as *Administrator*, you have given a hacker half the information he needs to access and obtain full rights to your system.
- Transactions that take place between applications, such as databases and Web-based forms, might allow interception.

To understand the risks that arise when an administrator accepts the default settings associated with a software program, consider the following scenario. Imagine that you have invited a large group of computer science students to tour your IT Department. While you're in the computer room talking about subnetting, a bored student standing next to a Windows 7 workstation that is logged on to the network decides to find out which programs are installed on the workstation. He discovers that this workstation has the SQL Server administrator

5.4 software installed. Your organization uses a SQL Server database to hold all of your employees' salaries, addresses, and other confidential information. The student knows a little about SQL Server, including the facts that the default administrator user ID is called *sa,* and that, by default, no password is created for this ID when someone installs SQL Server. He tries connecting to your SQL Server database with the *sa* user ID and no password. Because you accepted the defaults for the program during its installation, within seconds the student is able to gain access to your employees' information. He could then change, delete, or steal any of the data.

Risks Associated with Internet Access

Although the Internet has brought computer crime, such as hacking, to the public's attention, network security is more often compromised "from the inside" than from external sources. Nevertheless, the threat of outside intruders is very real.

Users need to be careful when they connect to the Internet. Even the most popular Web browsers sometimes contain bugs that permit scripts to access their systems while they're connected to the Internet, potentially for the purpose of causing damage. Users must also be careful about providing information while browsing the Web. Some sites will capture that information to use when attempting to break into systems. Bear in mind that hackers are creative and typically revel in devising new ways of breaking into systems. As a result, new Internet-related security threats arise frequently. By keeping software current, staying abreast of emerging security threats, and designing your Internet access wisely, users can prevent most of these threats.

Common Internet-related security issues include the following:

- A firewall may not provide adequate protection if it is configured improperly. For example, it may allow outsiders to obtain internal IP addresses, and then use those addresses to pretend that they have authority to access your internal network from the Internet—a process called **IP spoofing**. Alternately, a firewall may not be configured correctly to perform even its simplest function, which is preventing unauthorized packets from entering the LAN from outside. (You will learn more about firewalls later in this chapter.) Correctly configuring a firewall is one of the best means to protect your internal LAN from Internet-based attacks.
- When a user Telnets or FTPs to your site over the Internet, her user ID and password are transmitted in plain text—that is, unencrypted. Anyone monitoring the network (that is, running a network monitor program or a hacking program specially designed to capture logon data) can pick up the user ID and password and use it to gain access to the system.
- Hackers may obtain information about your user ID from newsgroups, mailing lists, or forms you have filled out on the Web.
- While users remain logged on to Internet chat sessions, they may be vulnerable to other Internet users who might send commands to their machines that cause the screen to fill with garbage characters and require them to terminate their chat sessions. This type of attack is called **flashing**.

5.4

- After gaining access to your system through the Internet, a hacker may launch denial-of-service attacks. A **denial-of-service attack** occurs when a system becomes unable to function because it has been inundated with requests for services and can't respond to any of them. As a result, all data transmissions are disrupted. This incursion is a relatively simple attack to launch (for example, a hacker could create a looping program that sends thousands of e-mail messages to your system per minute). One specific type of denial-of-service attack, known as a **smurf attack**, occurs when a hacker issues a flood of broadcast ping messages. In this case, the originating source address of the attack is spoofed to appear as a known host on the network. Because it's a broadcast transmission, all hosts on the subnet receive the ping messages and then generate more ICMP traffic by responding to it. Denial-of-service attacks can also result from malfunctioning software. Regularly upgrading software is essential to maintaining network security.

Now that you understand the variety of risks facing networks, you are ready to learn about policies that help mitigate these risks.

An Effective Security Policy

5.4

Network security breaches can be initiated from within an organization, and many depend on human errors. This section describes how to minimize the risk of break-ins by communicating with and managing the users in your organization via a thoroughly planned security policy.

A **security policy** identifies your security goals, risks, levels of authority, designated security coordinator and team members, responsibilities for each team member, and responsibilities for each employee. In addition, it specifies how to address security breaches. It should not state exactly which hardware, software, architecture, or protocols will be used to ensure security, nor how hardware or software will be installed and configured. These details change from time to time and should be shared only with authorized network administrators or managers.

Security Policy Goals

Before drafting a security policy, you should understand why the security policy is necessary and how it will serve your organization. Typical goals for security policies are as follows:

- Ensure that authorized users have appropriate access to the resources they need.
- Prevent unauthorized users from gaining access to the network, systems, programs, or data.
- Protect sensitive data from unauthorized access, both from within and from outside the organization.
- Prevent accidental damage to hardware or software.
- Prevent intentional damage to hardware or software.
- Create an environment in which the network and systems can withstand and, if necessary, quickly respond to and recover from any type of threat.
- Communicate each employee's responsibilities with respect to maintaining data integrity and system security.

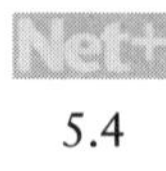

5.4

A company's security policy need not pertain exclusively to computers or networks. For example, it might state that each employee must shred paper files that contain sensitive data or that each employee is responsible for signing in his or her visitors at the front desk and obtaining a temporary badge for them. Noncomputer-related aspects of security policies are beyond the scope of this chapter, however.

After defining the goals of your security policy, you can devise a strategy to attain them. First, you might form a committee composed of managers and interested parties from a variety of departments, in addition to your network administrators. The more decision-making people you can involve, the more supported and effective your policy will be. This committee can assign a security coordinator, who will then drive the creation of a security policy.

To increase the acceptance of your security policy in your organization, tie security measures to business needs and clearly communicate the potential effects of security breaches. For example, if your company sells clothes over the Internet and a two-hour outage (as could be caused by a hacker who uses IP spoofing to gain control of your systems) could cost the company $1 million in lost sales, make certain that users and managers understand this fact. If they do, they are more likely to embrace the security policy.

A security policy must address an organization's specific risks. To understand your risks, you should conduct a posture assessment that identifies vulnerabilities and rates both the severity of each threat and its likelihood of occurring, as described earlier in this chapter. After risks are identified, the security coordinator should assign one person the responsibility for addressing that threat.

Security Policy Content

After you have identified risks and assigned responsibilities for managing them, you are ready to outline the policy's content. Subheadings for the policy outline might include the following: Password policy, Software installation policy, Confidential and sensitive data policy, Network access policy, E-mail use policy, Internet use policy, Remote access policy, Policies for connecting to customers' and vendors' networks, Policies for use of personal smartphones and laptops, and Computer room access policy. Although compiling all of this information might seem daunting, the process ensures that everyone understands the organization's stance on security and the reasons it is so important.

The security policy should explain to users what they can and cannot do and how these measures protect the network's security. A section aimed at users might organize security rules according to the particular function or part of the network to which they apply. This approach makes the policy easier for users to read and understand; it also prevents them from having to read through the entire document. For example, in the "Passwords" section, guidelines might include "Users may not share passwords with friends or relatives," "users must choose passwords that exceed ten characters and are composed of both letters and numbers," and "users should choose passwords that bear no resemblance to a spouse's name, pet's name, birth date, anniversary, or other widely available information."

Net+ 5.4 A security policy should also define what *confidential* means to the organization. In general, information is confidential if it could be used by other parties to impair an organization's functioning, decrease customers' confidence, cause a financial loss, damage an organization's status, or give a significant advantage to a competitor. However, if you work in an environment such as a hospital, where most data is sensitive or confidential, your security policy should classify information in degrees of sensitivity that correspond to how strictly its access is regulated. For example, top-secret data may be accessible only by the organization's CEO and vice presidents, whereas confidential data may be accessible only to those who must modify or create it (for example, doctors or hospital accountants).

Response Policy

Finally, a security policy should provide for a planned response in the event of a security breach. The response policy should identify the members of a response team, all of who should clearly understand the security policy, risks, and measures in place. Each team member should accept a role with certain responsibilities. The security response team should regularly rehearse their defense by participating in a security threat drill. Suggested team roles include the following:

- *Dispatcher*—The person on call who first notices or is alerted to the problem. The dispatcher notifies the lead technical support specialist and then the manager. He also creates a record for the incident, detailing the time it began, its symptoms, and any other pertinent information about the situation. The dispatcher remains available to answer calls from clients or employees or to assist the manager.
- *Manager*—This team member coordinates the resources necessary to solve the problem. If in-house technicians cannot handle the break-in, the manager finds outside assistance. The manager also ensures that the security policy is followed and that everyone within the organization is aware of the situation. As the response ensues, the manager continues to monitor events and communicate with the public relations specialist.

- *Technical support specialist*—This team member focuses on only one thing: solving the problem as quickly as possible. After the situation has been resolved, the technical support specialist describes in detail what happened and helps the manager find ways to avert such an incident in the future. Depending on the size of the organization and the severity of the incident, this role may be filled by more than one person.
- *Public relations specialist*—If necessary, this team member learns about the situation and the response and then acts as official spokesperson for the organization to the public.

After resolving a problem, the team reviews what happened, determines how it might have been prevented, and then implements those measures to prevent future problems. A security policy alone can't guard against intruders. Network administrators must also attend to physical, network design, and NOS vulnerabilities, as described in the following sections.

Physical Security

An important element in network security is restricting physical access to its components. Only trusted networking staff should have access to secure computer rooms, telco rooms, wiring closets, storage rooms, entrance facilities, and locked equipment cabinets. Furthermore, only authorized staff should have access to the premises, such as offices and data centers, where these rooms are located. If computer rooms are not locked, intruders may steal equipment or sabotage software or hardware. For example, a malicious visitor could slip into an unsecured computer room and take control of a server where an administrator is logged on, then steal data or reformat the server's hard disk. Although a security policy defines who has access to the computer room, locking the locations that house networking equipment is necessary to keep unauthorized individuals out.

Locks may be either physical or electronic. Many large organizations require authorized employees to wear electronic access badges. These badges can be programmed to allow their owner access to some, but not all, rooms in a building. Figure 11-1 depicts a typical badge access security system.

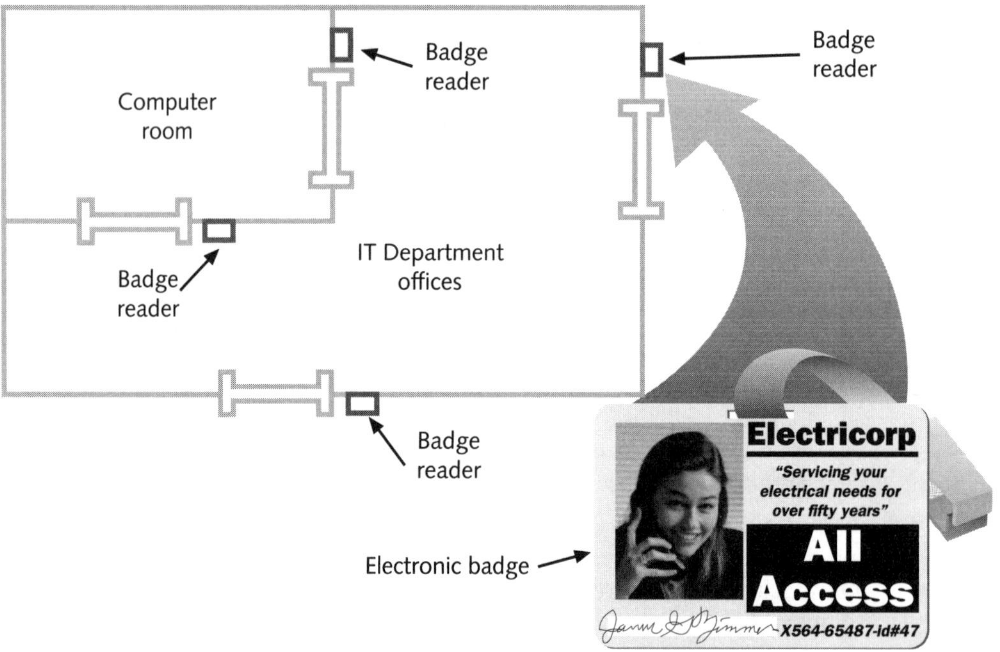

Figure 11-1 Badge access security system

A less-expensive alternative to the electronic badge access system consists of locks that require entrants to punch a numeric code to gain access. For added security, these electronic locks can be combined with key locks. A more-expensive solution involves **biorecognition access**, in which a device scans an individual's unique physical characteristics, such as the color patterns in her iris or the geometry of her hand, to verify her identity. On a larger scale, organizations may regulate entrance through physical barriers to their campuses, such as gates, fences, walls, or landscaping.

Many IT departments also use closed-circuit TV systems to monitor activity in secured rooms. Surveillance cameras can be placed in data centers, computer rooms, telco rooms, and data storage areas, as well as facility entrances. A central security office might display several camera views at once, or it might switch from camera to camera. The video footage generated from these cameras is usually saved for a time in case it's needed in a security breach investigation or prosecution.

As with other security measures, the most important way to ensure physical security is to plan for it. You can begin your planning by asking questions related to physical security checks in your security audit. Relevant questions include the following:

- Which rooms contain critical systems or data and must be secured?
- Through what means might intruders gain access to the facility, computer room, telecommunications room, wiring closet, or data storage areas (including doors, windows, adjacent rooms, ceilings, temporary walls, hallways, and so on)?
- How and to what extent are authorized personnel granted entry? (Do they undergo background or reference checks? Is their need for access clearly justified? Are their hours of access restricted? Who ensures that lost keys or ID badges are reported?)
- Are employees instructed to ensure security after entering or leaving secured areas (for example, by not propping open doors)?
- Are authentication methods (such as ID badges) difficult to forge or circumvent?
- Do supervisors or security personnel make periodic physical security checks?
- Are all combinations, codes, or other access means to computer facilities protected at all times, and are these combinations changed frequently?
- Do you have a plan for documenting and responding to physical security breaches?

Also consider what you might stand to lose if someone salvaged computers you discarded. To guard against the threat of information being stolen from a decommissioned hard disk, you can run a specialized disk sanitizer program to not only delete the hard drive's contents but also make file recovery impossible. Alternatively, you can remove the disk from the computer and erase its contents using a magnetic hard disk eraser. Some security professionals even advise physically destroying a disk by pulverizing or melting it to be certain data is unreadable.

Security in Network Design

Addressing physical access to hardware and connections is just one part of a comprehensive security approach. Even if you restrict access to computer rooms, teach employees how to select secure passwords, and enforce a security policy, breaches may still occur due to poor LAN or WAN design. In this section, you will learn how to address some security risks via intelligent network design.

Preventing external security breaches from affecting your network is a matter of restricting access at every point where your LAN connects to the rest of the world. This principle forms the basis of hardware- and design-based security.

Net+ Router Access Lists

5.2 Before a hacker on another network can gain access to files on your network's server, he
5.5 must traverse a switch or router. Although devices such as firewalls, described later in this
chapter, provide more tailored security, manipulating switch and router configurations

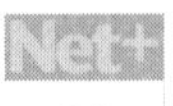

affords a small degree of security. This section describes a fundamental way to control traffic through routers.

5.2
5.5 A router's main function is to examine packets and determine where to direct them based on their Network layer addressing information. Thanks to a router's **ACL** (**access control list**, also known as an **access list**), routers can also decline to forward certain packets. An ACL instructs the router to permit or deny traffic according to one or more of the following variables:

- Network layer protocol (for example, IP or ICMP)
- Transport layer protocol (for example, TCP or UDP)
- Source IP address
- Source netmask
- Destination IP address
- Destination netmask
- TCP or UDP port number

Each time a router receives a packet, it examines the packet and refers to its ACL to determine whether the packet meets criteria for permitting or denying travel on the network. If a packet's characteristics match a variable that's flagged as "deny" in the ACL, the router drops the packet. If the packet's characteristics match a variable that's flagged as "permit," it forwards the packet.

An access list may contain many different statements. For example, it might include a statement to deny all traffic from source addresses whose netmask is 255.255.255.255 and another statement to deny all traffic destined for TCP port 23. Or it might include a statement to permit access to a console port from a certain subnet that is reserved for use by network administrators.

On most routers, each interface must be assigned a separate ACL. In addition, different ACLs may be associated with inbound and outbound traffic. Naturally, the more statements a router must scan (in other words, the longer the ACL), the more time it takes a router to act, and, therefore, the slower the router's overall performance.

An access list is not included on a router by default. If you install a router and do not create an ACL, you are allowing any kind of traffic to go in or out of that router. Once you create an ACL and assign it to an interface, you have explicitly permitted or denied certain types of traffic. Furthermore, any traffic that you do not explicitly permit in the ACL is implicitly denied.

An example of an access list configuration command that will allow traffic from users outside the LAN to pass through a Cisco router and access a Web server whose IP address is 10.250.1.10 is: `permit tcp any host 10.250.1.10 any eq www`. The command's syntax begins with a permit or deny statement (`permit`), followed by the Transport layer protocol (`TCP`), the source IP address (`any`), the destination's IP address (`10.250.1.10`), the source port number (`any`), and the destination's port number (`eq www`, which means the Web port 80).

Intrusion Detection and Prevention

5.6 Although a router's access list can block certain types of traffic, a more proactive security measure involves detecting suspicious network activity. In the world outside of computer

5.6 networks, a business owner might install closed-circuit TV cameras above her business's entrance and electrical sensors on its doors to monitor attempts to enter the building. Similarly, a network administrator might use techniques to monitor and flag any unauthorized attempt to access an organization's secured network resources using an **IDS (intrusion-detection system)**. An IDS exists as software running on a single computer, such as a server, or on a connectivity device, such as a switch. IDS that runs on a single computer, such as a client or server, and that has access to and allows access from the Internet, is known as **HIDS (host-based intrusion detection)**. Intrusion detection that occurs on devices that are situated at the edge of the network or that handle aggregated traffic is known as **NIDS (network-based intrusion detection)**. The most thorough security combines HIDS and NIDS to detect a wider scope of threats and provide multiple levels of defense. For example, an HIDS might detect an attempt to exploit an insecure application that an NIDS missed.

Major vendors of networking hardware, such as Cisco, HP, Juniper Networks, and Lucent sell IDS devices. Examples of popular open source IDS software, which can run on virtually any network-connected machine, include Tripwire and Snort.

One technique that an IDS may use to monitor traffic traveling carried by a switch is port mirroring. In **port mirroring**, one port is configured to send a copy of all its traffic to a second port on the switch. The second port issues the copied traffic to a monitoring program.

IDS software can be configured to detect many types of suspicious traffic patterns, including those typical of denial-of-service or smurf attacks, for example. For detecting unauthorized attempts to access a network, its sensors are installed at the edges of the network, the places where a protected, internal network intersects with a public network. A network's protective perimeter is known as the **DMZ**, or **demilitarized zone**. Alternately, an IDS can operate on a host to monitor suspicious attempts to log on or access the host's resources.

One drawback to using an IDS at a network's DMZ is the number of false positives it can log. For instance, it might interpret multiple logon attempts of a legitimate user who's forgotten his password as a security threat. If the IDS is configured to alert the network manager each time such an event occurs, the network manager might be overwhelmed with such warnings and eventually ignore all the IDS's messages. Therefore, to be useful, IDS software must be thoughtfully customized. In addition, to continue to guard against new threats, IDS software must be updated and rules of detection reevaluated regularly.

Although an IDS can only detect and log suspicious activity, an **IPS (intrusion-prevention system)** can react when alerted to such activity. For example, if a hacker's attempt to flood the network with traffic is detected, the IPS can detect the threat and prevent that traffic, based on its originating IP address, from flowing to the network. Thereafter the IPS will quarantine that malicious user. At the same time, the IPS continues to allow valid traffic to pass.

As with IDS, an IPS can protect entire networks through **NIPS (network-based intrusion prevention)** or only certain hosts, through **HIPS (host-based intrusion prevention)**. Using NIPS and HIPS together increases the network's security. For example, an HIDS running on a file server might accept a hacker's attempt to log on if the hacker is posing as a legitimate client. With the proper NIDS, however, such a hacker would likely never get to the server. Many vendors sell devices that integrate both IDS and IPS functions. As with an IDS, an IPS must be carefully configured to avoid an abundance of false alarms.

Net+ 5.6 Figure 11-2 illustrates the placement of an IDS/IPS device on a private network that's connected to the Internet. Note that such a device may be positioned between the firewall and the external network, as shown in Figure 11-2, or behind the firewall. This is an example of NIDS/NIPS. An IDS/IPS software running on the server or one of the clients within the internal LAN would be an example of HIDS/HIPS.

Intrusion-prevention systems were originally designed as a more comprehensive traffic analysis and protection tool than firewalls, which are discussed next. However, firewalls have evolved, and as a result, the differences between a firewall and an IPS have diminished.

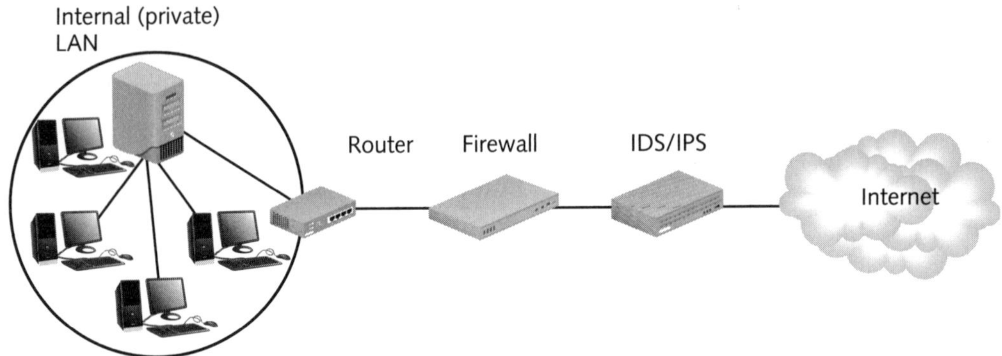

Figure 11-2 Placement of an IDS/IPS on a network

Firewalls

Net+ 5.5 A firewall is a specialized device, or a computer installed with specialized software, that selectively filters or blocks traffic between networks. A firewall typically involves a combination of hardware and software. The computer acting as a firewall may reside between two interconnected private networks or, more typically, between a private network and a public network (such as the Internet), as shown in Figure 11-3. This is an example of a **network-based firewall**, so named because it protects an entire network. Figure 11-4 shows a firewall designed for use in a business with many users. Other types of firewalls, known as **host-based firewalls**, only protect the computer on which they are installed.

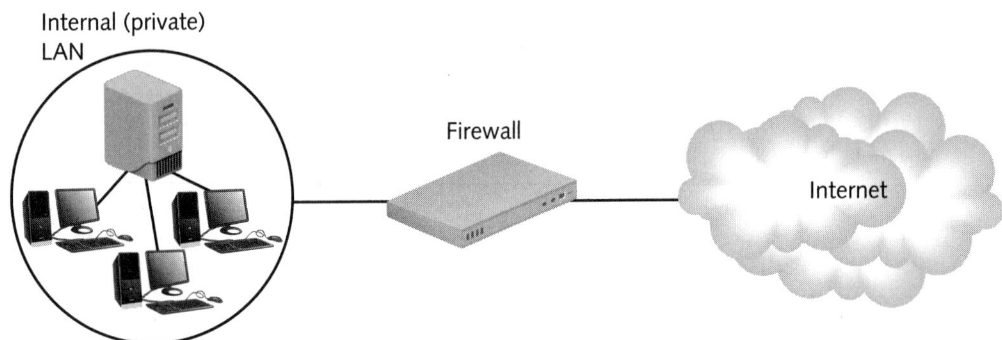

Figure 11-3 Placement of a firewall between a private network and the Internet

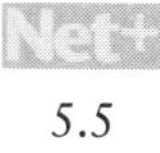
5.5

Figure 11-4 Firewall
Courtesy of NETGEAR

Many types of firewalls exist, and they can be implemented in many different ways. To understand secure network design and to qualify for Network+ certification, you should recognize which functions firewalls can provide, where they can appear on a network, and how to determine what features you need in a firewall.

5.2
5.5
The simplest form of a firewall is a **packet-filtering firewall**, which is a router (or a computer installed with software that enables it to act as a router) that examines the header of every packet of data it receives to determine whether that type of packet is authorized to continue to its destination. If a packet does not meet the filtering criteria, the firewall prevents the packet from continuing. However, if a packet does meet filtering criteria, the firewall allows that packet to pass through to the network connected to the firewall. In fact, nearly all routers can be configured to act as packet-filtering firewalls.

In addition to blocking traffic on its way *into* a LAN, packet-filtering firewalls can block traffic attempting to *exit* a LAN. One reason for blocking outgoing traffic is to stop worms from spreading. For example, if you are running a Web server, which in most cases only needs to respond to incoming requests and does not need to initiate outgoing requests, you could configure a packet-filtering firewall to block certain types of outgoing transmissions initiated by the Web server. In this way, you help prevent spreading worms that are designed to attach themselves to Web servers and propagate themselves to other computers on the Internet.

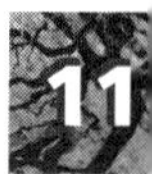

Often, firewalls ship with a default configuration designed to block the most common types of security threats. In other words, the firewall may be preconfigured to accept or deny certain types of traffic. However, many network administrators choose to customize the firewall settings, for example, blocking additional ports or adding criteria for the type of traffic that may travel in or out of ports. Some common criteria a packet-filtering firewall might use to accept or deny traffic include the following:

- Source and destination IP addresses
- Source and destination ports (for example, ports that supply TCP/UDP connections, FTP, Telnet, ARP, ICMP, and so on)
- Flags set in the IP header (for example, SYN or ACK)
- Transmissions that use the UDP or ICMP protocols
- A packet's status as the first packet in a new data stream or a subsequent packet
- A packet's status as inbound to or outbound from your private network

Based on these options, a network administrator could configure his firewall, for example, to prevent any IP address that does not begin with "196.57," the network ID of the addresses

5.2
5.5

on his network, from accessing the network's router and servers. Furthermore, he could disable—or block—certain well-known ports, such as the FTP ports (20 and 21), through the router's configuration. Blocking ports prevents *any* user from connecting to and completing a transmission through those ports. This technique is useful to further guard against unauthorized access to the network. In other words, even if a hacker could spoof an IP address that began with *196.57,* he could not access the FTP ports (which are notoriously insecure) on the firewall. Ports can be blocked not only on firewalls, but also on routers, servers, or any device that uses ports. For example, if you established a Web server for testing but did not want anyone in your organization to connect to your Web pages through his or her browsers, you could block port 80 on that server.

For greater security, you can choose a firewall that performs more complex functions than simply filtering packets. Among the factors to consider when making your decision are the following:

- Does the firewall support encryption? (You will learn more about encryption later in this chapter.)
- Does the firewall support user authentication?
- Does the firewall allow you to manage it centrally and through a standard interface?
- How easily can you establish rules for access to and from the firewall?
- Does the firewall support filtering at the highest layers of the OSI model, not just at the Data Link and Transport layers? For example, **content-filtering firewalls** can block designated types of traffic based on application data contained within packets. A school might configure its firewall to prevent responses from a Web site with questionable content from reaching the client that requested the site.
- Does the firewall provide logging and auditing capabilities, such as IDS or IPS?
- Does the firewall protect the identity of your internal LAN's addresses from the outside world?
- Can the firewall monitor a data stream from end to end, rather than simply examine each packet individually? If it can view a data stream, it's known as a **stateful firewall**. If not, it's known as a **stateless firewall**. Stateless firewalls perform more quickly than stateful firewalls, but are not as sophisticated.

You will recognize examples of firewall placement in most VPN architectures. For example, you might design a VPN that uses the Internet to connect your Houston and Denver offices. To ensure that only traffic from Houston can access your Denver LAN through an external connection, you could install a packet-filtering firewall between the Denver LAN and the Internet. Further, you could configure the firewall to accept incoming traffic only from IP addresses that match the IP addresses on your Houston LAN. In a way, the firewall acts like a bouncer at a private club who checks everyone's ID and ensures that only club members enter through the door. In the case of the Houston-Denver VPN, the firewall discards any data packets that arrive at the Denver firewall and *do not* contain source IP addresses that match those of Houston's LAN.

Some devices that provide firewall services are not called firewalls. For example, a small office or home office wireless router typically includes packet-filtering options. At the other end of the spectrum, devices made by Cisco for enterprise-wide security are known as security

appliances and can perform several functions, such as encryption, load balancing, and IPS, in
5.2 addition to packet filtering. Examples of software that enables a computer to act as a packet-
5.5 filtering firewall include iptables (for Linux systems), ZoneAlarm, and Comodo Firewall.
Some operating systems, including Windows 7, include firewall software.

Because you must tailor a firewall to your network's needs, you cannot simply purchase one, install it between your private LAN and the Internet, and expect it to offer much security. Instead, you must first consider what type of traffic you want to filter, and then configure the firewall accordingly. It may take weeks to achieve the best configuration—not so strict that it prevents authorized users from transmitting and receiving necessary data, yet not so lenient that you risk security breaches. Further complicating the matter is that you might need to create exceptions to the rules. For example, suppose that your human resources manager is working from a conference center in Salt Lake City while recruiting new employees and needs to access the Denver server that stores payroll information. In this instance, the Denver network administrator might create an exception to allow transmissions from the human resources manager's workstation's IP address to reach that server. In the networking profession, creating an exception to the filtering rules is called "punching a hole" in the firewall.

Because simple packet-filtering firewalls operate at the Network layer of the OSI model and examine only network addresses, they cannot distinguish between a user who is trying to breach the firewall and a user who is authorized to do so. For example, your organization might host a Web server, which necessitates accepting requests for port 80 on that server. In this case, a packet-filtering firewall, because it only examines the packet header, could not distinguish between a harmless Web browser and a hacker attempting to manipulate his way through the Web site to gain access to the network. For higher-layer security, a firewall that can analyze data at higher layers is required. The next section describes this kind of device.

Proxy Servers

4.1 One approach to enhancing the security of the Network and Transport layers provided by
firewalls is to combine a packet-filtering firewall with a proxy service. A **proxy service** is a software application on a network host that acts as an intermediary between the external and internal networks, screening all incoming and outgoing traffic. The network host that runs the proxy service is known as a **proxy server**. (A proxy server may also be called an **Application layer gateway**, an **application gateway**, or simply, a **proxy**.) Proxy servers manage security at the Application layer of the OSI model. To understand how they work, think of the secure data on a server as the president of a country and the proxy server as the secretary of state. Rather than have the president risk her safety by leaving the country, the secretary of state travels abroad, speaks for the president, and gathers information on the president's behalf. In fact, foreign leaders may never actually meet the president. Instead, the secretary of state acts as her proxy. In a similar way, a proxy server represents a private network to another network (usually the Internet).

Although a proxy server appears to the outside world as an internal network server, in reality it is merely another filtering device for the internal LAN. One of its most important functions is preventing the outside world from discovering the addresses of the internal network. For example, suppose your LAN uses a proxy server, and you want to send an e-mail message from your workstation to your mother via the Internet. Your message would first go to the proxy server (depending on the configuration of your network, you might or might not

Net+ 4.1 have to log on separately to the proxy server first). The proxy server would repackage the data frames that make up the message so that, rather than your workstation's IP address being the source, the proxy server inserts its own IP address as the source. Next, the proxy server passes your repackaged data to the packet-filtering firewall. The firewall verifies that the source IP address in your packets is valid (that it came from the proxy server) and then sends your message to the Internet. Examples of proxy server software include Squid (for use on UNIX or Linux systems) and Microsoft's Forefront Threat Management Gateway, which includes firewall features as well. Figure 11-5 depicts how a proxy server might fit into a WAN design.

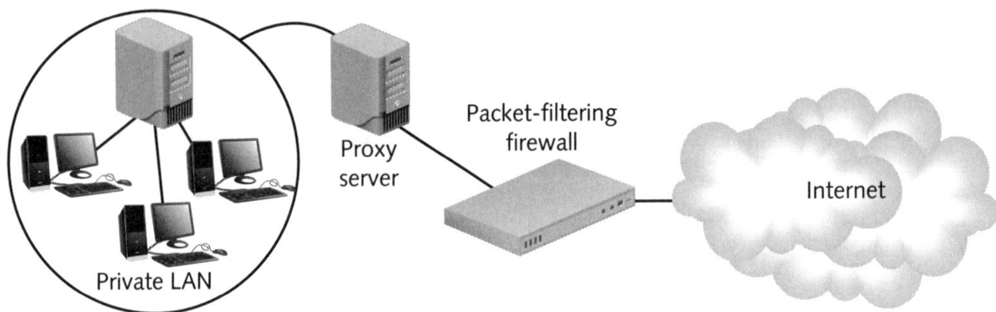

Figure 11-5 A proxy server used on a WAN

Proxy servers can also improve performance for users accessing resources external to their network by caching files. For example, a proxy server situated between a LAN and an external Web server can be configured to save recently viewed Web pages. The next time a user on the LAN wants to view one of the saved Web pages, content is provided by the proxy server. This eliminates the time required to travel over a WAN and retrieve the content from the external Web server.

Often, firewall and proxy server features are combined in one device. In other words, you might purchase a firewall and be able to configure it not only to block certain types of traffic from entering your network, but also to modify the addresses in the packets leaving your network.

Net+ Scanning Tools

5.6 Despite your best efforts to secure a network with router access lists, IDS/IPS, firewalls, and proxy servers, you might overlook a critical vulnerability. To ensure that your security efforts are thorough, it helps to think like a hacker. During a posture assessment, for example, you might use some of the same methods a hacker uses to identify cracks in your security architecture. Scanning tools provide hackers—and you—a simple and reliable way to discover crucial information about your network, including, but not limited to, the following:

- Every available host
- Services, including applications and versions, running on every host

- Operating systems running on every host
5.6
- Open, closed, and filtered ports on every host
- Existence and type of firewalls
- Software configurations
- Unencrypted, sensitive data

For example, a popular scanning tool called **NMAP (Network Mapper)** is designed to scan large networks quickly and provide information about a network and its hosts. NMAP, which runs on virtually any modern operating system, is available for download at no cost at *www.nmap.org*. NMAP began as a simple port scanning tool, but developers expanded its capabilities to include gathering information about hosts and their software. When running NMAP, you can choose what type of information to discover, thereby customizing your scan results.

Another tool, **Nessus**, from Tenable Security, performs even more sophisticated scans than NMAP. For example, among other things, Nessus can identify unencrypted, sensitive data, such as credit card numbers, saved on your network's hosts. The program can be purchased to run on your network or to run on off-site servers continuously maintained and updated by the developer. Because of its comprehensive nature and its use for revealing security flaws that must be addressed, Nessus and utilities like it are known as penetration-testing tools. Another penetration-testing tool, **metasploit**, combines known scanning techniques and exploits to result in potentially new hybrids of exploits.

Used intentionally on your own network, scanning tools improve security by pointing out insecure ports, software that must be patched, permissions that should be restricted, and so on. They can also contribute valuable data to asset management and audit reports. Used by hackers—or, more likely, bots—these tools can lead to compromised security. In other words, each of these tools has legitimate uses as well as illegal uses. However, even if the scanning tools are used against you, you can learn from them. For example, a properly configured firewall will collect information about scanning attempts in its log. By reviewing the log, you will discover what kinds of exploits might be—or have been—attempted against your network. Another way to learn about hackers is to lure them to your network on purpose, as described next.

Lures

Staying a step ahead of hackers and constantly evolving exploits requires vigilance. Those who want to learn more about hacking techniques or nab a hacker in the act might create a **honeypot**, or a decoy system that is purposely vulnerable. To make it attractive to hackers, the system might be given an enticing name, such as one that indicates its role as a name server or a storage location for confidential data. Once hackers access the honeypot, a network administrator can use monitoring software and logs to track the intruder's moves. In this way, the network administrator might learn about new vulnerabilities that must be addressed on his real networked hosts.

To fool hackers and gain useful information, honeypots cannot appear too blatantly insecure, and tracking mechanisms must be hidden. In addition, a honeypot must be isolated from secure systems to prevent a savvy hacker from using it as an intermediate host for other attacks. In more elaborate setups, several honeypots might be connected to form a **honeynet**.

5.6

Decoy systems can provide unique information about hacking behavior. But in practice, security researchers or those merely curious about hacking trends are more likely than overworked network administrators to establish and monitor honeypots and honeynets.

NOS (Network Operating System) Security

Regardless of whether you run your network on a Microsoft, Macintosh, Linux, or UNIX NOS, you can implement basic security by restricting what users are authorized to do on a network. Every network administrator should understand which resources on the server all users need to access. The rights conferred to all users are called public rights because anyone can have them and exercising them presents no security threat to the network. In most cases, public rights are very limited. They may include privileges to view and execute programs from the server and to read, create, modify, delete, and execute files in a shared data directory.

In addition, network administrators need to group users according to their security levels and assign additional rights that meet the needs of those groups. Creating groups simplifies the process of granting rights to users. For example, if you work in the IT Department at a large college, you will most likely need more than one person to create new user IDs and passwords for students and faculty. Naturally, the staff in charge of creating new user IDs and passwords need the rights to perform this task. You could assign the appropriate rights to each staff member individually, but a more efficient approach is to put all of the personnel in a group, and then assign the appropriate rights to the group as a whole.

Logon Restrictions

In addition to restricting users' access to files and directories on the server, a network administrator can constrain the ways in which users can access the server and its resources. The following is a list of additional restrictions that network administrators can use to strengthen the security of their networks:

- *Time of day*—Some user accounts may be valid only during specific hours—for example, between 8:00 a.m. and 5:00 p.m. Specifying valid hours for an account can increase security by preventing any account from being used by unauthorized personnel after hours.
- *Total time logged on*—Some user accounts may be restricted to a specific number of hours per day of logged-on time. Restricting total hours in this way can increase security in the case of temporary user accounts. For example, suppose that your organization offers an Adobe Photoshop training class to a group of high school students one afternoon, and the Photoshop program and training files reside on your staff server. You might create accounts that could log on for only four hours on that day.
- *Source address*—You can specify that user accounts may log on only from certain workstations or certain areas of the network (that is, domains or segments). This restriction can prevent unauthorized use of usernames from workstations outside the network.

- *Unsuccessful logon attempts*—Hackers might repeatedly attempt to log on under a valid username for which they do not know the password. As the network administrator, you can set a limit on how many consecutive unsuccessful logon attempts from a single user ID the server will accept before blocking that ID from even attempting to log on.

Another security technique that can be enforced by a network administrator through the NOS is the selection of secure passwords. The following section discusses the importance and characteristics of choosing a secure password.

Passwords

Choosing a secure password is one of the easiest and least expensive ways to guard against unauthorized access. Unfortunately, too many people prefer to use an easy-to-remember password. If your password is obvious to you, however, it may also be easy for a hacker to figure out. The following guidelines for selecting passwords should be part of your organization's security policy. It is especially important for network administrators to choose difficult passwords, and also to keep passwords confidential and to change them frequently.

Tips for making and keeping passwords secure include the following:

- Always change system default passwords after installing new programs or equipment. For example, after installing a router, the default administrator's password on the router might be set by the manufacturer to be "password".
- Do not use familiar information, such as your name, nickname, birth date, anniversary, pet's name, child's name, spouse's name, user ID, phone number, address, or any other words or numbers that others might associate with you.
- Do not use any word that might appear in a dictionary. Hackers can use programs that try a combination of your user ID and every word in a dictionary to gain access to the network. This is known as a **dictionary attack**, and it is typically the first technique a hacker uses when trying to guess a password (besides asking the user for her password).

- Make the password longer than eight characters—the longer, the better. Choose a combination of letters and numbers; add special characters, such as exclamation marks or hyphens, if allowed. Use a combination of uppercase and lowercase letters.
- Do not write down your password or share it with others.
- Change your password at least every 60 days, or more frequently. If you are a network administrator, establish controls through the NOS to force users to change their passwords at least every 60 days.
- Do not reuse passwords after they have expired.
- Use different passwords for different applications. For example, choose separate passwords for your e-mail program, online banking, VPN connection, and so on. That way, if someone learns one of your passwords, he won't necessarily be able to access all of your secured accounts.

Password guidelines should be clearly communicated to everyone in your organization through your security policy. Although users might grumble about choosing a combination of letters and numbers and changing their passwords frequently, you can assure them that the company's financial and personnel data is safer as a result.

Encryption

Encryption is the use of an algorithm to scramble data into a format that can be read only by reversing the algorithm—that is, by decrypting the data. The purpose of encryption is to keep information private. Many forms of encryption exist, with some being more secure than others. Even as new forms of encryption are developed, new ways of cracking their codes emerge, too.

Encryption is the last means of defense against data theft. In other words, if an intruder has bypassed all other methods of access, including physical security (for instance, he has broken into the data center) and network design security (for instance, he has defied a firewall's packet-filtering techniques), data may still be safe if it is encrypted. Encryption can protect data stored on a medium, such as a hard disk, or in transit over a communications channel. To protect data, encryption provides the following assurances:

- Data was not modified after the sender transmitted it and before the receiver picked it up.
- Data can only be viewed by its intended recipient or at its intended destination.
- All of the data received at the intended destination was truly issued by the stated sender and not forged by an intruder.

The following sections describe data encryption techniques used to protect data stored on or traveling across networks.

Key Encryption

The most popular kind of encryption algorithm weaves a **key**, or a random string of characters, into the original data's bits—sometimes several times in different sequences—to generate a unique data block. The scrambled data block is known as **ciphertext**. The longer the key, the less easily the ciphertext can be decrypted by an unauthorized system. For example, a 128-bit key allows for 2 possible character combinations, whereas a 16-bit key allows for 2^6 possible character combinations. Hackers may attempt to crack, or discover, a key by using a **brute force attack**, which means simply trying numerous possible character combinations to find the key that will decrypt encrypted data. Typically, a hacker runs a program to carry out the attack. Through a brute force attack, a hacker could discover a 16-bit key quickly and without using sophisticated computers, but would have difficulty discovering a 128-bit key.

Adding 1 bit to an encryption key makes it twice (2^1 times) as hard to crack. For example, a 129-bit key would be twice as hard to crack as a 128-bit key. Similarly, a 130-bit key would be four (2^2) times harder to crack as a 128-bit key.

The process of key encryption is similar to what happens when you finish a card game, place your five-card hand into the deck, and then shuffle the deck numerous times. After shuffling, it might take you a while to retrieve your hand. If you shuffled your five cards into four decks of cards at once, it would be even more difficult to find your original hand. In encryption, theoretically only the user or program authorized to retrieve the data knows how to unshuffle the ciphertext and compile the data in its original sequence. Figure 11-6 provides a simplified view of key encryption and decryption. Note that actual key encryption does not simply weave a key into the data once, but rather inserts the key, shuffles the data, shuffles the key, inserts another copy of the shuffled key into the shuffled data, shuffles the data again, and so on for several iterations.

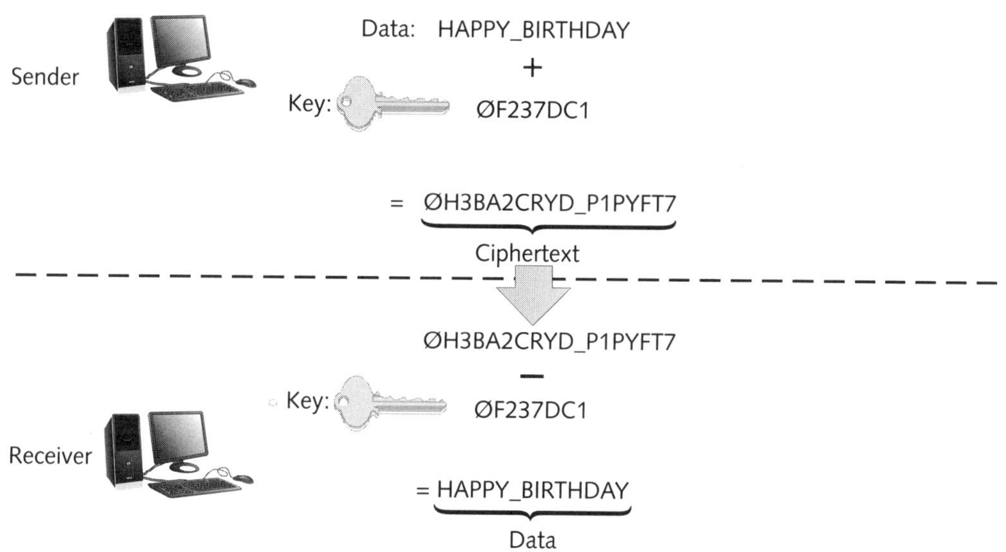

Figure 11-6 Key encryption and decryption

Keys are randomly generated, as needed, by the software that manages the encryption. For example, an e-mail program or a Web browser program may be capable of generating its own keys to encrypt data. In other cases, special encryption software is used to generate keys. This encryption software works with other types of software, such as word-processing or spreadsheet programs, to encrypt data files before they are saved or transmitted.

Key encryption can be separated into two categories: private key and public key encryption.

Private Key Encryption In **private key encryption**, data is encrypted using a single key that only the sender and the receiver know. Private key encryption is also known as **symmetric encryption** because the same key is used during both the encryption and decryption of the data.

Suppose Leon wants to send a secret message to Mia via private encryption. Assume he has chosen a private key. Next, he must share his private key with Mia, as shown in Step 1 of Figure 11-7. Then, Leon runs a program that encrypts his message by combining it with his private key, as shown in Step 2. Next, Leon sends Mia the encrypted message, as shown in Step 3. After Mia receives Leon's encrypted message, she runs a program that uses Leon's private key to decrypt the message, as shown in Step 4. The result is that Mia can read the original message Leon wrote.

The most popular private, or symmetric, key encryption is based on **DES** (pronounced *dez),* which stands for **Data Encryption Standard**. DES, which uses a 56-bit key, was

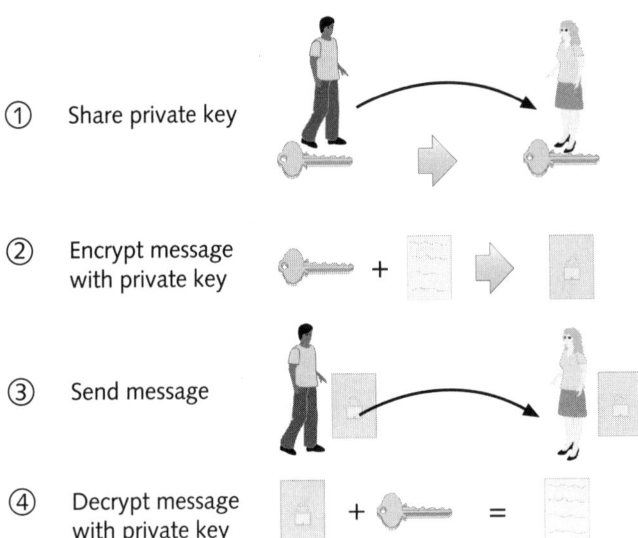
① Share private key
② Encrypt message with private key
③ Send message
④ Decrypt message with private key

Figure 11-7 Private key encryption

developed by IBM in the 1970s. When DES was released, a 56-bit key was secure; however, now such a key could be cracked within days, given sufficient computer power. For greater security, the modern implementation of DES weaves a 56-bit key through data three times, using two or three different keys. This implementation is known as **Triple DES (3DES)**.

A more recent private key encryption standard is the **AES (Advanced Encryption Standard)**, which weaves keys of 128, 160, 192, or 256 bits through data multiple times. The algorithm used in the most popular form of AES is known as Rijndael, after its two Belgian inventors, Dr. Vincent Rijmen and Dr. Joan Daemen. AES is considered more secure than DES and much faster than Triple DES. AES has replaced DES in situations such as military communications, which must have the highest level of security.

A potential problem with private key encryption is that the sender must somehow share his key with the recipient. For example, Leon could call Mia and tell her his key, or he could send it to her in an e-mail message. But neither of these methods is very secure. To overcome this vulnerability, a method of associating publicly available keys with private keys was developed. This method is called public key encryption.

Net+ 5.3

Public Key Encryption In **public key encryption**, data is encrypted using two keys: One is a key known only to a user (that is, a private key), and the other is a public key associated with the user. A user's public key can be obtained the old-fashioned way—by asking that user—or it can be obtained from a third-party source, such as a public key server. A **public key server** is a publicly accessible host (such as a server on the Internet) that freely provides a list of users' public keys, much as a telephone book provides a list of peoples' phone numbers.

Figure 11-8 illustrates the process of public key encryption.

Net+
5.3

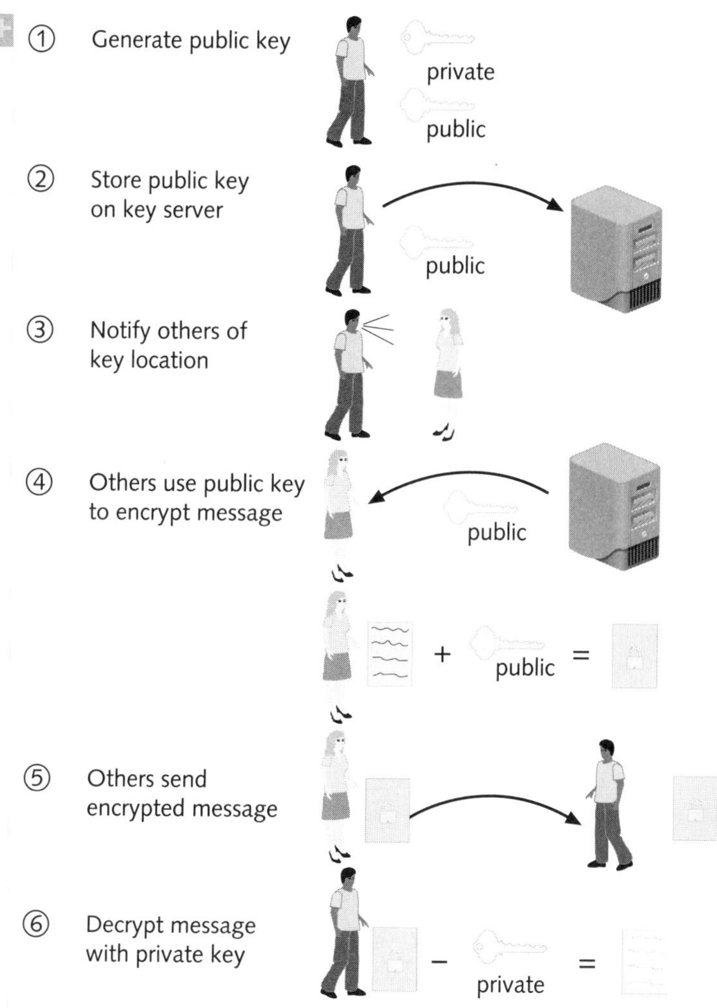
① Generate public key
private
public
② Store public key on key server
public
③ Notify others of key location
④ Others use public key to encrypt message
public
+
public
=
⑤ Others send encrypted message
⑥ Decrypt message with private key
–
private
=

Figure 11-8 Public key encryption

11

For example, suppose that Mia wants to use public key encryption to send Leon a message via the Internet. Assume Leon already established a private and a public key, as shown in Step 1 of Figure 11-8. He stores his public key on a key server on the Internet, as shown in Step 2, and keeps his private key to himself. Before Mia can send Leon a message, she must know his public key. Leon tells Mia where she can find his public key, as shown in Step 3. Next, Mia writes Leon a message, retrieves his public key from the public key server, and then uses her encryption software to scramble her message with Leon's public key, as shown in Step 4. Mia sends her encrypted message to Leon over the Internet, as shown in Step 5. When Leon receives the message, his software recognizes that the message has been encrypted with his public key. In other words, the public key has an association with the private key. A message that has been encrypted with Leon's public key can only be decrypted with his private key. The program then prompts Leon for his private key to decrypt the message, as shown in Step 6.

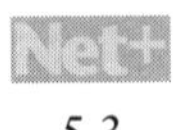
5.3 To respond to Mia in a publicly encrypted message, Leon must obtain Mia's public key. Then, the steps illustrated in Figure 11-8 are repeated, with Leon and Mia's roles reversed.

The combination of a public key and a private key is known as a **key pair**. In the private key encryption example discussed previously, Leon has a key pair, but only he knows his private key, whereas the public key is available to people, like Mia, who want to send him encrypted messages. Because public key encryption requires the use of two different keys, it is also known as **asymmetric encryption**.

Due to their semipublic nature, public keys are more vulnerable than private keys, and, therefore, public key algorithms generally use longer keys. The first public, or asymmetric, key algorithm, called **Diffie-Hellman**, was released in 1975 by its creators, Whitfield Diffie and Martin Hellman. However, the most popular public key algorithm in use today is **RSA** (named after its creators, Ronald Rivest, Adi Shamir, and Leonard Adleman), which was made public in 1977. In RSA, a key is created by first choosing two large prime numbers (numbers that cannot be divided evenly by anything but 1 or themselves) and multiplying them together. RSA is routinely used to secure e-commerce transactions. RSA may be used in conjunction with **RC4**, a key encryption technique that weaves a key with data multiple times, as a computer issues the stream of data. RC4 keys can be as long as 2048 bits. In addition to being highly secure, RC4 is fast.

With the abundance of private and public keys, not to mention the number of places where each may be kept, users need easier key management. One answer to this problem is using digital certificates. A **digital certificate** is a password-protected and encrypted file that holds an individual's identification information, including a public key. In the context of digital certificates, the individual's public key verifies the sender's digital signature. An organization that issues and maintains digital certificates is known as a **CA (certificate authority)**. For example, on the Internet, certificate authorities such as VeriSign will, for a fee, keep your digital certificate on their server and ensure to all who want to send encrypted messages to you (for example, an order via your e-commerce site) that the certificate is indeed yours. The use of certificate authorities to associate public keys with certain users is known as **PKI (Public-key Infrastructure)**.

The following sections detail specific methods of encrypting data as it is transmitted over a network. These methods use one or more of the encryption algorithms discussed in this section.

PGP (Pretty Good Privacy)

You have probably exchanged e-mail messages over the Internet without much concern for what happens with your message between the time you send it and when your intended recipient picks it up. In addition, you have probably read e-mails from friends without thinking that they might *not* be from your friends, but rather from other users who are impersonating your friends over the Internet. In fact, some e-mail communication is highly insecure. Depending on the mail server and client, messages may be sent in clear (that is, unencrypted) text, which makes it readable by anyone who can capture the message on its way from you to your recipient. In addition, a person with malicious intentions can easily pretend he is someone else. For example, if your e-mail address is *joe@example.com,* someone else could assume your address and send messages that appear to be sent by *joe@example.com.*

To secure e-mail transmissions, a computer scientist named Phil Zimmerman developed PGP in the early 1990s. **PGP (Pretty Good Privacy)** is a public key encryption system that can verify the authenticity of an e-mail sender and encrypt e-mail data in transmission. PGP, which is now administered at MIT, is freely available as both an open source and a proprietary software package. Since its release, it has become the most popular tool for encrypting e-mail. However, PGP can also be used to encrypt data on storage devices (for example, a hard disk) or with applications other than e-mail (for example, IP telephony).

Net+

SSL (Secure Sockets Layer)

5.2 **SSL (Secure Sockets Layer)** is a method of encrypting TCP/IP transmissions—including Web pages and data entered into Web forms—en route between the client and server using public key encryption technology. If you trade stocks or purchase goods on the Web, for example, you are most likely using SSL to transmit your order information. SSL is popular and used widely. The most recent versions of Web browsers, such as Google Chrome and Firefox, include SSL client support in their software.

You have probably noticed that URLs for most Web pages begin with the HTTP prefix, which indicates that the request is handled by TCP/IP port 80 using the HTTP protocol. When Web page URLs begin with the prefix **HTTPS** (which stands for **HTTP over Secure Sockets Layer** or **HTTP Secure**), they require that their data be transferred from server to client and vice versa using SSL encryption. HTTPS uses the TCP port number 443, rather than port 80.

Each time a client and server establish an SSL connection, they also establish a unique **SSL session**, or an association between the client and server that is defined by an agreement on a specific set of encryption techniques. An SSL session allows the client and server to continue to exchange data securely as long as the client is still connected to the server. An SSL session is created by the SSL handshake protocol, one of several protocols within SSL, and perhaps the most significant. As its name implies, the **handshake protocol** allows the client and server to introduce each other and establishes terms for how they will securely exchange data. For example, when you are connected to the Web and you decide to open your bank's account access URL, your browser initiates an SSL connection with the handshake protocol. The handshake protocol sends a special message to the server, called a **client_hello** message, which contains information about what level of security your browser is capable of accepting and what type of encryption your browser can decipher (for example, RSA or Diffie-Hellman). The client_hello message also establishes a randomly generated number that uniquely identifies your client and another number that identifies your SSL session. The server responds with a **server_hello** message that confirms the information it received from your client and agrees to certain terms of encryption based on the options your client supplied. Depending on the Web server's preferred encryption method, the server may choose to issue your browser a public key or a digital certificate at this time. After the client and server have agreed on the terms of encryption, they begin exchanging data.

SSL was originally developed by Netscape. Since that time, the IETF has attempted to standardize SSL in a protocol called **TLS (Transport Layer Security)**. TLS, which is supported by modern Web browsers, uses slightly different encryption algorithms than SSL, but otherwise is very similar to the most recent version of SSL.

Net+

SSH (Secure Shell)

5.2 Earlier in this book, you learned about Telnet, the TCP/IP utility that provides remote connections to hosts. For example, if you were a network administrator working at one of your company's satellite offices and had to modify the configuration on a router at the home office, you could telnet to the router and run commands to modify its configuration. However, Telnet provides little security for establishing a connection (authenticating) and no security for transmitting data (encryption). **SSH (Secure Shell)** is a collection of protocols that does both. With SSH, you can securely log on to a host, execute commands on that host, and copy files to or from that host. SSH encrypts data exchanged throughout the session. It guards against a number of security threats, including unauthorized access to a host, IP spoofing, interception of data in transit (even if it must be transferred via intermediate hosts), and **DNS spoofing**, in which a hacker forges name server records to falsify his host's identity. Depending on the version, SSH may use DES, Triple DES, RSA, Kerberos, or another, less-common encryption algorithm or method.

SSH was developed by SSH Communications Security, and use of their SSH implementation requires paying for a license. However, open source versions of the protocol suite, such as **OpenSSH**, are available for most computer platforms. To form a secure connection, SSH must be running on both the client and server. Like Telnet, the SSH client is a utility that can be run at the shell prompt on a UNIX or Linux system or at the command prompt on a Windows-based system. Other versions of the program come with a graphical interface. The SSH suite of protocols is included with all modern UNIX and Linux distributions and with Mac OS X Server and Mac OS X client operating systems. For Windows-based computers, you need to download a freeware SSH client, such as PuTTY.

Before you can establish a secure SSH connection, you must first generate a public key and a private key on your client workstation by running the `ssh keygen` command (or by choosing the correct menu options in a graphical SSH program). The keys are saved in two different, encrypted files on your hard disk. Next, you must transfer the public key to an authorization file on the host to which you want to connect. Finally, you are ready to connect to the host via SSH. On a computer running UNIX or Linux, this is accomplished by running the `slogin -l` *`username hostname`* command, where *username* is your client username and *hostname* is the name of the host to which you are trying to connect. The client and host then exchange public keys, and if both can be authenticated, the connection is completed. On a Windows-based computer, follow the menu options in the SSH client application.

SSH is highly configurable. For example, it can be configured to use one of several types of encryption for data en route between the client and host. It can be configured to require that the client enter a password in addition to a key. It can also be configured to perform **port forwarding**, which means it can redirect traffic that would normally use an insecure port (such as FTP) to an SSH-secured port. This allows you to use SSH for more than simply logging on to a host and manipulating files. With port forwarding, you could, for example, exchange HTTP traffic with a Web server via a secured SSH connection.

SCP (Secure CoPy) and SFTP (Secure File Transfer Protocol)

An extension to OpenSSH is the **SCP (Secure CoPy)** utility, which allows you to copy files from one host to another securely. SCP replaces insecure file copy protocols such as FTP, which do not encrypt usernames, passwords, or data while transferring them. Most modern OpenSSH packages, such as those supplied with the UNIX, Linux, and Macintosh OS X (client and server version) operating systems, include the SCP utility. Not all freeware SSH programs available for Windows include SCP, but separate, freeware SCP applications, such as WinSCP, exist.

SCP is simple to use. At the shell prompt of a UNIX or Linux system, type `scp filename1 filename2`, where *filename1* is the name of the file on the source host and *filename2* is the name of the file on the target host. Suppose you are copying a file from a server to your client workstation. In that case, you also need to include your username on the server and the server's host name in the command, as follows:

```
scp userid@hostname: filename1 filename2
```

In this command, *userid* is your username on the server, *hostname* is the server's fully qualified host name, *filename1* is the name of the file on the server, and *filename2* is what you want to call the file on your client workstation. On a Windows-based system, follow the menu options in your SSH or SCP client for copying files with SCP.

If your system uses the proprietary version of SSH, available from SSH Communications Security, you need to use **SFTP (Secure File Transfer Protocol)** to copy files rather than SCP. SFTP is slightly different from SCP, in that it does more than copy files. Like FTP, SFTP first establishes a connection with a host and then allows a remote user to browse directories, list files, and copy files. To open an SFTP connection from a UNIX or Linux system, type `sftp hostname` at a shell prompt, where *hostname* is the fully qualified host name of the computer to which you want to connect. To copy a file, type `get filename1 filename2`, where *filename1* is the name of the file on the source computer and *filename2* is what you want to call the file on the target computer. To close the SFTP connection, type `quit` and then press Enter. On a Windows-based system, follow the menu options in the SSH or SFTP client for copying files with SFTP.

The following section describes another technique for encrypting data in transit on a network.

IPSec (Internet Protocol Security)

5.2 **IPSec (Internet Protocol Security)** protocol defines encryption, authentication, and key management for TCP/IP transmissions. It is an enhancement to IPv4 and is native to IPv6. IPSec is somewhat different from other methods of securing data in transit. Rather than apply encryption to a stream of data, IPSec actually encrypts data by adding security information to the header of all IP packets. In effect, IPSec transforms the data packets. To do so, IPSec operates at the Network layer of the OSI model.

IPSec accomplishes authentication in two phases. The first phase is key management, and the second phase is encryption. **Key management** refers to the way in which two nodes agree on common parameters for the keys they will use. IPSec relies on **IKE (Internet Key Exchange)** to negotiate and authenticate keys. A separate service, **ISAKMP (Internet Security Association and Key Management Protocol)**, establishes policies for verifying the identity and the encryption methods that nodes will use for data transmission. After IKE has managed the shared keys and ISAKMP policies have ensured that both parties agree on the methods of secure transmission, IPSec invokes its second phase, encryption. In this phase, two types of encryption may be used: **AH (authentication header)** or **ESP (Encapsulating Security Payload)**. Both types of encryption provide authentication of the IP packet's

5.2

data payload through public key techniques. In addition, ESP encrypts the entire IP packet for added security.

IPSec can be used with any type of TCP/IP transmission. However, it most commonly runs on routers or other connectivity devices in the context of VPNs. As you learned in Chapter 10, VPNs are used to transmit private data over public networks. Therefore, they require strict encryption and authentication to ensure that data is not compromised.

Net+
4.1
5.2

On networks where more than a few simultaneous VPN connections must be maintained, a specialized device known as a **VPN concentrator** can be positioned at the edge of the private network to establish VPN connections, as shown in Figure 11-9. VPN concentrators authenticate VPN clients and establish tunnels for VPN connections. Their support of specific tunneling protocols, authentication mechanisms, and encryption algorithms vary from one manufacturer and model to another. Some support only IPSec or SSL, while others support both, for example. Some also provide enhanced features such as packet filtering.

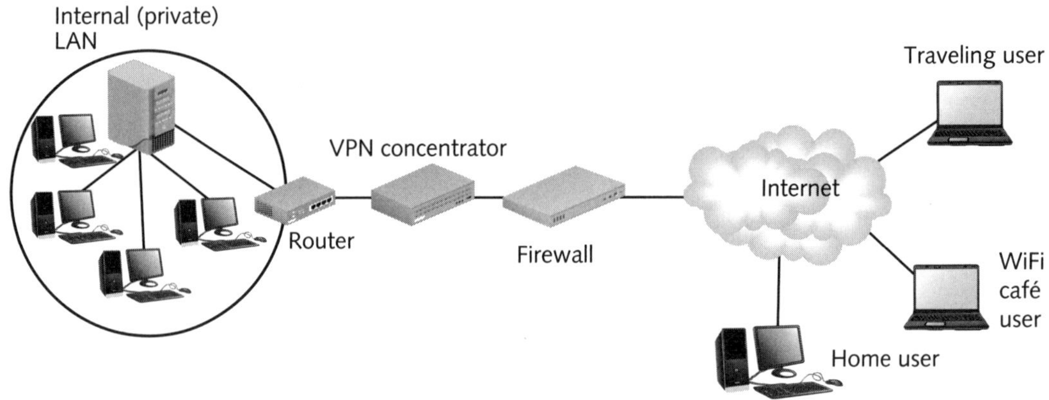

Figure 11-9 Placement of a VPN concentrator on a WAN

VPN concentrators are one type of encryption device. **Encryption devices** are computers, or, more often, specialized adapters within other devices, such as routers and servers, that perform encryption. Encryption devices encrypt and decrypt data faster than software running on other machines. As a result, they accelerate secure data transmission.

Authentication Protocols

5.3

You have learned that authentication is the process of verifying a user's credentials (typically a username and password) to grant the user access to secured resources on a system or network. **Authentication protocols** are the rules that computers follow to accomplish authentication. Several types of authentication protocols exist. They vary according to which encryption schemes they rely on and the steps they take to verify credentials. The following sections describe some common authentication protocols in more detail.

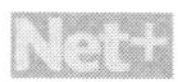

RADIUS and TACACS+

5.3 In environments that support many simultaneous connections and several user IDs and passwords, it makes sense to use a centralized service to manage access to resources. This section describes a category of protocols known as **AAA (authentication, authorization, and accounting)** that provides that service. AAA protocols first establish a client's identity by prompting a user for a username and password. Next, the protocols examine those credentials and based on their validity, allow or deny access to a system or network. Finally, AAA protocols track the client's system or network usage.

By far, the most popular AAA service is **RADIUS (Remote Authentication Dial-In User Service)**. RADIUS is a service defined by the IETF that runs over UDP and provides centralized network authentication, authorization, and accounting for multiple users. RADIUS can operate as a software application on a remote access server or on a computer dedicated to this type of authentication, called a **RADIUS server**.

Because RADIUS servers are highly scalable, many Internet service providers use a RADIUS server as a central authentication point for mobile or remote users. RADIUS may also be used to authenticate connections between wireless clients and access points or on cellular networks. Finally, they may operate in conjunction with other network servers. For example, an organization might combine a DHCP server with a RADIUS server to manage allocation of addresses and privileges assigned to each address on the network.

Figure 11-10 illustrates a RADIUS server used for remote access. RADIUS can run on UNIX, Linux, Windows, or Macintosh networks.

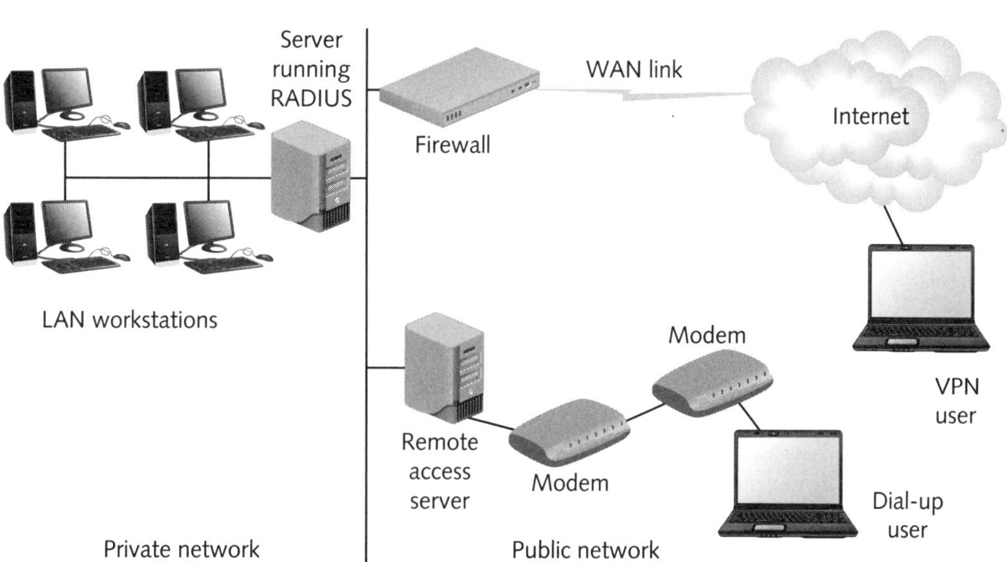

Figure 11-10 A RADIUS server on a network

5.3 Another AAA protocol, **TACACS+ (Terminal Access Controller Access Control System Plus)** offers network administrators the option of separating the access, authentication, and auditing capabilities. For instance, TACACS+ might provide access and accounting functions, but use another technique, such as Kerberos (discussed later in this chapter), to authenticate users. TACACS+ also differs from RADIUS in that it relies on TCP, not UDP, at the Network layer. TACACS+ is a proprietary protocol developed by Cisco Systems, Inc., and is typically installed on a router, rather than on a separate server.

Each of the protocols described in the following sections may play a role in the authentication step of AAA.

PAP (Password Authentication Protocol)

In Chapter 10's discussion of remote access protocols, you were introduced to PPP (Point-to-Point Protocol), which belongs to the Data Link layer of the OSI model and provides the foundation for connections between remote clients and hosts. PPP alone, however, does not secure connections. For this, it requires an authentication protocol.

In fact, several types of authentication protocols can work over PPP. One is **PAP (Password Authentication Protocol)**. After establishing a link with a server through PPP, a client uses PAP to send an authentication request that includes its credentials—usually a username and password. The server compares the credentials to those in its user database. If the credentials match, the server responds to the client with an acknowledgment of authentication and grants the client access to secured resources. If the credentials do not match, the server denies the request to authenticate. Figure 11-11 illustrates PAP's two-step authentication process.

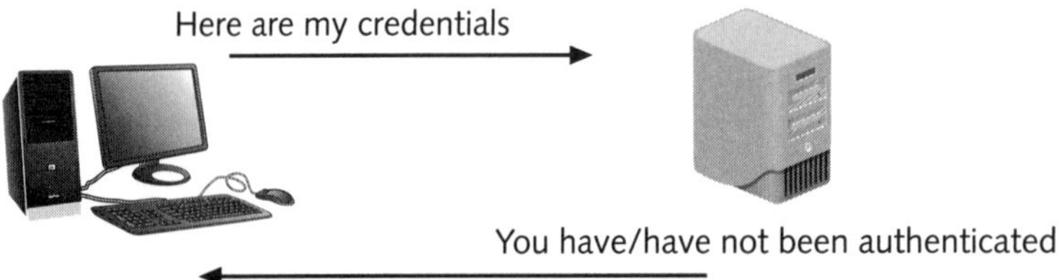

Figure 11-11 Two-step authentication used in PAP

Thus, PAP is a simple authentication protocol, but it is not very secure. It sends the client's credentials in clear text, without encryption, and this opens the way for eavesdroppers to capture a username and password. In addition, PAP does not protect against the possibility of a malicious intruder attempting to guess a user's password through a brute force attack. For these reasons, PAP is rarely used on modern networks. Instead, more sophisticated protocols, such as those described in the following sections, are preferred.

Net+

CHAP and MS-CHAP

5.3 **CHAP (Challenge Handshake Authentication Protocol)** is another authentication protocol that operates over PPP. Unlike PAP, CHAP encrypts usernames and passwords for transmission.

Net+ 5.3 It also differs from PAP in that it requires three steps to complete the authentication process. Together, these steps are known as a **three-way handshake**.

In CHAP, the authenticating device (for example, a remote access server) takes the first step in authentication after PPP establishes a connection between it and the computer requesting authentication (for example, a remote client). The server sends the client a randomly generated string of characters called the **challenge**. In the second step, the client adds its password to the challenge and encrypts the new string of characters. It sends this new string of characters in a response to the server. Meanwhile, the server also concatenates the user's password with the challenge and encrypts the new character string, using the same encryption scheme the client used. In the third step of the three-way handshake, the server compares the encrypted string of characters it received from the client with the encrypted string of characters it has generated. If the two match, it authenticates the client. But if the two differ, it rejects the client's request for authentication. Figure 11-12 illustrates the three-way handshake used in CHAP.

The benefit of CHAP over PAP is that in CHAP, a password is never transmitted alone, and never as clear text. This same type of security is offered in **MS-CHAP (Microsoft Challenge Handshake Authentication Protocol)**, a similar authentication protocol from Microsoft used with Windows-based computers. One potential flaw in CHAP and MS-CHAP authentication is that someone eavesdropping on the network could capture the string of characters that is encrypted with the password, decrypt that string, and obtain the client's password. To address this, Microsoft released **MS-CHAPv2 (Microsoft Challenge Handshake Authentication Protocol, version 2)**, which uses stronger encryption, does not use the same encryption strings for transmission and reception, and requires mutual authentication. In **mutual authentication**, both computers verify the credentials of the other—for example, the client authenticates the server just as the server authenticates the client. This is more secure than requiring only one of the communicating computers to authenticate the other.

11

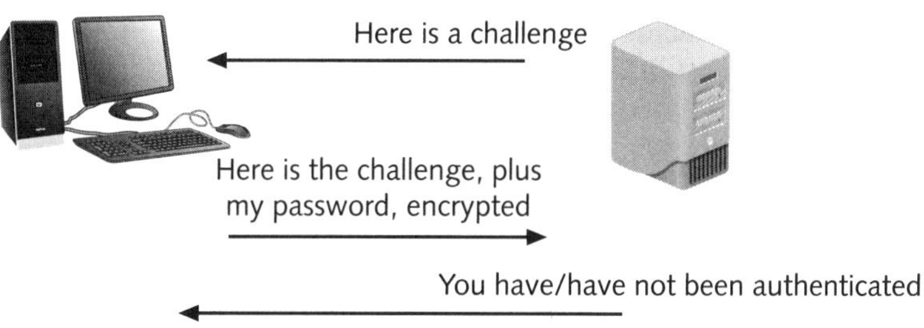
Here is a challenge
Here is the challenge, plus my password, encrypted
You have/have not been authenticated

Figure 11-12 Three-way handshake used in CHAP

MS-CHAPv2 is available for use with VPN and dial-up connections in the Windows client and network operating systems. Windows XP, Vista, and 7 clients support the use of PAP, CHAP, or MS-CHAPv2 when making dial-up connections.

An authentication protocol that is more secure than CHAP or MS-CHAP and is supported by multiple operating systems is EAP, discussed next.

Net+

EAP (Extensible Authentication Protocol)

5.3 **EAP (Extensible Authentication Protocol)** is another extension to the PPP protocol suite. It differs from the authentication protocols discussed previously in that it is only a mechanism for authenticating clients and servers; it does not perform encryption or authentication on its own. Instead, it works with other encryption and authentication schemes to verify the credentials of clients and servers.

Like CHAP, EAP requires the authenticator (for example, the server) to initiate the authentication process by asking the connected computer (for example, the client) to verify itself. In EAP, the server usually sends more than one request. In its first request, it asks the client's identity and indicates what type of authentication to use. In subsequent requests, it asks the client for authentication information to prove the client's identity. The client responds to each of the servers' requests in the required format. If the responses match what the server expects, the server authenticates the client.

One of EAP's advantages is its flexibility. It is supported by nearly all modern operating systems and can be used with any authentication method. For example, although the typical network authentication involves a user ID and password, EAP also works with biorecognition methods, such as retina or hand scanning. EAP is also adaptable to new technology. Therefore, no matter what future wireless encryption schemes are developed, EAP will support them.

In the case of wireless LANs, EAP is used with older encryption and authentication protocols to form a new, more secure method of connecting to networks from wireless stations. A distinct implementation of EAP, described next, forms the basis of one of the most secure wireless authentication techniques.

802.1x (EAPoL)

The **802.1x** standard, codified by IEEE, specifies the use of one of many authentication methods, plus EAP, to grant access to and dynamically generate and update authentication keys for transmissions to a particular port. Although it's primarily used with wireless networks now, it was originally designed for wired LANs; thus, it's also known as **EAPoL (EAP over LAN)**. 802.1x only defines a process for authentication. It does not specify the type of authentication or encryption protocols clients and servers must use. However, 802.1x is commonly used with RADIUS authentication. As you might expect, for nodes to communicate using 802.1x, they must agree on the same authentication method.

What distinguishes 802.1x from other authentication standards is the fact that it applies to communication with a particular port—for example, a physical switch port or a logically defined port on an access point. When a client wants to access the network, a port on the authenticator (such as a switch or access point) challenges the client to prove its identity. If the client is running the proper 802.1x software, the client will supply the authenticator with its credentials. The authenticator next passes on the client's credentials to an authentication server—for example, a RADIUS server. Only after the authentication server has verified a client's legitimacy will the switch or access point port be opened to the client's Layer 3 traffic. For this reason, 802.1x is sometimes also called **port authentication**, or **port-based authentication**. After the port is opened, the client and network communicate using EAP and an agreed-upon encryption scheme. Figure 11-13 illustrates the process followed by 802.1x when used with a WLAN (wireless LAN). You'll learn more about wireless network security techniques later in this chapter.

Net+
5.3

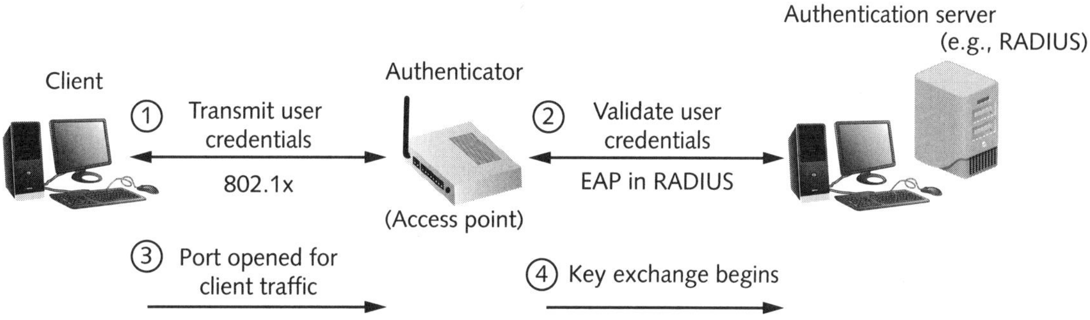

Figure 11-13 802.1x authentication process

Kerberos

Kerberos is a cross-platform authentication protocol that uses key encryption to verify the identity of clients and to securely exchange information after a client logs on to a system. It is an example of a private key encryption service. Kerberos provides significant security advantages over simple NOS authentication. Whereas an NOS client/server logon process assumes that clients are who they say they are and only verifies a user's name against the password in the NOS database, Kerberos does not automatically trust clients. Instead, it requires clients to prove their identities through a third party. This is similar to what happens when you apply for a passport. The government does not simply believe that you are "Leah Torres," but instead requires you to present proof, such as your birth certificate. In addition to checking the validity of a client, Kerberos communications are encrypted and unlikely to be deciphered by any device on the network other than the client. Contrast this type of transmission to the normally unencrypted and vulnerable communication between an NOS and a client.

To understand specifically how a client uses Kerberos, you need to understand some of the terms used when discussing this protocol. In Kerberos terminology, the server that issues keys to clients during initial client authentication is known as the **KDC** (**Key Distribution Center**). To authenticate a client, the KDC runs an **AS** (**authentication service**). An AS issues a **ticket**, which is a temporary set of credentials that a client uses to prove that its identity has been validated (note that a ticket is not the same as a key, which is used to initially validate its identity). A Kerberos client, or user, is known as a **principal**.

Now that you have learned the terms used by Kerberos, you can follow the process it requires for client/server communication. Bear in mind that the purpose of Kerberos is to connect a valid user with the *service* that user wants to access. To accomplish this, both the user and the service must register their keys with the authentication service. Suppose the principal is Jamal Sayad and the service is called "inventory." Jamal first logs on to his network as usual. Next, he attempts to log on to the "inventory" service with his Kerberos principal name and password. The KDC confirms that Jamal Sayad is in its database and that he has provided the correct password. Then, the AS running on the KDC randomly generates two copies of a new key, called the **session key**. The AS issues one copy to Jamal's computer and the other copy to the inventory service. Further, it creates a ticket that allows Jamal to use the inventory service. This ticket contains the inventory service key and can only be decrypted using Jamal Sayad's key. The AS sends the ticket to Jamal

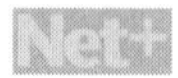

5.3 Sayad. Jamal's computer decrypts the session key with Jamal's personal key. It then creates a time stamp associated with his request, and encrypts this time stamp with the session key. The encrypted time stamp is known as the **authenticator**. This time stamp helps the service verify that the ticket is indeed associated with Jamal Sayad's request to use the inventory service. Next, Jamal's computer sends his ticket and authenticator to the service. The service decrypts the ticket using its own key and decrypts the authenticator using its session key. Finally, the service verifies that the principal requesting its use is truly Jamal Sayad as the KDC indicated.

The preceding events illustrate the original version of the Kerberos authentication process. The problem with the original version was that a user had to request a separate ticket each time he wanted to use a different service. To alleviate this inconvenience, Kerberos developers created the **TGS (Ticket-Granting Service)**, an application separate from the AS that also runs on the KDC. So that the client does not need to request a new ticket from the TGS each time it wants to use a different service on the network, the TGS issues the client a **TGT (Ticket-Granting Ticket)**. After receiving the TGT, anytime the user wants to contact a service, he requests a ticket not from the AS, but from the TGS. Furthermore, the reply is encrypted not with the user's personal key, but with the session key that the AS provided for use with the TGS. Inside that reply is the new session key for use with the regular service. The rest of the exchange continues as described previously.

Kerberos, which is named after the three-headed dog in Greek mythology who guarded the gates of Hades, was designed at MIT (Massachusetts Institute of Technology). MIT still provides free copies of the Kerberos code. In addition, many software vendors have developed their own versions of Kerberos.

Kerberos is an example of **single sign-on**, a form of authentication in which a client signs on one time to access multiple systems or resources. The primary advantage of single sign-on is convenience. Users don't have to remember several passwords, and network administrators limit the time they devote to password management. The biggest disadvantage to single sign-on is that once the obstacle of authentication is cleared, the user has access to numerous resources. A hacker needs fewer credentials to gain access to potentially many files or connections.

For greater security, some systems require clients to supply two or more pieces of information to verify their identity. For example, in a **two-factor authentication** scenario, a user might have to pass a fingerprint scan as well as provide his password. In general, an authentication process that requires two or more pieces of information is known as **multifactor authentication**. For example, multifactor authentication might require a password, fingerprint scan, plus a piece of information generated from a security token. A **security token** is a device or piece of software that stores or generates information, such as a series of numbers or letters, known only to its authorized user. One example of a hardware-based token is the popular SecurID key chain fob from RSA Security, as shown in Figure 11-14. The SecurID device generates a password that changes every 60 seconds. When logging in, a user provides the number that currently appears on the SecurID fob. Before he is allowed access to secured resources, his network checks with RSA Security's service to verify that the number is correct. Google Authenticator, Google's number generator service, provides free, software-based security tokens.

5.3

Figure 11-14 SecurID fob
Courtesy of RSA, The Security Division of EMC

Wireless Network Security

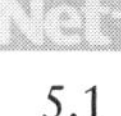

5.1 5.4 Wireless transmissions are particularly susceptible to eavesdropping. For example, a hacker could search for unprotected wireless networks by driving around with a laptop configured to receive and capture wireless data transmissions—a practice known as **war driving**. (The term is derived from the term *war dialing*, which is a similar tactic involving modems.) War driving is surprisingly effective for obtaining private information. Years ago, the hacker community publicized the vulnerabilities of a well-known store chain, which were discovered while war driving. The retailer used wireless cash registers to help customers make purchases when the regular, wired cash registers were busy. However, the wireless cash registers transmitted purchase information, including credit card numbers and customer names, to network access points in clear text. By chance, a person in the parking lot who was running a protocol analyzer program on his laptop obtained several credit card numbers in a very short time. The person alerted the retailer to the security risk (rather than exploiting the information he gathered). Needless to say, after the retailer discovered its error, it abandoned the use of wireless cash registers until after a thorough evaluation of its data security.

Once hackers discover vulnerable access points, they might make this information public through **war chalking**, or using chalk to draw symbols on the sidewalk or wall within range of an access point. The symbols, patterned after marks that hobos devised to indicate hospitable places for food or rest, indicate the access point's SSID and whether it's secured.

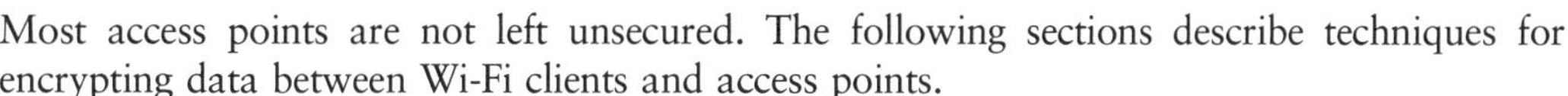

Most access points are not left unsecured. The following sections describe techniques for encrypting data between Wi-Fi clients and access points.

WEP (Wired Equivalent Privacy)

As you have learned, most organizations use one of the 802.11 protocol standards on their WLANs. By default, the 802.11 standard does not offer any security. In addition, most access points do not require a client to authenticate before it can communicate with the AP. The client only needs to know the access point's SSID, which many access points broadcast. Network administrators may prevent their access points from broadcasting the SSIDs, making them harder to detect. However, this does not provide true security.

For some measure of security, 802.11 allows for optional encryption using the **WEP (Wired Equivalent Privacy)** standard. WEP uses keys both to authenticate network clients and to encrypt data in transit. When configuring WEP, you establish a character string required to associate with the access point, also known as the **network key**. When the client detects the presence of the access point, the user is prompted to provide a network key before the client can gain access to a network via the access point. The network key can be saved as part of the client's wireless connection's properties.

The first implementation of WEP allowed for 64-bit network keys, and current versions of
5.1 WEP allow for more secure, 128-bit or even 256-bit network keys. Still, WEP's use of the
5.4 shared key for authenticating all users and for exchanging data makes it more susceptible to discovery than a dynamically generated, random, or single-use key. An exploit in which a hacker uses a program to determine a WEP key is known as **WEP cracking**. Even 128-bit network keys can be cracked in a matter of minutes. Moreover, because WEP operates in the Physical and Data Link layers of the OSI model, it does not offer end-to-end data transmission security. A better wireless security technique is 802.11i, which is discussed next.

IEEE 802.11i and WPA (Wi-Fi Protected Access)

A significant disadvantage to WEP is that it uses the same key for all clients and the key may never change. Due to this inherent insecurity, IEEE devised a new wireless security protocol, called **802.11i**, that uses 802.1x (EAPoL) to authenticate devices and dynamically assign every transmission its own key. 802.11i often relies on an encryption key generation and management scheme known as **TKIP (Temporal Key Integrity Protocol)**, pronounced *tee-kip*.

As you can imagine, EAPoL makes logging on to a wireless network more complex than it is with WEP. In 802.11i, a wireless station first issues a request to the access point. The access point functions as a proxy between the remote access server and station until the station has successfully authenticated with a remote access server. Meanwhile, the access point prevents any direct exchange of data between the two. After obtaining data from an unknown station, the access point repackages the data and then transmits it to the remote access server. It also repackages data from the remote access server before issuing it to the station. Thus, 802.11i requires mutual authentication—the station authenticates with the remote access server, and also, the remote access server authenticates with the station. After mutual authentication, the remote access server instructs the access point to allow traffic from the client into the network without first having to be repackaged. Next, the client and server agree on the encryption key they will use with the encryption scheme. Finally, they exchange data that has been encrypted through the mutually agreed-upon method. 802.11i specifies the AES encryption method and mixes each packet in a data stream with a different key. Because of its impressive security, 802.11i has replaced the less-secure WEP as the preferred means for protecting wireless transmissions from intruders.

WPA (Wi-Fi Protected Access) is a subset of the 802.11i standard endorsed by the **Wi-Fi Alliance**, an international, nonprofit organization dedicated to ensuring the interoperability of 802.11-capable devices. In fact, the Wi-Fi Alliance released WPA before 802.11i was ratified to quickly provide a more secure alternative to WEP. In WPA, authentication follows the same mechanism specified in 802.11i. The main difference is that WPA specifies RC4 encryption rather than AES. Since the 802.11i standard was approved, the Wi-Fi Alliance has released an updated version called **WPA2**. WPA2 includes support for the previously released WPA protocol. In all other ways, it is identical to 802.11i. The most secure Wi-Fi communication is made possible by combining a RADIUS server with WPA or WPA2, known as **WPA-Enterprise** or **WPA2-Enterprise**, respectively.

Although they are significantly more secure than WEP, WPA and WPA2 keys can be discovered through **WPA cracking** programs.

Table 11-1 summarizes the most important encryption and authentication methods discussed in this chapter.

Net+
5.1
5.2
5.3

Table 11-1 Notable encryption and authentication methods

Security method	Type	Primary use(s)	Notes
PGP	Encryption	E-mail, but also other applications and stored data	Uses public key encryption
SSL	Encryption	TCP/IP (Web) transmissions	Can use one of many encryption algorithms
SSH	Encryption	VPN	Can use public or private key exchange and one of many encryption algorithms
IPSec	Authentication	VPN	Uses IKE for key management, ISAKMP for secure associations, and AH or ESP for encryption; native to IPv6
RADIUS	Authentication, Authorization, and Accounting (AAA)	Remote access	Can use PPP, CHAP, and other protocols for authentication; relies on UDP at the Transport layer; supported by multiple platforms
TACACS+	Authentication, Authorization, and Accounting (AAA)	Remote access	Allows for separation of authentication, authorization, and accounting services; can use PPP, CHAP, and other protocols for authentication; relies on TCP at the Transport layer; Cisco proprietary
CHAP	Authentication	Remote access	Operates over PPP and requires a three-way handshake
MS-CHAP	Authentication	Remote access	Microsoft's version of CHAP
MS-CHAPv2	Authentication	Remote access	A revised version of MS-CHAP; requires mutual authentication between client and server
EAP	Authentication	Remote access	Operates over PPP; does not perform authentication or encryption, but provides framework for these
EAPoL (802.1x)	Authentication	Wi-Fi	Not a protocol, but a process for port-based authentication; EAPoL combines EAP plus one of many encryption algorithms
Kerberos	Authentication	Client logon to services	Uses private key encryption to allow single sign-on to multiple resources
WEP	Authentication	Wi-Fi	Uses symmetric, private key encryption; keys are statically assigned; easily thwarted
WPA	Authentication	Wi-Fi	Uses public key encryption (RC4) and EAPoL to authenticate devices and dynamically assign every transmission its own public key
WPA2	Authentication	Wi-Fi	Uses public key encryption (AES) and EAPoL to authenticate devices and dynamically assign every transmission its own key
WPA/WPA2-Enterprise	Authentication	Wi-Fi	Adds RADIUS to WPA or WPA2 authentication

Chapter Summary

- Every organization should assess its security risks by conducting a posture assessment that identifies vulnerabilities and rates the severity of threats and their potential consequences. Network administrators use the results of posture assessments to close gaps in security. If the assessment is conducted by a consulting company that has been accredited by an agency that sets network security standards, the assessment qualifies as a security audit.
- One of the most common methods by which an intruder gains access to a network is to simply ask users for their passwords. This strategy is commonly called social engineering because it involves manipulating social relationships to gain access. Phishing, a related tactic, involves luring users into revealing information that would allow intruders to gain access to secured network resources.
- Security risks that a network administrator must guard against include incorrectly configuring user accounts or groups and their privileges; overlooking security flaws in topology or hardware configuration; overlooking security flaws in operating system or application configuration; improperly documenting or communicating security policies; and leaving system settings at their default values.
- Some risks inherent in network transmission and design include leased lines that may allow for eavesdropping; unused router or server ports that can be exploited and accessed by hackers if not disabled; a router's configuration port, accessible by Telnet, that might not be adequately secured; routers that may not be properly configured to mask internal subnets or to deny access to certain hosts; and remote access servers used by telecommuting or remote staff that might not be carefully secured and monitored.
- Some risks pertaining to networking protocols and software include the following: inherent TCP/IP security flaws; trust relationships between one server and another; NOS "back doors" or security flaws; an NOS that allows server operators to exit to a command prompt; administrators who accept default operating system security; and transactions that take place between applications left open to interception.
- A security policy identifies an organization's security goals, risks, levels of authority, designated security coordinator and team members, responsibilities for each team member, responsibilities for each employee, and strategies for addressing security breaches.
- Only authorized personnel should be allowed into data centers, computer rooms, entrance facilities, and wiring closets. If these areas remain unsecured, intruders may easily enter and steal equipment or sabotage software and hardware.
- A router's ACL (access control list, also known as an access list) instructs it to decline to forward certain packets according to source IP address, source netmask, destination IP address, destination netmask, or TCP or UDP port, among other things.
- An IDS (intrusion-detection system) monitors traffic on a network or host for unauthorized attempts to access a network's resources. An IPS (intrusion-prevention system) can detect such attempts and automatically react to them—for example, by denying access to a host whose traffic triggers an alert.

- A firewall is a specialized device (typically a router, but possibly only a desktop computer running special software) that selectively filters or blocks traffic between networks. It can be placed between two interconnected private networks or, more typically, between a private network and a public network.
- The most common form of firewall is a packet-filtering firewall, which examines the header of every packet of data that it receives to determine whether that type of packet is authorized to continue to its destination.
- A proxy service is a software application on a network host that acts as an intermediary between the external and internal networks, screening all incoming and outgoing traffic. The host that runs the proxy service is known as a proxy server. A proxy server appears to external machines as a network server, but it is actually another filtering device for the internal LAN.
- Scanning tools such as NMAP (Network Mapper) and Nessus can quickly reveal comprehensive information about a network. Open ports, services, hosts, and even software configurations may be discovered. Used legitimately, scanning tools provide network administrators with valuable information that can help improve network security.
- To learn more about hackers' techniques or to catch a hacker in the act, some networking professionals use intentionally unsecured and isolated systems known as honeypots. Once a hacker has compromised the honeypot, his movements can be logged and his tactics examined. A network of honeypots is known as a honeynet.
- Every NOS provides at least some security by allowing you to limit users' access to files and directories on the network. In addition, network administrators can constrain how those with different types of user IDs can use the network by setting restrictions on, for example, time of day, total time logged on, source address, and number of unsuccessful logon attempts.

- Choosing secure passwords is one of the easiest and least expensive ways to guard against unauthorized access.
- Encryption is the use of an algorithm to scramble data into a format that can be read only by reversing the algorithm—or decrypting the data—to keep the information private. Many forms of encryption exist, with some being more secure than others.
- The most popular kind of encryption algorithm weaves a key, or a random string of characters, into the original data's bits, sometimes several times in different sequences, to generate a unique data block. The longer the key, the less easily the encrypted data can be decrypted by an unauthorized program.
- Key encryption comes in two forms: public and private key encryption. Popular private (symmetric) key encryption algorithms include DES (Data Encryption Standard), Triple DES (3DES), and AES (Advanced Encryption Standard). Popular public (asymmetric) key encryption algorithms include Diffie-Hellman, RSA, and RC4.
- Popular methods of encryption include PGP (Pretty Good Privacy), SSL (Secure Sockets Layer), SSH (Secure Shell) and OpenSSH, and IPSec (Internet Protocol Security). IPSec, which is native to IPv6, is a protocol used on many modern VPNs.

- SCP (Secure CoPy) and SFTP (Secure File Transfer Protocol) are ways of copying files securely via SSH or OpenSSH.
- Authentication protocols used with PPP connections include RADIUS (Remote Authentication Dial-In User Service), TACACS+ (Terminal Access Controller Access Control System Plus), PAP (Password Authentication Protocol), CHAP (Challenge Handshake Authentication Protocol), MS-CHAP (Microsoft Challenge Handshake Authentication Protocol), and MS-CHAPv2 (Microsoft Challenge Handshake Authentication Protocol, version 2). Other authentication protocols include EAP (Extensible Authentication Protocol), 802.1x (or EAPoL), and Kerberos.
- Wireless networks can use the WEP (Wired Equivalent Privacy) method of encrypting data in transit between stations and access points. WEP allows for keys as long as 256 bits. However, because WEP uses the same key for all stations attaching to an access point and for all transmissions, it is not very secure.
- A better wireless security solution than WEP is provided by IEEE's 802.11i standard, also known as TKIP (Temporal Key Integrity Protocol). In 802.11i, the 802.1x authentication method is combined with AES encryption. Each 802.11i transmission is dynamically assigned its own key for encryption.
- The Wi-Fi Alliance has released two wireless security standards: WPA and WPA2. WPA follows the same authentication and encryption processes as 802.11i, but uses RC4 encryption. WPA2 is identical to 802.11i, but provides backward compatibility for clients running WPA. The most secure Wi-Fi communication is made possible by combining a RADIUS server with WPA or WPA2, known as WPA-Enterprise or WPA2-Enterprise, respectively.

Key Terms

3DES *See* Triple DES.

802.11i The IEEE standard for wireless network encryption and authentication that uses the EAP authentication method, strong encryption, and dynamically assigned keys, which are different for every transmission. 802.11i specifies AES encryption and weaves a key into each packet.

802.1x A vendor-independent IEEE standard for securing transmission between nodes according to the transmission's port, whether physical or logical. 802.1x, also known as EAPoL, is the authentication standard followed by wireless networks using 802.11i.

AAA (authentication, authorization, and accounting) The name of a category of protocols that establish a client's identity; check the client's credentials and, based on those, allow or deny access to a system or network; and, finally, track the client's system or network usage.

access control list *See* ACL.

access list *See* ACL.

ACL (access control list) A list of statements used by a router to permit or deny the forwarding of traffic on a network based on one or more criteria.

Advanced Encryption Standard *See* AES.

AES (Advanced Encryption Standard) A private key encryption algorithm that weaves keys of 128, 160, 192, or 256 bits through data multiple times. The algorithm used in the most popular form of AES is known as Rijndael. AES has replaced DES in situations such as military communications, which require the highest level of security.

AH (authentication header) In the context of IPSec, a type of encryption that provides authentication of the IP packet's data payload through public key techniques.

application gateway *See* proxy server.

Application layer gateway *See* proxy server.

AS (authentication service) In Kerberos terminology, the process that runs on a KDC (Key Distribution Center) to initially validate a client who's logging on. The authentication service issues a session key to the client and to the service the client wants to access.

asymmetric encryption A type of encryption (such as public key encryption) that uses a different key for encoding data than is used for decoding the ciphertext.

authentication, authorization, and accounting *See* AAA.

authentication header *See* AH.

authentication protocol A set of rules that governs how servers authenticate clients. Several types of authentication protocols exist.

authentication service *See* AS.

authenticator In Kerberos authentication, the user's time stamp encrypted with the session key. The authenticator is used to help the service verify that a user's ticket is valid.

biorecognition access A method of authentication in which a device scans an individual's unique physical characteristics (such as the color patterns in her iris or the geometry of her hand) to verify the user's identity.

brute force attack An attempt to discover an encryption key or password by trying numerous possible character combinations. Usually, a brute force attack is performed rapidly by a program designed for that purpose.

CA (certificate authority) An organization that issues and maintains digital certificates as part of the Public-key Infrastructure.

certificate authority *See* CA.

challenge A random string of text issued from one computer to another in some forms of authentication. It is used, along with the password (or other credential), in a response to verify the computer's credentials.

Challenge Handshake Authentication Protocol *See* CHAP.

CHAP (Challenge Handshake Authentication Protocol) An authentication protocol that operates over PPP and that requires the authenticator to take the first step by offering the other computer a challenge. The requestor responds by combining the challenge with its password, encrypting the new string of characters and sending it to the authenticator. The authenticator matches to see if the requestor's encrypted string of text matches its own encrypted string of characters. If so, the requester is authenticated and granted access to secured resources.

ciphertext The unique data block that results when an original piece of data (such as text) is encrypted (for example, by using a key).

client_hello In the context of SSL encryption, a message issued from the client to the server that contains information about what level of security the client's browser is capable of accepting and what type of encryption the client's browser can decipher (for example, RSA or Diffie-Hellman). The client_hello message also establishes a randomly generated number that uniquely identifies the client, plus another number that identifies the SSL session.

content-filtering firewall A firewall that can block designated types of traffic from entering a protected network.

Data Encryption Standard *See* DES.

demilitarized zone *See* DMZ.

denial-of-service attack A security attack in which a system becomes unable to function because it has been inundated with requests for services and can't respond to any of them. As a result, all data transmissions are disrupted.

DES (Data Encryption Standard) A popular private key encryption technique that was developed by IBM in the 1970s.

dictionary attack A technique in which attackers run a program that tries a combination of a known user ID and, for a password, every word in a dictionary to attempt to gain access to a network.

Diffie-Hellman The first commonly used public, or asymmetric, key algorithm. Diffie-Hellman was released in 1975 by its creators, Whitfield Diffie and Martin Hellman.

digital certificate A password-protected and encrypted file that holds an individual's identification information, including a public key and a private key. The individual's public key is used to verify the sender's digital signature, and the private key allows the individual to log on to a third-party authority who administers digital certificates.

DMZ (demilitarized zone) The perimeter of a protected, internal network where users, both authorized and unauthorized, from external networks can attempt to access it. Firewalls and IDS/IPS systems are typically placed in the DMZ.

DNS spoofing A security attack in which an outsider forges name server records to falsify his host's identity.

EAP (Extensible Authentication Protocol) A Data Link layer protocol defined by the IETF that specifies the dynamic distribution of encryption keys and a preauthentication process in which a client and server exchange data via an intermediate node (for example, an access point on a wireless LAN). Only after they have mutually authenticated can the client and server exchange encrypted data. EAP can be used with multiple authentication and encryption schemes.

EAP over LAN *See* EAPoL.

EAPoL (EAP over LAN) *See* 802.1x.

Encapsulating Security Payload *See* ESP.

encryption The use of an algorithm to scramble data into a format that can be read only by reversing the algorithm—decrypting the data—to keep the information private. The most popular kind of encryption algorithm weaves a key into the original data's bits, sometimes several times in different sequences, to generate a unique data block.

encryption devices Computers or specialized adapters inserted into other devices, such as routers or servers, that perform encryption.

ESP (Encapsulation Security Payload) In the context of IPSec, a type of encryption that provides authentication of the IP packet's data payload through public key techniques. In addition, ESP also encrypts the entire IP packet for added security.

evil twin An exploit in which a rogue access point masquerades as a legitimate access point, using the same SSID and potentially other identical settings.

exploit In the context of network security, the means by which a hacker takes advantage of a vulnerability.

Extensible Authentication Protocol *See* EAP.

flashing A security attack in which an Internet user sends commands to another Internet user's machine that cause the screen to fill with garbage characters. A flashing attack causes the user to terminate her session.

FTP bounce A security exploit in which an FTP client specifies a different host's IP address and port number for the requested data's destination. By commanding the FTP server to connect to a different computer, a hacker can scan the ports on other hosts and transmit malicious code. To thwart FTP bounce attacks, most modern FTP servers will not issue data to hosts other than the client that originated the request.

hacker Traditionally, a person who masters the inner workings of operating systems and utilities in an effort to better understand them. More generally, an individual who gains unauthorized access to systems or networks with or without malicious intent.

handshake protocol One of several protocols within SSL, and perhaps the most significant. As its name implies, the handshake protocol allows the client and server to authenticate (or introduce) each other and establishes terms for how they securely exchange data during an SSL session.

HIDS (host-based intrusion detection) A type of intrusion detection that runs on a single computer, such as a client or server, that has access to and allows access from the Internet.

HIPS (host-based intrusion prevention) A type of intrusion prevention that runs on a single computer, such as a client or server, that has access to and allows access from the Internet.

honeynet A network of honeypots.

honeypot A decoy system isolated from legitimate systems and designed to be vulnerable to security exploits for the purposes of learning more about hacking techniques or nabbing a hacker in the act.

host-based firewall A firewall that only protects the computer on which it's installed.

host-based intrusion detection *See* HIDS.

host-based intrusion prevention *See* HIPS.

HTTP over Secure Sockets Layer *See* HTTPS.

HTTP Secure *See* HTTPS.

HTTPS (HTTP over Secure Sockets Layer) The URL prefix that indicates that a Web page requires its data to be exchanged between client and server using SSL encryption. HTTPS uses the TCP port number 443.

IDS (intrusion-detection system) A dedicated device or software running on a host that monitors, flags, and logs any unauthorized attempt to access an organization's secured resources on a network or host.

IKE (Internet Key Exchange) The first phase of IPSec authentication, which accomplishes key management. IKE is a service that runs on UDP port 500. After IKE has established the rules for the type of keys two nodes use, IPSec invokes its second phase, encryption.

Internet Key Exchange *See* IKE.

Internet Protocol Security *See* IPSec.

Internet Security Association and Key Management Protocol *See* ISAKMP.

intrusion-detection system *See* IDS.

intrusion-prevention system *See* IPS.

IPS (intrusion-prevention system) A dedicated device or software running on a host that automatically reacts to any unauthorized attempt to access an organization's secured resources on a network or host. IPS is often combined with IDS.

IPSec (Internet Protocol Security) A Layer 3 protocol that defines encryption, authentication, and key management for TCP/IP transmissions. IPSec is an enhancement to IPv4 and is native to IPv6. IPSec is unique among authentication methods in that it adds security information to the header of all IP packets.

IP spoofing A security attack in which an outsider obtains internal IP addresses and then uses those addresses to pretend that he has authority to access a private network from the Internet.

ISAKMP (Internet Security Association and Key Management Protocol) A service for setting policies to verify the identity and the encryption methods nodes will use in IPSec transmission.

KDC (Key Distribution Center) In Kerberos terminology, the server that runs the authentication service and the Ticket-Granting Service to issue keys and tickets to clients.

Kerberos A cross-platform authentication protocol that uses key encryption to verify the identity of clients and to securely exchange information after a client logs on to a system. It is an example of a private key encryption service.

key A series of characters that is combined with a block of data during that data's encryption. To decrypt the resulting data, the recipient must also possess the key.

Key Distribution Center *See* KDC.

key management The method whereby two nodes using key encryption agree on common parameters for the keys they will use to encrypt data.

key pair The combination of a public and private key used to decipher data that was encrypted using public key encryption.

man-in-the-middle attack A security threat that relies on intercepted transmissions. It can take one of several forms, but in all cases a person redirects or captures secure data traffic while in transit.

metasploit A penetration-testing tool that combines known scanning techniques and exploits to result in potentially new types of exploits.

Microsoft Challenge Handshake Authentication Protocol *See* MS-CHAP.

Microsoft Challenge Handshake Authentication Protocol, version 2 *See* MS-CHAPv2.

MS-CHAP (Microsoft Challenge Handshake Authentication Protocol) An authentication protocol provided with Windows operating systems that uses a three-way handshake to verify a client's credentials and encrypts passwords with a challenge text.

MS-CHAPv2 (Microsoft Challenge Handshake Authentication Protocol, version 2) An authentication protocol provided with Windows operating systems that follows the CHAP model, but uses stronger encryption, uses different encryption keys for transmission and reception, and requires mutual authentication between two computers.

multifactor authentication An authentication process that requires the client to provide two or more pieces of information, such as a password, fingerprint scan, and security token.

mutual authentication An authentication scheme in which both computers verify the credentials of each other.

Nessus A penetration-testing tool from Tenable Security that performs sophisticated scans to discover information about hosts, ports, services, and software.

network-based firewall A firewall configured and positioned to protect an entire network.

network-based intrusion detection *See* NIDS.

network-based intrusion prevention *See* NIPS.

network key A key (or character string) required for a wireless station to associate with an access point using WEP.

Network Mapper *See* NMAP.

NIDS (network-based intrusion detection) A type of intrusion detection that occurs on devices that are situated at the edge of the network or that handle aggregated traffic.

NIPS (network-based intrusion prevention) A type of intrusion prevention that occurs on devices that are situated at the edge of the network or that handle aggregated traffic.

NMAP (Network Mapper) A scanning tool designed to assess large networks quickly and provide comprehensive, customized information about a network and its hosts. NMAP, which runs on virtually any modern operating system, is available for download at no cost at *www.nmap.org*.

OpenSSH An open source version of the SSH suite of protocols.

packet-filtering firewall A router that examines the header of every packet of data that it receives to determine whether that type of packet is authorized to continue to its destination. Packet-filtering firewalls are also called screening firewalls.

PAP (Password Authentication Protocol) A simple authentication protocol that operates over PPP. Using PAP, a client issues its credentials in a request to authenticate, and the server responds with a confirmation or denial of authentication after comparing the credentials with those in its database. PAP is not very secure and is, therefore, rarely used on modern networks.

Password Authentication Protocol *See* PAP.

PGP (Pretty Good Privacy) A key-based encryption system for e-mail that uses a two-step verification process.

phishing A practice in which a person attempts to glean access or authentication information by posing as someone who needs that information.

PKI (Public-key Infrastructure) The use of certificate authorities to associate public keys with certain users.

port authentication A technique in which a client's identity is verified by an authentication server before a port, whether physical or logical, is opened for the client's Layer 3 traffic. *See also* 802.1x.

port-based authentication *See* port authentication.

port forwarding The process of redirecting traffic from its normally assigned port to a different port, either on the client or server. In the case of using SSH, port forwarding can send data exchanges that are normally insecure through encrypted tunnels.

port mirroring A monitoring technique in which one port on a switch is configured to send a copy of all its traffic to a second port.

port scanner Software that searches a server, switch, router, or other device for open ports, which can be vulnerable to attack.

posture assessment An assessment of an organization's security vulnerabilities. Posture assessments should be performed at least annually and preferably quarterly—or sooner if the network has undergone significant changes. For each risk found, it should rate the severity of a potential breach, as well as its likelihood.

Pretty Good Privacy *See* PGP.

principal In Kerberos terminology, a user or client.

private key encryption A type of key encryption in which the sender and receiver use a key to which only they have access. DES (Data Encryption Standard), which was developed by IBM in the 1970s, is a popular example of a private key encryption technique. Private key encryption is also known as symmetric encryption.

proxy *See* proxy server.

proxy server A network host that runs a proxy service. Proxy servers may also be called gateways.

proxy service A software application on a network host that acts as an intermediary between the external and internal networks, screening all incoming and outgoing traffic and providing one address to the outside world, instead of revealing the addresses of internal LAN devices.

public key encryption A form of key encryption in which data is encrypted using two keys: One is a key known only to a user, and the other is a key associated with the user and that can be obtained from a public source, such as a public key server. Some examples of public key algorithms include RSA and Diffie-Hellman. Public key encryption is also known as asymmetric encryption.

Public-key Infrastructure *See* PKI.

public key server A publicly available host (such as an Internet host) that provides free access to a list of users' public keys (for use in public key encryption).

RADIUS (Remote Authentication Dial-In User Service) A popular protocol for providing centralized AAA (authentication, authorization, and accounting) for multiple users. RADIUS runs over UDP and can use one of several authentication protocols.

RADIUS server A server that offers centralized authentication services to a network's access server, VPN server, or wireless access point via the RADIUS protocol.

RC4 An asymmetric key encryption technique that weaves a key with data multiple times as a computer issues the stream of data. RC4 keys can be as long as 2048 bits. In addition to being highly secure, RC4 is fast.

Remote Authentication Dial-In User Service *See* RADIUS.

RSA An encryption algorithm that creates a key by randomly choosing two large prime numbers and multiplying them together. RSA is named after its creators, Ronald Rivest, Adi Shamir, and Leonard Adleman. RSA was released in 1977, but remains popular today for e-commerce transactions.

SCP (Secure CoPy) A method for copying files securely between hosts. SCP is part of the OpenSSH package, which comes with modern UNIX and Linux operating systems. Third-party SCP applications are available for Windows-based computers.

Secure CoPy *See* SCP.

Secure File Transfer Protocol *See* SFTP.

Secure Shell *See* SSH.

Secure Sockets Layer *See* SSL.

security audit An assessment of an organization's security vulnerabilities performed by an accredited network security firm.

security policy A document or plan that identifies an organization's security goals, risks, levels of authority, designated security coordinator and team members, responsibilities for each team member, and responsibilities for each employee. In addition, it specifies how to address security breaches.

security token A device or piece of software used for authentication that stores or generates information, such as a series of numbers or letters, known only to its authorized user.

server_hello In the context of SSL encryption, a message issued from the server to the client that confirms the information the server received in the client_hello message. It also agrees to certain terms of encryption based on the options the client supplied. Depending on the Web server's preferred encryption method, the server may choose to issue your browser a public key or a digital certificate at this time.

session key In the context of Kerberos authentication, a key issued to both the client and the server by the authentication service that uniquely identifies their session.

SFTP (Secure File Transfer Protocol) A protocol available with the proprietary version of SSH that copies files between hosts securely. Like FTP, SFTP first establishes a connection with a host and then allows a remote user to browse directories, list files, and copy files. Unlike FTP, SFTP encrypts data before transmitting it.

single sign-on A form of authentication in which a client signs on once to access multiple systems or resources.

smurf attack A threat to networked hosts in which the host is flooded with broadcast ping messages. A smurf attack is a type of denial-of-service attack.

social engineering The act of manipulating personal relationships to circumvent network security measures and gain access to a system.

SSH (Secure Shell) A connection utility that provides authentication and encryption. With SSH, you can securely log on to a host, execute commands on that host, and copy files to or from that host. SSH encrypts data exchanged throughout the session.

SSL (Secure Sockets Layer) A method of encrypting TCP/IP transmissions—including Web pages and data entered into Web forms—en route between the client and server using public key encryption technology.

SSL session In the context of SSL encryption, an association between the client and server that is defined by an agreement on a specific set of encryption techniques. An SSL session allows the client and server to continue to exchange data securely as long as the client is still connected to the server. SSL sessions are established by the SSL handshake protocol.

stateful firewall A firewall capable of monitoring a data stream from end to end.

stateless firewall A firewall capable only of examining packets individually. Stateless firewalls perform more quickly than stateful firewalls, but are not as sophisticated.

symmetric encryption A method of encryption that requires the same key to encode the data as is used to decode the ciphertext.

TACACS+ (Terminal Access Controller Access Control System Plus) A Cisco proprietary protocol for AAA (authentication, authorization, and accounting). Like RADIUS, TACACS+ may use one of many authentication protocols. Unlike RADIUS, TACACS+ relies on TCP at the Network layer and allows for separation of the AAA services.

Temporal Key Integrity Protocol *See* TKIP.

Terminal Access Controller Access Control System Plus *See* TACACS+.

TGS (Ticket-Granting Service) In Kerberos terminology, an application that runs on the KDC that issues Ticket-Granting Tickets to clients so that they need not request a new ticket for each new service they want to access.

TGT (Ticket-Granting Ticket) In Kerberos terminology, a ticket that enables a user to be accepted as a validated principal by multiple services.

three-way handshake An authentication process that involves three steps.

ticket In Kerberos terminology, a temporary set of credentials that a client uses to prove that its identity has been validated by the authentication service.

Ticket-Granting Service *See* TGS.

Ticket-Granting Ticket *See* TGT.

TKIP (Temporal Key Integrity Protocol) An encryption key generation and management scheme used by 802.11i.

TLS (Transport Layer Security) A version of SSL being standardized by the IETF (Internet Engineering Task Force). With TLS, the IETF aims to create a version of SSL that encrypts UDP as well as TCP transmissions. TLS, which is supported by new Web browsers, uses slightly different encryption algorithms than SSL, but otherwise is very similar to the most recent version of SSL.

Transport Layer Security *See* TLS.

Triple DES (3DES) The modern implementation of DES, which weaves a 56-bit key through data three times, each time using a different key.

two-factor authentication A process in which clients must supply two pieces of information to verify their identity and gain access to a system.

VPN concentrator A specialized device that authenticates VPN clients and establishes tunnels for VPN connections.

vulnerability A weakness of a system, process, or architecture that could lead to compromised information or unauthorized access to a network.

war chalking The use of chalk to draw symbols on a sidewalk or wall within range of an access point. The symbols, patterned after marks that hobos devised to indicate hospitable places for food or rest, indicate the access point's SSID and whether it's secured.

war driving The act of driving while running a laptop configured to detect and capture wireless data transmissions.

WEP (Wired Equivalent Privacy) A key encryption technique for wireless networks that uses keys both to authenticate network clients and to encrypt data in transit.

WEP cracking A security exploit in which a hacker uses a program to discover a WEP key.

Wi-Fi Alliance An international, nonprofit organization dedicated to ensuring the interoperability of 802.11-capable devices.

Wi-Fi Protected Access *See* WPA.

Wired Equivalent Privacy *See* WEP.

WPA (Wi-Fi Protected Access) A wireless security method endorsed by the Wi-Fi Alliance that is considered a subset of the 802.11i standard. In WPA, authentication follows the same mechanism specified in 802.11i. The main difference between WPA and 802.11i is that WPA specifies RC4 encryption rather than AES.

WPA2 The name given to the 802.11i security standard by the Wi-Fi Alliance. The only difference between WPA2 and 802.11i is that WPA2 includes support for the older WPA security method.

WPA2-Enterprise An authentication scheme for Wi-Fi networks that combines WPA2 with RADIUS.

WPA cracking A security exploit in which a hacker uses a program to discover a WPA key.

WPA-Enterprise An authentication scheme for Wi-Fi networks that combines WPA with RADIUS.

zero-day exploit An exploit that takes advantage of a software vulnerability that hasn't yet become public, and is known only to the hacker who discovered it. Zero-day exploits are particularly dangerous, because the vulnerability is exploited before the software developer has the opportunity to provide a solution for it.

Review Questions

1. Which strategy is most commonly used by an intruder to gain access to a network?
   a. using malware
   b. social engineering
   c. man-in the middle attacks
   d. circumventing network hardware and design flaws

2. What is the type of risk when an Administrator accepts the default security options after installing an operating system or application?
   a. risks associated with Internet access
   b. risks associated with people
   c. risks inherent in network hardware and design
   d. risks associated with protocols and software
3. Which response team member is the person on call who first notices or is alerted to the problem?
   a. dispatcher
   b. technical support specialist
   c. manager
   d. public relations specialist
4. Which authentication protocol encrypts user names and passwords for transmission?
   a. CHAP
   b. PAP
   c. EAP
   d. PPP
5. By default, which standard does not offer any security?
   a. WPA
   b. WEP
   c. 802.11i
   d. 802.11
6. True or false? SSL (Secure Sockets Layer) is a method of encrypting TCP/IP transmissions - including Web pages and data entered into Web forms - en route between the client and server using public key encryption technology.
7. True or false? An IDS can detect, react to, and log suspicious activity.
8. True or false? When a firewall can view a data stream, it is known as a stateless firewall.
9. True or false? Encryption is the last means of defense against data theft.
10. True or false? RADIUS and TACACS+ belong to a category of protocols known as AAA (authentication authorization and accounting.)
11. A(n) ________________ is a thorough examination of each aspect of the network to determine how it might be compromised.
12. A(n) ________________ identifies your security goals, risks, levels of authority, designated security coordinator and team members, responsibilities for each team member, and responsibilities for each employee.

13. A(n) ________________ is a software application on a network host that acts as an intermediary between the external and internal networks, screening all incoming and outgoing traffic.

14. In ________________ encryption, data is encrypted using two keys.

15. ________________ is a key encryption technique for wireless networks that uses keys both to authenticate network clients and to encrypt data in transit.

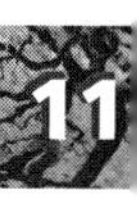

After reading this chapter and completing the exercises, you will be able to:

- Use terminology specific to converged networks
- Explain VoIP (Voice over IP) services, PBXs, and their user interfaces
- Explain video-over-IP applications and their user interfaces
- Describe VoIP and video-over-IP signaling and transport protocols, including SIP, H.323, and RTP
- Understand QoS (quality of service) assurance methods critical to converged networks, including RSVP and DiffServ

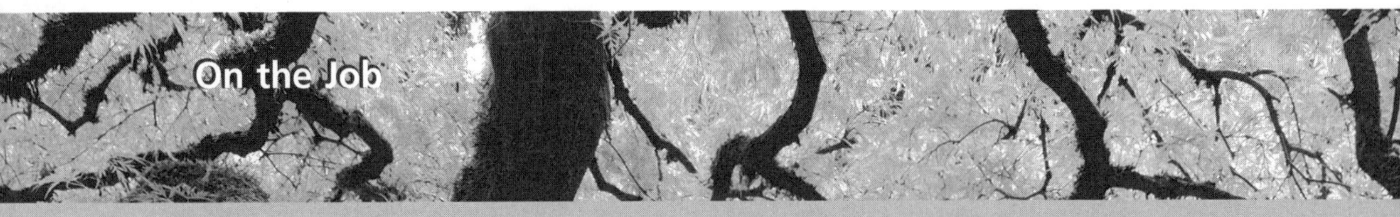

On the Job

The critical element in a stroke is time. Doctors have three hours from the onset of a stroke to deliver a lifesaving drug called tPA. Neurologists can cut this time by seeing patients through videoconferencing.

I provide support for the WAN and H.323 videoconferencing systems for Utah Telehealth Network's 49 sites. We recently installed a new H.323 videoconferencing codec in a doctor's home. Unlike the old unit, it kept randomly losing the far end's image. A second codec had the same problem. The troubleshooting process quickly turned interesting.

First, we made sure the network cable was secure by recrimping the ends. Next, we checked the router and switch for a data link. We also verified that speed and duplex were set correctly. No errors appeared in the counters.

Videoconferencing is often prone to IP addressing issues when using Network Address Translation, so we verified that both the private and public IP addresses were correct. When the problem continued, we applied a sniffer capture to the Internet side of the firewall. Its log showed that the firewall was not correctly converting private IP addresses to public addresses. Sessions would establish but then fail because the far end was trying to contact the private IP address rather than the near end's public address. We also tried changing the H.323 firewall's Application layer gateway settings. The adjustments let calls stay up, but we now lost far end camera control. This indicated that the firewall was affecting the Application layer as well.

I sent the packet captures to the firewall vendor, who claimed that Layer 3 routing caused the problem. However, thanks to those valuable logs, we proved that the firewall was not properly processing the H.323 application. Ultimately, we discovered that the firewall's firmware did not support the latest H.323 standards.

We chose to replace the firewall with a newer model that used the latest H.323 standards. The replacement worked fine with the codec. The increased maintenance costs taught us the hard way to evaluate every potential purchase in a test environment before putting it in production.

Jeff Shuckra
Network Engineer, Utah Telehealth Network

In Chapter 1, you learned that convergence is the use of one network to simultaneously carry voice, video, and data communications. For most of the twentieth century, voice and data signals traveled over separate networks. The PSTN (Public Switched Telephone Network), based on Alexander Graham Bell's circuit-switched model, carried telephone calls and fax transmissions. Packet-switched networks, such as the Internet, took care of e-mail, Web pages, file transfers, and access to other data resources. In the latter part of the twentieth century, the two types of networks began intersecting. However, this intersection is not necessarily seamless or efficient. In some cases, it requires modems to convert digital data into analog signals and vice versa. Networks achieve more unified integration, however, by packetizing voice—that is, digitizing the voice signal and issuing it as a stream of packets over the network.

In the last 15 years, telecommunications carriers, network service providers, data equipment manufacturers, and standards organizations have focused on ways to deliver voice, video, and data over the same networks. These converged networks, as they are called, may be cheaper and more convenient, but they also require new technology. This chapter describes a variety of voice and video-over-IP applications, plus the protocols and infrastructure necessary to deliver them.

Terminology

In discussions of convergence, the use of multiple terms to refer to the same or similar technologies is common. This is partly a result of a market that developed rapidly while many different vendors marketed their own solutions and applied their preferred terminology. The terms used throughout this chapter are those most frequently cited by standards organizations such as the ITU and IETF. Before you learn how voice and video-over-IP services work, it's useful to understand the meaning of these terms.

One important term is **IP telephony**, the use of any network (either public or private) to carry voice signals using the TCP/IP protocol. IP telephony is more commonly known as **VoIP (Voice over IP)**. VoIP can run over any packet-switched network. Virtually any type of data connection can carry VoIP signals, including T-carriers, ISDN, DSL, broadband cable, satellite connections, Wi-Fi, WiMAX, HSPA+, LTE, and cellular telephone networks.

When VoIP relies on the Internet, it is often called **Internet telephony**. But not all VoIP calls are carried over the Internet. In fact, VoIP over private lines is an effective and economical method of completing calls between two locations within an organization. And because the line is private, its network congestion can be easily controlled, which often translates into better sound quality than an Internet telephone call can provide. But given the Internet's breadth and low cost, it is appealing to consider the Internet for carrying conversations that we currently exchange over the PSTN.

Voice is not the only nondata application that can be carried on a converged network. Other applications include **IPTV (IP television)**, in which television signals from broadcast or cable networks travel over packet-switched networks. **Videoconferencing**, which allows multiple participants to communicate and collaborate at once through audiovisual means, is another example of using networks to carry video information. **Streaming video** refers to video signals that are compressed and delivered in a continuous stream. For example, when you choose to watch a television show episode on the Web, you are requesting a streaming video service. You don't have to download the entire episode before you begin to see and hear it. When streaming videos are supplied via the Web, they may be called **Webcasts**.

One way to distribute video signals over IP is multicasting. As described in Chapter 4, in multicasting, one node transmits the same content to every client in a defined group of nodes, such as a subnet. IPTV, videoconferencing, streaming video, and IP multicasting belong to the range of services known as **video over IP**.

Over time, voice and video services over packet-switched networks have matured, and as a result more users rely on them. These users, in turn, have demanded better integration with traditional data services, such as e-mail and Web browsing. In Chapter 1, you learned that unified communications (sometimes called **unified messaging**) is a service that makes several forms of communication available from a single user interface. In unified communications, a user can, for example, access the Web, send and receive faxes, e-mail messages, voice mail messages, instant messages, or telephone calls, and participate in videoconference calls—all from one console.

This overview of the terms used when discussing converged services gives you a sense of how many applications fall into this category. Now you are ready to learn how they work.

VoIP Applications and Interfaces

VoIP (pronounced "voyp") has existed in various forms for over a decade. Although organizations were slow to adopt it at first, as networks became faster, more reliable, and more accessible, use of VoIP increased dramatically. Significant reasons for implementing VoIP include the following:

- *Lower costs for voice calls*—In the case of long-distance calling, using VoIP over a WAN allows an organization to avoid paying long-distance telephone charges, a benefit known as **toll bypass**. For example, an organization that already leases T3s between its offices within a region can use the T3s to carry voice traffic between colleagues.
- *Supply new or enhanced features and applications*—VoIP runs over TCP/IP, an open protocol suite, whereas the PSTN runs over proprietary protocols. This means developers with enough skill and interest can develop their own VoIP applications, making the possibilities for new VoIP features and services endless. It also means that off-the-shelf VoIP applications can be modified to suit a particular organization's needs.
- *Centralize voice and data network management*—When voice and data transmissions use the same infrastructure, a network manager needs only to design, maintain, and troubleshoot a single network. Furthermore, on that network, VoIP devices can provide detailed information about voice transmissions, such as the date, time, and duration of calls, in addition to their originating number and caller names.

Voice and data can be combined on a network in several different configurations. VoIP callers can use either a traditional telephone, which sends and receives analog signals, a telephone specially designed for TCP/IP transmission, or a computer equipped with a microphone, speaker, and VoIP client software. And on any VoIP network, a mix of these three types of clients is possible. The following sections explain how analog and digital voice networks are integrated and describe equipment necessary to accomplish such integration.

Analog Telephones

If a VoIP caller uses a traditional telephone, signals issued by the telephone must be converted to digital form before being transmitted on a TCP/IP-based network. In fact, even if the entire VoIP connection is digital, voice signals still need to be converted from their natural, analog form into bits. This conversion involves first compressing and encoding analog signals, functions that occur at the Presentation layer of the OSI model. Any method for accomplishing this conversion is known as a **codec** (a word that derives from its function as a *coder/decoder*). Detailing the wide variety of voice and video codecs is beyond the scope of this book. However, to successfully implement converged networks, you should understand what types of equipment are necessary to accomplish analog-to-digital conversion.

One possibility is to connect an analog telephone to a VoIP adapter, sometimes called an **ATA (analog telephone adapter)**. The ATA might be a card within a computer workstation or an externally attached device that allows for one or more telephone connections. The traditional telephone line connects to an RJ-11 port on the adapter. The ATA, along with its device drivers and software on the computer, converts analog voice signals to IP packets and vice versa. Figure 12-1 shows an ATA that supports two telephone connections.

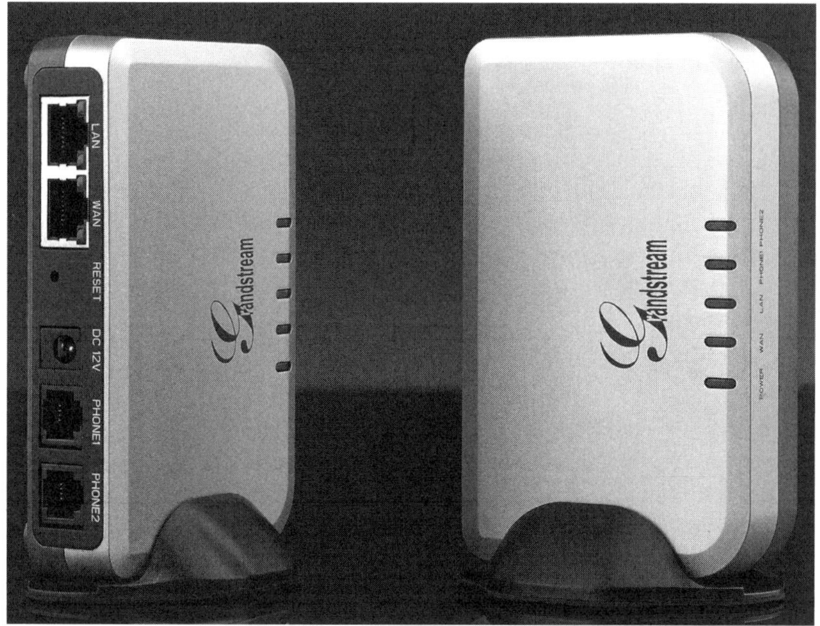

Figure 12-1 ATA (analog telephone adapter)
Courtesy of Grandstream Networks, Inc.

A second way to achieve this conversion is by connecting an analog telephone line to a switch, router, or gateway capable of accepting analog voice signals, converting them into packets, then issuing the packets to a data network—and vice versa. Like the switches, routers, and gateways you learned about earlier in this book, VoIP-enabled devices come with a variety of features, including support for NAT, VPN protocols, encryption, and more. Figure 12-2 shows a VoIP router that accepts up to four telephone lines. Next to the bank of eight RJ-11 ports for incoming analog lines are two RJ-45 ports to connect the router to an Ethernet network.

A third example of an analog-to-digital voice conversion device is a **digital PBX** or, more commonly, an **IP-PBX**. (**PBX** stands for **private branch exchange**, which is the term used to

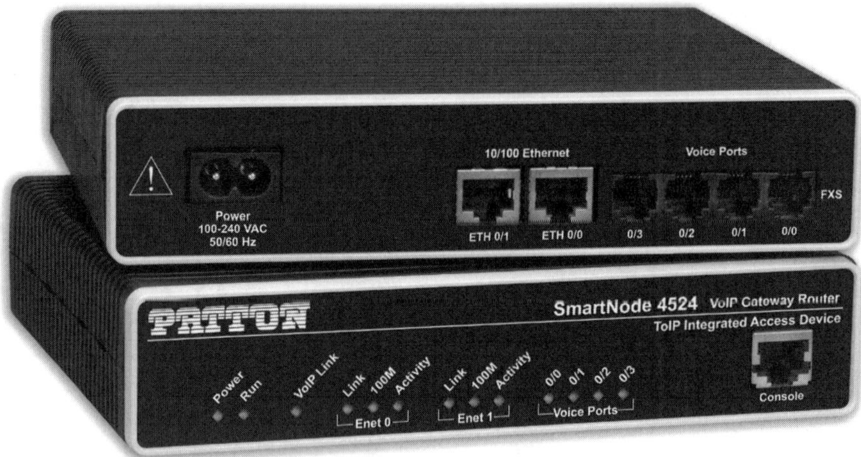

Figure 12-2 VoIP router

Photo of SmartNodeTM 4520 Analog VoIP Router from Patton Electronics, Co.

describe a telephone switch that connects and manages calls within a private organization.) In general, an IP-PBX is a private switch that accepts and interprets both analog and digital voice signals. Thus, it can connect with both traditional PSTN lines and data networks. An IP-PBX transmits and receives IP-based voice signals to and from other network connectivity devices, such as routers or gateways. Most IP-PBX systems are packaged with sophisticated software that allows network managers to configure and maintain an organization's phone system. For example, the system can be set up to ring a user's desk phone and cell phone simultaneously. And because an IP-PBX stores call information electronically, source and destination numbers, call times, durations, and voice-mail messages can be accessed via a Web interface.

Net+ A special type of IP-PBX is one that exists on the Internet. Instead of installing an IP-PBX on its
1.9 WAN, an organization might contract with a service provider for call management services in a **hosted PBX** arrangement. (Hosted PBXs may also be called **virtual PBXs**, although this term is a trademark of the VirtualPBX company.) Organizations that choose a hosted PBX don't need to install or maintain hardware or software for call completion and management.

Figure 12-3 shows an IP-PBX capable of managing up to 60 calls at once.

Figure 12-3 IP-PBX

© Courtesy of Epygi Technologies, Ltd

In a fourth scenario, the traditional telephone connects to an analog PBX, which then connects to a voice-data gateway. In this case, the gateway connects the traditional telephone circuits with a TCP/IP network (such as the Internet or a private WAN). The gateway digitizes incoming analog voice signals, compresses the data, assembles the data into packets, and then issues the packets to the packet-switched network. When transferring calls from a packet-switched network to a circuit-switched network (for example, if you call your home telephone number from your office's IP telephone), the gateway performs the same functions in the reverse order.

Figure 12-4 depicts the four different ways analog telephones can be used to access a VoIP network.

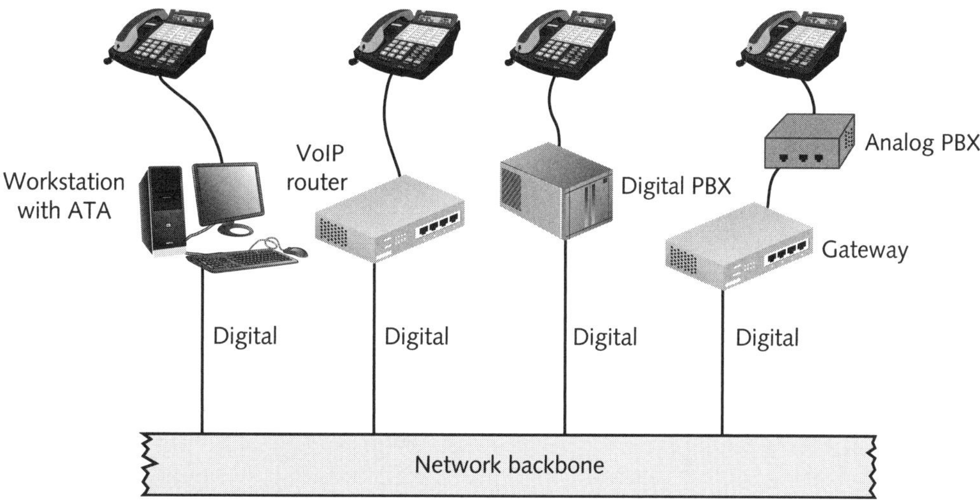

Figure 12-4 Integrating VoIP networks and analog telephones

IP Telephones

Most new VoIP installations use **IP telephones** (or **IP phones**), which, unlike traditional phones, transmit and receive only digital signals. When a caller uses an IP telephone, her voice is immediately digitized and issued from the telephone to the network in packet form. To communicate on the network, each IP telephone must have a unique IP address, just as any client connected to the network has a unique IP address. The IP telephone looks like a traditional touch-tone phone, but connects to an RJ-45 wall jack, like a computer workstation. Its connection may then pass through a connectivity device, such as a switch or router, before reaching the IP-PBX. An IP-PBX may contain its own voice-data gateway, or it may connect to a separate voice-data gateway, which is then connected to the network backbone. Figure 12-5 illustrates different ways IP telephones can connect with a data network.

IP telephones act much like traditional telephones. For example, they feature speed-dialing, call hold, transfer, and forwarding buttons, conference calling, voice-mail access, speakers and microphones, and an LCD screen that displays caller ID and call hold information. IP telephones come in both mobile and wired styles. More sophisticated IP telephones offer features not available with traditional telephones. Because IP telephones are essentially network clients, like workstations, the number and types of customized features that can be programmed for use with these phones is limitless. For example, IP telephone screens can act as Web browsers that allow users to complete a call by clicking on a telephone number.

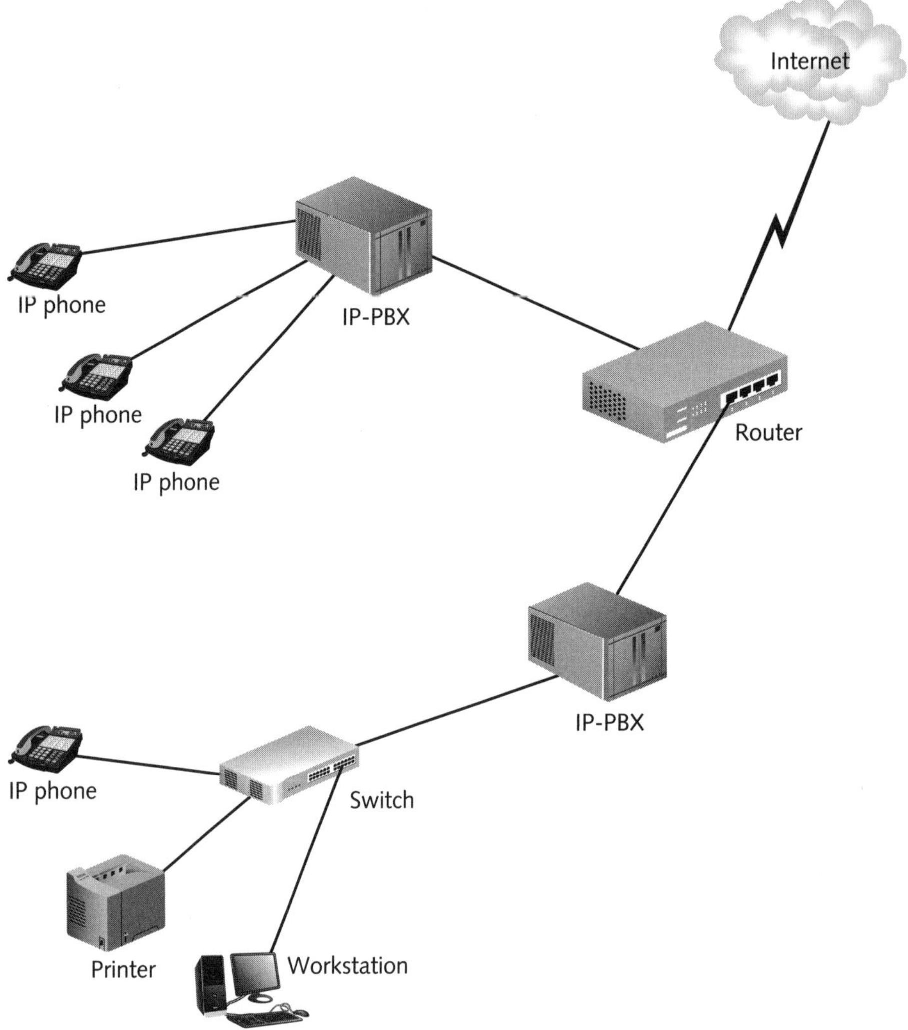

Figure 12-5 Accessing a VoIP network from IP phones

Another benefit of IP telephones is their mobility. Because IP telephones are addressable over a network, they can be moved from one office to another office, connected to a wall jack, and be ready to accept or make calls. Compare this with the traditional method of moving telephone extensions, which requires reprogramming the extension's location in a PBX database. A user would have to wait for the network administrator to perform this change before her telephone extension would work in a new location. With IP telephones, however, the user is free to move to any point on the network without missing a call.

One issue that faces IP telephones is the need for electric current. A conventional analog telephone obtains current from the local loop. This is necessary for signaling—for example, to make your phone ring and to provide a dial tone. However, IP telephones are not directly connected to the local loop. Instead, most obtain electric current from a separate power supply. This makes IP telephones susceptible to power outages in a way that analog telephones are not. It also points to the need for assured backup power sources in organizations that rely on IP telephones. In some VoIP installations, IP telephones obtain current via their Ethernet connection using PoE (Power over Ethernet). A typical IP phone is shown in Figure 12-6.

Figure 12-6 An IP phone

Courtesy of Grandstream Networks, Inc.

Using IP telephones is not the only way to benefit from a fully digital voice connection. Instead, an off-the-shelf workstation can be programmed to act like an IP telephone, as described in the next section.

Softphones

Rather than using traditional telephones or IP telephones, a third option is to use a computer programmed to act like an IP telephone, otherwise known as a **softphone**. Softphones and IP telephones provide the same calling functions; they simply connect to the network and deliver services differently. Before it can be used as a softphone, a computer must meet minimum hardware requirements (which any new workstation purchased at an electronics store would likely meet), be installed with an IP telephony client, and communicate with a digital telephone switch. In addition, softphone computers must have a sound card capable of full-duplex transmission, so that both the caller and the called party can speak at the same time. Finally, a softphone also requires a microphone and speakers or a headset. Skype, the popular Internet telephony software, is one type of softphone.

After a user starts the softphone client software, he is typically presented with a graphical representation of a telephone dial pad, as shown in Figure 12-7. The interface might also present a list of telephone numbers in the caller's address book, so that the caller can click on the number he wants to call. And like IP telephones, the program features buttons for call forwarding, speed dialing, conferencing, and so on—except that on a softphone, these buttons are clickable icons.

Figure 12-7 Softphone interface

Unlike many traditional phones, softphones allow the user to customize the graphical interface. For example, an administrative assistant who spends most of his time calling clients and vendors on behalf of his supervisor can position a list of clickable, frequently called numbers in the foreground of his default interface.

One difference between IP telephones and softphones is that a softphone's versatile connectivity makes it an optimal VoIP solution for traveling employees and telecommuters. For example, suppose you are a district sales manager with a home office and you supervise 32 sales representatives throughout the Pacific Northwest. Your company uses VoIP, with an IP-PBX connected to the company headquarters' LAN. At your home office, you have a desktop workstation equipped with a sound card, headset, and softphone software. You also lease a DSL connection to your local carrier, which allows you to log on to your company's LAN from home. After logging on to the LAN, you initiate the softphone client and then log on to the company's IP-PBX. By logging on to the IP-PBX, you access your personal call profile and indicate to the IP-PBX that your calls should be routed to your home computer. However, because you are a district sales manager, you only spend half of the time working from home. The other half of the time you travel to visit your sales representatives across the region. During that time, you use a laptop that, like your home workstation, is equipped with a sound card, headset, and the softphone client software. While on the road, you use remote connectivity software to access your company's LAN, then initiate your softphone client. Now your calls are directed to your laptop computer, rather than your home workstation. No matter where you are, you can establish a remote telephone extension, if the computer has the appropriate software and hardware installed. Figure 12-8 depicts the use of softphones on a converged network.

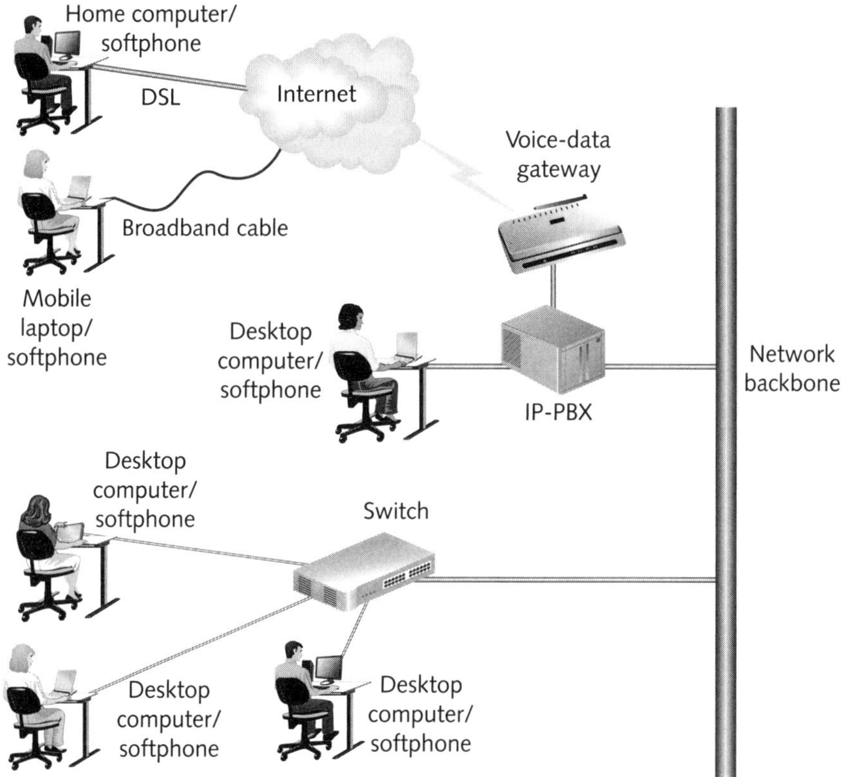

Figure 12-8 Connecting softphones to a converged network

Besides their extreme mobility, another advantage to softphones is the capability for convenient, localized call management. Like IP phones, softphone clients can easily track the date, time, and duration of calls, in addition to their originating number and caller names. A softphone user can also, for example, export call information to a billing or accounting program on the same workstation. This feature simplifies record keeping and billing for professionals—such as lawyers or consulting engineers—who bill their customers by the hour.

Now that you understand the variety of ways VoIP services may be implemented, you are ready to learn about the different types of video services that packet-switched networks may carry.

Video-over-IP Applications and Interfaces

Cisco Systems, the largest supplier of networking hardware in the world, estimates that by 2015, over two-thirds of the traffic carried by the Internet will be video traffic, with online video viewers totaling one billion people. This extraordinary growth is thanks to the large quantity of video content from providers such as Netflix and Hulu, the increasing volume of devices accessing the Internet, including smartphones and tablet PCs, plus the decreasing cost of bandwidth and equipment. Given these networking trends, it's important to understand the types of video services that TCP/IP networks can carry and the hardware and software they rely on.

The following sections divide video-over-IP services into three categories: streaming video, IPTV, and videoconferencing. However, divisions between these services are not always clear, as you'll learn. Also bear in mind that no matter what the application or distribution method, every video-over-IP transmission begins with digitizing the audio and visual signals using one of several popular video codecs, such as MPEG-4. Details of video codecs are beyond the scope of this book.

Streaming Video

You have already learned that streaming video is a service in which audiovisual signals are compressed and delivered over the Internet in a continuous stream. If you have watched a YouTube video on the Internet, you have used streaming video. Because most networks are TCP/IP-based, most streaming video belongs to the category of video over IP.

Among all video-over-IP applications, streaming video is perhaps the simplest. A user needs only to have a computer with sufficient processing and caching resources, plus the appropriate audiovisual hardware and software to view encoded video. On the transmission end, video can be delivered by any computer with sufficient capabilities to store and send the video. This might be a streaming server dedicated to the task or any computer that performs video streaming among other tasks. Streaming video can traverse any type of TCP/IP network, though it often relies on the Internet.

One popular way of providing video streams is to make them available as stored files (saved in any one of a number of popular video formats) on a server. The viewer then chooses to watch the video at his convenience, typically from a Web browser. Upon receiving a request, the server delivers the video to the viewer. This type of service, in which the video file remains on the server until it is specifically requested by the user, is known as **video-on-demand**. When you choose to watch a news report from your local TV channel's Web page, for example, you are making use of video-on-demand.

In another form of streaming video, the video is issued live—that is, directly from the source to the user as the camera captures it. For example, suppose you wanted to watch a political debate that's being broadcast by a TV network. You could access the network's Web site and watch the debate as it happens using live streaming video. One drawback to live streaming is that content cannot be edited before it's distributed. Another potential drawback is that viewers must connect with the stream as it occurs, whereas they can use video-on-demand at their convenience. In addition, video-on-demand allows viewers to control their viewing experience, for example, by pausing, rewinding, or fast-forwarding.

Figure 12-9 illustrates video-on-demand and live streaming video services.

The distinction between on-demand video and live streaming video is just the beginning. You also need to consider the number of clients receiving each service. For example, an IT manager in one office might use his laptop and its built-in camera to capture and issue a video of himself explaining a technical topic to one of his employees in another office. This is an example of point-to-point video over IP. Or he might issue the video stream to a whole group of employees in a point-to-multipoint manner.

You might recall the terms *unicast* and *multicast* from Chapter 4 and assume that point-to-multipoint streaming video means multicast transmission. That's not necessarily the case. In IP multicasting, a source issues data to a defined group of IP addresses. In fact, many streaming video services—and nearly all of those issued over a public network, such as the Internet—are examples of unicast transmissions. In a unicast transmission, a single node issues a stream of data

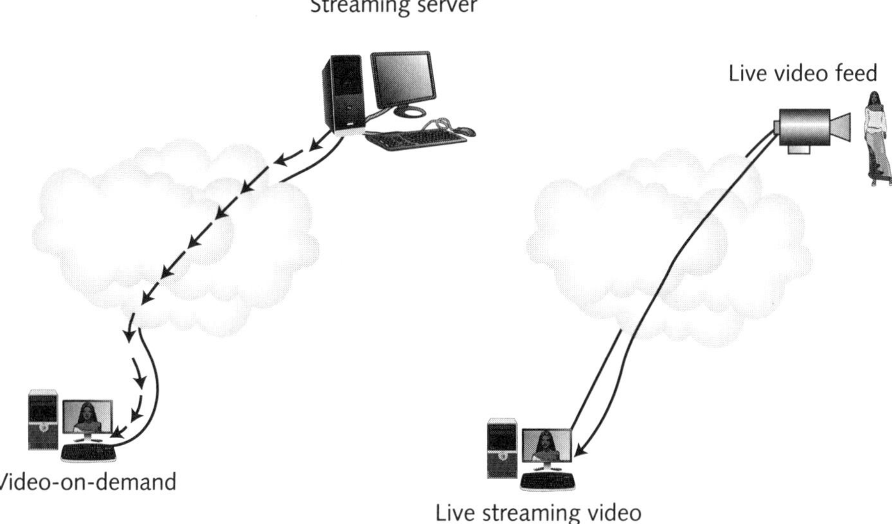

Figure 12-9 Video-on-demand and live streaming video

to one other node. In a VoIP call, for example, one IP phone addresses another in unicast fashion. If many Internet users watch CSPAN's streaming video on the Web simultaneously, the CSPAN source would issue encoded audiovisual signals to each viewer via separate unicast transmissions. In the example of an IT manager sharing a video discussion with his employees in another office, the transmission might be unicast or multicast, depending on how he configured it.

Finally, streaming video services may also be classified according to the type of network they use, private or public. Watching YouTube videos or TV episodes on Hulu are obviously cases of streaming video issued over a public network, the Internet. Examples of streaming video on private networks include educational videos delivered over the private networks of schools, businesses, or other organizations. For example, a guest speaker's presentation at a college's main campus auditorium could be filmed and transmitted via live streaming to classrooms in the colleges' satellite campuses, all without ever leaving the college's private network.

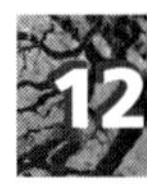

Most, though not all, examples of streaming video take place over public networks. The following section describes a video-over-IP service that typically makes use of private networks.

IPTV (IP Television)

In Chapter 7, you learned about the networks that telecommunications carriers and cable companies have established to deliver high-bandwidth Internet connections to their customers. These networks are now being used to deliver digital television signals using IPTV. In fact, because of digital video's value as an added service, your local telephone company is likely investing significant sums into the hardware and software that make IPTV possible. Because telecommunications carriers are leading the way with IPTV installation, this section concentrates on their network architecture and components, but bear in mind that cable companies are investing in this technology, too.

Several elements come together to deliver digital video to consumers, as shown in Figure 12-10. Each element and its role are described next.

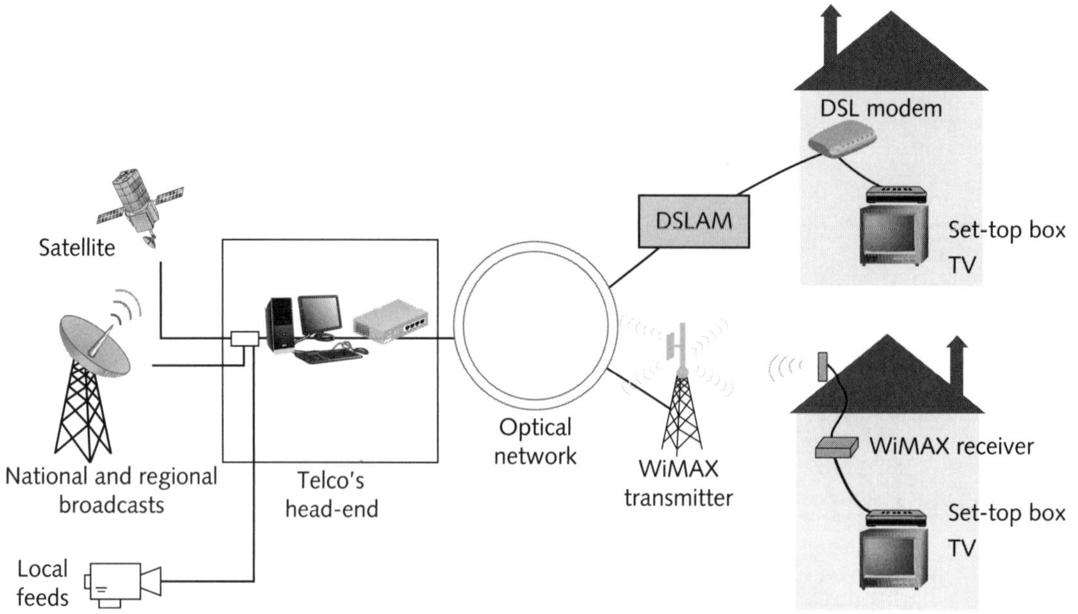

Figure 12-10 A telecommunications carrier's IPTV network

To begin, a telco accepts video content at a head-end. The content may include signals captured from satellite video feeds, national or regional broadcasts, or local content, such as live feeds of city council meetings. Typically, this content arrives in analog format, and at the head-end, an encoder converts it to digital format.

At the telco's CO (central office), one or more servers manage customer subscription information, encrypt video to comply with digital rights regulations, publish channel listing information, and associate each video input with its own channel, among other things. Also at the CO, each video channel is assigned to a multicast group.

Multicasting makes sense for delivering IPTV. First, it's a simple way of managing content delivery. For example, 2000 of the telco's customers might choose to watch a Monday night football game. Rather than supply the video via 2000 separate unicast transmissions, the carrier can issue one multicast transmission to the entire group of 2000 subscribers. The second advantage to using multicasting has to do with local loop capacity. As you know, fiber to the home is still rare in the United States, and most local loops rely on copper cabling. Therefore, throughput is limited. In an environment where customers may choose from hundreds of channels, supplying all the choices to every customer at all times would overwhelm the local loop's capacity. Even supplying more than a few channels would be too much. Instead, the telco transmits only the content a subscriber has chosen. When an IPTV user changes the channel, therefore, she is merely opting out of one IP multicast group and opting into another.

Recall from Chapter 4 that multicasting is managed by IGMP (Internet Group Management Protocol). Therefore, IGMP underlies all IPTV implementations at the Network layer of the OSI model. However, IGMP can only identify group members. To ensure efficient content delivery to a multicast group, routers communicate using a multicast routing protocol. Several multicast routing protocols exist. Which protocol the network uses is less important than the fact that all Layer 3 devices communicate using the same multicast routing protocol.

A compressed, digital video signal travels over the telco's network just as a data signal would. For example, if a subscriber obtains DSL service from the carrier, the signal would go from the telco's router to a DSLAM (DSL access multiplexer), either at the CO or at a remote switching facility, and then to the subscriber's DSL modem. If the subscriber obtains service wirelessly—for example, via WiMAX—the signal would be issued from the carrier's router to an antenna on a tower, and then to an antenna and WiMAX connectivity device at the subscriber's home. After passing through the DSL modem or home WiMAX device, the video signal is decoded and issued to a television by a **set-top box**. Besides decoding the video signal, set-top boxes communicate with content servers to manage video delivery. For example, the set-top box delivers TV program schedules from the content server to subscribers and sends a subscriber's channel request to the content server. In cases where IPTV providers allow pay-per-view or video-on-demand programming, set-top boxes manage requesting and delivering those services. Set-top boxes may also allow a user to browse the Internet from his TV. Figure 12-11 shows one type of set-top box.

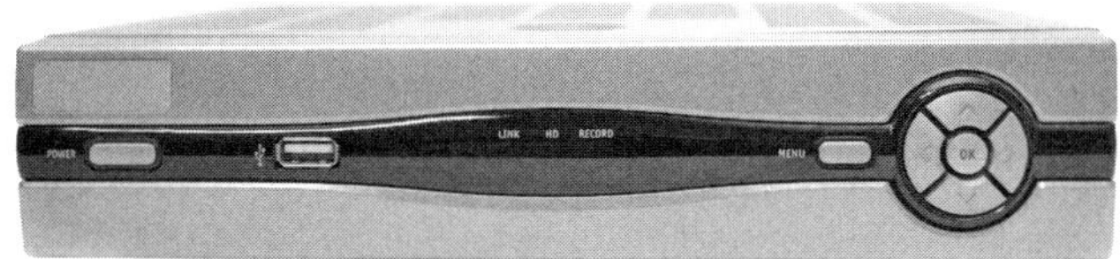

Figure 12-11 IPTV set-top box

A significant advantage of delivering video services over a telecommunications carrier's or cable company's network is that those firms control the connection end to end. This means they can better monitor and adjust its QoS (quality of service). Later in this chapter, you'll learn some techniques for controlling the QoS of voice and video transmissions. The next section describes a third popular video-over-IP service, videoconferencing.

Videoconferencing

So far in this chapter, you have learned about unidirectional video-over-IP services—that is, video delivered to a user who only watches the content, but does not respond with her own. In most examples of videoconferencing, connections are full-duplex, and participants may send and receive audiovisual signals. This allows two or more people in different locations to see and hear each other in real time. As you can imagine, the cost savings and convenience of such a service make it especially attractive to organizations with offices, clients, or consultants scattered across the nation or the globe. Besides replacing face-to-face business meetings and allowing collaboration, uses for videoconferencing include the following:

- *Telemedicine, or the provision of medical services from a distance*—For example, a physician can view and listen to a patient in another location. Often, the patient is accompanied by a nurse or physician's assistant, who might administer tests and supply information about the patient's condition. For patients who live far from major medical facilities, this saves the cost, time, and potential health risks of having to travel long distances. NASA is developing telemedicine capabilities for diagnosing patients in space.

- *Tele-education, or the exchange of information between one or more participants for the purposes of training and education*—A significant benefit of tele-education is the capability for one or a few experts to share their knowledge with many students.
- *Judicial proceedings, in which judges, lawyers, and defendants can conduct arraignments, hearings, or even trials while in different locations*—This not only saves costs, but may minimize potential security risks of transporting prisoners.
- *Surveillance, or remotely monitoring events happening at one or more distant locations*—Unlike previously mentioned videoconferencing applications, surveillance is typically unidirectional. In other words, security personnel watch (and perhaps also listen) to live video feeds from multiple locations around a building or campus, but do not send audiovisual signals to those locations.

Hardware and software requirements for videoconferences include, at minimum, a means for each participant to generate, send, and receive audiovisual signals. This may be accomplished by workstations that have sufficient processing resources, plus cameras, microphones, and videoconferencing software to capture, encode, and transmit audiovisual signals. Instead of a workstation, viewers may use a video terminal or a **video phone**, a type of phone that includes a screen, such as the one shown in Figure 12-12. These devices can decode compressed video and interpret transport and signaling protocols necessary for conducting videoconference sessions.

Figure 12-12 Videophone

When more than two people participate in a videoconference, for example, in a point-to-multipoint or multipoint-to-multipoint scenario, a video bridge is required. A **video bridge** manages multiple audiovisual sessions so that participants can see and hear each other. Video bridges may exist as a piece of hardware or as software, in the form of a conference server. For an organization that only occasionally uses videoconferencing, Internet-accessible video bridging services can be leased for a predetermined period. Organizations such as universities that frequently rely on videoconferencing might maintain their own conference servers or supply each auditorium, for example, with its own video bridge.

To establish and manage videoconferencing sessions, video bridges depend on signaling protocols, which are described in the following section.

Signaling Protocols

1.6 In VoIP and video-over-IP transmission, **signaling** is the exchange of information between the components of a network or system for the purposes of establishing, monitoring, or releasing connections as well as controlling system operations. Simply put, signaling protocols set up and manage sessions between clients. Some functions performed by signaling protocols include the following:

- Requesting a call or videoconference setup
- Locating clients on the network and determining the best routes for calls or video transmissions to follow
- Acknowledging a request for a call or videoconference setup and setting up the connection
- Managing ringing, dial tone, call waiting, and in some cases, caller ID and other telephony features
- Detecting and reestablishing dropped calls or video transmissions
- Properly terminating a call or videoconference

In the early days of VoIP, vendors developed their own, proprietary signaling protocols, which meant that if you wanted to use the Internet to call your neighbor, you and your neighbor had to use hardware or software from the same manufacturer. Now, however, most VoIP and video-over-IP clients and gateways use standardized signaling protocols. The following sections describe the most common of these.

On the circuit-switched portions of the PSTN, a set of standards established by the ITU known as **SS7 (Signaling System 7)** typically handles call signaling. You should be familiar with this term, as it might appear in discussions of interconnecting the PSTN with networks running VoIP.

H.323

H.323 is an ITU standard that describes an architecture and a group of protocols for establishing and managing multimedia sessions on a packet-switched network. H.323 protocols may support voice or video-over-IP services. Before learning about H.323 protocols, it's helpful to understand the set of terms unique to H.323 that ITU has designated. Elements of VoIP and video-over-IP networks have special names in H.323 parlance. Following are five key elements identified by H.323:

- ***H.323 terminal***—Any node that provides audio, visual, or data information to another node. An IP phone, video phone, or a server issuing streaming video could be considered an H.323 terminal.
- ***H.323 gateway***—A device that provides translation between network devices running H.323 signaling protocols and devices running other types of signaling protocols (for example, SS7 on the PSTN).
- ***H.323 gatekeeper***—The nerve center for networks that adhere to H.323. Gatekeepers authorize and authenticate terminals and gateways, manage bandwidth, and oversee call routing, accounting, and billing. Gatekeepers are optional on H.323 networks.
- ***MCU (multipoint control unit)***—A computer that provides support for multiple H.323 terminals (for example, several workstations participating in a videoconference) and manages communication between them. In videoconferencing, a video bridge serves as an MCU.
- ***H.323 zone***—A collection of H.323 terminals, H.323 gateways, and MCUs that are managed by a single H.323 gatekeeper. Figure 12-13 illustrates an H.323 zone comprising four terminals, one gateway, and one MCU.

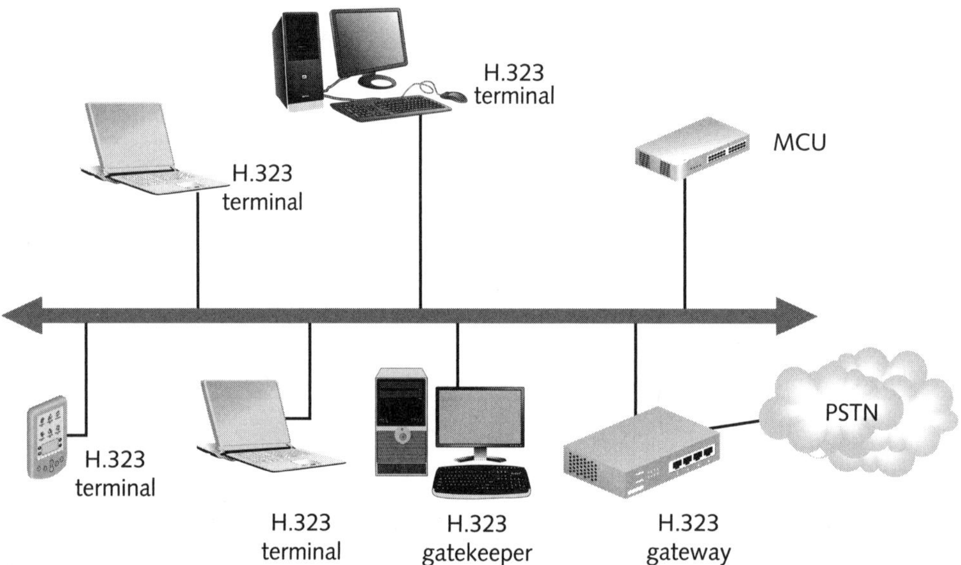

Figure 12-13 An H.323 zone

Now that you understand the elements that belong to an H.323 network, you are ready to learn about the H.225 and H.245 signaling protocols, which are specified in the H.323 standard. Both protocols operate at the Session layer of the OSI model. However, each performs a different function. **H.225** is the H.323 protocol that handles call or videoconference signaling.

For instance, when an IP telephone user wants to make a call, the IP telephone requests a call setup (from the H.323 gateway) via H.225. The same IP telephone would use the H.225 protocol to announce its presence on the network, to request the allocation of additional bandwidth, and to indicate when it wants to terminate a call.

Another H.323 Session layer protocol, **H.245**, ensures that the type of information—whether voice or video—issued to an H.323 terminal is formatted in a way that the H.323 terminal can interpret. To perform this task, H.245 first sets up logical channels between the sending and receiving nodes. On a VoIP or video-over-IP network, these logical channels are identified as port numbers at each IP address. One logical channel is assigned to each transmission direction. Thus, for a call between two IP telephones, H.245 would use two separate control channels. Note that these channels are distinct from the channels used for H.225 call signaling. They are also different from channels used to exchange the actual voice or video signals (for example, the words you speak during a conversation or the pictures transmitted in a videoconference).

In addition to the H.225 and H.245 signaling protocols, the H.323 standard also specifies interoperability with certain protocols at the Presentation layer, such as those responsible for coding and decoding signals, and at the Transport layer. Later in this chapter, you'll learn about the Transport layer protocols used with voice and video services.

ITU codified H.323 as an open protocol for multiservice signaling in 1996. Early versions of the H.323 protocol suffered from slow call setup, due to the volume of messages exchanged between nodes. Since that time, ITU has revised and improved H.323 standards several times, and H.323 remains a popular signaling protocol on large voice and video networks. After H.323 was released, however, another protocol for VoIP call signaling, SIP, emerged and attracted the attention of network administrators.

SIP (Session Initiation Protocol)

1.6 **SIP (Session Initiation Protocol)** is a protocol that performs functions similar to those performed by H.323. SIP is an Application layer signaling and control protocol for multiservice, packet-based networks. The protocol's developers modeled it on HTTP. For example, the text-based messages that clients exchange to initiate a VoIP call are formatted like an HTTP request and rely on URL-style addresses. Developers also aimed to reuse as many existing TCP/IP protocols as possible for managing sessions and providing enhanced services. Furthermore, they wanted SIP to be modular and specific. SIP's capabilities are limited to the following:

- Determining the location of an **endpoint**, which in SIP terminology refers to any client, server, or gateway communicating on a network; this means SIP translates the endpoint's name into its current network address
- Determining the availability of an endpoint; if SIP discovers that a client is not available, it returns a message indicating whether the client was already connected to a call or simply didn't respond
- Establishing a session between two endpoints and managing calls by adding (inviting), dropping, or transferring participants
- Negotiating features of a call or videoconference when it's established; for example, agreeing on the type of encoding both endpoints will employ
- Changing features of a call or videoconference while it's connected

1.6 SIP's functions are more limited than those performed by the protocols in the H.323 group. For example, SIP does not supply some enhanced features, such as caller ID, that H.323 does. Instead, it depends on other protocols and services to supply them.

As with H.323, a SIP network uses terms and follows a specific architecture mapped out in the standard. Components of a SIP network include the following:

- *User agent*—This is any node that initiates or responds to SIP requests.
- *User agent client*—These are end-user devices, which may include workstations, tablet computers, smartphones, or IP telephones. A user agent client initiates a SIP connection.
- *User agent server*—This type of server responds to user agent clients' requests for session initiation and termination. Practically speaking, a device such as an IP telephone can act as a user agent client and server, thus allowing it to directly contact and establish sessions with other clients in a peer-to-peer fashion. As you have learned, however, peer-to-peer arrangements are undesirable because they become difficult to manage when more than a few users participate. User agent clients and user agent servers are considered user agents.
- *Registrar server*—This type of server maintains a database containing information about the locations (network addresses) of each user agent in its domain. When a user agent joins a SIP network, it transmits its location information to the SIP registrar server.
- *Proxy server*—This type of server accepts requests for location information from user agents, then queries the nearest registrar server on behalf of those user agents. If the recipient user agent is in the SIP proxy server's domain, then that server will also act as a go-between for calls established and terminated between the requesting user agent and the recipient user agent. If the recipient user agent is not in the SIP proxy server's domain, the proxy server will pass on session information to a SIP redirect server. Proxy servers are optional on a SIP network.
- *Redirect server*—This type of server accepts and responds to requests from user agents and SIP proxy servers for location information on recipients that belong to external domains. A redirect server does not get involved in establishing or maintaining sessions. Redirect servers are optional on SIP networks.

Figure 12-14 shows how the elements of a SIP system may be arranged on a network. In this example, user agents connect to proxy servers, which accept and forward addressing requests and also make use of redirect servers to learn about user agents on other domains. For purposes of illustration, the registrar server, proxy server, and redirect server are shown as separate computers in Figure 12-14. However, on a SIP network all might be installed on a single computer.

Some VoIP vendors prefer SIP because of its simplicity, which makes SIP easier to maintain than H.323. And because it requires fewer instructions to control a call, SIP consumes fewer processing resources than H.323. In some cases, SIP is more flexible than H.323. For example, it is designed to work with many types of Transport layer protocols, not just one. One popular system based on SIP is Asterisk, an open source IP-PBX software package. Companies that provide telephone equipment, such as 3Com, Avaya, Cisco, and Nortel, also supply SIP software with their hardware.

Net+
1.6

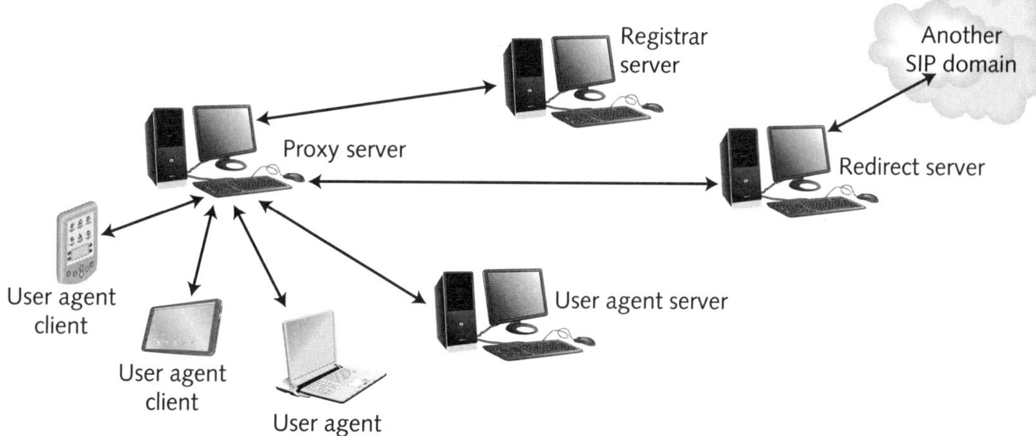

Figure 12-14 A SIP network

SIP and H.323 regulate call signaling and control for VoIP or video-over-IP clients and servers. However, they do not account for communication between media gateways. This type of communication is governed by one of two protocols, MGCP or MEGACO, which are discussed in the following sections.

MGCP (Media Gateway Control Protocol) and MEGACO (H.248)

You have learned about gateways in the context of WANs and VPNs. Gateways are also integral to converged networks. A **media gateway** accepts PSTN lines, converts the analog signals into VoIP format, and translates between SS7, the PSTN signaling protocol suite, and VoIP signaling protocols, such as H.323 or SIP.

You have also learned that information (or "payload," such as the speech carried by a VoIP network) uses different channels from and may take different logical or physical paths than control signals. In fact, to expedite information handling, the use of separate physical paths is often preferable. The reason for this is that if media gateways are freed from having to process control signals, they can dedicate their resources (for example, ports and processors) to encoding, decoding, and translating data. As a result, they process information faster. And as you have learned, faster data processing on a converged network is particularly important, given quality and reliability concerns.

However, gateways still need to exchange and translate signaling and control information with each other so that voice and video packets are properly routed through the network. To do so, gateways rely on an intermediate device known as an **MGC (media gateway controller)**. As its name implies, an MGC is a computer that manages multiple media gateways. This means that it facilitates the exchange of call signaling information between these gateways. It also manages and disseminates information about the paths that voice or video signals take between gateways. Because it is software that performs call switching functions, an MGC is sometimes called a **Softswitch**.

For example, suppose a network has multiple media gateways, all of which accept thousands of connections from both the PSTN and from private TCP/IP WAN and LAN links. When a media gateway receives a call, rather than attempting to determine how to handle the call, the gateway simply contacts the media gateway controller with a message that essentially says, "I received a signal. You figure out what to do with it next." The media gateway controller then determines which of the network's media gateways should translate the information carried by the signal. It also figures out which physical media the call should be routed over, according to what signaling protocols the call must be managed, and to what devices the call should be directed. After the media gateway controller has processed this information, it instructs the appropriate media gateways how to handle the call. The media gateways simply follow orders from the media gateway controller.

MGCs are especially advantageous on large VoIP networks—for example, at a telecommunications carrier's CO. In such an environment, they make a group of media gateways appear to the outside world as one large gateway. This centralizes call control functions, which can simplify network management. Figure 12-15 illustrates this model. (Note that in this figure, as on most large networks, the media gateways supply access services.)

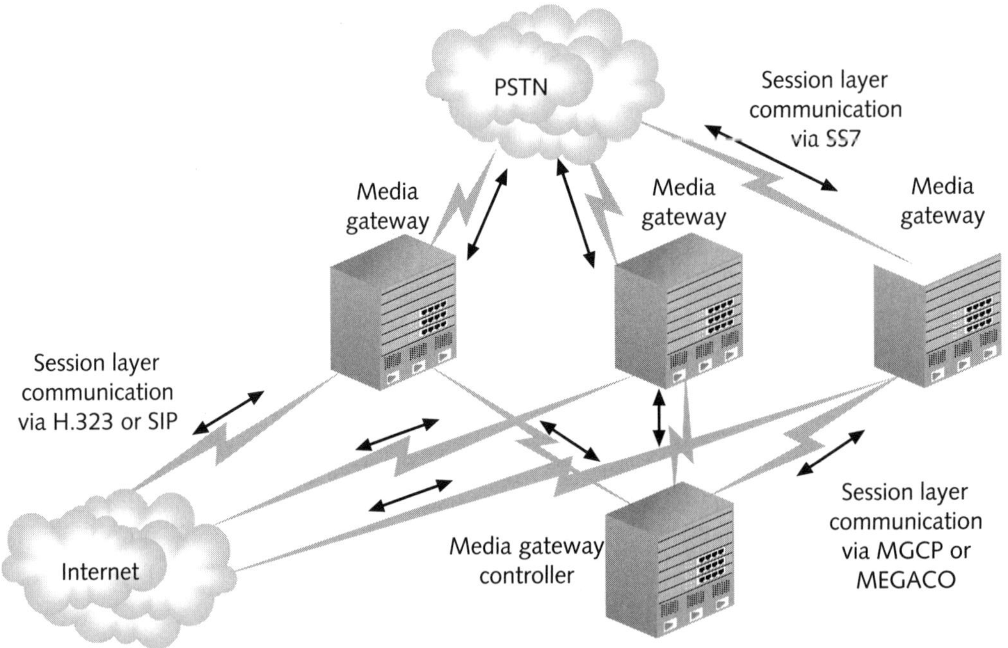

Figure 12-15 Use of an MGC (media gateway controller)

MGCs communicate with media gateways according to one of several protocols. The older protocol is **MGCP (Media Gateway Control Protocol)**. MGCP is commonly used on multiservice networks that support a number of media gateways. It can operate in conjunction with H.323 or SIP call signaling and control protocols.

A newer gateway control protocol is **MEGACO**. MEGACO performs the same functions as MGCP, but using different commands and processes. Like MGCP, MEGACO can operate with H.323 or SIP. Many network engineers consider MEGACO superior to MGCP because it supports a broader range of network technologies, including ATM. MEGACO was developed by cooperative efforts of the ITU and IETF, and the ITU has codified the MEGACO protocol in its **H.248** standard.

Bear in mind that this chapter describes only some of the signaling protocols used on converged networks. In fact, some softphones, VoIP servers, and videoconferencing software packages (for example, Skype) use proprietary protocols, which means that these devices or applications will only work with other devices or applications that use the same proprietary protocols.

Now that you are familiar with the most popular session control protocols used on converged networks, you are ready to learn about the transport protocols that work in tandem with those session control protocols.

Transport Protocols

Net+ The protocols you just learned about only communicate information about a voice or video
1.6 *session*. At the Transport layer, a different set of protocols is used to actually deliver the
4.6 voice or video payload—for example, the bits of encoded voice that together make up words spoken into an IP telephone.

Recall that on a TCP/IP network, the UDP and TCP protocols operate at the Transport layer of the OSI model. TCP is connection oriented and, therefore, provides some measure of delivery guarantees. UDP, on the other hand, is connectionless, and does not pay attention to the order in which packets arrive or how quickly they arrive. Despite this lack of accountability, UDP is preferred over TCP for real-time applications such as telephone conversations and videoconferences because it requires less overhead and, as a result, can transport packets more quickly. In transporting voice and video signals, TCP's slower delivery of packets is intolerable. However UDP's occasional loss of packets is tolerable—that is, as long as additional protocols are used in conjunction with UDP to make up for its faults.

RTP (Real-time Transport Protocol)

One protocol that helps voice and video networks overcome UDP's shortcomings is the **RTP (Real-time Transport Protocol)**. RTP operates at the Application layer of the OSI model (despite its name) and relies on UDP at the Transport layer. It applies sequence numbers to indicate the order in which packets should be assembled at their destination. Sequence numbers also help to indicate whether packets were lost during transmission. In addition, RTP assigns each packet a time stamp that corresponds to when the data in the packet were sampled from the voice or video stream. This time stamp helps the receiving node to compensate for network delay and to synchronize the signals it receives.

RTP alone does not, however, provide any mechanisms to detect whether or not it's successful. For that, it relies on a companion protocol, RTCP.

RTCP (Real-time Transport Control Protocol)

4.6 **RTCP (Real-time Transport Control Protocol,** or **RTP Control Protocol)** provides feedback on the quality of a call or videoconference to its participants. RTCP packets are transmitted periodically to all session endpoints. RTCP allows for several types of messages. For example, each sender issues information about its transmissions' NTP (Network Time Protocol) time stamps, RTP time stamps, number of packets, and number of bytes. Recipients of RTP data use RTCP to issue information about the number and percentage of packets lost and delay suffered between the sender and receiver. RTCP also maintains identifying information for RTP sources.

The value of RTCP lies in what clients and their applications do with the information that RTCP supplies. For example, if a call participant's software uses RTCP to report that an excessive number of packets are being delayed during transmission, the sender's software can adjust the rate at which it issues RTP packets.

RTCP is not mandatory on networks that use RTP. In fact, on large networks running high-bandwidth services, such as IPTV, RTCP might not be able to supply useful feedback in a timely manner. Some network administrators prefer not to use it.

It's important to realize that although RTP and RTCP can provide information about packet order, loss, and delay, they cannot do anything to correct transmission flaws. Attempts to correct these flaws, and thus improve the quality of a voice or video signal, are handled by QoS protocols, which are discussed next.

QoS (Quality of Service) Assurance

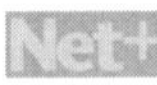

4.6 Despite all the advantages to using VoIP and video over IP, it is more difficult to transmit these types of signals over a packet-switched network than it is to transmit data signals. First, more so than data transmissions, voice and video can easily be distorted by a connection's inconsistent QoS. When you talk with your friend, you need to hear his syllables in the order in which he uttered them, and preferably, without delay. When you watch a movie over the Web, you want to see the scenes sequentially and without interruption. In general, to prevent delays, disorder, and distortion, a voice or video connection requires more dedicated bandwidth than a data connection. In addition, it requires the use of techniques that ensure high QoS.

QoS is a measure of how well a network service matches its expected performance. From the point of view of a person using VoIP or video over IP, high QoS translates into an uninterrupted, accurate, and faithful reproduction of audio or visual input. Low, or poor, QoS is often cited as a key disadvantage to using VoIP or video over IP. But although early attempts at converged services sounded and looked dreadful, thanks to technology improvements, these services now achieve quality comparable to the PSTN (in the case of VoIP) and cable television (in the case of video over IP).

Network engineers have developed several techniques to overcome the QoS challenges inherent in delivering voice and video over IP. The following sections describe three of these techniques, all of which are standardized by IETF.

RSVP (Resource Reservation Protocol)

4.6 **RSVP (Resource Reservation Protocol)**, specified in RFC 2205, is a Transport layer protocol that attempts to reserve a specific amount of network resources for a transmission before the transmission occurs. In other words, assuming it is successful, RSVP will create a path between the sender and receiver that provides sufficient bandwidth for the signal to arrive without suffering delay. You can think of RSVP as a technique that addresses the QoS problem by emulating a circuit-switched connection.

To establish the path, the sending node issues a PATH statement via RSVP to the receiving node. This PATH message indicates the amount of bandwidth the sending node requires for its transmission, as well as the level of service it expects. RSVP allows for two service types: guaranteed service and controlled-load service. Guaranteed service assures that the transmission will not suffer packet losses and that it will experience minimal delay. Controlled-load service provides the type of QoS a transmission would experience if the network carried little traffic.

Each router that the PATH message traverses marks the transmission's path by noting which router the PATH message came from. This process continues until the PATH message reaches its destination. But the reservation is not yet complete. After the destination node receives the PATH message, it responds with a Reservation Request (RESV) message. The RESV message follows the same path taken by the PATH message, but in reverse. It reiterates information about bandwidth requirements that the sending node transmitted in its PATH message. It also includes information about the type of service the sending node requested. Upon receiving the RESV message, each router between the destination node and the sender allocates the requested bandwidth to the message's path. This assumes that each router is capable of interpreting RSVP messages and also has sufficient bandwidth to allocate to the transmission. If routers do not have sufficient bandwidth to allocate, they reject the reservation request.

After each router in the established path has agreed to allocate the specified amount of bandwidth to the transmission, the sending node transmits its data. It's important to note that RSVP messaging is separate from the data transmission. In other words, RSVP does not modify the packets that carry voice or video signals. Another characteristic about RSVP is that it can only specify and manage unidirectional transmission. Therefore, for two users to participate in a VoIP call or a videoconference, the resource reservation process must take place in both directions.

Because it emulates a circuit-switched path, RSVP provides excellent QoS. However, one drawback to RSVP is its high overhead. It requires a series of message exchanges before data transmission can occur. Thus, RSVP consumes more network resources than some other QoS techniques. Although RSVP might be acceptable on small networks, it is less popular on large, heavily trafficked networks. Instead, these networks use more streamlined QoS techniques, such as DiffServ.

DiffServ (Differentiated Service)

DiffServ (Differentiated Service) is a simple technique that addresses QoS issues by prioritizing traffic. It differs significantly from RSVP in that it modifies the actual IP datagrams that contain payload data. Also, it takes into account all types of network traffic, not just the time-sensitive services such as voice and video. That way, it can assign voice streams a high priority and at the same time assign unessential data streams (for example, an employee surfing the

4.6 Internet on his lunch hour) a low priority. This technique offers more protection for the time-sensitive voice and video services.

To prioritize traffic, DiffServ places information in the DiffServ field in an IPv4 datagram. (For a review of the fields in an IP datagram, refer to Chapter 4.) In IPv6 datagrams, DiffServ uses a similar field known as the Traffic Class field. This information indicates to the network routers how the data stream should be forwarded. DiffServ defines two types of forwarding: **EF (Expedited Forwarding)** or **AF (Assured Forwarding)**. In EF, a data stream is assigned a minimum departure rate from a given node. This technique circumvents delays that slow normal data from reaching its destination on time and in sequence. In AF, different levels of router resources can be assigned to data streams. AF prioritizes data handling, but provides no guarantee that on a busy network packets will arrive on time and in sequence. This description of DiffServ's prioritization mechanisms is oversimplified, but a deeper discussion is beyond the scope of this book.

Because of its simplicity and relatively low overhead, DiffServ is better suited to large, heavily trafficked networks than RSVP.

MPLS (Multiprotocol Label Switching)

Another QoS technique that modifies data streams at the Network layer is MPLS (multiprotocol label switching). As described in Chapter 5, to indicate where data should be forwarded, MPLS replaces the IP datagram header with a label at the first router a data stream encounters. The MPLS label contains information about where the router should forward the packet next. Each router in the data stream's path revises the label to indicate the data's next hop. In this manner, routers on a network can take into consideration network congestion, QoS indicators assigned to the packets, plus other criteria.

MPLS forwarding is also fast. This is because, in MPLS, a router knows precisely where to forward a packet. On a typical packet-switched network, routers compare the destination IP address to their routing tables and forward data to the node with the closest matching address. With MPLS, data streams are more likely to arrive without delay. On a network supplying clients with voice and video services, fast transmission is desirable.

A network's connectivity devices and clients must support the same set of protocols to achieve their QoS benefits. However, networks can—and often do—combine multiple QoS techniques.

Chapter Summary

- The use of a network (either public or private) to carry voice signals using the TCP/IP protocol is commonly known as VoIP (Voice over IP). VoIP services can operate over any type of transmission medium and access method that support TCP/IP.
- When VoIP relies on the Internet, it is often called Internet telephony. But not all VoIP calls are carried over the Internet. In fact, VoIP over private lines is an effective and economical method of completing calls between two locations within an organization.
- An organization might use VoIP to save money on telephone calls, centralize management of voice and data services, or take advantage of customizable call features.

- Many types of clients and network designs are available with VoIP networks. Clients can be traditional analog telephones, IP telephones, or softphones (a computer running telephony software and connected to a microphone and headphones). In each case, analog voice signals are first converted to digital signals by a voice codec (coder/decoder).
- Analog VoIP clients may connect to IP networks in one of four ways: using an internal or external ATA (analog telephone adapter); connecting directly to a router or to a voice-data gateway that digitizes call information; connecting directly to an IP-PBX capable of handling both analog and digital voice connections; or connecting to an analog PBX, which then connects to a voice-data gateway.
- Digital VoIP clients typically connect to a digital PBX or other connectivity device with VoIP capabilities.
- A special type of digital PBX is one that is hosted by a service provider. Organizations that choose a hosted PBX don't need to install or maintain hardware or software for call completion and management. Hosted PBXs are also known as virtual PBXs.
- Rather than analog telephones, many VoIP installations use IP telephones, which transmit and receive only digital signals. To communicate on the network, each IP telephone must have a unique IP address. The IP telephone connects to an RJ-45 wall jack, like a computer workstation.
- One significant benefit to using IP telephones is their mobility. Because IP telephones are addressable over a network, they can be moved from one office to another office, be connected to a wall jack, and be ready to accept or make calls.
- Rather than using traditional telephones or IP telephones, a third option is to use a computer programmed to act like an IP telephone, otherwise known as a softphone. Softphones and IP telephones provide the same calling functions; they simply connect to the network and deliver services differently. A softphone's versatile connectivity makes it an optimal VoIP solution for traveling employees and telecommuters.

- Streaming video refers to video signals that are compressed and delivered in a continuous stream. It may be made available as files stored on a streaming server for video-on-demand or as real-time feeds in live streaming. Streaming video may be delivered in a point-to-point or point-to-multipoint fashion, though both types typically use unicast transmission.
- In IPTV (IP television), television signals from broadcast or cable networks travel over packet-switched connections. Telecommunications carriers and cable companies supply IPTV over their existing networks. They accept video content from satellite feeds, national or regional broadcasters, and local sources at a head-end. IPTV channels are delivered in multicast fashion to consumers, where they are decoded and issued to televisions by set-top boxes.
- Videoconferencing allows multiple participants to communicate and collaborate at once through audiovisual means. To view a videoconference, each participant must have at least a video terminal or video phone that can decode compressed video and interpret signaling protocols. To send and receive audiovisual signals, participants must also have a device equipped with a camera, microphone, and video-encoding capabilities.

- Videoconferences that are point to multipoint or multipoint to multipoint rely on video bridges to manage communication among participants. Video bridges may be hardware devices dedicated to this task or software running on conference servers.
- In VoIP and video-over-IP transmission, signaling is the exchange of information between the components of a network or system for the purposes of establishing, monitoring, or releasing connections as well as controlling system operations.
- Voice and video-over-IP services depend on signaling protocols to request a call or videoconference setup, locate clients on the network and determine the best routes for calls to follow, and acknowledge a request for a call or videoconference setup. Voice and video-over-IP services also depend on signaling protocols to set up the connection; manage ringing, dial tone, and other telephony features; detect and reestablish dropped calls or video transmissions; and properly terminate a call or videoconference.
- H.323 is an ITU standard that describes an architecture and a group of protocols for establishing and managing multimedia sessions on a packet-switched network.
- H.225 is the protocol specified by the H.323 standard that handles call or videoconference signaling. For instance, when an IP telephone user wants to make a call, the IP telephone requests a call setup (from the H.323 gateway) via H.225.
- Another H.323 Session layer protocol, H.245, ensures that the type of information—whether voice or video—issued to an H.323 terminal is formatted in a way that the H.323 terminal can interpret.
- SIP (Session Initiation Protocol) is an Application layer signaling and control protocol for multiservice, packet-based networks. SIP's developers modeled it on the HTTP protocol and aimed to reuse as many existing TCP/IP protocols as possible for managing sessions and providing enhanced services.
- SIP does not attempt to perform and control as many functions as the H.323 protocols. Its capabilities are limited to determining the location of an endpoint; determining the availability of an endpoint; establishing a session between two endpoints; managing calls by adding (inviting), dropping, or transferring participants; negotiating features of a call or videoconference when it's established; and changing features of a call or videoconference while it's connected.
- Some VoIP vendors prefer SIP because of its simplicity, which makes SIP easier to maintain than H.323. And because it requires fewer instructions to control a call, SIP consumes fewer processing resources than H.323.
- Media gateways rely on an intermediate device known as an MGC (media gateway controller) to exchange and translate signaling and control information with each other. An MGC facilitates the exchange of call signaling information between these gateways and manages and disseminates information about the paths that voice or video signals take between gateways.
- MGCs communicate with media gateways according to one of several protocols. The older protocol is MGCP (Media Gateway Control Protocol). MEGACO performs the same functions as MGCP, but uses different commands and processes. Many network engineers consider MEGACO superior to MGCP because it supports a broader range of network technologies, including ATM. The ITU has codified the MEGACO protocol in its H.248 standard.

- RTP (Real-time Transport Protocol) operates at the Application layer of the OSI model and relies on UDP at the Transport layer. It applies sequence numbers to indicate the order in which packets should be assembled at their destination and assigns each packet a time stamp that corresponds to when the data in the packet were sampled from the voice or video stream. This time stamp helps the receiving node to compensate for network delay and to synchronize the signals it receives.
- RTCP (Real-time Transport Control Protocol) provides feedback on the quality of a call or videoconference, such as the extent of delay or packet loss in a transmission.
- Network engineers have developed several techniques to overcome the QoS challenges inherent in delivering voice and video over IP. One, RSVP (Resource Reservation Protocol), is a Transport layer protocol that attempts to reserve a specific amount of network resources for a transmission before the transmission occurs.
- DiffServ (Differentiated Service) is a simple technique that addresses QoS issues by prioritizing traffic. DiffServ places information in the DiffServ field in an IPv4 datagram. In IPv6 datagrams, DiffServ uses a similar field known as the Traffic Class field. This information indicates to the network routers how the data stream should be forwarded.
- Another QoS technique that modifies data streams at the Network layer is MPLS (multiprotocol label switching). To indicate where data should be forwarded, MPLS replaces the IP datagram header with a label at the first router a data stream encounters. The MPLS label contains information about where the router should forward the packet next. Each router in the data stream's path revises the label to indicate the data's next hop. In this manner, routers on a network can take into consideration network congestion, QoS indicators assigned to the packets, plus other criteria.

Key Terms

AF (Assured Forwarding) In the DiffServ QoS technique, a forwarding specification that allows routers to assign data streams one of several prioritization levels. AF is specified in the DiffServ field in an IPv4 datagram.

analog telephone adapter *See* ATA.

Assured Forwarding *See* AF.

ATA (analog telephone adapter) An internal or externally attached adapter that converts analog telephone signals into packet-switched voice signals and vice versa.

Differentiated Service *See* DiffServ.

DiffServ (Differentiated Service) A technique for ensuring QoS by prioritizing traffic. DiffServ places information in the DiffServ field in an IPv4 datagram. In IPv6 datagrams, DiffServ uses a similar field known as the Traffic Class field. This information indicates to the network routers how the data stream should be forwarded.

digital PBX *See* IP-PBX.

EF (Expedited Forwarding) In the DiffServ QoS technique, a forwarding specification that assigns each data stream a minimum departure rate from a given node. This technique circumvents delays that slow normal data from reaching its destination on time and in sequence. EF information is inserted in the DiffServ field of an IPv4 datagram.

endpoint In SIP terminology, any client, server, or gateway communicating on the network.

Expedited Forwarding *See* EF.

H.225 A Session layer call signaling protocol defined as part of ITU's H.323 multiservice network architecture. H.225 is responsible for call or videoconference setup between nodes on a VoIP or video-over-IP network, indicating node status, and requesting additional bandwidth and call termination.

H.245 A Session layer control protocol defined as part of ITU's H.323 multiservice network architecture. H.245 is responsible for controlling a session between two nodes. For example, it ensures that the two nodes are communicating in the same format.

H.248 *See* MEGACO.

H.323 An ITU standard that describes an architecture and a suite of protocols for establishing and managing multimedia services sessions on a packet-switched network.

H.323 gatekeeper The nerve center for networks that adhere to H.323. Gatekeepers authorize and authenticate terminals and gateways, manage bandwidth, and oversee call routing, accounting, and billing. Gatekeepers are optional on H.323 networks.

H.323 gateway On a network following the H.323 standard, a gateway that provides translation between network devices running H.323 signaling protocols and devices running other types of signaling protocols (for example, SS7 on the PSTN).

H.323 terminal On a network following the H.323 standard, any node that provides audio, visual, or data information to another node.

H.323 zone A collection of H.323 terminals, gateways, and MCUs that are managed by a single H.323 gatekeeper.

hosted PBX A digital PBX service provided over the Internet.

Internet telephony The provision of telephone service over the Internet.

IP-PBX A private switch that accepts and interprets both analog and digital voice signals (although some IP-PBXs do not accept analog lines). It can connect with both traditional PSTN lines and data networks. An IP-PBX transmits and receives IP-based voice signals to and from other network connectivity devices, such as a router or gateway.

IP phone *See* IP telephone.

IP telephone A telephone used for VoIP on a TCP/IP-based network. IP telephones are designed to transmit and receive only digital signals.

IP telephony *See* Voice over IP.

IP television *See* IPTV.

IPTV (IP television) A service in which television signals from broadcast or cable networks travel over packet-switched networks.

MCU (multipoint control unit) A computer that provides support for multiple H.323 terminals (for example, several workstations participating in a videoconference) and manages communication between them. An MCU is also known as a video bridge.

media gateway A gateway capable of accepting connections from multiple devices (for example, IP telephones, traditional telephones, IP fax machines, traditional fax machines, and so on) and translating analog signals into packetized, digital signals, and vice versa.

Media Gateway Control Protocol *See* MGCP.

media gateway controller *See* MGC.

MEGACO A protocol used between media gateway controllers and media gateways. MEGACO is poised to replace MGCP on modern converged networks, as it supports a broader range of network technologies, including ATM. Also known as H.248.

MGC (media gateway controller) A computer that manages multiple media gateways and facilitates the exchange of call control information between these gateways.

MGCP (Media Gateway Control Protocol) A protocol used for communication between media gateway controllers and media gateways. MGCP is currently the most popular media gateway control protocol used on converged networks.

multipoint control unit *See* MCU.

PBX (private branch exchange) A telephone switch used to connect and manage an organization's voice calls.

private branch exchange *See* PBX.

proxy server On a SIP network, a server that accepts requests for location information from user agents, then queries the nearest registrar server on behalf of those user agents. If the recipient user agent is in the SIP proxy server's domain, then that server will also act as a go-between for calls established and terminated between the requesting user agent and the recipient user agent.

Real-time Transport Control Protocol *See* RTCP.

Real-time Transport Protocol *See* RTP.

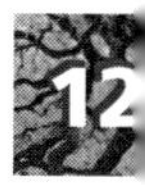

redirect server On a SIP network, a server that accepts and responds to requests from user agents and SIP proxy servers for location information on recipients that belong to external domains.

registrar server On a SIP network, a server that maintains a database containing information about the locations (network addresses) of each user agent in its domain. When a user agent joins a SIP network, it transmits its location information to the SIP registrar server.

Resource Reservation Protocol *See* RSVP.

RSVP (Resource Reservation Protocol) As specified in RFC 2205, a QoS technique that attempts to reserve a specific amount of network resources for a transmission before the transmission occurs.

RTCP (Real-time Transport Control Protocol) A companion protocol to RTP, RTCP provides feedback on the quality of a call or videoconference to its participants.

RTP (Real-time Transport Protocol) An Application layer protocol used with voice and video transmission. RTP operates on top of UDP and provides information about packet sequence to help receiving nodes detect delay and packet loss. It also assigns packets a time stamp that corresponds to when the data in the packet were sampled from the voice or video stream. This time stamp helps the receiving node synchronize incoming data.

RTP Control Protocol *See* RTCP.

Session Initiation Protocol *See* SIP.

set-top box In the context of IPTV, a device that decodes digital video signals and issues them to the television. Set-top boxes also communicate with content servers to manage video delivery.

signaling The exchange of information between the components of a network or system for the purposes of establishing, monitoring, or releasing connections as well as controlling system operations.

Signaling System 7 *See* SS7.

SIP (Session Initiation Protocol) An Application layer signaling and control protocol for multiservice, packet-based networks. With few exceptions, SIP performs much the same functions as the H.323 signaling protocols perform.

softphone A computer configured to act like an IP telephone. Softphones present the caller with a graphical representation of a telephone dial pad and can connect to a network via any wired or wireless method.

Softswitch *See* MGC.

SS7 (Signaling System 7) A set of standards established by the ITU for handling call signaling on the PSTN (Public Switched Telephone Network).

streaming video A service in which video signals are compressed and delivered over the Internet in a continuous stream so that a user can watch and listen even before all the data have been transmitted.

toll bypass A cost-savings benefit that results from organizations completing long-distance telephone calls over their packet-switched networks, thus bypassing tolls charged by common carriers on comparable PSTN calls.

unified messaging The centralized management of multiple types of network-based communications, such as voice, video, fax, and messaging services.

user agent In SIP terminology, a user agent client or user agent server.

user agent client In SIP terminology, end-user devices such as workstations, tablet computers, smartphones, or IP telephones. A user agent client initiates a SIP connection.

user agent server In SIP terminology, a server that responds to user agent clients' requests for session initiation and termination.

video bridge *See* MCU.

video-on-demand A service in which a video stored as an encoded file is delivered to a viewer upon his request.

video over IP Any type of video service, including IPTV, videoconferencing, and streaming video, that delivers video signals over packet-switched networks using the TCP/IP protocol suite.

video phone A type of phone that includes a screen and can decode compressed video and interpret transport and signaling protocols necessary for conducting videoconference sessions.

videoconferencing The real-time reception and transmission of images and audio among two or more locations.

virtual PBX *See* hosted PBX.

Voice over IP *See* VoIP.

VoIP (Voice over IP) The provision of telephone service over a packet-switched network running the TCP/IP protocol suite.

Webcast A streaming video, either on demand or live, that is delivered via the Web.

Review Questions

1. Which VoIP phone type allows a user to export call information to a billing or accounting program on the same workstation?
   a. digital PBX
   b. softphone
   c. traditional telephone
   d. IP telephone
2. Which video-over-IP service is useful in telemedicine applications?
   a. video-on-demand
   b. IPTV (IP television)
   c. videoconferencing
   d. streaming video
3. Which H.323 key element provides translation between network devices running H.323 signaling protocols and devices running other types of signaling protocols?
   a. H.323 gateway
   b. H.323 gatekeeper
   c. H.323 terminal
   d. H.323 zone

4. Which signaling protocol ensures that the type of information - whether voice or video - issued to an H.323 terminal is formatted in a way that the H.323 terminal can interpret?
   a. H.232
   b. H.325
   c. H.225
   d. H.245

5. Which transport protocol applies sequence numbers to indicate the order in which packets should be assembled at their destination?
   a. RTCP (Real-time Transport Control Protocol)
   b. RTP (Real-time transport protocol)
   c. RSVP (Resource Reservation Protocol)
   d. MGCP (Media gateway Control Protocol)
6. True or false? All VoIP calls are carried over the Internet.
7. True or false? Every video-over-IP transmission begins with digitizing the audio and visual signals using one of several popular video codecs, such as MPEG-4.
8. True or false? Because each IP telephone must have a unique IP address, they are stationary devices.
9. True or false? MEGACO (H.248) is a newer gateway control protocol that can also operate with H.323 or SIP.
10. True or false? Although RTP and RTCP can provide information about packet order, loss, and delay, they cannot do anything to correct transmission flaws.
11. The use of any network (either public or private) to carry voice signals using the TCP/IP protocol is ________________.
12. ________________ is an ITU standard that describes an architecture and a group of protocols for establishing and managing multimedia sessions on a packet-switched network.
13. ________________ is an Application layer signaling and control protocol for multiservice, packet-based networks.
14. An intermediate device, known as a(n) ________________, is used to exchange and translate gateway signaling and control information so that voice and video packets are properly routed through the network.
15. ________________, specified in RFC 2205, is a Transport layer protocol that attempts to reserve a specific amount of network resources for a transmission before the transmission occurs.

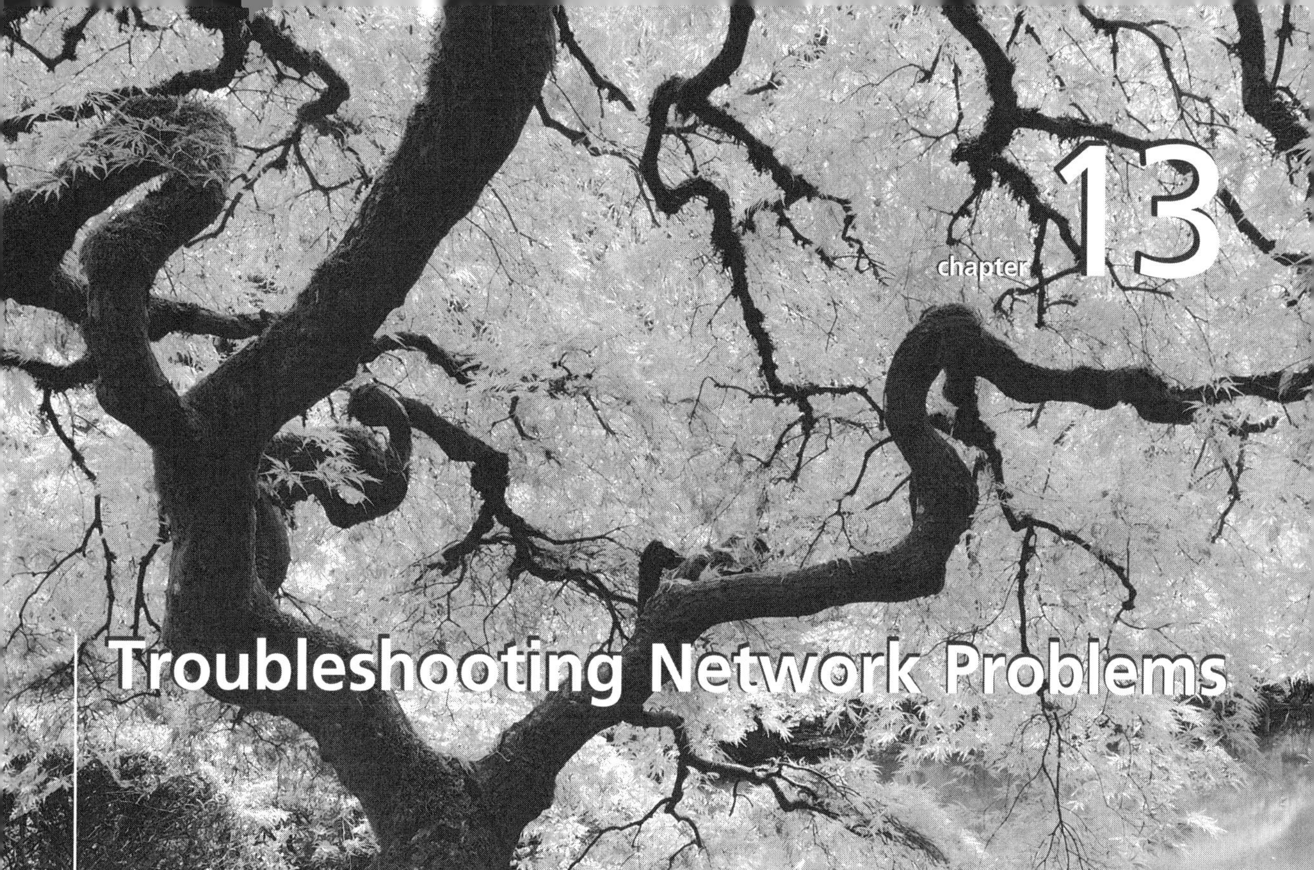

chapter 13

Troubleshooting Network Problems

After reading this chapter and completing the exercises, you will be able to:

- Describe the steps involved in an effective troubleshooting methodology
- Follow a systematic troubleshooting process to identify and resolve networking problems
- Document symptoms, solutions, and results when troubleshooting network problems
- Use a variety of software and hardware tools to diagnose problems

A customer called the managed security services firm I worked for and asked why one of his subnets was unable to reach the HTTP proxy service that was running on the inside interface of the Linux-based firewall we managed for him. I dutifully fired up tcpdump, an open source network diagnostic utility, and watched packets arriving from the subnet in question. The packets didn't look obviously malformed, and they were also correctly addressed for the proxy service on the firewall. Usually this sort of customer call resulted from a poorly configured automatic proxy configuration file, but not this time.

Puzzled, I watched as the customer removed the proxy address specification on a workstation in the affected network and was suddenly able to reach the world. This suggested that the problem was somehow related to the firewall. In each case, though, I would see the packets arrive on the inside interface of the firewall.

If the firewall were dropping the packets, I would have seen it in the logging. So I watched the socket state with netstat and saw that the proxy service never received the connection initiation segments (TCP SYN) from the problem subnet. Though I could see the packets arriving, the IP stack seemed to be ignoring them.

After examining the packet traces at various layers using tcpdump and Wireshark, I asked for another pair of eyes to help me. He noticed something I had overlooked. The 10th byte of the Ethernet frame destination address on the frame bound for the proxy service was wrong. This was the smoking gun. It meant that when packets passed through their switch to the Internet as a whole, the frame destination address was not mangled. But when packets passed through to the inside interface on the firewall, the switch was corrupting the frame destination address.

Our customer's network equipment vendor confirmed that the problem was the electronics on one of the switch ports. Sometimes another pair of eyes is all it takes.

Martin A. Brown
Renesys Corporation

By now, you know how networks *should* work. Like other complex systems, however, they don't always work as planned. Many things can go wrong on a network, just as many things can go wrong with your car, your house, or a project at work. In fact, a network professional probably spends more time fixing network problems than designing or upgrading a network. Some breakdowns (such as an overtaxed processor) come with plenty of warning, but others (such as a hard disk controller failure) can strike instantly.

The best defense against problems is prevention. Just as you maintain your car regularly, you should monitor the health of your network regularly. Of course, even the most well-monitored network will sometimes experience unexpected problems. For example, a utility company could dig a new hole for its cable and accidentally cut your dedicated link to the Internet. In such a situation, your network performance can go from perfect to disastrous in an instant. In this chapter, you will learn how to diagnose and solve network problems in a logical, step-by-step fashion, using a variety of tools.

Troubleshooting Methodology

Successful troubleshooters proceed logically and methodically. This section introduces a
1.8 basic troubleshooting methodology, leading you through a series of general problem-solving steps.

Following are steps for troubleshooting network problems as recommended by CompTIA. You should be familiar with these steps to demonstrate Network+ mastery:

- Identify the problem.
  - Gather information.
  - Identify symptoms.
  - Question users.
  - Determine if anything has changed.
- Establish a theory of probable cause.
  - Question the obvious.
- Test the theory to determine cause.
  - Once the theory is confirmed, determine the next steps to resolve the problem.
  - If the theory is not confirmed, reestablish a new theory or escalate.
- Establish a plan of action to resolve the problem and identify potential effects.
- Implement the solution or escalate as necessary.
- Verify full system functionality and, if applicable, implement preventive measures.
- Document findings, actions, and outcomes.

Bear in mind that experience in your network environment may prompt you to follow the steps in a different order or to skip certain steps entirely. For example, if you know that one segment of your network is poorly cabled, you might try replacing a section of cable in that area to solve a connectivity problem before attempting to verify the physical and logical integrity of the workstation's NIC. In general, however, it's best to follow each step in the order shown. Such a logical approach can save you from undertaking wasteful, time-consuming efforts such as unnecessary software or hardware replacements.

1.8

In addition to the organized method of troubleshooting described in this section, a good, general rule for troubleshooting can be stated as follows: Pay attention to the obvious! Although some questions might seem too simple to bother asking, don't discount them. You can often save much time by checking cable connections first. Many networking professionals can tell a story about spending half a day trying to figure out why a computer wouldn't connect to the network, only to discover that the network cable was not plugged into the wall jack or the device's NIC.

Identify the Problem and Its Symptoms

When troubleshooting a network problem, your first step is to identify the problem and its symptoms. Only after that can you can begin to deduce their cause. For example, suppose a user complains that he cannot save a file to a network drive. That's a symptom of a problem, which might be that his client cannot access the network drive. At that point, you can list several potential causes, including a faulty NIC, cable, switch, or router; an incorrect client software configuration; a server failure; or a user error. On the other hand, you can probably rule out a power failure, a printer failure, an Internet connectivity failure, an e-mail server failure, and a host of other problems.

Answering the following questions may help you identify symptoms of a network problem that aren't immediately obvious:

- Is access to the LAN or WAN affected?
- Is network performance affected?
- Are data or programs affected? Or are both affected?
- Are only certain network services (such as printing) affected?
- If programs are affected, does the problem include one local application, one networked application, or multiple networked applications?
- What specific error messages do users report?
- Is one user or are multiple users affected?
- Do the symptoms manifest themselves consistently?

One danger in troubleshooting technical problems is jumping to conclusions about the symptoms. For example, you might field 12 questions from users one morning about a problem printing to the network printer in the Facilities Department. You might have already determined that the problem is an addressing conflict with the printer and be in the last stages of resolving the problem. Minutes later, when a 13th caller says, "I'm having problems printing," you might immediately conclude that she is another Facilities staff member and that her inability to print results from the same printer addressing problem. In fact, this user may be in the Administration Department, and her inability to print could represent a symptom of a larger network problem. In another case, you might be dealing with multiple problems that present different, unrelated symptoms.

Take time to pay attention to the users, system and network behaviors, and any error messages. Treat each symptom as unique, but potentially related to others. In this way, you avoid the risk of ignoring problems or—even worse—causing more problems.

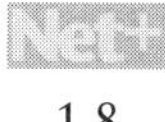
1.8

Take note of the error messages reported by users. If you aren't near the users, ask them to read the messages to you directly off their screens or, better yet, save an image of the screens that contain the error messages. For example, on computers running a Windows operating system, the Snipping Tool (accessed by clicking the Start button, pointing to All Programs, pointing to Accessories, and then clicking Snipping Tool) enables you to capture and save a screen image. On computers running Macintosh OS X, a variety of key combinations will capture a screen image, including Comand-Shift-3, which saves the image to the desktop. Several third-party screen capture utilities are available for all operating systems. After the user saves a screen image, keep it with your other troubleshooting notes for that problem for future reference.

Determine the Problem's Scope If a problem is not immediately obvious and requires further investigation, find out how many users or network segments are affected. For example, do the symptoms apply to:

- One user or workstation?
- A workgroup?
- A department?
- One location within an organization?
- An entire organization?

In addition, it is useful to narrow down the time frame during which the problem occurred. The following questions can help you determine the chronological scope of a problem:

- When did the problem begin?
- Has the network, server, or workstation ever worked properly?
- Did the symptoms appear in the last hour or day?
- Have the symptoms appeared intermittently for a long time?
- Do the symptoms appear only at certain times of the day, week, month, or year?

Similar to identifying symptoms, narrowing down the area affected by a problem can eliminate some causes and point to others. In particular, it can help distinguish workstation (or user) problems from network problems. If the problem affects only a department or floor of your organization, for example, you probably need to examine that network segment, its router interface, its cabling, or a server that provides services to those users. Or, you might trace a problem to a single user in that area—for example, an employee who watches video news reports from the Internet on his lunch hour, thereby consuming much of that segment's shared bandwidth. If a problem affects users at a remote location, you should examine the WAN link or its router interfaces. If a problem affects all users in all departments and locations, a catastrophic failure has occurred, and you should assess critical devices such as central switches and backbone connections.

With all network problems, including catastrophic ones, you should take the time to troubleshoot them correctly by asking specific questions designed to identify their scope. For example, suppose a user complains that his mail program isn't picking up e-mail. You should begin by asking when the problem began, whether it affects only that user

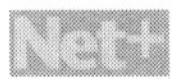
1.8

or everyone in his department, and what error message the user receives when he attempts to retrieve mail. In answering your questions, he might say, "The problem began about 10 minutes ago. Both my neighbors are having problems with e-mail, too. And as a matter of fact, a network technician was working on my machine this morning and installed a new graphics program."

As you listen to the user's response, you might need to politely filter out information that is unlikely to be related to the problem. In this situation, the user relayed two significant pieces of information: (1) The scope of the problem includes a group of users, and (2) the problem began 10 minutes ago. With this knowledge, you can then delve further in your troubleshooting. In this example, you would proceed by focusing on the network segment rather than on one workstation.

Discovering the time or frequency with which a problem occurs can reveal more subtle network problems. For example, if multiple users throughout the organization experience poor performance when attempting to log on to the server at 8:05 a.m., you might deduce that the server needs additional resources to handle the processing burden of accepting so many requests. If a network fails at noon every Tuesday, you might be able to correlate this problem with a test of your building's power system, which causes a power dip that affects the servers, routers, and other devices.

Identifying the affected area of a problem leads you to your next troubleshooting steps. The path might not always be clear-cut, but as the flowcharts in Figures 13-1 and 13-2 illustrate, some direction can be gained from narrowing both the demographic (or geographic) and the chronological scopes of a problem. Notice that these flowcharts end with the process of further troubleshooting. In the following sections, you will learn more about these subsequent troubleshooting steps.

One fascinating example of troubleshooting that began with determining a problem's chronological scope was experienced by a wireless networking engineer working on a small metropolitan area network. His spread-spectrum RF network links, which connected businesses to a carrier's facility via a transmitter and receiver on a hospital's roof, worked perfectly all day, but failed when the sun went down. When the sun came up the next morning, the wireless links worked again. The engineer confirmed that the equipment was fully operational, as he suspected, then talked with the hospital personnel. The hospital's director informed him that the hospital had installed security cameras on the outside of the building. The cameras used the same RF frequency as the network's wireless links. When the security cameras were activated at sunset, their signals interfered with the wireless network's signals, preventing data from reaching its destination.

Question Users You have probably experienced a moment in your dealings with computers in which you were certain you were doing everything correctly, but still couldn't access the network, save a file, or retrieve your e-mail. For example, you might have typed your case-sensitive network password without realizing that the Caps Lock function was turned on. As a result, even though you were certain that you typed the right password, you received a "password incorrect" error message each time you tried to enter it. All users experience such problems from time to time.

Net+
1.8

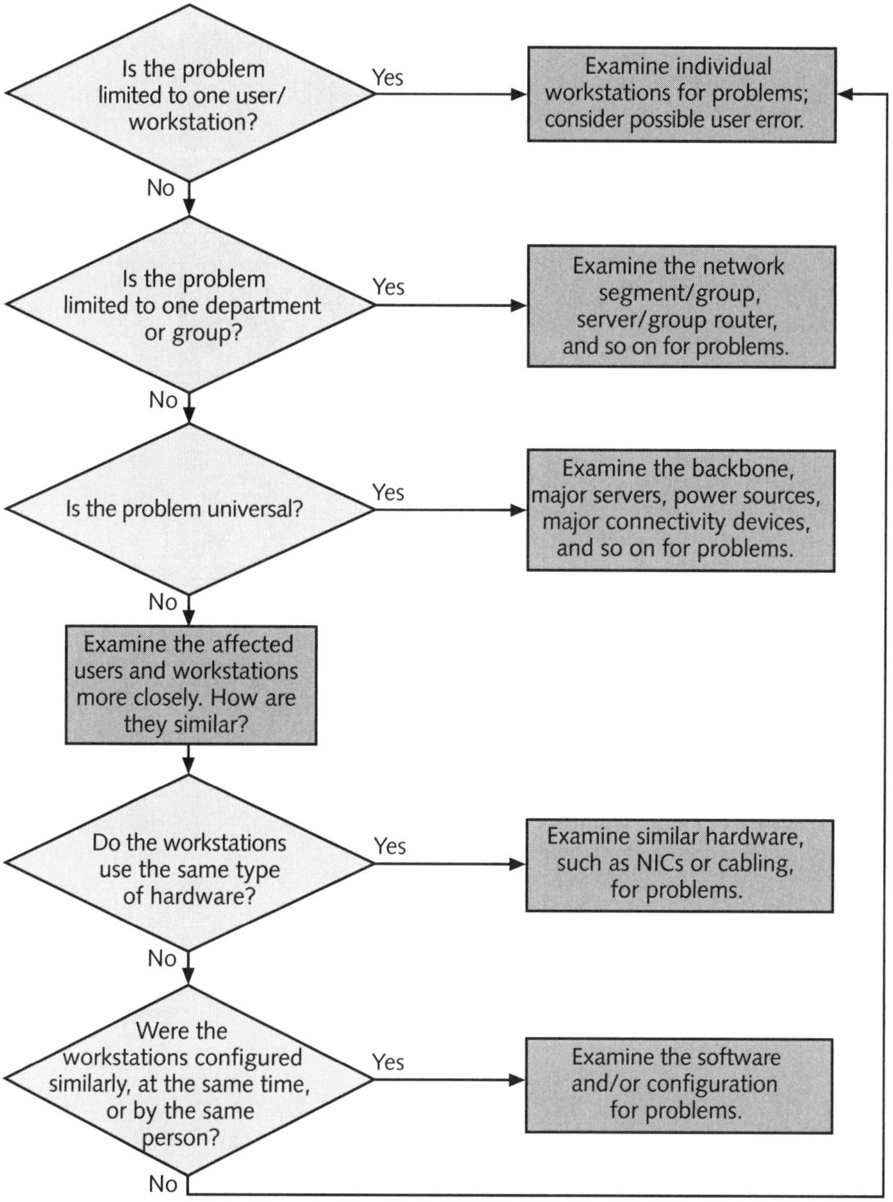

Is the problem limited to one user/ workstation?
Yes → Examine individual workstations for problems; consider possible user error.
No ↓

Is the problem limited to one department or group?
Yes → Examine the network segment/group, server/group router, and so on for problems.
No ↓

Is the problem universal?
Yes → Examine the backbone, major servers, power sources, major connectivity devices, and so on for problems.
No ↓

Examine the affected users and workstations more closely. How are they similar?
↓

Do the workstations use the same type of hardware?
Yes → Examine similar hardware, such as NICs or cabling, for problems.
No ↓

Were the workstations configured similarly, at the same time, or by the same person?
Yes → Examine the software and/or configuration for problems.
No → Examine individual workstations for problems; consider possible user error.

Figure 13-1 Identifying the area affected by a problem

It's natural for human beings to make mistakes. Thus, as a troubleshooter, one of your first steps is to ensure that human error is not the source of the problem. This approach saves you time and worry. In fact, a problem caused by human error is usually simple to solve. It's much quicker and easier to assist a user in remapping a network drive, for example, than to perform diagnostics on the file server.

One task that is commonly affected by user error is logging on to a network. Users become so accustomed to typing their passwords every morning and logging on to the network that, if

Net+ 1.8

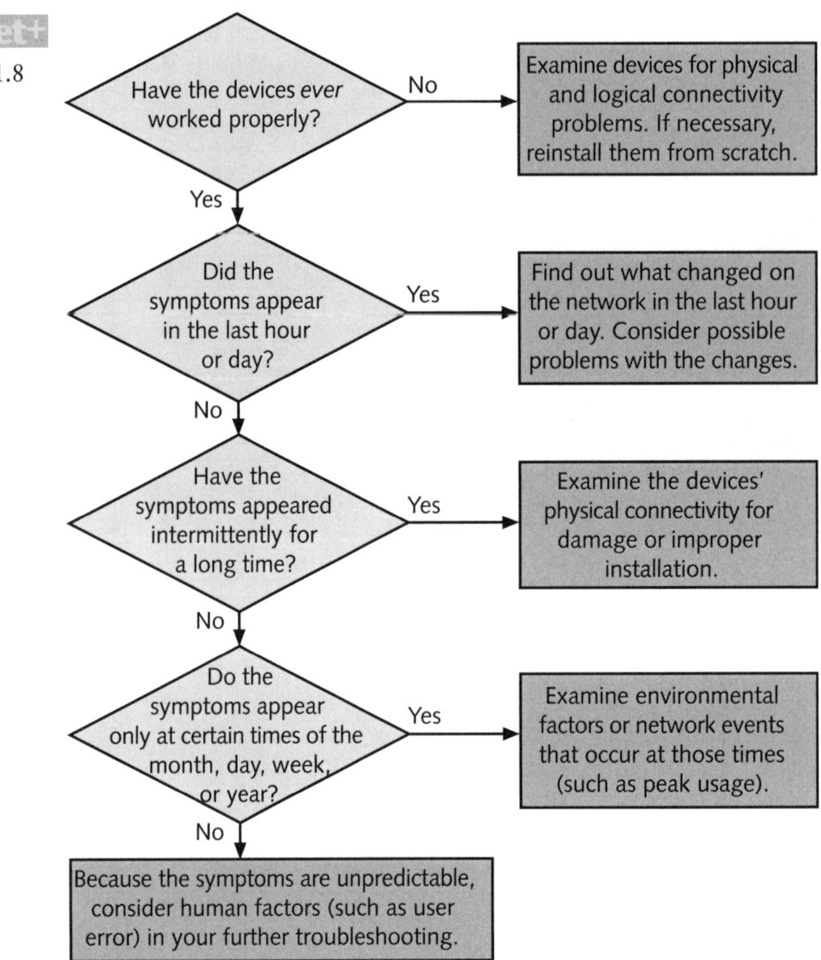

Figure 13-2 Identifying the chronological scope of a problem

something changes in the logon process, they don't know what to do. In fact, some users might never log off, so they don't know how to log on properly. Although these kinds of problems might seem simple to solve, unless a user receives training in the proper procedures and understands what might go wrong, she will never know how to solve a logon problem without assistance. Even if the user took a computer class that covered logging on, she might not remember what to do in unfamiliar situations.

The best way to verify that a user is performing network tasks correctly is to watch the user. If this isn't practical, the next best way is to connect to her computer using remote desktop software that allows you to view everything that appears on the user's screen or even control the computer from afar. Software can be controlled by the user, so she must consent to and cooperate in your troubleshooting efforts. If remote desktop software can't be used, talk with the user by phone while she tries to replicate the error. At every step, calmly ask the user to explain what appears on the screen and what, exactly, she is doing. Remind her to proceed slowly, according to your prompts, so that she doesn't rush ahead. After every

Net+ keystroke or command, ask the user again what appears on the screen. With this methodical
1.8 approach, you will have a good chance at catching user-generated mistakes. At the same time, if the problem does not result from human error, you will gain important clues for further troubleshooting.

Determine If Anything Has Changed As you begin troubleshooting, you should be aware of any recent changes to your network. The following questions could help you pinpoint a problem that results from a network change:

- Did the operating system or configuration on a server, workstation, or connectivity device change?
- Were new components added to a server, workstation, or connectivity device?
- Were old components removed from a server, workstation, or connectivity device?
- Were new users or segments added to the network?
- Was a server, workstation, or connectivity device moved from its previous location to a new location?
- Was a server, workstation, or connectivity device replaced?
- Was software installed or modified on a server, workstation, or connectivity device?
- Was old software removed from a server, workstation, or connectivity device?

If you suspect that a network change has generated a problem, you can react in two ways: You can attempt to correct the problem that resulted from the change, or you can attempt to reverse the change and restore the hardware or software to its previous state. Both options come with hazards. Of the two, reverting to a previous state is probably less risky and might take less time. However, correcting the problem is sometimes the best solution. For example, if you immediately suspect that a change-related problem can be fixed easily, try correcting the problem first. If it is impossible to restore a software or hardware configuration to its previous state, your only choice is to solve the problem.

Before changing a network device or configuration, develop a plan and gather the proper resources for reversing the change in case things go wrong. For example, if you upgrade the memory module in a server, you should keep the old memory module handy in case the new one has flaws. In another situation, you might keep a backup of device or application configurations—perhaps by making a copy of the directory that stores the target configuration.

Net+ To track what has changed on a network, you and your colleagues in the IT Department
1.8 should keep complete network change records. The more precisely you describe a change, its
4.5 purpose, and the time and date when it occurred in your records, the easier your troubleshooting will be if the change subsequently causes problems.

In addition to keeping thorough records, you must make them available to staff members who might need to reference them. For example, you might want to keep a record of changes in a database on a file server, and then use a Web-based form to retrieve and submit information from and to the database. That way, no matter where a network technician works in the organization, she can retrieve the information from any Web-enabled workstation. A simpler alternative is to keep a clipboard in the computer room with notes about changes.

1.8
4.5
Often, network changes cause unforeseen problems. For example, if you have narrowed a connectivity problem to a group of six users in the Marketing Department, you might refer to your network's change log and find that a switch in the Marketing Department's telecommunications closet was recently moved from one end of the closet to another. Reviewing the record of this change can help you more quickly pinpoint the switch as a possible cause of the problem. Perhaps the switch was incorrectly reconnected to the backbone after the move, or perhaps it became damaged in the move or lost its configuration.

Establish a Theory of Probable Cause

1.8 After you have identified the scope of the problem, questioned users, and analyzed recent changes to the network, you are close to determining the problem's cause. The following sections provide techniques on how to zero in on the most likely cause among several plausible scenarios.

Re-Create the Symptoms An excellent way to learn more about the causes of a problem is to try to re-create the symptoms yourself. If you cannot reproduce the symptoms, you might suspect that a problem was a one-time occurrence or that a user performed an operation incorrectly.

For example, suppose a user complains that he could edit a particular spreadsheet in the Accounting directory on the file server on Friday, but was unable to open the file on Monday. When you visit his workstation, you verify this sequence of events while logged on with his username. When you then log on as Administrator, however, you are able to open and edit the file. The difference in your experiences points to a user rights problem. At that point, you should check the user's privileges—especially whether they have changed since he could last retrieve the file. Perhaps someone removed him from a group that had Read and Modify rights to the Accounting directory.

Answering the following questions may help you determine whether a problem's symptoms are truly reproducible and, if so, to what extent:

- Can you make the symptoms recur every time or at all times? If symptoms recur, are they consistent?
- Can you make the symptoms recur some of the time?
- Do the symptoms happen only under certain circumstances? For example, does a WAN connection experience significant latency only if it follows a certain route?
- In the case of software malfunctions, are the symptoms consistent no matter how many and which programs or files the user has open?
- Do the symptoms *ever* happen when you try to repeat them?

When attempting to reproduce the symptoms of a problem, you should follow the same steps that the person reporting the symptoms followed. To reproduce a symptom reliably, ask the user precisely what she did before the error appeared. For example, if a user complains that her network connection mysteriously drops when she's in the middle of surfing the Web, try to replicate the problem at her workstation. Also, find out what else was running on the user's workstation or what kind of Web sites she was surfing.

1.8

Use good judgment when attempting to reproduce problems. In some cases, reproducing a problem could wreak havoc on the network, its data, and its devices; you should not attempt to reproduce such a problem. An obvious example involves a power outage in which your backup power source failed to supply power. After your network equipment comes back online, you would not cut the power again simply to verify that the problem derived from a faulty backup power source.

1.8
3.6

Verify Physical Layer Connectivity By some estimates, more than half of all network problems occur at the Physical layer of the OSI model, which includes cabling and network adapters. The Physical layer also controls signaling—both wired and wireless. Because Physical layer faults are so common and are often easily fixed, you should be thoroughly familiar with the symptoms of such problems.

Symptoms of Physical Layer Problems Often, physical connectivity problems manifest as a continuous or intermittent inability to connect to the network and perform network-related functions. Causes of unreliable network connectivity can include the following:

- Segment or network lengths that exceed the IEEE maximum standards (for example, an Ethernet 100Base-TX segment that exceeds 100 meters)
- Noise affecting a wireless or wire-bound signal (from EMI sources, improper grounding, or cross talk)
- Improper terminations, faulty connectors, loose connectors, or poorly crimped connections
- Damaged cables (for example, crushed, bent, nicked, or partially severed)
- Faulty NICs, GBICs, or SFPs

Physical connectivity problems do not typically result in software application anomalies, the inability to use a single application, poor network performance, protocol errors, software licensing errors, or software usage errors. Occasionally, however, software errors do point to a physical connectivity problem. For example, a user might be able to log on to his file server without problems. When he chooses to run a query on a database, however, his report software might produce an error message indicating that the database is unavailable or not found. If the database resides on a separate server, this symptom could point to a physical connectivity problem with the database server.

Diagnosing Physical Layer Problems Answering the following questions may help you identify a problem pertaining to physical connectivity:

- Is the device turned on?
- Is the NIC properly inserted?
- In the case of wireless NICs, is the antenna turned on?
- Is a device's network cable properly (that is, not loosely) connected to both its NIC and the wall jack?
- Do patch cables properly connect punch-down blocks to patch panels and patch panels to switches?

Net+

- Is the router or switch properly connected to the backbone?
- 1.8 Are all cables in good condition, without signs of wear or damage?
- 3.6 Are all connectors (for example, RJ-45) in good condition and properly seated?
- Do maximum network and segment lengths conform to the IEEE 802 specifications?
- Are all devices configured properly to work with your network type or speed?

A first step in verifying the physical integrity of a connection is to follow the cabling from one endpoint on the network to the other. For example, if a workstation user cannot log on to the network, and you have verified that he is typing his password correctly, check the physical connectivity from his workstation's NIC and patch cable. Follow his connection all the way through the network to the server that he cannot reach. Recently moved computers, recently recabled workgroups or nodes, and computers with cables in busy areas that could be unseated by bumping or pulling are prime candidates for errors caused by faulty connections.

In addition to verifying the connections between devices, you must verify the soundness of the hardware used in those connections. A sound connection means that cables are inserted firmly in ports, NICs, and wall jacks; NICs are seated firmly in the system board; connectors are not broken; and cables are not damaged. Damaged or improperly inserted connectivity elements may result in only occasional (and, therefore, difficult-to-troubleshoot) errors.

The flowchart in Figure 13-3 illustrates how logically assessing Physical layer elements can help you solve a network problem. The steps in this flowchart apply to a typical problem: a user's inability to log on to the network. They assume that you have already ruled out user error and that you have successfully reproduced the problem under both your and the user's logon ID.

Net+

Verify Logical Connectivity After you have verified the physical connections, you
1.8 must examine the firmware and software configurations, settings, installations, protocols, routes, and privileges. Depending on the type of symptoms, you might need to investigate networked applications, the network operating system, or hardware configurations. All of these elements belong in the category of "logical connectivity."

Answering the following questions may help you identify a problem with logical connectivity:

- Do error messages reference damaged or missing files or device drivers?
- Do error messages reference malfunctioning or insufficient resources (such as memory)?
- Has an operating system, configuration, or application been recently changed, introduced, or deleted?
- Does the problem occur with only one application or a few, similar applications?
- Does the problem happen consistently?
- Does the problem affect a single user, a group of users, or all users?

Net+
1.8
3.6

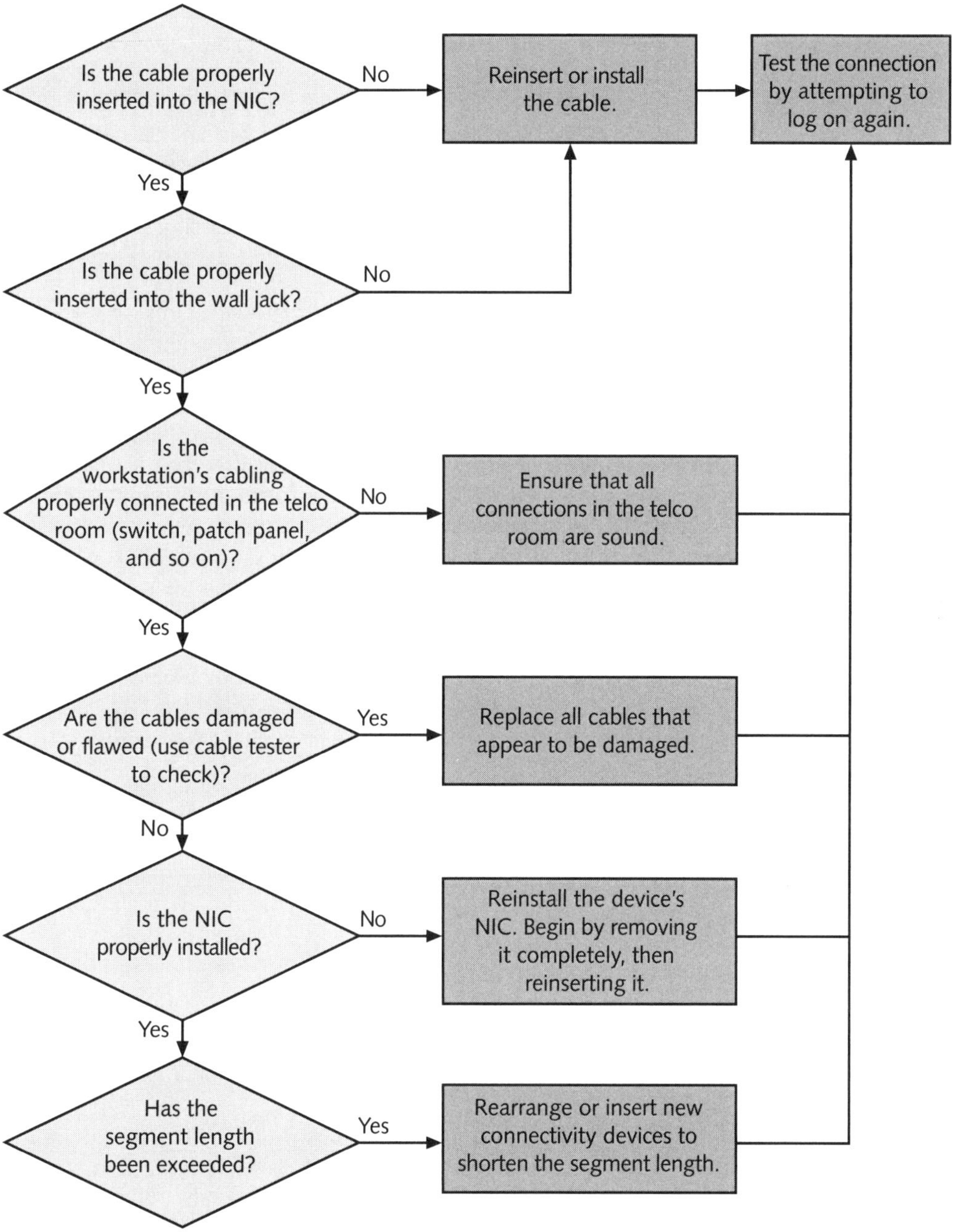

Is the cable properly inserted into the NIC?
No → Reinsert or install the cable. → Test the connection by attempting to log on again.
Yes ↓

Is the cable properly inserted into the wall jack?
No → Reinsert or install the cable.
Yes ↓

Is the workstation's cabling properly connected in the telco room (switch, patch panel, and so on)?
No → Ensure that all connections in the telco room are sound. → Test the connection by attempting to log on again.
Yes ↓

Are the cables damaged or flawed (use cable tester to check)?
Yes → Replace all cables that appear to be damaged. → Test the connection by attempting to log on again.
No ↓

Is the NIC properly installed?
No → Reinstall the device's NIC. Begin by removing it completely, then reinserting it. → Test the connection by attempting to log on again.
Yes ↓

Has the segment length been exceeded?
Yes → Rearrange or insert new connectivity devices to shorten the segment length. → Test the connection by attempting to log on again.

Figure 13-3 Verifying physical connectivity

4.3

As you learned in Chapter 4, a quick way to confirm that a node's network interface is responding and that its core TCP/IP protocols are properly installed is to ping the loopback address, 127.0.0.1. To perform this test on a host running IPv4, type `ping 127.0.0.1` and press Enter at a command prompt. To perform this test on a host running IPv6, type `ping -6 ::1` and press Enter at a command prompt. If you receive a positive response, you can expand the scope of your troubleshooting. If not, you need to determine why the node's network interface doesn't respond. Other troubleshooting utilities, such as traceroute, netstat, and dig are described in Chapter 9.

1.8
2.4

Logical connectivity problems often prove more difficult to isolate and resolve than physical connectivity problems because they can be more complex. For example, a user might complain that he has been unable to connect to the network for the last two hours. Some possible software-based causes for this include, but are not limited to, the following: an improperly configured NIC, improperly installed or configured client software, and improperly installed or configured network protocols or services. Suppose that, after you go to his workstation and confirm that it won't allow you or him to connect to the network, you check the functionality of his wireless NIC and its antenna. The NIC responds when you attempt to ping the loopback address, the antenna is on, and his workstation has associated with an access point. Next, you might ask the user whether anything changed on his machine approximately two hours ago. He tells you that he didn't do a thing to the machine—it just stopped working. At this point, you would probably examine the TCP/IPv4 configuration for his NIC. In doing so, you might determine that the incorrect DHCP server has been selected. This could happen with a wireless client, for example, if a rogue access point running the DHCP service is introduced on the network. After you change the DHCP setting, his workstation can communicate with the network.

Determining a likely cause is a process of narrowing down possibilities. Even after re-creating the problem and answering questions related to physical and logical connectivity, you might identify several plausible theories about the problem's cause. To further limit the possibilities, the next step is to pick a likely theory and test it.

Net+ Test the Theory to Determine Cause

1.8 In the case of simple network problems, testing your theory—for example, plugging in a disconnected patch cable—may also be the solution to the problem. However, given complicated problems, testing your theory will require more effort and analysis.

1.8
3.6

Test Physical Layer Theories If you suspect a problem lies with a faulty network component, you can assess the component individually to determine if it is the source of the problem. Examples of testing Physical layer theories include the following:

- Using a cable testing tool as described later in this chapter to test a cable's ability to transmit and receive data reliably
- Viewing the LED indicators on an interface to determine whether it is on and exchanging data
- Checking to make sure a NIC (whether on-board or peripheral), GBIC, or SFP is seated firmly in its slot
- Measuring cabling distance to ensure segments do not exceed length limits

- Using a wireless analyzer as described later in this chapter to confirm that all of an
1.8 access point's clients are within its range
- 3.6 Following cables from one node through connectivity devices to another node to verify end-to-end physical connectivity between them

Another way to determine whether a physical component is at fault is to exchange it for one that you know is functional. In many cases, such a swap resolves the problem very quickly, so you should try this tactic early in your troubleshooting process. It won't always work, of course, but with experience you will learn what types of problems are most likely caused by component failure.

For example, if a user cannot connect to the network, and you have checked to make sure all the connections are secure, the NIC is functional, and the logical connectivity elements are sound, you might consider swapping the user's network cable with a new one. As you know, network cables must meet specific standards to operate properly. If one becomes damaged (for example, by a chair repeatedly rolling over it), it will cause performance problems or prevent a user from connecting to the network. Swapping an old network cable with a new one is a quick test that could save you further troubleshooting.

In addition to swapping network cables, you might need to change a patch cable from one port in a switch to another, or from one data jack to another. Ports, data jacks, and SFP modules can be operational one day and faulty the next. You might also swap a network adapter from one machine to another, or try installing a new network adapter, making sure it's compatible with the client. Obviously, it's more difficult to swap a switch or router because of the number of nodes serviced by these components and the potentially significant configuration they require; if network connectivity has failed for an entire segment or network, however, this approach may provide a quicker answer than attempting to troubleshoot the faulty device.

A better—albeit more expensive—alternative to swapping parts is to build redundancy into your network. For example, you might have a server that contains two network adapters, allowing one network adapter to take over for the other if one adapter should fail. If properly installed and configured, this arrangement results in no downtime; in contrast, swapping parts requires at least a few minutes of service disruption. In the case of swapping a router, the downtime might last for several hours.

Before swapping any network component, make sure that the replacement has the same specifications as the original part. By installing a component that's different from the original device, you risk thwarting your troubleshooting efforts because the new component might not work in the environment. In the worst case, you may damage existing equipment by installing a component that isn't rated for it.

Test Logical Connectivity Theories As with testing theories about physical connec-
1.8 tivity problems, testing a theory about logical connectivity problems may end up solving the problem. For example, if you suspect a client's NIC driver is outdated, you can install the new driver to test your theory and the problem might be solved. More complicated logical connectivity problems, however, may require you to perform more sleuthing. Some examples of testing logical connectivity theories include the following:

- Viewing a switch configuration to determine which nodes are included in VLANs
- 1.8 Investigating user permissions on a server
- 2.5 Examining a NIC's configuration to check that the correct protocols (for example, TCP/IPv4 and/or TCP/IPv6) are installed and that the correct gateway, DHCP server, and name server are identified
- Reading a routing table to determine if any static entries point to routers that no longer exist
- Reviewing a router's access list or a firewall's policies to find out if legitimate traffic is being blocked
- Using tools such as ping, netstat, route, or traceroute to establish the condition of an interface or route
- Checking to make sure a wireless client's settings, including security method and passphrase, channel, and network type match those of its access point

As with Physical layer sleuthing, tools exist to help you test theories about logical connectivity problems. Later in this chapter, you will learn about protocol analyzers and network monitoring programs that enable you to examine network traffic and pinpoint a problem's cause.

Net+

Escalate If Necessary If you're unable to establish a cause despite your best efforts to
1.8 test likely theories, you might need to escalate the issue to a colleague with more experience or specialized knowledge. Many staff members can contribute to troubleshooting a network problem. Often, the division of duties is formalized, with a help desk acting as a single point of contact for users. A help desk is typically staffed with **help desk analysts**—people proficient in basic (but not usually advanced) workstation and network troubleshooting. Larger organizations might group their help desk analysts into teams based on their expertise. For example, a company that provides users with word processing, spreadsheet, project planning, scheduling, and graphics software might assign different technical support personnel at the help desk to answer questions pertaining to each application.

The help desk analysts are often considered **first-level support** because they provide the first level of troubleshooting. When a user calls with a problem, a help desk analyst typically creates a record for the incident and attempts to diagnose the problem. The help desk analyst might be able to solve a common problem over the phone within minutes by explaining something to the user. In the case of an extremely rare or complex problem, the first-level support analyst will refer, or **escalate**, the problem to a second-level support analyst.

A **second-level support** analyst is someone with specialized knowledge in one or more aspects of a network. For example, if a user complains that she can't connect to a server, and the first-level support person narrows down the problem to a failed file server, that first-level support analyst would then refer the problem to the second-level support person. Some organizations also have **third-level support** personnel who are highly skilled in one area of networking. Second-level analysts escalate only the most severe or complex issues to third-level support personnel. Such staff are typically not part of the help desk, but specialists in another area, such as routing and switching, server management, or security.

In addition to having first- and second-level support analysts, most help desks include a help desk coordinator. The **help desk coordinator** ensures that analysts are divided into the correct teams, schedules shifts at the help desk, and maintains the infrastructure to enable

1.8 analysts to better perform their jobs. They might also serve as third-level support personnel, taking responsibility for troubleshooting a problem when the second-level support analyst is unable to solve it.

When you're part of a troubleshooting team, you need to know when and how to escalate problems. For guidance, you might turn to a procedure that lists specific conditions under which escalation is critical. For example, suppose you work for an ISP with one large corporate customer whose income depends largely on Internet sales that are handled by servers and connections in your data center. Your organization might deem that anytime one of that company's servers fails to respond, a second-level support analyst is assigned to troubleshoot it. In other cases, you will have to use your judgment to determine whether a situation warrants escalation. You'll base your decision on several factors, including the number of users affected, the importance of the access or service affected, the familiarity of the problem, and your technical skills.

Establish a Plan of Action to Resolve the Problem

After you have thoroughly analyzed a network problem and identified its likely cause, you will be able to devise an action plan for solving it. First, however, you must consider how your solution might affect users and network functionality.

Scope One of the most important aspects to consider is the scope of your change. For example, replacing a cable that connects a workstation to a switch may affect only one user, but replacing a cable that connects a server to a switch affects all users who access that server. Assess the breadth of your solution—whether it is a single workstation, a workgroup, a location, or the entire network—before implementing that solution. If the problem does not pose an emergency, wait until no one is on the network before implementing solutions that affect many users. That way, you will have time to judge the solution's effects systematically and fix any new problems that might arise.

Trade-Offs Along with the scope, another factor to consider is the trade-off your solution might impose. In other words, your solution might restore functionality for one group of users, but remove it for others. For example, let's say you are a network technician at a stationery company that uses specialized software to program custom logos and control its embossing machines. When you add a group of new Windows 7 workstations to your network, you discover that these new workstations can't run the embossing control software properly. The software vendor tells you that to be compatible with Windows 7, you must install a new, Windows 7-compatible version of the software on your file server. You might be thrilled to hear of such a simple solution and install the updated embossing control software immediately. In the next half hour, you receive numerous phone calls from employees using Windows XP workstations who cannot properly use the embossing control software. Now, you have solved one problem, but created another. In this situation, it would have been wise to ask the software vendor about their upgrade's compatibility with all the other operating systems your company uses. If the vendor told you about a problem with Windows XP workstations, you could have kept the old installation on the server for these users, then installed a separate instance of the new version of the software for use by Windows 7 users.

Security Be aware of the security implications of your solution because it might inadvertently result in the addition or removal of network access or resource privileges for a user or group of users. One consequence might be that a user can no longer access a data file or

1.8 application he is accustomed to accessing. But a worse consequence is that you could create a security vulnerability that allows unauthorized people to access your network. Before installing a software upgrade or patch, for example, be sure to understand how it could change access for both authorized and unauthorized users.

Scalability Also consider the scalability of the solution you intend to implement. Does it position the network for additions and enhancements later on, or is it merely a temporary fix that the organization will outgrow in a year? Ideally, your solution would be perfectly suited to your network and allow for future growth. But a temporary fix is not necessarily wrong, depending on the scenario. For example, suppose you walk into the office one day to find that none of your users can access the network. You track down the problem as an internal hardware problem with your Internet gateway. Because the gateway is under warranty, you quickly call the manufacturer to get the gateway replaced or fixed immediately. The manufacturer tells you that although they don't have the identical gateway available in their local office, they can substitute a different, smaller model to get your users reconnected today, and meanwhile order the identical gateway that you can install when you have more time. In this situation, it's probably preferable to take the temporary gateway and restore functionality than to wait for the ideal solution.

Cost Another factor to consider when implementing your solution is cost. Obviously, replacing one patch cable or faulty SFP is a fairly inexpensive proposition, and you don't need to analyze cost in these cases. But if the solution you have proposed requires significant dollars for either software or hardware, weigh your options carefully. For example, suppose you discover a problem with performance on your network. After some investigation, you determine that the best solution is to replace all 400 workstations' network adapters with newer, faster network adapters. If you purchase quality NICs, this solution could cost over $5000 for the hardware alone, not to mention the time it will take technicians to replace the devices, which would cost more. Also you should consider when these workstations will be replaced and if you will have to either discard or remove the network adapters you just installed. It might be more prudent to identify where the network's performance is poor and address those areas separately—for example, by adding a switch to a busy segment or adding a more powerful server for a heavily used application.

Use Vendor Information Some networking professionals pride themselves in being able to install, configure, and troubleshoot devices without reading the instructions—or at least exhausting all possibilities before they submit to reading a manual. Although some manufacturers provide better documentation than others, you have nothing to lose by referring to the manual, except a little time. Chances are you will find exactly what you need—configuration commands for a router or switch, recommendations for remote access server setup, or troubleshooting tips for a network operating system function, to name a few examples.

In addition to the documentation that comes with hardware and software, most vendors provide free online troubleshooting information. For example, Microsoft, Red Hat, and Apple offer searchable databases in which you can type your error message or a description of your problem and receive lists of possible solutions. Reputable equipment manufacturers, such as 3Com, HP, Cisco, IBM, and Intel, also offer sophisticated Web interfaces for troubleshooting their equipment. If you cannot find the documentation for a networking component, you should try looking for information on the Web.

Call the vendor's technical support phone number only after you have read the product doc-
1.8 umentation and searched the vendor's Web page. With some manufacturers, you can talk to a technical support agent only if you have established and paid for a support agreement. With others, you must pay per phone call. Each vendor has a different pricing structure for technical support, so before you agree to pay for technical support, you should find out whether the vendor charges on a per-hour or per-problem basis.

Keep a list handy of the hardware and software vendors for your networking equipment; the list should include the company's name, its technical support phone number, a contact name (if available), its technical support Web site address, its policies for technical support, and the type of agreement you currently have with the vendor. Make sure the list is updated regularly and available to all IT personnel who might need it.

If you are uncertain whether your proposed solution is the *best* solution, even after your thorough diagnosis and research, seek advice from others, either within or outside your organization. Colleagues or consultants might share an experience that leads you to prefer one solution to another.

Implement the Solution or Escalate as Necessary

1.8 Finally, after you have established a plan for your proposed solution, you are ready to imple-
4.5 ment the solution. This step might be very brief (such as modifying a record in a routing table) or it might take a long time (such as replacing the hard disk of a server). In either case, implementing a solution requires foresight and patience. As with finding the problem, the more methodically and logically you can approach the solution, the more efficient the correction process will be. If a problem is causing catastrophic outages, however, you should solve it as quickly as possible.

The following steps will help you implement a safe and reliable solution:

- Alert all affected users of the planned change with as much advance notice as possible. Depending on the solution's scope and risk, those affected might include only a few users or the whole organization.
- Collect all the documentation you have about a problem's symptoms from your investigation and keep it handy while solving the problem.
- If you are reinstalling software on a device, make a backup of the device's existing software installation. If you are changing hardware on a device, keep the old parts handy in case the solution doesn't work. If you are changing the configuration of a program or device, take the time to print the program or device's current configuration. Even if the change seems minor, jot down notes about the original state.
- Perform the change, replacement, move, or addition that you believe will solve the problem. Record your actions in detail so that you can later enter the information into a database.
- Test your solution, as described in the section that follows.
- Before leaving the area in which you were working, clean it up. For instance, if you created a new patch cable for a telecommunications room, remove the debris left from cutting and crimping the cable.

1.8 4.5

- If the solution fixes the problem, record the details you have collected about the symptoms, the problem, and the solution in your organization's troubleshooting database.
- If your solution involved a significant change or addressed a significant problem (one that affected more than a few users), revisit the solution a day or two later to verify that the problem has, indeed, been solved and that it hasn't created additional problems.

In the case of large-scale fixes—for example, applying new configurations on a global VPN's routers because of a security threat—it's often best to roll out changes in stages. This approach allows you to find and correct any problem that occurs during the upgrade before it affects all users. It also allows you to test whether you're implementing the solution in the best possible way. In the example of reconfiguring routers, you could log on to the routers and apply configurations from a remote office, but in some cases this creates additional security concerns. You might prefer instead to visit the offices and apply the changes yourself or talk to a local IT employee who can make the changes on site.

Verify Full System Functionality

1.8 After implementing your solution, you must test its result and verify that you have solved the problem properly. Obviously, the type of testing you perform depends on your solution. For example, if you replaced a patch cable between a switch port and a patch panel, a quick test of your solution would be to determine whether you could connect to the network from the device that relies on that patch cable. If the device does not successfully connect to the network, you might have to try another cable, or reconsider whether the problem stems from physical or logical connectivity or some other cause. In that case, using the hardware and software troubleshooting tools discussed later in this chapter might lead to a more efficient evaluation of your solution.

Testing the results of your solution will also depend on the area affected by the problem. Suppose you replaced a switch that served four different departments in an organization. To test the result of your solution, you would need to verify connectivity from workstations in each of the four departments.

Keep in mind that you might not be able to test your solution immediately. In some cases, you might have to wait days or weeks before you know for certain whether it worked. For example, suppose you discovered that a server was sometimes running out of processor capacity when handling clients' database queries, causing users to experience unacceptably slow response times. To solve this problem, you added two processors and enabled the server's symmetric multiprocessing capabilities. But suppose that the timing of the database usage is unpredictable, however. This means you wouldn't find out whether the added processors eliminated the problem until a certain number of users attempted the operations that push the server to its peak processor usage.

Upon testing your solution, you should be able to determine how and why the solution was successful and what effects it had on users and functionality. For example, suppose you identified a symptom of excessively slow performance when saving and retrieving files to and from a server on your LAN. You determined that all users were affected by the problem and that it had worsened steadily in the past month. Your proposed solution was to replace the server with one that contained a faster processor, more memory, greater hard disk capacity, and

Net+ dual NICs. You implemented the solution and then tested its outcome to make sure all users
1.8 could save and retrieve files to and from the new server. If all went well, the effect of the solution might be an 80 percent increase in performance between clients and the server.

Most important, you want to avoid creating unintended, negative consequences as a result of your solution. For example, in the process of diagnosing a problem with a user's access to a mail directory, you might have reconfigured his mail settings to log on with your own user name to rule out the possibility of a physical connectivity error. After discovering that the problem was actually due to an IP addressing conflict, you might fix the IP addressing problem but forget that you changed the user's e-mail configuration. Having the user test your solution would reveal this oversight—and prevent you from having to return to the workstation to solve another problem.

After you verify system functionality, it's wise to consider how similar problems can be prevented in the future. Some network problems can be averted by network maintenance, documentation, security, or upgrades. Others can be avoided by thoughtful planning.For example, to avoid problems with users' access levels for network resources, you can comprehensively assess users' needs, set policies for groups, create a variety of groups, and explain the necessity for these groups to those who support the network. To prevent overusing network segments, you should perform regular network health checks—perhaps even continual network monitoring, with filters that isolate anomalous occurrences. Also, you should ensure that you have the means to either redesign the network to distribute traffic or purchase additional bandwidth well before utilization reaches critical levels. With experience, you will be able to add more suggestions for network problem prevention. When planning or upgrading a network, you need to consider how good network designs and policies can prevent later problems—not to mention, make your job easier and more fun.

After you have implemented and tested your solution and identified its results and effects, communicate your solution to your colleagues, thus adding to the store of knowledge about your network. The next section discusses how best to document your troubleshooting efforts and notify others of changes you've made.

Net+ Document Findings, Actions, and Outcomes

1.8 Whether you are a one-person network support team or one of 100 network technicians at
4.5 your organization, you should always document the symptoms and cause (or causes) of a problem and your solution. Given the volume of problems you and other analysts will troubleshoot, it will be impossible to remember the circumstances of each incident. In addition, networking personnel frequently change jobs, and everyone appreciates clear, thorough documentation. An effective way to document problems and solutions is in a centrally located database to which all networking personnel have online access.

For documenting problems, some organizations use a software program known as a **call tracking system** (also informally known as help desk software). Such programs provide user-friendly graphical interfaces that prompt the user for every piece of information associated with the problem. They assign unique identifying numbers to each problem, in addition to identifying the caller, the nature of the problem, the time necessary to resolve it, and the nature of the resolution.

Most call tracking systems are highly customizable, so you can tailor the form fields to your particular computing environment. For example, if you work for an oil refinery, you

1.8
4.5

might add fields for identifying problems with the plant's flow-control software. In addition, most call tracking systems allow you to enter free-form text explanations of problems and solutions.

If your organization does not have a call tracking system, you should at least keep records in a simple electronic form. A typical problem record form should include at least the following fields:

- The name, department, and phone number of the problem originator (the person who first noticed the problem)
- Information regarding whether the problem is software or hardware related
- If the problem is software related, the package to which it pertains; if the problem is hardware-related, the device or component to which it pertains
- Symptoms of the problem, including when it was first noticed
- The name and telephone number of the network support contact
- The amount of time spent troubleshooting the problem
- The resolution of the problem

As discussed earlier in this chapter, many organizations operate a help desk staffed with personnel who have only basic troubleshooting expertise and who record problems called in by users. To effectively field network questions, help desk staff must maintain current and accurate records for network support personnel. Furthermore, the IT Department should maintain a supported services list that help desk personnel can use as a reference. A **supported services list** is a document (preferably online) that lists every service and software package supported within an organization, plus the names of first- and second-level support contacts for those services or software packages. Increasing communication and availability of support information will expedite troubleshooting.

In addition to communicating problems and solutions to your peers whenever you work on a network problem, you should follow up with the user who reported the problem. Make sure that the client understands how or why the problem occurred, what you did to resolve the problem, and whom to contact should the problem recur. This type of education helps your clients make better decisions about the type of support or training they need, and also improves their understanding of and respect for your department.

After solving a particularly thorny network problem, record its resolution in your call tracking system and notify others of your solution and what, if anything, you needed to change to fix the problem. This communication serves two purposes: (1) It alerts others about the problem and its solution, and (2) it notifies others of network changes you made, in case they affect other services.

Large organizations often implement change management systems to methodically track changes on the network. A **change management system** is a process or program that provides support personnel with a centralized means of documenting changes to the network. The system might consist of a database package complete with graphical interfaces and customizable fields tailored to the computing environment. Whatever form a change management system takes, the most important element is participation. If networking personnel do not record their changes, even the most sophisticated software is useless.

Net+ The types of changes that network personnel record in a change management system include
1.8 the following:

4.5
- Adding or upgrading software on servers or connectivity devices
- Adding or upgrading hardware components on servers or connectivity devices
- Adding new hardware on the network (for example, a new firewall)
- Changing the properties or configurations of network devices (for example, changing the IP address or host name of a server or creating a new VLAN)
- Increasing or decreasing rights for a group of users
- Physically moving networked devices
- Moving user accounts and their files and directories from one server to another
- Making changes in processes (for example, a new backup schedule or a new contact for DNS support)
- Making changes in vendor policies or relationships (for example, a new cloud storage supplier)

It's generally not necessary to record minor modifications, such as changing a user's password, creating a new group for users, creating new directories, or changing a network drive mapping for a user. Each organization will have unique requirements for its change management system, and analysts who record change information should clearly understand these requirements.

Troubleshooting Tools

Net+ You have already learned about some utilities that can help you troubleshoot network pro-
4.2 blems. For example, you can learn many things about a user's workstation connection by attempting to ping different hosts on the network from that workstation. However, in some cases, the most efficient troubleshooting approach is to use a tool specifically designed to analyze and isolate network problems. Several tools are available, ranging from simple continuity testers that indicate whether a cable is faulty, to sophisticated protocol analyzers that capture and interpret all types of data traveling over the network. The tool you choose depends on the particular problem you need to investigate and the characteristics of your network.

The following sections describe a variety of network troubleshooting tools, their functions, and their relative costs. In the Hands-On Projects at the end of this chapter, you will have the opportunity to try some of these network troubleshooting tools.

Tone Generator and Tone Locator

Ideally, you and your networking colleagues would label each port and wire termination in a telecommunications closet so that problems and changes can be easily managed. However, because of personnel changes and time constraints, a telecommunications closet might be disorganized and poorly documented. If this is the case where you work, you might need a tone generator and a tone locator to determine where one pair of wires, possibly out of hundreds, terminates.

4.2 A **tone generator** (or **toner**) is a small electronic device that issues a signal on a wire pair. A **tone locator** (or **probe**) is a device that emits a tone when it detects electrical activity on a wire pair. They are sold together as a set, often called a toner and probe kit. By placing the tone generator at one end of a wire and attaching a tone locator to the other end, you can verify the location of the wire's termination. Figure 13-4 depicts the use of a tone generator and a tone locator. Of course, you must work by trial and error, guessing which termination corresponds to the wire over which you've generated a signal until the tone locator indicates the correct choice.

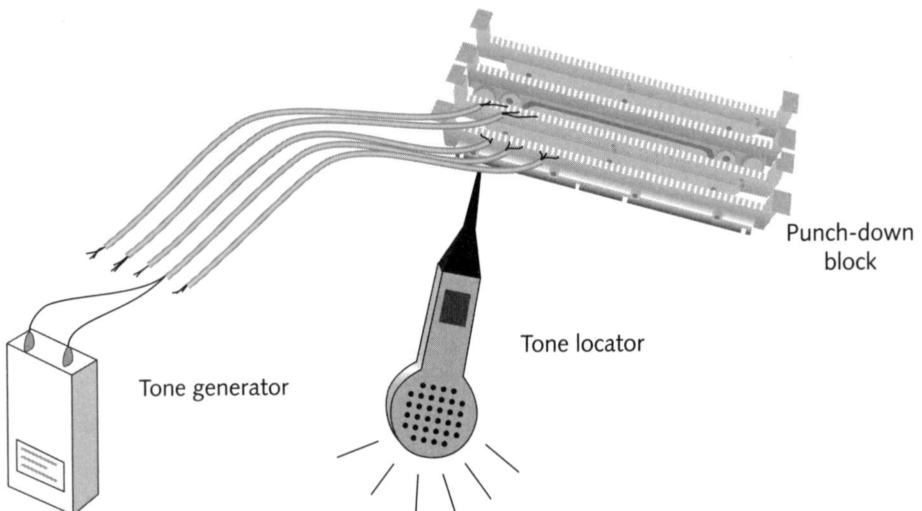

Figure 13-4 Use of a tone generator and tone locator

Tone generators and tone locators cannot be used to determine any characteristics about a cable, such as whether it's defective or whether its length exceeds IEEE standards for a certain type of network. They are only used to determine where a wire pair terminates.

A tone generator should never be used on a wire that's connected to a device's port or network adapter. Because a tone generator transmits electricity over the wire, it could damage the device or network adapter.

Multimeter

Cable testing tools are essential for both cable installers and network troubleshooters, as faulty cables are often the cause of network problems. Symptoms of cabling problems can be as elusive as occasional lost packets or as obvious as a break in network connectivity. You can easily test cables for faults with specialized tools. In this section and in the ones following, you will learn about different tools that can help isolate problems with network cables. The first device you will learn about is a **multimeter**, a simple instrument that can measure many characteristics of an electric circuit, including its resistance and voltage.

If you have taken an introductory electronics class, you are probably familiar with a **voltmeter**, the instrument that measures the pressure, or voltage, of an electric current. Recall that voltage is used to create signals over a network wire. Thus, every time data travel over a wire, the

4.2 wire carries a small voltage. In addition, each wire has a certain amount of resistance, or opposition to electric current. Resistance is a fundamental property of wire that depends on a wire's molecular structure and size. Every type of wire has different resistance characteristics. Resistance is measured in ohms, and the device used to measure resistance is called an **ohmmeter.** Another characteristic of electrical circuits is impedance—the resistance that contributes to controlling the signal. Impedance is also measured in ohms. Impedance is the telltale factor for ascertaining where faults in a cable lie. A certain amount of impedance is required for a signal to be properly transmitted and interpreted. However, very high or low levels of impedance can signify a damaged wire, incorrect pairing, or a termination point. In other words, changes in impedance can indicate where current is stopped or inhibited.

Although you could use separate instruments for measuring impedance, resistance, and voltage on a wire, it is more convenient to have one instrument that accomplishes all of these functions. The multimeter is such an instrument. Figure 13-5 shows a handheld digital multimeter.

Figure 13-5 A multimeter
Courtesy of Fluke Networks

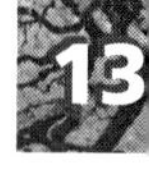

As a network professional, you might use a multimeter to do the following:

- Verify that a cable is properly conducting electricity—that is, whether its signal can travel unimpeded from one node on the network to another.
- Check for the presence of noise on a wire (by detecting extraneous voltage).
- Verify that the amount of resistance presented by terminators on coaxial cable networks is appropriate, or whether terminators are actually present and functional.
- Test for short or open circuits in the wire (by detecting unexpected resistance or loss of voltage).

Multimeters vary in their degree of sophistication and features. Some merely show voltage levels, for example, whereas others can measure the level of noise on a circuit at any moment with extreme precision. Costs for multimeters also vary; some, such as those available at any home electronics store, cost as little as $30, while others cost as much as $4000. Multimeters capable of the greatest accuracy are most useful to electronics engineers. As a

4.2 network technician, you won't often need to know the upper limit of noise on a cable within a small fraction of a decibel, for example. However, you do need to know how to check whether a cable is conducting current. Another instrument that can perform such a test is a continuity tester, which is discussed next.

Cable Continuity Testers

In troubleshooting a Physical layer problem, you may find the cause of a problem by simply testing whether your cable is carrying a signal to its destination. Tools used to make this determination are said to be testing the continuity of the cable and may be called **cable checkers** or **continuity testers**. They may also be called cable testers. The term **cable tester**, however, is a general term that also includes more sophisticated tools that can measure cable performance, as discussed in the following section.

When used on a copper-based cable, a continuity tester applies a small amount of voltage to each conductor at one end of the cable, and then checks whether that voltage is detectable at the other end. That means that a continuity tester consists of two parts: the base unit that generates the voltage and the remote unit that detects the voltage. Most cable checkers provide a series of lights that signal pass/fail. Some also indicate a cable pass/fail with an audible tone. A pass/fail test provides a simple indicator of whether a component can perform its stated function.

In addition to checking cable continuity, some continuity testers will verify that the wires in a UTP or STP cable are paired correctly and that they are not shorted, exposed, or crossed. Recall that different network models use specific wire pairings and follow cabling standards set forth in TIA/EIA 568. Make sure that the cable checker you purchase can test the type of network you use—for example, 10Base-T, 100Base-TX, or 1000Base-T Ethernet.

Continuity testers for fiber-optic networks also exist. Rather than issuing voltage on a wire, however, these testers issue light pulses on the fiber and determine whether they reached the other end of the fiber. Some continuity testers offer the ability to test both copper and fiber-optic cable.

Figure 13-6 depicts a continuity tester.

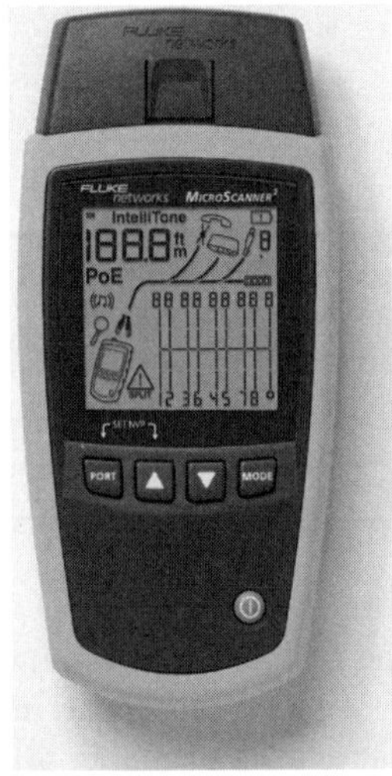

Figure 13-6 Cable continuity tester

Courtesy of Fluke Networks

Net+ 4.2 Whether you make your own cables or purchase cabling from a reputable vendor, test the cable to ensure that it meets your network's required standards. Just because a cable is labeled "Cat 6a," for example, does not necessarily mean that it will live up to that standard. Testing cabling before installing it could save many hours of troubleshooting after the network is in place.

Do not use a continuity tester on a live network cable. Disconnect the cable from the network, and then test its continuity.

For convenience, most continuity testers are portable and lightweight, and typically use one 9-volt battery. A continuity tester can cost between $30 and $300 and can save many hours of work. Popular manufacturers of these cable testing devices include Belkin, Fluke, and Paladin.

Cable Performance Testers

If you need to know more than whether a cable is simply carrying current, you can use a **cable performance tester**. The difference between continuity testers and performance testers lies in their sophistication and price. A performance tester accomplishes the same continuity and fault tests as a continuity tester, but can also perform the following tasks:

- Measure the distance to a connectivity device, termination point, or cable fault
- Measure attenuation along a cable
- Measure near-end cross talk between wires
- Measure termination resistance and impedance
- Issue pass/fail ratings for Cat 3, Cat 5, Cat 5e, Cat 6, Cat 6a, or Cat 7 standards
- Store and print cable testing results or directly save data to a computer database
- Graphically depict a cable's attenuation and cross talk characteristics over the length of the cable

A sophisticated performance tester will include a **TDR (time domain reflectometer)**. A TDR issues a signal on a cable and then measures the way the signal bounces back (or reflects) to the TDR. Connectors, crimps, bends, short circuits, cable mismatches, or other defects modify the signal's amplitude before it returns to the TDR, thus changing the way it reflects. The TDR then accepts and analyzes the return signal, and based on its condition and the amount of time the signal took to return, determines cable imperfections. In the case of a coaxial cable network, a TDR can indicate whether terminators are properly installed and functional. A TDR can also indicate the distance between nodes and segments.

In addition to performance testers for coaxial and twisted pair connections, you can also find performance testers for fiber-optic connections. Such performance testers use **OTDRs (optical time domain reflectometers)**. Rather than issue an electrical signal over the cable as twisted pair cable testers do, an OTDR transmits light-based signals of different wavelengths over the fiber. Based on the type of return light signal, the OTDR can accurately measure the length of the fiber; determine the location of faulty splices, breaks, connectors, or bends; and measure attenuation over the cable.

4.2 Because of their sophistication, performance testers for both copper and fiber-optic cables cost significantly more than continuity testers. A high-end unit could cost up to $30,000, and a low-end unit could sell for less than $4000. Figure 13-7 shows an example of a high-end cable performance tester that is capable of measuring the characteristics of both copper and fiber-optic cables.

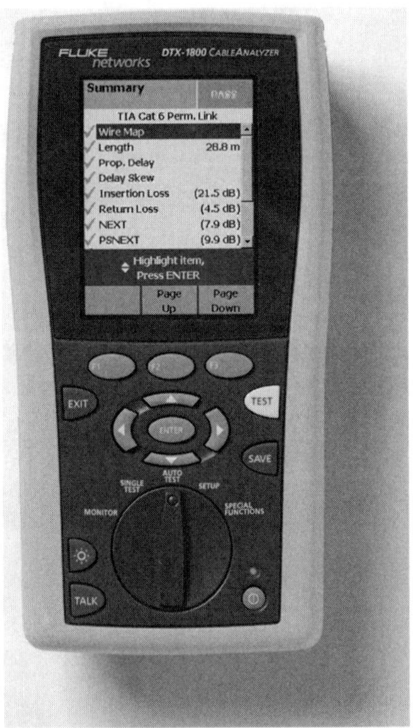

Figure 13-7 A high-end cable performance tester
Courtesy of Fluke Networks

Voltage Event Recorders

Hardware depends on a steady flow of electricity to function properly. The term **voltage event** refers to any condition in which voltage exceeds or drops below predefined levels. In Chapter 14, you will learn how inconsistent or insufficient power can cause problems for network devices. This section describes an instrument that allows you to monitor the electricity flowing to servers, routers, and switches.

This instrument, called a **voltage event recorder**, collects data about power quality. Left plugged into the same outlet that will be used by a network node, it gathers data about the power that outlet will provide to the node. This data is then downloaded to a workstation and analyzed by software that comes with the voltage event recorder. The software can check for and report on any voltage anomalies that exceed preset parameters. For example, you can configure the software to highlight any occasion on which the frequency of the power supplied by an outlet dips below 60 Hz (the standard for North American electrical outlets).

Net+ Voltage event recorders such as the one shown in Figure 13-8 can cost up to $5000.

4.2

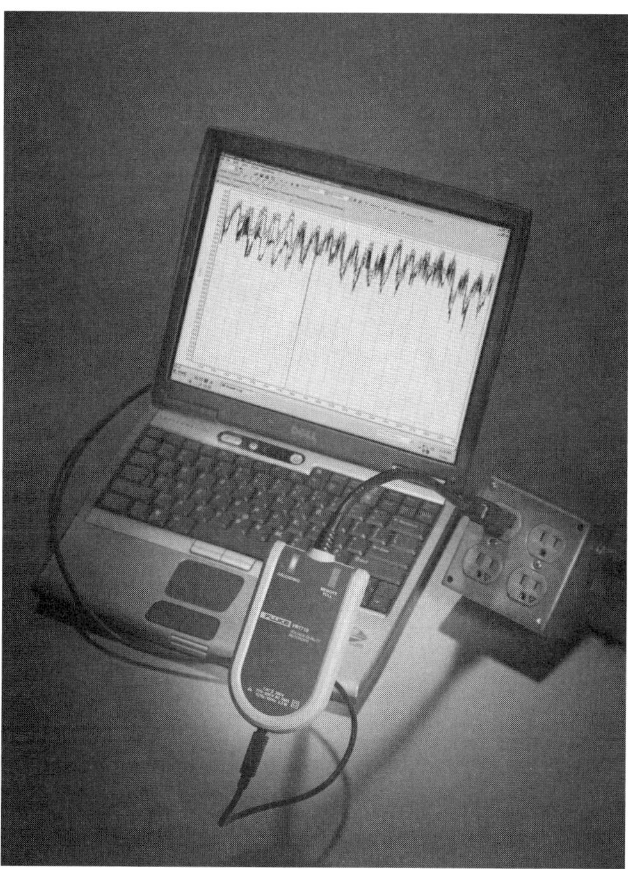

Figure 13-8 Voltage event recorder
Courtesy of Fluke Networks

Butt Set

If you have seen telephone technicians on the job, you have probably noticed the oversized telephone-like devices they carry. This device is known as a **lineman's handset**, a **telephone test set**, or, more commonly, a **butt set** because it can be used to butt into a telephone conversation. A butt set is essentially a rugged and sophisticated telephone. It helps a telephone technician working in the field to determine whether a line is functioning, not only by receiving the signal, but also by picking up any noise that might affect the signal. Some sophisticated butt sets can also perform rudimentary cable testing. For the most part, however, the butt set is a simple means of detecting dial tone on a line.

A butt set contains clips that fasten onto telephone transmission wires, thereby attaching to the local loop just as a telephone would. This connection can occur at the demarc, where a telephone line enters a residence, for example, or at a remote switching facility or at a CO. However, it can only function on lines that have already been demultiplexed. For example, you could not attach a butt set to the ends of a line carrying multiple channels and expect to test one of those channels.

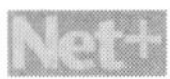 A butt set is shown in Figure 13-9.

4.2

Figure 13-9 Butt set
Courtesy of Fluke Networks

Network Monitors

4.2 4.4 A **network monitor** is a software-based tool that continually monitors network traffic from a server or workstation attached to the network. Network monitors typically can interpret up to Layer 3 of the OSI model. They can determine the protocols passed by each frame, but can't interpret the data inside the frame. By capturing data, they provide either a snapshot of network activity at one point in time or a historical record of network activity over a period of time.

Some NOSs come with network monitoring tools. Microsoft's **Network Monitor** is the tool that ships with Windows operating systems. In addition, you can purchase or download for free network monitoring tools developed by other software companies. Hundreds of such programs exist. After you have worked with one network monitoring tool, you will find that other products work in much the same way. Most even use very similar graphical interfaces.

4.2
4.4

To take advantage of network monitoring and analyzing tools, the network adapter installed in the machine running the software must support promiscuous mode. In **promiscuous mode**, a device driver directs the NIC to pick up all frames that pass over the network—not just those destined for the node served by the card. You can determine whether your network adapter supports promiscuous mode by reading its manual or checking with the manufacturer. Some network monitoring software vendors may even suggest which network adapters to use with their software.

All network monitoring tools can perform at least the following functions:

- Continuously monitor network traffic on a segment
- Capture network data transmitted on a segment
- Capture frames sent to or from a specific node
- Reproduce network conditions by transmitting a selected amount and type of data
- Generate statistics about network activity (for example, what percentage of the total frames transmitted on a segment are broadcast frames)

Some network monitoring tools can also perform the following functions:

- Discover all network nodes on a segment
- Establish a **baseline**, or a record of how the network operates under normal conditions, including its performance, collision rate, utilization rate, and so on
- Store traffic data and generate reports
- Trigger alarms when traffic conditions meet preconfigured conditions (for example, if usage exceeds 50 percent of capacity)

How can capturing data help you solve a problem? Imagine that traffic on a segment of the network you administer suddenly grinds to a halt one morning at about 8:00. You no sooner step in the door than everyone from the help desk calls to tell you how slowly the network is running. Nothing has changed on the network since last night, when it ran normally, so you can think of no obvious reasons for problems.

At the workstation where you have previously installed a network monitoring tool, you capture all data transmissions for approximately five minutes. You then sort the frames in the network monitoring software, arranging the nodes in order based on the volume of traffic each has generated. You might find that one workstation appears at the top of the list with an inordinately high number of bad transmissions. Or, you might discover that a server has been compromised by a hacker and is generating a flood of data over the network.

Before adopting a network monitor or protocol analyzer, you should be aware of some of the data errors that these tools can distinguish. The following list defines some commonly used terms for abnormal data patterns and packets, along with their characteristics:

- ***Local collisions***—Collisions that occur when two or more stations are transmitting simultaneously. A small number of collisions are normal on an Ethernet network. Excessively high collision rates within the network usually result from cable or routing problems.
- ***Late collisions***—Collisions that take place outside the window of time in which they would normally be detected by the network and redressed. Late collisions are usually

Net+ caused by one of several problems, including (1) a defective station (for example, a
4.2 card or transceiver) that is transmitting without first verifying line status, (2)
4.4 mismatched duplex settings between a sending and receiving node, or (3) failure to observe the configuration guidelines for cable length, which results in collisions being recognized too late.

- *Runts*—Packets that are smaller than the medium's minimum packet size. For instance, any Ethernet packet that is smaller than 64 bytes is considered a runt. Runts are often the result of collisions.
- *Giants*—Packets that exceed the medium's maximum packet size. For example, an Ethernet packet larger than 1518 bytes is considered a giant.
- *Jabber*—A device that handles electrical signals improperly, usually affecting the rest of the network. A network analyzer will detect a jabber as a device that is always retransmitting, effectively bringing the network to a halt. A jabber usually results from a bad NIC. Occasionally, it can be caused by outside electrical interference.
- *Negative frame sequence checks*—The result of the CRC (cyclic redundancy check) generated by the originating node not matching the checksum calculated from the data received. It usually indicates noise or transmission problems on the LAN interface or cabling. A high number of negative CRCs usually result from excessive collisions or a station transmitting bad data.
- *Ghosts*—Frames that are not actually data frames, but aberrations caused by a device misinterpreting stray voltage on the wire. Unlike true data frames, ghosts have no starting delimiter.

Network monitors are typically simple tools to master. The following section describes a similar type of tool that provides even more information about a network's traffic.

Net+ Protocol Analyzers

4.2 Similar to a network monitor, a **protocol analyzer** (or **network analyzer**) captures traffic. But
4.3 a protocol analyzer can also analyze frames, typically all the way to Layer 7 of the OSI model. For example, it can identify that a frame uses TCP/IP and, more specifically, that it is an ARP request from one particular workstation to a server. Analyzers can also interpret the payload portion of frames, translating from binary or hexadecimal code to human-readable form. As a result, network analyzers can capture passwords going over the network, if their transmission is not encrypted. Some protocol analyzer software packages can run on a standard workstation, but others require computers equipped with special network adapters and operating system software.

As with network monitoring software, a variety of protocol analyzer software is available. One popular example is the free program called Wireshark. You used this program in the Hands-On Projects in Chapters 5 and 11 to capture and view frames. Essentially, a protocol analyzer performs the same features as the network monitor software discussed previously, plus a few extras. It can also generate traffic in an attempt to reproduce a network problem and monitor multiple network segments simultaneously. Protocol analyzers typically support a multitude of protocols and network topologies. Those programs with graphical interfaces are especially helpful for revealing the traffic flow across the network.

Figure 13-10 illustrates the distribution of traffic captured by a protocol analyzer.

4.2
4.3

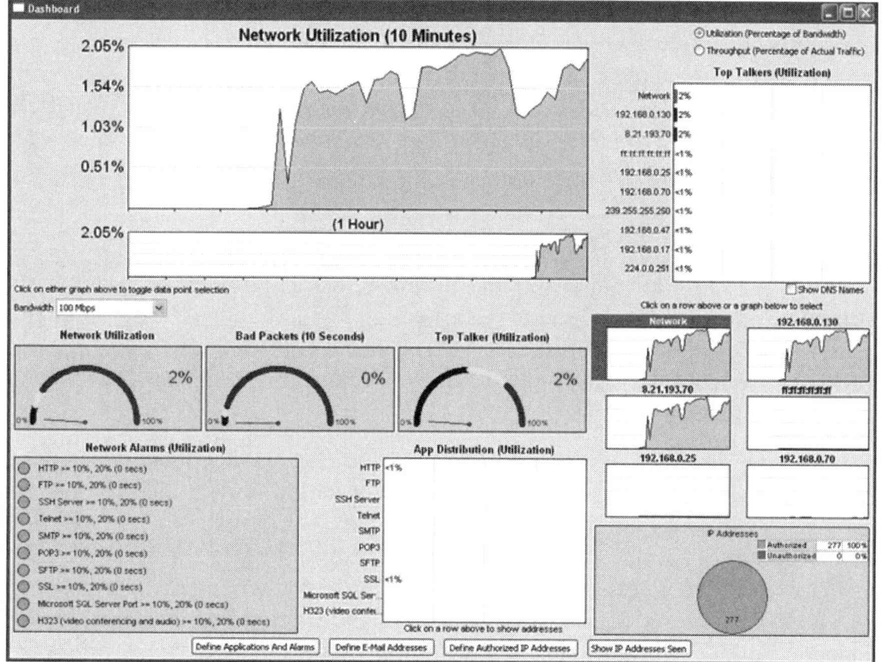

Figure 13-10 Traffic captured by a protocol analyzer

Courtesy of Frontline Test Equipment, Inc.

Before many companies developed protocol analyzing software, a hardware device dedicated to this task, sold by the company Sniffer Technologies and known under the brand name Sniffer, was popular. Just as the brand name Kleenex has become a substitute for the term *facial tissue,* network engineers today might call any protocol analyzer tool a **sniffer** or **packet sniffer**. And now, even the company that bought Sniffer Technologies, NetScout, only sells software-based protocol analyzers.

Protocol analyzers offer a great deal of versatility in the type and depth of information they can reveal. The danger in using this type of tool is that it could collect more information than you or the machine can reasonably process, thus rendering your exercise futile. To avoid this problem, you should set filters on the data gathered. For example, if you suspect that a certain workstation is causing a traffic problem, you should filter the data collection to accept only frames to or from that workstation's MAC address. If you suspect that you have a gateway-related TCP/IP problem, you should set a filter to capture only TCP/IP frames and to ignore other protocols from the gateway's MAC address.

1.4
2.5
4.2
4.3

Recall that using a switch logically separates a network into different segments. If a network is fully switched (that is, if every node is connected to its own switch port), your protocol analyzer can capture only frames destined for the port to which your node is connected. The increasing use of switches has made network monitoring more difficult, but not impossible. One solution to this problem is to reconfigure the switch to reroute the traffic so that your network analyzer can pick up all traffic—that is, to set up port mirroring.

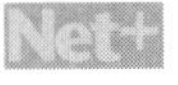

4.2 4.3 Before using a network monitor or protocol analyzer on a network, it's important to know what traffic on your network normally looks like. To obtain this information, you can run the program and capture data for a period of time on a regular basis—for example, every weekday between 8:00 a.m. and noon. You'll generate a lot of data, but you'll also learn a lot about your network. From this data, you can establish a baseline to use as a comparison with future traffic analyses.

Net+

Wireless Network Testers

2.4 Cable continuity and performance testers, of course, will tell you nothing about the wireless connections, stations, or access points on a network. For that, you need tools that contain wireless NICs and run wireless protocols. In fact, you can learn some things about a wireless environment by viewing the wireless network connection properties on your workstation, as you learned in Chapter 8.

However, viewing the status of the wireless connection on your workstation tells you only a little about your wireless environment—and this information only applies to one workstation. Many programs exist that can scan for wireless signals over a certain geographical range and discover all the access points and wireless stations transmitting in the area. This is useful for determining whether an access point is functioning properly, whether it is positioned correctly so that all the stations it serves are within its range, and whether stations and access points are communicating over the proper channels within a frequency band. Some programs can also capture the data transmitted between stations and access points. This information is useful for troubleshooting wireless connection problems (for example, poor performance or intermittent faults) after you've verified that connectivity is present. And some programs contain a **spectrum analyzer**, a tool that can assess the quality of the wireless signal. Spectrum analysis is useful, for example, to ascertain where interference is greatest.

Software that can perform wireless network assessment is often available for free and may be provided by the access point's manufacturer. Following is a list of specific capabilities common to wireless network testing tools:

- Identify transmitting access points and stations and the channels over which they are communicating
- Measure signal strength from and determine the range of an access point
- Indicate the effects of attenuation, signal loss, and noise
- Interpret signal strength information to rate potential access point locations
- Ensure proper association and reassociation when moving between access points
- Capture and interpret traffic exchanged between wireless access points and stations
- Measure throughput and assess data transmission errors
- Analyze the characteristics of each channel within a frequency band to indicate the clearest channels

Some companies have created testing instruments whose sole purpose is to assess the status of wireless networks. These tools can perform the same detection, data capture, and spectrum analysis functions as the software tools described previously. One advantage to using such devices, however, is that they are typically more portable than a laptop or desktop workstation. Second, they come installed with all the wireless network analysis tools you'll need, and

these are usually accessible from one simple, graphical interface. A third advantage is that
2.4 most wireless testing tools contain more powerful antennas than a workstation NIC. A more powerful antenna could mean the difference between assessing the wireless network for an entire building from your desk versus walking around to each floor with your laptop. Figure 13-11 shows one example of such a wireless network testing tool.

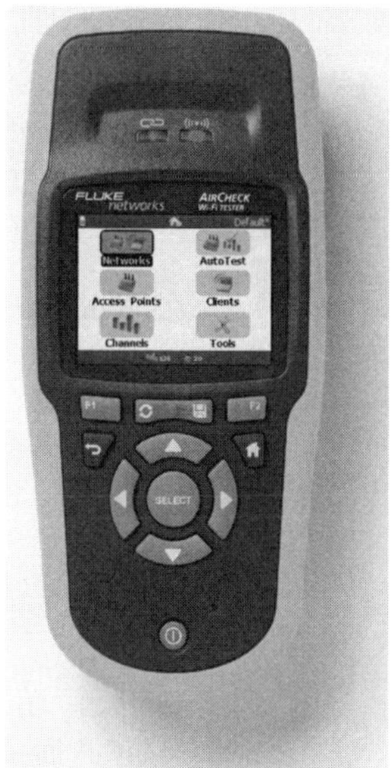

Figure 13-11 Wireless network testing tool
Courtesy of Fluke Networks

Chapter Summary

- The key to solving network problems is to approach them methodically and logically, using your experience to inform your decisions and knowing when to ask for someone else's help.
- The first step in troubleshooting is identifying the problem and its symptoms. Symptoms can include error messages, the inability to perform certain functions on the network, performance issues with connections or devices, or the inability to connect to a network. Record what you learn about symptoms.
- Part of identifying the problem is defining the affected area. In general, a network problem may be limited to one user; all users on a segment; all users on a network; certain types of users, departments, or locations; or certain times of the day or week. Also, question the user to make sure he is performing all functions correctly.
- At each point in the troubleshooting process, stop to consider what kind of changes have occurred on the network that might have created a problem. Changes pertaining to hardware may include the addition of a new device, the removal of an old device, a component upgrade, a cabling upgrade, or an equipment move. Changes pertaining to software may include an operating system upgrade, a device driver upgrade, a new application, or a changed configuration.

- After gathering information about a problem and its symptoms, attempt to re-create the problem and then assess physical and logical connectivity related to it. These steps help establish a theory of probable cause for the problem.
- Next, test your theory to determine whether it truly is the problem's cause. For example, check or try replacing physical components. Review client, server, and device configurations. Use tools such as ping and traceroute to test physical and logical connectivity.
- Establish a plan of action to resolve the problem. Assess the scope, trade-offs, security implications, scalability, and cost of your plan. Refer to vendor documentation. If necessary, review your plan with a more experienced colleague to be sure it is sound.
- Implement the solution or escalate the troubleshooting process. That is, decide whether you and other first-level support personnel can solve the problem or whether it should be transferred to second- or third-level support personnel. Whether or not the problem is escalated, you or the appropriate troubleshooting personnel should alert all users who might be affected by any changes. Keep notes about your troubleshooting handy and create ways of backing out of the change if something goes wrong (for example, store a copy of a switch's configuration before you make significant changes to it).
- After implementing a solution, verify full system functionality to ensure that you solved the problem and haven't created new problems. The type of testing you perform will depend on your solution. If the solution required significant network changes, revisit the solution a day or two after you implement it to verify that it has truly worked and not caused additional problems.
- Finally, document findings, actions, and outcomes. Some organizations use a software program for documenting problems, known as a call tracking system (or help desk software). These programs provide a user-friendly graphical interface that prompts the user for every piece of information associated with the problem.
- A tone generator and tone locator are used to identify the terminating location of a wire pair.
- A multimeter is a simple device that can measure the voltage, resistance, impedance, and other characteristics of an electrical circuit. On a network, it can, among other things, verify proper cable terminations and detect noise that might adversely affect a connection.
- Basic cable continuity testers determine whether your cabling can provide connectivity. In the case of copper-based cables, they apply a small voltage to each conductor at one end of the cable, and then check whether that voltage is detectable at the other end. A good cable checker will also verify that the wires are paired correctly and that they are not shorted, exposed, or crossed.
- A cable performance tester accomplishes the same continuity and fault tests as a continuity tester, but also ensures that the cable length is not too long, measures the distance to a cable fault, measures attenuation along a cable, measures near-end cross talk between wires, measures termination resistance and impedance, issues pass/fail ratings for Cat 3, Cat 5, Cat 5e, Cat 6, Cat 6a, and Cat 7 standards, and stores and prints test results.

- A voltage event recorder captures information about power quality. The data captured by the voltage event recorder can then be analyzed using the accompanying software. Analyzing the data allows you to pinpoint any power anomalies, such as excessive current or drops in voltage.
- A butt set is a common term for a telephone test set or lineman's handset, a tool that resembles an oversized telephone and allows technicians to access and test a local loop telephone connection.
- A network monitor is a software-based tool that monitors network traffic from a server or workstation attached to the network. Network monitors typically can interpret up to Layer 3 of the OSI model. They can determine the protocols passed by each packet, but can't interpret the data inside the packet.
- Protocol analyzers can typically interpret data up to Layer 7 of the OSI model. They can also interpret the payload portion of packets, translating from binary or hexadecimal code to human-readable form. Protocol analyzers may be software programs or devices dedicated to protocol analysis.
- Wireless network testing tools can be dedicated instruments or software that runs on a workstation (usually a laptop). They can discover wireless access points and stations, measure signal strength and interference, capture and interpret wireless data, measure throughput and identify data errors, and ensure proper association and reassociation between stations and access points.

Key Terms

baseline A record of how a network operates under normal conditions (including its performance, collision rate, utilization rate, and so on). Baselines are used for comparison when conditions change.

butt set A tool for accessing and testing a telephone company's local loop. The butt set, also known as a telephone test set or lineman's handset, is essentially a telephone handset with attached wires that can be connected to local loop terminations at a demarc or switching facility.

cable checker *See* continuity tester.

cable performance tester A troubleshooting tool that tests cables for continuity, but can also measure cross talk, attenuation, and impedance; identify the location of faults; and store or print cable testing results.

cable tester A device that tests cables for one or more of the following conditions: continuity, segment length, distance to a fault, attenuation along a cable, near-end cross talk, and termination resistance and impedance. Cable testers may also issue pass/fail ratings for wiring standards or store and print cable testing results.

call tracking system A software program used to document technical problems and how they were resolved (also known as help desk software).

change management system A process or program that provides support personnel with a centralized means of documenting changes made to the network.

continuity tester An instrument that tests whether voltage (or light, in the case of fiber-optic cable) issued at one end of a cable can be detected at the opposite end of the cable. A continuity tester can indicate whether the cable will successfully transmit a signal.

escalate In network troubleshooting, to refer a problem to someone with deeper knowledge about the subject. For example, a first-level support person might escalate a router configuration issue to a second- or third-level support person.

first-level support In network troubleshooting, the person or group who initially fields requests for help from users.

ghost A frame that is not actually a data frame, but rather an aberration caused by a device misinterpreting stray voltage on the wire. Unlike true data frames, ghosts have no starting delimiter.

giant A packet that exceeds the medium's maximum packet size. For example, any Ethernet packet that is larger than 1518 bytes is considered a giant.

help desk analyst A person who's proficient in basic (but not usually advanced) workstation and network troubleshooting. Help desk analysts are part of first-level support.

help desk coordinator A person who ensures that help desk analysts are divided into the correct teams, schedules shifts at the help desk, and maintains the infrastructure to enable analysts to better perform their jobs. They might also serve as third-level support personnel, taking responsibility for troubleshooting a problem when the second-level support analyst is unable to solve it.

jabber A device that handles electrical signals improperly, usually affecting the rest of the network. A network analyzer will detect a jabber as a device that is always retransmitting, effectively bringing the network to a halt. A jabber usually results from a bad NIC. Occasionally, it can be caused by outside electrical interference.

late collision A collision that takes place outside the normal window in which collisions are detected and redressed. Late collisions are usually caused by a defective station (such as a card or transceiver) that is transmitting without first verifying line status or by failure to observe the configuration guidelines for cable length, which results in collisions being recognized too late.

lineman's handset *See* butt set.

local collision A collision that occurs when two or more stations are transmitting simultaneously. Excessively high collision rates within the network can usually be traced to cable or routing problems.

multimeter A simple instrument that can measure multiple characteristics of an electric circuit, including its resistance and voltage.

negative frame sequence check The result of the CRC (cyclic redundancy check) generated by the originating node not matching the checksum calculated from the data received. It usually indicates noise or transmission problems on the LAN interface or cabling. A high number of (nonmatching) CRCs usually results from excessive collisions or a station transmitting bad data.

network analyzer *See* protocol analyzer.

network monitor A software-based tool that monitors traffic on the network from a server or workstation attached to the network. Network monitors typically can interpret up to Layer 3 of the OSI model.

Network Monitor A network monitoring program from Microsoft that comes with Windows operating systems.

ohmmeter A device used to measure resistance in an electrical circuit.

optical time domain reflectometer *See* OTDR.

OTDR (optical time domain reflectometer) A performance testing device for use with fiber-optic networks. An OTDR works by issuing a light-based signal on a fiber-optic cable and measuring the way in which the signal bounces back (or reflects) to the OTDR. By measuring the length of time it takes the signal to return, an OTDR can determine the location of a fault.

packet sniffer *See* protocol analyzer.

probe *See* tone locator.

promiscuous mode The feature of a network adapter that allows it to pick up all frames that pass over the network—not just those destined for the node served by the card.

protocol analyzer A software package or hardware-based tool that can capture and analyze data on a network. Protocol analyzers are more sophisticated than network monitoring tools, as they can typically interpret data up to Layer 7 of the OSI model.

second-level support In network troubleshooting, a person or group with deeper knowledge about a subject and to whom first-level support personnel escalate problems.

sniffer *See* protocol analyzer.

spectrum analyzer A tool that assesses the characteristics (for example, frequency, amplitude, and the effects of interference) of wireless signals.

supported services list A document that lists every service and software package supported within an organization, plus the names of first- and second-level support contacts for those services or software packages.

TDR (time domain reflectometer) A high-end instrument for testing the qualities of a cable. It works by issuing a signal on a cable and measuring the way in which the signal bounces back (or reflects) to the TDR. Many performance testers rely on TDRs.

telephone test set *See* butt set.

third-level support In network troubleshooting, a person or group with deep knowledge about specific networking topics to whom second-level support personnel escalate challenging problems.

time domain reflectometer *See* TDR.

tone generator A small electronic device that issues a signal on a wire pair. When used in conjunction with a tone locator, it can help locate the termination of a wire pair.

tone locator A small electronic device that emits a tone when it detects electrical activity on a wire pair. When used in conjunction with a tone generator, it can help locate the termination of a wire pair.

toner *See* tone generator.

voltage event Any condition in which voltage exceeds or drops below predefined levels.

voltage event recorder A device that, when plugged into the same outlet that will be used by a network node, gathers data about the power that outlet will provide the node.

voltmeter A device used to measure voltage (or electrical pressure) on an electrical circuit.

Review Questions

1. What is the first step when troubleshooting network problems as recommended by CompTIA?
   a. Establish a plan of action.
   b. Establish a theory of probable cause.
   c. Identify the problem.
   d. Verify full system functionality.
2. In determining the most probable cause of a problem, which step should be conducted first?
   a. Review and analyze recent changes.
   b. Determine what areas are affected.
   c. Identity the symptoms.
   d. Ensure that human error is not the source of the problem.
3. What type of personnel are highly skilled in one area of networking?
   a. First-level support
   b. Second-level support
   c. Third-level support
   d. Help desk coordinator
4. When troubleshooting a Physical layer problem, which tool would you use to test whether your cable is carrying a signal to its destination?
   a. Tone generator
   b. Continuity tester
   c. Tone locator
   d. Butt set
5. Which data error describes a packet that is smaller than the medium's minimum packet size?
   a. Jabber
   b. Ghosts
   c. Runts
   d. Bot
6. True or false? When attempting to reproduce the symptoms of a problem, you should follow the same steps that the person reporting the symptoms followed.

7. True or false? By some estimates, more than half of all network problems occur at the Logical layer of the OSI model.
8. True or false? Logical connectivity problems often prove more difficult to isolate and resolve than physical connectivity problems.
9. True or false? Tone generators and tone locators can be used to determine characteristics about a cable.
10. True or false? The difference between continuity testers and performance testers lies in their sophistication and price.
11. Some organizations use a software program for documenting problems, known as a(n) ________________ system.
12. A(n) ________________ is a simple instrument that can measure the voltage, resistance, impedance, and other characteristics of an electrical circuit.
13. A(n) ________________ is a software-based tool that continually monitors network traffic from a server or workstation attached to the network.
14. A(n) ________________ analyzer (or network analyzer) captures traffic and can analyze frames, typically all the way to Layer 7 of the OSI model.
15. A(n) ________________ is a tool that can assess the quality of the wireless signal.

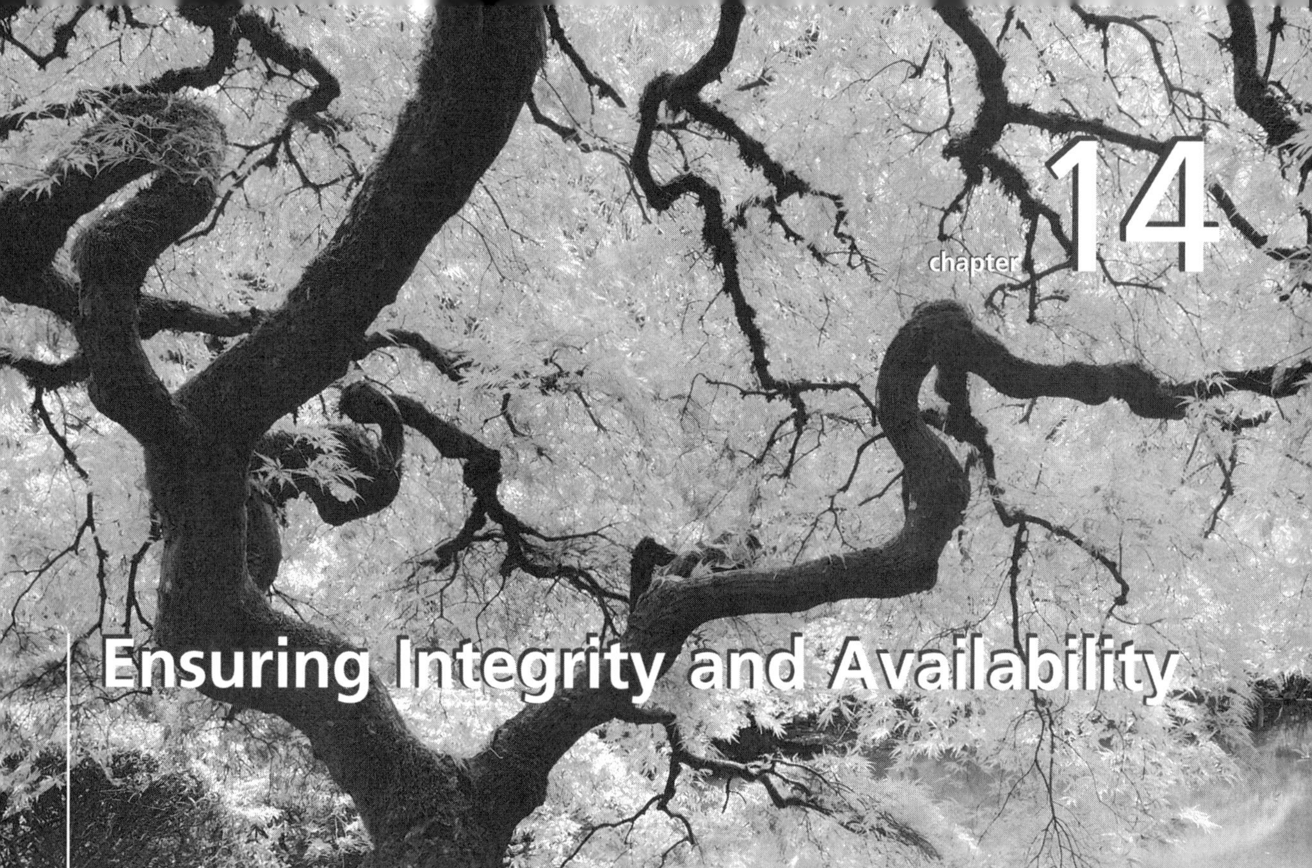

After reading this chapter and completing the exercises, you will be able to:

- Identify the characteristics of a network that keep data safe from loss or damage
- Protect an enterprise-wide network from malware
- Explain fault-tolerance techniques for storage, network design, connectivity devices, naming and addressing services, and servers
- Discuss best practices for network backup and recovery
- Describe the components of a useful disaster recovery plan and the options for disaster contingencies

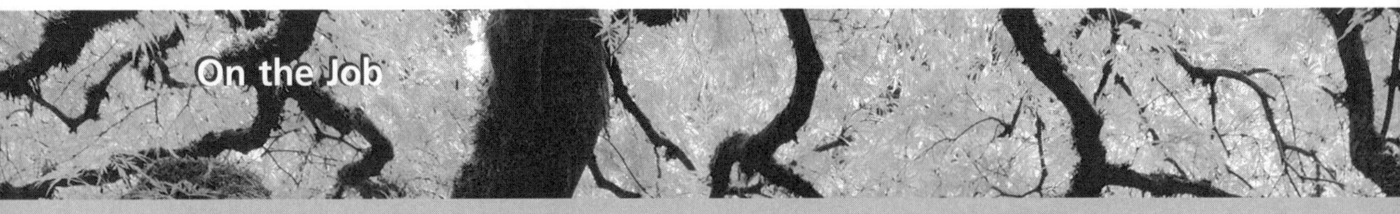

On the Job

Framus Video, a motion picture postproduction house, was in dire and fairly immediate need of more storage for a major movie studio project. At the time, I worked as National Sales Manager for a storage hardware vendor. I accompanied the dealer handling the company on a visit to the customer. My goal was to walk both the dealer and the customer through the decision-making process for acquiring storage. Frank, the customer's IT manager, was not conversant with issues related to storage, but he knew he needed more.

People constantly overcomplicate the storage buying process. Often, people want to buy the latest, fastest, and greatest storage, with no thought about cost. More often than not, they want a luxury car on a subcompact budget. This was the case here, a decision Frank made that resulted from conducting his own Internet research without fully understanding the issues.

The bottom line is that, when buying storage, you need to consider what your company really needs. The first question we considered was how much storage capacity Framus Video required. We needed to consider both the company's immediate and future needs. After talking it over, we decided that Framus needed 50 TB right away, expanding to 250 TB over the course of the ensuing year.

Performance requirements, the second consideration, are generally rated in terms of throughput (measured in terms of MB/s) and I/O (input/output transactions per second). Video applications, like those Framus was using, require throughput as well as larger capacities.

Operating systems and network environments were the next consideration. It turned out that the company's OS and network environment were both pure Mac. A single OS/network environment made storage planning much easier.

The last major consideration, of course, was budget. Could Framus Video afford a luxury car? No. We needed to look at what the company actually needed. A 250TB capacity might seem like a large amount of available storage. But in the movie industry, major studios will push 1 PB (petabyte) for a single movie. Because of the company's performance requirements, we settled on a Fibre Channel SAN, which would provide speed, bandwidth, and capacity, without disrupting the company's regular data network.

Within a week and a half, Framus was up and running. The company now has the ability to acquire more storage on the fly without disrupting the working environment.

Paul Snapp
Regional Manager, Infortrend Corporation

Because networks are a vital part of keeping an organization running, you must pay attention to measures that keep LANs and WANs safe and available. You can never assume that data is safe on the network until you have taken explicit measures to protect the information. In this book, you have learned about building scalable, reliable, enterprise-wide networks as well as selecting the most appropriate hardware, topologies, and services to operate your network. You have also learned about security measures to guard network access and resources. In this chapter, you will learn about protecting networks and their resources from the adverse effects of power flaws, hardware or system failures, malware, and natural disasters.

What Are Integrity and Availability?

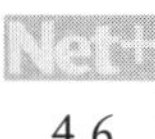

4.6

In the world of networking, the term **integrity** refers to the soundness of a network's programs, data, services, devices, and connections. To ensure a network's integrity, you must protect it from anything that might render it unusable. Closely related to the concept of integrity is availability. The term **availability** refers to how consistently and reliably a file or system can be accessed by authorized personnel. For example, a server that allows staff to log on and use its programs and data 99.99% of the time is considered highly available, whereas one that is functional only 98% of the time is less available. Another way to consider availability is by measuring a system or network's **uptime**, which is the duration or percentage of time it functions normally between failures. As shown in Table 14-1, a system that experiences 99.999% uptime is *unavailable*, on average, only 5 minutes and 15 seconds per year.

Table 14-1 Availability and downtime equivalents

Availability	Downtime per day	Downtime per month	Downtime per year
99%	14 minutes, 23 seconds	7 hours, 18 minutes, 17 seconds	87 hours, 39 minutes, 29 seconds
99.9%	1 minute, 26 seconds	43 minutes, 49 seconds	8 hours, 45 minutes, 56 seconds
99.99%	8 seconds	4 minutes, 22 seconds	52 minutes, 35 seconds
99.999%	.4 seconds	26 seconds	5 minutes, 15 seconds

On a computer running Linux or UNIX, you can view the length of time your system has been running by typing `uptime` at the command prompt and pressing Enter. Microsoft offers an uptime.exe utility that allows you to do the same from a computer running a Windows operating system.

A number of phenomena can compromise both integrity and availability, including security breaches, natural disasters, malicious intruders, power flaws, and human error. Every network administrator should consider these possibilities when designing a sound network. You can readily imagine the importance of integrity and availability of data in a hospital, for example, in which the network stores patient records and also provides quick medical reference material, video displays for surgical cameras, and control of critical care monitors.

Although you can't predict every type of vulnerability, you can take measures to guard against most damaging events. Later in this chapter, you will learn about specific approaches to data protection. Following are some general guidelines for keeping your network highly available:

4.6
5.4

- *Allow only network administrators to create or modify NOS (network operating system) and application system files*—Pay attention to the permissions assigned to regular users (including the groups "users" or "everyone" and the username "guest"). Bear in mind that the worst consequence of applying overly stringent file restrictions is an inconvenience to users. In contrast, the worst consequence of applying overly lenient file restrictions could be a failed network.
- *Monitor the network for unauthorized access or changes*—You can install programs that routinely check whether and when the files you've specified have changed. Such monitoring programs are typically inexpensive and easy to customize. Some enable the system to text or e-mail you when a system file changes.
- *Record authorized system changes in a change management system*—You have learned about the importance of change management when troubleshooting networks. Routine changes should also be documented in a change management system. Recording system changes enables you and your colleagues to understand what's happening to your network and protect it from harm. For example, suppose that the remote access service on a Linux server has stopped accepting connections. Before taking troubleshooting steps that might create more problems and further reduce the availability of the system, you could review the change management log. It might indicate that a colleague recently installed an update to the Linux NOS. With this information in hand, you could focus on the update as a likely source of the problem.
- *Install redundant components*—The term **redundancy** refers to an implementation in which more than one component is installed and ready to use for storing, processing, or transporting data. Redundancy is intended to eliminate single points of failure. To maintain high availability, you should ensure that critical network elements, such as your connection to the Internet or your file server's hard disk, are redundant. Some types of redundancy—for example, redundant sources of electrical power for a building—require large investments, so your organization should weigh the risks of losing connectivity or data against the cost of adding duplicate components.
- *Perform regular health checks on the network*—Prevention is the best weapon against network downtime. By establishing a baseline and regular network monitoring, you can anticipate problems before they affect availability or integrity. For example, if your network monitor alerts you to rapidly rising utilization on a critical network segment, you can analyze the network to discover where the problem lies and perhaps fix it before it takes down the segment.
- *Check system performance, error logs, and the system log book regularly*—By keeping track of system errors and trends in performance, you have a better chance of correcting problems before they cause a hard disk failure and potentially damage your system files. By default, all NOSs keep error logs. On a Linux server, for example, a file called "messages" located in the `/var/log` directory collects error messages from system services, such as DNS, and other programs also save log files in the /var/log directory. It's important that you know where these error logs reside on your server and understand how to interpret them.
- *Keep backups, system images, and emergency repair disks current and available*—If your file system or critical boot files become corrupted by a system crash, you can use backups or system images to recover the system. Otherwise, you might need to reinstall the software before you can start the system. If you ever face the situation of

recovering from a system loss or disaster, you must recover in the quickest manner
4.6 possible. For this effort, you need a backup strategy tailored to your environment.

5.4 • *Implement and enforce security and disaster recovery policies*—Everyone in your organization should know what he is allowed to do on the network. For example, if you decide that it's too risky for employees to download games off the Internet because of the potential for virus infection, you should inform them of a ban on downloading games. You might enforce this policy by restricting users' ability to create or change executable files that are copied to the workstation during the downloading of games. Making such decisions and communicating them to staff should be part of your IT policy. Likewise, key personnel in your organization should be familiar with your disaster recovery plan, which should detail your strategy for restoring network functionality in case of an unexpected failure. Although such policies take time to develop and might be difficult to enforce, they can directly affect your network's availability and integrity.

These measures are merely first steps to ensuring network integrity and availability, but they are essential. The following sections describe what types of policies, hardware, and software you can implement to achieve availability and integrity, beginning with malware detection and prevention.

Malware

5.4 **Malware** refers to any program or piece of code designed to intrude upon or harm a system or its resources. The term *malware* is derived from a combination of the words *malicious* and *software*. Included in this category are viruses, Trojan horses, worms, and bots, all of which are described in this section.

Strictly speaking, a **virus** is a program that replicates itself with the intent to infect more computers, either through network connections or through the exchange of external storage devices. Viruses are typically copied to a computer's storage device without the user's knowledge. A virus might damage files or systems, or it might simply annoy users by flashing messages or pictures on the screen, for example. In fact, some viruses cause no harm and can remain unnoticed on a system indefinitely.

Many other unwanted and potentially destructive programs are often called viruses, but technically do not meet the criteria used to define a virus. For example, a program that disguises itself as something useful but actually harms your system is called a **Trojan horse** (or simply, **Trojan**), after the famous wooden horse in which soldiers were hidden. Because Trojan horses do not replicate themselves, they are not considered viruses. An example of a Trojan horse is an executable file that someone sends you over the Internet, promising that the executable will install a great new game, when in fact it erases data on your hard disk or mails spam to all the users in your e-mail program's address book.

In this section, you will learn about the different viruses and other malware that can infect your network, their methods of distribution, and, most important, protection against them. Malware can harm computers running any type of operating system— Macintosh, Windows, Linux, or UNIX—at any time. As a network administrator, you must take measures to guard against them.

Malware Types and Characteristics

5.4 Malware can be classified into different categories based on where it resides on a computer and how it propagates itself. All malware belongs to one of the following categories:

- *Boot sector viruses*—**Boot sector viruses** position their code in the boot sector of a computer's hard disk so that when the computer boots up, the virus runs in place of the computer's normal system files. Boot sector viruses are commonly spread from external storage devices to hard disks. Boot sector viruses vary in their destructiveness. Some merely display a screen advertising the virus's presence when you boot the infected computer. Others do not advertise themselves, but stealthily destroy system files or make it impossible for the file system to access at least some of the computer's files. Examples of boot sector viruses include Michelangelo and the Stoned virus, which was widespread in the early 1990s (in fact, it disabled U.S. military computers during the 1991 Persian Gulf War) and persists today in many variations. Until you disinfect a computer that harbors a boot sector virus, the virus propagates to every external disk to which that computer writes information. Removing a boot sector virus first requires rebooting the computer from an uninfected, write-protected disk with system files on it. Only after the computer is booted from a source other than the infected hard disk can you run software to remove the boot sector virus.
- *Macro viruses*—**Macro viruses** take the form of a macro (such as the kind used in a word-processing or spreadsheet program), which can be executed as the user works with a program. For example, you might send a Microsoft Word document as an attachment to an e-mail message. If that document contains a macro virus, when the recipient opens the document, the macro runs, and all future documents created or saved by that program are infected. Macro viruses were the first type of virus to infect data files rather than executable files. They are quick to emerge and spread because they are easy to write, and because users share data files more frequently than executable files.
- *File-infector viruses*—**File-infector viruses** attach themselves to executable files. When an infected executable file runs, the virus copies itself to memory. Later, the virus attaches itself to other executable files. Some file-infector viruses attach themselves to other programs even while their "host" executable runs a process in the background, such as a printer service or screen saver program. Because they stay in memory while you continue to work on your computer, these viruses can have devastating consequences, infecting numerous programs and requiring that you disinfect your computer, as well as reinstall virtually all software.
- *Worms*—**Worms** are programs that run independently and travel between computers and across networks. They may be transmitted by any type of file transfer, including e-mail attachments. Worms do not alter other programs in the same way that viruses do, but they can carry viruses. Because they can transport and hide viruses, you should be concerned about picking up worms when you exchange files from the Internet, via e-mail, or through disks.
- *Trojan horse*—As mentioned earlier, a Trojan horse is a program that claims to do something useful but instead harms the computer or system. Trojan horses range from being nuisances to causing significant system destruction. The best way to guard against Trojan horses is to refrain from downloading an executable file whose origins you can't confirm. Suppose, for example, that you needed to download a new driver

Net+ for a NIC on your network. Rather than going to a generic "network support site" on
5.4 the Internet, you should download the file from the NIC manufacturer's Web site.
Most important, never run an executable file that was sent to you over the Internet
as an attachment to a mail message whose sender or origins you cannot verify.

- *Network viruses*—**Network viruses** propagate themselves via network protocols, commands, messaging programs, and data links. Although all viruses can theoretically travel across network connections, network viruses are specially designed to take advantage of network vulnerabilities. For example, a network virus may attach itself to FTP transactions to and from your Web server. Another type of network virus may spread through Microsoft Outlook messages only.
- *Bots*—Another malware category defined by its propagation method is a bot. In networking, the term **bot** (short for robot) means a program that runs automatically, without requiring a person to start or stop it. One type of bot is a virus that propagates itself automatically between systems. It does not require an unsuspecting user to download and run an executable file or to boot from an infected disk, for example. Many bots spread through the **IRC (Internet Relay Chat)**, a protocol that enables users running IRC client software to communicate instantly with other participants in a chat room on the Internet. Chat rooms require an IRC server, which accepts messages from an IRC client and either broadcasts the messages to all other chat room participants (in an open chat room) or sends the message to select users (in a restricted chat room). Malicious bots take advantage of IRC to transmit data, commands, or executable programs from one infected participant to others. After a bot has copied files on a client's hard disk, these files can be used to damage or destroy a computer's data or system files, issue objectionable content, and further propagate the malware. Bots are especially difficult to contain because of their fast, surreptitious, and distributed dissemination.

Certain characteristics can make malware harder to detect and eliminate. Some of these characteristics, which can be found in any type of malware, include the following:

- *Encryption*—Some viruses, worms, and Trojan horses are encrypted to prevent detection. Most anti-malware software searches files for a recognizable string of characters that identify the virus. However, an **encrypted virus**, for example, might thwart the antivirus program's attempts to detect it.

- *Stealth*—Some malware hides itself to prevent detection. For example, **stealth viruses** disguise themselves as legitimate programs or replace part of a legitimate program's code with their destructive code.
- *Polymorphism*—**Polymorphic viruses** change their characteristics (such as the arrangement of their bytes, size, and internal instructions) every time they are transferred to a new system, making them harder to identify. Some polymorphic viruses use complicated algorithms and incorporate nonsensical commands to achieve their changes. Polymorphic viruses are considered the most sophisticated and potentially dangerous type of virus.
- *Time dependence*—Some viruses, worms, and Trojan horses are programmed to activate on a particular date. This type of malware can remain dormant and harmless until its activation date arrives. Like any other malware, time-dependent malware can have destructive effects or might cause some innocuous event periodically. For

5.4 example, viruses in the "Time" family cause a PC's speaker to beep approximately once per hour. Time-dependent malware can include **logic bombs**, or programs designed to start when certain conditions are met. (Although logic bombs can also activate when other types of conditions, such as a specific change to a file, are met, and they are not always malicious.)

Malware can exhibit more than one of the preceding characteristics. The Natas virus, for example, combines polymorphism and stealth techniques to create a very destructive virus. Hundreds of new viruses, worms, Trojan horses, and bots are unleashed on the world's computers each month. Although it is impossible to keep abreast of every virus in circulation, you should at least know where you can find out more information about malware. An excellent resource for learning about new viruses, their characteristics, and ways to get rid of them is McAfee's Virus Information Library at *home.mcafee.com/virusinfo/*.

Malware Protection

You might think that you can simply install a virus-scanning program on your network and move to the next issue. In fact, protection against harmful code involves more than just installing anti-malware software. It requires choosing the most appropriate anti-malware program for your environment, monitoring the network, continually updating the anti-malware program, and educating users.

Anti-Malware Software Even if a user doesn't immediately notice malware on her system, the harmful software generally leaves evidence of itself, whether by changing the operation of the machine or by announcing its signature characteristics in the malware code. Although the latter can be detected only via anti-malware software, users can typically detect the operational changes without any special software. For example, you might suspect a virus on your system if any of the following symptoms appear:

- Unexplained increases in file sizes
- Significant, unexplained decline in system or network performance (for example, a program takes much longer than usual to start or to save a file)
- Unusual error messages appear without probable cause
- Significant, unexpected loss of system memory
- Periodic, unexpected rebooting
- Fluctuations in display quality

Often, however, you don't notice malware until it has already damaged your files.

Although malware programmers have become more sophisticated in disguising their software, anti-malware software programmers have kept pace with them. The anti-malware software you choose for your network should at least perform the following functions:

- Detect malware through **signature scanning**, a comparison of a file's content with known malware signatures (that is, the unique identifying characteristics in the code) in a signature database. This signature database must be frequently updated so that the software can detect new viruses as they emerge. Updates can be downloaded from the anti-malware software vendor's Web site. Alternatively, you can configure such updates to be copied from the Internet to your computer automatically, with or without your consent.

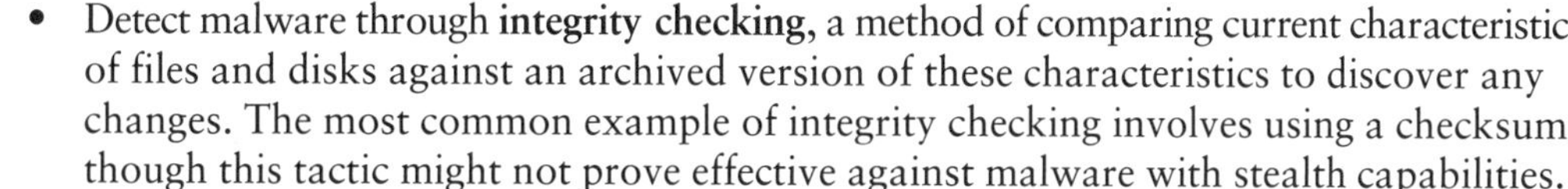

Net+ 5.4

- Detect malware through **integrity checking**, a method of comparing current characteristics of files and disks against an archived version of these characteristics to discover any changes. The most common example of integrity checking involves using a checksum, though this tactic might not prove effective against malware with stealth capabilities.
- Detect malware by monitoring unexpected file changes or viruslike behaviors.
- Receive regular updates and modifications from a centralized network console. The vendor should provide free upgrades on a regular (at least monthly) basis, plus technical support.
- Consistently report only valid instances of malware, rather than reporting false alarms. Scanning techniques that attempt to identify malware by discovering "malware like" behavior, also known as **heuristic scanning**, are the most fallible and most likely to emit false alarms.

Your implementation of anti-malware software depends on your computing environment's needs. For example, you might use a desktop security program on every computer on the network that prevents users from copying executable files to their hard disks or to network drives. In this case, it might be unnecessary to implement a program that continually scans each machine; in fact, this approach might be undesirable because the continual scanning adversely affects performance. On the other hand, if you are the network administrator for a student computer lab where potentially thousands of different users bring their own USB drives for use on the computers, you will want to scan the machines thoroughly at least once a day and perhaps more often.

When implementing anti-malware software on a network, one of your most important decisions is where to install the software. If you install anti-malware software only on every desktop, you have addressed the most likely point of entry, but ignored the most important files that might be infected—those on the server. If the anti-malware software resides on the server and checks every file and transaction, you will protect important files but slow your network performance considerably. To find a balance between sufficient protection and minimal impact on performance, you must examine your network's vulnerabilities and critical performance needs.

Anti-Malware Policies

Anti-malware software alone will not keep your network safe from malicious code. Because most malware can be prevented by applying a little technology and forethought, it's important that all network users understand how to prevent the spread of malware. An anti-malware policy provides rules for using anti-malware software, as well as policies for installing programs, sharing files, and using external disks such as flash drives. To be most effective, anti-malware policy should be authorized and supported by the organization's management. Suggestions for anti-malware policy guidelines include the following:

- Every computer in an organization should be equipped with malware detection and cleaning software that regularly scans for malware. This software should be centrally distributed and updated to stay current with newly released malware.
- Users should not be allowed to alter or disable the anti-malware software.
- Users should know what to do in case their anti-malware program detects malware. For example, you might recommend that the user stop working on his computer, and instead call the help desk to receive assistance in disinfecting the system.

5.4

- An anti-malware team should be appointed to focus on maintaining the anti-malware measures. This team would be responsible for choosing anti-malware software, keeping the software updated, educating users, and responding in case of a significant malware outbreak.
- Users should be prohibited from installing any unauthorized software on their systems. This edict might seem extreme, but in fact users downloading programs (especially games) from the Internet are a common source of malware. If your organization permits game playing, you might institute a policy in which every game must be first checked for malware and then installed on a user's system by a technician.
- System wide alerts should be issued to network users notifying them of a serious malware threat and advising them how to prevent infection, even if the malware hasn't been detected on your network yet.

When drafting an anti-malware policy, bear in mind that these measures are not meant to restrict users' freedom, but rather to protect the network from damage and downtime. Explain to users that the anti-malware policy protects their own data as well as critical system files. If possible, automate the anti-malware software installation and operation so that users barely notice its presence. Do not rely on users to run their anti-malware software each time they insert a USB drive or open an e-mail attachment because they will quickly forget to do so.

Fault Tolerance

4.6

Besides guarding against malware, another key factor in maintaining the availability and integrity of data is **fault tolerance**, or the capacity for a system to continue performing despite an unexpected hardware or software malfunction.

To better understand the issues related to fault tolerance, it helps to know the difference between failures and faults as they apply to networks. In broad terms, a **failure** is a deviation from a specified level of system performance for a given period of time. In other words, a failure occurs when something doesn't work as promised or as planned. For example, if your car breaks down on the highway, you can consider the breakdown to be a failure. A **fault**, on the other hand, involves the malfunction of one component of a system. A fault can result in a failure. For example, the fault that caused your car to break down might be a leaking water pump. The goal of fault-tolerant systems is to prevent faults from progressing to failures.

Fault tolerance can be realized in varying degrees; the optimal level of fault tolerance for a system depends on how critical its services and files are to productivity. At the highest level of fault tolerance, a system remains unaffected by even the most drastic problem, such as a regional power outage. In this case, a backup power source, such as an electrical generator, is necessary to ensure fault tolerance. However, less dramatic faults, such as a malfunctioning NIC on a router, can still cause network outages, and you should guard against them.

The following sections describe network aspects that must be monitored and managed to ensure fault tolerance.

Net+ Environment

4.2 4.6 As you consider sophisticated network fault-tolerance techniques, remember to analyze the physical environment in which your devices operate. Part of your data protection plan involves protecting your network from excessive heat or moisture, break-ins, and natural disasters. For example, you should make sure that your telecommunications closets and equipment rooms have locked doors and are air-conditioned and maintained at a constant temperature and humidity, according to the hardware manufacturer's recommendations. You can purchase temperature and humidity monitors that trip alarms if specified limits are exceeded. These monitors can prove very useful because the temperature can rise rapidly in a room full of equipment, causing overheated equipment to function poorly or fail outright.

Net+ Power

4.6 No matter where you live, you have probably experienced a complete loss of power (a **blackout**) or a temporary dimming of lights (a **brownout**). Such fluctuations in power are frequently caused by forces of nature, such as hurricanes, tornadoes, or ice storms. They might also occur when a utility company performs maintenance or construction tasks. The following section describes the types of power fluctuations that network administrators should prepare for. The next two sections describe alternate power sources, such as a UPS (uninterruptible power supply) or an electrical generator, that can compensate for power loss.

Power Flaws Whatever the cause, power loss or less than optimal power cannot be tolerated by networks. The following list describes power flaws that can damage your equipment:

- *Surge*—A momentary increase in voltage due to lightning strikes, solar flares, or electrical problems. Surges might last only a few thousandths of a second, but can degrade a computer's power supply. Surges are common. You can guard against surges by making sure every computer device is plugged into a **surge protector**, which redirects excess voltage away from the device to a ground, thereby protecting the device from harm. Without surge protectors, systems would be subjected to multiple surges each year.
- *Noise*—Fluctuation in voltage levels caused by other devices on the network or electromagnetic interference. Some noise is unavoidable on an electrical circuit, but excessive noise can cause a power supply to malfunction, immediately corrupting program or data files and gradually damaging motherboards and other computer circuits. If you've ever turned on fluorescent lights or a laser printer and noticed the lights dim, you have probably introduced noise into the electrical system. Power that is free from noise is called "clean" power. To make sure power is clean, a circuit must pass through an electrical filter.

- *Brownout*—A momentary decrease in voltage; also known as a **sag**. An overtaxed electrical system can cause brownouts, which you might recognize in your home as a dimming of the lights. Such voltage decreases can cause computers or applications to fail and potentially corrupt data.
- *Blackout*—A complete power loss. A blackout could cause significant damage to your network. For example, if a server loses power while files are open and processes are

4.6 running, its NOS might be damaged so extensively that the server cannot restart and its operating system must be reinstalled from scratch. A backup power supply, however, can provide power long enough for the server to shut down properly and avoid harm.

Each of these power problems can adversely affect network devices and their availability. It is not surprising then, that network administrators spend a great deal of money and time ensuring that power remains available and problem free. The following sections describe devices and ways of dealing with unstable power.

UPSs (Uninterruptible Power Supplies) To ensure that a server or connectivity device does not lose power, you should install a **UPS (uninterruptible power supply)**. A UPS is a battery-operated power source directly attached to one or more devices and to a power supply, such as a wall outlet, that prevents undesired features of the wall outlet's A/C power from harming the device or interrupting its services.

UPSs are classified into two general categories: standby and online. A **standby UPS** provides continuous voltage to a device by switching virtually instantaneously to the battery when it detects a loss of power from the wall outlet. Upon restoration of the power, the standby UPS switches the device back to A/C power. The problem with standby UPSs is that, in the brief amount of time that it takes the UPS to discover that power from the wall outlet has faltered, a device may have already detected the power loss and shut down or restarted. Technically, a standby UPS doesn't provide continuous power; for this reason, it is sometimes called an **offline UPS**. Nevertheless, standby UPSs may prove adequate even for critical network devices, such as servers, routers, and gateways. They cost significantly less than online UPSs.

An **online UPS** uses the A/C power from the wall outlet to continuously charge its battery, while providing power to a network device through its battery. In other words, a server connected to an online UPS always relies on the UPS battery for its electricity. Because the server never needs to switch from the wall outlet's power to the UPS's power, there is no risk of momentarily losing service. Also, because the UPS always provides the power, it can handle noise, surges, and sags before the power reaches the attached device. As you can imagine, online UPSs are more expensive than standby UPSs. Figure 14-1 shows standby and online UPSs.

UPSs vary widely in the type of power aberrations they can rectify, the length of time they can provide power, and the number of devices they can support. Of course, they also vary widely in price. UPSs intended for home use are designed merely to keep your workstation running long enough for you to properly shut it down in case of a blackout. Other UPSs perform sophisticated operations such as line filtering or conditioning, power supply monitoring, and error notification. To decide which UPS is right for your network, consider a number of factors:

- *Amount of power needed*—The more power required by your device, the more powerful the UPS must be. Suppose that your organization decides to cut costs and purchase a UPS that cannot supply the amount of power required by a device. If the power to your building ever fails, this UPS will not support your device—you might as well not have any UPS. Electrical power is measured in volt-amps. A **volt-amp (VA)** is the product of the voltage and current (measured in amps) of the electricity on a line.

4.6

Figure 14-1 Standby and online UPSs
Courtesy of Schneider Electric

To determine approximately how many VAs your device requires, you can use the following conversion: 1.4 volt-amps = 1 watt (W). A desktop computer, for example, may use a 200 W power supply, and, therefore, require a UPS capable of at least 280 VA to keep the CPU running in case of a blackout. If you want backup power for your entire home office, however, you must account for the power needs for your monitor and any peripherals, such as printers, when purchasing a UPS. A medium-sized server with a monitor and external tape drive might use 402 W, thus requiring a UPS capable of providing at least 562 VA power. Determining your power needs can be a challenge. You must account for your existing equipment and consider how you might upgrade the supported device(s) over the next several years. Consider consulting with your equipment manufacturer to obtain recommendations on power needs.

- *Period of time to keep a device running*—The longer you anticipate needing a UPS to power your device, the more powerful your UPS must be. For example, the medium-sized server that relies on a 574 VA UPS to remain functional for 20 minutes needs a 1100 VA UPS to remain functional for 90 minutes. To determine how long your device might require power from a UPS, research the length of typical power outages in your area.

- *Line conditioning*—A UPS should also offer surge suppression to protect against surges and line conditioning, or filtering, to guard against line noise. Line conditioners and UPS units include special noise filters that remove line noise. The manufacturer's technical specifications should indicate the amount of filtration required for each UPS. Noise suppression is expressed in decibel levels (dB) at a specific frequency (KHz or MHz). The higher the decibel level, the greater the protection.
- *Cost*—Prices for good UPSs vary widely, depending on the unit's size and extra features. A relatively small UPS that can power one server for five to 10 minutes

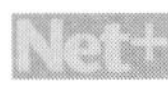

4.6 might cost between $100 and $300. A large UPS that can power a sophisticated router for three hours might cost up to $5000. Still larger UPSs, which can power an entire data center for several hours, can cost hundreds of thousands of dollars. On a critical system, you should not try to cut costs by buying an off-brand, potentially unreliable, or weak UPS.

As with other large purchases, you should research several UPS manufacturers and their products before selecting a UPS. Make sure the manufacturer provides a warranty and lets you test the UPS with your equipment. Testing UPSs with your equipment is an important part of the decision-making process. Popular UPS manufacturers are APC, Emerson, Falcon, and Tripp Lite.

After installing a new UPS, follow the manufacturer's instructions for performing initial tests to verify the UPS's proper functioning. Make it a practice to retest the UPS monthly or quarterly to be sure it will perform as expected in case of a sag or blackout.

Generators If your organization cannot withstand a power loss of any duration, either because of its computer services or other electrical needs, you might consider investing in an electrical generator for your building. Generators can be powered by diesel, liquid propane gas, natural gas, or steam. They do not provide surge protection, but they do provide electricity that's free from noise. In highly available environments, such as an ISP's or telecommunications carrier's data center, generators are common. In fact, in those environments, they are typically combined with large UPSs to ensure that clean power is always available. In the event of a power failure, the UPS supplies electricity until the generator starts and reaches its full capacity, typically no more than three minutes. If your organization relies on a generator for backup power, be certain to check fuel levels and quality regularly. Figure 14-2 illustrates the power infrastructure of a network (such as a data center's) that uses both a generator and dual UPSs.

Before choosing a generator, first calculate your organization's crucial electrical demands to determine the generator's optimal size. Also estimate how long the generator may be required to power your building. Depending on the amount of power draw, a high-capacity generator can supply power for several days. Gas or diesel generators may cost between $10,000 and $3,000,000 (for the largest industrial types). For a company such as a network service provider that stands to lose up to $1,000,000 per minute if its data facilities fail completely, a multi-million-dollar investment to ensure available power is a wise choice. Smaller businesses, however, might choose the more economical solution of renting an electrical generator. To find out more about options for renting or purchasing generators in your area, contact your local electrical utility.

Network Design

The key to fault tolerance in network design is supplying multiple paths that data can use to travel from any one point to another. Therefore, if one connection or component fails, data can be rerouted over an alternate path. The following sections describe examples of fault tolerance in network design.

Topology On a LAN, a star topology and a parallel backbone provide the greatest fault tolerance. On a WAN, a full-mesh topology offers the best fault tolerance. A partial-mesh

Net+
4.6

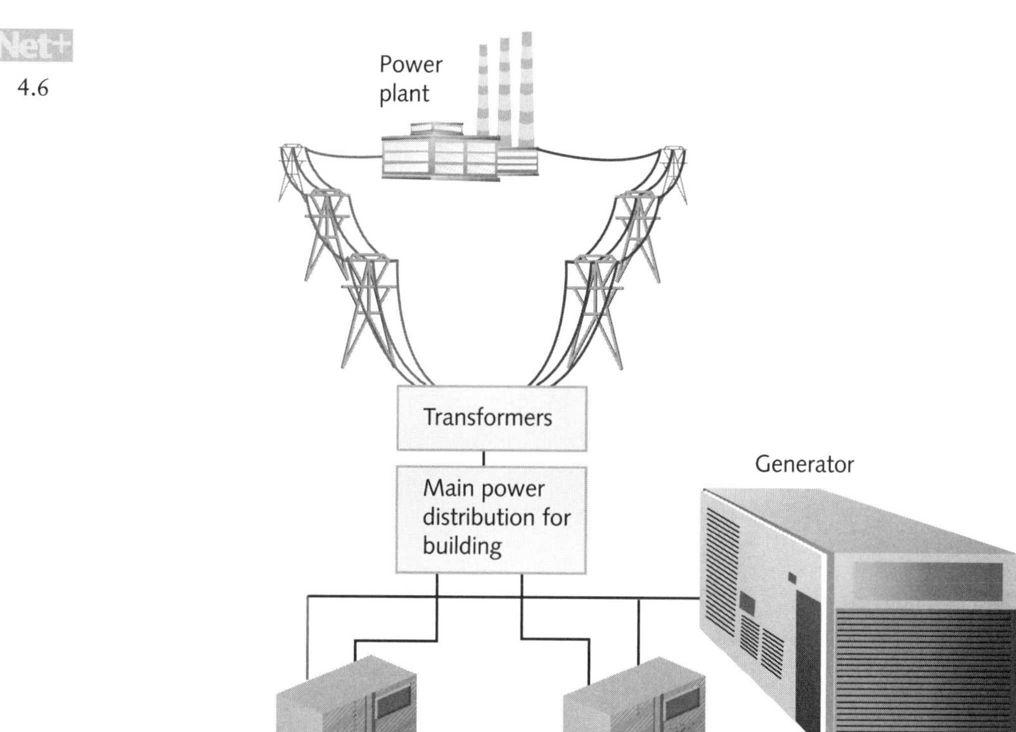

Figure 14-2 UPSs and a generator in a network design

topology offers some redundancy, but is not as fault tolerant as a full-mesh WAN because it offers fewer alternate routes for data. Figure 14-3 depicts a full-mesh WAN between four locations. Another highly fault-tolerant network is one based on SONET technology, which relies on a dual, fiber-optic ring for its transmission. Recall that because it uses two fiber rings for every connection, a SONET network can easily recover from a fault in one of its links.

Mesh topologies and SONET rings are good choices for highly available enterprise networks. But what about connections to the Internet or data backup connections? You might need to establish more than one of these links.

As an example, imagine that you work for a data services firm called PayNTime that processes payroll for a large oil company in the Houston area. Every day, you receive updated payroll information over a T1 link from your client, and every Thursday you compile this

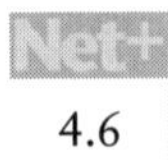

4.6

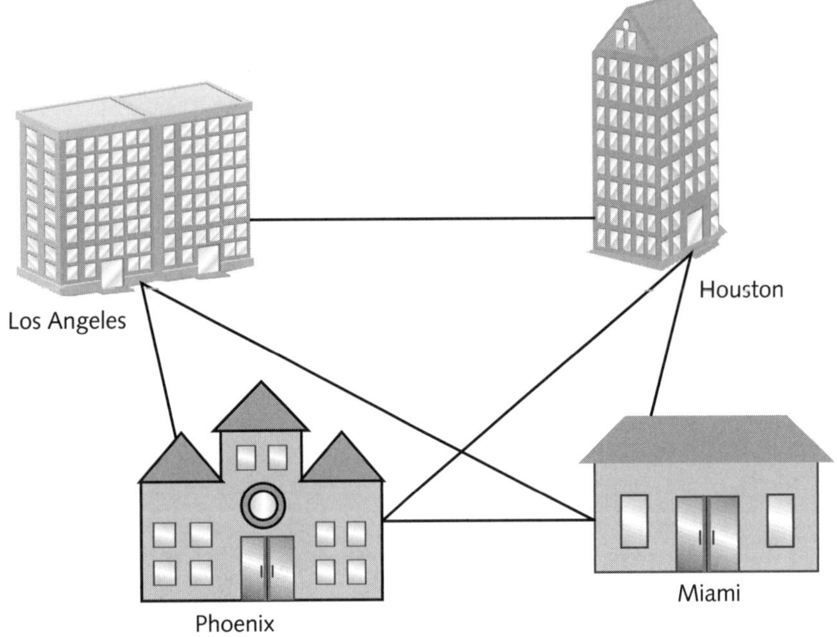

Figure 14-3 Full-mesh WAN

information and then issue 2000 electronic funds transfer requests to the oil company's bank. What would happen if the T1 link between PayNTime and the oil company suffered damage in a flood and became unusable on a Thursday morning? How would you ensure that the employees received their pay? If no redundant link to the oil company existed, you would probably need to gather and input the data into your system at least partially by hand. Even then, chances are that you wouldn't process the electronic funds transfers in time.

In this type of situation, you would want a redundant connection between PayNTime and the oil company's site. You might contract with two different service carriers to ensure that a problem with one carrier won't bring both connections down. Alternatively, you might arrange with one service carrier to provide two different routes. However you provide redundancy in your network topology, you should make sure that the critical data transactions can follow more than one possible path from source to target.

Redundancy in your network offers the advantage of reducing the risk of lost functionality, and potentially lost profits, from a network fault. As you might guess, however, the main disadvantage of redundancy is its cost. If you subscribed to two different service providers for two T1 links in the PayNTime example, you would probably double your monthly leasing costs of approximately $400. Multiply that amount times 12 months, and then times the number of clients for which you need to provide redundancy, and the extra layers of protection quickly become expensive. Redundancy is like a homeowner's insurance policy: You might never need to use it, but if you don't get it, the cost when you do need it can be much higher than your premiums. As a general rule, you should invest in connection redundancies where they are absolutely necessary.

Net+ 4.6 Now suppose that PayNTime provides services not only to the oil company, but also to a temporary agency in the Houston area. Both links are critical because both companies need their payroll processed each week. To address concerns of capacity and scalability, the company might want to consider partnering with an ISP and establishing secure VPNs with its clients. With a VPN, PayNTime could shift the costs of redundancy and network design to the service provider and concentrate on the task it does best—processing payroll. Figure 14-4 illustrates this type of arrangement.

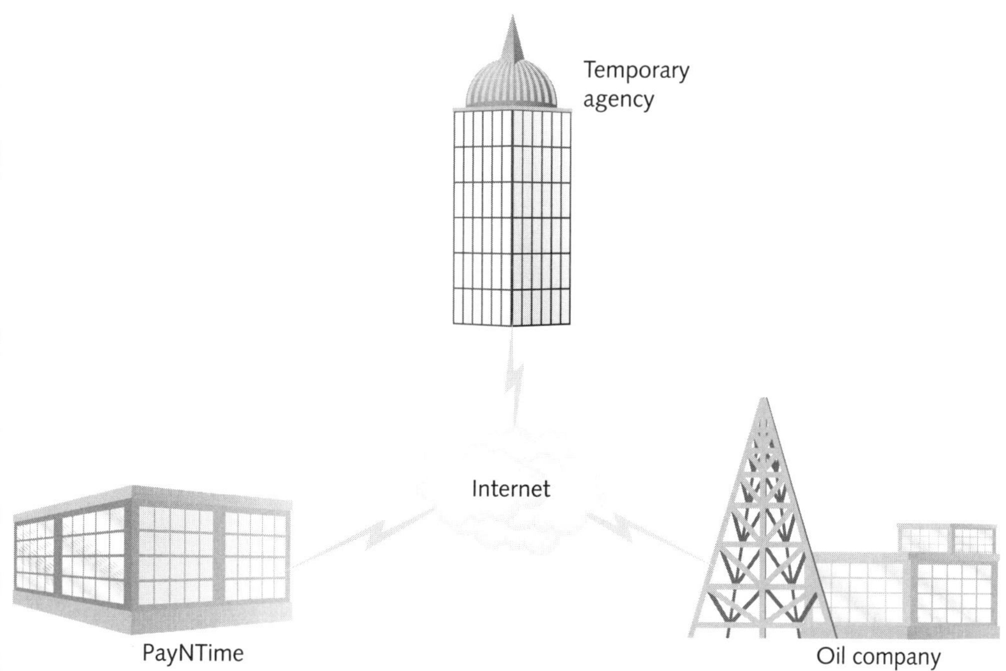

Figure 14-4 VPNs linking multiple customers

Achieving the utmost fault tolerance requires more than redundant connections, however. It also requires eliminating single points of failure in every piece of hardware from source to destination, as described next.

Devices and Interfaces Even when dedicated links and VPN connections remain sound, a faulty device or interface in the data path can affect service for a user, a whole segment, or the whole network. To understand how to increase the fault tolerance of a connection from end to end, let's return to the example of PayNTime. Suppose that the company's network administrator decides to establish a VPN agreement with a national ISP. PayNTime's bandwidth analysis indicates that a single T1 link is sufficient to transport the data of five customers from the ISP's office to PayNTime's data room. Figure 14-5 provides a detailed representation of this arrangement.

Net+ 4.6

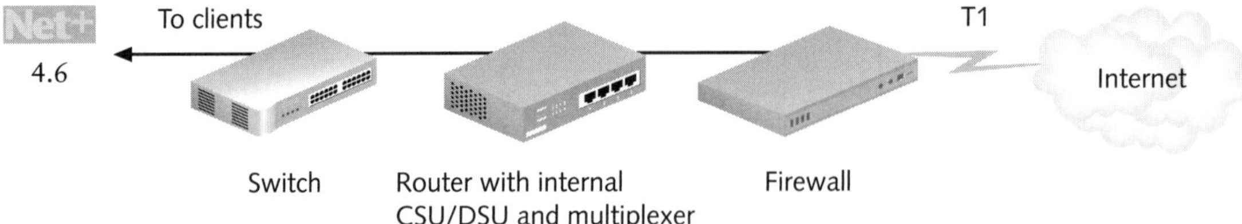

Figure 14-5 Single T1 connectivity

Notice the many single points of failure in the arrangement depicted in Figure 14-5. In addition to the T1 link failing—for example, if a backhoe accidentally cut a cable during road construction—any of the devices in the following list could suffer a fault or failure and impair connectivity or performance:

- Firewall
- Router
- CSU/DSU
- Multiplexer
- Switch

Figure 14-6 illustrates a network design that ensures full redundancy for all the components linking two locations via a T1.

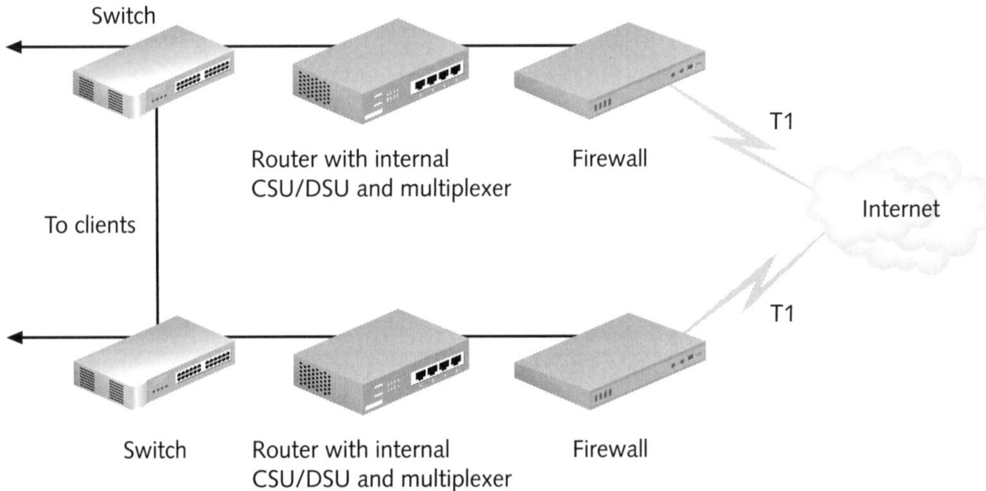

Figure 14-6 Fully redundant T1 connectivity

To achieve the utmost fault tolerance, each critical device requires redundant NICs, SFPs, power supplies, cooling fans, and processors, all of which should, ideally, be able to immediately assume the duties of an identical component, a capability known as automatic **failover**. If one NIC in a router fails, for example, failover ensures that the router's other NIC can automatically handle the first NIC's responsibilities.

4.6 In cases when it's impractical to have failover capable components, you can provide some level of fault tolerance by using hot swappable parts. The term hot swappable refers to identical components that can be changed (or swapped) while a machine is still running (hot). A hot swappable SFP or hard disk, for example, is known as a **hot spare**, or a duplicate component already installed in a device that can assume the original component's functions in case that component fails. In contrast, **cold spare** refers to a duplicate component that is not installed, but can be installed in case of a failure. Replacing a component with a cold spare requires an interruption of service. When you purchase switches or routers to support critical links, look for those that contain failover capable or hot swappable components. As with other redundancy provisions, these features add to the cost of your device purchase.

Using redundant NICs allows devices, servers, or other nodes to participate in link aggregation. **Link aggregation**, also known as **bonding**, is the seamless combination of multiple network interfaces or ports to act as one logical interface. In one type of link aggregation, **NIC teaming**, two or more NICs work in tandem to handle traffic to and from a single node. This allows for increased total throughput and automatic failover between the two NICs. It also allows for **load balancing**, or a distribution of traffic over multiple components or links to optimize performance and fault tolerance. For multiple NICs or ports to use link aggregation, they must be properly configured in each device's operating system.

Figure 14-7 illustrates how link aggregation provides fault tolerance and load balancing for a connection between a switch and a critical server.

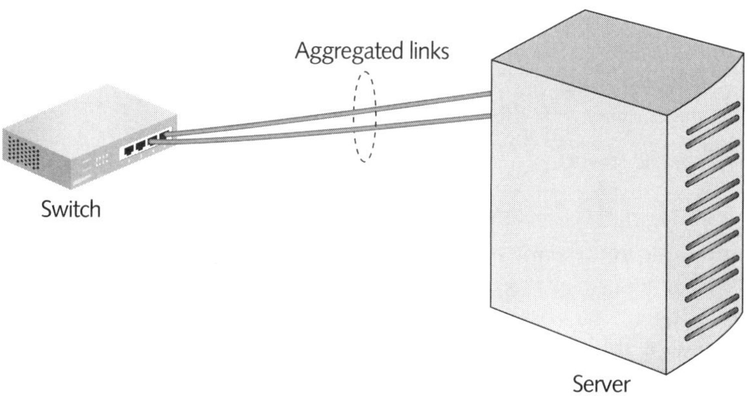

Figure 14-7 Link aggregation between a switch and server

Naming and Addressing Services When naming or addressing services, such as

1.7 DNS and DHCP, fail on a network, nearly all traffic comes to a halt. Therefore, it's impor-

4.6 tant to understand techniques for keeping these services available.

In Chapter 4, you learned that most organizations rely on more than one DNS server to make sure that requests to resolve host names and IP addresses are always satisfied. At the very least, organizations specify a primary name server and a secondary name server. **Primary name servers**, which are queried first when a name resolution that is not already cached is requested, are also known as **master name servers. Secondary name servers**, which can take the place of primary name servers, are also known as **slave name servers**.

Net+ 1.7 4.6

Network administrators who work on large enterprise networks are likely to add more than one slave name server to the DNS architecture. However, a thoughtful administrator will install only as many name servers as needed. Because the slave name servers regularly poll the master name servers to ensure that their DNS zone information is current, running too many slave name servers may add unnecessary traffic and slow performance. As shown in Figure 14-8, networks can also contain DNS caching servers, which save DNS information locally but do not provide resolution for new requests. If a client can resolve a name locally, it can access the host more quickly and reduce the burden on the master name server.

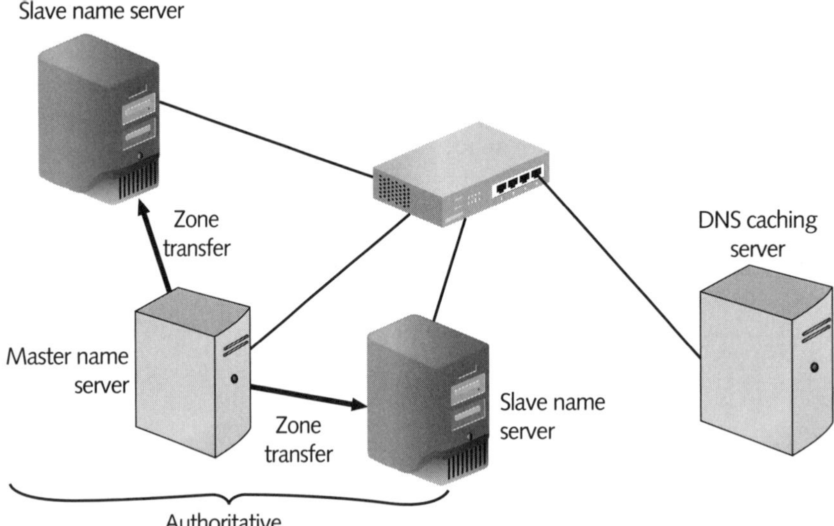

Figure 14-8 Redundant name servers

In addition to maintaining redundant name servers, DNS can point to redundant locations for each host name. For example, the master and slave name servers with the authority to resolve the *www.cengage.com* host name could list different IP addresses in multiple A records associated with this host. The portion of the zone file responsible for resolving the *www.cengage.com* location might look like the one shown in Figure 14-9. When a client requests the address for *www.cengage.com*, the response could be one of several IP addresses, all of which point to identical *www.cengage.com* Web servers. After pointing a client to one IP address in the list, DNS will point the next client that requests resolution for *www.cengage.com* to the next IP address in the list, and so on. This scheme is known as **round-robin DNS**. Round-robin DNS enables load balancing between the servers and increases fault tolerance. Notice that the sample DNS records in Figure 14-9 show a relatively low TTL of 900 seconds (15 minutes). Limiting the duration of a DNS record cache helps to keep each of the IP addresses that are associated with the host in rotation.

More sophisticated load balancing for all types of servers can be achieved by using a **load balancer**, a device dedicated to this task. A load balancer distributes traffic intelligently between multiple computers. Whereas round-robin DNS simply doles out IP addresses sequentially with every new request, a load balancer can determine which among a pool of servers is experiencing the most traffic before forwarding the request to a server with lower

Net+
1.7
4.6

#Host name	TTL		Type	IP address
www.cengage.com	800	IN	A	192.168.7.1
www.cengage.com	800	IN	A	192.168.7.2
www.cengage.com	800	IN	A	192.169.7.3
www.cengage.com	800	IN	A	192.168.7.4

Figure 14-9 Redundant entries in a DNS zone file

utilization. Naming and addressing availability can be increased further by using **CARP (Common Address Redundancy Protocol)**, which allows a pool of computers or interfaces to share one or more IP addresses. This pool is known as a group of redundancy. In CARP, one computer, acting as the master of the group, receives requests for an IP address, then parcels out the requests to one of several computers in a group. Figure 14-10 illustrates how CARP and round-robin DNS, used together, can provide two layers of fault tolerance for naming and addressing services. CARP is often used with firewalls or routers that have multiple interfaces to ensure automatic failover in case one of the interfaces suffers a fault.

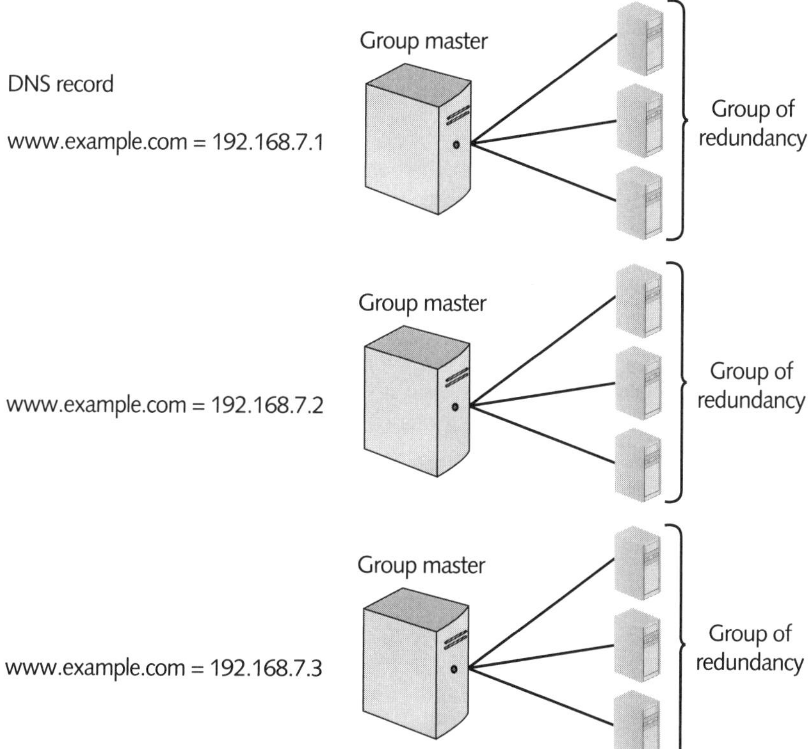

Figure 14-10 Round-robin DNS with CARP

Net+

Servers

4.6 As with other devices, you can make servers more fault tolerant by supplying them with redundant components. Critical servers often contain redundant NICs, processors, and hard disks. These redundant components provide assurance that if one item fails, the entire system won't fail. At the same time, redundant NICs and processors enable load balancing.

For example, a server with two 1-Gbps NICs might receive and transmit traffic at a rate of 460 Mbps during a busy time of the day. With additional software provided by either the NIC manufacturer or a third party, the redundant NICs can work in tandem to distribute the load, ensuring that approximately half the data travels through the first NIC and half through the second. This approach improves response time for users accessing the server. If one NIC fails, the other NIC automatically assumes full responsibility for receiving and transmitting all data to and from the server. Although load balancing does not technically fall under the category of fault tolerance, it helps justify the purchase of redundant components that do contribute to fault tolerance.

The following sections describe more sophisticated ways of providing server fault tolerance, beginning with server mirroring.

Server Mirroring

Mirroring is a fault-tolerance technique in which one device or component duplicates the activities of another. In **server mirroring**, one server continually duplicates the transactions and data storage of another. The servers involved must be identical machines using identical components. As you would expect, mirroring requires a high-speed link between the servers. It also requires software running on both servers that allows them to synchronize their actions continually and, in case of a failure, that permits one server to take over for the other. Server mirroring is considered to be a form of **replication**, a term that refers to the dynamic copying of data from one location to another.

To illustrate the concept of mirroring, suppose that you give a presentation to a large group of people, and the audience is allowed to interrupt you to ask questions at any time. You might talk for two minutes, wait while someone asked a question, answer the question, begin lecturing again, take another question, and so on. In this sense, you act like a primary server, busily transmitting and receiving information. Now imagine that your identical twin is standing in the next room and can hear you over a loudspeaker. Your twin was instructed to say exactly what you say as quickly as possible after you spoke, but to an empty room containing only a tape recorder. Of course, your twin must listen to you before imitating you. It takes time for the twin to digest everything you say and repeat it, so you must slow down your lecture and your room's question-and-answer process. A mirrored server acts in much the same way. The time it takes to duplicate the incoming and outgoing data detrimentally affects network performance if the network handles a heavy traffic load. But if you should faint during your lecture, for example, your twin can step into your room and take over for you in very short order. The mirrored server also stands ready to assume the responsibilities of its counterpart.

One advantage to mirroring is that the servers involved can stand side by side or be positioned in different locations—in two different buildings of a company's headquarters, or possibly even on opposite sides of a continent. One potential disadvantage to mirroring, however, is the time it takes for a mirrored server to assume the functionality of the failed server. This delay could last 15 to 90 seconds. Obviously, this downtime makes mirroring imperfect. When a server fails, users lose network service, and any data in transit at the

Net+ 4.6 moment of the failure is susceptible to corruption. Another disadvantage to mirroring is its toll on the network as data is copied between sites.

Although server mirroring software can be expensive, the hardware costs of mirroring also mount because you must devote an entire server to simply acting as a "tape recorder" for all data in case the other server fails. Depending on the potential cost of losing a server's functionality for any period of time, however, the expense involved may be justifiable.

You might be familiar with the term *mirroring* as it refers to Web sites on the Internet. Mirrored Web sites are locations on the Internet that dynamically duplicate other locations on the Internet, to ensure their continual availability. They are similar to, but not necessarily the same as, mirrored servers.

Clustering **Clustering** is a fault-tolerance technique that links multiple servers together to act as a single server. In this configuration, clustered servers share processing duties and appear as a single server to users. If one server in the cluster fails, the other servers in the cluster automatically take over its data transaction and storage responsibilities. Because multiple servers can perform services independently of other servers, as well as ensure fault tolerance, clustering is more cost effective than mirroring for large networks.

To understand the concept of clustering, imagine that you and several colleagues (who are not exactly like you) are simultaneously giving separate talks in different rooms in the same conference center. All of your colleagues are constantly aware of your lecture, and vice versa. If you should faint during your lecture, one of your colleagues can immediately jump into your spot and pick up where you left off, without the audience ever noticing. At the same time, your colleague must continue to present his own lecture, which means that he must split his time between these two tasks.

To detect failures, clustered servers regularly poll each other on the network, asking, "Are you still there?" They then wait a specified period of time before again asking, "Are you still there?" If they don't receive a response from one of their counterparts, the clustering software initiates the failover. This process can take anywhere from a few seconds to a minute because all information about a failed server's shared resources must be gathered by the cluster. Unlike with mirroring, users will not notice the switch. Later, when the other servers in the cluster detect that the missing server has been replaced, they automatically relinquish that server's responsibilities. The failover and recovery processes are transparent to network users.

Often, clustering is implemented among servers located in the same data room. However, some clusters can contain servers that are geographically distant from each other. One factor to consider when separating clustered servers is the time required for the servers to communicate. For example, Microsoft recommends ensuring a return-trip latency of less than 500 milliseconds for requests to clustered servers. Thus, clusters that must appear as a single storage entity to LAN clients depend on fast WAN or MAN connections. They also require close attention to their setup and configuration, as they are more complex to install than clusters of servers on the same LAN.

Clustering offers many advantages over mirroring. Each server in the cluster can perform its own data processing; at the same time, it is always ready to take over for a failed server if necessary. Not only does this ability to perform multiple functions reduce the cost of ownership for a cluster of servers, but it also improves performance.

4.6 Like mirroring, clustering is implemented through a combination of software and hardware. Microsoft Windows Server 2008 R2 incorporates options for server clustering. Clustering has been part of UNIX-type operating systems since the early 1990s.

Storage

Related to the availability and fault tolerance of servers is the availability and fault tolerance of data storage. In the following sections, you will learn about different methods for making sure shared data and applications are never lost or irretrievable.

RAID (Redundant Array of Independent [or Inexpensive] Disks) **RAID (Redundant Array of Independent [or Inexpensive] Disks)** refers to a collection of disks that provide fault tolerance for shared data and applications. A group of hard disks is called a disk **array** (or a drive). The collection of disks that work together in a RAID configuration is often referred to as the *RAID drive* or *RAID array*. To the system, the multiple disks in a RAID drive appear as a single logical drive. One advantage of using RAID is that a single disk failure will not cause a catastrophic loss of data. Other advantages are increased storage capacity and potentially better disk performance. Although RAID comes in many different forms (or levels), all types use shared, multiple physical or logical hard disks to ensure data integrity and availability.

RAID can be implemented as a hardware or software solution. **Hardware RAID** includes a set of disks and a separate disk controller. The hardware RAID array is managed exclusively by the RAID disk controller, which is attached to a server through the server's controller interface. To the server's NOS, a hardware RAID array appears as just another storage device.

Software RAID relies on software to implement and control RAID techniques over virtually any type of hard disk (or disks). Software RAID is less expensive overall than hardware RAID because it does not require special controller or disk array hardware. With today's fast processors, software RAID performance rivals that of hardware RAID, which was formerly regarded as faster. The software may be a third-party package, or it may exist as part of the NOS. On a Windows Server 2008 R2 server, for example, RAID drives are configured through the Disk Management snap-in, which is accessed through the Server Manager or Computer Management tool.

Several different types of RAID are available. A description of each RAID level is beyond the scope of this book, and understanding RAID types is not required to qualify for Network+ certification. If you are tasked with maintaining highly available systems, however, you should learn about the most popular RAID levels.

NAS (Network Attached Storage) **NAS (network attached storage)** is a specialized storage device or group of storage devices that provides centralized fault-tolerant data storage for a network. NAS differs from RAID in that it maintains its own interface to the LAN rather than relying on a server to connect it to the network and control its functions. In fact, you can think of NAS as a unique type of server dedicated to data sharing. The advantage to using NAS over a typical file server is that a NAS device contains its own file system that is optimized for saving and serving files (as opposed to also managing printing, authenticating logon IDs, and so on). Because of this optimization, NAS reads and writes from its disk significantly faster than other types of servers could.

Net+ 4.6 Another advantage to using NAS is that it can be easily expanded without interrupting service. For instance, if you purchased a NAS device with 400 GB of disk space, then six months later realized you need three times as much storage space, you could add the new 800 GB of disk space to the NAS device without requiring users to log off the network or taking down the NAS device. After physically installing the new disk space, the NAS device would recognize the added storage and add it to its pool of available reading and writing space. Compare this process with adding hard disk space to a typical server, for which you would have to take the server down, install the hardware, reformat the drive, integrate it with your NOS, and then add directories, files, and permissions as necessary.

Although NAS is a separate device with its own file system, it still cannot communicate directly with clients on the network. When using NAS, the client requests a file from its usual file server over the LAN. The server then requests the file from the NAS device on the network. In response, the NAS device retrieves the file and transmits it to the server, which transmits it to the client. Figure 14-11 depicts how a NAS device physically connects to a LAN.

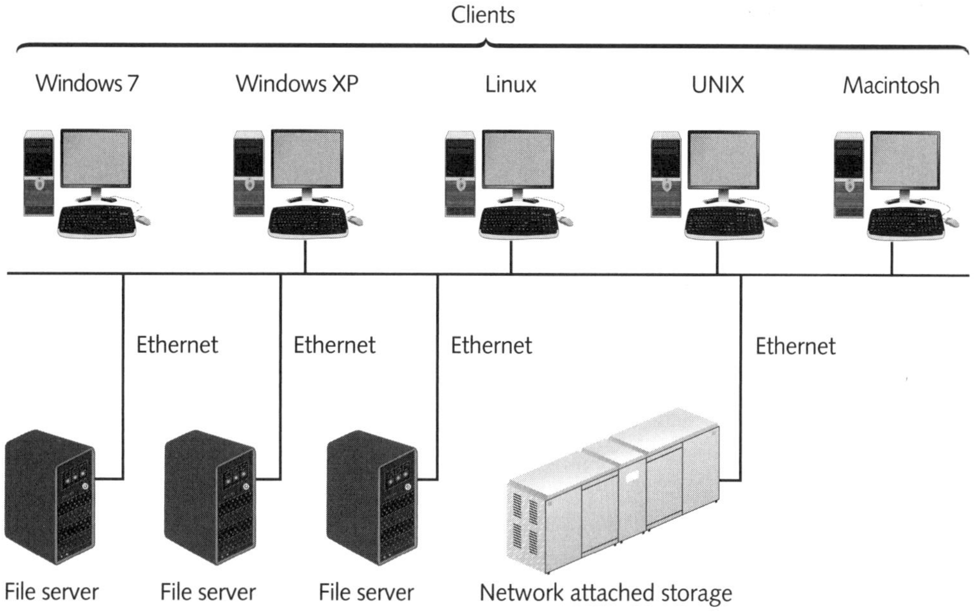

Figure 14-11 Network attached storage on a LAN

NAS is appropriate for enterprises that require not only fault tolerance, but also fast access for their data. For example, an ISP might use NAS to host its customers' Web pages. Because NAS devices can store and retrieve data for any type of client (providing it can run TCP/IP), NAS is also appropriate for organizations that use a mix of different operating systems on their desktops.

Large enterprises that require even faster access to data and larger amounts of storage might prefer storage area networks over NAS. You will learn about storage area networks in the following section.

Net+ 4.6

SANs (Storage Area Networks) As you have learned, NAS devices are separate storage devices, but they still require a file server to interact with other devices on the network. In contrast, **SANs (storage area networks)** are distinct networks of storage devices that communicate directly with each other and with other networks. In a typical SAN, multiple storage devices are connected to multiple, identical servers. This type of architecture is similar to the mesh topology in WANs, the most fault-tolerant type of topology possible. If one storage device within a SAN suffers a fault, data is automatically retrieved from elsewhere in the SAN. If one server in a SAN suffers a fault, another server steps in to perform its functions.

Not only are SANs extremely fault tolerant, but they are also extremely fast. Much of their speed can be attributed to the use of a special transmission method that relies on fiber-optic media and its own proprietary protocols. One popular SAN transmission method is called **Fibre Channel**. Fibre Channel connects devices within the SAN and also connects the SAN to other networks. Fibre Channel is capable of over 5 Gbps throughput. Because it depends on Fibre Channel, and not on a traditional network transmission method (for example, 1000Base-T), a SAN is not limited to the speed of the client/server network for which it provides data storage. In addition, because the SAN does not belong to the client/server network, it does not have to contend with the normal overhead of that network, such as broadcasts and acknowledgments. Likewise, a SAN frees the client/server network from the traffic-intensive duties of backing up and restoring data.

Figure 14-12 shows a SAN connected to a traditional Ethernet network.

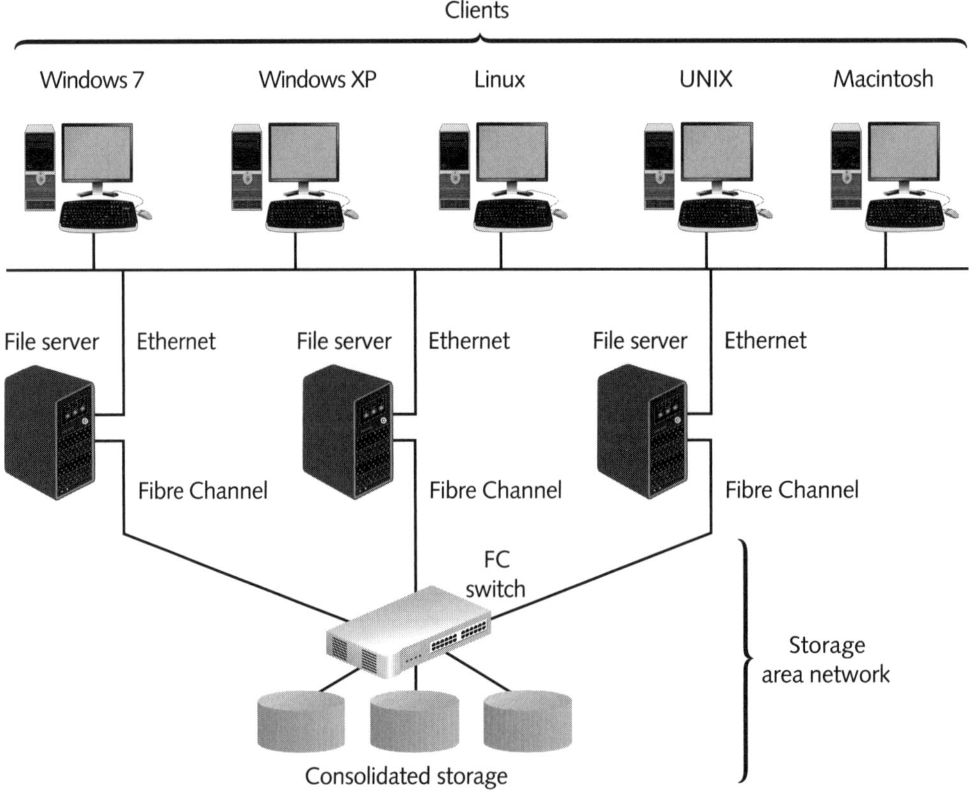

Figure 14-12 A storage area network

Net+ 4.6 Another advantage to using SANs is that a SAN can be installed in a location separate from the LAN it serves. Being in a separate location provides added fault tolerance. For example, if an organization's main offices suffered a fire or flood, the SAN and the data it stores would still be safe. Remote SANs can be kept in an ISP's data center, which can provide greater security and fault tolerance and also allows an organization to outsource the management of its storage, in case its own staff doesn't have the time or expertise.

Like NAS, SANs provide the benefit of being highly scalable. After establishing a SAN, you can easily add further storage and new devices to the SAN without disrupting client/server activity on the network. Finally, SANs use a faster, more efficient method of writing data than do both NAS devices and typical client/server networks.

SANs are not without drawbacks, however. One noteworthy disadvantage to implementing SANs is their high cost. A small SAN can cost $100,000, while a large SAN costs several millions of dollars. In addition, because SANs are more complex than NAS or RAID systems, investing in a SAN means also investing in long hours of training for technical staff before installation, plus significant administration efforts to keep the SAN functional—that is, unless an organization outsources its storage management.

Due to their very high fault tolerance, massive storage capabilities, and fast data access, SANs are best suited to environments with huge quantities of data that must always be quickly available. Usually, such an environment belongs to a very large enterprise. A SAN is typically used to house multiple databases—for example, inventory, sales, safety specifications, payroll, and employee records for an international manufacturing company.

Data Backup

You have probably heard or even spoken the axiom, "Make regular backups!" A **backup** is a copy of data or program files created for archiving or safekeeping. Without backing up your data, you risk losing everything through a hard disk fault, fire, flood, or malicious or accidental erasure or corruption. No matter how reliable and fault tolerant you believe your server's hard disk (or disks) to be, you still risk losing everything unless you make backups on separate media and store them off-site.

To fully appreciate the importance of backups, imagine coming to work one morning to find that everything disappeared from the server: programs, configurations, data files, user IDs, passwords, and the network operating system. It doesn't matter how it happened. What matters is how long it will take to reinstall the network operating systems; how long it will take to duplicate the previous configuration; and how long it will take to figure out which IDs should reside on the server, in which groups they should belong, and which permissions each group should have. What will you say to your colleagues when they learn that all of the data that they have worked on for the last year is irretrievably lost? When you think about this scenario, you quickly realize that you can't afford *not* to perform regular backups.

When identifying the types of data to back up, remember to include configuration files for devices such as routers, switches, access points, gateways, and firewalls.

Many different options exist for making backups. They can be performed by different types of software and hardware combinations and use one of many storage types or locations. They can be controlled by NOS utilities or third-party software. In this section, you will learn about the most common backup media, techniques for performing data backups, ways to schedule them, and methods for determining what you must back up.

Backup Media and Methods

When selecting backup media and methods, you can choose from several approaches, each of which comes with certain advantages and disadvantages. To select the appropriate solution for your network, consider the following questions:

- Does the backup storage media or system provide sufficient capacity?
- Are the backup software and hardware proven to be reliable?
- Does the backup software use data error-checking techniques?
- To what extent, if any, will the backup process affect normal system or network functioning?
- How much do the backup methods and media cost, relative to the amount of data they can store?
- Will the backup hardware and software be compatible with existing network hardware and software?
- Does the backup system require manual intervention? (For example, must staff members verify that backups completed as planned?)
- Will the backup methods and media accommodate your network's growth?

To help you answer these questions for your own situation, the following sections compare the most popular backup media and methods available today.

Optical Media

A simple way to save data is by copying it to **optical media**, which is a type of media capable of storing digitized data and that uses a laser to write data to it and read data from it. Examples of optical media include all types of CDs, DVDs, and Blu-Ray discs. Backing up data to optical media requires only a computer with the appropriate recordable optical storage drive and a utility for writing data to the media. Such utilities often come with a computer's operating system. If not, they are inexpensive and easy to find.

A **recordable DVD** can hold up to 4.7 GB on one single-layered side, and both sides of the disc can be used. In addition, each side can have up to two layers. Thus, in total, a double-layered, two-sided DVD can store up to 17 GB of data. Recordable DVDs, which are not the same as the video DVD that you rent from a movie store, come in several different formats. If you decide to back up media to DVDs, be sure to standardize on one manufacturer's equipment. **Blu-ray** is an optical storage format released in 2006 by a consortium of electronics and computer vendors. Blu-ray discs are the same size as recordable DVDs, but can store significantly more data, up to 128 GB on a quadruple-layer disc.

Because of their modest storage capacity, recordable DVDs and Blu-ray discs may be an adequate solution for a home or small office network, but they are not sufficient for enterprise networks. Another disadvantage to using optical media for backups is that writing data to them takes longer than saving data to some other types of media, such as tapes or disk drives, or to another location on the network. In addition, using optical media requires more human intervention than other backup methods.

Tape Backups In the early days of networking, the most popular method for backing up networked systems was tape backup, or copying data to a magnetic tape. **Tape backups** require the use of a tape drive connected to the network (via a system such as a file server or dedicated, networked workstation), software to manage and perform backups, and, of course, backup media. The tapes used for tape backups resemble small cassette tapes, but they are higher quality, specially made to reliably store data.

On a relatively small network, stand-alone tape drives might be attached to each server. On a large network, one large, centralized tape backup device might manage all of the subsystems' backups. This tape backup device usually is connected to a computer other than a busy file server to reduce the possibility that backups might cause traffic bottlenecks. Extremely large environments (for example, global manufacturers with several terabytes of inventory and product information to safeguard) may require robots to retrieve and circulate tapes from a tape storage library, also known as a vault, that may be as large as a warehouse.

Although many network administrators appreciate the durability and ease of tape backups, they are slower than other backup options.

External Disk Drives An **external disk drive** is a storage device that can be attached temporarily to a computer via its USB, PCMCIA, FireWire, or CompactFlash port. External disk drives are also known as **removable disk drives.** Small external disk drives are frequently used by laptop or desktop computer users to save and share data. After being connected to the computer, the external disk drives appear as any other drive, and the user can copy files directly to them. For backing up large amounts of data, however, network administrators are likely to use an external disk drive with backup control features, higher storage capacity, and faster read-write access.

One advantage to using external disk drives is that they are simple to use. Also, they provide faster data transfer rates than optical media or tape backups. However, on most networks, backing up data to a fixed disk elsewhere on the network, as explained in the next section, is faster.

Network Backups Instead of saving data to a removable disk or media, you might choose to save data to another place on the network. For example, you could copy all the user data from your organization's mail server to a different server on the network. If you choose this option, be certain to back up data to a different disk than where it was originally stored because if the original disk fails, you will lose both the original data and its backup. (Although disk locations on workstations are typically obvious, on a network they might not be.) If your organization operates a WAN, it's best to back up data to disks at another location. That way, if one location suffers an outage or catastrophe, the data will remain safe at the other location on the WAN. A sophisticated network backup solution would use software to automate and manage backups and save data to a SAN or NAS storage device. Most NOSs provide utilities for automating and managing network backups.

If your organization does not have a WAN or a high-end storage solution, you might consider online backups. An **online backup**, or **cloud backup**, saves data across the Internet to another company's storage array. Usually, online backup providers require you to install their client software. You also need a (preferably high-speed) connection to the Internet. Online backups implement strict security measures to protect the data in transit, as the information traverses public carrier links. Most online backup providers allow you to retrieve your data at any time of day or night, without calling a technical support number. Both the backup and restoration processes are entirely automated. In case of a disaster, the online backup company might offer to create DVDs or external storage drives containing your servers' data. When evaluating an online backup provider, you should test its speed, accuracy, security, and, of course, the ease with which you can recover the backed-up data. Be certain to test the service before you commit to a long-term contract for online backups.

Backup Strategy

After selecting the appropriate tool for performing your servers' data backups, devise a backup strategy to guide you and your colleagues in performing reliable backups that provide maximum data protection. This strategy should be documented in a common area where all IT staff can access it. The strategy should address at least the following questions:

- What data must be backed up?
- What kind of rotation schedule will backups follow?
- At what time of day or night will the backups occur?
- How will you verify the accuracy of the backups?
- Where and for how long will backup media be stored?
- Who will take responsibility for ensuring that backups occurred?
- How long will you save backups?
- Where will backup and recovery documentation be stored?

Different backup methods provide varying levels of certainty and corresponding labor and cost. An important concept to understand before learning about different backup methods is the archive bit. An **archive bit** is a file attribute that can be checked (or set to "on") or unchecked (or set to "off") to indicate whether the file must be archived. When a file is created or changed, the operating system automatically sets the file's archive bit to "on." Various backup methods use the archive bit in different ways to determine which files should be backed up, as described in the following list:

- *Full backup*—All data on all servers is copied to a storage medium, regardless of whether the data is new or changed. After backing up the files, a full backup unchecks—or turns off—the files' archive bits.
- *Incremental backup*—Only data that has changed since the last full or incremental backup is copied to a storage medium. An incremental backup saves only files whose archive bit is checked. After backing up files, an incremental backup unchecks the archive bit for every file it has saved.
- *Differential backup*—Only data that has changed since the last backup is copied to a storage medium, and that information is then marked for subsequent backup, regardless of whether it has changed. In other words, a differential backup does not uncheck the archive bits for files it backs up.

When managing network backups, you need to determine the best possible **backup rotation scheme**—you need to create a plan that specifies when and how often backups will occur. The aim of a good backup rotation scheme is to provide excellent data reliability without overtaxing your network or requiring a lot of intervention. For example, you might think that backing up your entire network's data every night is the best policy because it ensures that everything is completely safe. But what if your network contains 2 TB of data and is growing by 100 GB per month? Would the backups even finish by morning? How many tapes would you have to purchase? Also, why should you bother backing up files that haven't changed in three weeks? How much time will you and your staff need to devote to managing the tapes? How would the transfer of all of the data affect your network's performance? All of these considerations point to a better alternative than the "tape-a-day" solution—that is, an option that promises to maximize data protection but reduce the time and cost associated with backups.

When planning your backup strategy, you can choose from several standard backup rotation schemes. The most popular of these schemes, called **Grandfather-Father-Son,** uses daily (son), weekly (father), and monthly (grandfather) backup sets. As depicted in Figure 14-13, in the Grandfather-Father-Son scheme, three types of backups are performed each month: daily incremental (every Monday through Thursday), weekly full (every Friday), and monthly full (last day of the month).

	Monday	Tuesday	Wednesday	Thursday	Friday
Week 1	A	A	A	A	B
Week 2	A	A	A	A	B
Week 3	A	A	A	A	B
Week 4	A	A	A	A	B
Week 5	A	A	C		

One month of backups

A = Incremental "son" backup (daily)
B = Full "father" backup (weekly)
C = Full "grandfather" backup (monthly)

Figure 14-13 The Grandfather-Father-Son backup rotation scheme

After you have determined your backup rotation scheme, you should ensure that backup activity is recorded in a backup log. Your backup program should store details such as the backup date, media identification, type of data backed up (for example, Accounting Department spreadsheets or a day's worth of catalog orders), type of backup (full, incremental, or differential), files that were backed up, and backup location. Having this information available in case of a server failure greatly simplifies data recovery.

Finally, after you begin to back up network data, you should establish a regular schedule of verification. From time to time, depending on how often your data changes and how critical the information is, you should attempt to recover some critical files from your backup media. Many network administrators attest that the darkest hour of their career was when they were asked to retrieve critical files from a backup, and found that no backup data existed because their backup system never worked in the first place!

Disaster Recovery

Disaster recovery is the process of restoring your critical functionality and data after an enterprise-wide outage that affects more than a single system or a limited group of users. Disaster recovery must take into account the possible extremes, rather than relatively minor outages, failures, security breaches, or data corruption.

Disaster Recovery Planning

A disaster recovery plan accounts for the worst-case scenarios, from a far-reaching hurricane to a military or terrorist attack. It should identify a disaster recovery team (with an appointed coordinator) and provide contingency plans for restoring or replacing computer systems, power, telephone systems, and paper-based files. Sections of the plan related to computer systems should include the following:

- Contact names and phone and pager numbers for emergency coordinators who will execute the disaster recovery response in case of disaster, as well as roles and responsibilities of other staff.
- Details on which data and servers are being backed up, how frequently backups occur, where backups are kept (off-site), and, most important, how backed-up data can be recovered in full.
- Details on network topology, redundancy, and agreements with national service carriers, in case local or regional vendors fall prey to the same disaster.
- Regular strategies for testing the disaster recovery plan.
- A plan for managing the crisis, including regular communications with employees and customers. Consider the possibility that regular communications modes (such as phone lines) might be unavailable.

Having a comprehensive disaster recovery plan lessens the risk of losing critical data in case of extreme situations, and also makes potential customers and your insurance providers look more favorably on your organization.

Disaster Recovery Contingencies

An organization can choose from several options for recovering from a disaster. The options vary by the amount of employee involvement, hardware, software, planning, and investment each involves. They also vary according to how quickly they will restore network functionality in case a disaster occurs. As you would expect, every contingency necessitates a site other than the building where the network's main components normally reside. An organization might maintain its own disaster recovery sites—for example, by renting office space in a different city—or contract with a company that specializes in disaster recovery services to provide the site. Disaster recovery contingencies are commonly divided into three categories: cold site, warm site, and hot site.

A **cold site** is a place where the computers, devices, and connectivity necessary to rebuild a network exist, but they are not appropriately configured, updated, or connected. Therefore, restoring functionality from a cold site could take a long time. For example, suppose your small business network consists of a file and print server, mail server, backup server, Internet gateway/DNS/DHCP server, 25 clients, four printers, a router, a switch, two access points, and a connection to your local ISP. At your cold site, you might store four server computers on which your company's NOS is not installed, and that do not possess the appropriate configurations and data necessary to operate in your environment. The 25 client machines stored there might be in a similar state. In addition, you might have a router, a switch, and two access points at the cold site, but these might also require configuration to operate in your environment. Finally, the cold site would not necessarily have Internet connectivity, or at least not the same type as your network used. Supposing you followed good backup practices and stored your backup media at the cold site, you would then need to restore operating systems, applications, and data to your servers and clients; reconfigure your connectivity devices; and arrange with your ISP to have your connectivity restored to the cold site. Even for a small network, this process could take weeks.

A **warm site** is a place where the computers, devices, and connectivity necessary to rebuild a network exist, with some appropriately configured, updated, or connected. For example, a service provider that specializes in disaster recovery might maintain a duplicate of each of your servers in its data center. You might arrange to have the service provider update those duplicate servers with your backed-up data on the first of each month because updating the servers daily is much more expensive. In that case, if a disaster occurs in the middle of the month, you would still need to update your duplicate servers with your latest weekly or daily backups before they could stand in for the downed servers. Recovery from a warm site can take hours or days, compared with the weeks a cold site might require. Maintaining a warm site costs more than maintaining a cold site, but not as much as maintaining a hot site.

A **hot site** is a place where the computers, devices, and connectivity necessary to rebuild a network exist, and all are appropriately configured, updated, and connected to match your network's current state. For example, you might use server mirroring to maintain identical copies of your servers at two WAN locations. In a hot site contingency plan, both locations would also contain identical connectivity devices and configurations, and thus be able to stand in for the other at a moment's notice. As you can imagine, hot sites are expensive and potentially time consuming to maintain. For organizations that cannot tolerate downtime, however, hot sites provide the best disaster recovery option.

Chapter Summary

- Integrity refers to the soundness of your network's files, systems, and connections. To ensure their integrity, you must protect them from anything that might render them unusable, such as corruption, tampering, natural disasters, and malware. Availability refers to how consistently and reliably a file or system can be accessed by authorized personnel.
- Several basic measures can be employed to protect data and systems on a network: (1) Prevent anyone other than a network administrator from opening or changing the system files; (2) monitor the network for unauthorized access or changes; (3) record authorized system changes in a change management system; (4) use redundancy for

critical servers, cabling, routers, switches, gateways, NICs, hard disks, power supplies, and other components; (5) perform regular health checks on the network; (6) monitor system performance, error logs, and the system log book regularly; (7) keep backups, system images, and emergency repair disks current and available; and (8) implement and enforce security and disaster recovery policies.

- Malware is any type of code that aims to intrude upon or harm a system or its resources. Malware includes viruses, worms, bots, and Trojan horses.
- A virus is a program that replicates itself to infect more computers, either through network connections or through external storage devices passed among users. Viruses may damage files or systems, or simply annoy users by flashing messages or pictures on the screen or by causing the computer to beep.
- Any type of malware can have characteristics that make it hard to detect and eliminate. Such malicious code might be encrypted, stealth, polymorphic, or time dependent.
- A good anti-malware program should be able to detect malware through signature scanning, integrity checking, and heuristic scanning. It should also be compatible with your network environment, centrally manageable, easy to use (transparent to users), and not prone to false alarms.
- Anti-malware software is merely one piece of the puzzle in protecting your network from harmful programs. An anti-malware policy is another essential component. It should provide rules for using anti-malware software, as well as policies for installing programs, sharing files, and using external storage devices.
- A failure is a deviation from a specified level of system performance for a given period of time. A fault, on the other hand, is the malfunction of one component of a system. A fault can result in a failure. The goal of fault-tolerant systems is to prevent faults from progressing to failures.
- Fault tolerance is a system's capacity to continue performing despite an unexpected hardware or software malfunction. It can be achieved in varying degrees. At the highest level of fault tolerance, a system is unaffected by even a drastic problem, such as a power failure.
- As you consider sophisticated fault-tolerance techniques for servers, routers, and WAN links, remember to address the environment in which your devices operate. Protecting your data also involves protecting your network from excessive heat or moisture, break-ins, and natural disasters.
- Networks cannot tolerate power loss or less than optimal power and may suffer downtime or reduced performance due to blackouts, brownouts (sags), surges, and line noise.
- A UPS (uninterruptible power supply) is a battery power source directly attached to one or more devices and to a power supply that prevents undesired features of the power source from harming the device or interrupting its services. UPSs vary in the type of power aberrations they can rectify, the length of time they can provide power, and the number of devices they can support.
- A standby UPS provides continuous voltage to a device by switching virtually instantaneously to the battery when it detects a loss of power from the wall outlet. Upon restoration of the power, the standby UPS switches the device to use A/C power again.

- An online UPS uses the A/C power from the wall outlet to continuously charge its battery, while providing power to a network device through its battery. In other words, a server connected to an online UPS always relies on the UPS battery for its electricity.
- The most certain way to guarantee power to your network is to rely on a generator. Generators can be powered by diesel, liquid propane gas, natural gas, or steam. They do not provide surge protection, but they do provide noise-free electricity.
- Network topologies such as a full-mesh WAN or a star-based LAN with a parallel backbone offer the greatest fault tolerance. A SONET ring also offers high fault tolerance because of its dual-ring topology.
- Connectivity devices can be made more fault tolerant through the use of redundant components such as NICs, SFPs, and processors. Full redundancy occurs when components are hot swappable—that is, they have identical functions and can automatically assume the functions of their counterpart if it suffers a fault.
- You can increase the fault tolerance of important connections through the use of link aggregation, in which multiple ports or interfaces are bonded to create one logical interface. If a port, NIC, or cable connected to an interface fails, the other bonded ports or interfaces will automatically assume the functions of the failed component.
- Naming and addressing services can benefit from several fault-tolerance techniques, including the use of multiple name servers on a network. Also, you can assign each critical device multiple IP addresses in a zone file using round-robin DNS. In addition, you can use load balancers to intelligently distribute requests and responses among several identical interfaces. Finally, you can use CARP (Common Address Redundancy Protocol) to enable multiple computers or interfaces to share one or more IP addresses and provide automatic failover in case one computer or interface suffers a fault.
- Critical servers often contain redundant NICs, processors, and/or hard disks to provide better fault tolerance. These redundant components ensure that even if one fails, the whole system won't fail. They also enable load balancing and may improve performance.
- A fault-tolerance technique that involves utilizing a second, identical server to duplicate the transactions and data storage of one server is called server mirroring. Mirroring can take place between servers that are either side by side or geographically distant. It requires not only a link between the servers, but also software running on both servers to enable the servers to continually synchronize their actions and to permit one to take over in case the other fails.

- Clustering is a fault-tolerance technique that links multiple servers together to act as a single server. In this configuration, clustered servers share processing duties and appear as a single server to users. If one server in the cluster fails, the other servers in the cluster automatically take over its data transaction and storage responsibilities.
- An important storage redundancy feature is a RAID (Redundant Array of Independent [or Inexpensive] Disks). All types of RAID use shared, multiple physical or logical hard disks to ensure data integrity and availability. Some designs also increase storage capacity and improve performance. RAID is either hardware or software based. Software RAID can be implemented through operating system utilities.

- NAS (network attached storage) is a dedicated storage device attached to a client/server network. It uses its own file system but relies on a traditional network transmission method such as Ethernet to interact with the rest of the client/server network.
- A SAN (storage area network) is a distinct network of multiple storage devices and servers that provides fast, highly available, and highly fault-tolerant access to large quantities of data for a client/server network. A SAN uses a proprietary network transmission method (such as Fibre Channel) rather than Ethernet.
- A backup is a copy of data or program files created for archiving or safekeeping. If you do not back up your data, you risk losing everything through a hard disk fault, fire, flood, or malicious or accidental erasure or corruption. Backups should be stored on separate media (other than the backed-up server), and these media should be stored off-site.
- Backups can be saved to optical media (such as recordable DVDs or Blu-ray discs), tapes, external disk drives, a host on your network, or an online storage repository, using a cloud backup service.
- A full backup copies all data on all servers to a storage medium, regardless of whether the data is new or changed. An incremental backup copies only data that has changed since the last full or incremental backup, and unchecks the archive bit for files it backs up. A differential backup copies only data that has changed since the last full or incremental backup, but does not uncheck the archive bit for files it backs up.
- The aim of a good backup rotation scheme is to provide excellent data reliability but not to overtax your network or require much intervention. The most popular backup rotation scheme is called Grandfather-Father-Son. This scheme combines daily (son), weekly (father), and monthly (grandfather) backup sets.
- Disaster recovery is the process of restoring your critical functionality and data after an enterprise-wide outage that affects more than a single system or a limited group of users. It must account for the possible extremes, rather than relatively minor outages, failures, security breaches, or data corruption. In a disaster recovery plan, you should consider the worst-case scenarios, from a hurricane to a military or terrorist attack.
- To prepare for recovery after a potential disaster, you can maintain (or a hire a service to maintain for you) a cold site, warm site, or hot site. A cold site contains the elements necessary to rebuild a network, but none are appropriately configured and connected. Therefore, restoring functionality from a cold site can take a long time. A warm site contains the elements necessary to rebuild a network, and only some of them are appropriately configured and connected. A hot site is a precise duplicate of the network's elements, all properly configured and connected. This allows an organization to regain network functionality almost immediately.

Key Terms

archive bit A file attribute that can be checked (or set to "on") or unchecked (or set to "off") to indicate whether the file needs to be archived. An operating system checks a file's archive bit when it is created or changed.

array A group of hard disks.

availability How consistently and reliably a file, device, or connection can be accessed by authorized personnel.

backup A copy of data or program files created for archiving or safekeeping.

backup rotation scheme A plan for when and how often backups occur, and which backups are full, incremental, or differential.

blackout A complete power loss.

Blu-ray An optical storage format released in 2006 by a consortium of electronics and computer vendors. Blu-ray discs are the same size as recordable DVDs, but can store significantly more data, up to 128 GB on a quadruple-layer disc.

bonding *See* link aggregation.

boot sector virus A virus that resides on the boot sector of an external storage device and is transferred to the partition sector or the DOS boot sector on a hard disk when the machine starts.

bot A program that runs automatically. Bots can spread viruses or other malicious code between users in a chat room by exploiting the IRC protocol.

brownout A momentary decrease in voltage, also known as a *sag*. An overtaxed electrical system may cause brownouts, recognizable as a dimming of the lights.

CARP (Common Address Redundancy Protocol) A protocol that allows a pool of computers or interfaces to share one or more IP addresses. CARP improves availability and can contribute to load balancing among several devices, including servers, firewalls, or routers.

cloud backup *See* online backup.

clustering A fault-tolerance technique that links multiple servers to act as a single server. In this configuration, clustered servers share processing duties and appear as a single server to users. If one server in the cluster fails, the other servers in the cluster automatically take over its data transaction and storage responsibilities.

cold site A place where the computers, devices, and connectivity necessary to rebuild a network exist, but they are not appropriately configured, updated, or connected to match the network's current state.

cold spare A duplicate component that is not installed, but can be installed in case of a failure.

Common Address Redundancy Protocol *See* CARP.

differential backup A backup method in which only data that has changed since the last full or incremental backup is copied to a storage medium, and in which that same information is marked for subsequent backup, regardless of whether it has changed. In other words, a differential backup does not uncheck the archive bits for files it backs up.

disaster recovery The process of restoring critical functionality and data to a network after an enterprise-wide outage that affects more than a single system or a limited group of users.

encrypted virus A virus that is encrypted to prevent detection.

external disk drive A storage device that can be attached temporarily to a computer.

failover The capability for one component (such as a NIC or server) to assume another component's responsibilities without manual intervention.

failure A deviation from a specified level of system performance for a given period of time. A failure occurs when something doesn't work as promised or as planned.

fault The malfunction of one component of a system. A fault can result in a failure.

fault tolerance The capacity for a system to continue performing despite an unexpected hardware or software malfunction.

Fibre Channel A distinct network transmission method that relies on fiber-optic media and its own proprietary protocol. Fibre Channel is capable of over 5 Gbps throughput.

file-infector virus A virus that attaches itself to executable files. When the infected executable file runs, the virus copies itself to memory. Later, the virus attaches itself to other executable files.

full backup A backup in which all data on all servers is copied to a storage medium, regardless of whether the data is new or changed. A full backup unchecks the archive bit on files it has backed up.

Grandfather-Father-Son A backup rotation scheme that uses daily (son), weekly (father), and monthly (grandfather) backup sets.

hardware RAID A method of implementing RAID that relies on an externally attached set of disks and a RAID disk controller, which manages the RAID array.

heuristic scanning A type of virus scanning that attempts to identify viruses by discovering viruslike behavior.

hot site A place where the computers, devices, and connectivity necessary to rebuild a network exist, and all are appropriately configured, updated, and connected to match your network's current state.

hot spare In the context of RAID, a disk or partition that is part of the array, but used only in case one of the RAID disks fails. More generally, *hot spare* is used as a synonym for a hot swappable component.

incremental backup A backup in which only data that has changed since the last full or incremental backup is copied to a storage medium. After backing up files, an incremental backup unchecks the archive bit for every file it has saved.

integrity The soundness of a network's files, systems, and connections. To ensure integrity, you must protect your network from anything that might render it unusable, such as corruption, tampering, natural disasters, and viruses.

integrity checking A method of comparing the current characteristics of files and disks against an archived version of these characteristics to discover any changes. The most common example of integrity checking involves a checksum.

Internet Relay Chat *See* IRC.

IRC (Internet Relay Chat) A protocol that enables users running special IRC client software to communicate instantly with other participants in a chat room on the Internet.

link aggregation A fault-tolerance technique in which multiple ports or interfaces are bonded and work in tandem to create one logical interface. Link aggregation can also improve performance and allow for load balancing.

load balancer A device that distributes traffic intelligently between multiple computers.

load balancing The distribution of traffic over multiple links, hard disks, or processors intended to optimize responses.

logic bomb A program designed to start when certain conditions are met.

macro virus A virus that takes the form of an application (for example, a word-processing or spreadsheet) program macro, which may execute when the program is in use.

malware A program or piece of code designed to harm a system or its resources.

master name server An authoritative name server that is queried first on a network when resolution of a name that is not already cached is requested. Master name severs can also be called primary name servers.

mirroring A fault-tolerance technique in which one component or device duplicates the activity of another.

NAS (network attached storage) A device or set of devices attached to a client/server network, dedicated to providing highly fault-tolerant access to large quantities of data. NAS depends on traditional network transmission methods such as Ethernet.

network attached storage *See* NAS.

network virus A virus that takes advantage of network protocols, commands, messaging programs, and data links to propagate itself. Although all viruses could theoretically travel across network connections, network viruses are specially designed to attack network vulnerabilities.

NIC teaming A type of link aggregation in which two or more NICs work in tandem to handle traffic to and from a single node.

offline UPS *See* standby UPS.

online backup A technique in which data is backed up to a central location over the Internet.

online UPS A power supply that uses the A/C power from the wall outlet to continuously charge its battery, while providing power to a network device through its battery.

optical media A type of media capable of storing digitized data, which uses a laser to write data to it and read data from it.

polymorphic virus A type of virus that changes its characteristics (such as the arrangement of its bytes, size, and internal instructions) every time it is transferred to a new system, making it harder to identify.

primary name server *See* master name server.

RAID (Redundant Array of Independent [or Inexpensive] Disks) A server redundancy measure that uses shared, multiple physical or logical hard disks to ensure data integrity and availability. Some RAID designs also increase storage capacity and improve performance.

recordable DVD An optical storage medium that can hold up to 4.7 GB on one single-layered side. Both sides of the disc can be used, and each side can have up to two layers. Thus, in total, a double-layered, two-sided DVD can store up to 17 GB of data. Recordable DVDs come in several different formats.

redundancy The use of more than one identical component, device, or connection for storing, processing, or transporting data. Redundancy is the most common method of achieving fault tolerance.

Redundant Array of Independent (or Inexpensive) Disks *See* RAID.

removable disk drive *See* external disk drive.

replication A fault-tolerance technique that involves dynamic copying of data (for example, an NOS directory or an entire server's hard disk) from one location to another.

round-robin DNS A method of increasing name resolution availability by pointing a host name to multiple IP addresses in a DNS zone file.

sag *See* brownout.

SAN (storage area network) A distinct network of multiple storage devices and servers that provides fast, highly available, and highly fault-tolerant access to large quantities of data for a client/server network. A SAN uses a proprietary network transmission method (such as Fibre Channel) rather than a traditional network transmission method such as Ethernet.

secondary name server *See* slave name server.

server mirroring A fault-tolerance technique in which one server duplicates the transactions and data storage of another, identical server. Server mirroring requires a link between the servers and software running on both servers so that the servers can continually synchronize their actions and one can take over in case the other fails.

signature scanning The comparison of a file's content with known virus signatures (unique identifying characteristics in the code) in a signature database to determine whether the file is a virus.

slave name server A name server that can take the place of a master name server to resolve names and addresses on a network. Slave name servers poll master name servers to ensure that their zone information is identical. Slave name servers are also called secondary name servers.

software RAID A method of implementing RAID that uses software to implement and control RAID techniques over virtually any type of hard disk(s). RAID software may be a third-party package or utilities that come with an operating system NOS.

standby UPS A power supply that provides continuous voltage to a device by switching virtually instantaneously to the battery when it detects a loss of power from the wall outlet. Upon restoration of the power, the standby UPS switches the device to use A/C power again.

stealth virus A type of virus that hides itself to prevent detection. Typically, stealth viruses disguise themselves as legitimate programs or replace part of a legitimate program's code with their destructive code.

storage area network *See* SAN.

surge A momentary increase in voltage caused by distant lightning strikes or electrical problems.

surge protector A device that directs excess voltage away from equipment plugged into it and redirects it to a ground, thereby protecting the equipment from harm.

tape backup A relatively simple and economical backup method in which data is copied to magnetic tapes. In many environments, tape backups have been replaced with faster backup methods, such as copying to network or online storage.

Trojan *See* Trojan horse.

Trojan horse A program that disguises itself as something useful, but actually harms your system.

uninterruptible power supply *See* UPS.

UPS (uninterruptible power supply) A battery-operated power source directly attached to one or more devices and to a power supply (such as a wall outlet) that prevents undesired features of the power source from harming the device or interrupting its services.

uptime The duration or percentage of time a system or network functions normally between failures.

VA *See* volt-amp.

virus A program that replicates itself to infect more computers, either through network connections or through external storage devices, such as USB drives, passed among users. Viruses might damage files or systems or simply annoy users by flashing messages or pictures on the screen or by causing the keyboard to beep.

volt-amp (VA) A measure of electrical power. A volt-amp is the product of the voltage and current (measured in amps) of the electricity on a line.

warm site A place where the computers, devices, and connectivity necessary to rebuild a network exist, though only some are appropriately configured, updated, or connected to match the network's current state.

worm An unwanted program that travels between computers and across networks. Although worms do not alter other programs as viruses do, they can carry viruses.

Review Questions

1. Which type of malware is a program that claims to do something useful but instead harms the computer or system?
   a. Bot
   b. Worm
   c. Boot sector virus
   d. Trojan horse
2. Which factor is the most important decision to consider when implementing anti-malware software on a network?
   a. Where to install the software
   b. Ease of use for end-users
   c. Portability
   d. Disk space usage

3. Which type of power flaw is caused by a momentary decrease in voltage?
   a. Brownout
   b. Blackout
   c. Surge
   d. Noise

4. Which of the following is true regarding a software implementation of RAID?
   a. A software RAID array is managed exclusively by the RAID disk controller.
   b. Software RAID is less expensive overall than hardware RAID.
   c. Software RAID performance is much slower than that of hardware RAID.
   d. Software RAID must exist as part of the NOS.
5. Which type of backup does not uncheck the archive bits for files it backs up?
   a. Full
   b. Incremental
   c. Partial
   d. Differential
6. True or false? Macro viruses were the first type of virus to infect data files rather than executable files.
7. True or false? On a LAN, a star topology and a parallel backbone provide the greatest fault tolerance.
8. True or false? Clustering is a fault-tolerance technique that links multiple servers together to act as a single server.
9. True or false? SANs (storage area networks) are distinct networks of storage devices that communicate directly with each other and with other networks.
10. True or false? A hot site is a place where the computers, devices, and connectivity necessary to rebuild a network exist, with some appropriately configured, updated, or connected.
11. The term ________________ refers to the soundness of a network's programs, data, services, devices, and connections.
12. The term ________________ refers to how consistently and reliably a file or system can be accessed by authorized personnel.
13. ________________ viruses change their characteristics (such as the arrangement of their bytes, size, and internal instructions) every time they are transferred to a new system, making them harder to identify.
14. A(n) ________________ provides rules for using anti-malware software, as well as policies for installing programs, sharing files, and using external disks such as flash drives.
15. A(n) ________________ UPS provides continuous voltage to a device by switching virtually instantaneously to the battery when it detects a loss of power from the wall outlet.

Network Management

After reading this chapter and completing the exercises, you will be able to:

- Explain basic concepts related to network management
- Discuss the importance of documentation, baseline measurements, policies, and regulations in assessing and maintaining a network's health
- Manage a network's performance using SNMP-based network management software, system and event logs, and traffic-shaping techniques
- Identify the reasons for and elements of an asset management system
- Plan and follow regular hardware and software maintenance routines

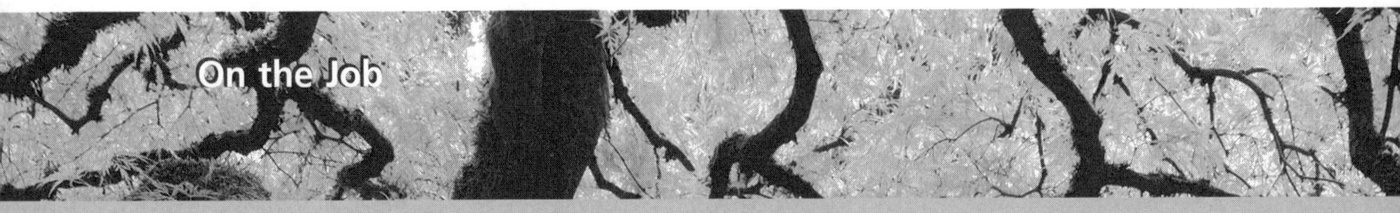

I used to work for a service provider whose shared network supplied switching, content distribution, and firewall protection for many medium-sized customer Web servers in our data center. We'd assigned one of our best network engineers a project that required a change to every firewall port opening statement on the network. That sort of work did appear on our list of preapproved routine changes, as long as the customer had provided written authorization for the security port opening. However, notifying all customers five days before the change, scheduling the change after hours, and management approval of a change record were not required.

But the network engineer had a complex project in mind. He was going to modify hundreds of lines of configuration at once on a redundant set of network devices that supported dozens of customers, and those lines of configuration were security related. Of course, this wasn't what I'd had in mind when I allowed this activity to be put on the preapproved changes list.

The network engineer had never done this kind of project before, so he mocked it up and tested it in our test lab. The lab maintained equipment and configurations for that purpose, but not a perfect copy of the production system with traffic.

During the middle of the day, the network engineer went ahead and implemented this "routine" change. It took down the whole network, including every one of those dozens of customers, for about 30 minutes. Worse, there was a brief period where some security rules at the firewall weren't working, exposing some ports.

Today, in networks for which I'm responsible for change management standards, I always include the following caveats for any preauthorization of routine changes:

1. If it's the first time we've done it, it isn't routine.
2. If it's not the version of the change that we do regularly, it isn't routine.
3. If it requires testing before performance, it isn't routine.

This network engineer and I both learned a lot after that change.

Brooke Noelke
CDW Hosting and Managed Services

In this book, you have learned the technologies and techniques necessary to design an efficient, fault-tolerant, and secure network. However, your work isn't finished once all the clients, servers, switches, routers, and gateways have been installed. After a network is in place, it requires continual review and adjustment. A network, like any other complex system, is in a constant state of flux. Whether the changes are caused by internal factors, such as increased demand on the server's processor, or external factors, such as the obsolescence of a router, you should count on spending a significant amount of time investigating, performing, and verifying changes to your network. In this chapter, you will learn about changes dictated by immediate needs as well as those required to enhance the network's functionality, growth, performance, or security. You'll also learn how best to implement those changes.

Fundamentals of Network Management

Net+ 4.5 Network management is a general term that means different things to different networking professionals. At its broadest, **network management** refers to the assessment, monitoring, and maintenance of all aspects of a network. It can include checking for hardware faults, ensuring high QoS (quality of service) for critical applications, maintaining records of network assets and software configurations, and determining what time of day is best for upgrading a router.

The scope of network management techniques differs according to the network's size and importance. On some large networks, for example, administrators run network management applications that continually check devices and connections to make certain they respond within an expected performance threshold. If a device doesn't respond quickly enough or at all, the application automatically issues an alert that pages the network administrator responsible for that device. On a small network, however, comprehensive network management might not be economically feasible. Instead, such a network might run an inexpensive application that periodically tests devices and connections to determine only whether they are still functioning.

Several disciplines fall under the heading of network management, including topics discussed in previous chapters, such as posture assessments. All share the goals of enhancing efficiency and performance while preventing costly downtime or loss. Ideally, network management accomplishes this by helping the administrator predict problems before they occur. For example, a trend in network usage could indicate when a switch will be overwhelmed with traffic. In response, the network administrator could increase the switch's processing capabilities or replace the switch before users begin experiencing slow or dropped connections. Before you can assess and make predictions about a network's health, however, you must first understand its logical and physical structure and how it functions under typical conditions.

Documentation

Throughout this book, you have witnessed and read about different types of network documentation. For example, in Chapter 13's discussion of troubleshooting, you learned that keeping a record of a problem and its solution helps to prevent similar problems from recurring, or at least helps technicians deal with it if it does recur. In this section and in the rest of this chapter, you'll learn about other types of documentation that contribute to sound network management.

The way you format and store your documentation can vary, but to adequately manage your network, you should at least record the following:

- *Physical topology*—Which types of LAN and WAN topologies does your network use: bus, star, ring, hybrid, mesh, or a combination of these? Which type of backbone does your network use—collapsed, distributed, parallel, serial, or a combination of these? Which type and grade of cabling does your network use? What types of cables are used and where are they located?

4.5

- *Access method*—Does your network use Ethernet (802.3), Wi-Fi (802.11), WiMAX (802.16), cellular, satellite, or a mix of transmission methods? What transmission speed(s) does it provide? Is it switched?
- *Protocols*—Which protocols are used by servers, nodes, and connectivity devices?
- *Devices*—How many of the following devices are connected to your network—switches, routers, gateways, firewalls, access points, servers, UPSs, printers, backup devices, and clients? Where are they located? Are they physical or virtual? If physical, what are their model numbers and vendors?
- *Operating systems*—Which network and desktop operating systems appear on the network? Which versions of these operating systems are used by each device? Which type and version of operating systems are used by connectivity devices such as routers?
- *Applications*—Which applications are used by clients and servers? Where do you store the applications? From where do they run?
- *Configurations*—What versions of operating systems and applications does each workstation, server, and connectivity device run? How are these programs configured? How is hardware configured? The collection, storage, and assessment of such information belongs to a category of network management known as **configuration management**. Ideally, you would rely on configuration management software to gather and store the information in a database, where those who need it can easily access and analyze the data.

If you have not already collected and centrally stored the answers to the questions just listed, it could take the efforts of several people and several weeks to compile them, depending on the size and complexity of your network. This evaluation involves visits to the telecommunications and equipment rooms, an examination of servers and desktops, a review of receipts for software and hardware purchases, and, potentially, the use of a protocol analyzer or network management software package. Though it requires effort, documenting all aspects of your network promises to save work in the future. After you have compiled the information, organize it into a database that can be easily updated and searched. That way, staff can access the information in a timely manner and keep it current.

Understanding conventions for network documentation can make your task easier. In this book, you have seen many instances of **network diagrams**, which are graphical representations of a network's devices and connections. Network diagrams can be as varied as the engineers who create them. Some adhere strictly to the network's physical layout and label each connection. Some represent only the logical topology. Others, like many of the figures in this book, are more general or designed to highlight one critical part of a network, such as its perimeter. These might depict an internal network of hundreds of clients with only a few clients within a circle labeled "internal network," for example.

You could sketch your network diagram on the back of a napkin or draw it on your computer using a graphics program. However, many people use software designed for mapping networks, such as Dia, Edraw, Gliffy, Microsoft Visio, or Network Notepad. Such applications come with icons that represent different types of devices and connections. Soon after entering the world of network engineering, you'll recognize certain icons that Cisco Systems has created and made popular. Because of its status in the networking world and the volume of networking hardware it sells, Cisco has set trends for network diagramming. Like the "Walk" or "Don't Walk" signs that are understood on street corners around the globe, Cisco's symbols for routers, switches, firewalls, and other devices are widely accepted and

4.5 understood in the networking field. Figure 15-1 shows a simplified network diagram that uses Cisco's iconography, with each device labeled. Notice that a router is represented by a hockey-puck shape with two arrows pointing inward and two arrows pointing outward. A wireless router looks the same, but has two antennas attached. A workgroup switch is represented by a small rectangular box, which also contains two arrows pointing inward and two arrows pointing outward.

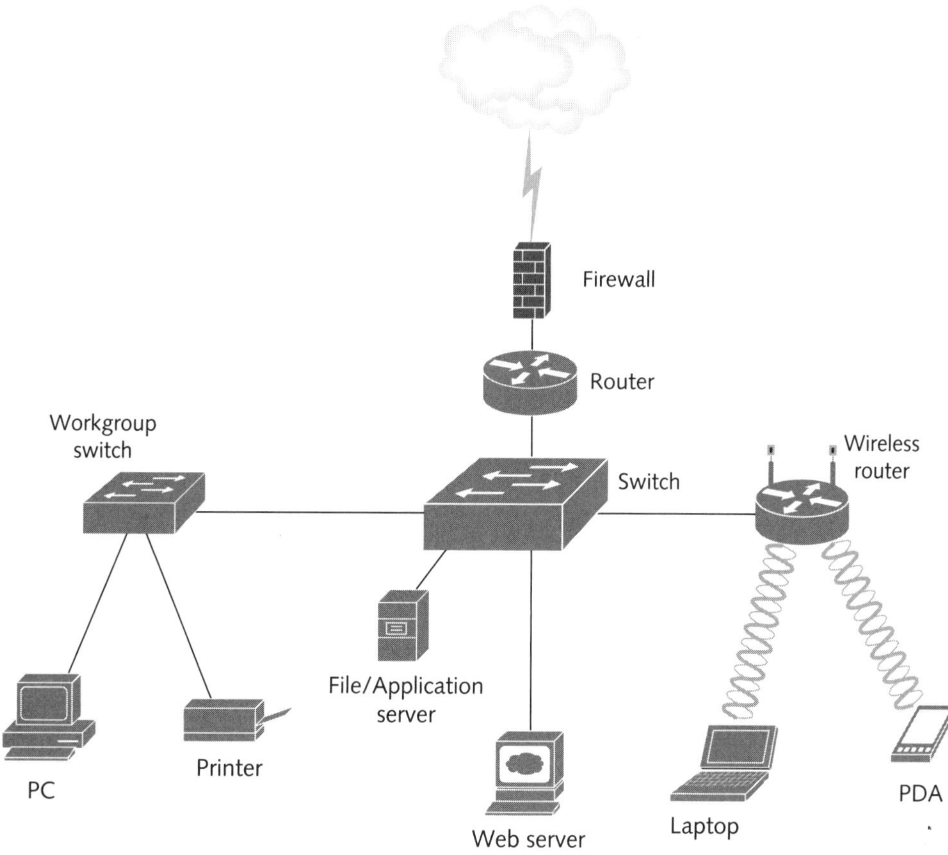

Figure 15-1 Network diagram using Cisco symbols

Most network diagrams provide broad snapshots of a network's physical or logical topology. This type of view is useful for planning where to insert a new switch or determining how a particular router, gateway, and firewall interact. However, if you're a technician who needs to find a fault in a client's wired connection to the LAN, a broad overview might be too general. Instead, you need a wiring schematic. A **wiring schematic** is a graphical representation of a network's wired infrastructure. In its most detailed form, it shows every wire necessary to interconnect network devices. Some less-detailed wiring schematics might use a single line to represent the group of wires necessary to connect several clients to a switch. Figure 15-2 provides an example of a detailed wiring schematic for a small office network connection that relies on cable broadband service to access the Internet.

Net+
4.5

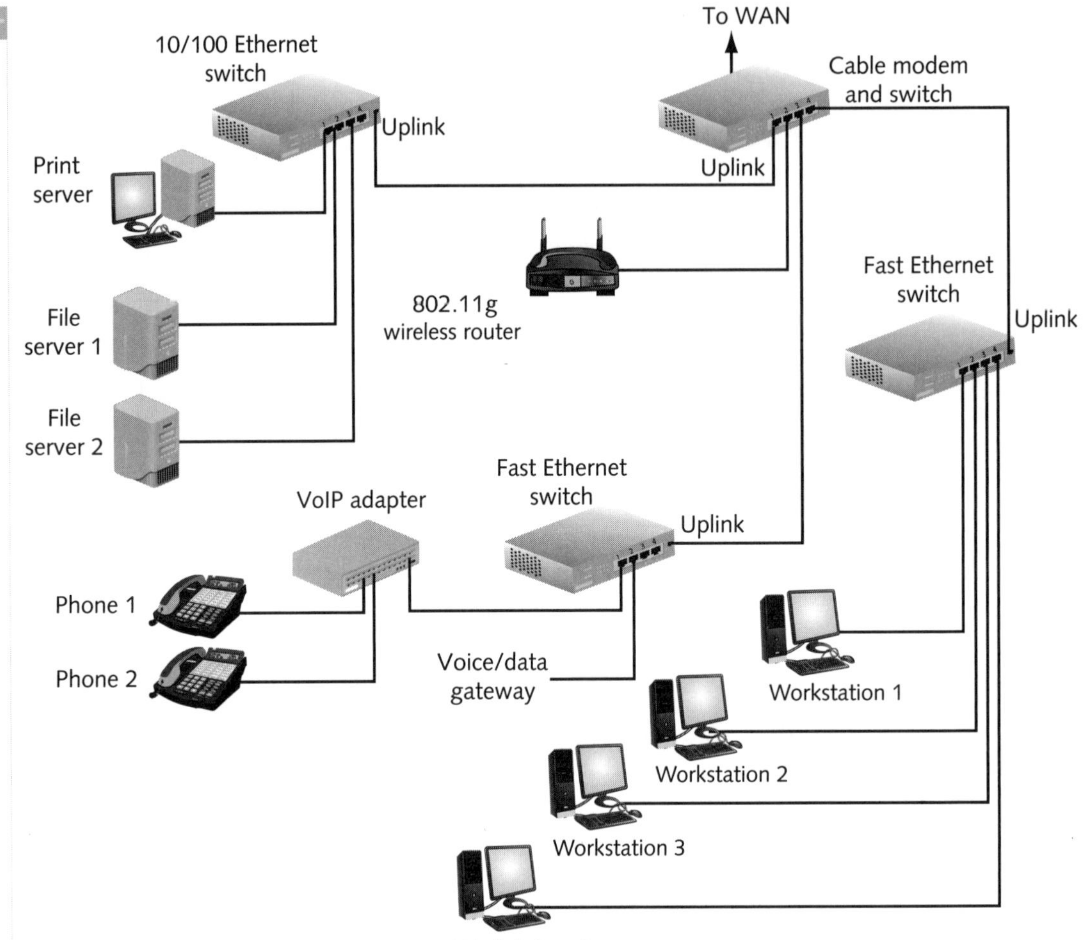

Figure 15-2 Wiring schematic

Documenting and capturing an accurate picture of your network's physical and logical elements are initial steps in understanding the network. Next you need to know how it routinely performs.

Baseline Measurements

As you learned in Chapter 13, a baseline is a report of the network's current state of operation. Baseline measurements might include the utilization rate for your network backbone, number of users logged on per day or per hour, number of protocols that run on your network, statistics about errors (such as runts, collisions, jabbers, or giants), frequency with which networked applications are used, or information regarding which users take up the most bandwidth. The graph in Figure 15-3 shows a sample baseline for daily network traffic over a six-week period.

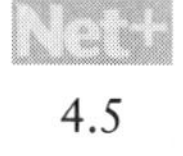
4.5

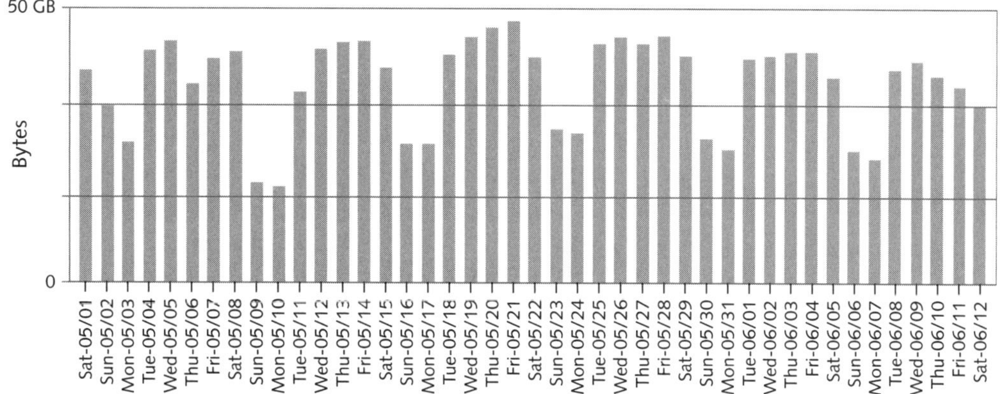

Figure 15-3 Baseline of daily network traffic

Baseline measurements allow you to compare future performance increases or decreases caused by network changes or events with past network performance. Obtaining baseline measurements is the only way to know for certain whether a pattern of usage has changed (and requires attention) or, later, whether a network upgrade made a difference. Each network requires its own approach. The elements you measure depend on which functions are most critical to your network and its users.

For instance, suppose that your network currently serves 500 users and that your backbone traffic exceeds 50% at 10:00 a.m. and 2:00 p.m. each business day. That pattern constitutes your baseline. Now suppose that your company decides to add 200 users who perform the same types of functions on the network. The added number of users equals 40% of the current number of users (200/500). Therefore, you can estimate that your backbone's capacity should increase by approximately 40% to maintain your current service levels.

The more data you gather while establishing your network's baseline, the more accurate your prediction will be. Network traffic patterns might be difficult to forecast because you cannot predict users' habits, effects of new technology, or changes in demand for resources over a given period of time. For instance, the preceding example assumed that all new users would share the same network usage habits as the current users. In fact, however, the new users may generate a great deal more, or a great deal less, network traffic.

How do you gather baseline data on your network? Although you could theoretically use a network monitor or network analyzer and record its output at regular intervals, several software applications can perform the baselining for you. These applications range from freeware available on the Internet to expensive, customizable hardware and software combination products. Before choosing a network-baselining tool, you should determine how you will use it. If you manage a small network that provides only one critical application to users, an inexpensive tool may suffice. If you work on a WAN with several critical links, however, you should investigate purchasing a more comprehensive package. The baseline measurement tool should also be capable of collecting the statistics needed. For example, only a sophisticated tool can measure traffic generated by each node on a network, filter traffic according to types of protocols and errors, and simultaneously measure statistics from several different network segments.

Policies, Procedures, and Regulations

Imagine you are the network administrator for a large enterprise network and that you supervise eight network technicians who are responsible for day-to-day installations, upgrades, and troubleshooting. Unless you and your technicians agree on policies for adding new users, for example, you might discover that some users have fewer access restrictions than they ought to have or that logon IDs don't follow a standard naming convention. The former could cause security vulnerabilities, and the latter could make future user management more challenging.

Following rules helps limit chaos, confusion, and possibly downtime for you and your users. Previous chapters of this book have described policies, procedures, and regulations that make for sound network management. They are summarized here:

- *Media installation and management*—Includes designing the physical layout of a cable or wireless infrastructure, choosing and following best practices for cable management, testing the effectiveness of cable or wireless infrastructure, and documenting cable layouts; see Chapters 3 and 8 for more information.
- *Network addressing policies*—Includes choosing and applying an addressing scheme, determining the use and limits of subnets, integrating an internal network's addressing with an external network's, and configuring gateways for NAT; see Chapters 4 and 9 for more information.
- *Security-related policies*—Includes establishing rules for passwords, limiting access to physical spaces such as the data center, limiting access to shared resources on the network, imposing restrictions on the types of files that are saved to networked computers, monitoring computers for malware, and conducting regular security audits; see Chapters 11 and 14 for more information.
- *Troubleshooting procedures*—Includes following a methodology for troubleshooting network problems and documenting their solutions; see Chapter 13 for more information.
- *Backup and disaster recovery procedures*—Includes establishing a method and schedule for making backups, regularly testing the effectiveness of backups, assigning a disaster recovery team and defining each member's role, and choosing a disaster recovery strategy and testing it; see Chapter 14 for more information.

In addition to internal policies, a network manager must consider state and federal regulations that might affect her responsibilities. In the United States, one such federal regulation is **CALEA (Communications Assistance for Law Enforcement Act)**, which requires telecommunications carriers and equipment manufacturers to provide for surveillance capabilities. CALEA was passed by Congress in 1994 after pressure from the FBI, which worried that networks relying solely on digital communications would circumvent traditional wiretapping strategies. In other words, a phone call made using VoIP over a private WAN cannot be intercepted as easily as a phone call made via the PSTN. Therefore, if you work at an ISP, for example, your switches and routers must provide an interface for electronic eavesdropping and your staff must be ready to allow authorities access to those devices when presented with a warrant.

A second significant federal regulation in the United States is **HIPAA (Health Insurance Portability and Accountability Act)**, which was passed by Congress in 1996. One aspect of this regulation addresses the security and privacy of medical records, including those stored or transmitted electronically. If you work at any organization that handles medical records, such as an insurance company, hospital, or transcription service, you must understand and follow federal standards for protecting the security and privacy of these records. HIPAA rules are very specific. They govern not only the way medical records are stored and transmitted, but also the policies for authorizing access and even the placement and orientation of workstations where such records might be viewed.

Many of the policies and procedures mentioned in this section are not laws, but best practices aimed at preventing network problems before they occur. The next section describes techniques for detecting and managing network problems before they significantly impair access or performance.

Fault and Performance Management

Net+ After documenting every aspect of your network and following policies and best practices,
4.4 you are ready to assess your network's status on an ongoing basis. This process includes both **performance management**, or monitoring how well links and devices are keeping up with the demands placed on them, and **fault management**, or the detection and signaling of device, link, or component faults.

Network Management Systems

To accomplish both fault and performance management, organizations often use enterprise-wide network management systems. Hundreds of such tools exist. All rely on a similar architecture, in which at least one network management console, which may be a server or workstation, depending on the size of the network, collects data from multiple networked devices at regular intervals, in a process called **polling**. Each managed device runs a network management **agent**, a software routine that collects information about the device's operation and provides it to the network management application running on the console. So as not to affect the performance of a device while collecting information, agents do not demand significant processing resources.

A managed device may contain several objects that can be managed, including components such as processor, memory, hard disk, NIC, or intangibles such as performance or utilization. For example, on a server, an agent can measure how many users are connected to the server or what percentage of the processor's resources are used at any time. The definition of managed devices and their data are collected in a **MIB (Management Information Base)**.

Agents communicate information about managed devices via any one of several Application layer protocols. On modern networks, most agents use **SNMP (Simple Network Management Protocol)**. SNMP is part of the TCP/IP suite of protocols and typically runs over UDP on port 161 (though it can be configured to run over TCP). Three versions of SNMP exist: SNMPv1, SNMPv2, and SNMPv3. **SNMPv1 (Simple Network Management Protocol version 1)** was the original version, released in 1988. Because of its limited features, it is rarely used on modern networks. **SNMPv2 (Simple Network Management Protocol version 2)** improved on SNMPv1 with improved performance and slightly better security, among other features. **SNMPv3 (Simple Network Management Protocol version 3)** is similar to

Net+ 4.4 SNMPv2, but adds authentication, validation, and encryption for packets exchanged between managed devices and the network management console. SNMPv3 is the most secure version of the protocol. However, some administrators have hesitated to upgrade to SNMPv3 because it requires more complex configuration. Therefore, SNMPv2 is still widely used. Most network management applications support multiple versions of SNMP. Some managed devices, however, support only one version.

Figure 15-4 illustrates the relationship between a network management application and managed devices on a network.

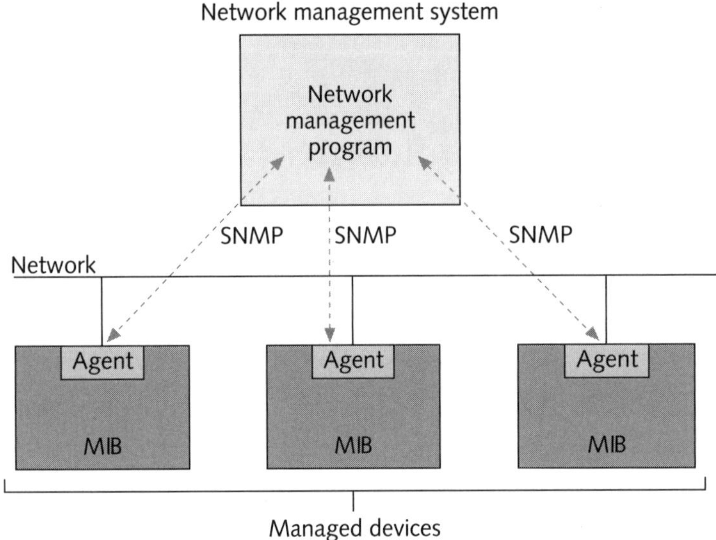

Figure 15-4 Network management architecture

After data is collected, the network management application can present an administrator with several ways to view and analyze the data. For example, a popular way to view data is in the form of a map that shows fully functional links or devices in green, partially (or less than optimally) functioning links or devices in yellow, and failed links or devices in red. An example of the type of map generated by a network performance monitor is shown in Figure 15-5.

Because of their flexibility, sophisticated network management applications are also challenging to configure and fine-tune. You have to be careful to collect only useful data and not an excessive amount of routine information. For example, on a network with dozens of routers, collecting SNMP-generated messages that essentially say "I'm still here" every five seconds would result in massive amounts of insignificant data. A glut of information makes it difficult to ascertain when a router in fact requires attention. Instead, when configuring a network management application to poll a router, you might choose to generate an SNMP-based message only when the router's processor is operating at 75% of its capacity or to measure only the amount of traffic passing through a NIC every five minutes.

Faults and conditions that exceed certain thresholds can trigger alarms in network management software. They can also be recorded by system and event logs, as described next.

Net+
4.4

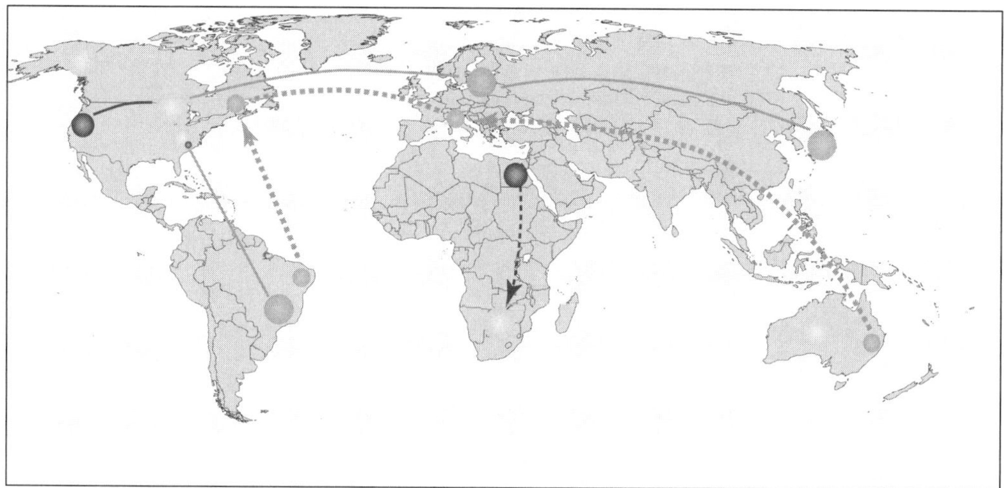

Figure 15-5 Map showing network status

System and Event Logs

Virtually every condition recognized by an operating system can be recorded. Records of such activity are kept in a log. For example, each time your computer requests an IP address from the DHCP server and doesn't receive a response, this can be recorded in a log. Likewise, a log entry can be added each time a firewall denies a host's attempt to connect to another host on the network that the firewall defends.

Different operating systems log different kinds of events by default. In addition, network administrators can customize logs by defining conditions under which new entries are created. For example, an engineer might want to know when the relative humidity in a data center exceeds 60%. If a device can monitor this information, the results can be written to a log.

On Windows-based computers, such a log is known as an **event log** and can be easily viewed with the **Event Viewer** application. Figure 15-6 provides an example of data collected in the event log on a workstation running the Windows 7 operating system. In the Hands-On Projects at the end of this chapter, you will view an event log using Windows Event Viewer.

Similar information is routinely recorded by computers running Linux or UNIX via the syslog function. **Syslog** is a standard for generating, storing, and processing messages about events on a system. It describes methods for detecting and reporting events and specifies the format and contents of messages. It also defines roles for each computer that participates in logging events. For example, the computer that is monitored by a syslog-compatible application and that issues event information is known as a generator. The computer that gathers event messages from generators is known as a collector. The syslog standard also establishes levels of severity for every logged event. For example, "0" indicates an emergency situation and "7" simply points to very specific information that might help in debugging a problem.

Computers running Linux and UNIX record syslog data in a **system log**. In general, newer versions of Linux typically write their system logs to the file `/var/log/messages`, while

Net+
4.4

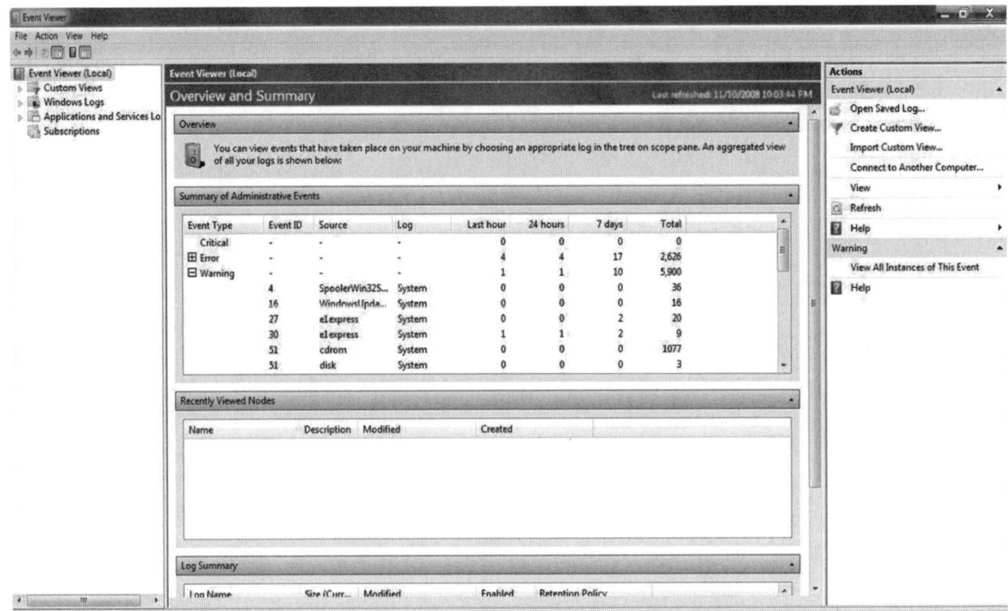

Figure 15-6 Event log on a workstation running Windows 7

older versions of UNIX often write to a system log in the file `/var/logs/syslog` and Solaris versions of UNIX write to a system log in the file `/var/adm/messages`. To find out where various logs are kept on your UNIX or Linux system, view the `/etc/syslog.conf` file (on some systems this is the `/etc/rsyslog.conf` file).

The `/etc/syslog.conf` file is also where you can configure the types of events to log and what priority to assign each event.

Bear in mind that the syslog function doesn't alert you to any problems, but it does keep a history of messages issued by the system. It's up to you to monitor the system log for errors. Most UNIX and Linux operating systems provide a GUI application for easily viewing and filtering the information in system logs. Other applications are available for sifting through syslog data and generating alerts. In the Hands-On Projects at the end of this chapter, you'll view and sort through data in a system log.

Much of the information collected in event logs and system logs does not point to a problem, even if it is marked with a warning. For example, you might have typed your password incorrectly while trying to log on to your computer, thus generating a log entry. Using these logs for fault management requires thoughtful data filtering and sorting.

Net+

Traffic Shaping

4.4 When a network must handle high volumes of network traffic, users benefit from a perfor-
4.6 mance management technique known as traffic shaping. **Traffic shaping** involves manipulating certain characteristics of packets, data streams, or connections to manage the type and amount of traffic traversing a network or interface at any moment. Its goals are to

Net+ assure timely delivery of the most important traffic while offering the best possible performance for all users.

4.4

4.6 Traffic shaping can involve delaying less-important traffic, increasing the priority of more-important traffic, limiting the volume of traffic flowing in or out of an interface during a specified time period, or limiting the momentary throughput rate for an interface. The last two techniques belong to a category of traffic shaping known as **traffic policing**. An ISP might impose a maximum on the capacity it will grant a certain customer. That way, it ensures that the customer does not tie up more than a certain amount of the network's overall capacity. Traffic policing helps the service provider predict how much capacity it must purchase from its network provider. It also holds down costs because the ISP doesn't have to plan for every client using all the throughput he could at all times (an unlikely scenario). An ISP that imposes traffic policing might allow customers to choose their preferred maximum daily traffic volume or momentary throughput and pay commensurate fees. A more sophisticated instance of traffic policing is dynamic and takes into account the network's traffic patterns. For example, the service provider might allow certain customers to exceed their maximums when few other customers are using the network.

Figure 15-7 illustrates how traffic volume might appear on an interface without limits compared with an interface subject to traffic policing.

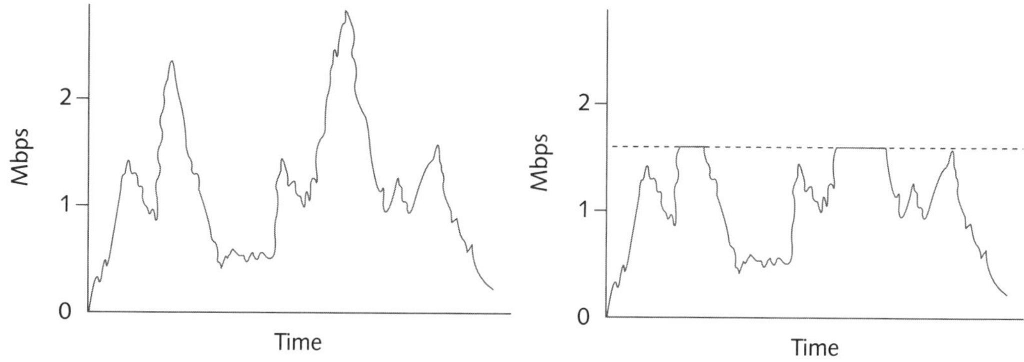

Figure 15-7 Traffic volume before and after applying limits

A controversial example of traffic shaping came to light in 2007. Comcast, one of the largest Internet service providers in the United States, was found to be clandestinely discriminating against certain types of traffic. For users uploading files to P2P (peer-to-peer) networks such as BitTorrent, Comcast was interjecting TCP packets with the RST (reset) field set. These packets were spoofed to appear as if they originated from the accepting site, and they cut the connection as the user attempted to upload files. Soon customers figured out the pattern and used packet analyzers such as Wireshark to reveal the forged TCP RST packets. They complained to authorities that Comcast had violated their user agreement. The FCC investigated, upheld the customers' claims, and ordered Comcast to stop this practice. Comcast chose a different method of traffic shaping. It assigned a lower priority to data from customers who generate a high volume of traffic when the network is at risk of congestion.

Several types of traffic prioritization—that is, treating more-important traffic preferentially—
4.4 exist. Software running on a router, multilayer switch, gateway, server, or even a client work-
4.6 station can prioritize traffic according to any of the following characteristics:

- Protocol
- IP address
- User group
- DiffServ (Differentiated Services) flag or TOS (type of service) field in an IP datagram
- VLAN tag in a Data Link layer frame
- Service or application

Depending on the traffic prioritization software, different types of traffic might be assigned priority classes, such as "high," "normal," "low," or "slow;" alternatively, it can be rated on a prioritization scale from 1 (lowest priority) to 7 (highest priority). For example, traffic generated by time-sensitive VoIP applications might be assigned high priority, while online gaming might be assigned low priority. Traffic prioritization is needed most when the network is busiest. It ensures that during peak usage times, the most important data get through quickly, while less-important data waits. When network usage is low, however, prioritization might have no noticeable effects.

Net+ Caching

4.6 In addition to traffic shaping, a network or host might use caching to improve performance. **Caching** is the local storage of frequently needed files that would otherwise be obtained from an external source. By keeping files close to the requester, caching allows the user to access those files quickly. As you'll learn, it can also save money for ISPs.

The most common type of caching is **Web caching**, in which Web pages are stored locally, either on a host or network, and then delivered to requesters. You might be familiar with the term *cache* from browsing the Web on your computer. A locally stored cache will keep copies of the Web pages you have viewed on your computer's hard drive. Later, when you want to view the page again, the browser will attempt to retrieve the page from your cache if the page hasn't changed since the last time you viewed it. Local caching is highly customizable. You can choose the size of your cache, the rules it uses to refresh its contents, and the conditions under which it clears its contents.

To an ISP, however, caching is much more than just a convenience. It prevents a significant volume of WAN traffic, thus improving performance and saving money. For example, if dozens of an ISP's subscribers read a popular news Web site each morning, the ISP can keep the entire Web site on its **cache engine**, a network device devoted to storage and delivery of frequently requested files. When the ISP's network receives a request for that Web site, the network examines the request and redirects it to a cache engine. The cache engine searches its files for the news Web site. If the cache engine doesn't have a current copy of the Web site, it requests the site from the news organization's server. In that case, the cache engine receives and stores the Web site for later delivery. When another user subsequently requests the same site, the network redirects the request to the cache engine, which delivers the Web site without having to request it from the originating server. The ISP need not spend any of its bandwidth to retrieve the site again until it has changed.

Asset Management

4.5

Another key component in managing networks is identifying and tracking its hardware and software through asset management. The first step in asset management is to take an inventory of each node on the network. This inventory should include the total number of components on the network, and also each device's configuration files, model number, serial number, location on the network, and technical support contact. You will also want to keep records of every piece of software purchased by your organization, its version number, vendor, licensing, and technical support contact.

The asset management tool you choose depends on your organization's needs. You might purchase an application that can automatically discover all devices on the network and then save that information in a database, or you might use a simple spreadsheet to save the data. In either case, your asset management records should be comprehensive and accessible to all personnel who may become involved in maintaining or troubleshooting the network. In addition, ensure that the asset management database is regularly updated, either manually or automatically, as changes to network hardware and software occur. The information you retain is useful only while it is current.

Asset management simplifies maintaining and upgrading the network chiefly because you know what the system includes. For example, if you discover that a router purchased two years ago requires an upgrade to its operating system software to fix a security flaw, you need to know how many routers are installed, where they are installed, and whether any have already received the software upgrade. An up-to-date asset management system allows you to avoid searching through old invoices and troubleshooting records to answer these questions.

In addition, asset management provides network administrators with information about the costs and benefits of certain types of hardware or software. For example, if you conclude that 50% of your staff's troubleshooting time is spent on one flawed brand of NIC, an asset management system can reveal how many NICs you would need to replace if you chose to replace those cards, and whether it would make sense to replace the entire installed base. Some asset management applications can even track the length of equipment leases and alert network managers when leases will expire.

The term *asset management* originally referred to an organization's system for keeping tabs on every piece of equipment it owned. This function was usually handled through the Accounting Department. Some of the accounting-related tasks included under the original definition for asset management, such as managing the depreciation on network equipment or tracking the expiration of leases, apply to asset management in networking as well.

Change Management

4.5

Network conditions are always in a state of flux. Technology advances, vendors come and go, and users' needs change. Managing change while maintaining your network's efficiency and availability requires good planning. The following sections describe how to approach the most common types of software and hardware changes, from installing patches to replacing a network backbone.

Net+

Software Changes

4.5 If you have ever supported desktop computers professionally or even maintained your own
5.4 computer at home, you know that an important part of keeping a system running optimally is upgrading its software. The following sections describe best practices for applying patches, application upgrades, and NOS upgrades.

Application Patches and Upgrades A **patch** is a correction, improvement, or enhancement to a software application. It differs from a revision or software upgrade in that it changes only part of an application, leaving most of the code untouched. Patches are often distributed at no charge by software vendors in an attempt to fix a bug in their code or to add slightly more functionality.

You'll encounter patches in all areas of routine networking maintenance. Among other things, network maintenance sometimes entails patching the server's operating system. For example, if your server runs Windows Server 2008 R2, you might need to apply a patch to close a security hole that allows remote users to hack into your server. Or you might have to patch the software on your Cisco switch to fix a vulnerability that makes it susceptible to denial-of-service attacks.

A software **upgrade** is a major change to a software package's existing code. Vendors might or might not offer upgrades for free. Also, the upgrade might or might not be comprehensive enough to substitute for the original application. In general, application upgrades are designed to add functionality and fix bugs in the previous version of the client. For example, an upgrade to a newer version of Google Chrome might incorporate features to protect you from Web sites that launch phishing attempts. The scope and purpose of client upgrades vary widely, depending on whether the upgrade is a redesign or simply a bug fix. An application upgrade might be transparent to users, or it might completely change the appearance of the application interface. Application upgrades typically overwrite some system files on the workstation, so their installation may affect other applications adversely. They might even prevent other applications from working as they did in the past.

Whereas patches are usually designed to correct a problem or vulnerability, upgrades are usually designed to enhance the application's functionality. For this reason, an application upgrade may be more a matter of convenience than necessity. Therefore, the time, cost, and effort involved in application upgrades should be weighed against the necessity of performing operating system or client upgrades. This consideration is especially important if a networking professional's time is limited (as it usually is).

Although the specifics vary for each type of software change, the general steps involved can be summarized as follows:

1. Determine whether the patch or upgrade is necessary.
2. Research the purpose of the change, its compatibility with current hardware and software, and its potential effects on other applications. If possible, install the software on a test system to make sure it acts as expected. Also determine whether and how the change can be reversed, in case troubles arise.
3. Determine whether the change should apply to some or all users. Also decide whether it will be distributed centrally or machine by machine.

Net+ 4.5 5.4

4. After choosing to implement the change, notify system administrators, help desk personnel, and users. Schedule the change for completion during off-hours (unless it is an emergency).
5. Back up the current system or software before making any modifications.
6. If necessary, prevent users from accessing the system or the part of the system being altered during the change.
7. Keep the software vendor's patch or upgrade instructions handy and follow them as you install the patch or revision.
8. Implement the change.
9. Test the system fully after the change, preferably exercising the software as a typical user would. Note any unintended or unanticipated consequences of the modification.
10. If the change was successful, reenable access to the system. If it was unsuccessful, revert to the previous version of the software following the process for reversing a software upgrade described later in this chapter.
11. Inform system administrators, help desk personnel, and users when the change is complete. If you had to reverse it, make this known and explain why.
12. Record your change in the change management system.

NOS (Network Operating System) Upgrades Perhaps the most critical type of software upgrade you'll perform is an upgrade to your NOS (network operating system). It usually involves significant, potentially drastic, changes to the way your servers and clients operate. As such, it requires plenty of forethought, product research, and rigorous testing before you implement it. In fact, for any network with more than a few users, you should create and follow a project plan for this undertaking. This plan should include all of the precautions typically associated with other software upgrades. In addition, you should consider the following:

- How will the upgrade affect user IDs, groups, rights, and policies?
- How will the upgrade affect file, printer, and directory access on the server?
- How will the upgrade affect applications or client interactions on the server?
- How will the upgrade affect configuration files, protocols, and services running on the server?
- How will the upgrade affect the server's interaction with other devices on the network?
- How accurately can you test the upgrade software in a simulated environment?
- How can you take advantage of the new operating system to make your system more efficient?
- What is your technical support arrangement with the operating system's manufacturer if you need help in the midst of the upgrade?
- Have you allotted enough time to perform the upgrade? (For example, would it be more appropriate to do it over a weekend rather than overnight?)
- During the upgrade, will old NOS files be saved, and can you reverse the installation if troubles arise?
- Have you ensured that the users, help desk personnel, and system administrators understand how the upgrade will affect their daily operations and support burdens?

4.5
5.4

These are only some of the critical questions you need to ask before embarking on an NOS upgrade. Your networking environment might warrant additional considerations. For example, suppose you are the network administrator for a company that is merging with a second company. Your two companies might use dissimilar NOSs, and the IT director might ask you to upgrade your NOS to match the other company's version. In this situation, you would not only have to consider the previous list of questions, but also a list of questions pertaining to the other company's operating system—for instance, how its NOS directories are organized. By addressing these questions before you upgrade your own NOS, you ensure that the merger of the two networks goes more smoothly.

An NOS upgrade is a complex and far-reaching change. It should not be undertaken with severe budgetary, resource, or time constraints. The following steps demonstrate how careful planning and a methodical process can help you accomplish an NOS upgrade. (Depending on your situation, the order and complexity of the steps could vary.)

1. *Research*—Gather information about the NOS from the manufacturer and from other sources, including online user groups, reputable journals, and other networking professionals. Evaluate the costs involved in upgrading. Also list the benefits and risks involved in embarking on this NOS upgrade.
2. *Project plan*—Before you have committed significant time and money to the project, devise a project plan. This plan should include the steps to follow, task assignments for staff, and a rough budget and timeline. Even if you decide not to upgrade the NOS after all, you must commit resources to proposing and evaluating the option.
3. *Proposal*—Write a proposal to evaluate the product, including a plan to purchase and implement it if the proposal is accepted. A proposal should include the following elements:
    - Questions to answer during evaluation, such as "Will the NOS work with my current network monitoring software?"
    - Names of personnel who will assist with evaluation and final approval
    - A rough timeline and plan for implementing the change if it is approved
    - A rough project plan for implementing the change if it is approved
    - Cost considerations
    - A review of the short- and long-term benefits and risks of the upgrade
    - A recommendation for or against performing the upgrade
    - A plan for purchasing the software and implementing the change
4. *Evaluation*—Assuming that the proposal indicates that you should proceed with an upgrade and that your superiors approve your recommendation, you are ready to begin the evaluation phase. First order an evaluation copy of the NOS. Then install the software on an unused server whose hardware is similar to the hardware of your production servers (making sure that the test server meets the NOS manufacturer's recommended hardware requirements). On the test system, create several mock user IDs and groups with varying privileges to simulate the real network environment. Also install the applications and services that the server will support if it goes into production.
5. *Testing*—Next, as part of your evaluation, distribute updated client software to a team of technical staff and project stakeholders and ask them to use the mock IDs and groups

Net+
4.5
5.4

to test the system. Over a given time period, they can test the system and keep notes on how the system meets the requirements specified in your proposal. The test team should pay particular attention to the new user interface for clients, the way in which your company's applications operate, the system's response time, and any new features provided by the upgrade. Meet regularly with the team during the evaluation period to discuss and compare experiences.

6. *Training*—If the results of the initial stages of evaluation lead you to decide to purchase the upgrade, make sure you and other networking staff are trained on how to work with the new NOS. Schedule training to take place only weeks before the anticipated implementation date so that your new skills are fresh when you begin the conversion.
7. *Preimplementation*—Before implementing the change, expand on the rough project plan for the upgrade. Ensure that your plan for transferring user accounts, groups, and their rights to the new system is sound. Decide how you want to reorganize the NOS directory, if necessary, and what types of volumes to create. In addition, review the existing servers to determine which applications, files, and directories should be transferred and which can be archived.

   Weeks before upgrading, inform users, help desk personnel, and other networking staff of the timeline and explain what changes to expect. Recommend that users clean up their data directories on the server and discard any unnecessary files. Similarly, ask networking staff to remove any nonessential applications or services they have installed on the server. If necessary, arrange to upgrade the client software on all workstations that will be affected by the operating system upgrade. A few days before the upgrade, issue a final warning to staff specifying when and for how long the server will be down to accomplish the upgrade.
8. *Implementation*—Perform the upgrade when few or no users will be on the network. Before beginning the upgrade, gather the software documentation and your project plan, along with the new NOS files and a bootable disk for the server. Just before taking the system down, broadcast a final warning to alert all users on the network that the server is going down soon. Then disable all logons to the network. Next, back up the entire server's hard disk. When the backup is complete, use your backup software to verify that critical files were successfully copied. Finally, perform the upgrade according to the manufacturer's instructions and your network's specifications.
9. *Postimplementation*—Test functions and applications on the upgraded server to verify the success of your upgrade. After you are satisfied that the upgrade is successful, reenable logons to the network and inform staff that the system is running again. Later, you can review the upgrade process with other networking staff to find out whether you learned any lessons that could make future server upgrades more efficient and less troublesome. Work with the help desk personnel to understand the kinds of support calls generated by the upgrade. Also continue testing the new operating system, fine-tuning when necessary, to fix problems or find errors before they become problems for users.

Reversing a Software Upgrade If the software upgrade you perform creates problems in your existing system, you should be prepared to reverse the process. The process of reverting to a previous version of software after attempting to upgrade it is known as **backleveling**. Most network professionals have been forced to backlevel at some point in their careers. The steps that constitute this process differ, depending on the complexity of the upgrade and the network environment involved.

Although no hard-and-fast rules for backleveling exist, Table 15-1 summarizes some basic sug-
4.5 gestions. Bear in mind that you must always refer to the software vendor's documentation to
5.4 reverse an upgrade. If you must backlevel a network operating system upgrade, you should also
consult with experienced professionals about the best approach for your network environment.

Table 15-1 Reversing a software upgrade

Type of upgrade	Options for reversing
Operating system patch	Use the patch's automatic uninstall utility.
Client software upgrade	Use the upgrade's automatic uninstall utility, or reinstall the previous version of the client on top of the upgrade.
Shared application upgrade	Use the application's automatic uninstall utility, or maintain a complete copy of the previous installation of the application and reinstall it over the upgrade.
Operating system upgrade	Prior to the upgrade, make a complete backup of the system; to backlevel, restore the entire system from the backup; uninstall an operating system upgrade only as a last resort.

Net+

Hardware and Physical Plant Changes

4.5 Hardware and physical plant changes might be required when a network component fails or malfunctions, but more often they are performed as part of an upgrade to increase capacity, improve performance, or add functionality to the network. In this section, you will learn about the simplest and most popular form of hardware change—adding more of what you already use, such as adding four more switches to the backbone or adding 10 new networked printers. You'll also learn about more complex hardware changes, such as replacing the entire network backbone with a more robust system.

Many of the same issues apply to hardware changes as apply to software changes. In particular, proper planning is the key to a successful upgrade. When considering a change to your network hardware, use the following steps as a guide:

1. Determine whether the change is necessary.
2. Research the upgrade's potential effects on other devices, functions, and users.
3. If you decide to implement the change, notify system administrators, help desk personnel, and users, and schedule it during off-hours (unless it is an emergency).
4. If possible, back up the current hardware's configuration. Ideally, you would have stored this information in a configuration management program. If that isn't the case, or if you want to be certain you have the most current information, you should collect it now. Most routers, switches, and servers have a configuration that you can easily copy to a disk.
5. Prevent users from accessing the system or the part of the system that you are changing.
6. Keep the installation instructions and hardware documentation handy.
7. Implement the change.

4.5

8. Test the hardware fully after the change, preferably putting a higher load on the device than it would incur during normal use in your organization. Note any unintended or unanticipated consequences of the change.
9. If the change was successful, reenable access to the device. If it was unsuccessful, isolate the device or reinsert the old device, if possible.
10. Inform system administrators, help desk personnel, and users when the change is complete. If it was not successful, make that known and explain why.
11. Record your change in the change management system.

Adding or Upgrading Equipment The difficulty involved in adding or upgrading hardware on your network depends largely on whether you have used the hardware in the past. For instance, if your organization always uses Cisco switches, adding one more Cisco switch to your second-floor telecommunications closet might take only a few minutes and cause absolutely no disruption of service to your users. On the other hand, even if your company uses Cisco switches, adding a Cisco VPN router to your network might be an entirely new experience. Therefore, take time to research, evaluate, and test any unfamiliar piece of equipment that you intend to add or upgrade on your network, even if it is manufactured by a vendor that supplies much of your other hardware.

With the rapid changes in the hardware industry, you might not be able to purchase identical hardware even from one quarter to the next. If consistency is a concern—for example, if your technical staff is familiar with only one brand and model of network printer, and you do not have the time or money to retrain personnel—you would be wise to purchase as much hardware as possible in a single order. If this approach is not feasible, purchase equipment from vendors with familiar products and solid reputations.

Each type of device that you add or upgrade on the network will have different preparation and implementation requirements. Knowing exactly how to handle the changes requires not only a close reading of the manufacturer's instructions, but also some experience with the type of networking equipment at hand. The following list provides a very general overview of how you might approach adding or upgrading devices on the network, from the least disruptive to the most complex types of equipment. The devices at the bottom of the list are not only the most disruptive and complex to add or upgrade, but also the most difficult to remove or backlevel.

- *Networked workstation*—A networked workstation is perhaps the simplest device to add. It directly affects only a few users, and does not alter network access for anyone else. If your organization has a standard networked workstation configuration (for example, a disk image, or a compressed snapshot of the workstation's contents, on the server), adding a networked workstation will be a quick operation as well. You can successfully add a networked workstation without notifying users or support staff and without worrying about downtime.

- *Networked printer*—A networked printer is easy to add to your network, too. Adding this equipment might be more complex than adding a workstation, however, because of its unique configuration process and because it is shared. Although it affects multiple users, a networked printer does not typically perform a mission-critical function in an organization, so the length of time required to install one does not usually affect productivity. Thus, although you should notify the affected users of a

4.5 networked printer addition, you do not need to notify all users and support staff. Likewise, you do not need to restrict access to the network or worry about downtime in this instance.

- *Workgroup switch or access point*—A single workgroup switch or access point might service as few as one or as many as 64 users. You do not have to worry about downtime or notifying users when *adding* a new workgroup switch or access point because it cannot affect anyone until it is actually in use. However, if you are upgrading or swapping out an existing workgroup switch or access point during working hours, you must notify the affected users because the upgrade or swap will create downtime, if only a few seconds. In addition, consider the traffic and addressing implications of adding or upgrading a workgroup switch or access point. For example, if you need to expand the capacity of a TCP/IP-based network segment from 24 users to 60 users, you can easily enough swap your 24-port switch with a 64-port switch. But before doing so, make sure that the segment has been allotted enough free IP addresses to service 60 users; otherwise, these users will not be able to access the network.
- *Server*—A server addition or upgrade can be tricky. Typically, this type of change (unless it is the replacement of a minor component) requires a great deal of foresight and planning. Before installing a new server, you need to consider the hardware and connectivity implications of the change, as well as issues relating to the NOS. Even if you are adding a server that will not be used immediately, you still need to plan for its installation. It's preferable to add the server while network traffic is low or nonexistent. Also, restrict access to the new server; otherwise, one of your users could find the server while browsing the network and try to save files to it or run an application from it.

  Upgrading the hardware (such as a NIC or memory) on an existing server may require nearly as much planning as adding an entirely new server. Schedule upgrades to an existing server for off-hours, so that you can shut down the server without inconveniencing any users who rely on it.
- *Backbone switches and routers*—Changing or adding backbone switches or routers to a network design can be complicated for several reasons. First, this type of change can be physically disruptive—for example, it might require the installation of new racks or other support frames in your telecommunications room. Second, backbone switches and routers usually affect many users—and might affect all users—on the network. For instance, if you must replace the Internet gateway for your organization's headquarters, you will cut every user's access to the Internet in the process (unless you have redundant gateways, which is the optimal setup if you rely on the Internet for mission-critical services). You should notify all users on the network about the impending change, even if you don't think they will be affected, because a backbone router or switch might affect segments of the network other than the one it services. In addition, you should plan at least weeks in advance for switch or router changes and expect at least several hours of downtime. Because enterprise switches and routers are expensive, take extraordinary care when handling and configuring this type of equipment. Also, because switches and routers serve different purposes, rely on the manufacturer's documentation to guide you through the installation process.

Net+
4.5

Bear in mind that adding a new processor to a server, a new NIC to a router, or more memory to a printer may affect your service or warranty agreement with the manufacturer. Before purchasing any components to add or replace in your network devices, check your agreement for stipulations that might apply. You may be allowed to add only components made by the same manufacturer, or risk losing all support from that manufacturer.

Above all, keep safety in mind when you upgrade or install hardware on a network. Never tinker with the insides of a device that is turned on. Make sure that all cords and devices are stowed safely out of the way and cannot cause trips or falls. Avoid wearing jewelry, scarves, or very loose clothing when you work on equipment; if you have long hair, tie it back. Not only will you prevent injury this way, but you will also be less distracted. By removing metal jewelry, you could prevent damage to the equipment caused by a short if the metal touches a circuit. If the equipment is heavy (such as a large switch or server), do not try to lift it by yourself. Finally, to protect the equipment from damage, follow the manufacturer's temperature, ventilation, antistatic, and moisture guidelines.

Cabling Upgrades Cabling upgrades, unless they involve the replacement of a single faulty patch cable, can require significant planning and time to implement, depending on the size of your network. Bear in mind that troubleshooting cabling problems can be made easier by maintaining current, accurate wiring schematics. If the network's cable layout is undocumented and poorly planned, particularly if it was installed years before and survived intact despite building changes and network growth, cabling changes will be more difficult. The best way to ensure that future upgrades go smoothly is to carefully document the existing cable *before* making any upgrades. If this assessment is not possible, you might have to compile your documentation as you upgrade the existing cabling.

Because a change of this magnitude affects all users on the network, consider upgrading the network cabling in phases. For example, schedule an upgrade of the first-floor east wing of your building one weekend, then the first-floor west wing of your building the next, and so on. Weigh the importance of the upgrade against its potential for disruption. For example, if the Payroll Department is processing end-of-month checks and having no difficulties other than somewhat slow response time, it is not critical to take away its access to install Cat 6a wiring. On the other hand, if the building maintenance staff needs a 1-Gbps connection to run a new HVAC control system, you will probably make it a priority to take down this access temporarily and replace the wiring. In this case, not only must you replace the wiring, but you might also need to replace switches and NICs.

For the most part, organizations that run very small networks are able to upgrade or install their own network cabling. Many other organizations rely on contractors who specialize in this service. Nevertheless, as a networking professional you should know how to run a cable across a room, either under a raised floor or through a ceiling plenum, in order to connect a device to the network.

Backbone Upgrades The most comprehensive and complex upgrade involving network hardware is a backbone upgrade. Recall that the network backbone is the main conduit for data on LANs and WANs, connecting major routers, servers, and switches. A backbone

4.5 upgrade requires not only a great deal of planning, but also the efforts of several personnel (and possibly contractors) and a significant investment. You may upgrade parts of the backbone—a NIC in a router or a section of cabling, for example—at any time, but upgrading the entire backbone changes the whole network.

Examples of backbone upgrades include migrating from token ring to Ethernet, migrating from a slower technology to a faster one, and replacing routers with switches (to make use of VLANs, for example). Such upgrades may satisfy a variety of needs: a need for faster throughput, a physical move or renovation, a more reliable network, greater security, more consistent standards, support of a new application, or greater cost-effectiveness. For example, the need for faster throughput may prompt an upgrade from an older Ethernet technology to Gigabit Ethernet. Likewise, the need to support videoconferencing may require a backbone upgrade from Cat 5 to fiber-optic cable.

Because backbone upgrades are expensive and time consuming, the first step in approaching such a project is to justify it. Will the benefits outweigh the costs? Can the upgrade wait a year or more? If so, you might be wise to wait and find out whether a cheaper or better technical solution becomes available later. Don't plan to wait until the technology "settles down" because networking progress never stands still. On the other hand, do wait to implement brand-new technology until you can find out how it has worked on other networks similar to your own or until the manufacturer eliminates most of the bugs.

The second step is to determine which kind of backbone design to implement. To make this decision, you must analyze the future capacity needs of your network, decide whether you want a distributed or collapsed backbone, determine whether you want to rely on switches or routers, decide whether to use subnetting and to what extent, and so on. Although some of these predictions will be guesswork, you can minimize the variables by examining the history of your organization's growth and needs.

After designing your backbone upgrade, develop a project plan to accomplish the upgrade. Given that you don't upgrade your backbone every day, you might want to contract this work to a firm that specializes in network design and upgrades. In that case, you will draft an RFP (request for proposal) to specify what that contractor should do. Regardless of whether you employ specialists, your project plan should include a logical process for upgrading the backbone one section at a time (if possible). Because this process causes network outages, determine how best to proceed based on users' needs. Choose a time when usage is low, such as over a holiday, to perform your upgrade.

Reversing Hardware Changes As with software changes, you should provide a way to reverse the hardware upgrade and reinstall the old hardware if necessary. If you are replacing a faulty component or device, this restoration, of course, is not possible. If you are upgrading a component in a device, on the other hand, keep the old component safe (for example, keep NICs in static-resistant containers) and nearby. Not only might you need to put it back in the device, but you might also need to refer to it for information. Even if the device seems to be operating well with the new component, keep the old component for a while, especially if it is the only one of its kind at your organization.

Chapter Summary

- Network management involves assessing, monitoring, and maintaining network devices and connections.
- Documenting all aspects of your network promises to save work in the future. Information to track includes, but is not limited to, physical topology, access method, protocols, devices, operating systems, applications, and configurations.
- Configuration management refers to the collection of information related to the versions of software installed on every network device and every device's hardware configuration.
- Network diagrams illustrate a network's physical or logical topology. A wiring schematic is a graphical representation of a network's wired infrastructure. Both are helpful for assessing a network's status and planning for its expansion.
- Baselining includes keeping a history of network performance and provides the basis for determining what types of changes might improve the network. It also allows for later evaluating how successful the improvements were.
- Policies, procedures, and regulations are important elements of sound network management. Elsewhere in this book, you have learned about media installation and management best practices, network addressing policies, resource sharing and naming conventions, security-related policies, troubleshooting procedures, and backup and disaster recovery procedures.
- CALEA (Communications Assistance for Law Enforcement Act) is a federal regulation that requires telecommunications carriers and equipment manufacturers to provide for surveillance capabilities. HIPAA (Health Insurance Portability and Accountability Act) addresses, among other things, the security and privacy of medical records, including those stored or transmitted electronically. These are just two laws that, depending on where you work, might affect your responsibilities as a network professional.
- Assessing a network's status on an ongoing basis includes performance management, or monitoring how well links and devices are keeping up with the demands placed on them, and fault management, or the detection and signaling of device, link, or component faults.
- Network management applications typically use SNMP (Simple Network Management Protocol) to communicate with agents running on managed devices. Agents can report information on a device's components or status (such as utilization or performance).

- The most recent version of SNMP is SNMPv3, which applies authentication, validation, and encryption to packets exchanged between managed devices and the network management console. SNMPv2, which is less secure, is also widely used.
- System logs and event logs keep a record of conditions reported by operating systems and applications. On a Windows-based computer, the Event Viewer allows you to review the computer's event log. UNIX and Linux systems run syslog, a standard for generating and collecting event information that stores messages in a system log. To find out where your computer's system log is kept, view the `/etc/syslog.conf` file.

- Traffic shaping helps ensure acceptable overall network performance by limiting the throughput or volume of traffic that may traverse certain network interfaces or by assigning variable priority levels to different types of traffic.
- Caching stores files locally that would otherwise be obtained from a remote source, such as a Web server across the country. An ISP uses cache engines on its network to store frequently accessed content and deliver it directly to requesters. In this way, the ISP improves response time and reduces WAN traffic and costs.
- An asset management system includes an inventory of the total number of components on the network as well as each device's configuration files, model number, serial number, location on the network, and technical support contact. In addition, it records every piece of software purchased by your organization, its version number, vendor, and technical support contact.
- A patch is an enhancement or improvement to a part of a software application, often distributed at no charge by software vendors to fix a bug, address a vulnerability, or add slightly more functionality.
- An application upgrade consists of modifications to all or part of an application that are designed to enhance functionality or fix problems with the software.
- Perhaps the most critical type of software upgrade you'll perform is an upgrade to your network operating system. This type of upgrade usually involves significant, potentially drastic, changes to the operation of your servers and clients. As such, it requires plenty of forethought, product research, and rigorous testing before you implement it. In fact, for any network with more than a few users, you should create and follow a project plan for this undertaking.
- Plan for the possibility that a software upgrade might harm your existing system, and be prepared to reverse the process. The restoration of a previous version of software after an attempted upgrade is known as backleveling.
- Hardware and physical plant changes might be required when your network has problems. More often, however, they are performed as part of a move to increase capacity, improve performance, or add functionality to the network.
- Research, evaluate, and test any unfamiliar piece of equipment you intend to add or upgrade on your network, even if it is manufactured by a vendor that supplies much of your other hardware. The process of implementing a hardware upgrade is very similar to that of carrying out a software upgrade, including notifying users and preparing to bring the system down during the change.
- Cabling upgrades are simpler and less error-prone if a network's cable plant is well documented. Also make sure to document new cable infrastructure after making changes. When embarking on a major cabling upgrade, such as a backbone replacement, it is advisable to upgrade the infrastructure in phases.
- The most comprehensive and complex upgrade involving network hardware is a backbone upgrade. The network backbone serves as the main conduit for data on LANs and WANs, connecting major routers, servers, and/or switches. A backbone upgrade not only requires a great deal of time to plan, but also the efforts of several staff members (and possibly contractors) and a significant investment.

- Allow for a way to reverse a hardware upgrade and replace it with the old hardware. If you are upgrading a component in a device, keep the old component safe and nearby. Not only might you need to put it back in the device, but you might also need to refer to it for information.

Key Terms

agent A software routine that collects data about a managed device's operation and provides it to a network management application.

backleveling To revert to a previous version of a software application after attempting to upgrade it.

cache engine A network device devoted to storage and delivery of frequently requested files.

caching The local storage of frequently needed files that would otherwise be obtained from an external source.

CALEA (Communications Assistance for Law Enforcement Act) A United States federal regulation that requires telecommunications carriers and equipment manufacturers to provide for surveillance capabilities. CALEA was passed by Congress in 1994 after pressure from the FBI, which worried that networks relying solely on digital communications would circumvent traditional wiretapping strategies.

Communications Assistance for Law Enforcement Act *See* CALEA.

configuration management The collection, storage, and assessment of information related to the versions of software installed on every network device and every device's hardware configuration.

event log The service on Windows-based operating systems that records events, or the ongoing record of such events.

Event Viewer A GUI application that allows users to easily view and sort events recorded in the event log on a computer running a Windows-based operating system.

fault management The detection and signaling of device, link, or component faults.

Health Insurance Portability and Accountability Act *See* HIPAA.

HIPAA (Health Insurance Portability and Accountability Act) A federal regulation in the United States, enacted in 1996. One aspect of this regulation addresses the security and privacy of medical records, including those stored or transmitted electronically.

Management Information Base *See* MIB.

MIB (Management Information Base) A database used in network management that contains a device's definitions of managed objects and their data.

network diagram A graphical representation of a network's devices and connections.

network management The assessment, monitoring, and maintenance of the devices and connections on a network.

patch A correction, improvement, or enhancement to part of a software application, often distributed at no charge by software vendors to fix a bug in their code or to add slightly more functionality.

performance management The ongoing assessment of how well network links, devices, and components keep up with demands on them.

polling A network management application's regular collection of data from managed devices.

Simple Network Management Protocol *See* SNMP.

Simple Network Management Protocol version 1 *See* SNMPv1.

Simple Network Management Protocol version 2 *See* SNMPv2.

Simple Network Management Protocol version 3 *See* SNMPv3.

SNMP (Simple Network Management Protocol) An Application layer protocol in the TCP/IP suite used to convey data regarding the status of managed devices on a network.

SNMPv1 (Simple Network Management Protocol version 1) The original version of SNMP, released in 1988. Because of its limited features, it is rarely used on modern networks.

SNMPv2 (Simple Network Management Protocol version 2) The second version of SNMP, which improved on SNMPv1 with faster performance and slightly better security, among other features.

SNMPv3 (Simple Network Management Protocol version 3) A version of SNMP similar to SNMPv2, but with authentication, validation, and encryption for packets exchanged between managed devices and the network management console. SNMPv3 is the most secure version of the protocol.

syslog A standard for generating, storing, and processing messages about events on a system. Syslog describes methods for detecting and reporting events and specifies the format and contents of messages.

system log On a computer running a UNIX or Linux operating system, the record of monitored events, which can range in priority from 0 to 7 (where "0" indicates an emergency situation and "7" simply points to information that might help in debugging a problem). You can view and modify system log locations and configurations in the file `/etc/syslog.conf` on most systems (on some systems, this is the `/etc/rsyslog.conf` file).

traffic policing A traffic-shaping technique in which the volume or rate of traffic traversing an interface is limited to a predefined maximum.

traffic shaping Manipulating certain characteristics of packets, data streams, or connections to manage the type and amount of traffic traversing a network or interface at any moment.

upgrade A significant change to an application's existing code, typically designed to improve functionality or add new features.

Web caching A technique in which Web pages are stored locally, either on a host or network, and then delivered to requesters more quickly than if they had been obtained from the original source.

wiring schematic A graphical representation of a network's wired infrastructure.

Review Questions

1. Which document is a graphical representation of a network's devices and connections?
   a. wiring schematic
   b. network diagram
   c. traffic shaping report
   d. configuration management documentation
2. Which category of network management tools is required to determine with certainty whether a pattern of usage has changed?
   a. performance management
   b. configuration management
   c. policies, procedures, and regulations
   d. baseline measurements
3. What is a correction, improvement, or enhancement to a software application called?
   a. upgrade
   b. revision
   c. patch
   d. update
4. Which device is the least disruptive type of equipment to add or upgrade?
   a. networked printer
   b. server
   c. networked workstation
   d. workgroup switch
5. On modern networks, most agents use ________________ to communicate information about managed devices.
   a. TCP
   b. SNMP
   c. MIB
   d. MRTG

6. True or false? The scope of network management techniques differs according to the network's size and importance.
7. True or false? On Windows-based computers, device monitor results are sent to a log is known as a system log.
8. True or false? To an ISP, caching is simply a convenience.
9. True or false? Good planning is necessary to manage change while maintaining a network's efficiency and availability.

10. True or false? The most comprehensive and complex upgrade involving network hardware is a backbone upgrade.

11. ________________ management involves assessing, monitoring, and maintaining network devices and connections.

12. ________________ involves manipulating certain characteristics of packets, data streams, or connections to manage the type and amount of traffic traversing a network or interface at any moment.

13. ________________ is the local storage of frequently needed files that would otherwise be obtained from an external source.

14. A(n) ________________ is a major change to a software package's existing code and is usually designed to enhance functionality.

15. ________________ is a standard for generating, storing, and processing messages about events on a system.

appendix A

Network+ Examination Objectives

This book covers material related to all of the Network+ examination objectives for exam N10-005, which were released by CompTIA (the Computing Technology Industry Association) in 2011. The official list of objectives is available at CompTIA's Web site, *www.comptia.org*. For your reference, the following tables list each exam objective and the chapter of this book that explains the objective, plus the amount of the exam that will cover each certification domain. Each objective belongs to one of five domains (or main categories) of networking expertise. For example, comparing and contrasting different 802.11 standards belongs to Objective 3.3 in the "Network Media and Topologies" domain, which accounts for 17% of the exam's content.

Domain	% of Examination
1.0 Network Concepts	21%
2.0 Network Installation and Configuration	23%
3.0 Network Media and Topologies	17%
4.0 Network Management	20%
5.0 Network Security	19%
Total	**100%**

Domain 1.0 Networking Concepts—21% of Examination

Network+ Examination Objectives—Networking Concepts

Objective	Chapter
1.1 Compare the layers of the OSI and TCP/IP models.	
• OSI model:	2, 4
• Layer 1—Physical	2, 4
• Layer 2—Data link	2, 4

Objective	Chapter
• Layer 3—Network	2, 4
• Layer 4—Transport	2, 4
• Layer 5—Session	2, 4
• Layer 6—Presentation	2, 4
• Layer 7—Application	2, 4
• TCP/IP model:	4
• Network Interface Layer	4
• Internet Layer	4
• Transport Layer	4
• Application Layer	4
(Also described as: Link Layer, Internet Layer, Transport Layer, Application Layer)	
1.2 Classify how applications, devices, and protocols relate to the OSI model layers.	
• MAC address	2
• IP address	4
• EUI-64	2
• Frames	2
• Packets	2, 4
• Switch	6
• Router	6
• Multilayer switch	6
• Hub	6
• Encryption devices	11
• Cable	3
• NIC	3
• Bridge	6
1.3 Explain the purpose and properties of IP addressing.	
• Classes of addresses	4, 9
• A, B, C and D	4, 9
• Public vs. Private	4, 9
• Classless (CIDR)	9
• IPv4 vs. IPv6 (formatting)	4, 9
• MAC address format	2
• Subnetting	9
• Multicast vs. unicast vs. broadcast	4, 9
• APIPA	4

Objective	Chapter
1.4 Explain the purpose and properties of routing and switching.	
• EIGRP	6
• OSPF	6
• RIP	6
• Link state vs. distance vector vs. hybrid	6
• Static vs. dynamic	6
• Routing metrics	6
• Hop counts	4, 6
• MTU, bandwidth	6
• Costs	6
• Latency	6
• Next hop	4, 6
• Spanning-Tree Protocol	6
• VLAN (802.1q)	6, 10
• Port mirroring	6
• Broadcast domain vs. collision domain	6
• IGP vs. EGP	6
• Routing tables	6, 9
• Convergence (steady state)	6
1.5 Identify common TCP and UDP default ports.	
• SMTP—25	4
• HTTP—80	4
• HTTPS—443	4
• FTP—20, 21	4
• TELNET—23	4
• IMAP—143	4
• RDP—3389	4
• SSH—22	4
• DNS—53	4
• DHCP—67, 68	4
1.6 Explain the function of common networking protocols.	
• TCP	2, 4
• FTP	4
• UDP	2, 4

Objective	Chapter
• TCP/IP suite	2, 4, 9
• DHCP	4
• TFTP	4
• DNS	4, 9, 14
• HTTPS	11
• HTTP	2, 4, 9
• ARP	2
• SIP (VoIP)	10
• RTP (VoIP)	10
• SSH	11
• POP3	9
• NTP	4
• IMAP4	9
• Telnet	4, 9
• SMTP	9
• SNMP2/3	15
• ICMP	4
• IGMP	4
• TLS	11
1.7 Summarize DNS concepts and its components.	
• DNS servers	4
• DNS records (A, MX, AAAA, CNAME, PTR)	4, 9
• Dynamic DNS	4
1.8 Given a scenario, implement the following network troubleshooting methodology:	
• Identify the problem:	13
• Information gathering	13
• Identify symptoms	13
• Question users	13
• Determine if anything has changed	13
• Establish a theory of probable cause	13
• Question the obvious	13
• Test the theory to determine cause:	13
• Once theory is confirmed determine next steps to resolve problem.	13
• If theory is not confirmed, re-establish new theory or escalate.	13

Objective	Chapter
• Establish a plan of action to resolve the problem and identify potential effects	13
• Implement the solution or escalate as necessary	13
• Verify full system functionality and if applicable implement preventative measures	13
• Document findings, actions and outcomes	13
1.9 Identify virtual network components.	
• Virtual switches	10
• Virtual desktops	10
• Virtual servers	10
• Virtual PBX	12
• Onsite vs. offsite	10
• Network as a Service (NaaS)	10

Domain 2.0 Network Installation and Configuration—23% of Examination

Network+ Examination Objectives—Network Installation and Configuration

Objective	Chapter
2.1 Given a scenario, install and configure routers and switches.	
• Routing tables	6, 9
• NAT	9
• PAT	9
• VLAN (trunking)	6, 10
• Managed vs. unmanaged	6
• Interface configurations	3, 6
• Full duplex	3, 6
• Half duplex	3, 6
• Port speeds	3, 6
• IP addressing	3, 6
• MAC filtering	3, 6
• PoE	6
• Traffic filtering	6, 11

Objective	Chapter
• Diagnostics	6, 15
• VTP configuration	6, 10
• QoS	6
• Port mirroring	6
2.2 Given a scenario, install and configure a wireless network.	
• WAP placement	8
• Antenna types	8
• Interference	8
• Frequencies	8
• Channels	8
• Wireless standards	8
• SSID (enable/disable)	8
• Compatibility (802.11 a/b/g/n)	8
2.3 Explain the purpose and properties of DHCP.	
• Static vs. dynamic IP addressing	4
• Reservations	4
• Scopes	4
• Leases	4
• Options (DNS servers, suffixes)	4, 9
2.4 Given a scenario, troubleshoot common wireless problems.	
• Interference	8, 13
• Signal strength	8, 13
• Configurations	8
• Incompatibilities	8, 13
• Incorrect channel	8
• Latency	8
• Encryption type	8, 11
• Bounce	8
• SSID mismatch	8
• Incorrect switch placement	8
2.5 Given a scenario, troubleshoot common router and switch problems.	
• Switching loop	6
• Bad cables/improper cable types	6

Objective	Chapter
• Port configuration	6
• VLAN assignment	6
• Mismatched MTU/MTU black hole	6
• Power failure	14
• Bad/missing routes	6, 9
• Bad modules (SFPs, GBICs)	3, 13
• Wrong subnet mask	4, 9
• Wrong gateway	6, 9
• Duplicate IP address	4
• Wrong DNS	4
2.6 Given a set of requirements, plan and implement a basic SOHO network.	
• List of requirements	6
• Cable length	3
• Device types/requirements	6, 8, 10
• Environment limitations	6, 8
• Equipment limitations	6, 10
• Compatibility requirements	3, 6, 8

Domain 3.0 Network Media and Topologies—17% of Examination

Network+ Examination Objectives—Network Media and Topologies

Objective	Chapter
3.1 Categorize standard media types and associated properties.	
• Fiber:	3
• Multimode	3
• Singlemode	3
• Copper:	3
• UTP	3
• STP	3
• CAT3	3
• CAT5	3

Objective	Chapter
• CAT5e	3
• CAT6	3
• CAT6a	3
• Coaxial	3
• Crossover	3
• T1 Crossover	7
• Straight-through	6
• Plenum vs. non-plenum	6
• Media converters:	3
• Singlemode fiber to Ethernet	3
• Multimode fiber to Ethernet	3
• Fiber to Coaxial	3
• Singlemode to multimode fiber	3
• Distance limitations and speed limitations	3
• Broadband over powerline	7
3.2 Categorize standard connector types based on network media.	
• Fiber:	3
• ST	3
• SC	3
• LC	3
• MTRJ	3
• Copper:	3
• RJ-45	3
• RJ-11	3
• BNC	3
• F-connector	3
• DB-9 (RS-232)	3
• Patch panel	3
• 110 block (T568A, T568B)	3
3.3 Compare and contrast different wireless standards.	
• 802.11 a/b/g/n standards	8
• Distance	8
• Speed	8
• Latency	8

Objective	Chapter
• Frequency	8
• Channels	8
• MIMO	8
• Channel bonding	8
3.4 Categorize WAN technology types and properties.	
• Types:	7
• T1/E1	7
• T3/E3	7
• DS3	7
• OCx	7
• SONET	7
• SDH	7
• DWDM	3
• Satellite	8
• ISDN	7
• Cable	7
• DSL	7
• Cellular	8
• WiMAX	8
• LTE	8
• HSPA+	8
• Fiber	7
• Dialup	7, 10
• PON	7
• Frame relay	7
• ATM	7
• Properties:	7
• Circuit switch	7
• Packet switch	7
• Speed	7
• Transmission media	7
• Distance	7

Objective	Chapter
3.5 Describe different network topologies.	
• MPLS	6, 12
• Point to point	7
• Point to multipoint	7
• Ring	5, 7
• Star	5, 7
• Mesh	5, 7
• Bus	5, 7
• Peer-to-peer	1
• Client-server	1
• Hybrid	5, 7
3.6 Given a scenario, troubleshoot common physical connectivity problems.	
• Cable problems:	3
• Bad connectors	3
• Bad wiring	3
• Open, short	3
• Split cables	3
• DB loss	3
• TXRX reversed	3
• Cable placement	3
• EMI/Interference	8, 13
• Distance	6, 8, 13
• Cross-talk	3
3.7 Compare and contrast different LAN technologies.	
• Types:	5
• Ethernet	5
• 10BaseT	5
• 100BaseT	5
• 1000BaseT	5
• 100BaseTX	5
• 100BaseFX	5
• 1000BaseX	5
• 10GBaseSR	5
• 10GBaseLR	5

Objective	Chapter
• 10GBaseER	5
• 10GBaseSW	5
• 10GBaseLW	5
• 10GBaseEW	5
• 10GBaseT	5
• Properties:	5
• CSMA/CD	5
• CSMA/CA	8
• Broadcast	3, 5, 6
• Collision	5, 6, 8
• Bonding	6, 8
• Speed	3, 5, 8
• Distance	3, 8
3.8 Identify components of wiring distribution.	
• IDF	3
• MDF	3
• Demarc	3
• Demarc extension	3
• Smart jack	7
• CSU/DSU	7

Domain 4.0 Network Management—20% of Examination

Network+ Examination Objectives—Network Management

Objective	Chapter
4.1 Explain the purpose and features of various network appliances.	
• Load balancer	14
• Proxy server	14
• Content filter	11
• VPN concentrator	10

Objective	Chapter
4.2 Given a scenario, use appropriate hardware tools to troubleshoot connectivity issues.	
• Cable tester	13
• Cable certifier	13
• Crimper	3
• Butt set	13
• Toner probe	13
• Punch down tool	3
• Protocol analyzer	6, 8, 11, 13
• Loop back plug	3
• TDR	13
• OTDR	13
• Multimeter	13
• Environmental monitor	13, 14
4.3 Given a scenario, use appropriate software tools to troubleshoot connectivity issues.	
• Protocol analyzer	13
• Throughput testers	13
• Connectivity software	13
• Ping	9, 13
• Tracert/traceroute	9, 13
• Dig	9, 13
• Ipconfig/ifconfig	4, 9, 13
• Nslookup	9, 13
• Arp	9, 13
• Nbtstat	9
• Netstat	9, 13
• Route	9, 13
4.4 Given a scenario, use the appropriate network monitoring resource to analyze traffic.	
• SNMP	15
• SNMPv2	15
• SNMPv3	15
• Syslog	15
• System logs	15
• History logs	15
• General logs	13, 15

Objective	Chapter
• Traffic analysis	13, 15
• Network sniffer	11, 13
4.5 Describe the purpose of configuration management documentation.	
• Wire schemes	15
• Network maps	15
• Documentation	15
• Cable management	15
• Asset management	15
• Baselines	13, 15
• Change management	13, 15
4.6 Explain different methods and rationales for network performance optimization.	
• Methods:	14
• QoS	14
• Traffic shaping	14
• Load balancing	14
• High availability	14
• Caching engines	14
• Fault tolerance	14
• CARP	14
• Reasons:	14
• Latency sensitivity	14
• High bandwidth applications (VoIP, video applications, unified communications)	12, 14
• Uptime	14

Domain 5.0 Network Security—19% of Examination

Network+ Examination Objectives—Network Security

Objective	Chapter
5.1 Given a scenario, implement appropriate wireless security measures.	
• Encryption protocols:	11
• WEP	11
• WPA	11

Objective	Chapter
• WPA2	11
• WPA Enterprise	11
• MAC address filtering	8
• Device placement	8
• Signal strength	8
5.2 Explain the methods of network access security.	
• ACL:	6, 11
• MAC filtering	6, 11
• IP filtering	6, 11
• Port filtering	6, 11
• Tunneling and encryption:	10, 11
• SSL VPN	11
• VPN	10, 11
• L2TP	10
• PPTP	10
• IPSec	11
• ISAKMP	11
• TLS	11
• TLS 1.2	11
• Site-to-site and client-to-site	10
• Remote access:	10
• RAS	10
• RDP	10
• PPPoE	10
• PPP	10
• ICA	10
• SSH	11
5.3 Explain methods of user authentication.	
• PKI	11
• Kerberos	11
• AAA (RADIUS, TACACS+)	11
• Network access control (802.1x, posture assessment)	11
• CHAP	11
• MS-CHAP	11

Objective	Chapter
• EAP	11
• Two-factor authentication	11
• Multifactor authentication	11
• Single sign-on	11
5.4 Explain common threats, vulnerabilities, and mitigation techniques.	
• Wireless:	11
• War driving	11
• War chalking	11
• WEP cracking	11
• WPA cracking	11
• Evil twin	11
• Rogue access point	8, 11
• Attacks:	11
• DoS	11
• DDoS	11
• Man in the middle	11
• Social engineering	11
• Virus	14
• Worms	14
• Buffer overflow	11
• Packet sniffing	11
• FTP bounce	11
• Smurf	11
• Mitigation techniques:	11, 14, 15
• Training and awareness	11, 14
• Patch management	11, 15
• Policies and procedures	11, 14, 15
• Incident response	11
5.5 Given a scenario, install and configure a basic firewall.	
• Types:	11
• Software and hardware firewalls	11
• Port security	11
• Stateful inspection vs. packet filtering	11

Objective	Chapter
• Firewall rules:	11
• Block/allow	11
• Implicit deny	11
• ACL	11
• NAT/PAT	9, 11
• DMZ	11
5.6 Categorize different types of network security appliances and methods.	
• IDS and IPS:	11
• Behavior based	11
• Signature based	11
• Network based	11
• Host based	11
• Vulnerability scanners:	11
• NESSUS	11
• NMAP	11
• Methods:	11
• Honeypots	11
• Honeynets	11

appendix B

Network+ Practice Exam

The following exam contains questions similar in content and format to what you will encounter on CompTIA's Network+ certification exam. The exam consists of 100 questions, all of which are multiple choice. Some questions have more than one correct answer. The number of questions on each topic reflects the weighting that CompTIA assigned to these topics in its N10-005 exam objectives, released in 2011. To simulate taking the CompTIA Network+ certification exam, allow yourself 90 minutes to answer all of the questions.

1. **You are modifying your core router's access list to prevent all FTP traffic from reaching your internal network. If the gateway's IP address is 192.168.1.1, which of the following commands would accomplish that?**
   a. `access-list 110 deny FTP 192.168.1.1 any eq TCP`
   b. `access-list 110 permit TCP any 192.168.1.1 not FTP`
   c. `access-list 110 deny FTP any 192.168.1.1 port 23`
   d. `access-list 110 deny TCP any any eq FTP`
   e. `access-list 110 permit FTP 192.168.1.1 any eq TCP`
2. **Your network manager has purchased a dozen new access points and all are configured to use the new 802.11n standard in the 2.4-GHz band. These access points will be capable of communicating with older access points that run which of the following standards?** (Choose all that apply.)
   a. 802.11g
   b. 802.11a
   c. 802.11b
   d. Bluetooth
   e. None of the above

3. Which of the following figures reflects the type of physical topology commonly used on a 100Base-T network?

a.

b.

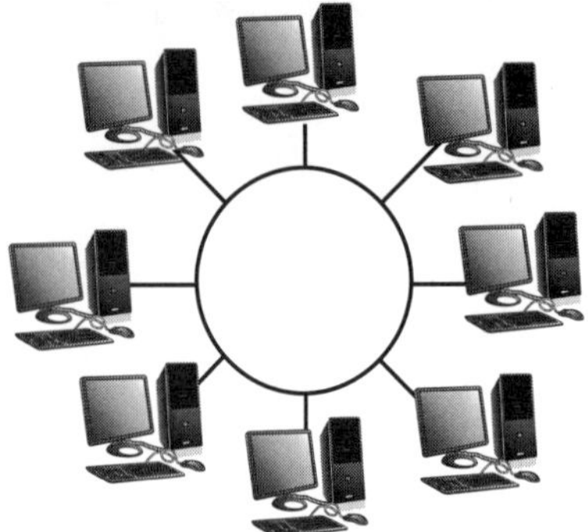

c.

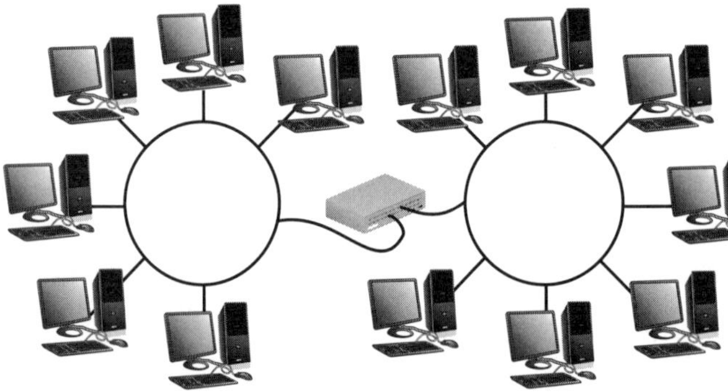

d.

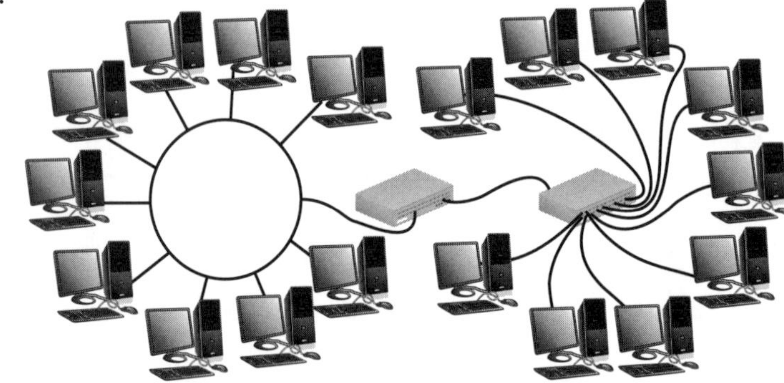

e.

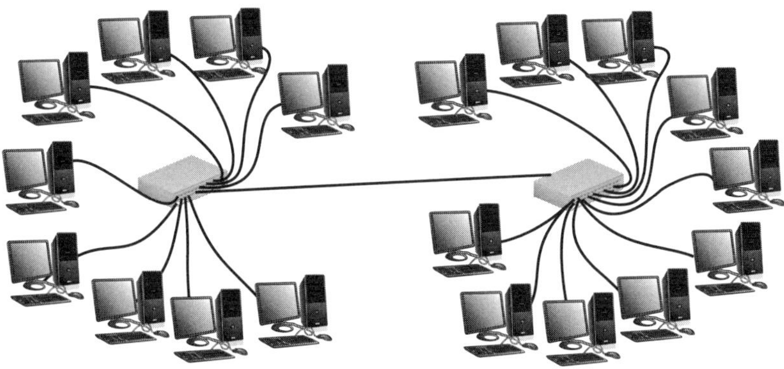

4. You have installed and configured two virtual Web servers and a virtual mail server on a physical server. What networking mode will you assign to each server's vNIC to ensure that the virtual machines hosts on the Internet can access the virtual machines?
   a. NAT
   b. Bridged
   c. Host-only
   d. Internal
   e. Grouped
5. Your organization contracts with a cloud computing company to store all of its data. The company promises 99.99% uptime. If it lives up to its claims, for how many minutes each year can you expect your data to be unavailable?
   a. Approximately 448 minutes
   b. Approximately 99 minutes
   c. Approximately 52 minutes
   d. Approximately 14 minutes
   e. Approximately 6 minutes
6. You are rearranging nodes on your Fast Ethernet network. Due to a necessarily hasty expansion, you have decided to supply power to a wireless router in a makeshift telco room using PoE. What is the minimum cabling standard you must use to connect this wireless router to the network's backbone?
   a. RG-6
   b. RG-59
   c. Cat 5
   d. SMF
   e. Cat 3

7. **To ensure that your private network is always protected, you decide to install three redundant firewalls. Which of the following would allow you to assign the same IP address to all three?**
   a. SMTP
   b. CARP
   c. SNMPv3
   d. IMAP
   e. NTP

8. **You are a networking technician in a radiology clinic, where physicians use the network to transmit and store patients' diagnostic results. Shortly after a new wing, which contains X-ray and magnetic resonance imaging (MRI) machines, is added to the building, computers in that area begin having intermittent problems saving data to the file server. After you have gathered information, identified the symptoms, questioned users, and determined what has changed, what is your next step in troubleshooting this problem?**
   a. Establish a plan of action to resolve the problem.
   b. Escalate the problem.
   c. Document findings, actions, and outcomes.
   d. Establish a theory of probable cause.
   e. Determine the next steps to resolve the problem.

9. **You are part of a team participating in a posture assessment of your company's WAN. Which of the following tools or strategies will help you gain a broad understanding of your network's vulnerabilities?**
   a. MIB
   b. War chalking
   c. NMAP
   d. WPA cracking
   e. PGP

10. **You work for an ISP. Several of your customers have called to complain about slow response from a popular Web site. You suspect that network congestion is at fault. Which TCP/IP utility would help you determine where the congestion is occurring?**
   a. FTP
   b. Nslookup
   c. Nbtstat
   d. Tracert
   e. Telnet

11. **Which of the following WAN topologies is the most fault tolerant?**
    a. Full mesh
    b. Bus
    c. Peer-to-peer
    d. Ring
    e. Hierarchical
12. **Which of the following is a valid MAC address?**
    a. C3:00:50:00:FF:FF
    b. 153.101.24.3
    c. ::9F53
    d. FE80::32:1CA3:B0E2
    e. D0:00:00:00
13. **What type of network could use the type of connector shown below?**

    a. 100Base-FX
    b. 100Base-TX
    c. l0Base-T
    d. 1000Base-T
    e. 10Base-2
14. **Your organization has just ordered its first T1 connection to the Internet. Prior to that, your organization relied on a DSL connection. Which of the following devices must you now have that your DSL connection didn't require?**
    a. Modem
    b. CSU/DSU
    c. Switch
    d. Hub
    e. Router

15. Which of the following wireless standards provides an entirely IP-based, packet-switched network for both voice and data transmissions? (Choose two.)
    a. LTE
    b. 802.16e
    c. 802.16m
    d. HSPA+
    e. 802.11n
16. You have created a new Web server on a computer running the Linux operating system and Apache Web server software. Which of the following programs will generate messages when modules don't load correctly or services encounter errors?
    a. Event Viewer
    b. IDS/IPS
    c. Packet Sniffer
    d. Network Monitor
    e. Syslog
17. You have been asked to provide a connectivity solution for a small, locally owned franchise of a national restaurant chain. The owners of the franchise want to send their confidential sales figures, personnel information, and inventory updates to the national office, which is 1200 miles away, once per week. Their total monthly data transfer will amount to almost 50 megabytes. The franchise owners do not plan to use the connection for any other purposes, and they do not have any IT staff to support the connection. Also, they do not want to spend more than $100 per month, nor more than $500 to install their connection. Considering cost, speed, reliability, technical expertise, distance, security, and the nature of their environment, what is the best solution for this client?
    a. A T1 that connects to the national office via a router at the local franchise and a router at the national office and that uses a VSN to ensure the security of the data en route
    b. A PSTN connection to a local Internet service provider that uses PPP to dial in to an access server and then sends data via e-mail to the national office
    c. A DSL connection to a local telephone and Internet service provider that uses IPSec to encrypt the data before it is sent to the national office's file server over the Internet
    d. A private SONET ring to connect with two local telephone and Internet service providers that connects to the national office's T3 and sends data via TCP/IP over ATM
    e. An ISDN connection to a local Internet service provider that allows employees to copy files to the national office's anonymous FTP site
18. You want to add the five virtual machines that exist on your host machine to the Staff VLAN at your office. Which of the following must your host machine's NIC support?
    a. CSMA/CA
    b. Channel bonding
    c. MIMO
    d. Trunking
    e. OSPF

19. **You have just rearranged the access points on your small office network. Now a group of employees often cannot get their workstations to connect with a new 802.11n access point. You have confirmed that the workstations are using the correct SSID, security type, and passphrase. You have also confirmed that the access point is on and functioning properly because when you stand in the computer room where it's located, you can connect to the access point from your smartphone. Which of the following is likely preventing the other users' workstations from associating with the new access point?**
    a. They are attempting to log on using incorrect user IDs.
    b. Their workstations are located beyond the access point's range.
    c. Their workstations are set to use 802.11g.
    d. They have turned off their wireless antennas.
    e. Their wired NICs are causing addressing conflicts with their wireless NICs.
20. **Which of the following wireless security techniques uses RADIUS and AES?**
    a. WEP
    b. WPA
    c. WPA2
    d. WPA-Enterprise
    e. WPA2-Enterprise
21. **You are the network administrator for a large college whose network contains nearly 10,000 workstations, over 100 routers, 80 switches, and 2000 printers. You are researching a proposal to both upgrade the routers and switches on your network and at the same time improve the management of your network. What type of protocol should you ensure that the new routers and switches can support in order to more easily automate your network management?**
    a. TFTP
    b. SMTP
    c. NNTP
    d. ICMP
    e. SNMP
22. **In the process of troubleshooting an intermittent performance problem with your network's Internet connection, you attempt to run a traceroute test to *www.microsoft.com*. The traceroute response displays the first 12 hops in the route, but then presents several "Request timed out" messages in a row. What is the most likely reason for this?**
    a. Your network's ISP is experiencing connectivity problems.
    b. The Internet backbone is experiencing traffic congestion.
    c. Your client's TCP/IP service limits the traceroute command to a maximum of 12 hops.
    d. Your IP gateway failed while you were attempting the traceroute test.
    e. Microsoft's network is bounded by firewalls that do not accept incoming ICMP traffic.

23. **What is the network ID for a network that contains the group of IP addresses from 194.73.44.10 through 194.73.44.254 and is not subnetted?**
    a. 194.1.1.1
    b. 194.73.0.0
    c. 194.73.44.1
    d. 194.73.44.255
    e. 194.73.44.0
24. **Which of the following 10-gigabit technologies has the longest maximum segment length?**
    a. 10Gbase-SR
    b. 10GBase-ER
    c. 10GBase-T
    d. 10GBase-LW
    e. 10GBase-SW
25. **Recently, your company's WAN experienced a disabling DDoS attack. Which of the following devices could detect such an attack and prevent it from affecting your network in the future?**
    a. A honeypot
    b. HIDS
    c. HIPS
    d. NIDS
    e. NIPS
26. **In NAT, how does an IP gateway ensure that outgoing traffic can traverse public networks?**
    a. It modifies each outgoing frame's Type field to indicate that the transmission is destined for a public network.
    b. It assigns each outgoing packet a masked ID via the Options field.
    c. It interprets the contents of outgoing packets to ensure that they contain no client-identifying information.
    d. It replaces each outgoing packet's Source address field with a valid IP address.
    e. It modifies the frame length to create uniformly sized frames, called cells, which are required for public network transmission.
27. **You have purchased an access point capable of exchanging data via the 802.11b or 802.11g wireless standard. According to these standards, what is the maximum distance, in meters, from the access point that wireless stations can travel and still reliably exchange data with the access point?**
    a. 20
    b. 50
    c. 75
    d. 100
    e. 400

28. Which of the following functions does SIP perform on a VoIP network? (Choose all that apply.)

a. Determines the locations of endpoints

b. Provides call waiting and caller ID services

c. Prioritizes calls for any single endpoint in a queue

d. Establishes sessions between endpoints

e. Encrypts VoIP signals before they are transmitted over the network

29. You suspect that a machine on your network with the host name PRTSRV is issuing excessive broadcast traffic on your network. What command can you use to determine this host's IP address?

a. `netstat PRTSRV`

b. `ipconfig PRTSRV`

c. `nslookup PRTSRV`

d. `ifconfig PRTSRV`

e. `nbtstat PRTSRV`

30. Which of the following allows a protocol analyzer on your network's backbone switch to monitor all the traffic on a VLAN?

a. Trunking

b. Port mirroring

c. Looping

d. Spanning Tree Protocol

e. Caching

31. What element of network management systems operates on a managed device, such as a router?

a. MIB

b. Polling

c. Agent

d. NMAP

e. Caching

32. Suppose you want to copy files from a Linux server at the office to your home computer, which also runs Linux, across a VPN. Both computers run OpenSSH. Which utility would you use to make sure these files are copied securely?

a. SCP

b. SFTP

c. FTP

d. TFTP

e. HTTP

33. Which of the following is a single sign-on authentication method?

a. IPSec

b. EAPoL

c. SSL

d. Kerberos

e. CHAP

34. You are a network administrator for a WAN that connects two regional insurance company offices—one main office and one satellite office—to each other by a T1. The main office is also connected to the Internet using a T1. This T1 provides Internet access for both offices. To ensure that your private network is not compromised by unauthorized access through the Internet connection, you install a firewall between the main office and the Internet. Shortly thereafter, users in your satellite office complain that they cannot access the file server in the main office, but users in the main office can still access the Internet. What two things should you check?

a. Whether the firewall has been configured to run in promiscuous mode

b. Whether the firewall is placed in the appropriate location on the network

c. Whether the firewall has been configured to allow access from IP addresses in the satellite office

d. Whether the firewall has been configured to receive and transmit UDP-based packets

e. Whether the firewall has been configured to allow Internet access over the main office's T1

35. What is one function of a VPN concentrator?

a. To prioritize traffic on a VPN

b. To consolidate multiple VPNs into a single, larger VPN

c. To cache a VPN's frequently requested content

d. To establish VPN tunnels

e. To collect traffic from multiple VLANs into a VPN

36. While troubleshooting a workstation connectivity problem, you type the following command: `ping 127.0.0.1`. The response indicates that the test failed. What can you determine about that workstation?

a. Its network cable is faulty or not connected to the wall jack.

b. Its TCP/IP protocol is not installed properly.

c. Its IP address has been prevented from transmitting data past the default gateway.

d. Its DHCP settings are incorrect.

e. Its DNS name server specification is incorrect.

37. **You are a support technician working in a telecommunications closet in a remote office. You suspect that a connectivity problem is related to a broken RJ-45 plug on a patch cable that connects a switch to a patch panel. You need to replace that connection, but you forgot to bring an extra patch cable. You decide to install a new RJ-45 connector to replace the broken RJ-45 connector. What two tools should you have to successfully accomplish this?**
    a. Punch-down tool
    b. Crimping tool
    c. Wire stripper
    d. Cable tester
    e. Multimeter
38. **What types of switches propagate flawed packets and, therefore, can contribute to greater network congestion?**
    a. Cut-through switches
    b. Transparent bridging switches
    c. Store-and-forward switches
    d. Content switches
    e. Trunking switches
39. **In IPv6, which of the following is the loopback address?**
    a. 1.0.0.1
    b. 127:0:0:0:0:0:0:1
    c. FE80::1
    d. ::1
    e. 127.0.0.1
40. **Which two of the following devices operate only at the Physical layer of the OSI model?**
    a. Hub
    b. Switch
    c. Router
    d. Bridge
    e. Repeater
41. **Which of the following is a reason for using subnetting?**
    a. To facilitate easier migration from IPv4 to IPv6 addressing
    b. To enable a network to use DHCP
    c. To make more efficient use of limited numbers of legitimate IP addresses
    d. To reduce the likelihood for user error when modifying TCP/IP properties
    e. To limit the number of addresses that can be assigned to one network interface

42. Which of the following is often used to secure data traveling over VPNs that use L2TP?
   a. PPTP
   b. PPoE
   c. Kerberos
   d. SSH
   e. IPSec

43. Which two of the following routing protocols offer fast convergence time and can be used on interior or border routers?
   a. RIP
   b. RIPv2
   c. OSPF
   d. BGP
   e. EIGRP

44. In the following network diagram, which network nodes could belong to a private network?

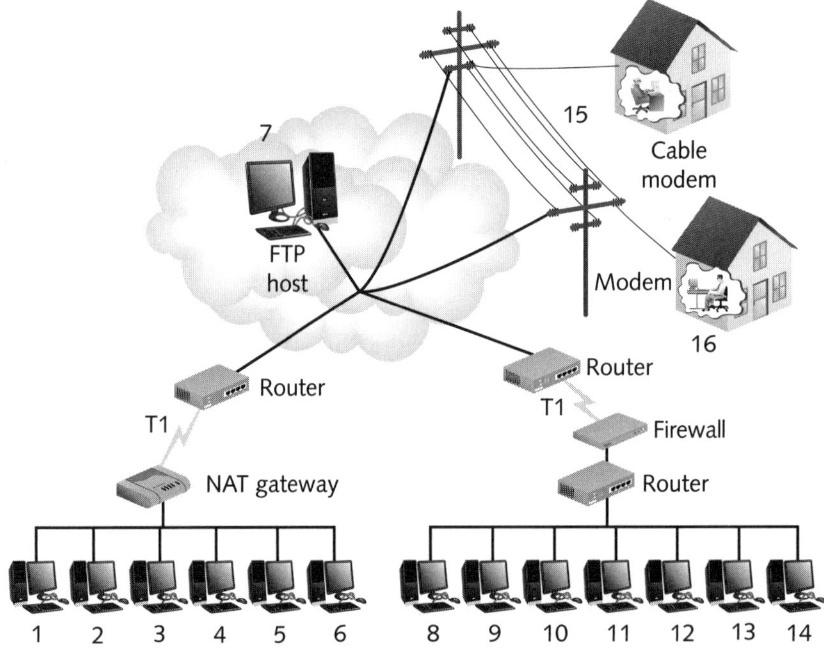

   a. Nodes 1 through 6 and nodes 8 through 14
   b. Nodes 1 through 6 only
   c. Nodes 8 through 14 only
   d. Nodes 1 through 7, plus 15 and 16
   e. All of the nodes could belong to a private network

45. Which of the following must be true for an evil twin attack to succeed?

a. The rogue access point must have the same SSID as the legitimate access point.

b. The rogue access point and legitimate access point must be in the same locale.

c. The rogue access point and legitimate access point must use the same security method.

d. The rogue access point and legitimate access point must use the same security key.

e. All of the above

46. Due to popular demand from employees who need to roam from one floor of your office building to another, you are expanding your wireless network. You want to ensure that mobile users enjoy uninterrupted network connectivity without having to reconfigure their workstations' wireless network connection settings. Which of the following variables must you configure on your new access points to match the settings on existing access points?

a. Administrator password

b. Scanning rate

c. SSID

d. IP address

e. Signal strength

47. Which transport protocol and TCP/IP port does the Telnet utility use?

a. UDP, port 23

b. TCP, port 21

c. UDP, port 22

d. TCP, port 23

e. UDP, port 21

48. What is the purpose of an AAAA resource record in your DNS zone file?

a. It identifies a host's IPv4 address.

b. It identifies a host's IPv6 address.

c. It identifies a host's MAC address.

d. It identifies a mail server address.

e. It indicates an alternate name for the host.

49. What protocol is used to transfer mail between a Sendmail server and a Microsoft Exchange server?

a. SMTP

b. SNMP

c. IMAP4

d. POP3

e. TFTP

50. **What would the command `route del default gw 192.168.5.1 eth1` accomplish on your Linux workstation?**
    a. Delete the default gateway's route to the host whose IP address is 192.168.5.1
    b. Remove the assignment of IP address 192.168.5.1 from the eth1 interface
    c. Remove the workstation's route to the default gateway whose IP address is 192.168.5.1
    d. Add a route from the workstation to the default gateway whose IP address is 192.168.5.1
    e. Remove the designation of default gateway, but keep the route for the host whose IP address is 192.168.5.1

51. **Your 100Base-T network is wired following the TIA/EIA 568B standard. As you make your own patch cable, which wires do you crimp into pins 1 and 2 of the RJ-45 connector?**
    a. White with green stripe and green
    b. White with brown stripe and brown
    c. White with blue stripe and blue
    d. White with red stripe and red
    e. White with orange stripe and orange

52. **A regional bank manager asks you to help with an urgent network problem. Because of a sudden and severe network performance decline, the manager worries that the bank's network might be suffering a DoS attack. Viewing which of the following types of network documentation would probably give you the quickest insight into what's causing this problem?**
    a. Wiring schematic
    b. Firewall log
    c. Logical network diagram
    d. The main file server's system log
    e. Physical network diagram

53. **You have connected to your bank's home page. Its URL begins with "https://." Based on this information, what type of security can you assume the bank employs for receiving and transmitting data to and from its Web server?**
    a. Kerberos
    b. SSL
    c. IPSec
    d. L2TP
    e. Packet-filtering firewall

54. What is the function of protocols and services at the Network layer of the OSI model?

a. To manage the flow of communications over a channel
b. To add segmentation and assembly information
c. To encode and encrypt data
d. To add logical addresses and properly route data
e. To apply electrical pulses to the wire

55. Which of the following utilities could you use to log on to a UNIX host?

a. NTP
b. ARP
c. PING
d. Telnet
e. SNMP

56. As a networking professional, you might use a multimeter to do which of the following? (Choose all that apply.)

a. Determine where the patch cable for a specific server terminates on the patch panel
b. Verify that the amount of resistance presented by terminators on coaxial cable networks is appropriate
c. Check for the presence of noise on a wire (by detecting extraneous voltage)
d. Confirm that a fiber-optic cable can transmit signals from one node to another
e. Validate the processing capabilities of a new router

57. A virtual switch includes several virtual ports, each of which can be considered a:

a. Virtual repeater
b. Virtual router
c. Virtual gateway
d. Virtual hub
e. Virtual bridge

58. What is the default subnet mask for the following IP address: 154.13.44.87?

a. 255.255.255.255
b. 255.255.255.0
c. 255.255.0.0
d. 255.0.0.0
e. 0.0.0.0

59. **Which of the following diagrams illustrates a SONET network?**

a.

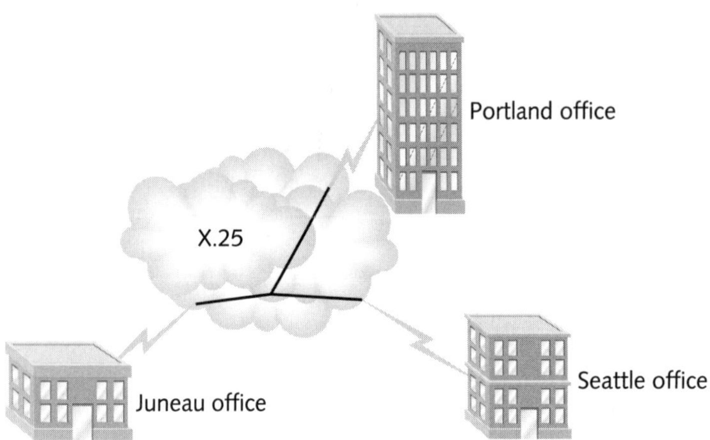

b.

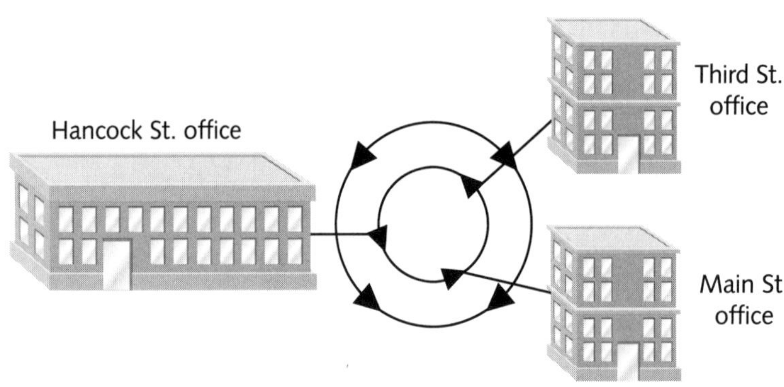

c.

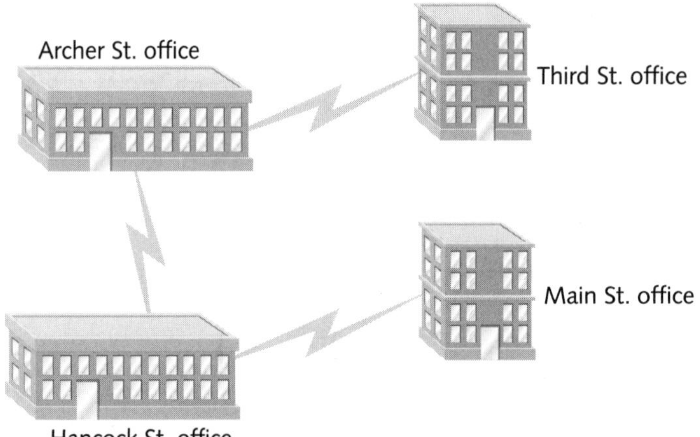

d.

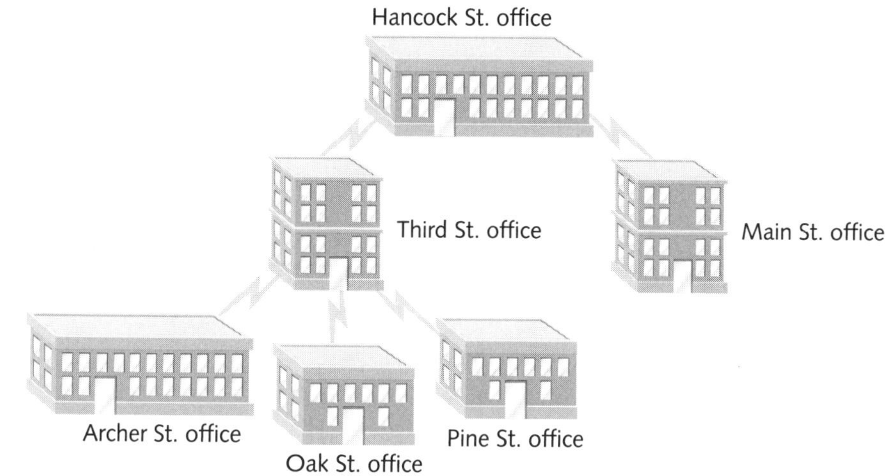

e.

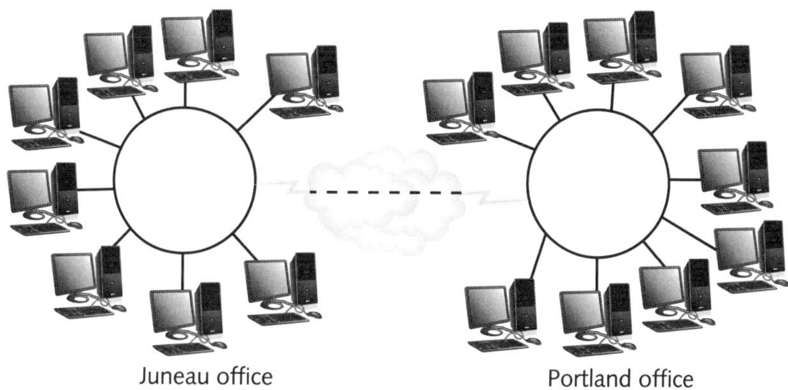

60. Where do you terminate Cat 6a cables in the cross-connect facility to complete a circuit?

a. Patch panel
b. Punch-down block
c. MDF
d. Smart jack
e. CSU/DSU

61. How do most modern FTP servers prevent FTP bounce attacks?

a. They will not issue data to hosts other than the client that originated the request.
b. They will deny requests to ports 21 or 22.
c. They will not allow anonymous logins.
d. They require clients to communicate using SSH.
e. They maintain an access list to determine which clients are legitimate.

62. At what layer of the TCP/IP model is routing information interpreted?

a. Network Interface layer

b. Data Link layer

c. Internet layer

d. Application layer

e. Transport layer

63. You have purchased a new router and are prepared to install it on your network, but have some concerns about security. By default, what kind of traffic policies will the new router's access list apply?

a. It will deny all inbound and outbound traffic.

b. It will deny all inbound traffic, but allow all outbound traffic.

c. It will allow all private outbound and inbound traffic, but deny any public inbound or outbound traffic.

d. It will allow all traffic inbound and outbound except for that directed at known, insecure ports.

e. By default, the router has no access list and will therefore allow any inbound or outbound traffic.

64. You have been asked to help improve network performance on a store's small office network, which relies on two hubs, two access points, and a router to connect its 18 employees to the Internet and other store locations. You decide to determine what type of traffic the network currently handles. In particular, you're interested in the volume of unnecessary broadcast traffic that might be bogging down shared segments. Which of the following tools will help you identify the percentage of traffic that comprises broadcasts?

a. Butt set

b. OTDR

c. Protocol analyzer

d. Multimeter

e. Cable tester

65. A colleague calls you for help with his home office Internet connection. He is using an 802.11n access point/router connected to a DSL modem. The access point/router's private IP address is 192.168.1.1 and it has been assigned an Internet routable IP address of 76.83.124.35. Your friend cannot connect to any resources on the Internet using his new Windows workstation.You ask him to run the `ipconfig` command and read the results to you. He says his workstation's IP address is 192.168.1.3, the subnet mask is 255.255.255.0, and the default gateway address is 192.168.1.3. What do you advise him to do next?

a. Display his DNS information.

b. Change his gateway address.

c. Change his subnet mask.

d. Try pinging the loopback address.

e. Use the `tracert` command to contact the access point/router.

66. **You are setting up a new Windows 7 client to connect with your LAN, which relies on DHCP. You made certain that the client has the TCP/IP protocol installed and is bound to its NIC. Which of the following must you do next to ensure that the client obtains correct TCP/IP information via DHCP?**
    a. Make certain the client's computer name and host name are identical.
    b. Enter the client's MAC address in the DHCP server's ARP table.
    c. Make sure the Client for Microsoft Networks service is bound to the client's NIC.
    d. Enter the DHCP server address in the Windows 7 TCP/IP configuration.
    e. Nothing; in Windows 7, the DHCP option is selected by default, and the client will obtain IP addressing information upon connecting to the network.
67. **You are a support technician trying to help a user configure a new graphics program she installed on her laptop. The laptop runs Ubuntu Linux. After some failed attempts at talking her through the process, you decide to remotely take over her workstation and walk her through the process. Which of the following open source software programs would allow you to do this?**
    a. Remote Desktop
    b. RealVNC
    c. OpenConnect
    d. ICA (Independent Computing Architecture) Client
    e. RAS (Remote Access Service)
68. **Which of the following devices separates broadcast domains?**
    a. Hub
    b. Switch
    c. Bridge
    d. Repeater
    e. Router
69. **Which one of the following media is most resistant to EMI?**
    a. Coaxial cable
    b. UTP cable
    c. STP cable
    d. Fiber-optic cable
    e. Microwave

70. **In the following figure, if router B suffers a failure, how will this failure affect nodes 1 through 9?**

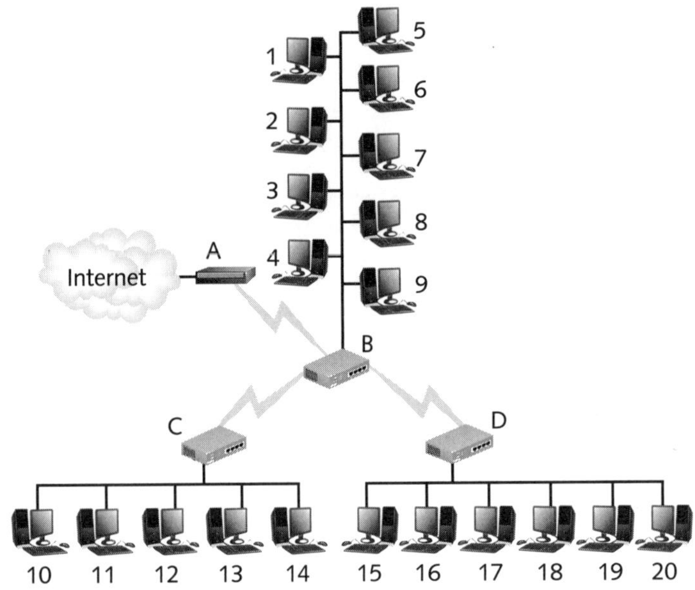

a. They will only be unable to access the Internet.

b. They will be unable to access the Internet and *either* nodes 10 through 14 or 15 through 20.

c. They will be unable to access the Internet, other nodes on the WAN, and other nodes on the LAN.

d. They will be unable to access the Internet and nodes 10 through 20.

e. Their connectivity will not be affected.

71. **Which of the following routing protocols has the poorest convergence time?**

a. RIP

b. EIGRP

c. OSPF

d. BGP

e. IGRP

72. **Which of the following ports would be used during a domain name lookup?**

a. 22

b. 23

c. 53

d. 110

e. 443

73. Suppose you have created six subnets on your network, which leases a group of Class C IPv4 addresses. What subnet mask must you specify in your clients' configurations to adhere to your subnetting scheme?
   a. 255.255.255.6
   b. 255.255.255.128
   c. 255.255.255.192
   d. 255.255.255.224
   e. 255.255.255.0
74. Which of the following protocols encapsulates data for transmission over VPNs?
   a. CHAP
   b. SNMP
   c. L2TP
   d. SFTP
   e. MPLS
75. You are configuring a DHCP server. Which of the following variables refers to the range of IP addresses that you will make available to all nodes on a segment?
   a. Scope
   b. Lease
   c. Zone
   d. Netmask
   e. Period
76. Which of the following wireless networking standards can reliably transmit data the farthest?
   a. Bluetooth
   b. 802.11a
   c. 802.11b
   d. 802.11c
   e. 802.11n
77. How does STP (Spanning Tree Protocol) prevent or stop broadcast storms?
   a. It examines the source IP address field in each broadcast packet and temporarily blocks traffic from that address.
   b. It enables routers to choose one set of best paths and ensures that alternate paths are used only when the best paths are obstructed.
   c. It enables switches to calculate paths that avoid potential loops and artificially blocks the links that would complete a loop.
   d. It enables firewalls to keep access lists that name hosts known for high-volume broadcast traffic and block those hosts from transmitting to the network.
   e. It helps routers define the boundaries of a broadcast domain.

78. Which of the following standards describes a security technique, often used on wireless networks, in which a port is prevented from receiving traffic until the transmitter's credentials are verified by an authentication server?

a. EAPoL

b. SSH

c. SSL

d. Kerberos

e. MS-CHAP

79. If a Windows workstation is configured to use DHCP, but cannot find a DHCP server, it will assign itself an address and subnet mask. Which of the following IPv4 addresses might it assign itself?

a. 129.0.0.1

b. 255.255.255.255

c. 123.45.67.89

d. 169.254.1.120

e. 987.65.432.1

80. Suppose your Windows workstation's wireless network adapter is configured to use the 802.11b wireless networking standard. Also, suppose a café you visit has an 802.11g access point. Assuming you have the correct SSID and logon credentials, what will happen when you attempt to associate with the cafés wireless network?

a. Your wireless networking client will be able to see the access point, but unable to associate with it.

b. Your wireless networking client will not be able to see the access point.

c. Your wireless networking client will be able to see the access point and attempt to associate with it, but the incompatible frequencies will prevent successful authentication.

d. Your wireless networking client will be able to see the access point and attempt to associate with it, but the incompatible security techniques will prevent successful authentication.

e. Your wireless networking client will be able to see the access point and successfully associate with it.

81. Routers use IGMP to:

a. Identify nodes belonging to a multicast group

b. Communicate with other routers about the best path between nodes

c. Reserve bandwidth for priority transmissions, ensuring high QoS

d. Filter out potentially harmful packets

e. Predict the expected round-trip time of a packet over a WAN

82. **A virtual PBX would provide your organization with which of the following services?**
   a. Data storage in the cloud
   b. VoIP call connection
   c. Expedited Internet routing
   d. QoS guarantees for video streaming
   e. Load balancing for WAN connections

83. **You work for a large fashion design firm. Because of a recent TV promotion, your company has received national recognition. At the same time, your WAN has received more security threats. To help fend off these threats, you decide to implement an IPS/IDS. Following is a simplified network diagram that represents your private network and its public network connection. Where on this diagram would you place the IPS/IDS device?**

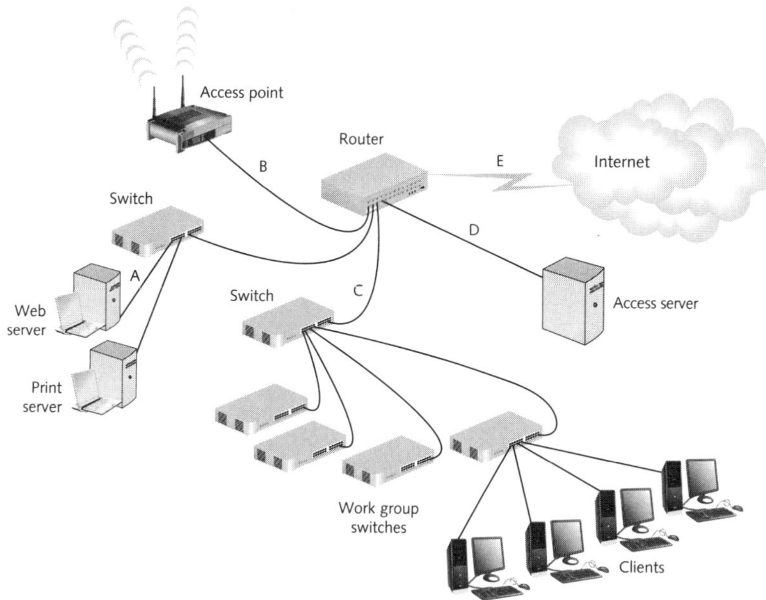

84. **A user watching an episode of a TV show over the Internet is an example of what type of communication?**
   a. Unicast
   b. Multicast
   c. Broadcast
   d. Point-to-multipoint
   e. Multipoint-to-point

85. You are configuring a connection between two backbone switches, and you want to make sure the connection doesn't fail or become overwhelmed by heavy traffic. Which of the following techniques would help you achieve both aims?
    a. Round-robin DNS
    b. CARP
    c. Clustering
    d. Trunking
    e. NIC teaming
86. Using RIP, what is the maximum number of hops a packet can take between its source and its destination?
    a. 3
    b. 5
    c. 10
    d. 15
    e. 18
87. You work for a telephone company that provides Internet service via dial-up and DSL connections. One day you have the chance to work in the field with an older telephone technician. You stop at an intersection and open a pedestal where telephone pairs terminate. Which of the following tools does the technician use to determine whether a customer's line is obtaining dial tone from the CO?
    a. OTDR
    b. Network monitor
    c. Protocol analyzer
    d. Butt set
    e. Cable continuity tester
88. Which of the following QoS techniques enables packet-switched technologies to travel over traditionally circuit-switched connections?
    a. ATM
    b. SONET
    c. MPLS
    d. Frame relay
    e. Clustering
89. How many bits are in an IPv6 address?
    a. 16
    b. 32
    c. 64
    d. 128
    e. 256

90. **Which of the following makes use of channel bonding to maximize throughput?**
   a. 802.11a
   b. 802.11b
   c. 802.11g
   d. 802.11n
   e. WiMAX

91. **The following graph, which represents traffic activity for an ISP's client, indicates that the ISP is utilizing what traffic-shaping technique?**

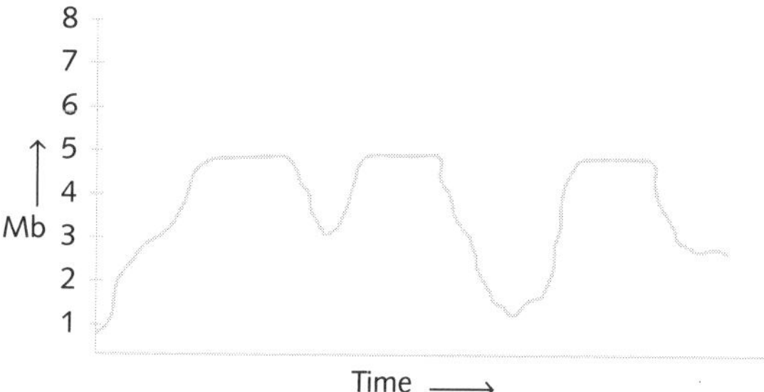

   a. Traffic policing
   b. Caching
   c. Load balancing
   d. Access list controls
   e. Fault tolerance

92. **Your company's network administrator has told you that you may operate a Web server for employees to access as long as it remains inside the demilitarized zone. What does he mean by this?**
   a. You may set up a Web server on your home network.
   b. You may set up a Web server on the company's access server, which allows clients from around the globe to connect to your WAN.
   c. You may set up a Web server at a hosting facility outside of the company's LAN or WAN.
   d. You may set up a Web server on the company's private LAN, which is protected by a firewall.
   e. You may not set up a Web server on the company's LAN or WAN.

93. Your organization is reassessing its WAN connections to determine how much more bandwidth it will need to purchase in the next five years. As a network administrator, which of the following data can you share that will help management make the right decision?

a. Wiring schematic

b. Logical network diagram

c. Syslogs

d. Baselines

e. Physical network diagram

94. If an organization follows structured cabling standards, where would its demarc be located?

a. Entrance facilities

b. MDF

c. IDF

d. Cross-connect facilities

e. Backbone

95. You are helping to troubleshoot a recurring problem related to obtaining and keeping a DHCP-distributed IP address on a colleague's Windows workstation. What application would allow you to configure the workstation to tally these errors and send you an e-mail message every time such a problem occurred?

a. Network and Internet Connections

b. System Logger

c. PuTTY

d. System Manager

e. Event Viewer

96. You are creating a new Linux server as a virtual machine on your Windows 7 workstation. Which of the following commands will tell you the IP address that is assigned to your virtual server?

a. `ipconfig /all` at the Windows command prompt

b. `ifconfig -a` at the Windows command prompt

c. `ethtool -a` at the Linux server's shell prompt

d. `ip addr` at the Windows command prompt

e. `ipconfig -a` at the Linux server's shell prompt

97. In IPv6 addressing, which of the following Format Prefixes indicates that an address belongs to a multicast group?

a. 00FF

b. 1F3E

c. FF02

d. 0001

e. FEC0

98. **Suppose your WAN contained a segment that relied on the 10GBase-EW standard. Which of the following transmission technologies might it use?**
    a. SONET
    b. Satellite
    c. Broadband cable
    d. DSL
    e. ISDN

99. **To provide some basic security for your small office network, you install software called IP Tables on an old Linux computer. This software examines each incoming datagram. Based on a set of criteria, including source IP address, source and destination ports, and protocols, it blocks or allows traffic. What type of system is this? (Choose all that apply.)**
    a. Content-filtering firewall
    b. Stateful firewall
    c. Stateless firewall
    d. Packet-filtering firewall
    e. Application layer firewall

100. **Ethernet and ATM both specify Data Link layer framing techniques. How do they differ?**
    a. Ethernet uses CRC fields to confirm the validity of the frame, whereas ATM uses no error detection.
    b. Ethernet uses variably sized packets, whereas ATM uses fixed-sized cells.
    c. Ethernet uses synchronous transmission, whereas ATM uses asynchronous transmission.
    d. Ethernet uses frame headers, whereas ATM does not.
    e. Ethernet offers no guarantee of timely delivery, whereas ATM ensures that packets are delivered within 10 ms.

appendix C

Visual Guide to Connectors

Throughout this book, you learned about several different cabling and connector options that may be used on networks. Some, such as RJ-45, are very common, whereas others, such as Fiber LC connectors, are used only on high-speed optical networks. So that you can compare such connectors and ensure that you understand their differences, this appendix compiles drawings of the connectors and a brief summary of their uses in a simple table. You must be familiar with the most popular types of connectors to qualify for Network+ certification. You can find more detail about these connectors and the networks on which they are used in Chapters 3, 6, and 7.

Table C-1 Network connectors and their uses

Specification	Male connector (front view)	Male connector (side view)	Female receptacle (front view)	Application
BNC			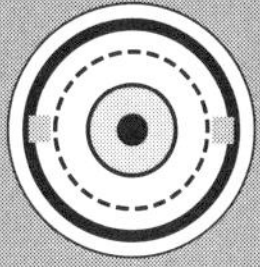	Used with coaxial cable for broadband cable connections; also used on old Ethernet networks such as Thinnet
RJ-11(registered jack 11)			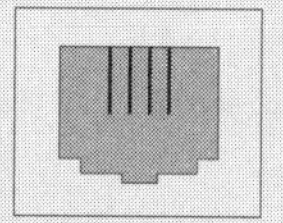	Used on twisted pair cabling for telephone systems (and some older twisted pair networks)
RJ-45 (registered jack 45) and RJ-48 (registered jack 48)	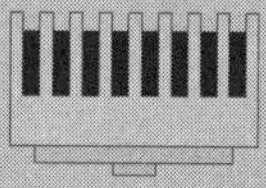		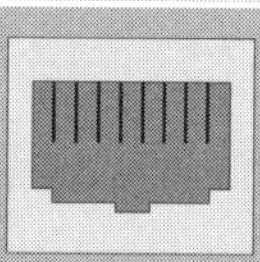	Used on twisted pair cabling for Ethernet and T-carrier connections
F-Type	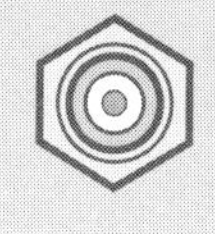	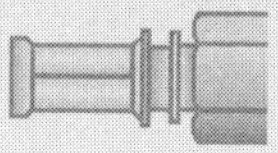	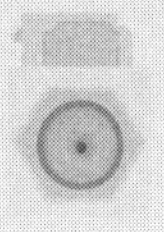	Used on coaxial cable suitable for use with broadband video and data applications

Table C-1 Network connectors and their uses (*continued*)

Specification	Male connector (front view)	Male connector (side view)	Female receptacle (front view)	Application
ST (straight tip)	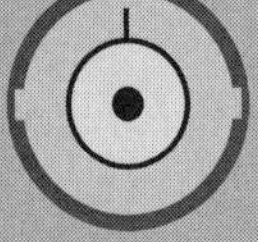			Used on fiber-optic cabling (for example, on 100Base-FX, Gigabit, and 10-GB Ethernet networks)
SC (subscriber connector or standard connector)		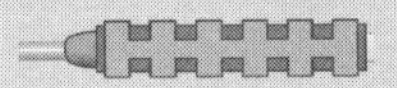		Used on fiber-optic cabling (for example, on 100Base-FX, Gigabit, and 10-GB Ethernet networks)
Fiber LC (local connector), single-mode			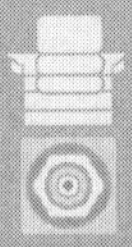	Used on fiber-optic cabling (for example, on 100Base-FX, Gigabit, and 10-GB Ethernet networks)
MT-RJ (mechanical transfer register jack)	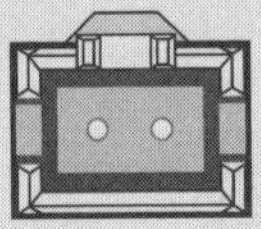	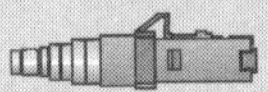	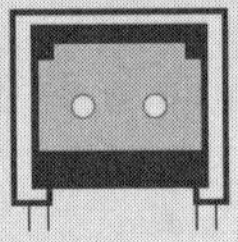	Used on fiber-optic cabling (for example, on 100Base-FX, Gigabit, and 10-GB Ethernet networks)
DB-9	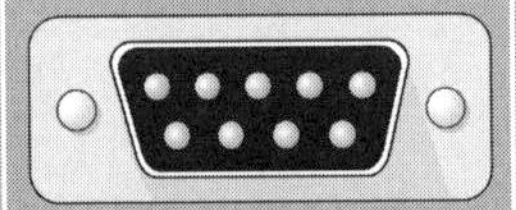		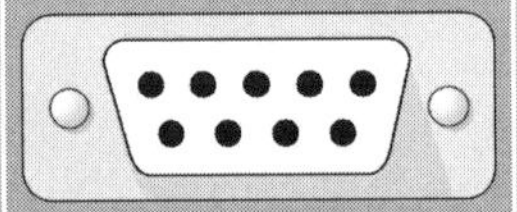	One of the RS-232 standard connectors used in serial connections
DB-25	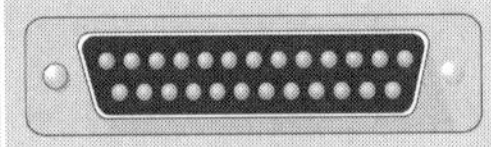		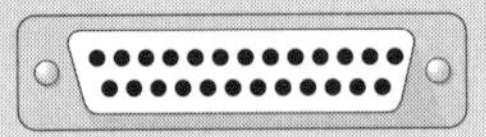	One of the RS-232 standard connectors used in serial connections
USB (Universal Serial Bus)				Used to connect external peripherals, such as modems, mice, audio players, NICs, cameras, PDAs, and smartphones

appendix D

Answers to Chapter Review Questions

Chapter 1

1. d
2. b
3. b
4. b
5. d
6. False
7. True
8. False
9. False
10. False
11. network
12. peer-to-peer
13. scalable
14. network services
15. certification

Chapter 2

1. b
2. c
3. d
4. a
5. d
6. True
7. False
8. False
9. True

10. False
11. Voluntary
12. RIR (Regional Internet Registry), Regional Internet Registry (RIR), RIR, Regional Internet Registry
13. OSI (Open Systems Interconnection), Open Systems Interconnection (OSI), OSI, Open Systems Interconnection
14. Application
15. Encapsulation

Chapter 3

1. c
2. c
3. b
4. c
5. d
6. True
7. True
8. False
9. True
10. True
11. Overhead
12. modulation
13. multiplexing
14. straight-through
15. RS-232 (Recommended Standard 232), RS-232, Recommended Standard 232 (RS-232), Recommended Standard 232

Chapter 4

1. c
2. b
3. c
4. a
5. d
6. False
7. False
8. True

9. True
10. True
11. routable
12. dotted decimal notation
13. subnet mask
14. APIPA (automatic Private IP Addressing), Automatic Private IP Addressing, APIPA
15. socket

Chapter 5

1. b
2. c
3. c
4. a
5. a
6. True
7. True
8. False
9. True
10. True
11. topology
12. logical topology
13. CSMA/CD (Carrier Sense Multiple Access with Collision Detection), CSMA/CD, Carrier Sense Multiple Access with Collisions Detection
14. Ethernet II (DIX), DIX, Ethernet II
15. PoE (Power over Ethernet), PoE, Power over Ethernet

Chapter 6

1. c
2. d
3. a
4. b
5. d
6. False
7. False
8. True
9. True

10. False
11. repeater
12. hub
13. bridge
14. cut-through, cut through
15. Gateways

Chapter 7

1. c
2. a
3. b
4. c
5. a
6. True
7. False
8. False
9. True
10. True
11. mesh, full-mesh
12. tiered
13. PSTN (Public Switched Telephone Network), PSTN, Public Switched Telephone Network, Public Switched Telephone Network (PSTN)
14. X.25
15. D

Chapter 8

1. b
2. c
3. a
4. b
5. c
6. False
7. False
8. False
9. False
10. False

11. mobile
12. FHSS (Frequency Hopping Spread Spectrum), Frequency Hopping Spread Spectrum (FHSS), FHSS, Frequency Hopping Spread Spectrum
13. site survey
14. WiMAX (Worldwide Interoperability for Microwave Access), WiMAX, Worldwide Interoperability for Microwave Access, Worldwide Interoperability for Microwave Access (WiMAX)
15. passive scanning

Chapter 9

1. d
2. d
3. b
4. b
5. b
6. False
7. True
8. False
9. True
10. False
11. Subnetting
12. CIDR (Classless Interdomain Routing), CIDR, Classless Interdomain Routing, Classless Interdomain Routing (CIDR)
13. NAT (Network Address Translation), NAT, Network Address Translation, Network Address Translation (NAT)
14. ICS (Internet Connection Sharing), ICS, Internet Connection Sharing, Internet Connection Sharing (ICS)
15. MIME (Multipurpose Internet Mail Extensions), MIME, Multipurpose Internet Mail Extensions, Multipurpose Internet Mail Extensions (MIME)

Chapter 10

1. b
2. c
3. d
4. c
5. b
6. True

7. False
8. True
9. True
10. True
11. VLAN
12. virtual appliance
13. SLIP (Serial Line Internet Protocol), SLIP, Serial Line Internet Protocol, Serial Line Internet Protocol (SLIP)
14. Naas (Network as a Service), Naas, Network as a Service, Network as a Service (Naas)
15. credentials

Chapter 11

1. b
2. d
3. a
4. a
5. d
6. True
7. False
8. False
9. True
10. True
11. posture assessment
12. security policy
13. proxy service
14. public key
15. WEP (Wired Equivalent Privacy)

Chapter 12

1. b
2. c
3. a
4. d
5. b
6. False
7. True

8. False
9. True
10. True
11. IP telephony
12. H.323
13. SIP (Session Initiation Protocol), SIP, Session Initiation Protocol (SIP), Session Initiation Protocol
14. MGC (Media Gateway Controller), MGC, Media Gateway Controller (MGC), Media Gateway Controller
15. RSVP (Resource Reservation Protocol), RSVP, Resource Reservation Protocol (RSVP), Resource Reservation Protocol

Chapter 13

1. c
2. d
3. c
4. b
5. c
6. True
7. False
8. True
9. False
10. True
11. call tracking
12. multimeter
13. network monitor
14. protocol
15. spectrum analyzer

Chapter 14

1. d
2. a
3. a
4. b
5. d
6. True

7. True
8. True
9. True
10. False
11. integrity
12. availability
13. Polymorphic
14. anti-malware policy
15. standby

Chapter 15

1. b
2. d
3. c
4. c
5. b
6. True
7. False
8. False
9. True
10. True
11. Network
12. Traffic shaping
13. Caching
14. upgrade
15. Syslog

1 gigabit per second (Gbps) 1,000,000,000 bits per second.

1 kilobit per second (Kbps) 1000 bits per second.

1 megabit per second (Mbps) 1,000,000 bits per second.

1 terabit per second (Tbps) 1,000,000,000,000 bits per second.

100-pair wire UTP supplied by a telecommunications carrier that contains 100 wire pairs.

1000Base-LX A Physical layer standard for networks that specifies 1-Gbps transmission over fiber-optic cable using baseband transmission. 1000Base-LX can run on either single-mode or multimode fiber. The *LX* represents its reliance on long wavelengths of 1300 nanometers. 1000Base-LX can extend to 5000-meter segment lengths using single-mode, fiber-optic cable. 1000Base-LX networks can use one repeater between segments.

1000Base-SX A Physical layer standard for networks that specifies 1-Gbps transmission over fiber-optic cable using baseband transmission. 1000Base-SX runs on multimode fiber. Its maximum segment length is 550 meters. The *SX* represents its reliance on short wavelengths of 850 nanometers. 1000Base-SX can use one repeater.

1000Base-T A Physical layer standard for achieving 1 Gbps over UTP. 1000Base-T achieves its higher throughput by using all four pairs of wires in a Cat 5 or better twisted pair cable to both transmit and receive signals. 1000Base-T also uses a different data encoding scheme than that used by other UTP Physical layer specifications.

100Base-FX A Physical layer standard for networks that specifies baseband transmission, multimode fiber cabling, and 100-Mbps throughput. 100Base-FX networks have a maximum segment length of 2000 meters. 100Base-FX may also be called Fast Ethernet.

100Base-T A Physical layer standard for networks that specifies baseband transmission, twisted pair cabling, and 100-Mbps throughput. 100Base-T networks have a maximum segment length of 100 meters and use the star topology. 100Base-T is also known as Fast Ethernet.

100Base-TX A type of 100Base-T network that uses two wire pairs in a twisted pair cable, but uses faster signaling to achieve 100-Mbps throughput. It is capable of full-duplex transmission and requires Cat 5 or better twisted pair media.

10Base-T A Physical layer standard for networks that specifies baseband transmission, twisted pair media, and 10-Mbps throughput. 10Base-T networks have a maximum segment length of 100 meters and rely on a star topology.

10GBase-ER A Physical layer standard for achieving 10-Gbps data transmission over single-mode, fiber-optic cable. In 10GBase-ER, the *ER* stands for *extended reach*. This standard specifies a star topology and segment lengths up to 40,000 meters.

10GBase-EW A variation of the 10GBase-ER standard that is specially encoded to operate over SONET links.

10GBase-LR A Physical layer standard for achieving 10-Gbps data transmission over single-mode, fiber-optic cable using wavelengths of 1310 nanometers. In 10GBase-LR, the *LR* stands for *long reach*. This standard specifies a star topology and segment lengths up to 10,000 meters.

10GBase-LW A variation of the 10GBase-LR standard that is specially encoded to operate over SONET links.

10GBase-SR A Physical layer standard for achieving 10-Gbps data transmission over multimode fiber using wavelengths of 850 nanometers. The maximum segment length for 10GBase-SR can reach up to 300 meters, depending on the fiber core diameter and modal bandwidth used.

10GBase-SW A variation of the 10GBase-SR standard that is specially encoded to operate over SONET links.

10GBase-T A Physical layer standard for achieving 10-Gbps data transmission over twisted pair cable. Described in its 802.3an standard, IEEE specifies Cat 6 or Cat 7 cable as the appropriate medium for 10GBase-T. The maximum segment length for 10GBase-T is 100 meters.

110 block Part of an organization's cross-connect facilities, a type of punch-down block designed to terminate Cat 5 or better twisted pair wires.

1G The first generation of mobile phone services, popular in the 1970s and 1980s, which were entirely analog.

2.4-GHz band The range of radio frequencies from 2.4 to 2.4835 GHz. The 2.4-GHz band, which allows for 11 unlicensed channels, is used by WLANs that follow the popular 802.11b and 802.11g standards. However, it is also used for cordless telephone and other transmissions, making the 2.4-GHz band more susceptible to interference than the 5-GHz band.

25-pair wire UTP supplied by a telecommunications carrier that contains 25 wire pairs.

2G Second-generation mobile phone service, popular in the 1990s. 2G was the first standard to use digital transmission, and as such, it paved the way for texting and media downloads on mobile devices.

3DES *See* Triple DES.

3G Third-generation mobile phone service, released in the early 2000s, that specifies throughputs of 384 Kbps and packet switching for data (but not voice) communications.

4G Fourth-generation mobile phone service that is characterized by an all-IP, packet-switched network for both data and voice transmission. 4G standards, released in 2008, also specify throughputs of 100 Mbps for fast-moving mobile clients, such as those in cars, and 1 Gbps for slow-moving mobile clients, such as pedestrians.

5-4-3 rule A guideline for 10-Mbps Ethernet networks stating that between two communicating nodes, the network cannot contain more than five network segments connected by four repeating devices, and no more than three of the segments may be populated.

5-GHz band A range of frequencies that comprises four frequency bands: 5.1 GHz, 5.3 GHz, 5.4 GHz, and 5.8 GHz. It consists of 24 unlicensed bands, each 20-MHz wide. The 5-GHz band is used by WLANs that follow the 802.11a and 802.11n standards.

802.11 The IEEE standard for wireless networking.

802.11a The IEEE standard for a wireless networking technique that uses multiple frequency bands in the 5-GHz frequency range and provides a theoretical maximum throughput of 54 Mbps. 802.11a's high throughput, compared with 802.11b, is attributable to its use of higher frequencies, its unique method of encoding data, and more available bandwidth.

802.11b The IEEE standard for a wireless networking technique that uses DSSS (direct-sequence spread spectrum) signaling in the 2.4–2.4835-GHz frequency range (also called the 2.4-GHz band). 802.11b separates the 2.4-GHz band into 14 overlapping 22-MHz channels and provides a theoretical maximum of 11-Mbps throughput.

802.11g The IEEE standard for a wireless networking technique designed to be compatible with 802.11b while using different encoding techniques that allow it to reach a theoretical maximum capacity of 54 Mbps. 802.11g, like 802.11b, uses the 2.4-GHz frequency band.

802.11i The IEEE standard for wireless network encryption and authentication that uses the EAP authentication method, strong encryption, and dynamically assigned keys, which are different for every transmission. 802.11i specifies AES encryption and weaves a key into each packet.

802.11n The IEEE standard for a wireless networking technique that may issue signals in the 2.4- or 5-GHz band and can achieve actual data throughput between 65 and 600 Mbps. It accomplishes this through several means, including MIMO, channel bonding, and frame aggregation. 802.11n is backward compatible with 802.11a, b, and g.

802.16 The IEEE standard for broadband wireless metropolitan area networking (also known as WiMAX). 802.16 networks may use frequencies between 2 and 66 GHz. Their antennas may operate in a line-of-sight or non-line-of-sight manner and cover 50 kilometers (or approximately 30 miles). 802.16 connections can achieve a maximum throughput of 70 Mbps, though actual throughput diminishes as the distance between transceivers increases. Several 802.16 standards exist. Collectively, they are known as WiMAX.

802.16e Currently, the most widely implemented version of WiMAX. With 802.16e, IEEE improved the mobility and QoS characteristics of the technology, making it better suited to VoIP and mobile phone users. 802.16e is capable of 70-Mbps throughput, but because bandwidth is shared and service providers cap data rates, most users actually experience 1- to 4-Mbps throughput.

802.16m Also known as WiMAX 2, the IEEE standard for a version of 802.16 that achieves theoretical throughputs of 330 Mbps with lower latency and better quality for VoIP applications than previous WiMAX versions. 802.16m has been approved as a true 4G technology. Manufacturers expect it to reach throughputs of 1 Gbps in the near future.

802.1D The IEEE standard that describes, among other things, bridging and STP (Spanning Tree Protocol).

802.1q The IEEE standard that specifies how VLAN and trunking information appears in frames and how switches and bridges interpret that information.

802.1w The IEEE standard that describes RSTP (Rapid Spanning Tree Protocol), which evolved from STP (Spanning Tree Protocol).

802.1x A vendor-independent IEEE standard for securing transmission between nodes according to the transmission's port, whether physical or logical. 802.1x, also known as EAPoL, is the authentication standard followed by wireless networks using 802.11i.

802.2 The IEEE standard for error and flow control in data frames.

802.3 The IEEE standard for Ethernet networking devices and data handling (using the CSMA/CD access method).

802.3ab The IEEE standard that describes 1000Base-T, a 1-gigabit Ethernet technology that runs over four pairs of Cat 5 or better cable.

802.3ae The IEEE standard that describes 10-Gigabit Ethernet technologies, including 10GBase-SR, 10GBase-SW, 10GBase-LR, 10GBase-LW, 10GBase-ER, and 10GBase-EW.

802.3af The IEEE standard that specifies a way of supplying electrical Power over Ethernet (PoE). 802.3af requires Cat 5 or better UTP or STP cabling and uses power sourcing equipment to supply current over a wire pair to powered devices. PoE is compatible with existing 10Base-T, 100Base-TX, 1000Base-T, and 10GBase-T implementations.

802.3an The IEEE standard that describes 10GBase-T, a 10-Gbps Ethernet technology that runs on Cat 6 or Cat 7 twisted pair cable.

802.3u The IEEE standard that describes Fast Ethernet technologies, including 100Base-TX.

802.3z The IEEE standard that describes 1000Base (or 1-gigabit) Ethernet technologies, including 1000Base-LX and 1000Base-SX.

802.5 The IEEE standard for token ring networking devices and data handling.

A+ The professional certification established by CompTIA that verifies knowledge about PC operation, repair, and management.

AAA (authentication, authorization, and accounting) The name of a category of protocols that establish a client's identity; check the client's credentials and, based on those, allow or deny access to a system or network; and, finally, track the client's system or network usage.

access control list *See* ACL.

access list *See* ACL.

access method A network's method of controlling how nodes access the communications channel. For example, CSMA/CD (Carrier Sense Multiple Access with Collision Detection) is the access method specified in the IEEE 802.3 (Ethernet) standard.

access point A device used on wireless LANs that transmits and receives wireless signals to and from multiple nodes and retransmits them to the rest of the network segment. Access points can connect a group of nodes with a network or two networks with each other. They may use directional or omnidirectional antennas.

access port The interface on a switch used for an end node. Devices connected to access ports are unaware of VLAN information.

access server *See* remote access server.

ACK (acknowledgment) A response generated at the Transport layer of the OSI model that confirms to a sender that its frame was received. The ACK packet is the third of three in the three-step process of establishing a connection.

acknowledgment *See* ACK.

ACL (access control list) A list of statements used by a router to permit or deny the forwarding of traffic on a network based on one or more criteria.

Active Directory The method for organizing and managing objects associated with the network in Windows Server NOSs.

active scanning A method used by wireless stations to detect the presence of an access point. In active scanning, the station issues a probe to each channel in its frequency range and waits for the access point to respond.

active topology A topology in which each workstation participates in transmitting data over the network. A ring topology is considered an active topology.

ad hoc A type of wireless LAN in which stations communicate directly with each other (rather than using an access point).

address A number that uniquely identifies each workstation and device on a network. Without unique addresses, computers on the network could not reliably communicate.

address management The process of centrally administering a finite number of network addresses for an entire LAN. Usually this task can be accomplished without touching the client workstations.

Address Resolution Protocol *See* ARP.

address resource record A type of DNS data record that maps the IP address of an Internet-connected device to its domain name.

addressing The scheme for assigning a unique identifying number to every workstation and device on the network.

ADSL (Asymmetric DSL) A variation of DSL that offers more throughput when data travel downstream, downloading from a local carrier's switching facility to the customer, than when data travel upstream, uploading from the customer to the local carrier's switching facility.

Advanced Encryption Standard *See* AES.

AES (Advanced Encryption Standard) A private key encryption algorithm that weaves keys of 128, 160, 192, or 256 bits through data multiple times. The algorithm used in the most popular form of AES is known as Rijndael. AES has replaced DES in situations such as military communications, which require the highest level of security.

AF (Assured Forwarding) In the DiffServ QoS technique, a forwarding specification that allows routers to assign data streams one of several prioritization levels. AF is specified in the DiffServ field in an IPv4 datagram.

agent A software routine that collects data about a managed device's operation and provides it to a network management application.

AH (authentication header) In the context of IPSec, a type of encryption that provides authentication of the IP packet's data payload through public key techniques.

AIX A proprietary implementation of the UNIX system distributed by IBM.

alias A nickname for a node's host name.

alien cross talk Electromagnetic interference induced on one cable by signals traveling over a nearby cable.

AM (amplitude modulation) A modulation technique in which the amplitude of the carrier signal is modified by the application of a data signal.

American National Standards Institute *See* ANSI.

American Wire Gauge *See* AWG.

amplifier A device that boosts, or strengthens, an analog signal.

amplitude A measure of a signal's strength.

amplitude modulation *See* AM.

analog A signal that uses variable voltage to create continuous waves, resulting in an inexact transmission.

analog telephone adapter *See* ATA.

ANDing A logical process of combining bits. In ANDing, a bit with a value of 1 plus another bit with a value of 1 results in a 1. A bit with a value of 0 plus any other bit results in a 0.

ANSI (American National Standards Institute) An organization composed of more than 1000 representatives from industry and government who together determine standards for the electronics industry in addition to other fields, such as chemical and nuclear engineering, health and safety, and construction.

anycast address A type of address specified in IPv6 that represents a group of interfaces, any one of which (and usually the first available of which) can accept a transmission. At this time, anycast addresses are not designed to be assigned to hosts, such as servers or workstations, but rather to routers.

Anything as a Service *See* XaaS.

AP *See* access point.

API (application programming interface) A set of routines that make up part of a software application.

APIPA (Automatic Private IP Addressing) A service available on computers running one of the Windows operating systems that automatically assigns the computer's network interface a link-local IP address.

application gateway *See* proxy server.

Application layer The seventh layer of the OSI model. Application layer protocols enable software programs to negotiate formatting, procedural, security, synchronization, and other requirements with the network.

Application layer gateway *See* proxy server.

application programming interface *See* API.

application switch A switch that provides functions between Layer 4 and Layer 7 of the OSI model.

archive bit A file attribute that can be checked (or set to "on") or unchecked (or set to "off") to indicate whether the file needs to be archived. An operating system checks a file's archive bit when it is created or changed.

ARP (Address Resolution Protocol) A core protocol in the TCP/IP suite that belongs in the Network layer of the OSI model. ARP obtains the MAC (physical) address of a host, or node, and then creates a local database that maps the MAC address to the host's IP (logical) address.

ARP cache *See* ARP table.

ARP table A database of records that maps MAC addresses to IP addresses. The ARP table is stored on a computer's hard disk where it is used by the ARP utility to supply the MAC addresses of network nodes, given their IP addresses.

array A group of hard disks.

AS (authentication service) In Kerberos terminology, the process that runs on a KDC (Key Distribution Center) to initially validate a client who's logging on. The authentication service issues a session key to the client and to the service the client wants to access.

asset management The process of collecting and storing data on the number and types of software and hardware assets in an organization's network. The data collection is automated by electronically examining each network node from a server.

association In the context of wireless networking, the communication that occurs between a station and an access point to enable the station to connect to the network via that access point.

Assured Forwarding *See* AF.

asymmetric encryption A type of encryption (such as public key encryption) that uses a different key for encoding data than is used for decoding the ciphertext.

Asymmetric DSL *See* ADSL.

asymmetric multiprocessing A multiprocessing method that assigns each subtask to a specific processor.

asymmetrical The characteristic of a transmission technology that affords greater bandwidth in one direction (either from the customer to the carrier, or vice versa) than in the other direction.

asynchronous A transmission method in which data being transmitted and received by nodes do not have to conform to any timing scheme. In asynchronous communications, a node can transmit at any time and the destination node must accept the transmission as it comes.

Asynchronous Transfer Mode *See* ATM.

ATA (analog telephone adapter) An internal or externally attached adapter that converts analog telephone signals into packet-switched voice signals and vice versa.

ATM (Asynchronous Transfer Mode) A Data Link layer technology originally conceived in the early 1980s at Bell Labs and standardized by the ITU in the mid-1990s. ATM delivers data using fixed packets, called cells, that each consist of 48 bytes of data plus a 5-byte header. ATM relies on virtual circuits and establishes a connection before sending data. The reliable connection ensured by ATM allows network managers to specify QoS levels for certain types of traffic.

attenuation The extent to which a signal has weakened after traveling a given distance.

attribute A variable property associated with a network object. For example, a restriction on the time of day a user can log on is an attribute associated with that user object.

augmented Category 6 *See* Cat 6a.

authentication The process of comparing and matching a client's credentials with the credentials in the NOS user database to enable the client to log on to the network.

authentication, authorization, and accounting *See* AAA.

authentication header *See* AH.

authentication protocol A set of rules that governs how servers authenticate clients. Several types of authentication protocols exist.

authentication service *See* AS.

authenticator In Kerberos authentication, the user's time stamp encrypted with the session key. The authenticator is used to help the service verify that a user's ticket is valid.

Automatic Private IP Addressing *See* APIPA.

Avahi A version of Zeroconf available for use with the Linux operating system.

availability How consistently and reliably a file, device, or connection can be accessed by authorized personnel.

AWG (American Wire Gauge) A standard rating that indicates the diameter of a wire, such as the conducting core of a coaxial cable.

B channel In ISDN, the "bearer" channel, so named because it bears traffic from point to point.

backbone The part of a network to which segments and significant shared devices (such as routers, switches, and servers) connect. A backbone is sometimes referred to as "a network of networks" because of its role in interconnecting smaller parts of a LAN or WAN.

backhaul An intermediate connection between subscriber networks and a telecommunications carrier's network.

backing up The process of copying critical data files to a secure storage area. Often, backups are performed according to a formulaic schedule.

backlevel To revert to a previous version of a software application after attempting to upgrade it.

backplane A synonym for motherboard, often used in the context of switches and routers.

backup A copy of data or program files created for archiving or safekeeping.

backup rotation scheme A plan for when and how often backups occur, and which backups are full, incremental, or differential.

bandwidth A measure of the difference between the highest and lowest frequencies that a medium can transmit.

base station *See* access point.

baseband A form of transmission in which digital signals are sent through direct current pulses applied to a wire. This direct current requires exclusive use of the wire's capacity, so baseband systems can transmit only one signal, or one channel, at a time. Every device on a baseband system shares a single channel.

baseline A record of how a network operates under normal conditions (including its performance, collision rate, utilization rate, and so on). Baselines are used for comparison when conditions change.

Basic Rate Interface *See* BRI.

basic service set *See* BSS.

basic service set identifier *See* BSSID.

beacon frame In the context of wireless networking, a frame issued by an access point to alert other nodes of its existence.

bend radius The radius of the maximum arc into which you can loop a cable before you will cause data transmission errors. Generally, a twisted pair cable's bend radius is equal to or greater than four times the diameter of the cable.

best path The most efficient route from one node on a network to another. Under optimal network conditions, the best path is the most direct path between two points. However, when traffic congestion, segment failures, and other factors create obstacles, the most direct path might not be the best path.

BGP (Border Gateway Protocol) A distance-vector routing protocol capable of considering many factors in its routing metrics. BGP, an Exterior Gateway Protocol, is the routing protocol used on Internet backbones.

BID (Bridge ID) A combination of a 2-byte priority field and a bridge's MAC address, used in STP (Spanning Tree Protocol) to select a root bridge.

binary A system founded on using 1s and 0s to encode information.

biorecognition access A method of authentication in which a device scans an individual's unique physical characteristics, such as the color patterns in her iris or the geometry of her hand, to verify the user's identity.

bit (binary digit) A bit equals a single pulse in the digital encoding system. It may have only one of two values: 0 or 1.

blackout A complete power loss.

block ID *See* OUI.

Blu-ray An optical storage format released in 2006 by a consortium of electronics and computer vendors. Blu-ray discs are the same size as recordable DVDs, but can store significantly more data, up to 128 GB on a quadruple-layer disc.

BNC (Bayonet Neill-Concelman, or British Naval Connector) A standard for coaxial cable connectors named after its coupling method and its inventors.

BNC connector A coaxial cable connector type that uses a twist-and-lock (or bayonet) style of coupling. It may be used with several coaxial cable types, including RG-6 and RG-59.

bonding 1) The process of combining more than one bearer channel of an ISDN line to increase throughput. For example, BRI's two 64-Kbps B channels are bonded to create an effective throughput of 128 Kbps. 2) *See* link aggregation

Bonjour Apple's implementation of the Zeroconf group of protocols.

boot sector virus A virus that resides on the boot sector of an external storage device and is transferred to the partition sector or the DOS boot sector on a hard disk when the machine starts.

Border Gateway Protocol *See* BGP.

border router A router that connects an autonomous LAN with an exterior network—for example, the router that connects a business to its ISP.

bot A program that runs automatically. Bots can spread viruses or other malicious code between users in a chat room by exploiting the IRC protocol.

bounce *See* reflection.

BPL (broadband over powerline) High-speed Internet access delivered over the electrical grid.

braiding A braided metal shielding used to insulate some types of coaxial cable.

branch A part of the organizational structure of an operating system's directory that contains objects or other organizational units.

BRI (Basic Rate Interface) A variety of ISDN that uses two 64-Kbps bearer channels and one 16-Kbps data channel, as summarized by the notation 2B+D. BRI is the most common form of ISDN employed by home users.

bridge A connectivity device that operates at the Data Link layer (Layer 2) of the OSI model and reads header information to forward packets according to their MAC addresses. Bridges use a filtering database to determine which packets to discard and which to forward. Bridges contain one input and one output port and separate network segments.

Bridge ID *See* BID.

broadband A form of transmission in which signals are modulated as radiofrequency analog pulses with different frequency ranges. Unlike baseband, broadband technology does not involve binary encoding. The use of multiple frequencies enables a broadband system to operate over several channels and, therefore, carry much more data than a baseband system.

broadband cable A method of connecting to the Internet over a cable network. In broadband cable, computers are connected to a cable modem that modulates and demodulates signals to and from the cable company's head-end.

broadband over powerline *See* BPL.

broadcast A transmission that involves one transmitter and multiple, undefined receivers.

broadcast domain Logically grouped network nodes that can communicate directly via broadcast transmissions. By default, switches and repeating devices such as hubs, extend broadcast domains. Routers and other Layer 3 devices separate broadcast domains.

brownout A momentary decrease in voltage, also known as a *sag*. An overtaxed electrical system may cause brownouts, recognizable as a dimming of the lights.

brute force attack An attempt to discover an encryption key or password by trying numerous possible character combinations. Usually, a brute force attack is performed rapidly by a program designed for that purpose.

BSS (basic service set) In IEEE terminology, a group of stations that share an access point.

BSSID (basic service set identifier) In IEEE terminology, the identifier for a BSS (basic service set).

bus 1) The single cable connecting all devices in a bus topology. 2) The type of circuit used by a computer's motherboard to transmit data to components. As the number of bits of data a bus handles increases, so too does the speed of the device attached to the bus.

bus topology A topology in which a single cable connects all nodes on a network without intervening connectivity devices.

bus topology WAN A WAN in which each location is connected to no more than two other locations in a serial fashion.

butt set A tool for accessing and testing a telephone company's local loop. The butt set, also known as a telephone test set or lineman's handset, is essentially a telephone handset with attached wires that can be connected to local loop terminations at a demarc or switching facility.

byte Eight bits of information. In a digital signaling system, broadly speaking, 1 byte carries one piece of information.

CA (certificate authority) An organization that issues and maintains digital certificates as part of the Public-key Infrastructure.

cable checker *See* continuity tester.

cable drop The fiber-optic or coaxial cable that connects a neighborhood cable node to a customer's house.

cable modem A device that modulates and demodulates signals for transmission and reception via cable wiring.

cable modem access *See* broadband cable.

cable performance tester A troubleshooting tool that tests cables for continuity, but can also measure cross talk, attenuation, and impedance; identify the location of faults; and store or print cable testing results.

cable plant The hardware that constitutes the enterprise-wide cabling system.

cable tester A device that tests cables for one or more of the following conditions: continuity, segment length, distance to a fault, attenuation along a cable, near-end cross talk, and termination resistance and impedance. Cable testers may also issue pass/fail ratings for wiring standards or store and print cable testing results.

cache engine A network device devoted to storage and delivery of frequently requested files.

caching The local storage of frequently needed files that would otherwise be obtained from an external source.

CALEA (Communications Assistance for Law Enforcement Act) A United States federal regulation that requires telecommunications carriers and equipment manufacturers to provide for surveillance capabilities. CALEA was passed by Congress in 1994 after pressure from the FBI, which worried that networks relying solely on digital communications would circumvent traditional wiretapping strategies.

call tracking system A software program used to document technical problems and how they were resolved (also known as help desk software).

capacity *See* throughput.

CARP (Common Address Redundancy Protocol) A protocol that allows a pool of computers or interfaces to share one or more IP addresses. CARP improves availability and can contribute to load balancing among several devices, including servers, firewalls, or routers.

Carrier Ethernet A level of Ethernet service that is characterized by very high throughput and reliability and is used between carriers, such as NSPs.

Carrier Sense Multiple Access with Collision Avoidance *See* CSMA/CA.

Carrier Sense Multiple Access with Collision Detection *See* CSMA/CD.

Cat Abbreviation for the word *category* when describing a type of twisted pair cable. For example, Category 5 unshielded twisted pair cable may also be called Cat 5.

Cat 3 (Category 3) A form of UTP that contains four wire pairs and can carry up to 10 Mbps, with a possible bandwidth of 16 MHz. Cat 3 was used for 10-Mbps Ethernet or 4-Mbps token ring networks.

Cat 5 (Category 5) A form of UTP that contains four wire pairs and supports up to 100-Mbps throughput and a 100-MHz signal rate.

Cat 5e (Enhanced Category 5) A higher-grade version of Cat 5 wiring that contains high-quality copper, offers a high twist ratio, and uses advanced methods for reducing cross talk. Enhanced Cat 5 can support a signaling rate of up to 350 MHz, more than triple the capability of regular Cat 5.

Cat 6 (Category 6) A twisted pair cable that contains four wire pairs, each wrapped in foil insulation. Additional foil insulation covers the bundle of wire pairs, and a fire-resistant plastic sheath covers the second foil layer. The foil insulation provides excellent resistance to cross talk and enables Cat 6 to support a signaling rate of 250 MHz and at least six times the throughput supported by regular Cat 5.

Cat 6a (Augmented Category 6) A higher-grade version of Cat 6 wiring that further reduces attenuation and cross talk and allows for potentially exceeding traditional network segment length limits. Cat 6a is capable of a 500-MHz signaling rate and can reliably transmit data at multi-gigabit per second rates.

Cat 7 (Category 7) A twisted pair cable that contains multiple wire pairs, each separately shielded then surrounded by another layer of shielding within the jacket. Cat 7 can support up to a 1-GHz signal rate. But because of its extra layers, it is less flexible than other forms of twisted pair wiring.

Category 3 *See* Cat 3.

Category 5 *See* Cat 5.

Category 6 *See* Cat 6.

Category 7 *See* Cat 7.

CCIE (Cisco Certified Internetwork Expert) An elite certification that recognizes expert-level installation, configuration, management, and troubleshooting skills on networks that use a range of Cisco Systems' devices.

CCNA (Cisco Certified Network Associate) A professional certification that attests to one's skills in installing, configuring, maintaining, and troubleshooting medium-sized networks that use Cisco Systems' switches and routers.

cell 1) A packet of a fixed size. In ATM technology, a cell consists of 48 bytes of data plus a 5-byte header. 2) In a cellular network, an area of coverage serviced by an antenna and base station.

central office *See* CO.

certificate authority *See* CA.

certification The process of mastering material pertaining to a particular hardware system, operating system, programming language, or other software program, then proving your mastery by passing a series of exams.

challenge A random string of text issued from one computer to another in some forms of authentication. It is used, along with the password (or other credential), in a response to verify the computer's credentials.

Challenge Handshake Authentication Protocol *See* CHAP.

change management system A process or program that provides support personnel with a centralized means of documenting changes made to the network.

channel A distinct communication path between two or more nodes, much like a lane is a distinct transportation path on a freeway. Channels may be separated either logically (as in multiplexing) or physically (as when they are carried by separate wires).

channel bonding In the context of 802.11n wireless technology, the combination of two 20-MHz frequency bands to create one 40-MHz frequency band that can carry more than twice the amount of data that a single 20-MHz band could. It's recommended for use only in the 5-GHz range because this band has more available channels and suffers less interference than the 2.4-GHz band.

channel service unit *See* CSU.

CHAP (Challenge Handshake Authentication Protocol) An authentication protocol that operates over PPP and that requires the authenticator to take the first step by offering the other computer a challenge. The requestor responds by combining the challenge with its password, encrypting the new string of characters and sending it to the authenticator. The authenticator matches to see if the requestor's encrypted string of text matches its own encrypted string of characters. If so, the requester is authenticated and granted access to secured resources.

checksum A method of error checking that determines if the contents of an arriving data unit match the contents of the data unit sent by the source.

child domain A domain established within another domain in a Windows Server domain tree.

CIDR (Classless Interdomain Routing) An IP addressing and subnetting method in which network and host information is manipulated without adhering to the limitations imposed by traditional network class distinctions. CIDR is also known as classless routing or supernetting. Older routing protocols, such as RIP, are not capable of interpreting CIDR addressing schemes.

CIDR block In CIDR notation, the number of bits used for an extended network prefix. For example, the CIDR block for 199.34.89.0/22 is /22.

CIDR notation In CIDR, a method of denoting network IDs and their subnet boundaries. Slash notation takes the form of the network ID followed by a slash (/), followed by the number of bits that are used for the extended network prefix.

CIFS (Common Internet File System) A file access protocol. CIFS runs over TCP/IP and is the standard file access protocol used by Windows operating systems.

ciphertext The unique data block that results when an original piece of data (such as text) is encrypted (for example, by using a key).

CIR (committed information rate) The guaranteed minimum amount of bandwidth selected when leasing a frame relay circuit. Frame relay costs are partially based on CIR.

circuit switching A type of switching in which a connection is established between two network nodes before they begin transmitting data. Bandwidth is dedicated to this connection and remains available until users terminate the communication between the two nodes.

Cisco Certified Internetwork Expert *See* CCIE.

Cisco Certified Network Associate *See* CCNA.

cladding The glass or plastic shield around the core of a fiber-optic cable. Cladding reflects light back to the core in patterns that vary depending on the transmission mode. This reflection allows fiber to bend around corners without impairing the light-based signal.

class A type of object recognized by an NOS directory and defined in an NOS schema. Printers and users are examples of object classes.

classful addressing An IP addressing convention that adheres to network class distinctions, in which the first 8 bits of a Class A address, the first 16 bits of a Class B address, and the first 24 bits of a Class C address are used for network information.

Classless Interdomain Routing *See* CIDR.

classless routing *See* CIDR.

client A computer on the network that requests resources or services from another computer on a network. In some cases, a client could also act as a server. The term *client* may also refer to the user of a client workstation or a client software application installed on the workstation.

client_hello In the context of SSL encryption, a message issued from the client to the server that contains information about what level of security the client's browser is capable of accepting and what type of encryption the client's browser can decipher (for example, RSA or Diffie-Hellman). The client_hello message also establishes a randomly generated number that uniquely identifies the client, plus another number that identifies the SSL session.

client/server architecture A network design in which client computers use a centrally administered server to share data, data storage space, and devices.

client/server network A network that uses centrally administered computers, known as servers, to enable resource sharing for and to facilitate communication between the other computers on the network.

client-to-site VPN A type of VPN in which clients, servers, and other hosts establish tunnels with a private network using a remote access server or VPN gateway. Each client on a client-to-site VPN must run VPN software to create the tunnel for, and encrypt and encapsulate data.

cloud backup *See* online backup.

cloud computing The flexible provision of data storage, applications, or services to multiple clients over a network. Cloud computing consolidates resources and is elastic, metered, self-service, multiplatform, and available on demand.

clustering A fault-tolerance technique that links multiple servers to act as a single server. In this configuration, clustered servers share processing duties and appear as a single server to users. If one server in the cluster fails, the other servers in the cluster automatically take over its data transaction and storage responsibilities.

CN (common name) In LDAP naming conventions, the name of an object.

CO (central office) The location where a local or long-distance telephone service provider terminates and interconnects customer lines.

coaxial cable A type of cable that consists of a central metal conducting core, which might be solid or stranded and is often made of copper, surrounded by an insulator, a braided metal shielding, called braiding, and an outer cover, called the sheath or jacket. Coaxial cable, called "coax" for short, was the foundation for Ethernet networks in the 1980s. Today it's used to connect cable Internet and cable TV systems.

cold site A place where the computers, devices, and connectivity necessary to rebuild a network exist, but they are not appropriately configured, updated, or connected to match the network's current state.

cold spare A duplicate component that is not installed, but can be installed in case of a failure.

collapsed backbone A type of backbone that uses a router or switch as the single central connection point for multiple subnetworks.

collision In Ethernet networks, the interference of one node's data transmission with the data transmission of another node sharing the same segment.

collision domain The portion of an Ethernet network in which collisions could occur if two nodes transmit data at the same time. Switches and routers separate collision domains.

command interpreter A program (usually text-based) that accepts and executes system programs and applications on behalf of users. Often, it includes the ability to execute a series of instructions that are stored in a file.

committed information rate *See* CIR.

Common Address Redundancy Protocol *See* CARP.

Common Internet File System *See* CIFS.

common name *See* CN.

Communications Assistance for Law Enforcement Act *See* CALEA.

company_id *See* OUI.

CompTIA An association of computer resellers, manufacturers, and training companies that sets industry-wide standards for computer professionals. CompTIA established and sponsors the A+ and Network+ (Net+) certifications.

conduit The pipeline used to contain and protect cabling. Conduit is usually made from metal.

configuration management The collection, storage, and assessment of information related to the versions of software installed on every network device and every device's hardware configuration.

connection oriented A type of Transport layer protocol that requires the establishment of a connection between communicating nodes before it will transmit data.

connectionless A type of Transport layer protocol that services a request without requiring a verified session and without guaranteeing delivery of data.

connectivity device One of several types of specialized devices that allows two or more networks or multiple parts of one network to connect and exchange data.

connectors The pieces of hardware that connect the wire to the network device, be it a file server, workstation, switch, or printer.

container *See* organizational unit.

content switch A switch that provides functions between Layer 4 and Layer 7 of the OSI model.

content-filtering firewall A firewall that can block designated types of traffic from entering a protected network.

continuity tester An instrument that tests whether voltage (or light, in the case of fiber optic cable) issued at one end of a cable can be detected at the opposite end of the cable. A continuity tester can indicate whether the cable will successfully transmit a signal.

convergence The use of data networks to carry voice (or telephone), video, and other communications services in addition to data.

convergence time The time it takes for a router to recognize a best path in the event of a change or network outage.

core The central component of a cable designed to carry a signal. The core of a fiber-optic cable, for example, consists of one or several glass or plastic fibers. The core of a coaxial copper cable consists of one large or several small strands of copper.

core gateway A gateway that operates on the Internet backbone.

cost In the context of routing metrics, the value assigned to a particular route as judged by the network administrator. The more desirable the path, the lower its cost.

country code TLD A top-level domain that corresponds to a country. For example, the country code TLD for Canada is .ca, and the country code TLD for Japan is .jp.

CRC (cyclic redundancy check) An algorithm (or mathematical routine) used to verify the accuracy of data contained in a data frame.

credentials A user's unique identifying characteristics that enable him to authenticate with a server and gain access to network resources. The most common type of credentials are a username and password.

crossover cable A twisted pair patch cable in which the termination locations of the transmit and receive wires on one end of the cable are reversed.

cross talk A type of interference caused by signals traveling on nearby wire pairs infringing on another pair's signal.

CSMA/CA (Carrier Sense Multiple Access with Collision Avoidance) A network access method used on 802.11 wireless networks. In CSMA/CA, before a node begins to send data it checks the medium. If it detects no transmission activity, it waits a brief, random amount of time, and then sends its transmission. If the node does detect activity, it waits a brief period of time before checking the channel again. CSMA/CA does not eliminate, but minimizes, the potential for collisions.

CSMA/CD (Carrier Sense Multiple Access with Collision Detection) A network access method specified for use by IEEE 802.3 (Ethernet) networks. In CSMA/CD, each node waits its turn before transmitting data to avoid interfering with other nodes' transmissions. If a node's NIC determines that its data have been involved in a collision, it immediately stops transmitting. Next, in a process called jamming, the NIC issues a special 32-bit sequence that indicates to the rest of the network nodes that its previous transmission was faulty and that those data frames are invalid. After waiting, the NIC determines if the line is again available; if it is available, the NIC retransmits its data.

CSU (channel service unit) A device used with T-carrier technology that provides termination for the digital signal and ensures connection integrity through error correction and line monitoring. Typically, a CSU is combined with a DSU in a single device, a CSU/DSU.

CSU/DSU A combination of a CSU (channel service unit) and a DSU (data service unit) that serves as the connection point for a T1 line at the customer's site. Most modern CSU/DSUs also contain a multiplexer. A CSU/DSU may be a separate device or an expansion card in another device, such as a router.

cut-through mode A switching mode in which a switch reads a frame's header and decides where to forward the data before it receives the entire packet. Cut-through mode is faster, but less accurate, than the other switching method, store-and-forward mode.

cyclic redundancy check *See* CRC.

D channel In ISDN, the "data" channel is used to carry information about the call, such as session initiation and termination signals, caller identity, call forwarding, and conference calling signals.

daisy chain A group of connectivity devices linked together in a serial fashion.

Data Encryption Standard *See* DES.

Data Link layer The second layer in the OSI model. The Data Link layer bridges the networking media with the Network layer. Its primary function is to divide the data it receives from the Network layer into frames that can then be transmitted by the Physical layer.

Data Link layer address *See* MAC address.

data propagation delay The length of time data take to travel from one point on the segment to another point. On Ethernet networks, CSMA/CD's collision detection routine cannot operate accurately if the data propagation delay is too long.

data service unit *See* DSU.

datagram *See* packet.

DB-9 connector A type of connector with nine pins that's used in serial communication that conforms to the RS-232 standard.

DB-25 connector A type of connector with 25 pins that's used in serial communication that conforms to the RS-232 standard.

DC (domain component) In LDAP naming conventions, the name of any one of the domains to which an object belongs.

DDNS (Dynamic DNS) A method of dynamically updating DNS records for a host. DDNS client computers are configured to notify a service provider when their IP addresses change, then the service provider propagates the DNS record change across the Internet automatically.

dedicated A continuously available link or service that is leased through another carrier. Examples of dedicated lines include ADSL, T1, and T3.

default gateway The gateway that first interprets a device's outbound requests, and then interprets its inbound requests to and from other subnets. In a Postal Service analogy, the default gateway is similar to a local post office.

default router *See* default gateway.

demarc *See* demarcation point.

demarcation point (demarc) The point of division between a telecommunications service carrier's network and a building's internal network.

demilitarized zone *See* DMZ.

demultiplexer (demux) A device that separates multiplexed signals once they are received and regenerates them in their original form.

demux *See* demultiplexer.

denial-of-service attack A security attack in which a system becomes unable to function because it has been inundated with requests for services and can't respond to any of them. As a result, all data transmissions are disrupted.

dense wavelength division multiplexing *See* DWDM.

DES (Data Encryption Standard) A popular private key encryption technique that was developed by IBM in the 1970s.

device driver The software that enables an attached device to communicate with the computer's operating system.

device ID *See* extension identifier.

DHCP (Dynamic Host Configuration Protocol) An Application layer protocol in the TCP/IP suite that manages the dynamic distribution of IP addresses on a network. Using DHCP to assign IP addresses can nearly eliminate duplicate-addressing problems.

DHCP scope The predefined range of addresses that can be leased to any network device on a particular segment.

DHCP server A server that manages IP address assignment, maintaining information about which addresses are allowable, which are available, and which have already been associated with a host.

DHCPv4 The version of DHCP used with IPv4. DHCPv4 uses port number 67 for client-to-server communications and port number 68 for server-to-client communications.

DHCPv6 The version of DHCP used with IPv6. DHCPv6 uses port number 546 for client-to-server communications and port number 547 for server-to-client communications.

dial-up A type of connection in which a user connects to a distant network from a computer and stays connected for a finite period of time. Most of the time, the term *dial-up* refers to a connection that uses a PSTN line.

dial-up networking The process of dialing into a remote access server to connect with a network, be it private or public.

dictionary attack A technique in which attackers run a program that tries a combination of a known user ID and, for a password, every word in a dictionary to attempt to gain access to a network.

differential backup A backup method in which only data that has changed since the last full or incremental backup is copied to a storage medium, and in which that same information is marked for subsequent backup, regardless of whether it has changed. In other words, a differential backup does not uncheck the archive bits for files it backs up.

Differentiated Service *See* DiffServ.

Diffie-Hellman The first commonly used public, or asymmetric, key algorithm. Diffie-Hellman was released in 1975 by its creators, Whitfield Diffie and Martin Hellman.

diffraction In the context of wireless signal propagation, the phenomenon that occurs when an electromagnetic wave encounters an obstruction and splits into secondary waves. The secondary waves continue to propagate in the direction in which they were split. If you could see wireless signals being diffracted, they would appear to be bending around the obstacle. Objects with sharp edges—including the corners of walls and desks—cause diffraction.

DiffServ (Differentiated Service) A technique for ensuring QoS by prioritizing traffic. DiffServ places information in the DiffServ field in an IPv4 datagram. In IPv6 datagrams, DiffServ uses a similar field known as the Traffic Class field. This information indicates to the network routers how the data stream should be forwarded.

dig (domain information groper) A TCP/IP utility that queries the DNS database and provides information about a host given its IP address or vice versa. Dig is similar to the nslookup utility, but provides more information, even in its simplest form, than nslookup can.

digital As opposed to analog signals, digital signals are composed of pulses that can have a value of only 1 or 0.

digital certificate A password-protected and encrypted file that holds an individual's identification information, including a public key and a private key. The individual's public key is used to verify the sender's digital signature, and the private key allows the individual to log on to a third-party authority who administers digital certificates.

digital PBX *See* IP-PBX.

digital subscriber line *See* DSL.

directional antenna A type of antenna that issues wireless signals along a single direction, or path.

direct-sequence spread spectrum *See* DSSS.

directory In general, a listing that organizes resources and correlates them with their properties. In the context of NOSs, a method for organizing and managing objects.

disaster recovery The process of restoring critical functionality and data to a network after an enterprise-wide outage that affects more than a single system or a limited group of users.

diskless workstation A workstation that doesn't contain a hard disk, but instead relies on a small amount of read-only memory to connect to a network and to pick up its system files.

distance-vector The simplest type of routing protocols, these determine the best route for data based on the distance to a destination. Some distance-vector routing protocols, like RIP, only factor in the number of hops to the destination, while others take into account latency and other network traffic characteristics.

distinguished name *See* DN.

distributed backbone A type of backbone in which a number of intermediate connectivity devices are connected to one or more central connectivity devices, such as switches or routers, in a hierarchy.

distributed denial of service (DDoS) attack A security attack in which multiple hosts simultaneously flood a target host with traffic, rendering the target unable to function.

distribution The term used to refer to the different implementations of a particular UNIX or Linux system. Debian, Gentoo, Red Hat, SUSE, and Ubuntu are just a few examples of Linux distributions.

DMZ (demilitarized zone) The perimeter of a protected, internal network where users, both authorized and unauthorized, from external networks can attempt to access it. Firewalls and IDS/IPS systems are typically placed in the DMZ.

DN (distinguished name) A long form of an object's name in Active Directory that explicitly indicates the object name, plus the names of its containers and domains. A distinguished name includes a DC (domain component), OU (organizational unit), and CN (common name). A client uses the distinguished name to access a particular object, such as a printer.

DNAT (Dynamic Network Address Translation) A type of address translation in which a limited pool of Internet-valid IP addresses is shared by multiple private network hosts.

DNS (Domain Name System or Domain Name Service) A hierarchical way of tracking domain names and their addresses, devised in the mid-1980s. The DNS database does not rely on one file or even one server, but rather is distributed over several key computers across the Internet to prevent catastrophic failure if one or a few computers go down. DNS is a TCP/IP service that belongs to the Application layer of the OSI model.

DNS cache A database on a computer that stores information about IP addresses and their associated host names. DNS caches can exist on clients as well as on name servers.

DNS server *See* name server.

DNS spoofing A security attack in which an outsider forges name server records to falsify his host's identity.

DNS zone A portion of the DNS namespace for which one organization is assigned authority to manage.

domain 1) A group of computers that belong to the same organization and have part of their IP addresses in common. 2) In the context of Windows Server NOSs, a group of users, servers, and other resources that share account and security policies through a Windows Server NOS.

domain component *See* DC.

domain controller A computer running a version of the Windows Server NOS that contains a replica of the Active Directory database.

domain information groper *See* dig.

domain model In Microsoft terminology, the type of client/server network that relies on domains, rather than workgroups.

domain name The symbolic name that identifies a domain. Usually, a domain name is associated with a company or other type of organization, such as a university or military unit.

Domain Name Service *See* DNS.

Domain Name System *See* DNS.

domain tree A group of hierarchically arranged domains that share a common namespace in a Windows Server Active Directory.

dotted decimal notation The shorthand convention used to represent IPv4 addresses and make them more easily readable by humans. In dotted decimal notation, a decimal number between 0 and 255 represents each binary octet. A period, or dot, separates each decimal.

downlink In the context of wireless transmission, the connection between a carrier's antenna and a client's transceiver—for example, a smartphone.

downstream A term used to describe data traffic that flows from a carrier's facility to the customer. In asymmetrical communications, downstream throughput is usually much higher than upstream throughput. In symmetrical communications, downstream and upstream throughputs are equal.

driver *See* device driver.

DS0 (digital signal, level 0) The equivalent of one data or voice channel in T-carrier technology, as defined by ANSI physical layer standards. All other signal levels are multiples of DS0.

DSL (digital subscriber line) A dedicated WAN technology that uses advanced data modulation techniques at the Physical layer to achieve extraordinary throughput over regular phone lines. DSL comes in several different varieties, the most common of which is Asymmetric DSL (ADSL).

DSL access multiplexer *See* DSLAM.

DSL modem A device that demodulates an incoming DSL signal, extracting the information and passing it to the data equipment (such as telephones and computers), and modulates an outgoing DSL signal.

DSLAM (DSL access multiplexer) A connectivity device located at a telecommunications carrier's office that aggregates multiple DSL subscriber lines and connects them to a larger carrier or to the Internet backbone.

DSSS (direct-sequence spread spectrum) A transmission technique in which a signal's bits are distributed over an entire frequency band at once. Each bit is coded so that the receiver can reassemble the original signal upon receiving the bits.

DSU (data service unit) A device used in T-carrier technology that converts the digital signal used by bridges, routers, and multiplexers into the digital signal used on cabling. Typically, a DSU is combined with a CSU in a single device, a CSU/DSU.

dual-stack A type of network that supports both IPv4 and IPv6 traffic.

duplex *See* full-duplex.

DWDM (dense wavelength division multiplexing) A multiplexing technique used over single-mode or multimode fiber-optic cable in which each signal is assigned a different wavelength for its carrier wave. In DWDM, little space exists between carrier waves to achieve extraordinary high capacity.

dynamic ARP table entry A record in an ARP table that is created when a client makes an ARP request that cannot be satisfied by data already in the ARP table.

Dynamic DNS *See* DDNS.

Dynamic Host Configuration Protocol *See* DHCP.

Dynamic Host Configuration Protocol version 4 *See* DHCPv4.

Dynamic Host Configuration Protocol version 6 *See* DHCPv6.

dynamic IP address An IP address that is assigned to a device upon request and may change when the DHCP lease expires or is terminated. BOOTP and DHCP are two ways of assigning dynamic IP addresses.

Dynamic Network Address Translation *See* DNAT.

Dynamic Ports TCP/IP ports in the range of 49,152 through 65,535, which are open for use without requiring administrative privileges on a host or approval from IANA.

dynamic routing A method of routing that automatically calculates the best path between two nodes and accumulates this information in a routing table. If congestion or failures affect the network, a router using dynamic routing can detect the problems and reroute data through a different path. Modern networks primarily use dynamic routing.

E1 A digital carrier standard used in Europe that offers 30 channels and a maximum of 2.048-Mbps throughput.

E3 A digital carrier standard used in Europe that offers 480 channels and a maximum of 34.368-Mbps throughput.

EAP (Extensible Authentication Protocol) A Data Link layer protocol defined by the IETF that specifies the dynamic distribution of encryption keys and a preauthentication process in which a client and server exchange data via an intermediate node (for example, an access point on a wireless LAN). Only after they have mutually authenticated can the client and server exchange encrypted data. EAP can be used with multiple authentication and encryption schemes.

EAP over LAN *See* EAPoL.

EAPoL (EAP over LAN) *See* 802.1x.

echo reply The response signal sent by a device after another device pings it.

echo request The request for a response generated when one device pings another device.

EF (Expedited Forwarding) In the DiffServ QoS technique, a forwarding specification that assigns each data stream a minimum departure rate from a given node. This technique circumvents delays that slow normal data from reaching its destination on time and in sequence. EF information is inserted in the DiffServ field of an IPv4 datagram.

EGP (Exterior Gateway Protocol) A routing protocol that can span multiple, autonomous networks. BGP and EIGRP are examples of Exterior Gateway Protocols.

EIA (Electronic Industries Alliance) A trade organization composed of representatives from electronics manufacturing firms across the United States that sets standards for electronic equipment and lobbies for legislation favorable to the growth of the computer and electronics industries.

EIGRP (Enhanced Interior Gateway Routing Protocol) A routing protocol developed in the mid-1980s by Cisco Systems that has a fast convergence time and a low network overhead, but is easier to configure and less CPU-intensive than OSPF. EIGRP also offers the benefits of supporting multiple protocols and limiting unnecessary network traffic between routers.

elastic A characteristic of cloud computing that means services can be quickly and dynamically—sometimes even automatically—scaled up or down.

electromagnetic interference *See* EMI.

Electronic Industries Alliance *See* EIA.

EMI (electromagnetic interference) A type of interference that may be caused by motors, power lines, televisions, copiers, fluorescent lights, or other sources of electrical activity.

encapsulate The process of wrapping one layer's PDU with protocol information so that it can be interpreted by a lower layer. For example, Data Link layer protocols encapsulate Network layer packets in frames.

Encapsulating Security Payload *See* ESP.

encrypted virus A virus that is encrypted to prevent detection.

encryption The use of an algorithm to scramble data into a format that can be read only by reversing the algorithm—decrypting the data—to keep the information private. The most popular kind of encryption algorithm weaves a key into the original data's bits, sometimes several times in different sequences, to generate a unique data block.

encryption devices Computers or specialized adapters inserted into other devices, such as routers or servers, that perform encryption.

endpoint In SIP terminology, any client, server, or gateway communicating on the network.

Enhanced Category 5 *See* Cat 5e.

Enhanced Interior Gateway Routing Protocol *See* EIGRP.

enterprise An entire organization, including local and remote offices, a mixture of computer systems, and a number of departments. Enterprise-wide computing takes into account the breadth and diversity of a large organization's computer needs.

entrance facilities The facilities necessary for a service provider (whether it is a local phone company, Internet service provider, or long-distance carrier) to connect with another organization's LAN or WAN.

escalate In network troubleshooting, to refer a problem to someone with deeper knowledge about the subject. For example, a first-level support person might escalate a router configuration issue to a second- or third-level support person.

ESP (Encapsulation Security Payload) In the context of IPSec, a type of encryption that provides authentication of the IP packet's data payload through public key techniques. In addition, ESP also encrypts the entire IP packet for added security.

ESS (extended service set) A group of access points and associated stations (or basic service sets) connected to the same LAN.

ESSID (extended service set identifier) A special identifier shared by BSSs that belong to the same ESS.

Ethernet A networking technology originally developed at Xerox in the 1970s and improved by Digital Equipment Corporation, Intel, and Xerox. Ethernet, which is the most common form of network transmission technology, follows the IEEE 802.3 standard.

Ethernet II The original Ethernet frame type developed by Digital Equipment Corporation, Intel, and Xerox, before the IEEE began to standardize Ethernet. Ethernet_II is distinguished from other Ethernet frame types in that it contains a 2-byte type field to identify the upper-layer protocol contained in the frame. It supports TCP/IP and other higher-layer protocols.

ethtool A popular tool for viewing and modifying network interface properties on Linux computers.

EUI-64 (Extended Unique Identifier-64) The IEEE standard defining 64-bit physical addresses. In the EUI-64 scheme, the OUI portion of an address is 24 bits in length. A 40-bit extension identifier makes up the rest of the physical address to total 64 bits.

event log The service on Windows-based operating systems that records events, or the ongoing record of such events.

Event Viewer A GUI application that allows users to easily view and sort events recorded in the event log on a computer running a Windows-based operating system.

Everything as a Service *See* XaaS.

evil twin An exploit in which a rogue access point masquerades as a legitimate access point, using the same SSID and potentially other identical settings.

expansion board A circuit board used to connect a device to a computer's motherboard.

expansion card *See* expansion board.

expansion slot A receptacle on a computer's motherboard that contains multiple electrical contacts into which an expansion board can be inserted.

Expedited Forwarding *See* EF.

explicit one-way trust In the context of Windows Server NOSs, a type of trust relationship in which two domains that belong to different NOS directory trees are configured to trust each other.

exploit In the context of network security, the means by which a hacker takes advantage of a vulnerability.

ext4 The name of the primary file system used in most Linux distributions.

extended network prefix The combination of an IP address's network ID and subnet information. By interpreting the address's extended network prefix, a device can determine the subnet to which an address belongs.

extended service set *See* ESS.

extended service set identifier *See* ESSID.

Extended Unique Identifier-64 *See* EUI-64.

Extensible Authentication Protocol *See* EAP.

extension identifier A unique set of characters assigned to each NIC by its manufacturer. In the traditional, 48-bit physical addressing scheme, the extension identifier is 24 bits long. In EUI-64, the extension identifier is 40 bits long.

Exterior Gateway Protocol *See* EGP.

exterior router A router that directs data between nodes outside a given autonomous LAN, for example, routers used on the Internet's backbone.

external disk drive A storage device that can be attached temporarily to a computer.

fading A variation in a wireless signal's strength as a result of some of the electromagnetic energy being scattered, reflected, or diffracted after being issued by the transmitter.

failover The capability for one component (such as a NIC or server) to assume another component's responsibilities without manual intervention.

failure A deviation from a specified level of system performance for a given period of time. A failure occurs when something doesn't work as promised or as planned.

Fast Ethernet A type of Ethernet network that is capable of 100-Mbps throughput. 100Base-T and 100Base-FX are both examples of Fast Ethernet.

fault The malfunction of one component of a system. A fault can result in a failure.

fault management The detection and signaling of device, link, or component faults.

fault tolerance The capability for a component or system to continue functioning despite damage or malfunction.

FCS (frame check sequence) The field in a frame responsible for ensuring that data carried by the frame arrives intact. It uses an algorithm, such as CRC, to accomplish this verification.

FDM (frequency division multiplexing) A type of multiplexing that assigns a unique frequency band to each communications subchannel. Signals are modulated with different carrier frequencies, then multiplexed to simultaneously travel over a single channel.

ferrule A short tube within a fiber-optic cable connector that encircles the fiber strand and keeps it properly aligned.

FHSS (frequency hopping spread spectrum) A wireless signaling technique in which a signal jumps between several different frequencies within a band in a synchronization pattern known to the channel's receiver and transmitter.

fiber to the home *See* FTTH.

fiber to the premises *See* FTTP.

fiber-optic cable A form of cable that contains one or several glass or plastic fibers in its core. Data is transmitted via pulsing light sent from a laser or light-emitting diode (LED) through the central fiber (or fibers). Fiber-optic cables offer significantly higher throughput than copper-based cables. They may be single-mode or multimode and typically use wave-division multiplexing to carry multiple signals.

Fibre Channel A distinct network transmission method that relies on fiber-optic media and its own proprietary protocol. Fibre Channel is capable of over 5-Gbps throughput.

file access protocol A protocol that enables one system to access files on another system.

file globbing A form of filename substitution, similar to the use of wildcards in Windows and DOS.

file server A specialized server that enables clients to share applications and data across the network.

file services The functions of a file server that allow users to share data files, applications, and storage areas.

file system An operating system's method of organizing, managing, and accessing its files through logical structures and software routines.

File Transfer Protocol *See* FTP.

file-infector virus A virus that attaches itself to executable files. When the infected executable file runs, the virus copies itself to memory. Later, the virus attaches itself to other executable files.

filtering database A collection of data created and used by a bridge that correlates the MAC addresses of connected workstations with their locations. A filtering database is also known as a forwarding table.

firewall A device (either a router or a computer running special software) that selectively filters or blocks traffic between networks. Firewalls are commonly used to improve data security.

first-level support In network troubleshooting, the person or group who initially fields requests for help from users.

fixed A type of wireless system in which the locations of the transmitter and receiver are static. In a fixed connection, the transmitting antenna focuses its energy directly toward the receiving antenna. This results in a point-to-point link.

flashing A security attack in which an Internet user sends commands to another Internet user's machine that cause the screen to fill with garbage characters. A flashing attack causes the user to terminate her session.

flow A sequence of packets issued from one source to one or many destinations. Routers interpret flow information to ensure that packets belonging to the same transmission arrive together. Flow information may also help with traffic prioritization.

flow control A method of gauging the appropriate rate of data transmission based on how fast the recipient can accept data.

FM (frequency modulation) A method of data modulation in which the frequency of the carrier signal is modified by the application of the data signal.

forest In the context of Windows Server NOSs, a collection of domain trees that use different namespaces. A forest allows for trust relationships to be established between trees.

Format Prefix A variable-length field at the beginning of an IPv6 address that indicates what type of address it is (for example, unicast, anycast, or multicast).

forwarding table *See* filtering database.

FQDN (fully qualified domain name) A host name plus domain name that uniquely identifies a computer or location on a network.

fractional T1 An arrangement that allows a customer to lease only some of the channels on a T1 line.

fragmentation A Network layer service that subdivides segments it receives from the Transport layer into smaller packets.

frame A package for data that includes not only the raw data, or "payload," but also the sender's and recipient's addressing and control information. Frames are generated at the Data Link layer of the OSI model and are issued to the network at the Physical layer.

frame check sequence *See* FCS.

frame relay A digital, packet-switched WAN technology whose protocols operate at the Data Link layer. The name is derived from the fact that data is separated into frames, which are then relayed from one node to another without any verification or processing. Frame relay offers throughputs between 64 Kbps and 45 Mbps. A frame relay customer chooses the amount of bandwidth he requires and pays for only that amount.

frequency The number of times that a signal's amplitude changes over a fixed period of time, expressed in cycles per second, or hertz (Hz).

frequency division multiplexing *See* FDM.

frequency hopping spread spectrum *See* FHSS.

frequency modulation *See* FM.

FTP (File Transfer Protocol) An Application layer protocol used to send and receive files via TCP/IP. FTP uses port 21 for data and port 22 for file transfer control information.

FTP bounce A security attack in which an FTP client specifies a different host's IP address and port number for the requested data's destination. By commanding the FTP server to connect to a different computer, a hacker can scan the ports on other hosts and transmit malicious code. To thwart FTP bounce attacks, most modern FTP servers will not issue data to hosts other than the client that originated the request.

FTTH (fiber to the home) A service in which a residential customer is connected to his carrier's network with fiber-optic cable.

FTTP (fiber to the premises) A service in which a residential or business customer is connected to his carrier's network using fiber-optic cable.

F-Type connector A connector used to terminate coaxial cable used for transmitting television and broadband cable signals.

full backup A backup in which all data on all servers is copied to a storage medium, regardless of whether the data is new or changed. A full backup unchecks the archive bit on files it has backed up.

full-duplex A type of transmission in which signals may travel in both directions over a medium simultaneously. May also be called, simply, "duplex."

full-mesh WAN A version of the mesh topology WAN in which every site is directly connected to every other site. Full-mesh WANs are the most fault-tolerant type of WAN.

fully qualified domain name *See* FQDN.

fully qualified host name *See* FQDN.

gateway A combination of networking hardware and software that connects two dissimilar kinds of networks. Gateways perform connectivity, session management, and data translation, so they must operate at multiple layers of the OSI model.

gateway router *See* border router.

GBIC (Gigabit interface converter) A standard type of modular interface designed in the 1990s for Gigabit Ethernet connections. GBICs may contain RJ-45 or fiber-optic cable ports (such as LC, SC, or ST). They are inserted into a socket on a connectivity device's backplane.

GEO (geosynchronous earth orbit) The term used to refer to a satellite that maintains a constant distance from a point on the equator at every point in its orbit. Geosynchronous orbit satellites are the type used to provide satellite Internet access.

geosynchronous earth orbit *See* GEO.

ghost A frame that is not actually a data frame, but rather an aberration caused by a device misinterpreting stray voltage on the wire. Unlike true data frames, ghosts have no starting delimiter.

giant A packet that exceeds the medium's maximum packet size. For example, any Ethernet packet that is larger than 1518 bytes is considered a giant.

Gigabit Ethernet A type of Ethernet network that is capable of 1000-Mbps, or 1-Gbps, throughput.

Gigabit interface converter *See* GBIC.

globally unique identifier *See* GUID.

Grandfather-Father-Son A backup rotation scheme that uses daily (son), weekly (father), and monthly (grandfather) backup sets.

graphical user interface *See* GUI.

group A means of collectively managing users' permissions and restrictions applied to shared resources. Groups form the basis for resource and account management for every type of NOS.

guest In the context of virtualization, a virtual machine operated and managed by a virtualization program.

GUI (graphical user interface) A pictorial representation of computer functions and elements that, in the case of NOSs, enables administrators to more easily manage files, users, groups, security, printers, and other issues.

GUID (globally unique identifier) A 128-bit number generated and assigned to an object upon its creation in Active Directory. Network applications and services use an object's GUID to communicate with it.

H.225 A Session layer call signaling protocol defined as part of ITU's H.323 multiservice network architecture. H.225 is responsible for call or videoconference setup between nodes on a VoIP or video-over-IP network, indicating node status and requesting additional bandwidth and call termination.

H.245 A Session layer control protocol defined as part of ITU's H.323 multiservice network architecture. H.245 is responsible for controlling a session between two nodes. For example, it ensures that the two nodes are communicating in the same format.

H.248 *See* MEGACO.

H.323 An ITU standard that describes an architecture and a suite of protocols for establishing and managing multimedia services sessions on a packet-switched network.

H.323 gatekeeper The nerve center for networks that adhere to H.323. Gatekeepers authorize and authenticate terminals and gateways, manage bandwidth, and oversee call routing, accounting, and billing. Gatekeepers are optional on H.323 networks.

H.323 gateway On a network following the H.323 standard, a gateway that provides translation between network devices running H.323 signaling protocols and devices running other types of signaling protocols (for example, SS7 on the PSTN).

H.323 terminal On a network following the H.323 standard, any node that provides audio, visual, or data information to another node.

H.323 zone A collection of H.323 terminals, gateways, and MCUs that are managed by a single H.323 gatekeeper.

hacker Traditionally, a person who masters the inner workings of operating systems and utilities in an effort to better understand them. More generally, an individual who gains unauthorized access to systems or networks with or without malicious intent.

half-duplex A type of transmission in which signals may travel in both directions over a medium, but in only one direction at a time.

handoff The transition that occurs when a cellular network client moves from one antenna's coverage area to another.

handshake protocol One of several protocols within SSL, and perhaps the most significant. As its name implies, the handshake protocol allows the client and server to authenticate (or introduce) each other and establishes terms for how they securely exchange data during an SSL session.

hardware address *See* MAC address.

hardware RAID A method of implementing RAID that relies on an externally attached set of disks and a RAID disk controller, which manages the RAID array.

head-end A cable company's central office, which connects cable wiring to many nodes before it reaches customers' sites.

Health Insurance Portability and Accountability Act *See* HIPAA.

help desk analyst A person who's proficient in basic (but not usually advanced) workstation and network troubleshooting. Help desk analysts are part of first-level support.

help desk coordinator A person who ensures that help desk analysts are divided into the correct teams, schedules shifts at the help desk, and maintains the infrastructure to enable analysts to better perform their jobs. They might also serve as third-level support personnel, taking responsibility for troubleshooting a problem when the second-level support analyst is unable to solve it.

hertz (Hz) A measure of frequency equivalent to the number of amplitude cycles per second.

heuristic scanning A type of virus scanning that attempts to identify viruses by discovering viruslike behavior.

HFC (hybrid fiber-coax) A link that consists of fiber cable connecting the cable company's offices to a node location near the customer and coaxial cable connecting the node to the customer's house. HFC upgrades to existing cable wiring are required before current TV cable systems can provide Internet access.

HIDS (host-based intrusion detection) A type of intrusion detection that runs on a single computer, such as a client or server, that has access to and allows access from the Internet.

hierarchical file system The organization of files and directories (or folders) on a disk in which directories may contain files and other directories. When displayed graphically, this organization resembles a treelike structure.

HIPS (host-based intrusion prevention) A type of intrusion prevention that runs on a single computer, such as a client or server, that has access to and allows access from the Internet.

High Speed Packet Access Plus *See* HSPA+.

HSPA+ (High Speed Packet Access Plus) A 3G mobile wireless technology released in 2008 that uses MIMO and sophisticated encoding techniques to achieve a maximum 84-Mbps downlink throughput and 11-Mbps uplink throughput in its current release. Advances in more efficiently using limited channels and incorporating more antennas in MIMO promise to push the maximum downlink data rate to 336 Mbps.

HIPAA (Health Insurance Portability and Accountability Act) A federal regulation in the United States, enacted in 1996. One aspect of this regulation addresses the security and privacy of medical records, including those stored or transmitted electronically.

honeynet A network of honeypots.

honeypot A decoy system isolated from legitimate systems and designed to be vulnerable to security exploits for the purposes of learning more about hacking techniques or nabbing a hacker in the act.

hop A term used to describe each trip a unit of data takes from one connectivity device to another. Typically, *hop* is used in the context of router-to-router communications.

hop limit *See* TTL.

host 1) A TCP/IP utility that at its simplest returns either the IP address of a host if its host name is specified or its host name if its IP address is specified. 2) A computer that enables resource sharing by other computers on the same network. 3) In the context of virtualization, the physical computer on which virtualization software operates and manages guests.

host file A text file that associates TCP/IP host names with IP addresses.

host name A symbolic name that describes a TCP/IP device.

host-based firewall A firewall that only protects the computer on which it's installed.

host-based intrusion detection *See* HIDS.

host-based intrusion prevention *See* HIPS.

hosted PBX A digital PBX service provided over the Internet.

hostname A TCP/IP utility used to show or modify a client's host name.

hosts The name of the host file used on UNIX, Linux, and Windows systems. On a UNIX-or Linux-based computer, hosts is found in the `/etc` directory. On a Windows-based computer, it is found in the `%systemroot%\system32\drivers\etc` folder.

hot site A place where the computers, devices, and connectivity necessary to rebuild a network exist, and all are appropriately configured, updated, and connected to match your network's current state.

hot spare In the context of RAID, a disk or partition that is part of the array, but used only in case one of the RAID disks fails. More generally, *hot spare* is used as a synonym for a hot-swappable component.

hot-swappable The feature of a component that allows it to be installed or removed without disrupting operations.

HTTP (Hypertext Transfer Protocol) An Application layer protocol that formulates and interprets requests between Web clients and servers. HTTP uses the TCP port number 80.

HTTP over Secure Sockets Layer *See* HTTPS.

HTTP Secure *See* HTTPS.

HTTPS (HTTP over Secure Sockets Layer) The URL prefix that indicates that a Web page requires its data to be exchanged between client and server using SSL encryption. HTTPS uses the TCP port number 443.

hub A connectivity device that belongs to the Physical layer of the OSI model and retransmits incoming data signals to its multiple ports. Typically, hubs contain one uplink port, which is used to connect to a network's backbone.

hybrid fiber-coax *See* HFC.

hybrid topology A physical topology that combines characteristics of more than one simple physical topology.

Hypertext Transfer Protocol *See* HTTP.

Hyper-V Microsoft's virtualization software package. Hyper-V operates with Windows Server 2008 and Windows Server 2008 R2.

hypervisor The element of virtualization software that manages multiple guest machines and their connections to the host (and by association, to a physical network). A hypervisor is also known as a virtual machine manager.

IAB (Internet Architecture Board) A technical advisory group of researchers and technical professionals responsible for Internet growth and management strategy, resolution of technical disputes, and standards oversight.

IANA (Internet Assigned Numbers Authority) A nonprofit, United States government-funded group that was established at the University of Southern California and charged with managing IP address allocation and the Domain Name System. The oversight for many of IANA's functions was given to ICANN in 1998; however, IANA continues to perform Internet addressing and Domain Name System administration.

ICA (Independent Computing Architecture) The software from Citrix Systems, Inc., that, when installed on a client, enables the client to connect with a host computer and exchange keystrokes, mouse clicks, and screen updates. Citrix's ICA client can work with virtually any operating system or application.

ICANN (Internet Corporation for Assigned Names and Numbers) The nonprofit corporation currently designated by the United States government to maintain and assign IP addresses.

ICMP (Internet Control Message Protocol) A core protocol in the TCP/IP suite that notifies the sender that something has gone wrong in the transmission process and that packets were not delivered.

ICMPv6 The version of ICMP used with IPv6 networks. ICMPv6 performs the functions that ICMP, IGMP, and ARP perform in IPv4. It detects and reports data transmission errors, discovers other nodes on a network, and manages multicasting.

ICS (Internet Connection Sharing) A service provided with Windows operating systems that allows one computer, the ICS host, to share its Internet connection with other computers on the same network.

ICS host On a network using the Microsoft Internet Connection Sharing service, the computer whose Internet connection other computers share. The ICS host must contain two network interfaces: one that connects to the Internet and one that connects to the LAN.

IDF (intermediate distribution frame) A junction point between the MDF and concentrations of fewer connections—for example, those that terminate in a telecommunications closet.

IDS (intrusion-detection system) A dedicated device or software running on a host that monitors, flags, and logs any unauthorized attempt to access an organization's secured resources on a network or host.

IEEE (Institute of Electrical and Electronics Engineers) An international society composed of engineering professionals. Its goals are to promote development and education in the electrical engineering and computer science fields.

IETF (Internet Engineering Task Force) An organization that sets standards for how systems communicate over the Internet (for example, how protocols operate and interact).

ifconfig A TCP/IP configuration and management utility used with UNIX and Linux systems.

IGMP (Internet Group Management Protocol or Internet Group Multicast Protocol) A TCP/IP protocol used on IPv4 networks to manage multicast transmissions. Routers use IGMP to determine which nodes belong to a multicast group, and nodes use IGMP to join or leave a multicast group.

IGP (Interior Gateway Protocol) A routing protocol, such as RIP, that can only route data within an autonomous (internal) network.

IKE (Internet Key Exchange) The first phase of IPSec authentication, which accomplishes key management. IKE is a service that runs on UDP port 500. After IKE has established the rules for the type of keys two nodes use, IPSec invokes its second phase, encryption.

IMAP (Internet Message Access Protocol) A mail retrieval protocol that improves on the shortcomings of POP.

The single biggest advantage IMAP4 has relative to POP is that it allows users to store messages on the mail server, rather than always having to download them to the local machine. The most current version of IMAP is version 4 (IMAP4).

IMAP4 (Internet Message Access Protocol, version 4) The most commonly used form of the Internet Message Access Protocol (IMAP).

impedance The resistance that contributes to controlling an electrical signal. Impedance is measured in ohms.

incremental backup A backup in which only data that has changed since the last full or incremental backup is copied to a storage medium. After backing up files, an incremental backup unchecks the archive bit for every file it has saved.

information node *See* inode.

infrastructure WLAN A type of WLAN in which stations communicate with an access point and not directly with each other.

inherited A type of permission, or right, that is passed down from one group (the parent) to a group within that group (the child).

inode (information node) A UNIX or Linux file system information storage area that holds all details about a file. This information includes the size, the access rights, the date and time of creation, and a pointer to the actual contents of the file.

Institute of Electrical and Electronics Engineers *See* IEEE.

Integrated Services Digital Network *See* ISDN.

integrity The soundness of a network's files, systems, and connections. To ensure integrity, you must protect your network from anything that might render it unusable, such as corruption, tampering, natural disasters, and viruses.

integrity checking A method of comparing the current characteristics of files and disks against an archived version of these characteristics to discover any changes. The most common example of integrity checking involves a checksum.

Interior Gateway Protocol *See* IGP.

interior router A router that directs data between nodes on an autonomous LAN.

intermediate distribution frame *See* IDF.

Intermediate System to Intermediate System *See* IS-IS.

International Organization for Standardization *See* ISO.

International Telecommunication Union *See* ITU.

Internet A complex WAN that connects LANs and clients around the globe.

Internet Architecture Board *See* IAB.

Internet Assigned Numbers Authority *See* IANA.

Internet Connection Sharing *See* ICS.

Internet Control Message Protocol *See* ICMP.

Internet Control Message Protocol version 6 *See* ICMPv6

Internet Corporation for Assigned Names and Numbers *See* ICANN.

Internet Engineering Task Force *See* IETF.

Internet Group Management Protocol *See* IGMP.

Internet Group Multicast Protocol *See* IGMP.

Internet Key Exchange *See* IKE.

Internet Message Access Protocol *See* IMAP.

Internet Message Access Protocol, version 4 *See* IMAP4.

Internet Protocol *See* IP.

Internet Protocol address *See* IP address.

Internet Protocol Security *See* IPSec.

Internet Relay Chat *See* IRC.

Internet Security Association and Key Management Protocol *See* ISAKMP.

Internet service provider *See* ISP.

Internet services The services that enable a network to communicate with the Internet, including Web servers and browsers, file transfer capabilities, Internet addressing schemes, security filters, and a means for directly logging on to other computers.

Internet Society *See* ISOC.

Internet telephony The provision of telephone service over the Internet.

Internetwork To traverse more than one LAN segment and more than one type of network through a router.

intrusion-detection system *See* IDS.

intrusion-prevention system *See* IPS.

IP (Internet Protocol) A core protocol in the TCP/IP suite that operates in the Network layer of the OSI model and provides information about how and where data should be delivered. IP is the subprotocol that enables TCP/IP to internetwork.

IP address (Internet Protocol address) The Network layer address assigned to nodes to uniquely identify them on a TCP/IP network. IPv4 addresses consist of 32 bits divided into four octets, or bytes. IPv6 addresses are composed of eight 16-bit fields, for a total of 128 bits.

IP datagram *See* IP packet.

IP masquerading *See* DNAT.

IP next generation *See* IPv6.

IP packet The IP portion of a TCP/IP frame that acts as an envelope for data, holding information necessary for routers to transfer data between subnets.

IP phone *See* IP telephone.

IP spoofing A security attack in which an outsider obtains internal IP addresses and then uses those addresses to pretend that he has authority to access a private network from the Internet.

IP telephone A telephone used for VoIP on a TCP/IP-based network. IP telephones are designed to transmit and receive only digital signals.

IP telephony *See* Voice over IP.

IP television *See* IPTV.

IP version 4 Link Local *See* IPv4LL.

ipconfig The utility used to display TCP/IP addressing and domain name information in the Windows client operating systems.

IPng *See* IPv6.

IP-PBX A private switch that accepts and interprets both analog and digital voice signals (although some IP-PBXs do not accept analog lines). It can connect with both traditional PSTN lines and data networks. An IP-PBX transmits and receives IP-based voice signals to and from other network connectivity devices, such as a router or gateway.

IPS (intrusion-prevention system) A dedicated device or software running on a host that automatically reacts to any unauthorized attempt to access an organization's secured resources on a network or host. IPS is often combined with IDS.

IPSec (Internet Protocol Security) A Layer 3 protocol that defines encryption, authentication, and key management for TCP/IP transmissions. IPSec is an enhancement to IPv4 and is native to IPv6. IPSec is unique among authentication methods in that it adds security information to the header of all IP packets.

IPTV (IP television) A service in which television signals from broadcast or cable networks travel over packet-switched networks.

IPv4 (IP version 4) The Internet Protocol standard released in the 1980s and still commonly used on modern networks. It specifies 32-bit addresses composed of four octets. It lacks the security, automatic addressing, and prioritization benefits of IPv6. It also suffers from a limited number of addresses, a problem that can be resolved by using IPv6 instead.

IPv4LL (IP version 4 Link Local) A protocol that manages automatic address assignment among locally connected nodes. IPv4LL is part of the Zeroconf group of protocols.

IPv6 (IP version 6) A standard for IP addressing that is gradually replacing the current IPv4 (IP version 4). Most notably, IPv6 uses a newer, more efficient header in its packets and allows for 128-bit source and destination IP addresses. The use of longer addresses allows for many more IP addresses to be in circulation. IPv6 also provides automatic addressing, better security, and prioritization features.

IRC (Internet Relay Chat) A protocol that enables users running special IRC client software to communicate instantly with other participants in a chat room on the Internet.

ISAKMP (Internet Security Association and Key Management Protocol) A service for setting policies to verify the identity and the encryption methods nodes will use in IPSec transmission.

ISDN (Integrated Services Digital Network) An international standard that uses PSTN lines to carry digital signals. It specifies protocols at the Physical, Data Link, and Transport layers of the OSI model. ISDN lines may carry voice and data signals simultaneously. Two types of ISDN connections are used in North America: BRI (Basic Rate Interface) and PRI (Primary Rate Interface). Both use a combination of bearer channels (B channels) and data channels (D channels).

IS-IS (Intermediate System to Intermediate System) A link-state routing protocol that uses a best-path algorithm similar to OSPF's. IS-IS was originally codified by ISO, which referred to routers as "intermediate systems," thus the protocol's name. Unlike OSPF, IS-IS is designed for use on interior routers only.

ISO (International Organization for Standardization) A collection of standards organizations representing 162 countries with headquarters located in Geneva, Switzerland. Its goal is to establish international technological standards to facilitate the global exchange of information and barrier-free trade.

ISOC (Internet Society) A professional organization with members from 90 chapters around the world that helps to establish technical standards for the Internet.

ISP (Internet service provider) A business that provides organizations and individuals with Internet access and often, other services, such as e-mail and Web hosting.

ITU (International Telecommunication Union) A United Nations agency that regulates international telecommunications and provides developing countries with technical expertise and equipment to advance their technological bases.

iwconfig A command-line utility for viewing and setting wireless interface parameters on Linux and UNIX workstations.

jabber A device that handles electrical signals improperly, usually affecting the rest of the network. A network analyzer will detect a jabber as a device that is always retransmitting, effectively bringing the network to a halt. A jabber usually results from a bad NIC. Occasionally, it can be caused by outside electrical interference.

jamming A part of CSMA/CD in which, upon detecting a collision, a station issues a special 32-bit sequence to indicate to all nodes on an Ethernet segment that its previously transmitted frame has suffered a collision and should be considered faulty.

KDC (Key Distribution Center) In Kerberos terminology, the server that runs the authentication service and the Ticket-Granting Service to issue keys and tickets to clients.

Kerberos A cross-platform authentication protocol that uses key encryption to verify the identity of clients and to securely exchange information after a client logs on to a system. It is an example of a private key encryption service.

kernel The core of a UNIX or Linux system. This part of the operating system is loaded and run when you turn on your computer. It mediates between user programs and the computer hardware.

kernel module A portion of the kernel that you can load and unload to add or remove functionality on a running UNIX or Linux system.

Kernel-based Virtual Machine *See* KVM.

key A series of characters that is combined with a block of data during that data's encryption. To decrypt the resulting data, the recipient must also possess the key.

Key Distribution Center *See* KDC.

key management The method whereby two nodes using key encryption agree on common parameters for the keys they will use to encrypt data.

key pair The combination of a public and private key used to decipher data that was encrypted using public key encryption.

KVM (Kernel-based Virtual Machine) An open source virtualization package designed for use with Linux systems.

L2TP (Layer 2 Tunneling Protocol) A protocol that encapsulates PPP data, for use on VPNs. L2TP is based on Cisco technology and is standardized by the IETF. It is distinguished by its compatibility among different manufacturers' equipment; its ability to connect between clients, routers, and servers alike; and also by the fact that it can connect nodes belonging to different Layer 3 networks.

label A character string that represents a domain (either top-level, second-level, or third-level).

LAN (local area network) A network of computers and other devices that is confined to a relatively small space, such as one building or even one office.

LAN Emulation *See* LANE.

LANE (LAN Emulation) A method for transporting token ring or Ethernet frames over ATM networks. LANE encapsulates incoming Ethernet or token ring frames, then converts them into ATM cells for transmission over an ATM network.

last mile *See* local loop.

late collision A collision that takes place outside the normal window in which collisions are detected and redressed. Late collisions are usually caused by a defective station (such as a transceiver) that is transmitting without first verifying line status or by failure to observe the configuration guidelines for cable length, which results in collisions being recognized too late.

latency The delay between the transmission of a signal and its receipt.

Layer 2 Tunneling Protocol *See* L2TP.

Layer 3 switch A switch capable of interpreting data at Layer 3 (Network layer) of the OSI model.

Layer 4 switch A switch capable of interpreting data at Layer 4 (Transport layer) of the OSI model.

LC (local connector) A connector used with single-mode or multimode fiber-optic cable.

LDAP (Lightweight Directory Access Protocol) A standard protocol for accessing network directories.

leaf object An object in an operating system's directory, such as a printer or user, that does not contain other objects.

lease The agreement between a DHCP server and client on how long the client can use a DHCP-assigned IP address. DHCP services can be configured to provide lease terms equal to any amount of time.

license tracking The process of determining the number of copies of a single application that are currently in use on the network and whether the number in use exceeds the authorized number of licenses.

Lightweight Directory Access Protocol *See* LDAP.

line printer daemon *See* `lpd`.

lineman's handset *See* butt set.

line-of-sight *See* LOS.

link aggregation A fault-tolerance technique in which multiple ports or interfaces are bonded and work in tandem to create one logical interface. Link aggregation can also improve performance and allow for load balancing.

link segment *See* unpopulated segment.

link-local address An IP address that is automatically assigned by an operating system to allow a node to communicate over its local subnet if a routable IP address is not available. ICANN has established the range of 169.254.0.0 through 169.254.254.255 as potential link-local IPv4 addresses. IPv6 link-local addresses begin with FE80.

link-state A type of routing protocol that enables routers across a network to share information, after which each router can independently map the network and determine the best path between itself and a packet's destination node.

Linux An open source operating system modeled on the UNIX operating system. Finnish computer scientist Linus Torvalds originally developed it.

LLC (Logical Link Control) sublayer The upper sublayer in the Data Link layer. The LLC provides a common interface and supplies reliability and flow control services.

load balancer A device that distributes traffic intelligently between multiple computers.

load balancing The distribution of traffic over multiple links, hard disks, or processors intended to optimize responses.

local area network *See* LAN.

local collision A collision that occurs when two or more stations are transmitting simultaneously. Excessively high collision rates within the network can usually be traced to cable or routing problems.

local connector *See* LC.

local loop The part of a phone system that connects a customer site with a telecommunications carrier's switching facility.

logic bomb A program designed to start when certain conditions are met.

logical address *See* network address.

Logical Link Control sublayer *See* LLC (Logical Link Control) sublayer.

logical topology A characteristic of network transmission that reflects the way in which data are transmitted between nodes. A network's logical topology may differ from its physical topology. The most common logical topologies are bus and ring.

Long Term Evolution *See* LTE.

loopback adapter *See* loopback plug.

loopback address An IP address reserved for communicating from a node to itself, used mostly for troubleshooting purposes. The IPv4 loopback address is always cited as 127.0.0.1, although in fact, transmitting to any IP address whose first octet is 127 will contact the originating device. In IPv6, the loopback address is represented as ::1.

loopback plug A connector used for troubleshooting that plugs into a port (for example, a serial, parallel, or RJ-45 port) and crosses over the transmit line to the receive line, allowing outgoing signals to be redirected back into the computer for testing.

loopback test An attempt to contact one's own machine for troubleshooting purposes. In TCP/IP-based networking, a loopback test can be performed by communicating with an IPv4 address that begins with an octet of 127. Usually, this means pinging the address 127.0.0.1.

LOS (line-of-sight) A wireless signal or path that travels directly in a straight line from its transmitter to its intended receiver. This type of propagation uses the least amount of energy and results in the reception of the clearest possible signal.

lpd (line printer daemon) A UNIX service responsible for printing files placed in the printer queue by the `lpr` command.

lpr A UNIX command that places files in the printer queue. The files are subsequently printed with `lpd`, the print service.

LTE (Long Term Evolution) A 4G cellular network technology that achieves downlink data rates of up to 1 Gbps and uplink rates up to 500 Mbps. AT&T and Verizon have adopted LTE for their high-speed wireless data networks.

MAC (Media Access Control) sublayer The lower sublayer of the Data Link layer. The MAC appends the physical address of the destination computer onto the frame.

MAC address *See* physical address.

Mac OS X Server A proprietary NOS from Apple Computer that is based on a version of UNIX.

macro virus A virus that takes the form of an application (for example, a word-processing or spreadsheet) program macro, which may execute when the program is in use.

mail server A server that manages the storage and transfer of e-mail messages.

mail services The network services that manage the storage and transfer of e-mail between users on a network. In addition to sending, receiving, and storing mail, mail services can include filtering, routing, notification, scheduling, and data exchange with other mail servers.

main bus *See* bus.

main cross-connect *See* MDF.

main distribution frame *See* MDF.

malware A program or piece of code designed to harm a system or its resources.

MAN (metropolitan area network) A network that is larger than a LAN, typically connecting clients and servers from multiple buildings, but within a limited geographic area.

For example, a MAN could connect multiple city government buildings around a city's center.

man pages (manual pages) The online documentation for any variety of the UNIX operating system. This documentation describes the use of the commands and the programming interface.

Management Information Base *See* MIB.

management services The network services that centrally administer and simplify complicated management tasks on the network. Examples of management services include license tracking, security auditing, asset management, address management, software distribution, traffic monitoring, load balancing, and hardware diagnosis.

man-in-the-middle attack A security threat that relies on intercepted transmissions. It can take one of several forms, but in all cases a person redirects or captures secure data traffic while in transit.

manual pages *See* man pages.

map The action of associating a disk, directory, or device with a drive letter.

mask *See* subnet mask.

master name server An authoritative name server that is queried first on a network when resolution of a name that is not already cached is requested. Master name servers can also be called primary name servers.

maximum transmission unit *See* MTU.

MCITP (Microsoft Certified IT Professional) A professional certification established by Microsoft that demonstrates in-depth knowledge about Microsoft products.

MCU (multipoint control unit) A computer that provides support for multiple H.323 terminals (for example, several workstations participating in a videoconference) and manages communication between them. An MCU is also known as a video bridge.

MDF (main distribution frame) Also known as the main cross-connect, the first point of interconnection between an organization's LAN or WAN and a service provider's facility.

mechanical transfer-registered jack *See* MT-RJ.

Media Access Control sublayer *See* MAC (Media Access Control) sublayer.

media converter A device that enables networks or segments using different media to interconnect and exchange signals.

media gateway A gateway capable of accepting connections from multiple devices (for example, IP telephones, traditional telephones, IP fax machines, traditional fax machines, and so on) and translating analog signals into packetized, digital signals, and vice versa.

Media Gateway Control Protocol *See* MGCP.

media gateway controller *See* MGC.

MEGACO A protocol used between media gateway controllers and media gateways. MEGACO is poised to replace MGCP on modern converged networks, as it supports a broader range of network technologies, including ATM. Also known as H.248.

member server A type of server on a Windows Server 2003, Server 2008, or Server 2008 R2 network that does not hold directory information and, therefore, cannot authenticate users.

mesh topology WAN A type of WAN in which several sites are directly interconnected. Mesh WANs are highly fault tolerant because they provide multiple routes for data to follow between any two points.

metasploit A penetration-testing tool that combines known scanning techniques and exploits to result in potentially new types of exploits.

metropolitan area network *See* MAN.

MGC (media gateway controller) A computer that manages multiple media gateways and facilitates the exchange of call control information between these gateways.

MGCP (Media Gateway Control Protocol) A protocol used for communication between media gateway controllers and media gateways. MGCP is currently the most popular media gateway control protocol used on converged networks.

MIB (Management Information Base) A database used in network management that contains a device's definitions of managed objects and their data.

Microsoft Certified IT Professional *See* MCITP.

Microsoft Challenge Handshake Authentication Protocol *See* MS-CHAP.

Microsoft Challenge Handshake Authentication Protocol, version 2 *See* MS-CHAPv2.

middleware The software that sits between the client and server in a 3-tier architecture. Middleware may be used as a messaging service between clients and servers, as a universal query language for databases, or as means of coordinating processes between multiple servers that need to work together in servicing clients.

MIME (Multipurpose Internet Mail Extensions) A standard for encoding and interpreting binary files, images, video, and non-ASCII character sets within an e-mail message.

MIMO (multiple input-multiple output) In the context of 802.11n wireless networking, the ability for access points to issue multiple signals to stations, thereby multiplying the signal's strength and increasing their range and data-carrying capacity. Because the signals follow multipath propagation, they must be phase-adjusted when they reach their destination.

mini GBIC *See* SFP.

mirroring A fault-tolerance technique in which one component or device duplicates the activity of another.

MMF (multimode fiber) A type of fiber-optic cable that contains a core with a diameter between 50 and 100 microns, through which many pulses of light generated by a light-emitting diode (LED) travel at different angles.

mobile A type of wireless system in which the receiver can be located anywhere within the transmitter's range. This allows the receiver to roam from one place to another while continuing to pick up its signal.

mobile switching center *See* MSC.

mobile telecommunications switching office *See* MSC.

modal bandwidth A measure of the highest frequency of signal a multimode fiber-optic cable can support over a specific distance. Modal bandwidth is measured in MHz-km.

modem A device that modulates analog signals into digital signals at the transmitting end for transmission over telephone lines, and demodulates digital signals into analog signals at the receiving end.

modulation A technique for formatting signals in which one property of a simple carrier wave is modified by the addition of a data signal during transmission.

motherboard The main circuit board that controls a computer.

mount The process of making a disk partition available.

MPLS (multiprotocol label switching) A type of switching that enables any one of several Layer 2 protocols to carry multiple types of Layer 3 protocols. One of its benefits is the ability to use packet-switched technologies over traditionally circuit-switched networks. MPLS can also create end-to-end paths that act like circuit-switched connections.

MSC (mobile switching center) A carrier's facility to which multiple cellular base stations connect. An MSC might be located inside a telephone company's central office or it might stand alone and connect to the central office via fiber-optic cabling or a microwave link. Equipment at an MSC manages mobile clients, monitoring their location and usage patterns, and switches cellular calls. It also assigns each mobile client an IP address.

MS-CHAP (Microsoft Challenge Handshake Authentication Protocol) An authentication protocol provided with Windows operating systems that uses a three-way handshake to verify a client's credentials and encrypts passwords with a challenge text.

MS-CHAPv2 (Microsoft Challenge Handshake Authentication Protocol, version 2) An authentication protocol provided with Windows operating systems that follows the CHAP model, but uses stronger encryption, uses different encryption keys for transmission and reception, and requires mutual authentication between two computers.

mtr (my traceroute) A route discovery and analysis utility that comes with UNIX and Linux operating systems. Mtr combines the functions of the ping and traceroute commands and delivers an easily readable chart as its output.

MT-RJ (mechanical transfer-registered jack) A connector used with single-mode or multimode fiber-optic cable.

MTSO (mobile telecommunications switching office) *See* MSC.

MTU (maximum transmission unit) The largest data unit a network (for example, Ethernet or token ring) will accept for transmission.

multicast address A type of address in the IPv6 that represents multiple interfaces, often on multiple nodes. An IPv6 multicast address begins with the following hexadecimal field: FF0*x*, where *x* is a character that identifies the address's group scope.

multicasting A means of transmission in which one device sends data to a specific group of devices (not necessarily the entire network segment) in a point-to-multipoint fashion.

multifactor authentication An authentication process that requires the client to provide two or more pieces of information, such as a password, fingerprint scan, and security token.

multimeter A simple instrument that can measure multiple characteristics of an electric circuit, including its resistance and voltage.

multimode fiber *See* MMF.

multipath The characteristic of wireless signals that follow a number of different paths to their destination (for example, because of reflection, diffraction, and scattering).

multiple input-multiple output *See* MIMO.

multiplexer A device that separates a medium into multiple channels and issues signals to each of those subchannels.

multiplexing A form of transmission that allows multiple signals to travel simultaneously over one medium.

multipoint control unit *See* MCU.

multiprocessing The technique of splitting tasks among multiple processors to expedite the completion of any single instruction.

multiprotocol label switching *See* MPLS.

Multipurpose Internet Mail Extensions *See* MIME.

multitenant A feature of cloud computing in which multiple customers share storage locations or services without knowing it.

multitasking The ability of a processor to perform multiple activities in a brief period of time (often seeming simultaneous to the user).

mutual authentication An authentication scheme in which both computers verify the credentials of each other.

NaaS (Network as a Service) A type of cloud computing that offers clients a complete set of networking services—for example, mail, Web, DNS, DHCP, and remote access services, plus LAN and WAN connectivity.

name server A server that contains a database of TCP/IP host names and their associated IP addresses. A name server supplies a resolver with the requested information. If it cannot resolve the IP address, the query passes to a higher-level name server.

namespace The database of Internet IP addresses and their associated names distributed over DNS name servers worldwide.

narrowband A type of wireless transmission in which signals travel over a single frequency or within a specified frequency range.

NAS (network attached storage) A device or set of devices attached to a client/server network, dedicated to providing highly fault-tolerant access to large quantities of data. NAS depends on traditional network transmission methods such as Ethernet.

NAT (Network Address Translation) A technique in which IP addresses used on a private network are assigned a public IP address by a gateway when accessing a public network.

nbtstat A TCP/IP troubleshooting utility that provides information about NetBIOS names and their addresses. If you know the NetBIOS name of a workstation, you can use nbtstat to determine its IP address.

near-end cross talk *See* NEXT.

negative frame sequence check The result of the CRC (cyclic redundancy check) generated by the originating node not matching the checksum calculated from the data.

Nessus A penetration testing tool from Tenable Security that performs sophisticated scans to discover information about hosts, ports, services, and software.

net mask *See* subnet mask.

NetBIOS A protocol that runs in the Session and Transport layers of the OSI model and associates NetBIOS names with workstations. NetBIOS alone is not routable because it does not contain Network layer information. However, when encapsulated in another protocol such as TCP/IP, it can be routed.

netstat A TCP/IP troubleshooting utility that displays statistics and the state of current TCP/IP connections. It also displays ports, which can signal whether services are using the correct ports.

network A group of computers and other devices (such as printers) that are connected by and can exchange data via some type of transmission media, such as a cable, a wire, or the atmosphere.

network adapter *See* NIC.

network address A unique identifying number for a network node that follows a hierarchical addressing scheme and can be assigned through operating system software. Network addresses are added to data packets and interpreted by protocols at the Network layer of the OSI model.

Network Address Translation *See* NAT.

network analyzer *See* protocol analyzer.

Network as a Service *See* NaaS.

network attached storage *See* NAS.

network class A classification for TCP/IP-based networks that pertains to the network's potential size and is indicated by an IP address's network ID and subnet mask. Network Classes A, B, and C are commonly used by clients on LANs; network Classes D and E are reserved for special purposes.

network diagram A graphical representation of a network's devices and connections.

Network File System *See* NFS.

network ID The portion of an IP address common to all nodes on the same network or subnet.

network interface card *See* NIC.

network interface unit *See* NIU.

network key A key (or character string) required for a wireless station to associate with an access point using WEP.

Network layer The third layer in the OSI model. Protocols in the Network layer translate network addresses into their physical counterparts and decide how to route data from the sender to the receiver.

Network layer address *See* network address.

network management The assessment, monitoring, and maintenance of the devices and connections on a network.

Network Mapper *See* NMAP.

network monitor A software-based tool that monitors traffic on the network from a server or workstation attached to the network. Network monitors typically can interpret up to Layer 3 of the OSI model.

Network Monitor A network monitoring program from Microsoft that comes with Windows operating systems.

network number *See* network ID.

network operating system *See* NOS.

network prefix *See* network ID.

network service provider *See* NSP.

network services The functions provided by a network.

Network Termination 1 *See* NT1.

Network Termination 2 *See* NT2.

Network Time Protocol *See* NTP.

network virus A virus that takes advantage of network protocols, commands, messaging programs, and data links to propagate itself. Although all viruses could theoretically travel across network connections, network viruses are specially designed to attack network vulnerabilities.

Network+ (Net+) The professional certification established by CompTIA that verifies broad, vendor-independent networking technology skills, such as an understanding of protocols, topologies, networking hardware, and network troubleshooting.

network-based firewall A firewall configured and positioned to protect an entire network.

network-based intrusion detection *See* NIDS.

network-based intrusion prevention *See* NIPS.

New Technology File System *See* NTFS.

NEXT (near-end cross talk) Cross talk, or the impingement of the signal carried by one wire onto a nearby wire, that occurs between wire pairs near the source of a signal.

NFS (Network File System) A popular remote file system created by Sun Microsystems, and available for UNIX and Linux operating systems.

NIC (network interface card) The device that enables a workstation to connect to the network and communicate with other computers. NICs are manufactured by several different companies and come with a variety of specifications that are tailored to the workstation's and the network's requirements. NICs are also called network adapters.

NIC teaming A type of link aggregation in which two or more NICs work in tandem to handle traffic to and from a single node.

NIDS (network-based intrusion detection) A type of intrusion detection that occurs on devices that are situated at the edge of the network or that handle aggregated traffic.

NIDS (network-based intrusion prevention) A type of intrusion prevention that occurs on devices that are situated at the edge of the network or that handle aggregated traffic.

NIU (network interface unit) The point at which PSTN-owned lines terminate at a customer's premises. The NIU is usually located at the demarc.

NMAP (Network Mapper) A scanning tool designed to assess large networks quickly and provide comprehensive, customized information about a network and its hosts. NMAP, which runs on virtually any modern operating system, is available for download at no cost at *www.nmap.org*.

node A computer or other device connected to a network, which has a unique address and is capable of sending or receiving data.

noise The unwanted signals, or interference, from sources near network cabling, such as electrical motors, power lines, and radar.

nonbroadcast point-to-multipoint transmission A communications arrangement in which a single transmitter issues signals to multiple, defined recipients.

NOS (network operating system) The software that runs on a server and enables the server to manage data, users, groups, security, applications, and other networking functions. The most popular network operating systems are UNIX, Linux, and Microsoft Windows Server 2008 R2.

nslookup A TCP/IP utility that allows you to look up the DNS host name of a network node by specifying its IP address, or vice versa. This ability is useful for verifying that a host is configured correctly and for troubleshooting DNS resolution problems.

NSP (network service provider) A carrier that provides long-distance (and often global) connectivity between major data-switching centers across the Internet. AT&T, Verizon, and Sprint are all examples of network service providers in the United States. Customers, including ISPs, can lease dedicated private or public Internet connections from an NSP.

NT1 (Network Termination 1) A device used on ISDN networks that connects the incoming twisted pair wiring with the customer's ISDN terminal equipment.

NT2 (Network Termination 2) An additional connection device required on PRI to handle the multiple ISDN lines between the customer's network termination connection and the local phone company's wires.

NTFS (New Technology File System) A file system developed by Microsoft and used with its Windows NT, Windows 2000 Server, Windows Server 2003, Windows Server 2008, and Windows Server 2008 R2 operating systems.

NTP (Network Time Protocol) A simple Application layer protocol in the TCP/IP suite used to synchronize the clocks of computers on a network. NTP depends on UDP for Transport layer services.

object A representation of a thing or person associated with the network that belongs in the NOS directory. Objects include users, printers, groups, computers, data files, and applications.

object class *See* class.

OC (Optical Carrier) An internationally recognized rating that indicates throughput rates for SONET connections.

octet One of the 4 bytes that are separated by periods and together make up an IPv4 address.

offline UPS *See* standby UPS.

ohmmeter A device used to measure resistance in an electrical circuit.

OLT (optical line terminal) A device located at the carrier's endpoint of a passive optical network. An OLT contains multiple optical ports, or PON interfaces and a splitter that subdivides the capacity of each port into up to 32 logical channels, one per subscriber.

omnidirectional antenna A type of antenna that issues and receives wireless signals with equal strength and clarity in all directions. This type of antenna is used when many different receivers must be able to pick up the signal, or when the receiver's location is highly mobile.

on-board NIC A NIC that is integrated into a computer's motherboard, rather than connected via an expansion slot or peripheral bus.

on-board port A port that is integrated into a computer's motherboard.

online backup A technique in which data is backed up to a central location over the Internet.

online UPS A power supply that uses the A/C power from the wall outlet to continuously charge its battery, while providing power to a network device through its battery.

ONU (optical network unit) In a passive optical network, the device near the customer premises that terminates a carrier's fiber-optic cable connection and distributes signals to multiple endpoints via fiber-optic cable, in the case of FTTP, or via copper or coax cable.

Open Shortest Path First *See* OSPF.

open source The term that describes software whose code is publicly available for use and modification.

Open Systems Interconnection model *See* OSI (Open Systems Interconnection) model.

OpenSSH An open source version of the SSH suite of protocols.

Optical Carrier *See* OC.

optical line terminal *See* OLT.

optical loss The degradation of a light signal on a fiber-optic network.

optical media A type of media capable of storing digitized data, which uses a laser to write data to it and read data from it.

optical network unit *See* ONU.

optical time domain reflectometer *See* OTDR.

organizational unit *See* OU.

Organizationally Unique Identifier *See* OUI.

OSI (Open Systems Interconnection) model A model for understanding and developing computer-to-computer communication developed in the 1980s by ISO. It divides networking functions among seven layers: Physical, Data Link, Network, Transport, Session, Presentation, and Application.

OSPF (Open Shortest Path First) A routing protocol that makes up for some of the limitations of RIP and can coexist with RIP on a network.

OTDR (optical time domain reflectometer) A performance testing device for use with fiber-optic networks. An OTDR works by issuing a light-based signal on a fiber-optic cable and measuring the way in which the signal bounces back (or reflects) to the OTDR. By measuring the length of time it takes the signal to return, an OTDR can determine the location of a fault.

OU (organizational unit) A logical receptacle for holding objects with similar characteristics or privileges in an NOS directory. Containers form the branches of the directory tree.

OUI (Organizationally Unique Identifier) A 24-bit character sequence assigned by IEEE that appears at the beginning of a network interface's physical address and identifies the NIC's manufacturer.

overhead The nondata information that must accompany data for a signal to be properly routed and interpreted by the network.

P2P network *See* peer-to-peer network.

packet A discrete unit of information sent from one node on a network to another.

Packet Internet Groper *See* PING.

packet sniffer *See* protocol analyzer.

packet switching A type of switching in which data are broken into packets before being transported. In packet switching, packets can travel any path on the network to their destination because each packet contains a destination address and sequencing information.

packet-filtering firewall A router that examines the header of every packet of data that it receives to determine whether that type of packet is authorized to continue to its destination. Packet-filtering firewalls are also called screening firewalls.

padding The bytes added to the data (or information) portion of an Ethernet frame to ensure this field is at least 46 bytes in size. Padding has no effect on the data carried by the frame.

page file A file on the hard drive that is used for virtual memory.

paging The process of moving blocks of information, called pages, between RAM and into a page file on disk.

paging file *See* page file.

PAP (Password Authentication Protocol) A simple authentication protocol that operates over PPP. Using PAP, a client issues its credentials in a request to authenticate, and the server responds with a confirmation or denial of authentication after comparing the credentials with those in its database. PAP is not very secure and is, therefore, rarely used on modern networks.

parallel backbone A type of backbone that consists of more than one connection from the central router or switch to each network segment.

partial-mesh WAN A version of a mesh topology WAN in which only critical sites are directly interconnected and secondary sites are connected through star or ring topologies. Partial mesh WANs are less expensive to implement than full-mesh WANs.

partition An area of a computer's hard drive that is logically defined and acts as a separate disk drive.

passive optical network *See* PON.

passive scanning In the context of wireless networking, the process in which a station listens to several channels within a frequency range for a beacon issued by an access point.

passive topology A network topology in which each node passively listens for, then accepts, data directed to it. A bus topology is considered a passive topology.

Password Authentication Protocol *See* PAP.

PAT (Port Address Translation) A form of address translation that uses TCP port numbers to distinguish each client's transmission, thus allowing multiple clients to share a limited number of Internet-recognized IP addresses.

patch A correction, improvement, or enhancement to part of a software application, often distributed at no charge by software vendors to fix a bug in their code or to add slightly more functionality.

patch cable A relatively short section (usually between 3 and 25 feet) of cabling with connectors on both ends.

patch panel A wall-mounted panel of data receptors into which cross-connect patch cables from the punch-down block are inserted.

pathping A command-line utility that combines the functionality of the tracert and ping commands (similar to UNIX's mtr command) and comes with Windows operating systems.

PBX (private branch exchange) A telephone switch used to connect and manage an organization's voice calls.

PCI Component Interconnect Express *See* PCIe.

PCIe (PCI Component Interconnect Express) A 32-bit bus standard capable of transferring data at up to 1 Gbps per data path, or lane, in full-duplex transmission. PCIe is commonly used for expansion board NICs.

PD (powered device) On a network using Power over Ethernet, a node that receives power from power sourcing equipment.

PDU (protocol data unit) A unit of data at any layer of the OSI model.

peer-to-peer network A network in which every computer can communicate directly with every other computer. By default, no computer on a peer-to-peer network has more authority than another. However, each computer can be configured to share only some of its resources and keep other resources inaccessible to other nodes on the network.

per seat In the context of applications, a licensing mode that limits access to an application to specific users or workstations.

per user A licensing mode that allows a fixed quantity of clients to use one software package simultaneously.

performance management The ongoing assessment of how well network links, devices, and components keep up with demands on them.

permanent virtual circuit *See* PVC.

PGP (Pretty Good Privacy) A key-based encryption system for e-mail that uses a two-step verification process.

phase A point or stage in a wave's progress over time.

phishing A practice in which a person attempts to glean access or authentication information by posing as someone who needs that information.

physical address A 48- or 64-bit network interface identifier that includes two parts: the OUI, assigned by IEEE to the manufacturer, and the extension identifier, a unique number assigned to each NIC by the manufacturer.

Physical layer The lowest, or first, layer of the OSI model. Protocols in the Physical layer generate and detect signals so as to transmit and receive data over a network medium. These protocols also set the data transmission rate and monitor data error rates, but do not provide error correction.

physical memory The RAM chips installed on the computer's system board that provide dedicated memory to that computer.

physical topology The physical layout of the media, nodes, and devices on a network. A physical topology does not specify device types, connectivity methods, or addressing schemes. Physical topologies are categorized into three fundamental shapes: bus, ring, and star. These shapes can be mixed to create hybrid topologies.

ping To send an echo request signal from one node on a TCP/IP-based network to another, using the PING utility. *See also* PING.

PING (Packet Internet Groper) A TCP/IP troubleshooting utility that can verify that TCP/IP is installed, bound to the NIC, configured correctly, and communicating with the network. PING uses ICMP to send echo request and echo reply messages that determine the validity of an IP address.

ping6 The version of the PING utility used on Linux computers that run IPv6.

pipe A character that enables you to combine existing commands to form new commands. The pipe symbol is the vertical bar (|).

pipeline A series of two or more commands in which the output of prior commands is sent to the input of subsequent commands.

PKI (Public-key Infrastructure) The use of certificate authorities to associate public keys with certain users.

plain old telephone service (POTS) *See* PSTN.

plenum The area above the ceiling tile or below the subfloor in a building.

PoE (Power over Ethernet) A method of delivering current to devices using Ethernet connection cables.

point-to-multipoint A communications arrangement in which one transmitter issues signals to multiple receivers. The receivers may be undefined, as in a broadcast transmission, or defined, as in a nonbroadcast transmission.

point-to-point A data transmission that involves one transmitter and one receiver.

Point-to-Point Protocol *See* PPP.

Point-to-Point Protocol over Ethernet *See* PPPoE.

Point-to-Point Tunneling Protocol *See* PPTP.

polling A network management application's regular collection of data from managed devices.

polymorphic virus A type of virus that changes its characteristics (such as the arrangement of its bytes, size, and internal instructions) every time it is transferred to a new system, making it harder to identify.

PON (passive optical network) A network in which a carrier uses fiber-optic cabling to connect with multiple endpoints—for example, many businesses on a city block. The word *passive* applies because in a PON no repeaters or other connectivity devices intervene between a carrier and its customer.

POP (Post Office Protocol) An Application layer protocol used to retrieve messages from a mail server. When a client retrieves mail via POP, messages previously stored on the mail server are downloaded to the client's workstation, and then deleted from the mail server.

POP3 (Post Office Protocol, version 3) The most commonly used form of the Post Office Protocol.

populated segment A network segment that contains end nodes, such as workstations.

Port Address Translation *See* PAT.

port authentication A technique in which a client's identity is verified by an authentication server before a port, whether physical or logical, is opened for the client's Layer 3 traffic. *See also* 802.1x.

port forwarding The process of redirecting traffic from its normally assigned port to a different port, either on the client or server. In the case of using SSH, port forwarding can send data exchanges that are normally insecure through encrypted tunnels.

port mirroring A monitoring technique in which one port on a switch is configured to send a copy of all its traffic to a second port.

port number The address on a host where an application makes itself available to incoming data.

port scanner Software that searches a server, switch, router, or other device for open ports, which can be vulnerable to attack.

port-based authentication *See* port authentication.

Post Office Protocol *See* POP.

Post Office Protocol, version 3 *See* POP3.

posture assessment An assessment of an organization's security vulnerabilities. Posture assessments should be performed at least annually and preferably quarterly—or sooner if the network has undergone significant changes. For each risk found, it should rate the severity of a potential breach, as well as its likelihood.

POTS *See* PSTN.

Power over Ethernet *See* PoE.

PowerPC The brand of computer central processing unit invented by Apple Computer, IBM, and Motorola, Inc., and used in IBM servers.

power sourcing equipment *See* PSE.

powered device *See* PD.

PPP (Point-to-Point Protocol) A communications protocol that enables a workstation to connect to a server using a serial connection. PPP can support multiple Network layer protocols and can use both asynchronous and synchronous communications. It performs compression and error correction and requires little configuration on the client workstation.

PPPoE (Point-to-Point Protocol over Ethernet) PPP running over an Ethernet network.

PPTP (Point-to-Point Tunneling Protocol) A Layer 2 protocol developed by Microsoft that encapsulates PPP data for transmission over VPN connections. PPTP operates with Windows RRAS access services and can accept connections from multiple different clients. It is simple, but less secure than other modern tunneling protocols.

preamble The field in an Ethernet frame that signals to the receiving node that data are incoming and indicates when the data flow is about to begin.

preemptive multitasking The type of multitasking in which tasks are actually performed one at a time, in very brief succession. In preemptive multitasking, one program uses the processor for a certain period of time, then is suspended to allow another program to use the processor.

Presentation layer The sixth layer of the OSI model. Protocols in the Presentation layer translate between the application and the network. Here, data are formatted in a schema that the network can understand, with the format varying according to the type of network used. The Presentation layer also manages data encryption and decryption, such as the scrambling of system passwords.

Pretty Good Privacy *See* PGP.

PRI (Primary Rate Interface) A type of ISDN that uses 23 bearer channels and one 64-Kbps data channel, represented by the notation 23B+D. PRI is less commonly used by individual subscribers than BRI, but it may be used by businesses and other organizations needing more throughput.

primary name server *See* master name server.

Primary Rate Interface *See* PRI.

principal In Kerberos terminology, a user or client.

print services The network service that allows printers to be shared by several users on a network.

printer queue A logical representation of a networked printer's functionality. To use a printer, clients must have access to the printer queue.

private address An IP address used only on an organization's internal network. Certain IP address ranges are reserved for private addresses. Private addresses cannot be used to communicate over the Internet.

private branch exchange *See* PBX.

private cloud An arrangement in which shared and flexible data storage, applications, or services are managed on and delivered via an organization's internal network.

private key encryption A type of key encryption in which the sender and receiver use a key to which only they have access. DES (Data Encryption Standard), which was developed by IBM in the 1970s, is a popular example of a private key encryption technique. Private key encryption is also known as symmetric encryption.

private network A network whose access is restricted to only clients or machines with proper credentials.

Private Port *See* Dynamic Ports.

probe 1) In 802.11 wireless networking, a type of frame issued by a station during active scanning to find nearby access points. 2) *See* tone locator.

process A routine of sequential instructions that runs until it has achieved its goal. For example, a spreadsheet program is a process.

promiscuous mode The feature of a network adapter that allows it to pick up all frames that pass over the network—not just those destined for the node served by the card.

proprietary UNIX Any implementation of UNIX for which the source code is either unavailable or available only by purchasing a licensed copy.

protocol A standard method or format for communication between network devices. For example, some protocols ensure that data are transferred in sequence and without error from one node on the network to another. Other protocols ensure that data belonging to a Web page is formatted to appear correctly in a Web browser window. Still others encode passwords and keep data transmissions secure.

protocol analyzer A software package or hardware-based tool that can capture and analyze data on a network. Protocol analyzers are more sophisticated than network monitoring tools, as they can typically interpret data up to Layer 7 of the OSI model.

protocol data unit *See* PDU.

proxy *See* proxy server.

proxy server 1) A network host that runs a proxy service. Proxy servers may also be called gateways. 2) On a SIP network, a server that accepts requests for location information from user agents, then queries the nearest registrar server on behalf of those user agents. If the recipient user agent is in the SIP proxy server's domain, then that server will also act as a go-between for calls established and terminated between the requesting user agent and the recipient user agent.

proxy service A software application on a network host that acts as an intermediary between the external and internal networks, screening all incoming and outgoing traffic and providing one address to the outside world, instead of revealing the addresses of internal LAN devices.

PSE (power sourcing equipment) On a network using Power over Ethernet, the device that supplies power to end nodes.

PSTN (Public Switched Telephone Network) The network of lines and carrier equipment that provides telephone service to most homes and businesses. Now, except for the local loop, nearly all of the PSTN uses digital transmission. Its traffic is carried by fiber-optic or copper twisted pair cable, microwave, and satellite connections.

public address An IP address that is valid for use on public networks, such as the Internet. An organization assigns its hosts public addresses from the range of addresses assigned to it by Internet numbering authorities.

public cloud An arrangement in which shared and flexible data storage, applications, or services are managed centrally by service providers and delivered over public transmission lines, such as the Internet. Rackspace and Amazon (with its EC2 offering) are leading public cloud service providers.

public key encryption A form of key encryption in which data is encrypted using two keys: One is a key known only to a user, and the other is a key associated with the user and that can be obtained from a public source, such as a public key server. Some examples of public key algorithms include RSA and Diffie-Hellman. Public key encryption is also known as asymmetric encryption.

Public-key Infrastructure *See* PKI.

public key server A publicly available host (such as an Internet host) that provides free access to a list of users' public keys (for use in public key encryption).

public network A network that any user can access with no restrictions. The most familiar example of a public network is the Internet.

Public Switched Telephone Network *See* PSTN.

punch-down block A panel of data receptors into which twisted pair wire is inserted, or punched down, to complete a circuit.

PVC (permanent virtual circuit) A point-to-point connection over which data may follow any number of different paths, as opposed to a dedicated line that follows a predefined path. X.25, frame relay, and some forms of ATM use PVCs.

QoS (quality of service) The result of specifications for guaranteeing data delivery within a certain period of time after their transmission.

quality of service *See* QoS.

radiation pattern The relative strength over a three-dimensional area of all the electromagnetic energy an antenna sends or receives.

radio frequency interference *See* RFI.

RADIUS (Remote Authentication Dial-In User Service) A popular protocol for providing centralized AAA (authentication, authorization, and accounting) for multiple users. RADIUS runs over UDP and can use one of several authentication protocols.

RADIUS server A server that offers centralized authentication services to a network's access server, VPN server, or wireless access point via the RADIUS protocol.

RAID (Redundant Array of Independent [or Inexpensive] Disks) A server redundancy measure that uses shared, multiple physical or logical hard disks to ensure data integrity and availability. Some RAID designs also increase storage capacity and improve performance.

range The geographical area in which signals issued from an antenna or wireless system can be consistently and accurately received.

Rapid Spanning Tree Protocol *See* RSTP.

RAS (Remote Access Service) The dial-up networking software provided with Microsoft Windows 95, 98, NT, and 2000 client operating systems. RAS requires software installed on both the client and server, a server configured to accept incoming clients, and a client with sufficient privileges (including username and password) on the server to access its resources. In more recent versions of Windows, RAS has been incorporated into the RRAS (Routing and Remote Access Service).

RC4 An asymmetric key encryption technique that weaves a key with data multiple times as a computer issues the stream of data. RC4 keys can be as long as 2048 bits. In addition to being highly secure, RC4 is fast.

RDN (relative distinguished name) An attribute of an object that identifies the object separately from its related container(s) and domain. For most objects, the relative distinguished name is the same as its common name (CN) in the distinguished name convention.

RDP (Remote Desktop Protocol) An Application layer protocol that uses TCP/IP to transmit graphics and text quickly over a remote client-host connection. RDP also carries session, licensing, and encryption information.

Real-time Transport Control Protocol *See* RTCP.

Real-time Transport Protocol *See* RTP.

reassembly The process of reconstructing data units that have been segmented.

reassociation In the context of wireless networking, the process of a station establishing a connection (or associating) with a different access point.

Recommended Standard 232 *See* RS-232.

recordable DVD An optical storage medium that can hold up to 4.7 GB on one single-layered side. Both sides of the disc can be used, and each side can have up to two layers. Thus, in total, a double-layered, two-sided DVD can store up to 17 GB of data. Recordable DVDs come in several different formats.

redirect server On a SIP network, a server that accepts and responds to requests from user agents and SIP proxy servers for location information on recipients that belong to external domains.

redirector A service that runs on a client workstation and determines whether the client's request should be handled by the client or the server.

redundancy The use of more than one identical component, device, or connection for storing, processing, or transporting data. Redundancy is the most common method of achieving fault tolerance.

Redundant Array of Independent (or Inexpensive) Disks *See* RAID.

reflection In the context of wireless, the phenomenon that occurs when an electromagnetic wave encounters an obstacle and bounces back toward its source. A wireless signal will bounce off objects whose dimensions are large compared with the signal's average wavelength.

regeneration The process of retransmitting a digital signal. Regeneration, unlike amplification, repeats the pure signal, with none of the noise it has accumulated.

Regional Internet Registry *See* RIR.

registered jack 11 *See* RJ-11.

registered jack 45 *See* RJ-45.

registered jack 48 *See* RJ-48.

Registered Ports The TCP/IP ports in the range of 1024 to 49,151. These ports are accessible to network users and processes that do not have special administrative privileges. Default assignments of these ports must be registered with IANA.

registrar server On a SIP network, a server that maintains a database containing information about the locations (network addresses) of each user agent in its domain. When a user agent joins a SIP network, it transmits its location information to the SIP registrar server.

relative distinguished name *See* RDN.

remote access A method for connecting and logging on to a LAN from a workstation that is remote, or not physically connected, to the LAN.

remote access server A server that runs communications services that enable remote users to log on to a network. Also known as an access server.

Remote Access Service *See* RAS.

Remote Authentication Dial-In User Service *See* RADIUS.

Remote Desktop A feature of Windows operating systems that allows a computer to act as a remote host and be controlled from a client running another Windows operating system.

Remote Desktop Protocol *See* RDP.

remote user A person working on a computer on a different network or in a different geographical location from the LAN's server.

removable disk drive *See* external disk drive.

repeater A device used to regenerate a signal. Repeaters operate at the Physical layer of the OSI model.

replication 1) A fault-tolerance technique that involves dynamic copying of data (for example, an NOS directory or an entire server's hard disk) from one location to another. 2) In the context of Microsoft Windows Server NOSs, the process of copying Active Directory data to multiple domain controllers. This ensures redundancy so that in case one of the domain controllers fails, clients can still log on to the network, be authenticated, and access resources.

Request to Send/Clear to Send *See* RTS/CTS.

resolver Any host on the Internet that needs to look up domain name information.

resource record The element of a DNS database stored on a name server that contains information about TCP/IP host names and their addresses.

Resource Reservation Protocol *See* RSVP.

resources The devices, data, and data storage space provided by a computer, whether stand-alone or shared.

restoring The process of retrieving files from a backup. It is necessary to restore files if the original files are lost or deleted.

RFI (radio frequency interference) A kind of interference that may be generated by broadcast signals from radio or TV antennas.

RG-6 A type of coaxial cable with an impedance of 75 ohms and that contains an 18 AWG core conductor. RG-6 is used for television, satellite, and broadband cable connections.

RG-8 A type of coaxial cable characterized by a 50-ohm impedance and a 10 AWG core. RG-8 provided the medium for the first Ethernet networks, which followed the now-obsolete 10Base-5 standard.

RG-58 A type of coaxial cable characterized by a 50-ohm impedance and a 24 AWG core. RG-58 was a popular medium for Ethernet LANs in the 1980s, used for the now-obsolete 10Base-2 standard.

RG-59 A type of coaxial cable characterized by a 75-ohm impedance and a 20 or 22 AWG core, usually made of braided copper. Less expensive but suffering greater attenuation than the more common RG-6 coax, RG-59 is used for relatively short connections.

ring topology A network layout in which each node is connected to the two nearest nodes so that the entire network forms a circle. Data are transmitted in one direction around the ring. Each workstation accepts and responds to packets addressed to it, then forwards the other packets to the next workstation in the ring.

ring topology WAN A type of WAN in which each site is connected to two other sites so that the entire WAN forms a ring pattern.

RIP (Routing Information Protocol) The oldest routing protocol that is still widely used, RIP is a distance-vector protocol that uses hop count as its routing metric and allows up to only 15 hops. It is considered an IGP. Compared with other, more modern, routing protocols, RIP is slower and less secure.

RIPv2 (Routing Information Protocol version 2) An updated version of the original RIP routing protocol that makes up for some of its predecessor's overhead and security flaws. However, RIPv2's packet forwarding is still limited to a maximum 15 hops.

RIR (Regional Internet Registry) A not-for-profit agency that manages the distribution of IP addresses to private and public entities. ARIN is the RIR for North, Central, and South America and sub-Saharan Africa. APNIC is the RIR for Asia and the Pacific region. RIPE is the RIR for Europe and North Africa.

RJ-11 (registered jack 11) The standard connector used with unshielded twisted pair cabling (usually Cat 3 or Level 1) to connect analog telephones.

RJ-45 (registered jack 45) The standard connector used with shielded twisted pair and unshielded twisted pair cabling.

RJ-48 (registered jack 48) A standard for terminating wires in an 8-pin connector. RJ-48 is the preferred connector type for T1 connections that rely on twisted pair wiring.

roaming In wireless networking, the process that describes a station moving between BSSs without losing connectivity.

root bridge The single bridge on a network selected by the Spanning Tree Protocol to provide the basis for all subsequent path calculations.

root domain In Windows Server NOS terminology, the single domain from which child domains branch out in a domain tree.

root server A DNS server maintained by ICANN and IANA that is an authority on how to contact the top-level domains, such as those ending with .com, .edu, .net, .us, and so on. ICANN oversees the operation of 13 root servers around the world.

round-trip time *See* RTT.

round-robin DNS A method of increasing name resolution availability by pointing a host name to multiple IP addresses in a DNS zone file.

routable The protocols that can span more than one LAN because they carry Network layer and addressing information that can be interpreted by a router.

route 1) A utility for viewing or modifying a host's routing table. 2) To intelligently direct data between networks based on addressing, patterns of usage, and availability of network segments.

route prefix The prefix in an IPv6 address that identifies a route. Because route prefixes vary in length, slash notation is used to define them. For example, the route prefix indicated by 2608:FE10::/32 includes all subnets whose prefixes begin with 2608:FE10 and, consequently, all interfaces whose IP addresses begin with 2608:FE10.

router A multiport device that operates at Layer 3 of the OSI model and uses logical addressing information to direct data between networks or segments. Routers can connect dissimilar LANs and WANs running at different transmission speeds and using a variety of Network layer protocols. They determine the best path between nodes based on traffic congestion, available versus unavailable routes, load balancing targets, and other factors.

Routing and Remote Access Service (RRAS) The software included with Windows operating systems that enables a server to act as a router, firewall, and remote access server. Using RRAS, a server can provide network access to multiple remote clients.

Routing Information Protocol *See* RIP.

Routing Information Protocol version 2 *See* RIPv2.

routing metric The method used by routing protocols to determine the best path for data to follow over a network. Routing metrics may be calculated using any of several variables, including number of hops, bandwidth, delay, MTU, cost, and load.

routing protocols The means by which routers communicate with each other about network status. Routing protocols determine the best path for data to take between nodes.

routing switch *See* Layer 3 switch.

routing table A database stored in a router's memory that maintains information about the location of hosts and best paths for forwarding packets to them.

RRAS *See* Routing and Remote Access Service.

RS-232 (Recommended Standard 232) A Physical layer standard for serial communications, as defined by EIA/TIA.

RSA An encryption algorithm that creates a key by randomly choosing two large prime numbers and multiplying them together. RSA is named after its creators, Ronald Rivest, Adi Shamir, and Leonard Adleman. RSA was released in 1977, but remains popular today for e-commerce transactions.

RSTP (Rapid Spanning Tree Protocol) As described in IEEE's 802.1w standard, a version of the Spanning Tree Protocol that can detect and correct for network changes much more quickly.

RSVP (Resource Reservation Protocol) A QoS technique that attempts to reserve a specific amount of network resources for a transmission before the transmission occurs.

RTCP (Real-time Transport Control Protocol) A companion protocol to RTP, RTCP provides feedback on the quality of a call or videoconference to its participants.

RTP (Real-time Transport Protocol) An Application layer protocol used with voice and video transmission. RTP operates on top of UDP and provides information about packet sequence to help receiving nodes detect delay and packet loss. It also assigns packets a time stamp that corresponds to when the data in the packet were sampled from the voice or video stream. This time stamp helps the receiving node synchronize incoming data.

RTP Control Protocol *See* RTCP.

RTS/CTS (Request to Send/Clear to Send) An exchange in which a wireless station requests the exclusive right to communicate with an access point and the access point confirms that it has granted that request.

RTT (round-trip time) The length of time it takes for a packet to go from sender to receiver, then back from receiver to sender. RTT is usually measured in milliseconds.

runt An erroneously shortened packet.

sag *See* brownout.

Samba An open source software package that provides complete Windows-style file- and printer-sharing capabilities.

SAN (storage area network) A distinct network of multiple storage devices and servers that provides fast, highly available, and highly fault-tolerant access to large quantities of data for a client/server network. A SAN uses a proprietary network transmission method (such as Fibre Channel) rather than a traditional network transmission method such as Ethernet.

SC (subscriber connector or standard connector) A connector used with single-mode or multimode fiber-optic cable.

scalable The property of a network that allows you to add nodes or increase its size easily.

scanning The process a wireless station undergoes to find an access point. *See also* active scanning and passive scanning.

scattering The diffusion of a wireless signal that results from hitting an object that has smaller dimensions compared with the signal's wavelength. Scattering is also related to the roughness of the surface a wireless signal encounters. The rougher the surface, the more likely a signal is to scatter when it hits that surface.

schema The description of object types, or classes, and their required and optional attributes that are stored in an NOS's directory.

SCP (Secure CoPy) A method for copying files securely between hosts. SCP is part of the OpenSSH package, which comes with modern UNIX and Linux operating systems. Third-party SCP applications are available for Windows-based computers.

SDH (Synchronous Digital Hierarchy) The international equivalent of SONET.

secondary name server *See* slave name server.

second-level support In network troubleshooting, a person or group with deeper knowledge about a subject and to whom first-level support personnel escalate problems.

Secure CoPy *See* SCP.

Secure File Transfer Protocol *See* SFTP.

Secure Shell *See* SSH.

Secure Sockets Layer *See* SSL.

security audit An assessment of an organization's security vulnerabilities performed by an accredited network security firm.

security auditing The process of evaluating security measures currently in place on a network and notifying the network administrator if a security breach occurs.

security policy A document or plan that identifies an organization's security goals, risks, levels of authority, designated security coordinator and team members, responsibilities for each team member, and responsibilities for each employee. In addition, it specifies how to address security breaches.

security token A device or piece of software used for authentication that stores or generates information, such as a series of numbers or letters, known only to its authorized user.

segment 1) A unit of data that results from subdividing a larger protocol data unit. 2) A part of a network. Usually, a segment is composed of a group of nodes that share the same communications channel for all their traffic.

segmentation The process of decreasing the size of data units when moving data from a network that can handle larger data units to a network that can handle only smaller data units.

self-healing A characteristic of dual-ring topologies that allows them to automatically reroute traffic along the backup ring if the primary ring becomes severed.

sequencing The process of assigning a placeholder to each piece of a data block to allow the receiving node's Transport layer to reassemble the data in the correct order.

serial A style of data transmission in which the pulses that represent bits follow one another along a single transmission line. In other words, they are issued sequentially, not simultaneously.

serial backbone A type of backbone that consists of two or more internetworking devices connected to each other by a single cable in a daisy chain.

serial cable A cable, such as an RS-232 type, that permits serial data transmission.

Serial Line Internet Protocol *See* SLIP.

server A computer on the network that manages shared resources. Servers usually have more processing power, memory, and hard disk space than clients. They run network operating software that can manage not only data, but also users, groups, security, and applications on the network.

server_hello In the context of SSL encryption, a message issued from the server to the client that confirms the information the server received in the client_hello message. It also agrees to certain terms of encryption based on the options the client supplied. Depending on the Web server's preferred encryption method, the server may choose to issue your browser a public key or a digital certificate at this time.

Server Message Block *See* SMB.

server mirroring A fault-tolerance technique in which one server duplicates the transactions and data storage of another, identical server. Server mirroring requires a link between the servers and software running on both servers so that the servers can continually synchronize their actions and one can take over in case the other fails.

service set identifier *See* SSID.

session A connection for data exchange between two parties. The term *session* may be used in the context of Web, remote access, or terminal and mainframe communications, for example.

Session Initiation Protocol *See* SIP.

session key In the context of Kerberos authentication, a key issued to both the client and the server by the authentication service that uniquely identifies their session.

Session layer The fifth layer in the OSI model. The Session layer establishes and maintains communication between two nodes on the network. It can be considered the "traffic cop" for communications, such as videoconferencing, that require precisely coordinated data exchange.

set-top box In the context of IPTV, a device that decodes digital video signals and issues them to the television. Set-top boxes also communicate with content servers to manage video delivery.

SFD (start-of-frame delimiter) A 1-byte field that indicates where the data field begins in an Ethernet frame.

SFP (small form-factor pluggable) transceiver A standard hot-swappable network interface used to link a connectivity device's backplane with fiber-optic or copper cabling. SFPs are known as mini GBICs because they perform a similar function as GBICs, but have a smaller profile. Current SFP standards enable them to send and receive data at up to 10 Gbps.

SFP GBIC *See* SFP.

SFTP (Secure File Transfer Protocol) A protocol available with the proprietary version of SSH that copies files between hosts securely. Like FTP, SFTP first establishes a connection with a host and then allows a remote user to browse directories, list files, and copy files. Unlike FTP, SFTP encrypts data before transmitting it.

sheath The outer cover, or jacket, of a cable.

shell Another term for the UNIX command interpreter.

shield *See* braiding.

shielded twisted pair *See* STP.

signal bounce A phenomenon, caused by improper termination on a bus-topology network, in which signals travel endlessly between the two ends of the network, preventing new signals from getting through.

signal level An ANSI standard for T-carrier technology that refers to its Physical layer electrical signaling characteristics.

DS0 is the equivalent of one data or voice channel. All other signal levels are multiples of DS0.

signaling The exchange of information between the components of a network or system for the purposes of establishing, monitoring, or releasing connections as well as controlling system operations.

Signaling System 7 *See* SS7.

signature scanning The comparison of a file's content with known virus signatures (unique identifying characteristics in the code) in a signature database to determine whether the file is a virus.

Simple Mail Transfer Protocol *See* SMTP.

Simple Network Management Protocol *See* SNMP.

Simple Network Management Protocol version 1 *See* SNMPv1.

Simple Network Management Protocol version 2 *See* SNMPv2.

Simple Network Management Protocol version 3 *See* SNMPv3.

simplex A type of transmission in which signals may travel in only one direction over a medium.

single sign-on A form of authentication in which a client signs on once to access multiple systems or resources.

single-mode fiber *See* SMF.

SIP (Session Initiation Protocol) A set of Application layer signaling and control protocols for multiservice, packet-based networks. With few exceptions, SIP performs much the same functions as the H.323 signaling protocols perform.

site license A type of software license that, for a fixed price, allows any number of users in one location to legally access a program.

site survey In the context of wireless networking, an assessment of client requirements, facility characteristics, and coverage areas to determine an access point arrangement that will ensure reliable wireless connectivity within a given area.

site-to-site VPN A type of VPN in which VPN gateways at multiple sites encrypt and encapsulate data to exchange over a tunnel with other VPN gateways. Meanwhile, clients, servers, and other hosts on a site-to-site VPN communicate with the VPN gateway.

slash notation *See* CIDR notation.

slave name server A name server that can take the place of a master name server to resolve names and addresses on a network. Slave name servers poll master name servers to ensure that their zone information is identical. Slave name servers are also called secondary name servers.

SLIP (Serial Line Internet Protocol) A communications protocol that enables a workstation to connect to a server using a serial connection. SLIP can support only asynchronous communications and IP traffic and requires some configuration on the client workstation. SLIP has been made obsolete by PPP.

small form-factor pluggable transceiver *See* SFP.

smart jack A termination for T-carrier wire pairs that is located at the customer demark and which functions as a connection protection and monitoring point.

SMB (Server Message Block) A protocol for communications and resource access between systems, such as clients and servers. SMB originated at IBM and then was adopted and further developed by Microsoft for use on its Windows operating systems. The current version of SMB is known as the CIFS (Common Internet File System) protocol.

SMF (single-mode fiber) A type of fiber-optic cable with a narrow core that carries light pulses along a single path data from one end of the cable to the other end. Data can be transmitted faster and for longer distances on single-mode fiber than on multimode fiber. However, single-mode fiber is more expensive.

SMTP (Simple Mail Transfer Protocol) The Application layer TCP/IP subprotocol responsible for moving messages from one e-mail server to another.

smurf attack A threat to networked hosts in which the host is flooded with broadcast ping messages. A smurf attack is a type of denial-of-service attack.

SNAT (Static Network Address Translation) A type of address translation in which each private IP address is correlated with its own Internet-recognized IP address.

sneakernet A way of exchanging data between computers that are not connected on a network. The term *sneakernet* was coined before the widespread use of networks, when data was copied from a computer to a removable storage device such as a floppy disk, carried (presumably by someone wearing sneakers) to another computer, then copied from the storage device onto the second computer.

sniffer *See* protocol analyzer.

SNMP (Simple Network Management Protocol) An Application layer protocol in the TCP/ IP suite used to convey data regarding the status of managed devices on a network.

SNMPv1 (Simple Network Management Protocol version 1) The original version of SNMP, released in 1988. Because of its limited features, it is rarely used on modern networks.

SNMPv2 (Simple Network Management Protocol version 2) The second version of SNMP, which improved on SNMPv1 with faster performance and slightly better security, among other features.

SNMPv3 (Simple Network Management Protocol version 3) A version of SNMP similar to SNMPv2, but with authentication, validation, and encryption for packets exchanged between managed devices and the network management console. SNMPv3 is the most secure version of the protocol.

social engineering The act of manipulating personal relationships to circumvent network security measures and gain access to a system.

socket A logical address assigned to a specific process running on a computer. Some sockets are reserved for operating system functions.

soft skills The skills such as customer relations, oral and written communications, dependability, teamwork, and leadership abilities, which are not easily measured, but are nevertheless important in a networking career.

softphone A computer configured to act like an IP telephone. Softphones present the caller with a graphical representation of a telephone dial pad and can connect to a network via any wired or wireless method.

Softswitch *See* MGC.

software distribution The process of automatically transferring a data file or installing a software application from the server to a client on the network.

software RAID A method of implementing RAID that uses software to implement and control RAID techniques over virtually any type of hard disk(s). RAID software may be a third-party package or utilities that come with an operating system NOS.

Solaris A proprietary implementation of the UNIX operating system by Sun Microsystems.

SONET (Synchronous Optical Network) A high-bandwidth WAN signaling technique that specifies framing and multiplexing techniques at the Physical layer of the OSI model. It can integrate many other WAN technologies (for example, T-carriers, ISDN, and ATM technology) and allows for simple link additions and removals. SONET's topology includes a double ring of fiber-optic cable, which results in very high fault tolerance.

source code The computer instructions written in a programming language that is readable by humans. Source code must be translated into a form that is executable by the machine, typically called binary code (for the sequence of zeros and ones) or target code.

spam Unsolicited, unwanted e-mail.

Spanning Tree Protocol *See* STP.

spectrum analyzer A tool that assesses the characteristics (for example, frequency, amplitude, and the effects of interference) of wireless signals.

spread spectrum A type of wireless transmission in which lower-level signals are distributed over several frequencies simultaneously. Spread-spectrum transmission is more secure than narrowband.

SS7 (Signaling System 7) A set of standards established by the ITU for handling call signaling on the PSTN (Public Switched Telephone Network).

SSH (Secure Shell) A connection utility that provides authentication and encryption. With SSH, you can securely log on to a host, execute commands on that host, and copy files to or from that host. SSH encrypts data exchanged throughout the session.

SSID (service set identifier) A unique character string used to identify an access point on an 802.11 network.

SSL (Secure Sockets Layer) A method of encrypting TCP/IP transmissions—including Web pages and data entered into Web forms—en route between the client and server using public key encryption technology.

SSL session In the context of SSL encryption, an association between the client and server that is defined by an agreement on a specific set of encryption techniques. An SSL session allows the client and server to continue to exchange data securely as long as the client is still connected to the server. SSL sessions are established by the SSL handshake protocol.

ST (straight tip) A connector used with single-mode or multimode fiber-optic cable.

stand-alone computer A computer that uses applications and data only from its local disks and that is not connected to a network.

standard A documented agreement containing technical specifications or other precise criteria that are used as guidelines to ensure that materials, products, processes, and services suit their intended purpose.

standard connector *See* SC.

standby UPS A power supply that provides continuous voltage to a device by switching virtually instantaneously to the battery when it detects a loss of power from the wall outlet. Upon restoration of the power, the standby UPS switches the device to use A/C power again.

star topology A physical topology in which every node on the network is connected through a central device. Any single physical wire on a star network connects only two devices, so a cabling problem will affect only two nodes. Nodes transmit data to the device, which then retransmits the data to the rest of the network segment where the destination node can pick it up.

star topology WAN A type of WAN in which a single site acts as the central connection point for several other points. This arrangement provides separate routes for data between any two sites; however, if the central connection point fails, the entire WAN fails.

star-wired bus topology A hybrid topology in which groups of workstations are connected in a star fashion to connectivity devices that are networked via a single bus.

star-wired ring topology A hybrid topology that uses the physical layout of a star and the token-passing data transmission method.

start-of-frame delimiter *See* SFD.

stateful firewall A firewall capable of monitoring a data stream from end to end.

stateless firewall A firewall capable only of examining packets individually. Stateless firewalls perform more quickly than stateful firewalls, but are not as sophisticated.

static ARP table entry A record in an ARP table that someone has manually entered using the ARP utility. Static ARP table entries remain the same until someone manually modifies them with the ARP utility.

static IP address An IP address that is manually assigned to a device and remains constant until it is manually changed.

Static Network Address Translation *See* SNAT.

static routing A technique in which a network administrator programs a router to use specific paths between nodes. Because it does not account for occasional network congestion, failed connections, or device moves and requires manual configuration, static routing is not optimal.

station An end node on a network; used most often in the context of wireless networks.

statistical multiplexing A method of multiplexing in which each node on a network is assigned a separate time slot for transmission, based on the node's priority and need.

stealth virus A type of virus that hides itself to prevent detection. Typically, stealth viruses disguise themselves as legitimate programs or replace part of a legitimate program's code with their destructive code.

storage area network *See* SAN.

store-and-forward mode A method of switching in which a switch reads the entire data frame into its memory and checks it for accuracy before transmitting it. Although this method is more time consuming than the cut-through method, it allows store-and-forward switches to transmit data more accurately.

STP (shielded twisted pair) A type of cable containing twisted-wire pairs that are not only individually insulated, but also surrounded by a shielding made of a metallic substance such as foil.

STP (Spanning Tree Protocol) A switching protocol defined in IEEE 802.1D. STP operates in the Data Link layer to prevent traffic loops by calculating paths that avoid potential loops and by artificially blocking links that would complete a loop. Given changes to a network's links or devices, STP recalculates its paths.

straight tip *See* ST.

straight-through cable A twisted pair patch cable in which the wire terminations in both connectors follow the same scheme.

streaming video A service in which video signals are compressed and delivered over the Internet in a continuous stream so that a user can watch and listen even before all the data have been transmitted.

structured cabling A method for uniform, enterprise-wide, multivendor cabling systems specified by the TIA/EIA 568 Commercial Building Wiring Standard. Structured cabling is based on a hierarchical design using a high-speed backbone.

subchannel One of many distinct communication paths established when a channel is multiplexed or modulated.

subnet A part of a network in which all nodes shares a network addressing component and a fixed amount of bandwidth.

subnet mask In IPv4 addressing, a 32-bit number that, when combined with a device's IP address, indicates what kind of subnet the device belongs to.

subnet prefix The 64-bit prefix in an IPv6 address that identifies a subnet. A single IPv6 subnet is capable of supplying 18,446,744,073,709,551,616 IPv6 addresses.

subnetting The process of subdividing a single class of network into multiple, smaller networks.

subprotocols The specialized protocols that work together and belong to a protocol suite.

subscriber connector *See* SC.

supernet In IPv4, a type of subnet that is created by moving the subnet boundary to the left and using bits that normally would be reserved for network class information.

supernet mask A 32-bit number that, when combined with a device's IPv4 address, indicates the kind of supernet to which the device belongs.

supernetting *See* CIDR.

supported services list A document that lists every service and software package supported within an organization, plus the names of first- and second-level support contacts for those services or software packages.

surge A momentary increase in voltage caused by distant lightning strikes or electrical problems.

surge protector A device that directs excess voltage away from equipment plugged into it and redirects it to a ground, thereby protecting the equipment from harm.

SVC (switched virtual circuit) A logical, point-to-point connection that relies on switches to determine the optimal path between sender and receiver. ATM technology uses SVCs.

swap file *See* page file.

switch 1) A connectivity device that logically subdivides a network into smaller, individual collision domains. A switch operates at the Data Link layer of the OSI model and can interpret MAC address information to determine whether to filter (discard) or forward packets it receives. 2) The letters or words added to a command that allow you to customize a utility's output. Switches are usually preceded by a hyphen or forward slash character.

switched virtual circuit *See* SVC.

switching A component of a network's logical topology that manages how packets are filtered and forwarded between nodes on the network.

symmetric encryption A method of encryption that requires the same key to encode the data as is used to decode the ciphertext.

symmetric multiprocessing A method of multiprocessing that splits all operations equally among two or more processors.

symmetrical A characteristic of transmission technology that provides equal throughput for data traveling both upstream and downstream and is suited to users who both upload and download significant amounts of data.

symmetrical DSL A variation of DSL that provides equal throughput both upstream and downstream between the customer and the carrier.

SYN (synchronization) The packet one node sends to request a connection with another node on the network. The SYN packet is the first of three in the three-step process of establishing a connection.

SYN-ACK (synchronization-acknowledgment) The packet a node sends to acknowledge to another node that it has received a SYN request for connection. The SYN-ACK packet is the second of three in the three-step process of establishing a connection.

synchronization *See* SYN.

synchronization-acknowledgment *See* SYN-ACK.

synchronous A transmission method in which data being transmitted and received by nodes must conform to a timing scheme.

Synchronous Digital Hierarchy *See* SDH.

Synchronous Optical Network *See* SONET.

syslog A standard for generating, storing, and processing messages about events on a system. Syslog describes methods for detecting and reporting events and specifies the format and contents of messages.

system bus *See* bus.

system log On a computer running a UNIX or Linux operating system, the record of monitored events, which can range in priority from 0 to 7 (where "0" indicates an emergency situation and "7" simply points to information that might help in debugging a problem). You can view and modify system log locations and configurations in the file `/etc/syslog.conf` on most systems (on some systems this is the `/etc/rsyslog.conf` file).

T1 A digital carrier standard used in North America and most of Asia that provides 1.544-Mbps throughput and 24 channels for voice, data, video, or audio signals. T1s rely on time division multiplexing and may use shielded or unshielded twisted pair, coaxial cable, fiber optics, or microwave links.

T3 A digital carrier standard used in North America and most of Asia that can carry the equivalent of 672 channels for voice, data, video, or audio, with a maximum data throughput of 44.736 Mbps (typically rounded up to 45 Mbps for purposes of discussion). T3s rely on time division multiplexing and require either fiber-optic or microwave transmission media.

TA (terminal adapter) A device used to convert digital signals into analog signals for use with ISDN phones and other analog devices. TAs are sometimes called ISDN modems.

TACACS+ (Terminal Access Controller Access Control System Plus) A Cisco proprietary protocol for AAA (access, authentication, and authorization). Like RADIUS, TACACS+ may use one of many authentication protocols. Unlike RADIUS, TACACS+ relies on TCP at the Network layer and allows for separation of the AAA services.

tape backup A relatively simple and economical backup method in which data is copied to magnetic tapes. In many environments, tape backups have been replaced with faster backup methods, such as copying to network or online storage.

T-carrier The term for any kind of leased line that follows the standards for T1s, fractional T1s, T1Cs, T2s, T3s, or T4s.

TCP (Transmission Control Protocol) A core protocol of the TCP/IP suite. TCP belongs to the Transport layer and provides reliable data delivery services.

TCP/IP (Transmission Control Protocol/Internet Protocol) A suite of networking protocols that includes TCP, IP, UDP, and many others. TCP/IP provides the foundation for data exchange across the Internet.

TCP/IP core protocols The major subprotocols of the TCP/IP suite, including IP, TCP, and UDP.

TDM (time division multiplexing) A method of multiplexing that assigns a time slot in the flow of communications to every node on the network and, in that time slot, carries data from that node.

TDR (time domain reflectometer) A high-end instrument for testing the qualities of a cable. It works by issuing a signal on a cable and measuring the way in which the signal bounces back (or reflects) to the TDR. Many performance testers rely on TDRs.

TE (terminal equipment) The end nodes (such as computers and printers) served by the same connection (such as an ISDN, DSL, or T1 link).

telecommunications closet Also known as a "telco room," the space that contains connectivity for groups of workstations in a defined area, plus cross-connections to IDFs or, in smaller organizations, an MDF. Large organizations may have several telecommunications closets per floor, but the TIA/EIA standard specifies at least one per floor.

Telecommunications Industry Association *See* TIA.

telephone test set *See* butt set.

Telnet A terminal emulation protocol used to log on to remote hosts using the TCP/IP protocol.

Temporal Key Integrity Protocol *See* TKIP.

terminal A device with little (if any) of its own processing or disk capacity that depends on a host to supply it with applications and data-processing services.

Terminal Access Controller Access Control System Plus *See* TACACS+.

terminal adapter *See* TA.

terminal equipment *See* TE.

terminator A resistor that is attached to each end of a bus-topology network and that causes the signal to stop rather than reflect back toward its source.

TFTP (Trivial File Transfer Protocol) A TCP/IP Application layer protocol that enables file transfers between computers. Unlike FTP, TFTP relies on UDP at the Transport layer using port 69, and it does not require a user to log on to the remote host.

TGS (Ticket-Granting Service) In Kerberos terminology, an application that runs on the KDC that issues Ticket-Granting Tickets to clients so that they need not request a new ticket for each new service they want to access.

TGT (Ticket-Granting Ticket) In Kerberos terminology, a ticket that enables a user to be accepted as a validated principal by multiple services.

Thicknet An IEEE Physical layer standard for achieving a maximum of 10-Mbps throughput over coaxial copper cable. Thicknet is also known as 10Base-5. Its maximum segment length is 500 meters, and it relies on a bus topology.

thin client A client that relies on another host for the majority of processing and hard disk resources necessary to run applications and share files over the network.

Thinnet An IEEE Physical layer standard for achieving 10-Mbps throughput over coaxial copper cable. Thinnet is also known as 10Base-2. Its maximum segment length is 185 meters, and it relies on a bus topology.

third-level support In network troubleshooting, a person or group with deep knowledge about specific networking topics to whom second-level support personnel escalate challenging problems.

thread A well-defined, self-contained subset of a process. Using threads within a process enables a program to efficiently perform related, multiple, simultaneous activities. Threads are also used to enable processes to use multiple processors on SMP systems.

three-tier architecture A client/server environment that uses middleware to translate requests between the client and server.

three-way handshake A three-step process in which Transport layer protocols establish a connection between nodes. The three steps are: Node A issues a SYN packet to node B, node B responds with SYN-ACK, and node A responds with ACK.

throughput The amount of data that a medium can transmit during a given period of time. Throughput is usually measured in megabits (1,000,000 bits) per second, or Mbps. The physical nature of every transmission media determines its potential throughput.

TIA (Telecommunications Industry Association) A subgroup of the EIA that focuses on standards for information technology, wireless, satellite, fiber optics, and telephone equipment. Probably the best known standards to come from the TIA/EIA alliance are its guidelines for how network cable should be installed in commercial buildings, known as the "TIA/EIA 568-B Series."

ticket In Kerberos terminology, a temporary set of credentials that a client uses to prove that its identity has been validated by the authentication service.

Ticket-Granting Service *See* TGS.

Ticket-Granting Ticket *See* TGT.

tiered topology WAN A type of WAN in which sites that are connected in star or ring formations are interconnected at different levels, with the interconnection points being organized into layers to form hierarchical groupings.

time division multiplexing *See* TDM.

time domain reflectometer *See* TDR.

Time to Live *See* TTL.

time sharing *See* preemptive multitasking.

TKIP (Temporal Key Integrity Protocol) An encryption key generation and management scheme used by 802.11i.

TLD (top-level domain) The highest-level category used to distinguish domain names—for example, .org, .com, and .net. A TLD is also known as the domain suffix.

TLS (Transport Layer Security) A version of SSL being standardized by the IETF (Internet Engineering Task Force). With TLS, the IETF aims to create a version of SSL that encrypts UDP as well as TCP transmissions. TLS, which is supported by new Web browsers, uses slightly different encryption algorithms than SSL, but otherwise is very similar to the most recent version of SSL.

token A special control frame that indicates to the rest of the network that a particular node has the right to transmit data.

token ring A networking technology developed by IBM in the 1980s. It relies upon direct links between nodes and a ring topology, using tokens to allow nodes to transmit data.

toll bypass A cost-savings benefit that results from organizations completing long-distance telephone calls over their packet-switched networks, thus bypassing tolls charged by common carriers on comparable PSTN calls.

tone generator A small electronic device that issues a signal on a wire pair. When used in conjunction with a tone locator, it can help locate the termination of a wire pair.

tone locator A small electronic device that emits a tone when it detects electrical activity on a wire pair. When used in conjunction with a tone generator, it can help locate the termination of a wire pair.

toner *See* tone generator.

top-level domain *See* TLD.

topology The physical layout of computers on a network.

tracepath A version of the traceroute utility found on some Linux distributions.

traceroute (tracert) A TCP/IP troubleshooting utility that uses ICMP to trace the path from one networked node to another, identifying all intermediate hops between the two nodes. Traceroute is useful for determining router or subnet connectivity problems. On Windows-based systems, the utility is known as tracert.

traffic The data transmission and processing activity taking place on a computer network at any given time.

traffic monitoring The process of determining how much data transfer activity is taking place on a network or network segment and notifying administrators when a segment becomes overloaded.

traffic policing A traffic-shaping technique in which the volume or rate of traffic traversing an interface is limited to a predefined maximum.

traffic shaping Manipulating certain characteristics of packets, data streams, or connections to manage the type and amount of traffic traversing a network or interface at any moment.

transceiver A device that transmits and receives signals.

transmission In networking, the application of data signals to a medium or the progress of data signals over a medium from one point to another.

Transmission Control Protocol *See* TCP.

Transmission Control Protocol/Internet Protocol *See* TCP/IP.

transmission media The means through which data are transmitted and received. Transmission media may be physical, such as wire or cable, or wireless, such as radio waves.

transmit To issue signals to the network medium.

transponder The equipment on a satellite that receives an uplinked signal from Earth, amplifies the signal, modifies its frequency, then retransmits it (in a downlink) to an antenna on Earth.

Transport layer The fourth layer of the OSI model. In the Transport layer, protocols ensure that data are transferred from point A to point B reliably and without errors. Transport layer services include flow control, acknowledgment, error correction, segmentation, reassembly, and sequencing.

Transport Layer Security *See* TLS.

tree A logical representation of multiple, hierarchical levels in a directory. It is called a tree because the whole structure shares a common starting point (the root), and from that point extends branches (or containers), which may extend additional branches, and so on.

Triple DES (3DES) The modern implementation of DES, which weaves a 56-bit key through data three times, each time using a different key.

Trivial File Transfer Protocol *See* TFTP.

Trojan *See* Trojan horse.

Trojan horse A program that disguises itself as something useful, but actually harms your system.

trunk port The interface on a switch capable of managing traffic from multiple VLANs.

trunking The aggregation of multiple logical connections in one physical connection between connectivity devices. In the case of VLANs, a trunk allows two switches to manage and exchange data between multiple VLANs.

trust relationship The relationship between two domains on a Windows Server network that allows a domain controller from one domain to authenticate users from the other domain.

TTL (Time to Live) A number that indicates the maximum duration that a packet can remain on the network before it is discarded. Although this field was originally meant to represent units of time, on modern networks it represents the number of router hops a datagram has endured. The TTL for datagrams is variable and configurable, but is usually set at 32 or 64. Each time a datagram passes through a router, its TTL is reduced by 1. When a router receives a datagram with a TTL equal to 1, the router discards that datagram.

tunnel A secured, virtual connection between two nodes on a VPN.

tunneling The process of encapsulating one type of protocol in another. Tunneling is the way in which higher-layer data is transported over VPNs by Layer 2 protocols.

twist ratio The number of twists per meter or foot in a twisted pair cable.

twisted pair A type of cable similar to telephone wiring that consists of color-coded pairs of insulated copper wires, each with a diameter of 0.4 to 0.8 mm, twisted around each other and encased in plastic coating.

two-factor authentication A process in which clients must supply two pieces of information to verify their identity and gain access to a system.

two-way transitive trust The security relationship between domains in the same domain tree in which one domain grants every other domain in the tree access to its resources and, in turn, that domain can access other domains' resources. When a new domain is added to a tree, it immediately shares a two-way trust with the other domains in the tree.

UDP (User Datagram Protocol) A core protocol in the TCP/IP suite that sits in the Transport layer of the OSI model. UDP is a connectionless transport service.

unicast address A type of IPv6 address that represents a single interface on a device.

unified communications The centralized management of multiple types of network-based communications, such as voice, video, fax, and messaging services.

unified messaging The centralized management of multiple types of network-based communications, such as voice, video, fax, and messaging services.

uninterruptible power supply *See* UPS.

UNIX A client or server operating system originally developed by researchers at AT&T Bell Laboratories in 1969. UNIX is a proprietary operating system, but similar operating systems, such as Linux, are freely distributable.

unpopulated segment A network segment that does not contain end nodes, such as workstations. Unpopulated segments are also called link segments.

unshielded twisted pair *See* UTP.

upgrade A significant change to an application's existing code, typically designed to improve functionality or add new features.

uplink In the context of wireless transmission, the connection between a client's transceiver and a carrier's antenna.

uplink port A port on a connectivity device used to connect it to another connectivity device.

UPN (user principal name) The preferred Active Directory naming convention for objects when used in informal situations. This name looks like a familiar Internet address, including the positioning of the domain name after the @ sign. UPNs are typically used for e-mail and related Internet services.

UPN (user principal name) suffix The portion of a universal principal name (in Active Directory's naming conventions) that follows the @ sign.

UPS (uninterruptible power supply) A battery-operated power source directly attached to one or more devices and to a power supply (such as a wall outlet) that prevents undesired features of the power source from harming the device or interrupting its services.

upstream A term used to describe data traffic that flows from a customer's site to a carrier's facility. In asymmetrical communications, upstream throughput is usually much lower than downstream throughput. In symmetrical communications, upstream and downstream throughputs are equal.

uptime The duration or percentage of time a system or network functions normally between failures.

user A person who uses a computer.

user account A record of a user that contains all of her properties, including rights to resources, password, username, and so on.

user agent In SIP terminology, a user agent client or user agent server.

user agent client In SIP terminology, end-user devices such as workstations, tablet computers, smartphones, or IP telephones. A user agent client initiates a SIP connection.

user agent server In SIP terminology, a server that responds to user agent clients' requests for session initiation and termination.

User Datagram Protocol *See* UDP.

user principal name *See* UPN.

UTP (unshielded twisted pair) A type of cabling that consists of one or more insulated wire pairs encased in a plastic sheath. As its name implies, UTP does not contain additional shielding for the twisted pairs. As a result, UTP is both less expensive and less resistant to noise than STP.

VA *See* volt-amp.

vertical cross-connect Part of a network's backbone that supplies connectivity between a building's floors. For example, vertical cross-connects might connect an MDF and an IDF or IDFs and telecommunications closets within a building.

video bridge *See* MCU.

video over IP Any type of video service, including IPTV, videoconferencing, and streaming video, that delivers video signals over packet-switched networks using the TCP/IP protocol suite.

video phone A type of phone that includes a screen and can decode compressed video and interpret transport and signaling protocols necessary for conducting videoconference sessions.

videoconferencing The real-time reception and transmission of images and audio among two or more locations.

video-on-demand A service in which a video stored as an encoded file is delivered to a viewer upon his request.

virtual adapter *See* vNIC.

virtual address *See* network address.

virtual appliance An image that includes the appropriate operating system, software, hardware specifications, and application configuration necessary for a prepackaged solution to run properly on a virtual machine.

virtual bridge An interface connecting a vNIC with a virtual or physical network, or a port on a virtual switch.

virtual circuit A connection between network nodes that, although based on potentially disparate physical links, logically appears to be a direct, dedicated link between those nodes.

virtual desktop A desktop operating environment that is hosted virtually, on a different physical computer from the one the user interacts with.

virtual local area network *See* VLAN.

virtual machine *See* VM.

virtual machine manager *See* hypervisor.

virtual memory The memory that is logically carved out of space on the hard drive and added to physical memory (RAM).

Virtual Network Computing *See* VNC.

virtual network interface card *See* vNIC.

virtual PBX *See* hosted PBX.

virtual private network *See* VPN.

virtual server A server that exists as a virtual machine, created and managed by virtualization software on a host, or physical, computer.

virtual switch A logically defined device that is created and managed by virtualization software and that operates at the Data Link layer. Ports on a virtual switch connect virtual machines with a network, whether virtual or physical, through the host's physical NIC.

virtual workstation A workstation that exists as a virtual machine, created and managed by virtualization software on a host, or physical, computer.

VirtualBox A virtualization software platform from Oracle.

virtualization The emulation of a computer, operating system environment, or application on a physical system.

virus A program that replicates itself to infect more computers, either through network connections or through external storage devices, such as USB drives, passed among users. Viruses might damage files or systems or simply annoy users by flashing messages or pictures on the screen or by causing the keyboard to beep.

VLAN (virtual local area network) A network within a network that is logically defined by grouping its devices' switch ports in the same broadcast domain. A VLAN can consist of any type of network node in any geographic location and can incorporate nodes connected to different switches.

VLAN trunking protocol *See* VTP.

VM (virtual machine) A computer that exists in emulation on a physical computer, or host machine. Multiple VMs may exist on one host where they share the physical computer's CPU, hard disk, memory, and network interfaces.

VMware A vendor that supplies the most popular types of workstation and server virtualization software. Used casually, the term *VMware* may also refer to the virtualization software distributed by the company.

VNC (virtual network computing) An open source system that enables a remote client (or viewer) workstation to manipulate and receive screen updates from a host. Examples of VNC software include RealVNC, TightVNC, and UltraVNC.

vNIC (virtual network interface card) A logically defined network interface associated with a virtual machine.

Voice over IP *See* VoIP.

VoIP (Voice over IP) The provision of telephone service over a packet-switched network running the TCP/IP protocol suite.

volt The measurement used to describe the degree of pressure an electrical current exerts on a conductor.

voltage The pressure (sometimes informally referred to as the strength) of an electrical current.

voltage event Any condition in which voltage exceeds or drops below predefined levels.

voltage event recorder A device that, when plugged into the same outlet that will be used by a network node, gathers data about the power that outlet will provide the node.

volt-amp (VA) A measure of electrical power. A volt-amp is the product of the voltage and current (measured in amps) of the electricity on a line.

voltmeter A device used to measure voltage (or electrical pressure) on an electrical circuit.

VPN (virtual private network) A logically constructed WAN that uses existing public transmission systems. VPNs can be created through the use of software or combined software and hardware solutions. This type of network allows an organization to carve out a private WAN through the Internet, serving only its offices, while keeping the data secure and isolated from other (public) traffic.

VPN concentrator A specialized device that authenticates VPN clients and establishes tunnels for VPN connections.

VTP (VLAN trunking protocol) Cisco's protocol for exchanging VLAN information over trunks. VTP allows one switch on a network to centrally manage all VLANs.

vulnerability A weakness of a system, process, or architecture that could lead to compromised information or unauthorized access to a network.

WAN (wide area network) A network that spans a long distance and connects two or more LANs.

WAN link A point-to-point connection between two nodes on a WAN.

WAP (wireless access point) *See* access point.

war chalking The use of chalk to draw symbols on a sidewalk or wall within range of an access point. The symbols, patterned after marks that hobos devised to indicate hospitable places for food or rest, indicate the access point's SSID and whether it's secured.

war driving The act of driving while running a laptop configured to detect and capture wireless data transmissions.

warm site A place where the computers, devices, and connectivity necessary to rebuild a network exist, though only some are appropriately configured, updated, or connected to match the network's current state.

wavelength The distance between corresponding points on a wave's cycle. Wavelength is inversely proportional to frequency.

wavelength division multiplexing *See* WDM.

WDM (wavelength division multiplexing) A multiplexing technique in which each signal on a fiber-optic cable is assigned a different wavelength, which equates to its own subchannel. Each wavelength is modulated with a data signal. In this manner, multiple signals can be simultaneously transmitted in the same direction over a length of fiber.

Web caching A technique in which Web pages are stored locally, either on a host or network, and then delivered to requesters more quickly than if they had been obtained from the original source.

Web server A computer that manages Web site services, such as supplying a Web page to multiple users on demand.

Webcast A streaming video, either on demand or live, that is delivered via the Web.

Well Known Ports The TCP/IP port numbers 0 to 1023, so named because they were long ago assigned by Internet authorities to popular services (for example, FTP and Telnet), and are, therefore, well known and frequently used.

WEP (Wired Equivalent Privacy) A key encryption technique for wireless networks that uses keys both to authenticate network clients and to encrypt data in transit.

WEP cracking A security exploit in which a hacker uses a program to discover a WEP key.

wide area network *See* WAN.

Wi-Fi *See* 802.11.

Wi-Fi Alliance An international, nonprofit organization dedicated to ensuring the interoperability of 802.11-capable devices.

Wi-Fi Protected Access *See* WPA.

WiMAX *See* 802.16.

WiMAX 2 *See* 802.16m.

Wired Equivalent Privacy *See* WEP.

wireless A type of signal made of electromagnetic energy that travels through the air.

wireless access point *See* access point.

wireless gateway An access point that provides routing functions and is used as a gateway.

wireless LAN *See* WLAN.

wireless router An access point that provides routing functions.

wireless spectrum A continuum of electromagnetic waves used for data and voice communication. The wireless spectrum (as defined by the FCC, which controls its use) spans frequencies between 9 KHz and 300 GHz. Each type of wireless service can be associated with one area of the wireless spectrum.

wiring schematic A graphical representation of a network's wired infrastructure.

WLAN (wireless LAN) A LAN that uses wireless connections for some or all of its transmissions.

workgroup In Microsoft terminology, a group of interconnected computers that share each other's resources without relying on a central file server.

workstation A computer that runs a desktop operating system and connects to a network.

Worldwide Interoperability for Microwave Access (WiMAX) *See* 802.16.

worm An unwanted program that travels between computers and across networks. Although worms do not alter other programs as viruses do, they can carry viruses.

WPA (Wi-Fi Protected Access) A wireless security method endorsed by the Wi-Fi Alliance that is considered a subset of the 802.11i standard. In WPA, authentication follows the same mechanism specified in 802.11i. The main difference between WPA and 802.11i is that WPA specifies RC4 encryption rather than AES.

WPA2 The name given to the 802.11i security standard by the Wi-Fi Alliance. The only difference between WPA2 and 802.11i is that WPA2 includes support for the older WPA security method.

WPA2-Enterprise An authentication scheme for Wi-Fi networks that combines WPA2 with RADIUS.

WPA cracking A security exploit in which a hacker uses a program to discover a WPA key.

WPA-Enterprise An authentication scheme for Wi-Fi networks that combines WPA with RADIUS.

X Window system A GUI environment for UNIX and Linux systems.

X.25 An analog, packet-switched WAN technology optimized for reliable, long-distance data transmission and standardized by the ITU in the mid-1970s. The X.25 standard specifies protocols at the Physical, Data Link, and Network layers of the OSI model. It provides excellent flow control and ensures data reliability over long distances by verifying the transmission at every node. X.25 can support a maximum of only 2-Mbps throughput.

XaaS (Anything as a Service, or Everything as a Service) A type of cloud computing in which the cloud assumes functions beyond networking, including, for example, monitoring, storage, applications, and virtual desktops.

xDSL The term used to refer to all varieties of DSL.

Xen An open source virtualization software platform from Citrix Systems.

Zero configuration *See* Zeroconf.

Zeroconf (Zero configuration) A collection of protocols that assigns link-local addresses, performs DNS functions, and discovers services, such as print services, available to the node.

zero-day exploit An exploit that takes advantage of a software vulnerability that hasn't yet become public, and is known only to the hacker who discovered it. Zero-day exploits are particularly dangerous, because the vulnerability is exploited before the software developer has the opportunity to provide a solution for it.

zipcord cable A relatively short fiber-optic cable in which two strands are arranged side by side in conjoined jackets, enabling full-duplex communication.

zone file A text file associated with a DNS zone that contains resource records identifying domains and their IP addresses.

zone transfer In DNS, the act of copying a primary name server's zone file to the secondary name server to ensure that both contain the same information.

appendix F

Answers to Network+ Practice Exam Questions

1. d. `access-list 110 deny TCP any any eq FTP`
2. a. 802.11g, c. 802.11b
3. e.

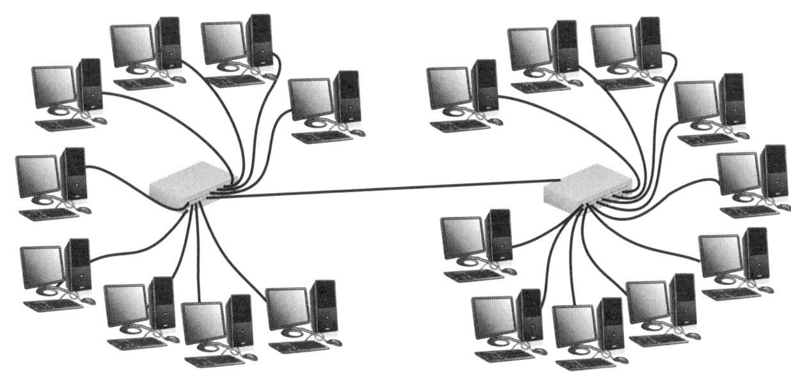

4. b. Bridged
5. c. Approximately 52 minutes
6. c. Cat 5
7. b. CARP
8. d. Establish a theory of probably cause
9. c. NMAP
10. d. Tracert
11. a. Full mesh
12. a. C3:00:50:00:FF:FF
13. a. 100Base-FX
14. b. CSU/DSU
15. a. LITE, c. 802.16m

16. e. Syslog
17. a. A T1 that connects to the national office via a router at the local franchise and a router at the national office and that uses a VSN to ensure the security of the data en route.
18. d. Trunking
19. b. Their workstations are located beyond the access point's range.
20. e. WPA2-Enterprise
21. e. SNMP
22. e. Microsoft's network is bounded by firewalls that do not accept incoming ICMP traffic.
23. e. 194.73.44.0
24. b. 10GBase-ER
25. e. NIPS
26. d. It replaces each outgoing packet's Source address field with a valid IP addres.
27. d. 100
28. a. Determines the locations of endpoints, d. Establishes sessions between endpoints
29. c. `ifconfig PRTSRV`
30. b. Port mirroring
31. c. Agent
32. a. SCP
33. d. Kerberos
34. b. Whether the firewall is placed in the appropriate location on the network,
    c. Whether the firewall has been configured to allow access from IP addresses in the satellite office
35. d. To establish VPN tunnels
36. b. Its TCP/IP protocol is not installed properly.
37. b. Crimping tool, c. Wire stripper
38. a. Cut-through switches
39. d. ::1
40. a. Hub, e. Repeater
41. c. To make more efficient use of limited numbers of legitimate IP addresses
42. e. IPSec
43. c. OSPF, e. EIGRP
44. e. All of the nodes could belong to a private network
45. e. All of the above
46. c. SSID
47. d. TCP, port 23

48. b. It identifies a host's IPv6 address.

49. a. SMTP

50. c. Remove the workstation's route to the default gateway whose IP address is 192.168.5.1

51. e. White with orange stripe and orange

52. b. Firewall log

53. b. SSL

54. d. To add logical addresses and properly route data

55. d. Telnet

56. b. Verify that the amount of resistance presented by terminators on coaxial cable networks is appropriate,
    c. Check for the presence of noise on a wire (by detecting extraneous voltage)

57. e. Virtual bridge

58. c. 255.255.0.0

59. b.

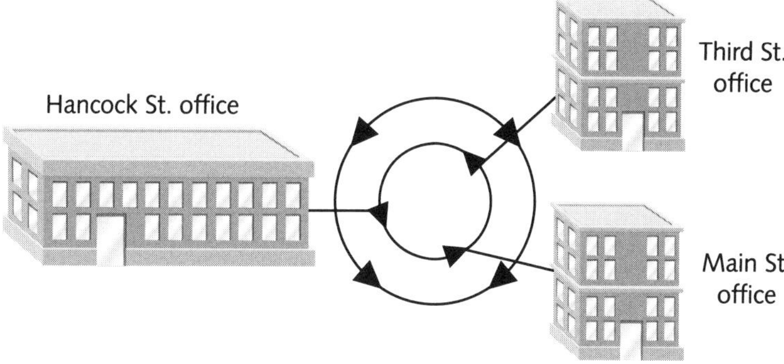

60. b. Punch-down block

61. a. They will not issue data to hosts other than the client that originated the request.

62. c. Internet layer

63. e. By default, the router has no access list and will therefore allow any inbound or outbound traffic.

64. c. Protocol analyzer

65. b. Change his gateway address.

66. e. Nothing; in Windows 7, the DHCP option is selected by default, and the client will obtain IP addressing information upon connecting to the network.

67. b. RealVNC

68. e. Router

69. d. Fiber-optic cable

70. c. They will be unable to access the Internet, other nodes on the WAN, and other nodes on the LAN.
71. a. RIP
72. c. 53
73. d. 255.255.255.224
74. c. L2TP
75. a. Scope
76. e. 802.11n
77. c. It enables switches to calculate paths that avoid potential loops and artificially blocks the links that would complete a loop.
78. a. EAPoL
79. d. 169.254.1.120
80. e. Your wireless networking client will be able to see the access point and successfully associate with it.
81. a. Identify nodes belonging to a multicast group
82. b. VoIP call connection
83. At point E
84. a. Unicast
85. e. NIC teaming
86. d. 15
87. d. Butt set
88. c. MPLS
89. d. 128
90. d. 802.11n
91. a. Traffic policing
92. d. You may set up a Web server on the company's private LAN, which is protected by a firewall.
93. d. Baselines
94. a. Entrance facilities
95. e. Event Viewer
96. a. `ipconfig /all` at the Windows command prompt
97. c. FF02
98. a. SONET
99. c. Stateless firewall, d. Packet-filtering firewall
100. b. Ethernet uses variably sized packets, whereas ATM uses fixed-sized cells

appendix **G**

Network Operating System Basics

A server's NOS (network operating system) manages resource sharing, user permissions, network access, addressing, and security and might perform other functions. CompTIA's Network+ exam does not require knowledge of NOSs; however, during your career as a networking professional, you will need to understand how NOSs are structured and how they accomplish their tasks. This appendix introduces the basic concepts related to NOSs. It also identifies features of the most popular NOSs: Windows Server 2008 R2, UNIX, and Linux. To learn more about NOSs, master the material required for CompTIA's Linux+ certification and Microsoft's Server certifications.

Characteristics of Network Operating Systems

Recall that most networks are based on a client/server architecture, in which a server enables multiple clients to share resources. Such sharing is managed by the NOS. However, that's not all an NOS provides. Among other things, an NOS must do the following:

- Centrally manage network resources, such as programs, data, and devices (for example, printers).
- Secure access to a network.
- Allow remote users to connect to a network.
- Allow users to connect to other networks (for example, the Internet).
- Back up data and make sure it's always available.
- Allow for simple additions of clients and resources.
- Monitor the status and functionality of network elements.
- Distribute programs and software updates to clients.
- Ensure efficient use of a server's capabilities.
- Provide fault tolerance in case of a hardware or software problem.

Not all of these functions are built in to every NOS installation; some are optional. When installing an NOS, you can accept the default settings or customize your configuration to more closely meet your needs. You can also take advantage of special services or enhancements that come with a basic NOS. For example, if you install Linux with only its minimum components, you may later choose to install the clustering service, which enables multiple servers to act as a single server, sharing the burden of NOS functions. The components included in each NOS and every version of a particular NOS vary. This variability is just one reason that you should plan your NOS installation carefully.

In this appendix, the word *server* refers to the hardware on which an NOS runs. In the field of networking, the word *server* may also refer to an application that runs on this hardware to provide a dedicated service. For example, although you may use an HP server as your hardware, you could run the Sendmail application as your mail server on that hardware. Some specialized server programs come with an NOS—for example, many versions of Linux include the Apache Web server program.

Although every NOS discussed in this appendix supports file and print sharing, plus a host of other services, NOSs differ in how they achieve those functions, what type of environment they suit, and how they are administered. Next, you will learn how to evaluate an NOS for use on your network.

Network Operating Systems and Servers

Most networks rely on servers that exceed the minimum hardware requirements suggested by the software vendor. Every situation will vary, but to determine the optimal hardware for your servers, be sure to ask the following questions:

- What kinds of applications will run on the server?
- How many clients will connect to the server?
- How much storage space will each user need?
- How many virtual machines will the server support?
- What types of interfaces does the network require?
- How much downtime, if any, is acceptable?
- What can the organization afford?

The first question in this list is perhaps the most important. For example, you can purchase an inexpensive, low-end server that runs Linux adequately and suffices for resource sharing and simple application services. However, to perform more advanced functions and run resource-intensive applications on your network, you would need to invest in a server that has significantly more processing power and memory. Every application comes with different processor, RAM, and storage requirements. Before purchasing or upgrading a server, consult the installation guide for each application you intend to run. Also, analyze your plans for growth before making a hardware purchasing decision. Whereas high-end servers with massive processing and storage resources plus fault-tolerant components can cost as much as $10,000, your department may need only a $1000 server.

No matter what your needs, ensure that your hardware vendor has a reputation for high quality, dependability, and excellent technical support. Although you might be able to trim your costs on workstation hardware by using generic models, you should spend as much as necessary for a reliable server. A component failure in a server can cause problems for many people, whereas a workstation problem will probably affect only one person.

Client Support

The primary reason for using networks is to enable clients to communicate and share resources efficiently. Therefore, client support is one of the most important functions an NOS provides. Client support includes the following tasks:

- Creating and managing client accounts
- Enabling clients to connect to the network
- Allowing clients to share resources
- Managing clients' access to shared resources
- Facilitating communication between clients

You are already familiar with the way lower-layer protocols assist clients and servers in communication. The following discussion provides a general view of client/server communication from the higher layers of the OSI model.

Client/Server Communication Both the client software and the NOS participate in logging a client on to the server. Although clients and their software may differ, the process of logging on is similar in all NOSs, no matter what clients are involved. First, the user launches the client software from his desktop. Then, he enters his credentials (normally, a username and password) and presses the Enter key. At this point, a service on the client workstation, called the **redirector**, intercepts the request to determine whether it should be handled by the client or by the server. A redirector belongs to the Presentation layer of the OSI model. It's a service of both the NOS and the client's desktop operating system. After the client's redirector decides that the request is meant for the server, the client transmits this data over the network to the server. (If the redirector had determined that the request was meant for the client, rather than the server, it would have issued the request to the client's processor.) For security's sake, most modern clients will encrypt username and password information before transmitting it to the network media. Encryption is another Presentation layer function.

At the server, the NOS receives the client's request for service and decrypts it, if necessary. Next, it attempts to authenticate the user's credentials. If authentication succeeds, the NOS responds to the client by granting it access to resources on the network, according to limitations specified for this client. Figure G-1 depicts the process of a client connecting to an NOS.

After the client has successfully logged on, the client software communicates with the NOS each time the client requests services from the server. For example, if you wanted to open a file on the server's hard drive, you would interact with your workstation's operating system to make the file request; the file request would then be intercepted by the redirector and passed to the server via the client software. To expedite access to directories whose files you frequently require, you can **map** a drive to that directory. Mapping involves associating a letter, such as *M* or *T*, with a disk, directory, or other resource (such as a CD-ROM tower). Logon scripts, which run automatically after a client authenticates, often map drives to directories on the server that contain files required by client applications.

In the early days of networking, client software from one manufacturer could not always communicate with network software from another manufacturer. One difference between

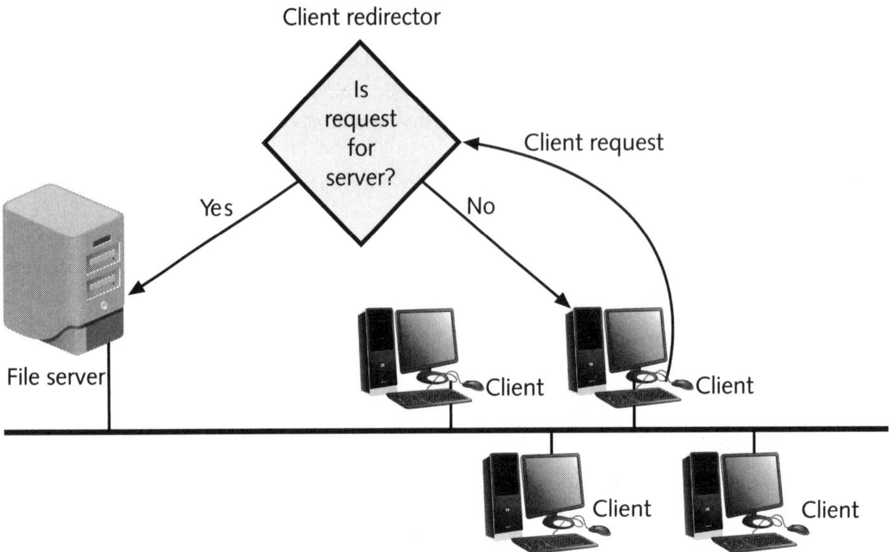

Figure G-1 A client connecting to an NOS

NOSs is the **file access protocol** that enables one system to access resources stored on another system on the network. For example, a Windows client typically communicates with a Windows server using the **CIFS (Common Internet File System)** file access protocol. CIFS was developed by Microsoft as a way for clients to request file and print services from servers. It's a more recent version of an older client/server communications protocol, **SMB (Server Message Block)**, which originated at IBM and then was adopted and further developed by Microsoft.

Thanks in part to broader support of multiple file access protocols, now most every type of client can authenticate and access resources via any NOS. Usually, the NOS manufacturer supplies a preferred client software package for each popular type of client. For example, Microsoft requires Windows workstations connecting to its Windows Server NOSs to have Client for Microsoft Networks running. Client software other than that recommended by the NOS manufacturer might work, but it's wise to follow the NOS manufacturer's guidelines.

In some instances, a piece of software called **middleware** is necessary to translate requests and responses between the client and server. Middleware prevents the need for a shared application to function differently for each different type of client. It stands between the client and the server and performs some of the tasks that an application in a simple client/server relationship would otherwise perform. Typically, middleware runs as a separate service—and sometimes on a separate physical server—from the NOS. To interact with the middleware, a client issues a request to the middleware. Middleware reformats the request in such a way that the application on the server can interpret it. When the application responds, middleware translates the response into the client's preferred format and issues the response to the client. Middleware may be used as a messaging service between clients and servers, as a universal query language for databases, or as a means of coordinating processes between multiple servers that need to work together in servicing clients.

For example, suppose a library's database of materials is contained on a UNIX server. Some library workstations run the Macintosh desktop operating system, while others run Windows 7 and Linux. Each workstation must be able to access the database of materials. Ideally, all client interfaces would look similar, so that a patron who uses a Macintosh workstation one day could use a Linux workstation the next day without even noticing the difference. Further, the library can only manage one large database; it cannot maintain a separate database for each different type of client. In this case, a server running the database middleware can accept the queries from each different type of client. When a Linux workstation submits a query, the database middleware interprets the Linux instruction, reformats it, and then issues the standardized query to the database. The database middleware server might next accept a query from a Macintosh computer, which it then reformats into a standardized query for the database. In this way, the same database can be used by multiple different clients.

A client/server environment that incorporates middleware in this fashion is said to have a **three-tier architecture** because of its three layers: client, middleware, and server. To take advantage of a three-tier architecture, a client workstation requires the appropriate client software, for example, a Web browser or remote Terminal Services client. Figure G-2 illustrates the concept of middleware.

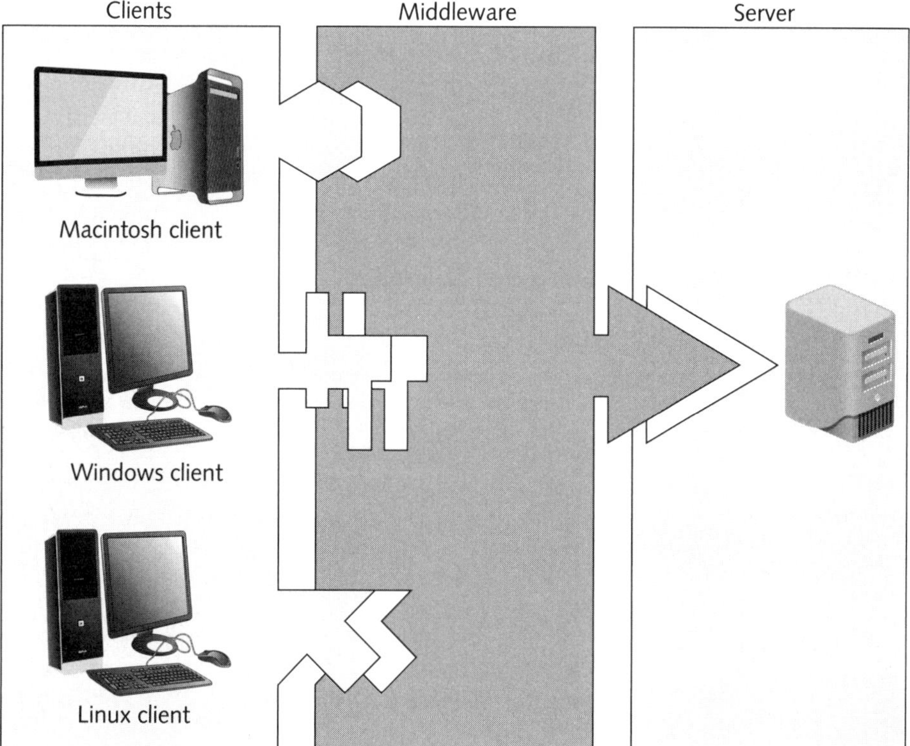

Figure G-2 Middleware between clients and a server

Users and Groups After an NOS authenticates a client, it grants the client access to the services and resources it manages. The type of access a client (or user) has depends on her **user account** and the groups to which she's assigned. The most privileged user account on a system is the administrator. On a UNIX or Linux system, the account is also known as root. The administrator, or root, has unlimited rights to resources and objects managed by a server or domain. When you install an NOS, this account is created by default.

You have probably worked with enough computers and networks to know why usernames are necessary: to grant each user on a network access to files and other shared resources. To manage network access more easily, you can combine users with similar needs and restrictions into groups.

In every NOS, **groups** form the basis for resource and account management. Many network administrators create groups according to department or, even more specifically, according to job function within a department. They then assign different file or directory access rights to each group. For example, on a high school's network, the administrator may create a group called Students for the students and a group called Teachers for the teachers. The administrator could then easily grant the Teachers group rights to view all attendance and grade records on the server, but deny the same access to the Students group.

To better understand the role of groups in resource sharing, first consider their use on a relatively small scale. Suppose you are the network administrator for a public school system. You might want to give all teachers and students access to run instructional programs from a network directory called PROGRAMS. In addition, you might want to allow teachers to install their own instructional programs in this same directory. Meanwhile, you need to allow teachers and principals to record grade information in a central database called GRADES. Of course, you don't want to allow students to read information from this database. Finally, you might want principals to use a shared drive called STAFF to store the teachers' performance review information, which should not be accessible to teachers or students. Table G-1 illustrates how you can provide this security by dividing separate users into three groups: teachers, students, and principals.

Table G-1 Providing security through groups

Group	Rights to PROGRAMS	Rights to GRADES	Rights to STAFF
Teachers	Read, modify	Full control	No access
Students	Read	No access	No access
Principals	No access	Read, modify	Full control

Plan your groups carefully. Creating many groups (for example, a separate group for every job classification in your organization) might impose as much of an administrative burden as not using any groups.

After an NOS authenticates a user, it checks the username against a list of resources and their access restrictions list. If the username is part of a group with specific access permissions or restrictions, the system will apply those same permissions and restrictions to the user's account.

For simpler management, groups can be nested (one within another) or arranged hierarchically (multiple levels of nested groups) according to the type of access required by different types of users. The way groups are arranged will affect the permissions granted to each group's members. For example, if you created a group called Assistants within the Teachers group for classroom assistants, the Assistants group would be nested within the Teachers group and would, by default, share the same permissions as the Teachers group. Such permissions are called **inherited** because they are passed down from the parent group (Teachers) to the child group (Assistants). If you wanted to restrict the Assistants users from seeing student grades, you would have to separately assign restrictions to the Assistants group for that purpose. After you assign different rights to the Assistants group, you have begun creating a hierarchical structure of groups. NOSs differ slightly in how they treat inherited permissions, and enumerating these differences is beyond the scope of this book. However, if you are a network administrator, you must thoroughly understand the implications of hierarchical group arrangements.

After the user and group restrictions are applied, the client is allowed to share resources on the network, including data, data storage space, applications, and peripherals. To understand how NOSs enable resource sharing, it's useful to first understand how they identify and organize network elements.

Directory Services

Modern NOSs follow similar patterns for organizing information about network elements, such as users, printers, servers, data files, and applications. This information is kept in a directory. A **directory** is a list that organizes resources and associates them with their characteristics. One example of a directory is a file system directory, which organizes files and their characteristics, such as file size, owner, type, and permissions. You may be familiar with this type of directory from manipulating or searching for files on your workstation. NOSs do use file system directories. However, these directories are different from and unrelated to the directories used to manage network clients, servers, and shared resources.

Modern versions of all popular NOSs use directories that adhere to standard structures and naming conventions set forth by **LDAP (Lightweight Directory Access Protocol)**, which is a protocol used to access information stored in a directory. By following the same directory standard, different NOSs can easily share information about their network elements.

According to the LDAP standard, a thing or person associated with the network is represented by an **object**. Objects may include users, printers, groups, computers, data files, and applications. Each object may have a multitude of **attributes**, or properties, associated with it. For example, a user object's attributes may include a first and last name, location, mail address, group membership, access restrictions, and so on. A printer object's attributes may include a location, model number, printing preferences (for example, double-sided printing), and so on.

In LDAP-compatible directories, a **schema** is the set of definitions of the kinds of objects and object-related information that the directory can contain. For example, one type of object is a printer, and one type of information associated with that object is the location of the printer. Thus, "printer" and "location of printer" would be definitions contained within the schema.

A directory's schema may contain two types of definitions: classes and attributes. **Classes** (also known as **object classes**) identify what type of objects can be specified in a directory. User account is an example of an object class. Another object class is Printer. An attribute is a characteristic associated with an object. For example, Home Directory is the name of an attribute associated with the User account object, whereas Location is an attribute associated with the Printer object. Classes are composed of many attributes. When you create an object, you also create a number of attributes that store information about that object. The object class and its attributes are then saved in the directory. Figure G-3 illustrates some schema elements associated with a User account object.

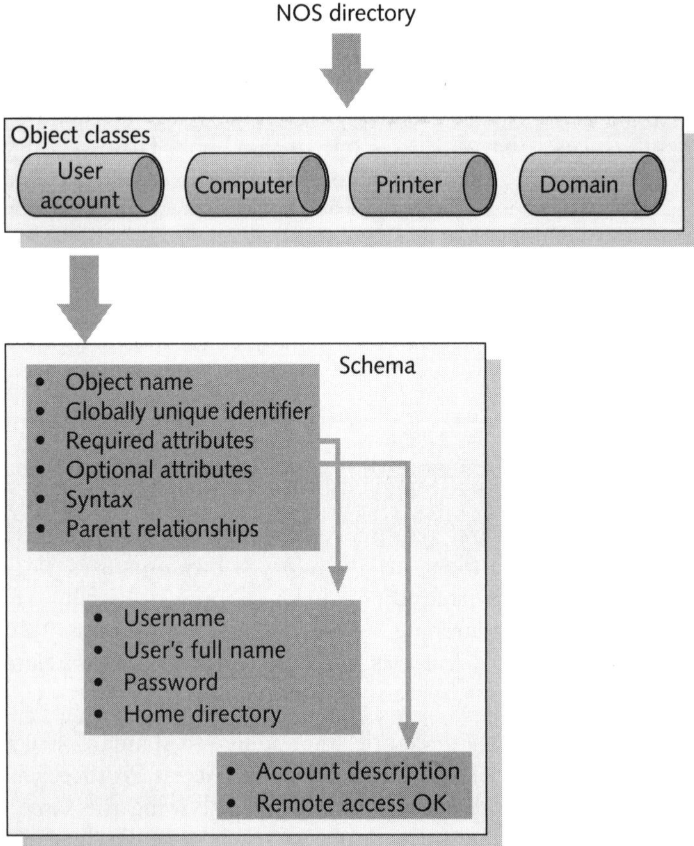

Figure G-3 Schema elements associated with a User account object

To better organize and manage objects, a network administrator places objects in **containers**, or **OUs** (**organizational units**). OUs are logically defined receptacles that serve only to assemble similar objects. Returning to the example of a school network, suppose each student, teacher, and principal were assigned a username and password for the network. Each of these users would be considered an object, and each would require an account. (An account is the record of a user that contains all of his properties, including rights to resources, password, name, and so on.) One way of organizing these objects is to put all the user objects in one OU called "Users."

Suppose the school provided a server and a room of workstations strictly for student use. The use of these computers would be restricted to applications and Internet access during only certain hours of the day. As the network administrator, you could gather the student usernames (or the Students group), the student server, the student printers, and the student applications in an OU called Students. You could associate the restricted network access (an attribute) with this OU so that these students could access the school's applications and the Internet only during certain hours of the day.

An OU can hold multiple objects. Also, an OU is a logical construct—that is, a means of organizing other things; it does not represent something real. An OU is different from a group because it can hold and apply parameters for many different types of objects, not only users.

In the LDAP standard, directories and their contents form trees. A **tree** is a logical representation of multiple, hierarchical levels within a directory. The term *tree* is drawn from the fact that the whole structure shares a common starting point (the root) and from that point extends **branches** (or containers), which may extend additional branches, and so on. Objects are the last items in the hierarchy connected to the branches and are sometimes called **leaf objects**. Figure G-4 depicts a simple directory tree.

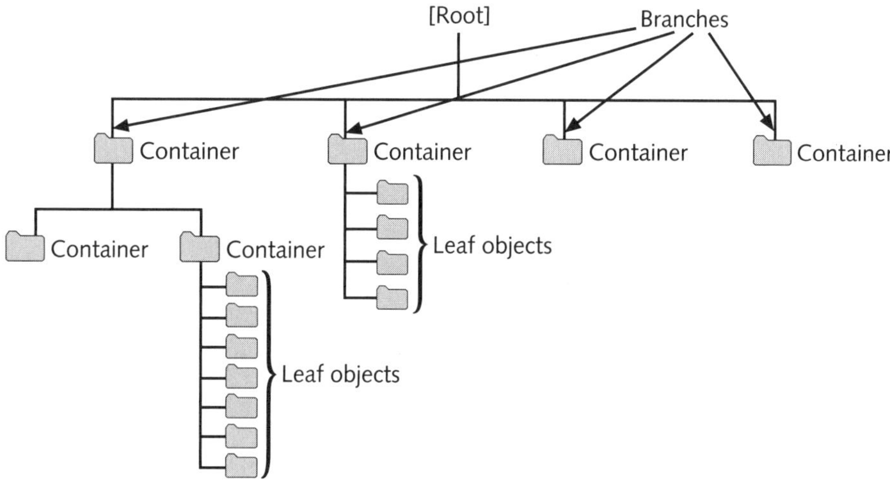

Figure G-4 A directory tree

Before you install an NOS, be sure to plan the directory tree with current and future needs in mind. For example, suppose you work at a new manufacturing firm, called Circuits Now, which produces high-quality, inexpensive circuit boards. You might decide to create a simple tree that branches into three OUs: users, printers, and computers. But if Circuits Now plans to open new manufacturing facilities sometime in the future (for instance, one devoted to making memory chips and another for transistors), you might want to call the first OU in the tree "circuit boards." This would separate the existing circuit board business from the new businesses, which would employ different people and require different resources. Figure G-5 shows both possible trees.

Directory trees are very flexible and, as a result, are usually more complex than the examples in Figure G-5. Chances are that you will enter an organization that has already established its tree, and you will need to understand the logic of that tree to perform your tasks. Later, you will learn about Active Directory, which is the LDAP-compatible directory used by the Windows Server 2003, Server 2008, and Server 2008 R2 NOSs.

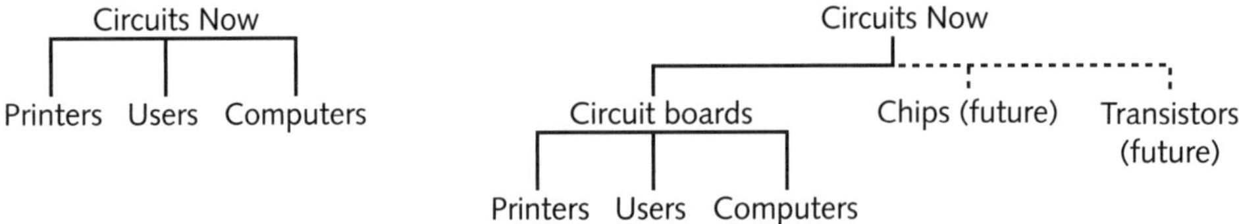

Figure G-5 Two possible directory trees for the same organization

Sharing Applications

One of the significant advantages of the client/server architecture is the ability to share resources, thereby reducing costs and the time required to manage the resources. In this section, you will learn how an NOS enables clients to share applications.

Shared applications are often installed on a file server that is specifically designed to run applications. In a small organization, however, they might be installed on the same server that provides other functions, such as Internet, security, or remote access services. In the case of proprietary software, you must purchase a license for the application that allows it to be shared among clients. In other words, you cannot legally purchase one licensed copy of Microsoft Word, install it on a server, and allow hundreds of your users to share it.

Software licensing practices vary from one vendor to another. A software vendor might sell an organization a fixed quantity of licenses, which allows only that number of clients to use the application simultaneously. This type of licensing is known as **per user** licensing. For example, suppose a life sciences library purchases a 20-user license for a database of full-text articles from a collection of *Biology* journals. If 20 users are running the database, the 21st person who attempts to access the database will receive a message announcing that access to the database is prohibited because all of the licenses are currently in use. Other software vendors sell a separate license for each *potential* user. Regardless of whether the user is accessing an application, a license is reserved so that the user will not be denied access. This practice is commonly known as **per seat** licensing. For example, if the life sciences library wanted to make sure each of its 15 employees could access the *Biology* journal database at any time, it would choose to purchase licenses for each of the employees. The application on the server could verify the user through a logon ID or the workstation's network address, for example. A third licensing option is the **site license**, which for a fixed price allows an unlimited number of users to legally access an application. In general, a site license is most economical for applications shared by many people (for example, if the life sciences library shared its *Biology* journal database with all of the students on a university campus), whereas for small numbers of users, per seat or per user licenses are more economical.

After you have purchased the appropriate type and number of licenses, you are ready to install the application on a server. Before doing so, however, make sure your server has enough free hard drive space, memory, and processing power to run the application. Then follow the software manufacturer's guidelines for a server installation. Depending on the application, this process might be the same as installing the application on a workstation or it might be much different.

After installing the software on a server, you are ready to make it available to clients. Through the NOS, assign users rights to the directories where the application's files are installed. Users will at least need rights to access and read files in those directories. For some applications, you might also need to give users rights to create, delete, or modify files associated with the application. For example, a database program may create a small temporary file on the server when a user launches the program to indicate to other potential users that the database is open. If this is the case, users must have rights to create files in the directory where this temporary file is kept. An application's installation guidelines will indicate the rights you need to assign users for each of the application's directories.

Next, you will need to provide users with a way to access the application. For example, you can create an icon on the user's desktop that is associated with the application file. When the user double-clicks the icon, her client software issues a request for the server to open the application. In response, the NOS sends a part of the program to her workstation, where it will be held in RAM. This allows the user to interact with the program quickly, without having to relay every command over the network to the server. As the user works with the application, the amount of processing that occurs on her workstation versus the amount of processing that the server handles will vary according to the network architecture.

You might wonder how an application can operate efficiently or accurately when multiple users are simultaneously accessing its files. After all, an application's program file is a single resource. If two or more network users double-click their application icons simultaneously, how does the application know which client to respond to? In fact, the NOS is responsible for arbitrating access to these files. In the case of multiple users simultaneously launching a network application from their desktop icons, the NOS will respond to one request, then the next, then the next, each time issuing a copy of the program to the client's RAM. In this way, each client is technically working with a separate instance of the application.

Shared access becomes more problematic when multiple users are simultaneously accessing the same data files as well as the same program files. For example, consider an online auction site, which accepts bids on many items from many Internet users. Imagine that an auction is nearing a close with three users simultaneously bidding on the same flat-screen TV. How does the auction site's database accept bid data for that TV from multiple sources? One solution to this problem is middleware. The three Internet bidders cannot directly modify the database located on the auction site's server. Instead, a middleware program on the server accepts data from the clients. If the database is not busy, the middleware passes a bid to the database. If the database is busy (or open), the middleware queues the bids (forces them to wait) until the database is ready to rewrite its existing data, then passes one bid, then another, and another, to the database until its queue is empty. In this way, only one client's data can be written to the database at any point in time.

Sharing Printers

Sharing peripherals, such as printers, can increase the efficiency of managing resources and reduce costs for an organization. In this section, you will learn how networks enable clients to share printers. Sharing other peripheral devices, such as plotters, works in a similar manner.

In most cases, an organization designates a server as the print server—that is, as the server in charge of managing print services. A printer may be directly attached to the print server or, more likely, be attached to the network in a location convenient for the users. A printer directly attached to the network requires its own NIC and network address, as with any network node. In other cases, shared printers may be attached to networked workstations. For these printers to be accessible, the workstation must be turned on and functioning properly. Figure G-6 depicts multiple ways to share printers on a network.

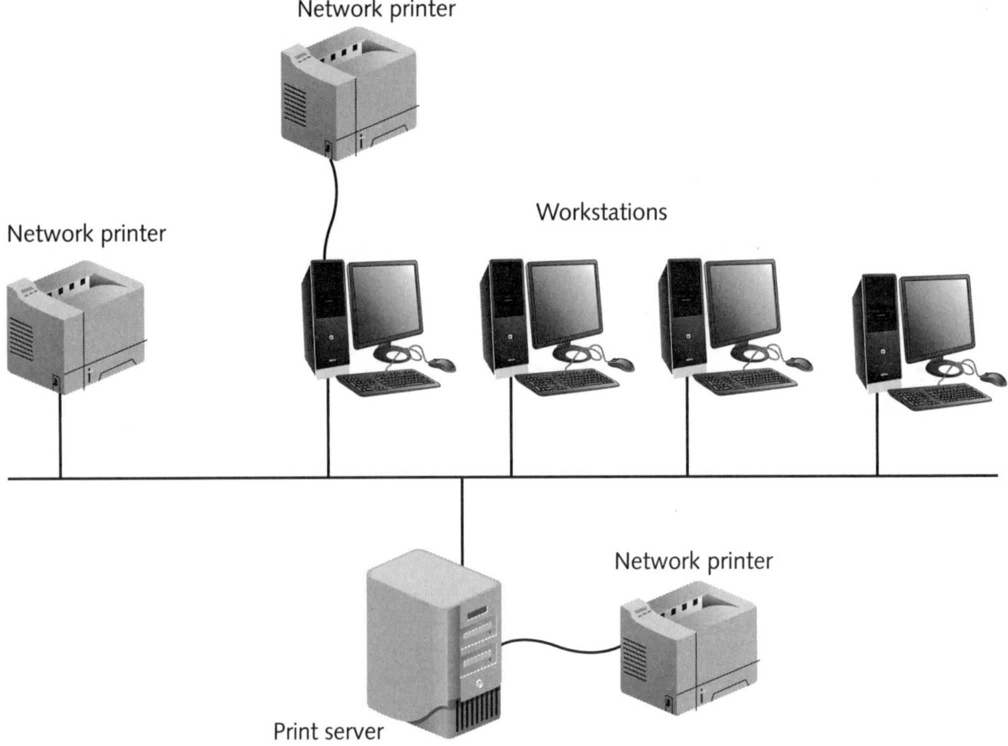

Figure G-6 Shared printers on a network

After the printer is physically connected to the network, it needs to be recognized and managed by the NOS before users can access it. Different NOSs present different interfaces for managing printers, but all NOSs can do the following:

- Create an object that identifies the printer to the rest of the network.
- Assign the printer a unique name.
- Install drivers associated with the printer.
- Set printer attributes, such as location and printing preferences.
- Establish or limit access to the printer.
- Remotely test and monitor printer functionality.
- Update and maintain printer drivers.
- Manage print jobs, including modifying a job's priority or deleting jobs from the queue.

As you create a new printer, the NOS will require you to install a printer driver, unless one is already installed on the server. This makes the printer's device driver files accessible to users who want to send jobs to that printer. Before users can access the printer, however, you must ensure that they have proper rights to the printer's queue. The **printer queue** (or *share,* as it is known in Microsoft terminology) is a logical representation of the printer's input and output.

That is, a queue does not physically exist, but rather acts as a sort of virtual in-box for the printer. When a user prints a document, he sends the document to the printer queue. To send it to the printer queue, he must have rights to access that queue. As with shared data, the rights to shared printers can vary. Users might have minimal privileges that allow them to simply send jobs to the printer, or they might have advanced privileges that allow them to change the priority of print jobs in the queue, or even (in the case of an administrator) change the name of the queue.

Networked printers appear as icons in the Printers folder on Windows and Macintosh workstations, just as local printers would appear. After they have found a networked printer, users can send documents to that printer just as they would send documents to a local printer. When a user chooses to print, the client redirector determines whether the request should be transmitted to the network or remain at the workstation. On the network, the user's request gets passed to the print server, which puts the job into the appropriate printer queue for transmission to the printer.

Managing System Resources

Because a server's system resources are limited and are required by multiple users, it is important to make the best use of them. Modern NOSs have capabilities that maximize the use of a server's memory, processor, bus, and hard drive. The result is that a server can accommodate more client requests faster—thus improving overall network performance. In the following sections, you will learn about some NOS techniques for managing a server's resources.

Memory From working with computers, you might already be familiar with the technique of using virtual memory to boost the total memory available to a system. Servers can use both physical and virtual memory, too, as this section describes.

Physical memory refers to the RAM chips that are installed on the computer's system board and whose sole function is to provide memory to that machine. The amount of physical memory required by your server varies depending on the tasks that it performs. For example, the minimum amount of physical memory required to run the Standard Edition of Windows Server 2008 R2 (the version of Windows Server 2008 R2 designed to meet the needs of most businesses) is 512 MB. However, if you intend to host virtual machines and run file and print sharing, Internet, and remote access services on one server, additional physical memory will ensure better performance. Microsoft recommends using at least 2 GB for optimal performance.

Another type of memory may be logically carved out of space on the hard drive for temporary use. In this arrangement, both the space on the hard drive and the RAM together form **virtual memory**. Virtual memory is stored on the hard drive as a **page file** (also known as a **paging file** or a **swap file**), the use of which is managed by the operating system. Each time the system exceeds its available RAM, blocks of information, called pages, are moved out of RAM and into virtual memory on disk. This technique is called **paging**. When the processor requires the information moved to the page file, the blocks are moved back from virtual memory into RAM.

Virtual memory is both a blessing and a curse. On the one hand, if your server has plenty of hard drive space, you can use virtual memory to easily expand the memory available to server applications. This is a great advantage when a process temporarily needs more memory than the physical memory can provide. Virtual memory is typically engaged by default; it requires no user or administrator intervention and is accessed without the clients' knowledge. (However, as a network administrator, you can modify the amount of hard drive space available for virtual memory.) On the other hand, using virtual memory slows operations because accessing a hard drive takes longer than accessing physical memory. Therefore, an excessive reliance on virtual memory will cost you in terms of performance.

Multitasking Another technique that helps servers use their system resources more efficiently is **multitasking**, which is the execution of multiple tasks at one time. The ability to multitask enables a processor to perform many different operations in a very brief period of time. If you have used multiple programs on a desktop computer, you have taken advantage of your operating system's multitasking capability. All of the major NOSs are capable of multitasking. If they weren't, network performance would be considerably slower because busy servers are continually receiving and responding to multiple requests.

Note that multitasking does not mean performing more than one operation simultaneously. A computer can only process multiple operations simultaneously if it has more than one processor. In UNIX, Linux, Windows Server 2008, and Windows Server 2008 R2, the server performs one task at a time, allowing one program to use the processor for a certain period of time, and then suspending that program to allow another program to use the processor. Thus, each program has to take turns loading and running. Because no two tasks are ever actually performed at one time, this capability is more accurately referred to as **preemptive multitasking**—or, in UNIX terms, **time sharing**. Preemptive multitasking happens so quickly, however, that the average user would probably think that multiple tasks were occurring simultaneously.

Multiprocessing Before you learn about the next method of managing system resources, you need to understand the terms used when discussing data processing. A **process** is a routine of sequential instructions that runs until it has achieved its goal. When it is running, a word-processing program's executable file is an example of a process. A **thread** is a self-contained, well-defined task within a process. A process may contain many threads, each of which may run independently of the others. All processes have at least one thread—the main thread. For example, to eliminate the waiting time when you save a file in your word processor, the programmer who wrote the word-processor program might have designed the file save operation as a separate thread. That is, the file save part of the program happens in a thread that is independent of the main thread. This independent execution allows you to continue typing while a document is being written to the disk, for example.

On systems with only one processor, only one thread can be handled at any time. Thus, if a number of programs are running simultaneously, no matter how fast the processor, a number of processes and threads will be left to await execution. Using multiple processors allows different threads to run on different processors. The support and use of multiple processors to handle multiple threads is known as **multiprocessing**. Multiprocessing is often used on servers as a technique to improve response time. To take advantage of more than one processor on a computer, its operating system must be capable of multiprocessing. Depending on the edition, Windows Server 2008 R2 may support up to 64 processors.

Multiprocessing splits tasks among more than one processor to expedite the completion of any single instruction. To understand this concept, think of a busy metropolitan freeway during rush hour. If five lanes are available for traffic, drivers can pick any lane—preferably the fastest lane—to get home as soon as possible. If traffic in one lane slows, drivers may choose another, less-congested lane. This ability to move from lane to lane allows all traffic to move faster. If the same amount of traffic had to pass through only one lane, everyone would go slower and get home later. In the same way, multiple processors can handle more instructions more rapidly than a single processor could.

Modern NOSs support a special type of multiprocessing called **symmetric multiprocessing**, which splits all operations equally among two or more processors. Another type of multiprocessing, **asymmetric multiprocessing**, assigns each subtask to a specific processor. Continuing the freeway analogy, asymmetric multiprocessing would assign all semitrucks to the far-right lane, all pickup trucks to the second-to-the right lane, all compact cars to the far-left lane, and so on. The efficiency of each multiprocessing model is open to debate, but, in general, symmetric processing completes operations more quickly because the processing load is more evenly distributed.

Multiprocessing offers a great advantage to servers with high processor usage—that is, servers that perform numerous tasks simultaneously. If an organization uses its server merely for occasional file and print sharing, however, multiple processors might not be necessary. Therefore, carefully assess your processing needs before purchasing a server with multiple processors. Some processing bottlenecks are not actually caused by the processor—but rather by the time it takes to access the server's hard drives or by problems related to cabling or connectivity devices.

Windows Server 2008 R2

Windows Server 2008 R2 is the latest version of Microsoft's NOS. It's an enhancement of its predecessor, Windows Server 2008, though many of the older NOS's features remain in the newer version. In particular, Windows Server 2008 R2 provides enhanced virtualization and power management features. Windows-based NOSs are known for their intuitive graphical user interface, multitasking capabilities, and compatibility with a huge array of applications. A **GUI** (**graphical user interface**; pronounced "gooey") is a pictorial representation of computer functions that, in the case of NOSs, enables administrators to manage files, users, groups, security, printers, and so on. Windows Server 2008 R2 comes in several editions. Although special-purpose versions also exist, the most commonly installed versions are Standard Edition, Enterprise Edition, and Datacenter Edition. Differences between these editions can be summarized as follows:

- *Standard Edition*—Provides essential resource sharing and management features necessary for most businesses, plus Web and limited virtualization services; includes support for up to 32 GB of RAM and four processors performing symmetric multiprocessing
- *Enterprise Edition*—Provides all the services provided by the Standard Edition, plus sophisticated VPN services and failover clustering for high-availability environments; includes support for up to 1 TB of RAM and eight processors performing symmetric multiprocessing
- *Datacenter Edition*—Provides all the services provided by the Enterprise Edition, plus unlimited virtualization; includes support for up to 64 processors, up to 2 TB of RAM

Some general benefits of the Windows Server 2008 R2 NOSs include the following:

- Support for multiple processors, multitasking, and symmetric multiprocessing
- A comprehensive system for organizing and managing network objects, called Active Directory
- Simple centralized management of multiple clients, resources, and services
- Centralized management of all server functions through a single interface known as the Server Manager
- Multiple, integrated Web development and delivery services that incorporate a high degree of security and an easy-to-use administrator interface
- Support for modern protocols and security standards
- Excellent integration with other NOSs and support for many different client operating systems
- Integrated remote client services—for example, automatic software updates and client assistance
- Provisions for monitoring and improving server performance
- Sophisticated power consumption management for servers using multiple processors
- Support for high-performance, large-scale storage devices

Hardware Requirements

You have learned that servers generally require more processing power, memory, and hard drive space than do client workstations. In addition, servers may contain redundant components, such as multiple hard drives, self-monitoring firmware, multiple processors and NICs, or peripherals other than the common DVD-ROM drives. The type of servers you choose for your network will depend partly on your NOS. Each NOS demands specific server hardware.

An important resource for determining what kind of hardware to purchase for your Windows server is the Windows Server Catalog. The Windows Server Catalog lists all computer components proven to be compatible with Windows Server 2008 R2, and it can be found online at *www.windowsservercatalog.com*. Always consult this list before buying new hardware. Although hardware that is *not* listed on the Web site might work with Windows Server 2008 R2, Microsoft's technical support won't necessarily help you solve problems related to such hardware.

Table G-2 lists Microsoft's minimum server requirements for Windows Server 2008 R2, Standard Edition.

Minimum requirements specify the least amount of RAM, hard drive space, and processing power you must have to run the NOS. Your applications and performance demands, however, may require more resources. Some of the minimum requirements listed in Table G-2 (for example, the 1.4 GHz processor) may apply to the smallest test system but not to a realistic networking environment. Be sure to assess the optimal configuration for your network's server based on your environment's needs before you purchase new hardware. For instance, you should make a list of every application and utility you expect the server to run in addition to the NOS. Then look up the processor, memory, and hard drive requirements for each of those programs and estimate how significantly their requirements will affect your server's overall hardware requirements. It is easier and more efficient to perform an analysis before you install the server than to add hardware after your server is up and running.

Table G-2 Minimum hardware requirements for Windows Server 2008 R2, Standard Edition

Component	Requirement
Processor	1.4 GHz (x64) or Itanium processor (2 GHz or faster processor recommended).
Memory	512 MB of RAM is the absolute minimum, but at least 2 GB is recommended.
Hard drive	A hard drive supported by Windows Server 2008 R2 (as specified in the Windows Server Catalog) with a minimum of 10 GB of free space available for system files; 40 GB or more is recommended.
NIC	Although a NIC is not required by Windows Server 2008 R2, it is required to connect to a network. Use a NIC found in the Windows Server Catalog. The NOS supports the use of multiple NICs.
DVD-ROM	A DVD-ROM drive found in the Windows Server Catalog is required unless the installation will take place over the network.
Pointing device	A mouse or other pointing device found in the Windows Server Catalog.

NTFS (New Technology File System)

Windows Server 2008 R2 supports several **file systems**, or methods of organizing, managing, and accessing its files through logical structures and software routines. By default, however, this NOS establishes **NTFS** (**New Technology File System**) when installed on a server. Microsoft designed NTFS expressly for its Windows NT platform, which preceded earlier Windows Server versions.

To understand file systems, you must first understand the distribution of data on a disk. Disks are divided into allocation units (also known as clusters). Each allocation unit represents a small portion of the disk's space; depending on your operating system, the allocation unit's size might or might not be customizable. A number of allocation units combine to form a **partition**, which is a logically separate area of storage on the hard drive. Each partition can be installed with any type of file system that your NOS can interpret.

NTFS is secure, reliable, and makes it possible to compress files so they take up less space. At the same time, NTFS can handle massive files, and allow fast access to data, programs, and other shared resources. It is used on all versions of the Windows operating system since Windows NT. If you are working with Windows Server 2008 R2, Microsoft recommends choosing NTFS for your server's file system. Therefore, you should familiarize yourself with the following NTFS features:

- NTFS filenames can be a maximum of 255 characters long.
- NTFS stores file size information in 64-bit fields.
- NTFS files or partitions can theoretically be as large as 16 exabytes (2^{64} bytes).
- NTFS is required for Macintosh connectivity.

- NTFS incorporates sophisticated, customizable compression routines. These compression routines reduce the space taken by files by as much as 40 percent. A 10-GB database file, for example, could be squeezed into 6 GB of disk space.
- NTFS keeps a log of file system activity to facilitate recovery if a system crash occurs.
- NTFS is required for encryption and advanced access security for files, user accounts, and processes.
- NTFS improves fault tolerance through RAID and system file redundancy.

Note that NTFS partitions cannot be read by older operating systems, such as Windows 95, Windows 2000 Professional, and early versions of UNIX. However, owing to all the benefits listed previously, the only instance in which you should *not* use NTFS is if one of your server's applications is incompatible with this file system.

Active Directory

Earlier, you learned about directories, the methods for organizing and managing objects on the network. Windows Server NOSs use a directory service called **Active Directory**. This section provides an overview of how Active Directory is structured and how it uses standard naming conventions to better integrate with other networks. You'll also learn how Active Directory stores information for Windows domains.

Workgroups A Windows Server 2008 R2 network can be set up in a workgroup model or a domain model. This section describes the workgroup model. In the next section, you will learn about the more popular domain model.

A **workgroup** is a group of interconnected computers that share each other's resources without relying on a central server. In other words, a workgroup is a type of peer-to-peer network. As in any peer-to-peer network, each computer in the workgroup has its own database of user accounts and security privileges.

Because each computer maintains its own database, each user must have a separate account on each computer he wants to access. This decentralized management results in significantly more administration effort than a client/server Windows Server 2008 R2 network would require. In addition, workgroups are only practical for small networks with very few users. On the other hand, peer-to-peer networks such as a Windows Server 2008 R2 workgroup are simple to design and implement and may be the best solution for home or small office networks in which security concerns are minimal.

Domains In Windows Server terminology, the term **domain model** refers to a type of client/server network that relies on domains rather than on workgroups. A **domain** is a group of users, servers, and other resources that share a centralized database of account and security information. The database that domains use to record their objects and attributes is contained within Active Directory. Domains are established on a network to make it easier to organize and manage resources and security. For example, a university might create separate domains for each of the following colleges: Life Sciences, Humanities, Communications, and Engineering. Within the Engineering domain, additional domains such as Chemical Engineering, Industrial Engineering, Electrical Engineering, and Mechanical Engineering may be created, as shown in Figure G-7. In this example, all users, workstations, servers, printers, and other resources within the Engineering domain would share a distinct portion of the Active Directory database.

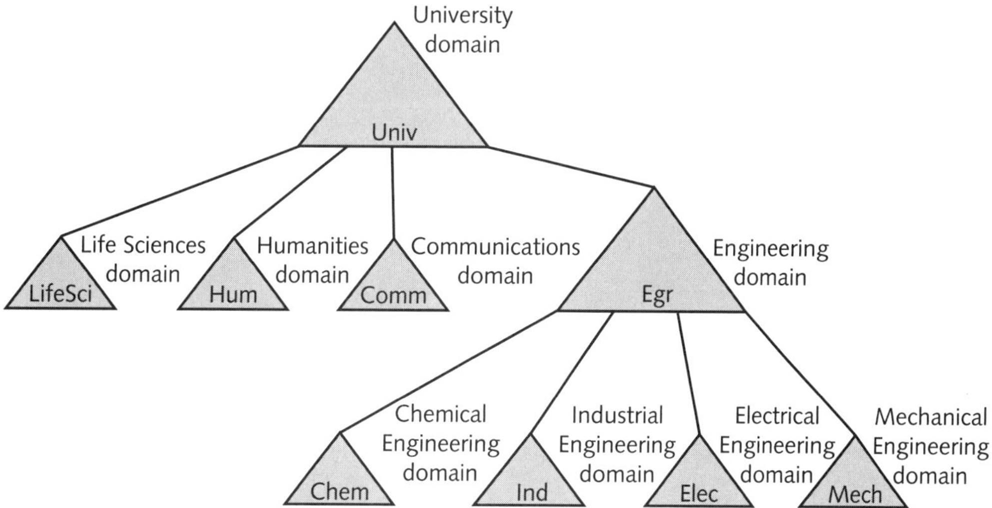

Figure G-7 Multiple domains in one organization

Keep in mind that a domain is not confined by geographical boundaries. Computers and users belonging to the university's Engineering domain may be located at five different campuses across a state, or even across the globe. No matter where they are located, they obtain their object, resource, and security information from the same database and the same portion of Active Directory.

Depending on the network environment, an administrator can define domains according to function, location, or security requirements. For example, if you worked at a large hospital whose WAN connected the city's central healthcare facility with several satellite clinics, you could create separate domains for each WAN location, or you could create separate domains for each clinical department, no matter where they are located. Alternately, you might choose to use only one domain and assign the different locations and specialties to different organizational units within the domain.

The directory containing information about objects in a domain resides on computers called **domain controllers**. A Windows Server 2008 R2 network may use multiple domain controllers. In fact, you should use at least two domain controllers on each network so that if one domain controller fails, the other will continue to retain your domains' databases. Windows Server 2008 R2 computers that do not store directory information are known as **member servers**. Because member servers do not contain a database of users and their associated attributes (such as password or permissions to files), member servers cannot authenticate users. Only domain controllers can do that. Every server on a Windows Server 2008 R2 network is either a domain controller or a member server.

When a network uses multiple domain controllers, a change to the database contained on one domain controller is copied to the databases on other domain controllers so that their databases are always identical. The process of copying directory data to multiple domain controllers is known as **replication.** Replication ensures redundancy so that, in case one of the domain controllers fails, another can step in to allow clients to log on to the network, be authenticated, and access resources. Figure G-8 illustrates a Windows Server 2008 R2 network built using the domain model.

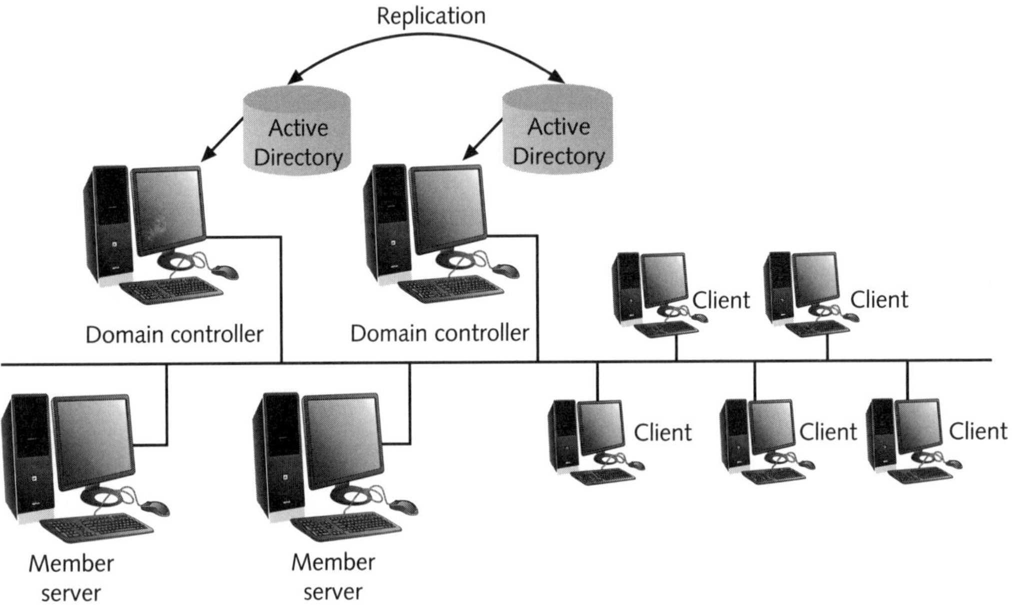

Figure G-8 Domain model on a Windows Server 2008 R2 network

OUs (Organizational Units) Earlier, you learned that NOSs use OUs (organizational units) to hold multiple objects that have similar characteristics. In Windows Server 2008 R2, an OU can contain several million objects. And each OU can contain multiple OUs. For example, suppose you were the network administrator for the university described previously, which has the following domains: Life Sciences, Humanities, Communications, and Engineering. You could choose to make additional domains within each college's domain. But suppose instead that the colleges weren't diverse or large enough to warrant separate domains. In that case, you might decide to group objects according to organizational units. For the Life Sciences domain, you might create the following OUs that correspond to the Life Sciences departments: Biology, Geology, Zoology, and Botany. In addition, you might want to create OUs for the buildings associated with each department. For example, Schroeder and Randall for Biology, Morehead and Kaiser for Geology, Randall and Arthur for Zoology, and Thorne and Grieg for Botany. The tree in Figure G-9 illustrates this example. Notice that Randall belongs to both the Biology and Zoology OUs.

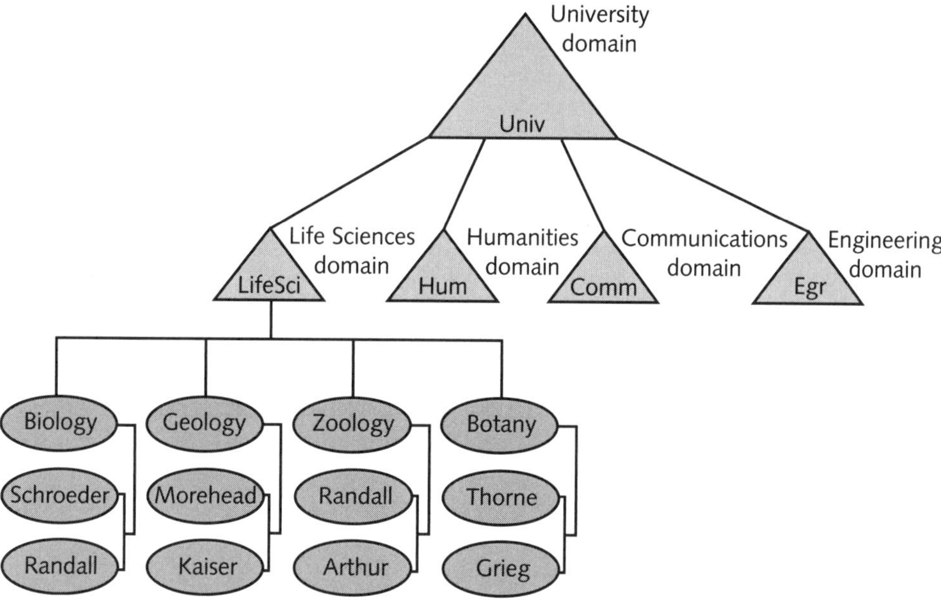

Figure G-9 A tree with multiple domains and OUs

Collecting objects in organizational units allows for simpler, more flexible administration. For example, suppose you want to restrict access to the Zoology printers in the Arthur building so that the devices are only available between 8:00 a.m. and 6:00 p.m. To accomplish this, you could apply this policy to the OU that contains the Arthur building's printer objects.

Trees and Forests Now that you understand how an NOS directory can contain multiple levels of domains and organizational units, you are ready to learn the structure of the directory that exists above domains. It is common for large organizations to use multiple domains in their Windows Server 2008 R2 networks. Active Directory organizes multiple domains hierarchically in a **domain tree** (or simply, tree). Active Directory's domain tree is an example of a typical NOS tree. At the base of the Active Directory tree is the **root domain**. From the root domain, **child domains** branch out to separate groups of objects with the same policies, as you saw in Figure G-7. Underneath the child domains, multiple organizational units branch out to further subdivide the network's systems and objects.

A collection of one or more domain trees is known as a **forest**. All trees in a forest share a common schema. Domains within a forest can communicate, but only domains within the same tree share a common Active Directory database. In addition, objects belonging to different domain trees are named separately, even if they are in the same forest.

Trust Relationships For your network to work efficiently, you must give some thought to the relationships between the domains in a domain tree. A relationship between two domains in which one domain allows another domain to authenticate its users is known as a **trust relationship**. Active Directory supports two types of trust relationships: two-way transitive trusts and explicit one-way trusts. Each child and parent domain within a domain tree and each top-level domain in a forest share a **two-way transitive trust** relationship. This means that a user in domain A is recognized by and can be authenticated by domain B, and vice versa. In addition, a user in domain A may be granted rights to any of the resources managed by domain B, and vice versa.

When a new domain is added to a tree, it immediately shares a two-way trust with the other domains in the tree. These trust relationships allow a user to log on to and be authenticated by a server in any domain within the domain tree. However, this does not necessarily mean that the user has privileges to access any resources in the tree. A user's permissions must be assigned separately for the resources in each different domain. For example, suppose Irina is a research scientist in the Mechanical Engineering Department. Her user account belongs to the Engineering domain at the university. One day, due to construction in her building, she has to temporarily work in an office in the Zoology Department's building across the street. The Zoology Department OU and all its users and workstations belong to the Life Sciences domain. When Irina sits down at the computer in her temporary office, she can log on to the network from the Life Sciences domain, which happens to be the default selection on her logon screen. She can do this because the Life Sciences and Engineering domains have a two-way trust. After she is logged on, she can access all her usual data, programs, and other resources in the Engineering domain. But even though the Life Sciences domain authenticated Irina, she will not automatically have privileges for the resources in the Life Sciences domain. For example, she can retrieve her research reports from the Mechanical Engineering Department's server, but unless a network administrator grants her rights to access the Zoology Department's printer, she cannot print the document to the networked printer outside her temporary office.

Figure G-10 depicts the concept of a two-way trust between domains in a tree.

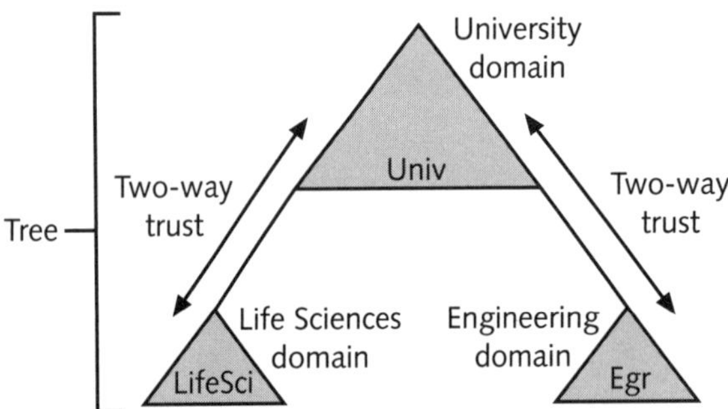

Figure G-10 Two-way trusts between domains in a tree

The second type of trust relationship supported by Active Directory is an **explicit one-way trust**. In this scenario, two domains that are not part of the same tree are assigned a trust relationship. The explicit one-way trust does not apply to other domains in the tree, however. Figure G-11 shows how an explicit one-way trust can enable domains from different trees to share resources. In this figure, notice that the Engineering domain in the University tree and the Research domain in the Science Corporation tree share a one-way trust. However, this trust does not apply to parent or child domains associated with the Engineering or Research domains. In other words, the Research domain could not have access to the entire University domain (including its child domains such as Life Sciences).

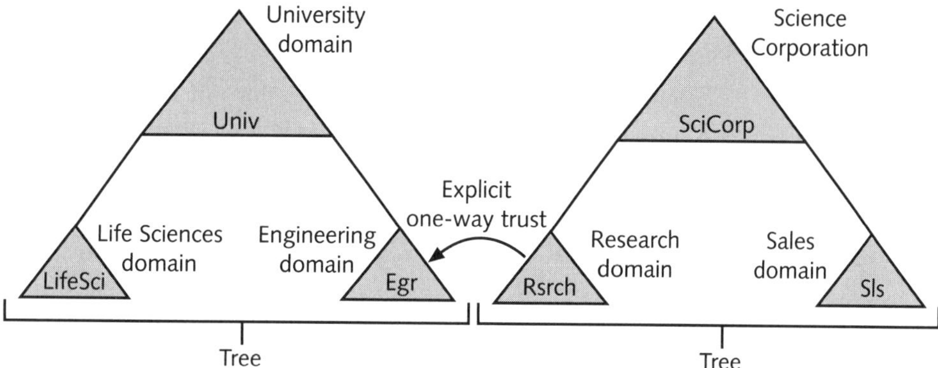

Figure G-11 Explicit one-way trust between domains in different trees

This section introduced you to the basic concepts of a Windows Server 2008 R2 network structure. If you are charged with establishing a new network that relies on Windows Server 2008 R2, you will need to learn a lot more about Active Directory. In that case, you'll want to buy a book on the topic, and perhaps take a class exclusively devoted to Active Directory.

Naming Conventions In the preceding section, you learned to think about domains in terms of their hierarchical relationships. Getting to know the structure of a network by studying its domain tree is similar to understanding your ancestry by studying a genealogical chart. Another way to look at ancestors is to consider their names and their relationship to you. For example, suppose a man named John Smith walks into a room full of relatives. The various people in the room will refer to him in various ways, depending on their relationship to him. One person might refer to him as "Uncle John," another as "Grandpa John," and another as "My husband, John." In the same way, different types of names, depending on where in the domain they are located, may be used to identify objects in a domain.

Naming (or addressing) conventions in Active Directory are based on the LDAP naming conventions. Because it is a standard, LDAP allows any application to access the directory of any system according to a single naming convention. Naming conventions on the Internet also follow LDAP standards. In Internet terminology, the term **namespace** refers to the complete database of hierarchical names used to map IP addresses to their hosts' names. The Internet namespace is not contained on just one computer. Instead, it is divided into many smaller pieces on computers at different locations on the Internet. In the genealogy analogy, this would be similar to having part of your family records in your home file cabinet, part of them in the state historical archives, part of them in your country's immigration files, and part of them in the municipal records of the country of your ancestors' origins. Somewhere in the Internet's vast, decentralized database of names and IP addresses (its namespace), your office workstation's IP address indicates that it can be located at your organization and, further, that it is associated with your computer.

In Active Directory, the term *namespace* refers to a collection of object names and their associated places in the Windows Server 2008 R2 network. In the genealogy analogy, this would be similar to having one relative (the Active Directory) who knows the names of each family member and how everyone is related. If this relative recorded the information about every relative in a database (for instance, Mary Smith is the wife of John Smith and the mother of Steve and Jessica Smith), this would be similar to what Active Directory does through its namespace.

Because the Active Directory namespace follows the conventions of the Internet's namespace, when you connect your Windows Server 2008 R2 network to the Internet, these two namespaces are compatible. For example, suppose you work for a company called Trinket Makers, and it contracted with a Web development firm to create a Web site. Further, suppose that the firm chose the Internet domain name trinketmakers.com to uniquely identify your company's location on the Internet. When you plan your Windows Server 2008 R2 network, you will want to call your root domain trinketmakers to match its existing Internet domain name (the .com part is assumed to be a domain). That way, objects within the Active Directory namespace can be assigned names related to the trinketmakers.com domain name, and they will match the object's name in the Internet namespace, should that be necessary.

Each object on a Windows Server 2008 R2 network can have three different names. The following list describes the formats for these names, which follow LDAP specifications:

- *DN (distinguished name)*—A long form of the object name that explicitly indicates its location within a tree's containers and domains. A distinguished name includes a **DC (domain component)** name, the names of the domains to which the object belongs, an OU (organizational unit) name, the names of the organizational units to which the object belongs, and a **CN (common name)**, or the name of the object. A common name must be unique within a container. In other words, you could have a user called "Msmith" in the Legal container and a user called "Msmith" in the Accounting container, but you could not have two users called "Msmith" in the Legal container. Distinguished names are expressed with the following notation: DC=domain name, OU=organizational unit name, CN=object name. For example, the user Mary Smith in the Legal OU of the trinketmakers domain would have the following distinguished name: DC=com, DC=trinketmakers, OU=legal, CN=msmith. Another way of expressing this distinguished name would be trinketmakers.com/legal/msmith.
- *RDN (relative distinguished name)*—A name that uniquely identifies an object within a container. For most objects, the relative distinguished name is the same as its CN in the distinguished name convention. A relative distinguished name is an attribute that belongs to the object. This attribute is assigned to the object when the administrator creates the object. Figure G-12 provides an example of an object, its distinguished name, and its relative distinguished name.
- *UPN (user principal name)*—The preferred naming convention for users in e-mail and related Internet services. A user's UPN looks like a familiar Internet address, including the positioning of the domain name after the @ sign. When you create a user account, the user's logon name is added to a **UPN suffix**, the portion of the user's UPN that follows the @ sign. A user's default UPN suffix is the domain name of her root domain. For example, if Mary Smith's username is msmith and her root domain is trinketmakers.com, her UPN suffix is trinketmakers.com and her UPN is *msmith@trinketmakers.com.*

In addition to these names, each object has a **GUID (globally unique identifier)**, a 128-bit number that ensures that no two objects have duplicate names. The GUID is generated and assigned to an object upon its creation. Rather than use any of the alphabetical names, network applications and services communicate with an object via the object's GUID.

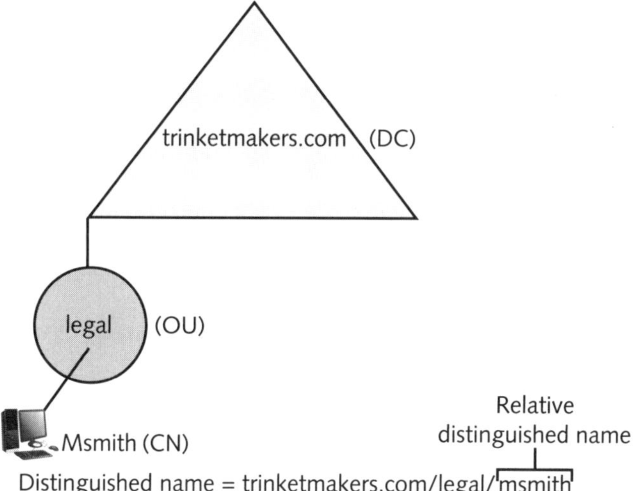

Figure G-12 Distinguished name and relative distinguished name

UNIX and Linux

UNIX and Linux differ in fundamental ways from Windows Server NOSs. Researchers at AT&T Bell Laboratories developed **UNIX** in 1969. In fact, UNIX preceded and led to the development of the TCP/IP protocol suite in the early 1970s. **Linux** is a popular example of a freely available and nonproprietary operating system that resembles UNIX. Today, most Internet servers and many servers on private WAN and LANs rely on UNIX or Linux. Fortunately, the differences between UNIX and Linux varieties are relatively minor. If you understand how to use one, with a little effort you can understand how to use another. The following sections introduce the UNIX operating system in general and then describe Linux in more detail.

Common Characteristics of UNIX and Linux

Today, the UNIX operating system comes in many varieties, or **distributions**. Before learning about their differences, however, you should know that all varieties of the UNIX and Linux operating system share the following features:

- The ability to support multiple, simultaneously logged-on users
- The ability to coordinate multiple, simultaneously running tasks (or programs)
- The ability to **mount**—or to make available—disk partitions upon demand
- The ability to apply permissions for file and directory access and modification
- A uniform method of issuing data to or receiving data from hardware devices, files, and running programs
- The ability to start a program without interfering with a currently running program
- Hundreds of subsystems, including dozens of programming languages
- Programs necessary for routing, firewall protection, DNS services, and DHCP services

- Source code portability, or the ability to extract code from one UNIX system and use it on another
- Window interfaces that the user can configure, the most popular of which is the **X Window system**

NOTE

The term **source code** refers to computer instructions written in a programming language that is readable by humans. Source code must be translated into a form that is executable by the machine, typically called binary code (for the sequence of zeros and ones) or target code.

Types of the UNIX operating system can be divided into two main categories: proprietary and open source. The following sections describe characteristics of each category and offer examples of UNIX versions in both categories. Note that some versions of UNIX will operate only on certain types of computers. Examples of such UNIX varieties and their unique hardware requirements are also described next.

Versions of UNIX and Linux

Many companies market both hardware and software based on the UNIX operating system. An implementation of UNIX for which the source code is either unavailable or available only by purchasing a licensed copy is known as **proprietary UNIX**. By most counts, the three most popular vendors of proprietary UNIX are Apple Computer, Sun Microsystems, and IBM. Apple's proprietary version of UNIX, **Mac OS X Server**, runs on computers that use Intel processors. Sun's proprietary version of UNIX, called **Solaris**, runs on the company's proprietary SPARC-based (the CPU invented by Sun Microsystems) workstations and servers, as well as Intel-based Pentium-class workstations and servers. IBM's proprietary version, **AIX**, runs on its PowerPC-based computers. (**PowerPC** is a brand of computer central processing unit invented by Apple Computer, IBM, and Motorola, Inc., and used in IBM servers.) Many other organizations have licensed the UNIX source code and created proprietary UNIX versions that run on highly customized computers (that is, computers that are appropriate for very specific tasks).

Choosing a proprietary UNIX system has several advantages:

- *Accountability and support*—An organization might choose a proprietary UNIX system so that when something doesn't work as expected, it has a resource on which to call for assistance.
- *Optimization of hardware and software*—Workstation vendors who include proprietary UNIX with the computers they sell invest a great deal of time in ensuring that their software runs as well and as fast as possible on their hardware.
- *Predictability and compatibility*—Purveyors of proprietary UNIX systems strive to maintain backward compatibility with new releases. They schedule new releases at regular, predictable intervals. Customers usually know when and how things will change with proprietary UNIX systems.

One drawback of choosing a proprietary UNIX system, however, relates to the fact that the customer has no access to the system's source code and, thus, cannot customize the operating system. Open source UNIX solves this problem.

Open source versions of UNIX include GNU, BSD, and Linux. These systems, in turn, come in a variety of implementations, each of which incorporates slightly different features and capabilities. For example, the different types of Linux include Debian, Gentoo, Red Hat, SUSE, Ubuntu, and a host of others.

The key difference between freely distributable UNIX and proprietary implementations relates to the software license. Proprietary UNIX includes agreements that require payment of royalties for each system sold and that forbid redistribution of the source code. A primary advantage of open source UNIX and Linux is that users can modify their code and thereby add functionality not provided by a proprietary version of UNIX. Another potential advantage of using a freely distributable version of UNIX or Linux is that, in general, these varieties run on a wider range of systems.

Linux follows standard UNIX conventions, is highly stable, and is free. Linus Torvalds developed it in 1991 when he was a second-year computer science student in Finland. After developing Linux, Torvalds posted it on the Internet and recruited other UNIX aficionados and programmers to help enhance it. Today, Linux is used for file, print, and Web servers across the globe. Its popularity has even convinced large corporations that own proprietary UNIX versions, such as IBM, Hewlett-Packard, and Sun Microsystems, to publicly embrace and support Linux.

Now that you have been introduced to the types of UNIX of Linux, you are ready to learn more details about these NOSs, beginning with hardware requirements.

Hardware Requirements

Hardware requirements for UNIX and Linux systems are very similar to those for Windows Server versions. One key difference, however, is that any UNIX or Linux operating system can act as a workstation or server operating system. Therefore, the computer's minimum hardware requirements depend partly on which version of UNIX or Linux you are installing and partly on how you intend to use the system.

A further difference is that in all UNIX distributions, the use of a GUI (graphical user interface) remains optional—that is, you can choose to use the GUI, a command-line interface, or a combination of the two. By contrast, with most Windows Server versions, you *must* use the GUI for many operations. Some network administrators regard the choice of using a GUI or a command-line interface in UNIX and Linux as an advantage. For example, you might choose to use the GUI for operations that require a great deal of interaction, such as adding new users or configuring services. However, for server operations that run unattended, it often makes sense to use the command-line interface. Doing so consumes less of the computer's memory and other resources.

As you have learned, no single "right" server configuration exists. You might need to add more memory and more disk space according to your networking environment and users' needs. For example, if you intend to install virtual machines on your UNIX or Linux server, increase the amount of RAM and hard disk space accordingly. Unfortunately, you sometimes cannot learn the memory requirements of an application until you actually run it on the server. In these instances, it is always better to overestimate your needs than to underestimate them.

Minimum hardware requirements for UNIX and Linux vary to some extent based on the distribution you are installing. For example, the minimum hardware requirements for an Ubuntu Linux server are as follows:

- 1 GHz processor
- 1 GB of RAM
- 15 GB of disk space

- Graphics card and monitor capable of 640 x 480
- CD-ROM, DVD-ROM, or USB drive for system installation

Adding high-performance video cards, sound cards, and other I/O devices to your UNIX or Linux server is optional.

Multiprocessing

A process represents an instance of a program running in memory (RAM). In addition to processes, UNIX and Linux also support threads, which are self-contained subsets of a process. Any modern NOS must handle multiple processes and threads in an efficient manner. UNIX and Linux allocate separate resources (such as memory space) to each process as it is created. They also manage all programs' access to these resources. This approach enables partitioning of processes in memory, thereby preventing one program from disrupting the operation of the entire system. When one program ends unexpectedly on a UNIX or Linux system, it doesn't cause the whole computer to crash.

As with modern Windows Server NOSs, modern UNIX and Linux systems support SMP (symmetric multiprocessing). Different distributions of UNIX and Linux support different numbers of processors. You must know how your servers will be used and plan for multiprocessing servers according to your estimated application-processing loads.

Memory Allocation

From early on, UNIX systems were created to use both physical and virtual memory efficiently. Similar to Windows Server 2008 R2, UNIX and Linux allocate a memory area for each application. All of these operating systems attempt to decrease the inefficiency of this practice, however, by sharing memory between programs wherever they can. For example, if five people are using FTP on your UNIX server, five instances of the FTP program will run. In reality, only a small part of each FTP program (called the private data region—the part that stores the username, for example) will receive its own memory space; most of the program will remain in a region of memory shared by all five instances of the program. In this case, rather than using five times the memory required by one instance of the program, a UNIX or Linux system sets aside only a little more memory for five FTP users than it does for one FTP user.

Most UNIX and Linux systems run on CPUs that employ 64-bit addresses, enabling programs to access more than 18 exabytes (2^{64} bytes) of memory. Virtual memory in a UNIX or Linux server can take the form of a disk partition or it can be in a file, much like the virtual memory file pagefile.sys in Windows Server 2008 R2.

The Kernel

The core of all UNIX and Linux systems is called the **kernel**. The kernel is loaded into memory and runs when you turn on your computer. Its primary function is to coordinate access to all your computer's hardware, such as the disks, memory, keyboard, and monitor. You can add or remove functionality on a running UNIX or Linux system by loading and unloading kernel modules. A UNIX **kernel module** is a file that contains instructions for performing a specific task such as reading data from and writing data to a hard drive. The Solaris kernel is derived from the original AT&T UNIX software from Bell Labs. The Linux kernel is the software Linus Torvalds wrote and released to the public in 1991.

File and Directory Structure

UNIX was one of the first operating systems to implement a **hierarchical file system** (a method of organizing files and directories on a disk in which directories may contain files and other directories). The notion of a file system organized in this way was considered revolutionary at the time of UNIX's inception. Today, most operating systems, including all Microsoft operating systems, use hierarchical file systems. Figure G-13 shows a typical UNIX file system hierarchy.

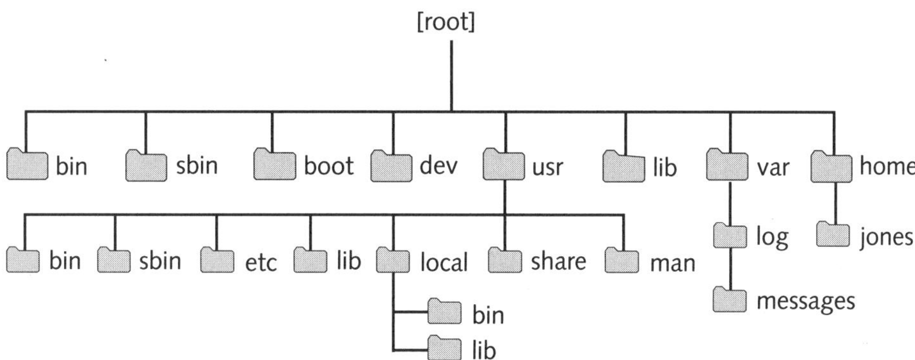

Figure G-13 UNIX file system hierarchy

On a UNIX or Linux system, the `/boot` directory contains the kernel and other system initialization files. Applications and services are stored in the `/bin` and `/sbin` directories. (The applications and services in the `/sbin` directory support the system initialization process; you'll rarely use these programs.) The `/var` directory holds variable data, such as log files, users' unread e-mail, and print jobs waiting to be printed. The file `/var/log/messages`, for example, stores system log messages, such as a notification of a disk drive that is running out of space. Users' login directories typically appear in `/home`. When you create a new user account, the system assigns a directory in `/home` to that user. The login (or home) directory matches the account's username. Thus, `/home/jones` is the login (or home) directory for the username jones on a UNIX system.

File Systems

UNIX and Linux file systems fall into two broad categories: disk file systems and network file systems. Disk file systems are used to organize the information on a hard drive. Network file systems enable users to access files on other servers via the network.

Disk File Systems The UNIX or Linux disk file system is the operating system's facility for organizing, managing, and accessing files through logical structures and software routines. Just as Windows Server 2003, Server 2008, and Server 2008 R2 support NTFS and other file systems, UNIX and Linux systems also support multiple file system types. The **ext4**, or fourth extended file system, is the file system native to most current versions of Linux.

On UNIX and Linux systems, you can access disk partitions formatted with NTFS file systems. This applies to partitions on disks that are physically attached to computers that are running a UNIX or Linux system. Over a network, UNIX and Linux systems have access to nonnative file system types, using network file systems, as described next.

Network File Systems Computers running UNIX or Linux also make use of network file systems, which are analogous to Windows shares. From a UNIX host, the network file system allows you to attach shared file systems (or drives) from Windows or other UNIX servers and share files with users on other computers. Sun Microsystems' **NFS (Network File System)** is a popular remote file system type supported by UNIX and Linux. Sun Microsystems published the specification for NFS, and most vendors of UNIX and Linux systems include NFS applications for sharing and accessing files over a network. Another network file system, called **Samba**, is an open source application that implements the Windows SMB and CIFS file system protocols. Samba is included with Solaris and most Linux distributions by default.

A UNIX and Linux Command Sampler

For many years, the command line was the primary method of interacting with a computer running the UNIX or Linux NOS, and to this day, many system administrators prefer this method. Even when you're running a GUI, the GUI merely executes commands in response to your mouse clicks. This section discusses the basics of the UNIX user interface and provides a sample of fundamental UNIX commands.

The program that accepts the commands you type on the keyboard and runs the commands for you is called a **command interpreter**. Also known as a **shell**, a command interpreter translates your typed commands into machine instructions that a UNIX or Linux system can understand. In other words, the command interpreter is a program that runs other programs. UNIX command interpreters also perform file globbing (described later) and keep track of what commands you've entered previously. The primary UNIX command interpreter is the file `/bin/sh`. To use the shell effectively, you should be familiar with at least some basic commands.

Every UNIX and Linux system contains full documentation of UNIX commands in the **man pages** (or **manual pages**). The man pages describe each command's function and proper execution. Although their organization differs slightly in various flavors of UNIX, man pages are typically arranged in nine sections:

- *Section 1*—Covers the commands that you most typically enter while typing in a command window
- *Sections 2 through 5*—Document the programmer's interface to the UNIX system
- *Section 6*—Documents some of the amusements and games that are included in the UNIX system
- *Section 7*—Describes the device drivers for the system
- *Section 8*—Covers the commands used by administrators to manage the system
- *Section 9*—Documents the UNIX kernel functions programmers use when writing device drivers

You access man pages by entering the `man` command in a UNIX command window. For example, to read the man page entry for the `telnet` command, you would type `man telnet` in a command window, and then press Enter.

Although the UNIX man pages are accurate and complete, UNIX newcomers often complain that they can't find the appropriate man page if they don't know the name of the command they want to use. That's why the `apropos` command exists. It enables you to find possible man page entries for the command you want to use. For example, you might type `apropos list` and then press Enter to search for a command that lists files. The `apropos` command would then display all commands and programming functions that include the keyword `list` in their man page entries.

Type `man` *`command`* (where *`command`* is a command name displayed by `apropos`), and press Enter when you find a command name that looks like it might do what you want.

Commands function in much the same way as sentences in ordinary language. Some of these sentences are one-word directives to the system requesting that it perform a simple task on your behalf (such as `date` for "tell me the current date and time"). Other sentences are detailed instructions to the system containing the equivalent of nouns, adjectives, and adverbs and creating a precise description of the task you want the system to perform. For example, to instruct the system to "display the names of all files in the current directory that have been accessed in the past five days," you would type `find . -type f -atime -5 -print` and press Enter.

Commands, command options, and filenames in UNIX and Linux are all case sensitive. Be certain to use uppercase and lowercase as appropriate each time you type a command in a UNIX or Linux command window.

A few rules exist to guide your use of UNIX commands and, as you might expect, exceptions to most of the rules also exist. Most commands (though not all) are lowercase alphabetic characters. Using the analogy of a sentence, the command itself would be the verb—that is, the action you want the system to take (for example, `ls` to list information about files). The things on which you want the system to operate (often files) would be the nouns. For example, you would type `ls index.html` to list a file named index.html. Options to the commands are analogous to adjectives and adverbs—that is, modifiers that give more specifics about the command. To specify an option, you usually type a hyphen (-) followed by a letter. For example, if you want to list files in a directory and also list details about the files, such as their size and creation date, you type `ls -l`. You can make commands even more specific by using **file globbing**—the equivalent to using wildcards in Windows and DOS. On a UNIX or Linux system, this operation is also called filename substitution. For example, `ls -l a*` would produce a detailed listing of all files beginning with the letter *a*.

A significant (and perhaps initially confusing) difference between the UNIX and Windows command-line interfaces relates to the character you use to separate directory names when you type in a command window. The Windows separator character is the backslash (\ ). The equivalent UNIX directory separator character is the forward slash (/). For example, in a Windows Command Prompt window, you type the `telnet` command as `\windows\system32\telnet.exe`. The `telnet` command in UNIX is `/usr/bin/telnet`.

Table G-3 lists some common UNIX commands and provides a brief description of each.

Table G-3 Commonly used UNIX commands

Command	Function
`date`	Display the current date and time
`ls -la`	Display with details all the files in the current directory
`ps -ef`	Display details of the current running programs
`find dir` *`filename print`*	Search for *`filename`* in the directory *`dir`* and display the path to the filename on finding the file
`cat` *`file`*	Display the contents of *`file`*
`cd` *`/d1/d2/d3`*	Change the current directory to *`d3`*`, located in` *`/d1/d2`*
`cp` *`file1 file2`*	Make a copy of *`file1`*, named *`file2`*
`rm` *`file`*	Remove (delete) *`file`* (Note that this is a permanent deletion; there is no trash can or recycle bin from which to recover the deleted file.)
`mv` *`file1 file2`*	Move (or rename) *`file1`* to *`file2`*
`mkdir` *`dir`*	Make a new directory named *`dir`*
`rmdir` *`dir`*	Remove the directory named *`dir`*
`who`	Display a list of users currently logged on
`vi` *`file`*	Use the "visual" editor named `vi` to edit *`file`*
`lpr` *`file`*	Print *`file`* using the default printer; `lpr` actually places *`file`* in the printer queue; the file is actually printed by `lpd (line printer daemon)`, the UNIX printer service
`grep` *`"string" file`*	Search for the string of characters in *`string`* in the file named *`file`*
`ifconfig`	Display the network interface configuration, including the IP address, MAC address, and usage statistics for all NICs in the system
`netstat -r`	Display the system's TCP/IP network routing table
`sort` *`filename`*	Sort alphabetically the contents of *`filename`*
`man` *`command`*	Display the man page entry for *`command`*
`chmod` *`rights file`*	Change the access rights (the mode) of *`file`* to *`rights`*
`chgrp` *`group file`*	Change the group to which the *`file`* belongs to *`group`*
`telnet` *`host`*	Start a virtual terminal connection to *`host`* (where *`host`* may be an IP address or a host name)
`ftp` *`host`*	Start an interactive file transfer to (or from) *`host`* using the FTP protocol (where *`host`* may be an IP address or a host name)
`startx`	Start the X Window system
`kill process`	Attempt to stop a running program with the process ID *`process`*
`tail` *`file`*	Display the last 10 lines of *`file`*
`exit`	Stop the current running command interpreter; log off the system if this is the initial command interpreter started when logging on

The most frequently used UNIX command is `ls`. By entering `ls` (and specifying `-l`, the detailed listing option), you learn everything about a file except its contents. UNIX and Linux systems maintain the following information about each file:

- The filename
- The file size (in bytes)
- The date and time that the file was created
- The date and time that the file was last accessed (viewed or printed)
- The date and time that the file contents were last modified (created, edited, or changed in any way)
- The number of "aliases" or links to the file
- The numeric identifier of the user who owns the file
- The numeric identifier of the group to which the file belongs
- The access rights for the owner, the group, and all others

For each file, the system stores all of this information (except the filename) in a file **inode (information node)**. The beginning of each disk partition contains reserved space for all inodes on that partition. Inodes also contain pointers to the actual file contents on the disk. The file's name is stored in the directory that contains the file. To learn about the inode information, use the `ls` command. Figure G-14 shows a sample list generated by `ls -l`.

```
% ls -l
total 154
drwxr-xr-x   2 root root  4096 Nov 14 15:31 bin
drwxr-xr-x   4 root root  1024 Nov 14 15:21 boot
drwxr-xr-x   9 root root  3920 Nov 20 19:55 dev
drwxr-xr-x  74 root root 12288 Nov 20 20:16 etc
drwxr-xr-x   3 root root  4096 Nov 19 15:35 home
drwxr-xr-x   2 root root  4096 Aug 12 12:02 initrd
drwxr-xr-x  11 root root  4096 Nov 14 15:28 lib
drwx------   2 root root 16384 Nov 14 09:03 lost+found
drwxr-xr-x   3 root root  4096 Nov 20 19:55 media
drwxr-xr-x   2 root root  4096 Oct 15 19:21 misc
drwxr-xr-x   2 root root  4096 Aug 12 12:02 mnt
drwxr-xr-x   2 root root  4096 Aug 12 12:02 opt
dr-xr-xr-x  67 root root     0 Nov 20 13:49 proc
drwxr-x---   7 root root  4096 Nov 20 20:11 root
drwxr-xr-x   2 root root 12288 Nov 14 15:26 sbin
drwxr-xr-x   1 root root     0 Nov 20 13:49 selinux
drwxr-xr-x   2 root root  4096 Aug 12 12:02 srv
drwxr-xr-x   9 root root     0 Nov 20 13:49 sys
drwxrwxrwt   5 root root  4096 Nov 20 20:13 tmp
drwxr-xr-x  14 root root  4096 Nov 14 15:19 usr
drwxr-xr-x  20 root root  4096 Nov 14 15:23 var
% _
```

Figure G-14 Sample output from `ls -l`

In Figure G-14, the letters in the far-left column (for example, drwxr-xr-x) make up the access permissions field. The first character in the access permissions field (on the far left) indicates the file type. Files type designations include the following:

- d for directories
- -, a hyphen, for regular files, such as word-processing files or spreadsheet files—that is, those which, as far as the operating system is concerned, contain unstructured data
- l for symbolic link files (much like Windows shortcuts)
- b for block device files—for example, disk partitions
- c for character device files—for example, serial ports

The remaining letters in the access permissions field—for example, rwxr-xr-x represent the permissions that users and groups have to access each file. The meaning of these letters is described in the output of ls -l shown in Figure G-15.

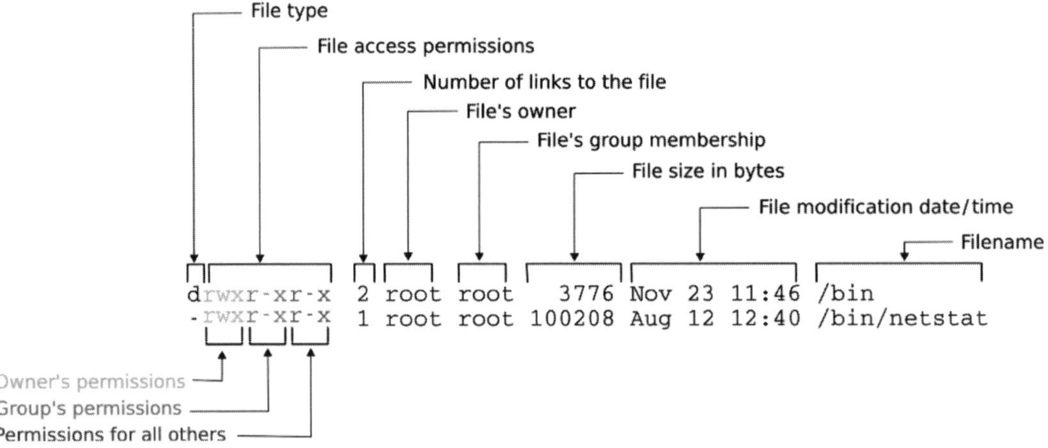

Figure G-15 Anatomy of ls -l output

Windows and UNIX systems share the powerful ability to direct output from one command to the input of another command. In UNIX, you combine commands using a **pipe**, which is entered as a vertical bar (|). (Think of data "flowing" through a pipe from one command to another.) Two or more commands connected by a pipe are called a **pipeline**. UNIX pipes make it possible to create sequences of commands that might require custom programming on other systems. For example, you can learn the process ID number assigned to a running program by combining two simple UNIX commands as follows: ps -ef|grep "/bin/sh". In UNIX, most commands that display output in a command window allow you to direct the output to another command. Most commands that accept typing from your keyboard also accept input from other commands.

Key Terms

Active Directory The method for organizing and managing objects associated with the network in Windows Server NOSs.

AIX A proprietary implementation of the UNIX system distributed by IBM.

asymmetric multiprocessing A multiprocessing method that assigns each subtask to a specific processor.

attribute A variable property associated with a network object. For example, a restriction on the time of day a user can log on is an attribute associated with that user object.

branch A part of the organizational structure of an operating system's directory that contains objects or other organizational units.

child domain A domain established within another domain in a Windows Server domain tree.

CIFS (Common Internet File System) A file access protocol. CIFS runs over TCP/IP and is the standard file access protocol used by Windows operating systems.

class A type of object recognized by an NOS directory and defined in an NOS schema. Printers and users are examples of object classes.

CN (common name) In LDAP naming conventions, the name of an object.

command interpreter A program (usually text-based) that accepts and executes system programs and applications on behalf of users. Often, it includes the ability to execute a series of instructions that are stored in a file.

Common Internet File System *See* CIFS.

common name *See* CN.

container *See* organizational unit.

DC (domain component) In LDAP naming conventions, the name of any one of the domains to which an object belongs.

directory In general, a listing that organizes resources and correlates them with their properties. In the context of NOSs, a method for organizing and managing objects.

distinguished name *See* DN.

distribution The term used to refer to the different implementations of a particular UNIX or Linux system. Debian, Gentoo, Red Hat, SUSE, and Ubuntu are just a few examples of Linux distributions.

DN (distinguished name) A long form of an object's name in Active Directory that explicitly indicates the object name, plus the names of its containers and domains. A distinguished name includes a DC (domain component), OU (organizational unit), and CN (common name). A client uses the distinguished name to access a particular object, such as a printer.

domain A group of users, servers, and other resources that share account and security policies through a Windows Server NOS.

domain component *See* DC.

domain controller A computer running a version of the Windows Server NOS that contains a replica of the Active Directory database.

domain model In Microsoft terminology, the type of client/server network that relies on domains, rather than workgroups.

domain tree A group of hierarchically arranged domains that share a common namespace in a Windows Server Active Directory.

explicit one-way trust A type of trust relationship in which two domains that belong to different NOS directory trees are configured to trust each other.

ext4 The name of the primary file system used in most Linux distributions.

file access protocol A protocol that enables one system to access files on another system.

file globbing A form of filename substitution, similar to the use of wildcards in Windows and DOS.

file system An operating system's method of organizing, managing, and accessing its files through logical structures and software routines.

forest In the context of Windows Server NOSs, a collection of domain trees that use different namespaces. A forest allows for trust relationships to be established between trees.

globally unique identifier *See* GUID.

graphical user interface *See* GUI.

group A means of collectively managing users' permissions and restrictions applied to shared resources. Groups form the basis for resource and account management for every type of NOS.

GUI (graphical user interface) A pictorial representation of computer functions and elements that, in the case of NOSs, enables administrators to more easily manage files, users, groups, security, printers, and other issues.

GUID (globally unique identifier) A 128-bit number generated and assigned to an object upon its creation in Active Directory. Network applications and services use an object's GUID to communicate with it.

hierarchical file system The organization of files and directories (or folders) on a disk in which directories may contain files and other directories. When displayed graphically, this organization resembles a treelike structure.

information node *See* inode.

inherited A type of permission, or right, that is passed down from one group (the parent) to a group within that group (the child).

inode (information node) A UNIX or Linux file system information storage area that holds all details about a file. This information includes the size, the access rights, the date and time of creation, and a pointer to the actual contents of the file.

kernel The core of a UNIX or Linux system. This part of the operating system is loaded and run when you turn on your computer. It mediates between user programs and the computer hardware.

kernel module A portion of the kernel that you can load and unload to add or remove functionality on a running UNIX or Linux system.

LDAP (Lightweight Directory Access Protocol) A standard protocol for accessing network directories.

leaf object An object in an operating system's directory, such as a printer or user, that does not contain other objects.

Lightweight Directory Access Protocol *See* LDAP.

line printer daemon *See* lpd.

Linux An open source operating system modeled on the UNIX operating system. Finnish computer scientist Linus Torvalds originally developed it.

lpd (line printer daemon) A UNIX service responsible for printing files placed in the printer queue by the lpr command.

lpr A UNIX command that places files in the printer queue. The files are subsequently printed with lpd, the print service.

Mac OS X Server A proprietary NOS from Apple Computer that is based on a version of UNIX.

man pages (manual pages) The online documentation for any variety of the UNIX operating system. This documentation describes the use of the commands and the programming interface.

manual pages *See* man pages.

map The action of associating a disk, directory, or device with a drive letter.

member server A type of server on a Windows Server 2003, Server 2008, or Server 2008 R2 network that does not hold directory information and, therefore, cannot authenticate users.

middleware The software that sits between the client and server in a three-tier architecture. Middleware may be used as a messaging service between clients and servers, as a universal query language for databases, or as a means of coordinating processes between multiple servers that need to work together in servicing clients.

mount The process of making a disk partition available.

multiprocessing The technique of splitting tasks among multiple processors to expedite the completion of any single instruction.

multitasking The ability of a processor to perform multiple activities in a brief period of time (often seeming simultaneous to the user).

namespace The complete database of hierarchical names (including host and domain names) used to resolve IP addresses with their hosts.

Network File System *See* NFS.

New Technology File System *See* NTFS.

NFS (Network File System) A popular remote file system created by Sun Microsystems, and available for UNIX and Linux operating systems.

NTFS (New Technology File System) A file system developed by Microsoft and used with its Windows NT, Windows 2000 Server, Windows Server 2003, Windows Server 2008, and Windows Server 2008 R2 operating systems.

object A representation of a thing or person associated with the network that belongs in the NOS directory. Objects include users, printers, groups, computers, data files, and applications.

object class *See* class.

organizational unit *See* OU.

OU (organizational unit) A logical receptacle for holding objects with similar characteristics or privileges in an NOS directory. Containers form the branches of the directory tree.

page file A file on the hard drive that is used for virtual memory.

paging The process of moving blocks of information, called pages, between RAM and into a page file on disk.

paging file *See* page file.

partition An area of a computer's hard drive that is logically defined and acts as a separate disk drive.

per seat In the context of applications, a licensing mode that limits access to an application to specific users or workstations.

per user A licensing mode that allows a fixed quantity of clients to use one software package simultaneously.

physical memory The RAM chips installed on the computer's system board that provide dedicated memory to that computer.

pipe A character that enables you to combine existing commands to form new commands. The pipe symbol is the vertical bar (|).

pipeline A series of two or more commands in which the output of prior commands is sent to the input of subsequent commands.

PowerPC The brand of computer central processing unit invented by Apple Computer, IBM, and Motorola, Inc., and used in IBM servers.

preemptive multitasking The type of multitasking in which tasks are actually performed one at a time, in very brief succession. In preemptive multitasking, one program uses the processor for a certain period of time, then is suspended to allow another program to use the processor.

printer queue A logical representation of a networked printer's functionality. To use a printer, clients must have access to the printer queue.

process A routine of sequential instructions that runs until it has achieved its goal. For example, a spreadsheet program is a process.

proprietary UNIX Any implementation of UNIX for which the source code is either unavailable or available only by purchasing a licensed copy.

RDN (relative distinguished name) An attribute of an object that identifies the object separately from its related container(s) and domain. For most objects, the relative distinguished name is the same as its common name (CN) in the distinguished name convention.

redirector A service that runs on a client workstation and determines whether the client's request should be handled by the client or the server.

relative distinguished name *See* RDN.

replication The process of copying Active Directory data to multiple domain controllers. This ensures redundancy so that in case one of the domain controllers fails, clients can still log on to the network, be authenticated, and access resources.

root domain In Windows Server NOS terminology, the single domain from which child domains branch out in a domain tree.

Samba An open source software package that provides complete Windows-style file- and printer-sharing capabilities.

schema The description of object types, or classes, and their required and optional attributes that are stored in an NOS's directory.

Server Message Block *See* SMB.

shell Another term for the UNIX command interpreter.

site license A type of software license that, for a fixed price, allows any number of users in one location to legally access a program.

SMB (Server Message Block) A protocol for communications and resource access between systems, such as clients and servers. SMB originated at IBM and then was adopted and further developed by Microsoft for use on its Windows operating systems. The current version of SMB is known as the CIFS (Common Internet File System) protocol.

Solaris A proprietary implementation of the UNIX operating system by Sun Microsystems.

source code The computer instructions written in a programming language that is readable by humans. Source code must be translated into a form that is executable by the machine, typically called binary code (for the sequence of zeros and ones) or target code.

swap file *See* page file.

symmetric multiprocessing A method of multiprocessing that splits all operations equally among two or more processors.

thread A well-defined, self-contained subset of a process. Using threads within a process enables a program to efficiently perform related, multiple, simultaneous activities. Threads are also used to enable processes to use multiple processors on SMP systems.

three-tier architecture A client/server environment that uses middleware to translate requests between the client and server.

time sharing *See* preemptive multitasking.

tree A logical representation of multiple, hierarchical levels in a directory. It is called a tree because the whole structure shares a common starting point (the root), and from that point extends branches (or containers), which may extend additional branches, and so on.

trust relationship The relationship between two domains on a Windows Server network that allows a domain controller from one domain to authenticate users from the other domain.

two-way transitive trust The security relationship between domains in the same domain tree in which one domain grants every other domain in the tree access to its resources and, in turn, that domain can access other domains' resources. When a new domain is added to a tree, it immediately shares a two-way trust with the other domains in the tree.

UNIX A client or server operating system originally developed by researchers at AT&T Bell Laboratories in 1969. UNIX is a proprietary operating system, but similar operating systems, such as Linux, are freely distributable.

UPN (user principal name) The preferred Active Directory naming convention for objects when used in informal situations. This name looks like a familiar Internet address, including the positioning of the domain name after the @ sign. UPNs are typically used for e-mail and related Internet services.

UPN (user principal name) suffix The portion of a universal principal name (in Active Directory's naming conventions) that follows the @ sign.

user account A record of a user that contains all of her properties, including rights to resources, password, username, and so on.

user principal name *See* UPN.

virtual memory The memory that is logically carved out of space on the hard drive and added to physical memory (RAM).

workgroup In Microsoft terminology, a group of interconnected computers that share each other's resources without relying on a central file server.

X Window system A GUI environment for UNIX and Linux systems.

Index

A

C

D

E

F

N

O

Q

R

S

U

X

Z